To Andrew
from his friend

22/9/09

Why the European Union?

Is the future of Europe bright or dark?

Francis S. E. Codjoe. Jnr

ORIGINAL WRITING

ISBN: 978-1-907179-24-2

A cip catalogue for this book is available from the National Library.

Printed in Great Britain by MPG Books Group, Bodmin and Kings Lynn.
Published by Original Writing Ltd., Dublin, 2009

Copyright and Permissions

Dedication

This book is dedicated to the memory of the Eminent Victorian- the "Anglicanised Irishman of Scotch extraction".

1841-1918
The Prince of Detectives: Head of Scotland Yard
The Knight Commander of (the Order of) Bath
The Assistant Commissioner of Metropolitan Police
A Barrister and Distinguished Public Servant
An Intellectual among Intellectuals
A Giant among Giants, A Literary Recluse
The Stalwart Defender of the Christian Faith
The Zealous Champion of Christian Causes
A Theologian among Theologians
A Preacher, a Witness and an Author
Mr Valliant for the Truth
The Man who refuses to lift the flag of truce before a foe
A Man of Peace who never shirks a fight
The Giant among Giants who 'knocked down' the Champion of Darwinism and 'destroyed' Darwin's 'bulldog.'
"The true test of a man is not what he does, but what, with the principles he holds, he would do, and if this be true of individuals, it is still more intensely true of communities"

Acknowledgements

Without Mark Whitby, Chairman of Ramboll UK Ltd, this book would not have been produced. Mark laid at my disposal the company's Information Technology infrastructure to produce the script for this work. Thank you Mark, the youngest man to hold the Presidency of the Institute of Civil Engineers in the United Kingdom.

Special recognition to Charlie Tonkis, Dina Bhudia, Kevin Alavoine, Zaheer Malak, Oladotun Shonowo and their colleagues at the Information Technology Department of Ramboll for their technical support. I thank all the staff at Ramboll for their encouragement. I appreciate the labour of Phil Lebar, the printing services manager, and his colleagues Peter Grant, Vince Quinne and Stuart Faulds for producing the Portable Data Format (PDF) files for Public presentation of this project.

I would like to thank Claire Jennings and her partner, Ian Turner, for producing some of the charts in this book.

I am grateful to my wonderful friends, Susan Chandler-Brown and Julia Evans, and my wife Gertrude Naadu Lartey–Codjoe. They read successive drafts of this work and helped me with their inputs. They were always around when I needed their advice.

I am deeply indebted to Dr. Chuck Missler, the Information Technology Scientist, who introduced me to the Knight Commander (of the Order) of Bath. The Knight, who was a Counsellor and Helper of many, 'carried me on his broad shoulders' when I started this project.

I appreciate the contribution my precious associates Alan Day, Marilyn Day and Ferne Abbott have made to this work.

Finally, and most importantly, I bow before the Almighty God for using Brother Joseph Jackson Amankwaa to rescue me from the 'pit of darkness.' Brother Joseph introduced me to the Lord Jesus Christ whom I am not ashamed to proclaim as the Messiah, the Lord of lords, the King of kings, the Beginning and the End. I praise you, Lord, for your Mercy and Kindness. Great is Your faithfulness. Amen!

About the Author

Francis S E Codjoe was born in Ghana. He was educated by Irish Priests at St Augustine's College in Cape Coast. He worked for Her Majesty Revenue and Customs (HMRC) in London.

Francis is not a politician or a political activist. He is neither a businessman nor a pastor. Through unusual circumstances he found himself researching the significance of European integration. He shares with you his 9-year labour.

Apology

The script was not edited. All the errors in this book are the responsibility of the author. I have indulged in repetitions to emphasise significant points. Please accept my apology.

"Postcard photography HARLINGUE VIOLLET
"Mister Europe": The "Practical Apostle of
European Unity" and the "Revolutionary"

Jean Monnet: "Europe of sovereign states was incapable of, despite its leaders' goodwill, of reaching the sensible decisions that were needed for the common good. It would be quite another matter, however, once the power of decision was entrusted to institutions serving the general interest and applying the will of the majority in a system of common rules" (Memoirs 1978)

Jean Monnet: "Once a Common Market has been created, then a political union will come naturally."

The "Unknown Truth" about Jean Monnet's Labour to Create a Federal Europe;
Monnet, unconsciously, toiled for a 'master' he never knew. The French statesman was just an instrument to bring to pass what a British public servant wrote about a political union of European nations: how it would develop, its character and future prospects before he himself was born in 1888.

Contents

APPENDICES

Preface

We Must be Silent No More

"The truest test of a man is not conduct, but character; not what he does, but what he is. Human judgement must, of course, be guided by a man's acts and words. But God is not thus limited. Man judges by conduct; God judges by character. Therefore it is that "what is highly esteemed among men is abomination in the sight of God."

("For Us Men" – RA)

Great Britain and Ireland are at crossroads – a critical point in the history of their blessed nations. Should Britain and Ireland be at the 'heart of Europe' as suggested by politicians and commentators, or they should withdraw from the European Union? Politicians have failed to convince the British and the Irish people that their destiny lies in the European Union. On account of this failure, *The Observer*, in its 2 September 2007 edition, published an article entitled "This cowardly refusal to make a political case for Europe." The newspaper made this significant comment: "If the European Union didn't exist, politicians would have to invent it. It would be an epic project. The British government would have to ask voters for permission. The Fundamental truth is that the European integration started out as a free-trade agreement that has evolved into a political entity. That process demands public consent. The mandate Harold Wilson won to stay in the European Economic Community in 1975 cannot be stretched to cover the union that exists now. ..The argument about Britain's place in Europe has to start now. A referendum on the constitution would have been an opportunity to do just that."

This leads to the following questions:

- "Why have succeeding British governments, since 1975, deliberately denied Britons their legitimate and democratic rights to decide on their long-term relationship with the European Union?
- "Why did Gordon Brown, the British Prime Minister, and his 'lieutenants' - David Miliband, the Foreign Secretary, and Jim Murphy, the then Europe Minister, and his allies in the British Parliament - commit the British people to the Lisbon Treaty – a legal document that transfers more powers from the elected and accountable British politicians to unelected strangers in Brussels who are not accountable to any one?

Gordon Brown's refusal to call for a public vote on a treacherous document that would impact the lives of the British people, prompted an appropriate response from Matthew d'Ancona, Editor of *The Spectator*. In his article, *"After this, we can't believe a word you say, Gordon,"* he writes: "This latest betrayal will compound the question that all voters now ask about all politicians: why can't they keep a promise?"

The pages before you are my contribution to the debate: "Should Great Britain and Ireland remain in the European Union or withdraw from it"? "Let the issue be put and let the battle be joined", says Tony Blair, the former British Prime Minister. The battle begins now.

I believe it was not by coincidence, but by providence that Ireland was the only member state of the European Union to have voted on the Lisbon Treaty and rejected it. They should not be ashamed of dumping the Lisbon Treaty in June 2008. The people of Ireland did the right thing. They, unconsciously, acted on the advice their "Forgotten Father" recorded in the 19th century about the future prospects of a confederation of European nations. Ireland is a tiny country. Yet Ireland -'a small axe' - can cut down the 'big tree' - the European Union. Ireland is a 'David" that can easily "slaughter" EU- the "European giant' - provided the Irish people would "listen" to the prophetic voice of the "Seer of Dublin" and not blindly follow the "children" of Jean Monnet and Konrad Adenauer. These European statesmen hated the concept of national sovereignty.

I hope the information in this book would strengthen the Irish to have the confidence to reject the Lisbon Treaty and also motivate the British people to force their politicians to allow them a vote on the Treaty of Lisbon.

Politicians, political commentators and academics in America, Britain, Europe and Ireland and the rest of the world know one side of the European 'political phenomenon' – the evolution of an economic and political alliance of European nations from the ashes of the Second World War. For example, the official history of the European Union published on *Europa* Website states: "After the First and Second World Wars a number of Europeans became convinced that the only way to secure a lasting peace between European countries was to unite them economically and politically...The historic roots of the European Union lie in the Second World War...The end of World War II marked the beginning of the European Construction."

The fact is there is another side to the story of European Construction which I would share with you. The European "political phenomenon" - the so-called "extraordinary political project" of our time - has, indeed, captivated politicians and political intellectuals in the Western World to the extent that some Universities in America, England, Europe, Ireland, Scotland and other parts of the globe subscribed to *Jean Monnet Centres of Excellence.* These "Centres" are dedicated to the memory of Jean Monnet, the "spiritual godfather" of the European Project. The *Jean Monnet Centres of Excellence* are subsidised by the European Commission. These "Centres" organise *Jean Monnet Programme for understanding European integration* – "with projects across the five continents and reaching 250000 students every year."

The progress of the European Union would have a significant impact on every soul on planet earth. We must, therefore, examine this "political phenomenon" of our time to appreciate its true purpose, character and future prospects. In Britain, those who don't subscribe to Monnet's vision of a united Europe have been ridiculed as 'backward looking' and "xenophobic."

The ingrained perception is that politicians, political commentators and scholars are better-informed on European integration than the public. The reality is these 'experts' prey on the ignorance of the masses and impose on them their own opinions on European Construction. The "EU Specialists" support the disposal of the sovereign rights of "ignorant" Britons and Irish to unelected and unaccountable officials in Brussels who have no idea what the European Union is for. Supporters of the European Project have applied their limited knowledge on European integration to, consciously or unconsciously; perpetrate a gigantic deception on the masses about the merits of European integration to seduce them to board Jean Monnet's "Great Titanic."

In his article, *"It takes an Irish poet to remind us of the grandeur of the European project",* Professor Timothy Garton Ash writes: "...Will the future of Europe be decided by the voice of a poet? In a rare and moving intervention, Ireland's greatest living poet, Seamus Heaney, has come out plainly for a yes to the Lisbon Treaty and raised the whole debate to a different level." The Professor goes on: "There are many reasons for ratifying the Lisbon Treaty, reasons to do with our political and economic wellbeing, but the poem speaks mainly for our honour and identity as Europeans." (*The Guardian* 24 June 2009)

The "unknown truth" hidden from scholars and poets is that a brilliant Irish barrister wrote about the future of Europe before Jean Monnet, the master builder of European Construction, was even conceived in 1888. In fact the whole debate on the Lisbon Treaty and Ireland's long-term relationship with the European Union would be raised to an extraordinarily high level if the Irish examine the works of the "Sage of Ulster."

And according to an article in the 4 July 2009 edition of *The Irish Times,* Deaglan De Breadun writes: "He (Timothy Garton Ash) sees the EU as vital to Ireland's survival in a world where the Irish would otherwise be crushed between the superpowers of the US and China." This assertion leads to the question: is the future of EU itself bright for Ireland to secure its future in the EU?

Bruce Arnold expressed a different and realistic view of Ireland's relationship with the European Union in his article *"We are no longer crucial. We are marginal again – unless we say 'No' to the Lisbon Treaty."* The columnist writes: "Germany is at the heart of the European Union and the Lisbon Treaty undoubtedly strengthens its power – at the expense of Ireland....While Germany has considered, in the Karlsruhe Judgment, its relationships with the EU and with the treaty, our leaders, Brian Cowen and Michael Martin, have acted like corner boys and rabble-rousers, rushing to Europe for a quick fix designed to get a 'Yes' vote. There was no serious thought or dignity at all.....They espouse a wishful idea of Ireland at the centre of Europe. This will never be. Ireland is small and peripheral. It has slavishly attended EU meeting looking for a cheap set of answers for a rerun of a totally unchanged Lisbon Treaty. Mr Arnold goes on: "Our interest and Germany's are quite clearly opposed. Germany will be strengthened by what is happening, Ireland will be weakened. Their voting strength is enhanced, ours is lessened. They want to be at the heart of Europe, and can be. They are already dominant there. We want to be at the heart of Europe without knowing what it means, still less knowing how we achieve it." (*Irish Independent* 4 July 2009).

In the same 4 July 2009 edition of *Irish Independent*, Conor O'Sullivan wrote a letter to the Editor about Ireland's relationship with the European Union. Under the title *"We need real debate on Europe's future"*, he stated: "When has there been a full public debate on where Ireland is going along with the European project? What is the national strategy?....Could it not be debated on, whether we wish to be an independent State, economically tied to Europe, or be part of a United States of Europe? Then the referendum would be a ratification of that national decision.... European integration and its internal market are put ahead of national societies' requirements. Is this what we want as a nation?"

In England, Ruth Lea, an Economist and Director of Global Vision, wrote on Britain's relationship with the European Union. In an article titled, *"Why most British people want to pull back from Europe,"* she stated: "Almost every aspect of our lives is influenced by the law-makers in Brussels. Our Parliament, when dealing with legislation from Brussels, can do little more than give it the nod...It is in the British people's interests to be free of the bureaucrats of Brussels." (The SUN 15 March 2007).

And the result of a Global Vision ICM Survey Poll, which was published in The

Sunday Telegraph on 8 June 2008, indicated that 41% of Britons wanted only trade relationship with Europe. 27% wanted Britain to stay a full EU member. 26% wanted withdrawal from EU. If trade-only options were offered in a referendum 64% said they would vote in favour. If Britain sought to negotiate a looser relationship but other nations blocked the move, 57% said the U.K. should leave the EU, while 33% said it should stay in." Ruth Lea summed it up: "A looser relationship, based on trade and co-operation, rather than full political and economic integration, is consistently the option of the British people."

Whatever the results of all the numerous polls that have been conducted about Britain's relationship with the European Union, the fact remains that majority of British people think Britain has not benefited from its membership of the European Union, and they hate being ruled by strangers whom they have not elected and are not accountable to them and have no power to remove them. Unfortunately, their opposition to Jean Monnet's vision of a federal Europe has incurred the wrath of political elites. Some of these 'experts' on European Construction have trampled upon the public by insulting them as 'racists', 'lunatics' and 'ignorant.' For example, it was reported that Denis MacShane, the former Labour Minister for Europe, branded 29 million Britons who oppose a European superstate "racists." According to this EU 'Expert', "Euroscepticism is misnomer. What we are talking about is hatred of Europe. We have got a dark streak of xenophobia and racism in our mentality." (THE SUN Wednesday 11 August 2004).

Such irresponsible comments from a Labour Party politician lead to the question: "Do politicians and political commentators have monopoly of scholarship on the significance of European integration? The fact is these 'experts' have no clue what the European Union is for. Do they know the future of the European Union? After all, who among the 'experts' was able to predict with certainty in 2000, that there would be a global financial crisis that would result in the collapse of Banks, the nationalisation of some major financial institutions in Britain and America, and a summit of 20 world leaders in America and Britain to find a global solution to a global economic crisis in a 'global society'?

- Which politician foresaw that the value of the British Pound Sterling would one day fall almost to the value of the euro?
- Which politician in Ireland foresaw the Irish economy would face a severe crisis in 2008 and 2009?
- Which political scientist predicted that the great "Wall Street" would crawl to American taxpayers for a rescue to prevent the "Wall" tumbling down?
- Which Economists foresaw that a barrel of oil would rise up to $150 and fall to about $40 dollar and rise again?

Gordon Brown, the "saviour", admitted that he did not foresee the financial storm which resulted in his Labour Government pumping billions into the British economy to save it from collapse. Prime Minister Brown said: "What we did not see, or nobody saw was the possibility of market failure." Mr. Brown added: "the global financial crisis was completely new territory." Angela Merkel, the German chancellor, described the global economic crisis an "extraordinary international crisis" (Financial Times 26 February 2009).

If Gordon Brown and Angela Merkel and other politicians in Britain, Europe and Ireland could not foresee the global economic storm on the horizon, what convinced them to suggest that the Lisbon Treaty would be beneficial to Europeans and therefore the Treaty must be imposed on them to commit their future to the European Union whose future is unknown to politicians? If politicians, political intellectuals and Economists cannot predict future events, then we must ask the question: "Why are they dragging the citizens of Europe to board Jean Monnet's "EU Titanic?"

In a lecture, ***The Europe We Need,*** which was delivered at the Institute of International and European Affairs in Dublin on 23 June 2009, Professor Timothy Garton Ash declared: "We are launched on big and stormy seas. We need a bigger and better boat, and there are also still some monsters in the deep." What would be the destination of this "bigger European boat"? Do politicians and political commentators and academics know the destination of the "European boat?"

The fact is it suits politicians to board Monnet's "luxurious boat" - to entertain themselves at the expense of the voters who subsidise the "European Titanic" of the 21st century. Observe the words of Peter Hitchens in his article *How will we be able to look at our grandchildren in the face when they ask: What did you do to stop Britain being taken over by a foreign power?:* "Political elites in all the parties love the EU, not because it is good for the country, but because it is good for them. They love its regular service of gravy trains, carrying failed Ministers off to a life of high salaries, big expenses and huge pensions, plus an almost total absence of responsibility. They don't mind at all that it deprives them of the power to do very much. They are for the most part, short of ideas and lazy and happy to be able to pass the buck to Brussels while enjoying their pay and perks." (*The Mail on Sunday* 4 November 2007)

WHY SHOULD EUROPE BE A "DANGEROUS SUBJECT" FOR TORY LEADER AND A "MARGINAL ISSUE" FOR THE BRITISH PUBLIC

On 26 July 2008, George Parker, political editor for Financial Times, commented on Britons attitude towards the European Union. In his article, *"The Sceptical Isle,"* he stated: "Cameron understands that while most of his party dislike Brussels, and the public and press are generally sceptical, Europe remains a dangerous subject for a Tory leader. Eurosceptics like to point to polls showing headline hostility towards the EU, but deeper analysis shows that the public regard Europe as a marginal issue in their daily lives." He continued: "In June this year (2008), it was only the 18th most mentioned issue facing Britain," says Helen Coombs, deputy head of research at Ipsos MORI, the polling organisation. She says it was higher in the 1990s, when Britain was agonising over whether to join the euro, but even the row over the Lisbon Treaty has failed to push Europe up the agenda. "It's simply not something that people vote on in general elections,"

The problem is that the British people have not been properly educated on Europe and the Lisbon Treaty. Before the above report, Ed Miliband, a 'disciple' of Gordon Brown, had already subscribed to the notion that the British public is not interested in the European project. On BBC Question Time, the Labour politician, 'boasted' of Britons' apathy to the European Union: "I don't think these issues (referring to a discussion on the Lisbon Treaty and Britain's relationship with the EU) are issues which people in my constituency want to have a referendum on. If you're interested in improving democracy in this country, having a referendum on issues that don't speak to people's lives is not the way to achieve it."
Such comments portray the ignorance of politicians about the significance of the European Union. It is a pity that an issue that must be on top of the political agenda has become an irrelevance. Politicians prefer not to talk about the European Union, and they are satisfied that voters consider "Europe" a marginal issue in their lives. The truth is that politicians have failed to educate the masses on the implications of Britain's membership of the European Union because of their own petty knowledge on European integration. Without any doubt, Britain's membership of the European Union - a project which is being directed by the French and the Germans - is an issue which should be the major concern of Britons and the Irish. Who in his right mind would like to be ruled by strangers and to be instructed how many hours he or she should labour to support his family?

Brian Sewell made the point in his article, "*Why our voices must be heard.*" He stated: "Deprived of any further opportunities to vote on European matters, the nation has become steadily less well-informed. Maastricht was a well kept mystery...Without the stimulus of debate we have been denied information; without the stimulus of a referendum at any further stage in the development of the EU, we have slipped into ignorance, indifference and mistrust. All governments since 1975 wanted it this way: "Leave it for us." (*Evening standard* 3 June 2003).

POLITICIANS MUST 'GO BACK TO SCHOOL' ON EUROPEAN INTEGRATION

Had British and Irish politicians done their "homework" on European integration, they would have learnt that, in the 19th century, a British public servant, who was a native of Dublin and educated at Trinity College, wrote about a confederation of European nations: how it would develop through an European crisis, its character and destiny even before the French Founding Fathers of European Community, Jean Monnet and Robert Schuman, were born in 1888 and 1886. The Irishman predicted this European confederacy would be the next major political feature in history after the restoration of the Jews to Palestine. He made this prediction even before Theodre Herzl, the Founding Father of Zionism, formed the Zionist Movement in 1896. The state of Israel was reborn on 14 May 1948. Two years later, on 9 May 1950, the European Union was born with the Schuman Plan exactly as the Irishman had predicted.

Such information would have motivated British politicians to put "European Construction" on top of their political agenda and educate the public accordingly. Unfortunately, because most politicians are not well-informed on the significance of Jean Monnet's project, they lack the confidence to alert the public about the impact the European project would have on their lives. Consequently, the British and the Irish people, who have invested their trust in politicians to educate them on European integration, have been betrayed. They have become less-informed to the point that 'Europe' has become a 'non-issue' to Britons in particular. This is a tragedy; not a situation politicians and political commentators should be 'proud' of. British politicians must 'go back to school' to learn more about the true significance of the European Project and its future.

British politicians have taken the 'silent majority,' who resent being ruled from Brussels, for granted. A typical example was demonstrated in the attitude of the former Minister of Europe, Carolyn Flint. This Labour Party politician was responsible for promoting the Lisbon Treaty in Britain, and yet she did not study this important document. She had the impudence to criticise the Irish people who rejected the Lisbon Treaty in a popular vote.

It is time for the British and the Irish people to know the "unknown truth" and the "forgotten truth" about the political integration of European nations for these two truths to set us all free from 'slavery' in Jean Monnet's 'slave market' in Brussels. The truth is that the French 'master builder' of European Community, who has been described a 'prophet,' a 'revolutionary' and a 'genius', did not merit any of these titles. Monnet had a blurred vision of a federal Europe without knowing the future prospects of his vision.

In his essay, *The Man from Gognac: Jean Monnet and the Anglo-American Mindset,* Dr Henry H H Remark, Professor of Comparative Literature and West European Studies at Indiana University, sang the praises of Jean Monnet with these words: "How this unlikely person with an unlikely education from an unlikely corner of France was able to achieve, against all odds, what nobody else has been able to do since Charlemagne: the functioning structure of a European Community (EC). Not alone, certainly, but without him it would not have happened. And the longer I plunged into this....unique phenomenon, the more surprised....I have been to discover how instrumental.....the Anglo-American model and reality have been for Monnet in laying the groundwork for a federated Europe. Due to his (Monnet's) intervention and his ability to motivate crucial allies and implementers, this is no longer a vision, a dream, let alone an illusion, but a reality, if only the first though crucial step toward a more fully integrated United States of Europe." (Source: *The European Union From Jean Monnet to Europe* pages 57-59).

The reality is that, in his labour to construct the European Community – the "unique phenomenon" - Jean Monnet, unconsciously, toiled to bring to pass what an extraordinary brilliant Irishman had already written about his European project and its destiny before he himself was even conceived. Who was a true 'prophet' and a "genius"? The French architect of European Construction or the Irishman? In the 19th century it was written of this Ulsterman: "His views are worthy of the utmost respect and consideration...The well-being of Ireland was to him a matter standing above politics in the ordinary sense...He is one of the men to whom the country, without knowing it, owes a great deal...his name will go down to generations yet unborn."

COMMON SENSE IS NOT ALWAYS COMMON IN BRITAIN'S HOUSE OF COMMONS

Great Britain belongs to Britons not the few politicians who debate in the House of Commons where common sense is not always common. For a British politician once said he was ashamed to be a member of British Parliament. And the British Prime Minister, Gordon Brown, once labelled Members of Parliament 'selfish' for demanding 10 percent payrise whereas public servants were being offered less than 3 percent payrise *(The Daily Telegraph 24 December 2007).* Witness Stephen Glover's comments in his essay *Bare-faced lies and why we let all politicians get away with them.* He writes: "Politicians are addicted to lying because they believe that telling the truth in a difficult situation, or apologising involves a loss of face. They understand that we may see through their deceptions but they calculate that we will not mind very much as long as we reap the benefits of their lies. Politicians would think twice about telling lies if they feared they would be punished for it....We have entered into a dishonest contract with our rulers, tolerating a degree of deception so long as the economy continues to grow, and we are at least half competently governed." *(Daily Mail 10 October 2007)*

Our "dishonest contract with our rulers" was laid bare in May 2009; *The Daily Telegraph* published a series of political corruption in the House of Commons. Some politicians were exposed as "thieves, liars and tax fiddlers." They abused their privileges and fought hard to prevent the publication of the scale of their greed and fraud that tainted the reputation of the Mother of all Parliaments.

The future belongs to our children. We should not sit back and allow 'selfish' politicians to authorise bureaucrats in Brussels to 'poison' our sons and daughters with distorted information about the European Union. It is our responsibility to provide our children with sound education on European integration - to equip them to discern truth from falsehood. For example, the official explanation of the significance of the EU symbol - a circle of 12 gold stars - is a distortion of truth. I would deal with this subject.

Jose Manuel Barroso, the President of European Commission, and his officials in Brussels seem to have made the case for a deeper political integration of European nations and no one should question them. The fact is experts are seldom good judges. The proper place for Mr. Barroso, the leading 'expert' on European integration, is not on the judgement seat in Brussels, but in the witness chair at Wembley Stadium in London to be 'cross-examined' by the 'ignorant' Britons. The "Seer of Dublin" who, before the First World War, wrote about European Union, recorded: "No one who has much experience of judicial inquiries is ever surprised to find that a case which seems convincing when presented *ex-parte*, breaks down under cross-examination or shattered by an opposing evidence."

The Green Politician, Cem Oezdemir, a member of the European Parliament who sits in the legislature's foreign affairs committee, argued the case for Turkey's membership of the European Union. In an article titled *Turkish EU Entry is in Europe's interest*, he stated: "For me, today's Europe is a vision and a project that would not be conceivable without the catastrophe of World War II. To me, Europe and the EU symbolize the ideals of peace, democracy and freedom of opinion. The realization of these ideals on a daily basis is meant to prevent such a catastrophe from ever happening again in Europe."

Is this 'expert' on "Europe and the EU" aware that before the First World War, a servant of the British Crown had already mentioned that Spain, Portugal, Greece and Turkey would become members of a political alliance of European nations that would develop through an European crisis? And this Irishman predicted that the European confederacy would be the next major political feature in history after the restoration of the Jews to Palestine. Has the Irishman been proved right?
Here is the uncomfortable truth for Europeans. Britain and Ireland are unique

among the member states of the European Union, They share common heritage. For it was their brilliant 'father' who recorded how Jean Monnet's project would come into existence before the "Pride of France" and the 'Giant of Europe' was born. In view of this truth, and coupled with what the British public servant recorded about the future of Europe, the British and the Irish have a simple, but an awkward choice to make. They can follow blindly Jean Monnet's vision of a federated Europe, or the Irishman's extraordinary vision of the destiny of political Europe and withdraw from the European Union.

I would encourage politicians, political commentators and political intellectuals in America, Britain, Europe and Ireland to 'consult' the "Forgotten Ulsterman" to improve their understanding of the European project and its future prospects.
Frederick Forsyth writes: "Our country used to be abolished on a monthly basis. Then it was weekly. Now it is daily. When will the Tories say enough is enough?" (*Daily Express* 25 July 2008). Britain is not the property of politicians for them to sell it to aliens in Europe. *The British Constitution Group* declares: "It is the British people's right to govern themselves, and not to be dictated to by an unelected European elite, which has no understanding of, or sympathy for our historic customs, our way of life, our system of governance, our laws, or our British Constitution. For several decades now, behind a shield of lies and deceit, the collective political establishment in Great Britain has conspired to deny us our democratic right to decide who will govern us; they have destroyed our legal system, vandalised our constitution that protects our freedoms, and repackaged them with a new legal and political order for which we have never asked, nor do we want. Whilst politicians are rewarded for their betrayal, the British people, in stark contrast, have had their rights, freedoms and liberties tossed aside. If we do not have the courage and fortitude to stand up for our freedoms, then we surely deserve to lose them. In that unhappy case, how will we face our children, our dependents and the memory of those that have died in defence of our freedoms?"

Now is the time for patriotic Britons, to push aside the corrupt politicians who have turned the Mother of Parliaments into a House of Shame, and reclaim our blessed country from the parasites in Europe. We must act now. We must not procrastinate our withdrawal from the European Union. The strife to procrastinate is the stride to fail. For procrastination leaves traces of regrets behind its heels.

If we want to free ourselves from the tentacles of Brussels, then let us reflect on the advice the Texas congressman Ron Paul offered to Americans. In Paul's *The Revolution* he writes: "Ours is not a fated existence, for nowhere is our destiny etched in stone. In the final analysis, the last line of defence in support of freedom and the Constitution consists of the people themselves. If the people want to be free, if they want to lift themselves out from underneath a state apparatus that threatens their liberties, squanders their resources on needless wars, destroys the value of their dollar, and spews forth endless propaganda about how indispensable it is and how lost we would all be without it, there is no force that can stop them. If freedom is what we want, it is ours for the taking. Let the revolution begin." We must be silent no more.

THE "SEER OF DUBLIN" AND DARWIN'S THEORY OF EVOLUTION
The "Unknown Truth" about the Evolution and Creationism Controversy

The "Unknown Irishman" made a contribution to the Evolution and Creationism controversy. Since the controversy is still raging on - with a discovery of "the fossilised remains of a small, lemur-like creature in Germany, believed to be some 43 million years old, which scientists claim could be the key to answering the ultimate question about human evolution - it is worthwhile to share with you, briefly, what the "Seer of Dublin" wrote on Charles Darwin's Theory of Evolution. This was a subject that captivated Victorians in the 19th century. It was the result of the debate between the scientist, Professor Thomas Huxley, and Bishop Samuel Wilberforce.

In the 21st century Charles Darwin is still held in high esteem by scientists, politicians and some Christians. The controversy surrounding his Theory of Evolution continues to capture our attention. In America, the debate on Evolution and Creationism is fierce. It was reported, that in 2005, a CBS poll found that 51 percent of Americans reject the theory of Evolution. As a result, "an exhibition celebrating the life of Darwin at the American Museum in New York failed to find a corporate sponsor for its £1.7million operating costs because companies were anxious not to take sides in the debate. Meanwhile, the creationists Museum in Cincinnati, Ohio, attracted £3million in donations." And according to "a study... by opinion panel research, nearly one in three students in Britain shuns scientific evidence of the origin of man; while 56 per cent believe in evolution theory." (Source: METRO 26 September 2006 *Losing faith in Science*)

Even some Christian churches and religious leaders in America and Britain adore Charles Darwin. In 2008, the Church of England made an unreasonable apology to Darwin for "misunderstanding" him. In Britain we have Darwin's image on our £10 note. In 2009, the world celebrated Darwin's 200th anniversary of his birth with Cultural Exhibitions and Radio and Television programmes. A commemorative coin was also issued in Britain to mark the anniversary.

Darwin's great-great-grandchild, the poet Ruth Padel, contributed an essay in honour of his ancestor. This piece of writing was published in the 12 December 2008 edition of *The Independent* newspaper. In this special essay, entitled *"Darwin's descendant,"* Ms Padel describes "her forebear as an extraordinary human being as well as the man who gave us the theory of evolution." She writes: "The debate about human origins was taken up by younger biologist like TH Huxley so that by the time Darwin addressed it in *The Descent of Man* (1874) all responsible thinkers had accepted evolution - including leaders of the Church. The Poet continues, "Lord Harris, a former Bishop of Oxford, whom I interviewed for my radio programmes, pointed out that in 1860, only one year after *Origin* came out – the year of Huxley's clash at Oxford with Bishop Wilberforce – a sermon was preached by Frederick Temple, headmaster of Rugby and later Archbishop of Canterbury, which effortlessly squared evolution with religion." Ms Padel then declared: "In 2009, we need to know Darwin better..."

Another Essay to honour Charles Darwin was published in the 27 December 2008 edition of *Daily Mail*. In this essay - *A HERO FOR OUR AGE* - Britain's leading anthropologist, Desmond Morris, "salutes Darwin" with this comment: "The point is, Charles Darwin was one of those rare individuals who devoted themselves entirely to the pursuit of knowledge, to the detriment of everything else in their lives. He was, and remains, one of our greatest ever thinkers – a man whose discovery changed the way we see the world."

We must ask the following questions:

- "Is it true that all "responsible thinkers" and scientists in the Victorian era submitted to Darwin's Theory of Evolution?
- "Why did Darwin's great-great-grandchild and the anthropologist Morris make no reference to the 'Great Tournament' between Gladstone and Huxley and the "Seer of Dublin"?

The reality is that, in the 21st century, the person the world needs to know better is NOT the agnostic Charles Darwin, but the great scholar among scholars, the Irishman who discredited Darwin's Theory of Evolution and 'destroyed' Darwin's bulldog, Professor Thomas Huxley. The world needs to know better the Knight Commander, the really 'wonderful man, who wrote about European Union, "the rarest of all political phenomenon" in history, before it materialised.

In his article, *We squander the great legacy of the Victorians at our peril,* Simon Heffer writes: "Those who fought Darwin, such as Bishop Wilberforce, were quickly and terminally wounded; this was the triumph of rationalism." (*The Daily Telegraph* 14 January 2009). The fact is not all who fought Darwin were wounded. It was "Darwin's bulldog," Professor Huxley, who was terminally wounded by an eminent Victorian.

On 10 March 2009, Andrew Marr began a three-part series on Darwin's Theory of Evolution which was screened on BBC. In the first episode, "Darwin's Dangerous Idea," Marr also spoke about the 1860 confrontation between Professor Huxley and Bishop Samuel Wilberforce. The outcome of the confrontation popularised Darwin's Theory of Evolution because of how the "hypocrite" Huxley was perceived to have 'floored' the Anglican Bishop. Marr concluded his documentary by telling the world: "Man is the great truth-seeking primate. Darwin has given us a great truth. And there is no going back."

I ask the question: "Why did Andrew Marr fail to mention Professor Huxley's confrontation with Prime Minister William Gladstone, and Huxley's "tournament" with the Prince of Detectives. Had Marr done his home-work on the Evolution and Creationism Controversy, he would have learnt that "Darwin's rottweiler" was destroyed by an intellectual among intellectuals. The fact is Darwin's so-called "Dangerous Idea" is just an idea - an agnostic's mental impression of the origin of man - and nothing more. Charles Darwin has given a BIG LIE to ignorant scientists and "blind" Church leaders - the Pharisees of the 21st century - who do not understand the Holy Bible.

In page 83-84 of *T H Huxley Scientist, Humanist and Educator*, which was first published in 1959, Dr Cyril Bibby writes: "It is easy today to conclude that two great minds might well have found something more important to debate than the details of pentateuchal cosmogony, but it is not difficult to understand why the clash was so sensational and led to such a vast subsidiary correspondence in the daily and periodical Press. The issue was at that time a major one: Gladstone sought to prove that the ground which science had made its own was of no strategic importance to religion, which indeed had prepared the way for the advance; Huxley replied that the Church was slyly seeking to cover an important retreat by glossographic smokescreen. Those who admitted that Genesis was in conflict with science Huxley regarded as honest and enlightened, those who maintained the literal infallibility of scripture he regarded as honest if impervious to argument, but those who tried to keep a foot in both camps he held in contempt."

In this biography of Thomas Huxley, Dr Bibby made much of Huxley's intelligence and his "attack on the Church for "intellectual dishonesty", and his 'destruction' of Gladstone and Bishop Wilberforce. On Gladstone, Dr Bibby writes: "…..when the French theologian Reville presented the Genesis story of creation as merely a charming primitive tradition, Gladstone claimed that its account of the serial production of the earth and its various orders of living things was affirmed by science itself. Unfortunately for Gladstone, his knowledge of geology was markedly inferior to Huxley's knowledge of Biblical exegesis, and the contest was too uneven." Dr Bibby went on to record how Huxley ridiculed Gladstone's intelligence. He writes: "…he (Gladstone)… displayed a far from average knowledge both of palaeontology and of textual criticism. Humbly admitting that it would be presumptuous (for him, Huxley) to instruct his adversary (Gladstone) on Indian and Greek philosophy, he (Huxley) nevertheless managed to suggest that Mr Gladstone could benefit consult that most excellent and by no means recondite source of information, the Encyclopaedia Britannica.' And, all in all, he (Huxley) managed to make the Prime Minister look something of a fool." (Source: *T H Huxley Scientists, Humanist and Educator* 1959)

On Huxley's clash with Bishop Samuel Wilberforce at Oxford Zoological Museum in 1860, Dr Bibby writes: "Soapy Sam spoke for full half an hour with inimitable spirit, emptiness and unfairness. And he made the fatal error of an offensive personal inquiry about Huxley's own simian ancestry. "The Lord hath delivered him into mine hands," the young biologist muttered to his neighbour, and he proceeded to enlist against his adversary the Victorians' high regard for truthfulness and good taste. His quiet gravity contrasting with the Bishop's smiling insolence, Huxley triumphed completely."

According to Dr Bibby, "The many accounts of the episode differ in detail, but nothing conflicts with that which Huxley himself sent to his friend in South Wales: *"Samuel thought it was a fine opportunity for chaffing a savan - However he performed the operation vulgarly & I determined to punish him - partly on that account and partly because he talked pretentious nonsense. So when I got up I spoke pretty much to the effect - that I had listened with great attention to the Lord Bishop's speech but had been unable to discover either a new fact or a new argument in it ---except indeed the question raised as to my personal predictions in the matter of ancestry----That it would not have occurred to me to bring forward such a topic as that for discussion myself, but that I was quite ready to meet the Right Revd. Prelate even on that ground----If then, said I the question is put to me would I rather have a miserable ape for a grandfather or a man highly endowed by nature and possessed of great means of influence & yet who employs those faculties & that influence for the mere purpose of introducing ridicule into a grave scientific discussion - I unhesitatingly affirm my preference for the ape. Whereupon there was inextinguishable laughter among the people - and they listened to the rest of my argument with the great attention.....I think Samuel will think twice before he tries a fall with men of science again.....I believe I was the most popular man in Oxford for full four & twenty hours afterwards." (*Source: *T H Huxley SCIENTIST, HUMANIST AND EDUCATOR)*

What amazes me is that Dr Bibby, like all the admirers of Professor Huxley, never mentioned a single word on Huxley's 'Tournament' with the "Seer of Dublin" on the very issue Gladstone raised - that Science and Genesis were perfectly in accord as regards the order in which life appeared upon our globe. In this particular 'confrontation' between Huxley and the "Forgotten servant of the British Crown" which took place in 1892, the "Unknown Irishman" exposed Huxley's ignorance on Sacred Scriptures and "floored" the Champion of Darwinism and put down "Darwin's bulldog." I urge the reader to examine chapter VII of the Irishman's book *In Defence: A Plea for the Faith.* The Knight Commander met Professor Huxley, the ablest and most bitter assailant of Genesis the world has ever known, on the ground of his own choosing and routed him. I hope this particular book and the other works of the Irishman, which I would share with you, would strengthen your faith in the Book of Genesis to dismiss the scientific community which claims man - a being with conscience - evolved from a brute. Has an animal any sense of right or wrong? Doesn't a seed produce its kind?

On 10 July 2009, Colm Keena reported in the Irish Times that Professor Janet Browne, a graduate in Zoology from Dublin's Trinity College, now the Aramont professor in the history of science at Harvard University, has become a leading authority on Darwin. Professor Browne told an audience in Trinity College, Dublin: "Evolutionary biology is the hottest topic alive at the moment. Stunning advances are being made. The momentum is great and increasing." The Harvard Professor was awarded an honorary degree at Trinity College. The leading authority on Darwin would be interested to know that, in the 19th century a Law graduate from Trinity College discredited Charles Darwin's theory of Evolution. This graduate subsequently "knocked out" the Champion of Darwinism, Professor Thomas Huxley, in a "tournament." He "slaughtered" Darwin's bulldog.

The works of this Irish scholar from Trinity College would bring to light the "unknown truth" about the Evolution and Creationism controversy - how the proud Champion of Darwinism, Professor Thomas Huxley, was defeated. The "Hero for our Age" is not Charles Darwin, but the Knight Commander who 'killed' Darwin's bulldog. The Future is uncertain to the world that believes in Darwin's Theory of Evolution. The future is certain to those who believe in the Knight's classic work which was published a year before Darwin passed away.

Finally, I hope this book would motivate the British and the Irish to have the confidence to confront their selfish politicians, who are determined to sell them into 'slavery' in Brussels and demand their release from 'bondage.' The Republic of Ireland might have gained economically from its membership of the European Union. The question is: "Is the future of the European Union bright or dark?" Would the Irish people be 'saved' in Europe if they commit their future to Jean Monnet's project? The European Union is the 'Trojan horse' of the 21st century. The Irish should reflect on the saying: "Fear the Greeks even when they offer gifts."

Francis S E Codjoe Jnr
London
September 2009

Before Theodor Herzl formed the Zionist Movement in 1896, an Irish had already written that the Jews would return to Palestine , and a political union of European nations would also follow.

The Nation of Israel was created in May 1948

The European Union was born in May 1950 with the Schuman Plan

The "Seer of Dublin": "Through the gradual unfolding, it may be of influences even now in operation; or far more probably as the outcome of some great Europe crisis in the future, this confederation of (European) nations shall be developed, and thus the stage will be prepared..."

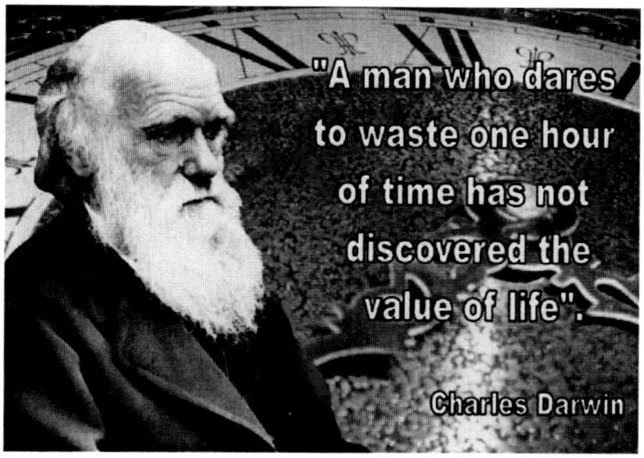

"EVOLUTION AND CREATIONISM CONTROVERSY":

The "Unknown Truth"
In the 19th century, the Scholar among Scholars "destroyed" 'Darwin's Bull-dog, Professor T Huxley.
"Huxley used pretentious phrases about science, and ungenerous sneers at those who believe the Bible. Huxley, the ablest and most bitter assailant of Genesis...was met on the ground of his own choosing and routed":

The "Seer of Dublin" writes: "Regarded as a theory to account for life, evolution is the widest folly; but as an hypothesis to account for the varied forms of life, it claims a hearing on its merits...The man who can give no account of his own existence is a fool; and he who denies a God can give no account of his existence."

"The horse may have been developed from a pig-like animal, and man may be "descended from a hairy quadruped furnished with a tail and pointed ears." But what direct proof is there that either the horse or the man was, in fact, developed or evolved in this way? The answer must be, Absolutely none. It is a matter of inference only..."

"How did life begin? And here evolution affords no answer, and must stand aside. Let the existence of life be taken for granted, and evolution may explain the rest....in the presence of a question that lies across the threshold of knowledge, science, the very personification of knowledge , turns agnostic and is dumb...."

The Prince of Detectives: "Darwin declares in the closing sentence of his treatise, "Man still bears in his bodily frame the indelible stamp of his lowly origin." But what account can be given of his moral nature? And what of his spiritual nature? To dismiss such considerations with few high-sounding phrases is to stultify ourselves by mere words. No reasonable account of them has ever been attempted. The phenomena of language again present insuperable difficulties which evolutionists studiously ignore. If man were the product of evolution we should confidently expect to find that, with advancing civilization. language would ever tend to gain in precision, to acquire new powers, and to become more elaborate; whereas it is well known fact that its tendency is to change in a direction the very opposite. Nor is this a peculiar feature of one language, but the universal law of all..." ***(The Buddha of Christendom.)***

"If the hypothesis of evolution be true, living matter must have arisen from not-living matter. Therefore life did originate thus, and the truth of evolution is established. Thus argues the professor and scientist. But the man who considers, reflects, hesitates, doubts, will call for the evidence; and finding there is none, he will reject the conclusion, and also, if necessary, the dependent hypothesis...... Besides being absolutely without evidence to give it external support, this hypothesis cannot support itself internally---cannot be framed into a coherent thought. It is one of those illegitimate symbolic conceptions, because they remain untested. Immediately an attempt is made to elaborate the idea into anything like a definite shape, it proves to be a pseud-idea, admitting of no definite shape. It implies the establishment of a relation in thought between nothing and something - a relation of which one term is absent - an impossible relation. The case is one of those where men do not believe, but rather believe they believe. For belief, properly so called, implies a mental representation of the thing believed; and no such representation is here possible." ***(A Doubter's Doubts About Science and Religion)***

The Evolution and Creationism Controversy was settled in the 19th century. Charles Darwin and his Theory of Evolution and all his "disciples" are irrelevant in the 21st century. What is relevant in our generation are the European Union and the works of the "Seer of Dublin."

Charles Darwin described Thomas Huxley "The king of men"

Prof. T Huxley: the Scientist, Humanist and Educator. "Darwin's bulldog"

Prime Minister William E. Gladstone

H. Spencer: The man who coined the phrase: "survival of the fittest"

The "Seer of Dublin" A scholar among scholars: "A man who cannot give no account of his own existence is a fool..."

He 'destroyed' Darwin's bulldog who was regarded a brilliant man.

Dr Cyril Bibby writes: "Huxley regarded those who admitted that Genesis was in conflict with science Huxley as honest and enlightened, those who maintained the literal infallibility of scripture he regarded as honest if impervious to argument, but those who tried to keep a foot in both camps he held in contempt." (T H Huxley 1959)

Scholars only comment on Huxley's clash with Bishop Wilberforce at Oxford Zoological Museum in 1860 and his attack on Gladstone – making Gladstone looked like a "fool." What about Huxley's tournament with the "Seer of Dublin"? The Champion of Darwinism was "knocked down."

The Prince of Detectives dismissed Prof. Huxley's assertion that Science is not accord with Genesis. He exposed Huxley's ignorance on Scriptures.

Introduction

"If the knowledge of the past be important, a knowledge of the future must be of far higher value still, in enlarging the mind and raising it above the littlenesses produced by a narrow and unenlightened contemplation of the present."
(RA)

In his biography of Jean Monnet, THE FIRST STATESMAN OF INTERDEPENCE, Francois Duchene writes: "the European Union is "the rarest of all phenomena" in history. And the former French Prime Minister, Dominique de Villepin, in an interview with the Financial Times, described the European Union as "the greatest political historic adventure of the last century."(Source Financial Times, 7 February 2007: *Europe 'must seize chance to get back to top'*).

The European Union has also been hailed the greatest success political story of our time. The American *TIME* magazine described the European Union "the Quiet miracle" that has brought 50 years of peace and prosperity into Europe. *TIME* added: "Today's Europe is the largest expanse of peace and widely shared prosperity in the world." According to *Newsweek*, another influential American magazine, "Europe is now a global super-power of world-historic importance, second to none in economic clout." And according to Stephen A Schuker, Professor of History at Virginia University, Alan Milward described the European Union "a rescuer of the nation-state." In view of the achievements of the European Union, "Can we be hopeful about Europe's future?" This was the question Pascal Lamy, a former EU Commissioner, raised in an article published in the Financial Times on 21 March 2007.

We know the past. We are familiar with the present. We don't know the future. Since we thirst to know the future, curiosity drives us to apply what we do know to attempt to discover what we don't know. Hence, in our anxiety to know what the future holds, some of us seek guidance from Palm Readers, Fortune tellers and Astrologers. Some consult mystics. Others daily patronise "Your Stars" column in our newspapers and magazines.

"Finis opus coronat." This is the classic saying which means "The end crowns the work." If this is the reality of all human endeavours, then we must ask these questions about the European Union – "The Quiet Miracle":

- What is the future of this "Quiet Miracle"- "the greatest political historic adventure?"
- What is the fate of the 500 million consumers in the biggest economic market in the world?
- What impact would the European Union have on the United States of America in particular, and mankind in general?
- What is the 'Soul of Europe' and the "Schuman Caveat"?
- Is the European Union 'alive' or 'dead'?

The answers to these questions were published in the 19th century by the native of Dublin. I have earlier mentioned that it was an Irishman who wrote about a political union of European nations: how it would develop, its character and future prospects before the French founding fathers of the European Community, Jean Monnet and Robert Schuman, were born in 1888 and 1886. This Ulsterman declared: *"If a knowledge of the past be important, a knowledge of the future is of far higher value still, in enlarging the mind and raising it above the littlenesses produced by a narrow and unenlightened contemplation of the present."*

We must, therefore, ask the following questions:

- Can we be hopeful of Europe's future?
- Is the future of the European Union bright or dark"?
- Does the future of Ireland and Great Britain lie in the European Union?"
- Should Great Britain and Ireland move to the "centre of Europe" to be at the "heart" of the European Project as suggested by politicians and political commentators?

Duchene, Jean Monnet's biographer, also writes: "Monnet's role in the birth of the European Community was an even complex phenomenon." The question persists: What is the future of this "complex phenomenon"? I would share with you what the 'Forgotten British public servant' recorded concerning the character and destiny of political Europe before the 'master builder' of European Community was conceived.

GOLBAL WARMING: THE THREAT FACING MANKIND?

It has been suggested by 'experts' that the single most important threat facing the human race and its future is "Climate Change" from global warming. I do not share this view. The critical issue of our time is the development of the European Union. It is this political alliance of European nations that would pose the supreme menace to mankind. The world would realise the danger when the European Union reaches its maturity and crowns its powerful Emperor. The Lisbon Treaty, which European leaders signed on 13 December 2007, has paved the way for the

King of Europe to enter the political arena to assume his 'majestic' role. Later on I will explain why "Climate Change" is not the major threat to our existence, and why the European Project is not the world's best hope for preventing the so-called global catastrophe from 'global warming' as suggested by some scientists, politicians and political commentators.

In his *Introduction to the European Union*, Dick Leonard tells the reader that Adolf Hitler was the "Catalyst" of the European Community and Jean Monnet was the "Architect." It was Jean Monnet who provided the seeds of European Union to the French Foreign Minister, Robert Schuman, to sow them. Schuman planted the seeds on 9 May 1950 when he unveiled the plan for the formation of the European Coal and Steel Community. France and Germany started this Enterprise. Later on, Belgium, Italy, Luxembourg and The Netherlands joined the project.

Francois Dutchene described Jean Monnet the "Spiritual Father of Europe"– the brain behind the European Project. The fact is the idea of European integration had already been discussed before the advent of Jean Monnet. Prominent among the pioneers of a federal Europe were the Austro-Hungarian diplomat, Richard Kouden hoave-Kalergi, Konrad Adenauer, the first Chancellor of the Federal Republic of Germany, and the French statesman Aristide Briand. It was after the Second World War that the 'soil' for European integration became fertile for Jean Monnet to provide the seeds of this "fruit" (European Union) to be planted by Robert Schuman.

In view of the 'success' of the European Project, Duchene described Jean Monnet as "probably the one thoroughgoing internationalist so far who has made a marked impact on history." The French statesman has also been described "the apostle of European unity". Preaching his 'prophetic gospel' of a federal Europe, Monnet declared: "Once a Common Market has been created, then a political union will come naturally." And Walter Hallstein, a German Economist, and a former European Commission President, endorsed Monnet's 'wisdom' and Adenauer's vision of a United States of Europe. He declared: "Make no mistake, we are not in business, we are in politics. We are building the United States of Europe." (*TIME* Magazine)

In his *Introduction* to Jean Monnet's Memoirs, which was published in 1978, George W Ball, the American Lawyer and undersecretary of state for John F. Kennedy and Lyndon B. Johnson, who became an advisor to the European Economic Community, writes: "Jean Monnet's transcendent purpose was to transform Europe and he has quite literally succeeded. Not only has he been the architect of the European Economic Community but also its master builder." Jean Monnet has become the "god of Europe".

Here is an extract from the Introduction to the book *Testimonials in Memory of Jean Monnet* to confirm Monnet's status in Europe. "In 1988, on the occasion of the 100th anniversary of Jean Monnet's birth, the European Community decreed the "Jean Monnet European year" and empowered the Friends of Jean Monnet Association to communicate any information which would increase the awareness of Jean Monnet's work and to ensure that his name live on. Francois Mitterrand, the President of France, decided to transfer his ashes to the Pantheon. The ceremony took place on 9th November 1988 in the presence of the Chiefs of State and of Government of all the European Community countries. The Association persuaded more than 1500 French and European cities to name public places after Jean Monnet. Among them were many high schools and secondary schools."

THE INTRIGUING QUESTION: WHY WAS JEAN MONNET NOT CONSIDERED FOR SAINTHOOD?

The French founding fathers of the European Union, Jean Monnet and Robert Schuman, were Roman Catholics. The Vatican once attempted to put Schuman on a "fast track" to sainthood for being a "deeply religious" man and for his contribution towards European unity – a project which Vatican is enthusiastically associated with. For Pope Benedict XVI has already confirmed the Roman Catholic Church's support for the European Project. For example, in a visit to Austria in September 2007, the spiritual leader of the 1.2 billion Catholics told the world that the purpose of his trip was "partly in order to underline the essential contribution that the Catholic Church is able and willing to give to European unification….."

A section of the French community, bolstered by the support of President Chirac, vigorously campaigned for Schuman's sainthood. Perhaps they needed Vatican to bless their European project. After all, most of the leading statesmen who advocated for a federal Europe were Catholics. Among them were Paul Henri-Spaak, former Prime Minister of Belgium, Alcide de Caperi, former Prime Minister of Italy and Dr. Konrad Adenauer, the first German Chancellor.

We must ask the questions: "Why was Jean Monnet not recommended for sainthood? Why was he denied that honour? Monnet was also a Catholic like Schuman. Moreover, Monnet was the master-brain behind the "European phenomenon," not Schuman. I will throw a light on this "seemingly" unfair treatment of the "spiritual god-father" of European Community.

THE FUTURE OF EUROPE

59 years after the birth of the European Union, political leaders in Europe are still struggling to determine the future of the European Enterprise. 59 years after the dawn of the European "phenomenon," Europeans still do not understand the European Project. 59 years after the European Construction "the people of Europe are reluctant to credit the EU with their good fortune" (Financial Times 23 March 2007) Why? Because, European leaders, who were supposed to have been well-informed on the European Project, lacked understanding of the project due to their superficial knowledge on European integration. Consequently, they have failed to explain in detail the purpose of the European Union and its future prospects.

Not surprisingly, Chancellor Angela Merkel, in a significant speech in the German Parliament, said: "We must...critically review the state of the European project. We need to put people at the centre and explain what Europe means for their jobs, prosperity, social security, health-care and old age...I don't want to dramatise things, but I believe a new rationale is more necessary than ever" (Source: The Guardian Friday 12 May 2006: *Merkel calls for fundamental review of European Mission).*

We must ask the following questions:

- Why didn't Angela Merkel initiate the "new rationale" herself? Or the "new rationale" was Merkel's plot with the European leaders to rebrand the discredited European Constitution and impose it on the people of Europe.
- "Did European leaders put "people at the centre" when they denied Europeans a say on the Lisbon Treaty - a document that would have impact on their lives?

Words are vague and valueless if they do not serve as portraits of living acts.

Premier Tony Blair, also confirmed the uncertain future of the European Union. On 16 June 2006, he told an EU summit in Brussels: "The EU needed a new set of rules" to stop it grinding to a halt with 27 or more members." (Source: Financial Times, 17 – 18 June 2006 *Europe's summiteers duck the big issues*). Since his speech, what significant contribution was Blair able to make to prevent "EU grinding to a halt"?

On 19 May 2006, Peter Riddell, a political analyst for *The Times,* highlighted the unknown future of the European Union in his article *"Europe will not go away, so let's start discussing its future."* And the former French Prime Minister, Dominique de Villepin, having listed some of the crisis facing the European Union, declared:

"There is crisis about the meaning of Europe: Is the European project just about the opening up of a big single market, or does Europe still have a real political vocation and ambition?" (Financial Times 7 February 2007). What contribution did Dominique de Villepin make to resolve the "crisis about the meaning of Europe"? I repeat: words are vague and valueless if they do not serve as portraits of living acts.

After the launch of "The Schuman Plan," which created the European Coal and Steel Community, Konrad Adenauer confessed the uncertain future of Europe. In his Memoirs, Dr. Adenauer records: "It is my opinion and belief that the parliaments of six European Countries (Belgium, France, Italy, Germany, Luxembourg and the Netherlands) which will have to deal with this European Coal and Steel Community realise exactly what it is all about and that in particular they realise that the political goal, the political meaning of the European Coal and Steel Community, is infinitely larger than its economic purpose ....I believe that for the first time in history....countries want to renounce part of their sovereignty, voluntarily and without compulsion, in order to transfer the sovereignty to a supranational structure...In my opinion the European Union had a past but no future." The German Chancellor continues: "I regarded The Schuman Plan and the European Defence Community as preliminary steps to a political unification of Europe."

The future of the European Union - "the rarest of all political phenomena in history," has become elusive to Europeans and their political leaders. Because of this problem, Minette Marrin posed a question in the 29 May 2005 edition of *The Sunday Times*. In an article titled *"It is getting hard to avoid the question: what **is** Europe for?"* the Columnist asked: "What is Europe for? She continued: "That is the simple question which underlines the whole project but is rarely asked and rarely answered...If you ask Europhiles what the European project is for; they will respond with incredulity and perhaps even with mild contempt..." And the Columnist, Andrew Rawnsley, made the same observation with his remark: "When I ask politicians in London how they will sell practical benefits from the European constitution to the typical British voter, they almost invariably sigh and change the subject." (*The Observer,* 2 May 2005). Why the evasion?

Dr. Timothy Garton Ash, in his article, *"Today's European Union is 27 states in search of a story,* writes: "...Everyone knows that, beneath the surface, political Europe is not in a party mood about itself. The Community is morose, ill-tempered and uncertain of its future" (*The Guardian,* 4 January 2007). It is clear from the above commentaries that European politicians have no hint what Europe is for and they have no clear view of its future. This ignorance stems from their superficial knowledge of the source of the European Union. They have been "blinded" by the popular view: "European Union evolved from the wreckage of the Second World War."

The truth is that Jean Monnet and all the European Statesmen who dreamt of a federal Europe did not have a clue where their "Great Titanic" would land. Jean Monnet and his 'disciples' knew what they planed to achieve, and yet did not understand what they were planning. With all their efforts to construct a United States of Europe, they were not aware that they were unconsciously acting as instruments to bring to pass what a brilliant Irish lawyer had already published about Europe and its destiny.

NEW LIGHT IN EUROPE

Brian Sewell, in his article, "*Why our voices must be heard,*" writes: "On 5 June 1975 the British voted in their first and only referendum to confirm our union with the European Economic Community. It was hotly and publicly debated....Deprived of any further opportunities to vote on European matters, the nation has become less well-informed. Without the stimulus of debate we have been denied information; without the stimulus of a referendum...we have slipped into ignorance, indifference and mistrust." Mr Sewell continues; "Europe is a matter far beyond party politics, as was recognised by the referendum of 1975. But since then no one much under 50 has been allowed to express an opinion through the ballot box" (*Evening Standard* 3 June 2003). Why have politicians denied the British people a say on their membership of a political union?

It seems politicians and the 'experts' at the heart of the European project in Brussels have made the case for the existence of the European Union and it is not to be disputed. I repeat the words of the "Unknown" British public servant: "No one who has much experience of judicial inquiries is ever surprised to find that a case which seems convincing when presented *ex-parte* breaks down under cross-examination or is shattered by opposing evidence." The British and the Irish must know the 'opposing evidence' to the 'case' made by the 'experts' on European integration. It is my burden to help. For the Good Book says: "The first to present his case seems right, till another comes forward and questions him" (Proverbs 18:17).

To every problem there is a solution. But where a particular problem cannot be solved, it means the requisite knowledge out of which the solution could be drawn has not yet been acquired. I will throw a new light on the European Project for the benefit of Americans, Europeans, and the rest of the world, and in particular for the Irish and my fellow British citizens, who have been unfairly labelled the "most ignorant" and "isolated" in Europe, because of their strong euro-scepticism. This information would assist Britons to uphold their 'contempt' for the European Project which lacks democratic legitimacy and political accountability. This "new light" on the European Enterprise would also help Americans, Europeans and political intellectuals to have a different perspective of Jean Monnet's vision of a "federated Europe."

Britain's deep euro-scepticism might have caused her "isolation" in Europe and the loss of influence in the corridors of power in Brussels. However, Britain's "isolation" does not necessarily imply that all the British people are ignorant of the truth: what the European Union is for and its future. Truth is always isolated from falsehood. For truth is an 'island of light' which is secluded from the 'sea of darkness' to shine brightly in the fog of falsehood. Our "tiny island" risks its existence if it jumps into the "Great European Ocean" which is infested with "sea monsters." By providence, nature created our great 'Island' to protect it from "infection."

JEAN MONNET: THE "SPIRITUAL GOD-FATHER" OF EUROPEAN COMMUNITY

The popular view among historians, politicians and most political commentators is that the French Statesman, Jean Monnet, was the master-brain behind the European Project. Henry H. H. Remark, Professor of West European Studies at Indiana University, writes: *"...against all odds", Monnet was able to achieve "what nobody else has been able to do since Charlemagne: the functioning structure of European Community (EC)....without him it would not have happened."* (Source: The European Union From Jean Monnet to the Euro pages 57-58).

Because of Jean Monnet's status as "The Father of Europe," and having been also described as "the Father of transatlantic partnership," French politicians have assumed prominent roles in the affairs of the European Union. For example, the columnist, Peter McKay, wrote: "France created the EU principally to serve France" (*Daily Mail* 27 March 2006). And a leading article in the 29 May 2005 edition of *The Sunday Times* stated: "...For more than 50 years France has been at the forefront of European integration. Charles de Gaulle's haughty rejection of Britain's attempts to join in the 1960's showed that the real power in Europe lay in Paris not Brussels....The EU constitution was drawn under the haughty Valery Giscard d'Estaing, and its intent was to secure France's role at the heart of Europe". And when the European Constitution was initially rejected in 2005 by the French and the Dutch, the same French were given a crucial role to salvage parts of the abandoned constitution. This French role in the European project was confirmed at a secret Europe Ministers' meeting held in Madrid on 26 January 2007 to plan the revival of the discredited EU constitution. The Spanish Europe Minister, Alberto Navarro, declared: "The position of the French and the Dutch are crucial. They are founder members of the EU. If their objections can be reconciled with those of the 18 that have ratified, the remaining nations will be under pressure to follow suit."
And Gideon Rachman, commenting on the criticisms Nicolas Sarkozy and Segolene Royal made against the European single currency (the euro) during the 2007 French Presidential election campaign, reported: "The French created the European Union, so it would be appropriate if they destroyed it". According to the

Columnist, if you listened to the arguments made by the two presidential candidates, it would sound as if they intended "taking a sledgehammer to the Common European home built by their compatriots Jean Monnet, Robert Schuman and Jacques Delors." Mr Rachman concluded his article with this interesting remark: "France is married to the euro and the EU - and divorce is still far too big a step to contemplate. But the French are behaving like a spouse who has fallen out of love and is not shy of letting everybody know about it. The long-term outlook for marriage like that is rarely good." (Source: *Financial Times* 10 April 2007 *"How the French are falling out of love with the eurozone"*)

In Jean Monnet's biography, *The First Statesman on Interdependence,* Francois Duchene writes: "Monnet... alone linked up the whole European chain of being the conceptual background to the tiniest tactical detail...He coloured the European idea to an exceptional degree with his personality....Monnet proved the most creative of this small band...He was arguably the one thoroughgoing internationalist so far who has made a marked impact on history."

Who was Jean Monnet? What was "Monnet's personality" which coloured the European idea? I will examine these issues in due course.

The late American President, John F Kennedy, also admired John Monnet. According to Duchene, in 1963, Kennedy declared: "By a constructive idea, Monnet had done more to unite Europe in twenty years than all the conquerors in a thousand." In that year (1963) the American President awarded Monnet the Freedom Medal as founder of the European Coal and Steel Community." (Source: *European Union From Jean Monnet to the Euro* page 94) In 1975, Dr

Henry Kissinger, the former US Secretary of State, presented the Grenville Clark Prize to Jean Monnet in Paris. Kissinger applauded the French statesman: "I want to tell you (Jean Monnet) that the men of the present generation who are in charge of political affairs regard your vision as well-founded. They see that it is on the point of being fulfilled as you originally conceived it. The creation of a united Europe seems imminent. The United States gives it full support." (Source: Jean Monnet: Memoirs 1978 page 498). In his 15 November 1975 speech to present the prize to Jean Monnet, Dr. Henry Kissinger said: *"There are few men or women of whom one can say that their life gave a new turning point to the time in which they lived. There are still fewer who were able to rise above dealing with daily affairs to conceive of an ideal to which they then worked to give substance. I believe that we can say, without the risk of error, that no man in the world has marked and modified the political life of our time more than the one whom we are honouring today. The great works of history have never been anything other than dreams before becoming realities. At the end of the War, Mister Monnet had dreamed that from destruction and ruins a united Europe might emerge; and that in concert with the United States, it would work in a spirit of independence allied to a desire for cooperation aimed at the greatest good for all free peoples. What was in 1946 only an absurd idea is today a tangible reality. All those among us whom Mister Monnet charmed, criticized, inspired and led in his wake when our imagination was unable to entirely follow his own, are entitled to be proud on this occasion. [...]. We are all grateful to you not only for what you have accomplished on the political level, but for having demonstrated so many human qualities; and for having shown such wisdom and such patience."* (Source: *Testimonials in Memory of Jean Monnet*)

And *TIME* Magazine described Jean Monnet as a person who had no formal education. Yet, "the world's most brilliant economists" regarded him as their "peer." According to *TIME,* Monnet "never joined a political party, but parliamentarians all over Europe flocked to his sermons." Jean Monnet's portrait was painted on postage stamps in France, Spain, Germany, Luxembourg and other nations in Europe.

We must ask the question: "Was Jean Monnet really a man of vision who should be adored in America, Britain, Europe, Ireland and around the globe? Because of Jean Monnet's perceived prominent role in the creation of the European Community, this 'apostle of European unity' has become an "immortal soul" in European institutions and politics. Monnet is 'worshipped' by those who subscribe to European integration as the 'best thing' to have happened to Europeans and Americans. For George Ball, the politician who worked with Johnson and Kennedy, and became a personal lawyer for Monnet, had a conviction that "an integrated Europe in partnership with the United States of America was the best way of defending the West". Brussels finance all kinds of educational programmes in honour of "Mister Europe." We have "The Jean Monnet Action" that covers about 60 countries throughout the world. They offer Jean Monnet courses as part of their curricula. And it is not surprising that *Jean Monnet Centre of Excellence* is also established in Russia.

THE 'UNKNOWN TRUTH' ABOUT EUROPEAN UNION AND THE 'FORGOTTEN SON' OF IRELAND

Sometimes truth hurts, but it also soothes. The truth about why an economic community of 6 European countries has developed into a political union – a *"United kingdom of Europe"* - was foretold by an Irishman before "Mister Europe" was born in 1888. This "Forgotten Irish" wrote with absolute confidence that a confederation of European nations would be developed through an European crisis before the Americans launched the Marshall Plan in 1947 after the Second World War. It was The Marshall Plan that urged Europeans to unite to rebuild their shattered economy. This eventually paved the way for the creation of the European Coal and Steel Community – an economic platform for the political unification of Europe. Witness the words of Schuman: *"The pooling of coal and steel production should immediately provide for the setting up of common foundations for economic development* ***as a first step in the federation of Europe,*** *and will change the destinies of those regions which have long been devoted to the manufacture of munitions of war, of which they have been the most constant victims."* (Emphasis mine)

This "Unknown Ulsterman" did not only predict the European confederacy before it became a reality. He recorded that a political union of European nations would be preceded by a major political event in history - the rebirth of the nation of Israel. He foretold the restoration of the Jews to Palestine even before the concept of "Political Zionism" was espoused in 1882 by the Russian Jew, Leo Pinsker. This concept lead to the establishment of Zionist Movement in 1896 by Theodor Herzl. And the Balfour Declaration of 2 November 1917 eventually resulted in the reincarnation of the state of Israel in 1948. Whatever this Irishman published about political integration of European nations and its character has been fulfilled. We can conclude that by virtue of his unusual foresight, it is likely what he recorded about the future of Europe would also come to pass. I have already stated the Lisbon Treaty has created the avenue for his prediction of Europe's future to be fulfilled. The Treaty of Lisbon (The European Constitution) is the last "piece" which perfectly fits the "European Jig-Saw Puzzle."

THE ENGLISH AND THE IRISH "TRUTH"

I would now share with the French and the Germans, the two prominent founding members of the European Union, the English and Irish "truth" about their project - what the "Unknown Ulsterman" recorded about the restoration of the Jews to Palestine and the development of an European confederacy before Jean Monnet, the French architect of European Community, was conceived, and when the German Statesman, Dr Konrad Adenauer, was about six years old. By bringing this "inconvenient truth" to light, I hope the French would not boast about France's contribution to the European Union, and German politicians would think twice before 'bullying' the Irish and the British.

Had European leaders and political commentators and intellectuals in America, Britain, Europe and Ireland together with the Roman Catholic Church analysed what the "Sage of Ulster" published_concerning European integration and its destiny.

- Pope John Paul II would have thought twice before advocating for "a new united Europe from the Atlantic to the Urals" during his visit to Austria in 1983. The Pontiff would not have repeated the same theme in his address to the European Parliament in Strasbourg in 1988.
- Pope Benedict XVI would not have expressed any opinion on Turkey's membership of the European Union. And neither would he have supported the European Constitution by suggesting that the signing of the Lisbon Treaty was a step to boost the process of building the "European home..."
- Cardinal Cormac Murphy-O'Connor, the former spiritual leader of Roman Catholics in England and Wales, would not have suggested in his Cumberland Lodge lecture on 14 April 2007, that "The Church and State should help Europe grow" (Source: The Times).
- The Catholic Archbishop of Dublin, Most Rev. Diarmuid Martin, would not have suggested that the future and identity of Ireland are "clearly and irrevocably bound with that of Europe," and that "Ireland cannot evade its European calling nor shrink from its European responsibilities." (Irish Times Saturday, 15 November 2008)
- President Barack Obama would not have expressed any view on Turkey's membership of the European Union to incur the "wrath" of President Nicolas Sarkozy, that the American President should not poke his nose into European Union business. (Source: The Times 6 April 2009 *"Leave Turkey's bid to join EU to us, Sarkozy warns Obama."*)
- Charles de Gaulle would not have rejected Britain's applications to join the Common Market in 1963 and 1967.
- Dean Acheson, the post-war US Secretary of State, would not have thought that Britain made a historic error by not joining the European Coal and Steel Community (*TIME* 19 March 2007).
- President John F Kennedy would not have awarded the Freedom Medal to Jean Monnet in 1963. And Dr Henry Kissinger would also not have presented the Grenville Clark Prize to Monnet in 1975.
- A Spanish Prime Minister would not have patronised the French by saying: "Europe cannot advance without France."
- Jacques Chirac, the former French President, would not have walked out from an European Union summit because a Frenchman decided to express himself in English instead of French. Chirac would also not have

threatened to "scrap Britain's hard-fought exemption from European Union rules governing the maximum working week..." (Financial Times 8 November 2006).

- Giscard d'Estaing, the "Father of the European Constitution," would not have suggested that France and the Dutch should be given a second opportunity to vote on a rejected constitution (*Financial Times* 23 May 2006). And he would not have boasted about the repackaged EU Constitution which was imposed on the masses.
- The former French Interior Minister, now President Nicholas Sarkozy, would not have proudly suggested that a mini European treaty should be introduced and ratified by politicians without a mandate from the electorate. Sarkozy would also not have suggested that Britain and Ireland should share one Commissioner. This is a politician who emblazoned his party's message on flip-flops and condoms (Source: The Guardian 23 August 2006*: "Sarkozy woos French voters with flops and signed condoms*). And President Sarkozy and his EU partners would have trembled to suggest that Ireland should vote again when they rejected the Lisbon Treaty in a popular vote. Sarkozy would not have dared to insult the Irish as "fools" for dumping the Lisbon Treaty.
- Romano Prodi, the former Italian prime minister, who was once the President of the European Commission, would also have thought twice before patronising France that without them it would be "impossible to have any progress" on relaunching the rejected European Constitution. (Source: Financial Times 7 November 2006: *EU needs to press on with enlargement, Prodi warns*)
- The Labour Government of Tony Blair and Gordon Brown would not have planned to spend "millions in a bid to brainwash" a jaded British electorate with superficial and irrelevant issues for them to embrace the European Union (Source: The Mail on Sunday *"You WILL love Europe…by order of the PM"*.
- Gordon Brown would have instructed his Foreign Secretary, David Miliband, to tear the Lisbon Treaty into pieces.
- German politicians would not have threatened a British Prime Minister with an ejection to an outer circle of Europe, if Britain rejected a revised constitution – "a deceased parrot". What is in the "inner circle of Europe"? (The Daily Telegraph 7 December 2007).
- The German Ambassador, Wolfgang Ischinger, would not have insulted the British public by saying the German Chancellor, Angela Merkel, plans to deny voters a chance to reject the Brussels' master-plan by saying: "We want to preserve significant portions of the document without a second referendum." (This was a document two of the founding nations of the European Project rejected in a popular vote) (The Sun, Wednesday, January 3, 2007: *German plot over EU treaty*).

- The British Labour Government would not have entertained the idea of replacing the United Kingdom flag with the European Union flag (Daily Express 7 March 2007). The EU Flag has the "spell" of the "Great Harlot."
- Denis MacShane, the former Europe Minister, would not have considered Sir Anthony Eden's decision to veto Britain negotiating and signing the Treaty of Rome in 1957 a "blunder" (The Independent 21 March 20047). The blunder of all blunders would be for British politicians to ignore what a distinguished British public servant wrote about European integration and its future. Had Mr MacShane read what this brilliant servant of the British Crown published on "European confederacy and its prospects, he would have examined his thoughts before describing himself "an unashamed enthusiast for Europe."
- Sir Stephen Wall, who formerly advised Tony Blair on European Union, would not have quoted Jean Monnet's criticism of Britain, that in not joining the original European Community in 1957, Britain has paid the "price of victory" (Financial Times 21 March 2007). Monnet only had a blurred vision of European unity. Had "Mister Europe" read the 14th edition of the Irishman's work, which was released in the same year the Treaty of Rome was signed, he would not have criticised Britain.
- The Independent newspaper would not have adorned the front page of its 21 March 2007 edition with the 12 stars of Europe with this message: *"As the European Union celebrates its anniversary 50 reasons to love the EU"*. I respond: "There is one simple reason to hate the "EU Titanic." It was doomed before its construction began on 9 May 1950. For the "50 reasons" to love the European Union are just "extravagant cargo" on Jean Monnet's luxurious "Titanic" steaming towards an "ice-berg."

Had President Sarkozy studied what the British Secret Service Agent wrote about political Europe and its future before his 'Father', Jean Monnet, was born, he would not have dared to lecture Britons about remaining outside the euro and the Schengen zone during his visit to England in March 2008. And Gordon Brown would have dismissed Nicolas Sarkozy's rhetoric: "We need Britain and France at the heart of Europe, a global Europe that is reforming, open, flexible, outward-looking." Question: "What is the heart of Europe"?

- Had the intelligent and 'widely-read' Gordon Brown read what the 'Anglicanised Irishman of Scotch extraction' published on political Europe and its destiny, he would have withdrawn Britain from the European Union the minute he entered Number 10 Downing Street.

BARROSO'S FLATTERY AND PATRONAGE

Had Jose Manuel Barroso, the President of the European Commission, studied the works of the "Sage of Ulster," the political scientist from Portugal would have examined his thoughts before patronising Britain in his Hugo Young Memorial Lecture: *"Seeing through the Hallucinations: Britain and Europe in the 21st century."* In his speech at Chatham House, the Portuguese declared: "Britain is a lead player in Europe. On climate change...the UK's support was vital....On security and defence the UK was...the biggest contributor of troops to European security. The next head of the EU's military staff will be British... On Africa, Prime Minister Blair has shown a clear commitment, making it a priority of the British presidency of the EU and G8...On open economies and competitiveness, the UK was a driving force for the creation of the single market and has been a leader in pushing for open trade...."

Barroso continued with his flattery, "...The UK is playing a central role. That is good for the EU, and I think good for the UK....The UK now finds itself at the centre of efforts to build a successful open and global Europe. ...The UK's role in developing Europe is a vital role and the UK can take pride in its contribution. And yet it sometimes seems reluctant to do so. This may be because of your native modesty... The UK will always have influence in Europe. Its size, its economic power and its international networks will ensure that".

The European Union Chief concluded his clever "sales presentation" with the following questions:

- "Does the UK want to shape a positive agenda which reflects its own agenda, or be dragged along as a reluctant power?
- "Does the United Kingdom want to continue to drive from the centre or return to sulking from the peripheral?

The choice is ours to make; but not the one Barroso would like. The United Kingdom does not need to be dragged into a "Project" which neither its architect nor his 'disciples' have a clue of its future." Mr Barroso: The choice is ours: Britain does not need to be either at the centre or the peripheral of an undemocratic political union which operates in secrecy and is not accountable to the people who feed it. The British people do not need Monnet's "Luxurious Titanic." I repeat: had the President of the European Commission studied the brilliant Barrister's publication on European integration before his "hero," Jean Monnet, was born, he would not have asked the questions he raised. Is Barroso aware that this Irish Barrister listed Portugal and Spain as members of a political union of European nations over 105 years before these two countries joined the European Community in 1986? Barroso should have done his homework on European integration before giving a lecture at Chatham House.

During his lecture, the Boss of European Bureaucracy in Brussels (BEBB) was selective in mentioning Robert Schuman's contribution to the European Project. Mr. Barroso referred to only a section of "The Schuman Plan." The ultimate aim of the "Schuman Plan" was to lay the foundation for a federal Europe. The economic plan which created the European Coal and Steel Community was, in the words of Schuman, "the preliminary step to the political unification of Europe." Schuman echoed the voice of his predecessor, Aristide Briand, the French Foreign Minister, who, in 1929, declared: "Among people who are geographically grouped together like the peoples of Europe, there must exist a sort of federal link." And in 1952, after Schuman had launched his economic plan, Dr. Konrad Adenauer confirmed the idea of European Federation with this statement: "...I regarded the Schuman Plan and the European Defence Community as a preliminary step to a political unification of Europe."

JEAN MONNET'S VISION

We know Jean Monnet was the brain behind the Schuman Plan. And the goal of Schuman's proposal for the creation of the European Cole and Steel Community was to lay the foundation for a federal Europe. Monnet wanted Europe to be "fused" together. His vision was: "Once a Common Market has been created, then a political union will come naturally". In his Memoirs, Monnet writes: *"I have no doubt, for my part, that a confederation will one day lead to a federation. But for the moment, is it possible to go further? I cannot say that it is. Meanwhile, the confederation would have the very great advantage of assuring public opinion in our countries that they have joined an entity which is not only economic but political, and that they are* therefore *part of something bigger than any of their countries alone."*

Witness the comments some scholars recorded in *The European Union: From Jean Monnet to the Euro.* Joan Hoff, Director of the Contemporary History Institute and Professor of History at Ohio University and Richard K Vedder, a distinguished Professor of Economics at the same University, stated: "As early as 1943, Monnet, an official in the exiled French Liberation movement, wrote to Charles de Gaulle urging the establishment of a European "federation" or some form of European unity encompassing a common economic unit." And Professor Henry H H Remak, Professor of Comparative Literature, Germanic and West European Studies at Indiana University, also recorded: "Monnet laid the ground work for a federated Europe."

A federal Europe has been the ultimate ambition of European politicians - including Romano Prodi, the former Italian Prime Minister, and Dominic de Villepin, the former French Cabinet Minister. They have openly expressed their views about the federal goal of Europe. In an interview with the Financial Times on 6 February 2007, Mr de Villepin commented on the crisis that had engulfed the

European Project. He declared: "Is the European project just about the opening up of a big single market, or does Europe still have a real political vocation and ambition?"

Because of the cynical purpose of the Schuman Plan, Jean Monnet concealed it from the British Prime Minister Clement Atlee. Monnet feared that Britain would sabotage his Federal dream. For Christopher Booker and Dr Richard North revealed in *The Great Deception*, that it was Paul-Henri Spaak, the Belgian Prime Minister, "who urged on his friend Monnet the idea, that the most effective way to disguise their project's political purpose was to conceal it behind a pretence that it was concerned only with economic co-operation, based on dismantling trade barriers, a Common Market". It was this same Spaak, who once said: "We (the European institutions) do not want committee. We have too many already. What we want is a man of sufficient stature to hold the allegiance of all people, and to lift us out of the economic morass in which we are sinking. Send us such a man and he be god or the devil, we will receive him." Yes! Europe will receive their hero at the appointed time. The Lisbon Treaty has created the platform for the arrival of the 'man of sufficient stature,'-the political genius - to lead Europe to the Wonder Land of Peace and Prosperity.

From what we have learnt about the Schuman Plan and its main goal, it is, therefore, disingenuous for British politicians to create the impression that the European Union is just an economic project. The fact is the goal of Jean Monnet's vision of a united Europe was to create a federal Europe with a President. And Monnet made this clear in his Memoirs with this remark: *"Since nothing could be done for the present, why not construct grandiose plans for the distant future? Our approach was very different. We believed in starting with limited achievements, establishing de facto solidarity, from which a federation would gradually emerge. I have never believed that one day Europe would be created by some political mutation, and I thought it wrong to consult the peoples of Europe about the structure of a community of which they had no practical experience."* Witness the comments Jose Manuel Barroso made about Jean Monnet: "Monnet's idea of European unity was seized upon by French Foreign Minister Robert Schuman and German Chancellor Konrad Adenauer... The power of Monnet's gradualist vision means that it still serves as a blueprint for European integration today." (TIME *60 Years of Heroes* 13 November 2006). This is precisely what the Lisbon Treaty was designed to achieve – to create a federated Europe with its President and Foreign Minister – so called High Representative - to fool the British, the Irish and Europeans.

JOSE MANUEL BARROSO AND THE HUGO YOUNG MEMORIAL LECTURE

Let us return to Barroso's lecture at Chatham House. The head of the European machinery in Brussels rightly mentioned Jean Monnet as a co-founding father of the European Enterprise. Why didn't he reveal in his *Hugo Young Lecture* that Robert Schuman was not dedicated to Monnet's "big idea" of a United States of Europe? For in Monnet's biography, Duchene writes: "He (Schuman) and Monnet were not at one on supranationality. For Schuman, the plan existed to solve the immediate Franco-German problem. For Monnet it was a first step to a united Europe. Schuman accepted supranationality for the plan because there was no alternative, but ***was not committed.***" (Emphasis mine)

Jose Manuel Barroso (the "BEBB") was anxious about how Britain would pull its weight behind Brussels to make the European Union work. But I find it puzzling that the President of the European Commission, an 'expert' on European integration, did not mention a single word in his 4388 word-speech on the crucial advice Robert Schuman delivered to the European Parliament in 1958. This "advice", which I term it "The Schuman Caveat", was vital for the survival of the European Project. Why did the EU Boss fail to make any reference to "The Schuman Caveat"? Was it ignorance or a deliberate attempt to deny the British public a significant information about the European Enterprise? Robert Schuman did not give Europe a "blank cheque" when, on 9 May 1950, he endorsed Monnet's plan for a federal Europe. We will learn more about "The Schuman Caveat."

THE PURPOSE OF THE "CORE PURPOSE" AND THE ABSURDITY OF ALL ABSURDITIES

The former Portuguese Prime Minister, in his *Hugo Young Memorial Lecture,* outlined the main challenges facing Europe. Prominent among them were: tackling climate change, fighting global poverty (especially in Africa), immigration, boosting Europe's security, globalisation and economic prosperity. Whatever the core purpose of Europe for the 21st century might be, the actual purpose of the 'core purpose' of the European Union is to pave the way for a genius to enter the political scene to lead Europe to the paradise of "carbon-free where prosperity, peace and security prevail. The Good Book says: "While people are saying, Peace and safety," destruction will come on them suddenly, as labour pains on a pregnant woman and they will not escape." (1 Thessalonians 5:3).

In his speech of "Patronage and flattery," which was probably intended to seduce 'ignorant' Britons to jump from the 'little Island' to board Monnet's "Titanic" floating on the "Big Sea", the Head of the European juggernaut remarked: "If there was ever a case to argue that the agendas of the UK and the EU were distinct, that is now quite simply absurd." What is rather absurd – the absurdity of all absurdities - is UK blindly following Monnet's fuzzy vision of a fused Europe and ignoring the extraordinary vision of their brilliant 'father.'

"FEDERATED EUROPE": THAT WAS JEAN MONNET'S VISION

United Kingdom and Europe may share the same "vocation" of ensuring "open and global Europe – delivering 21st century solutions to 21st century concerns." But the brutal truth is that the agenda of Europe is different from that of United Kingdom. Jean Monnet's project in Brussels is committed to a United States of Europe. Majority of British people do not want to become "slaves" in a "federated Europe" to be 'bullied' by aliens.

Without any doubt, the primary aim of the European Project is to become the government of Europe with a President and Foreign Minister to usurp the sovereign rights of member states without the consent of the masses. This is evident in a statement Monnet made in his memoirs: *"Europe of sovereign states was incapable of, despite its leaders' goodwill, of reaching the sensible decisions that were needed for the common good. It would be quite another matter, however, once the power of decision was entrusted to institutions serving the general interest and applying the will of the majority in a system of common rules."* And Konrad Adenauer also made it plain in his interview with the American Journalist, Kingsley-Smith. The German Chancellor revealed that the Union between France and Germany would eventually lead to political unification of European nations.

Dr Adenauer expressed his regret about Britain's refusal to join the European Coal and Steel Community. In an address to The Bundestag concerning Germany's decision to join the Council of Europe, Adenauer declared: *"I was in full agreement with the French Government that the significance of the Schuman's proposal was first and foremost political and not economic. A careful perusal of the declarations by the French cabinet of 9 May 1950 showed that the intention that this Plan was to be the beginning of a federal structure of Europe was mentioned explicitly in several places. The political importance had been underlined as strongly as possible and I could confirm from* personal *conversations with Monnet that the political element carried the most weight in the balance of French considerations....Not to enter the Council of Europe and to refuse the invitation would be a repudiation of this French proposal, for the political purpose of the French proposal was the creation of a federated Europe."* (Adenauer Memoirs: 1945-53 pages -264-265) The British and the Irish must realise that they are being forced to become citizens of a federal Europe, and their countries becoming just provinces or states of United States of Europe. The issue is: did the British and the Irish join a political union of European nations in 1973, or they became members of an European Economic Community?

In *Principality and Power of Europe*, Adrian Hilton commented on the Democratic Deficit in the European Project. He stated: "The principles of democracy are completely undermined by an European oligarchy where the supreme powers of state and government are in the hands of a small body of individuals – the commissioners...the European government machine has little to do with democracy or justice, and everything to do with power...the lack of political accountability and democratic justification for the EU's federal aspirations, and the transferring of powers away from national parliaments to a centralising core, is anti-freedom, undemocratic and unconstitutional...Each successive treaty has been concerned with the amalgamation of power into a centralised, unaccountable body."

In Britain, the majority do not want to be ruled from overseas by strangers who meet in secret to formulate laws and impose them. For example:

- Why should Brussels attempt to pass a law to force British motorists to switch on their lights irrespective of weather conditions?
- Why should EU plan to force thousands of British citizens to retake their driving test? (*Daily Mail* 4 November 2006)
- Why should bureaucrats in Brussels even suggest that the EU flag should be hoisted on EU birthdays?
- Why should unelected officials in Brussels who are not accountable to Britons dictate to Britons how to protect their children in their cars?
- Why Should Brussels introduce EU Directives 97/67/EC and 2002/38/EC that forced the break up of the Royal Mail and the closure of Post Offices in Britain?
- Why should Brussels pass laws that strangle British businesses with increase costs? (*"Single EU trade are threatens City growth": Financial Times* 4 December 2006) And why should the EU impose unnecessary and costly regulations on British businesses? According to *Open Europe* report: "EU regulations introduced since 1998 have...cost the UK economy almost £107 billion – far more than the UK's total gross contributions to the EU budget over the same period."
- Why should European Parliament and the bureaucrats in Brussels dictate to British people how many hours they should work for a living? British workers do not enjoy the lucrative benefits and huge salaries and pensions politicians and officials in Brussels are entitled to. It is therefore irrational for politicians in Europe to dictate to Britons the numbers of hours they must labour to survive. This is DICTATORSHIP. No reasonable democratic nation would tolerate such interference in its national affairs by aliens. So, why have British politicians succumbed to aliens in Brussels? They lack the confidence to confront the "bullies" in Brussels.

The patriotic Sun newspaper summed up Brussels interferences in the affairs of Britain in its editorial of 26 May 2009. Under the title *"Obscene bill...and for what?"* The Sun says: "If you think our greedy MPs are up to their snouts in taxpayers' money, just look what their cousins are up to in Brussels! Free meals, free travel, free dental treatment...free mudbaths...The perks are so generous that MEPs routinely qualify as millionaires after one five-year term in this cesspit of corruption. And what do we get in return? An avalanche of meddling directives dictating the way we live, eat, work and go about our business. The EU intrudes into every nook and cranny of our daily lives, from human rights for paedophile prisoners to the garbage we put in our bins and the defence of the realm. And if the hated EU Constitution becomes law....500million EU citizens will lose all further direct say – forever."

The EU's meddling in the lives of Britons prompted a British judge to question the intrusion of the European Court into the domestic affairs of the British people. In an article titled *Top British judge accuses Human Rights Court of creating a 'federal law of Europe*, Jonathan Petre and Simon McGee reported on how one of Britain's most senior judges launched an attack on the European Court of Human Rights. The judge, Lord Hoffmann, said: "It (the European Court of Human Rights) had been unable to resist the temptation to aggrandise its jurisdiction and impose uniform rules on member states." He told the Judicial Studies Board: "The European Human Rights Court (which consists of judges selected by people with no legal qualifications) considers itself the equivalent of the Supreme Court of the United States, laying down a federal law of Europe." (*The Mail on Sunday* 5 April 2009)

Unfortunately, through ignorance, British politicians have transferred powers that were entrusted to them temporarily to Brussels. Alan Duncan, the Conservative Party's trade and Industry spokesman, commenting on how the Labour Government struggled to opt out of silly Brussels directives on working hours, rightly said: "It is absurd and perverse that our rules on how long we work and how we balance our lives should be decided in a grubby trade off deal..." (Source: "Brussels wants 60-hour limit on working week *The Daily Telegraph* 21 October 2006). And in December 2008, the European Parliament – "Employees of the Rubber Stamp Factory" – voted to make it illegal for Britons to work more than 48 hours a week.

The *Daily Mail* responded to this irrational vote: "Not only is this decision morally wrong (if a person wants to work overtime and their employer wishes them to do so, it is no business of the state, let alone the EU, to interfere), it is enormously damaging to our fragile economy, which so badly needs the flexibility the opt-out provides" (Daily Mail 18 December 2008). And according to *Open Europe*, the end to the United Kingdom's opt-out from the European Union's 48 hours working week, would cost the UK about £2300 per household by 2020. In view of the detrimental effect the European Parliament's decision on working hours would have on Britons, it is ridiculous for corrupt politicians, who devote their time fiddling their parliamentary expenses, to be drumming into the ears of Britons that Britain must be at the "heart of Europe" to influence and reform the European Union. Do politicians know the "heart of Europe"? Has the EU got a "soul"? I will deal with these subjects.

"BORDERING ON THE ABSURDITY"

Is it not bizarre that Brussels secretly appointed an alien from France to rule British citizens without their consent? The Sunday Express brought this sneaking EU plan to our attention. In an article titled: *The Frenchman who now rules British citizens*, the Deputy Political Editor, Kirsty Buchanan, writes: "Under a barmy Brussels plot to Balkanise Britain, a vast swathe of England has been joined together with west Belgium and Northern France to create Europe's first "trans-national Region." And this region would be ruled by a stranger from France, Monsieur Le Vern.

The political editor continued to unveil what the eurocrats in Brussels had plotted: "Under the plans, western Britain will be grouped with parts of France, Spain and Portugal to form the Atlantic Region. Eastern Britain will continue with parts of Sweden, Denmark, Germany, Belgium, the Netherlands and Norway to form the North Sea region. There is an Ireland and Wales region while most of Scotland will combine with Norway, Greenland, Iceland, Sweden and Finland to become the Northern Periphery."

If all these demarcations were being constructed for the interest of Britain, as the Labour Government suggested, why in secret? Why were the British people not consulted? This is sheer tyrannical rule which majority of Britons detest. And the arrogant bureaucrats in Europe demanded that member states should redraw their national maps to suit Brussels specifications. Who granted Brussels the right to enforce their specifications on Britain? Brussels, the Capital City of EU, was without a government for over 9 months because of divisions among 'patriotic' Belgian politicians. If the centre cannot hold, what happens? "Things fall apart," says Chinua Achebe.

Commenting on dictatorship at the 'heart of the European project,' Eric Pickles, shadow local government minister, branded "Arc Manche" the political equivalent of Frankenstein's monster. He writes: "Taxpayers will be alarmed that their hard-earned cash is now being spent on wiping England off the map and handling power to foreign politicians who they never elected." Mr Pickles continued: "This Labour-EU project needs to be stopped before these trans-national regions grab real power and funding" (*Sunday Express* 22 October 2006).

The editorial in the Sunday Express summed up the conceit and the autocratic 'phenomenon' in Brussels. In its leading article, *Bordering on the absurd*, the paper reported: "A shadowy Frenchman called Alian Le Vern had a meeting in Sussex.... where he introduced himself as the new "President" for Arc Manche. This new territory incorporates much of southern England with parts of France. Other new Anglo-French, Spanish and Portuguese regions are due to follow. What nonsense is this? These mad bureaucrats say they are extending "trans-nationality." Who asked them to? And why are they wasting so much of our money trying to turn Britain into the Balkans."

THE GERMANS WERE FULFILLING THE DREAM OF THEIR "FATHER" – KONRAD ADENAUER

On 3 September 2006, The Sunday Telegraph also reported on Brussels diabolical plan to break Great Britain into "pieces." In a space captioned *New EU map makes Kent part of same 'nation' as France*, Jasper Copping and Melisa Kite wrote: "They have tried to re-draw the map of Europe before. Now a German led 'conspiracy of cartographers' stands accused of trying to use a new EU directive to give Brussels the powers to change national boundaries....This, according to the Tories, could be the first step of a Berlin-inspired master plan to create a United States of Europe divided, not into nation states, but instead a series of 'transnational' regions, the templates for which have already been drawn...They seek to break Britain into regions that cross national boundaries.. Erick Pickles, a Conservative Party spokesman on Local Government, said: "There is an agenda to undermine national identities and impose a United States of Europe by stealth. Conservatives will fight these attempts to balkanise Britain." According to the article, the Germans are the most vocal supporter of transnationality. No wonder a German politician made this declaration: "There is the great hope underlying the goal of a united Europe that we can permanently overcome our borders."

It is time British and Irish politicians, who are scared of their counterparts in France and Germany, realised that the Germans were eager to fulfil the dream of their "Father", Konrad Adenauer. It was this first Chancellor of West Germany who, after the First World War, advocated for a United States of Europe. German politicians hate the concept of national sovereignty. For Konrad Adenauer considered the Schuman Plan the beginning of European unification. In his Memoirs, he writes: "I saw the signing of the ECSC treaty as the opening of a new epoch in the history of Europe." The Germans have already made a provision in their Basic Law that enabled the Federal Republic to transfer sovereign rights to supranational institutions.

I quote verbatim from Adenauer's Memoirs to indicate how German politicians despise the concept of national sovereignty: "Since their inception, the German

Federal parliament and the Federal Government had seen one of their noblest tasks in repeated appeals for the creation of a European community and in attempts to bring it about. On 26 July 1950, the Bundestag passed a resolution which read: *Convinced that the present fragmentation of Europe into sovereign states must lead the peoples of Europe further into distress and bondage every day, the Bundestag of the Republic of Germany, duly constituted after free elections, appeals for a European pact of federation as envisaged by the Preamble and Article 24 of the Basic Law for the Federal Republic of Germany.*
This European pact is to:

1. *create a supranational federal authority founded on universal, direct and free elections and endowed with legislative, executive and judicial powers;*
2. *equip this authority with all the prerogatives needed to bring about economic unity on a basis of social justice, to facilitate a common European foreign policy serving the peace of the world, to define and safeguard equal rights for all European nations, to guarantee and put under legal protection the basic rights and human freedoms of citizens of Europe."* (Adenauer Memoirs 1943-23 page 330)

So, it was not surprising when, on 30 June 2009, Germany's highest court dismissed a case brought by 50 German politicians against the Lisbon Treaty. The politicians argued that approval of the Lisbon Treaty (that transfers more powers from national parliaments to the EU) would threaten the national sovereignty of Germany. The court ruled that the Lisbon Treaty is compatible with German constitution. According to Judge Andreas Yosskuhle, "The basic German law says yes to the Lisbon Treaty."

In view of European political elites' dislike for national sovereignty - an issue which Paul Henri Spaak, the Belgian Euro-zealot, also considered it an 'outmoded concept' - the British and the Irish and Europeans should not have been surprised at German-inspired sneaky efforts to re-draw the map of Europe. The Germans, on the other hand, must realise that in their attempt to create new boundaries and regions in the Continent of Europe, and coupled with the expansion of the Schengen Zone to bring practical meaning to European integration, they and the busy-bodies in Brussels were, unconsciously, bringing to pass what the British public servant wrote about political integration of European nations and its destiny when Dr. Konrad Adenauer was six years old.

I urge European leaders and their 'employees' in Brussels, who are desperate to reconstruct the boundaries of Europe to suit their agenda of creating a Federal Republic of Europe, to examine what the "Forgotten Irishman" recorded concerning political Europe before the First World War erupted. I quote: " ....*That there should be a commonwealth of nations living side by side at peace was a concep-*

tion that nothing in the history of the world could have suggested…… It is impossible to foretell how far kingdoms may be consolidated, and boundaries may be changed… In forecasting the fulfilment of these, we are dealing with events which, while they may occur within the lifetime of living men, may yet be delayed for centuries…we may rest content with the certainty that…their fulfilment will be clear; not merely to minds educated in mysticism, but to all who are capable of observing public facts…. This confederation of [European]nations shall be developed and….." The "Seer of Dublin" went on to document the character and future prospects of this European confederacy.

The important fact is, events associated with the development of the European Union and its make-up have confirmed what the native of Dublin published on European integration over 128 years ago. I would encourage the President of European Commission and his officials to study the Irishman's works on political Europe. They would learn that the very words and phrases he used in the 19th century to describe a confederation of European nations have been used today, in the 21st century, to portray the European Union. Later on I would share with you the classic works of the "Seer of Dublin."

ALL THAT GLITTERS IS NOT GOLD

It is time the pompous politicians in Brussels, who have assumed unnecessary powers over the British people, realised that they do not owe Britons. Great Britain does not need the European Union to survive. And neither does the European Union need Britain to survive. Let's go our separate ways. The selfish British politicians must also realise that, without the explicit consent of the British people, they have no right to sell their sovereign rights to foreigners in Europe who are not accountable to them. Politicians cannot hide behind the concept of 'Parliamentary democracy' to treat Britons with contempt and sell them into 'slavery' in Monnet's 'slave market' in Brussels. Is it consistent with the concept of democracy for the degraded British Parliament to force Britons to become European citizens without their permission? After all, Norway and Switzerland are not bankrupt outside the European Union. They would make a grave error if they are tempted by economic factors, whatever they might be, to jump into Monnet's "Titanic." Norway, Switzerland and Iceland must find out the future prospects of the European Union before considering membership of "That Thing" in Brussels. All that glitters is not gold.

THE PATRIOT POWELL AND THE "PROPHET" LORD DENNING

I exhort British politicians to reflect on the comments the true British patriot, Enoch Powell, made about the Common Market in 1992: "What the EEC (now the European Union) is bent upon", says Powell, "has nothing to do with free trade or free anything. It is a naked assertion of the will to power, the will to create a unified state to which, instead of our own national organs of representation and government, we are all to be subordinated." Enoch Powell has been vindicated. For about 80 percent of British laws have been imposed on Britons by busy-bodies in Brussels? Now witness the prophetic words of the legal genius, Lord Denning, Master of the Rolls: "No longer is European Law an incoming tide flowing up the estuaries of England. It is now like a tidal wave bringing down our sea walls and flowing inland over fields and houses, to the dismay of us all." When would greedy British politicians return the 'Trojan horse' of the 21st century, which has been deposited in the House of Indulgence, to its owners in France and Germany? Majority of Britons do not want that 'deadly gift.' Would the Irish return the "European Trojan Horse" to its owners in Europe?

"THEFT OF DEMOCRATIC RIGHTS"

I would now focus on Mr Barosso's comments on sovereignty during his Lecture at Chatham House. On this issue, it was misguided for the President of the European Commission, who was labelled "incompetent" by Joschka Fischer, a former German Foreign Minister, to have quoted Harold Macmillan's view on "sovereignty": "Ascension...would not involve a one-sided surrender of sovereignty.... In renouncing some of our sovereignty we would receive a share of the sovereignty renounced by others." The truth is that a nation's sovereignty is not the property of its politicians. As servants of the people who put them in power, politicians cannot trade the sovereign rights of Britons in a "slave market" without their mandate. In an article for The Sun newspaper, titled *Don't deny voters' rights*, the former Labour politician, Tony Benn, writes: "Electors are sovereign. They only lend their power for up to 5 years to MPs they elect. To transfer that power to those we don't elect is a theft of democratic rights."

I ask the question: "Having quoted Macmillan on the issue of sovereignty, what prevented Mr. Barroso from quoting Sir Winston Churchill's view on European Unity: "We are with Europe but not of it. We are linked but not comprised. We are interested and associated but not absorbed...I love France and Belgium, but we (the British people) must not allow ourselves to be pulled down to that level." For the record: Churchill did not advocate for Britain to join a United States of Europe. In *Principality and Power of Europe*, Adrian Hilton reminds us how Churchill's statement on European integration was misrepresented as his belief in Britain's participation in the European project. Hilton quoted Churchill: "Great Britain, the British Commonwealth of Nations, mighty America....must be friends and sponsors of the new Europe"- indicating a supporting role for Britain in European integration, but not participation. Hilton then quoted the words of Jacques Delors to confirm Churchill's position on European Unity: "Even that great European, Winston Churchill, envisaged European integration only for the countries of the European continent, not for Britain."

The fact is both Harold Macmillan and Edward Heath did not, initially, present to the British people the truth relating to Britain's membership of the Common Market. Why was the true import of the *Werner Report,* which was produced by the Prime Minister of Luxembourg in 1970, hidden from the British people? The facts of their deceptions are in the public domain. I urge you to get a copy of *The Great Deception* by Christopher Booker and Dr. Richard North.

In his 'clever' speech at Chatham House, Joe Manuel Barroso created the impression that it is the business of British politicians to convince Britons of their need for Europe. Europe exits; and Europe will continue to exist and expand into more than 30 countries to fulfil the purpose of its existence as predicted by the "Forgotten British public servant". However, whether Britons need Europe or not is not the responsibility of degraded British politicians to decide, particularly since most politicians do not know the purpose of the European Union, and have no clue of its future prospects and do not know the "Captain" who will 'pilot' Monnet's Luxurious "Titanic" to its fateful port.

Politicians do not know everything about European integration, hence their inability to 'sell' Europe to British voters. The 2 September 2007 edition of *The Observer* newspaper published an article that confirmed the ignorance of politicians. The title says it all: *"This cowardly refusal to make the political case for Europe."* Destitute of conviction to make the political case for Europe, it is clear that the once planned attempt by the British Labour Government to use public money in a "multi-million pound propaganda war to force the British people to love the European Union and Brussels bureaucrats" was misguided. (The Mail on Sunday 3 December 2006). The plain truth is that politicians in the House of Shame, who lack understanding of the significance of European integration and, therefore, unable to make the case for Europe, have no moral authority to impose their opinions on the European Project on Britons. "Opinions are our own; we must not hold them firmly. He who forces his opinions on others is a boor; and he who dies for his opinions is a fool", says the "Seer of Dublin."

THE "PROFESSIONAL EUROPEAN SALESMAN"

Let us, again, return, to Barroso's 'sermon' at Chatham House. The "Leading European Salesman" suggested that British politicians should sell Jean Monnet's project to Britons. Was the President of European Commission seriously suggesting that if a plumber, a nurse, a lawyer or a medical surgeon, who has had no knowledge on European integration, wins an election and enters the British Parliament, this "instant politician" automatically becomes an 'expert' on European politics to "sell" EU to Britons? This is absurd. The brutal truth is that neither a tradesman nor a professional lawyer, or a scientist, who becomes a politician, is necessarily qualified to advocate for Britain to dispose of its sovereignty to aliens in Brussels. Even a Doctorate degree in Political Science does not guarantee expertise on European integration. I would support my claim later on.

JOSE MANUEL BARROSO: THE "PASSIONATE EUROPEAN SALESMAN"

After the President of the European Commission had extolled the virtues of his "product" (European integration), the "slick European salesman" from Brussels (whom the British people voted in a BBC Radio 4 poll, which was published on 2 January 2006, as the most powerful man in Britain) closed his "sales Presentation" to the 'sceptical' British 'customers' with this remark: "I am passionate about Europe, its values, its history, its truly extraordinary achievements in the last 60 years. No-one is forced to love Europe. What I ask is that the United Kingdom demands more from Europe, and keeps giving more in return. It is no longer a question of whether people are pro or anti-Europe. These are the debates of the last century. The question is: do you want to make the European Union work? I know that Hugo Young's answer was "yes". In the years to come, let that voice be heard louder, not less, in Britain's political arena".

Had the Portuguese political scientist done his 'homework' on European integration before his 'sermon' at Chatham House, which was described as Barroso's 'venture into the 'lion's den,' the EU Chief would not have made that request to Britons. Majority of British people, who do not want to be ruled by foreigners, would answer "No" to his request. Of course, every salesman is passionate about his product. But not every prospective customer would be passionate about a salesman's product – most particularly when the salesman doesn't know much about the product he is selling. The issue is: love for Europe should be conditional. The political elites in Europe cannot force European citizenship on Britons. Not all Britons would like to become 'adopted children' of a man who had no shame in 'stealing' someone's wife.

The debate about whether people are pro or anti Europe is not confined to the last century as Mr Barroso suggested. The debate still continues in the 21st century. Because European politicians have not made the case for EU; they keep running away from the electorate. Had Europeans known the root of the European Union and its ordained purpose; and the character of the coming Emperor of Europe and how he would govern from his palatial palace, they would have trembled at the European Project. The "passengers" on Jean Monnet's "Titanic" should consider their positions: whether to continue enjoying their 'trip' on the "luxurious ship", or jump from the "floating palace" before it sinks.

Hugo Young might have answered "Yes" to Brussels. However, Hugo Young would not have necessarily responded on behalf of all Britons. In the years to come, the voice to be heard louder, not less, and not only in Britain's political arena but also in Ireland, America, Europe and around the four corners of planet earth, is the prophetic voice of the "Forgotten servant" of the 'Sceptical Island.' It was this "Unknown Irishman" who wrote about European integration - how it would develop and its future prospects before the "Catalyst" of the European Community, Adolf Hitler, and the "architect" of the European Project, Jean Monnet, and the "sower" of the seed of federal Europe, Robert Schuman, were all born.

I would now support my claim that not all bureaucrats in Brussels and political leaders in Europe, Britain and Ireland are properly educated on the significance of European integration. On 5 September 2007, Mr. Derk-Jan Eppink who, for over 7 years, was a senior official with the European Commission, launched his best-selling' book, *"Life of a European Mandarin: Inside the Commission"* at the Foreign Press Association, 11 Carlton House Terrace, London SW1Y 5AJ. I was among the audience. After the Dutch author had made his sales-pitch – trying to sell the European Project to 'sceptical' Britons, he invited questions. I asked Mr. Eppink two questions:

- "What advice did the first President of the European Parliament offer to Europeans concerning the survival of the European Project?"
- Do you know that a Briton wrote about European integration, its character and future before Jean Monnet, the architect of the European Union, was born in 1888?

Mr. Eppink paused for sometime. After taking a deep breath he confessed: "I don't know." The issue is: if a former EU expert, with about 7 years experience at the heart of the European Project, could not answer two questions about the Project, thereby proving his limited knowledge on European Construction, how could politicians who have had no experience in Brussels deal with issues about the EU? Mr Eppink's 'best-seller' was reviewed in the 26 November 2007 edition of the Financial Times.

The fact is Britain would be better off leaving "That Thing" in Brussels. 99% of Sunday Express' readers once voted for Britain to leave the European Union when they expressed their views on "The Arc Manche region - Europe's first 'transnational region' - which joins together southern England, west Belgium and northern France" (*Sunday Express* 29 October 2006). Here is an extract from Mr R Millichip's letter to the Sunday Express: "The majority of the British people want out of Europe. We will have to make sacrifices but I am sure we will gladly suffer them if the millions of pounds which Europe takes from us go towards retaining our identity and sovereignty as a nation. Instead, we have become a laughing stock of Europe and the rest of the world. This (Labour) government adheres to every stupid idea the EU comes up with, while other countries ignore any new rules and regulations unless it financially benefits them." Mr Millichip then urged the *Sunday Express* to initiate a campaign to pull Britain out of the European Union. I will support the campaign to remove the "load" the "parasites" in Brussels have laid on Britons.

IS THE FRENCH MAN NICOLAS SARKOZY QUALIFIED TO LECTURE BRITONS ON EUROPEAN INTEGRATION?

When President Sarkozy visited London in March 2008, he praised Gordon Brown for denying the British people a vote on the Lisbon Treaty. Sarkozy had the audacity to suggest that Britain should consider joining the euro to be at the heart of his 'father's' Project, if Britain does not want to be at the peripheral of Europe. How well-informed is Sarkozy on European integration to lecture Britons? Britain does not need the European Union and its euro to survive. Does Sarkozy know the future of Jean Monnet's project? Is Sarkozy aware that a British public servant wrote about European Union and its future before his 'father', Jean Monnet, the master builder of EU, was born?

If Britain is pushed to the peripheral of Europe by not joining the euro because of its lukewarm attitude towards the European Enterprise, the British people would not chew stones outside Europe. Britons would not crawl with empty bowls to bow before Brussels to beg for bread. It would be better for Britons to fish from the 'little pond' and catch small cods, than to be abducted and dragged into the Deep European Sea which is infested with "sharks". The fact is Britain is not part of the continent of Europe. Nature created Britain an island to be free from 'infection.' We must be proud of our nation and fight to restore its glory. On the merits of EU and its Euro, Great Britain does not need lectures from the French President Nicolas Sarkozy.

I repeat: had President Sarkozy studied what the "forgotten servant of the British Crown" recorded concerning political Europe and its future prospects before his 'Father', the 'obstinate' Monnet, was even conceived, he would have shivered and mourned over France and Europe. And had Gordon Brown also done his 'homework' on European integration by studying what his well-informed "Presbyterian Father" published concerning European confederacy, its nature and destiny, he would have rather lectured President Sarkozy on the real significance of the 'European phenomenon.' After all, if the European Union were a Public Limited Company, it would have been struck off from the Register of Companies. Why? Because for the 14th year in succession the Court of Auditors failed to approve the Accounts of Europe because of errors, fraud, financial mismanagement and missing documents.

THE ARROGANCE OF THE IGNORANT

Political elites at home and away have always schemed and forced their views on European integration upon the masses. It is time patriotic Britons and Irish knew the spirit behind Jean Monnet's project and its destiny. Arrogance has blinded the bureaucrats in Brussels and their political masters to claim monopoly of knowledge on European Union. And for this reason, a slimmed-down EU treaty, which was engineered by the political elites in France and Germany, was pushed through national Parliaments without the consent of the people and imposed it on them. I ask again: "Are politicians better-informed on European integration than the electorate? I have already stated, that the place of the 'experts' on European integration is not on the judgement seat in Brussels, but in the witness box at Wembley Stadium in London to be cross-examined by Britons. I repeat the words of the "Seer of Dublin": "A case which seems convincing when presented *ex-parte* breaks down under cross-examination or is shattered by opposing evidence."

ATTEMPT TO "BRIBE" A BRITISH PRIME MINISTER AND THE CATHOLIC POPE

On 27 October 2006, the Financial Times reported on how Brussels wanted to strike a deal with Gordon Brown, the then Chancellor of the Exchequer, (If he becomes a Prime Minister) to accept a new treaty without the consent of the British people. In a space titled *Bored by 'results', Europe regains its taste for grand plans,* the newspaper revealed that when aides of the "cunning salesman of Europe", Mr Barroso, met Gordon Brown in London in October 2006, they detected that the British Chancellor, "the Scot", doesn't like the constitution much." However they felt Mr. Brown cared "passionately about reforming the EU budget and dismantling the Common Agricultural Policy, the farm subsidy regime he blames for distorting world trade and harming poor countries." In view of this observation, the bureaucrats felt that a deal could be struck with Mr Brown to accept a treaty on behalf of the British people".

The newspaper added: "When Mr Brown met Ms Merkel earlier in 2006, her aides started speaking of a possible broader deal: in exchange for signing up to a revised constitution, Mr Brown could demand a modernisation of the EU budget, reform of farm support and regional aid for innovation and research". The report continued: "Mr Barroso and Ms Merkel plainly think Mr Brown might accept a new treaty updating the EU's constitution if he could present it as part of a package embracing enlargement, a 21st century budget and a new mandate for the free-market…." This cynical plan to 'bribe' a future British Prime Minister to adopt a discredited constitution on behalf of the British people without their consent demonstrates the arrogance of politicians in Brussels, and their contempt for Britons. If the Eurocrats in Brussels sincerely believed they were pursuing the interest of the British people, why did they plan to bribe a future British Prime Minister? They should have been bold to present their case to the electorate for them to decide whether to embrace the European Project or reject it. This behaviour exposes the intellectual and moral bankruptcy behind the whole European Project.

Great Britain is not the property of Gordon Brown. Britons elect politicians to safeguard their sovereignty - not to dispose off their rights on the altar of political expediency to non-British citizens in Europe who are not accountable to Britons. No one in Britain is above the destiny of Great Britain. So, we must not allow selfish and discredited politicians to sell Britain into 'slavery' in Brussels. I repeat the words of Tony Benn: "Electors are sovereign. They only lend their power for up to 5 years to MPs they elect. To transfer that power to those we don't elect is a theft of democratic rights."

Apart from the contemptuous attempt by eurocrats to 'bribe' a future British Prime Minister, it was also reported that the German Chancellor contemplated to "bribe' the Pope to somehow endorse the rejected European Constitution which had no room for God and the Lord Jesus Christ. In his article *Europe: the issue that dare not speak its name*, the pompous Denis MacShane, writes: "In Berlin, Chancellor Angela Merkel says that when Germany takes over the six-month EU presidency…she will seek to breathe life into the constitution and add a reference to Christianity to please the Pope" (*The Independent* 26 September 2006). What an insult to Christians who are not under the authority of the Bishop of Rome, who is the 'life-chairman' of 'Vatican PLC'!

The Church of Christ is not the Roman Catholic Church that places its traditions on equal footing with Sacred Scriptures, and its *The New Jerusalem Bible* claims the Book of Daniel is an "edifying fiction." The Pope is the head of 1.2 billion Roman Catholics. He does not represent all Christians. The notion that the head of the Roman Catholic Church could be 'bribed' to endorse a godless project is not surprising. For if the Catholic Church were spiritually inclined, they would not have consecrated Europe to the Virgin Mary in 1309. Secondly, had

Pope Benedict XVI truly understood the significance of the European Project, he would not have commented on Turkey's membership of the European Union. Whether the European Union embraces or rejects Turkey should not have been the concern of a spiritual leader of a Christian denomination. It should be the sole business of politicians. And thirdly, Pope Benedict XVI would not have called on the Irish to adopt the Lisbon Treaty had he understood the spiritual implications of this particular Treaty. And the Archbishop of Dublin, the Most Reverend Diarmuid Martin, would not have joined the 'Europa bandwagon' to influence the Irish to commit their future to the European Union whose future remains "uncertain," according to Timothy Garton Ash. Why should Christian leaders in the Roman Catholic Church joined atheists to promote the European Union – a project that has no space for the Lord Jesus Christ? It amazes me; but so should it be for Scriptures to be fulfilled.

DAVID MILIBAND AND EU AND CHRISTIANITY

The British Foreign Secretary, David Miliband, in his attempt to press for Turkey's membership of the European Union, made this disparaging comment: "Shared values had to be embodied in institutions rather than simply being asserted. Europe can't be a closed Christian club" (Source: Financial Times 26 September 2007: *Time to learn and move on, says Miliband)*

I ask Mr. Miliband: "Has the EU ever been a Christian club?" The EU has never been a Christian club. It was, therefore, unnecessary for the atheist Miliband to have associated that corrupt project in Brussels with Christianity. The godless EU is unfit for the Lord Jesus Christ? Is the atheist Miliband aware that over 128 years ago a brilliant British public servant, who was not an atheist, recorded that Austria, Belgium, England, France, Germany, Greece, Italy, Portugal, Spain and Turkey, would become members of a political alliance of European nations?

When did Miliband become an 'expert' on European integration to lecture Britons on the merits of Britain's participation in the European Union, and then denied Britons a say on a Treaty that would usurp their sovereign rights? Does Miliband know the qualification of the Irishman who wrote about Britain's membership of the European confederacy before De Gaulle rejected Britain's 1963 and 1967 applications to join the European Common Market? Had Miliband done his 'homework' on European integration before becoming the Foreign Secretary, he would not have dared to associate Christianity with that 'godless thing' in Europe. A Doctorate Degree in Political Science does not guarantee expertise on European integration. Because of ignorance British politicians are blindly following the 'children' of Jean Monnet and Konrad Adenauer. In their blindness, they are dragging Britons to board Monnet's "European Titanic" which was doomed before it started its "maiden voyage" from France on 9 May 1950.

The autocratic attitudes of politicians in Europe depict the European Union an undemocratic project. The Daily Telegraph confirmed it in its 30 May 2005 edition. Commenting on France's rejection of the European Constitution in its editorial, *"Mere democracy won't stop the EU machine"*, the newspaper reported: "It is hard to think of a graver crisis of legitimacy for the EU, if even France, Europe's most loyal daughter, wants no more of the racket....On any normal measure, the EU has lost the confidence of its citizens...Euro-elites will carry on as if nothing has happened. But the project was never meant to be democratic. From the first, the EU's founding fathers understood that it needed to be immune to public opinion. The genius of Jean Monnet and Robert Schuman was to design a system in which supreme power was wielded by unelected officials, and in which the peoples were presented with a series of *faits accomplait*.....Since 1975 the British people have not had the opportunity to vote on European integration..."

British politicians are not entitled to negotiate deals with Brussels to force EU treaties on Britons. Politicians should not treat those who put them in power with contempt. The masses may be "old and uneducated with few academic qualifications". However, not all of them are less-informed on the European Project and the shady-dealings in Brussels. Wisdom and common sense to discern truth from falsehood are not taught in universities or any institution of Higher Education. They are also not common in the House of Commons – now the "House of Shame."

I ask: are the university-educated politicians properly-educated on European integration? Do these professional politicians know the future of Europe? If they knew the fate of the European Project, Peter Riddell would not have written an article entitled "Europe will not go away, so let's start discussing its future" (The Times 19 May 2006). If "a core group" in Europe want to fly with a supersonic jet into the European wonderland, Britain would be better off riding on a bicycle. It would be safer for Britons to crawl in a slow lane to reach safely, because the "European supersonic jet" doesn't know its destination. It could land anywhere and crash.

A PROPHET IS OF NO HONOUR IN HIS OWN COUNTRY

British politicians should have been grateful to President de Gaulle for rejecting their 1963 and 1967 applications to join the Common Market. Unfortunately, political leaders at that time were not aware of what a British public servant had already written on European integration and its future. It is unfortunate to notice that, even today, British politicians are crawling before European politicians. They are eager to please the French and the Germans. They are running helter-skelter in Europe and seeking to form alliances in the European Parliament whereas they should have relaxed in London for Europeans to run to them for advice on the

mentioned explicitly in several places. The political importance had been underlined as strongly as possible and I could confirm from personal conversations with Monnet that the political element carried the most weight in the balance of French considerations.... Not to enter the Council of Europe and to refuse the invitation would be a repudia-

European Enterprise and its prospects. What a sad spectacle! And why this episode? Because, a prophet is of no honour in his own country and among his own people.

According to "experts," the history of the European Union is deeply rooted in the

WHY THE EUROPEAN UNION? IS THE FUTURE OF EUROPE BRIGHT OR DARK?

Britain's employment laws, the 19th edition of the Irishman's prediction of a commonwealth of European nations living side by side at peace was published.

In 1972, the European Communities Act was signed. In that very year the 18th edition of the Irishman's work on how a political Europe would develop, its nature and future prospects were published. Had British and Irish politicians read this particular edition, they would not have joined the Common Market in 1973.

In 1957, the six founding members of the European Coal and Steel Community (Belgium, France, Germany, Italy, Luxembourg and the Netherlands) met in Rome to sign their historic Treaty to move the European Project forward to its ultimate goal. In that very year the 14th edition of the "Seer of Dublin's" prediction of European confederacy and its prospects was published. According to Professor Irene Fine–Honigman, Professor in the MBA Programme at John Hopkins University, "de Gaulle believed that Europe would become a confederation but only within a long–term historical political framework". She quoted de Gaulle: "I don't exclude, a far later, a confederation which would be the crowning point of a patient effort to bring forth a common policy, common diplomacy, common security at the end of a long period when the six nations (Belgium, France, Germany, Italy, Luxembourg and the Netherlands) have become accustomed to living together." Had President de Gaulle read the 14th edition of the Ulsterman's work, he would have learnt that, before he was born in 1890, this British public servant had already stated: "a confederation of European nations" would develop through an "European Crisis."

Finally, it would be of interest to Europeans and Americans and the world to learn that in 1889, the year Adolf Hitler, the "Catalyst" of European Community was born, the third edition of the Ulsterman's work on how a political union of European nations and its future would develop from an European crisis, was published.

posed this question to Britons: "*May we not indulge the hope that however far our nation may lapse in evil days to come from the high place which, with all her faults, she has held as the champion of freedom and of truth, she will be saved from the degradation of participating in the vile confederacy of the latter days?*"

THE "ROOT" OF THE EUROPEAN UNION

We know it was the horrors of the First and Second World Wars and probably the military might of the then Soviet Union, that motivated some European politicians in the 1920's to conceive the idea of a United States of Europe. Jean Monnet only proceeded with the concept of European federation when the opportunity presented itself after the Second World War. Monnet declared: "There will not be peace in Europe if the states of Europe rebuild themselves on the basis of national sovereignty....The states of Europe must therefore form a federation or an European entity that would make them into a common economic unit...There is no future for the people of Europe other than in union. To create Europe is to create peace..."

We know "The Schuman Plan", launched in 1950, put Jean Monnet's vision of United States of Europe into operation. In 1952 the 'saviour' of Europe revealed his ambition for creating a federal Europe by declaring that the nations of Europe must be "fused" together. Observe what the French Statesman recorded in his Memoirs: "*Europe of sovereign states was incapable of, despite its leaders' goodwill, of reaching the sensible decisions that were needed for the common good. It would be quite another matter, however, once the power of decision was entrusted to institutions serving the general interest and applying the will of the majority in a system of common rules.*"

Today, Europe may not be "federated"; but tomorrow it will be "fused" together. This was the aim of the pioneers of European integration. And it remains the mission of the officials in Brussels - to create a United States of Europe by stealth. Environmentalism (the pursuit of the protection of mother earth) has become one of the instruments Brussels is employing to achieve the goal of their 'patrons'-Jean Monnet and Konrad Adenauer. For Adenauer confirmed Monnet's plan for a federal Europe in a lecture to the German Parliament. I repeat the address:

"*I was in full agreement with the French Government that the significance of the Schuman's proposal was first and foremost political and not economic. A careful perusal of the declarations by the French cabinet of 9 May 1950 showed that the intention that this Plan was to be the beginning of a federal structure of Europe was mentioned explicitly in several places. The political importance had been underlined as strongly as possible and I could confirm from personal conversations with Monnet that the political element carried the most weight in the balance of French considerations.... Not to enter the Council of Europe and to refuse the invitation would be a repudia-*

tion of this French proposal, for the political purpose of the French proposal was the creation of a federated Europe." Dr Adenauer added: *"The Council of Europe was a first attempt to federate. All were convinced that if the Federal Republic of Germany did not participate in it (The Council of Europe), the Council was finished and the attempt to bring about a European federation had foundered."* (Adenauer Memoirs 1945-53 Pages 264-265)

The "dictators" in Brussels, on their "war-path" to create a "federated Europe," to fulfil the dreams of their patrons, planned to introduce "green crimes" with criminal penalties and jail sentences for those who break environmental laws in Europe. Dr. Syed Kamall, a Conservative Member of European Parliament, commenting on Brussels encroachment on the sovereign rights of member states to deal with criminals according to their own national laws, said: "The Commission is using the environmental agenda as an excuse to massively increase its powers at the expense of national parliaments. This is a very slippery slope" (Source: The Daily Telegraph 8 February 2007: *"Brussels to list 'green crimes'.*). Politicians should not be surprised. The "green agenda," adopted by Brussels, is a cynical ploy to "fuse" European nations to achieve the federal goal of Konrad Adenauer and Jean Monnet.

About 68 years after the "Forgotten Irishman" had written about the certainty of the restoration of the Jews to Palestine, the nation of Israel was reborn against all expectations. On 14 May 1948, David Ben Gurion proclaimed the existence of the Independent State of Israel. And 70 years after the Irishman had written, *"This confederation of [European] nations shall be developed ...."* the European Coal and Steel Community (the forerunner of the European Union) was also born on 9 May 1950. In 1957 the Treaty of Rome was signed to lay down the foundation stone upon which a "federated Europe" would be built. And on 13 December 2007, the Treaty of Lisbon was signed as the last "piece" to fit the "European jig-saw puzzle", and to pave the way for the "Seer of Dublin's" prediction of Europe's future to be fulfilled.

A point of interest: When writing about European confederacy, the "Forgotten servant" of the 'Little Pond' listed Austria, Belgium, England, Greece, France, Germany, Italy, Portugal, Spain and Switzerland as potential members of the political union. He also mentioned Turkey and Egypt as members of this confederacy before Turkey applied to join the European Community in 1963, and before Brussels also suggested the *Wider Neighbourhood Policy* which could offer membership of the European Union to countries in North African - including Egypt and Tunisia.
An American political commentator, who was among the journalists who discussed Turkey's membership of the European Union in a BBC24 Dateline Programme, said "...Let's face it; it's going to happen ....Turks will be in Europe." The other experts at the "Dateline" table advanced arguments in favour of Turkey's mem-

bership of the European Union. One of them, Yasmin Alibhai-Brown, addressing the Austrians who have been perceived to be "hostile" to Turkey's membership of the EU, declared: "If you do not want a wedge, a really challenging wedge to develop between Iran, Syria, and then Turkey; if you do not want a clash of civilisations, grow up..." I would , again, remind these 'experts' on European integration, that it was an Irishman who wrote about Turkey's membership of a political Europe before Turkey applied to join the European Community in 1963. When Americans and Europeans and the rest of the world examine the works of the "unknown Irishman," they would regard the "giant" of Europe, Jean Monnet, a 'pygmy' before the "Irish Knight." At the end of this book I will put these two "giants"- Jean Monnet and the "Forgotten Ulsterman"- in a scale for the world to weigh them.

PRESIDENT CHARLES DE GAULLE AND BRITAIN AND THE COMMON MARKET

In 1963 Charles de Gaulle rejected Britain's first application to join the Common Market. Politicians should have welcomed the decision with joy. The French President, unconsciously, helped Britain to stay away from Europe. For in that same year of 1963, the prophetic word about the European Union and its future had been reproduced for the 15th time. In 1967, De Gaulle said "Non" to Britain's second application to join the European Community. In that very year the 16th edition of the prophetic word regarding the European Union and its destiny was released.

Had President de Gaulle read at least the 15th and the 16th editions of the "Unknown Irishman's" work about European integration and its future, which were published in 1963 and 1967, he would have trembled at the sight of Britain's applications to join the Common Market. The French President would not have humiliated Britain on 27 November 1967 when he assembled diplomats, civil servants, ministers and journalists to accuse Britain of a "deep-seated hostility" towards European construction. De Gaulle would not have dared to warn Belgium, Germany, Italy, Luxembourg and the Netherlands that if they attempted to impose Britain's membership of the Common Market on France, it would result in the breakdown of the European Community. On the other hand, Great Britain would have saved herself from embarrassment had British politicians examined what the distinguished British public servant wrote about European integration. And the British Prime Minister, Harold Wilson, and his followers at Westminster would not have mourned in the House of Commons when the big-headed Frenchman rejected their applications to join Jean Monnet's Club.

In 1969, when the haughty De Gaulle fell from power, the 17th edition of the "Unknown Ulsterman's" work on the moral fibre and destiny of the European Project was released. In 1975, when Britons voted in a referendum to join a Common Market, not a political union of European nations that would dictate

Britain's employment laws, the 19th edition of the Irishman's prediction of a commonwealth of European nations living side by side at peace was published.

In 1972, the European Communities Act was signed. In that very year the 18th edition of the Irishman's work on how a political Europe would develop, its nature and future prospects were published. Had British and Irish politicians read this particular edition, they would not have joined the Common Market in 1973.

In 1957, the six founding members of the European Coal and Steel Community (Belgium, France, Germany, Italy, Luxembourg and the Netherlands) met in Rome to sign their historic Treaty to move the European Project forward to its ultimate goal. In that very year the 14th edition of the "Seer of Dublin's" prediction of European confederacy and its prospects was published. According to Professor Irene Fine–Honigman, Professor in the MBA Programme at John Hopkins University, "de Gaulle believed that Europe would become a confederation but only within a long–term historical political framework". She quoted de Gaulle: "I don't exclude, a far later, a confederation which would be the crowning point of a patient effort to bring forth a common policy, common diplomacy, common security at the end of a long period when the six nations (Belgium, France, Germany, Italy, Luxembourg and the Netherlands) have become accustomed to living together." Had President de Gaulle read the 14th edition of the Ulsterman's work, he would have learnt that, before he was born in 1890, this British public servant had already stated: "a confederation of European nations" would develop through an "European Crisis."

Finally, it would be of interest to Europeans and Americans and the world to learn that in 1889, the year Adolf Hitler, the "Catalyst" of European Community was born, the third edition of the Ulsterman's work on how a political union of European nations and its future would develop from an European crisis, was published.

JEAN MONNET AND HIS "VAGUE" VISION

Jean Monnet, the 'chief mover' of the Schuman Plan, had no idea of the future prospects of his vision of a "federated Europe." Could this be the reason why Monnet left the goal of the European project "vague" as suggested in *Why Europe will run the 21st century?* In this book Mark Leonard, writes: "Monnet's contribution was a vision of how not to have a vision...He let the fear of conflict drive European unity and left its goal vague, allowing everyone to feel that Europe was going their way. To this day, Europe is a journey with no final destination, a political system that shies away from the grand plans and concrete certainties that define American politics." The reality is that European Union has a "final destination." This fact was recorded in the 19th century before the European Union came into existence in the 20th century. The question is: how could a lack of vision for a project become its strength? The Lord says: My people are destroyed from lack of knowledge" (Hosea 4:6). And "where there is no vision people perish" (Proverbs 29:18).

Jean Monnet did not know the fate of his project. Is it any wonder that European politicians are still struggling to 'sell' the European project to Europeans who are not excited about Monnet's Project? In his article, *"Unloved and mistrusted, even by the French: the EU at 50"*, Niall Ferguson, Professor of History at Harvard University, writes: "So totally has life in Europe been transformed that you might expect the European Union to be universally adored at 50. Yet only 46 percent of its citizens have a positive view of the EU, while more than a third believe their country has not benefited from EU membership. Support for the EU is lowest in Britain, where just one in three people regard membership in a positive light, and barely one in four trusts the European Commission or Parliament."(*The Sunday Telegraph,* 25 March 2007). This analysis confirms the comments Ruth Lea recorded in her article *"Why most British people want to pull back from Europe"* (*The Sun* 15 March 2007).

EUROPEAN UNION AND THE 'BRAINWASHING' OF CHILDREN

Despite their lack of understanding of the European Project, the British Labour politicians were determined to sell the European union to our children. On 2 August 2006, Daily Mail published an article entitled *Pupils need to learn how the EU benefits us.* The opening paragraph read: "Children could be forced to learn about the supposed benefits of the European Union under Government plans." I ask the question: Why should the Labour government plan to compel our children to learn about the "benefits" of a political union which the government itself has no clue of its actual purpose and future?

Responding to Geoff Hoon's strategy to introduce European Education in the British National Curriculum, Christopher Booker writes: "The EU has become the way our country is run…It is responsible for more than half of our major new laws….It is right that we should all be much more aware of this than we are – not just children, but all of us who remain amazingly ignorant of how much power to decide how our country is governed has now been handed over to Brussels." Brussels still want to appropriate more powers to itself by forcing the British people to surrender their judicial powers to unaccountable institutions, hence the introduction of the Lisbon Treaty.

THE BURDEN OF THE AUTHOR

In view of the subtle attempt by the British government to "brainwash" children about the merits of the European Project, and the persistent misguided arguments that the destiny of Britain lies at the "heart of Europe," there is an urgent need for a proper education on the implication of Jean Monnet's vision of a federal Europe and its future. For Brian Sewell, in his article for the Evening Standard, *Why our voices must be heard*, stressed the importance for the Blair government to call for a referendum on the EU Constitution which was agreed in 2004. He reminded us how Britons engaged in a fierce debate in their 1975 referendum to confirm our membership of the Common Market.

According to Mr Sewell, our nation had the opportunity to be well-informed. However, since 1975 "no debate of such intensity has happened." I repeat his lamentation: "Deprived of any further opportunities to vote on European matters, the nation has become steadily less-informed. Maastricht was a well-kept secret. Without the stimulus of debate we have been denied information; without the stimulus of a referendum at any further stage in the development of the European Union, we have slipped into ignorance, indifference and mistrust. All governments since 1975 wanted it this way: "Leave it for us." Mr Sewell added, "Europe is a matter far beyond party politics". The columnist then made this significant statement: *"Any empire that embraces too many nations, cultures, languages and economies cannot be held together in perpetuity. I doubt if a united Europe will last long."* Surely, the European Empire would have a brief life-span when its Emperor is crowned. Monnet's "EU Titanic" was destined to sink even before its architect was conceived.

It is my burden to stimulate debate on Britain and Ireland's withdrawal from the European Union by sharing with my fellow countrymen and the Irish people, who have been taken for granted for so long, the following information:

- The "Unknown UIrishman" who wrote about European integration, its character and future prospects before the French Founding Fathers of the European Community, Jean Monnet and Robert Schuman, were born in 1888 and 1886.

- The actual purpose of the European Union.
- The "strong emperor" who will lead the European Empire to solve its economic, political and security problems.
- The prospects of the European Union, and its long term implications for Europeans and the world.

BRITAIN'S MEMBERSHIP OF THE EUROPEAN UNION SUITS POLITICIANS NOT THE ELECTORATE

We know in 1975 Britain voted in a referendum to continue its membership of a Common Market. The Common Market has now developed into a political union which imposes laws and regulations on British people. It is, therefore, logical for Britons to decide whether they would continue their membership of such a project to become 'citizens' of Europe to be ruled by foreigners. After all, citizenship is acquired voluntarily, not under compulsion. But it seems unprincipled and selfish British politicians have colluded with their European partners to impose European citizenship on British people. If politicians claim it benefits Britain to remain in the European Union, why have succeeding British governments failed to publish the cost/benefit analysis of Britain's membership of the European Union?

The reason is simple. Britain's membership of the European Union suits the 'greedy' politicians not the voters who put them in power. Peter Hitchens explained it eloquently for us: I repeat his words: "Political elites in all the parties love the European Union, not because it is good for the country, but because it is good for them. They love its regular service of gravy trains, carrying failed Ministers off to a life of high salaries, big expenses and huge pensions, plus an almost total absence of responsibility. They don't mind at all that it deprives them of the power to do very much. They are for the most part, short of ideas and lazy, and happy to be able to pass the buck to Brussels while enjoying their pay and perks" (*The Mail on Sunday* 4 November 2007).

THE END CROWNS THE WORK

The British and the Irish might have gained from their membership of the European Union. However, they should consider the long-term consequences of their relationship with the European Union, and not to be blinded by the short-term benefits of participating in the "greatest political adventure of the last century" and the biggest economic market in the world. After all, it is the end that crowns the work. Is the future of Europe bright or dark? Let me illustrate the point. What benefit would it serve a 100–meter sprinter who leads a race to the 90-metre spot and falls down? Would he receive a gold medal? What satisfaction would a 110 x 4 relay-team gain, if, having led the race, the anchor man drops the baton a meter before the finishing line? Would this team receive a crown of glory from the goddess "Nike" for not breaking the tape?

We must ask another question: "If the passengers who perished on the great Titanic had known that the "unsinkable" ship would sink, would they have boarded the vessel? The Titanic started well on its maiden journey from Southampton to New York. But did it end well? Would the European "magnificent Vessel" - with its 'expensive cargo' ('Enlargement', Common Agricultural Policy, Common Fisheries Policy, The Human Rights Act, The European Central Bank, the 'mighty euro', The EU Flag and Anthem, the European Court of Justice, the Lisbon Treaty etc) reach its destination safely? The interest of the British and the Irish in the European Project should be based on its future prospects, and not on the short-term benefits gained from Brussels – the financing of prestigious and bizarre projects in member countries.

EUROPEAN UNION AND THE ENVIRONMENT

Some politicians and political commentators maintain the European Union is better placed to help combat the threat of global warming. For example, Adrian Hamilton writes; " The simple point about the EU is that, on most major issues which affect citizens today – the environment, security, energy, economic growth, trade negotiations and monopoly regulation – the European context is the only one that makes sense" (*The Independent* 11 May 2006). Another political commentator confirmed it: "Only a supranational union of nations could possibly effect the collective action needed to bring down carbon emissions" (Jonathan Freedland, The Guardian 4 October 2006). And it was even reported in *The Guardian* that British ministers "believe an opportunity has risen to rebrand the EU as the best protector of the Environment, energy, security, and a way of spreading democracy" (Source: *The Guardian* 3 November 2006, *"Hoon risks row with plan to reform EU").*

Because of this perception, the European Union, in its zeal to be the 'protector of the environment' to save the world, considered EU green legislation that even threatens the closure of some British industries because of the cost in compliance. This was reported in an article "Industry fears over EU green legislation" (Financial Times 7 January 2008). Brussels has been emboldened by the Green Revolution even to attempt to seek powers to jail polluters who break environmental laws. It was reported in the national newspapers that the then European Commissioner for Justice and Home Affairs, Franco Frattini, believed that Europeans would support Brussels usurpation of sovereign rights of member states to imprison "environmental criminals" because of their concern of the damage being inflicted on the environment.

Global warming, economic prosperity, energy and social security may be the pressing problems facing the European Union - with climate change on top of the agenda since this is perceived to be the greatest threat facing mankind today. But the pressing question is: what is this European Union that could possibly 'solve' all the problems facing Europe – including the threat from global warming? We must first establish the actual purpose for which the European Union was created, before we can determine whether it could solve the problems confronting Europe.

Secondly, European leaders must first ascertain the future of the European Project before thinking about how to solve the problems caused by global warming – a future phenomenon. If the future of the European Union is "uncertain" as remarked by Timothy Garton Ash in his article, *Today's European Union is 27 states in search of a story,* (The Guardian 4 January 2007), how could this European Union, whose future is uncertain, solve a problem of the future? Does it make sense for the European Union to claim that it could help solve the effects of global warming since the European Union cannot predict its own future?

The European Union has warned the world of global climate chaos (*The Guardian* 11 January 2007). But is this political union qualified to warn mankind that climate change could lead to regional conflicts, famines and immigration? With or without global climate change, there would be poverty, pestilences, famines, wars, and earthquakes. Today, Britons, the Irish and Europeans are depending on the European Union and its scientists to save them from destruction from climate change. However, a day is fast approaching when men would yearn to die from climate change, but death would elude them (Revelation 9:6). The European Empire would not be able to solve any of the problems facing the world until its charismatic and intelligent Emperor is crowned by the powerful leaders in the revived Roman Empire.

THE DESTINY OF EUROPE

The view that the historic roots of the European Union lie in the Second World War was again confirmed in a series of BBC Radio 4 programme – *Forging the Union.* This was aired in August 2006. Listeners were told that the European Union evolved from the ruins of the Second World War. A text on the BBC Radio 4 website read: "Allan Little looks at how the European Union was created, from the devastation of the Second World War to its current incarnation as a new kind of super power…"

TIME Magazine, in its Special Report, *"What's Europe Done For You?"* stated: "After the carnage of the World War II, it was as much as American minds and muscle as European ones that determined that Europe needed new institutions binding nations together if it was to avoid the catastrophes of war." And *Newsweek* Magazine also confirmed the source of EU with this declaration in its Special Report: *Europe at 50*: "Europe arose from the ashes of the Great Depression and World War II to become whole and free. Half a century ago, only an utopian would have predicted that, today, one can traverse Europe from Sicily to Sweden without encountering a border control...and using a single European Currency."

This leads to the question: was the British public servant who, before the First World War, recorded that a confederation of European nations would be developed through an European crisis, an utopian? We must ask the question: "What stirred the native of Dublin to predict that a confederation of European nations would follow the rebirth of the nation of Israel since the two World Wars of 1914 and 1939 had not even occurred? Another question: "What motivated this servant of the British Crown to predict with confidence, that the next major political feature of the future, after the restoration of the Jews to Palestine, would be a confederation of European nations? He made this prediction even before the Russian Jew, Leo Pinsker suggested, in 1882, that the Jews must find their own home not necessarily in Palestine, which was the land of their ancestors.

And if the Irishman's predictions of these two major political events in history have been fulfilled, then we can rest assured that what he recorded about the future of Europe will also come to pass. The Lisbon Treaty, signed on 13 December 2007, has paved the way for his prediction of the fate of Europe to be fulfilled. At the time of writing preparations were being made to welcome the King of Europe. It was suggested that the King needs a sumptuous palace, a retinue of about 22 staff with personal Jet to rival Air Force 1 - the private plane for American Presidents. Whether the Lisbon Treaty is ratified or abandoned, the King of Europe would be enthroned to lead Europe to the "Promised Land of Carbon-Free" – full of peace and prosperity."

According to *Daily News,* a publication in the nineteen century, this "Unknown Irishman", who predicted a political Europe and its future, "writes forcibly, eloquently, with much knowledge of what others think and say, and with profound conviction and confidence." And to the Ulsterman's credit, another newspaper reported: "His views are worthy of the utmost respect and consideration." You will meet the "Unknown Ulsterman."

As we progress with our study, I would examine whether the destiny of Great Britain and Ireland lie in Jean Monnet's fuzzy vision of a "fused" Europe, or in the extraordinarily bright vision of the "Seer of Dublin." I repeat. I will put Jean Monnet, the 'giant' of Europe, and the "Forgotten Irishman" in a scale for Americans and Europeans, and the rest of the world to measure them. The results of the assessment would determine whether it would be safer for Great Britain and

Ireland to jump from their little 'islands' into the 'sea' which is flooded with "sea monsters"? Would Britons and the Irish survive in the 'sea of sharks'?

You might have known or read about Jean Monnet, the "Spiritual god-father" of the European Project, the "tutelary genius," the "thoroughgoing internationalist who has made a marked impact on history." Monnet has even been described as a "prophet" and a "revolutionary." We must ask the question: how should politicians, political commentators and political scientists in America and Europe, who 'worship' Jean Monnet, describe the Irishman who wrote about European Union: how it would develop, its nature and future prospects before the "prophet" Monnet, the "Practical apostle of European unity," was born in 1888?

THE EUROPEAN 'MONSTER'

In a newspaper article, *Party leaders run scared as European monster awakens,* Andrew Grice writes: "Europe is the sleeping giant of British politics. It often suits our leaders not to talk about it. Just when they think the issue is dead, a monster awakens, goes on the rampage, divides their parties and damages them in the eyes of the voters" (The Independent 17 June 2006). And Melanie Phillips confirmed this fact in her article - *The dirty little secret is that our MPs hardly matter any more."* She writes: "The EU is the issue that all politicians are ignoring in the hope that we will forget about it. They hope we have forgotten to be concerned about the European constitution, which would bring into being an unprecedented bureaucratic super-state and end once and for all what remains of the independence of EU member states. The EU is fundamentally anti-democratic project based on the belief that the individual nation is the source of the ills of the world and that by contrast supra-national institutions offer the solution to all its problems. The absence of democratic accountability is now corrupting not just European politics but our own" (*Daily Mail* 9 June 2008). She has been proved right. In May 2009 some politicians in the British Parliament were exposed in the national newspapers as fiddlers and tax evaders who defrauded the British people and turned the House of Commons into a "House of Shame."

If Europe is a "giant", then little "David" must collect 5 smooth stones from the small "Island" and sling one of them at the forehead of the "giant". If Europe is a "monster", then little "David" must use the sword of the Knight to cut off its "*7 heads*" and "*10 horns*". (I will explain this figure of speech later on).

EURO COINS: THE GREEK 2 EURO CENTS AND THE ITALIAN 5 EURO CENTS:

A Spanish politician once declared that it is upon the European currency, the Euro, would the political union of Europe be built. We know the cultures of Rome and Greece are the foundations upon which Western Civilisation was built. Greek and Roman politics, philosophy, art, drama, science, architecture, law, dance and mathematics form the basis of European culture and civilisation. For this reason, whatever is associated with the Roman and Greek cultures has a bearing on the development of the European Union and its future.

If the 'Euro' is the foundation stone upon which the glory of the European Union would shine, then we must examine what lies behind this 'mighty currency' of Europe, which some experts suggest would one day overthrow the American Dollar. The designs on national currencies and coins are significant. They relate to either a history or a culture of the people who use such currencies and coins. In view of this truism, I will examine the significance of the portraits on the Greek 2 Euro cents and the Italian 5 Euro cents. I have selected these two particular coins because the illustrations on them are connected to the culture and history of the Greeks and the Romans from which European and Western civilisations evolved.

For example, the pictures on the Roman coinage, "IVDAEA CAPTA" (*Judea captured)*, were struck by Emperor Vespasian in AD71 to commemorate the defeat and the capture of the Jews in AD70. The portraits also served another purpose. They reminded the Romans of their gallantry in the destruction of Judea and its Temple in Jerusalem. At the same time they served as a warning to the Jews against further rebellion. Likewise, the illustrations on the Greek 2 Euro cents and the Italian 5 Euro cents are symbols which remind us of how an historic event, which took place in the second century BC, was repeated in the first century AD. And I boldly declare that the same histories would be repeated when the Emperor of the revived Roman Empire is crowned to lead *Europa* to the "Carbon-Free" Land of Peace and Prosperity.

Later on, I will lay the Greek 2 Euro cents under a special "microscope" for a detailed 'three-dimensional high definition picture' to provide us with an additional insight into the European Project and its destiny.

EUROPEAN UNION AND TURKEY AND THE ROMAN CATHOLIC CHURCH

Some Church leaders and Christians 'shed tears' when the architects of the European Constitution rejected their plea to mention God and Christianity in the Blue-print of Europe. On the other hand, when the Archbishop of Canterbury, Dr

Rowan Williams, visited Brussels in 2005, he expressed the view that the Anglican Church was not greatly concerned with the omission of God and Christianity in the preamble to the first European Constitution. However Dr Williams mentioned that he wanted "to better understand the European Union and its role and moral purpose." (*Daily Mail*, 9 November 2005).

The question is: was it necessary for the Roman Catholic Church to have pleaded with the experts who drafted the European Constitution to make references to God and Christianity in their document? Does the Lord Jesus Christ need the European Union? "Was it also essential for a Roman Catholic Cardinal to have questioned the merits of Turkey's membership of the European Union?" Speaking on BBC Radio 4, the former Archbishop of Westminster, Cardinal Cormac Murphy-O'Connor, questioned Tony Blair's enthusiasm for Turkey's membership of the European Union. The Cardinal told listeners: "There may be another view that the mixture of cultures is not a good idea. I think the question is for Europe. Will the admission of Turkey to the European Union be something that benefits a proper dialogue or integration of a very large, predominantly Islamic, country in a continent that, fundamentally, is Christian?" (*The Times* 22 September 2006).

A servant cannot be greater than his master. May be the then spiritual leader of Roman Catholics in England and Wales was following the foot-steps of his master, Pope Benedict XVI. Before his ascension to the Papal throne, the then Cardinal Joseph Alois Ratzinger, in 2004, expressed concern about Turkey's membership of the European Union. He, the Vatican's doctrinal watchdog, declared that "European Union should not admit Turkey as a member because Turkey had always been "in permanent contrast to Europe" (*Financial Times* 27 November 2006). However, in 2006, during his visit to Turkey, the same Pope Benedict XVI advocated for Turkey to be admitted into the European Union. The Pontiff's change of position on Turkey's membership of the European Club earned him the title a "Flip-flop" Pope – "A vicar of doctrine who becomes a diplomat" (*TIME* 25 December 2006). Would the former Cardinal of Westminster also change his mind on Turkey's membership of the European Union now that his 'master' has changed his position on the issue?

Europe may be a 'fundamentally Christian continent' as suggested by Cardinal Cormac Murphy-O'Connor. But the question is: "Is the European Union a 'Christian Club' which should not accommodate a Muslim nation?" I will examine this religious controversy and the relationship between the European Union and Christianity. I will also discuss the role the European Union would play to 'resolve' the conflict in the Middle East and its implications for the United States of America and the rest of the world.

"THE SCHUMAN CAVEAT": A CONSPIRACY OF SILENCE OR IGNORANCE?

In the development of European integration historians, intellectuals, politicians and political commentators have given prominence (and rightly so) to "The Schuman Plan" which was launched on 9 May 1950. This date is significant to the bureaucrats in Brussels to the extent that it has been earmarked the birth day of Europe. In his "Hugo Young's Lecture" at Chatham House, Jose Manuel Barroso, referred to "The Schuman Plan" but failed to say a single word about "The Schuman Caveat." Why?

The 13 November 2006 edition of *TIME* marked its 60 years of publishing in Europe. The cover story read: "60 YEARS OF HEROES" In this Anniversary publication, the President of the European Commission described Jean Monnet, the architect of European Construction, as one of the heroes of our time, whose "*vision still serves as a blue-print for European integration today*". The Boss of European Bureaucracy in Brussels ("BEBB") trumpeted the achievements of "Mister Europe" by referring to the praises the late President John F Kennedy showered on Jean Monnet.

Mr Barroso reminded the world that Jean Monnet's idea of European integration, through the pooling together of the coal and steel resources of France and Germany under a supranational high authority, "was seized upon by French Foreign Minister, Robert Schuman, and the first German Chancellor, Konrad Adenauer." I ask the following questions:

- Why did the expert on European integration fail to mention "The Schuman Caveat" which is vital for the survival of Monnet's "gradualist vision" of a federal Europe?
- Why has "The Schuman Caveat" been ignored by officials in Brussels?
- Why have politicians and political commentators eliminated "The Schuman Caveat" from the debate on European integration and its enlargement?

The "forgotten fact" is that after Robert Schuman launched the European Coal and Steel Community, he subsequently endorsed the "Plan" for a federal Europe with a "caveat." Schuman, initially, disclosed this *"caveat"* to the European Parliament in 1958. He highlighted the significance of the "caveat" in his last book which was published in the 1960's. Is it a conspiracy of silence or ignorance that has resulted in the exclusion of "The Schuman Caveat" in all the debates about the future of Europe? We will examine the implications of this "Caveat."

EUROPEAN UNION, THE CLINTON GLOBAL INITIATIVE AND THE MIDDLE EAST CRISIS

One of the main aims of the European Union is to help resolve the age-old warfare between the Jews and their Arab neighbours - to bring peace to the Middle East. After the 34-day Lebanon War between Israel and Hezbollah in 2006, the popular view shared among political commentators was: "Hezbollah defeated the Israelis." The general perception was America lost its credibility in the eyes of the Muslim world for its blind support of the Jews. In the process, the European Union emerged as the credible "honest broker" with the clout to solve the Middle East conflict. I will deal with the role the European Union would play in the Middle East politics to produce the master politician who will bring 'peace' to the troubled Mediterranean Region.

On 24 September 2006, a global summit titled, *In the name of God,* was organised by the Clinton Global Initiative to discuss a plan to end the fighting between the Jews and the Palestinians. The summit, which was televised on CNN, was hosted by its Chief International Correspondent, Christiane Amanpour. Two of the distinguished quests: Her Majesty Queen Rania of Jordan and a former United Nations Special Adviser, Ambassador Lakhder Brahim, made significant statements that shed a light on how the Jews and the Arabs could meet at a negotiating table for the final peace treaty that would end the blood-feud between the 'two brothers'.

It was also reported in the 24 October 2006 edition of the Financial Times, that George Soros, the millionaire philanthropist, was "considering giving his support to a new initiative that could help resolve the conflict between the Israelis and the Palestinians. In an article titled "*Jewish lobby for peace with Palestinians gather pace in US,"* Gay Dinmore reported on how some Israelis were planning to support a new initiative, "Israel Project", which "could prove a counterweight to more traditional voices" that are also seeking to bring peace into the Middle East. A supporter of the "Israel Project", Jeremy Ben-Ami, who was once an advisor to the former President of the United States of America, Bill Clinton, said, the Lebanon conflict provided a sense of urgency to discussion. The discussion represented "a new effort to promote the perspective in the Jewish community that Israel's security depends on ending this [Palestinian] conflict peacefully. We deeply care for Israel. The Lebanon conflict shows the dangers facing Israel and its need for peace as quickly as possible." The Financial Times' article reported that Mr Soros, who funded the Democratic 2004 presidential campaign, "was vocal in his criticism of Israel's tactics against Hizbollah." He has "called for an end to the vicious circle of escalating violence by reaching a political settlement with the Palestinians."

We will study the implications of the contribution the Queen of Jordan and the former UN Ambassador made towards a solution to the Middle East crisis in the global summit – *In the name of God.* I will throw a light on how a political settlement between the Jews and the Arabs could be achieved "quickly" to bring peace between the warring factions. The world should wait for a while. "Peace" would be restored in the Middle East at the appointed time. The political genius to broker the "peace" deal is on the horizon.

With or without an European Constitution, the European juggernaut would continue to roll on with great velocity. When France and The Netherlands rejected the EU Constitution the Eurocrats paused to plan how they would repackage the discredited Constitution and impose it on the peoples of Europe. Without any doubt, politicians would employ fair and foul means and legitimate and illegitimate means to revive the dead Roman Empire for the purpose foretold by the "Sage of Ulster." In summary: the European leaders are in a hurry to bring to pass what the "Unknown Ulsterman" wrote about the future of Europe.

Britain and Ireland must not co-operate with Europe to 'resurrect' the dead Roman Empire. The life span of this 'non-imperial Empire' would be far shorter in comparison to the years the preceding empires of Rome, Greece, Medo-Persia and Babylon ruled the earth. However far our nation might have fallen in these 'evil days', we must not participate in the reconstruction of the old Roman Empire. Supporters of the European Union claim Britain must be at the "heart of Europe". The question is: What is this "heart of Europe"? Is the European Project a living 'organism' or a body without a 'soul'? The fate of the revived Roman Empire has already been determined by a "*Rolling Stone.*" It takes a wise man to avert a prophecy.

THE MAJOR THREAT FACING MANKIND IS THE PROGRESSION OF THE EUROPEAN UNION AND NOT CLIMATE CHANGE

On 30 October 2006, the former World Bank chief economist, Sir Nicholas Stern, produced a report on "Climate Change." The document warned of global catastrophe if countries failed to spend about £184billion to reduce the amount of carbon dioxide and other pollutants pumped into the atmosphere. The Report, which was commissioned by the Labour Government, was launched in a glaze of publicity. The then Prime Minister, Tony Blair, declared at the launch: "This is the most important report on the future published by this government....It is not in doubt that if the science is right, the consequences for our planet are literally disastrous." Question: "What about if the science is wrong?"

Today, the perception is that human beings, who don't know what would happen to them in the next minute, can save the planet by reducing the quantity of poisonous gases thrown into the air. We delude ourselves. To begin with, the

"Stern Report" is not the most important document about the future of planet earth. And no human being on planet earth could produce a credible report about the future of mankind. The future of our planet has already been recorded in a Unique Book which the confused world claims it is out of date. Yet, without any doubt, this Book is the most important and reliable document ever produced. What is this book? You may guess.

Secondly, I defy all scientists who subscribe to the view that if we do not cut carbon emissions, there would be a global disaster within the next 10 to 50 years. I defy the scientists who claim climate change "is like nuclear war." The fact is not all scientists support such alarmist view of our planet. The truth is: Scientists cannot predict the future because they don't know the future. Their knowledge is limited. Was it a scientist who predicted the restoration of the Jews to Palestine before the Zionist Movement was launched in 1896 and the state of Israel was created in May 1948? Again, was it a scientist who predicted a confederation of European nations and its character before the founding Fathers of European Community were born in 1888 and 1886?

In February 2008, an earthquake that measured 5.2 on the Richter scale shook Britain. This was believed to be the largest tremor since 1984 when an earthquake, measuring 5.4 on the Richter scale, shook North Wales. The question is: which scientist predicted in 2007 that in 2008 an earthquake would be felt from Southampton to Scotland, with the epicentre in Market Rasen in Lincolnshire? None. Yet some of these scientists, who could not even forecast what would happen a year ahead, claim that the earth would be destroyed within 10 to 50 years if carbon emission into the air is not reduced. Should these scientists be taken seriously with their message of doom? I repeat: scientists do NOT know the future. Which scientist or politician predicted in the 20th century that there would be a global financial crisis that would result in the collapse of Lehman Brothers and the nationalisation of major financial institutions in Britain and America?

This whole "climate change thing", which, according to Jose Manuel Barroso, has become a "defining issue for EU", "is a fairy tale." Give me a break'– to borrow the words of Bill Clinton. Professor Richard Lindzen dismissed the fallacy of the global threat from climate change in his article *"Global warming is the religion of our age: self-righteous, intolerant of dissent and based on superstition"* (Daily Mail 8 March 2007). The Science Professor poured scorn on the Stern Report with this remark: "The lack of understanding of science shines through every chapter of his report. He is guilty of misreading data, of distorting the evidence to suit his political masters' dogma, of throwing numbers about with reckless abandon of promoting alarmism in place of rational discussion, and of reinventing history...Far from being the powerful masterpiece that Blair claimed, Stern's report is manifestly incompetent. It is another doggy dossier, where assertions are presented as facts and data is twisted to suit a political purpose..."

And it was reported in the 7 March 2007 edition of The Times, that in February 2007 the Czech President, Vaclav Klaus, described global warming as "a false myth perpetuated by politicised scientists." Then appeared Al Gore's "Inconvenient Truth": the doom-laden Climate Change film that warns the destruction of the earth if men fail to reduce Carbon Dioxide into the atmosphere. According to a British Judge, Mr Gore's doom-laden documentary contains about nine errors. Error is an error. "Among the children of error there is no cohesion, save their hostility to truth", says the "Seer of Dublin."

Again, another scientist dismissed the 'climate change' threat. In an article, *Global warming? No it's getting colder*, Tony Bonnici quoted the view of the scientist Philip Stott. According to this emeritus professor of biogeography at the University of London, "The world has been warming up since the end of little ice age some time around 1880. There has been a gradual rise in temperatures – with a few ups and downs along the way – and the world is now 0.74C warmer...There was a cooling period between 1947 and 1970 followed by a warming period. But since 1998 there has been no global warming. At the same time we have seen a rise in the levels of carbon dioxide."

The Reporter then quoted the comments of another Austrian scientist which seemed to support the view of professor Stott. The Australian Scientist, Bob Carter, professor of paleoclimatologist, stated: "The cause of many rapid climate changes remains unknown but it's unlikely that greenhouse gas fluctuations are responsible for them." He added, Greenhouse gases might be baneful "for raising Earth's average temperature from a chilly -18C to the estimated modern value of about 15C" (*Daily Express* 10 April 2008). It is clear from this article that scientists are divided on this "Climate Change" thing. Not all of them share the pessimistic view that "Global warming" would cause havoc around the world.

The awkward truth is that whether politicians spend trillions of pounds to reduce emissions of carbon dioxide from motor vehicles, aircrafts, ships and industrial plants to zero, or whether atmospheric pollutants increase to trillions of tons, the earth would be renewed with fire by the direct hand of the Almighty God – the One who made the heavens and the earth. There would be no human intervention. The disaster that is coming upon the earth would not be the result of the carbon dioxide we pumped into the atmosphere. For the Good Book has already predicted the fate of planet earth: *"The day of the Lord will come like a thief. The heavens will disappear with a roar; and the earth and everything in it will be laid bare...That day will bring about the destruction of the heavens by fire, and the elements will melt away in the heat", and there will be a new heaven and a new earth* (2 Peter 3:10-13). This would surely happen because the Omnipotent has decreed that not a single word from his Mouth would return void. It is the Lord who will create a new heaven and a new earth (Isaiah 65:17).

GOD KEEPS HIS WORD

When God revealed to Enoch, the 7th generation of mankind, that He would wipe out all life on earth because of the wickedness of men, the Almighty waited patiently for 969 years before using the flood of waters to destroy the world. This happened in the days of Noah, which was the 10th generation of mankind. We will learn more about the significance of the first 10 generations of mankind – the genealogy of Adam to Noah - and the importance of the order the Patriarch Jacob blessed his 12 sons. The implications of these scriptures, which are recorded in Genesis 5 and Genesis 49 respectively, would confirm that the Bible is not an ordinary human book. It is a Divine revelation.

God will renew His polluted earth not with the floods of water as it happened in the days of Noah, but with fire. The regeneration of our planet with inferno would be preceded by the last 7- year reign of human governments on earth. The European Union would be the catalyst for the renewal of all things on planet earth. The extent to which we associated ourselves with the coming leader of the "political phenomenon" in Europe would determine our eternal destiny: whether we will escape the wrath of God or be thrown into the lake of burning sulphur. Our fate would not be determined by our "carbon foot-prints" – the amount of carbon dioxide we have released to contaminate the air.

The Almighty, who knows the end from the beginning, lectured us on "climate change" thousands of years ago. He stated: *"As long as the earth endures, seed-time and harvest, cold and heat, summer and winter, day and night will never cease"* (Genesis 8:22*).* Scriptures are more credible than any scientific research work. The Bible predicts future events with 100 percent accuracy. The Lord Jesus Christ is more reliable than scientists, economists, philosophers, politicians and Eco-Warriors. It would be far more profitable for us to listen to what the Lord of lords, the King of kings says about the future of our planet.

Let us examine what the Book of Revelation says about the Lord pouring His 7 bowls of judgement on earth. The contents of the "7th Bowl" would be "flashes of lightning, rumblings, peals of thunder and a severe earthquake. No earthquake like it has ever occurred since man has been on earth, so tremendous would be the quake that every island would flee away. The mountains would disappear. From the sky huge hailstones of about a hundred pounds would fall upon men. And men "would curse God on account of the plague of hail because the plague would be terrible" (Revelation 16:17-21). There would be a day when men would yearn to die from climate change, but death would elude them (Revelation 9:6).

On account of the above Scriptures, I, again, defy the "Scare-Mongering Scientists" (SMS) who have predicted a worldwide calamity of faming, poverty, diseases, rising sea levels, rising temperatures and floods if we do not ease emissions of Carbon Dioxide. Why couldn't the sophisticated scientists predict the Global Financial Crisis of 2007-2008 which resulted in the collapse and nationalisation of financial institutions in America and Britain? The answer is simple. Scientists have no 'eyes' to see future events. Scientists: witness what the Bible says about our Planet: "First of all, you must understand that in the last days scoffers will come, scoffing and following their own evil desires.....But they deliberately forget that long ago by God's word the heavens existed and the earth was formed out of water and by water. By these waters also the world of that time was deluged and destroyed. By the same word the present heavens and earth are reserved for fire, being kept for the day of judgement and destruction of ungodly men." (2 Peter 3:3-7)

And over 2000 years ago, the Lord Jesus Christ predicted that before He returns, "Nation will rise against nation, and kingdom against kingdom. There will be great earthquakes, famines and pestilences in various places, and fearful events and great signs from heaven" (Luke 21:10-11). In view of the Lord's proclamation (He who is the TRUTH, the LIFE and the WAY), we do not need scientists to frighten us of universal tragedy of floods, famine, drought and epidemic diseases if we do not curb greenhouse gases from our motor vehicles, aircrafts, ships and industrial plants.

WATCH OUT FOR THE FATEFUL 'SIGN' ASSOCIATED WITH THE EUROPEAN UNION

The Lord Jesus Christ made this bold statement: "Heaven and earth will pass away, but my words will not pass away." We should rather keep watch for the last momentous sign the Lord predicted would appear before He returns to judge mankind. This important sign is associated with the development of the European Union. What is the sign? It is *"the abomination that causes desolation."* It would be seen in the Jerusalem Temple (Matthew 24:15) to mark the genesis of the last 3½ years of this age which would be under the control of the Emperor of the revived Roman Empire.

The European Union would play the leading role to bring about this final "sign" to close the era of Gentile supremacy on earth. This would culminate in unspeakable disasters. Our focus must be on the progress of the European Project, not on the percentage of carbon dioxide we pour into the atmosphere. For the Lord has already declared that He would not destroy the world again with flood of waters (Genesis: 9:12-16). He will clean the mess in His creation with fire. Our eternal destiny would, therefore, be determined on how we associated ourselves with this "sign" – the "Abomination that causes desolation."

The European Union is eager for the rest of the world to adopt its rules (Financial Times 19 February 2007). The European Union might have been proud of its role in the negotiations to create the Kyoto treaty which would bind countries to reduce carbon emissions to "save" the planet. The reality is that Kyoto Treaty and all human treaties on climate change would not succeed in preventing the calamity that is coming upon the earth. New technologies and eco-taxes to reduce carbon emission would not help either. The 'religion of Climate Change' has diverted the minds of men from the most significant event in history that would determine our eternal destiny on earth. This 'religion for the salvation of mother earth' is the deception of the 21st century.

The Lord Jesus Christ tells us: "I am the truth, the way and the life." This means, His warning concerning planet earth would surely come to pass. No scientist, no economist, no philosopher and no politician can claim to be the "truth, the way and life." Scientists and politicians don't know the future. These 'experts' are not men of vision. They are 'men of circumstances' – driven by events and always at the mercy of events. For example, how many scientists predicted in 1900 that that Britain would experience a major earthquake on 27 February 2008? How many politicians predicted in 2000 that The Northern Rock Bank would be 'nationalised' by the Labour government in 2008? How many politicians predicted the 'credit crunch' of 2008? How many politicians predicted that some of their colleagues would be exposed and shamed as "fiddlers" and "tax dodgers" Yet these same politicians, who have no clue of what is happening around them, boast they can save the world. They have joined the 'blind' scientists to put fear in the public that within 10-50 years the earth would 'collapse' if we do not reduce carbon emissions.

In an article titled *Eco-loonies reject an inconvenient truth*, Littlejohn quoted an American scientist, John Coleman, who claimed the great global warming scare is a huge scam. He made this remark at a conference on Climate Change. Most prominent newspapers and magazines did not cover his comments on the climate change scam. Littlejohn continued: "Politicians have vested interest in peddling this swindle. It's the latest way of bullying us and picking our pockets" (Daily Mail 18 March 2008). This is the truth about the "economics of climate change."

Nigel Lawson, the former Chancellor of the Exchequer, in his essay, *The real inconvenient truth*, writes, "Global warming is the new religion and any heretic who questions it is demonised. He explains that with the collapse of Marxism, and other forms of socialism coupled with the dislike of the excesses of capitalism, and the rejection of religion, men have now embraced the religion of Climate Change to fill the vacuum. Commenting on how the European Union has become the 'Vatican of Climate Change Religion', Mr. Lawson writes: "... I suspect it is no accident that it is in Europe that eco-fundamentalism in general and global warming absolutism in particular has found its most fertile soil. For ... Europe has become the most secular society in the world, where the traditional religion have the weakest hold....It is that quasi-religion of green alarmism, of which global warming issue is the most striking example, which has filled the vacuum, with reasoned questioning of its mantras regarded as little short of sacrilege." Nigel Lawson concludes his essay by declaring that even if this so-called threat to human existence from climate change could be averted, "it is clear that the would-be saviours of the planet are, in practice, the enemies of poverty reduction in the developing world. So, the new religion of global warming, however convenient it may be to the politicians.... indeed, the more one examines it, the more it resembles a Da Vince Code of environmentalism. It is a great story, and a phenomenal best-seller. It contains a grain of truth – and a mountain of nonsense."

The Green Revolution has become 'fashionable clothes' to be put on by the modern man. We must depend on what the Lord says about the future of our planet not what 'pendulum' politicians and "blind" scientists speculate. We will learn more about the last "sign" - *"the abomination that causes desolation"* - as we progress with our study.

When an issue suits the agenda of politicians it is proclaimed on the mountain top. But when a subject undermines their programme it is put under a bushel. Labour politicians put the *Stern Report* on the environment on a hill top. Why didn't politicians display the *Werner Report* on the Common Market on the rooftop for the British public to see it, but was hidden from them? I repeat: our focus must be centred on the development of the European Union. Because it is the coming emperor of the European Empire who will eventually, but temporarily, steer events in this world. And it is vital we recognise this last Kaiser of the revived Roman Empire when he arrives on the political scene. The Lisbon Treaty has paved the way for the Emperor to be crowned.

At this point I would make my position clear. I am not suggesting we live irresponsibly by dumping rubbish around and driving in motor vehicles which are not roadworthy – belching out fumes. All of us will die. This is the reality of human existence. But our eventual demise does not mean we should be careless with our lives. We should not hasten our death by indulging in excessive alcoholic beverages, smoking of tobacco and bad eating habits. We should not be reckless to jump in front of trucks. Neither should we dive onto electrified rail lines. Similarly, the earth would be renewed with fire as decreed by the Lord Jesus Christ. That does not mean we should plunder it. So long as we are spending our days on planet earth, we must take care of our environment. But the notion that we can somehow save the planet to save ourselves by spending trillions to clean the air and plant billions of trees in the forest is ridiculous. We must not worship the environment. What is called "Mother Earth" should not be deified. Politicians don't know what is happening in their political parties. Events control them; they are not in control. Yet they proudly proclaim: "We are going to save the planet with "Green policies." This is sheer arrogance that generates from ignorance. Let politicians around the globe first solve rising crimes, and violence in their streets. Let them prevent teenage pregnancies and abortions. Let them prevent anti-social behaviours and global financial crisis.

Sadly, some church leaders and Christians have jumped on the green bandwagon to pursue the "Green revolution". Pope Benedict has become the first "Green Pope". These Christian leaders have abandoned their primary assignment, the proclamation of the Gospel of Christ: "Repent for the Kingdom of God is at hand", and have become assistant eco-warriors who are 'worshipping' the earth. The environment is not God; it is the hand-work of the Almighty. The Anglican Bishop of Liverpool, the Rt. Reverend James Jones, cautioned Christians: "Forget Heaven, we must save the earth" (The Times 27 November 2003). The scriptural truth is that man cannot save himself. So, if a creature of dust cannot save himself, how can this frail human being rescue planet earth? If even the earth is 'terminally ill', how can a mortal being heal it? Does the man of dust know the foundations of the earth? The earth belongs to the Lord and everything in it (Psalm 24:1). It is the Lord who will renew His earth which we have 'polluted' it with violence, greed, immoralities, wickedness and our numerous vices.

Christians should not blindly follow 'blind' politicians. Church leaders should rather stress the elimination of the real "*pollutants*" that "pollute" our "environment." It is these "*pollutants*": murder, sexual immoralities, anger, pride, theft, slander, adultery, fornication, drunkenness, envy, lewdness and other vices that would defile us to make us unclean to enjoy eternal life in the Kingdom of God, not the 'external pollutants' (Matthew 15:10-20). We must be clean in the 'inside' to know how to clean the 'outside'. If Church leaders do not believe in this scriptural truth, they must leave their glittering robes behind the altars and the pulpits and become full time 'environmental warriors.' The 'Sophisticated Theologians' among them should go back to universities and seminaries to teach "Lology."

Lamenting on the state of Christianity in his days, the "Seer of Dublin" wrote: "Illumination is much needed at this moment, when the church is honeycombed by scepticism – scepticism, moreover which is the outcome, not of fuller knowledge or matured thought, but of intellectual conceit and levity which are the marked characteristics of the age."

YESTERDAY, TODAY AND TOMORROW

Supporters of the European Enterprise are witnesses of the confusion and the divisions that have plagued the European Project. And European leaders have no hint where the European Vessel is heading. It was therefore not surprising when the Belgian Prime Minister, Paul-Henri Spaak, who was once the President of the Consultative Assembly of the Council of Europe, and chaired the Assembly of European Coal and Steel Community, made this 'prophetic' statement in 1952: *"We do not want another committee. We have too many already. What we want is a man of sufficient stature to hold the allegiance of all people, and to lift us out of the economic morass in which we are sinking. Send us such a man and he be God or the devil, we will receive him."* Surely, a time is fast approaching when Europe will have such a leader. Their Lisbon Treaty has paved the way for the "man of sufficient stature" to appear to lift Europe from its woes.

So far as the European Construction is concerned, politicians and political commentators are familiar with its past: the development of European Community from the debris of the Second World War. The euro-enthusiasts always quote "The Schuman Plan" which laid the foundation for the economic and political union of European nations. Strangely, these 'experts' on European integration have not mentioned a single word on "The Schuman Caveat" which is about the future prospects of the European project. European leaders: witness these words of the "Seer of Dublin": *"If a knowledge of the past be important, a knowledge of the future must be of far higher value still, in enlarging the mind and raising it above the littlenesses produced by a narrow and unenlightened contemplation of the present.*

When the French and the Dutch rejected the European Constitution in 2005, BBC Radio 4 produced a programme that discussed the direction of the European Project. The host, Quentin Peel, international affairs editor of the Financial Times, opened the discussion with this statement: "The European Union is in a profound political crisis. It is a challenge that calls into question not just what the Union does, but what is it for and how it should work". A panellist followed up: "I think it's time for a radical reform of what the European Union is about….it's clear an awful lot of people are not happy with it. How we unscramble it is going to be the great debate." Another panellist, Pascal Lamy, French political advisor, declared: "The French referendum, the Dutch referendum and what you see after the financial perspectives later on is for me a symptom that the 25 member states do not anymore agree on the bulk of what they want to do together: among them enlargement; among them immigration; among them certain aspects of internal market; among them the lack of real European economic policy; among them the lack of security…"

The question still remains. How is it that for the past 58 years, since the birth of the European Union, politicians and commentators do not know what the European Union is for? Is it not curious, that the 'children' of Jean Monnet, the master builder of European Community, have no idea of the direction and the future prospects of the 'Enterprise' which their 'father' built?

"SEDUCTION" BY BARROSO CONTINUES

Before the summit in Berlin to celebrate the 50th anniversary of the Treaty of Rome, Jose Manuel Barroso, once again, attempted to seduce Britons to jump into the "Deep-sea" in Brussels to be consumed by "sea-monsters." On 2 March 2007, Mr Barroso held a pre-summit meeting with the then British Prime Minister, Tony Blair. The Chief "Euro-salesman" made one of his "slick presentations": "The Europe of the 21st century takes its inspiration in many ways from Britain." This perceived compliment was an attempt to influence Tony Blair to sell Britons to 'slave traders' in Monnet's "slave market" in Brussels. Mr Barroso continued with his seduction: "We need Britain in Europe for many reasons" – probably to help solve the problems of climate change, terrorism and poverty in Africa.

On 3 March 2007, *The Times* commented on Mr Barroso's conference with Tony Blair. In its leading article, "Declaration of what?" the editorial rightly voiced this caution: "Blair and Britain must avoid being ambushed in Berlin." The popular view is that the Common Agricultural Policy, the Common Fisheries Policy, the Enlargement of the European Union, and the development of a Single Market with its Single Currency are some of the major success stories of the European Union. These achievements have precipitated the perception that the European Union is an 'Unsinkable ship.' This 'luxurious vessel' (EU) has captivated British and Irish politicians to the extent that they would even indulge in 'misleading advertisements' to get Britons and the Irish to board the lavish boat. However, the tragedy of the "Unsinkable" Titanic of the 20th century should be a lesson to all politicians who have "closed their eyes" to jump into Jean Monnet's "magnificent boat." They have been "tempted" with 'discounted first class tickets' from 'ticket masters' in Brussels to 'pay' for the people of Britain and Ireland to join them on the "doomed vessel."

On 28 February 2007, *speakout.co.uk* sponsored a full page advertisement in *The* Daily Telegraph on Britain's participation in the European Union. The advert featured the portraits of the then leaders of the three main political parties: Tony Blair (Labour), David Cameron (Conservatives), and Sir Menzies Campbell (Liberal Democrats). The text read: "A migrant a minute is entering Britain. Without a debate or vote in Parliament our elected MPs have handed control of our borders to the European Union, allowing unlimited immigration into Britain from EU countries. 88% of you, the people, want a vote on getting your borders back. Write to your MP and demand a referendum NOW."

On the same day (28 February 2007) the *speakout.co.uk* poster was painted in The Daily Telegraph, another interesting poster on European Union was also published in the Financial Times. This particular advertisement invited the public to FT debate on the European Union. The title of the poster read: The EU: blessing or curse? The theme of the debate was: *"Thank God for Brussels".* The discussion, which was scheduled to mark the 50th anniversary of the Treaty of Rome, was intended to answer the following questions:

- Has the EU strengthened its member countries or sapped them with bureaucracy?
- What is European Union really for, and where should it be heading?

The unknown and inconvenient truth is that the answers to the above questions were first published by the "Unknown Irishman" in the 19th century before the European Union's 'prophet', Jean Monnet, was even conceived in 1888. And the same "answers" were again published in 1957, the very year the Treaty of Rome was signed to bring the European Economic Community into existence which has now developed into a political union of 27 European nations.

It is interesting to observe that Financial Times - a newspaper which supports the development of the European Union - acknowledges a God who deserves thanksgiving. But do Brussels and the EU "Do God"? The plain truth is that the 'Directors' of "EU PLC" in Belgium have no room for the gracious God whom "thanksgiving" is due. This fact was confirmed in the 20 March 2007 edition of The Independent newspaper. In a column titled *EU celebrates its 50th birthday – with a row about religion*, the paper noted: "Neither God nor Christianity will feature in a 50th birthday celebration for the EU which will highlight European values and list key challenges for the future such as climate change." The fact is the European Union is not a Christian Club, so there is no need for Christianity to be associated with the European Project. Secondly, God and the Lord Jesus Christ do not need the European Union. Yet, they need the European Union for a purpose. We will learn more about this "purpose" as we progress with our study

THE EUROPEAN UNION IS A "FLOATING PALACE"

On 21 March 2007, The Independent newspaper concluded its leading article, *"A potent symbol of peace and unity,"* with this tribute to the European Union: "In its 50 years, the EU has shown more cohesion than division, sometimes surprising itself. And it has become a model for international association that is admired around the world. Seen from the inside, it might seem short of efficiency, democracy and common purpose, but too often our critical introspection blinds us to its merits. The best testimonial for the European Union at 50 is the queue of would-be members clamouring to join."

This is my response: The "passengers" in the long queue to board the "Great Titanic" of the 21st century are not aware that the EU is a "floating palace" steaming towards an "ice-berg." It is not too late for the 'would-be passengers of Monnet's vessel' to heed the warning the "Unknown Ulsterman" gave about European integration before the "EU Titanic" was constructed in 1950. Without a comprehensive knowledge of the actual purpose of the European Union and its future prospects, "passengers" would be attempted to board a "luxurious "vessel" which was doomed even before the architect who designed it was conceived. It is the man in the street who would be mesmerised by EU - the "potent symbol of peace and unity" - to board the "European Titanic." The Good Book says: "While people are saying 'peace and safety,' destruction will come upon them suddenly, as labour pains on a pregnant woman and they will not escape." (1 Thessalonians 5:3).

This leads to the question: "If the European Union has become a model for international association that is admired around the world, and if because of this "political phenomenon" its French architect, Jean Monnet, is regarded a 'genius' and a 'prophet,' then how should Americans and Europeans and the rest of the world describe the Irishman who wrote about this "phenomenon" and its character before Jean Monnet was born?

THE 50th ANNIVERSARY OF THE TREATY OF ROME

On Sunday, 25 March 2007, the 27 leaders of the European Union gathered at the German Historic Museum in Berlin to celebrate the 50th anniversary of the Treaty of Rome. This Treaty was the second step in the construction of the European Empire. The first step was The Schuman Plan which created the European Coal and Steel Community.

Prior to the climax of the celebration (the signing of the Berlin Declaration) Angela Merkel, the German Chancellor, Jose Manuel Barroso, the President of European Commission, Romano Prodi, then the Italian Prime Minister, and Hans Gert Pottering, the then President of the European Parliament, made patronising speeches. They trumpeted the successes of the European Project - "Peace, Prosperity, the Development of a Single Market and the Enlargement of the European Community". The European "Quartet" concluded their rhetoric by highlighting the challenges of the future - globalisation, immigration, global warming and terrorism. Without a surprise, not a single speaker made any reference to the crucial advice the first President of the European Parliament gave to Europeans concerning the survival of the European enterprise. Why? Was it ignorance or conspiracy of silence?

PETER MANDELSON AND LEON BRITTAN AND THEIR CONTEMPT FOR BRITONS

After the speeches at the German Historic Museum, the celebration reached its peak when the EU 'Trio' (Angela Merkel, Jose Manuel Barroso, and Hans Gert Pottering) signed the Berlin Declaration. The purpose of this document, which was drafted in secrecy, was to lay the foundation for the repackaging of the rejected European Constitution and how it should be imposed on the peoples of Europe. Peter Mandelson, the then EU Trade Commissioner, was quoted to have suggested that "the changes that would be proposed would not require the endorsement of the British people in a vote" (Source: Daily Mail 26 March 2007, *EU constitution back on the Table).* That was an exhibition of arrogance and contempt for the British people.

I ask the following questions:

- "When did Peter Mandelson become an 'expert' on European integration to lecture Britons?"
- "Why were Britons not given the chance to endorse or reject a constitution which was intended to make them 'slaves' to strangers in a foreign country?"

Without any surprise, Leon Brittan, a former 'employee' of "EU Corporation," made a ridiculous statement on the Lisbon Treaty. He suggested: "It would be piquant....for an unelected House of Lords to seek to impose a referendum, the ultimate manifestation of popularist democracy, where the elected house has declined it". Did the elected "House of Fiddlers" have a mandate from the British people who lent them their power to transfer those powers to aliens? In his wisdom, Leon Brittan was comfortable for unelected and uncountable officials in EU Headquarters, who have no clue what the European Enterprise is for, to impose laws on elected politicians who are accountable to the British people.

Had the "learned" Leon Brittan done his 'homework' on European integration, and analysed what a brilliant Irish Barrister wrote about political Europe and its future prospects before the French Founding Fathers of the European Union were conceived, he would have had a different perspective of Jean Monnet's project. Leon Brittan would have learnt that the Lisbon Treaty was something to be 'afraid' of, and that the British people should have been given their democratic and moral rights to throw the Lisbon Treaty into a dust-bin. However, it was not surprising that Leon Brittan supported the transfer of powers to undemocratic institutions in Europe. As a former EU Commissioner he is under obligation to sing his masters;' voice – to promote the interest of the European Union - a body which lacks political accountability and democratic legitimacy for its existence - a political project "made by deceit and lies" (Fredrick Forsyth: *Daily Express* 11 April 2008). The question remains: How well-informed are politicians on European integration to treat the electorate with contempt?

THE TREATY OF ROME AND THE PREDICTION OF EUROPEAN CONFEDERACY

Had the European leaders who gathered in Berlin read the 14th edition of the "Forgotten Ulsterman's" work on political union of European nations, they would not have spent millions to celebrate the 50th anniversary of the Treaty of Rome. The Bland Berlin Declaration (BBD) would not have been necessary. The text, which ended with a meaningless statement, "For we know, Europe is our future" worth less than the value of the paper it was written on. Not surprisingly, the spectacle at the German Historic Museum in Berlin was a "blind" woman leading 26 strong "blind" men with a "group passport" to board Monnet's "Doom Titanic."

Was it a coincidence that the 14th edition of the "Seer of Dublin's" prediction of the development of a confederation of European nations and its future was published in the same year the Treaty of Rome was signed as the second major step towards a "federated Europe"? The Berlin Declaration was not necessary, because an Irishman published the future of political European in the 19th century before the European Union even evolved from the wreckage of the Second World War in the 20th century.

EU LEADERS COPY THE TACTICS OF THEIR PATRONS

It was insulting to Europeans for politicians, who cannot discern the purpose and the future of the European Union, to have planned in secret to impose a discredited constitution on them – a document which two of the founding members of the European Union had already rejected in a popular vote in 2005. We must not be surprised by the diabolical tactics European leaders adopted to force the Lisbon Treaty on the peoples of Europe. They followed the footsteps of their patrons. Witness the comments Paul Henri Spaak made when the initial plan for creating an European Defence Community failed: "Our recent set back in connection with the European Defence Community had proved that it was premature to try and build a united Europe by….the most logical and speedy method….the constitutional method….. We consider that having failed on the political plane, we should take up the question on the economic plane."
The Belgian Spaak, who was a signatory to the Treaties of Paris and Rome, added: *"Political union which had to follow economic union was no longer to be imposed by treaties that proved too bold for the public to swallow….Under the new tactics it was to be imposed by the pressure of facts created by the gradual abolition of economic*

frontiers between the Six. Union was no longer to be proclaimed, it was to be insinuated into old divided Europe, to be smuggled in by the back door, to flow naturally, spontaneously and irresistibly from the necessities created by total economic disarmament." (Messina Conference June 1955 Source: *A political Biography of Paul Henri Spaak by J H Huizinga*).

It is clear from Spaak's comments that deceit and secrecy are the hallmarks of the European project. And Peter McKay confirmed it in his article "A vampire feeding on our misery." He writes: "Deceit and hypocrisy are as common in politics as in everyday life." (Daily Mail 17 November 2008).

The European leaders spent millions of euro to entertain themselves on the "unsinkable" ship to celebrate the Treaty of Rome. That was their 'wise' decision. However, they should not drag innocent citizens to board Monnet's 'cruise ship' – the magnificent palace on the storming seas, which is destined to sink beneath the waves. The British and the Irish must jump off the 'EU Boat' before it sinks.

To dispel any fears that Britons and the Irish would "drown" by leaping off Monnet's 'luxurious boat', I would remind the reader what Charles Moore, former Editor of The Daily Telegraph, wrote in his article *Happy birthday to EU, happy birthday to EU, happy...?* He stated: "Most of this country's moves towards greater European integration have been born of weakness. The theory, in our economic decadence of the 1960s and 1970s, was that when you want a seat in the lifeboat, you don't haggle about the price. Today, we don't need the lifeboat. More money is managed and traded in London than in the entire euro zone put together. There is nothing that more European integration could bring us that we cannot get by other means." After highlighting the "fuzzy language" of the Berlin Declaration and the autocratic attitude of the Eurocrats, Mr Moore concluded, "The Eurosceptic task now is not to shout abuse from the bank, but to persuade the rulers of Europe that unless they go with the flow, they will drown." (The Daily Telegraph 26 March 2007). Unfortunately, nothing would persuade the rulers of Europe to change course. The "Magnificent Titanic" of the 21st century is on course to sink. That is its destiny. What the "Forgotten Irishman" published on European confederacy and its character has been fulfilled. What he recorded about the future of this 'political phenomenon in history' is on course to be fulfilled. The Lisbon Treaty has paved the way for the 'Experienced Captain' to pilot Monnet's 'unsinkable' ship to its destination.

To every problem there is a solution. But where a problem cannot be solved, it means the requisite knowledge out of which the solution could be drawn has not yet been acquired. My burden is to unveil the "Unknown Truth", the "Forgotten Truth" and the "Distorted Truth" relating to the European Project for these "three truths" to set Britons and the Irish free from 'bondage' in Brussels.

THE VALUE OF THE "KEY" THAT "UNLOCKS" THE "TITANIC" OF THE 21st CENTURY

Between March and April 2007, most London newspapers reported that a letter which was written by a passenger who died on the Titanic became a treasure worth about £60000. The man –Alfred Rowe, confided to his wife Constance that "he thought the ship too big and a positive danger" (The Times 30 March 2007). This "precious" letter was posted on 11 April 1912 from Queenstown, the Titanic's last stop, and was discovered for the first time in 95 years. It was also reported that the keys and the chain to the Titanic's mail room, which was found hanging on the frozen body of the Post room clerk, Scott Woody, a week after the ship was buried in the Atlantic, had been discovered. And this relic was valued about £50000.

If £60000 was the estimated value for a letter written on the doomed Titanic, and £50000 was the expected value of the rusty keys to the Titanic post room, then what price should we place on the Ulsterman's book that unlocks the future of the European Union - the political phenomenon of our time - which is the "Titanic of the 21st century"? This classic book about European integration and its future was first published in 1881 before the "Unsinkable" Titanic set sail from Southampton to New York in 1912. The third edition was released in 1889; the year Adolf Hitler, the "Catalyst of the European Community, was born, and when Jean Monnet, the chief designer of the "European vessel", was a year old; and Robert Schuman, the politician who launched the European Coal and Steel Community, was a three year old toddler. I have already mentioned of further editions which were published in 1895, 1903, 1914, 1957, 1963, 1967, 1969, 1972, 1975 and 1977. I have seen copies of the Second, Third, Fifth, Sixth, Seventh, Tenth, Eleventh, Twelfth, Thirteenth, Fourteenth and the Nineteenth editions of this classic book. The Irish author, who was described as a "literary recluse," autographed one of the editions for a friend.

Here is a clue that could help you identify the "Seer of Dublin" who had a bright vision of how the European Union would develop. He was "a student entirely free from professional bias and trained in a severe school of legal and judicial investigation to sift witnesses and weigh evidence." William Gladstone, the renowned British Prime Minister who was well-read, read one of his classics and wrote to the "Seer." The "Seer" published this particular book anonymously because he did not place much value on it. He did not give a copy to Gladstone and neither was he aware that the Prime Minister had one. In this book, the "Seer" 'slaughtered' Darwin's bulldog – Professor Thomas Huxley – who has "reincarnated" in the person of Professor Richard Dawkins, the 21st century champion of Darwinism, who sneers at Christians for believing it was God who created man.

On 19 April 2007, Alan Milburn, a former Cabinet Minister in the Labour Government, criticised Angela Merkel's attempt to rebrand the European Constitution which was rejected in 2005. He also expressed dismay about the complacency of the supporters of the European Union who had failed to question the direction of the European Enterprise. In an interesting article, *New grand design for Europe is doomed to fail – again,* Mr Milburn brought the character of the European Union into sharp focus. He stated: "The EU speaks a bureaucratic language that is foreign to the public. Too often it seems as if unaccountable elite takes decisions behind closed doors. Scepticism isn't peculiar to Britain. Elsewhere in Europe public antipathy is common place. The results of the 2005 constitution referendums gave it voice.....The EU needs to stop pointing and start examining its own part in the gulf that exists between the public and Europe...."

Mr Milburn continued with his incisive examination of the failings of the European Project: "It is not just what Europe does but how it does it that has failed to keep pace with the times", he said. "Europe's institutions were born out of post-war adversity." Mr Milburn stressed that in an age where the public is well-informed; the masses are not prepared to tolerate "unaccountable decision-making" by the political elite. He added: "So Tony Blair is right to demand a rethink about what Europe is for and to reorientate it's spending and policy priorities". He concluded: "Unless the EU is prepared to address the gulf between rulers and governed we risk a bureaucrats' Europe, not a people's Europe. It is time for Europe to face outwards not inwards, to empower the public not the politicians. Elitism is out. Engagement is in. Europe needs to learn the lesson." (The Times 19 April 2007). Unfortunately, Mr Miliburn's request would fall on deaf ears. Nothing would steer the "EU Titanic" from its fate. It is destined to sink.

EUROPE'S "DEATH WARRANT"

On 13 December 2007, the 27 European leaders signed the 'death warrant' of Europe when they met in Lisbon to endorse the so-called Reformed EU Treaty. Had the people of Portugal examined what the great Irishman recorded about the future of Europe, they would not have allowed the treaty to be signed on their soil. They would have urged their politicians to return the repackaged European Constitution to France where it originated from. Had the former Irish Prime Minister, Bertie Ahern, and his successor, Brian Cowen, studied what the native of Dublin wrote about political Europe before the European Union evolved from the debris of the Second World War, they would not have bothered the Irish people with a referendum on the Lisbon Treaty. And had the 'widely-read' Gordon Brown also read the works of the "Forgotten Anglicanised Irishman of Scotch extraction," he would have snubbed the Lisbon EU-Summit, just as how he snubbed the EU-African summit. And having learnt the nature of the European Project and its destiny, the British Prime Minister would have torn the Lisbon

Treaty into pieces to save Great Britain from sinking with Monnet's luxurious boat. Mr Brown would also have saved the House of Commons and the House of Lords from wasting precious hours debating on the "unreadable" Lisbon Treaty.

THE EU FLAG AND ANTHEM

That the European Union is a 'Nation' by itself cannot be questioned. It has all the symbols and trappings of nationhood: Flag, Anthem, Currency, Bank, Court of Justice, Common Agricultural and Fisheries Policies, a draft Constitution (Lisbon Treaty) that would make the EU a legal personality with its own President to sign international treaties on behalf of its 'provinces', and a Foreign Minister who heads Diplomatic Offices around the world. The EU is planning for its own army.

The European flag and anthem were excluded from the original text of the Lisbon Treaty to prevent the document being classified an European Constitution, thereby avoiding the need of national referenda. This was evident in David Miliband's address to the House of Commons: "It is good that the symbols, flags and anthems, which distracted attention from the discussion of the European constitutional treaty, are done away with so that we can focus on what will make the EU useful to this country ⊠ jobs, climate and energy ⊠ the issues that matter to ordinary people."

Without any surprise, Germany and France managed to include the EU flag and its pagan anthem in the final text of the Lisbon Treaty as a subsidiary clause. Members of the European Parliament supported the move with this declaration: "Symbols are vital elements of any communication. They convey an emotional image of the underlying values of the organisations they represent." The question is: what values do the EU symbol portray? In their attempt to be clever and to fool the masses by including the EU flag and anthem into the Lisbon Treaty through the back door, German and French politicians and the European Parliament have confirmed the character of the European Union which the European emblem signifies.

Symbols and signs are significant. They play vital role in our society. For example, if a motorist is not familiar with Road Signs or ignores them, chances are he could be involved in a fatal accident. The official explanation of the EU symbol states that the circle of 12 stars on a blue background means 'perfection and dependency among the member countries of the European Union.' Is this the true significance of the EU emblem? We will learn more about the European symbol as we progress with our study.

ANALYSIS OF THE LISBON TREATY

Professor Anthony Coughlan, Secretary of the National Platform for EU Research and Information Centre in Dublin, analysed the significance of the Lisbon Treaty for the benefit of the layman. I would share with you an extract from his analysis: "It is hard to think of a State which the new European Union will not have once the Lisbon Treaty is ratified....The Treaty provides that the EU may go to war while individual Member States may "conceivably abstain".....The new European Union will have its own government, with a legislative, executive and judicial arm, its own political President, its own citizens and citizenship, its own human and civil rights code, its own currency, economic policy and revenue, its own international treaty-making powers, foreign policy, foreign minister, diplomatic corps and United Nations voice, its own crime and justice code and Public Prosecutor. It already possesses such normal State symbols as its own flag, anthem, motto and annual holiday...."

Professor Coughlan continued: "All the classical Federal States which have been formed on the basis of power being surrendered by lower constituent states to a higher Federal authority have developed in a gradual way, just as has happened in the case of the European Union.....Indeed the EU has accumulated its powers much more rapidly than some of these Federal States – Canada, USA and Australia – in the short historical time-span of some sixty years.

The Key difference between these classical Federations and the new European Union is that the former, once their people had settled, share a common language, history, culture and national solidarity that gave them a democratic basis and made their State authority popularly legitimate and acceptable. All stable States are founded on such communities where people speak a common language and mutually identify with one another as one people – a "We". In the EU there are no European people or "*demos*", except statistically. The Lisbon Treaty is an attempt to construct a highly centralised European federation artificially, from the top down, out of Europe's many nations, peoples and states, without their free consent and knowledge.....By giving a Constitution indirectly rather than directly to the new European Union which it will establish, the Lisbon Treaty sets in place what Belgian Primer Minister Guy Verhofstadt has called the "*capstone of a European Federal State.*" For the Euro-federalist political elites who have been driving this process over decades, this is the culmination of what started nearly 60 years ago when the 1950 Schuman Declaration, which is commemorated annually on 9 May, Europe Day, proclaimed the European Coal and Steel Community to be the "*first step in the federation of Europe.*"
He concludes: "The peoples of Europe do not want this kind of highly centralised Federal European Union whose most striking feature is that it is run virtually entirely by committees of politicians, bureaucrats and judges, none of whom are directly elected by the people. The Constitutional Treaty setting it up has

already been rejected by the French and the Dutch in 2005, as French President Nicolas Sarkozy has admitted. For fear of being rejected again, Prime Ministers and Presidents in Europe agreed among themselves not to have referendums on the rebranded European Constitution. Only the Irish people were allowed to have their say on the Lisbon Treaty because their constitution permits it. This has been made possible by the case taken before the Supreme Court by the late Raymond Crotty. That action by that great Irishman stopped the State's politicians of that time from ratifying a previous European treaty, the Single European Act, in an unconstitutional manner."

SUMMARY OF 13 CRITICAL FACTS ABOUT THE LISBON TREATY

Before the second Irish referendum on the Lisbon Treaty was held in October 2009, Dr Coughlan listed thirteen crucial things the Lisbon Treaty would do if the once rejected European Constitution is ratified by all the 27 member states of the European Union. The summary was prepared with the help of authorities on Irish constitutional and European law, The following are the main reasons why the Lisbon Treaty, if ratified, would be bad for Ireland and the rest of EU states. The Lisbon Treaty would:

1. Be a power-grab by the Big States for control of the EU.

At present EU laws are made by a simple majority of Member States (14 out of 27), so long as between them they have a qualified majority of 255 votes out of 345. Under this Nice Treaty system the Big States have 29 votes each and Ireland has 7, one quarter of each Big State. Under Lisbon future EU laws would be made by 55% of Member States, i.e. 15 out of 27, so long as they have 65% of the total EU population between them. By basing EU law-making primarily on *population size,* the Lisbon Treaty would double Germany's relative voting strength on the EU Council of Ministers from its present 8% of the total votes to 17% on a population basis, and increase France's, Britain's and Italy's by half, from 8% to 12% - while halving Ireland's vote from 2% to 0.8% (Art.16, *Treaty on European Union* / TEU). How does having 0.8% of a vote in making EU laws put us *"at the heart of Europe"?* Taoiseach Brian Cowen's "guarantees" do not explain how having half as much influence in the EU as Ireland has today would induce other Member States to listen to our concerns on unemployment and help to resolve the economic crisis in the interest of Irish companies, workers and farmers. *(*See Note 1 below on the voting rules for making EU laws)*

2. Copperfasten the Laval and related judgements of the EU Court of Justice.

This would put the competition rules of the EU market above the right of Trade Unions to enforce pay standards higher than the minimum wage for migrant workers. At the same time Lisbon would give the EU full control of immigration policy (Art.79 TFEU). This combination threatens the pay and working conditions of many Irish people. A Protocol in a new Treaty different from Lisbon would be needed to set aside the recent Laval, Rüffert and other EU Court judgements, but the EU Prime Ministers refused that.

3. Permit the post-Lisbon EU to impose Europe-wide taxes directly on us for the first time without need of further Treaties or referendums.
This could be any kind of tax - income tax, sales tax, property tax - so long as it was unanimously agreed by EU Governments. If Lisbon were to be ratified, Government Ministers would have every incentive to agree to give the EU much increased" *own resources"* by introducing its own taxes to finance the many new functions the EU would obtain under the Treaty.

4. Amend the existing treaties to give the EU exclusive power as regards rules on foreign direct investment and give the Court of Justice the power to order the harmonisation of national indirect taxes...
This amendment and the new Protocol No. 27 on the Internal Market and Competition would strengthen the hand of the Court in using the EU's internal market rules to subvert Ireland's low 12.5% company tax rate, which is the principal reason foreign firms come to Ireland and stay here when they come. Compare Germany's 30% company tax rate. Commission plans for a harmonised tax base in the EU, the precursor of harmonised tax rates, have been put on the back-burner until after Lisbon Two for fear they would alarm Irish voters.

5. The Commission, which is appointed not elected, has the monopoly of proposing all European laws.
The Lisbon Treaty would abolish our present right to "propose" and decide who Ireland's Commissioner is, by replacing it with a right to make "suggestions" only, leaving it up to the incoming Commission President to decide (Art.17.7 TEU; cf.Art.214 TEC). Our No vote of last year secured us a commitment to a permanent Commissioner, but what is the point of every EU State continuing to have its own Commissioner post-Lisbon when it can no longer decide who that Commissioner will be? Under the present Nice Treaty Ireland would continue to decide who should be our Commissioner, and can continue to have an Irish Commissioner indefinitely as well.

6. Give the legally new EU which it would establish its own State Constitution, which would be superior to the Irish and other national Constitutions.
The Lisbon Treaty would abolish the existing European Community which Ireland joined in 1973 and transfer all of its powers and institutions to the new post-Lisbon Union. It would give the European Union its own legal personality for the first time, which would be constitutionally separate from and superior to its 27 Member States, so that it could sign international Treaties with other

States in all areas of its powers (Arts.1 and 47 TEU; Declaration No.17 concerning Primacy). This post-Lisbon EU would have the same name but would be constitutionally very different from the present EU, which was founded by the 1992 Maastricht Treaty.

In constitutional terms Lisbon would thereby turn Ireland into a regional or provincial state within this new Federal-style Union, with the EU's Constitution and laws having legal primacy over the Irish Constitution and laws in any cases of conflict between the two. The EU Court of Justice, as the Supreme Court of the new post-Lisbon Union, would decide such conflicts. Constitutionally and in the eyes of others this would be the end of Ireland's position as an independent sovereign State in the international community of States. Although we would retain some of the trappings of independent statehood from pre-Lisbon days, in reality we would be more like a regional or provincial state such as Bavaria inside Federal Germany or Massachusetts or Texas inside the USA. From the inside the EU would seem to be based on a Treaty between States, but from the outside it would look like a State itself. The only major power of a State which the post-Lisbon European Union would lack would be the power to force its members to go to war against their will, although they could go to war voluntarily on the EU's behalf.

7. Turn us all into real citizens for the first time of this new post-Lisbon European Union, owing obedience to its laws and loyalty to its authority over and above our obedience and loyalty to Ireland and the Irish Constitution and laws in the event of any conflict between the two. One can only be a citizen of a State. And all States must have citizens. Article 9 TEU would give us an *"additional"* EU citizenship, on top of our Irish citizenship. This would be a real EU citizenship for the first time, with associated citizens' rights and duties, and would be quite different from the notional or symbolical EU "citizenship" of today. We would still retain our Irish citizenship, but it would be subordinate to our EU citizenship in any case of conflict between the two, as is the case with citizens of such Federal States as Germany, the USA, Switzerland, and Canada. The EU Court of Justice would decide on any such conflicts.

8. Give the EU Court of Justice the power to decide our rights as EU citizens by making the EU Charter of Fundamental Rights legally binding for the first time.
The Charter includes such rights as free speech, the right to fair trial, the right to life, the rights of the child, the right to strike, property rights etc. - all of these rights the people of Ireland already have under the Irish Constitution, but which it would fall to the EU Court of Justice, not Ireland's courts, to interpret and decide for people **in their capacity as citizens of the post-Lisbon EU** if Lisbon should be ratified. This would enable the EU judges to use its case-law to lay down a uniform standard of rights for the 500 million citizens of the post-Lisbon Union

in the name of a common EU citizenship in the years and decades to come. It would open the possibility of clashes with national human rights standards in sensitive areas where Member States differ from one another at present, e.g. trial by jury, the presumption of innocence until proven guilty, *habeas corpus,* the legalisation of hard drugs, euthanasia, abortion, labour law, succession law, marriage law, children's rights etc. Ireland's Supreme Court and the Court of Human Rights in Strasbourg would no longer have the final say on what our rights are.

9. Ireland would lose the national veto it has at present by handing over to the EU the power to make laws binding on us in 32 new policy areas, including public services, crime, justice and policing, immigration, energy, transport, tourism, sport, culture, public health, the EU budget and international measures on climate change The Dáil (the Irish Parliament) and Irish voters who elect the Dáil would no longer decide laws or policy for the areas transferred.

10. Reduce the power of National Parliaments to make laws in relation to 49 policy areas or matters, and increase the influence of the European Parliament in making EU laws in 19 new areas.
Lisbon would entitle one-third of the National Parliaments or 1 million EU citizens to request the EU Commission to propose a new EU law or to abandon a proposed law, but the Commission need not accede to any such request; Protocol No. 2 on Subsidiarity and Proportionality). Lisbon underlines the implicitly subordinate role of National Parliaments in the institutional structure of the post-Lisbon Union by laying down that *"National Parliaments contribute actively to the good functioning of the Union."* Members of the European Parliament (MEPs), who at present are *"representatives of the peoples of the Member States brought together in the Community."* would under Lisbon become *"representatives of the Union's citizens."* This change illustrates the constitutional revolution Lisbon would bring about.

11. Be a self-amending Treaty:
The Lisbon Treaty would permit the EU Prime Ministers and Presidents to shift most remaining EU policy areas where unanimity is required and a national veto still exists - e.g. on tax harmonisation - to qualified majority voting on the Council of Ministers, without need of further EU Treaties or referendums. In addition, the so-called "Flexibility Clause", which allows the EU to take action and adopt measures to attain one of the EU's objectives even if *"the Treaties have not provided the necessary powers,"* would be extended by Lisbon to all areas of the Treaty and not just the internal market rules as before. This would open the floodgates to more political integration, i.e. centralisation, by means of this article, which is already widely used.

12. Enable the 27 EU Prime Ministers and Presidents to appoint an EU President for up to five years without allowing voters any say as to who he or she would be.

This would abolish the six-monthly rotating EU presidencies. Appointment rather than democratic election to this and other top EU jobs, such as the proposed EU "Foreign Minister"/ High Representative typifies the undemocratic nature of the proposed Lisbon Constitution. It is the Prime Ministers and Presidents of the Big States who would have the key say in these appointments because of the big increase in their voting power under Lisbon.

13. Militarize the EU further:

The Treaty would require Member States *"progressively to improve their military capabilities"* and to aid and assist other Member States experiencing armed attack *"by all the means in their power."*

Explanation to Note 1:

When Ireland joined the then EEC in 1973 Germany, France, Britain and Italy had 10 votes each in making European laws and Ireland had 3 - one-third that of the Big States. Under the present Nice Treaty the Big States have 29 votes each and Ireland has 7 - one quarter of the Big States. Under Lisbon Germany's votes would be 20 times Ireland's, for it has 80 million people as against Ireland's 4 million, and France, Britain and Italy, with their average populations of 60 million, would each have 15 times more votes than Ireland. Germany and France between them have one-third of the EU's population of near 500 million. Under the Lisbon rules they would need only two small countries to vote with them to block any EU law they did not like.

Turning the EU into a State:

In summary: the Lisbon Treaty would be a giant step in turning the EU into a supranational Federal-style State, in which Ireland would effectively be reduced to regional or provincial status. It would give Government Ministers and the Big EU States huge new powers, while taking power away from ordinary citizens across the EU, and from the National Parliaments they elect. Because of Irish's Constitution, only Ireland was allowed a vote on it. According to Dr Coughlan, "Only we Irish can save democracy in the EU by refusing to allow ourselves be pressurised into overturning our rejection of Lisbon in 2008. If we vote No again in Lisbon Two we hold the door open to our fellow countrymen and women in Northern Ireland and give them the chance of having a say in a UK referendum next year.

Dr Coughlan advised the public, "The most urgent task for those of us who want to defend Irish democracy, national independence and our ability to defend our economic interests in face of Lisbon is to take the initiative in sharing this information with our friends and neighbours before the referendum date." I would urge you to read the full text on the Lisbon Treaty recorded on the National Platform for EU Research and Information Centre website. It provides detailed analysis and explanatory notes to the summary I have outlined above.

2 OCTOBER 2009: IRELAND'S DAY OF DESTINY

On 8 July 2009, the Irish Prime Minister Brian Cowen set 2 October 2009 as the date for the second referendum on the Lisbon Treaty. On the referendum, the Foreign Minister Michael Martin said Brian Cowen's "Government will not resign in terms of the outcome. This is not about the Government. This is about the future of the Irish people and the future of Irish society within the European Union. It transcends every particular party. This issue is now a matter for every citizen to make up his or her mind as to where they want their country to be in the future." According to Mr Martin, in his view a "Yes" vote would put Ireland at the heart of Europe. A "No" vote does marginalise the country and puts it on the periphery of Europe. Of that, I have no doubt. So I'm simply saying this is a referendum that transcends political parties and it's something that is personal and very important to each individual in society." (Source: Irish Independent 9 July 2009).

The Foreign Minister's sentiments about the outcome of the Lisbon Referendum raise the following questions:

- What is the "heart of Europe"? Is Europe alive or "dead"?
- What is the future of Europe? Is it bright of dark?

The Irish people would be pleased to know, that their "Forgotten Father" - the "Seer of Dublin" - recorded the answers to the above questions even before the European Union evolved from the debris of the Second World War.

According to the 9 July 2009 Editorial of the Irish Times, the "defining issue for Lisbon, second time round, is whether Ireland wants to stand financially isolated or part of a strong and supportive European Union.". Eoin O Broin rightly responded: "Surely the issue is whether or not the content of the Lisbon Treaty is good for Ireland and the European Union? He goes on: "Unfortunately your Editorial ignored this important question, attempting instead to scare rather than inform your readers." (Irish Times 11 July 2009).

The fact is politicians, political commentators and all Europeans must view the Lisbon Treaty from two perspectives – Jean Monnet's vision of a "federated Europe" and the "Seer of Dublin's" vision of the future of Europe. In the eyes of the supporters of the European Project (whom I describe as the "children" of

Jean Monnet and Konrad Adenauer), the Lisbon Treaty is the last "piece" that solves the " European Jig-Saw Puzzle" – the crowing glory of Jean Monnet and Konrad Adenauer's vision of turning the European Coal and Steel Community into a political federation – a "federated Europe". Apparently, the Lisbon Treaty turns Jean Monnet and Konrad Adenauer's dream of a United States of Europe into a reality. However, in reality, the Lisbon Treaty paves the way for the "Seer of Dublin's" prediction of the future of Europe to be fulfilled.

It was not by an accident that only the Irish people had the opportunity to vote on the Lisbon Treaty and rejected it on 12 June 2008. This result temporarily saved Britain and Ireland from committing national suicide. For the Irish, unconsciously, acted on the warning their brilliant "Father" gave about the destiny of Europe. The Irish should be proud that it was their "father" who, in the 19th century, wrote about European integration and its future before Sarkozy's "Father," Jean Monnet, the master architect of European Construction, was even conceived. Sadly, the "sons" and "daughters" of the "Seer of Dublin" were "bullied" by the 'children' of Jean Monnet and Konrad Adenauer to ignore their democratic decision to reject a dubious European Constitution that would make them 'slaves' in Europe and to vote again to adopt the Lisbon Treaty. The Irish would commit the blunder of all blunders if they are influenced by the threat of "isolation" from Europe and the collapse of the Irish economy outside the EU to vote "Yes" to adopt the Lisbon Treaty. It is time the Irish knew that Jean Monnet, the "Spiritual godfather" of the 'godless' European Union, would not have qualified to polish the shoes of their brilliant "father." The French President and his people would find this fact hard to swallow. Facts are stubborn, independent and unyielding.

The truth about European integration cannot be settled by a plebiscite. For the "Sage of Ulster" recorded in one of his classics this truism: *"Truth has always been in the minority. But there is no element of cohesion in error. Among the children of error there is no bond of unity save such as depends on common hostility to truth."* By denying Britons and Europeans the opportunity to vote on the European Constitution (so-called the Lisbon Treaty), a document that would consign them into 'slavery', the European Union has, indeed, confirmed its character as described by the "Seer of Dublin". The EU preaches democracy to other nations, yet it has no democratic legitimacy for its existence.. For the few who administer the "Government of Europe" are not accountable to the majority who feed them and finance the "European Government." The EU is hostile to democracy; it is a dictatorship. It is fitting I close the overview of this book with the Irishman's word about democracy: *"Democracy, not despotism is the goal towards which civilisation is tending... But democracy in its full development is one of the surest roads to despotism.* ***First, the revolution; then the plebiscite; then the despot."***

We must now ask these questions:

- How was the Irishman able to predict with certainty, in the 19th century, and even before the Zionist Movement was formed in 1896, that a confederation of European nations would be the next major political feature in history after the restoration of the Jews to Palestine?
- How was the "Anglicised-Irishman of Scotch extraction" able to forecast with confidence, even before the First World War began in 1914, that a political union of European nations would develop through an European Crisis?
- How was this Irishman - who became a distinguished public servant in England - able to predict the character of European Union?
- Would the native of Dublin's prediction of the future of Europe be fulfilled?

The answers are in the pages before you.

Part 1

European Union: the climax of history; the critical issue of our time

CHAPTER ONE

The History of the world empires foretold

"The times of the span of moments cast no shadows behind them; but the times of the span of movements in moments cast shadows of their deeds in the light of moments yet to be born."
("Pieces of Wood" JJA)

I have already mentioned that the Lisbon Treaty is the last "piece" that fits the "European Jig-Saw Puzzle." To understand the real significance of this particular "piece", we need a comprehensive knowledge and understanding of the European Union: - where this "unique phenomenon" came from; its purpose and future prospects. So, in view of the extraordinary significance of the subject before us, I would spend time to lay a foundation that would help us to build our understanding of the political integration of European nations. We will know the 'source' of the 'European political phenomenon,' where this "political and historic adventure of the last century" is heading towards, the powerful leader who will lead Europe to the Promised Land of "Carbon Free" where Peace and Prosperity prevail, and the impact the reign of the Emperor of Europe would have on Europeans and mankind.

This foundation would also serve as an amour to deflect the arrows of misleading information about Jean Monnet's vision of a "federated Europe" that has been imposed on the "ignorant" public. These seemingly sharp "arrows," which are just "blunt" darts, have been designed by politicians, political scientists and political commentators to 'frighten' the electorate to love the European Union unconditionally.

Since the beginning of time nothing has happened by chance. For example, today's explosion of knowledge and the ease with which we travel from one country to another in our technologically advanced generation were all foretold in the Good Book. Witness the prophetic revelation recorded in the Old Testament Book of Daniel 12:4: *"Many shall run to and fro and knowledge shall increase."*

It is a plain truth that over the years we have witnessed an increase in international travel on land, sea and in the air. More roads and airports are being built to cope with the increased volume of traffic. We have planes that can fly around the world in 24 hours. European scientists have now built a Super–Jumbo plane A380, which boasts of casinos, cocktail bars, gyms and even a library. This aircraft "is as tall as eight-storey building, has enough room on its wings to park 70 family vehicles and on take off will generate as much thrust as 3,500 cars" (Daily Express 18 January 2005). Scientific learning has also increased dramatically. Scientists are probing the space with visits to the moon and mars. They have built spacecrafts to circle around the sun three times to collect billions of delicate solar atoms for research. Today, some scientists are even suggesting it might be likely for human beings to escape from the earth to live on planet Mars. Scientists now claim they have discovered water on planet Mars – an evidence of 'life on Mars'.

About 500,000 new books are published every day. In an article, Religious publishers versus 'spiritualism,' which was published in The Times on 27 March 2003, Gregg Watts reported: "According to a survey by Book Marketing Ltd, 277 Million books were sold in Britain in 2002. Out of this, an estimated four million were religious or spiritual titles." The Word of God has surely come to pass. International travel has become easier, and knowledge and education have increased. Consider the internet – the speed with which information is being transmitted today. The Lord is on the Throne. At the appointed time He will visit the earth and all eyes will see Him (Revelation 1:7). Amen!

THE QUESTION IN *"QUO VADIS"*

The sign of the appointed time is upon us. In the classic film *Quo vadis?* Robert Taylor witnessed the destruction of Nero's Rome by fire, and the mauling of Christians by hungry lions. The leading actor then posed this question: "Babylon, Greece and Rome: what next?" The answer: the "resurrection" of the "dead" Roman Empire, which is in its infancy as the European Union. The President of the European Commission, Jose Manuel Barroso, consciously or unconsciously confirmed it in a newspaper article titled *Barroso hails the European 'empire'*. The Boss of EU bureaucracy boasted: "Unlike old super-state empire, the European Union was based on a voluntary surrender of sovereignty, not military conquests. What we have now is the first non-imperial empire. We are a very special construction unique in history. Sometimes I like to compare the European Union as a creation to the organisation of empire. We have the dimension of empire" (The Daily Telegraph 11 July 2007).

The development of EU - a political union of European nations - was not by chance. Just as how the fate of Alexander the Great was foretold hundreds of years before the Greek Warrior was born in 356BC and died at a young age in 323BC, and before his Grecian Empire was taken over by the Romans, so was the destiny of the "first non-imperial empire" (the revived Roman Empire) published over 2600 years before the European Union came into existence.

We know the world is indebted to the civilisations of the Greeks and the Romans. The Preamble to the original proposed European Union Constitution confirmed it. For this reason, before we can understand the significance of the European Union and the future prospects of this 'political phenomenon,' it is necessary we establish the actual "source" of this European project since the European culture is influenced by Greek and Roman civilisations.

THE VISION AND PROPHECY OF DANIEL

After the death of Alexander the Great, according to history, his four generals divided his Grecian Empire into four parts – the kingdom of Ptolemy (Egypt), of Cassander (Macedonia), of Lysimachus (Asia Minor) and of Seleucus (Syria). The Book of Daniel foretold this four part division of Alexander's Empire (Daniel 8:8). Before Alexander the Great was born in 356BC, and before the empires of Babylon, Medo-Persia, Greece and Rome ruled the world in succession, the Bible had already predicted the reign of these empires. In about 552BC, almost 200 years before the Greek Warrior was born, the prophet Daniel saw a vision of how 4 great Empires would rule the world in succession.

Furthermore, Daniel foresaw how the Babylonian Empire would be conquered by the Medo-Persians; how the Medo-Persians would be overthrown by the Greeks, led by Alexander the Great; how the Greek warrior would suddenly die at the zenith of his power, and how his Grecian Empire would be divided into 4 kingdoms by Alexander's 4 generals. Daniel, again, saw in a vision a beast which looked like a leopard. It "had on its back four wings like those of a bird. The beast had four heads, and it was given authority to rule" (Daniel 7:6). This "beast" symbolised Alexander the Great's Grecian empire. And the "four heads of this monster" represented the four generals who succeeded the Greek warrior and divided his empire into four kingdoms.

KING NEBUCHADNEZZAR AND HIS DREAM OF A GREAT HUMAN IMAGE

Before Daniel witnessed the vision of the 4 Empires, which were symbolised by four cruel beasts (lion, bear, leopard and a fierce monster with iron teeth) coming out of the sea (Daniel 7:1-21), king Nebuchadnezzar of Babylon had already seen in a dream a human statue which was awesome in appearance (Daniel 2:31). "The head of this effigy was made of pure gold, its chest and arms were of silver, its belly and thighs were of bronze, its legs were of iron, and the feet were partly of iron and partly of clay" (Daniel 2:32). The mysterious dream troubled the Babylonian King to the extent that he might have forgotten it. The magicians, the astrologers and all the wise men in Babylon could not recount the dream and explain it to their Emperor. In his fury, Nebuchadnezzar threatened to sentence the wise men to death. The King was advised that the young Hebrew captive in his court, Daniel, would be able to tell him the dream and its meaning.

Daniel was summoned before Nebuchadnezzar. The Emperor asked him: "Are you able to tell me what I saw in my dream and interpret it?" Daniel requested for time to pray about it. During one night the mystery was revealed to him in a vision. Daniel returned to the Emperor with the answer: He told Nebuchadnezzar, "No wise man, enchanter, magician or diviner can explain to the King the mystery he has asked about, but there is a God in heaven who reveals mysteries. He has shown King Nebuchadnezzar what will happen in days to come. Your dream and the vision that passed through your mind as you lay on your bed are these:

"As you were lying there, O King, your mind turned to things to come, and the revealer of mysteries showed you what is going to happen. As for me, this mystery has been revealed to me, not because I have greater wisdom than other living men, but so that you, O King, may know the interpretation and that you may understand what went through your mind.

"You looked, O King, and there before you stood a large statue---an enormous, dazzling statue, awesome in appearance. The head of the statue was made of pure gold, its chest and arms of silver, its belly and thighs of bronze, its legs of iron, its feet partly of iron and partly of baked clay. While you were watching, a rock was cut out, but not by human hands. It struck the statue on its feet of iron and clay and smashed them. Then the iron, the clay, the bronze, the silver and the gold were broken to pieces at the same time and became like chaff on a threshing-floor in the summer. The wind swept them away without leaving a trace. But the rock that struck the statue became a huge mountain and filled the whole earth." (Daniel 2:29-35)

Daniel then interpreted the dream to Nebuchadnezzar: "You, O king, are the king of kings. The God of heaven has given you dominion and power and might and glory; in your hands he has placed mankind and the beasts of the field and the birds of the air. Wherever they live, he has made you ruler over them all.

After you, another kingdom will rise, inferior to yours. Next a third kingdom, one of bronze, will rule over the whole earth. Finally, *there will be a fourth kingdom, strong as iron----for iron breaks things to pieces,* so *it will crush and break all the others. Just as you saw the feet and the toes were partly of baked clay and partly of iron, so this will be a divided kingdom yet it will have some of the strength of iron in it, even as you saw the iron mixed with clay. As the toes were partly iron and partly clay, so this kingdom will be partly strong and partly brittle. And just as you saw the iron mixed with baked clay,* so *the people will be a mixture, and will not remain united any more than iron mixes with clay.....The great God has shown the king what will take place in the future. The dream is true and the interpretation is trustworthy."* (Daniel 2:36-45) Amen!

On hearing this message, King Nebuchadnezzar fell before Daniel. He honoured the Jewish captive and lavished him with many gifts. The Emperor told Daniel: "Surely, your God is the God of gods and the Lord of kings and a revealer of mysteries, for you were able to reveal this mystery." Consequently, Nebuchadnezzar honoured Daniel. He made the young Hebrew ruler over the entire province of Babylon and placed him in charge of all its wise men (Daniel 2:46-48).

THE VISION OF 4 BEASTS: THE EUROPEAN UNION IN PROPHECY

Daniel's vision of the 4 cruel beasts, which is recorded in chapter 7 of the Book of Daniel, was a parallel to the 4 metals king Nebuchadnezzar saw in his dream in Daniel chapter 2. Daniel saw 4 ferocious beasts coming out of the "troubled" Mediterranean Sea. .

- The first beast looked like a lion. It corresponds to the head of gold of the great human image in Daniel 2:36-38. This lion symbolises the Empire of Babylon with its founder King Nebuchadnezzar
- .The second beast looked like a bear. It corresponds to the breast and arms of silver of the human statue in Daniel 2:31. This represents the Empire of Medo-Persia, which defeated the Babylonians.
- The third beast seemed like a leopard. It corresponds to the abdomen and thighs of bronze of the human statue in Daniel 2:32. This symbolises the Macedonian–Grecian Empire with its king, Alexander the Great.
- The fourth beast was hideous without a name. It "was terrifying and frightening and very powerful. It had large iron teeth; it crushed and devoured its victims and trampled underfoot whatever was left. It was different from all the former beasts, and it had *ten horns*" (Daniel 7:7). This fourth beast corresponds to the 2 legs of iron and the 10 toes of the human statue. We know the 10 toes were partly of baked clay and partly of iron.

According to the explanation the Lord gave to Daniel, "The fourth beast is a fourth kingdom that would appear on earth. It would be different from all the other kingdoms and will devour the whole earth, trampling it down and crushing it." What does this fourth beast with iron teeth symbolise? Rome. It was the Romans who defeated the Greeks and dominated the whole earth with iron fist.

In about 397AD, the Roman Empire was divided into two - the Eastern section with its capital in Constantinople, and the Western segment with Rome as its capital. These two divisions of the Roman Empire correspond to the two legs of iron of the human statue. The 10 toes of this effigy match up to the 10 horns on the fourth beast; and they represent 10 kings who will come from this fourth kingdom. (Daniel 7:23-24, Rev. 17:12-13). We will learn more about the *"10 horns"* on the terrible beast with iron teeth as we progress with our study.

THE REVELATION ABOUT THE EUROPEAN UNION

Now, let us listen again to how Daniel explained to king Nebuchadnezzar the significance of the *"10 toes"*, which were part of the fourth section of the human statue the king of Babylon saw in his dream: "Just as you (Nebuchadnezzar) saw that the feet and toes were partly of baked clay and partly of iron, so this will be ***a divided kingdom;*** yet it will have some of ***the strength of iron in it,*** even as you saw iron mixed with clay. As the toes were partly iron and partly clay, so this ***kingdom will be partly strong and partly brittle.*** And just as you saw the iron mixed with baked clay, so ***the people will be a mixture and will not remain united,*** any more than iron mixes with clay" (Daniel 2:41-43).

This prophetic revelation which relates to the significance of the feet and the ten toes of the human statue, and which corresponds to the fourth empire in Nebuchadnezzar's dream, is being fulfilled today. We see its fulfilment in European integration: the economic and political union of European nations that has developed from six countries to twenty seven. The membership of this political union will continue to grow to become a mighty empire. Later on I will share with you, in detail, how this prophecy about the *"Ten toes"* of the human statue, which were partly of baked clay and partly of iron, has been fulfilled in the growth of the European Union.

AN OVER-VIEW OF WORLD POWERS BEFORE THE ROMAN EMPIRE CAME INTO EXISTENCE: THE FIGHTING BETWEEN A RAM AND MALE GOAT

Chapter 8 of the Book of Daniel is a record of another vision Daniel saw. This prophetic revelation was about a fierce fighting between a ram with two horns and a male goat with its successor. The two horns of the ram signify the kings of Mede and Persia, which formed the Empire of Medo-Persia. In this particular vision, Daniel saw the ram pushing westward, northward and southward. This signifies that the Medo-Persians conquered Babylon on the West, Assyria on the North and Egypt on the South.

THE DEFEAT OF THE BABYLONIAN EMPIRE

The overthrow of the Babylonian Empire by the Medo-Persians was by the hand of God. It took place during the reign of King Belshazzar, the last king of Babylon, who was a descendant of King Nebuchadnezzar. Belshazzar was killed by Darius the Mede when Belshazzar was feasting with his wives and concubines. Belshazzar had no regard for God. He and his mistresses drank wine from the silver and golden vessels King Nebuchadnezzar plundered from the Temple in Jerusalem in about 586BC. While they were feasting with the sacred vessels, the pagan King and his guests praised their gods of silver and gold and bronze.

The desecration of the sacred utensils from the House of God offended the Almighty. As a result, God revealed to King Belshazzar what would befall on him and his kingdom with this message on a wall: *"MENE, MENE, TEKEL, PARSIN"*. The King could not understand the writing on the wall. He invited Daniel to explain the inscription. This was the message:

"Mene: God has numbered the days of your reign and brought it to an end.

"Tekel: You have been weighed on the scales and found Wanting.

"Peres: Your kingdom is divided and given to the Medes and Persians."
(Daniel 5:25-28).

The Bible tells us the very night when Belshazzar was overeating and drinking with his lords and concubines, Darius the Mede, who was 62 years old, slew the king of Babylon and took over the kingdom. (Daniel 5:30-31). This incident fulfilled God's Word to Jeremiah concerning the end of Israel's 70-year servitude in Babylon: *"This whole country (Israel) will serve the king of Babylon seventy years. But when the seventy years are fulfilled, I will punish the king of Babylon and his nation, the land of the Babylonians for their guilt....and will make it desolate forever"* (Jeremiah 25:11-12). And the prophet Isaiah also foretold how God would raise Cyrus to release the Jews from captivity to return to Jerusalem to rebuild the Temple which Nebuchadnezzar destroyed in 587BC (Isaiah 44:27-28, 45:1-3).

It is clear, the death of Belshazzar and the overthrow of the Babylonian Empire by the Medo-Persians were not accidents. It was by God's providence to punish the heathen king because of his debauchery, and at the same time to hand over the Babylonian Empire to Cyrus, so that this new king would release the children of Israel to return to their homeland to fulfil God's word in Isaiah 45:27-28: "Cyrus, He is my shepherd and will accomplish all that I please: he will say of Jerusalem, "Let it be rebuilt," and of the temple, "Let its foundations be laid....Cyrus whose right hand I take hold to subdue nations before him." Praise the Lord. He is in control of world events. His word never returns to him void. It accomplishes the purpose for which He desires (Isaiah 55:11). Amen!

THE CONQUEST OF MEDO–PERSIA AND THE RISE OF ALEXANDER THE GREAT

Medo-Persia emerged as a great Empire. However, the Medes and the Persians were godless and arrogant. They showed no regard for God. It was their king, Darius, who issued an edict that no one should pray to any God except the king. (Daniel 6:6-7). And when Daniel disobeyed and prayed to the God of heavens, he was arrested and thrown into a den of lions. But God delivered his servant from the hungry lions (Daniel 6:16-21).

Because of their ungodliness, the Lord punished the Medes and the Persians by raising Alexander the Great to demolish their empire. The collapse of the Medo-Persian Empire was prophetically described in a fierce symbolic fighting between a male goat and a ram. In chapter 8 of the Book of Daniel we read that a male goat came from the west and furiously attacked a ram, striking the ram and shattering his two horns. (Daniel 8:6-7). This male goat, coming from the west to crush the ram, signified how Alexander the Great, who came from Europe which is west of the Mediterranean Sea, attacked and defeated the Medo-Persians. The conquest of the Medo-Persians was illustrated on one of the silver coins that bore the image of Alexander the Great. The other side of the coin depicts Zeus on a throne holding an eagle and a sceptre. Beneath the throne is a ram.

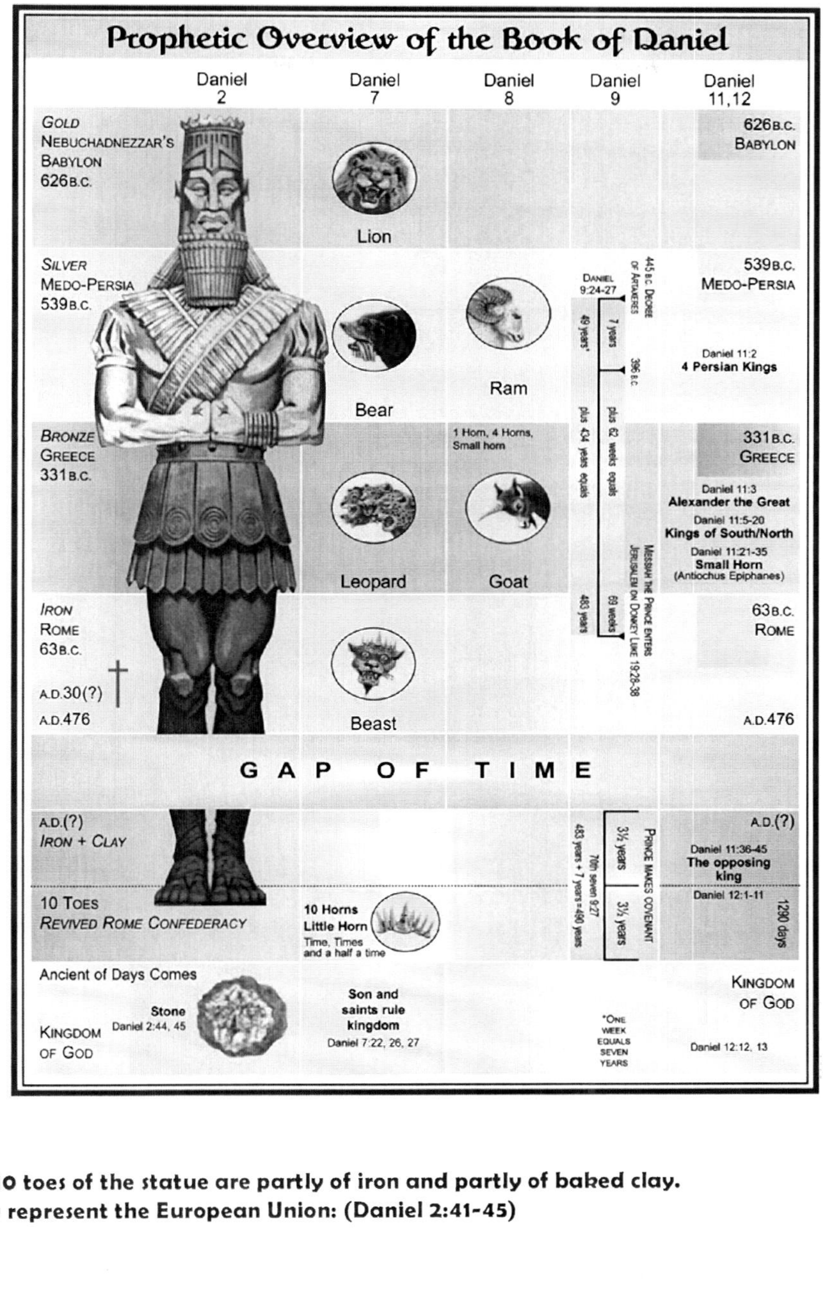

The 10 toes of the statue are partly of iron and partly of baked clay. They represent the European Union: (Daniel 2:41-45)

European Union:
The "10 Toes" of the Great Human Image
***"Before things happened, I (God) announced them"* (Isaiah 48:5)**

"Just as you (Nebuchadnezzar) saw that the feet and toes were partly of baked clay and partly of iron, so this will be a **divided kingdom**; yet it will have some of the **strength of iron** in it, even as you saw iron mixed with clay. As the toes were partly iron and partly clay, so this kingdom will be partly **strong** and partly **Brittle**. And as you saw the iron mixed with baked clay, so the **people will be a mixture and will NOT remain united** any more than iron mixes with clay..... The great God has shown the king what will take place in the future. The dream is true and the interpretation is trustworthy" (Daniel 2:41-45).

Prophecy Fulfilled:
EU: A Divided Kingdom
EU: A kingdom of Strong and Weak nations
EU: A Kingdom of Mixed People who are not united.

"My thoughts are not your thoughts....As the rain and the snow come down from heaven; and do not return to it without watering the earth and making it bud and flourish, so that it yields seed for the sower and bread for the eater, so is my word that goes out from my mouth; It will not return to me empty, but will accomplish what I desire and achieve the purpose for which I sent it.... Before things happened, I (God) announced them to you" (Isaiah 55:8-11

THE PROPHETIC WORD ABOUT THE RISE AND FALL OF ALEXANDER THE GREAT

The conquest of the Medo-Persian Empire by Alexander the Great; his sudden death at the pinnacle of power, and the division of his Grecian Empire into 4 kingdoms by his 4 generals were all revealed to Daniel about 200 years before Alexander himself was born. Let us listen to what the angel Michael told Daniel: "I tell you the truth; three more kings will appear in Persia, and then a fourth, who will be far richer than all the others. When he has gained power by his wealth, he will stir up everyone against the kingdom of Greece. Then *a mighty king will appear, who will rule with great power and do as he pleases.* After he has appeared, his kingdom will be broken up and parcel out towards the four winds of heaven. It will not go to his descendants, nor will it have the power he exercised, because his empire will be uprooted and given to others (Daniel 11:2-4). The "mighty king" in this Scripture was Alexander the Great. After his death he was not succeeded by his children or relatives.

Now, let us study closely how Daniel described the prophetic vision concerning Alexander the Great's military conquest of the world, how he would overcome the Medo-Persians, and how he would suddenly die in his youth at the peak of his power:

"....Suddenly a goat with a prominent horn between his eyes came from the west, crossing the whole earth without touching the ground. He came towards the two-horned ram (*Medo-Persia*) I had seen....and charged at him in great rage. I saw him attack the ram furiously, striking the ram and shattering his two horns (*Medo-Persia*). The ram *(Medo-Persia)* was powerless to stand against him (*Alexander the Great*). The goat (*Alexander the Great*) knocked him *(Medo-Persia)* to the ground and trampled over him, and none could rescue the ram (*Medo-Persia*) from his (*Alexander*) power. The goat (*Alexander*) became very great, but at the height of his power his large horn was broken off, and in its place four prominent horns grew up towards the four winds of heavens" (Daniel 8:5-8).

Hallelujah! Praise the Lord of heavens. He knows the end from the beginning. It is only the Almighty God who writes history before history is written. Before things happened, He announced them. Amen! (Isaiah 48:5). Man does not know the future, so he guesses the future. But the Creator of the Universe knows the future from the beginning. This is one of the Divine Attributes of the Omniscience God. That is why the Lord Jesus Christ claims: "I am the Alpha and the Omega, the First and the Last, the Beginning and the End" (Revelation 22:13). Which Politician, Scientist, Philosopher, Economist, Environmentalist, Barrister, Medical Practitioner, Engineer, Militant Atheist, Darwinist or a Politician could have made such a bold claim? NONE.

Let us examine Daniel's vision of the ***"male goat"*** and its practical meaning in the context of history and contemporary events. According to Daniel 8:5, *"A goat with a prominent horn between his eyes came from the west, crossing the whole earth without touching the ground."* This text signifies that Alexander the Great was an intelligent man with deep understanding of military welfare. With extraordinary skills, the young Alexander was able to conquer the world in rapid succession as history tells us. The speed of his conquest was likened to how a leopard chases its prey. Hence, the Lord used leopard to describe Alexander the Great's Grecian Empire (Daniel 7:6).

THE SUDDEN DEATH OF ALEXANDER THE GREAT IS NOT A MYSTERY TO BIBLE-BELIEVING CHRISTIANS

According to Daniel 8:8, "The goat became very great, but at the height of his power his large horn was broken off, and in its place four prominent horns grew up towards the four winds of heaven." This Scripture prophetically described how Alexander became powerful and died at a young age, and how after his death his four generals – Cassander, Lysimachus, Ptolemy and Seleucus – divided his Macedonian–Grecian Empire into four kingdoms in Macedonia, Asia Minor, Egypt and Syria. According to history these four empires later merged into two empires – one in the south, Egypt, and the other in the north which is Syria.

The sudden death of Alexander the Great at the height of his power and fame might be a puzzle and mystery to the world to solve. But with Bible-believing Christians it is not. Because, we have learnt that before Alexander the Great was born in 356BC, the God of the Bible whom we love and worship, had already revealed it to his servant Daniel, about 200 years earlier, how Alexander the Great would suddenly die at a tender age, and how his Grecian Empire would be divided into four kingdoms by his four generals. The Lord says: ***"Before things happened, I announced them"*** (Isaiah 48:5). Amen! Whether Alexander the Great died from fever or poison is not material. The fact is the Greek Warrior died at a young age at the height of his power exactly as predicted in the Book of Daniel.

THE VISION OF A RAM AND A MALE GOAT

The Lord explained to Daniel the significance of the ram and the goat: "I am going to tell you what will happen later in the time of wrath, because the vision concerns the appointed time of the end. The two-horned ram that you saw represents the king of Media and Persia. The shaggy goat is the king of Greece and the large horn between his eyes is the first king. The four horns that replaced the one that was broken off represents four kingdoms that will emerge from his nation but will not have the same power" (Daniel 8:19-22). According to history, the four generals who succeeded Alexander the Great were not of Alexander's calibre.

What a fulfilment of Bible prophecy! The Bible was hundred percent accurate in predicting Alexander the Great's military conquests of the world; his defeat of the Medo-Persians; his sudden death in his youth at the height of his power; the succession of his four generals after his death, and the subsequent division of his empire into four kingdoms. This was the vision of the events Daniel saw in about 552 BC, over 200 years before they actually took place. And we know from Alexander the Great's "*death certificate*" at the British Museum that the Greek Warrior died on 11 June 323BC. Again, were the intellectual gurus, Darwin and Freud, able to see what would happen even a day ahead of their time? The Bible has no equal. Praise the Lord! His Word is true and reliable. Amen!

HISTORY CONFIRMS THE PROPHETIC WORD OF THE BIBLE

In *Truth Lesson, Level One, Volume 2,* Witness Lee, the great Bible teacher, writes: "....G.H Pember, in his writing on the prophecies, says that signs of a ram could be found everywhere in Persia, especially in its capital. Ancient Greece also abounded with signs of a goat. The Bible symbolizes Persia by a ram and Greece by a he-goat. The he-goat refers to Alexander the Great."

Goat was also associated with the land of Macedonia where Alexander was born. Pre-historic period records that, "The history of Macedonia may be said...somewhere around the beginning of the 7th century BC....Stock breeding, based on the raising of goats and sheep, was one of the prime Macedonia's development..." Macedonian coins used goat symbols from 500 – 146BC. And Alexander the Great himself claimed he was a descendant of Jupiter Ammon, whose symbol was goat. It is recorded in history that when Alexander the Great marched into Macedonia, he wore a crown with a he-goat's horn. This information clearly confirms how prophetic Daniel's description of Alexander the Great and the kingdom of Greece was. After a twelve- year reign, Alexander the Great died suddenly before the age of thirty three.

According to Josephus, the renowned Jewish historian who witnessed the destruction of Jerusalem by the Romans in AD70, when Alexander the Great passed through the Jewish state, he was shown a copy of the Book of Daniel. He was astonished by the prophecy which referred to him. Because of this revelation, Alexander treated the Jews kindly, unlike Antiochus Epiphanies who killed thousands of Jews and desecrated their Temple with the blood of a sow and erected the god Zeus in the Holy Place.

The Bible is God speaking. It is not a human literature like the principles of Economics, Accounting and Physics, Law or any other worldly discipline. The principles governing worldly subjects are changing every hour to meet the demands of our changing culture. Laws and policies framed by politicians today would be changed tomorrow. The laws of men change from day to day, and from generation to generation. The popular song of politicians is: "Change, Change, Change;"; "Reform, Reform, Reform" And the "changes" and "reforms" never materialise. However the precepts of the Bible are "carved in granite". They do not change.

THE BIBLE IS NEITHER FOR THE WISE NOR FOOLS

From what we have learnt so far, is it intellectually nonsense to believe in the Bible as militant atheists, led by Professor Richard Dawkins, suggest? Is it intellectually reasonable to believe in the philosophies and laws of men - men who are always crying for "change, change, change". Militant atheists: witness the words of the "Seer of Dublin" who wrote about European integration before European Community came into existence: *"The Bible was not written for the wise of this world, and neither for fools. It was written for men with spiritual intelligence and common sense which is not common in our institutions of learning."*

SUMMARY

We have discovered from the Book of Daniel how it prophetically described the military conquest of the Medo-Persians by Alexander the Great. The same Book also predicted the sudden death of Alexander the great at a young age at the peak of his power. It also foretold the division of Alexander the Great's Empire into four kingdoms by his four generals. Were these accurate predictions in the Hebrew Scriptures not extraordinary? Yet, modern educated men - the university professors and theologians with hundreds of alphabets after their names - claim the Bible is a myth; belief in religion is intellectual backwardness; religious thought is incoherent and irrational; and belief in God is a delusion, because scientific logic does not support it.

Question: Is it logical for a human being with a conscience to have developed from a brute with no conscience that attacks and maul a human being to death? (*Crazy to share your home with a chimp*: The Sun 21 February 2009) I repeat: scientists don't know the future. They cannot predict what would happen in the next minute. They are "blind" men with no clue of what is happening in the world. These "Lisbon" scientists, who are 'hostile' to the Bible, are just 'clones' of Professor T Huxley – Darwin's rottweiler – who was a bitter enemy of the Book of Genesis.

God is above scientific logic. Is it not amazing for a history to be written before the events of that history actually took place two hundred years after the history had already been recorded? How would agnostics, militant atheists, sceptics, humanists, animists, Darwinists, liberal theologians and doubting clergymen, bishops, Archbishops and Cardinals describe the Bible? Would they be able to produce a book to compare the Bible? Since time began, which Professor in Science has produced a book which is 100 % accurate in its prediction? None. Yet ignorant and deluded intellectuals, who do not know the Bible, hide their ignorance behind university degrees and, with slovenly thinking, ridicule Bible-believing Christians. Common sense and wisdom are not thought in universities. They are not available in scientific laboratories.

"DULL STUPIDITY OF IGNORANT UNBELIEF"

The wisdom of men is foolishness in the sight of God (1 Corinthians 1: 20-21). Do we have a book in history that accurately predicted the conquests of Alexander the Great and his sudden death before Alexander himself was born? No. It is also clear from our discussion, that the Bible even went further to foretell what would happen after the death of Alexander the Great – the division of his Grecian Empire into four kingdoms by his four generals. The works of historians Diodorus and Plaitarch confirm these Biblical facts.

In page 261 of *The Bible and Modern criticism*, the author writes: "While an intelligent scepticism will apply the severest tests to anything claiming to be Divine revelation, the rejection of it on a *priori* grounds is nothing but the dull stupidity of an ignorant unbelief." He added: "The Bible was not written for the wise of this world; still less for fools. To understand it aright we need both spiritual intelligence and common sense."

The pompous scientists, who 'worship' Darwin, witness what an intellectual among intellectuals wrote about you - the rationalists: ".. Lord Kelvin's dictum… gave these men an opportunity of "glorying in their shame"; and they eagerly availed themselves of it. His (Lord Kelvin's) assertion that, "Scientific thought" compelled belief in God set the whole pack in full cry. The acknowledgement even of "a direct force," they declared, "in effect wipes out the whole position won for us by Darwin…" The brilliant scholar continues: "This clearly indicates that the only value they (the rationalists and scientists) put upon their hypothesis is that it enables them to get rid of God….. What must be the moral, or indeed the intellectual condition of men who regard the negation of God as "a position won for them"! But, it may be asked, what about evolution? The materialistic evolution of Herbert Spencer is as dead as its author. And even *Darwin's more enlightened biological scheme is now discredited.* For it is recognised that something more than Darwinism offers is needed to account for the phenomenon of life. The evolution hypothesis is thoroughly philosophical; and that is all that can be said for it, for it is unproved and seemingly incapable of proof..." I will not continue. However in a note, the barrister added: "I may add that a friend of mine who was much with Darwin during his last illness assures me that he expressed the greatest reverence for the Scriptures and bore testimony to their value." (Pages 80– 82 of A *Doubter's Doubt About Science and Religion*)

THE AUTHENTICITY OF THE BOOK OF DANIEL

Before we continue with our discussion on the significance of the European Union and its future, I would like to make a vital point about the Book of Daniel. Because of the extraordinary accuracy of the predictions in this Book, a pagan Greek philosopher, Porphyry Malchus, attempted to discredit it. Porphyry, the hostile enemy of Christians, suggested that the Book of Daniel was a literal fraud written in 2nd century BC after the events had already taken place. Sceptical Bible scholars, fashionable clergymen and Bishops in England adopted the preposterous suggestion of the pagan Porphyry to undermine the integrity of this Old Testament Manuscript. The fact is it was German infidels who initially followed the atheist Porphyry to discredit the Bible. And English University Professors and clergymen also joined the bandwagon. Prominent among them were Professor S R Driver of Oxford and Dr Dean Farrar, an Anglican Archdeacon.

And it is beyond belief that even today, theologians of a Christian denomination (let me be specific: the Roman Catholic Church) have followed the worn out path of the pagan dreamer and used the discredited arguments of his "blind" disciples of the *School of Higher Criticism* to produce a Bible that claims the Book of Daniel is an *"edifying fiction"*- full of "inaccuracy and vagueness of historical detail" - written during the persecution of the Jews by the despicable Syrian king, Antiochus Epiphanes (167-164BC) In effect, Christians have a Bible that undermines the Bible. And it is a pity that the hierarchy of the Roman Catholic Church has endorsed such a Bible as worthy to be used for religious education in Schools, Colleges, and Universities. After endorsing *The New Jerusalem Bible* with their "Nihil obstat" and "Imprimatur," the experts who approved of its usage by Catholics and in Catholic institutions put up a"political statement": "It is not implied that those who have granted the Nihil obstat and Imprimatur agree with the contents, opinions or statement expressed." The fact is *The New Jerusalem Bible* is a Roman Catholic Bible not a Protestant Bible.

I would briefly share with you the errors of the critics of Daniel. In *The Bible and Modern criticism*, after the "Seer of Dublin" has torn into pieces one of the so-called "historical errors" purported to discredit the Book of Daniel, he writes: "This historical error is a blunder so glaring that a schoolboy might well be ashamed of it. And yet it is gravely adopted and reproduced by English ecclesiastics and Professors for the enlightenment of a much deluded public." He continued: "If only these men (the prominent critics of the Book of Daniel) could be "got into court", and subjected to cross-examination, they would lose not their case but their reputation." After dismissing the "language" argument against the Book of Daniel, the "Seer" added: "The remaining question is one of evidence of a wholly different kind; and no university professor, however eminent, is as fit to deal with it as the trained lawyer or the experienced juryman." He continued: "Those who study the Daniel controversy will recognise the truth of Hengstenberg's statement, that the attack upon the book originated in a prejudged determination to eliminate the supernatural element from the Bible."

The German Eichhorn spearheaded the attack on the Old Testament Books, especially the five Books of Moses, by downplaying the supernatural events recorded in them in the hope of winning back the educated classes. Eichhorn's business was to eliminate the miraculous elements in the Bible. The "Seer of Dublin" responded: "The rationalism of Germany at the close of the eighteenth century would accept the Bible only on the terms of bringing it down to the level of a human book, and the problem which had to be solved was to get rid of the element of miracle which pervades it."

In Christ and Criticism, the Irishman dismissed the "historical error" theory against the Book of Daniel. Witness his words: "Here is another typical item in the Critics' indictment of Daniel. The book opens by recording Nebuchadnezzar's siege of Jerusalem in the third year of Jehoiakim, a statement the correctness of which is confirmed by history, sacred and secular. Berosus, the Chaldean historian, tells us that during this expedition Nebuchadnezzar received tidings of his father's death, and that, committing to others the care of his army and of his Jewish and other prisoners, "he himself hastened home across the desert." But the German sceptics, having decided that Daniel was a forgery, had to find evidence to support their verdict. And so they made the brilliant discovery that Berosus was here referring to the expedition of the following year, when Nebuchadnezzar won the battle of Carchemish against the army of the king of Egypt, and that he had not at that time invaded Judea at all. But Carchemish is on the Euphrates, and the idea of "hastening home" from there to Babylon across the desert is worthy of a schoolboy's essay! That he crossed the desert is proof that he set out from Judea; and his Jewish captives were, of course, Daniel and his companion princes. His invasion of Judea took place before his accession, in Jehoiakam's third year, whereas the battle of Carchemish was fought after his accession, in the king of Judah's fourth year, as the biblical books record. But this grotesque blunder of Bertholdt's "Book of Daniel" in the beginning of the nineteenth century is gravely reproduced in Professor Driver's "Book of Daniel" at the beginning of the twentieth century." And liberal theologians, Bishops, Archbishops and priests of today have also reproduced the same 'error' to 'blindfold' Christians who have pinned their understanding of the Bible on Bible scholars.

It is therefore, shameful, deceitful, unscriptural and theological dishonesty for the Roman Catholic Church to endorse "*The New Jerusalem Bible.*" This is a Bible which claims the Book of Daniel is a religious fiction, and the only Daniel known in history is not the one in the Book of Daniel, and neither the one in Ezekiel14:19-20, nor the "Daniel" the Lord Jesus spoke about in Matthew 24:15, but rather a "sage Daniel" who was "revered in the ancient Near East?" I repeat: this is sheer intellectual and theological dishonesty – an attempt to undermine the supernatural character of the Book of Daniel.

The Irish Barrister, defending the Book of Daniel, wrote: "The critics maintain that the definiteness of the predictions of Daniel is due to the fact that the book was written after the events referred to; and further, that its "vision" cease with the reign of Antiochus Epiphanes. The main issues of fact, therefore, to be decided at such a trial would be these:-

1 Was the Book of Daniel in existence in pre-Maccabean days? And
2 Was any one of its visions fulfilled in latter times? And if either of these issuers should be found against the critics their whole case would be shattered."

Pope Benedict XVI must now declare to the 1.2 billion Roman Catholics whether the Book of Daniel is a divine revelation or an "edifying fiction" - a religious fraud composed in the 2nd century BC as suggested in the Catholic Bible. The world is waiting for an answer.

I will make a contribution towards the defence of the Integrity of the marvellous Book of Daniel in Volume 2 of this work. In the meantime I have reproduced the list of the so-called historic errors that "discredit" the Book of Daniel. I copied this list from Appendix II of *Daniel in the Critics Den*. "God's Barrister" defended the Book of Daniel in this work.

"PROFESSOR DRIVER'S INDICTMENT OF DANIEL

THE following is a brief summary of Professor Driver's indictment of the Book of Daniel. He enumerates under nine heads "facts of a historical nature" which point to an author later than Daniel (pp. xlvii—ivi).

These are :—

1. The position of the Book in the Jewish Canon. (As to this see pp. 57—61, and 103—108, ante.)
2. The omission of his name from Ecclesiasticus. (See pp. 57, 98 n., ante.)
3. That the Book of Kings is silent as to the siege mentioned in Dan. i. 1. (See p.15 and App. I., ante.)
4. The use of the term "Chaldean." (See p. 45 a., ante.)
5. That Belshazzar is spoken of as king, and as son of Nebuchadnezzar. (See p. 23 if., ante.)
6. The mention of Darius the Mede as King of Babylon. (See p. 31ff. and i65, ante.)

7. The mention of "the books" in Dan. ix. 2.
   The word sepher means simply a scroll It often denotes a book; often a letter (as, e.g., Jer. xxix. i, or Isa.
   xxxvii. 14.) Then again Jer. xxxvi. I, 2 records that Jeremiah's prophecies up to that time were recorded in a "book." And ten years later a further "book" of them was sent to Babylon (Jer. ii. 60, 61).
   Or if anyone insists that "the books" must here mean a recognised canon, where is the difficulty? The statement that no such "collection" existed in B.C. 536 is one of those wanton assertions that abound in this controversy. It may "safely be affirmed" with certainty that the scrolls of the Law were kept together. And there was no man on earth more likely to possess them than the great prophet-prince of the Captivity.
8. "The incorrect explanation of the name Bel-shazzar in iv. 8." (As Dr. Driver goes on to describe this as "doubtful" (p. liv.), I have not deemed it necessary to notice it.)
9. The "improbability" that strict Jews would have accepted a position among the "wise men" (see p. 13, ante), and other like "improbabilities." (As Dr. Driver goes on to admit that these do not possess weight, and "should be used with reserve," I have not dwelt upon them.) His second ground of attack is the language of the book (lvi.-lxiii.). This has been fully discussed in these pages (ch. iv.).

And the third ground is "the theology of the book." After deprecating the "exaggerations of the rationalists" under this head, he proceeds: - "It is undeniable that the conception of the future Kingdom of God, and the doctrines of angels, of the resurrection, and of a judgment on the world, appear in Daniel in a more developed form than elsewhere in the Old Testament." Far be it from me to deny it! It is largely on this very account that the Christian values the book, remembering as he does, what Professor Driver ignores, that its teaching in all these respects is definitely adopted and developed in the New Testament. And if he finds that the later Jewish apocalyptical literature resembles the book in some respects, he has no difficulty in accounting for the resemblance. (See p. 57, ante.)

I make the critic a present of the entire argument under this head of "the theology of the book," save on three points. And they are points which would never have been urged by an English Christian writer save under the influence of German infidelity.

It is not true that the interest of the book culminates in the history of Antiochus. As all Christian expositors with united voice maintain, it culminates in the prophecy of Messiah's advent and death. And as all students of prophecy recognise, it reaches on to the time of the treat Antichrist of whom Antiochus was but a type.

- Daniel's passionately earnest prayer recorded in ch. ix. is a complete answer to the statement that he took "little interest in the welfare and prospects of his contemporaries."

- We are told that "the minuteness of the predictions embracing even special events in the distant future, is also out of harmony with the analogy of prophecy." If this were sustained it would not affect the book as a whole, but serve merely to accredit the suggestion urged by some writers that part of chap. xi. is an interpolation. But in view of the facts this allegation is as strange as that under (2) supra, and as many others in Professor Driver's book. What about the minute predictions scattered through the Old Testament respecting the Nativity and the Passion? And the last eight chapters of Ezekiel contain a mass of predictions which still await fulfilment, as minute as anything in Daniel. This is all that the Higher Criticism has to urge against the Book of Daniel."

CHAPTER 2

European Union: The "Dead" Roman Empire Resurrected

"...There are the religious teachers .....whose role it appears to be to import the raw material of German rationalism and to retail it with a veneer of British piety to suit the British market. And secondly, there are the scientists of the materialistic school, to whom the very name of God is intolerable..."

(A Doubter's Doubt about Science and Religion - RA)

I will now share with the militant atheists, the fashionable theologians, the doubting clergymen and bishops, who have joined forces with the pagan Porphyry to undermine the divine character of the Bible with human philosophies, the awkward truth in the Scriptures which is unfolding in our generation. This particular truth would lead to the conclusion that the Bible is still relevant today, and it is far clearer in our days than it was over 2600 years ago.

This truth, which is "hidden" in the Scriptures, is the answer to the question Robert Taylor raised in the Biblical epic film *Quo vadis?* After the leading actor had witnessed the burning of Rome and the killing of Christians by hungry lions in a Roman arena, Robert Taylor posed this question: "Babylon, Greece, Rome; what next?" What follows Rome is the Revival of the "dead" Roman Empire which is now being constructed by the bureaucrats in Brussels.

What we are about to learn - the progress of the economic and political union of European nations - would be of great help to politicians, political scientists and political commentators and all who dwell on planet earth. According to European politicians the birth of the European Union was of great historic event. The late Francois Duchene, who witnessed the birth of the European Community, described it as "the rarest of all phenomena in history." And Dominique de Villlepin, a former French Prime Minister, also described the European Union "the greatest political and historic adventure of the last century." Indeed, the development of the European Union is a significant phenomenon. This political phenomenon will affect the lives of every soul in Africa, Antarctica, Asia, Australia, Europe and North and South America.

In this study we will discover that the current news and contemporary events, as well as all future events were written in the Bible thousands of years before they became news for our newspapers to publish them. In other words, today's newspapers were published thousands of years ago. Yesterday's newspapers were also printed in the Bible thousands of years ago before we read them. And tomorrow's newspapers had already been published thousands of years ago. We praise the Lord for His Infallible Word. "Before things happened the Almighty announced them (Isaiah 48:5). Amen!

THE "REVIVED ROMAN EMPIRE" – THE EMPIRES OF GREECE AND ROME ARE "ALIVE" TODAY

About 27BC Caesar Augustus was installed the Emperor of the Roman Empire. It was this realm that succeeded the Grecian Empire as the 4th powerful empire to rule the world. And history also tells us how God, in His sovereignty, used the Roman Empire to kill the Lord Jesus by crucifixion to fulfil the prophetic vision: *"...after three score and two weeks shall Messiah be cut off, but not for himself..."* (Daniel 9:26).

The Roman Empire collapsed in about 476AD. Yet, despite its demise, the Roman culture, law, politics and custom continue to influence our lives. Look at the western nations and many other countries around the world – their laws, politics and systems of government are primary based on how the Romans, the Greeks and the Persians governed themselves. After all, some of the words in the English Language, the most popular language and medium of communication in the world, have their roots in Latin and Greek.

DEMOCRACY: "THE BEAUTIFUL BRIDE" IS NOT A "PEREFECT" WOMAN

Consider the political concept of "democracy", which is virtually universally respected as the best or right form of government. It was the Greeks who gave the nations of the world this 'beautiful bride' called "Democracy." Democracy has become the 'charming and respectful woman' the world is chasing to marry. The appeal and beauty of this *"lady"* (Democracy) is irresistible. Two powerful western nations, United States of America and Britain, have already fallen in love with *her,* and attempting to force this "beautiful lady" on countries which they regard as undemocratic and a "threat" to world peace. Could one force a beautiful woman to be the bride of a man, if such a "bachelor" did not fancy the charm of this 'pretty woman' because of her vile character?

After all, this "attractive lady" (Democracy) is not a perfect woman. Samuel Brittan, in his article *Democracy alone is simply not enough,* quoted the words of

Sir Winston Churchill: "Democracy is absurd, but all other systems are worse" (Financial Times Friday, May 13, 2005). In his letter to the Financial Times on 20 May 2005, Michael Smith, a former British Ambassador to Tajikistan, commented on democracy. He stated: "The political correctness that surrounds the word 'democracy' these days is depressing. "Democracy" as a goal lends cover to many a dictator while obscuring the central issue, which is accountability..." And the "Forgotten son of Ulster" summed up the character of the world's most "beautiful lady": "Democracy, not despotism, is the goal towards which civilization is tending. But democracy in its full development is one of the surest roads to despotism..."

The Greeks have also presented another gift to mankind - the Olympic Games. The nations of the world have embraced this precious "gift." Every four years they honour it. What lessons do we learn from the following facts?

- Democracy has been adopted by many nations.
- The Nations of the world participate in Olympic Games.
- The English Language (the most popular language and medium of communication in the world) has its roots in Latin and Greek.

It is clear the Greek and Roman Empires are still in 'existence.' Though these Empires fell centuries ago, they are still "alive". We are witnesses of how our society is under the influence of Greek and Roman cultures.

On 10 February 2003, a leading article in The Times read: "*LIFE AFTER DEATH: A welcome revival in the popularity of Latin and Greek.*" This article, in a sense, confirmed that the Empires of Greek and Rome are still "*reigning*". Here is an extract from the article "...The best reason for encouraging these subjects (Latin and Greek) is the more straight forward. Latin and Greek are great. They are the foundations of western civilisation: politics, philosophy, drama, art, architecture, law, science, mathematics and dance. They are our inheritance from our founding fathers. Their surviving literature include the foundation masterpieces.....It can only be hoped that this boom, which proves that there is life after death for languages, will be repeated in the state sector.". The editorial indicated a rising popularity of Latin and Greek in independent schools.

The weight of Roman culture on our lives was again highlighted in an article titled *Latin fights back in computer age.* The author, Susan Elkin, writes: "The word 'computer' comes from Latin (literally it means a thinker)...Latin underpins more than half of the English language. Without some Latin you will never understand precisely how English works. It helps you to deduce word meanings, and it provides a systematic grounding in grammar....Knowing some Latin also makes it easier to get to grips with modern languages such as French, Germany,

Italian, and Spanish. And for many centuries Latin was the common language of public life across Europe." She added: "It makes good sense to rescue Latin", because the lack of education in this subject has contributed to the "worsening quality of writing and communication" in our society.(Source: Daily Mail 11 July 2006). And it was reported that the European Union Socrates Programme has funded the CIRCLE project with a grant of about £200000 to create electronic resources to "make it easier to teach Latin, Greek, and Classical Civilisation. The acronym CIRCLE stands for "Classics and ICT Resource Course for Europe."

THE EUROPEAN UNION: AN "EXTENSION" OF GREEK AND ROMAN EMPIRES

From what we have learnt so far, it is obvious the glory of Greece and the splendour of Rome are shining upon us today. Our society is under the influence of Greek and Roman cultures. The Roman Empire, the fourth and the last world power which was revealed to the King of Babylon in a dream as 2 legs of iron of a dazzling human statue, is still "ruling." Daniel saw the powerful Roman Empire as a terrifying beast with iron teeth.

A section of the preamble to the European Constitution which was rejected by the French and the Dutch in 2005 confirms that we are still in the Roman Empire: "....Europe is a continent that has brought forth civilisations.... Since the first stages of mankind, have gradually developed the values underlying humanism, equality of person, freedom, respect for reason.....Drawing inspiration from the cultural, religious and humanist inheritance of Europe which, **nourished first by the civilisations of Greek and Rome,** characterised by spiritual impulse always present and later by the philosophical currents of the Enlightenment...." (Financial Times 29 May 2003).

This text, which is part of the Mission Statement of the European Union, clearly confirms that, in a sense, **the European Union is an extension of Greek and Roman cultures.** This was foretold in Daniel 7:12: *"As for the rest of the beasts, they had their dominion taken away, yet their lives were prolonged for a season."* The "beasts" in this text were Lion, which represented the Babylonian Empire; a Bear, which corresponded to the Medo-Persian Empire, and a Leopard, which signified the Grecian Empire of Alexander the Great. Thus, according to this Scripture, even though the Empires of Babylon, Medo-Persia and Greece have ceased to exist, their cultures continue to influence our lives.

Moreover, the Continent of Europe derived its name from Greek mythology. Europe, the sixth largest continent, was named after a woman called *Europa.* She was a Greek mythical figure, a beautiful Phoenician Princess, who attracted the Greek god, Zeus. *Europa* and other girls were gathering flowers at seashore when

Zeus saw them from heaven. Zeus was captivated by the extraordinary beauty of *Europa* to the extent that he transformed himself into a magnificent white bull and swam to the shore. All the girls were absorbed by the handsome bull and began playing with it. Zeus, now a bull, enticed the beautiful *Europa* to sit at his back. The bull immediately abducted *Europa* into the sea - carrying her off. After *Europa* had overcome her initial fears, she thought this was not an ordinary bull. She pleaded with the bull not to harm her. The bull then revealed himself as Zeus, the greatest of all the gods. Zeus expressed his love for *Europa*. He assured her of safety, and escorted her to Crete, his own island. Zeus and *Europa* shared bed together and the couple gave birth to three sons. To demonstrate his love for *Europa,* Zeus offered this "beautiful woman" three precious gifts. It is interesting to note that one of the gifts was a magical man made of bronze. For we know that the bronze section of the dazzling statue Nebuchadnezzar saw in his dream referred to Alexander's Grecian Empire.

I conclude this chapter with an extract from TIME Special Report on Jean Monnet and European Community that confirms the European Union is the revived Roman Empire as predicted in Daniel 2:40-45: "Like many revolutionary ideas, united Europe is not a new union but an old one revived. The dream of order and unity once embodied in the Rome of the Caesars lived on through the Middle Ages, not only in the Roman Catholic Church but in that embattled but strangely viable anachronism, the Holy Roman Empire. Even after it disintegrated, and the last remnants of feudal internationalism gave way to popular nationalism, the European idea remained; and even if Europeans themselves at times forgot it, the rest of the world would not. For most of 2000 years the culture, commerce and conquests of the peoples of Western Europe shaped the world's destinies. European traders and explorers knit the world. European armies subdued it. European adventurers settled it. European artists and philosophers remade its esthetic norms. European artisans launched the Industrial Revolution, and European Capital carried it to the ends of the earth. But as Europe's influence grew, so did the scale of its conflicts." (TIME 6 October 1961).

CHAPTER 3

The Myth will become a reality

The Greek Mythology: Zeus turns into a handsome white bull. Zeus abducts *Europa* – the beautiful Phoenician Princess – to Crete. The Greek god seduces *Europa*. They produced three sons.

The Continent of Europe was named after this mythical woman.
This mythical story is a design on the Greek 2 euro cents.

A seed produces its kind.
The "Myth" became a "Reality" and the "Reality" will be repeated.

"The natural attitude of a thinking mind towards the supernatural is that of scepticism." Scepticism, not agnosticism. The sceptic halts at the cross-roads to take his bearings; but at the sight of a cross-road the agnostic gives up his journey altogether. True scepticism connotes intellectual caution, but agnosticism is intellectual suicide."

(RA)

We have learnt that the continent of Europe was named after an imaginary woman - *Europa* - whose lover was a Greek god. And it is interesting to note that the Greek 2 euro cents has a portrait of *Europa* sitting at the back of a bull. This Greek mythology: a naked woman ridding on a beast, would become a reality when the European Union reaches its maturity. Another EU coin, the Italian 5 euro cents, shows the Flavius Amphitheatre. It was the Roman Emperor, Flavius Vespasian, who started to build this magnificent arena in around 75AD. His son, Titus Vespasian, inaugurated the Colloseum in 80AD. The meaning of the portraits on these two euro coins would provide an insight into the significance of the European Union and the effect this political alliance of European nations would have on mankind. We will discuss the implication of these two euro coins in due course.

The designs on these 2 Euro coins, again, confirm how the Western culture is an amalgamation of the Greek and the Roman civilisations. The truth is that from the biblical perspective the whole world is part of the western culture, which is the Roman culture. But this Roman culture is the consummation of the Greek, the Persian and the Babylonian cultures. And this, I repeat, fulfils the prophetic word in Daniel 7:12: *"The other beasts had been stripped of their authority, but were allowed to live for a period"*. I have already indicated that the *"Other beasts"* refer to the Grecian, Medo-Persian and Babylonian Empires. They correspond to the three nasty beasts - the leopard, the bear and the lion - which Daniel saw in a vision. This revelation is recorded in (Daniel 7:1-6).

The vision of the 4 cruel beasts was unveiled to Daniel in the first year of king Belshazzar of Babylon. This was about 555BC before the Persian King, Cyrus, released the Jews from servitude in about 536BC. Even though these three empires, Babylon, Medo – Persia and Greece, are no longer in existence, yet their cultures continue to triumph in our generation. They have become part of our way of life in the "Roman Empire" of today. For example, Astrology was first practised by the Babylonians. Today, in our Age of Enlightenment, Astrology is being taught and practised. In *THE LATE GREAT PLANET EARTH,* Hal Lindsey explained it: "The Babylonian kings did not make a move without consulting their astrologers, and the Medo-Persians who conquered the Babylonians did the same thing. They, too, had their court astrologers and wisemen. When the Greek, Alexander the Great, conquered the Medo-Persian Empire he also began to follow astrologers and their wisdom. The practice was transported to Rome where we see the Caesars consulting the augurs, who were experts in astrology, spiritism, and the black arts." Clearly, despite the fact that these three Empires (Greece, Medo-Persia and Babylon) are no more in existence, what they practised (Astrology) is being practised in our generation. Later on we will discover how the leopard, the bear and the lion represent the Empires of Greece, Medo – Persia and Babylon respectively.

THE "DEAD" ROMAN EMPIRE REVIVED IN THE "UNSTABLE" WORLD

We have learnt that, even though in the eyes of men the Roman Empire ceased to exist in about 476AD, in the sight of God the Roman Empire is still in "existence." We know it was during the first year of King Belshazzar's reign that Daniel saw a vision of 4 cruel beasts (lion, bear, leopard and frightening beasts with iron teeth) rising from the Mediterranean Sea. These four vicious beasts represented the 4 world powers (Babylon, Medo-Persia, Greece and Rome) that have ruled the world in succession.

Before we proceed, I would explain the significance of the *"sea"* from which the 4 wicked beasts emerged. In the Bible *"sea"* signifies "peoples, multitudes, tongues and nations" (Revelation 17:15). The roaring waves of the sea swirl around to the shore and return into the sea. For this reason, the sea is noted for its restlessness and instability. This is the suggestive metaphor. In the unstable and chaotic world have emerged 'wild beasts' – wicked men who have dominated the earth with iron fists. History tells us how tyrants like Hitler, Napoleon and Mussolini emerged from chaotic political systems and national economic breakdowns to rule. In the developing world we notice how dictators have sprung up from unstable political systems to control the masses. From our present turbulent world, which is plagued with wars, famine, poverty, epidemic diseases and political and economic crisis, would appear a brutal dictator who would rule the world with an iron fist.

The Roman Empire, which was the fourth world power to rule the world, was symbolised by the fourth beasts with "ten horns." According to Daniel 7:7, this particular beast was terrifying and frightening and very powerful. It crushed and devoured its victims. And Daniel 7:23 tells us that the hideous monster (the Roman Empire) was "*different from all the other kingdoms and will devour the whole earth, trampling down and crushing it.*" Historical facts confirm how the Caesars of Rome ruthlessly ruled the world. One of these Caesars was the wicked Emperor Nero. He burned Christians alive and offered them to hungry lions. The *"ten horns"* on this 4th cruel beast (the Roman Empire) are very significant. We will learn more about them as we progress.

In the Bible the number 4 stands for planet earth (Ezekiel 7:1-2). From the scriptural standpoint this means the Roman Empire, which was the 4th world power after the Grecian Empire of Alexander the Great, would be the last Empire to rule the earth. No other political power will rise up to become the 5th Empire. The Roman Empire died centuries ago. However, the dead Roman Empire is being revived through the development of the European Union. I repeat: the President of the European Commission, Jose Manuel Barroso, has already described the European Union the world's "first non imperial empire." And when the Treaty of Rome was signed in 1957, Paul-Henri Spaak, the Belgian statesman, declared: "....we have today been putting the first stone of a **new Roman Empire,** and this time without firing a shot?" We all felt like Romans that day." (TIME 5 June 2005)

THE WORLD IS "BABYLON" COME OUT OF BABYLON

I have already mentioned that the Roman Empire, which was symbolised by the 4th beast in Daniel's vision of 4 cruel beasts (Daniel 7:3-7), corresponds to the two legs of iron of the human statue Nebuchadnezzar saw in a dream (Daniel 2:32-33). We know the head of this human image was of pure gold. It represented the Babylonian Empire of which Nebuchadnezzar was its Emperor (Daniel 2:36-38). What does this head of gold of the human image signify? Let us find out.

The New Testament teaches that the Lord Jesus Christ is the Head of the Church, and the Church is the Body that fully expresses the Lord. (Ephesians. 1:23; 3:13). Similarly, if the head of the human statue Nebuchadnezzar saw was Babylon, then the body of the statue was also Babylon. This means, the Empires of Medo-Persia, Greece and Rome, which respectively formed the chest and arms (silver), the belly and thighs (bronze) and the legs of iron and the toes of iron and clay of this statue, are all Babylonian. Hence, these three Empires (Medo-Persia, Greece and Rome) fully express the head, which is Babylon. As the nature of a body takes the nature of the head, it implies the 'Revived Roman Empire," which is yet to manifest fully through the European Union, is "Babylonian."

We know the nations of the world are indebted to the civilisations of Greece and Rome, because, they have married their cultures: politics, drama, art, architecture, law, philosophy, science, mathematics and dance. And if the Grecian and Roman Empires were all Babylonian, then by implication, the world of today is "Babylonian." Babylon, which was the head of human government, was symbolised by "pure gold" of the dazzling human statue Nebuchadnezzar saw (Daniel 2:32). This same Babylon was also symbolised by a lion with the wings of an eagle (Daniel 7:4). Gold is a glittering precious substance. And lion, the king of the forest, is a ferocious beast that suddenly pounces on its prey. By implication, human governments have stunning outward appearances. Consider the ceremonies that are put on display to welcome heads of states and kings and Queens, and reflect on the grandeur surrounding American political conventions that nominate presidential candidates. Yet, immediately the pageantries are over, the 'beasts' return to the 'jungle' to devour themselves. Political institutions all over the world are infested with "wild beasts."

Politicians promised so much during their campaigns. After gaining power, politicians fail to deliver their promises. In some countries politicians loot the coffers of the nation and live in luxury while the masses starve. In other countries they become corrupt and swim in the sea of nepotism - favouring those who had financed their campaigns with business contracts. While the public is advised to tighten their belts by accepting low wages, the elected politicians appropriate to themselves higher remuneration and other benefits and privileges. In summary, once in power, politicians pursue their selfish interests – eager to make name for themselves and to leave their 'legacies' behind. Is this not apparent in our so-called civilised societies?

THE "LION," THE "BEAR" AND THE "LEOPARD" POLITICIANS

It is obvious to anyone who has observed political campaigns and "point-scoring", that the political systems of the world are jungles populated with "feral beasts". This was evident in the 2008 US Presidential campaign. Presidential candidates for the Republicans and Democrats 'devoured' each other in debates and advertisements. And in Britain when politicians confront each other during "Question time", they 'devour' one another with accusations and counter- accusations. Politics in the civilised world is a forest inhabited by "wild beasts". We have "Lion politicians". They suddenly spring and attack their 'enemies' – political opponents. There are "Bear politicians" who trample upon their opponents. We have "Leopard politicians." They ruthlessly devise schemes to stay in power to control the masses. If you cast your mind around political institutions in the world, you would recollect how politicians "devour" themselves with accusations and counter-accusations.

In *Daniel Speaks today,* C Ernest Tatham relates the four wild beasts, which correspond to the sparkling metals of gold, silver, bronze and iron of the human statue, to the political systems and practices of the world. He writes: "In the second chapter of the Book of Daniel, the four world-empires are seen from man's point of view; in the seventh they are presented as God sees them. To man these empires are dominant, impressive, and awe-inspiring, but to heaven they are fierce; unclean, and carnivorous beasts of prey." Today, in our 'confrontational politics of points-scoring', the nations of the world have become vast jungle of "untamed beasts - snapping and snarling at one another and ready to spring, devour and conquer. Surely, God revealed to Daniel what would happen in the world of Babylon. God's figures of speech are always accurate. Godless Gentile Nations are populated by Ruthless Feral Beasts."

This 'huge forest of wild animals' is the political Babylon the Lord Jesus Christ spoke about in Revelation 18. The king of this jungle is the vicious lion which devours its prey. The Lord warns us: *"Come out of her (Babylon) so that you will not share in her sins, so that you will not receive any of her plagues; for her sins are pilled up in heaven"* (Revelation 18:4-5). In this particular chapter you would see a picture of the 2007-2008 financial and economic crisis which is about to become a reality at the appointed time.

If we, therefore, consider the advice the Lord Jesus gave us concerning our coming out of Babylon, it becomes clear that Christians should not entertain the idea that they can enter the dark world of politics to change the ideologies of politicians with their Christian principles and values. They risk being isolated and influenced by the humanistic philosophies of secular politicians. The Philosophy of "Political Correctness" usually undermines Christian values. How many Christian politicians have resigned from Parliaments or Congresses because their political parties enacted laws that contradicted the teachings of the Bible?

For example, how many Christian politicians resigned because their respective political parties supported the legalisation of same-sex marriages – a lifestyle which contradicts what the Bible teaches? A Labour Party politician, who is a Christian, was asked a simple question: "Do you think homosexuality is a sin?" She hesitated. She was pressed for a simple answer to which she responded: "I don't think it is right for politicians to start making moral judgements about people. What I think the question is, is what my political views are? As a politician, those are the ones that I am accountable for to the public". The same Christian politician "repeatedly declined to say whether she agreed that same-sex couples should be permitted to adopt children" (*The Independent* 10 May 2006). This politician could not give a simple, clear answer: "Yes" or "No" to a simple question. Perhaps, for fear she might cause offence to become unpopular and possibly lose her job at that time , she stumbled.

We must take the advice of the Lord Jesus seriously: *"Come out of Babylon so that you will not share in her sins, so that you will not receive any of her plagues; for her sins are pilled up in heaven"*(Revelation 18:4-5). As Christians, who are members of the Body of Christ, it is our duty to advise our political leaders with the 'truth' that is enshrined in Sacred Scriptures. It is not our business to get involved in politics to change the political systems of the world to make the world a better place. We cannot change the political system. Who can persuade European leaders to mention God and the Lord Jesus Christ in their Constitution? The Roman Catholic Church tried and failed; yet Vatican is still in 'love' with the godless European Union. Why? We shall find out.

No human being can make this world, which would be judged, a better place. At the appointed time the King of kings will return to restore normality and eternal righteousness in our confused, immoral and wicked world. Our business is to proclaim the Gospel and teach the TRUTH to make disciples for the Lord. The "stone cut without human hands" is rolling to crush the human statue from its toes of baked clay and iron. This is why the "Stone" advises us to get out of Babylon. I repeat, as Christians, it is our responsibility to share the TRUTH with our politicians. It would be their decision to accept or reject the GOSPEL TRUTH. However, if a Christian feels he/she has been called to enter the political arena to change the political system; he/she must heed the call.

CHAPTER 4

The Source of Babylon

"Critics are specialists, and it is proverbial that specialists are bad judges. The place of the experts is in the witness box not on the judgement seat." **(RA)**

The Lord Jesus Christ warned us about our relationship with *Babylon.* Since some of us are still in *Babylon,* it is important we identify the source of *Babylon* to help us severe our relationship with *her.* The origin of Babylon was the city and the Tower of Babel - the place where confusion of tongues occurred (Genesis 11:1-9). Nimrod was the brain behind the city of Babel. Babel is the Hebrew word for Babylon. The meaning of Babylon is explained by the Hebrew word -*"balal,"* which means "to confuse," or "mix". According to Penguin English Dictionary, the Word "Babel" means a scene of noise or confusion, especially from many voices. It also explains "Babble" as to utter meaningless or unintelligible sounds, or to talk foolishly.

Is the whole world not in confusion? Examine the political systems and their institutions around the world, and you would notice how politicians have no idea of what is happening. They are not in control of events. They have been overwhelmed by events. And in their reaction to unforeseen circumstances, they promise solutions to the economic, social, and political and security problems that engulf them. They keep on promising: "Reform, Reform, Reform"; "Change, Change, Change." But "Reformation" eludes them. The "Change" is never realised, and in vain they search for solutions. They clutch at straws; 'blind' men groping in darkness. "They look for light, but all is darkness; for brightness, but they walk in deep shadows. Like the blind they grope along the wall, feeling their way like men without eyes. At midday they stumble as if it were twilight." (Isaiah 59:9-10)

The confusion among nations was manifested when the United Nations world summit in September 2005 "failed to deliver an agreed definition of terrorism." (Financial Times Editorial, Monday September 19, 2005). If the United Nations could not even define "terrorism," what chances do members of this body have in eradicating terrorism? No doubt, the world is "Babylonian." It is interesting to note that our English words "Bable" and "Babble" are derived from an event that took place more than two thousand years before the Lord Jesus Christ was born.

THE ENTREPRISE AT BABEL IS BEING REPEATED IN EUROPE

In chapters 10 and 11 of the Book of Genesis we read about how Nimrod, a great hunter, decided that a union of men with the same tongue (knowledge) should plan the building of a tower that could reach the heavens. Their aim was to make a name for themselves, and to be independent in their own kingdom. The Lord of the heavens foiled the project at Babel and scattered the people around the earth. The Tower of Babel enterprise, which men planned it to satisfy their ego, plunged into confusion. And since that historic day - through wars, treaties, alliances and marriages - nations in certain parts of the world are seeking to be unified again, just as it was in the days of Nimrod, during which time men planned to unite to construct a city for themselves and a Tower to symbolise their achievement. It may interest you to know that today we have a fleet of Bomber Planes called "Nimrods". On 12 June 2005, a headline in The Sunday Times read: "RAF Nimrods may become bomber force."

The "hunters" of old - Charlemagne and Hitler of Germany, the Italian Mussolini and the French Napoleon - did not succeed in their attempt to 'fuse' Europe, just as how the hunter Nimrod failed to unite mankind at Babel. Napoleon declared: "What does it matter whether two nations are separated by rivers or mountains or that they speak different idioms? Europe is but one province of the world: when we make war, we make civil war. I should have liked to have made these peoples one single and uniform body."

History is repeating itself. The enterprise at Babel is being duplicated in our generation. Today, there are economic and political unions of nations around the world. We have Organisation of African Union (OAU) of 53 states, The Commonwealth of 53 states, Economic Community of West African States (ECOWAS), The Arab League of 22 states, and The North American Free Trade Association (NAFTA) of three states. The most significant of these alliances is the European Union (EU) – which has been described as one of the great successes of the post 1945 world – a unique geopolitical experiment that has spread peace and prosperity across a continent that, within living memory, had little of either" (Carla Power *TIME* August 11 2009). At present the European Union boasts of 27 members with prospective members in a queue. So, where the French dictator, Napoleon, failed, it seems the French 'schemer', Jean Monnet. has 'succeeded' to unite the peoples of Europe. And finally, we have the United Nations, an international body of almost all the nations on planet earth.

UNIFICATION WITHOUT GOD IS CONFUSION

Men started the Tower of Babel Project to become independent of God. It ended in chaos. And so would all political and economic unions of nations, which have been designed to be independent of God, end in confusion. The truth is that any human enterprise - whether for political, social security or economic purposes -without the sanction of God through the Lord Jesus Christ, would not survive. Why? Because, such projects would have inherited the 'spirit of Babel', which is confusion. The Bible says: *"Unless the Lord builds the house, they labour in vain who build it, unless the Lord guards the city, the watchmen stay awake in vain"* (Psalm 127:1). So, in vain would be Jean Monnet's vision of peace in a united (federal) Europe.

In his booklet *"Farewell Europe"* Horst Schaffranek, a renowned German Bible teacher, writes: "God packed the world into boxes. If this fact is ignored, a mess results as in the case of former Yugoslavia....God made sure that nations are separated from one another since Babel – and not melted altogether in a big pot". The European Union has become a 'melting pot' of different tongues. Jean Monnet, in his wisdom, thought he could 'fuse' European nations to suit his vision of a federal Europe. Monnet's toil to unite Europe was to bring to pass what an Irishman wrote about his 'vision' of a political Europe and its future before he, Monnet, was born.

In an article *Never mind the treaty squabbles, Europe's real problem is Babel* (The Guardian 18 October 2007), Timothy Garton Ash, Professor of European Studies in University of Oxford, writes: "The chief lesson of a unique project is that the EU's greatest worry is not Brussels – it's 23 different languages.....The heart of Europe's democracy problem is not Brussels but Babel". The question is: "What happened to the Tower of Babel Project and the "10 toes" of the great human image which were partly of baked clay and partly of iron"? For the answers please refer to Genesis 11:1-9 and Daniel 2: 31-35.

"HUMANISM" WAS BORN AT BABEL: THE PLACE OF CONFUSION

At Babel, men decided *"to build themselves a city with a tower that reaches to the heavens, so that they make a name for themselves"* (Genesis 11:4). The followers of Nimrod did not need God just like the European Union of today that has no room for God. According to history, portraits of idols were inscribed on the Tower at Babel. We can conclude rightly that at Babel men opposed God; worshipped idols, and decided to make name for themselves. These are the characteristics of Babylon. These features are prominent in both the political system and the apostate church (the religious Babylon). Laws initiated by the political Babylon, and the practices and some of the doctrines of the degraded church (the religious Babylon) undermine what the Bible teaches. The two "Babylon" exalt men. They crave for status, lust after wealth, and approve and condone sexual immoralities. The enlightened men of today's Babylon have substituted the precepts of the Bible with human philosophies to the extent that the Bible has become an offence and must be removed from public buildings.

The Lord Jesus Christ, the Central Character of the Bible, has also become an offence to men. His "Cross" has no place in crematoriums. His name has no place on Christmas cards – cards which were supposed to commemorate the *date* of His birth. "Now NHS (our National Health Service) says a Christian blessing is offensive to minorities" (Daily Mail 28 November 2005). The Christmas Season has been renamed winter holidays to avoid offending non-Christians. And on Friday 4 November 2005, the confused men of the world were exposed on the front page of the DAILY EXPRESS with this text: "NOW CHRIST IS BANNED – BC (Before Christ) is out...it has to be BP (Before Present)."

In this front page story, the newspaper reported: "Museum Bosses are trying to erase Jesus Christ from the pages of history. In the latest ludicrous attempt to tear down traditions, curators have banned the phrase BC – Before Christ – and insist in using BP – Before Present – to avoid offending other faiths." This outrageous decision prompted Church of England spokesman, Steve Jenkins, to say: "I always thought BP was where you go to fill up with petrol, I just can't understand the point of introducing other initials and I'm sure no one else can. It's unnecessary and incredibly silly." And the historian, Dr. Starkey, dubbed it "infantile". He added, "I am not a Christian, indeed I am anti-Christian, but BC is an essential feature of our history and to dispense of our history with it in such a frivolous way is very foolish." Such was the display of the intelligence of humanism in the propagation of the doctrine of "Political correctness." What a confusion!

The spirit of "Humanism" was born at the Tower of Babel. This spirit – *"Let us make name for ourselves"*; *"We don't need God"; "We don't do God"; "God is dead"; Belief in God is intellectual backwardness"* - has influenced the projects of men. Ray C Stedman aptly described it: "I am always amazed to see how many public edifices made a plague somewhere on which the names of all the public officials who were in power when it was built are inscribed; the major, the head of public works, etc. "Let us make name for ourselves," is a fundamental urge of a fallen race. It reveals one of the basic philosophies of humanism: "Glory to man in the highest, for man is the master of things." That is the central thought of humanism, glory to mankind."

THE SIGN OF BABEL IN THE EUROPEAN UNION

In *Babylon in Europe* David Hathaway tells us how the European Parliament in Brussels was built to symbolise "European political unity." He writes; "The building in Strasbourg is modelled on Brueghel's famous Tower of Babel paintings to depict religious themes, modelled the tower on the shape of the ruins of the

Colloseum in Rome, in order to emphasise not only God's judgement on the Babylonian Empire! This begs the question - is the EU the spiritual descendant of the original Babel, and is the EU attempting to rebuild what God once destroyed? He continued: "When looked at (the European Parliament) from the *outside,* the new building in Strasbourg represents the Tower of Babel, and from the *inside* the Colloseum – Babylon and Rome. When you enter the Parliament "the building has an oval area open to the sky, precisely like the Colloseum." The evangelist then reminds us how the Colloseum was inaugurated in AD80 to celebrate the defeat of the Jews and the destruction of their Temple in AD70.

THE REVIVED ROMAN EMPIRE IN PROPHECY

Without a surprise, today, the philosophy of humanism, the 'Babel spirit', is the *diet* that feeds and nourishes the entire confused world. This same 'Babel spirit' is the "light" that guides the dark world which is under the rule of the "Roman Empire." We know the "two legs of iron" of the magnificent human statue which Nebuchadnezzar saw in his dream, signify the Eastern and the Western segments of the Roman Empire. We have also discovered that the Roman Empire was divided into two in 395AD. The Eastern half of the Empire continued as the Byzantine Empire with Constantinople as the capital. And the Western half had Rome as its capital. The 10 toes of the human statue, which were partly of iron and partly of baked clay, represent the Eastern and the Western European countries that constitute the European Union. The Omnipotent and Omniscience God writes history before history is written.

In 2004 the world witnessed how some of the Eastern European countries, which were formerly under the communist rule, joined the Western European countries to form an enlarged European Union. This EU 'success story,' which has been described as the creation of the world's non-imperial empire, is serving as the foundation stone upon which the "dead" Roman Empire would be "revived." The coming King of Men would emerge from this revived Roman Empire. This last Caesar shall reign with the support of the powerful leaders of the European Empire (Revelation 17:12-14).

In concluding *The Dream of* Rome, Boris Johnson writes: "One thing we in Europe must perhaps accept is that we will never recover that vast sense of political unity, with the face of every citizen turned like a sunflower towards the political centre. That was pre-eminently the achievement of Augustus, and it seems very unlikely to be repeated. To do so would involve the creation of an emperor, with semi-divine status, having a direct relationship with every citizen in his divinely ordained empire. No, we will never reproduce the Roman Empire, with its huge and peaceable unity of races and nations. But if history teaches us anything it is that we are fated never to stop trying."

I agree with Mr. Johnson that perfect political unity would not be achieved in Europe. However, there would be an Emperor with a "semi-divine status" to lead the European Union and rule the world. Mankind would love this last Caesar of the Revived Roman Empire. Europe and the world will worship the charismatic Caesar – a political genius who will exhibit extraordinary intelligence to 'solve' the economic, political and religious problems facing the 'global society.' We will learn more about this last Emperor of the European Empire as we progress with our study. The Lisbon Treaty has paved the way for the Emperor to be crowned.

CHAPTER 5
The "10 Toes" of the Human Statue

"There is a point beyond which unbelief is impossible, and the mind in refusing truth must needs take refuge in a misbelieve which is sheer credulity" **(RA)**

The "ten toes" of the human statue which were partly of iron and partly of baked clay (Daniel 2:41), have two-fold symbolism. Firstly, they signify the last stages of the revived Roman Empire. Secondly, these *10 toes*, which correspond to the *10 horns* on the 4th cruel beast Daniel saw in his vision (Daniel 7:7, 20, 24), represent the 10 powerful European Leaders who will emerge from the European Empire. Chapter 17 of the Book of Revelation confirms this prophetic word in the Book of Daniel. And this particular chapter is a record of Apostle John's vision of a woman ridding on a scarlet beast with seven heads and ten horns. The Angel explained to John: *"The ten horns which you saw are ten kings who have received no kingdom as yet, but they receive authority for one hour as kings with the beast"* (Revelation 17:12). We will learn more about this prophetic passage in Appendix.1

In the Bible the number 10 symbolises power, authority and fullness. We know iron is stronger than clay. This means the 10 toes of the human statue, which were partly of iron and partly of baked clay, represent the small and big nations; the weak and powerful nations, and the poor and rich nations in the European Union.

EVIDENCE OF SMALL AND BIG NATIONS, WEAK AND POWERFUL NATIONS AND POOR AND RICH COUNTRIES IN THE EUROPEAN UNION

Without any doubt, the European Union is a confederation of small and weak nations, big and powerful nations and poor and rich countries. These constitute the "toes of iron and clay" of the great human statue. I have selected the following extracts from our newspapers to confirm the fulfilment of the prophetic revelation that relates to the "feet and toes which were partly iron and partly clay" of the human image Nebuchadnezzar saw in his dream" *(*Daniel 2:42-43).

- On 10 October 2002, Daily Mail published an article entitled *The Euro Empire: Ten of the continent's poorest nations are embraced by Brussels – but the Irish could still wreck the party.* According to the writer, Steeve Doughty, "Ten countries were given the go ahead to join the European Union…creating an empire that could stretch from Galway to Gdansk… The total bill for letting some of the Europe's poorest countries join a rich man's club will be enormous…."
- Here is a quote from an article published in the Financial Times on 17 September 2003: "Tensions in the existing Club (the European Union) are growing: between big member states and small, between new members and old and between the wealthier northern fringes, who pay big net contributions to the budget, and the poorer southerners such as Greece, Spain and Portugal, who still receive large net subsidies." (The big and wealthier countries in this text are the *"toes of iron."* The small and poorer countries are the toes of "*baked clay.*")
- On 30 January 2004, The Times published an article titled *Fears in Europe over dictatorship by the "big three."* It was reported Britain, France and Germany (the European Union's most powerful nations) decided to take an initiative to discuss policies on the Union's economic growth, immigration and its constitution. The initiative by these countries "alarmed other European nations who fear the "big three" will dictate to them."

A diplomat from a smaller EU country expressed his concern: "...We cannot accept that they (Britain, France and Germany) decide and then come to Brussels with the decision." And another diplomat also remarked: "If they (the "Big Three") come and tell us, this is what Europe will do, that is not a good thing." (The "big Three" are the *"toes of Iron";* and "Us" (the small countries) are the *"toes of baked clay"*)

THE EUROPEAN UNION: AN "EMPIRE" WHICH IS PARTLY STRONG AND PARTLY WEAK

Let us also examine the following newspaper headlines and articles and relate them to the prophetic significance of Daniel 2:42 which says: *"As the toes were partly iron and partly clay, so this kingdom* (The European Union) *will be partly strong and partly brittle".*

1. *"Continent grumbles at concessions that favour bigger nations"* (The Times 27 May 2003). It was reported the smaller nations in the European Union were upset that they were being downgraded in favour of big national allies in the Club.

2. *"Finn gives voice to the fears of EU's small states"* (Financial Times 9 September 2003). This title was related to the European Union's draft constitution. The paper reported that a political leader, who was an expert on European Union, was "resolute in his determination to protect the position of the smaller EU countries ("the toes of clay") and ensure that the equality of member states be maintained."
3. *"Big six split with smaller nations over constitution"*
4. This title which appeared in The Times on 15 May 2003, confirms "the toes of iron" (The "Big six") and "the toes of clay" (the smaller nations) in the European Empire.
5. *"Breaking the pact: as France and Germany abandon the fiscal rules, divisions widen over Europe's future"* (The Times 27 September 2003). It was reported: "The European Union has rules, but not everyone obeys them." According to the report, even before the breaking of the Stability Pact, "some smaller countries (*"the toes of clay"*) .... warned of the problems of negotiating a treaty against a backdrop of big countries ("the toes of iron") breaking the rules. Gerrit Zaim, the Dutch finance minister, said: "...Everything is now going to be more difficult. After what has happened, many countries are not going to put themselves in the hands of the big states (*"the toes of iron*)**."**
6. *"Bullying by large countries could split Europe"* (Financial Times 24 November 2003). This article reported how Europe had been experiencing many divisions in its history, but managed to avoid a split between small and large countries" [*the feet and toes partly of clay and partly of iron*] The report added, "The group of large countries can block anything it likes, but its combined voting weight is not sufficient to adopt a proposal against a united front of small countries (the toes of clay*).* But some of the small and medium-sized countries are getting nervous..... France and Germany ("the toes of iron"), instead of using their powers to assuage those fears, are exacerbating them with their bullying tactics and persistent breaches of the Stability Pact."
7. *"Winning at catch-up will take more than just Club membership"* (Financial Times 26 April 2004). Under this title the newspaper reported: "All the 10 new members of the European Union are poorer than all but one of the existing members (the exception is Greece). The Czech Republic, Slovakia, Poland, Hungary, Latvia and Lithuania are poorer, relative to rich members of the EU, than were any previous members on accession....." In this article we noticed the ***"toes of clay"*** (the poorer nations) and the ***"toes of iron"*** (the rich nations) in the ***two legs of the human image***, which represent the revived Roman Empir*e* – The European Union.
8. *"Barroso accused of currying favour with bigger states" The president's*

apparent willingness to cave in to Paris and Berlin worries some commissioners" (Financial Times, 22 December 2006). According to the newspaper, some of the EU commissioners accused the President of the Commission of his "tendency to cave in too readily to pressure from big member-states." According to the report, one of the Commissioners, Mr McGreevy…called on the president not to cut "secret deals" with large states…and warned of a backlash from smaller member states." The Report added: "Mr McCreevy's intervention was triggered by a German request that the Commission halt two infringement procedures pending against Berlin."

What we have learnt clearly confirms the co-existence of small and big countries, poor and rich countries as well as weak and powerful nations in the European Union. This information fulfils the prophetic message in Daniel 2:42: "As the toes were partly iron and partly clay, so this kingdom (The European Union, soon to be the revived Roman Empire) will be partly strong and partly brittle".

THE PROPHETIC SIGNIFICANCE OF THE "10 TOES OF IRON AND CLAY"

Let us now examine Daniel's interpretation of *the 10 toes* of the dazzling human image king Nebuchadnezzar saw (Daniel 2:31-32), and then consider its implications. The prophet explained to the Emperor: "Just as you (Nebuchadnezzar) saw that the feet and toes were partly of baked clay and partly of iron, so this will be a *divided kingdom;* yet it will have some of the strength of iron in it, even as you saw iron mixed with clay. As the toes were partly iron and partly clay, so *this kingdom will be partly strong and partly brittle.* And just as you saw the iron mixed with baked clay, so *the people will be a mixture and will not remain united*, any more than iron mixes with clay" (Daniel 2:41-43). What a prophetic revelation about the European Union. For the EU is a divided "kingdom" with powerful and weak nations; a "kingdom" of mixed people (French, Germans, Italians, Portuguese, Britons, Irish, Bulgarians, Romanians etc with different languages, culture and history) who are not united!

Daniel's interpretation of the feet and the 10 toes of the human image, which were partly of iron and partly of baked clay, is a crucial passage in the Hebrew Scriptures. It will affect every soul on planet earth. We can appreciate the practical meaning of the symbolism of "the toes of baked clay and iron" in the context of history and contemporary events in Europe.

"The feet and the ten toes" of the great human image

The last section of the human statue Nebuchadnezzar saw signifies the last stages of the Roman Empire and the development of the European Union which would be the revival of the 'dead' Roman Empire. The European Union was born on 9 May 1950 with the Schuman Plan. The Treaty of Rome, which was signed on 25 March 1957 by the six founding members (Belgium, France, Germany, Italy, Luxembourg and the Netherlands), created the European Economic Community or The Common Market. This economic entity has now developed into a political union of 27 members. Other countries are yearning to join the political phenomenon. The role the city of Rome played in the progress of the European Union from its "childhood" as the European Coal and Steel Community is very significant. Because, the Book of Revelation teaches about this great city. We will learn more about Rome when we discuss "The Woman and the Beast" in Appendix 1.

The Commonwealth of European Nations (the EU) has its own currency (the Euro), a flag, an anthem, Common Agricultural and Fishery Policies, a Parliament, a Central Bank, a Court of Justice that imposes laws on member-states, and a Constitution – rebranded the Lisbon Treaty. The European Union would eventually grow to become a Mighty Empire ruling the world. This was made clear in the article, "Brussels to expand its empire", which was published in The Times on 4 May 2004. And it was also reported in the 19 February 2007 edition of the Financial Times that the European Union wanted the rest of the World to adopt its rules.

PIONEERS OF EUROPEAN INTEGRATION

Before we continue with our study, it is important for us to know some of the prominent personnel who have contributed to the development of the political integration of European nations. Before the birth of the European Union on 9 May 1950, many politicians had earlier proposed the formation of a United States of Europe. Among the early proponents of this political union were the first German Chancellor, Konrad Adenauer, Austro-Hungarian diplomat, Richard Koudenhove-Kalergi, a French Foreign Minister. Aristide Briand and Italian Prime Minister, Alcide De Gasperi.

After the First World War, **Richard Koudenhove-Kalergi** was motivated to fight for a united Europe. He founded the Pan-European Movement to bring together politicians in the First pan-European Congress held in Vienna. In his first book, this diplomat wrote: "Europe as a political concept does not exist. This part of the world includes nations and states installed in the chaos, in a barrel of gunpowder on international conflicts in the field of future conflicts. This is the European question, the mutual hate of the Europeans that poison the atmosphere....The European Question will only be solved by means of the union of Europe's nations....The biggest obstacle to the accomplishment of the United Sates of Europe is the one thousand years old rivalry between the two most populated nations of Pan-Europe: Germany and France."

In 1929 the French foreign minister, **Aristide Briand**, advocated for a federal

Europe. He stated: "Among peoples who are geographically grouped together like the peoples of Europe, there must exist a sort of federal link. It is this link which I wish to endeavour to establish. Evidently the association will act mainly in the economic sphere. That is the most pressing question. But I am sure also that from a political point of view and from a social point of view the federal link, without infringing the sovereignty of any of the nations which might take part in such an association, could be beneficial."

Edouard Herriot, a compatriot of Briand, supported the idea of a "Federal link". In 1930 he proposed the formation of United States of Europe. Unfortunately, other politicians did not show enthusiasm for the idea. In latter years, faced with the growing international conflicts during and after the First and Second World Wars, the need for peace in Europe became paramount. The Italian Prime Minister, **Alcide De Gasperi**, a Roman Catholic, became a leading proponent of the formation of a federation of democratic European States. He worked closely with Robert Schuman and Konrad Adenauer to set up the conditions for the advancement of European integration.

Konrad Adenauer, another Roman Catholic, also advocated a plan for an organic integration of the French, Belgian and German economies to safeguard peace in Europe. He recorded in his memoirs: "If Britain, too, were to decide to participate in this economic integration, we would be much closer to the ultimate goal of a union of states of Western Europe". He added: "The unification of Europe seemed far more feasible now (1945-1953) than in the 1920's...The idea of international co-operation between peoples must succeed...In a future United States of Europe I saw great hope for Europe and thus for Germany. We had to try to remind France, Holland, Belgium, and the other European countries that they are and will remain forever our neighbours" (Memoirs 1945-1953).

Finally, two Italians also had visions for a federal Europe. They were **Giovanni Agnelli** and **Altiero Spinelli**. Agnelli was born in 1866. As a businessman he was attracted by American business ethics. He introduced Henry Ford's Mass Production technique into Italy. In 1918 he became interested in politics. He campaigned against the League of Nations and advocated for a federal Europe under a central control. It was his belief that only a federation of European nations would prevent war and bolster economic development.

Altiero Spinelli was born in 1907. In 1924, aged 17, he joined the Italian Communist Party. Spinelli spent about 15 years in Mussolini's prisons. Spinelli ensured that the 1947 Italian constitution included a clause saying that Italy wanted to be part of a federal Europe. It was in confinement on the island of Ventotene that he had the inspiration to pursue an agenda of a federal Europe after he had studied the text of Anglo-Saxon federalists. This motivated him to dump his communist inclinations to clinch to federal system of government. Along with Ernesto Rossi and Eugenio Colorni, he drew up the Ventotene Manifesto in 1941. *According to the ex-communist a federal Europe would require a new type of political organisation in Europe that should not yield to national interests.*

THE FUZZY VISION OF THE 'DREAMER' JEAN MONNET

It was Jean Monnet, an eye witness of the two world wars, who developed the plan to initiate the process towards a federal Europe. His vision was to use economic instrument to fuse Europe together. Jean Monnet was born in Cognac on 9 November 1888. He was also a Roman Catholic. On 5 August 1943, Monnet addressed a gathering of the National Liberation Committee, the French government which was in exile in Algiers. He told the assembly that peace in Europe could only be achieved through unity among European States. He declared, "There will be no peace in Europe if the states rebuild themselves on the basis of national sovereignty, with its implications of prestige policies and economic protection.....The countries of Europe are not strong enough individually to be able to guarantee prosperity and social development for their peoples. The states of Europe must therefore form a federation or a European entity that would make them into a common economic unit." (Memoirs 1978)

Prompted by his view that, "there is no future for the people of Europe other than in union," Jean Monnet outlined his vision of an 'autocratic' political Europe with this statement: *"Europe of sovereign states was incapable of, despite its leaders' goodwill, of reaching the sensible decisions that were needed for the common good. It would be quite another matter, however, once the power of decision was entrusted to institutions serving the general interest and applying the will of the majority in a system of common rules*" (Monnet Memoirs 1978).

Monnet, like Adenauer and Spaak, hated the principle of national sovereignty. The closing remarks of his Memoirs bear it out: "The sovereign nations of the past can no longer solve the problems of the present. They cannot ensure their own progress or control their own future. And the community itself is only a stage on the way to the organised world of tomorrow." In view of Monnet's crude philosophy on 'sovereignty', we should, therefore, not be surprised that French and German politicians are hostile to the concept of national sovereignty. They are desperate to eliminate nation states by redrawing the map of Europe to fulfil the vision of their patrons.

In 1946, Sir Winston Churchill, who had earlier, in June 1940, objected to Monnet's proposal for a political union between France and Britain with a common citizenship, made a noteworthy speech at Zurich University on the need to "create the European family....and to provide it with a structure under which it can dwell in peace, in safety and in freedom." Churchill declared: "We must build a kind of United States of Europe.....The first step in the recreation of the European Family must be a partnership between France and Germany."

I would make a vital point about Churchill's attitude to a federal Europe. Officials in Brussels have construed Churchill's speech about United Europe to imply his support for a United States of Europe of which Britain should become part of it. In his speech, Churchill advocated that Britain should only offer a supporting role to a United States of Europe. He did not suggest that Great Britain should become a province of Europe. Jacques Delors, a former President of European Commission, confirmed Churchill's intention with this statement: "Even that great European, Winston Churchill, envisaged European integration only for the countries on the European continent, not for Britain." On European integration Churchill himself made his position clear with a comment he made in 1952: "I love France and Belgium but we must not allow ourselves to be pulled down to that level." Churchill, unconsciously, echoed the voice of the "Forgotten British public servant" who warned Britain would not be saved in a political union of European nations.

JEAN MONNET: THE MASTER BUILDER OF EUROPEAN COMMUNITY AND THE SCHUMAN PLAN

Jean Monnet contended that the unification of Europe could only be achieved with an initiative from France. His belief was that coal and steel were the key to economic power and the raw materials for forging weapons of war. So, if France and Germany pooled their coal and steel resources together under a common control, it would 'reduce their malign prestige and turn them instead into a guarantee of peace'. Monnet then presented his idea for European integration to Robert Schuman, France's Foreign Minister.

Schuman welcomed Monnet's plan. He agreed with the proposal that a united Europe would prevent another war, and France should take the initial steps. He sold the idea to Konrad Adenauer. Schuman then launched the plan by proposing that France and Germany should bury their differences over the control of the Ruhr, the vital coal and steel region, and take the initiative to work towards a United States of Europe. He suggested that these two countries should place the production of their coal and steel under a common administration in such a way that would allow other European countries to join. Thus, the pooling of France's and Germany's coal and steel production together would provide the foundation upon which economic unity could be built and developed as a first step towards the creation of a federal Europe.

"THE SCHUMAN PLAN"
Summary

With the agreement of the West German Chancellor, Konrad Adenauer, Schuman made this declaration on 9 May 1950 on behalf of the French government: "Europe will not be made at once, or according to a single plan. It will be built through concrete achievements which first create a de facto solidarity. The coming together of the nations of Europe requires the elimination of the age-old opposition of France and Germany. Any action taken must in the first place concern these two countries. With this aim in view, the French Government proposes that Franco-German production of coal and steel as a whole be placed under a common High Authority, within the framework of an organisation open to the participation of the other countries of Europe. The pooling of coal and steel production should immediately provide for the setting up of common foundations for economic development as a first step in the federation of Europe."

After Schuman's declaration, the Federal Republic of Germany, Italy, Belgium, Luxembourg and the Netherlands joined France. The European Coal and Steel Community was born. This economic community of six European nations laid the foundation stone for the European Community (EC). In 1952 Jean Monnet was appointed the first president of the High Authority. Schuman also became the first president of the European Parliament. It is clear from Schuman's declaration that the proposed economic project would eventually lead to a political union of European nations to preserve peace in Europe. That was Jean Monnet's aim. In his Memoirs Monnet stated: "I have never doubted that one day this process will lead us to the United States of Europe, but I see no point in trying to imagine today what political form it will take."

WAS SCHUMAN COMMITTED TO A FEDERAL EUROPE?

Robert Schuman was born in Luxembourg on 29 June 1886. At the age of 32 he became a French citizen. Initially, Schuman was not committed to the idea of a United States of Europe. In Jean Monnet's Biography, *The First Statesman of Interdependence,* Francois Duchene, writes: "...Schuman was still wary in May 1950. In the first place, he was wary on principle. On top of that, he and Monnet were not at one on supranationality. For Schuman, the plan existed to solve the immediate Franco-German problem. For Monnet, it was the first step to a united Europe. Schuman accepted supranationality for the plan because there was no alternative, but was not committed. Schuman was very different from Monnet. He was "a deeply religious bachelor...."

According to Duchene, when Schuman was once having a launch with Monnet, the latter praised Schuman: "You have great asset. You look honest...I am not joking, you look honest. It is a priceless asset as a politician. People will believe what you say". Schuman also described Monnet: "Very obstinate, but plays fair". Now the intriguing questions:

- Why did Monnet describe Schuman an "honest" man?
- Why such a compliment?
- Did Monnet feel some uneasiness about his own intentions regarding the whole idea of European integration?

It was Monnet's conviction that European nations had to unite to survive. On 2 April 1976, the heads of states at the European Council in Luxembourg honoured Jean Monnet. He was made an "Honorary Citizen of Europe." Before his death in 1979, Monnet declared: "Continue, continue, there is no future for the people of Europe other than in union....Make men work together, show them that beyond their differences and geographical boundaries there lies a common interest."

EUROPEAN UNION AND SOVEREIGNTY

On 12 July 1952, after the Treaty of Paris, which established the European Coal and Steel Community, was signed, Konrad Adenauer made a significant speech. The German Chancellor supported the political union of European nations which was advanced in The Schuman Plan with this statement: "It is my opinion and belief that the parliaments of the six European countries (France, Germany, Italy, Belgium, Luxembourg and the Netherlands) which will have to deal with this European Coal and Steel Community realise exactly what it is all about and that in particular they realise that *the political goal, the political meaning of the European Coal and Steel Community, is infinitely larger than its economic purpose... ...I believe that for the first time in history....countries want to renounce part of their sovereignty, voluntarily and without compulsion, in order to transfer the sovereignty to a supranational structure."* (Emphasis mine)

In his memoirs, Konrad Adenauer declared: "In my opinion the European nation states had a past but no future.....I regarded The Schuman Plan and the European Defence Community as preliminary steps to a political unification of Europe."

I ask these questions:

- "Did Konrad Adenauer ever mention the advice which his friend, Robert Schuman, gave to the European Parliamentarians in 1958 relating to the survival of the European Project?
- "Did Jean Monnet ever talk about the significance of Schuman's "Advice" when he (Monnet) was eager to see his idea of a "federal Europe" come into fruition?

- "Why the silence on Schuman's "Advice" which I term: "The Schuman Caveat"? I will examine "The Schuman Caveat" and its implication in due course.

Britain was not keen in joining the European Coal and Steel Community. In fact Britain ignored Monnet's invitation to join the club. In *Guide to the European Union* Dick Leonard writes: "The U.K did not regard itself primarily as being a European nation, and adopted a superior attitude to the new organisation (the European Coal and Steel Community) as evidenced by the private remark of Churchill to his doctor in 1952: "I love France and Belgium but we must not allow ourselves to be pulled down to that level." Was Churchill right? And was Dean Acheson, the American Secretary of State after the Second World War, justified with his assessment that Britain made a historic error when they snubbed the European Coal and Steel Community? The answers would become clear as we progress with our study.

BRITAIN AND THE COMMON MARKET AND DE GAULLE

Britain made attempts in 1963 and 1967 to join the European Economic Community. Even though five member states of the Community favoured Britain's participation, including Jean Monnet, who had earlier concealed "the Schuman Plan" from Britain, the French President, Charles de Gaulle, objected to Britain's membership. De Gaulle was suspicious of Britain's commitment to the Community because of its special and close relationship with the United States of America. On 27 November 1967, the French President warned Belgium, Germany, Italy, Luxembourg and the Netherlands that if they tried to impose British membership on France, it would result in the breakdown of the Community. Before an assembly of Diplomats, Civil Servants, Journalists and Ministers, de Gaulle accused Britain of a "deep-seated hostility" towards the European Project. According to the French President, London showed a "lack of interest" in the Common Market, and would require a "radical transformation" before joining the European Economic Community.

Questions: Why the arrogance of the French President? Was de Gaulle well-informed of the significance of European integration and its implications? Had the haughty French President read the 15th and 16th editions of the "Unknown Briton's" work about political union of European nations, its character and future prospects, which were published in 1963 and 1967, he would have thought twice at the sight of Britain's applications to join the Common Market. The French President would not have had the impudence to humiliate Britain. After all, it was a British public servant who wrote about European integration and its future before the French founding fathers of European Community were even conceived. Had De Gaulle done his 'homework' on European Community, He would have learnt that, in 1969, when he fell from power, that same year, the 17th edition of the

Londoner's work on political integration of European nations was released.

In 1972 the 18th edition of the Irishman's work on European integration was published. Had Prime Minister Edward Heath read this particular edition, he would not have dared to deceive the British people and dragged them to board Monnet's vessel of doom. In his *The Course of my life,* the late Edward Heath revealed that the 'clever' Jean Monnet repeatedly advised him that Britain should sign the treaties of Paris and Rome. His contention was that if Britain would join immediately as a member of the Community, they could seek to influence decisions of the Institutions so that their policies could meet their needs.

The reality is that Jean Monnet did not understand his vision of European unity. Had Monnet also done his 'homework' and read any of the editions of the Briton's work on European integration, he would have realised that he was only a 'slave' toiling to bring to pass what his 'master' – a servant of the British Crown ⊠ had already recorded before his mother conceived him. With his passion for a united Europe, and his tireless efforts to build a United States of Europe, Monnet unconsciously laboured to fulfil the vision of a British public servant.

Here is a brief summary of the growing stages of the European Empire:

- ***THE TREATY OF PARIS:***

In 1950 Robert Schuman proposed the establishment of the European Coal and Steel Community. On 18 April 1951 The Treaty of Paris was signed to formally establish the European Coal and Steel Community, which became the first and founding instrument of the European Union. The Treaty came into force on 25 July 1952. The purpose of this Community was to integrate the coal and steel industries of France, West Germany, Italy, Belgium, the Netherlands, and Luxembourg under an independent authority.

- ***THE TREATY OF ROME:***

Following the success of the European Coal and Steel Community, The Treaty of the European Economic Community (EEC) was signed in Rome on 25 March 1957. The Treaty came into force on 1 January 1958. The EEC was to develop the economies of the member states into one large common market and build a political union of the nations of Western Europe. Hence the EEC was also known as the Common Market. The EEC also sought to establish a single commercial policy toward non-member countries. In 1993 the EEC was renamed the European Community (EC) (Why this new name? It was a signal towards a political union of European nations)

- ***THE SINGLE EUROPEAN ACT:***

The Single European Act introduced measures which were aimed at achieving an internal market and institutional changes. It also provided legal form for European Political Cooperation. The Single European Act was signed in February 1986. It came into force on 1 July 1987.

- ***THE MAASTRICHT TREATY:***

The European Union was developed out of the European Community, which was the new name for the European Economic Community. Because the European Community became successful, its member countries decided to embark upon greater integration to cooperate in matters of security, foreign policy and justice issues. And one of the major aims of the whole European Project was to create a common currency to replace member countries national currencies. Thus, The Treaty on European Union initiated the road to political and economic and monetary union. It was drafted at a significant time in history – during the reunification of Eastern and Western Germany, and the collapse of the Soviet block. This made it necessary for re-evaluation of the European project. Among some of the important innovations were the concepts of European citizenship and the European Monetary Union. This Treaty was signed on 7 February 1992, and it came into force on 1 November 1993. (The ambition for a United States of Europe became obvious).

- ***THE AMSTERDAM TREATY:***

The enlargement towards the East in addition to other issues on the European Union programme prompted the negotiation of the Treaty of Amsterdam. This Treaty opened the way towards closer cooperation. It was signed on 2 October 1997. It came into force on 1 May 1999. In this same year the Single Currency for the European Union was launched. In 2000 Euro Currency (the "glory of Europe") was introduced.

- ***THE NICE TREATY:***

This particular treaty was signed on 26 February 2001 to deal with the institutional adaptations required for the expansion of the Union to 25 Member States. The Treaty came into force on 2 February 2003.

- ***THE CONSTITUTION OF EUROPE:***

In 2003 a draft constitution for the European Union was published. However, the member states of the Union could not agree to adopt the draft on 13 December 2003. On 1 May 2004, ten countries joined the European Union. They were: Cyprus (Greek part), the Czech Republic, Estonia, Hungary, Latvia, Lithuania, Malta, Poland, Slovakia and Slovenia. On 13 June 2004, the draft constitution was adopted by all the 25member countries of the European Union. In October 2004, European leaders met in Rome to sign the constitutional treaty, which ought to be ratified by all the members later on. In 2005, the European Constitution was rejected by France and the Netherlands. The Constitution was put on a "life-support" system. Euro politicians, led by Angela Merkel, planned in secret to rebrand the discredited constitution and force it on the masses without their consent. So much for the Champion of Democracy (the European Union) that wants to spread democracy.

SUSPENSION OF THE RATIFICATION OF THE EUROPEAN CONSTITUTION.

At a summit in Brussels (from 16 to 17 June 2005), the European leaders decided to suspend the ratification of the European Constitution due to its rejection by two founding members of the Union – France and The Netherlands. France voted "No" in a referendum on 29 May 2005 to throw out the constitution. And the Dutch also voted "No" on 1 June 2005 to dump the constitution – the Pride of France. When Germany took over the EU presidency on 1 January 2007, Angela Merkel made it her priority to revive the dead constitution and impose it on member states with rubber stamps from national parliaments. The then British Prime Minister, Tony Blair, followed the "blind" Merkel and refused to grant the British people a vote on the new EU treaty – a treaty which would consign Britons into 'slavery' in Brussels. Had Mr Blair also read what the brilliant servant of the British Crown published on European integration, when Angela Merkel's 'father', Konrad Adenauer, was only 6 years old, he would not have supported Merkel and her 'brothers' to "spit in the face" of the British people by denying them their sovereign rights to decide whether they preferred to be ruled by strangers in Europe.

TONY BLAIR'S CONTEMPT FOR BRITONS AND THE CRY OF 'SUN' READERS

Readers of *The Sun* newspaper expressed their concern about the attitude of Tony Blair. In the letter's column titled *"Blair EU deal is a betrayal"*:

- Peter Stratton of Lincoln writes: "The plan to sign a backdoor deal on the EU constitution is a disgrace."

- Alan Foster of Southampton expressed the frustration of the British people: "Blair has been a bare-faced liar over the EU treaty. How did British politics sink this low?"
- Charlie Guthrie of Corringham voiced his concern: "Is there nothing we can do to stop Blair smuggling this treaty through without giving the British people the right to vote in a referendum?"
- Mike Barry of Crayford also added his voice: "Why does Blair have total contempt for Britain? He promises no back door deals on the EU, then promptly goes to Germany to do one."
- And Ronald Pieles cried out: "The PM's actions are not those of a leader who cares for his country, its people, or way of life, but more those of a petulant loser. He concluded: "This treaty must be stopped or we had best get set for the asset-strippers because they clean the UK out." (The Sun Monday, 30 April 2007)

Tony Blair, who is not well-informed on the significance of European integration, just like all the political leaders in America and Europe, was determined to impose his opinion on Monnet's Project on the British people. The "Forgotten British public servant" once said: "Anyone who forces his opinion on others is a boor. And a man who dies for his opinion is a fool."

The Lisbon Treaty

The rejected European Constitution was subsequently repackaged as a new Treaty. On 13 December 2007, EU leaders signed the document to be imposed on the people who "feed" them. On 12 June 2008, Ireland rejected the crooked Treaty in a referendum that caused panic among European leaders.

I would make a point before we proceed. Politicians, political scientists, political commentators in Europe and American and the rest of the world would understand where the European Union came from, the actual purpose of its existence and its destiny, if they appreciate the significance of the magnificent human statue King Nebuchadnezzar saw in his dream. The history and the destiny of the 4 major empires that have ruled the world since the servitude of the Jews in Babylon were coded in the stunning statue which was crowned with gold and decorated with precious metals: silver, bronze, iron and clay. In about 604BC, God revealed the destiny of human governments to the King of Babylon, who was the ruler of the world at that period in history. Witness what Daniel told the King of Babylon: "You, O King, are the king of kings. The God of heaven has given you dominion and power and might and glory. In your hands he has placed mankind and the beasts of the field and the birds of the air. Wherever they live, he has made you ruler over them all. You are the head of Gold." (Daniel 2:36-38)

THE SHORT REIGN OF HUMAN GOVERNMENTS

When the children of Israel rebelled against God, the Lord transferred the sceptre of earthly rule from Judah to the Gentile King of Babylon. In accordance with His Sovereign Will, the Almighty gave His people over to King Nebuchadnezzar to deport them to Babylon to serve pagan kings for 70 years (Daniel 1:1-2). It was in the era of servitude that God revealed to King Nebuchadnezzar the destiny of the 4 major empires that would rule the world consecutively for a limited period. It was also shown to the Babylonian Emperor, that at the prearranged time these human governments would be destroyed by God. And the Lord of lords, the King of kings would descend to establish His eternal Kingdom of righteousness (Daniel 2:44). World power would continue to remain in the hands of Gentiles until the appointed time when the Lord returns. Witness the prophetic word of our Divine Lord: *"Jerusalem will be trampled on by the Gentiles until the times of the Gentiles are fulfilled"* (Luke 21:24).

Presidents, Prime Ministers, Kings and Queens should realise that whatever powers they wield today have been delegated to them for a season. The Lord sets kings and He overthrows them at His pleasure. For Daniel 2:21– 22 tells us: *"God changes the times and the seasons; He removes Kings and raises up Kings. He gives wisdom to the wise and knowledge to those who have understanding. He reveals deep and secret things; He knows what is in the darkness. And light dwells with Him."* Amen! Politicians are not in control of events. They are at the mercy of events. European politicians have no idea where their "EU Titanic" is heading towards. Is the future of the "indestructible" European Project bright or dark?

PROPHECY FULFILLED

The admission of Eastern European countries into the European Union fulfilled the prophetic significance of the *two feet and the ten toes* of the human statue king Nebuchadnezzar saw in his dream. In the light of contemporary events, let us now focus on how Daniel's interpretation of the *feet and the toes* of the magnificent image relates to another aspect of the development of the European Union. In Daniel 2:41 the prophet told King Nebuchadnezzar: *"Just as you saw that the feet and toes were partly of baked clay and partly of iron, so this will be a divided kingdom; yet it will have some of the strength of iron in it..."* This prophetic word has now been fulfilled in the European Union. It is interesting to note what Boris Johnson writes in his *The Dream of Rome:* "The word Rome may come from the Greek word meaning strength". In the next chapter we will consider more facts that relate to the prophetic revelation concerning the European Union as portrayed in the "10 toes" of the human statue.

Chapter 6

The European Union: A "Divided Kingdom" With Mixed People

"The sceptic is like the obstinate juror who puts his back against the wall and refuses to believe the evidence" (RA)

Apparently, in the sight of men, the European Union is a *"united kingdom"* of 27 nations with its own trappings of nationhood. Actually, in the sight of God, the European Union is a *"divided kingdom."* Some member states are eager to pursue different economic, foreign, defence and immigration policies for the benefit of their respective citizens. For example, some single currency member-states accused other members in the *kingdom* for "Undermining the EU Stability Pact, the keystone of monetary union" (Sunday Telegraph 7 September 2003).

Camilla Cavendish, in her article, *Killing with kindness; the human cost of Britain's naïve embrace of Eastern Europe,* highlighted the pursuit of national interests among the member-states of the European Union. According to her, there is "a... more cynical approach to European enlargement than is usually implied by rhetoric about re-unifying Europe and rectifying historic injustices....Policy makers talk of bringing stability to Eastern Europe, but the EU admits only countries that have stable democracies. The French have never wanted to expand the club. The British have pushed enlargement in order to dilute French influence. The Germans once shared that aim and felt a historic call to embrace the East, but are more worrying about the bill. This lack of common purpose explains why the prosperous states have failed to adopt common stance on immigration" (The Times 22 January 2004).

EVIDENCE OF A "DIVIDED KINGDOM"

On 4 October 2002, Daily Mail published an article titled *The Euro Empire.* Within this article Steve Doughty commented on the admission of new countries into the European Union. He revealed one of the major issues that divides the European Union : "The most obvious problem facing the EU as it enlarges is the

Common Agricultural Policy...Within the EU, the Belgian government, among others, has insisted that the CAP is reformed at the time of enlargement, or its cost will rise from £40 billion a year .... to an unsustainable £60billion a year. But France and other countries that benefit most from CAP handouts... blocked any change. Therefore failure of the deal may be welcomed in France but it would be a blow to Britain, which has relied on enlargement to weaken the EU's centralising pull towards a superstate."

On 17 September 2003, Financial Times released an article on the European Union titled *"A fractured Europe: divisions deepen between big and small countries, north and south, elites and their electors."* The newspaper highlighted many areas of divisions in the European Empire. Here are two of them:

1. "The most serious divide....is between the largest states, France, Germany, Britain, Italy and the smaller ones. It is a dispute that has been brewing for years, as smaller countries such as Belgium, Austria, Finland and Portugal have built up resentments over perceived bullying of the big countries".
2. "Another divide is between new member states and old, aggravated by the disputes over Iraq. The former Soviet block members all backed the US-led invasion, along with Britain, Spain and Italy, and against the objection of EU founder members such as France and Germany."

Here are other aspects of divisions in the European Union that fulfil the prophetic revelation about the EU: *"A divided kingdom"* (Daniel 2:41).

- Among the European Union there are federalist-minded countries and sovereignty-sensitive countries. Some countries do not want the term constitution; they prefer to call it a new "treaty".
- Some countries in the European Union were not happy with the expected retention of veto over tax decisions and foreign policy (The Times 27 May 2003).
- Even though some member states have adopted the single currency of the Union, yet majority of them preferred their original national currencies. For example, on 6 October 2003, Daily Mail published an article captioned: *"NEIN! Most Germans wish they hadn't been lumbered with the euro and want the deutschmarks back."* Steve Doughty, the Social Affairs Correspondent, stated: "A HUGE majority of Germans have turned against the euro – and their hostility to the single currency now matches that of Briton." Seven out of ten German voters would reject the euro if they had a chance to vote on it in a referendum ... a poll for the Daily Mail reveals. French voters too would now vote to keep the franc, it shows. The findings revealed that initially, the euro dramati-

cally failed to win public support even in the countries that did most to generate the single currency."

On 28 December 2006, The Daily Telegraph reported how the French have turned against the monetary union. In a column titled *French hostility to the euro begins to gather pace,* the newspaper gave account of how 71% of blue-colour workers claimed the euro has hurt them personally. And a quarter of Frenchmen still think in francs "the whole time" when shopping. Again, on 18 January 2007, Telegraph informed readers about how some Germans have rebelled against the Euro to the extent that some regions have started printing their own currencies. In an article titled *Germans get by without the euro*, it was reported that there would soon be "66 regional currencies operating" alongside the euro currencies. The euro currency rebels claimed: "For us it is more a way to build regional strength. We're not enemies of Europe."

Other member-states of the European Union are yet to decide whether it would be in their national interest to adopt the common currency of the Union. In every European Union member-state there are those who support the Euro and those who oppose it. For example, on 26 April 2005, a column in *The Times* newspaper read: ***"Brown takes euro off agenda.".*** It was reported that Gordon Brown, the then British Chancellor of the Exchequer, regarded Britain's membership of the euro as *"being off for the foreseeable future."* Mr Brown, in his address to the London Chamber of Commerce, said, "While we support the euro in principle, we have been determined that to ensure stability, any decision must be based on the national economic interest and be clear and unambiguous." In the view of the author of this article, Philip Webster, it appeared Mr Brown had kicked "the euro into the long grass." Michael Howard, the former Conservative Party leader, who addressed the same conference, suggested that Britain should look to the United States and not to Europe as the model for its economy...Europe should be a market for British business not an economic model." Mr Howard went on: "We (the British) have dropped from fourth to eleventh in the world competitive league. I don't want the British economy to follow the European model".

- Some countries wanted God and Christianity explicitly mentioned in the European Constitution. Others objected to it. Those who drafted the Constitution argued: *"Explicit references to Christianity would be insensitive to Europe's other religious group..."* (Financial Times 29 May 2003).

On 5 October 2003, this article appeared in The Sunday Times: *"Little and Large of EU slug it."* The columnists, Peter Conradi and Hilary Clarke, highlighted some of the divisions in the European Empire:

- Britain is fighting to defend its national Veto on tax.
- Spain and Portugal want to keep a large number of votes in the Council of Ministers.
- Smaller members want each country to have its own commissioner.
- Catholic countries want a reference to God in the preamble to the treaty.

Even a text in the preliminary statements of the draft Constitution admits the actual division in an apparent "*United Kingdom of Europe.*" Consider this text in the preamble: "...While remaining proud of their own national identities and history; the people of Europe are determined to transcend their ancient divisions and unite in an ever closer fashion to forge a common identity." (Financial Times 29 May 2003.

ADDITIONAL EVIDENCE TO SUPPORT BIBLE PROPHECY THAT THE EUROPEAN UNION WOULD BE A "DIVIDED KINGDOM"

On 8 December 2003, Financial Times published an article: "*Challenge to EU plans for defence.*" According to the writer, Judy Dempsey, the four neutral countries of the European Union (Austria, Finland, Ireland and Sweden) "joined forces to challenge attempts by Britain, France and Germany to include a mutual defence clause in the EU's new constitutional treaty. The proposed clause, similar to Nato's article five, spells out that if a member state is attacked, other member countries are automatically obliged to provide assistance in accordance with the United Nations charter." However, these four neutral countries were not happy with such a clause because it would undermine their neutrality.

The article confirmed the neutrality of the 4 countries by reporting what Brian Cowen, the then Irish foreign minister (now the Irish Prime Minister), said: "The different security policy traditions of Ireland, Finland, Sweden, and Austria make it impossible for us to accept the presidency proposal as currently drafted....We cannot participate in a common or mutual defence arrangement unless approved by the people in referendum."

The question is: how could a "United Kingdom of Europe" (the European Union) have member-states that are neutral, and are not prepared to support other members of the "kingdom" when an enemy attacks them? Does this case portray the European Union a "united kingdom," or a "divided kingdom"?

On 8 December 2003, Financial Times commented briefly on The Nice Treaty 2000 in an article titled "*Power sharing row could scupper new Union.*" It was reported that this particular Treaty was an attempt to revamp the EU's institutions to prepare for their expansion from 15 to 25 countries. The negotiations, which were marked with bitterness partly because of the French government's attempt to maintain equal share of votes with Germany, "produced a Council of Minister's voting system that is still being contested."

This Nice Treaty gave Spain, a country with a population of 40 million, 27 votes, almost as many as Germany with its population of 82 million. Poland, with a population of about 40 million, was also given 27 votes, As a result of this disproportional allotment of votes, one German diplomat expressed his misgivings: "The idea of Poland and Spain having 54 votes between them and Germany just 29 is totally unacceptable. Our public opinion would never wear it." Here, we notice the existence of *"the feet and toes which are partly of baked clay and partly of iron"* (Daniel 2:41-42).

On 15 December 2003, a column in The Times read: *"Glee in Polish camp at debut victory."* This news item was about the collapse of the negotiations in Brussels on 13 December 2003 to adopt the draft constitution for the European Union. The newspaper reported what Pierre Lequiller, a European politician, said after the collapse of the summit. According to Mr. Lequille, "The split in Europe was not between the old member-states from the East. The division is between those who want a political Europe and those who do not want one. We are at a turning point. There is no reason why the foot-draggers should force those who want to go faster and farther to wait." Once again, we witness a divided "kingdom of Europe."

On 24 June 2004 Anatole Kaletsky wrote an article for The Times: *"Let France and Germany build their superstate."* The columnist highlighted some of the divisions in the European Empire. He stated: "Political rhetoric has always presented the "European project" as a great journey, giving rise to metaphors of missed buses, slow lanes and fast lanes, second–class passengers and bicycles which will fall over if they stop moving...The leaders of France and Germany along with Belgium, Luxembourg and possibly Austria and the Netherlands want to extend European authority into all possible fields of government...foreign policy ... defence, to law enforcement, macroeconomics and even sports promotion. Britain of course, holds exactly opposite view.....It is clearer than ever that different European countries want to move in diametrically opposite directions...."

DIVISION IN THE EUROPEAN UNION ABOUT TURKEY'S ENTRY INTO THE "INCLUSIVE CLUB"

On 13 December 2002, The Sun newspaper published an article about the British Prime Minister's warning to the European Union summit on Turkey's prospective membership of the European Club. According to the Political Editor, Trevor Kavanagh, "Tony Blair warned that Europe must welcome 70million Turkish citizens into the Euro club – or risk inflaming the Islamic world." Mr Blair told the Copenhagen Summit: "Turkey's membership is not just important in its own right, but as a signal to the wider Islamic world that we want to engage." Mr Kavanagh continued: "Britain now risks a head-on collision with France and Germany who vehemently oppose Turkey's membership. Former French President, Giscard d'Estaing, warned it could destroy Europe. Germany feared it would lose its place as the biggest nation - outstripped by Turkey, which has one of the world's highest birth rates."

In contrast to Tony Blair's enthusiasm for the European Union to admit Turkey, Anthony Browne, The Times Europe Correspondent, painted a different picture about the consequences of Turkey's entry into the European Union. In his article, *"Europe will rue the day that it admits Turkey to the club"* (The Times 26 March 2004), Mr. Browne highlighted concerns relating to Turkey's admission into the European "phenomenon." He reported: "It is not the new constitution that is the biggest – and most divisive – issue facing the European Union, but rather the looming decision whether to let Turkey join....With its population growing by nearly a million a year, Turkey would be the most populous country in the EU by the time it joined. It would have a bigger vote than Germany, France or Britain.... Turkey has so little in common with the current member states that further policy integration would be impossible. The prospect of allowing an almost entirely Asian developing country to become the biggest member of the EU prompted the former French President, Valerie Giscard d'Estaing, to predict "the end of Europe" – which is why so many Europhiles are opposed, and British Euro-sceptics in favour...The EU project is already haemorrhaging..."

Finally, the introduction of the Lisbon Treaty, which was signed by the 27 EU leaders on 13 December 2007, provoked bitter debate among those who supported it and those who opposed it. The supporters claimed the Treaty would enable the European Project to function smoothly – with Europe speaking with one voice. Those who objected to its implementation claimed it would transfer more powers to unaccountable and unelected officials in Brussels, and that the EU would eventually become a United States of Europe with its own President and Diplomatic offices around the globe.

PROPHECY OF A "DIVIDED KINGDOM" FULFILLED

It is clear from the newspapers headlines and the articles we have read, that the European Union is a "Divided Union". The division in this apparent *"United Kingdom of Europe"* fulfils the prophetic word in Daniel 2:41: "Just as you (king Nebuchadnezzar) saw that the feet and toes were partly of baked clay and partly of iron, so this will be a *divided kingdom...*" The fulfilment of this prophecy perfectly fits the motto of the European Union – *"Unity in diversity"* – a supposedly 'united empire,' but, in reality, a 'divided empire.'

In his *The Dream of Rome*, Boris Johnson, consciously or unconsciously, summarised the prophetic revelation relating to the European Union as foretold in Daniel 2:41-43. In page 23 of his book, Mr Johnson writes: "The trouble is that this project (the European Union) so big and in some ways so noble – is not always popular. It is not democratic. It seems to evoke national feelings of resentment even among the French and the Dutch, both founder members of the EU, who in 2005 threw out the proposed European Constitution." And in Page 25 the author (a Member of the Conservative Party who became Major of London), further portrayed the European Union as a divided kingdom with mixed people. He writes: "We modern Europeans are divided. All the polls say so. We are divided into Euro-philes and Euro-sceptics, people who are pleased at the idea of forming a single unit out of the disparate European nations, and people who much prefer to keep their national traditions and to maintain the primacy of national governments." It is interesting to note that *The Dream of Rome* compares the Roman Empire to the European Union. This writer adds: The comparison would become a reality.

On Friday 16 June 2006, it was published in the *Evening Standard*, that the President of the European Commission, Jose Manuel Barroso, was seen reading *The Dream of Rome.* Perhaps, the Chief EU bureaucrat was seeking inspiration from Mr. Johnson's book to motivate and guide him to lead EU (the revived Roman Empire) to the Promised Land of Peace and Prosperity.

THE EUROPEAN UNION – A "STRONG" AND A "WEAK" KINGDOM

The Book of Daniel also predicted that the European Union would be a kingdom of strong and weak nations. Witness the prophetic word in Daniel 2:41: *"As the toes were partly iron and partly clay, so this kingdom will be partly strong and partly brittle....a divided kingdom; yet it will have some of the strength of iron in it".* The "toes of clay and iron" in the European Union were evident in the comments Romano Prodi made before the former communist countries joined the European Union in 2004. In an article titled *"Poor nations will not drag us down",* the then European Commission President said: "The new countries are generally far poorer (The 'toes of clay' of the human statue) than the current members of the EU (The 'toes of Iron')....eight were on the other side of the iron curtain. The ten will make 20% of the EU population but bring just 5% or 6% of the revenue."(The Times 2 December 2003).

The same prophetic word in Daniel 2:41 was also confirmed in David Marsh's article *Only the strong may survive in the euro area* (Daily Mail 23 February 2009). Commenting on the "ravages of the world recession," the Chairman of London & Oxford Capital Markets writes: "Reflecting the increasing tensions in the euro block, Germany... revealed it would be willing to bail out weaker-performing

EMU members to protect the 10-year-old system from calamitous failure... Because weaker nations can no longer devalue their way out of trouble, there is a risk these imbalances will worsen - bringing pressures that could ultimately cause the break-up of the euro." He added: "The weakest economies' external deficits have widened sharply because of these countries' poor competitiveness . . .." Messrs. Prodi and Marsh comments clearly confirm the prophetic word relating to the character of the European Union namely, *"... this kingdom will be partly strong and partly brittle....a divided kingdom; yet it will have some of the strength of iron in it."*

THE EUROPEAN UNION – THE FUTURE SUPER POWER

We know the European Union is an "*Empire*" of big, strong, rich and powerful nations. It is also a "*kingdom*" of small, weak, and poor nations. Despite the weaknesses of the poor and least developed member-states in the European Union, which are *"the toes of clay"*, the European Union would still remain a powerful "Empire." For instance, "a new foreign minister will be created to try and strengthen Europe's voice in the world" (Financial Times 28 August 2003). The Lisbon Treaty has created this position together with an office of a President. And this powerful man would sign treaties on behalf of the member-states of the European Union.

Also the European Commission has plans to engage in "heavy spending to help the European Union meets its target of overtaking the United States as the world's most competitive economy..." (*Financial Times* 19 January 2004). The European Union is now leading the world to fight a new kind of "global terrorism" – the so-called global warming which, according to some scientists, is about to destroy the "Mother Earth" within 20-50 years if carbon emissions from motor vehicles, aeroplanes and ships are not reduced. Clearly, the European Union has the ambition to become the most powerful *"Empire"* on planet earth. At present it is the biggest economic market in the world with about 500 million consumers.

The European Union demonstrated its power when America failed to prevent the EU from establishing its own military planning agency independent of the Nato alliance (and thus Washington). In an article *"How America became the world's dispensable nation,"* the author, a Senior Fellow at the New America Foundation in Washington DC, stated: "Europe is building up its own rapid reaction force. And despite US resistance, the EU is developing Galileo, its own Satellite network which will break the monopoly of the US global positioning Satellite System" (Financial Times, 25 January 2005).

When Dr Condoleezza Rice, the former US Secretary of State, expressed her support for a common European Foreign Policy, "she was ill rewarded by Herr

Schroder's assertion in Munich that Nato was no longer the transatlantic co-ordination of strategy, and that it was an EU bent on developing its own independent military wing….." But George Bush, the then American President, disagreed (The Times 21 February 2005).

THE EUROPEAN UNION – A POTENTIAL MILITARY SUPER-POWER

In February 2005, the US President, George W Bush, paid a four-day visit to Europe. During his meetings with European leaders he stressed that Nato was "the cornerstone of the transatlantic relationship." But President Chirac of France did not share President Bush's view. The then French leader rather supported the vision of the former German Chancellor, Herr Schroder, whose view was, "the EU should increasingly become the forum for Europe and the US to discuss their security." Schroder stated: "Europe is steadily building up its defence capability. This development is a positive opportunity for our alliance. For a stronger, more united Europe implies a stronger more effective alliance." (The Times 23 February 2005). The creation of European Army was one of President Sarkozy's aims when France assumed the EU Presidency in 2008.

We must ask the question: who would be the effective "strong leader" to lead the United States of Europe to solve its security, political and economic problems"? The Lisbon Treaty has paved the way for the powerful man to emerge. That the ultimate aim of the European Union to become a world-super power to replace the United Sates of America was again highlighted in a newspaper column titled *High-tech weapons help Europe to close military gap with US.* It was reported, "The European Union is to develop unmanned drones, new armoured vehicles and advanced communications systems in a strategy to become a military superpower and close the defence technological gap with the United States…..They are aimed at transforming the EU from being a political power, in charge of policies such as agriculture and trade, to a military one, capable of sending troops around the world to enforce a foreign policy agreed by its member states" (The Times 2 March 2005).

The European Union once again demonstrated its independence from America by defying the United States to lift its arms embargo against China. This decision caused President George Bush to stress that it could result in US Congressional restrictions on technology transfer to Europe.

The target of the European Union to become the most powerful "Empire" on earth was also unveiled in a newspaper article headed *Brussels plans to expand its empire again* (The Times 4 May 2004). In this article Anthony Browne highlighted the aspiration of the European Union to become the Mighty Empire on planet earth. It was published that after the ten new countries joined the then existing

15 countries, the European officials began to prepare "more ambitious plans to expand the Brussels Empire across North Africa, the Middle East and Asia.... The EU's executive body, will launch a strategy document setting out details of an effective enlargement of the EU over decades across all the Muslim countries lining the Mediterranean from Morocco to Syria, as well as Israel, Lebanon and all the former parts of the Soviet Union that are in Europe including Russia."

There were also "well-advanced plans for..... all the Balkan countries, including Albania, Croatia, Bosnia and Serbia" to become members of the Club. The Correspondent continued: "Under the New Neighbourhood Policy (also called the Wider Europe policy) countries such as Egypt, Algeria, Libya, Ukraine and Russia would become full members of the single market, with open borders for trade and investment, with their citizens given the full right to live and work in the European Union. The policy has been agreed in principle by the national governments of the EU." The Times Correspondent revealed: "In a further development Georgia, Armenia and Azerbaijan, former Soviet republics in the Caucasus region between the Black Sea and Caspian Sea, will be told....that they, too, eventually will be eligible for the New Neighbourhood Policy. The three countries have said that they want full membership of the EU...."

Mr Anthony Browne's article paints a clear picture of the objective of the European Union to become a grand Empire of strong and weak nations ruling the world. And this objective would be fulfilled to fulfil the prophetic message in Daniel 2:41: *"As the toes were partly iron and partly clay, so this kingdom will be partly strong and partly brittle....a divided kingdom; yet it will have some strength of iron in it."*

"Europe must do more to embrace its neighbours." This was the title of an article published in the 12 December 2006 edition of Financial Times. Charles Grant, writes: "The EU cannot afford to be indifferent to the arc of instability that runs from Belarus to North Africa, through Ukraine, Maldova, the western Balkans, the Caucasus and the Middle East. Unless the EU takes responsibility for steering its neighbourhood towards prosperity and good governance, it could pay a heavy price: Political instability, religious extremism, ethnic conflict, organise crime and illegal immigration could all spill over from the neighbourhood to the union and in some cases already are."

When France took over the EU Presidency in 2008, President Sarkozy held a Mediterranean Union Summit in Paris. According to Sarkozy's vision, the Med-Union "would have a mission to reunite Europe and Africa around the countries along the Mediterranean rim and to set up a partnership on an equal footing between the countries." The Mediterranean Project will focus on "peace, development and respect for the environment." About 42 world leaders attended the conference.

THE WORD OF GOD MUST COME TO PASS

"Enlargement" of the European Union from 6 founder countries in 1952 to 27 members in 2007 has been cited as the most successful foreign policy of the European Project. I quote again the words of *TIME* Correspondent, Carla Power: *"The E.U. is one of the great successes of the post-1945 world – a unique geopolitical experiment that has spread prosperity across a continent that, within living memory, had little of either."* This must be the case to bring to pass what the "Seer of Dublin" wrote about political union of European nations. And this would result in the "resurrection" of the "dead" Roman Empire which would eventually fulfil the prophetic revelation encoded in the *10 toes of baked clay and iron* of the magnificent human statue King Nebuchadnezzar saw in his dream ((Daniel 2:40-43).

OLYMPIC GAMES AND THE ASPIRATIONS OF THE EUROPEAN UNION

Let us examine another subject that underlines the ambition of the European Union to become the world superpower. During the 2004 Olympic Games in Greece, the countries of the European Union won 286 medals. 82 were gold. The United States of America, the current world superpower and leading sports nation, took 103 medals of which 35 were gold. China accumulated 32 gold medals. Russia won 27 gold medals, and Australia had 17 Gold medals. After the Games, an European Commissioner suggested that in future Olympics, participating nations from the European Union should compete under the European Flag. What was the purpose behind this suggestion? You may guess.

On Tuesday, 31 August 2004, a space in the *Daily Mail* read" **"*NOW EU BIDS TO HIJACK OLYMPIC GLORY*".** According to the paper, "EU leaders want all member countries to carry the blue 12-Star banner as well as their own flags, starting at the next Games in Beijing. Behind the move is a desire to present the United States of Europe as the world's major sporting power. EU nations won 286 medals in Athens compared 103 for US".

On this same day, 31 August 2004, *The Sun* also commented on the Eurocrats diabolical plan to usurp the sovereignty of EU member states. In a column titled *EU claims it won the Olympics,* the newspaper reported that Mr Prodi (the then EU Commissioner) turned the Athens games into a political football claiming that our (British athletes') bag of 30 gold medals helped the EU trounce America and China." And according to another article in The Times newspaper, EU officials claimed "The European Union was the true champions of the Olympic Games not the USA or China." They justified their ridiculous claim by citing the total haul of more than 280 medals the 25 member states of the European Union won. This attitude of political elites in Brussels demonstrates how desperate they are to portray the EU as a super-power.

Furthermore, Britain, France and Germany – the three most powerful nations of the European Union - were planning "on how the European Union could create an independent planning unit for any military missions carried out separately from Nato...The US, however, remains strongly against any EU operational planning unit, fearing it would eventually lead to a European defence policy independent of Nato" (Financial Times 27 November 2003).

On 16 November 2004, The Times correspondent, Charles Bremner, wrote on the French President's visit to London. This was published in an article titled "Britain cannot be an honest broker between Europe and US." In this news report, the French President, Jacques Chirac, asserted his vision of a separate Europe balancing the influence of the United States of America. According to the French Statesman, "The evolution of the world towards a multipolar situation is inevitable. That is part of human history. In consequence there will be a great American pole, a great European pole, a Chinese one, an Indian one, eventually a South American pole. These great poles have to live together. "

President Chirac's remarks should not surprise us. In her book, *Eurabia – The Euro-Arab Axis,* Bat Ye'or explained that under France initiative, Euro-Arab dialogue was established for economic and political purposes to undermine American supremacy. In pages 40-41 of her monumental work, Bat Ye'or writes: "Haj Amin's calls for an active Franco-Arab alliance were abetted by influential French politicians and intellectuals who urged the government to adopt a coherent policy toward the Muslim world. They cherished France's ambition since the days of Bonaparte and Napoleon III.....They believed that France's association with a Muslim federation extending over North Africa and the Middle East would bring it an ascendancy that would impress the Soviet Union and rival the United States." *Eurabia* reveals that the Europeans had a sinister motive. They sought co-operation from the Muslims to build the European Union for it to be a counterweight to America not an ally. She states one of the five pillars of "Eurabian doctrine" was "hostility to America and obstruction of its influence in the Middle East."

JEAN MONNET ON THE UNITED STATES OF AMERICA, EUROPE AND PEACE

We must, therefore, not be surprised by the ambition of European politicians, especially the French and the Germans, to overthrow America's supremacy. This was also the vision of their patron - Jean Monnet. Monnet made this clear in his interview with Leonard Gross to mark his 80th birthday. In an article for *Look,* entitled *Jean Monnet talks of the U.S., Europe and peace*, the European Editor writes: "As long as Europe remains divided, it is no match for the Soviet Union. Europe must unite. Then, and only then, can it deal as an equal with U.S. Then, and only then, can the U.S and Europe, together, confront the Communist world." According to Gross, Monnet was confident the process would take place. Commenting on The Common Market, Jean Monnet said: *"The Common Market changed the attitude of the producers. A static society gets transformed if you touch the right point – and we touched the right point…As the process grows, the inevitable necessity of some kind of political authority emerges. You can't do without it. In fact, it already exists….If we don't unite, then there's no doubt in my mind that….America will come to dominate Europe." Leonard Gross concluded his interview with "Mister Europe" by asking Monnet: "Would Europe unite in time?" He responded: "My dear sir, my answer is always the same. Necessity. Union among men is not natural. Necessity is always required."* (*Look* 26 November 1968)

Indeed, a day is fast approaching when Monnet's vision would be 'realised' - when a man with extraordinary political skills and power leads "united Europe" to 'solve' the problems of the world. The Lisbon Treaty has prepared the ground for the King of Europe to take up his throne.

IMMIGRANTS TO EUROPE MUST TAKE EURO-EXAM

The determination of the European Union to become a "United Kingdom of Europe" with one body and one mind, to make Jean Monnet's 'vision' of a United States of Europe a reality, was reported in The Times. In an article entitled, *EU chiefs want all immigrants to take entry exam***,** Rory Watson and Anthony Browne wrote: "Immigrants arriving in Europe could be forced to sit a test demonstrating their knowledge of their host country under plans discussed by interior ministers from the European Union's six largest members." This, according to the reporters, was "the latest step in the development of a common immigration policy in Europe….to ensure that immigrants accept Western values and become integrated into the host society." The values immigrants were expected to embrace, according to Charles Clarke, the former British Home Secretary, were "democracy, respect for other faiths, free speech, the rule of law, and free media…."

The question is: how democratic is the European Union? Did the European leaders offer their people a chance to vote on the Lisbon Treaty that transfers more powers from national parliaments to unelected and unaccountable officials in Brussels? Was it not the intention of the European leaders to impose the so-called new EU Treaty on the masses, fearing that it would be rejected in a popular vote? The European Union is not qualified to preach democracy to any nation. The EU is a 'dictatorship'. For the "Seer of Dublin" wrote: "Democracy, not despotism is the goal towards which civilization is tending; but democracy in its full development is one of the surest roads to despotism….The true test of a man is not what he does, but what, with the principles he holds, he would do, and if this be true of individuals, it is still more intensely true of communities." Does the EU practice what it preaches? The EU is 'hostile' to democratic values. The EU, whose institutions are not accountable to the voters who finance them, has no worthwhile "core values" worth emulating by other nations. That is the reality.

THE FULFILMENT OF THE EUROPEAN DREAM

The various newspaper reports we have examined indicate how the prophetic revelation relating to the European Union in Daniel 2:41 is being fulfilled: "*...a divided kingdom, yet it will have some of the strength of iron in it.*" It is also clear from these articles and the comments made by European Union officials that the European Union craves to become the world superpower overtaking the United States of America - not only in military and economic terms, but also in sports. Without any doubt, the European Union is desperate to become a Mighty Empire ruling the world. This would certainly be fulfilled to welcome the *"small horn whose eyes would be the eyes of a man, and with the mouth that could speak great things...."* (Daniel 7:8, Daniel 7:7, Daniel 7:23-24 and Revelation 17:12-13).

According to political commentators, if the European Union Constitution is ratified and adopted, the European Union would become a sovereign kingdom with political identity. The fact is whether the European constitution is adopted, rebranded, slimmed down or rejected, the European Union would still become a Mighty Empire. The Lisbon Treaty has made this possible with a clause that confers legal personality on EU with the mandate to sign international treaties which would be binding on EU member-states.

THE QUIET SUPERPOWER WITH SOFT POWER

Before Europe celebrated the 50th anniversary of the Treaty of Rome in Berlin on 25 March 2007, most of the leading international magazines (TIME, NEWSWEEK, THE ECONOMIST) and newspapers highlighted the achievements of the European Union. Prominent among the success stories were the creation of a Single Market with a common currency, The Common Agricultural Policy and the enlargement of the Union from 6 members to 27countries comprising of about 500million consumers – the largest trading block in the world. Financial Times summarised the achievements in its 23 March 2007 edition. Under the title *The case for an adult, outward-looking EU,* the editorial reported: "One of the EU's most striking successes has been the ability to promote peace and prosperity within its ever-expanding borders. The original six pioneers have attracted 21 additional members to their club – creating what has been called the first "voluntary empire" in history. Political stability and prosperity have been entrenched in the Iberian Peninsula. Democracy and the rule of law have been returned to many of the new member states of central Europe."

A section of the media that supports the European Project arrived at the conclusion that the EU is now a "Quiet superpower" with a "Soft power". But it must "compliment its soft power by developing more hard power to help deal with common security threats and crises." *Newsweek* magazine, in its Special Report, "Europe at 50", highlighted the successes of the European Union. *Newsweek* noted: "Europe is now a global superpower of world historic importance, second to none in economic clout. It has constructed one of the most successful systems of government – the modern social welfare state, which for all its flaws has brought unprecedented prosperity and security to Europe's people. It is the single most successful advance in voluntary international cooperation in modern history." The report further described how the original 6 club members have increased their membership to 27 with others in a long queue. The values of the EU, according to *NEWSWEEK*, "are spreading across the globe - far more attractive, in many respects, than those of America....When it comes to the instruments needed to engineer peace, the softer tools of civilian power, Europe far exceeds America. It is the "quiet superpower"...The EU is the largest trading and investment partner of every nation in the Middle East....The EU has emerged as Europe's most innovative and significant contribution to modernity."

The Report added the sentiments of the financier George Soros - how the multimillionaire was planning to finance a "new European Council on Foreign Relations on the notion that U.S foreign policy "has left the world leaderless and in disarray." According to Soros, "Europe and a revitalized EU offer a better model and motive force for addressing the global challenges of modern era". *NEWSWEEK* concluded: "True or not, it's significant that 50 years after the EU's march to unity began, it is now Europe, not the United States, that's held as a new lamp unto nations." And Dr Alexander Stubb, Finland's Foreign Minister, also echoed European Union's potential superpower status in his address at the *Carnegie Endowment for International Peace.* Proud to be an Euro-federalist, Dr Stubb boasted to his audience that the "EU is the largest coalition or political union in the world - there is no system akin to it in the world... EU is the biggest single market in the world – bigger than the United States, much bigger than China, and 15 times bigger than Russia. And the EU is the biggest donor of aid in the world."

It is curious to note that, Dr Stubb, an expert on European integration, uttered not a single word on corruption in the European Union. For fraud is written in the DNA of the European Project. Secondly, Dr. Stubb did not make any reference to the crucial advice the first President of the European Parliament offered to Europeans concerning the survival of the European project. Why? Was it ignorance or a conspiracy of silence among European politicians to conceal a vital truth from the electorate? Was Dr. Stubb aware that before the French founding fathers of the European Community were born in 1888 and 1886, a British public servant had already written about a confederation of European nations which would develop through an European crisis?

POLITICIANS AND POLITICAL COMMENTATORS SHOULD NOT GLOAT ABOUT THE 'ACHIEVEMENTS' OF THE EUROPEAN UNION

Supporters of Jean Monnet's vision of a federal Europe should not boast about the achievements of the European Union. I would remind them it was an Irishman who predicted that a political union of European nations would be the next major political phenomenon in history after the rebirth of the nation of Israel. Even the very words and phrases the Ulsterman used in the 19th to describe the European confederacy were used by Jean Monnet, in the 20th century, to describe his vision of a federal Europe.

Let us examine some of Jean Monnet's comments about his vision and compare them with what the native of Dublin wrote about political Europe before Monnet himself was born.

The voice of Jean Monnet: "I have always believed that Europe will be established through ***crisis*** and not the sum of the outcome of those ***crisis.***" There will be no peace in Europe if the states of Europe rebuild themselves on the basis of national sovereignty... I have no doubt that a *confederation* will one day lead to a federation...The ***confederation*** will have the great advantage of assuring public opinion in our countries that they have joined an entity which is not only economic but political, and that they are therefore part of ***something bigger*** than any of their countries alone" (Memoirs 1978)

The voice of the "Unknown Ulsterman": "Next to the restoration of the Jews to Palestine, the most ***prominent political feature in history*** would be the partition of Roman earth.....It is impossible to foretell how far kingdoms may be consolidated and boundaries may be changed...In forecasting the fulfilment of these we are dealing with events, which, while they may occur within the life time of living men, may yet be delayed for centuries. We may rest content with the certainty that their fulfilment will be clear to all those who are capable of observing public facts. ..Through the gradual unfolding....or far more probably as the outcome of some great ***European crisis*** in the future, this ***confederation*** of ***[European] nations*** shall be developed and..."(1881).

The "Seer of Dublin" went on to record the future prospects of political Europe. He then predicted Greece and Turkey would join the European confederacy. This was 100 years before Greece joined the European Community in 1981, and 82 years before Turkey first applied for membership of the European club in 1963. He also listed Belgium, France, Germany, Italy, Portugal and Spain as some of the leading members. He warned England would not be saved in this political alliance of European nations. The "Seer" did not expect Ireland to join the European confederacy.

I have already stated that Jean Monnet, in his attempt to build a federal Europe, toiled as a 'slave' to fulfil the extraordinary vision of an Irish 'master' he never knew. The French architect of European Construction, the "practical apostle of European unity," was no 'genius.' This leads to the question: if the creation of the European Union is a "Quiet Miracle", as published in *TIME* magazine, and if Jean Monnet is regarded as a man who has made an impact on history, then how should politicians and political commentators in America, Britain, Europe and Ireland describe the Irishman who predicted this 'Quiet Miracle' in the 19th century before the "Quiet Miracle" manifested in the 20th century? The world is waiting for an answer.

I repeat: the aspirations of the European Union would materialise whether its new constitution (re-packaged as The Lisbon Treaty) is ratified, modified or rejected. The European Union would develop to be the re-incarnation of the "dead" Roman Empire. And from this resurrected Roman Empire would emerge a strong leader. The "Unknown Irishman" described the powerful leader of the European Empire an "awful Being." This charismatic leader of Europe would be the political genius who would make his mark in history by employing his extraordinary intelligence and political acumen to 'solve' the Middle East crisis. This would mark the beginning of the end of human governments on earth. We will learn more about this coming king of Europe in due course.

EUROPEAN UNION: AN EMPIRE OF MIXED PEOPLE

So that you would appreciate the supernatural character of the Book of Daniel, I would again refer to additional newspaper reports that confirm the nature of the revived Roman Empire as predicted in Daniel 2:43: *"And just as you saw the iron mixed with baked clay, so the people will be a mixture and will not remain united any more than iron mixes with clay"* (Daniel 2:43). If we relate this prophetic word to another aspect of the development of the European Union, we would appreciate how the prophetic message, *"the people will be a mixture and will not remain united any more than iron mixes with clay,* has been fulfilled in the Continent of Europe.

We know the citizens of this apparent *"United Kingdom of Europe"* (The European Union) are men and women with different nationalities, cultures and traditions. They speak different languages. A political commentator summed it up: "It will certainly be a feast for translators when the Lithuanian President's speech has to be turned simultaneously into Polish, Hungarian and Maltese" (31 December 2003).

"Club Europe will now speak 20 languages." This was the title of a column in the 2 December 2003 edition of The Times before the 10 new countries joined the European Club in May 2004. And there was an article in *The Economist* that confirmed how different languages in the European Empire have fulfilled the prophetic word in Daniel 2:41-43. Under the title "Babelling on," *The Economist* reported: "In their loftier moments Brussels politicians say that languages are an expression of the European Union's unity in diversity. What they seldom admit is that languages are a logistical and expensive headache, as well as a cause of nationalistic squabbles.....A plan in 2002 to simplify European patents failed when some countries blocked it because the new patent would be only in English, French and German" (The Economist December 16TH - 22ND 2006).

Furthermore, some members of the European Union have experienced communist rule. In this "political kingdom of Europe" there are Christians and non Christians. Even among the Christians there is a "mixture". We have Roman Catholics, Anglicans, Methodists, Presbyterians, Calvinists, Lutherans, Pentecostals, Charismatics and other different denominations. In the "United Kingdom of Europe" there are Muslims, Jews, agnostics, humanists, Darwinists, animists and atheists. And we know the occasional disputes among the different religious groups, as well as political conflicts among politicians of different ideological persuasions..

Some members of Jean Monnet's Project have banned the wearing and displaying of religious symbols in public schools. A section of the population in these countries opposed such religious restrictions. The banning of Islamic veils, the Jewish yarmulkes and the wearing of large crucifixes created tension in France. In Britain the public were divided on the same issues. There were 'conflicts' between politicians. Even religious leaders were divided. Some supported the wearing of veils in public; others claim "wearing veils doesn't conform to norms of decency." Clearly, the 'sons' and 'daughters' of Jean Monnet have different religious and political persuasions. All these facts prove the European Union is an "Empire" of mixed people who are not united. And these issues fulfil the prophetic word in Daniel 2:43 *"So the people will be a mixture and will not remain united any more than iron mixes with clay."*

EU: "A DIVIDED UNION"

"The Economist", in its September 25th - October 1st 2004 edition, published a 14 page special report on the state of Europe. The front cover read: "Europe's Divided Union." Inside the magazine was a group photograph of European politicians. Beneath the portrait was the inscription: ***"a divided Union."*** In this Special Report, the influential Journal provided analysis of how the European Union is deeply divided among its politicians and citizens on a whole range of political, social and economic issues. I quote from the report which partly summarises a divided European "kingdom":

"Nearly half a century after its birth, the EU's approval ratings remain pretty feeble. In the most recent Eurobarometer, just 43% of EU citizens said they had a positive image of the Union, against 21% with a negative. Even in Germany, one of the weightiest founder members, only 39% thought the country had benefited from EU membership, against 38% who thought it had not. A previous Eurobarometer found that almost half of EU voters would not mind, or indeed would be "very relieved", if the EU were simply to disappear. Evidence from the ballot box is not much more encouraging. Sweden and Denmark both voted in referendums against adopting the euro. (Most countries embraced the euro without referendum). Even Ireland, which has arguably benefited more from EU membership than any other nation, initially voted to reject the Nice treaty that paved the way for EU enlargement, and had to stage a second referendum before coming up with the "right" answer."

The report went on to discuss other divisive issues. According to *The Economist,* because the European Union has increased its hold on social policy, this has resulted in "a clash of political philosophies between free-market Anglo-Saxons and welfare-minded continentals that can leave both sides unhappy. It is an article of faith in France that Britain practises "social dumping," undermining French industry by refusing to impose decent minimum standards on employers. The British, for their part, are convinced that the French and the Germans, finding themselves unable to reform their welfare systems, are seeking to impose their own inefficiencies on everybody else through EU regulations..."

This Report also confirms the fulfilment of the prophetic revelation in Daniel 2:41-43, which says: "Just as ...the feet and toes of the human statue were partly of baked clay and partly of iron, so this (the European Union which is the foundation stone of the revived Roman Empire) will be a divided kingdom...And just as the iron is mixed with baked clay, so the people will be a mixture and will not remain united any more than iron mixes with clay." Praise the Lord. For His Word that goes out from His mouth will not return to Him empty. It will accomplish what He desires and achieves the purpose for which He sent it. Amen! (Isaiah 55:11).

THE POLITICS OF "CAT AND MOUSE" AND "HIDE AND SEEK" - THE EUROPEAN UNION A DIVIDED KINGDOM WITH MIXED PEOPLE WHO ARE NOT UNITED

"The clash of political philosophies between free-market Anglo-Saxons and welfare-minded continentals" was laid bare during Economic Summit of European leaders in Brussels on 22 March 2005. The Summit discussed many issues. Among them were how to promote economic growth and employment; how to relax the Stability and Growth Pact, and how to enforce the Services Directives.

The Services Directives were intended to open up Europe's services market, so that anyone who is legally allowed to offer a service in one member-state would be able to do so in another on a temporary basis without meeting local legal requirements. However, because of the perceived disadvantages the implementation of this Service Directives would have had on France and Germany, the Directives were watered down in their favour. The then British Prime Minister, Tony Blair, supported the dilution of the Directives, even though he was an ardent supporter of liberalising the Economy of Europe to create more jobs for Europeans.

The attitude of France and Germany, in pursuing their national interests at the expense of that of the smaller nations of Eastern Europe, prompted this headline in the Financial Times: *"Europhile hearts miss a beat as Berlin and Paris turn on Brussels. Politicians in two countries that planted the seeds of European integration have turned into agitators of dissent over draft services directives and the stability pact."* The paper reported: "Mr Chirac has rallied against the EU's services directives, a text, Gerhard Schroder, the Germany Chancellor, said was spreading "fear and terror in his country.....The Franco-German couple's new bare-knuckle approach to EU affairs has caused frustration beyond Brussels, particularly in Poland and other new East European members who fear the EU's agenda is being warped to benefit older members" (Financial Times 23 March 2005).

On this same day (23 March 2005), a column in The Times read *Blair backs down as French resist greater freedoms for EU workers.* According to the newspaper the British Prime Minister gave in to "French demands for a far reaching revision of controversial regulations across the EU after President Chirac of France declared that the free market policies advocated by Britain were "the new communism of our age." The Times reported that Mr Blair agreed, after a major row, to water down the proposals to open up Europe's market in services to help the French Government avoid defeat in the May's referendum on the European Constitution and to protect the European Social Model...The conflict between Britain's support for free markets and the protective labour policies championed by France came to a head over proposals backed by UK to enable everyone from mechanics to architects to work without hindrance across the European Union. The article also revealed that the plans to create a single market in services were needed to create about 600,000 jobs in Europe and to boost economic growth. However, these plans were a source of grievances and worry among Trade Unions in France, who claimed the Services Directives "would destroy jobs, and create lower wages."

Just hours after the British Prime Minister had supported the French President to win concessions on the proposed EU directives to open Europe's market in services, which the French and Germans feared could lead to increase "social dumping" (the flooding of their countries with cheap labour from the relatively poor Eastern European countries that could lead to increase in unemployment), President Chirac demanded that Britain should give up its £3billion rebate from the European Union budget.

This demand from the French President, according to Daily Mail, was "Chirac's stab in the back for Blair over £3bn." The newspaper noted that the Prime Minister offered help to the French President, because Blair did not want "to be seen harming Chirac's chances of winning a Yes vote in the French referendum on the European Constitution in May 2005." President Chirac, again, twisted the knife further into Britain over a remark he made at a dinner. He astonished other leaders by saying Mr Blair's free-market philosophy was as dangerous to Europe as Communism, declaring, "Ultra-liberalism is the communism of our current days" (Daily Mail 24 March 2005).

THE RETALIATION IN A DIVIDED KINGDOM WITH MIXED PEOPLE WHO ARE NOT UNITED

President Chirac's demand that Britain should sacrifice its £3billion rebate from the European Union, because it could no longer be justified, prompted the then British Foreign Secretary, Jack Straw, to insist, "he would block any attempt to end the rebate which was originally granted to balance the effects of the Common Agricultural Policy: We have an absolute veto, and we would use it" (Daily Mail, 24 March 2005).

Furthermore, Chirac's perceived hostile attack on Britain, and his seemingly ungrateful attitude towards the British Prime Minister who helped his chances of winning the French referendum by supporting the watering down of the Services Directives to favour France and Germany, prompted a response from Mr Blair. This was published in an article entitled *"Blair plans reprisal for Chirac's coup over reform of EU."* It stated, "TONY BLAIR hit back ....at Jacques Chirac's claim to have won a Gallic victory over EU employment rules by insisting that France would ultimately be outvoted on the issue." (The Times 25 March 2005)

Mr. Blair told MPs that his vision of liberalised EU jobs and services market had been backed in private discussions by many other EU governments and would eventually prevail. As M. Chirac boasted to his Cabinet of the concessions he had won on Wednesday EU council, Mr Blair was telling MPs that "the final decision will be by qualified majority voting" - meaning that France would eventually be unable to veto liberalisation measures". It was further reported that the British Prime Minister, who "left Brussels without comment, took his revenge on M. Chirac by associating France with those resisting the modernisation of the EU. He also made it clear that a majority of European leaders were prepared to force through Britain's view of a free market approach."

It is obvious from what we have learnt about the controversy surrounding the liberalisation of commerce between European Union member states, and the hostility between French and British leading politicians, that the European Union is a "divided kingdom". It is also apparent that the European Union is a "kingdom" in which the interests of big countries (*the toes of iron)* tend to prevail over that of smaller countries (the *toes of clay*).

This fact is supported by a leading article published in 24 March 2005 editorial of Financial Times. The title read *EU's big boys behaving badly: France and Germany may rue beating up on Brussels.* According to the editorial, "Not only have the French and German leaders continued the trend of big EU states (*the toes of iron)* dictating to the Commission, to the dismay and anger of smaller and newer states (*the toes of clay)* which naturally look to the EU executive for protection and leadership. ......To the dismay, again, of smaller members of the eurozone *(the toes of clay),* France and Germany (*the toes of iron)* were also dealt a get-out-of-fiscal-jail card with the summit's relaxation of the stability pact's disciplines and widening of the excuses for avoiding them. Since Germany was the principal father of the pact, this was more an act of infanticide than of Brussels-bashing…." (The "toes of clay and iron" were inserted by the author to confirm the existence of small and big countries, weak and strong nations in the European Union as foretold in Daniel 2:41-43).

The division in the European Union and the pursuit of national interests of the big nations ***(the toes of iron)*** at the expense of the smaller countries ***(the toes of clay)*** were highlighted in a column titled *EU concerns over Chirac's high-risk feud with Barroso* (Financial Times 29 March 2005). It was mentioned Mr. Barroso, the President of the European Commission, made a "thinly veiled criticisms of Mr Chirac for failing to understand that Europe had changed, and that the single market was open to all 25 members of an enlarged union." The EU Chief declared: "Some people think of the Commission as being there to protect the 15 against the 10 – it is not". The report added: ".... he (Mr. Barroso) tried to make sense of Europe's baffling political alignments, where centre-left leaders such as

Tony Blair of Britain or Marek Belka of Poland supported liberal reforms, while centre-right politicians such as Mr Chirac opposed them. Mr Barroso remarked, "The real divide is not between left and right. It is between modernisers and reactionaries." The report concluded that Gunter Verheugen, Mr Barroso's German vice-president, urged the warring factions to calm down. The vice-president further declared: "the Commission cannot win if it starts an open war with the leaders of the bigger countries."

Finally, on 30 June 2005, The Times Columnist, Anatole Kaletsky, brought to light how the European Union is a "divided Kingdom." In his article, *Eureka! Blair's perfect (but eccentric) answer to the European conundrum,* Mr Kaletsky made a reference to Tom Kremer's book – *The Missing Heart of Europe.* He stated: "Kremer explains with ....eloquence why diversity, rather than integration, is likely to be the outcome of a more democratic Europe. He suggests there are broadly two polities in Europe, divided not just by history, but by culture and even by humour. On one side there are French-style "concentric" countries, respectful of order and authority, rigorously rational and politically centralised. On the other side are British-style "eccentric" countries, characterised by liberal individualism, pragmatism, grassroots democracy and disdain for authority. The differences go as far as linguistic structure; the open vocabulary and unstructured grammar of English contrasts with French linguistic rigour, as supervised by the Acedemie Francaise..."

And here is additional information that fulfils the prophetic word: *"This kingdom will be partly strong and partly brittle....the people will not remain united..."* (Daniel 2:42-43). The European Union's common values are defined as, "equality of persons, freedom and respect and a mission to protect the *weakest and most deprived.".* And an European politician once said: "The Union's small countries are needed by the big countries as a buffer to prevent open clashes between them, and this gives them the opportunity to send messages and wield influence on policy." (Financial Times 1 September 2003). I summed it up with this headline: *"New 'Iron Curtain' will split EU's rich and poor."* (The Times 2 March 2009)

BIBLE PROPHECY FULFILLED

What we have read about the European Union in *The Economist;* the information we have received from the various newspapers relating to the controversies surrounding the liberalisation of trade among European Union member-states, and the initial refusal of the British Government to forfeit its £3billion rebate as demanded by the French President, that the "*cheque britannique*" was no longer justified, again sum up the fulfilment of Bible prophecy in Daniel 2:41-43 (On the issue of the British rebate the British government subsequently surrendered it to please their masters in Brussels.)

In summary, the following articles:

- The Economist report on "a divided Union",
- "Blair backs down as French resist greater freedoms for EU workers" (The Times March 23,2005)
- "Europhile hearts miss as Berlin and Paris turn on Brussels" (Financial Times 23 March 2005)
- "Blair plans reprisal for Chirac's coup over reform of EU" (The Times March 25, 2005),"
- "Chirac's stab in the back for Blair over £3bn rebate"(Daily Mail, March 24, 2005)
- "EU's big boys behaving badly"(Financial Times 24 March 2005),
- "EU concerns over Chirac's high-risk feud with Barroso" (Financial Times March 29, 2005), together with all the previous articles we have read about the European Union, confirmed the prophetic message in Daniel's interpretation of *the toes of clay and iron* of the magnificent human image king Nebuchadnezzar saw in his dream:

Let us, again, reflect on the explanation Daniel gave to the King of Babylon concerning the prophetic significance of the "10 toes" of the splendid human statue he dreamt of: "Just as you (King Nebuchadnezzar) saw that the feet and toes were partly of baked clay and partly of iron, so this (The Revived Roman Empire) will be *a divided kingdom,* yet it will have some of the strength of iron in it; even as you saw iron mixed with clay. As the toes were partly iron and partly clay, *so this kingdom will be partly strong and partly brittle.* And just as you saw the iron mixed with baked clay, so the people will be a ***mixture*** and ***will not remain united,*** any more than iron mixes with clay" (Daniel 2:41-43). What a perfect description of the European Union.

Remember what Daniel told Nebuchadnezzar after he had explained the dream that troubled him: "The great God has shown the king what will take place in the future. The dream is true and the interpretation is trustworthy" (Daniel 2:45) Praise the Lord! Before things happened, the Almighty, the Omniscience, announced them (Isaiah 48:5) to demonstrate that HE alone is outside time; and HE alone records history in advance. Amen!

In October 2004, the then 25 European leaders met in Rome and signed the treaty for adopting the European Constitution. At that time all the 25 member countries of the Union were expected to ratify the constitutional treaty for it to take effect. Some countries adopted the treaty through national parliaments without giving their people the opportunity to debate on it – probably for fear of the constitution being rejected. I support my assertion with reference to an article published in the Daily Mail on 13 May, 2005. The title read *82m Germans have no say as MPs back the EU constitution*. According to the report, "The German people were denied a referendum by their country's constitution, despite mounting pressure .....for such a vote to take place". And when Peter Gauweiler, a German Member of Parliament, and others sponsored a move to get the German constitution changed to allow a referendum on the treaty, the German highest court rejected his application. Mr Gauweiler then "argued that a vote would have shown up a deep-rooted disaffection among Germans with the EU." The European Constitution was imposed on the Germans. Was this an exhibition of true democracy? No. The reality is that the political leaders in Europe were in haste to fulfil the prophetic revelation about European integration. The Word of God must come to pass.

In Britain, the Labour Government, led by Tony Blair, had wanted to adopt the European Constitution without granting the British people a vote on it. Under mounting pressure from the Press, Blair changed his mind to allow the ratification of the Treaty to be decided in a referendum. Britons were denied opportunity to vote on the Constitution because it was rejected by the French and the Dutch. However, in 2007, when the German Chancellor, Angela Merkel, planned to impose the rebranded treaty on the masses, Tony Blair declined to give the British people a chance to vote on the new treaty. The question is: If British and European politicians believed that the new treaty was truly for the interest of the masses but not for their 'selfish interest', what prevented them to allow the voters to decide on a document that would govern them? Are politicians better informed on European integration than the masses? Do they hold monopoly of scholarship on the significance of Jean Monnet's project?

THE FRENCH REFERENDUM

On 27 May 2005, the European constitution was ratified by the German parliament in a move designed to influence the French to vote yes in their referendum. However, on 29 May 2005, the French voted NO to reject the Charter of Europe of which their former president, Valery Giscard d'Estaing, was the principal architect. Before the French voted, all the opinion polls suggested the electorate would throw out the constitution. The European Union headquarters in Brussels, faced with the "unacceptable rejection" of the EU Constitutional treaty by France, a founder member of the European project, applied all the economic instruments to flatter the French to vote "YES" to accept the Blue-print for Europe.

For example, on 24 April 2005, a column in The Times read *EU defers wine duty to help Chirac*. It explained how Brussels attempted to influence the vote in France. According to the report, "The proposals to introduce European duty on wine were shelved until a later date." Why? Because, if such a duty were to have been imposed on French wine, the French would have regarded it an assault on their culture. And this, perhaps, could irritate the French to reject the constitution.

The article noted that Joachin Almunia, the Monetary Affairs Commissioner, was "unusually quiet at the prospect of France breaching the eurozone's deficit rules, even though he criticised Italy...for failing to get grips with its public debt."

Before Brussels attempted to influence the French to adopt the constitution, all the EU foreign ministers laboured, in various ways, to manipulate the French to vote "Yes". On 18 April 2005, an article in the Financial Times read "*Europe rallies to save French referendum.*" It was reported: "Europe's foreign ministers ... rallied around the embattled French campaign for the European constitution, arguing that a "No" vote on the May 29 referendum would set back the European Union's drive to play a bigger part on the world stage." The article added that many EU officials feared a "French rejection of the treaty could prove fatal for the constitutional treaty. And this would probably "halt the EU's enlargement drive – sometimes dubbed "The most successful foreign policy in the world." However, the same "successful foreign policy" (EU enlargement) became a thorn in the flesh of EU politicians. In an article headed "EU expansion halted over fears of unrest," Bruno Waterfield reported: "European Union enlargement has been put on hold over fears of a growing backlash against migrant workers." (The Daily Telegraph 25 February 2009)

In Britain, the then Foreign Secretary, Jack Straw, pleaded with the French to adopt the European Constitution. His intervention in French politics caused a controversy, because the British Government had already promised not to interfere in French politics. When reporters challenged Mr Straw's behaviour, he admitted that it was none of Britain's business. Yet he went on to say: "We hope there is a Yes vote. This is a matter for the French people. We need a Yes vote because we believe the Constitution is in the interest of all the people of Europe. If there is a No vote by France or any member state, the EU has a problem..." (Source: Daily Mail 24 May 2005: "Straw urges the French to vote Yes (Only days after Number Ten promised not to interfere") Did Blair and Straw offer Britons the chance to vote on the European Constitution? Hypocrites. They pretend to know all about European integration.

THE SCARE TACTICS

Some European politicians and businessmen even used bullying and intimidating tactics to influence voters to accept the European constitution. On 19 May 2005, Daily Mail reported on how Brussels were twisting arms. According to the paper, the Brussels hierarchy attempted to blackmail voters into backing the constitution of Europe. The EU President, Jose Manuel Barroso, warned France,: "A No vote would have dire political and economic consequences throughout Europe. There would be more uncertainty on the economy which could be bad for consumption and investment."

Valery Giscard d'Estaing, the architect of the Constitution, also cried out: "it is impossible to improve on his design". Gerhard Schroder, the then German Chancellor, told French voters that it was a pure illusion to believe that there is a Plan B. Even terrorist threats were employed to influence the French to vote Yes. Business leaders warned: "Rejection of the treaty would hurt business."

THE PROPHECY OF A DIVIDED KINGDOM WITH MIXED PEOPLE WHO ARE NOT UNITED MUST BE FULFILLED

What happened on the fateful day when the French went to the polls to decide the fate of the proposed European Constitution? 55 percent voted No to reject the treaty, and 45 percent voted Yes. Despite all the pressure from European politicians, who used the "Europe Machinery" to influence the outcome of the vote to suit their prejudices, majority of the French rejected the Blue-print of Europe. It is clear, the 'European machine' failed to swing the vote despite the threats. The inability of European leaders to make intelligent argument to convince their peoples to adopt a document that was intended to make them prosperous and safe from terrorists, demonstrates the moral and intellectual bankruptcy behind Jean Monnet's vision of a federal Europe.

Melanie Phillips' commentary on the French referendum highlighted divisions in the European kingdom that fulfils the prophetic word in Daniel 2:40-43 – a political union of "divided people" with "mixed people who are not united". In her article, *This vote reveals the lies at the heart of the European project,* the columnist wrote: "The French campaign dramatically exposed the profound fault-lines and contradictions at the heart of the whole EU project....Millions of European voters have grasped that the EU project is a swindle. It was sold to them on the false prospectus that it would bring prosperity. Instead, they find their countries are crippled by economic sclerosis.....many do not understand why this has happened. Many French voters who voted 'non' did so for wrong reasons. They believed that the constitution would foist upon them Anglo-Saxon market discipline and expose them to the chill winds of competition from foreign workers. Ironically, this position is the diametric opposite of the British 'no' voters, who rightly fear that further integration with Europe would destroy our economic advantage and leave us similarly crippled. What the French 'non' voters don't seem to grasp is that the whole EU edifice rests on a set of fantasy foundation. The first is the premise that the nation states of Europe have common interests. In fact, they have rather more irreconcilable social, political and cultural differences --- and their economic interests lie in being in competition with each other, the very thing the EU is in business to stifle." (Daily Mail 30 May 2005).

And on Saturday 28 May 2005, The Times published an article which also emphasised the fact that the European Union is a "Kingdom" of mixed people who are

not united. The title of the report read *"All together now: French rivals sing resounding chorus of 'non': The two extremes of French politics find themselves on the same side of the argument."* According to the reporter, Ben Macintyre, "Millions of mainstream voters opposed to the constitution ..... a baffling array of nay-sayers, from disgruntled farmers to trade unionists, from revolutionary Communists to ardent nationalists. An inchoate group, mutually contradictory and deeply divided, the rejectionists have nothing in common save their shared antipathy to constitutional treaty laid out by European bureaucrats and backed by the French elite."

Javier Solana, the European Union foreign policy representative, commented on the negative sentiments about the European project with this declaration: "Europeans are suffering from self-doubt at a moment when the world needs Europe all the more". And Benita Ferrero –Waldner, the EU External Relations Commissioner, also remarked: "If we want Europe to play a role in the world, it is necessary to be in favour of the constitution."

We must ask the question: "On what ground has the European Union's enlargement become the "most successful foreign policy in the world?" Surely, the world would need Europe *"all the more"*, but for a different reason which European politicians have not envisaged, and which the "master builder" of the European Enterprise, Jean Monnet, did not have a clue. The prophetic messages in Daniel 2:36 – 48 about the *"10 toes"* of the human statue; the *"10 horns"* of a *"beast"* in Daniel 7:7; the beast with *"7 heads"* and *"10 horns"* in Revelation 13:1, and the *"10 kings,"* in Revelation 17:12-13 must be fulfilled. For this reason the European Union must be enlarged to play a bigger role in the world to bring the Word of God to pass. Because, the coming King of Men, who will rule the world, would hail from the revived Roman Empire of which the European Union is its foundation block.

THE DUTCH REFERENDUM

On Wednesday, 1 June 2005, the people of Netherlands also voted to throw out the constitutional treaty. The referendum process to endorse or reject the European constitution exposed divisions among national and international politicians, political commentators, business leaders and the ordinary citizens of Europe. Without any doubt, there were individuals who supported the constitution and those who opposed it – a picture of a divided kingdom with divided people who are not united. The prophetic word in Daniel 2:41-43 has been fulfilled.

DIFFERENT VIEWS ON THE EUROPEAN CONSTITUTION AND DIVISIONS AMONG NATIONAL POLITICIANS

On 18 January 2005, a title in the Financial Times Leader and Letters column read: "Instead of a constitution or a treaty, the EU has produced an inaccessible impractical mess." And on 1 February 2005, another column in the same newspaper read: "Treaty will help simplify officialdom."

Before the German Members of Parliament voted on 12 May 2005 to back the controversial EU constitution, the German Chancellor, Gerhard Schroeder, told them: "Don't bother with the details....I would like to ask you in this moment, not to be too petty or too obsessed by detail in staring at the odd half-sentence in the odd paragraph that may not meet our expectations." However, a conservative Member of the Parliament, Peter Gauweiler, responded, "It (the constitution) certainly doesn't meet my expectations. I believe the devil is in the detail, and always have done." (Daily Mail, Friday May, 13, 2005).

The question is: "Who, in his right mind, would sign a contract without bothering to scrutinize the odd half-sentence in the odd paragraph?" Yet, this was exactly the case with German Parliamentarians. The ruling elite wanted to force the Germans to accept the European Constitution without any discussion. This is the "True" democracy the European Union boasts of - the "beacon of light" that is shining from the "political phenomenon" created by the "smuggler" Jean Monnet to illuminate the "dark" world. What an illusion!

On 10 February 2005, The Sun newspaper published an article titled: *"LABOUR CLASH ON EU CONSTITUTION – STRAW V BLAIR."* It painted different views on the Constitution among British politicians, as well as differences between the British and the French governments. According to The Sun, Jack Straw, the British Foreign Secretary, told BBC Radio, "This constitution is a victory for Britain and the British view of Europe. Mr Straw went further: "...the document (the European Constitution) CURBS the EU's powers to set British laws....It was a major victory for Britain over Europeans....What this does is say, "This far and no further and actually brings back influence to the nation states." Mr. Straw's comments directly clashed with Mr Blair's position who, in November 2002, declared the exact opposite. At a speech in Cardiff, the Prime Minister said, "We must end the nonsense of "This far and no further." The question is: "Which of these British politicians was right?" This was a clear demonstration of division among domestic politicians who were confused about the whole EU Project.

The British Government's policy on the European constitution was again plunged into confusion when Mr. Straw was contradicted by his own deputy. The then Foreign Secretary claimed the treaty would end future negotiations on the balance of power. But his deputy, the then EU Minister, Denis MacShane, had said few weeks earlier, that "Europe is very young – this won't be the last word." The Sun further reported: "Mr Straw told MPs, Britain risked being isolated by rejecting the constitution in a referendum. But the then Shadow Foreign Secretary, Michael Ancram, blasted ministers for lying about the extent of the constitution's power grab." This, again, was another demonstration of division among national politicians who have no idea what the European Union is for.

DIVISIONS AMONG EUROPEAN GOVERNMENTS:
The Battle between Britain and France

The Sun also highlighted the different views on the European Constitution by British and French governments. According to the British Foreign Secretary, "This constitution is a victory for Britain and the British view of Europe". However, few weeks before Mr Straw's declaration, the French President, Jacques Chirac, announced that "the EU treaty was a huge triumph for his country." The constitution, according to the French President, "represented a significant defeat for British interests." Mr Chirac described the constitution on his website: "the crowning of what one could call the French vision for Europe, against the Anglo-Saxon vision. This constitution was wanted by France. No other country has played a more important role in its creation and its elaboration." We have seen a picture of a "divided "European Union. The prophetic Word of God in Daniel 2:40-43 must be fulfilled: This "kingdom" will be divided**,** the people will be a "mixture**"** and will "not remain united, just as iron does not mix with clay."

THE FOOLISH AND PERILOUS PRIDE OF THE FRENCH

Why did the French President boast about France's contribution to the European Constitution? Was Chirac aware that before Jean Monnet, the French architect of European Community, the "god of Europe," was born in 1888, a British public servant had already written about a political alliance of European nations and its future? Had the French President read what the "unknown Irishman" wrote about European integration: how it would develop, its nature and future prospects before the French "genius", Jean Monnet, was conceived, he would have kept mute. The 'obstinate' Monnet was only an instrument to bring to pass what the British "giant" had already written about Europe. The French 'apostle of European unity' was just a "labourer" who toiled to create a United States of Europe to fulfil the vision of his British "master" whom he never knew. "Mister Europe" would not have qualified to stoop and untie the bootstraps of the British 'giant.' It is time the French remained silent and stopped boasting about the 'obstinate' Jean Monnet, and their contribution towards "the vile confederacy of the latter days." At the end of our discussion I will put Jean Monnet (the French 'prophet' and 'revolutionary') and the "Forgotten son" of Britain (the Anglo-Saxon visionary) on a scale for the world to 'weigh' them.

DIVISIONS AMONG BUSINESS COMMUNITY

The business community also held conflicting views on the significance of the European Constitution. Some British businessmen claimed in a letter to the Financial Times on 25 February 2005, that the British people should welcome the Constitution, "because it will make it easier to do business throughout the world's largest trading block – a market into which more than 50 percent of our goods are exported and upon which more than 3million jobs in our country depend. It will also ensure that Britain remains at the top table, taking a leading role in the decision–making processes on key issues that affect our country, our businesses and the people who work in them." This view was subsequently challenged and undermined.

On 2 March 2005, a title in the letters column of Financial Times read: "Top table status in the EU does not ensure tastiest deals." This title contradicted the positive economic benefits which had been expressed by Euro-phile business men. G M Simon expressed his economic view on the European Constitution in a letter to the Financial Times. He stated: "FT commented on the fact that Britain's multi-billion pound art market was in danger of moving to New York because of new regulations imposed by the European Commission. Perhaps the signatories to the letter (Dated 25 February 2005, which claimed Britain's ratification of the constitution would ensure Britain remains at the top table in European discussions) would now write to you explaining how it is that, notwithstanding the top table status, such decisions are taken to the disadvantage of UK interests. It would seem that sitting at the top table does not ensure a palatable menu" (G M Simon, Moreton-in-Marsh, Gloss).

Again, the positive view of the European Constitution was disputed in an article published in the 27 January 2005 edition of the Daily Mail. In a column titled "*Selling Britain down the river,*" Edward Heathcoat-Amory, a Conservative Party Member of Parliament, and a former delegate to the Convention on the Future of Europe, reported: "This country (Britain) has surrendered to Brussels...that Britain has no right to block legislation we no longer have a veto." And commenting on the Constitution, the Daily Mail editorial recorded: "This constitution doesn't simply involve a massive loss of national independence over immigration. It will strip us of power to control our economy, foreign policy, criminal justice and much else – all contentious issues."

Peter Hain, a Labour politician, once described the European constitution as a "tidying-up exercise." But political commentator, Peter Riddell, contrasted this view by stating the EU constitution "is more than tidying – up, it is not a centralised European state. It is a compromise between closer integration to take account of enlargement to 25 members..." (The Times, 3 February 2005)

On 23 March 2005, Roland Vaubel, Professor of Economics at the University of Mannheim, sent a letter on behalf of the *European Constitutional Group* to the Financial Times to express their opposition to the Constitution. There were more than 100 signatories of academics to this letter. These intellectuals united in rejecting the agreement reached by heads of states on the proposed European Constitution on the following grounds:

1. The proposed constitution paves the way for ever more matters to be decided at an ever-increasing distance from the citizen…
2. The proposed constitution opens up numerous new avenues for increased regulation in Europe's competitiveness in the world economy…
3. By centralising policymaking, the proposed constitution gives the state more power over the citizens and suppress international differences..
4. The constitution was a complicated and ambiguous document.
5. The letter went on: "important matters such as whether or not the Union has the power to tax or how the charter of rights is to be applied have been left deliberately obscure, or have become hopelessly over-complicated."

The letter concluded, "We do not deny that the proposed constitution contains some positive elements. But on balance it clearly makes things worse. It pushes people still further away from those who exercise power in their name. It must be rejected."

From the differing views expressed by British politicians, political commentators, European politicians, business communities and academics, could we say the European Union is a "United kingdom with united people", or the European Union is a "divided kingdom with divided people who remain un-united"? Daniel 2:41-43 provided the answer over 2600 years before Jean Monnet helped Robert Schuman to sow the seed of European Union on 9 May 1950.

DIVISIONS AMONG EUROPEAN GOVERNMENTS

Finally, before Spain voted in a referendum on 20 February 2005 to endorse the European constitution, The Times published an article *"EU truth has many faces as polls get rivals into a state."* The correspondents, Charles Bremmer, Roger Boyes and Adam LeBor, also highlighted the diverse views European politicians and the electorate held on the European Union and its proposed constitution.

According to the political commentators, "From Dublin to Warsaw, governments are tailoring their portrayals of the constitution to maximise its appeal to their particular electorates, while opponents are doing exactly the opposite…" They stated:

- The most glaring contrast lied between Britain and France. President Chirac played up the treaty as the consecration of Europe as a super welfare state along French lines. Tony Blair, by contrast, depicted it as a guarantee of British sovereignty, complete with vetos and inviolable "red lines."
- Many Danes and Dutch regarded the treaty as a dangerous open door to Turkey and Muslim immigration...Dutch resistance sprang less from what is in the constitution than from national identity crisis over immigration, and anger at France and Germany's flouting of eurozone budget rules.
- In Luxembourg, the treaty was viewed as a welcome step towards political union. That opinion was shared in Germany.
- In Germany, the public saw the constitution as the creation of a political voice for Europe to face down the United States.
- For the Irish, the constitution was a promise of further aid-driven prosperity, but opponents saw its defence element as a threat to the neutrality of the Irish.
- Wolfgang Schuessed, Austria's Chancellor, argued that the constitution protected smaller member states. "If the constitution fails," he said, "the big countries will be able to carry out plans that we have been wanting to prevent."
- ...In Prague, President Klaus, one of the Union's biggest sceptics, saw the constitution as a dangerous infringement of sovereignty, while Stanislav Gross, the Prime Minister and his political opponent, said the Czech Republic badly needed it because "if we say no, we will stand alone."
- In Poland, happiness over European largesse for its farmers was helping to boost the generally positive view of the constitution. Traditionalists, however, saw the absence of allusion to Europe's Christianity as a blow against Poland's Roman Catholic roots.
- In France, critics claimed the constitution would kill "Social Europe" by turning it into an unregulated free-trading zone. Powerful opponents from the French Right and Left branded it a British blueprint for an Americanised Union.
- British Euro-sceptics painted the treaty, which was drafted under the leadership of the former French President, Valery Giscard d'Estaing, as a French-inspired plot for a federal super-state".

On 1 March 2005, a space in the Financial Times read *Danes set date for EU constitution vote.* It was reported the European constitution was "supported by more than four-fifths of the Danish Parliament. An Eurobarometer poll published in December put Danish voter support at 44 percent, opposition at 26 percent and those undecided at 30 percent." It was also reported that opponents of the constitutional treaty, which included Pa Kjaersgaard, the Danish People's Party.... criticised the new treaty as "an elitist project" aimed at creating a "United States of Europe." "I am convinced that the Danish people do not want to be part of an EU state", a politician concluded. And another Danish politician, "Ole Krarup, a member of the European parliament for the People's Movement against the EU, said the constitutional treaty was "the final step to a militarised EU superstate aiming to control Denmark down to the tiniest detail."

"ARE WE FOOLS LED BY LIARS?"

Again, all these articles and reports paint a picture of a "United Kingdom of Europe" whose leaders and citizens are divided on an issue that should have united them. William Ress-Mogg summed up the different views on the European Constitution MK1 in his article *"Are we fools led by liars?"* He posed the question: "WHO'S GOT it right? The German Minister for Europe, Hans Martin Bury, or the Foreign Secretary of the United Kingdom, Jack Straw?....Herr Bury told the Bundestag that the constitution of the European Union is more than a 'milestone', it is "the birth certificate of the United States of Europe". But previously, "Mr Straw said, the constitutional treaty signalled "thus far and no further on European integration." Is the treaty a boundary marker for European integration or is it a birth certificate for "a single European state bound by one European constitution," to use the language of the German Foreign Minister, Joschka Fischer?" (The Times Monday, 28 February 2005).

The different opinions expressed on the Constitution of Europe by political leaders and their electorate exposed the European Union as a divided kingdom with people of different tongues and culture who are not united. This situation, again, confirms the prophetic significance of the "*10 toes*" of the human image Nebuchadnezzar saw. "As the toes were partly iron and partly clay, so ...this kingdom will be a divided kingdom....so the people will be a mixture and will not remain united any more than iron mixes with clay" (Daniel 2:43).

THE LUXEMBOURG REFERENDUM

On 10 July 2005, the people of Luxembourg, who are compelled by law to vote, endorsed the European Constitutional treaty by 56.52 percent to 43.48. Even in Luxembourg, a founding member of the European Union, there were division. The vote took place under a threat from the Luxembourg Prime Minister, Jean-Claude Juncker, that he would resign if the people voted "No" to reject the constitution. The result of the Luxembourg vote meant that 13 out of the then 25 member-states of the European Union ratified the constitutional treaty.

The Luxembourg ratification of the Constitution was seen to have injected life into the *corpse.* Why? Because, the constitution was pronounced dead when the French and the Netherlands rejected it. However, opponents of the European Constitution insisted the Constitution was dead. In an article entitled: "EU constitution gets a little boost after Luxembourg says yes – just", the writer, Anthony Browne, quoted the words of Neil O'Brien, the campaign director of the "no" campaign in Britain: "If supporters of the constitution think "yes" vote in Luxembourg somehow cancels out the French and Dutch votes, they have completely lost touch with reality" (The Times Monday July 11, 2005). Once again we witness a "divided kingdom," with mixed people who are not united.

The European Union, which was initially an Economic Community of 6 Western European countries, but now a political union of 27 Eastern and Western European countries (with other countries waiting to join), is gradually heading towards the complete fulfilment of the prophetic message coded in the 10 toes of the magnificent statue which were partly of baked clay and partly of iron. (Daniel 2:41-43). These "ten toes" correspond to the "ten horns on the 4th dreadful beast in Daniel 7:7. The same "ten toes" correspond to the "ten horns of the beast" in Revelation 13:1 and also the beast with seven heads and ten horns in Revelation 17:3. The same 10 horns of the beast are related to the "10 horns" of the enormous red dragon in Revelation 12:3.

The question is: what are these "10 horns on the 4th beast?" Daniel 7:23-25 explains it: "The fourth beast shall be the fourth kingdom upon earth, which shall be diverse from all kingdoms, and shall devour the whole earth, and shall tread it down, and break it in pieces. And **the ten horns** out of this kingdom are **ten kings** that shall arise: and another shall rise after them; and shall be diverse from the first and he shall subdue three kings. And he shall speak great words against the Most High, and shall wear out the saints of the Most High, and think to change times and laws; and they shall be given into his hand until a time and times and the dividing of time (3½ years KJ)." As we progress with our study, we will learn more about the significance of the relationship between the "ten toes" of the great human image and the "ten horns of the fourth beast."

THE SIGNIFICANCE OF THE "10 TOES" AND THE RATIONALISTS

I have shared with you the meaning of the "10 toes" of the human image. So that you might not be deceived by misleading interpretation of the "10 toes" by some so-called Bible experts, I will close this chapter by dismissing a particular argument that has been advanced by trendy theologians to undermine the implication of the "10 toes" of the human statue Nebuchadnezzar saw.

We have discovered how the Book of Daniel prophetically described in detail the development of the European Union and its character. This divine revelation of the next major political feature in history after the restoration of the Jews to Palestine is seen in the "10 toes" of the magnificent statue which were partly of baked clay and partly of iron. I have already mentioned that because of the extraordinary accuracy of the predictions in the Book of Daniel, this Old Testament Book has become the subject of hostile attacks by liberal theologians, bishops and clergymen. Their champion in England was Professor S R Driver, a nineteen century scholar at Oxford University. Professor Driver was the first English Bible scholar, who in 1892, published his *Book of Daniel* to undermine the genuineness and Divine character of the Book of Daniel.

'Sophisticated' intellectuals, using their rational minds, argued that the Book of Daniel was a religious novel, an "edifying fiction", which was written in the second century after the events had already taken place. So, to defend their "edifying fiction" theory, they attempted to undermine the prophetic message scripted in the *"10 toes"* of baked clay and iron of the statue by excluding the Roman Empire from the fourth section of the dazzling human image which is symbolised by the two legs of iron and the fourth dreadful beast with iron teeth which Daniel saw (Daniel 7:7). According to the 'blind' Rationalists, who only read the black letters in the Bible, this horrible beast did not represent the Roman Empire but the Grecian Empire of Alexander the Great. With this false interpretation they suggested that the "10 toes" of clay and iron symbolised the 10 kingdoms of the Seleucidae – one of the 4 kingdoms that evolved from the Grecian empire after the death of Alexander the Great.

If Scripture should be interpreted with Scripture, but not with 'university knowledge,' then Scripture does not support the Rationalists interpretation of the two legs of iron of the human image which are symbolised by the fourth terrible beast. For scripture clearly teaches, that the "10 toes" of the human statue correspond to the "10 horns" of the dreadful beasts, and these "10 horns" represent "10 kings" (Daniel 7:24). By interpreting Scripture with Scripture, we notice that these same "10 horns" and "10 kings" appear in the Book of Revelation. For Revelation 13:1 and Revelation 17:12 tell us Apostle John saw "10 horns" on a beast, and these horns represent "10 kings." Witness the words of the Angel of the Lord: "*The ten horns you saw are ten kings who have not received a kingdom, but who for one hour will receive authority as kings with the beast.*" It is clear from this Scripture that when John saw the vision in about 90AD, the "10 kingdoms" have not come into existence. So, how could these ten kingdoms refer to the ten kingdoms of the Seleucide, since these kingdoms evolved from Alexander the Great's Macedonian-Grecian Empire? It was after the death of the Greek warrior that his four generals divided his empire into 4 kingdoms of which the Seleucide was one of them.

In the 19th century, Dr Edward Pusey rightly dismissed the Rationalists misleading interpretation of the "10 toes". In Lecture II of Dr. Pusey's *Daniel the Prophet*, the

Regius Professor of Hebrew at Oxford, writes: "The kingdoms of the Seleucidae and the Ptolemies, ever at variance with one another, had no unity, they were in no sense a kingdom, except as they were connected with the great Empire–plan of Alexander. They were continuous of the Greek predominance over the nations of Oriental character in Asia Minor, Egypt, Assyria."

Dr Pusey went on to comment on the fourth empire which was symbolised by the 2 legs of iron of the human statue and its ten toes of clay and iron. The Oxford Professor recorded: "In the fourth Empire we have again strength yet greater than in the third Empire, ending in greater division; yet, even in its division, retaining to the end, in its several portions, its original iron might......" Dr Pusey continued with an explanation of the fourth kingdom of Iron, Rome: "Twofold in its form, as the Roman power, itself one, came to be divided into East and West, it ends in yet further division into ten kingdoms; and iron commingles itself with a material as plastic, as itself is unyielding, potter's clay. This as Daniel interprets it, expresses partly the mingled strengths and weakness of the later condition of the empire, strong as before, in some parts, yet side by side with weakness, partly the union of this fourth empire with that which was foreign from itself, through intermarriages, *the seed of men*, whereby however the two powers do not cohere. History down to Antiochus Epiphanes exhibits nothing of this sort. There was no such subdivision into ten; no three which were uprooted. A union moreover between the Seleucidae and Ptolemies by intermarriages would have been an union of like, not of unlike, materials. It would have been a cementing of kingdom within itself, iron with iron, not iron with clay..."

When Dr Pusey's series of lectures on the Book of Daniel were published in 1885 as a complete Book titled *Daniel the prophet,* the "10 toes of iron and clay" have not manifested. However, in 1881, the "Forgotten Ulsterman', who was a lay Christian, had already written that the *"10 toes of iron and clay"* would manifest after the rebirth of the nation of Israel. Let's listen to the "Prophet of Linden Gardens":
"Next to the restoration of the Jews to Palestine, the most prominent political feature of the future is the partition of the Roman earth....It is impossible to foretell how far kingdoms may be consolidated and boundaries may be changed. In forecasting the fulfilment of these...we are dealing with events which, while they may occur within the lifetime of living men, may yet be delayed for centuries...we may rest content with the certainty that...their fulfilment will be clear...to all who are capable of observing public facts......Through the gradual unfolding it may be of influences even now in operation; or far more probably as the outcome of some great European crisis in the future. This confederation of (European) nations shall be developed and thus ...." I will continue with this prophetic word later on.

Chapter 7
What is European Union for?

"..Just as the studies which charm the naturalist are an unknown world to those who are ignorant of the book of nature, so also are elements which make the Bible a fascinating volume to the believer do not exist for those who fail to possess the clew to its mysteries. Truth brings out the hidden harmony, where unbelief can only with a dull dogmatism deny" **(A Doubter's Doubts about Science and Religion: RA)**

I would, again, refer to the question Minette Marrin posed in the 29 May 2005 edition of The Sunday Times. "It's getting hard to avoid the question: what is Europe for?" This is the simple question which underlines the whole project but is rarely asked and rarely answered....If you ask Europhiles what the European project is for, they will respond with incredulity and perhaps even mild contempt..."

The issue is: if "the European Union is the rarest of all phenomena in history" as suggested by Francois Duchene, the Internationalist who witnessed the birth of the European Union; if the European Union is the biggest political alliance in the world and the largest economic market right on our doorstep, of which it would be an act of extraordinary foolishness for Britain as a country to withdraw from it, as suggested by Tony Blair (Daily Mail 16 June 2004), then it is imperative we answer the question: "What is Europe for?"

In view of contemporary events, and from the context of history and spiritual perspective, let us examine the actual purpose of an Economic Community of six European nations that has now developed into a political union of 27 nations. We know in 1929 a French patriot, Aristide Briand, proposed a "federal link between the peoples of Europe". Before Briand's proposal, the Austro-Hungarian Diplomat, Richard Koudenhove-Kalergi, had, in 1923, raised the issue of European integration: "The European Question will only be solved by means of the Union of European nations," he declared.

We have also learnt that in 1943 Jean Monnet propounded his philosophy: "To create Europe is to create peace". The 'apostle of European unity' delivered his 'prophetic sermon': "Once a common market has been created, then a political union will come naturally.... I have no doubt, for my part, that a confederation [of European nations] will one day lead to a federation" (Memoirs 1978). Monnet presented his idea of European unity to Robert Schuman after previous inaction by the League of Nations. In 1946, Sir Winston Churchill made a speech in Zurich about the plight of Europe – a continent with some smaller states. His sovereign remedy was to re-create European Family – to build a kind of United States of Europe which would "champion its right to live and shine."

I have already mentioned that European politicians and some political commentators have construed Churchill's view as being in favour of Britain's participation in a United States of Europe. For example, Professor Ulrich Beck, in his essay, "Nation-state politics can only fail the problems of the modern world" (The Guardian 15 January 2007), quoted Winston Churchill to somehow suggest the British Statesman favoured a federal Europe of which Britain would become a province. Winston Churchill did not advocate for Britain to join a United States of Europe. Remember what he said in 1952: "I love France and Belgium, but we must not allow ourselves to be pulled down to that level."

In 1950, Robert Schuman, the French foreign minister who was once put "on the path to sainthood" by the Catholic Church (The Times 3 March 2004), planted the seeds of political unification of European nations with an economic plan – the pooling together of the coal and steel resources of France, Germany, Italy, Belgium, Netherlands and Luxembourg – under a common administration.

The Treaty of Paris in 1951 created The European Coal and Steel Community. In 1952 this Community was established to bring together the member-states' resources of coal, steel and iron-ore into a single market. This was the foundation block for the European Economic Community. After the Treaty of Paris, Konrad Adenauer, the first Chancellor of the Federal Republic of Germany (West Germany) supported the political union of European nations by declaring, "In my opinion and belief....the political meaning of the European Coal and Steel Community is infinitely larger than its economic purpose."

In 1957 the Treaty of Rome was signed to give birth to the Common Market. In 1961 the six countries declared their desire for a closer political union. The seed of a "Mighty Political kingdom" was sown. This fact was confirmed by Dietrich Von Kyaw in his article: *"Don't stretch Europe's promised Land"*. He declared: **"....**We have to accept that these days the EU is no longer merely an economic union of countries that share common interests and values. It has also become a_political union that brings stability to the continent**....**" (Financial Times 7 November 2003). This statement confirmed Konrad Adenauer's view of European integration. In a speech made on 12 July 1952, the German stated that in his opinion the six members of the European Coal and Steel Community should realise that the political meaning of the European Coal and Steel Community is larger than its economic purpose.

In 1962 The Common Agricultural Policy was introduced. The purpose of this Policy was to protect European farmers so that the Community would not depend on imports from overseas. The farmers were assured a fair price for their produce.

Between 1972 and 1973 Britain, Ireland and Denmark joined the Community. Greece joined in 1981. And in 1986 Spain and Portugal became members. In 1998 The Single European Act was agreed, and a year later The European Monetary Union and the Social Chapter were introduced. In 1992 The Maastricht Treaty on closer union took place. In that same year of 1992, all trade barriers within the European Economic Community had been abolished. A single European Market was created. The aim was to ensure that goods, money and citizens of the Community would enter national frontiers without restrictions. At the same time Custom Duties were imposed on all goods imported from outside the Community. Each member country was obliged to return the revenue from such duties into the Community to help finance it. At this point it is obvious the European Economic Community, which was initially created for economic purpose, had a hidden motive to turn it into super-state controlled by unelected strangers accountable to no one. Jean Monnet made it plain in his interview with Leonard Gross. "Mister Europe" stated: "The Common Market changed the attitude of the producers. A static society gets transformed if you touch the right point – and we touched the right point...As the process grows, the inevitable necessity of some kind of political authority emerges. You can't do without it. In fact, it already exists...." (*Look* 26 November 1968)

In 1995, Austria, Finland and Sweden joined the Community. In 1998 The European Central Bank was established. Over the years membership of the Community increased from six nations to fifteen states to form the European Union. In 1999 a single currency for the Union was launched in Austria, Belgium, Finland, France, Germany, Ireland, Italy, Luxembourg, The Netherlands, Portugal and Spain. Negotiation then began to enlarge the Community by welcoming countries from Eastern Europe. The seed of a "kingdom", which was sown in 1961, has started to shoot.

THE BIRTH OF A GREAT EMPIRE

In 2000, The Nice Treaty paved the way for the enlargement of the European kingdom. In the same year Euro Currency (the glory of Europe) was introduced, and the first meeting took place on the future of Europe, whereby it was decided to draw up a draft constitution for the European Union. It was also agreed that Cyprus (Greek part), the Czech Republic, Estonia, Hungary, Latvia, Lithuania, Malta, Poland, Slovakia and Slovenia should join the Union.

In December 2003 a draft constitution for the European Union was prepared. On 1 May 2004 the countries from Eastern Europe joined the Union. On 13 June 2004 the draft constitution of Europe was adopted. A Great Political kingdom was born – "creating an empire that could stretch from Galway to Gdansk" (Daily Mail, 4 October 2002*)*. The tiny seed sown in 1952, which started to shoot in 1961, finally produced a "fruit." The "fruit" is gradually ripening.

In summary: from 1951 up to 2004 a Community of six nations increased its membership to become a Political Union of twenty five members. In January 2007 Bulgaria and Romania joined the European Union. Membership of the Empire increased to twenty seven. Prospective members including Croatia, Macedonia and Turkey are on the waiting list to join the political phenomenon and the largest trading-block of the 21st century. On 13 December 2007 the 27 EU leaders signed the Lisbon Treaty. This was the discredited constitution repackaged to fool the masses as a new treaty which did not merit a referendum.

On 20 May 2005, Dr. D R Cooper wrote to Financial Times to express his concern about how the European Constitution and its laws would have primacy over national and constitutional laws of the member-states. He exposed the cynical and deceptive intention of the political elite behind the European Enterprise. He wrote: "Before Britain joined the European Economic Community, we were assured that we would simply be transferring from one international trading block, European Free Trade Area, to a better alternative...we expected to follow EEC rules, and we later agreed to follow World Trade Organisation rules..."

THE PURPOSE OF EUROPE

The European Economic Community, an economic seed sown in 1950, has now grown to become an European Union, a "delicious political fruit," in 2008. A seed must produce its kind. We must ask the question: "Why has a Community of six European nations, which came together to form the European Coal and Steel Community for economic reasons, has now developed into a political "Empire" of twenty seven Western and Eastern European countries – with all the symbols of nationhood: a single currency, a common flag, an anthem, a Parliament, a Court of Justice, a Common Agricultural Policy, a Central Bank and a Constitution? The answer is simple: to bring to pass what a British public servant wrote in 1881 about a political union of European nations that would develop through an European crisis.

EUROPEAN UNION: "THE FEET AND TOES - PARTLY CLAY AND PARTLY IRON – TO FULFIL BIBLE PROPHECY

In the eyes of politicians and political intellectuals the European Union was created to enhance political, economic and social co-operation among its members, and to bring peace, prosperity and security to its citizens. Today, this political union is seen, primarily by the French and the Germans, as a fulfilment of the dreams of their 'Patrons' Jean Monnet, Robert Schuman and Konrad Adenauer. According to Jean Monnet, whom Dag Hammarskjöld described as a "revolutionary", peace in Europe could only be achieved through political unity among European states. And Konrad Adenauer, also declared: "A union between France and Germany would give new life and vigour to Europe that is seriously ill….In the future United States of Europe, I saw great hope for Europe…"

Notwithstanding the 'visions' of the French and German statesmen, the reality is that the European Union developed from the ashes of the Second World War to bring to pass what an Irishman had already written about political Europe and its future. Ultimately, political Europe would fulfil the prophetic message coded in *"The feet and toes of the human statue which were partly of baked clay and partly of iron."* We know it was this vision of a magnificent human sculpture that troubled King Nebuchadnezzar of Babylon to the extent that he threatened to kill the astrologers, magicians and the wise men who could not explain the vision to him (Daniel 2:10-33).

Nothing on planet earth happens by chance. The Heavens rule; not 'blind' politicians who 'cry': "Change, Change, Change"; "Reform, Reform, "Reform", and do not know where the "Change" and the "Reform" would come from because they don't know the future. The Sovereignty of God is behind all political, social and economic events. The world Empires - from the Babylonian Empire to the present "European Empire" - are under the rule of God (Daniel 4:34-35) to accomplish His eternal purpose.

THE DESTINY OF THE EUROPEAN UNION AND HUMAN GOVERNMENTS

We have learnt from the Book of Daniel how the European Union, the revived Roman Empire, is symbolised by the 10 toes of the splendid human image which were partly of baked clay and partly of iron. (Daniel 2:41-43). This means the fate of the human statue King Nebuchadnezzar saw in his dream, would also determine the destiny of the European Empire. In other words, the providence of the European Union is directly linked to the destiny of all the world powers that have ruled on earth since the Jews were deported to Babylon in 606BC. The fate of these Empires (Babylon, Medo-Persia, Greece and Rome) was revealed to Daniel when the meaning of King Nebuchadnezzar's dream was explained to him.

WHY "TOES OF BAKED CLAY' AND NOT OF ANY OTHER SUBSTANCE?

Before we examine the destiny of human governments, including the European Union, which is the revived Roman Empire in its infancy, it is important for us to establish the significance of the "baked clay" in the "10 toes" of the magnificent human image. The Bible teaches that God used stiff, sticky earth (clay) to form man (Genesis 2:7). The prophet Isaiah declared: "....O Lord thou art our Father, we are the clay, and thou our potter. And we are all the works of thy hand" (Isaiah 64:8 KJ). It is clear from this scripture that clay, the substance of human body, is a symbol for the frail, mortal man. This means the "baked clay" in the "10 toes" of the human statue signifies how the 10 powerful leaders in the European Empire of mixed people who are not united would use human philosophies which are not reliable (fragile like clay) - and not the perfect commandments of God - to govern Europeans.

And just as how the "clay-man" (Adam) fell because of his disobedience and was driven out from the Paradise of eternal life to sweat for his daily bread and to return to the dust from which he was created, so would the kingdoms of men collapse. Why? Because human governments apply human intelligence and wisdom, which are foolishness in the sight of God (1 Corinthians 1:20-25), to rule. The inevitable destruction of worldly powers (the political Babylon) was also revealed to Nebuchadnezzar in his dream. The Emperor of Babylon saw a 'stone' striking the toes of the human statue and the whole effigy breaking into pieces. For Daniel 2:34-36 tell us, while King Nebuchadnezzar was watching the enormous human statue, "a rock ... cut out ... not by human hands .... struck the statue on its feet of iron and clay and smashed them. Then the iron, the clay, the bronze, the silver, and the gold were broken to pieces at the same time and became like chaff on a threshing-floor in the summer. The wind swept them away without leaving a trace. But the rock that struck the statue became a huge mountain and filled the whole earth." And this is Daniel's interpretation of this portion of Nebuchadnezzar's dream: "In the time of those kings, the God of heavens will set up a kingdom that will never be destroyed, nor will it be left to another people. It will crush all these kingdoms and bring them to an end, but it will itself endure for ever. This is the meaning of the vision of the rock cut out of mountain, but not by human hands - a rock that broke the iron, the bronze, the clay, the silver and the gold to pieces." (Daniel 2:44-45). Thereafter, Daniel addressed King Nebuchadnezzar: "The great God has shown the king what will take place in the future. The dream is true and the interpretation is trustworthy" (Daniel 2:45).

WHAT IS THIS 'ROCK'?

The question is: what is this "rock cut out of mountain, but not by human hands that broke the iron, the bronze, the clay, the silver and gold of the human statue to pieces"? Scripture interprets itself. Let us, therefore, search through Scriptures for an answer.

According to the Gospels, when the chief priests and the elders questioned the Lord Jesus Christ by what authority did He perform miracles and teach, the Lord replied among other things saying; *"Have you never read the Scriptures: "The stone the builders rejected has become the capstone;......He who falls on this stone will be broken into pieces, but he on whom it falls will be crushed"* (Matthew 21:42-44). With this response to the doubting scribes and elders, it is obvious the Lord Jesus Christ referred to Himself as the "Stone" that would crush people into pieces. By implication, our Divine Lord is the "stone cut without human hands" which would crush the "human statue" on its feet of iron and clay, and break the whole human effigy into pieces to become like chaff on a threshing-floor in the summer to leave no trace of them. This means, at the appointed time, the Lord of lords and the King of kings will return to overthrow human governments that have rebelled against Him. This WILL SURELY HAPPEN.

GOD CANNOT BE MOCKED

Why such a drastic action by a loving and merciful God? The answer is simple: God cannot be mocked. All national governments – whether of the first world, the second world, the third world or the fifth world – do not serve God. They do not promote the interest of their Creator. They claim there is no God. There is no Creator. Man evolved from an ape, and the "brute-man" must be glorified by virtue of his intelligence and achievements. Most policies and laws of all political systems undermine the Commandments of God. Thus human governments - from the age of Tower of Babel - have been opposing God. So, in His fury, the "Rock of Ages" will crush those who ridiculed and opposed Him into powder. There would be no trace of them. The Lord declares: "Woe to the obstinate children, to those who carry out plans that are not mine, forming an alliance, but not by my Spirit, heaping sin upon sin; who go down to Egypt without consulting me; who look for help to Pharaoh's protection..." (Isaiah 30:1-2).

The apostate church, the religious Babylon, the "bride" of the political Babylon, would also face the fury of the Lord. The degraded Church has also condoned with the world to undermine the Commandments of the Creator of Heaven and Earth. The Lord warns us: "Come out of her (Babylon) my people, so that you will not share in her sins, so that you will not receive any of her plagues" (Revelation 18:4). Judgement begins with the family of God (1 Peter 4:17). It takes a wise man to avert a prophecy.

"888" WILL DESTROY "666"

Because human governments resist God and formulate laws that undermine His Commandments, the Lord Jesus Christ, the "Stone cut without human hands", will destroy all worldly powers. Let us witness a 'film' of the destruction of world powers which was "screened" in the Book of Samuel. This "film" would become a reality. The Old Testament Book of Samuel teaches that the Philistine giant, Goliath, defied the army of God. The pagan brute taunted the Israelites to select one of their soldiers to face him. To the surprise of this heathen monster, he was confronted by a young shepherd boy, David. This Hebrew lad slew Goliath with a single stone from the five stones he had collected from a stream.

According to 1 Samuel 17:4, Goliath was 6 cubits in height (9 feet). In the Bible the number 6 stands for man. 9 feet equals 108 inches. 108 inches consist of 18 sixes - 666 666 666 666 666 666. Goliath's number is "666". David was the 8th son of Jesse. His number is "8". The name "Jesus" in Greek is *"Iesous"*. The numerical significance of "*Iesous*" is "888". Here is the explanation:

Iota	10
Eta	8
Sigma	200
Omicron	70
Upsilon	400
Sigma	200
Total	888

(Source: *Unveiling End Times in our Time* by Dr Adrian Rogers)

We have learnt the Lord Jesus Christ is a "Stone", and on whoever this "Stone" falls, would be crushed into powder and scatter like chaff (Matthew 21: 42-44). We also know the number of the "beast," the Antichrist, is "666" (Revelation 13:18). He will be crowned by the powerful leaders of the revived Roman Empire (Revelation 17:.12-14). Goliath, the uncircumcised Philistine who mocked the children of God, was a picture of Antichrist *(666)*, the coming world leader, who will also blaspheme God, desecrate His temple and wage war against the saints – the faithful Jews and Christians (Daniel 9:27, Revelation 13:5-7). So, just as David (the number 8) slew Goliath (the number "666"), in like manner would the Lord Jesus Christ (the number "888") slaughter Antichrist (the number "666") and his rebellious followers who have opposed God and slandered His Holy Name. At the final battle at Armageddon, the "888" will cast the "666" and his army into the fiery lake of burning sulphur (Revelation 19:20-21, 20:7-15).

"GOLIATHS" OF TODAY

The heathen world should realise that the Church (not the "compromised church") is the Body of Christ. And according to Ephesians 6:10-18, the Church is a warrior – the army of Christ. Her weapon is the Sword of the Spirit, the Word of God, which is the Lord Jesus Christ, whose number is **"888."** Arrogant men, who mock the Church (the Body of Christ) and blaspheme the Lord Jesus Christ, are the "Goliaths" of today. Their numbers are "666 666 666 666 666 666". The "Stone" (888) will crush them into dust.

Remember, King Nebuchadnezzar of Babylon, the head of human governments, built a golden statue and commanded all men to worship it. This statue was ninety feet high and nine feet wide (Daniel 3:1-6). The number of this sculpture is 666, 666. 666, 666, 666. 666 (10) which was a portrait of Antichrist whose number is "666". Just as King Nebuchadnezzar, the head of then world government, commanded men to worship a statue of 666, 666, 666....so would Antichrist, the coming world leader whose number is ***"666"***, command the world to worship his image which would be installed in the Jerusalem Temple. The penalty for disobedience is death, just as Nebuchadnezzar ordered the slaughter of those who refused to adore his golden stature (Revelation 13:15-18, Daniel 3:1-6).The world is on notice. History will repeat itself.

IS GOD OMNIPOTENT OR IMPOTENT?

Today, it seems there is no Omnipotent God, but just an impotent God. The 'impotent' God has "encouraged" the rise of militant atheism and the driving of many Christians and their leaders to infidelity. Witness what the 'Sage of Ulster" recorded in his *The Silence of God:* 'When we turn to Holy Writ this mystery of a silent Heaven....seems to become more utterly insoluble....A silent Heaven! Yes, but it is not the silence of callous indifference or helpless weakness; it is the silence of a great sabbatical rest, the silence of a peace which is absolute and profound – a silence which is the public pledge and proof that the way is open for the guiltiest of mankind to draw near to God. When faith murmurs, and unbelief revolts, and men challenge the Supreme to break that silence and declare Himself, how little do they realise what the challenge means! It means the end of the reign of grace; it means the closing of the day of mercy and the drawing of the day of wrath." God is silent because He has spoken His last Word through His Son, the Lord Jesus Christ.

In the next chapter we will examine the European Union from the Christian perspective. Before we discuss this subject, I would draw your attention to a significant event that took place in Brussels in February 2005. It was a picture of what is yet to come.

THE "10 HORNS"; THE "10 KINGS" "THE 10 LEADERS AND THE 4 MINUTES"

The former United States President, George W Bush, visited Europe in February 2005. Some political commentators described his visit as "a Mending Fences visit – reaching out to European leaders to heal the rift that was created between America and Europe during the American and British invasion of Iraq in 2003". On Wednesday, 23 February 2005, The Times correspondents, Anthony Browne and Roland Watson, reported President Bush's visit to North Atlantic Treaty Organisation and European Union's headquarters in Brussels. According to these correspondents, "At Nato, leaders spoke in order of their length of service......Each leader talked about what they wished.....The meeting overran by 30 minutes....At the more disciplined EU, a free-for all was avoided by giving 10 of the 25 leaders a topic to talk about, and limiting them to four minutes each." This arrangement meant President Chirac of France addressed the meeting on Nato and EU reforms. And Tony Blair, the British Prime Minister, spoke about Iraq and Israel.

It is interesting to note that at the EU meeting, only 10 of the 25 EU leaders were chosen to speak for 4 minutes each? Why were only 10, but not any other number of leaders selected to speak, and not for any length of time but 4 minutes? Whatever is associated with the European Union has its spiritual significance. This means whatever reason that might have been alluded to this number of selection and the allotted speaking time for each leader, had its spiritual implications. It was a pointer to the prophetic message concerning the 10 powerful leaders of the Revived Roman Empire, who would delegate their power and authority to Antichrist to rule the world. The world number is 4.

This prophetic message is recorded in Daniel 7:7, 23-24, Revelation 13:1 and Revelation 17:4, 12.

- In Daniel 7:7, 23-24, the prophet tells us: "In my vision I saw a fourth beast terrifying and very frightful, it was different from all the other beasts, and it had ten horns ......I wanted to know the true meaning of the fourth beast. I also wanted to know about the 10 horns on its head....." The Lord explained to Daniel: The fourth beast is a fourth kingdom that will appear on earth....The 10 horns are the 10 kings who will come from this kingdom". This 4th kingdom is the Roman Empire, which is symbolised by the 2 legs of iron of the human image Nebuchadnezzar saw (Daniel 2:31-33). And the 10 kings are the 10 powerful leaders who will emerge from the revived Roman Empire. These 10 kings are signified by the 10 toes of the great human statue which were partly of iron and partly of baked clay (Daniel 2:41-43).

- Revelation 13:1 tells us what apostle John witnessed in a vision: "I (John) saw a beast coming out of the sea. He had 10 horns and 7 heads, with 10 crowns on his horns. And on each head a blasphemous name."
- In Revelation 17:4, 12 we read of another prophetic vision: "...I (John) saw a woman sitting on a scarlet beast that was covered with blasphemous names; having 7 heads and 10 horns......The 10 horns which you saw are 10 kings, who have received no kingdom as yet, but they receive authority for one hour as kings with the beast."
- Revelation 12:3 says: "Then another sign appeared in heaven; an enormous red dragon with **7** heads and 10 horns and 7 crowns on his head." The 10 horns on this red dragon are associated with the 10 kings who have not received a Kingdom.

We will examine the significance of ***the 10 horns, the 10 kings and the beast*** in Revelation 17 in much detail when we discuss *"The Woman and the beast"* in the Appendix. I conclude this section of the book with two illustrations that would throw an additional light on what the European Union is for. The first diagram illustrates the significance of two particular euro coins. The second diagram summarises the history and destiny of world powers as revealed in the magnificent human statue King Nebuchadnezzar saw in his dream.

Europa abducted by Zeus:
The Design on the 2 Greek euro cents

The Colloseum:
The Design of the Italian 5 euro cents

Chapter 8

The Two Euro Coins: The Greek 2 Euro Cents and the Italian 5 Euro Cents

"Divine prophecies have springing and germinant accomplishment throughout many ages, though the height or fullness of them may belong to some one age" (Lord Bacon)

We know Greek and Roman cultures are the basis of our Western civilisation. This was confirmed in a leading article - *LIFE AFTER DEATH* (The Times 10 February 2003).The article states: "Latin and Greek....are great.... They are the foundation of Western Civilisation, politics, philosophy, drama, art, law, science, dance, mathematics and architecture. They are our inheritance from our founding fathers." In view of this historical fact, I would share with you the significance of the portraits on the Greek 2 euro cents and the Italian 5 euro cents, in so far as the development of the European Union and its future prospects are concerned.

THE GREEK 2 EURO CENTS

In the beginning of this chapter we learnt that the Continent of Europe was named after a Greek mythical Phoenician Princess called *Europa*. We discovered how the Greek god, Zeus, deceived the beautiful *Europa*. Zeus abducted the Princess to Crete and seduced her to produce three sons. The Greek 2 euro cents, which depicts the portrait of the naked *Europa* riding on a beast, is a prophetic revelation of how the Revived Roman Empire would operate in its final 3½ years.

According to history, Antiochus Epiphanes, a Syrian King who was a descendant of one of the four kingdoms which evolved from Alexander the Great's Grecian Empire, invaded Judea in about 170BC. This immoral king persecuted and killed thousands of Jews. He outlawed the Jewish religion and custom by putting to death those who practiced circumcision. In 168BC Antiochus desecrated the Jewish Temple with the blood of a sow (a female pig), and built the idol of Zeus and set it upon the altar. He even encouraged fornication in the Temple. All these were abomination before God.

We have already learnt that the "10 toes" of the human statue King Nebuchadnezzar saw represent the 10 powerful leaders of the European Empire. And these 10 influential 'kings' of the Roman earth would assign their authority to a genius who will lead the revived Roman Empire (Revelation 17:12-14). The charisma and extraordinary intelligence of this personage would convince Europeans that at long last "we have now got the MAN to solve our problems. The Prophetic cry of the Belgium Prime Minister, Paul Henri-Spaak: - "Give us a devil to solve our problems"- would come to pass. This King of Men, the last Caesar, will sign a 7 year peace treaty with Israel and its Arab neighbours to bring peace to the Middle East (Daniel 9:27) [Remember, the Lisbon Treaty makes provision for the European Union to become a legal personality with a President who will sign international treaties on behalf of all the EU member states. And we are aware of the initiatives the European Union has been taking to solve the Middle East crisis – to help create a Palestinian state alongside the state of Israel].

The charismatic leader of Europe will break the peace treaty after three and half years. Like the tyrant Antiochus Epiphanes, the Emperor of the revived Roman Empire would persecute the faithful Jews and Christians as predicted in Daniel 7:21 and Revelation 13:5-7. He will also abolish the Jewish religion. He will corrupt the Jewish Temple with his statue, and demand the world to worship him. This would be the "abomination" spoken of by the prophet Daniel (Daniel 9:27). The Lord Jesus Christ referred to this idol of Antichrist in the Jerusalem Temple as the "Abomination of the desolation." (Matthew 24:15-17). Apostle Paul also confirmed the degradation of the temple by the Man of Lawlessness in 2 Thessalonians 2:1-4.

Just as Zeus deceived the beautiful *Europa* and seduced her, so would the coming Emperor of Europe deceive the European Union and the whole world with his outstanding personality, eloquence and amazing intelligence. Men would put their faith in this political genius to lead them to the "Promised Land of Peace and Prosperity." And just as the despicable Antiochus Epiphanes desecrated the Jewish Temple with the idol of Zeus, so would this world leader, with the support of the "10 toes," desecrate the Temple in Jerusalem with his idol, which would be built by the false prophet – the beast from the earth (Revelation 13:5-14, Daniel 9:27 and 2 Thessalonians 2:1-4).

In summary, the Greek 2 Euro cents, which depicts a mythical woman on a beast, would become a reality. We will learn more about this "reality" when we discuss "the woman and the beast" in the Appendix.

THE ITALIAN 5 EURO CENTS: THE COLLOSEUM

The Italian 5 euro cents bears a picture of the Flavius Amphitheatre. It was Emperor Vespasian who started its construction in about AD75. Vespasian's son, Titus, inaugurated the magnificent theatre in AD80. There were 100 days celebration during which thousands of animals were killed. Hundreds of Christians perished in the arena of the Colloseum. Arena means "Sand" in Latin. It was a perfect description of the area in the Amphitheatre where innocent people shed their blood. The arena was covered with sand to soak the blood of slaughtered Christians and deceased gladiators and dead animals. The Flavius Amphitheatre on the Italian 5 euro cents is a symbol of torture and blood-shed.

For us to appreciate the significance of this Italian 5 euro cents, it is necessary we examine the symbolism of the bronze coins Flavius Vespasian produced after the conquest of Judea and the destruction of the Jerusalem Temple. To commemorate their glorious victory over the Jews, Emperor Vespasian, in AD71, struck a series of coins with the inscription ***IVDAEA CAPTA*** which means *"Judea captured."* Below are examples of such coins.

"Ivdaea Capta" (Judea Captured)

The Emperor Vespasian created this bronze coin in AD71 to celebrate the conquest of the Jews and the destruction of their temple in Jerusalem. His son, Titus destroyed the city and the temple in AD70. The coin depicts a Jewish woman in sorrow. A Jewish man with his hands tied at his back. The Palm Tree is a symbol of Judea.

"Ivdaea Capta" (Judea Captured)

Nike- Goddess of Victory writing on a shield attached to a palm tree. Her foot on her helmet. The Palm Tree is a symbol of Judea.

A Jewish woman mourning on the ground sitting under a palm tree. The Emperor Vespasian is on the left with a spear, full military dress and his foot on his helmet

The portraits and inscriptions on these *"Judea captured"* coins were intended to commemorate the defeat of the Jews, and also to send a warning signal to other nations that they would be crushed like the Jews if they rebelled against the might of Imperial Rome. In effect, the Roman invasion of Judea and the destruction of the Jerusalem Temple and the raiding of its treasures, which took place about 38 years after the death of the Lord Jesus Christ, was a repetition of an historic event that occurred about 168 years before the Lord Jesus Christ was born.

Similarly, the portrait on the Italian 5 euro cents is a symbol to remind our generation of how the same history would be repeated just before the Lord Jesus Christ returns. And Just as the *"Judea captured"* Roman coins served as a warning to potential rebels, so does the Amphitheatre on the Italian 5 euro cents serve as a warning to those who would "rebel" against the last Caesar of the revived Roman Empire – the unusual political showman who would lead Europe to the "Promised Land of Carbon-Free" where peace and prosperity prevail.

From what we have learnt about the images on the Greek 2 euro cents and the Italian 5 euro cents, it is clear these symbols - *Europa* sitting on a beast and the Roman Amphitheatre which was inaugurated by the Roman Prince, Titus, have one thing in common. They are associated with the persecution of the Jews and the desecration of their Temple. And this would be the ambition of the King of Men when he leads Europe and the world with the support of the "10 toes." The histories of 168BC and AD70 would be repeated. It will certainly happen. But no one knows the date. The Lisbon Treaty signed on 13 December 2007 has paved the way for the Emperor of Europe to enter the political scene and takes his crown from European leaders. Whether the European Constitution (renamed Lisbon Treaty) is abandoned or become binding on Europeans or not, the Kaiser would surely take up his throne.

According to Daniel 9:26-27, the desecration of the Jerusalem Temple and the persecution of the Jews would happen. The Lord Jesus Christ Himself confirmed it in Matthew 24:15-21: "So when you see standing in the holy place 'the abomination that causes desolation' spoken of through the prophet Daniel - let the reader understand - then let those who are in Judea flee to the mountains. Let no-one on the roof of the house go down to take anything out of the house....For there will be great distress, unequalled from the beginning of the world until now - and never to be equalled again." Apostle Paul also reminded us of this event in 2 Thessalonians 2:3-10. And the Lord Jesus Christ, again, confirmed it to Apostle John in chapters 13 and 17 of the Book of Revelation. We will learn more about the "10 toes" in the next section.

The total value of the 2 euro coins under examination is 7 cents. This has its significance. In the Bible the number 2 stands for witness. The number 7 is the perfect number which symbolises completeness. We have learnt that the development of the European Union was a prophetic revelation in the Book of Daniel which is being fulfilled. So, what prophetic message do we receive from the value of these two euro coins (the Greek 2 euro cents and the Italian 5 euro cents?) The picture on the Greek 2 euro cents (a woman on a beast) and the image on the Italian 5 euro cents (the Roman Amphitheatre) bear witness (2) of God's complete and final (7) revelation about the career of the coming world leader. Having been crowned by European leaders, the powerful political genius will deceive the world. He will violate the 7-year peace treaty with Israel and its Arab neighbours. The Kaiser will blaspheme God, desecrate the Temple in Jerusalem and persecute the faithful Jews and Christians. Revelation 13:5-8 tells us. *"And the beast was given the power of speech, uttering boastful and* blasphemous words, and he was given freedom to exert his authority and to exercise his will during forty-two months (Three and half years Daniel 7:8). And he opened his mouth to speak slanders against God, blaspheming His name and His abode, (Even vilifying) those who live in heaven. He was further permitted to wage war on God's holy people (the saints) and to overcome them. And power was given him, to extend his authority over every tribe and people and tongue and nation." (The Amplified Bible).

Before the concluding word, I would summarise the prophetic significance of the two Euro coins (the Greek 2 euro cents and the Italian 5 euro cents) with this illustration:

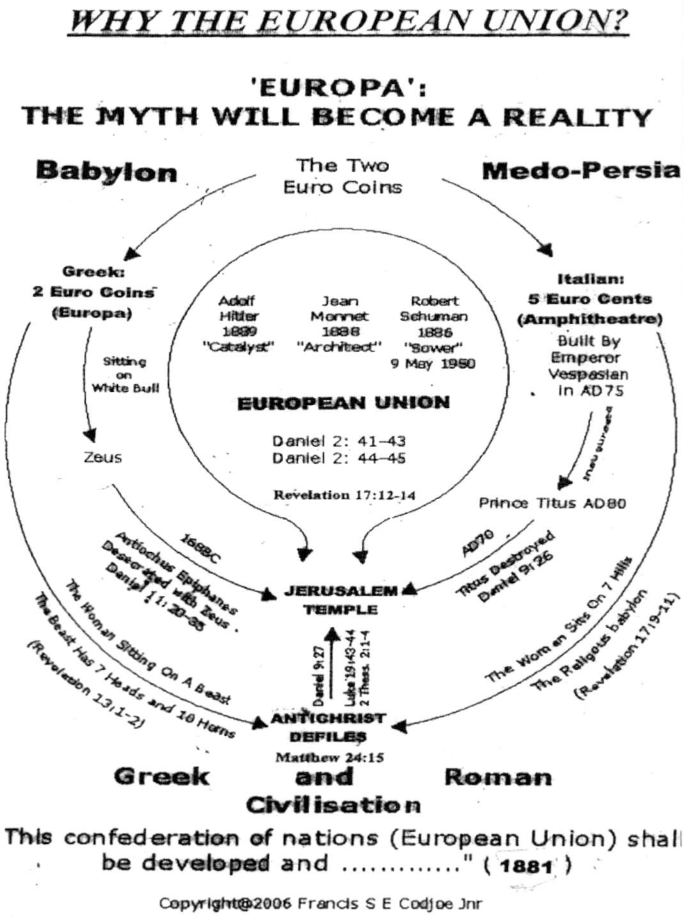

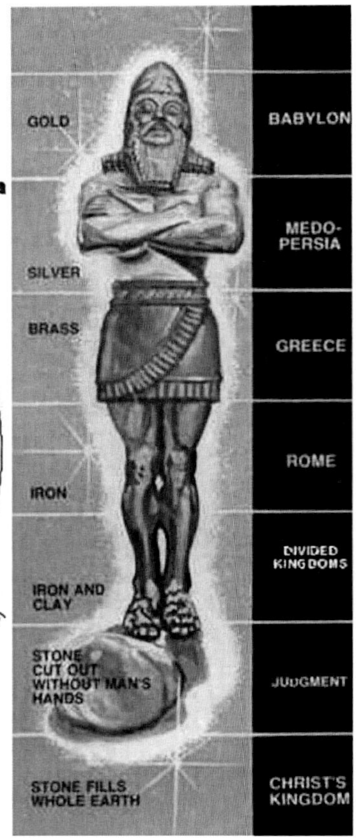

"Before things happened, I announced them..." (Isaiah 48:5)

SUMMARY OF THE PROPHETIC REVELATION IN THE TWO EURO COINS

- The Continent of Europe was named after *"Europa"* – a Greek Mythical Princess.
- The Greek god, **Zeus**, turned into a beast (a white bull) to deceive *Europa*. Zeus abducted Europa to Crete. He seduced *Europa*.
- Antiochus Epiphanes, a Syrian King, arose from one of the 4 kingdoms that evolved from Alexander the Great's Grecian Empire. He seized the kingdom by deception. He invaded Judea; abolished the Jewish religion and the practice of circumcision. He desecrated the Jewish Temple with the blood of a female pig and the statue of Zeus.
- In AD75, Emperor Vespasian started to build the Amphitheatre in Rome. In AD80, his son Titus, inaugurated the auditorium
- It was the same Roman Prince, Titus, who invaded Judea in AD70. Like Nebuchadnezzar, Titus also besieged Judea for some months. He killed many Jews and destroyed their holy Temple (Daniel 9:27). The Jews were scattered across many nations to fulfil the Word of God in Deuteronomy 28:62-66.

The Greek 2 euro cents and the Italian 5 euro cents have one thing in common: the desecration of the Temple of God in Jerusalem. The Temple will be rebuilt before the end of this age. TIME magazine once reported the plans for the rebuilding of the Jerusalem Temple. And it was also reported in *Israel & Christians Today*, how a "delegation of 34 people from Papua New Guinea visited the Western Wall in 2007 and donated a kilo of gold and several thousand dollars to the Temple Institute, an organisation dedicated to rebuilding the Temple. In an article *Gold donated for new temple*, Kobi Nahshoni reported that the delegates, who call themselves members of "The Bible Circle," told the Temple Institute that having studied the prophecy of Zechariah, where it says: "And they that are far off shall come and build in the Temple of the Lord, and ye shall know the Lord of hosts hath sent me unto you", they decided to follow the verse and go to Israel. According to the Papuans, in future they would send valuable wood for the construction of the new Temple.

THE CONCLUDING WORD:

JEAN MONNET: THE "SPIRITUAL GOD-FATHER" OF EUROPEAN COMMUNITY, THE "GENIUS" AND THE "HONORARY CITIZEN OF EUROPE"

In Jean Monnet's biography, the late Francois Duchene writes: "Monnet's role on the birth and rise of the European Community was an even more complex phenomenon…..Becoming the father of the Community involved more than inventing it. Jean Monnet is the tutelary genius of the European Community today, this is because he shaped the idea of Europe as no one else even tried to do and became its spiritual father…Monnet was the clarifying force. He narrowed the starting point of integration to the sectors of coal and steel…..Monnet also insisted on supranationality. Monnet gave the intellectual, practical and political lead…He was uniquely identified with European Union." He continued: "Monnet… alone linked up the whole European chain of being, from the conceptual background to the tiniest tactical detail. As a result he coloured the European idea to an exceptional degree with his personality and concepts." According to Duchene, "In the year after the war", Spaak wrote, "He (Monnet) played a preponderant role in the building of Europe…" Monnet proved the most creative…he was probably the one thorough going internationalist so far who has made a marked impact on history….His supreme achievement was to bring a new European political system into being… …..Judged by works, he is one of the few who have changed the modern world.".

Duchene concluded "Mister Europe's" biography with these words: "European Union, raised in special circumstances……..is not in any simple way a model for such a world, but it is the boldest instance yet of a civil answer to the threat of chaos. If Monnet had not launched it when he did, there is every sign no one else would have done so. He seized a brief opportunity to achieve one of the rarest feats in history, the deliberate introduction of a new theme."

QUESTION: HOW SHOULD WE DESCRIBE THE IRISHMAN WHO WROTE ABOUT EUROPEAN COMMUNITY: HOW IT WOULD DEVELOP; ITS CHARACTER AND FUTURE PROSPECTS BEFORE JEAN MONNET WAS BORN IN 1888?

If Jean Monnet "shaped the idea of Europe to create peace in Europe by bringing a new European political system into being; if Jean Monnet was a "tutelary genius", because he shaped the idea of Europe as no one else even tried to do, and became its spiritual father as well"; if Jean Monnet has achieved "one of the rarest feats in history; if Jean Monnet was described as a "revolutionary" and "one of the most extraordinary personalities of modern times," and if Robert Schuman, the man who sowed the seed of European Union, was put "on the path to sainthood" by the Roman Catholic Church, then the following questions must claim our attention:

- "How should we describe the native of Dublin who, before Jean Monnet and Robert Schuman were born, wrote: ***"This confederation of*** [European] ***nations shall be developed***....?"
- "How should we describe the "Anglicanised Irishman of Scotch extraction" who, before the creation of the European Coal and Steel Community, listed all the current leading nations in the European Union?"
- "How should we describe the British public servant who, 100 years before Greece joined the European Union in 1981, predicted that Greece would become a member of a political alliance of European nations?"
- "How should we describe the Detective who, in 1881, predicted that the next prominent political feature in history after the restoration of the Jews to Palestine would be the development of a confederation of European nations?"
- "And how should we describe the Ulsterman who, before Turkey applied to become a member of the European Community in 1963, listed Turkey as one of the members of a political Europe?"

This "Unknown Irishman, Englishman and Scot" was certain of the formation of a political alliance of European nations, that he listed the major founding members of the European Coal and Steel Community together with all the powerful nations in the present European Union including Belgium, the headquarters of the European Union. He was confident of European political integration that he even mentioned Turkey and Egypt as prospective members of political Europe. We know Turkey's admission into the European Union has become a controversial and divisive issue. And Egypt is one of the countries which "would become full member of the Single Market under the New Neighbourhood Policy also called the Wider Europe policy" (*Brussels plans to expand its empire again* The Times 4 May 2004).

In his *"Guide to the European Union,"* Dick Leonard writes: "Adolf Hitler was the main catalyst of the European Community.....If Hitler provided the impetus towards the European Unity, Monnet was indisputably the principal architect". The fact, is when Hitler was not in his mother's womb to become the "catalyst" of European Community; when Jean Monnet was not in existence to become the "architect" of European Community; and when Robert Schuman was also not in the womb, for him to come out to launch Jean Monnet's economic plan on 9 May 1950 to lay the foundation for a federal Europe, a Londoner had already written:

"This confederation of]European] ***nations shall be developed and........".*** He went on to describe the character of this political entity and who will lead it to its destiny.

The question still remains: who was this servant of the British Crown who wrote about European Union and its future before the founding fathers of European Community, Jean Monnet and Robert Schuman – were born in 1888 and 1886? "What motivated him to write: "*This confederation of (European) nations shall be developed through a European crisis....*" Again, what motivated this Irishman to predict with certainty the restoration of Israel, over 67 years, before Israel was reborn on 14 May 1948? If whatever this Ulsterman wrote about European integration has come to pass, then what he recorded about the future of Europe must be taken seriously. Who was this native of Dublin? I will introduce him as we progress with our study.

WAS ROBERT SCHUMAN COMMITTED TO THE IDEA OF A FEDERAL EUROPE?

Before we proceed to the next section, I urge you to reflect on this issue. Jean Monnet, the "revolutionary" and the principal architect of the European Construction, described Robert Schuman an "honest" politician whom people would believe whatever he said. The question is: why have politicians, political commentators and political scientists ignored the crucial "advice" Robert Schuman offered to the European Parliament relating to the survival of the European Enterprise?

NOTES

Part 2

European Union (The "10 Toes") and Christianity

Chapter 9

EUROPEAN CONSITUTION AND CHRISTIANITY

"Illumination is much needed at this moment, when the church is honeycombed by scepticism – scepticism, moreover which is the outcome, not of fuller knowledge or matured thought, but of intellectual conceit and levity which are the marked characteristics of the age."

"Treat your Bible as you would treat a friend. A friendship that cannot bear the strain of a misunderstanding does not deserve the name; nor a faith that gives way in presence of a difficulty. But with many the place the Bible holds resembles that not of a friend at all, but rather that of a mere acquaintance. For proofs that it is the Word of God are clear and abundant. But they do not lie open on the surface. Gold and diamonds are not picked up upon the highway; men need to dig for them. Even nature hides her treasures from the trifler. God is a "rewarder of them that seek Him diligently."
(The Bible and Modern criticism - RA)

Apart from politics, another major issue which divides the member states of the European Union is religion. The *Religious Tolerance.org* published on its website the opposing views which were expressed on the issue of religion in the European Union under the subject: *"DO 'GOD' AND 'CHRISTIANITY' HAVE A PLACE IN THE EUROPEAN UNION CONSTITUTION?"*

I have outlined below some of the comments that favoured the inclusion of God and Christianity in the European Constitution and those that were against.

COMMENTS IN FAVOUR OF GOD AND CHRISTIANITY

- "According to *Agence France Presse* the Polish primate, Cardinal Josef Glemp, said he supported EU entry "But only with God". The same news source quoted the Roman Catholic primate in Hungary, Monsignor Peter Erdoe, as saying, "Without Christianity, the heart of Europe would be missing."

- Bishop Joseph Duffy of Cloger, who represented the Irish Catholic Church, in his meeting with the then European Commission President, Romano Prodi, was quoted to have said: "Religion is part of our identity. You can't understand the history of Europe without acknowledging the impact of religion, which has made an enormous contribution to the identity of Europe. Prodi was trying to impress on us that we are at a very, very significant juncture, which means a new Europe. He is sympathetic to the Churches and sees that they have a contribution to make on the question of EU identity. The question of God would be a matter for the preamble, rather than the text of the constitution. We would be looking for an invocation Dei, but we would not be looking for a reference to Christ because we respect those who are not Christians."
- "The Catholic Bishops' Conference in England and some Jewish, Muslim and Protestant faith groups...also advocated inclusion of Christianity and God."
- Elmar Brol, an European deputy from Germany, who chaired the caucus of the conservative European People's Party at the convention, expressed his belief that "reference to a Christian God would strengthen European identity" He said, "Europe as a whole is based on a Christian heritage"
- The late Pope John Paul II lobbied European leaders for "a clear reference to God and Christian faith to be formulated in the European constitution."

COMMENTS AGAINST GOD AND CHRISTIANITY IN THE EUROPEAN CONSTITUTION

- According to WorldNetDaily: the editorial of Scandinavia's largest daily newspaper, the Swedish Aftonbladet, said, "referring to Christian values in the constitution and placing them above other values would be a huge mistake because it would exclude groups and raise new walls."
- Terry Sanderson, vice president of the UK's National Secular Society, told EUobserver: "We are very glad a reference to God has been left out, it would have created unnecessary barriers in Europe....Europe has to be secular for it to be really unified."
- A British gay-positive group, the *Gay and Lesbian Humanist Association* (GALHA) stated that because of "increased secularization of morality and public life," they considered it pointless to include God in the new charter. Spokesperson Terry Sanderson said: "We are not opposed to a clause that would establish the freedom to practice religion." What we don't want to see is religion moving out of the area of freedom and becoming predominant right there in the beginning. Religion is dying throughout Europe." He blamed "the church" for the suffering of gays

and lesbians "over the last millennium." GHALA wrote: "To include references to God or 'our Christian heritage' would be to start turning back on our 500-year journey from the Enlightenment. Instead, we should be proud of our progress, and growing humanity."

- Socialist French deputy, Oliver Duhamel, suggested that mention of Christianity and God is "absurd," because it would exclude Muslims and others of non-Christian faiths, as well as those Europeans who do not believe in God.
- Linda McAvan, a British Labour MEP, argued that a specific mention of Christianity "would offend those many millions of people of different faiths or no faith at all."
- A Humanist Convention member from Ireland, Dublin MEP Proinsias De Rossa, suggested that the inclusion of God would be divisive: "It would be a mistake; it's a serious mistake."

Some who suggested an inclusive approach

- Louis Michel, the Belgium Foreign Minister, said the EU should be inclusive. He stated: "Europe is not mono-religious."
- Jean-Luc Dehaene, vice-president of the Convention and a former Belgium prime minister, said that any religious reference would have to be general and pluralist, like that of the EU's Charter of Fundamental Rights which states that "the Union shall respect cultural, religious, and linguistic diversity."

The member states of the European Union were generally divided on whether "God" and "Christianity" should have a place in the constitution of Europe. For example, before the European leaders adopted the first European Constitution in Rome in 2004, Poland and Italy, in particular, wanted God and Christianity mentioned in the Constitution. However, other countries including Britain, Germany and France were not keen on the idea. Why? Because, "God and Christianity" would cause offence to potential members of the Union who were not Christians and do not believe in God. And it would also forestall the enlargement of the Union since some of the prospective members, especially Turkey, were not Christian countries.

For example, a leading article, *Talking Turkey,* which was published in The Times newspaper on 17 May 2004, stated: "...His (the former British Prime Minister, Tony Blair) support for Turkish entry into the European Union has been longstanding, consistent and crucial. He has said for years that Turkey.......deserves to be considered seriously as a candidate by the EU. He has spoken strongly against those who raise Turkey's Muslim heritage as a barrier, as though Europe were some kind of a Christian Club".
On 25 May 2004, in an article titled *Seven hold out for a Christian constitution*, The

Times reported on a dispute which erupted during an emergency meeting of EU foreign ministers on whether "the proposed constitution should refer to Europe's Christian heritage." According to the report, "The preamble to the European constitution refers only to the "cultural, religious, and humanist inheritance of Europe". It was revealed in this column that seven countries: Italy, Poland, Lithuania, Malta, Portugal, the Czech Republic and Slovenia, signed a letter to the chairman of the negotiation, Brian Cowen, the then Irish foreign minister, "to demand that a reference to Europe's Christian roots be inserted" in the European Constitution.

According to the publication, the issue was highly controversial because "many countries, including Britain, were opposed to making the European Union a "Christian club" which would complicate negotiations on admitting Muslim Turkey." On the other hand, Italian and Polish politicians felt that a reference to Christianity in the European Union Constitution could influence the Pope (the late Pope John Paul II) to make the ratification of the constitutional treaty easier - probably in countries where Roman Catholics are the majority.

On 5 July 2004, an article in Financial Times read *False obstacles to Turkey's EU bid.* The writer, Kirsty Hughes, argued the case for Turkey to be admitted to the European Union. She explained that religion should not be a criterion for membership qualification to join the European Union. According to the article, "The EU is a secular state – as Turkey is a secular state....by its own rules the EU should be blind to religion.....Turkey is also a Mediterranean country, joining the EU for political as well as economic reasons – similar to Spain or Portugal." The report concluded: "there should therefore, be no intrinsic barriers to Turkish membership, if it met European Union's political and economic criteria".

On 24 September 2004, The Times published an article entitled *EU unites under threat as Turks clamour to join."* The writer, Anthony Browne, discussed the implications of Turkey's membership of the European Union. He wrote: "....Britain and the United States are passionate supporters of Turkey, arguing that embracing a Muslim nation in the EU's Christian club would show the Islamic world that there is no clash of civilisations....Rejecting Turkey after decades of promises, say London and Washington, could force it into the hands of Islamic terrorists."

And before the European Union leaders met at a summit in Brussels on 17 December 2004 to decide on Turkey's membership of the Union, the Turkish Prime Minister expressed his views on those member-states which were reluctant to embrace Turkey on religious grounds. On 13 December 2004, an article in The Times read *Turkish leader warns of terror wave if EU rejects membership.* In this article, "RECEP TAYYIP ERDOGAN, the Turkish Prime Minister ... told European Union leaders that they would pay a heavy price in continued violence from Islamic extremists if the EU rejected Turkey as a member and confirmed as a Christian Club". Mr Erdogan continued with his veil threat: "Accepting a country (Turkey) that has brought together Islam and democracy will bring about harmony between civilisations. If on the other hand, it is not welcomed, the world will have to put up with the present situation…There is nothing we can do if the EU feels that it can live with being simply a Christian club"?

And David Miliband, the British Foreign Secretary, in supporting Turkey's membership of the Europe Union, blindly joined the "anti-Christian" chorus. In an article captioned *Time to learn and move on, says Miliband* (Financial Times 26 September 2007), the Labour politician displayed no original thought on European integration. The atheist parroted the anti-christian sentiments of his former boss, Tony Blair, and Romano Prodi, with these words: "shared values had to be embodied in institutions rather than simply asserted. Europe can't be a closed Christian club". I ask the question: "From where did the atheist Miliband get the idea that somehow the European Union has been a "Christian club?"

THE EUROPEAN UNION IS NOT A "CHRISTIAN CLUB" THE EU DOES NOT QUALIFY TO BE A "CHRISTIAN CLUB" AND THE EU WILL NEVER QUALIFY TO BE A "CHRISTIAN CLUB"

I would assure the Turkish Prime Minister that the European Union is not a Christian Club and the European Union has never been a Christian Club. After all, Tony Blair, in his 'glorious days', suggested that the EU is not a Christian Club. So, whether the former Prime Minister of Britain and the former President of the United States of America, George Bush, later considered the EU a Christian club that should welcome Turkey to prove that the EU is an "inclusive" political Union to avoid the clash of civilisation; and whether the Italian and Polish politicians considered it necessary for Christianity to be mentioned in the European Constitution to win the approval of the Pope to make the ratification of the constitution easier, the truth is that the European Union is NOT a Christian club in any shape or form. The European Union does not qualify to be a Christian club. And the European Union will never qualify as a Christian club. Therefore, Christianity should not be a factor to influence the decision on Turkey's admission into the political phenomenon of the 21st century. It is sad and ironic that the late Pope John Paul II was eager to see Christianity mentioned in the European Constitution.

Since the European Union is concerned about the effects of global warming, and the security and prosperity of its citizens, those member-states and politicians who object to Turkey's membership of EU, as though the European Union was somehow a Christian club, should cast away their misplaced conception. They should rather heed the warning of the Turkish Prime Minister, that the European

Union would "pay a heavy price ...if the EU rejects Turkey as a member and confirms itself as a Christian club....and if the EU feels that it can live with being a Christian Club", and admit Turkey into their fold.

Why should Christianity be an issue in European Union's deliberations? If the European Union were a Christian club, the architects of the Blueprint of Europe would have mentioned the Lord Jesus Christ in the text. Rather, the framers of the European Constitution claimed it would be insensitive for them to mention the Lord Jesus and Christianity in the constitution, because, such references would cause offence to non Christians and atheists. The issue is that any true "Christian club" would not deny the Precious Name of its Founder, the Lord Jesus Christ, in its constitution. After all, some European politicians claimed it would have been a "huge mistake" and "absurd" to have mentioned "God" and "Christianity" in the European Constitution.

Again, if the European Union were a Christian club, Poland, Italy, Malta, Portugal, Lithuania and the Czech Republic would not have pleaded in vain for Christianity to be mentioned in the Constitution of Europe. If the European Union were a Christian club, the architects of the Constitution would have stated in their draft, that "adultery is a sin"; "sexual relationship among same-sex is also a sin", and same-sex marriages are forbidden among European citizens". Rather, the European Constitution does not condemn adultery, or sexual relationships between the same sexes, nor same-sex marriages. The European Union rather supports all forms of sexual relationships.

For example, when Rocco Buttiglione, an Italian prospective candidate for the European Commissioner for justice and home affairs, expressed his Christian views that homosexuality is a sin and marriage is the best environment in which to bring up children (Daily Mail Editorial 2004), most Members of the European Parliament objected to Buttiglione's comments as offensive. They demanded his exclusion from any office in the European project. According to the 29 October 2004 issue of the Economist: "On October 11th, he (Rocco Buttiglione) became the first commission nominee to be rejected by a European Parliament committee, when the civil-liberties committee voted 27-26 to reject his nomination to the justice and home affairs portfolio. The majority's ire was roused by his comment, in response to the committee's questions that "I may think homosexuality is a sin, but this has no effect on politics unless I say homosexuality is a crime." Stephen Glover also commented on the treatment of Rocco Buttiglione in an article titled *The fascists are back in Europe.* He wrote: "The silencing of this EU commissioner for holding personal views shared by countless millions is nothing less than intellectual Nazism."

On 13 September 2005, the European Court ruled that it is perfectly legitimate for a woman to marry her father-in-law. After the ruling, these headlines appeared in our newspapers:

- *"Now you can marry your mother-in-law"* (Daily Mail Wednesday, September 14, 2005).
- *"Woman wins right to wed father-in-law"*, with a sub headline: *"A ban designed to protect the integrity of the family has been ruled illogical by the European Court"* (The Times, Wednesday September 14, 2005). Under this title, Frances Gibb wrote: "A LITTLE-KNOWN law that prevents people marrying their sons, or daughters-in-law is likely to be scrapped after a European Court ruling ...that it breaches human rights. The European Court of Human Rights in Strasbourg said that to deny in-laws the right to wed was a breach of their human rights to marry and found a family.".

If the European Union were a Christian Club, it would not have approved a marriage between a woman and her father-in-law. The Christian Constitution, the Holy Bible, forbids such marriages (Leviticus 20:14). It is clear from the actions of the European Parliament and the European Court of Justice, that the European Union is NOT a Christian club. The European Constitution may approve all kinds of sexual relationships and different forms of marriages, but the Christian Constitution – the Holy Bible - does not approve sexual behaviour and marriages that are inconsistent with its precepts.

HYPOCRISY OF THE UNGODLY EU

The rejection of Rocco Buttiglione because of his Christian views on homosexuality was a clear breach of the fundamental principles of the European Union. The discriminating behaviour of the "children" of Jean Monnet was exposed in the 31 October 2004 edition of The Sunday Times by the Columnist Minette Marrin. Under a title *In one bloody bout Brussels reveals its true hypocrisy*, she writes, "They (The Members of the European Parliament and the Brussels establishment) are convinced that their public rejection of Rocco Bouttiglione because of his views is a triumph both for democracy and for the European Union and everything it stands for. Yet in bringing down Buttiglione, they were and are in flagrant breach of the fundamental principles of the EU. It is very odd".

The Columnist explained that the principles the EU Bureaucrats and the Parliament breached are clearly outlined in their own Charter of Fundamental Rights of the European Union. "Article 10 guarantees freedom of thought, conscience and religion, including the freedom to "manifest" one's beliefs not only in worship, but also in "teaching, practice and observance." Article 11 guarantees freedom of expression to hold opinions and exchange them "without" interference by public authority." Article 21 states that any discrimination based on any ground such as a religious belief, political or any other opinion shall be prohibited." And finally, Article 22 declares that the EU shall respect cultural and religious diversity." Before concluding her article, Minette Marrin stated: "The Buttiglione fiasco is an elegant demonstration of what is wrong with the new European high culture as demonstrated in Brussels. It is riddled with hypocrisy and confusion and the kind of totalitarian attitudes that the EU was created to resist. "This whole thing is a fairy tale" - to borrow the words of Bill Clinton.

THE SPIRIT OF HUMANISM IN THE EU CONSTITUTION

It is obvious from how Mr Buttiglione was treated and disqualified from taking a position in the European Project, that the European Union has no respect for any cultural or religious diversity. "That Thing" in Brussels is NOT a Christian club. That, the European Union is not, and cannot be a Christian club is not an exaggeration from the author's point of view. The very emphasis of *"Humanism"* in the Constitution of Europe clearly portrays the European Union as atheistic.

A section of the preamble to the old Constitution (now the Lisbon Treaty) states: "...Europe is a continent that has brought forth civilisations....Since the first stages of mankind, have gradually developed the values underlying humanism, equality of person, freedom, respect for reason......Drawing inspiration from the cultural, religious and humanist inheritance of Europe, which nourished first by the civilisations of Greek and Rome, characterised by spiritual impulse....and... by the philosophical currents of Enlightenment..."

A close study of this text reveals the non-Christian character of the European Union. After all, what is this *humanism* that features prominently in the preamble to the original EU constitution which was rejected by the French and the Dutch in 2005 and later repackaged as a new Reform Treaty? According to *Encyclopaedia Britannica,* "In recent years the term humanism has often been used to refer to value systems that emphasise the personal worth of each individual but that do not include a belief in God."

Norman Geisler, a Christian apologist, summarising the Humanist Manifesto II of The American Humanist Association in Professor Harold Berry's book, *WHAT THEY BELIEVE SECULAR HUMANISM,* stated: "Like its predecessor....the second Manifesto is atheistic, naturalistic, evolutionistic, socialistic, relativistic, and still optimistic that man can save himself....Humanism traces its roots from ancient China, classical Greece and Rome, through the Renaissance and the Enlightenment, to the scientific revolution of the modern world."

Professor Berry of Grace College of the Bible at Omaha, Nebraska, in the United States, writes: "Secular humanism places trust in human intelligence rather in divine guidance. The secular humanists deify man by placing his needs and experiences above the authority of God's Word. They boldly declare: "We believe ....that traditional dogmatic or authoritarian religions that place revelation, God, ritual, or creed above human needs and experience do a disservice to the human species." Delos Mckown, the Humanist, states: "Secular humanists, in short, are agnostic or atheistic". And *The Oxford Companion to Philosophy* explains "Humanism" as, "The tendency to emphasise man and his status, importance, powers, achievements, interests or authority....Humanism is also associated with the Renaissance, when it denoted a move away from God to man as the centre of interest..."

It is clear, the prominence of secular humanism in secular Europe conflicts with Biblical Christianity. If the European Union were not atheistic, then the question arises: "Why did the architects of the European constitution fail to explicitly mention God in their document?" The simple answer is: Because God was not at the centre of the European Project, the God-incarnate, the Lord Jesus Christ, was eliminated from the preamble to Euro-Constitution.

THE MISSION STATEMENT OF THE "CHRISTIAN CLUB"

The Mission Statement of the Lord Jesus Christ, the Founder of the true "Christian Club", was and is and will always be: *"Repent, for the kingdom of heaven is near"* (Matthew 4:17). The constitution of the European Union does not make any reference to "Repentance" and the "kingdom of heaven". The European Union CANNOT be a "Christian Club", and it does NOT deserve to be a "Christian Club." The Lord Jesus Christ, speaking with authority, declared: *"Whosoever confesses Me before men, him I will also confess before My Father who is in heaven. But whoever denies Me before men, him I will deny before My Father who is in heaven"* (Matthew 10:32-33). And, *"He who is not with Me is against Me, and he who does not gather with Me scatters"* (Luke 11:23).

The Constitution for the Lord Jesus' Kingdom is recorded in chapters 5 to 7 of the Gospel of Matthew. When the Lord inaugurated the Constitution for His "Club" on a mountain, He told His audience, "You have heard that it was said, "Do not commit adultery". But I tell you that anyone who looks at a woman lustfully has already committed adultery in his heart". Our Divine Lord declared He did not come to abolish the Law and the prophets. This means, the Lord Jesus Christ upheld the Old Testament teachings, which clearly say adultery and homosexuality are unlawful sexual relationships (Leviticus 20:10-13) which the members of His "Club" (Christians) must not practise. However, such sexual relationships are not unlawful acts in the European Union constitution and the apostate Church. The Lord Jesus Christ also cautioned the members of His "Club" (the Church) against diplomatic language and ambiguous speeches. He advised them that their answers to closed questions must be either "Yes" or "No". Anything beyond this comes from the devil (Matthew 5:37). But politicians in the European "kingdom", like all politicians, at times indulge in fudges and ambiguous language. They are not used to saying "Yes" or "No" to simple, closed questions.

THE CHURCH: THE ONLY "CHRISTIAN CLUB"

The only "Christian club" which is recognised by God, is the Church, which His Son, the Lord Jesus Christ, shed His Precious Blood to establish it. The mission of the "Christian Club" is to proclaim the Gospel of Christ. The Lord Jesus Christ commanded the members of His "Club": "Go and make disciples of all nations, baptising them in the name of the Father and of the Son and of the Holy Spirit, and teaching them to obey everything I have commanded you..." (Matthew 28:19-20). Is this the 'mission' of the European Union? No. The mission statement of the European Project is to prevent global warming, enhance political, economic and social cooperation among the member-states, and bring material prosperity, peace and security to its citizens. The preaching of "repentance and forgiveness of sins" is not in the vocabulary of the European Union. After all, in secular humanism man is supreme.

MORALITY IS IRRELEVANT IN POLITICS

The fact is, in the political arena, moral issues are not the standards by which politicians are judged on their qualification for a particular office. What politicians do in secret would not determine their suitability for public office. This means, in politics you can build a steel wall between your private life and public life. You can have multiple sexual relationships in and outside marriage. You can fornicate and commit adultery and still be an excellent politician. Your public job is always safe irrespective of your moral conduct. A leading politician (to be specific) Gordon Brown, once said: Politicians do not make "moral judgement". But this same man talked about "moral compass." And he deemed it necessary to preach in St Paul's' Cathedral about moral values that could save the "global age" from economic ruins.

In the "Christian Club", which is the Church, a Christian has one life – a life in Christ. A faithful Christian has neither a private nor a public life. Christians cannot build iron walls between what they do in private and in public. Christians cannot lead double lives. Christians cannot fornicate or live adulterous lives and be excellent Christians. Moral conduct determines your qualification for the 'Christian Job' - the proclamation of the Gospel to call unbelievers to repent and accept the Lord Jesus Christ as their Saviour. A Christian cannot have multiple sexual partners in or outside marriage and be an effective and excellent labourer for the Lord Jesus Christ. We cannot bridge the gulf between Christianity and politics. The Gospel was not given to save the "human statue" from destruction. It was given to save man from the wreckage of civilisation promoted by the political systems of the world.

CHRISTIANS SHOULD NOT MOURN THE EXCLUSION OF GOD AND CHRISTIANITY FROM THE EUROPEAN CONSTITUTION

The European Union is a political entity – a worldly "Empire" with an "Emperor" who is on the horizon. It CANNOT be a Christian club. The seeds for the European Project were sown on 9 May 1950 to produce Economic and Political fruits, not to yield the fruit of "Repentance for the kingdom of God is at hand". For this reason the European Union does NOT qualify to be a Christian club. However, European politicians should realise that it was a Christian who, in the 19th century, confidently predicted in one of his classic books, that the development of a confederation of European nations would be the next major political feature in history after the phenomenon of Israel – the restoration of the Jews to Palestine. This Christian even listed all the current leading member states of the European Union when the "Fathers of European Community," Jean Monnet and Robert Schuman, had not been conceived. And one hundred years after he had predicted that Greece would join the European confederacy, Greece joined the club in 1981. This is the inconvenient truth about European integration which pompous politicians and atheists should grapple with it.

IS THE FUTURE UNKNOWN?

"No one can see the future", says 19 March 2007 edition of *TIME* magazine. And an advert in the 9 October 2006 edition of Financial Times also read: "But if one person could reliably predict just a few minutes into the future, he or she would dominate the entire world within a few days...So, if we know one thing, it is that the future is essentially unknowable. Yet we strive to guess it or at least to affect it..." We must then ask the question: "How was it possible for a Christian from Dublin to predict with certainty that next to the restoration of the Jews to Palestine, the prominent political feature in history would be a political union of European nations that would develop through an European crisis? In other words, how was this Irishman able to forecast with accuracy that the scattered Jews would settle in Palestine about 68 years before the nation of Israel was reborn? And how could he also foretell that the next major political phenomenon in history, after the creation of the state of Israel, would be a confederation of European nations that would be developed through an European crisis?

The Ulsterman wrote about European integration: how it would be developed, its character and future prospects even before Adolf Hitler was also conceived, and before Hitler grew to outline his plans to conquer the world at the "FAher Conference in November 1937, and thus becoming the "Catalyst" for European Community. Jean Monnet, the "practical apostle of European unity", conceived his plan for a federal Europe after the army of Hitler had invaded Poland on 1 September 1939, which sparked France and England to declare war on Germany. I repeat the question: What compelled the Christian from Ireland to predict the development of a political alliance of European nation and even listed Turkey as a member of this confederacy before Turkey first applied in 1963 to join the European Community.

Before Schuman launched his plan in 1950 to create the European Coal and Steel Community (the forerunner of the European Union), Aristide Brian, a former French Prime Minister, in 1929, made this statement in relation to political union of Europe: "Among peoples who are geographically grouped together like the peoples of Europe there must exist a sort of federal link. It is this link which I wish to endeavour to establish. Evidently the association will act mainly in the economic sphere. That is the most pressing question. But I am sure also that from a political point of view, and from a social point of view the federal link, without infringing the sovereignty of any of the nations which might take part in such an association, could be beneficial."

JEAN MONNET HATES THE 'CONCEPT' OF SOVEREIGNTY

On 5 August 1943 the French master builder of the European project, Jean Monnet, made this statement: "There will be no peace in Europe if the states rebuild themselves on the basis of national sovereignty, with its implications of prestige policies and economic protection...The countries of Europe are not strong enough individually to be able to guarantee prosperity and social development for their peoples. The states of Europe must therefore form a federation or an European entity that would make them into a common economic unit." He added: "Europe of sovereign states was incapable of, despite its leaders' goodwill, of reaching the sensible decisions that were needed for the common good. It would be quite another matter, however, once the power of decision was entrusted to institutions serving the general interest and applying the will of the majority in a system of common rules" The "practical apostle of European unity" concluded his Memoirs with this 'significant' remark: "But time is passing, and Europe is moving only slowly on the course to which she is so deeply committed....We cannot stop ...the community we have created is not an end in itself...Like the provinces of the past, our nations must learn to live together under common rules and institutions freely arrived at. The sovereign nations of the past can no longer solve the problems of the present; they cannot ensure their own progress or control their own future. And the community itself is only a stage on the way to the organized world of tomorrow.

"Mister Europe" declared: "I have no doubt, for my part, that a confederation will one day lead to a federation. But for the moment, is it possible to go further? I cannot say that it is. Meanwhile, the confederation would have the very great advantage of assuring public opinion in our countries that they have joined an entity which is not only economic but political, and that they are therefore part of something bigger than any of their countries alone" (*Source: Jean Monnet Memoirs 1978)*

It was therefore not surprising when, in September 2008, Valery Giscard d'Estaing, the arch federalist, addressing a conference in London on Britain's future relationship with the European Union, echoed the voice of his 'master', Jean Monnet: "Integration is vital European; it is a question of scale that will become vital in the world of tomorrow. The EU has already come too far with the project of closer integration to stop now."

The question is: "Did Jean Monnet really understand his vision of a united – federal Europe?" The "apostle of European unity" toiled to fulfil the real vision of the Irish master he never knew. The French and the Germans should also realise that before their 'hero', Jean Monnet, was even conceived, the "Seer of Dublin" used the prominent word *"confederation"*- which Monnet associated it with his vision of a United States of Europe. Writing in the 19th century about political Union of European nations and its future, the "man of true vision" stated: "Through the gradual unfolding...or far more probably as the outcome of some great European crisis in the future, this confederation of [European] nations shall be developed and..." After listing the prominent members of this European political phenomenon, the Irishman warned Britain would not be saved in the European alliance. He described political Europe "The vile confederacy of the latter days."

Again, on the issue of European integration, Sir Winston Churchill made the following speech at Zurich University on 19 September 1946: "I wish to speak to you today about the tragedy of Europe...Yet all the while there is a remedy which, if it were generally and spontaneously adopted by the great majority of people in many lands, would as if by a miracle transform the whole scene, and would in a few years make all Europe, or the greater part of it, as free and as happy as Switzerland is ....What is this sovereign remedy? It is to create the European family, or as much of it as we can, and to provide it with a structure under which it can dwell in peace, in safety and in freedom. We must build a kind of United States of Europe....The first step in the creation of the European Family must be a partnership between France and Germany."

Before these prominent personalities dreamt of a political union of European nations that would bring peace and prosperity to the peoples of Europe, a British public servant had already predicted, *"This confederation of nations shall be devel-*

oped...." The pertinent question remains. What prompted this Christian to make this prediction? And we must also ask the question: "From where did this man get his information about a "confederation of European nations"?

Is it not extraordinary, that before the circumstances that motivated Aristide Briand, Konrad Adenauer, Jean Monnet and Sir Winston Churchill, to suggest the idea of a united Europe that could live in peace and prosperity, a Christian had already written about how this political alliance of European nations would be developed, its character and future prospects? Christians should not weep over the exclusion of God, the Lord Jesus Christ and Christianity from the European Constitution. By the grace of God we, the Bible-believing Christians, know more about the European Union and its destiny than all the brains behind the construction of the European Project and its constitution.

WOULD THE "UNKNOWN IRISHMAN" - WHO PREDICTED THE EU BEFORE THE EU WAS BORN - NOW DOMINATE THE WORLD?

I repeat the advertisement that was posted in the Financial Times on 9 October 2006: "If one person could reliably predict just two minutes into the future, he or she would dominate the entire world within a few days. So if we know one thing, it is that the future is essentially unknowable. Yet we strive to guess it or at least to affect it."

The question still remains. "How was it that a servant of the British Crown did not guess the development of two major political events in Europe and Palestine, but wrote with absolute certainty, that "a confederation of (European) nations shall be developed," and it would be the next major political feature in history after the restoration of the Jews to Palestine? And behold, the state of Israel was created in Palestine on 14 May 1948, about 68 years after his prediction. And two years later, on 9 May 1950, the European Union was also born. The question is: "Would this "Unknown Irishman," who laboured for Great Britain, now dominate the entire world?

A summary

Before we proceed, I would review the significant points we must bear in mind:

- The European Union was created from the wreckage of the Second World War (1939-45)
- Jean Monnet, the French statesman, was the brain behind European integration as Jose Manuel Barroso, the President of European Commission, puts it: "Monnet's idea of European unity was seized upon by French Foreign Minister Robert Schuman and German Chancellor Konrad Adenauer....The power of Monnet's gradualist vision means that it still serves as a blueprint for European integration today" (*TIME* 13 November 2006).
- A Christian wrote about political union of European nations even before the First World War began in 1914, and before Jean Monnet was born in 1888, and before the European Union was born on 9 May 1950. He even mentioned Austria, Egypt, Greece, Spain, Belgium, Portugal, England, Italy, Germany, France and Turkey as prospective members of the European confederacy. (Please notice how Niall Ferguson, a Professor of History at Harvard University, described the European Union in an article for the Daily Telegraph: "...The customs union has become a (still imperfect) single market. Yet, at the root the EU remains not the federal super-state, but a *confederation* whose primary concern is trade policy" (The Daily Telegraph 25 March 2007)
- This Christian also predicted the restoration of the Jews to Palestine about 68 years before the nation of Israel was reborn on 14 May 1948.

We know the European Union is the foundation block upon which the "dead" Roman Empire would be "resurrected". From this revived Roman Empire would emerge the world leader who would have no desire for women (Daniel 11:37). But this coming King of Men, with an unusual cleverness and personality, will promise the world social security, political stability, economic prosperity and peace. This is the man who would confirm a seven-year peace treaty with the nation of Israel and its Arab neighbours. But three and half years later breaks the treaty.

The Emperor of Europe would establish one world religion. He will oppose God, blaspheme the name of God. He will compel the world to worship his image in the Temple of Jerusalem, which had been erected under the guidance of the false prophet – the "beast from the earth," the apostate Jew, (Revelation 13:11-15). The Strong Leader of Europe shall make war against the faithful Jews and Christians who refuse to worship him. (Daniel 9:27 Revelation 13:7). The Lord Jesus Christ referred to the "idol" of this world leader in the Jerusalem temple as "*the abomina-*

tion that causes desolation standing in the holy place spoken of by the prophet Daniel" (Matthew 24:15, Daniel 9:27).

It is interesting to note, that a Jewish rabbi suggested the formation of one world religion. In an article titled *Talk, not tanks, will bring us peace,* Yona Metzger, a charismatic Jewish Rabbi, described as one of the 12 most influential religious leaders in the world, proposed the setting up of a "United Nations of religions" – One World Religion. He says: "Every country will send a religious ambassador and we shall meet round the table and talk, even countries that do not have diplomatic relations." His vision is that such a United Nations of Religion could prevent another Holocaust (The Times 26 January 2008).

Certainly there would be a "peace" agreement between the Jews and their Arab neighbours. The question is: who is going to negotiate this "peace deal" which has eluded politicians? (Daniel 9:27) On the issue of a "United Nations of Religion," Revelation 13 says, the "beast out of the earth," made the whole world worship the beast from the sea. He ordered mankind to set up an image in honour of the beast that was wounded by the sword and yet lived. All who refuse to worship the image of the beast will be killed."

With this information before us, how could the European Union, whose coming leader will persecute Christians and fight the Lord Jesus Christ, be a Christian club? I repeat: the Lord Jesus Christ established a Church – those whom He has called out of the wicked and corrupt world to be His followers. Their assignment is not to build a political empire, but to proclaim His message of "Repentance and forgiveness of sins". The Lord of lords and the King of kings did not institute a worldly Club. The "Constitution" of the Church, which is the Holy Bible written under divine inspiration, is different from the constitution of the European Union, which was written under compromises.

The former German leader, Chancellor Gerhard Schroder, confirmed this fact. In an article titled *82 million Germans have no say as MPs back the EU constitution,* Gerhard Schroder, after he had told the German Members of Parliament, "Don't bother with the details" of the European constitutional treaty, made this statement: "The treaty is not a one-size-fits-all document. It is a human work. Of course it doesn't fulfil every hope and it doesn't banish every fear. The text of the constitution is a very good and fair compromise (Daily Mail, Friday 13 May 2005). The Lord Jesus Christ does not seek comprise. You are with Him or against Him.

The European Union, by its nature and practices, does not qualify to be a Christian club. Therefore, there was no need for some Christians and church leaders to have expressed concern on the subject of the omission of God and Christianity from the Constitution of Europe. Sadly, Italy and Poland held the impression that a reference to Christianity in the European constitution could influence the head of the Roman Catholic Church (then Pope John Paul II) to influence the Catholic nations to embrace the constitution.

THE "FLIP-FLOP" POPE

The Roman Catholic Church was so distressed by the omission of God and Christianity in the European constitution, that "in an highly unusual step..... Cardinal Joseph Ratzinger (the then Catholic Church top theologian, but now Pope Benedict XVI) warned against Turkish membership of the EU" (Financial Times 30 August 2004). The warning was not necessary. There was no need for a church leader to have pleaded with European politicians to include God and Christianity in the European constitution.

Strangely, Pope Benedict XVI changed his position on Turkey's membership of EU during his visit to Turkey in November 2006. This change of stance on a political issue prompted an article in *TIME* magazine with the title "A Vicar of Doctrine Becomes a Diplomat." Within this article, David van Biema writes: "Benedict, 79, by publicly supporting Turkey's entry into the European Union and praying in Istanbul's Sultan Ahmet....Mosque, the man who had seemed one of the Roman Catholic Church's most inflexible prelates appeared to flip-flop both on his prepapal, keep-Europe-Christian stance and his previously expressed distaste for interfaith." (*TIME* December 25, 2006 - January 1, 2007).

This leads to the question: "What has changed in the character of Europe and Turkey to influence Pope Benedict XVI to modify his position on Turkey's membership of the political phenomenon of the 21st century?" Pope Benedict XVI should have distanced himself from the business of the European Union. What was his reason for commenting on Turkey's membership of the European Union – a project that has no room for the Lord Jesus Christ? Christians should not wail over the exclusion of God and the Lord Jesus Christ from the Blue-print of Europe. After all, it was a Christian who predicted the development of political Europe, its nature and future prospects before the European Union came into existence.

THE SAD IRONY:
THE CHURCH HAS BECOME A "SLAVE" TO A POLITICAL UNION THAT HAS REJECTED GOD AND THE LORD JESUS CHRIST

On 21 May 2005, before the French voted in a referendum on the European constitutional treaty, the Financial Times published an article titled *Europe's healthy religious tension.* It was reported: "Most French politicians admit that if God had been included in the EU constitution, the likelihood of a No vote on May 29 would have been far greater. The secular establishment would have been galvanised. So France got its way." It is clear, French politicians felt in order to secure a victory in their referendum on the European Constitution, it was necessary to eliminate God and the Lord Jesus Christ from the draft treaty. To this founder member of the European Union (France), God, the Lord Jesus Christ and Christianity were not needed for the cause of Europe. They were liabilities in the "Consolidated Balance Sheet" of Euro PLC's "Consolidated Financial Accounts" that had not been approved for 14 consecutive years. Major James Buffy-Maun reminded us in his letter to the *Metro* newspaper that "The EU is unable to sign off its accounts due to rampant abuses and fraud."

And when the teachings of the Bible were replaced with humanistic philosophies to bolster the chances of French politicians winning their referendum, what happened on the fateful day of 29 May 2005 when France voted on the European constitution? The masses, whom the politicians wanted to please by removing the Lord Jesus Christ from the Constitution of Europe, voted *"Non"* overwhelmingly to reject the document. The Lord Jesus Christ was not an impediment to the campaign organised by French politicians. On 1 June 2005, the Dutch, another founding member of the European Union, also voted *"NEE"* in greater numbers than the French to dumb the European constitution. As a result of the rejection of the European Blue-print, the whole European Project was thrown into confusion. Some of the European leaders, who proudly endorsed the EU constitutional treaty in Rome in October 2004, began to write the obituary of their handiwork.

VATICAN'S 'DEAL' WITH THE EUROPEAN UNION

The Financial Time's article on *Europe's healthy religious tension* reported: "...In the EU constitution...there may be no mention of God, but the churches have won, for the first time, a special right to consultation with European institutions, and a guarantee that the EU will not prejudice their national status." According to an European politician, "the Vatican was happy with the deal".

To begin with: Vatican, which does not believe in the authenticity of the Bible, does not act on behalf of all Christians. Now the question arises: If Vatican truly believes in the Sacred Scriptures, of which the Lord Jesus Christ is the Central Character, how could the Catholic Church have become happy in a deal with European institutions – a political body that snubbed the Lord Jesus Christ and rejected Him from its Constitution? In whose name did the Vatican bargain such a deal? The European politicians deemed it necessary to protect their interests by rejecting the King of kings, the Lord of lords. But the Vatican and other churches were happy to enter into a deal with a political union that has no room for the Lord Jesus Christ. Sadly, today, the Church has become a "slave" to the world –

following its humanistic philosophies that undermine the integrity of the Bible and the Divinity of the Lord Jesus Christ. So that Sacred Scriptures might be fulfilled, I would remind the Vatican that the real deal between the Church of Rome and the European Empire would be struck when the true leader of Europe is installed by the "ten toes" (Revelation 17:3, 12). *Verbum sapientis est.* The Lisbon Treaty has paved the way for the Emperor of Europe to be crowned.

WOULD HISTORY REPEAT ITSELF IN THE "MARRIAGE" BETWEEN THE EUROPEAN UNION AND THE ROMAN CATHOLIC CHURCH?

The Vatican and other churches ensured that the deal they made with the European Union would bring about a special right to have consultation with the European Union institutions, and their rights to keep their national status. But why did the churches establish a "deal" with a political system that has rejected the Lord Jesus Christ? Could it be anything to do with the past? Could it be anything to do with fear? King Solomon tells us, there is nothing new under the sun. So, what historical event could have, perhaps, motivated the churches, consciously or unconsciously, to strike a deal with 'That Thing' in Brussels? Would the "deal" survive? History, at times, repeats itself.

Let us recall the life and times of Henry VIII that was screened on the HISTORY CHANNEL. In the year 1509, King Henry VIII, just eighteen, married the widow of his late brother, Arthur. The woman was Catherine of Aragon, a Spanish Princess. Catherine was five years older than Henry when they married. The marriage was one that many historians claimed was for love. It was a happy marriage from the beginning. In 1516 Catherine bore Henry a daughter, whom they named Mary. Henry, though grateful for a healthy child, really desired a male heir. He believed the next child would be a boy.

Henry knew there was nothing wrong with his fertility; he had sired Mary plus various illegitimate children. So, when Catherine continued to have miscarriages and finally stopped producing children, Henry believed something was wrong with the marriage itself. Originally, Catherine had come to England to be the wife of Arthur, but just after four months of marriage, Arthur died. Henry reflected on this thought when he found a portion of Scripture in Leviticus 20:21 which states: *"If a man takes his brother's wife it is an unclean thing. He has uncovered his brother's nakedness. They shall remain childless".* This text provided Henry with a route to escape from the marriage to enable him marry a younger and a healthier Anne Boleyn.

Henry instructed Cardinal Wolsey to obtain an Annulment sealed by the only authority - the Roman Catholic Church. Catherine was a devout Catholic. This might have put the then Pope, Clement VII, in a dilemma about what to do with this faithful Catholic woman – especially since Catherine was adamant that she and Arthur had never consummated their marriage, and the previous Pope had given Henry and her right to marry after the death of Arthur. After years of trials, rebuttals and legal wrangling, Pope Clement refused to give Henry the dissolution he sought.

Henry realised that the Pope would never grant the Annulment he wanted. He was doomed to spend the rest of his life without a male heir. It was Henry's desire for a son, more than anything else that prompted him to start a reform that would eventually bring a new religious era in England. He had heard about the Protestant faith – a name derived from the protests against Catholic practices. In Germany, Martin Luther was expounding this new message: a Pope was not needed to contact God. Individuals were qualified, just like the Pope, to seek God personally without any intermediary.

The Roman Catholic Church was also pardoning sins for money. King Henry seized upon these corrupt practices to disassociate himself from the Church in Rome. The King would not only be part of a new religion in England, but would become the Supreme Head of the Church of England. This would pave the way to grant himself a divorce from the infertile Catherine and marry an already pregnant Anne Boleyn.

Henry's "sermon" was: "priests and monks were liars, who kept riches for themselves and left their flock in poverty. These religious men perpetrated stories of having relics-phials, filled with the blood of Christ, and pieces of items from the lance that pierced the side of the Lord. In their deceit, Catholic priests encouraged the poor and the uneducated to pay for such dubious relics. Ultimately, Henry had his soldiers travelled all over England desecrating Catholic Churches, killing their monks and ceasing the riches they had hoarded over the centuries.

Many Catholics who opposed Henry were murdered or burnt at the stake. One famous devout Catholic who was executed on Henry's orders was Sir Thomas Moore. He could not accept Henry as the Supreme Head of the Church of England. In his estimation, only the Pope had this "divine entitlement." But Moore himself was not righteous. He had perpetrated the torture and execution of those who worshipped God through the new religion. He branded them heretics. Henry's crusade affected the Roman Catholic Church. Their riches and lands were seized. The whole era was known as the time of The Reformation. To put it bluntly: it was a revolt against ecclesiastic dictatorship. In the end King Henry VIII initiated a trend in England that was to have repercussions all over the world for centuries to come. He might have done it for his own interests, but at least it allowed England to be educated by studying the Bible – something the Catholic Sir Thomas Moore had many people burnt for doing.

Now the question arises. "Is this one of the reasons why the Vatican and other churches have chosen to secure a pact with the European Union - to ensure that a new "Henry VIII" (disguised as the European Union) does not destroy and rob them of their riches?

THE PROPHETIC DEATH OF HENRY VIII AND ITS IMPLICATIONS

Henry's desire for a male child was met in his third marriage to Jane Seymour. His son, Edward, died at the age of 15 years. Henry could not produce the dynasty he longed for. He died in 1547. It has been suggested that in 1532, Friar Peto predicted that Henry would die and dogs would lick up his blood just as what happened to biblical character king Ahab, if he, Henry, should ever leave Catherine of Aragon for Anne Boleyn. It is reported that Henry's casket, containing the weight of a decomposing corpse, exploded while it was being transported to Windsor for burial. The sentries found dogs licking up his blood the next morning when the workers came to repair the casket.

Would such a fate that fell upon Henry VIII (metaphorically speaking) happen to the European Union because of its handing of power and authority to the coming king of Men, once the "beast" has dealt with the Catholic Church and other churches by destroying it? I am not surprised that Vatican and other churches have co-operated with the European Institutions to strike a "deal." How can the established churches entered into a transaction with the bureaucrats of Europe who have eliminated the Lord Jesus Christ from the constitution of Europe – a constitution which was described by some of those who were involved in its drafting as *"confused and confusing"*.

The Vatican and other churches that struck a 'deal' with the EU institutions must listen to what Lord Kerr of Kinlochart, who was intimately involved in drafting the European constitution, described the Blue-print of Europe: "It (the EU constitution) got out of control" and the EU's current predicament is a mess." The Times Editorial, commenting on the European constitution (which has been repackaged as the Lisbon Treaty) stated: "…This constitution is the wrong way to set about reforming and reinvigorating the EU. The constitution's opacities would render the EU even more incomprehensible to its citizens; and its ambiguities favour further empire building by Brussels; and it can lay no claim to responding sensibly and swiftly to enlargement…."

VATICAN AND OTHER CHURCHES' 'DEAL' WITH THE EUROPEAN UNION MUST TAKE PLACE

I repeat: how could Vatican and the 'other churches' have struck a deal with European Institutions whose constitution is deeply flawed from Christian perspective? The Churches should have had the sight to "see" what the European Union is for and its destiny. The reality is that their "deal" with the European Union must take place to serve as a picture of the real deal that should fulfil the prophetic words in chapters 17 and 18 of the Book of Revelation. Whatever guarantees Vatican and the other churches might have secured from the European institutions would be a temporary phenomenon. At the appointed time, the King of Europe would expose the "*deal*" as a sham. For the Lord Jesus Christ revealed to Apostle John what is to come: *"The beast and the ten horns you saw will hate the prostitute. They will bring her to ruin and leave her naked; they will eat her flesh and burn her with fire. For God has put it into their hearts to accomplish his purpose by agreeing to give the beast their power to rule, until God's words are fulfilled. The woman you saw is the great city that rules over the kings of the earth" (Revelation 17:15-18).* We must ask: Who is this "woman"? What is this "great city"? We will learn about them in the Appendix.

"SOUL" FOR SALE

It is worthy to note that before Vatican and 'other churches' entered into a 'deal' with the European Union, both the Vatican and the Church of England had already benefited financially from the European Union. These churches advocated support for Jean Monnet's vision of a united Europe. In his *The Principality and Power of Europe,* Adrian Hilton explains how the Catholic Church had been a vocal voice for the unification of Europe. He writes: "Since World War II, each Pope has thrown his weight behind moves toward the creation of a supra-national European Union. Pope John XXIII insisted that Roman Catholics should be 'in the front ranks' of the unification effort. In 1963, Pope Paul VI declared: "Everyone knows the tragic history of our century. If there is a means of preventing this from happening again, it is the construction of a peaceful, organic, united Europe."

Mr. Hilton further described how the European Union offered financial assistance to the Roman Catholic Church to finance one of their projects. He writes: "Europe was consecrated to Mary by the Vatican in 1309 and placed under her patronage. The Shrine of 'Our Lady of Europe', in Gibraltar, was instituted at the consecration. This shrine has been renovated with a £200,000 grant from the EU, about which the Vatican announced: 'It is the prayer of His Holiness that the shrine will be an evermore effective centre of unification, a place where under the patronage of Mary, the human family will be drawn evermore closely into a fraternal unity and peaceful co-existence." Even the European flag of 12 stars have been attributed to the woman with a crown of 12 stars in Revelation 12. The Roman Catholic Church claims this "woman" represents Blessed Virgin Mary. This is false theology. There are two "women" in Revelation 12. None of them represents Mary. Later on I will explain the significance of the European Flag with its 12 ring of stars.

If the Roman Catholic Church has consecrated Europe to the Blessed Virgin Mary, why is it that during the Austrian EU presidency the European leaders attempted to use pornographic images, not the image of the Virgin Mary, as posters to entice Europeans to "love" Europe? And secondly, why was the imagery of a mythical woman, *Europa,* sitting at the back of a beast (the pagan god Zeus) also used to rekindle interest in the European project? According to the Austrian foreign minister, Hans Winkler, "The best way to nurture a feeling for and interest in Europe is to discover its sensuous and cultural diversity." Why did this politician not recommend Europeans to visit the "Shrine of Our Lady of Europe" at Gibraltar and pray to her?

Again, an inspiring essay was produced by Jiri Grusa, the President of International PEN club, to motivate Europeans to embrace the European project. Why were Europeans not encouraged to seek guidance from the Blessed Virgin Mary by praying: "Hail Mary full of Grace….." The whole episode of European politicians using pornographic images and sensuous materials to promote Jean Monnet's vision of a federal Europe was a slap in the face of Vatican. Has Vatican sold its soul to EU for 30 pieces of silver? "This whole thing is a fairy tale, give me a break". I borrowed these words from Bill Clinton.

EUROPEAN UNION AND THE CHURCH OF ENGLAND

The Catholic Church is not alone in courting the European Union and promoting its values. The same could be said of the Anglican Church. Under the subject "Soul for Europe" in *The Principality and Power of Europe,* Mr. Hilton writes: "The Church of England has been complicit in promoting Britain's membership of the EU through the 'Soul for Europe' project". This project is part of the EU commission to promote itself. The project declares: "The building of Europe has a spiritual dimension. The objective of the 'Soul for Europe' is to encourage contribution to the unification of Europe. Mr. Hilton quoted the sentiments of the then President of the EU Commission, Jacques Santer: "The dialogue between the churches and the Commission is one of the most positive achievements." Mr. Santer praised those churches that promoted European Unity. He offered them grant aid for their labour and faithfulness to the European Project – a political project that is corrupt and with no democratic legitimacy; a godless enterprise that has no space for the Lord Jesus Christ.

According to Mr Hilton, "Applications for funding were filtered through the "Soul for Europe" screening committee, whose membership is secret. The criteria for eligibility include an intrinsic 'religious or ethical inspiration' giving meaning to the process of European unification; they must explicitly promote the integration of Europe; and they must publicly acknowledge that assistance has been received from the EU." This sinister agenda, according to Mr Hilton, was consistent with the words of the then German Chancellor, Helmut kohl, to the Pope, that 'it is the Christian duty of every citizen to work in order to build Europe." A Christian, who believes in the Bible and the genuineness of the Book of Daniel as a supernatural Book, but not a "pious fiction", as the Catholic Bible (*The New Jerusalem Bible)* claims, would not associate himself with the European Union.

Adrian Hilton tells us in *The Principality and Power of Europe:* "Soul for Europe" was estimated to have received £25 million from Europe to be distributed to "organisations which were either ecumenical or multi-faith, and who supported the abolition of the nation state." The author reveals how the then President of "Christianity and the Future of Europe," the Bishop of Ely, received seven grants for the propagation of "his Europe Agenda, including provision of help with parish twinnings." This, according to Adrian Hilton, "explains why Lord Brittan, former EU Trade Commissioner, was invited to speak at Ely Cathedral about the future of the EU, and letters to their church newsletter questioning the event were not printed because they were deemed to be 'political.' This prompted a remark from a member of the congregation: "Sir Leon can give a political lecture to a congregation in a Cathedral on a contentious issue, but no right of reply is allowed.....I would have thought this was a case of double standards lacking Christian values."

What a pity! A bishop, who is supposed to teach politicians where the European Union came from, where the European Union is going, and its future prospects, rather invites a politician with no clue of where the European Union is heading towards to lecture Christians about the future of Jean Monnet's project. What a betrayal of the "sheep" to the "wolves"! This is the case of the blind leading the blind to the pit. Have Roman Catholic and Anglican Churches "sold" their "souls" to the European Union that has no soul of itself? We are in the Age of Enlightenment in which "money talks." So, I ask the Established Churches: "Is it soul for sale at any price?" I encourage the reader to get a copy of *The Principality and Power of Europe.* It will open your eyes about the character of "That Thing" which is based in Brussels.

IF THE EUROPEAN UNION IS NOT A CHRISTIAN CLUB, WHAT IS IT?

In November 2002, Pope John Paul II, in an address to the Italian Parliament, urged Europe to mention Christianity in the European Constitution Mark 1. He pleaded with Giscard d'Estaing to ensure that the Constitution makes reference to Europe's Christian root. Vatican was disappointed when the French man told *La Republica*, an Italian newspaper, that he did not regard a reference to God as opportune since Europe was populated with Muslims, Jews, atheists as well as Christians (The Times 6 February 2003).

- If God and the Lord Jesus Christ are 'liabilities' in the "Balance Sheet" of the European Union Accounts;
- if "the EU is a Supranational organisation where religion is supposed to play no role";
- if religion is not a criterion for membership qualification to the European Union;
- if the EU is a secular organisation and by its own rules should be blind to religion,
- and if the European Union is not a "Christian club" as suggested by Tony Blair and other leading politicians, then what is the European Union?

Whatever the European Union is, it is certainly not for the Lord Jesus Christ. And the Lord warns: "He who is not with me is against me, and he who does not gather with me scatters" (Matthew 12:30). We must ask the questions:

- How on earth should the Roman Catholic and the Anglican Churches associate themselves with the European Union?
- Do leaders of these two Christian denominations not understand the Scriptures?
- Have The Catholic Church and the Church of England forgotten the warning of the Lord Jesus Christ? "
- How could the Church, which is supposed to be the Bride of Christ, share the same bed with the European Union which has no room for Christ?
- How could the former spiritual head of Roman Catholics in England and Wales, Cardinal Cormac Murphy O'Connor, suggest in a lecture that the Church and the State should help Europe to grow? This was an error - an irresponsible suggestion which is spiritual adultery of which the Church should be ashamed of. "O my people, your guides lead you astray; they turn you from the path, says the Lord. (Isaiah 3:12).

In His letter to the "Church in Thyatira," the Lord Jesus Christ writes: *"I have this against you. You have tolerated that woman Jezebel, who calls herself a prophetess. By her teaching she misleads my servants into sexual immorality and the eating of food sacrifice to idols. I have given her time to repent of her immorality and she is unwilling. So I will cast her on a bed of suffering and I will make those who commit adultery with her suffer intensely, unless they repent of her ways. I will strike her children dead. Then all the churches will know that I am he who searches hearts and minds..."* (Revelation 2:20-23). This is a sombre warning to the apostate church.

Let us witness how Timothy Garton Ash, the Oxford Professor in European Studies, described Europe in his article ***Islam and us:*** "...European fundamentalist secularists think that all religion is blindness and stupidity, a kind of mental affliction...The one form of evangelism which is still acceptable on the European left is evangelical Darwinism. Its fundamental belief is that all other forms of belief are symptoms of intellectual backwardness ... Europe is the place where post-Darwinian secularisation is most advanced. It's now the most secular continent on earth" (The Guardian 6 March 2003)

And in his article – *Requiem for a great leader* – Timothy Garton Ash, again, describes the secular condition in Europe. "Europe today is increasingly secular and materialistic", he writes. "The Holy Roman Empire has become the post-modern empire of consumerism. Far from being a "Christian club," as some Turks fear, the European Union would not even put a mention of God into the preamble to its constitutional treaty. If anything, it's a secular club..." (*Evening Standard* Friday, 8 April 2005).

We must, therefore, not be surprised that the Antichrist, the Man of Lawlessness, the Man of Sin, the Son of Perdition, would emerge from one of the secular nations in Europe. That *"Awful Being"* would have no regard for God or any desire for women (Daniel 11:37). This implies, the "Man of Lawlessness" would be ungodly – a celibate or a sodomite. The King of Europe, the personage with unusual charisma and political acumen, would grace our television screens, the Internet and the front pages of our newspapers and magazines. His voice would reverberate on all Radio Stations. This would be the eloquent political whiz kid who will fill the vacuum of political leadership in Europe and the Middle East. This WILL surely happen. The Lisbon Treaty – signed on 13 December 2007 – has prepared the grounds for European leaders to crown the powerful Kaiser who will lead Europe and the world to the "Carbon-Free Paradise of Peace and Prosperity."(CFPPP)

THE ANSWER TO THE QUESTIONS: "WHAT NOW FOR EUROPE?" "WHAT NEXT FOR A BROKEN EUROPE?"

We know on 1 June 2005, the Dutch delivered a fatal blow to the European Project. They rejected the constitutional treaty by an overwhelming majority of 62 percent to 38 percent. Their dumping of the European Constitution took place three days after the French rejected the same constitution by a majority of 54 percent to 36 percent. When these two founding members of the European Union from the "opposite sides of the ideological divide between the federal interventionist camp and the Atlanticists, who favour a looser, less regulated Europe", rejected the constitution of Europe, it was greeted with the following headlines:

- "After fatal French blow, the Dutch hammer final nail in the Constitution" (Daily Mail, Thursday, June 2 2005*)*.
- "Europe in turmoil as the Dutch vote No" (Financial Times, Thursday, June 2, 2005).
- "Fight to save constitution after Dutch Vote "Nee" (The Times 2 June 2005). And the editorial stated: "Dutch courage – The Netherlands has discredited the EU constitution more than France"
- "EUROPE IN CRISIS: POOL AXED - Our (British) EU vote shelved as 63% of Dutch say no" (THE SUN 2 June 2005).

On this same day, 2 June 2005, the front page of The Independent newspaper posed the crucial question, "WHAT NOW FOR EUROPE?" in 19 different languages of the European Union. And on the following day, 3 June 2005, The Times also asked the question: "WHAT NEXT FOR A BROKEN EUROPE?"

Here is the answer. Whether the frustrated and divided political leaders of Europe tear up the European Constitution or patch it; whether the enlightened politicians, who drafted the Constitution for the European Empire (which had no room for the Lord Jesus Christ), would treat their Blue-print as a corpse and bury it; whether the European leaders, who thought the Constitution was too complex for their people to have voted on it, would breathe life into the "corpse" and adopt it through the back door, or through the front door, or through the side door, or through the roof; whether Ireland is forced to adopt the Lisbon Treaty or dump it, the European Union would still function and grow. The "EU Titanic" would continue to sail. The 'experience Captain' is on his way to pilot Monnet's luxurious Titanic to its appointed destination to fulfil the Bible prophecy in Daniel 2 and Revelation 13 and 17.

After France rejected the Constitution, The Daily Telegraph published a commentary in its leading article, *"Mere Democracy won't stop the EU machine"*. According to the editorial, "...The French have reviled their own creation....It is hard to think of a graver crisis of legitimacy for the EU, if even France, Europe's most loyal daughter, wants no more of the racket...On any normal measure, the EU has lost the confidence of its citizens. But the project was not meant to be democratic. From the first, the EU's founding fathers understood that it needed to be immune from public opinion. The genius of Jean Monnet and Robert Schuman was to design a system in which supreme power was wielded by unelected officials, and in which the peoples were presented with a series of *faits accomplish.* When in 1992, they got their first No vote in Denmark's referendum on Maastricht, our masters were too set in their ways to consider respecting the result, and so pushed on regardless. They will do the same thing today" (The Daily Telegraph 30 May 2005). Indeed, true to their character, the EU leaders succeeded in rebranding the rejected Constitution as a new EU Treaty – playing with words to confuse the 'ignorant' Europeans and Britons.

The political elites in Europe and Britain thought they were "smart" – taking the electorate for granted. However, with their arrogance, and blinded by 'ignorance', they were bringing to pass what a brilliant "Anglicanised Irishman of Scotch extraction" had already written about Europe and its future. And this would fulfil the prophecy revealed to the young Hebrew Prince who was in exile in Babylon. This was about 2612 years ago when Daniel was serving in the court of King Nebuchadnezzar. Without any question, the construction of the European Project would be completed for a purpose which its "Master builder", Jean Monnet, did not know.

A political commentator put it clearly: "The constitution may be dead, but Europe will survive" (The Times 2 June 2005). Yes, Europe will survive to be led by the last Caesar of the revived Roman Empire. And the stage will be prepared for the 'Rolling Stone' to descend to fulfil the prophetic messages in the Books of Daniel and Revelation: "A divided kingdom with strong and weak nations; A divided kingdom with a divided people; A divided kingdom with mixed people who will not remain united"...and the stone cut without human hands will struck the dazzling statue from its toes of iron and clay to its head of gold... (Daniel 2:39-43). "The ten horns ...are ten kings who have not yet received a kingdom, but who for one hour will receive authority as kings along with the beast. They have one purpose and will give their power and authority to the beast" (Rev. 17:12-13).

The prophetical description of the complexion of the European Union, which is recorded in Daniel 2:39-43, was partly highlighted in the editorial of The Independent newspaper: "...The reasons for the French and Dutch rejections have been so disparate. In both countries the "no" vote combined a host of factors, from dissatisfaction with the current state of their countries and their present governments to the effects, as they saw them, of Europe's rapid expansion. The far right in France joined with the communists and socialist left to reject a treaty they saw as representing the interests of small elite. The Dutch middle class rejected the treaty in part because they felt the character of their country was changing in ways they found unacceptable. Others objected to the price rises and economic instability they associated with the euro." This, undoubtedly, is a clear picture of the European Union: a divided kingdom with mixed people who are not united.

And the Financial Times also highlighted some of the prophetic aspects relating to the European Union that were recorded in Daniel 2:39-43 (A divided Kingdom of big and small countries; a Kingdom with divided people). In a column titled *Dutch find 20 reasons to reject EU treaty,* the newspaper reported: "Heading the list of reasons was a fear that the Netherlands would lose influence in a Europe that would favour large countries. Close behind came domestic concerns...the view that Dutch political leaders have failed to consult the public and have run a woeful campaign to encourage ratification. More than a quarter of No voters.....opposed Turkey's application for EU membership, and nearly as many feared an European superstate...Others simply said they disliked politics....."

The Times newspaper also published some of the comments of those who voted on the constitution to confirm the biblical prophecy relating to the European Union as a divided "kingdom" with mixed people who are not united: Here are they:

- "I voted "no." I believe the current treaty is not democratic enough.
- "Referendums are always a bad idea because peoples' vote are guided by emotions. They don't want change."
- "This is a free country. We do not want Europe to come and change it."
- A Dutch man said: "They want to make it one country like America, and that's not good. I like being a Dutchman. Each country has its own rules – a Dutchman and an Englishman are different. Our identity, our laws, what we are proud of will disappear."

Political leaders in Europe were also divided. These headlines confirmed it:

- "Around Europe a deep division clearly exists" (The Guardian May 31, 2005). Under this headline, Nicholas Watt and Luke Harding wrote: "Divisions between "old" Europe and "new" Europe were highlighted ....as leaders across the continent clashed in the wake of the French rejection of the EU constitution. Gerhard Schroder, the German Chancellor, spoke up for the EU's six founding members when he hailed the Franco-German alliance and called for the ratification of the constitution to continue. In the new corner, the Czech president, Vaclav Klaus, echoed the private thoughts of British ministers by dismissing the constitution as "a thing of the past."

- *"Blair and Schroder at odds on EU treaty"* (Financial Times 3 June 2005). Under this title, Daniel Dombey and George Parker reported: "Divisions over the fate of the European constitution deepened .....as Germany and Britain embarked on opposing diplomatic initiatives amid revelations that senior commissioners have been privately pushing for the treaty to be suspended." What an irony! A constitutional treaty, which the leaders of Europe enthusiastically endorsed it to mark the beginning of a new dawn for the European Empire, later became a thorn in their flesh that some struggled to remove it.

EUROPE'S TORTUOUS JOURNEY TO THE "PROMISED LAND"

On 29 October 2004, in the city of Rome, amid great excitement, leaders of the then 25 member-states of the European Union signed the constitutional treaty of Europe. On 30 October 2004, The Times published an article "*West meets East for an historic EU signing*". Richard Owen described Europe's day of destiny when the European leaders "put a seal on Europe's Constitution." He stated: "At an historic and lavish ceremony on Capitol Hill, in the room where the EU's founding treaty was signed by just six nations, prime ministers, and foreign ministers celebrated the reunion of East and West against a backdrop of Roman Statues and Renaissance frescoes".

The summit host, the Italian Prime Minister Silvio Berlusconi, declared: "Never before in history have we seen an example of nations voluntarily deciding to exercise their sovereign powers jointly in the exclusive interests of their peoples, thus overcoming age-old impulses of rivalry and distrust". At the same summit, President Ciampi of Italy boasted about the endorsement of the European constitution. He declared: "It is a birth of a political union, not only an economic and social union; an event unique in the history of our Continent, a turning point in the history of humanity". And Mr. Jan Peter Balkenende, the Prime Minister of the Netherlands, added his compliments: "Integration had turned Europe into a realm of peace and co-operation that is the envy of nations".

To these political elites Jean Monnet's gradualist vision of a federal Europe was being realised. The reality is the European leaders were unconsciously bringing into fruition what an "Unknown British public servant" had already written about Europe before Jean Monnet was born. The unknown and uncomfortable truth is that, and I repeat: The "god of Europe", Jean Monnet, was just a 'slave' who toiled for the British 'master' he never knew. And had nations understood the implications of the European Union and known its future prospects, they would not have envied the European Union. The EU is a 'big empty barrel' making lots of noises. The European Project is a 'big tree' to be cut down with a 'small axe'. It is the 'uninformed' who envies Monnet's "Luxurious Titanic" and yearns to board it to his own detriment.

The Italian Prime Minister persuaded the European leaders to hold the signing ceremony in Rome for reasons of history. Signor Berlusconi "vowed that Italy would be the first to ratify the Constitution, using a parliamentary vote instead of a referendum." This historic event, which took place in Rome in particular, is very significant. Why? Because of the role the city of Rome would play before the end of this generation. We will learn more about Rome when we discuss the "Woman on the Beast" in the Appendix.

The 25 European leaders committed themselves to debating and ratifying the treaty by November 2006. The signed document was intended to guide Europeans to the "Promised Land of Security, Peace and Economic Prosperity." But in June 2005, some of these leaders, who had celebrated the endorsement of the EU constitution as an excellent blue-print for Europeans, were plotting to kill and bury the very document which was to become the beacon of light for Europe and the world. These political leaders of the biggest economic market in the world could not foresee that within just 8 months from the day they signed the constitutional treaty as the "Light of Europe", two of the founding members of the European Project, France and the Netherlands, would reject the constitution. The Times editorial of 31 May 2005 described this document as "incomprehensible and self-indulgent."

THE "AGE OF ENLIGHTENMENT" AND THE "AGE OF DARKNESS"

- Where was the "foresight" of the enlightened politicians in the Age of Enlightenment, who claimed the Lord Jesus Christ would be a stumbling block in the pursuit of the European Dream of peace, economic prosperity and security?
- Why were the architects of the European constitution, who eliminated God from their document, unable to foresee that the French and the Dutch would reject their "excellent document" to cause a "political earthquake" that would create confusion and divisions among the peoples of Europe?
- Where was the "sight" of the European leaders who sanctioned the constitution and praised its merits as the framework that would help deliver prosperity to all the citizens of the member-states?

However, Daniel, who was confined in Babylon in the "Dark Age" of the 6th century, was able to foresee over 2612 years ahead of him, and to record the present divided state of the European Union of weak and strong nations - a divided kingdom of mixed people who would remain divided. Daniel also recorded the future of the Revived Roman Empire.

The crisis that engulfed Europe due to the rejection of the European constitution MK1 by France and the Netherlands clearly demonstrated the limitation of human knowledge and the flaws in our human intelligence. Blinded by pride and prejudice, some pompous intellectuals rely on their intellect to ridicule Christians by claiming, "It is intellectual nonsense to believe in religion", and a "belief in religion is intellectual backwardness". Why couldn't these super intellectuals have the foresight to advise their political masters, that the European constitution would be dumped by two of its founding members?

Where were those European scientists, who rejected any idea of a Creator, but subscribed to Darwin's fable that they descended from apes? Why didn't the intellectuals use their super computers to advice their political masters that France and the Netherlands would reject their blue-print so they should not conduct any referendum to derail the European Project?

THE FOOLISH PRIDE OF POMPOUS INTELLIGENT MEN

The disciples of Darwin should recoil into their laboratories. Scientists do not know everything. They don't know the future. After all, it was a "super scientist" who fooled the world and threw the scientific community into chaos when he presented false research on human cloning. This headline, "*Snuppy the puppy was cloned, but everything else was a fake*", which appeared in The Times of 11 January 2006, told the story of deceit. "HE CLONED a dog, but not much else. While Woo Suk Hwang (a professor in science) did create the first cloned puppy, his human cloning was revealed....to be one of the greatest frauds in modern science..."

Before this Korean scientist was exposed, the world adored him as a "saviour" who had pioneered a research to help cure incurable diseases. The Bible asks, "Where is the wise man" in our age of Enlightenment? "Where is the scholar" in our Age of Enlightenment? "Where is the philosopher" in our Age of Enlightenment? "Has God not made foolish the wisdom of the world? The Lord says: "I will destroy the wisdom of the wise; the intelligence of the intelligent I will frustrate". (1 Corinthians 1:19-20). According to the "Seer of Dublin", the Bible was not written for the wise of this world, neither for fools. It was written for men with spiritual intelligence and common sense.

When human beings were used as guinea pigs to test a new drug, what happened? The volunteers nearly lost their lives. Science is not "under threat from rising tide of religious fundamentalism" as suggested by Britain's most senior scientist, Lord

May (Source: Financial Times 30 November 2005). The threat to Science comes from bogus scientific claims and dubious medical drugs, not from those of us who firmly believe the world was created in SIX LITERAL DAYS by the Omniscience God through His Beloved Son, the Lord Jesus Christ, the King of kings and the Lord of lords. Amen!

The Bible says: "He (the Lord Jesus Christ) was in the beginning with God. Through Him all things were made; without Him nothing was made that has been made. In Him was life, and that life was the light of men. The light shines in the darkness, but the darkness has not understood it" (John 1:2-5). The Lord Jesus Christ is credible than all the Super scientists and intellectuals and politicians of the Age of Enlightenment. The Lord Jesus Christ boldly proclaims: "I am the light of the world" (John 9:5) "I am the bread of life" (John 7:48). "I am the way, the truth and the life." "I am the resurrection and the life" (John 11:25). Who on planet earth can make such claims? NONE. Evolution is Darwin's gift to the ignorant scientists and 'blind' clergymen. These intelligent men removed their designer wrist watches; remove the contents into a bowl and reach the 'wise' decision that their designer watches were accidents. The brilliant Irish scholar wrote: "A man who cannot give account of his own existence is a fool. And he who denies God cannot give account of his existence."

Let us return to the critical question which needs an answer: "Why did the political leaders of 25 different countries in Europe, with millions of people who are divided by history, culture, and values, sign a document to commit these poor souls with different languages and traditions to form a United States of Europe?" The answer is simple: to fulfil the prophetic Word of the Lord Jesus Christ in the Books of Daniel and Revelation.

Before we continue with our discussion I would pause to remind the arrogant intellectuals who ridicule Christians of being "intellectually backward", that it was not a scientist, but a Christian – an intellectual among intellectuals, a giant among giants, not a 'pigmy' among today's 'pigmies' – who was the first to simultaneously predict the rebirth of the nation of Israel in Palestine and the birth of a confederation of European nations before these two political phenomena in history took place in May 1948 and May 1950 respectively. Where was the principal architect of the European project, the Frenchman Jean Monnet, the "god" of Brussels, when a Christian intellectual published that the political union of European nations would be the next major "political feature" in history after the restoration of the Jews to Palestine?

European scientists and their political leaders have no clue of the destination of their European Titanic. I challenge the Super Secular Scientists (SSS) to apply their scientific knowledge to predict where the European Vessel would land, and who will fill the leadership vacuum in Europe, and who will solve the Middle East crisis to bring 'everlasting peace and security' not only to the Mediterranean Region but the entire world. The superficial knowledge of European scientists and politicians about the source of the European Union has blinded them from the truth about what the European Union is for and its future. Hence the question posed by Minnete Marrin; "What is Europe for?

WHEN NEGATIVE IS POSITIVE TO FULFIL BIBLE PROPHECIES

Even when the French and the Dutch dumped the EU Constitution, and some Europeans expressed lack of interest in the European Enterprise (so that the Scriptures might be fulfilled), European leaders were divided into two camps: those who wanted to kill the constitution and bury it, and those who wanted to continue with the ratification of the treaty. The confusion and the division among European leaders and political commentators were such that, some politicians interpreted France and the Netherlands "No" to the EU constitution as a "Yes" – thereby giving them the mandate to continue with the building of the European Empire.

This was how The Times confirmed the ambition of the European leaders to create the European Empire to fulfil the prophetic word in the Bible: "Although 57 percent of the French voted "non", and 62 percent of the Dutch said "nee," few were prepared to admit that Europe's elite had lost touch with the people, and that in their relentless drive for integration, they had left their citizens behind. In the Alice-in-Wonderland world of Brussels, "no" has been interpreted as "yes".

The Times further reported how Margot Wallstrom, the Commissioner's Swedish vice-president, produced a poll showing that 57 percent of the French who rejected the constitution actually wanted more European integration. "A majority who said "no" are favourable to the whole European project." It is not that they have said "no" to the idea of European integration. It is not a rejection of the European project." And even after the Dutch "rejected the European constitution in far greater numbers than the French.....European political leaders insisted that the vote was not against the constitution. The European Green Party rushed out a statement saying, "No" in France and Holland does not mean "no" to the European constitution." Grazia Francescato, the party spokesman added: "It is evident that this "No" is not a real "No" against the constitution, but a vote of protest against..... the neo-liberal policies of their governments".

After France and Holland had overwhelmingly rejected the proposed European Constitution, one would have expected the European leaders not to have implemented any of the "Packages" that was rejected in a democratic vote. Yet, the political leaders of Europe, who claim to know better than their citizens, turned a deaf ear to the voice of the masses. They began to implement parts of the discarded constitution. This was revealed in a newspaper column headlined: *Rejected by two nations, but bureaucracy still rolls on - Officials are already implementing parts of the constitution before it has been ratified.* (The Times 8 June 2005). Under this headline, Anthony Browne wrote: "The European constitution may have been rejected by France and Netherlands, and been put on ice by Britain, but in Brussels the work of implementing it is forging ahead. European officials started working on many of the constitution's innovations as soon as it was written, insisting that they should not wait until it was ratified......EU officials are already setting up the offices of Europe's first permanent president, an appointed post established by the constitution to replace the rotating six- month presidency, which is held by Europe's elected heads of government......The EU is forging ahead with a diplomatic service officially called an External Action Service, with EU embassies and ambassadors in every country to project EU foreign policy and issue EU visas. The service, which some governments hope will replace national diplomatic services, will answer to the European foreign minister, a post created by the constitution, but to which Javier Solana, the EU's current head of foreign policy has already been appointed." Indeed the Lisbon Treaty, signed on 13 December 2007, confirmed these powerful positions in the European Union.

Mr Desmond Sawyne, reporting on "the degree of Euro-scepticism in the Conservative Party said, "The EU constitution is being implemented not so much by stealth but quite openly, even if incrementally." (The Guardian 12 July 2006)

The undemocratic approach by the European leaders to implement sections of a constitution, which had already been rejected by two of the founding members of the European Union, prompted this response: "Opponents of the constitution condemned the pre-emptive implementation. Timothy Kirkhope, the leader of the Conservatives in the European Parliament, said: "There is no subtlety to this process; the constitution's defenders are not even attempting to disguise their efforts to implement it one way or another. It is both extremely arrogant and contemptuous of democracy." Anthony Browne further reported: "The document's supporters insist that even if it is dead, it could still be justified to bring in the best part of it..."

It is clear, the European Union is hostile to democracy. Yet, it preaches democracy and supervises elections in third world countries whereas it refuses Europeans to vote on a document that would affect their lives. The EU personifies dictatorship of the 21st century. It has no democratic legitimacy and no political accountability. But this is what it should be so that what the great Irishman recorded about the character of political Europe would be fulfilled. He described political Europe the *"vile confederacy of the latter days."* On democracy, he wrote: "Democracy is the goal towards which civilization is tending; but democracy in its full development is one of the surest roads that leads to despotism."

Politicians always attempt to find their own way where there is no way. In July 2006, the Financial Times reviewed a book titled *The Constitution for Europe* in a space titled "*Politicians will not take Non for an answer.*" The review states: "One year after those double "No" votes, Europe's ruling classes are busy devising ways to bring the constitution treaty back to life, with the aim of reviving all or part of it by 2009. In Brussels the No votes of Spring 2005 are often portrayed as an "accident." France and the Netherlands did not really mean to reject a treaty designed to refound and modernise the European Union for the 21st century."

According to the review, the task of salvaging the wrecked constitution was trusted to a French legal brain, "a renowned fixer," to find "the wording to soothe member states..." In the opinion of the author of *The Constitution for Europe,* Europeans "can be persuaded to think again about a new treaty, but only after several years of confidence-building by the EU through policy delivery in areas such as the single market, illegal migration and energy security..."

I ask the question: "Had the majority of French and Dutch voted "YES" to ratify the constitution, would they have allowed a "fixer" from the "No" camp to argue that the "Yes" voters should be given a chance to change their minds? Had the constitution been accepted by France and Holland, the bureaucrats in Brussels would have rejoiced with this song: "A new era has dawn for Europe." The "all-knowing" Eurocrats do not take "No" for an answer. They always find ways to override the wishes of the masses to suit their interests. The political elites, in their haste to bring to pass what a Christian had predicted about their project, unconsciously, did whatever possible to introduce the discredited constitution through the back door. And they succeeded with the Lisbon Treaty. And it is this treaty which paves the way for Europe's bleak future to come to pass, as predicted by the "Seer of Dublin".

It is hypocritical for the European Union to claim to be a beacon of democracy to the world. How democratic is the European Union for the President of the European Commission to criticise Russia: "For me it's not yet clear, honestly, if Russia will be a full democracy in the way we see it in the EU. This is not yet clear" (Source: The Independent 13 July 2006: *"Russia is not a democracy, says Barroso")*

The opponents of the European Constitution should not be surprised by the arrogance of those European leaders who implemented parts of the rejected constitution which all the member-states of the Union should have ratified it. I repeat: in their zeal and desperate attempts to fulfil their dream of building a Mighty European Empire from the North to South, and from East to West, these European leaders were rather in a hurry, unconsciously, to fulfil the prophetic messages which had been written about the revived Roman Empire over 2600 years ago.

"TIME FOR REFLECTION"

Whenever European leaders reflect on course they have taken to lead Europeans to the Promised Land of "Carbon-Free", they should also reflect on what Daniel wrote in chapters 2 and 7 of his Book, and what Apostle John recorded in chapters 13 and 17 of the Book of Revelation. It takes a wise man to avert a prophecy.

A DESPERATE CRY FOR LEADERSHIP IN EUROPE

Most Europeans have lost confidence in their leaders. To some, their political masters have "shun responsibility" to lead them. The reality is none of the current European politicians possesses the qualities to escort Europeans to the "Promised Land." That is why the masses are wailing for a powerful leader to guide them to their "destiny." This fact was made clear in various newspaper articles. Even before the French and the Dutch rejected the European constitution, the masses cried for new leadership in Europe.

Let me share with you some of the desperate cries for leadership in Europe. They are significant.

- On 21 March 2005, the title of a leading article in the Financial Times read *How Europe has lost its way. The EU suffers from a lack of political leadership.* According to this article, "The EU conveys the impression of an organisation that has lost its sense of purpose and direction. It is no surprise that this has led to a rise in political infighting and mutual recriminations among its leaders...At the heart of Europe's state of confusion is a lack of political leadership....It is the lack of leadership from France and Germany that is more directly responsible for many of the EU's problems. The two countries used to be the engine of European integration. But both appear to have lost some of their enthusiasm for the "European project"...Both countries have become inward looking and defensive...The trouble is that EU leaders are unlikely to do more than paper the cracks. What the EU is crying out for is not another series of promises, but a leadership committed to genuine reforms".
- On 24 May 2005, a title in the editorial column of the Financial Times read: *Gridlocked Europe – And no sign of the leadership the EU needs to break out of it.* According to this article, "...The challenges the EU faces are so formidable and the socio-political backdrop is so unpropitious that it is hard to think of any other country that would do better, at least with the present crop of European leaders. It is, in any case, not just a question of leadership but also of the increasingly cantankerous popular mood....Europe's political elite sometimes seems like those Bourbon kings who learned nothing and forgot nothing. It still believes the secret

of EU integration is smart drafting of laws and treaties, mostly behind closed doors, and timely if unseemly horse-trading (ditto). That formula needed high levels of popular confidence in political leaderships – definitely not the case now".

- On 25 May 2005, there was another cry for leadership in Europe in an article published in the Financial Times. The titled read*: Europe urgently needs leadership.* The writer, Stephen Wall, commented on how the British and French governments should co-operate to face, "most of the big external challenges facing Europe – climate change, world poverty, international peacekeeping, the Middle East, Iran and relations with China ..." He stated: "Neither economically nor politically can Europe afford a split over its future, especially when there is no one country of the Union whose view amounts to a vision. But it is the lack of that vision that imperils the constitution, not its anodyne provisions. And the danger for Europe is not that we are embarked on an Anglo-Saxon dismantling of what the French must like, or some supranational super-state which some in Britain most fear. The real danger is that we muddle querulously along, neither delivering the competitive edge we need for our own prosperity nor the leadership the world needs for peace and stability..."
- Still on the need for leadership in Europe. Lord Douglas Hurd, a former British Foreign Secretary, who, in the 1990's, threatened to quit the Major Cabinet over a row about European Union, wrote an article titled *Two men and a woman who can save Europe"* (The Sunday Telegraph 29 May 2005). In this article, which was written before the French rejected the European constitution, Lord Hurd attempted to identify the leaders who could possibly rescue the EU from its crisis. He stated: "A "No" vote, whatever the motives of the voters, will in effect be a vote to keep the EU as it is today. This conclusion will be fiercely resisted by those who want to press forward in a different direction and by those who want to turn back". Lord Hurd added: "Skilled and brave leadership is exactly what we do not have. Or rather, the skills of our leaders are devoted to self-preservation. The Leaders of the four major countries of Europe, Britain, France, Italy and Germany are, in Disraeli's phrase, exhausted volcanoes. We see the occasional puff of smoke, but nothing of purpose. These are men without credit, without the power any longer to move and persuade". Lord Hurd identified potential leaders of Europe: Angela Merkel, a German politician, whom he regarded as "a woman of talent, shrewdness and integrity: ..a genuine nice person". Lord Hurd was then not clear whether Nicholas Sarkozy, the then French Interior Minister, or Gordon Brown, the British Chancellor of the Exchequer could be the next "to reach the top."
- On 31 May 2005, after the French decisively dumped the European con-

> stitution, there was another desperate cry for someone to lead Europe. A space in the Financial Times read: *"ROOM AT THE TOP – Union in crisis looks for strong leadership to fill the vacuum"*. The author of this article, commenting on the ineffective leaders in the European Union, concluded: "With a power vacuum in France and Germany, an inexperienced president at the European Commission and weak leaders clinging to power across many EU countries, Europe has seldom been so lacking in political direction".

On the issue of leadership in Europe, Jim Dougal, a former head of EU Commissioner's UK representation in London, highlighted the problem in a column titled *Working for Brussels bureaucracy became intolerable* (Financial Times 1 July, 2005). Commenting on his 7 years experience in the "Bureaucratic nightmare" that prevailed in the European Commission, Mr Dougal stated: "The crisis into which the EU has fallen since the French and Dutch referendums is not new. The Union and the Commission in particular, have been in permanent crisis for at least 10 years. Lack of leadership has become a way of life…..The citizens want to concentrate on economics not politics. To succeed it needs a credible voice and leadership..."

According to Mr. Dougal, Europeans want their leaders to "concentrate on economics not on politics." His observation was confirmed by Mr. Peter Gregory of Northwood in his contribution to a BBC Newsnight debate on *"How would you fix Europe?"* Mr. Gregory stated: "The original idea for the European countries under the Treaty of Rome was for it to be an European Economic Community….. But most of the peoples of those countries want to maintain the sovereignty of their own Democratic Institutions, which is something that the politicians and eurocrats don't understand or even wish to understand. They have created a monster that is already out of control, and do not seem to realise that they have for years now been seeking a form of political unity which is currently impossible. It is impossible because if two founder members have already voted no in referenda, what chance of being able to mould the thoughts and aspirations of the EEC, some of whom have had no time at all to rationalise their positions".

Anatole Kaletsky also raised the leadership issue in Europe. In his article *"The people of Europe have voted for paralysis – and perhaps obliteration"* (The Times, Thursday October 13, 2005), he commented on the new German election which ended in a deadlock without any outright winner (but eventually had a new woman Chancellor appointed under a grand coalition of the two major political parties), Mr. Kaletsky wrote: "After this…creation of a German government in which Angela Merkel will not even control the Finance and Foreign ministries, all three of the great European nations that have dominated the Continent's history for 2000 years --- Germany, France and Italy – are effectively leaderless. They will almost certainly remain politically paralysed at least until the French presidential election of 2007. The power vacuum now covering the whole of continental Europe is almost unprecedented, at least since the disastrous period between the two world wars..."

Another commentator, Effrey Gedmin, also commented on the German general election which ended in a political stalemate on 18 September 2005. He raised the leadership issue in his article titled *The price of Germany's indecision."* Mr. Gedmin stated: "...Europe desperately needs strong leadership, but it is hard to imagine a weak, inward-looking German government offering much promise" (Financial Times, Wednesday, 21 September 2005).

From the various newspaper articles we have read, it is clear Europe needs a skilled, brave and an intelligent person with a talent to pilot the "European Titanic." According to experts on European integration, the prospective leader of the European Union must be shrewd with integrity; a genuine and nice person with a vision to offer a political direction by steering the rudderless European ship to safety. Who is the qualified person to lead Europe? He would be the Last Caesar of the Revived Roman Empire. The powerful King of Men to 'solve' all the European problems is on the horizon. He would use his charm to seduce the European leaders to crown him as the emperor of the world's first 'non imperial empire.' But it would end in tears.

Despite the concerns of some Europeans about the creation of a federal Europe, their leaders are determined to promote a United States of Europe. For example, the former French Prime Minister, Mr. Dominique De Villepin, laid out his vision of a political Europe in an article titled *United way to a new political Europe.* This was published in the Financial Times on Wednesday, June 29, 2005. According to Mr. De Villepin, "....All around us, states (India, China, Brazil, South Africa)... conduct one-third of their foreign trade with each other. South American countries are developing economic ties. We must be able to defend our political, economic and social interests, presenting a united front." Mr. De Villepin added, "political unity in Europe is imperative for the defence of our values: democracy, human rights and cultural diversity ...the founding characteristics of our common project. Either we give ourselves the resources to build this new political Europe, or we resign ourselves to making our continent a vast free-trade area, governed by the rules of competition. Everyone must put an end to the ambiguity through action. We need ambitious projects....Europe is the world's leading trade power. Twelve member-states, including France, have created a stable currency: the euro....."

"So what?" I repeat the "Unknown truth" about political Europe that would make the French and the Germans feel "uncomfortable". A servant of the British Crown wrote about political unity in Europe and its future before the French founding fathers of the European Community, Jean Monnet and Robert Schuman, were born, and when the German Chancellor, Konrad Adenauer, was about six years old.

In the light of the former French Prime Minister's rhetoric about "political unity of Europe" and the desperate cry for a leader with muscle to lead the European Empire, we must ask the question: "Why are political leaders of Europe anxious to create a"United States of Europe" with its own currency, Central Bank, Parliament, Court of Justice, flag, anthem, military and police forces, a Constitution, a President and Diplomatic Offices around the world? Why were political elites in haste to rebrand a rejected constitution and impose it on the masses? The answer is simple. They must fulfil the prophetic word in Daniel 2:39-43. Surely, a United States of Europe – a strong political union of different countries of big and small nations, strong and weak nations, rich and poor states with mixed people who are not united – needs a strong leader with a credible voice. But the qualified man to lead Europe and the world is not known to Europeans. He is about to enter the political scene. The Lisbon Treaty has paved the way for his arrival.

SOLUTION TO THE LEADERSHIP CRISIS IN EUROPE

I would share with you a clue that could help Europeans and the rest of the world identify the strong leader of Europe. When a man appears on the political scene in Europe who looks like a "*leopard, with a feet like those of a bear and a mouth like that of a lion*" (Revelation 13:1), then mankind should wake up and rejoice, for their 'redemption' is near. The characteristics of the "beast from the sea" (Revelation 13:1-2) are what Europe and mankind are looking for to solve their political, social and economic and security problems.

The qualities of the 'politician' to lead Europe were partly described in a leading article published in The Times newspaper on Monday, 18 December 1876: "... What is it that all Europe is looking for? It is the KING of MEN, the great head of the Hellenic race, the man whom a thousand galleys and a hundred thousand men submitted to on a simple recognition of his personal qualities, and obeyed for ten long years..." He must be "a scholar, a statesman, a man of unflinching courage and irresistible enterprise, full of resources, and ready to look in the face of a rival or a foe...the man who can challenge for his own the Shield of AGAMEMNON, now waiting for the challenge, is the true Emperor of the East, and our easiest escape from our present difficulties".

Europeans should exercise patience. At the appointed time their 'prayers' would be answered. Their "saviour"– a commanding and fascinating man – a political whiz kid who is capable of unlocking complex problems with his amazing insight of science and technology (Daniel 7:8, 25) would merge to lead Europe to the "Promised

Land" of security, economic prosperity and peace. The future leader of Europe would be the embodiment of the virtues of King Nebuchadnezzar of Babylon (*Lion*), Darius of Medo-Persia (*Bear)*, Alexander the Great of the Macedonian-Grecian Empire (*Leopard)*, and the Caesars of Rome.

THE MOTHER OF ALL DECEPTIONS

I have already mentioned the coming world leader would be enthroned by the 10 powerful leaders in the United States of Europe (Revelation 17:12-13). He will pick up all the pieces from the wreckage and restored them. The road to world peace leads through Jerusalem. Without the end to the Israeli-Palestinian conflict, the world would not know peace. It is the last Caesar of the revived Roman Empire who would establish a 7- year peace treaty with the Jews and the Arabs. The world would experience 'peace and prosperity'. After three and half years of tranquillity, the mother of all deceptions would take place. The King of Men will break the peace covenant with Israel and her Arab neighbours (Daniel 9:27). The political genius will blaspheme the God of heaven, and claim to be God. His agent, "the beast from the earth" (the false prophet, Revelation 13:11) will perform extraordinary miracles that would attract the attention of the world to follow "the beast from the sea". The Emperor will demand homage to his idol in the Jerusalem temple. This icon would have been built by the "*False prophet*", the apostate Jew. And those who ignore his instructions would incur the wrath of the "Awful Being". In those days no one would be able to engage in any enterprise: buy or sell, without the stamp of his approval, which would be ***"666".*** (Revelation 13:13-18). It would all end in tears, and the world would experience the deception of all deceptions.

PAUL SPAAK'S 'PRAYER' WOULD BE ANSWERED

Between 1949-1951, Paul Henri Spaak, then Prime Minister of Belgium, was also the President of the Consultative Assembly of the Council of Europe. In his desperate search for a solution to the problems facing Europe, he boldly declared: "We do not want another committee. We have too many already. What we want is a man of sufficient stature to hold the allegiance of all people, and to lift us out of the economic morass in which we are sinking. Send us such a man and, he be god or the devil, we will receive him." The 'prayer' of Paul Spaak would be 'answered'. Europe will surely get such a man – a political showman, energised by Satan, and enthroned by the powerful leaders of the European Union. The King of Men, the man of stature, the Great Deceiver, would make a promising start to impress Europeans and the world. This political genius is what the Bible describes as the "Man of Lawlessness" (2 Thessalonians 2:7-9). The Lisbon Treaty has paved the way for the advent of the 'saviour' of Europe.

ARROGANCE AND IGNORANCE IN THE "VILE CONFEDERACY OF THE LATTER DAYS"

We have read how some Europeans and politicians opposed to God and Christianity being mentioned in the European constitution. When their desire was granted, they boasted: "We are very glad a reference to God has been left out....Religion is dying throughout Europe." Others chanted: "It would have been absurd to have God and Christianity in the EU constitution." Some danced: "God in the European Union constitution would have offended millions of people of different faiths and those who had no faith at all". The rest poured scorn on the Lord: "Inclusion of God would have been divisive; it would have been a mistake – a serious mistake."

I would raise these questions:

- Do these arrogant personalities know the source of the European Union?
- What is special about the European Enterprise?
- What is extraordinary about this EU Club, which has no credible leader?
- Are Europeans proud of a "project" whose accounts have not been approved for fourteen consecutive years because of fraud, errors and financial irregularities?
- What is unique about a political project which uses pornographic images to advertise its 'business' to win "sceptical customers"?

In the Age of Enlightenment, sex sells. So the European Union has adopted the 'commercial spirit' of the day - "Sex", to woo customers. What a pity! And after all, Robert Schuman who launched the European Project was neither an atheist nor agnostic. He was a committed Christian. The 'Father of Europe', Jean Monnet, described Schuman an "honest politician whom people would believe in whatever he said". And Dr. Konrad Adenauer described Schuman "a saint in business suit." Which of those who pour scorn on God and Christianity could claim to be an 'honest' politician?

FRAUD, CORRUPTION, NEPOTISM AND HYPOCRISY IN EU

On Wednesday, 16 November 2005, a column in The Times read: *"EU accounts still riddled with fraud and errors say auditors."* The Columnist explained how Europe's official financial watchdog refused to approve the European Union accounts for the eleventh year in a row because they were full of fraud and errors. According to the Brussels Correspondent, Anthony Browne, "The European Court of Auditors refused to give a statement of assurance on €100 billion (£67 billion) budget for 2004 because the vast majority of the payment budget was again materially affected by errors of legality and regularity."

Carl Mortished also commented on the same un-audited European Union accounts in The Times In an article headed *Another 'nul points' for the EU's book-keeping,* Mr Mortished compared the European Union to a Public Limited Company. He asked the question, "Would you invest in a company that for 11 consecutive years had failed to produce a clean set of Accounts?" Would you feel comfortable doing business with one of its local subsidiaries knowing that it was exercising unbridles authority to manage its own expenditure with no control and review from head office?" The columnist told Britons: "Whether you like it or not, you are that investor because the European Commission still has not a clue how tax euros are being spent." He concluded his commentary on EU accounts with the statement Herbert Weber, the President of the European Court of Auditors, made when presenting his report to the European Parliament: "... annual award of "nul points" to the EU accounts was proving embarrassing to some politicians."

Stephen Pollard also reported on the European Union's deceptive accounting practices in an article titled *Why can't this fraud be halted?* Writing in the 16 November 2005 edition of the Daily Mail, Mr. Pollard compared the European Union accounts to a self-employed who, having failed to complete his Tax Returns for several years, tells the Tax Inspector, "I have not got the slightest idea how much money I have received; no idea how I have spent it; could not care less where the money had gone, and couldn't be bothered to co-operate with the Tax Inspector's attempt to find out." Such a sole trader would find himself in prison for tax fraud. According to Mr. Pollard, having examined some of the reports for the past eleven years, "the scale of the fraud becomes shocking. For example, the Italians favourite scam claiming money for non-existent olive farms (there aren't enough olive trees in the whole of Italy to cover a fraction of the subsidies claimed) – appears to be spreading. In Austria, the extent of eligible Alpine pasture was overestimated by more than 60 percent – according to the auditors' report. Thirty percent of Greek subsidy grants are for maize which has never existed. On and on, it goes, paragraph after paragraph of brazen fraud perpetrated shamelessly."

The columnist concluded his commentary with this statement: "The damning truth is that fraud runs through the very heart of the EU. And whether it's subsidies for growing real food and then letting it rot, or the fraud highlighted in the auditors' report, someone has to pay. And that someone is you."

The fraudulent practices in the European Union continued. In October 2006, the Court of Auditors again refused to sign off the European Union accounts for the 12th year. The Times reported this fact in a column headed: *New Europeans use imaginary cattle to milk EU subsidies.* According to the report, Slovenia, which joined the EU

Club only two years, proved to be "imaginative as Italian olive growers when claiming Brussels subsidies."

Rory Watson, who supplied the information from Brussels, stated: "Inspectors found that half the cattle Slovene farmers said they owned, so qualifying them for special EU cow and beef grants, did not exist. A quarter of their sheep and goats were equally invisible...The auditors discovered that two thirds of the 95 EU-financed regional projects that they examined, which include new roads and bridges, contained "material errors." These ranged from a lack of proper invoices for expenditure being reclaimed to declaring costs that had no relation to the scheme being funded." The Court of Auditors' president, Hubert Weber, when presenting his findings declared: "The underlying reason why most errors occur is that beneficiaries - farmers, local authorities, project managers - claim more than they have the right to claim. They did so either through neglect, error or attempt to defraud."

The European Union Administrative, Audit and Anti-fraud Commissioner, Slim Kallas, reacted angrily to the criticism, He attacked the ways the Auditors interpreted their errors. The fact is in 2007, the same Auditors did not approve the accounts of the European Union because of fraud and financial mismanagement. This failure prompted a British politician to describe the EU as a "Banana Republic" (Sunday Express 11 November 2007). And in November 2008, the EU accounts were not approved again because of fraud and mistakes. Whatever be the case, since the EU Accounts have not been accepted by their own Auditors for fourteen consecutive years, had the European Union been a Public Limited Company, it would have been struck off from the Register of Companies. There would have been no legal justification for its existence as a viable business.

The "vile" character of the European Union was again exposed in an article entitled *EU accused of artificially inflating its aid figures* (The Independent, Friday 11 May 2007). According to the article, "Charities across Europe accused their governments of making misleading claims about their aid figures by including items which should not be counted as development aid...France and Austria were named as the two worst offenders for exaggerating their aid figures, with inflating accounting for at least half of the amount they give. UK ....met its promised targets..." The report continued: "Four countries, Spain, Portugal, Greece and Italy failed to even reach their promised 2006 targets in the first place. Italy remained the smallest contributor of aid."

The "abominable" nature of the European Union was again demonstrated in an art exhibition which was held in Rome in March 2007 to mark the 50th anniversary of the Treaty of Rome. Austria's contribution was a naked woman with legs apart waiting for anyone to walk in. This pornographic art portrays the moral and intellectual bankruptcy behind the European project.

The European Union is also known for its nepotism and job for the boys. In his *The Principality and Power of Europe,* Adrian Hilton reminded us how in 1998 twenty EU commissioners were forced to resign for cronyism and corruption. These officials awarded themselves "£130000 per annum for three years, received full salaries while in their caretaker administration, and retained full pension rights." Paul van Buitenen, who exposed fraud in the Commission, was suspended on half pay. A leading Labour MEP Pauline Green urged the European Parliament not to reinstate him. Mr. Hilton further wrote that Van Buitenen uncovered massive fraud in the Commission's biggest projects, involving millions of pounds. It was close friends and family members of the Commission who regularly won the contracts.

The job for reforming the Commission accused of nepotism and favouritism was given to men who were themselves no better. The New Commission which replaced the old one, according to Mr. Hilton, "consisted of a Belgian under investigation for fraud, a Spaniard suspected of complicity in the abuse of EU subsidies, a Dutchman who fiddled fines while working for Jacques Delors, and the then President of the Commission, Romano Prodi, who was himself accused of failing to declare taxes." A German newspaper wrote: "No-one wants to mess with the powerful people in Paris and Berlin. Everything remains as before."

"THIS WHOLE EUROPEAN UNION THING IS A FAIRY TALE"

The hypocrisy of the European Union was exposed in a newspaper column headlined: *The dirty secret of the Brussels limos.* It was reported that the European Commission admitted on 7 September 2006, that the limousines their senior staff use create "twice as much pollution as the limits Brussels is forcing on car makers. The EU Commission had threatened to impose legislation to reduce carbon dioxide emissions in new cars to 120 grammes per kilometre by 2012. But the 85 vehicles used by commissioners and other senior staff produce more than 258 grammes. Chris Davies, the Liberal Democrat MEP and the party's environmental spokesman who revealed the figures, said, "It's all deeply embarrassing. It is no longer acceptable for Brussels to insist that people should do as we say rather than do as we do. It is time we practiced what we preached" (Daily Mail Friday, 8 September 2006). This is the EU which is leading the world to reduce carbon dioxide to prevent environmental catastrophe from global warming. To borrow the words of Bill Clinton: "This whole thing is a fairy tale. Give me a break." No sane investor would risk his hard-earned money on shares in "EU PLC." Yet, Britain pours billions into EU PLC. Why?

The final testament: *"Europe's errant entrants: Brussels struggles to confront corruption within the new two"* (Financial Times, Wednesday 13 June 2007.) The EU was aware that Bulgaria and Romania had crime and corruption problems. Yet,

Brussels, in their haste to build an Empire to fulfil the prophetic word of the "Seer of Dublin," ignored the high-level rate of crime and corruption in these countries and welcomed them into their fold. The fact is the EU has no credibility to reject Bulgaria and Romania. After all, a seed produces its kind and light attracts light. And Birds of the same feathers flock together.

On 23 April 2008, this title appeared in the London Evening Standard: *"MEPs refuse to publish report on expenses."* It was reported Members of the European Parliament voted to refuse to divulge details of the millions of euros they claimed as 'legitimate' expenses. Expressing his concern about the behaviour of his colleagues in the 'Brussels Rubber-Stamp Factory', Chris Davies said: "These votes bring discredit and dishonour upon the entire Parliament. Far from cleaning up their act, a majority of MEP's seemed intent on allowing greed and self-interest to triumph over the proper financial management of public money". The fact is these MEP's have no shame just like their 'father' Jean Monnet, the architect of EU. The EU is morally bankrupt, intellectually bankrupt and spiritually bankrupt. It is 'Unfit for Purpose,' yet 'Fit for the Purpose.' This is the European Union which claimed to have mentioned God and Christianity in their constitution would have been "divisive", an "absurdity" and a "serious mistake." This is the European Union, led by the German Chancellor, Angela Merkel, who deemed it unnecessary to feature God and Christianity in the celebration of EU's 50th birthday. Does the Lord Jesus Christ need recognition from the European Union?

The financial mismanagement, the fraud, the corruption, the nepotism, the cronyism and the hypocrisy that are endemic in the European Union fulfil the "Seer of Dublin" prophetic description of political Europe: *"the vile confederacy of the latter days"*. You will soon meet the "Seer" who painted this picture of the European Union before the "Spiritual Father" of European Community, the honorary citizen of Europe, the French 'giant', Jean Monnet, was born. Monnet's portrait on a German postal stamp reads: *"Ehrenburger von Europa"*

THE LORD JESUS CHRIST DOES NOT NEED THE EUROPEAN UNION;
YET THE LORD NEEDS THE EUROPEAN UNION

We have learnt some politicians suggested God was not needed in the Euro-Constitution. Because, His presence would have been "divisive" to foil their goal of bringing into fruition the "fused" Europe which was the "gradualist vision" of their 'father', Jean Monnet. Bible-believing Christians should not take these politicians serious. They have no idea of the nature of their 'Project' and its prospects. As 'passengers' on the "European Titanic," they have no clue where their "luxurious ship" would land. I repeat: the superficial knowledge on European integration has blinded politicians from the truth about Jean Monnet's vision of a federal Europe. I boldly declare: "God is not interested to associate Himself with a "corporation" whose accounts are riddled with fraud and errors. The Lord Jesus Christ would not invest in a "company" whose directors are not accountable to its shareholders. The Lord would not become a "Chairman" of a Public Limited Company which uses pornographic materials to promote its business. The Lord does NOT need the European Union; yet the Lord NEEDS the European Union for His purpose.

Do pompous politicians and Europeans understand the significance of their opposition to God and Christianity? Let me repeat: it was a Christian, not an atheist, who first wrote about Jean Monnet's vision of a united Europe and its future before Monnet himself was even conceived. It was this same Christian who listed all the leading members of the European Union, and recorded that Austria, Egypt, Greece, Portugal, Spain and Turkey would become members of a confederation of European nations.

The Lord Jesus Christ needs the European Union to fulfil the prophetic message in the Books of Daniel and Revelation - which state the European Union would become the foundation stone upon which the "dead" Roman Empire would be "revived", and the 10 powerful leaders of this European Empire would delegate their power and authority to the "Man of Sin" who would deceive them with his charisma, eloquence, and political and scientific skills; and He, the Lord of lords, the King of kings, would come down like a "Stone" to crush the 'Magnificent edifice' from its toes of baked clay and iron to its head of gold. He, who has ear, let him hear what the scriptures say.

Secondly, the Lord Jesus Christ does not need the European Union. Why? Because, the European Union is not "fit for purpose" (to borrow the words of Dr. John Reid) – to proclaim His Gospel of "Repentance and forgiveness of sins", which brings lost souls into His eternal kingdom of righteousness. The Lord Jesus Christ has delegated the responsibility and authority for the execution of His "Business" (the Preaching of the Gospel) to the members of His "Club" - those who have been called out of the "sea" (the corrupt world) and have surrendered their lives under His authority."

The preaching and teaching of the Gospel of Christ are not the business of the apostate church which is 'married' to the eco-world; sold its soul to the European Union for 'thirty pieces of silver'; and apologised to Darwin. The apostate Church is the "Church in Ephesus" (which has lost its first love for Christ); it is the "Church in Pergamos" (which is married to the world); it is the "Church in Thyatira" (which is full of rituals, false teachings and sexual immoralities); it is the "Church in Sardis" (which is dead), and it is also the "Church in Laodicea" (the Luke-warm Church which is filled with arrogance, and is useless to the Lord to the extent that He will spit her from His Mouth) (Revelation 2 -3).

I repeat: the "Business" of the Lord Jesus Christ - the preaching of His Gospel - is not for the European Union and her "eco- bride", the degraded Church. This "odd couple" have no room for the Lord of lords and the King of kings. Their laws and teachings undermine Sacred Scriptures, which bear testimony of the Lord Jesus Christ. For example, they have rejected the Lord's teaching on creation in Matthew 19:4-6 and put their faith in Darwin's fairy tale of evolution, which, according to the "Seer of Dublin," it is "*first, merely a philosophic theory, second, that it is unproven; third it is inadequate and fourth...it is unnecessary, except of course those scientists who cling to any plank that will save them from having to acknowledge the existence of God.*" (A Doubter's Doubt About Science and Religion)

CHRISTIANS SHOULD NOT MOURN OVER THE EXCLUSION OF CHRISTIANITY IN THE EUROPEAN CONSTITUTION

On 29 September 2004, The Times newspaper published an article titled *European Union entry might fail to delight the Turkish.*" Carl Mortished made this statement: "....Turkey is patriarchal, family- oriented and devout. Europe---as exemplified by the core states of Britain, France and Germany --- is materialistic, libidinous and (largely) atheistic". This complexion of the European Union disqualifies her to be a "Christian club" to promote the Lord Jesus Christ in our dying world. For this reason, we, the Bible-believing Christians, do not envy the European Union despite its economic 'successes', and the trillions of euros it has poured into Europe for prestigious and bizarre projects to win the hearts of Europeans. Just as the Titanic of the 20th century was doomed before it set sail on its maiden voyage in 1912, so was the "EU Titanic" of the 20th century doomed before it "set sail on its maiden voyage" on 9 May 1950.

In our Age of Enlightenment the popular political and social "Song" is: "Change, Change, Change; "Reform, Reform, Reform"; "Economy, Economy, Economy"; "Money Talks, Money Rules" and Sex Sells." But the Lord tells us: "What will it profit a man if he gains the whole world, and loses his own soul. Or what will a man give in exchange for his soul" (Mark 8:36-37). We appreciate the development of the European Union from its incubation in 1950 to its present "majestic" form of 27 nations with more nations in haste to join. The reality is the existence of this political and economic phenomenon of the 21st century proves the accuracy of Bible prophecy as we have discovered it in Daniel 2:41-43. We praise the Lord for the progress of "*the vile confederacy of the latter days*" which strengthens our faith in His Word. Amen!

Faithful Christians should not be disappointed and mourn over the failure of European politicians to mention God and Christianity in their constitution. And

Christians should neither have rejoiced were God and Christianity had taken the centre stage in the Charter of Europe. Why? Because, the European Union is NOT a Christian club by any standard. Even their own politicians preferred the European Enterprise to remain a non-Christian club so that it would become attractive, and not a stumbling block, to non-Christian nations that are queuing to join the political phenomenon of the 21st century and the biggest economic market in the world. And had even God and Christianity been mentioned in the European constitution, it would not have made the European Union a "Christian club" in any shape or form to preach "Repentance, for the kingdom of God is at hand". As the columnist, Rosemary Righter, reported in the 28 May 2004 edition of The Times: *"Let the Turks in: the EU isn't a club for Christians."*

The former British Foreign Secretary, Jack Straw, in giving his "full support to Turkey (to become a member of the European Union) insisted that proving the EU was not a Christian club would help to resolve the *"clash of civilisations"* and win the war on terrorism" (*The Times* 26 March 2004). The truth is that there is nothing to be proved about European Union's relationship with Christianity. The fact is: the EU is NOT a Christian club by any imagination. The Lord Jesus Christ, Who built His "Club" (the Church), does not regard the EU as His *"Own"*. The European Union conducts its business in secrecy to impose laws on its member states. The EU is hostile to truth and democracy. True Christianity conducts its "business" in the open. Because the Lord Jesus Christ advised the disciples to proclaim from the roof-top whatever He had taught them in secret. Christianity should never have been an issue to engage the attention of European politicians in deciding whether to admit Turkey into their 'fabulous club' or not.

If politicians and political commentators believe admitting Turkey into the biggest economic market in the world could help prevent the so-called "clash of civilisations" and win their war against terrorism, then "Let the Turks in: the EU isn't a club for Christians." Politicians should not have dragged Christianity into EU politics regarding Turkey's membership of their club.

The hours European politicians and their intellectuals spent on arguing whether God and Christianity should have been included or excluded from the European constitution, would have been fruitful had they devoted those precious hours in educating Europeans about the workings of the European Project, and the impact the then 350-page *"Birth certificate"* (the European constitution which has now been rebranded the Lisbon Treaty) would have on their lives. Why? Because, millions of Europeans are largely ignorant of the workings of the European Union and the real impact European legislations have on their lives. If "Turkey's loss will be another strategic defeat for the West, as argued by Philip Stephens (Financial Times 15 December 2005), then the political leaders of Europe should "Let the Turks in: the EU is not a Christian club for Christians."

CONFUSION AND IGNORANCE

Most Europeans did not understand the implications of the European constitution which they were expected to adopt. For example, on 12 February 2005, the editorial of The Daily Telegraph, when commenting on the Spanish attitude to the European constitution before they voted to accept it, stated: "....There has been no debate about the constitution. As the justice minister, Juan Fernando Lopez Aguilar, put it, "You don't have to read the European Constitution to know it's a good thing". Which is just as well, from his point of view, since more than 90 percent of Spanish voters say they know next to nothing about the document.... They have not been offered an argument between two points of view". Due to lack of understanding of the constitution, only 42.3 percent of Spain's 34.6 million people voted in the referendum on 20 February 2005.

On 10 February 2005, an article entitled *End the conspiracy of silence over Europe* was published in the Financial Times. It commented on the attitude of British people towards the European Union. Among other things, the writer stated: "British voters are consistently revealed to be among the most ignorant in Europe about all matters to do with Europe, including the constitutional treaty, attempts to provide them with better information have been almost non-existence in Europe...The only country in the union where opponents outnumbered supporters was the United Kingdom, with 20 percent in favour and 30 percent against. The European Union average was 49 percent in favour, and 26 percent against...." Why this 'condemnation' of Britons? After all, how well-informed are Europeans and political commentators on the significance of Jean Monnet's project. What new thoughts have they brought into the European debate save their reactions to events and comments made by politicians? It is time the 'ignorant' Britons are left alone. They don't need lectures from those who have sold their souls to Brussels and blindly support the European Union that ignores the democratic decisions of the masses who subsidise it.

In another article published in the Financial Times, the British Broadcasting Corporation was "accused of ignorance, bias and stereotyping over coverage of Europe." According to this article, dated 28 January 2005, "United Kingdom officials at the European Parliament also condemned aspects of BBC coverage. In a submission, Dermot Scot, director of the parliament's U.K office, said the BBC "reinforced ignorance by presenting arguments as if the main issues were about membership of the European Union or single currency".

On 17 February 2005, a column in The Times newspaper read *EU's poll data propaganda: "Millions are to be spent on promoting the constitution among member states."* It was reported the European Commission was aware of a high level of ignorance about the EU constitution. The EU then planned to spend about £5.5

million to educate its citizens about the new European constitution before referendums were held. To quote the writer: "Commission funds will pay for leaflets, videos, and even other presentations to be targeted at countries with high level of ignorance about the constitution".

The Financial Times also published a full page comment and analysis of the European constitutional treaty. The title read *"A vote in the void: referendums take European politics into the unknown."* This article also highlighted different opinions and widespread ignorance about the European Project and its constitution. The columnists, George Parker and Leslie Crawford, reported: "If one or more countries reject the treaty, legally it would be dead. Five years of political reality is about to be exposed with dangerous consequences for the EU.....The referendums are the biggest test yet of public opinion on what the EU has become and what it aspires to be...Much of this political activity in Brussels has left voters confused or cold.......a poll found that more than half of Europeans knew little about the constitution and a third of the total had never heard of it.....A No vote in the UK is the biggest danger to the treaty and the future success of the EU".

THE "VIRTUES" OF THE WORLD'S MOST "BEAUTIFUL WOMAN" ON DISPLAY

Why wouldn't most Europeans be ignorant about a constitutional treaty that was expected to govern their lives? The problem is before France and Dutch voted "No" to reject the European constitution, German politicians considered it a wise move not to have allowed Germans to vote on a document that was to govern them. In an article headed *Silence is golden as Germany avoids treaty vote* (Financial Times April, 21 2005), Bertran Benoit wrote: "No referendum, no debate, no problem; while the European constitutional treaty inflames passions in France, across the Rhine in Germany the issue is largely passing people by....With opinion polls suggesting French voters will vote No – and do so for reasons that have little to do with the constitution – Chancellor Gerhard Schroder's refusal to hold a referendum now appears as wise as French President Jacques Chirac's decision to go for a vote seems misguided".

Martin Koopman, head of the Franco-German programme of the German Council on Foreign Relations, declared: "I am not glad that we are not having a public debate here. But I am certainly glad we are not having a referendum." Is this true democracy – the "beautiful bride" the world is in love with to the extent that the Lord Jesus Christ would become a stumbling block in Europe's pursuit of the most "attractive woman" in the universe? This is the portrait of a confused world. The enlightened world extols the virtues of the "beautiful lady" – Democracy. Yet, when a democratic nation, like Germany, refused to allow its citizens to vote on a document that would have impact on their lives, it was considered a wise move. The enlightened Europe then regarded it a foolish move when a democratic country like France allowed its citizens to vote on the constitution which would manage them. The "attractive lady" (Democracy) was displaying "her" attributes. Why all these contradictions? Because, politicians were desperate to impose their will on the masses for their selfish interests. In their cleverness to bully the people who feed them, European politicians were unconsciously bringing to pass what the "Seer of Dublin" wrote about the character of political Europe: *"the vile confederacy of the latter days."*

And finally, Andrew Rawnsley confirmed the confusion and ignorance among European political leaders on the European Constitution. In his article, *"How Europe's leaders lost the plot,"* (The Observer 22 May 2005), Mr Rawnsley reported: "What hasn't been mastered by Europe's leadership is any case for the constitution because it will improve the lives of their people. French and Dutch politicians have proved to be incapable of articulating why voting 'Yes' would be an advantage to the average citizen. When I ask politicians in London how they would sell practical benefits from the constitution to the typical British voter, they almost invariably sigh and change the subject."

What a pity! We had European "manufacturers" (politicians) who could not explain the benefits of their 'products' to their customers (the citizens of Europe). Here were "professional salesmen" who could not sell their 'goods' to prospective customers. And here were "architects" who failed to recommend their "building plans" to prospective homeowners. Yet, despite these "flaws" in the European Union, the Vatican and 'other churches' became 'satisfied customers' of the European "product" without having used the "product" itself. They bought a "building plan" from an architect who was not sure of the quality of his own handiwork. What a shame! Vatican and 'other churches' were in a better position to have known the quality of the "European product" they were buying, and the building plan the "European architects" provided for them. Unfortunately, they had already 'abandoned the tool' – the Holy Scriptures - that would have guided them to appreciate the 'quality' of the products they were buying.

The Church of England, in its blindness, decided to bow to Charles Darwin than acknowledging the teachings of the Lord Jesus Christ on creation. Darwin would not have qualified to use the pen of the eminent Victorian who wrote about European Union: how it would develop, its character and future prospects even before the founding fathers of European Community – Jean Monnet and Robert Schuman – were born in 1888 and 1886.

The Vatican and the "other churches" possess the Holy Bible - the source of Absolute Truth, and yet they have placed their own dogmas above the Scriptures. Since "The Catholic Church no longer swears by the truth of the Bible" (The

FRANCE

La Figaro: "Behind the Media punch-up between Blair and Chirac, which is so personal that there is something almost monarchical about it, two conceptions of Europe are in deep collision."

Le Nouvel Observateur: "In this clash, the British Prime Minister is, barring unforeseen incidents, best-placed to win the cup".

Liberation: "There are no sacred cows any more since the French referendum if Europe wants to recover a raison d'etre".

ITALY

La Republica: "Tony Blair, strengthened by his electoral victory, has shown one way ahead: a Europe which is more liberal and Atlanticist. The truth is that Chirac has no convincing counter-proposal."

GERMANY

Berliner Zeltung: "Blair is pursuing a policy which is to be paid for by others. Margaret Thatcher blackmailed her way into the rebate 21 years ago. The reasoning was absurd even then."

Frankfurter Allgemelne: "Schroder can no longer mediate between London and Paris. He has drawn too close to Chirac. The EU is no longer being led."

Die Weit: "The Chancellor still believes that Europe can be led by the German-French alliance. But he should have seen that the unconditional partnership with France creates the danger of blocking the EU, dividing it and ultimately destroying it."

POLAND

Gazeta Wyborcza: "How can you ask the EU citizens to decide whether they agree with a treaty if its text is regarded by French Socialists as the door to a liberal corporate Europe, and by British neo-liberals as a vehicle for a neo-socialist Europe?" (Source: *The Times,* 20 June 2005).

SPAIN

In a space entitled "PRIME MINISTER GARNERS GRUDGING PRAISE AS COMMENTATORS TURN ON EUROPE'S LEADERS", the Financial Times reported: "The Spanish press was scathing of the EU's collective leadership failure. "Europe's leaders have offered a pitiful spectacle, full of insults and the defence of national interests", said *El Mundo*, a Madrid daily." (21 June 2005)

The information I have shared with you plainly confirmed widespread ignorance and confusion about the European Union. The confusion was such that some Europeans, particularly the Germans and the Italians, planned to restore their respective national currencies – the Deutschmarks and the Lira. For example, on 20 June 2005, a column in The Times read ***Separatists seek to ditch euro and bring back lira."*** Under this title Richard Owen wrote: "MINISTERS in the Italian coalition Government...opened a campaign for referendum to force Italy to ditch the euro or to revive the lira as a "parallel currency."

There was also a 'revolt' in certain regions of Germany where the residents printed their own currencies. On Tuesday, 18 January 2007, a column in the Business Section of The Daily Telegraph read: "Germans get by without the euro: There will soon be 65 regional currencies in operation alongside the EU's, but the financial authorities are not worried". And on 29 January 2007, the Financial Times also commented on how some Europeans view the euro. In an article titled *Europeans still take dim-view of the euro,* the paper reported: "More than half of citizens using the euro say they prefer their former national currency. Almost two thirds of Germans say they prefer their former currency - the D-Mark. The report added that more than two thirds of the French, Italians and Spanish – and more than half of Germans believe the single currency has had a "negative impact."

FRANCE: CRYING OVER SOVEREIGNTY?

Before the German 'revolt', France also turned against the euro. The Daily Telegraph reported in its 28 December 2006 edition: "The French people have now turned against the euro...A poll released by *Le Pelerin* magazine found that a majority of the French public now regard the euro as a bad thing, blaming it for price jumps and job losses. 71% of blue-collar workers now say the euro hurt them personally. A quarter of all French still think in francs "the whole time" when shopping. The former French Premier, Dominic de Villepin, said: "We must clarify matters in exchange rate policy, which means taking our sovereignty back." Was it not the same prime minister who hailed the EU as the greatest political adventure in history?

What has become of the "gradualist vision" of de Villepin's 'father', Jean Monnet, the "apostle of European Unity"? Why was de Villepin complaining about loss of sovereignty? It was Jean Monnet who poured contempt on national sovereignty with this remark: "Europe of sovereign states was incapable of, despite its leader's goodwill, of reaching the sensible decisions that were needed for the common good. It would be quite another matter, however, once the power of decision was entrusted to institutions serving the general interest and applying the will of the majority in a system of common rules" (Jean Monnet Memoirs 1978). And according to the President of European Commission, Jose Manuel Barroso, Monnet's vision "still serves as a blue-print for European integration today"? (TIME 60th Anniversary Edition 31 October 2006). The French should not complain of 'taking our sovereignty back' from European institutions. Because, Jean Monnet's vision of a federal Europe would not be realised without the destruction of national sovereignties. The French cannot have it both ways.

BRITAIN AND THE 'MIGHTY' EURO

In June 2008, the European Central Bank celebrated the 10th anniversary of the European Single Currency – the Euro. Hitherto, some commentators have argued that within a decade or two the Euro would replace the American Dollar as the most reliable and powerful currency in the world. A Professor of European political economy at the London School of Economics, Willem Buiter, argued: "There is no excuse for Britain not to join the euro." In making his case for Britain's entry into the eurozone he stated: "There are political arguments for joining the euro area. The future of Europe is federal. The euro is a symbolic step towards deeper political integration. The UK can continue acting as it has since the European Union ….was created: stand on the sidelines, snipe, join late and reluctantly and then moan about how things are turning out. Or it could be at the heart of Europe, shaping its institutions. The UK punches below its weight because it is not a full member of the EU: if you are not in the euro group, you do not count. So macroeconomic stability, the defence of London's status as a global financial centre and the political logic of deeper European integration all call for the dumping of sterling and adoption of the euro. Just do it." (Financial Times 3 June 2008) Does this professor of economics really understand the significance of European integration? Does he know the future of Jean Monnet's project?

On the other side of the debate, Sean O'Grady argued in The Independent that it might have been a disaster had Britain joined the single currency. Martin Wolf argued against Britain's entry into the eurozone in his article *Britain is better off outside the euro* (Financial Times 30 May 2008). He stated: "Not long ago, some argued that the fact that sterling had been stable against the euro from early 2003 to late 2007 was a reason for joining. Now people argue that sterling should join the eurozone because it is weak…..There is no evidence that being outside the eurozone has imposed a performance penalty upon the UK economy". He added there might be countries interested to join the eurozone but Britain is better off outside it. "That is the end of this story." If Britain is better off outside the euro, is Britain better off inside the EU?

The debate of Britain abandoning the Sterling to embrace the Euro was resurrected in November 2008, when the global financial crisis erupted. Again, commentators argued for and against Britain's entry into the euro-zone. One of the supporters of Britain's membership of the euro-club, who was reacting to the financial crisis - a crisis which was the result of reckless banking practices and consumers living above their means - stated: "It might be politically toxic – but we must join the euro now."

Whatever the merits of the euro, and whatever the arguments for or against Britain adopting "Mister Europe's" currency, the vital question remains: "What is the future of European Union"? After all it is the end that crowns the work. The euro might have started well on its glorious journey. But do experts know the destination? Would euro's journey end well? The Great Titanic began its maiden voyage from Southampton to New York with great expectation. But did the passengers on board the lavish vessel enjoy the trip? Did the Titanic reach safely? If the passengers had known that the 'unsinkable' ship would hit an iceberg to sink, would they have joined the luxurious vessel?

Jean Monnet's "EU Titanic" might have started sailing well. But did the 'master builder' of the "EU Ship" know where it would land? The Lisbon Treaty has paved the way for the 'experienced Captain' to pilot Jean Monnet's "Luxurious Titanic" to its 'destination.' It does not matter how well you start a journey. What matters is how the journey ends. The uncomfortable truth is that Monnet's "European Titanic" was doomed before its construction began on 9 May 1950, and even before the French architect of the "European Titanic" himself was born. I would encourage politicians and political intellectuals to consult the works of the "Seer of Dublin" to know the fate of their "European Titanic."

THE CRITICAL QUESTION FACING EUROPE

Now, the crucial question: if Europeans are ignorant and confused about the workings of their "Empire" and its constitution; if political leaders in Europe are divided on the vision of Europe; if European leaders are struggling to determine the future direction and expansion of their Project (all of these which are just the physical aspects of European integration), how could the 500 million citizens in Europe and their leaders appreciate the spiritual implications of the construction of the "European Empire"? Things we see are temporary, but things unseen are eternal.

CHRISTIANS MUST NOT BE IN THE DARK ABOUT THE DIRECTION OF THE EUROPEAN UNION

The world may be in the dark with different views on political integration of European nations. Europeans may be ignorant and confused about the development of their "Empire" and its constitution, which was once "dead in snow" and now brought back to life. The European constitution was once in limbo, just as how the Roman Catholic "Limbo" doctrine is in limbo. According to our Lord Jesus Christ, who announced things before they happened (Isaiah 48:5), we, Christians, are "The light of the world" (Matthew 5:14). Our status implies that if the world is in darkness about the future of the European Union, we must have a clear view of this political phenomenon. The truth is from the spiritual standpoint, the existence of the European Union is destined to fulfil Bible prophecy – to become the foundation stone upon which the *dead* Roman Empire would be revived, and from which ten of their powerful leaders would bestow their power and authority to the coming Antichrist to rule the world (Daniel 2:40-43, Daniel 7:7, 24; Revelation 17:7 and Revelation 17:12-13). And the Lisbon Treaty has created the platform for the Man of Lawlessness to take up his throne in Europe.

So, we, the Bible-believing Christians ("The Camels in the desert who chew the cud"), should not be in the dark about the fate of Jean Monnet's "Titanic" which is steaming towards an 'ice-berg'. No one can save the "EU Titanic" from sinking beneath the waves. It is therefore an absurdity for some British politicians and commentators to suggest that Britain should remain in the EU and reform it. Who is capable of reforming Monnet's project? Have British politicians able to influence the reformation of the "dirty CAP" – the Common Agricultural Policy that consumes about 40 percent of the EU budget and benefits the French the most? British politicians are always 'bullied' by the French and the Germans.

THE TWO MAJOR POLITICAL EVENTS IN HISTORY PREDICTED IN THE BIBLE MUST BE FULFILLED

A careful study of the Holy Scriptures would reveal that 2 major political events would take place before the Lord Jesus Christ returns to strike the great human image from its toes of baked clay and iron to clear the mess we have created in His creation. One of these events (the rebirth of the nation of Israel) had already been fulfilled. The second (the revival of the Roman Empire) is being fulfilled before our eyes.

According to symbolic meaning of numbers in the Bible, the number 2 stands for "Witness". The fulfilments of these two prominent political events were destined before the foundation of the world, to bear witness to mankind of God's

Sovereignty and Providence. The Creator of the universe is the Lord of lords, the King of kings. He is in control of all events. He writes history before history is written by men. "Before things happened, the Sovereign Lord announced them" (Isaiah 48:5). After his humiliation, the proud King Nebuchadnezzar testified that the Heavens rule (Daniel 4:34-35), and the Most High is Sovereign over the kingdoms of men and gives them to anyone he wishes (Daniel 4:32). So, in the 19th century, before the First World War, a prominent British public servant, who loved the Lord Jesus Christ, reminded the world of these 2 significant political events which must evolved before the Lord Jesus Christ returns to judge all men. These predicted events, which are recorded in the Old Testament books of Jeremiah, Ezekiel, Daniel and Zechariah, were the restorations of the nation of Israel and the revival of the dead Roman Empire.

THE RESTORATION OF THE JEWS TO PALESTINE

We know the Jews have been restored to Palestine. This has fulfilled the rebirth of the nation of Israel. It took place in May 1948. Because of the unfaithfulness of the children of Israel, God delivered His people into the hands of the heathens (Daniel 1:1-2), to punish and scatter them among the Gentile nations. The Sovereign Lord declared: "Because you people have brought to mind your quilt by your open rebellion, revealing your sins in all that you do – because you have done this, you will be taken captive" (Ezekiel 21:24). The Lord had earlier declared in chapter 28 of the Book of Deuteronomy that if the Children of Israel disobeyed Him, He would first drive them to a nation unknown to them and their fathers (Deut. 28:36), and then "scatter them among all nations, from one end of the earth to the other" (Deut. 28:64).

The Gentile nations persecuted the Jews. For example, they were deported to Babylon. The servitude in the land of idols began in about 606BC when King Nebuchadnezzar took away the Jewish Royal family and the Temple vessels. Among the first deportees were Daniel, Hananiah, Mishael and Azzariah. In about 596BC Nebuchadnezzar invaded Jerusalem again. He captured the politicians and the rest of the upper class. Ezekiel was among these exiles. And in about 587BC the Babylonians invaded Jerusalem. This time they burnt the city and destroyed the Temple. This was the first destruction and the desecration of the Temple of God.

Between 170 and 168BC the Syrian tyrant, Antiochus Epiphanes, a descendant from one of the 4 kingdoms that evolved from Alexander the Great's Grecian Empire, also invaded Judea. He killed thousands of Jews. He abolished their religion and their custom of circumcision. He desecrated their temple with the blood of female pigs. He erected the Greek god, Zeus, in the temple. This was the second destruction and desecration of the Temple of God in Jerusalem.

In AD 70, the Roman army led by Prince Titus, besieged Jerusalem. The Romans destroyed the city and its temple, and killed thousands of Jews and took some as slaves (Daniel 9:26). The ruins of the temple are visible today. This was the third destruction and desecration of the Temple. The Temple would be rebuilt and desecrated for the 4th and final time. Indeed, the Lisbon Treaty has paved the way for this to be fulfilled.

True to God's word, the Jews were scattered among the Gentiles. Consequently the nation of Israel ceased to exist. Their dispersion was only temporarily as God promised He would restore them to their land. So, the sceptre of earthly power, which should have remained with the Jews, was transferred to the Gentiles. Let us listen to what Daniel told King Nebuchadnezzar, the head of the Gentile kingdom, after he had explained the meaning of his vision of a human statue. "You, O king, are king of kings. The God of heaven has given you dominion and power and might ...In your hands he has placed mankind and the beasts of the field and the birds of the air. Wherever they live, he has made you ruler over them" (Daniel 2:37-38).

The worldly powers would remain in the hands of Gentiles until the appointed time when the Lord Jesus Christ returns to restore all things. Witness the prophetic word of the Lord: *"And they* (the Jewish people) *will fall by the edge of the sword, and be left captives into many nations. And Jerusalem will be trampled by Gentiles until the times of the Gentiles are fulfilled"* (Luke 21: 24). We know it was Emperor Hadrian who expelled the Jews from Judea and renamed their land "Syria Palestina". This took place between 132 – 135AD after the Jews had revolted against the pagan statue Hadrian constructed in the ruins of their temple which was destroyed by Titus Vespasian in AD70.

THE "DEAD BONES" CAME OUT ALIVE

In the sight of God, the persecuted and scattered Jews were "dead bones in a valley". But the Faithful God, in accordance with His promise to restore His people to their homeland, has clothed these "dead bones". The Lord has put flesh on the "dry bones" and breathed life into them, hence the mysterious rebirth of the nation of Israel on 14 May 1948. This was foretold in Ezekiel 37:1-14: "...I will bring you (the Jews) back to the land of Israel. Then you, my people, will know that I am the Lord... I will settle you in your own land. Then you will know that I the Lord have spoken, and I have done it." Against all odds, the Jews won a 6-day war in 1967 to gain Jerusalem. This victory, according to commentators, was miraculous. Scripture must be fulfilled. Amen!

Plans were made for the estimated 20,000 Jews living in Ethiopia to return to the land of their forefathers. "Jewish federation in North America voted to raise

£56 million to help Ethiopian Jews to emigrate to Israel…" (FAITH NEWS: The Times Saturday June 11, 2005).
On Wednesday, 27 December 2005, The Times reported that Jews in Britain were immigrating to Israel. In an article titled *Britons head for the Promised Land as Israel faces a population threat,"* the paper published figures of the number of Jews who had returned to Israel. And in a column headed "The importance of 'Aliyah' ('Aliyah' is a Hebrew term which means "going up"), Times recorded the following figures of Jewish immigration:

- 3 million immigrants to Israel since 1948
- 1.2 million Went to Israel from the Soviet Union.
- 75,000 came from Ethiopia,
- 30.000 came from the United Kingdom.
- 200,000 immigrants arrived in 1990. eight times the 1989 total
- 50 percent rise in immigration in the years after the Six Day War in 1967
- 1.18 population growth in percent
- 76 percent of Israelis are Jewish (Source: Israel Government World Fact Book)

According to the Jewish emigrants, the reasons for their immigration to Israel are the customary ones: Zionism and spiritual. They claimed: "We feel like God is returning His children to his home."

Whatever the odds, no human being can uproot the Jews. The nation of Israel shall continue to exist until the Lord Jesus Christ returns. Let us listen to the prophet Jeremiah: "This is what the Lord says, he who appoints the sun to shine by day, who decrees the moon and the stars to shine by night, who stirs up the sea so that its waves roar – the Lord Almighty is his name: Only if these decrees vanish from my sight …will the descendants of Israel cease to be a nation before me.….Only if the heavens above can be measured and the foundations of the earth below be searched out will I reject all the descendants of Israel because of all they have done." (Jeremiah 31:35-37). The question is: would the moon, the sun and the stars ever fail to shine? Would the sea cease to roar? The nation of Israel would only cease to exist when the heavenly bodies fail to shine, and the waves in the ocean cease to roar.

David Noakes summed up the fulfilled prophecy relating to the rebirth of Israel in an article "The Restoration of All Things". This was published in a newsletter "Israel & Christians Today." According to Mr Noakes, "Never in recorded history has any other nation dispersed into exile retained a sense of national identity through twenty centuries and returned to its original land and language; yet this has happened before our eyes in our own generation. To those who deny that this is a work of God, the same reply is appropriate as that which Jesus gave in his response to the unbelieving Sadducees: "You are in error because you do not know the Scriptures or the power of God" (Matthew 22:29, NIV) (Extract from the book "CONTOURS – HIS PEOPLE, HIS LAND And HIS HISTORY).

The "Fig tree" that was cursed because it had no fruit, but only leaves, (Matthew 21:18-19), is now becoming tender and putting forth leaves. We must know 'summer is near' (Matthew 24:32-33). The 'fig tree' is a symbol of the nation of Israel (Jeremiah 24:1-9). The world should examine the significance of this prophetic word from the Lord Jesus Christ.

THE RESTORATION OF THE "DEAD" ROMAN EMPIRE

Just as the nation of Israel was recreated on 14 May 1948 from "wreckage," so is the "dead" Roman Empire being revived from the ashes of the Second World War. The Lord Jesus Christ first visited the earth during the days of the Roman Empire. His second arrival would also take place during the era of the revived Roman Empire. Without any doubt, the "dead" Roman Empire shall be "resurrected". The European Union has become the instrument for this "resurrection". And the "corpse" is gradually coming back to life. The Lisbon Treaty has made this possible.

Indeed, the rebirth of the Roman Empire, as predicted by the "Seer of Dublin" before the European Union was born, was confirmed in a book reviewed in the 2 February 2008 edition of The Guardian newspaper. Beneath a portrait of five EU leaders, dressed as "Caesars", was this inscription: *"While Britain frets about EU expansion, Europe is overtaking its rivals to become the world's most successful empire. US scholar Parag Khanna on the rise of the new Rome: The Empire strikes back."* According to the American author: "For over half a century, European nations have been pooling their power, eventually giving small and shattered post-Second World War countries a new lease of life....Europe has its own vision of what world order should look like...the EU is now the most confident economic power in the world, regularly punishing the United States in trade disputes". He continued: "EU expansion is a gamble more expensive than America's war in Iraq, but one that is actually paying off....*The EU is easily the most popular and successful empire in history,* for it does not dominate, it disciplines...." Parag Khanna concluded his review of *The Second World: Empires and Influence in the new Global Order* with this statement: "As with all empires, the EU rubber band will stretch until it no longer can, growing until it has fully replaced and dismantled Soviet Union across Europe's east, creating a borderless and contiguous 'pas Europae' of about 35 countries, an imperial blanket covering close to 600 million....." (Emphasis mine)

I would remind the American scholar that the EU expansion is not a 'gamble', and the EU, being the most popular and successful empire in history, is also not surprising. For Sir Robert Anderson confidently predicted this European empire even before the founding fathers of this empire were conceived and before Adolf Hitler, the "catalyst" of European Community, was born in 1889. In the next chapter I shall introduce the "Seer of Dublin". He was a scholar among scholars and a 'giant' among 'giants.'

We have already learnt that ten powerful leaders would emerge from the revived Roman Empire to delegate their power and authority to the last Caesar. The question is: who would be the leaders to cooperate with the most powerful Caesar to lead Europe and the rest of the world to the Promised Land of Peace and Prosperity? The Lisbon Treaty signed on 13 December 2008 has paved the way for the last commanding Emperor to be crowned.

Chapter 10

THE FORESIGHT OF THE BRITISH PUBLIC SERVANT

"The specialist is always apt to exaggerate the importance of his own testimony and to betray impatience when evidence of another kind is allowed legitimate weight" **(RA)**

About 128 years ago the "Seer of Dublin" published *THE COMING PRINCE.* In this popular work, which explains the significance of the vision of 70 Weeks recorded in Daniel 9:24-27, the author also recorded how a political union of European nations would develop through a European crisis. The "Seer" listed 10 countries that could become the leading nations in this political alliance of European nations. According to the Irishman, these powerful nations in the European confederacy would give their powers and authority to a political genius to 'save' Europe. This 'genius' would eventually lead the "global society" to a catastrophic end. The native of Dublin was inspired by the following Scriptural passages in Daniel 2:4-43, Daniel 7:24-25 and Revelation 13 and 17:12-13 to make the prediction.

In view of these scriptures, which are bound to be fulfilled, the Ulsterman expressed his fears about his native land, Ireland, and England, the country he served with his heart and soul, becoming members of this European confederacy. This political Union would cooperate with the fascinating and the extremely gifted Caesar to seize the kingdom of the world by deception, and make war against the faithful Jews and Christians (Revelation 13:5).

When *The Coming Prince* was first published in 1881, which was before the First World War, the idea of an economic and political union of European nations had not even been conceived by the pioneers of a Federal Europe. Among them were Richard Koudenhove – Kalergi (Austro-Hungarian Diplomat), Aristide Briand, former French Prime Minister, Konrad Adenauer, first Chancellor of the Federal Republic of Germany and Alcide Gasperi, former Italian Prime Minister. The French Statesmen, Jean Monnet and Robert Schuman, the founding fathers of the European Community, had not even been conceived. This means, Jean Monnet, the "apostle of European unity," had not given the seeds of European Union to Robert Schuman to sow them.

It was, therefore, sheer ignorance and foolish pride for European politicians to have boasted that it would have been "divisive", a "serious mistake" and an "absurd" to have mentioned God and Christianity in their Constitution. The inconvenient truth for politicians and political commentators is that it was a servant of Christ who wrote about their European Project, its nature and future prospects before their 'hero' - the so-called 'tutelary genius' - Jean Omer Marie Gabriel Monnet - was born.

THE "BRAVE WARRIOR" 'WEEPS': The "Fears and Tears" of the "Seer of Dublin"

I have already mentioned that the "Seer of Dublin", Sir Robert Anderson, prophetically listed in his *The Coming Prince* some of the major countries in the European confederacy (now the European Union), which would eventually form the foundation block for the revived Roman Empire. It was Sir Robert's prayer that Ireland, the land of his birth, and England, the country he served with distinction, would not join this political alliance of European nations to empower the last Caesar, the "Man of Lawlessness," to deceive mankind and make war against the Lord Jesus Christ and His followers.

Let us carefully examine what Sir Robert Anderson recorded concerning a political union of European nations: *"Of the great political changes which must precede his advent* (the coronation of the last Caesar of the revived Roman Empire), *the most conspicuous are the restoration of the Jews to Palestine, and the predicted division of the Roman earth...... The attempt to enumerate the ten kingdoms of the future would involve a profitless inquiry. History repeats itself; and if there be any element of periodicity in the political diseases by which nations are afflicted, Europe will inevitably pass through another crisis such as that which darkened the last decade of the eighteen century....It is impossible to foretell how far kingdoms may become consolidated and boundaries may be changed. Moreover in forecasting the fulfilment of these prophecies, we are dealing with events which, while they may occur within the lifetime of living men, may yet be delayed for centuries. .*

Our part is not only to prophecy, but only to interpret; and we may well rest content with the certainty that when the Apocalyptic visions are in fact fulfilled, their fulfilment will be clear, not merely to minds educated in mysticism, but to all who are capable of observing public facts......

..... . .Through the gradual unfolding, it may be, of influences even now in operation; or far more probably as the outcome of some great European crisis in the future, this_confederation of nations shall be developed, and thus the stage will be prepared on which shall appear that awful Being, the great leader of men in the eventful days

which are to close the era of Gentile supremacy......"

In the Appendix to *The Coming Prince*" , Dr, Anderson wrote: "*Next to the restoration of the Jews, the most prominent political feature of the future, according to Scripture, is the tenfold partition of the Roman earth ......That there should be a commonwealth of nations living side by side at peace, was a conception that nothing in the history of the world could have suggested....The principal clew which Scripture affords upon the subject is the connection between these kingdoms and the Roman Empire (Daniel 7:24)*

But some latitude must probably be allowed as to boundaries, otherwise we should have to choose between two equally... alternatives, namely either that our nation shall have sunk to the position of a province, not even Ireland remaining under her sway (Ireland was entirely, and Scotland was in part, outside the territorial limits of the Roman Empire), or else England which is to be numbered among the ten kingdoms will include the vast empire of which this island is the heart and centre. May we not indulge the hope that however far our nation may lapse in evil days to come from the high place which, with all her faults, she has held as the champion of freedom and of truth, she will be saved from the degradation of participating in the vile confederacy of the latter days?"

These considerations as to boundaries apply also to *Germany. Though in a lower degree; and Russia is clearly out of the reckoning altogether....But there is no doubt that Egypt, Turkey, and Greece will be numbered among the ten kingdoms....Turning again to the West, the names of France, Austria, Italy, and Spain present themselves; and seven of the kingdoms are thus accounted for. Can the list be completed? Belgium, Switzerland, and Portugal remain, and these too would claim a place were we dealing with the Europe of today; but as it is the future we are treating of, any attempt to press the matter further seems futile.*
.....Is it possible that the most powerful nations of the world, England, Germany, and Russia, are to have no part in the great drama of the last days? But it must be remembered, first, that the relative importance of the great Powers may be different at the time when these events shall be fulfilled".

We have witnessed what Dr Anderson recorded in the 19th century concerning a political alliance of European nations: how it would develop, its character and future prospects. Let us also examine how the European Union developed: what Jean Monnet, its master builder, wrote about it; and the comments political commentators and intellectuals have published about the European Union. We would then compare their commentaries with Dr. Anderson's prediction.

JEAN MONNET AND HIS "DISCIPLES"

We know the European Union evolved from the crisis that erupted after the Second World War. This was evident from the Marshal Plan which was launched in 1947 to save Europe from social, economic and political collapse. And Jean Monnet, the principal architect of European Construction, whose career began in the 1930's, himself declared: "I have always believed that Europe will be established through ***crisis*** and not the sum of the outcome of that crisis" Again, he stated: "To create Europe is to create peace." In his Memoirs, published in 1978, Monnet wrote: "I have no doubt, for my part, that a ***confederation*** will one day lead to a ***federation.*** But for the moment, is it possible to go further? I cannot say that it is. Meanwhile, the ***confederation*** would have the very great advantage of assuring public opinion in our countries that they have joined an entity which is not only economic but political and that they are therefore part of something bigger than any of their countries alone."

The "practical apostle of European unity" concluded his 'sermon' (memoirs) with these significant words: "But time is passing, and Europe is moving only slowly on the course to which she is so deeply committed....We cannot stop ...the community we have created is not an end in itself...Like the ***provinces of the past***, our nations must learn to live together under common rules and institutions freely arrived at. The sovereign nations of the past can no longer solve the problems of the present; they cannot ensure their own progress or control their own future. And the community itself is only a stage on the way to the organized world of tomorrow."

Questions: "Did Jean Monnet really understand his remarks?" Did he know the future of his project? Was "Mister Europe" aware that before he was born, an Irishman had already written about a confederation of European nations that would develop through a European crisis and eventually lead to an European empire?

Commentaries

- At the 50th anniversary of the Treaty of Rome the Editorial of The Independent newspaper read *European Union: A potent symbol of peace and unity.*
- NEWSWEEK magazine, in a Special Report to mark the anniversary, recorded: "Europe arose from the ashes of the Great Depression and World War II to become whole and free......Europe is now a ***global super-power*** of world-historic importance, second to none in economic clout. It has constructed one of the most successful systems of government...which has brought prosperity and security to Europe's people. It is the single most successful advance in voluntary international cooperation in modern history."

- In Monnet's biography Francois Duchene writes: European Union is "***the rarest of all political phenomena in history"!***
- Ulrich Beck, a German Professor, in his article, "Nation states can only fail the problems of the modern world" (The Guardian 15 January 2008), writes: "Europe remains to be understood and conceptualised. ***This historically unique form of international community*** cannot be explained in terms of the traditional concepts of methodological nationalism..."
- Harvard Professor of History, Niall Ferguson, in his article *"Unloved and mistrusted, even by the French: the EU at 50"* writes: "The Treaty of Rome (1957) actually committed six countries to create a customs union and common agriculture, transport and social policies. That was all. And the institutions it established (The European Commission and court) were designed merely to achieve these limited goals...The six has become twenty seven. Thirteen of them have acquired a common currency. European law reigns supreme. And the customs union has become a (still imperfect) single market. Yet at root the European Union remains not the federal super-state of conservative nightmares, but a ***confederation*** whose primary concern is trade" (The Daily Telegraph 25 March 1957). Is it really the case?
- A title in the 22 October 2006 edition of Sunday Express read *Bordering on the absurd.* The paper commented: "EU officials had secret plans to redraw the map of Britain. A shadowy Frenchman had a meeting in Sussex where he introduced himself as the new "President" for Arc Manche. This new territory incorporates much of southern England with parts of France. Other new Anglo-French, Spanish and Portuguese regions are due to follow
- The Daily Telegraph also published an article titled *New EU map makes Kent part of same 'nation' as France.* The paper recorded: "A German led conspiracy of cartographers stands accused of trying to use a new EU directive to give Brussels powers to ***change national boundaries***...This according to the Tories, could be the first step of a Berlin-inspired master plan to create a United States of Europe divided, not into states, but instead a series of "transnational" regions....They seek to break Britain into regions that cross national ***boundaries.*** A German minister said**:** **"**There is the great hope underlying the goal of a united Europe that we can permanently overcome our borders.**"**
- On 1 August 2007, the Daily Express published a letter in a column headlined *Westminster Scots cabal out to destroy us.* The author, Mark Taylor, expressing his concern about the possible loss of our independence and sovereignty to unelected and unaccountable officials in Brussels, writes: "Mr Brown's aim was to makeover of England. This includes the snapping of county Councils, to be replaced with nine

Euro-approved ***regions*** answerable to Brussels"

- During Britain's EU presidency in 2004, Turkey was formally allowed to begin negotiation to become a full member of the European Union. This decision was reported in an article titled *EU makes historic offer to begin negotiations for Turkey* (The Times December 2004). The unknown truth is that before Turkey first applied for membership of the European Union, Sir Robert Anderson had already written in 1881 that Turkey would join an European confederacy. Incidentally, the 14th edition of his prophetic work about political Europe was published in 1963, the very year Turkey became associated with the European Project.

THE MORALLY BANKRUPT EU

- It is well known that fraud, corruption and nepotism are widespread in the European Union; Here are a few headlines:
- "EU accounts still riddled with fraud and errors, say Auditors" (The Times 16November 2006)
- "Why can't this fraud be halted" (Daily Mail 16 November 2005)
- The Financial Times published an European Union corruption chart in its 13 June 2007 edition:
- "Brussels corruption scandal could lead to more arrests" (Financial Times 30 March 2007)
- "Brussels struggles to confront corruption within the new two" (Bulgaria and Romania) (Financial Times 13 June 2007)
- "EU fraud costs £1million a day" (Daily Express 10June 2007). In this article, Macer Hall reported that according to a Brussels report, EU fraud is costing taxpayers more than £1miilion a day. Neil O'Brien, the Spokesman for the Open Europe think-tank said; "The EU continues to lose vast sums of money to fraud. If the people in charge of the EU were running a business they would have been sacked years ago."
- "Outrage as porn posters of the Queen promote EU presidency (The Times 30 December 2006)
- "EU tries seduction to rekindle voters' ardour" (The Times 28 April 2006.)
- In June 2007, after European leaders had already entered into shady deals to rebrand the rejected EU constitution as a new Treaty to govern the masses, the EU posted a pornographic film on its website to boost interest in the workings of their corrupt project. The video showed 18 couples having sex. This dirty film portrays the EU as a 'vile' project. Which reputable Public Limited Company would use pornography to promote its business to gain more customers?

From the above newspaper articles and headlines, we notice that the following words and phrases are associated with the European Union: Peace, Crisis, Confederation, Boundaries, Regions, Province, Treaty, Turkey, Corruption, Fraud, Pornography the "rarest of all political phenomena", and "historically unique form of international community."

SIR ROBERT ANDERSON: A MAN OF VISION Britain a "Province" of Europe

If we carefully examine what Sir Robert Anderson wrote about European confederacy in the 19th century, we would notice that the "Seer of Dublin" associated the same words and similar phrases I have listed above with the political union of European nations. Examine the commentaries I have listed below, which were made in 21st century about Britain becoming a "Province" of Europe, and compare them with what Dr Anderson wrote in 19th century about Britain: *"But some latitude must probably be allowed as to boundaries, otherwise we should have to choose between two equally...alternatives*, namely either our *nation shall shave sunk to the position of a province....of the "vile confederacy of the latter days."*

Peter Hitchens, in his article, *Will Europe's spoilt children put us to shame by saying No?*, writes: "To the secret horror of the real rulers of Europe, one tiny country is letting its people vote on whether it should give up its independence for ever. The other 26 members of the Franco-German Empire have meekly agreed to accept their new status as ***provinces"*** (The Mail on Sunday 25 May 2008).

Melanie Phillips, in her article, *Contempt, apathy and lie – why Britain is crying out for our own 'pitbull with lipstick'*, writes, "Middle Britain mourns that its country is being transformed by mass immigration; it is demonised for saying so. *It is aghast that it no longer governs itself but is becoming a ***province of Euroland***; it is scorned as xenophobic." (Daily Mail 8 September 2008).

Leo McKinstry, in his article, *National spirits are high yet Brown is about to sell our soul to Brussels*, writes, "Equally important is the unceasing drive for European integration under rule from Brussels. The commissars of the EU utterly despise traditional concepts of national identity and independence, believing that all borders must be removed as we are forced to submit to governance by a new federal superstate. In their view, France and England should disappear as sovereign entities, becoming nothing more than the ***provinces of the EU's new empire."*** (Daily Express)

William Rees-Mogg, in his article, *If Scotland got its vote, then so should we: Beware, Mr Brown, the English are proud patriots too*, writes: "Certainly, the English people, however much they might object to becoming one of the ***western provinces of the European Empire***, will be allowed no chance to decide the matter for themselves. It is extraordinary how many Scots are involved in the end game of English Independence" (The Times 17 September 2007).

Dr. Anthony Coughlan, Secretary EU Research and Information Centre in Dublin, commented on Ireland's rejection of the implications of Lisbon Treaty. He wrote: "The Referendum Commission in Ireland thus failed to inform voters that the legally new European Union which would be established by Lisbon would, unlike the present EU, have the constitutional form of a supranational Federation in which Ireland and the other EU Member States would have the constitutional status of regional or ***provincial states,*** and of which we would all be made real citizens for the first time, rather than our being just notional, symbolic or honorary EU "citizens" as at present... But it would be ludicrous if the peoples of Europe were to consent to turn their countries into ***state-provinces*** of an EU federation, and themselves into real citizens of it, without their realising that is what they are being asked to do."

Is it not amazing, that the word **"province"** which Sir Robert Anderson used in the 21st century to describe the status of Britain in a political Europe, has been used today, in the 21s century, to describe Britain and Ireland's eventual position in the European Union when the Lisbon Treaty becomes legally binding on all the EU member states. The 'obstinate' Jean Monnet would not have qualified to untie the boot-straps of the 'decent' Knight Commander.

Britain and Ireland would commit national suicide if they ignore Sir Robert Anderson's warning about the fate of Europe, and blindly follow the 'children' of the 'blind smuggler', Jean Monnet – whose fuzzy vision of a "fused" Europe continues to be the blueprint of European integration today. We would regret if we allow our 'blind' and 'greedy' politicians to drag us to board Monnet's '***Luxurious Titanic***' which was doomed before its construction began on 9 May 1950.

When Sir. Robert Anderson predicted in 1881 the restoration of the Jews to Palestine and the creation of a confederation of European nations from which its ten powerful leaders would emerge to hand over their power and authority to Antichrist, the "Father of Europe", Jean Monnet, who dreamt the European vision, had not been born. The European Union was not in existence any shape or form. What Sir Robert Anderson predicted over 128 years ago about a confederation of European nations, has now become a reality in the existence of the European Union with all the symbols and trappings of an Empire: a single currency, a flag, an anthem, a Court of Justice, a Parliament, a Central Bank, a Common Agricultural Policy, a Common Fishery Policy and a constitution named the Lisbon Treaty which would formally confer a legal personality on the EU with a President signing international treaties on behalf of the Empire, and a Foreign Minister overseeing its diplomatic offices around the globe.

THE PLACE OF THE EU EXPERTS IS NOT AT THE "JUDGEMENT SEAT" IN BRUSSELS BUT IN THE "WITNESS BOX" IN LONDON

The manner in which the Lisbon Treaty was formulated and introduced depicted the despicable character of Jean Monnet's project. Even some EU leaders openly declared that the treaty was about 90 percent of the rejected Constitution. Without any shame, just like their 'father' Monnet who, without shame, 'abducted' a married woman to Moscow for a quick divorce and remarriage, European leaders boasted of their deceit. Jose Manuel Barroso, the President of European Commission, had the impudence to advise Tony Blair – the then British Prime Minister – to ignore the concerns of the British people. The place of the EU 'Expert' – Jose Manuel Barroso - is not on the 'safe judgement seat' in Brussels, but in the 'hostile witness box' in London to be cross-examined and confronted with the "Unknown truth" and "Forgotten truth" about European integration. The "ignorant" Britons would have the opportunity to dismiss the 'case' Barroso and his experts have made for a deeper political integration of European nations. Sir Robert Anderson writes: "No one who has much experience of judicial inquiries is ever surprised to find that a case which seems convincing when presented *ex-parte* breaks down under cross-examination or is shattered by opposing evidence." And Proverbs 18:17 says; "The first to present his case seems right, till another comes forward and questions him."

The European Constitution (the Lisbon Treaty) was deliberately drafted only in French and its translation into English deliberately delayed, and its contents made unreadable to prevent people from understanding it. Valery Giscard d'Estaing, the architect of the Constitution, without any shame, openly admitted that the whole Lisbon project was a deception. And Ms. Gisela Stuart, a former Labour Party minister, commented on how the European Council has been incorporated into the formal institution of the European project. According to her, the European Council used to be a body where heads of states met to co-ordinate the interests of the nation states. But, "under this new structure, that body where heads of states meet will become subordinate to the union's interests. They will now have a duty to represent the interests of the union, not the interests of the member state. It's a consolidation of the way the union work; into a structure which is much more like a government."

On the same so-called Reformed Treaty, the Vice President of the European Commission, Ms Wallstrom, voiced her concern. According to her, the European Council prepared a readable version of the Jargon-filled Reform Treaty but refused her requests to publish it until the treaty had been ratified by all the 27 members of the European Union. Her indictment was that everything that takes place behind closed doors was not good for Europe. What a 'devious' Euro-project. Sir Robert Anderson aptly described the European confederacy the *"vile confederacy of the latter days"*.

The question is: How was Sir Robert Anderson able to predict, with accuracy, the development of a political alliance of European nations and its "vile" character before Hitler became the "catalyst" for the creation of this "European Empire"? From where did Dr. Anderson get his information about the European confederacy and its future? The answer is simple: from the Old Testament Book of Daniel – a Book which the Roman Catholic Bible – *The New Jerusalem Bible (The Reader's and the Popular Editions)* – describe it as an "Edifying Fiction" - a religious novel written in about 200BC after the events had already taken place.

It is clear from Sir Robert's writing, that he was concern about Britain's participation in the abominable "Alliance of European Nations." I quote the question the servant of the British Crown posed: *"May we not indulge the hope that however far our nation may lapse in evil days to come from the high place which, with all her faults, she has held as the champion of freedom and of truth, she will be saved from the degradation of participating in the vile confederacy of the latter days"?* If Jean Monnet is highly honoured in Europe as a political genius, a 'prophet' and a 'revolutionary', and *Centres of Excellence* have been created in Universities around the world in his honour; and if the European Union has been described a "Quiet miracle"; and the Roman Catholic Church put Robert Schuman on the path to sainthood for his contribution to the European project, we must ask the question: How should the world describe Sir Robert Anderson?

SIR ROBERT ANDERSON 'WEEPS' OVER IRELAND

Sir Robert was born in Dublin. Sadly, it was during Ireland's six months presidency of the European Union that the Union was enlarged - when in May 2004 ten new countries, mostly of the former Communist block, were admitted into the European Club to join the then existing fifteen members to create a "kingdom" of twenty five countries. Also, it was Dublin's presidency that played a leading role in persuading all the then 25 member-countries of the European Union to agree on the text for the first constitutional treaty for the European Empire.

Ireland's "achievement" in the history of the European Union took place on Friday, 18 June 2004. According to Financial Times, it was "Bertie Ahern, the then Ireland's prime minister's...greatest political triumph." Premier Ahern and his officials celebrated their success with lots of champagne bottles. The newspaper reported: "In the early hours of Saturday morning (19 June 2004), Mr Ahern's motor- cade swept past the designer shops of *Cartier quartier*.......to the Conrad Hotel. The opulent Bar of the Brussels' Hotel was suddenly a Dublin pub as the Irish holders of the European Union's rotating presidency toasted the agreement on a new constitutional treaty, a text designed to define the EU's ambitions – and its limits – for a generation" (Financial Times 21 June 2004).

Again, how ironic, that Ireland (the birth place of Sir Robert Anderson) the nation which he thought would not become a member of the "vile confederacy of the latter days", rather contributed to the "resurrection" of the "dead" European constitution. And sadly, it was the Irish Foreign Minister, Brain Cowen (now the Irish Prime Minister) to whom seven members of the European Union petitioned in vain that a reference to Europe's Christian roots be inserted in the constitution of Europe. God, the Lord Jesus Christ and Christianity were eliminated from the vocabulary of the European Constitution lest they offended non-Christians of the European Kingdom.

Even when France, a founding member of the European Union, killed the European constitution, it was an Irish Prime Minister who vowed to help resurrect the "corpse" by voicing his support for the European project. For a column in the 31 May 2005 edition of the Metro newspaper read *Ahern: We'll Vote on EU constitution.* According to this article, "Mr Ahern insisted Irish voters would get the chance to have their say on the controversial 380-page document even though it has been dubbed dead. And the Taoiseach, during whose presidency the European constitution was agreed, declared there was little hope of renegotiating or redrafting the constitution," Mr Ahern said, "We are still committed to the European Constitution – I hope all member states are."

The Irish Premier further expressed his confidence, that the rest of Europe would accept the constitution, "as the best way forward" - a constitution which had been rejected by the French and the Dutch. The Prime Minister of Ireland 'disappointed' Sir Robert Anderson. And how sad it is, that a Humanist Convention member from Ireland, a Dublin Member of the European Parliament, suggested it would have been divisive and a "serious mistake" to have mentioned God and Christianity in the European Constitution. Had Bertie Ahern and Irish politicians read what the brilliant Irishman wrote about the European project and its destiny before the French architect of European Construction was born, they would have torn the EU Constitution into pieces and withdrawn Ireland from the European Union. Ireland might have gained economically from the European Union. However, it is the end that crowns the work. The Irish people must remember the classic saying: "Beware of the Greeks even when they offer gifts." It was written of Sir Robert Anderson: "The well-being of Ireland was to him a matter standing above politics in the ordinary sense."

THE NOBLE KNIGHT 'WEEPS' OVER GREAT BRITAIN

And what about England, the country Sir Robert served with his heart and soul? Sadly, Britain is one of the 'three powerful engines' driving the European Train. Incidentally, Britain contributes substantially to sustain the "United kingdom of Europe" – an "Empire" which was built on deceit and lies. And it was a British

Prime Minister, Tony Blair, who in his zeal to champion the cause of Turkey's membership of the European Union, claimed the European Union is not a Christian club. What an irony!

Again, it was a British Foreign Secretary, David Miliband, who, in his enthusiasm to be seen as a 'credible' and 'progressive' politician, also joined the popular song: "The EU is not a Christian Club to become a stumbling block to Turkey's membership of the EU." Were Blair and Miliband aware of the credentials of the politician who launched the European Coal and Steel Community, the forerunner of the European Union"? Schuman was a Lawyer and a Roman Catholic. He was a committed Christian – not an atheist. Jean Monnet, the 'Father of Europe' described Schuman 'an honest' politician whom people would believe in whatever he said.

I would also remind the arrogant politicians, who despise the notion of God and Christianity being associated with the European project, to reflect on the compliments Dr. Konrad Adenauer, the great German Statesman, paid to Americans after the "great Satan" had pumped billions of dollars into Europe to rescue the continent from its economic mess after the Second World War. "Germany must declare herself wholeheartedly for the Christian world of the West and all it stands for", declared Adenauer. "The world must be convinced of American strength....The US has today perhaps the mightiest mission in history. In a human and historic sense America has a duty.... to see that the light never goes out on our earth.....I (Konrad Adenauer) want to see a united Europe. Only then can my country be free. To that we need the help of the best Europeans of all – the Americans." (*TIME* December 5, 1949). What a tribute to Great America, and what a slap in the face of those pompous politicians who sneer at Christianity. Unfortunately, today, Americans, led by their politicians, have rejected the commandments of God and the teachings of the Lord Jesus Christ to follow the agnostic Charles Darwin. Americans are paying the price for their folly.

It was reported in an article entitled *UK "bankrolling growing EU,* that "The EU's annual accounts revealed that ....the UK was the second largest net contributor in absolute terms – at 2billion pounds...the second largest behind Germany at 5.9 billion pounds. Without the rebate the UK net contribution would have been 6 billion pounds- the largest of any member state"(Daily Mail 8 September 2004).

Even the British Government, on 9 June 2005, confirmed that it contributed substantially to the European budget. Listen to Tony Blair's response to the request made by the French President to sacrifice Britain's rebate of £3billion it receives from the European Union: "Britain has been making a gesture....over the past ten years, even with the British rebate, we have been making a contribution into Europe two and half times that of France. Without the rebate, it would have been 15 times as much as France. That is our gesture". (Daily Mail Friday June 10, 2005).

The ruling Labour Government, in early 2004, had already expressed its commitment to encourage the British people to be at the "Heart of Europe", because that is where our destiny lies. And also, it was Prime Minister Blair, who, in his enthusiasm to commit Britain to the European confederacy, declared: "I think it would be an act of extraordinary foolishness for us as a country in early 21st century to withdraw from the biggest political alliance in the world and the biggest economic market right on our doorstep" (Daily Mail Wednesday, June 16, 2004). And the same Prime Minister was among other EU leaders who firmly opposed to the European Union being labelled a "Christian club". Had Tony Blair done his 'homework' on European integration, and examined the works of Dr. Anderson, he would have learnt that it would be an act of an extraordinary blunder - the blunder of all blunders - for Britain to remain in the European Union. He would have withdrawn Great Britain from Jean Monnet's Project.

THE BRITISH PRESIDENCY OF THE EUROPEAN UNION

On 1 July 2005, the British Prime Minister took over the 6-month rotating EU Presidency. Few days before he assumed 'office', Blair shifted his position of not negotiating away the £3billion Britain receives from the European budget. On June 18, 2005 he declared: "The British rebate is an anomaly that has to go". Prior to this announcement, Tony Blair had already made the following statements:

- On 8 June 2005, he told Members of the British Parliament: "The UK rebate will remain and we will not negotiate it away – period".
- The following day, 9 June 2005, he cried: "The rebate exists because otherwise there would be this quite unfair proportion of British contribution."
- On 13 June 2005, Blair shouted: "We cannot discuss the existence of the British rebate unless we discuss the whole of the financing of the European Union".
- On 14 June 2005, he proclaimed: "This (rebate) is not some special thing that has been given as a privilege to Britain. It is a mechanism to correct what would otherwise be grossly unfair – there cannot be an agreement that does not involve reconsideration of the fundamentals."

But, on 21 June 2005, the Daily Mail reported that, "following a meeting with the Danish Prime Minister, Goran Person (one of Britain's few ally in the rebate battle), the British Prime Minister, in a response to a question about the collapse of the European Union budget at the Brussels summit on 17 June, 2005, replied with a concession: "We have made it clear that we are prepared not just to discuss and negotiate, but to recognise that the rebate is an anomaly that has to go - but it has to go in the context of the other anomaly being changed away." According to the report this statement contrasted Tony Blair's statement to the Parliament when he was challenged whether the rebate was "non-negotiable. To which he told the MP's: "The UK rebate will remain and we will not negotiate it away: period."

HAS BRITAIN BENEFITTED FROM ITS MEMBERSHIP OF THE EUROPEAN UNION?

According to Daily Mail, the Office of the Prime Minister "admitted that British tax payers could send billions of pounds more to Europe even if Mr Blair wins his battle for EU budget reform. His official spokesman insisted this would be a price worth paying.....If people see it is fair and results in a more prosperous Europe they will accept it's a price worth paying". The question remains: How prosperous has Britain become by virtue of its membership of the EU? Have British Governments ever published the cost/benefit analysis of Britain's membership of the European Union?

For example, the extent to which Britain has lost out from its relationship with the European Union was published in an article entitled *£33million child benefit paid to foreign children who live abroad.* (Daily Mail 2 June 2008). Within this article, Glive Owen reported how Polish and other EU nationals in Britain have gained at the expense of British taxpayers: "Larger amounts are paid out to East European workers in child tax credits, but the Government has refused to put a figure on that liability..." The UK welfare benefit is so attractive because it is £977 a year for the first child and £652 for younger siblings – as opposed to £160 for each child in Poland. But the reciprocal agreement under European law means that Britons working in that country get only the £160 from the Warsaw government. Opposition MPs demanded the Government get a grip on the runaway payouts. But, according to lawyers, the only answer is for Britain to negotiate a new deal among the 27 European Union countries. Why such negotiation? Because, politicians who have no clue what the EU is for, have 'sold' Britain to strangers in Europe. The fact is Britain is not part of the Continent of Europe. We can trade with European countries. We cannot surrender our sovereignty to corrupt institutions in Europe that are not accountable to Britons.

And how is it that because of our involvement with the European Union, unelected judges in the "European kingdom" could "intervene in British laws and lay down criminal penalties to be handed down by British courts, even if the British Government does not agree. And the EU Commission will be able to set the punishments that apply, if Britons break laws based on EU policy." Dr. Liam Fox, the then Shadow Foreign Secretary, commenting on Brussels power to put British citizens in jail, declared, "This is a very dangerous precedent that opens the way to our legal traditions being asset stripped by the power-hungry European Union......the UK is bit by bit losing control over our ability to make our own laws" (Daily Mail Wednesday September 14, 2005). And during the Conservative Party Conference, which was held in Brighton on 5 October 2005, Dr. Fox told the delegates, "Conservatives must never accept that Britain's destiny lies in a "United States of Europe".

Camilla Cavendish wrote on the same issue: the European Union's usurpation of the rights of British people to govern themselves with their own laws. In her article, *The March of the machines,* which was published in The Times on Wednesday, 15 September 2005, she reported: "The bureaucrats of the EU…have a life of their own: our leaders are incapable of taming them….The new transfer of power to Brussels has again wrong-footed politicians focusing on lofty Millennium Goals, not on bread-and butter sovereignty. Few Europeans even know the names of those who sit on Europe's Court of Justice. Yet it's ruling …obviously abolished another national veto…Judicial creep is the inevitable result of federalism."

With all the disadvantages suffered by Britain by virtue of our membership of the European Union, Gordon Brown claimed if Britain were to leave the European Union, 3 million jobs would suffer. We would lose exports. What about the billions Britain pumps into the EU some of which find its way into the pockets of politicians in the European Parliament? Would an "investor" Brown buy shares in a Public Limited Company that has failed to file audited accounts with the Registrar of Companies for 14 consecutive years? How would the "prudent" Gordon Brown rate a company whose Board of Directors are "morose", ignore its shareholders and uncertain of the company's future prospects?

I would encourage you to read Gerard Batten's 31-page booklet "*How much does the European Union cost Britain*"? You would learn in detail how Britain has suffered financially since joining the Common Market in 1973. Mr Batten, who is a Member of European Parliament, introduces the 2008 Edition of his treatise with this statement: "The cost of EU membership is inexorably rising and Britain will bear an ever-increasing burden of direct and indirect costs – for no discernable benefits. This pamphlet is one of the few serious attempts to quantify the cost of EU membership to Britain and I have made every effort to keep its contents fair and accurate. If anything I have erred on the side of caution and quoted only those figures which are quantifiable and verifiable from official or respected sources. The real cost of EU membership is in all likelihood much higher than my estimates." The three main political parties have still not published the cost/benefit analyses of Britain's membership of the European Union. Why?

British Governments, without exception, have 'disappointed' Sir Robert Anderson. How could the nation he loved and risked his life to serve pumped billions to finance a "vile' project in Europe which would fight the Lord Jesus Christ after its 'Emperor' had deceived the world? How could a nation, whose Queen and King honoured him with Knighthood, surrender the right to govern itself to strangers in a foreign land?

Who was this Sir Robert Anderson? I know you are eager to meet him. Please hold your breath.

Chapter 11

BRITAIN AND TURKEY'S MEMBERSHIP OF THE EUROPEAN UNION AND CHRISTIANITY

"The Critics are men who empty the works of watch into a bowl, and then after examining them in detail arrive at the sapient conclusion that present no proof of unity of design" **(RA)**

When Britain took over the EU presidency in 2005, one of its priorities was to persuade member-states of the Union to embrace Turkey. A meeting was scheduled on 3 October 2005 to approve the formal negotiations of Turkey's membership of the Great European Club. On 1 October 2005, two days before the meeting, Ben Macintyre published in The Times his second essay which argued the case for and against Turkey's EU membership. In his article, *A bridge between two cultures, two continents and two futures* with a subtitle *Letting Turkey into the club Europe would be politically astute and demonstrates fairness"*, Mr Macintyre reported: "...On the eve of opening negotiations, Mr Eridogan (Prime Minister of Turkey) was blunt: "If the EU is not a Christian club it should prove it....By doing so, the EU could build a bridge with the 1.5 billion Muslims of the world."

This was not the first time the Prime Minister of Turkey has raised the issue of Christianity on Turkey's membership of the European Union. It seemed this Prime Minister has the impression that European Union is a Christian club, and as a result would be unwilling to accept Turkey, a Muslim country, to become a member of an "exclusive Christian club". I would submit to Mr Erdogan and the politicians who entertain the notion that the European Union is somehow a Christian club with no space for a Muslim country, that Jean Monnet's project is NOT a Christian club in any shape or form. I assure the Prime Minister of Turkey that the EU does not qualify to be a Christian club, and would never be a Christian club.

It is not my business whether European politicians admit Turkey into their Club or not. However, since the Prime Minister of Turkey and some politicians and political commentators are fond of linking Christianity with the European Union, it is my business, as a committed Christian who is not ashamed of the Lord Jesus Christ, to correct the erroneous impression that the European Union is somehow a Christian club that has become an hindrance to a Muslim country that aspires to join the greatest political alliance in the world and the biggest economic market of the 21st century. If "letting Turkey into the European club would be politically astute" to solve the security problems facing Europe and mankind, then European politicians should make their decision on Turkey's membership of their club purely on political grounds, without pretending that Christianity is also an issue to be considered.

In the same newspaper, the American government expressed its desire for Turkey to join the European Union. Under the title *America intervenes to warn of rejection disaster,* Diplomatic Editor, Richard Beeston, reported: "The Bush Administration intervened in the debate about Turkey's entry into the EU, warning Brussels of disastrous consequences if Ankara's membership bid is turned down." According to the report, "Eric Edelman, a member of Pentagon, and the US Ambassador to Ankara said, "refusing Turkey's entry would not just stabilise strategic region on Europe's border but also set back efforts to encourage democratic reform across the Muslim world." And President Obama also confirmed America's support for Turkey's membership of the European Union in his address to Turkish Parliament in April 2009.

If America and Britain and other European countries feel Turkey's membership of the EU would solve their security problems, and also make that "beautiful lady" (Democracy) attractive to prospective "bridegrooms" in the Muslim world, then the European Union should wholeheartedly accept Turkey. Christianity should not be used in any way to prevent a Muslim country joining a secular European club that has no room for the Lord Jesus Christ.

FROM DEADLOCK TO "SQUALID" DEAL

On 2 October 2005, the eve before the European leaders met in Luxembourg to discuss the negotiations about Turkey's membership, the European foreign ministers held a preliminary meeting to open the way for the negotiations. The meeting ended in a deadlock. Austria's foreign minister, Ursula Plassnik, insisted that the negotiations should centre on Turkey being offered a "Privileged Partnership" instead of full membership. Jack Straw, the then British Foreign Secretary, who chaired the meeting, was disappointed by Austria's position. He felt it would prevent the British Presidency from achieving one of its main goals.

Mr Straw warned failure to open the negotiations that would pave the way for Turkey's membership of the European Union, could lead to an unprecedented "clash of civilisations" between the Christian and Muslim worlds. I quote the comments Mr Straw made on BBC24 News: "This would be the best available way of binding these two great religions together....two of the three great religions of the book – Christianity and Islam." According to the Foreign Secretary it would represent a failure if the European Union failed to accept Turkey.

I have already explained that the EU is NOT a Christian club. If the European Union were a Christian club, the Lord Jesus Christ would have been mentioned in the European Constitution. Rather, the architects of the European Constitution felt that mentioning "Jesus Christ" in the Blue-print of Europe would be offensive and divisive. For example, a Dublin Member of the European Parliament even went to the extent of suggesting that the inclusion of God in the European Constitution "would be a mistake; a serious mistake." A British Labour Member of Parliament also argued that a specific mention of Christianity "*would offend those many millions of people of different faiths or no faith at all.*". And a Socialist French deputy also suggested that to have mentioned Christianity and God in the European Constitution would have been "*absurd*" because, it would exclude Muslims and others of non-Christian faiths, as well as citizens who do not believe in God.

In view of the 'hostility' towards the Lord Jesus Christ, and the cry to exclude God and Christianity from the Constitution of Europe, why did Jack Straw, and other European politicians associate the European Union with Christianity? Again, if the European Union were a Christian club, the Lord's Prayer would be said before and after every EU summit. Has the Bible got a place in the European Union? No. It was, therefore, an unnecessary threat from Jack Straw that there would be a "clash of civilisations" if Turkey, a Muslim country, were to be rejected by the European Union – a 'Christian club'. The destiny of the world does not depend on whether the European Union accepts or rejects Turkey. However, the end of Gentile supremacy on earth is associated with the European Empire - the "10 toes of clay and iron of the human statue" described in Daniel 2:41-45.

When the emergency talks, which were initiated by the British Foreign Secretary, collapsed on 2 October 2005, Anthony Browne commented on it in The Times. In a column titled *Turkey left out in cold as Austria digs in heels over EU entry talk,* the Brussels Correspondent wrote: "Before the talks, Mr Straw gave warning about the impact it would have on relations between Islam and the West if Austria wielded its veto: "This is a crucial meeting for the future of the European Union ....We are concerned about this theological–political divide, which could open up even further the boundary between so-called Christian-heritage states and those of Islamic heritage. The heavy responsibility rests on all member states".

THE EUROPEAN UNION IS NOT A CHRISTIAN CLUB

Mr Erdogan declared on Turkish television: "Either the EU will decide to become a world force and a world player, which would show its political maturity, or it will limit itself to a Christian club." Once again, I would remind the Turkish Prime Minister that the European Union is NOT a Christian club. The truth is that the Lord Jesus Christ does not need the European Union that has no room for Him. However, the Lord needs the European Union to fulfil His prophetic Word in chapter 2:41-43 of the Book of Daniel. Whether European Union becomes a "world force and a world player" or not, will not depend on its association with Christianity. After all, the Lord Jesus Christ has warned His followers to come out of the political Babylon (Revelation 18:1-4). The European Union is part of this Babylon. Their Parliament in Strasbourg looks like the Tower of Babel as illustrated in Brueghel's painting.

I would also remind the Prime Minister of Turkey, that the former British Prime Minister, Tony Blair, once implied that the EU is not a Christian club. During the campaign before the British General election, which was held on 5 May 2005, Tony Blair objected to religion being dragged into politics. It was, therefore, disingenuous for Jack Straw to have suggested, somehow, that if the "EU Christian club" does not welcome Turkey, a Muslim country; there will be a clash of civilisations." What kind of "clash of civilisation" Jack Straw alluded to?

Here is my question to Jack Straw, the British Government and all the European leaders: "When did the European Union become a Christian club?" European politicians should leave Christianity alone and pursue their dream of Carbon Free world where their citizens would live in peace and prosperity. However, the Credible Lord Jesus Christ cautions us: *"Without Me you can do nothing"* (John 15:5).

On 3 October 2005, an article in Financial Times read *EU without Turkey will be just a Christian club*. Did this announcement imply that, currently, without Turkish membership of the European Union, the EU is a Christian Club? The plain truth is, the EU, without Turkey, is not a Christian club. And the EU with Turkey will continue to be a non-Christian club. So long as political commentators and politicians keep on associating the European Union with Christianity, I would continue to remind them that the European Union has no qualification to be a Christian club. The Lord does not need the European Union, yet the Lord needs 'That Thing' in Brussels. Has the Bible got a "seat" in the European Parliament? Would the Bible not cause offence to non-Christians and atheists in the European Parliament? For the Bible says: "Jesus Christ is the way, the truth and the life. No one comes to the Father except through Him?" (John 14:6). I repeat: The Lord Jesus Christ does NOT need the EU, yet the Lord NEEDS the

EU to fulfil His Word to come as a "*Stone cut without human hands*" to crush the human statue from its 'toes of clay and iron' to its 'head of gold' to close the era of Gentile supremacy on earth (Daniel 2:41-45).

THE LUXEMBOURG DEAL: THE "LONDON-ANKARA-WASHINGTON-AXIS"

Deep in the night of 3 October 2005, the European foreign ministers finally agreed to start talks that could allow Turkey to join the European Union. This decision resulted from a series of "frantic and acrimonious shuttle of diplomacy" which was initiated by the British foreign secretary. The Austrian Government, whose people oppose to Turkey's membership of the Union, and whose foreign minister had earlier insisted that Turkey should not be offered full membership of EU, was eventually bought off.

Austria was promised that its ally, Croatia, would also get the opportunity to join the European Union after it was revealed that Croatia had agreed to haunt down war criminals from the conflict in Bosnia. Hitherto, the European Union had already postponed talks with Croatia in March 2005, because Croatia was deemed to be protecting a leading war crimes suspect. But suddenly, while the negotiations were still dragging on, Carla del Ponte, the United Nations chief prosecutor for former Yugoslavia, cleared the way for Croatia by informing the EU that Croatia was complying. This "mysterious" intervention was enough for the European Union to remove the obstacle facing Croatia, and at the same time paved the way for Austria to shift its previous position on Turkey's membership. A deal was struck to please the "belligerents".

On 4 October 2005, appropriate headlines appeared in some of the national newspapers to reflect the 'Luxembourg deal'.

- "Crisis fears fade as Straw wins EU deal for Turkey" (Daily Mail).
- "Deal saves talks on Turkey's EU entry", "Path to EU opens for Turkey after last minute deal" (The Times).
- On the "Luxembourg deal" Financial Times reported: "The European Union ...cleared the way for membership talks with Turkey after a day of high drama in which failure was only narrowly averted and even foreign ministers were left in the dark about the proposed deal."

This "Luxembourg Deal" was achieved with the intervention of the American Government. The Financial Times exposed the American involvement in EU affairs in its 5 October 2005 Editorial. Under a title *Diplomats raise eyebrows over US involvement in deal-making,* the leading article reported "....Amid the exhilaration of the British and the European Commission delegations, other diplomats sounded a sour note about what some portrayed as a London-Ankara-Washington axis". According to the editorial, one of EU official from "a heavyweight country" said, "The British consulted the Turks and the Americans before they consulted us". Condoleezza Rice, the then US Secretary of State, played a key role. She spoke to Mr Straw by phone very early in the Washington morning, as well as to Recep Tayyip Erdogan.

The final deal was completed in a call between Mr Erdogan and Tony Blair. It was reported that many of the 25 EU foreign ministers at the meeting in Luxembourg were kept in the dark about the ongoing arrangement. "The roles of Turkey and US were particularly controversial. The American interest in the deal was based on their perception that, "a Turkey firmly anchored in Europe will be an even more reliable partner for the transatlantic family and a positive force for advancing peace, prosperity and democracy." On April 2009, President Obama also articulated this view when he told the Turkish Parliament: "Turkey is a critical ally. Turkey is an important part of Europe. And Turkey and the United States must stand together — and work together — to overcome the challenges of our time."

On 5 October 2005, The Times again commented on the "Luxembourg deal". In an editorial captioned, *"THE ONUS ON ZAGREB: Croatia must justify an unwelcome EU decision to open accession talks,"* the paper stated: "However welcome the compromise that finally broke the Austrian veto on opening accession talks with Turkey, the European Union's decision to start simultaneous talks with Croatia is disturbing. Yugoslavia republic forced its way back to the table as a result of a squalid deal and brazen brinkmanship by its neighbour and former imperial ruler; but, in overturning the suspension imposed on talks with Croatia until a war crimes suspect was handed over, the EU has sent an unwelcome signal to those countries, Serbia and Bosnia in particular, unwilling to accept responsibility for past atrocities or take the steps essential for lasting reconciliation." The editorial continued: "Austria's intransigence in making the Turkish talks - already previously agreed - dependent on a switch in EU policy sets a bad precedent..."

Would the Lord Jesus Christ associate Himself with a confederation of nations that indulges in "squalid deals"? No. Yet, the Turkish prime minister, once again, associated the European Union with Christianity when his country won the chance to start negotiations under the Luxembourg "squalid deal" to get the opportunity to enjoy the fruits of the biggest economic market in the world." On 5 October 2005, Daily Mail reported the Turkish prime minister's comments in an article titled, "Turkey will have to earn its place warns EC chief." According to the report, "When the architect of the European constitution, Valery Giscard d'Estaing, said he was surprised by the decision to launch accession talks....the Turkish premier said the decision had been a victory over prejudice in the mainly Christian EU." "On what grounds?" I ask Mr Erdogan.

I would again remind Mr Erdogan, that his views on EU's association with Christianity are misplaced. The EU does NOT proclaim the Gospel of Christ (Mathew 4:17). Secondly, which of the European Union leaders is committed to the Great Commission from the Lord Jesus Christ: *"Go and make disciples of all nations, baptising them in the name of the Father and of the son and of the Holy Spirit, and teaching them to obey everything I have commanded you…?"* (Matthew 28:19-20) None! Is the European Parliament committed to this "Great Commission"? Absolutely not! After all, the European Anthem is atheistic. The lyrics are about universal brotherhood with references to pagan shrine and gods. Secondly, the European Parliament looks like the Tower of Babel – the avenue where men rebelled against God and were scattered. Has the EU not even ignored the crucial godly advice the first President of the European Parliament offered to Europeans concerning the survival of the European Union?

Emma Nicholson, the Vice-Chairman of the Foreign Affairs Committee in the European Parliament in Brussels, confirmed the unchristian nature of the European Union in her letter to The Times on Wednesday, October 5, 2005. Under the subject *Turkey faces the bumpy road to a European future,* she wrote: "The deal struck is a great success for both the British presidency and of course, for Europe. But it is also a success for Europe…The opening of negotiations is a clear message that Europe is an outward looking and inclusive club. After all, the EU is not about religion or language – it is about core values, which Turkey shares."

If the "EU is not about religion…" as declared by an EU official, why is the Turkey prime minister fond of associating the European Union with the Christian Religion"? And why should Jack Straw also declared on BBC 24 News: "This (the eventual EU membership of Turkey) would be the best available way of binding these two great religions together….Christianity and Islam." Was it not some of the members of his Labour Party who boasted: *"We don't do God"?* Was it not the leader of his Government, Tony Blair, who cried during the campaign for the 5 May 2005 General Election that religion, should not be brought into politics when some church leaders raised the issue of abortion? Politicians are confused. When religion suits politicians it is entertained in politics. When religion doesn't suit politicians they object to it. The double-standards politicians: you cannot have it both ways.

THE NEW DAWN FOR EUROPE

Eventually the British EU presidency made a 'history'. It created a new dawn in European politics by succeeding in brokering a "squalid deal" that would bring Turkey to the EU negotiation table. Turkey, therefore, became the first Muslim country to be granted the opportunity to formally seek membership of the European Inclusive Club (EIC). The British foreign Secretary, as Chairman of the meetings, was desperate to broker a deal to "rescue Britain's EU presidency from oblivion". Because, Tony Blair's EU Presidency had been criticised by diplomats, media and think-tanks for lack of vision and direction. For example, the French newspaper, *Le Figaro,* on 21 September 2005, accused the British Prime Minister of "leading a British Presidency that was invisible and inaudible. The relaunch of political Europe is not on London agenda". And a diplomat also declared, "We do not see or feel the British Presidency". Finally, *The Times* Correspondents, Anthony Browne and Charles Bremner, writing about the criticisms of British leadership of the EU for pursuing a national agenda, stated: "Marco Incerti of the Centre for European Policy Studies, said: "The famous speech by Tony Blair raised expectations but those that criticised Blair for just saying nice words are being proved right. In an apparent swipe at the British Presidency, Jose Manuel Barroso, the "Buffoon of Brussels," who has no respect for Britons, said on 21 September 2005, "We are in this pause for reflection, but there has not been much reflection so far. What European debate has actually been launched?"

A "DEAL", BUT NOT A "BIG DEAL"

Understandably, it was a relief for the British foreign secretary when the "Luxembourg deal" was struck – a pact which enabled the Britain's EU Presidency to achieve one of its top priorities. Jack Straw declared: "We have just made history. The EU and Turkey agree we want ever closer relationship. It means we have an EU founded on values, not history" (*The Times* 4 October 2005). After the 30 hours of negotiations Mr Straw remarked, "We owe this to Turkey…its going to be a long road ahead but bringing Turkey into the EU is a prize worth striving for." The deal to launch formal talks on Turkey's membership of the European Union was hailed as "one of the biggest steps in its 50 year history". In the end Britain's EU Presidency attained its prime objective.

Question: "Were Jack Straw and Tony Blair, in their enthusiasm to help Turkey's membership of the European Union, aware they were unconsciously hasting the fulfilment of the brilliant Barrister's prediction, that Turkey would become one of the members of a political union of European nations? The British so-called "success" in making it possible for Turkey to join the European Union was not surprising. It was not a 'big deal'. Because, in the 19th century a British public servant predicted Turkey's membership of a political union of European nations before the European Community was born in the 20th century.

On 4 October 2005, the Financial Times commented on the British success in its editorial. Under the title "*Stalking Turkey*" with a subtitle "*Political courage is needed to sell the EU enlargement story,*" the paper reported: "Full membership for Turkey in the EU would be an extraordinary achievement, of huge benefit to both sides. It would demonstrate that the Union is not an exclusive Christian club, but is capable of accepting an overwhelmingly Muslim nation. It would bring in a dynamic economy and a young population, as well as a country that plays an important strategic role in the Middle East and central Asia". The editorial concluded: "Opening the door to Turkey is an essential step and one to be welcomed, not begrudged".

I ask the question: Has the European Union ever been an "exclusive Christian Club" since its creation? No! The Lord Jesus Christ has never regarded the European Union as His "club." The Lord's exclusive Club is the Church – not Cathedrals and imposing buildings with "blind" leaders. The Church is the organic body of men and women who have been called out from the *"sea"*- the corrupt world - to follow the Lord Jesus Christ in spirit and in truth. In view of this Scriptural truth, European politicians and political commentators should not waste their time and energy in bringing Christianity into their equation when attempting to solve their "Turkey problem". The EU is NOT a Christian club. The EU has NEVER been a Christian club. European leaders have even ignored the godly advice one of its founding fathers offered them to ensure the survival of their Project. I would share this 'advice' with you later on.

THE CASE FOR TURKEY'S MEMBERSHIP OF THE EUROPEAN UNION

Before the decision was made by the European Commission to open the gate for Turkey to start negotiating its membership of the "Progressive Club" of Europe, a major discussion was held on the BBC Dateline Programme. Gavin Esler hosted the debate for the 4 panellists. An American political commentator was the first to present the case for Turkey's membership: "There are geo-political facts here that would make things happen," He said. "Whether Europe decides to let Turkey in or not....Let's face it: it's going to happen...Turks will be in Europe. They will be working in Europe. Europe needs workers desperately. Spain needs a million new workers a year to keep its economy going. This is inevitable. Europe invited Turkey to begin thinking about this in the 1960's."

The Times correspondent in India made her contribution by stating that for the past 42 years Turkey has been on a long winding road to become a member of EU. For the past 20 years the Turks have been working very hard. She however stressed that because of the rate of increase in its population, which would be about 83 million by the time Turkey joins, the Dutch, the French, the Austrians, the Danes and the Swedes might not like it.

At this point, Yasmin Alibhai-Brown, The Independent columnist, also made her case: "They (the Dutch, the French, the Austrians, the Danes and the Swedes) like the Turks very much when they worked for them for nothing. They liked them very much when they go and destroy their most beautiful places on holidays; it stinks of racism." Addressing the Austrians, who are perceived to be the most hostile people to Turkey's membership of the EU, she said: "We remember what you gave world history. You should be very careful about how you play this one....If you don't want a wedge, a really challenging wedge to develop between Iran, Iraq, Syria and then Turkey; if you don't want a clash of civilisations, grow up." She concluded her argument by stressing that even though the intellectuals in Turkey believed it would be good for Turkey to join the EU, they felt so humiliated by the intransigents of the Austrians and others that they have reached the point where they say: "Fine, not interested."

The fourth panellist made his case for Turkey in Europe by suggesting that the Foreign Ministers must think very carefully before they make any decision on Turkey. For, "If they say "no" to Turkey, it would be catastrophic to the entire Europe and the EU countries. You would be saying to Turkey "No" as if you are saying, "No", because you are a Muslim; this is very dangerous." He pressed his case: "Turkey deserves a place in Europe. Turkey, since the collapse of the Ottoman Empire, has always presented itself to the world as part of the Western world of Europe and NATO. Just think of the immensely good message Europe could deliver to the world by accepting Turkey. When Turkey joins Europe it will border Syria, Iraq and Iran. These will be neighbouring countries to Europe. That would give these countries and others in the region a very good example on human rights, democracy and culturally."

The panel agreed that Turkey needs to reform in certain areas. However, they felt it would be offensive to the millions of Muslims in Europe to be treated as second class citizens if the EU decides to offer Turkey "Privilege Partnership" instead of full membership status in the "Exclusive club." The arguments the panellists advanced to support Turkey's membership of the EU collaborated with what Rosemary Righter highlighted in her article, *Let the Turks in: the EU isn't a club for Christians.* The columnist reported: "...The truth is no one wants Turkey in because no one wants the EU's most populous state....which it would rapidly become ..... Muslim. But there is no reason why a moderate Muslim nation cannot flourish within a European partnership. It will be costly to absorb Turkey; it will be difficult; it must be done. For the strategic prize is a grand one: the reinforcement of a civilising influence on Islam, right across the great arc stretching from Damascus deep into central Asia." She continued: "Were EU governments to go back on their word, Turks would put that down to invincible anti-Muslim prejudice. An alienated, destabilised, probably radicalised country of 70 million on Europe's doorstep would be in prospect. The price of keeping Europe "European" could be terrifying high" (The Times Friday 28 May 2004).

On 6 October 2004, the EU Commission recommended the opening of accession talks with Turkey. In his article "Why we need Turkey to join Europe", Anatole Kaletsky, first outlined the concerns of those countries that opposed Turkey's membership. He then argued that in the long run Europe would become a safer place, if Turkey, having joined the EU, becomes more prosperous and this prosperity "rippled out into other Muslim countries on Europe's Periphery: Morocco, Tunisia, Algeria, Libya, even the ultimate prize, Egypt...Making Turkey and ultimately the whole Mediterranean basin more European offers the best hope of reversing the spread of militant Islam and averting a global war of religion" (*The Times* Thursday 7 October 2004).

I repeat: it is none of my business whether European Union embraces Turkey or abandon their NATO ally. I express no opinion on Turkey's membership of the European Union. However, since some politicians and political commentators in Europe and Britain constantly associate the European Union with Christianity, and attempt to suggest that the European Union is somehow a Christian Club which disqualifies Turkey's membership, I am prompted to ask the question again: "When did the European Union become an exclusive Christian "club" to become a road block to Turkey's journey to the Euro-land to enjoy the fruits of the largest economic market in the world? Call it Lisbon Treaty, Reformed Treaty or a Constitution whatever you prefer, the Lord Jesus Christ was not mentioned in the preamble to the European Constitution? Would the name "Jesus Christ" not have caused an offence? Didn't a French politician suggest that it would have been "absurd" for God and Christianity to have been mentioned in the European Constitution? Furthermore, when Rocco Buttiglione, an European Commissioner nominee, expressed his Christian view on homosexuality and marriage, the European Parliament voted against his nomination. He was found unworthy to work for the European Enterprise because his Christian views contradict the secular views of the European Parliament.

If "the price of keeping Europe 'European' could be terrifying high," because there would be on Europe's doorstep "an alienated, destabilised, probably radicalised country of 70 million", then European leaders should heed the advice of the "Experts" and accept Turkey, and refrain from pretending that the EU is a Christian Club which has no room for a Muslim country. It is time politicians and commentators stopped associating "That Thing" in Brussels with Christianity. The EU is NOT a Christian club. However, If "the time has come for Europe to open the gates to Islam" (Financial Times 7 October 2005); and if welcoming Turkey into the EU would combat the spread of militant Islam and so prevent catastrophe in Europe; and if the "children" of Jean Monnet don't want "a clash of civilisations," then Europe should welcome Turkey to save themselves from creating a "really challenging wedge between Iran, Iraq and Syria."

THE "UNKNOWN TRUTH" ABOUT TURKEY'S MEMBERSHIP OF THE EUROPEAN UNION

I would remind political intellectuals and politicians that it was a committed Christian, Dr Robert Anderson, who, before the European Union came into existence recorded that Turkey would become a member of a political alliance of European nations. There is, therefore, nothing extraordinary about the EU welcoming Turkey into its fold. What is extraordinary about Turkey's membership of the European Union is that a British public servant predicted it even before Turkey first applied for membership of European Community in 1963. This is the 'extraordinary' event in history, not what happened at Luxembourg. For the "squalid deal" that paved the way for Turkey's membership of the European Union was an event that rather paved the way for the Prince of Detective's prediction about Turkey's membership of political Europe to be fulfilled.

ROMAN CATHOLIC CHURCH AND THE EUROPEAN UNION AND TURKEY

Perhaps, the reason why politicians and political commentators associate Christianity with the European Union is the attitude of Roman Catholic Popes and Bishops. The problem is that the hierarchy of the Roman Catholic Church is constantly interfering with the affairs of the European Union to influence some of its decisions. For example, on Turkey's membership of EU, Pope Benedict XVI was once against it. Cardinal Cormac Murphy-O'Connor also objected to it. Later on the same Pope Benedict XVI changed his position and supported Turkey's membership. The question is: "Why should Christian leaders associate themselves with the European Union that has no room for the Lord Jesus Christ?" This seems puzzling; but it should not be. Because, the Church of Rome would share the same 'bed' with the last Caesar of the Revived Roman Empire. "*Verbum sapientist est.* I would deal with this subject in the Appendix.

THE LORD JESUS CHRIST IS AN 'EXTREMIST.' HE MAKES NO DEALS. YOU ARE EITHER WITH HIM OR AGAINST HIM

The European Union and its institutions strive on deals and compromises to survive. The Lord Jesus Christ does not make 'deals'. Neither does the Lord compromise on His Word. The Lord Jesus Christ is an "Extremist." You are either with Him or you are against Him. The Lord of lords is not a politician. He is not of the "centre - right". He neither occupies the "left of the centre" nor the 'Right of the Centre, or the "Middle Ground". The King of kings is after souls not votes. Our Divine Lord sits at the Right Hand of God Almighty (Colossian 3:1, 1 Peter 3:22). Witness how the Lord Jesus responded to the high priest who questioned

Him on an oath whether He was the Christ, the Son of God: *"I say to all of you: In the future you will see the Son of Man sitting at the right hand of the Mighty One and coming on the cloud of heaven"* (Matthew 26:63-64). And Apostle Peter told the Jews: "..*God raised Jesus from the dead and exalted him to His own right hand as Prince and Saviour...*" (Acts 5:30-31).

When a rich, young ruler ignored the Lord Jesus' advice, and turned his back on Him because he could not dispose of his wealth and give them to the poor to become a disciple to gain treasures in heaven, our Divine Lord did not strike any deal with this wealthy aristocrat to keep his riches and still become His disciple. Even though the Lord loved this affluent man, He did not compromise His Word. He allowed the rich man to go his way (Mark 10:17-22). Similarly, the Lord Jesus Christ does not expect members of His "Club" (the Church) to make "squalid deals" and compromise His teachings to attract crowd to His "Club". The European Union, which is described as "say-one-thing-do another double-speak" does not deserve to be a Christian Club. I repeat: It is time European politicians and political commentators stopped associating that "Autocratic Thing" in Brussels with Christianity.

BIBLE PROPHECY FULFILLED

From the events that led to the "Luxembourg squalid deal" (that overcame Austria's opposition of Turkey's full membership of the EU), it is clear the European Union is a "divided Kingdom" with "mixed people" who are "not united". This, again, fulfils the prophetic word in Daniel 2:41-43: "Just as you (King Nebuchadnezzar) saw that the feet and toes were partly of baked clay and partly of iron, so this will be a *divided kingdom*.......And just as you saw the iron mixed with baked clay, so the *people will be a mixture and will not remain united* any more than iron mixes with clay". What a prophecy! A word which was recorded over 2600 years ago in the Book of Daniel is now being fulfilled. Is the Book of Daniel a 'religious novel' in the Bible? Certainly not! Yet, the Catholic Bible – "The New Jerusalem Bible – Reader's Edition" - describes the Book of Daniel an "Edifying fiction."

THE CLIMAX OF BRITAIN'S EU PRESIDENCY

The beginning of the end of Britain's EU presidency started with a two day EU summit in Brussels on 15 December 2005. Before the European leaders met to negotiate the EU budget for 2007 to 2013, Mr. Kaletsky wrote an interesting article that reflected the prophetic word in Daniel 2:40-43 – a divided kingdom with divided people who are not united. The article was titled "Hoist the white flag Tony; get rid of the rebate millstone around our neck." Mr Kaletsky further expressed his concern on how "British politicians and diplomats have failed to defend Britain's vital interest against the ruthless nationalism of France, Spain,

Italy, and other shamelessly self-serving European powers." Despite his concerns about the European Union and its institutions, he wanted the British prime minister to surrender part of the special rebate won by Margaret Thatcher in 1984 from her European "partners" to compensate for Britain with its small agricultural sector." Mr Kaletsky then shared his view with readers: "Mr. Blair should pluck the courage to sacrifice Mrs Thatcher's rebate – and to face the inevitable cries of treason from the Tories and the popular press – partly because a budget deal is essential to make a success of the EU's eastward enlargement." He added, "If Mr Blair refuses to negotiate on the British refund, he will seriously damage the alliances he skilfully created in the early years of this decade with Poland and other Central European countries which will bear most of the costs of a continuing budget deadlock." It is precisely this alliance of European nations that Sir Robert Anderson wrote about in the 19th century before the "apostle of European unity," Jean Monnet and his "children" schemed to bring it into fruition in the 20th and 21st centuries.

THE EUROPEAN UNION BUDGET

When the British government initially proposed that the European Union budget for 2007 to 2013 should be cut by €24.7 billion from the €871 billion previously proposed to €845.6 billion, the head of European Commission accused Britain of "fuelling Euroscepticism and damaging the credibility of the process of enlargement." A spokesman for Jose Manual Barroso also attacked the British prime minister of "trying to do Europe on the cheap." The President of the European Commission had earlier, unfairly criticised the British prime minister of being EU's Robin Hood in reverse – implying that Britain (the "toes of iron") was robbing the poor countries (the toes of clay) to be given to rich countries, which are the toes of iron of the magnificent human statue King Nebuchadnezzar saw(Daniel chapter 2)

The Hungarian Prime Minister, Ferene Gyurcsany, also warned: "If wealthy European states (the toes of iron) were not generous to the poorer east (the toes of clay), they faced the prospect of the most possible conflicts between the different parts of Europe." The Financial Times reported these comments in its 30 November 2005 edition, under a title "Hungary warns western states of budget conflict**."** The Hungarian Premier issued the threat of possible conflict after most of the east European states (the toes of clay) that joined the European Union in 2004 categorically rejected the budget plans put forward by the United Kingdom. The Hungarian then cried out: "The European Union's stability could not be taken for granted. And if there is an unbearable differences between countries, it will prompt large scale migration and it will jeopardise social stability." Was this "threat" an attempt to blackmail the "toes of iron of the dazzling human statue"? It was this same prime minister of Hungary who was subsequently accused of having misled Hungarians about the state of their economy to win re-election. The Hungarians felt cheated. Their anger boiled into lawlessness which resulted in the destruction of properties and the burning of cars. It was the worse street violence in the Hungarian capital since the fall of communism. The prime minister resisted calls to resign. Despite having deceived his people, the European Union bureaucrats considered him to be the credible politician to save Hungary. This incident was published in the 20 September 2006 edition of the Financial Times in a column headed *Gyurcsany may still offer best hope, says EU.* The newspaper reported: "Hungary's prime minister has not just deceived his voters since coming to power in 2004: he also tried to hoodwink the markets, Brussels and the European Central Bank into believing he had his country's finances under control."

In spite of his deception, according to the report, "many in the international community were still prepared to believe Ferenc Gyurcsany was the best person to get Hungary out of its fiscal hole." This is the man who "lied in the morning and lied in the evening" to Hungarian voters to win power and threatened that if Britain and other rich nations (the toes of iron) did not increase their funding of the EU Project to assist the poor nations (the toes of clay), there would be conflict between parts of Europe.

Here is an extract from the Hungarian Prime Minister's speech, which was delivered to his political party on May 26, 2006. The speech, that sparked the rioting in Hungary, was secretly recorded and leaked to the press.

- "I almost died when I had to pretend for 1½ years (before April elections) as if we were governing. Instead we lied in the morning, we lied in the evening. I am through with this. We either do it and then you've got your man, or you pick someone else."
- "It was absolutely clear that what we were saying was not true....And all this time we have done nothing for four years. Nothing. You cannot mention a single government measure that we could be proud of."
- "We don't have much choice because we have screwed it up. Not just a bit, but big time. No country in Europe has acted as brazenly as we did." (Source: www.porfolio.hu/en (Financial Times 20 September 2006).

THE WORD OF GOD HAS COME TO PASS

From what we have learnt so far, it is evident how the European Union has become an "Empire" of weak and strong nations, poor and rich countries with divided peoples of different cultures and tongues who are not united. Once again, we have witnessed the accomplishment of God's prophetic word in Daniel 2:41-43: "Just as you (King Nebuchadnezzar) saw that the feet and toes were partly of baked clay and partly of iron, so this will be a divided kingdom.....As the toes were partly iron and partly clay, so this kingdom will be partly strong and partly brittle. And just as you saw the iron mixed with baked clay, so the people will be a mixture and will not remain united any more than iron mixes with clay."

At this point it would be appropriate to share with you Brian Sewell's comments on the European Union. They are prophetic description of the fate of the great human statue recorded in Daniel 2:41-45. In his article, "Why our voices must be heard", Mr. Sewell writes: "It is in the nature of empires to expand too quickly and then fragment. Any empire that embraces too many nations, cultures, languages and economies cannot be held in perpetuity...Europe with a single currency...will tumble *like Humpty-Dumpty from his wall, never to be reassembled...I doubt if a united Europe will last long...Like the Titanic the EU will become a universal symbol of hubris*" (Emphasis mine. Evening Standard 3 June 2003). Indeed, the "European phenomenon", the revived Roman Empire, would certainly collapse. It would last only 7 years when its powerful Emperor is enthroned. Its glory would shine for just 3½ years (Daniel 9:27). A word to the wise is enough.

THE EUROPEAN UNION SUMMIT ON 15 DECEMBER 2005 AND THE COMMON AGRICULTURAL POLICY (THE 'DIRTY' CAP)

Let us return to the last days of Britain's EU Presidency. The first day of the European Union Budget Summit ended without any agreement on how the political leaders would finance the EU Project from 2007 to 2013. On 16 December 2005, The Times reported that day's proceedings in an article titled *Blair and Chirac go head to head over agriculture.* According to the political correspondents Philip Webster and Anthony Browne, Tony Blair, and the French President, Jacques Chirac (who are no longer in office), remained locked in a battle of wills... as Britain insisted that it would veto any budget that did not allow the prospect of changes to agricultural spending before 2014. France hit back by saying it would not allow the review of the Common Agricultural Policy spending in 2008 if the changes were not postponed until 2014. According to the Correspondents, "France and other countries piled the pressure on Mr Blair to give up more of the British rebate." We were informed British dispute with France appeared to be the biggest obstacle to finalise the budget deal. President Chirac demanded Britain to make "big sacrifices" from its £3.4 billion rebate. But the French President refused to offer any meaningful review of the Common Agriculture Policy which favoured French farmers.

The Budget for the Common Agricultural Policy was described by a British diplomat as "The most stupid, immoral state-subsidised policy in human history, give or take communism." And according to a new report on reforming Europe's farm policy by Jack Thurston for the Centre for European Reform, a London-based think tank, "The present system remains an emblem of inefficiency and inequality...it distorts the EU single market; it fails to increase the efficiency of European farming, and it principally benefits the biggest farms in the richest EU countries,"(the "toes of iron") (The Times, Tuesday, December 13, 2005).

During the budget negotiation Poland, an ally of Britain, teamed up with France to provide the toughest opposition to Britain in the budget dispute. Poland was labelled an "Awkward customer." In a newspaper article entitled *Awkward Poland makes alliance with the French,* the Poles were further described as having "complicated views on the EU itself." After the initial German-Franco pact, which dominated the direction of the European Project, we had a new Franco-Polish pact – an alliance within the alliance of European nations - to pursue their national interests at the expense of other countries, especially Britain. Such divisions and disagreements, based on the pursuit of national interests in the European Union, which were on display at the end of the first day of the EU budget summit, once again fulfilled the prophetic word in Daniel 2:41-43: "And just as you saw the iron mixed with baked clay, so the people will be a mixture and will not remain united, any more than iron mixes with clay."

THE 2007 – 2013 BUDGET DEAL

Eventually, on the final day of the summit, the deadlock was broken. A deal to continue financing the *Titanic of the 21st century* from 2007 to 2013 was achieved when the "stumbling block" (the reduction of the British rebate) was removed. Britain agreed to surrender part of its EU budget rebate by £1 billion a year. Britain made this sacrifice without any commitment from France on early reform of the subsidies it receives for its farmers. According to The Daily Telegraph, Tony Blair "bowed to a Franco-German demand, backed by farming nations and new members from East and Central Europe *(the toes of clay)*, to abandon calls for budget discipline and expand EU spending dramatically during the next budget period from 2007 until 2013."

The Daily Telegraph's Correspondents, David Rennie and Tony Helm, wrote: "Although Mr Blair chaired the Brussels summit of European Union leaders, he was concerned by a twin assault from established EU farming nations and from his much-vaunted allies in eastern and central Europe." The correspondents continued, "....A French-led block of farming nations, including Spain, Austria and Italy, handed him (Mr Blair) an ultimatum that he makes deep permanent cuts to the rebate. Behind that demand laid the public threat of a French veto if he (the British prime minister) pushed for reforms of the Common Agricultural Policy at any time before the end of 2007 – 2013 period."
The pursuit of national interests in the European Union was summarised in a letter which Mr Riccardo Illy, President of the Assembly of European Regions,

wrote to the Financial Times. This epistle was published in a column headed *Leaders must fund political ambitions for European Union as a whole.* Mr Illy stated: "The negotiations on the financial perspectives 2007-2013 have severely damaged Europe's credibility and raised additional doubts for the citizens on the future of the European Union. They also showed that even after 50 years of European construction, of the creation of a wide area of peace and stability, national interests still prevail in Europe, able to cause an ambitious project of a united and enlarged Europe to regress."

And Mr William Hague, the shadow foreign secretary, also expressed his view on the budget deal: "The British prime minister's approach had got the eastern Europeans alienated, everyone in Europe upset, no concessions from the French, but quite a slice of the British rebate being put on the table." Mr Hague told the BBC Radio, "I think we are seeing here some of the real fundamental contradictions in the way Europe works at the moment. How do we support the new countries coming in when so much EU money goes to the CAP? Unless that is addressed we are not going to get anywhere in the long run, so they really need to go back to that theme." Mr William Hague, again, accused Mr Blair of caving in over the rebate secured by Margaret Thatcher in 1984, without gaining any concessions in return. He said, "Seldom in the course of European negotiations has so much been surrendered for so little. It is amazing how the government has moved miles while the French have barely moved a centimetre." However, according to the 18 December 2005 edition of The Sunday Times, Mr Blair insisted that reaching a deal was crucial to bolster the enlargement of the EU to 25 member states. It would "enhance Britain's reputation in Europe." And failing to reach a deal would have done "an immense damage" to the national interest.

I raise these questions: "What kind of "Britain's reputation" was Tony Blair referring to? "Why should Britain sacrifice its financial interest to please the 'sons and daughters' of Jean Monnet who, together with their 'father', have no clue what the EU is for?" Tony Blair's view was not shared by other politicians. Mr Bill Cash, a Conservative Member of British Parliament, declared, "Tony Blair has handed Gordon Brown (the then Chancellor of the Exchequer) a poisoned chalice with this deal. He will have to find an extra £1 billion a year, money that could have gone on hospitals and schools. This will spell real trouble for Brown and I can see why he would be angry."

The Sunday Times continued, "To add to Blair's woes, France....claimed victory in its battle to defend Europe's £30 billion a year farm budget. Jacques Chirac, the French President, said his nation had "got what it wanted" in principle, and goaded Blair by heaping praise on him for displaying "much courage" in his difficult political gesture."
The attitude of France during and after the budget negotiations was summarised by Simon Jenkins in his article *Blair set out for Waterloo and found himself at*

Dunkirk. Mr Jenkins wrote: "The CAP, and France as its great beneficiary, remains supreme.....No European state plays this game of self interest better than France. For half a century Paris has squeezed Brussels for all it is worth and has been granted immunity from the economic forces swirling across Europe." Mr Blair's defence of the budget deal was, "We cannot ask the poorer countries *(the toes of clay of the human image)* to pay the rebate on British spending because that would be wrong."

The editorial of The Sunday Times summarised the outcome of the British surrender of part of its rebate "A costly climb-down." According to the leading article, "Britain will pay more into the EU, our net contribution rising from £3.5 billion to £6 billion a year. The British rebate has been shelved by £1 billion a year. And for what? Next to nothing. It would have been better for Mr Blair to walk away than agree this deal. He, however, was anxious not to be seen as an EU wrecker – that would not be good for his so called "legacy". Next door in 11 Downing Street, as he watches the prime minister negotiating away Britain's interest, Gordon Brown is fuming. He is right to be." The editorial concluded.

THE CHARACTER OF THE EUROPEAN UNION

The 'successful summit' which agreed the EU budget for 2007 – 2013, was greeted with this headline, *"Aftermath of EU deal turns ugly"* (The Times 19 December 2005.) The text effectively summed up the character of the European Union.

Tony Blair negotiated the 2007 – 2013 budget deal in good faith. The refusal of the British Government to agree to the reduction of its rebate during the previous EU budget summit under the Luxembourg Presidency, was blamed for the collapse of the summit in failing to reach an agreement on how to finance the European "Empire" from 2007 – 2013. So, to remove "the stumbling block" to pave the way for an agreement on how to finance Jean Monnet's "Great Titanic" for 2007 – 2013, Mr Blair agreed to surrender a portion of the rebate Britain receives from EU, on the understanding that the Common Agricultural Policy, which consumes a higher proportion of the EU budget, and which favours France the most, would be reviewed with a view to reducing the funds allocated to the 'sacred cow' (the Common Agricultural Policy) by 2009. But no sooner had the summit agreed on the budget deal than France and Ireland (the two countries that benefit greatly from farm subsidies) threatened to veto any attempt to reduce the spending on the Common Agricultural Policy before 2014.

According to The Times Correspondent, "President Chirac of France and Bertie Ahern, the Irish Prime Minister, both emerged triumphantly from the budget negotiations insisting that the EU's agricultural spending has been secured until 2014, the start of the next budget period. France is the biggest overall recipient of farm subsidies, getting about £6 billion a year, while Ireland is the biggest per capita". The report indicated that, their "insistence that the Common Agricultural Policy had been kept intact was a huge embarrassment for Mr Blair, who justified the surrendering of £7 billion of the British rebate by saying, he had secured a wide-ranging review of EU finances in 2008 – 2009.

Mr Anthony Browne continued with his report: "Mr Blair had always insisted that he would only accept cuts in the (British) rebate in return for cuts in farm spending, and said after the summit that the review opened the way to curbing the EU's £198 billion agricultural budget. However, M. Chirac and Mr. Ahern pointed out that despite the review, the level of farm subsidies would stay at the current levels until 2014, because the subsidies could be cut only with the unanimous agreement of all countries."

In spite of Mr Blair acting 'reasonably' to prevent another budget deadlock that could have been detrimental to the poorer countries (*the toes of clay)*, French newspapers poured scorn on the British Prime Minister's failure to secure cuts in farm subsidies. *Le Dimache* said that farm subsidies "will not fall between now and 2013, despite the wishes of Tony Blair." The Sunday edition of *Le Parisien* declared President Chirac "won the march against Tony Blair on the British rebate without yielding on the Common Agricultural Policy." While newspapers in France were ridiculing the British prime minister's gesture, the Prime Minister of Greece, Costas Karamanlis, appreciated it by saying, "The British presidency deserves praise for its constructive role in a complicated negotiation and for the courage it showed in giving up part of its rebate." Britain was a laughing stock in Europe.

"KNOWLEDGE IS POWER; IGNORANCE IS WEAKNESS"

What a Pity! Had Tony Blair studied what Sir Robert Anderson published on European confederacy, its character and future prospects before the French architect of the European Project, was born in 1888, he would not have tolerated the arrogant French President. Mr. Blair would not even have attended the summit in the first place. He would have learnt from Sir Robert's works that Britain would not be saved in Europe. This information would have motivated Blair to withdraw Britain from the European Union the second he entered No 10 Downing Street. Unfortunately, due to ignorance, Prime Minister Blair thought the fate of Britain rests in the European Union. So, he blindly followed the 'children' of Jean Monnet to board the 'doomed Titanic.' "Knowledge is power; ignorance is weakness", says the "Seer of Dublin."

What a pity" Why should a British Prime Minister be humiliated by a French President, whose 'Father', Jean Monnet, the architect of European Construction, unconsciously toiled to bring to pass what Mr. Blair's 'father,' a brilliant lawyer, had already written about European Union and its demise before the French architect of EU was even conceived.

A PROPHET IS OF NO HONOUR IN HIS OWN COUNTRY AND AMONG HIS OWN PEOPLE

Great Britain, a blessed country that should have known better about the European Union and its future prospects, became an object of ridicule among 'blind' men who have no idea what the European Union is for. What an irony! Had the British "prophet" been honoured in his own country, France, Ireland, and the beneficiaries of the corrupt Common Agricultural Policy would not have dared to poke fun at a British Prime Minister. Tony Blair was weak in the negotiations because he did not 'fortify' himself with the knowledge his 'father' had already provided about political Europe and its future. The French, who poked fun at the British Premier, should realise that their "scheming" 'Father', Jean Monnet, might have been the "Trusty Eckhart" of an European idea, but he was no genius. The "honorary citizen of Europe" was only a 'slave' who laboured to fulfil the extraordinary vision of his British 'master.' And had the then Irish Premier, Bertie Ahern, also read what the native of Dublin, wrote about Europe and its destiny, he would have thought twice before getting excited about the benefits Ireland enjoyed from putting up the 'dirty' CAP. The Irish Premier would have recommended the withdrawal of Ireland from that "vile thing" in Brussels. And how sad it is, that the 'sons' and 'daughters' of Monnet and Adenauer are dragging the Irish people to board the doomed EU Titanic. The Irish have ignored their 'Father'. For, a prophet is of no honour in his country and among his own people.

DIVISIONS AMONG POLITICAL PARTIES

In Britain, politicians of the three main political parties – Conservatives, Labour and Liberal Democrats – were divided on the merits of the budget deal negotiated by Tony Blair which resulted in Britain's net contribution to the European Union rising to about £6 billion a year – about £100 per British citizen. Some of the politicians claimed the surrendering of the British rebate would affect the government's spending on public services – schools, hospitals and transport.

Even among politicians of the ruling Labour Government, there were disagreements about the budget deal. In a newspaper article captioned "Brown refuses to endorse the P. M's surrender over EU rebate," Daily Mail highlighted the disagreements: "There was deep anger in Downing Street that, far from rallying behind Mr Blair in his hour of need, Mr Brown has gone out of his way to distance himself from the deal – and highlight its impact on public spending. Number 10 hit back.....by stressing that Jon Cunliffe, the head of treasury's macro-economic policy and international directorate, was part of the team of British officials in

Brussels which drew up the budget deal." Daily Mail added, "Despite Downing Street's comments, supporters of Mr Brown argued that Mr Cunliffe was just one man in the midst of a 50–strong negotiating team dominated by number 10." The report concluded with the comments made by Sir Menzies Campbell, a Liberal Democrat spokesman: "It is fundamental and profound disappointment that a (British) presidency which began with such high hopes has resulted in the agreement we now know about."

THE FUTURE OF BRITAIN DOES NOT LIE IN EUROPE

We must ask the question: Did Gordon Brown, the then 'Iron Chancellor' really care about Britain's national interest, when he appeared not to have endorsed Tony Blair's surrender of Britain's rebate? Was it not the same Gordon Brown, the "obstinate juror," who 'sold' Britons to Brussels by forcing the Lisbon Treaty through the "House of Indulgence" without any serious scrutiny of the European Constitution, and by refusing Britons a vote on a wretched document that would usurp their sovereign rights? Some politicians are hypocrites. If the "Dirty CAP" fits you, wear it.

And finally, when Tony Blair ended Britain's EU presidency with an address to the Members of the European Parliament, further divisions in the "European Empire" came to light. On Wednesday, 21 December 2005, this headline, "Blair deflects EU fire with attack on 'reactionaries,' appeared in The Times. Rory Watson and Phillip Webster reported: "TONY BLAIR brought down the curtain on Britain's European Union presidency with a ferocious attack on Euro-sceptics 'reactionaries'. He described them as being trapped in the mentality of the Second World War." Most members of the European Parliament complained that the budget agreed for 2007 – 2013 was too small.

According to The Times, "Nigel Farage, the UKIP leader in the European Parliament, complained that Mr Blair had been outclassed by President Chirac of France and had been forced to give away £7 billion without receiving anything in return". The UKIP leader was booed when he posed the question: "Why should our (British) money go to new sewers in Budapest and a new underground in Warsaw when public services in London are crumbling?"

Another Conservative Party Member of the European Parliament, Mr Roger Helmer, attacked the reduction of the British rebate negotiated by the Prime Minister. He said, "This is treachery, prime minister. You are giving away a huge sum of money simply as a big leaf for your failure. You boasted that the British rebate was not on the table, period. Then you did put it on the table and you are now selling it in salami slices, with nothing in return but fool's gold and vacuous promises." Mr Blair responded to the criticism by accusing his 'enemies' of being "reactionaries." And when the socialist members of the European Parliament applauded Mr Blair, he confronted them: "You sit there with our country's flag, but you do not represent our country's interests. This is the year 2005, not 1945. We are not fighting each other any more. These are our partners, our colleagues and our future lies in Europe." (Daily Mail 21 December 2005).

The question is: What convinces Tony Blair to suggest that the future of Great Britain lies in Europe? The future of Blair may be tied to the European Union. But the future of Great Britain does not lie in a project which uses immoral methods - pornographic film and nude posters and art - to promote it and has no room for the Lord Jesus Christ, the King of kings. Even before the European Union evolved from the ashes of the Second World War, Sir Robert Anderson, the Prophet of Linden Gardens, warned Britain would not be saved by participating in a political union of European nations.

According to The Times, during the two-hour meeting with the Members of the European Parliament, "Mr Blair was frequently applauded when he admitted that the budget was far from perfect, but was essential to make enlargement a success and to channel investment and funding to the new member states." The MEP's made it clear that they would press Austria to increase the budget of £586 billion when it takes over the EU presidency from Britain on 1 January 2006.

I ask these questions:
What is the ultimate purpose of EU enlargement?
What is the British interest in a project which was sold to them through deception?"
What is the future of EU - a "divided kingdom" of "mixed people," who are not united?
The answers lie in the "ten toes of the human image "King Nebuchadnezzar saw in his dream in about 604BC. The "stone cut without human hands will strike the statue on its feet of iron and clay and smashed them. As a result, the iron, the clay, the bronze, the silver and the gold of the effigy would be broken into pieces and become like chaff on a threshing-floor in the summer. The wind will sweep them away without leaving a trace. But the rock that struck the statue would become a huge mountain to fill the whole earth." (Daniel 2:34-35). Does the future of Great Britain lie in the "ten toes of baked clay and iron"? Should Britain be at the heart of the "toes of baked clay and iron? It takes a wise man to avert a prophecy.

THE WORD OF GOD IS TRUE

From what we have learnt so far, it is obvious the path that led to the successful budget deal for 2007 - 2013, and the events that took place thereafter clearly confirm the vile nature of the European Union. It is a disunited "kingdom" of rich and poor nations, strong and weak countries with mixed people who are not united pursuing their national interests.

In summary, the British EU presidency, which began in June 2005 and ended in December 2005, brought to light what God, over 2600 years ago, revealed to a pagan king in a pictorial form of "ten toes" of a dazzling human statue which were partly of baked clay and partly of iron. It was this vision that prompted Sir Robert Anderson to predict with absolute confidence that a confederation of European nations would be developed to pave the way for the "Man of Lawlessness" to be crowned as the last Caesar of the revived Roman Empire to close the era of Gentile supremacy. The Lisbon Treaty has created the platform for the King of Men to be enthroned.

BRITAIN CANNOT BE AT THE "HEART OF EUROPE" TO REFORM THE EU AND ITS 'SACRED COW' – THE COMMON AGRICULTURAL POLICY

In concluding this chapter, I would highlight an issue to dismiss the ridiculous notion entertained by British politicians, that Great Britain must be at the "heart of Europe" to influence the direction of the European Project by reforming it.

We have learnt Prime Minister Blair justified his surrendering of the British rebate by claiming he had secured a wide-ranging review of European Union finances in 2008-09. What happened when a review of the financing of the Common Agricultural Policy was discussed in November 2008 during France's EU Presidency? No reform to the Common Agricultural Policy was made. France led the way to defeat Britain's proposal for reform of the 'Dirty CAP.' The outcome of the negotiation prompted this headline; *"French wreck EU farm cash reforms"* (The Daily Telegraph, 21 November 2008).

Reporting on the issue, Telegraph's Brussels' Correspondent, Bruno Waterfield, stated: "Vested interests in France, Germany and Italy...blocked European Union farm subsidies that cost the average British family more than £300 a year. Britain was outmanoeuvred by France", which was holding the EU's rotating presidency, and left isolated in a battle over Europe's £42billion Common Agricultural Policy (CAP)." Mr Waterfield continued: "Hilary Benn, the Minister for the Environment, Food and Rural Affairs, had supported a package of farm reforms as part of Britain's strategy to reduce EU spending on agriculture, which accounts for 40 percent of the Brussels budget. After all night negotiations, Mr Benn was defeated when a "qualified majority" of EU countries, led by France – with support from Germany – overruled Britain to preserve lucrative CAP subsidies for their farmers." Mr Benn complained: "The CAP creates vested interests which distort things and slow the progress of reform." He also expressed concern over "back door" measures that will allow France and others to recycle unspent farm subsidy cash – worth £254million for the French every year – into extra payments to their farmers." The Correspondent concluded his article with a reference to the comments Jim Paice, a Conservative Party's spokesman made on the issue. According to the Tory MP, the Labour Party, under Tony Blair, surrendered "a chunk of Britain's rebate from Brussels for promises of future CAP reform. The Government gave up £7billion of taxpayers' money for CAP reform which it has failed to materialise."

This leads to the following questions:

Was the British Government able to influence the financing of the "Dirty Cap"? Would British politicians still insist Britain should be at the "heart of Europe" to reform the EU? The truth is that the EU cannot be reformed. Politicians "roar" as lions in the "House of Indulgence", but become "toothless mute dogs" in Europe. They shiver when they see their masters in Brussels. What a pity! Why should the "children" of a "brave Knight" quail before the "children" of a "smuggler."

'EU PLC': NOT WORTH INVESTING IN IT

Supporters of the European Project suggest that the British people should "invest" in Europa ***PLC.*** How could we invest in a 'company' whose accounts have not been acknowledged by its own auditors for several years because of fraud? Without any surprise, in November 2008, it was reported in the national newspapers, that the EU Court of Auditors could not endorse the EU accounts for the 14th year in succession because of mistakes and financial irregularities. The Daily Mail provided the public with the following information in an article titled, "*We have been tangoed: EU gave £850000 of our cash to teach Finns dance, and millions to bizarre projects.*"

- £60million to an Italian consortium that invented businesses. It spent most of the money on cars, motorcycles and yachts. One member, a dentist, had a yellow Ferrari and 55 other luxury cars.
- £10million to Charlerol in Belgium. It went on eating, drinking. And a hunting trip to Belarus for councillors.
- £1million on project to train TV showgirls in Naples.
- £250,000 was diverted by an Italian social democrat senator to relatives. He also received £8,500 for a silk worm breeding consortium that never existed.

- £40,000 to former major of Chirivel, Spain, to a riding school. When he was refused a licence, he made the site a hostess club called Seventh Heaven.

Mats Persson, Chief Research Officer of Open Europe, stated: "The inability of the EU to have its accounts signed off is becoming a familiar story....The responsibility for this spectacular failure lies partly at the door of member states, but overwhelmingly with the Commission." He added, "Until byzantine spending schemes such as the CAP and Structural Funds system are fundamentally reformed, or scrapped altogether, fraud will continue. The EU funds are supposed to help create jobs and boost Europe's competitiveness, but far too often money is being wasted on projects ranging from the inefficient to the downright bizarre. Surely, while facing recession, we can think of better ways to spend £100billion a year (Daily Mail 10 November 2008).

On 11 November 2008, The Times also reported on EU's failure to submit clean accounts. In an article titled Record €6bn goes astray as EU grants are overpaid, the newspaper outlined the following reasons:

- There were numerous cases of overclaiming from the EU's budget of £93billion, especially in regional projects designed to raise living standards in poorer areas, as well as "serious failure to respect procurement rules."
- At least 11 percent of the €42billion budget for regional and social funds should not have been paid out---the largest area of mismanagement and one for which the 27 member states and the European Commission are jointly responsible.
- There were also irregularities of between 2 per cent and 5 per cent in the €51billion agricultural budget.

The Court of Auditors added: "In general, errors are often due to farmers overclaiming and/or entitlements being wrongly calculated. The Court found errors related to farmers overclaiming or exaggerating land area or the number of animals." Commenting on this shameful episode, Mark Francois, the Shadow Europe Minister, said: "This depressing annual ritual has got to stop. As taxpayers across the EU feel the effects of the credit crunch they may well ask why the European Union is still failing to put its financial house in order." Truly, the European Union is "The vile confederacy of the latter days": The word of the "Seer of Dublin" has been fulfilled. He warned Britain would not be saved in this political alliance of European nations.

This leads to the following questions: "How could Britain invest in Europe PLC where some of its 'management team' fiddle expenses and the 'board of directors' refuse to expose them to the 'shareholders'? "Why should Britons continue buying shares in ***Euro PLC*** whose managers do not know the future prospects of their Enterprise? Any serious investor would first analyse a company's financial records lodged with the Company House; examine the calibre of its management, and consider the company's future prospects before risking his money to buy shares in the company.

"Europa PLC" should have been struck off. It is not a company worth investing in it. It is intellectually bankrupt; it is morally bankrupt and spiritually bankrupt. Jean Monnet's luxurious *Titanic* was doomed to sink before its construction began on 9 May 1950. Had the passengers who perished on the Great *Titanic* have known the "unsinkable" ship would sink, would they have wasted their money on tickets? The fate of the 'unsinkable' Titanic should be a warning to politicians who are dragging Britons and the Irish to board Monnet's "Luxurious Titanic." Britain and Ireland MUST LEAVE the "Euro Titanic." It is heading towards an 'iceberg.'

Chapter 12

THE GERMAN EU PRESIDENCY AND THE REFORMED EU TREATY

"The German people have been taught to regard the most sacred of all sacred words as merely 'a scrap of paper.' And this is the kultur which has changed a frat and God-fearing nation into the Germany of this infamous war. And as the moment is rapidly leavening the Protestant Churches of Britain it is high time to give warning of its effect" **(R.A 1915**)

The "success" of the German Presidency: The Brussels Summit and the EU-Reformed Treaty: The beginning of the end of the "vile confederacy of the latter days"

On 22 June 2007 Germany ended its 6-months rotating EU presidency at a 2-day summit in Brussels. The German presidency left a "legacy of deceit" spearheaded by the German Chancellor, Angela Merkel. Being a faithful "daughter" of her "father," Konrad Adenauer, the First German Chancellor who advocated for a United States of Europe after the First World War, Ms Merkel adopted all sorts of treachery for the rejected constitution to be imposed on the peoples of Europe. The "success" of the summit, which Pope Benedict XVI expressed an interest in it when he met Tony Blair at the Vatican, marked the crowning glory of Angela Merkel's stewardship. The German Chancellor, following the foot-steps of her adopted "father" - the "scheming" Jean Monnet - cynically spearheaded the rebranding of the European Constitution which had been rejected by France and the Netherlands.

Before the summit, Angela Merkel secretly wrote to all the EU leaders that a cosmetic surgery would be performed on the discarded Constitution: terminology would be weakened and decorated but no substantive changes would be made. And this repackaged constitution would be released as a brand new treaty to govern the citizens of the European Empire. What a "clever" woman. The world should not have been surprised of Merkel's manoeuvre. The German Chancellor was fulfilling the dream of her "father," Konrad Adenauer who dreamt of a United States of Europe. In his memoirs Adenauer writes: "After the First World War I advocated for an organic integration of the French, Belgian and German economies for the safeguarding of a durable peace....The unification of Europe seemed far more feasible now than in the 1920...The idea of international cooperation between peoples must succeed....In a future United States of Europe I saw great hope for Europe and thus for Germany..." (Memoirs 1945 – 1953).

Merkel's 'Reformed EU Constitution' was cynically produced and endorsed by politicians in the EU "jungle" which is infested with "wild beasts." The new EU treaty took more powers away from member states to build the European Empire with its own President and a Foreign Minister disguised under the title High Representative for Foreign Affairs and Security. The New EU Nation would become a legal personality qualified to negotiate treaties and represents the European Union in international bodies. The EU finally demonstrated its 'devilish' nature to confirm what Sir Robert Anderson wrote about the character of European confederacy. The "Seer of Dublin" made his prediction when Dr. Konrad Adenauer was six years old

Christopher Booker commented on the reformed EU treaty, which evolved from a "clumsy deal." In his article, *EU treaty: the great double deception,* the columnist writes: "The layer of spin and deceit that surround this wretched EU treaty are so convoluted that it takes some working out to disentangle the contradictions, U-turns and straight lies it has come to involve." Mr Booker explained how European politicians were determined "to foist on the peoples of Europe the final components of a supranational government, as agreed in their constitution, without giving the peoples of Europe any say on the matter. Ever since the constitution was rejected by the peoples of France and Holland, they have been trying to find a way of smuggling it back in by pretending it was something else" (The Sunday Telegraph 8 July 2007).

A SEED PRODUCES ITS KIND

Well done EU leaders. You have proved that you are truly the "sons" and "daughters" of the "obstinate" Jean Monnet. For your "father' schemed to steal someone's wife. The 'spiritual godfather' of European unity had no scruples in forcing a married woman to leave her husband. Likewise, Monnet's 'children' had no twinges of conscience to deceive Europeans. Monnet had no shame for grabbing Silvia from her husband. His 'children" also had no shame for their treachery and boasting, that they deceived the people who put their trust in them. What a shame! A seed produces its kind. The 'sons' and 'daughters' of Monnet have confirmed Sir Robert Anderson's prophetic description of their EU Project: *"the vile confederacy of the latter days."*

The powers European institutions have been wrestling away from member states are part of the "expensive luxurious cargo" on board Jean Monnet's *"Titanic"* of the 21st century which was destined to sink before its construction began on 9 May 1950. The reality is that the EU President and his Foreign Minister would become the shadow of the Real Powerful Caesar of the Revived Roman Empire who would lead Europe and the world to the Promised Land of Carbon Free and prosperity. But this leadership would end in the greatest deception of all time. I would encourage politicians who are interested to become the first EU President to examine what the Books of Daniel and Revelation teach about the last Caesar of the revived Roman Empire. It would be wise not to accept the positions of EU President or Foreign Minister in the "vile confederacy of the latter days."

The EU President would be appointed by EU leaders. The masses would have no say in the appointment of a President who would speak on their behalf. This is interesting. In creating this powerful position in the European Union, the European leaders would paint a "picture" of how the 10 powerful leaders of the Revived Roman Empire would delegate their powers to the "King of Men" to rule the world. This charismatic and intelligent leader of Europe would be the most fascinating and intelligent politician the world has ever known. Initially he will team up with the Great Harlot who sits on 7 hills to control the world. Eventually this Emperor would expose the "Mother of all prostitutes" and burn her (Revelation 17: 10-18). This powerful Caesar is the *"Awful Being"* Sir Robert Anderson wrote about. His 7-year reign would mark the beginning of the end of Gentile supremacy on earth (Daniel 9:27).

THE "WILD BEASTS" DEVOURED ONE ANOTHER IN THE JUNGLE

Before the crucial summit in Brussels to consider the revival of the dead European Constitution, the 'beasts' in the "jungle" "schemed" and "fought" one another. The French President, Nicholas Sarkozy – whose name "Nicolas" means he who conquers *(Nico)* the ordinary people (*Laos*) – engaged with Tony Blair and Gordon Brown with a view to persuading them to surrender more powers to Brussels. Sarkozy succeeded. He then mocked Tony Blair who allowed him to remove the competitive clause in the founding treaty of the European Community.

Sarkozy's attack on this particular clause in the Treaty of Rome prompted the former European Competition Commissioner, Marion Monti, to declare that the move initiated by the French president was a "distinct signal of the beginning of the disintegration of the European Union." The Times editorial, commenting on Sarkozy's move to ditch the competitive spirit among EU member states, stated: "In EU, principles are traded away while words are sought that may mean slightly different things in different languages to different politicians united only in mutual fear of their electorates".

The same Nicolas Sarkozy flew to Poland to influence the Polish Prime Minister to surrender a portion of his country's voting power in the EU project. The Polish Premier later expressed his outrage at the attempts by the German Presidency to dilute the voting power of the Poles. He attacked the Germans that had they not killed millions of Poles in the Second World War, they would have had more voting rights in the European Union. The Premier felt that the Germans wanted to dominate the EU by increasing their share of votes while reducing that of Poland.

The Daily Mail commented on the "Rumble in the EU Jungle" in an article headed: *Poland's Nazi taunt inflames EU summit.* The Polish attack raised the temperature in the 'jungle.' The ferocious "beasts" snarled at each other. First, Angela Merkel, the referee in the "Jungle," responded: "Every country will be taken seriously as regards their concerns." Other nations condemned the Poles for breaching EU etiquette. The Danish Premier pounced on Poland: "The idea of basing today's decision on voting rights on World War Two is absurd". Luxembourg "beast" joined the hostilities. He roared: "The bitter arguments on the Polish side are not acceptable. Germany has never been a better neighbour to Poland than it is today." When the Polish Prime Minister, Jaroslaw Kaczynski, threatened to wreck the EU summit, he was threatened his country would lose money. Since "money talks" in Babylon Mr Kaczynski backed down. He was consoled with a promise that the loss of his country's voting power would be postponed until sometime in 2014. What a shabby deal! Once again, the "Seer of Dublin's" description of the character of political Europe (the *"vile confederacy of the latter days"*) has been justified.

This is the proud EU which claimed it would have been "absurd", "divisive" and a "serious mistake" to have mentioned God and Christianity in their degraded constitution. European leaders listen: The Lord Jesus Christ does not need the "vile" EU. Yet the Lord needs the "abominable" EU for His own purpose – to prove that the Word that goes out of His Mouth would never return void but would accomplish whatever it was intended to do (Isaiah 55:10-11). Amen!

THE CALL FOR A REFERENDUM IN BRITAIN
Barroso "Bullies" Blair

Before Tony Blair, joined the "wild beasts" in the "jungle," Jose Manuel Barroso, the EU chief bureaucrat, had the audacity of a dead cockroach to instruct the then British Prime Minister to ignore the concerns of Britons over Brussels' treachery to revive the dead European Constitution and to enforce it on them. With his trade mark of flattery, Barroso, the "showman from Brussels," the "expert" on European integration, showed utter contempt for the British public. Addressing an assembly of national and Euro-parliamentarians, he said: "You know about UK and the respect I have for your country, we have to stand up in front of our national public opinions and give up to some of the populism we have in our member states". What qualifies Barroso and his 'disciples' to stand up and dictate to Britons about European integration? How well-informed is Barroso on European integration?

Without a surprise, Tony Blair obliged to his "master" Barroso. For at the negotiating table the British Prime Minister also showed utter contempt for the British people by surrendering powers that did not belong to him to unelected and unaccountable eurocrats in Europe. Blair and his Foreign Secretary, Margaret Beckett, conceded that more powers had been handed over to Brussels, The new Foreign Secretary, David Miliband, also confirmed a massive transfer of powers to undemocratic institutions in Brussels. The arrogance and contempt of this "odd couple" (Barroso and Blair) was greeted with calls for a referendum – to give British people the opportunity to vote on "Merkel's Treacherous Treaty"(MTT) to decide whether they wanted to be ruled by 'blind' and arrogant "tyrants" in Brussels who have no hint what their EU project is for and its future prospects.

The following headlines appeared in British newspapers:

- "Clumsy EU deal is better than none" (Financial Times 25 June 2007)
- "Now a vote on Europe" (The Sunday Times 24 June 2007_
- "Our new Prime Minister must call a referendum" (The Sunday Telegraph 24 June 2007)
- "EU traitor: Blair surrenders key British powers and leaves Brown with a referendum headache" (News of the World, 24 June 2007)
- "After Blair betrays our nation: Give us the vote on the EU treaty" (Daily Express 25 June 2007). Under this title Leo Mckinstry explained to the British people that Tony Blair, who negotiated the "clumsy deal" in the 'jungle of cruel bests,' "hastened the destruction of our country's liberty under the steamroller of the unelected bureaucratic European Union." Mr. Mckinstry continued: "The treaty he (Blair) endorsed is no minor tidying up exercise. It is the blue-print of a new political entity, the United States of Europe, complete with a president, foreign policy, defence system, executive diplomatic service and laws, which will override the autonomy of member states....Britain is rapidly becoming little more than a region within the nation Europe."

This is exactly what Sir Robert Anderson wrote about in 1881 - the development of a confederation of European nations which would be the next major political feature in history after the restoration of the Jews to Palestine. He predicted Britain would become a province of an European Government. Witness the words of the "Seer of Dublin": "*That there should be a commonwealth of nations living side by side at peace, was a conception that nothing in the history of the world could have suggested. The principal clew which Scripture affords on the subject is the connection between these kingdoms and the Roman Empire, But some latitude must probably be allowed as to boundaries, otherwise we should have to choose between equally improbable alternatives namely; either that our own nation shall have sunk to the position of a province.....or else that the England which is to be numbered among the ten kingdoms will include the vast empire of which this island is the heart and centre. May we not indulge the hope that however far our nation may lapse in evil days to come from the high place which, with all her faults, she has held as the champion of freedom and of truth, she will be saved from the degradation of participating in the vile confederacy of the latter days"?*

THE EUROPEAN EMPIRE: SIR ROBERT ANDERSON'S WORD ABOUT EUROPEAN INTEGRATION IS CONFIRMED

Jose Manuel Barroso, the captain of the bureaucrats of the "vile confederacy of the latter days", finally made a significant announcement to confirm Sir Robert Anderson's prophetic word about Europe. On 10 July 2007, the Portuguese proclaimed to mankind that Britain was now part of a new European empire. Addressing a media in the "Jungle," the President of the European Commission declared to the world that his Commission was proud of the creation of an European Empire through "Merkel's Treacherous Treaty" which gave Brussels the trappings of an Empire – a full time President and a Foreign Minister who would speak on behalf of European citizens. The European "Sales Director," whose "Board of directors" would have been sacked and their company struck off for failure to published audited accounts for 14 consecutive years due to errors, fraud and financial mismanagement, boasted: "We should not have doubts about the EU's future – it is what it has always been. It is the world's first non-imperial Empire...."

In an article titled *Barroso hails the European empire,* The Daily Telegraph recorded Barroso's comments: "We are a very special construction unique in the history of mankind. Sometimes I like to compare the EU as a creation to the organisation of empire. We have the dimension of empire. What we have is the first non-imperial empire. We have 27 countries that fully decided to work together and to pool their sovereignty. I believe it is a great construction and we should be proud of".

In his excitement about the creation of an European empire, which is "unique in the history of mankind," the President of European Commission did not realise he was bringing to pass what Sir Robert Anderson recorded about a political alliance of European nations before the founding fathers of the "European Empire" - Jean Monnet and Robert Schuman, were even conceived. Thirty three years before the First World War the British public servant wrote: *"Next to the restoration of the Jews to Palestine the most prominent political feature in history would be a confederation of European nations....Through the gradual unfolding, it may be, of influences even now in operation; or far more probably as the outcome of some great European crisis in the future, this confederation of nations shall be developed....I say nations, not kingdoms, advisedly, for though they will ultimately be kingdoms, that is , under monarchical government, yet before the advent of the Kaiser (the new Emperor of the European Empire) such may not be the case.....This division of the Roman earth will take place before his appearance......but whether a year, a decade or a century...we do not know".* The word of the "Seer of Dublin" – spoken in the 19th century ⊠ has been fulfilled in the 21st century.

I would advise the President of European Commission and his colleagues in Brussels to read *The Coming Prince* to gain a better understanding of where the European Union actually came from, the character of this political union and the future prospects of Jean Monnet's vision of a federal Europe. *The Coming Prince* would also benefit Barroso's political masters - Angela Merkel and Nicolas Sarkozy.

EUROPEANS WAKE UP!

"Merkel's Treacherous Treaty" which abolishes the sovereignty of member states should not be a surprise. The clever Angela, putting on the "shoes" of the beautiful Phoenician Princess, "*Europa*", who was abducted by Zeus, planned for the old constitution to be re-introduced by stealth by presenting it as nothing more than a new simple treaty. Mr Mckinstry writes, "So, with the connivance of the rest of Europe's leaders, she (Angela Merkel) pulled it off this coup, consigning our national identities to the dustbin of history". The Daily Express Columnist tells us the British government does not want the electorate to vote on the treaty because politicians know we would reject the treaty. "Such reasoning only shows that the EU is a gigantic exercise in the abuse of power. This is what the European Union has been destined for. The public were told in the 1970's they were joining a free trade association, not "an embryonic United States of Europe. We have been living with deception and duplicity ever since as our country disappears."

Those who supported the European project openly confessed that they had succeeded in imposing the discredited constitution on the masses through the back door without the hassle of seeking a mandate from the people. For when the treaty was adopted in the EU "Jungle", some of the leaders, without any shame, admitted that the constitution, which was thrown into the dust-bin by France and the Netherlands, have been picked up and thrown upon the peoples of Europe.

Here are some of the comments made by European leaders:

- Finland Europe Minister, Astrid Thors, said: "there is nothing from the original institutional package that has been changed."
- Angela Merkel, the brain behind the "treachery," boasted that the fun-

damentals of the dumped constitution have been maintained in large part. Only the less significant symbolic parts, the flag, and the anthem which make people think the EU is superstate, have been removed. What a "deceitful" woman and an unprincipled politician. (The EU flag and anthem were subsequently re-instated through the back-door. The European flag will be displayed in all European Parliament meeting rooms and official events. The pagan anthem (Ode to Joy) will be performed at the opening ceremonies following each European election and at official meetings)

- The Irish Premier, Bertie Ahern, said: "ninety percent of the constitution is still alive." But the spokesman for the Spanish Socialist Party Diego Lopez Gorrido, declared: "Ninety nine percent of the original constitution has survived". This is more than what the Irish prime minister had suggested.
- The Spanish Prime Minister, Jose Zapatero, joined the chorus: "A great part of the content of the European Constitution is captured in the new treaties."
- The European Parliament President, the Mr 'know–all' Hans-Gert Pottering, said: "The substance of the constitution is retained."
- French President, Nicolas Sarkozy, mocked Tony Blair (whom he Sarkozy had earlier suggested could become the first EU President), that he had won his battle to remove from "Merkel's Treacherous Treaty" the competitive clause enshrined in the Treaty of Rome.
- Finally, the author of the flopped constitution, Valery Giscard d'Estaing, declared the treaty agreed by Tony Blair and the twenty six EU leaders was a revival of the rejected constitution. Having compared his role in the drafting of the dumped constitution to that of the American founding fathers, the Frenchman said, "This text is in fact a rerun of a great part of the substance of the constitutional treaty.

Despite these plain confessions, Gordon Brown, the new British Prime Minister, was adamant that the reformed treaty had changed drastically from the old constitution that there was no need for the British people to vote on it. Parliament is the proper place for discussing the treaty not the public arena. What an insult to the intelligence of the electorate. How well-informed are politicians to exclude the public from deciding their future in the vile European Union? What a blatant deception by Brown and his colleagues in Europe. What integrity have they got? The British people are no fools. Great Britain is not the property of "greedy" politicians in the "House of Indulgence" with a "smeargate."

"KNOWLEDGE IS POWER; IGNORANCE IS WEAKNESS"

In the face of the deception engineered by the "wild beasts" in Brussels, when Tony Blair was requested to call for a referendum for the British people to decide whether they would prefer to be ruled by unprincipled, unelected and unaccountable strangers in Brussels, the former prime minister, cloaked in his arrogant dress, rejected the call as "utterly absurd". What was "utterly absurd" was for a British prime minister who blindly follows the vague vision of a "schemer" and a "smuggler" Jean Monnet to drag Britons to board Monnet's doomed "luxurious Titanic." I repeat: had Tony Blair examined Dr. Robert Anderson's work on European confederacy, he would have withdrawn Britain from "That Thing" in Brussels.

Brussels dismissed Tony Blair's claim that he had secured some exemptions for the British people. The Eurocrats poured scorn on Blair. This was highlighted in a newspaper column titled *Blair's opt-out on EU is worthless.* According to the paper, on 11 July 2007, "Senior European Union officials confirmed that Britain's 'red line' opt-out from the Fundamental Rights is not worth the paper it is written on. Margot Wallstrom, the European Commission Vice president, who endorsed a pornographic film to promote the EU, "insisted that the charter will apply to huge swathes of British law, the 75 percent or more is derived from EU legislation". What a pity! Why should Britain accommodate such nonsense from a corrupt and morally and intellectually bankrupt EU? Because, a prophet is of no honour in his own country and among his own people.

POMPOUS POLITICIANS AND THE ABSURDITY OF ALL ABSURDITIES

When Jim Murphy, the then Europe Minister, was confronted with a call for a referendum on the monstrous Lisbon Treaty, he blindly followed the footsteps of his former "boss", Tony Blair. He repeated the chorus: "It would be 'frankly absurd' to ask the electorate to vote on an EU treaty which had been rejected by France and Holland." What is "absurd" is less-informed politicians blindly following the distorted vision of a "blind" smuggler. What is "absurd" is for British politicians to ignore the Bright Vision of their brilliant "father", Sir Robert Anderson, and sheepishly follow the hazy vision of Monnet which would 'muscle' Britain. What is 'absurd' is 'blind' and pompous, politicians groping in darkness, and selling Britons into "slavery" in a strange land in Brussels.

THE "GIANTS" OF BRITISH POLITICS AND EUROPEAN CONSTRUCTION

Tony Blair and his "disciples" should rather have followed the amazing vision of Sir Robert Anderson, the Prince of Detectives, and ignored the Frenchman Monnet, whose misty vision of a "fussed" Europe, according to Jose Manuel Barroso, is still serving as the blue-print of European integration today. Unfortunately Gordon Brown, who succeeded Tony Blair, supported his former master's arrogant position. Had these two "giants" of British politics (Blair and Brown) read what Dr Anderson published on European integration before the seeds of European Union were sown on 9 May 1950, they would not have joined the "roaring" of the "wild beasts" in the EU "jungle". They would have "slain" them with the 'unknown truth' about the European Union. Unfortunately the two "giants" lacked the power for such a feat. "Knowledge is power; ignorance is weakness".

Again, had Tony Blair examined what this "forgotten father" recorded about European integration, its character and future prospects, before Sarkozy's "father", Jean Monnet, was conceived, he would have rather put a heat on all the EU leaders and left the "jungle" of "feral beasts" and sparred himself a humiliation from Nicolas – *'he who lords over the people'*. Tony Blair's lack of knowledge of what the brilliant servant of the British Crown wrote about the "vile confederacy of the latter days" made him weak to uphold British interest. "Britain does not belong to its prime minister and his political party. They have no right to dispose the sovereign rights of the British people on the altar of political expediency for their selfish ends without a mandate from the voters.

Christopher Booker also expounded on the moral fibre of the shameful EU treaty which evolved from a "clumsy deal". In a column headlined *EU treaty: the great double deception*, he writes: "The layer of spin and deceit that surround this wretched treaty are so convoluted that it takes some working out to disentangle the contradictions, U-turns and straight lies it has come to involve". He further explained how EU leaders – a project infested with about 2050 criminal fraud cases costing over £225million – were determined "to foist on the peoples of Europe the final components of a supranational government, as agreed in their constitution, without giving the peoples of Europe any say on the matter. Ever since the constitution was rejected by the peoples of France and Holland, they have been trying to find a way of smuggling it back in by pretending it was something else" (The Sunday Telegraph 8 July 2007).

And in an essay titled *If Gordon Brown forces this EU treaty on us, you can kiss goodbye to democracy* (Daily Mail 7 August 2007), Mr Booker explained how the European Union would empower the European Council with unlimited powers to impose laws and raise their own taxes. The European Council was set up by the "smuggler" Monnet' in 1974 as a 'shadow' cabinet for the eventual government of Europe. And this 'unseen' cabinet would now force European leaders to promote the interests, values and objectives of the European Project which is intellectually bankrupt, morally bankrupt and spiritually bankrupt.

In her article *Even by the EU's squalid standards, this treaty plumbs new depths of mendacity. What is at stake is democracy,* Melanie Phillips summed up the filthy character of the European Project. She commented on the squalid deals hatched in Brussels which resulted in 26 "blind" men endorsing "Merkel's Treacherous Treaty." The Columnist writes: "The plain fact is that, true to type, the EU set out to smuggle in a constitution by stealth---and it is now brazenly doing precisely that. Even by its own ruthless standards, the scale of the intended deceit and the railroading of its own proceedings to ensure that it gets away with it are truly remarkable". She added, the manner the reformed treaty was pushed through "takes the undemocratic ruthlessness of the EU to new depths...Who can be surprised? Mendacity and hostility to democracy are written into the very DNA of the European project. It always was a scheme to destroy the sovereignty of member states while pretending to act in their interests. It always involved a wholesale deceit of the peoples of Europe, because it was always understood that none of them would knowingly vote for their countries to commit national suicide. At every single stage, we have been told that the EU's progressive erosion of national sovereignty was a scare story invented by swivel-eyed xenophobes. At every single stage, we have lost more and more of our independence. At every single stage we have been lied to" (Source: Daily Mail 25 June 2007).

At the end of the "Rumble in the Jungle," the "cunning referee", Angela Merkel, boasted that the European Union have avoided a disaster. She claimed the EU leaders had achieved what they set out to do. According to "Europa Angela" the new treaty was designed to be more modest to avoid the need of referendums. This shows that Europe came together at the end. What a delusion! The "wisdom" of "Princess Angela" will deceive her. She and her "brothers in arms" did a "wonderful" job by following the footsteps of their "scheming father", Jean Monnet, who smuggled a beautiful married woman to Moscow for a quick divorce and re-marriage.

What the autocrats succeeded was to bring to pass Sir Robert's prophetic description of the European project. Before the European Union was born, Sir Robert Anderson labelled it *"The vile confederacy of the latter days".* What the "blind" EU leaders succeeded in the "jungle of wild beasts" was to deceive their people to deceive themselves, and to pave the way for the "Awful Being" - the "great deceiver" to take the Throne of Europe and deceive Europe and the world with his charisma, eloquence and political skills. Well done Europa!

As Mr. Mckinstry told us, "The era of the nation state is over in Europe. We are now to be governed by a new German-led bureaucratic empire." The reality is that the creation of European Empire would proceed - with or without MTT – "Merkel's Treacherous Treaty". According to the Portuguese Prime Minister, Jose Socrates, who took over the EU rotating presidency in July 2007, the "MTT' would be "set in stone". Mr. Socrates was a "dreamer". The reality is that the Magnificent Edifice of Europe, which was built on the "sand of deception", would be blown away by a "Rolling Stone" at the appropriate time. This SHALL surely happen. It's not late for Britons and the Irish, and those Europeans who care for their lives, to disembark and allow the EU leaders to their fate on Jean Monnet's "magnificent ship.'

DEMOCRACY: THE SUREST ROAD TO DESPOTISM

Congratulations to Angela Merkel and her brothers, who 'smuggled' a rejected constitution and forced it on the peoples of Europe. They have proved that they are truly the "children" of a "smuggler". For their 'father,' Jean Omer Marie Gabriel Monnet, had no scruples in forcing a married woman to divorce her husband. When the woman failed to break the marriage in Italy, the "obstinate" Monnet "smuggled" the beautiful lady to Moscow. There she obtained a quick divorce. The "practical apostle of European unity" then managed to marry someone's wife without any shame. History, at times, repeats itself. The mythical story of the abduction of the beautiful Phoenician Princess, *Europa,* by the deceiving Zeus, became a reality. The real incident took place from Italy to Moscow. Is it any wonder that the spirit of deception permeates through the European Project? To repeat: the Mother of all deceptions in EU would take place when the last Emperor of the European Empire is welcomed by the 10 powerful leaders of the restored Roman Empire. We live in an exciting, critical and challenging time.

With their treachery and arrogance to deny Europeans a say on a constitution that would deprived them of their dignity, European Leaders should ponder on these words of Sir Robert Anderson. "Democracy, not despotism, is the goal towards which civilisation is tending. But the democracy in its full development is one of the surest roads to despotism. First, the revolution; then the plebiscite; then the despot. The Caesar owes his sceptre to the mob." How true today are the words of the British "Giant" whom Jean Monnet would not have qualified to untie his bootstraps.

To conclude this chapter, let us examine the significant words in Dr. Anderson's view on Democracy ("Revolution", "Plebiscite" and "Despotism") and how they apply to the European Union of the 20th and 21st centuries:

- *Revolution*: The European Union evolved from the ashes of the Second World War. Jean Monnet, the principal architect of the European Construction, declared: "The unification of Europe, like all peaceful *revolutions*, takes time – time to persuade people; time to change people's mind; time to adjust to the need of major transformations" (Jean Monnet Memoirs 1978)
- *The Plebiscite* : In 1975 the British people voted in a *referendum* to join European Economic Community – a Common Market – not a political union.
- *Despotism:* Since 1975 successive British governments have denied Britons a say on their future relationship with the European Union, The Common Market has now become a political entity with laws framed in Europe and imposed on Britons. The Lisbon Treaty, that transfers more powers from the British parliament to strangers who are not accountable to Britons, was imposed on them by "selfish" politicians. Politicians have become "despots."

"Democracy, not despotism, is the goal towards which civilisation is tending. But democracy in its full development is one of the surest roads to despotism." This "CAP" fits the European Union that refused to accept the democratic verdict of the Irish people on the Lisbon Treaty in a referendum held on 12 June 2008.

Chapter 13

PORTUGAL'S EU PRESIDENCY AND THE TREATY OF LISBON

"There would be a time when it is no longer a confederacy of nations bound together by treaty, with a Napoleon rising up in the midst of them and struggling for supremacy; but a confederacy of kings who are the lieutenants of one great kaiser, a man whose transcendent greatness has secured to him an undisputed pre-eminence....
"I say nations, not kingdoms, advisedly, for though they will ultimately be kingdoms, that is, under monarchical government, yet before the advent of the Kaiser (the new Emperor of the European Empire) such may not be the case.....This division of the Roman earth will take place before his appearance......but whether a year, a decade or a century...we do not know...The opportunity too must synchronise with his coming. But the voice of prophecy is clear, that the HOUR is coming and the MAN".
(THE COMING PRINCE: RA)

The Lisbon Summit: 18 -19 October 2007

On 19 October 2007, the 27 European leaders met at a Summit in Lisbon to agree the text of the new EU treaty. Before the meeting, most Europeans called for a referendum on the Treaty which was merely the old discredited European Constitution rebranded. According to a Financial Times Harris Poll published on 18 October 2007, 76% of Germans, 75% of Britons, 72% of Italians and 63% of French voters cried for a say on how they would be governed by a Constitution which was rejected by the French and the Dutch in 2005 and had been repacked as a new EU Treaty. Some politicians warned European leaders, that "by avoiding referendum and making the treaty a complicated document that amends earlier EU treaties, the EU will reinforce the idea among European citizens that the European Construction is a mechanism organised behind their backs by jurists and diplomats."

The truth is that "scheming" and "deception" were the methods the master architect of European Construction, the "smuggler" Jean Monnet, and his 'disciples' employed to promote his blurred vision of a United States of Europe. The "obstinate" Monnet hated national vetoes. On 5 August 1943 he declared: "There will not be peace in Europe if the states of Europe rebuild themselves on the basis of national sovereignty, with its implications of prestige policies and economic protection". He went on: "The states of Europe must form a federation or a European entity that would make them into a common economic unit.... Europe of sovereign states was incapable of, despite its leaders' goodwill, of reaching the sensible decisions that were needed for the common good. It would be quite another matter, however, once the power of decision was entrusted to institutions serving the general interest and applying the will of the majority in a system of common rules" (Memoirs 1978). The fact is Jean Monnet did not have a clue of what he suggested.

On the issue of supranationality that abolishes nation states, Monnet's biographer, Francois Duchene, writes; "Schuman was still wary in May 1950....He was wary on principle. On top of that, he and Monnet were not at one on supranationality. For Schuman, the plan existed to solve the immediate Franco-German problem. *For Monnet, it was the first step to a united Europe.* Schuman accepted supranationality for the plan because there was no alternative, but was not committed." [Emphasis Mine]

I ask the questions again: "Why did Jose Manuel Barroso, the 'expert' on European integration, fail to mention in his Hugo Young Lecture at Chatham House, that Robert Schuman was not committed to Jean Monnet's idea of a United States of Europe? Why did the "mouth-piece" of Europe fail to mention the "Schuman Caveat" which is vital for the survival of Jean Monnet's vision of a united Europe?

In Britain, Prime Minister Gordon Brown maintained that there was no need for a referendum on the new EU Treaty because of Britain's "opt-out" clauses and 'red-lines.' Secondly, in Brown's estimation the new treaty was substantially different from the constitution that was rejected in 2005. This was ridiculous and insulting. Because, even the Labour dominated European Security Committee suggested that the "red-lines" were drawn in sand, and they could be washed away by the European Court of Justice. This should not surprise us because the EU edifice was constructed on the "sand of deception" which would be blown away into pieces at the appointed time. William Hague, the Shadow Foreign Secretary, responded to Mr Brown's flimsy excuses by saying, Gordon Brown was cynically putting these "red-lines" to wriggle out of his manifesto. Hence like the Maginot Line they do not live up their "billing". The message was clear as The Sun newspaper explained it for us: "The impregnable Maginot Line was intended to stop Hitler's army invading France in World War II. In the end, German tanks drove round it and were in the streets of Paris" (The sun 17 October 2007)

THE "VILE" EUROPEAN UNION AND ITS "BLIND" LEADERS DUG THE "GRAVE" FOR EUROPE

After the text of the repackaged European Constitution was agreed, the arrogant Valery Giscard d'Estaing, the brain behind the discredited European Constitution, admitted that the EU leaders rewrote the document in a different order to avoid the need for referendums. In a letter to the French newspaper *Le Monde,* the former French president boasted of the treachery he and the EU leaders perpetrated on the peoples of Europe. "The institutional proposals of the constitutional treaty are found complete in the Lisbon Treaty only in a different order and inserted in former treaties", said Giscard d'Estaing. He continued: "Above all, it is to avoid having referendums thanks to the fact that the articles are spread out and constitutional vocabulary has been removed. The Proposals in the original constitutional treaty are practically unchanged...Just lift the lid and look in the toolbox – all the same innovative and effective tools are there, just as they were carefully crafted by the European Convention: a stable presidency, a streamlined Commission, a Parliament with genuine legislative rights, a Foreign Minister, even if he has been given another, inadequate title...and the most advanced charter of fundamental rights in the world." In his "blindness," without any twinges of conscience, Giscard concluded his boasting: "When the day comes that men and women with sweeping ambitions for Europe decide to make use of this treaty, they will be able to rekindle from the ashes of today the flame of a United Europe."_

On November 2007, the pompous Giscard d'Estaing again boasted on BBC Radio 4's *Today* programme, that the Lisbon Treaty was "absolutely similar" to his EU Constitution which was rejected by his own people and the voters in Holland. The French statesman was excited the corrupt treaty was "unreadable" - deliberately drafted as such to prevent referendum. In his ignorance, Valery Giscard d'Estaing deceived himself. And the EU leaders who adopted the "crooked" treaty also deceived themselves to be deceived and "bullied" by the coming emperor of the European Empire. Had the French architect of the crooked EU treaty and the European leaders examined what the brilliant Briton, Dr. Robert Anderson, wrote about European integration, its make-up and prospect before their French hero, Jean Monnet, was born in Cognac, they would have realised that they were "labourers" who were toiling to pave the way for what the distinguished British public servant published about the future of Europe to be fulfilled. Giscard and his followers might have fooled Europeans, but in reality they fooled themselves to dig their own "graves." And sadly they are dragging the masses into the pit. The time is fast approaching when the coming "saviour" of Europe, whom Dr Anderson described as the "awful Being", would deceive the European leaders. Their laughter would turn into tears and their joy into mourning. IT SHALL SURELY HAPPEN.

GORDON BROWN AND HIS "RED-LINES"

Despite the admission of the architect of the European Constitution that Europeans have been deceived with a re-branded document, together with his confession on BBC Radio 4 that the Lisbon Treaty was "absolutely similar" to the old EU Constitution rejected by the French and the Dutch, Gordon Brown and his Foreign Secretary, David Miliband, stubbornly maintained that the text of the reformed EU Treaty, approved in Lisbon, was fundamentally different from the abandoned Constitution and did not merit a referendum in Britain. This was insulting. Instead of Brown and Miliband having the courage to confront Giscard and his "disciples" in Brussels about their "treachery", and invite the British people to vote on the "deception", they just kept mute and blindly followed the "blind" EU leaders like sheep through a gap. It is time the Prime Minister and his foreign secretary and all British politicians realised that Great Britain is not their property to be sold to the "sons" and "daughters" of Jean Monnet and Konrad Adenauer who are not accountable to Britons.

British politicians have turned into "dictators" who impose their shallow opinions on European integration on the electorate. They have no respect for any concept of democracy. They have turned the House of Commons - a place of honour - into a "Den of Indulgence." Peter Hitchens aptly described it in his searching article: *"Our political parties are corpses and democracy as we used to know it is quite dead. We the voters, simply give it a new funeral every few years"* (The Mail on Sunday, 21 September 2008). British politicians: reflect on these words from the pen of Sir Robert Anderson: "Democracy, not despotism is the goal towards which civilization is tending. But democracy in its full development is one of the surest roads to despotism." Have British politicians become "despots"?

Despite Angela Merkel's claims that, "the substance of the constitution is preserved", and Jose Luis Zapatero assertion: "We have not let a single substantive point go," Prime Minister Brown stubbornly refused to accept the fact that the new EU Treaty was just a copy of the rejected European Constitution. Brown's contempt for the British public prompted a rebuke in the leading column of the 29 July 2007 edition of The Sunday Telegraph: "It is not the lie that offends so much as the brazenness. When Gordon Brown claims that the EU's Reform Treaty is different from the rejected constitution, he is making a claim so risible that an eight year-old would see through it." Gordon Brown's reluctance to call for a referendum on his clumsy excuse insulted the intelligence of the majority of Britons.

That Gordon Brown's so-called "red-lines" and "opt-out" clauses would be eventually ignored is no secret. In *Principality and Power of Europe*, Adrian Hilton reminded us how the Danes, after they had rejected the Maastricht Treaty, were bribed with tax cuts in return for a "Yes" vote. Mr Hilton writes: "In order to achieve the treaty's ratification, the Danish government submitted a series of opt-outs to the electorate, including clauses on the Single Currency, citizenship of the Union, immigration and defence. The propaganda machine warned of all the dire consequences of rejecting the treaty a second time. Yet even as this national government assured its sovereign people of the legitimacy of these opt-outs, Germany's chancellor was pointing out that such opt-outs had no legal binding." In their estimation few Danish voters would not be allowed to wreck Monnet's Project. Jacques Delor went further to abuse any EU opponents within France, displaying a complete contempt for democracy by declaring, "There is no place in a democracy for people who call for a *'Non'*, for the sorcerer's apprentices, for those who wake phantoms. I will say to them they should get out of politics". The fact is politics in the 21st century stinks which needs cleansing. It is a jungle of ferocious beasts. Who would like to enter this 'stinking jungle' to be devoured by 'wild beasts'?

The "intellectually bankrupt" European leaders, who lacked the confidence to persuade their electorates to the European Project, in their desperation, often resorted to abuses and intimidation when they were confronted with the truth about their despicable enterprise. For example, a British politician, Denis MacShane, once labelled *The Sun* newspaper readers, who hate the corrupt European Project, as "racists." Another Labour Party politician also painted them as "lunatics." And an Italian politician also described opponents of the crooked EU treaty as "terrorists." This is the "vile" character of political Europe which the "Seer of Dublin" wrote about in the 19th century before the European Union was born in the 20th century. The EU does not want to be accused; yet the EU is blended with the "terms of accusation."

After the 2-day Summit in Lisbon, Gordon Brown joined the 26 EU leaders to celebrate the adoption of the degraded EU Treaty. He was later branded a "Traitor" – a "Judas" who betrayed the British people at the "sordid Last Supper" at Lisbon. The British Prime Minister, who is not well-informed on the significance of European integration, joined in a Champagne celebration after he had agreed to surrender huge swathes of British powers to Brussels. Destitute of confidence, Mr. Brown patronised the Portuguese Premier Jose Socrates, who forced the EU Treaty on the European leaders to endorse it. "You've done brilliantly", says Mr Brown. "We're very proud of you. You did very well, that was very difficult. I don't know how you managed it but that was a great success."

Had the 'widely-read' Brown read what the brilliant scholar, Dr Robert Anderson, whose parents hailed from Scotland, published on European integration, he would not have praised the Portuguese. He would have snubbed the Lisbon Summit and pledged to withdraw Great Britain from that "vile thing" in Brussels. Unfortunately due to ignorance, Gordon Brown exhibited his weakness by patronising Jose Socrates who had no understanding of what the European Union is for, and the true significance of the Treaty of Lisbon. Sadly, Gordon Brown's smiles and congratulations to the Portuguese Premier were signs of weakness. It portrayed a "seasoned" politician with limited knowledge on the significance of European integration. "Knowledge is power; ignorance is weakness."

THE "SERMON AT STRASBOURG"

Without any surprise, on 24 March 2009, Gordon Brown went to the European Parliament in Strasbourg to expose his ignorance about the implication of the European project. For in his attempt to 'sell' his economic plan to save the global society from economic ruins -the "international Hurricane that was sweeping the world" - the Prime Minister patronised the sycophants in Strasbourg by heaping praises on them. *"Thanks to the work of all of you and the generations whose work we build on that today we enjoy a Europe of peace and unity which will truly rank among the finest achievements of human history and which is today a beacon of hope for the whole world,"* says the "shameless" Gordon Brown. *"So I stand here, proud to be British and proud to be European, representing a country that does not see itself as an island adrift from Europe, but as a country at the centre of Europe, not in Europe's slip-stream but in Europe's mainstream....And that is why I am also proud that by a large majority our British Parliament ratified the Lisbon Treaty. And I believe that we in Europe are uniquely placed to lead the world in meeting the wholly new and momentous challenges of globalisation ahead. We are uniquely placed because of what we have achieved in our union and I want to thank the members of this European Parliament, you should all be proud of what together we have achieved - the greatest and biggest single market in the world, now bringing opportunities to 500 million people, the most successful endeavour in economic cooperation anywhere in the world and you should be proud that this is an achievement of the European Union...."*

That was the "cynicism of politics." Gordon Brown, the politician who was timid to join his colleagues to sign the European Constitution, boasted to the "employees" of the "Rubber Stamp Factory" of his feat for pushing the "unreadable" Lisbon Treaty down the throats of Britons. Again, had Gordon Brown studied Sir Robert Anderson's works and what he wrote about the future of Europe, he would not have entered the 21st century "Tower of Babel" in Strasbourg.

Few days after Gordon Brown had boasted about the ratification of the Lisbon Treaty in the British parliament - turned into a "House of Shame" - his Minister for Europe, Caroline Flint, admitted in the "House of Sleaze" that she had not fully studied the Lisbon Treaty, even though a copy was given to her when she was promoted. Ms Flint confessed: "I have read some of it but not all of it." Her confession prompted the following responses. Mark Francois, the Conservative

Party's spokesman on Europe, said: "It is not every day that someone will admit they haven't read the most important document for their job. Her astonishing admission does leave some questions. How does she know if the Treaty is good for Britain if she had not read it" (Parliamentary Committee debate, 30 March; Mail Telegraph Sun, 1 April 2009)

- Lorraine Mullally, director of *Open Europe*, remarked: "This is an unbelievable admission. It is extremely worrying that the minister responsible for promoting the treaty in this country has no idea what it actually says. Perhaps this explains why she is against giving the British people the vote on it they were promised – she simply has no idea how important it is."
- Nigel Farage, UK Independence Party leader, added: "A minister being in this position of simply not being bothered is staggeringly insulting to the people she is supposed to represent. She joins a long list of distinguished politicians who have urged us to vote for or accept such EU treaties without straining their intellects by reading or understanding them." (Rosa Prince, Political Correspondent 31 March 2009)

And it was this "lazy" Flint who criticised the Irish people that they were ignorant for rejecting the Lisbon Treaty. What a hypocrite! The reality is that the "obstinate juror" led "selfish" and "lazy" British politicians to "steal" the democratic rights of the people who feed them, and then transferred their powers to strangers in Europe. Dan Hannan, a member of the European Parliament, criticised Gordon Brown's "Sermon at Strasbourg" saying, "Prime Minister, I see you have already mastered the essential craft of the European politician, namely the ability to say one thing in this chamber and a very different thing to your home electorate...Perhaps you would have more moral authority in this house if your actions matched your words." He went on to describe Mr Brown as "the devalued Prime Minister of a devalued Government."

With his enthusiasm for the European Union, the "obstinate juror" became an "adopted son" of the "obstinate" Jean Monnet. He was excited to cruise on the "Magnificent Ship" of his "step-father." However, Mr. Brown and his followers cannot drag all Britons to join them on Monnet's "magnificent vessel" which was doomed to sink before its construction began. The British people don't hate Europeans. But majority of Britons hate the corrupt EU, because they don't want to be ruled by aliens who are not accountable to them. Not every Briton wants to become an "adopted" child of a "smuggler." They prefer to fish in their own "tiny Island." They don't want to cast their nets into the "sea" which is infested with "sea-monsters." The Patriot Stuart Wheeler writes: "The EU is a disaster, even worse than the recession because the recession will end some time but the EU may not… The country has not been successfully invaded since William the Conqueror in

1066, yet most of our laws are now made in Brussels by unelected commissioners, who impoverish the people of the EU, while making fortunes themselves...The EU costs about £1000 per annum for every man, woman, child and baby in this country. How can this conceivably be worth it? What are the colossal benefits?" (News of the World, 29 March 2009).

Gordon Brown has been described as an intellectual heavyweight - a 'widely-read' Prime Minister since William Ewart Gladstone. Had the "widely-read" Brown analysed what Sir Robert Anderson, a son of an elder in the Presbyterian Church of Ireland, published on European confederacy and its destiny, he would have torn the Lisbon Treaty into pieces, removed Britain from the "centre of Europe" and mourned over Europe. Premier Brown would have saved himself the constant taunt for failing to call for a referendum on the fraudulent Lisbon Treaty. Secondly, Brown would have saved the British taxpayers' money for employing the services of lawyers to defend himself in a legal suit in the High Court for not honouring the Labour Party's manifesto pledge of a referendum on the European Constitution. What a tragedy! How could a British Prime Minister abandon the extraordinary bright vision of a prominent servant of the British Crown to follow blindly Jean Monnet's misty vision of a federal Europe which, according to Jose Manuel Barroso, "still serves as the blue-print for European integration today" (*TIME* 60 Years Anniversary issue, 13 November 2006).

RT. HON. WILLIAM EWART GLADSTONE AND SIR ROBERT ANDERSON

It may be of interest to Prime Minister Gordon Brown and British politicians to know William Gladstone's impression of Sir Robert Anderson. The 'widely-read' Gladstone read Sir Robert's book: *A Doubter's Doubts about Science and Religion.* Sir Robert published this work anonymously to indicate how little he thought of it. Yet, Premier Gladstone treasured that book to the extent that he wrote to the author. The letter was dated 18 December 1889 - the occasion of Parnell's historic visit to Hawarden. That day was devoted to reviewing and reconsidering the whole Irish question and discussing it with the Irish leaders. And yet on that very day Prime Minister Gladstone found leisure to read Sir Robert's book. According to Dr. Anderson, he did not send a copy to Gladstone and neither was he aware that he possessed one. Here is the opening and closing paragraphs of Gladstone's letter to Dr. Robert Anderson:

Hawarden
December 18, 1889

Dear Sir
I do not know whom I have the honour of addressing, but I wish to thank you for your *Doubter's Doubts,* and to say that I have read it with a great deal of sympathy

and concurrence in the main argument.....
I presume to hope that you will follow up the subjects of your volume with the same care, force and exactitude which in it you have bestowed especially upon the treatment of the main argument.

I remain, dear Sir
Your faithfully and obedient
W E Gladstone

The Author
A Doubter's Doubts

This letter was written in the very year Adolf Hitler, the "Catalyst" of European Community, was born. Jean Monnet, the "Master builder," of the European Community, was only a year old. In the *"Doubter's Doubts About Science and Religion"*, Dr. Robert Anderson discredited Darwin's Theory of Evolution and tamed Darwin's "bulldog," Professor Thomas Huxley. Dr Anderson entered into a series of correspondence with Professor Huxley on the controversial subject: "Evolution and Creationism." In the end Mr Huxley 'ran away.' You may read *"A Doubter's Doubt of Science and Religion,"* and then refer to Dr. Anderson's correspondence with Professor Thomas Huxley. They were published in The Times of January 23 and 26 and February 1, 3, 4, 8 and 11 in 1892.

I would urge Prime Minister Gordon Brown, his Foreign Secretary, David Miliband, and David Cameron, Leader of the Conservative Party and Nick Clegg, Leader of the Liberal Democrats and all British politicians to scrutinise what the illustrious public servant wrote about European integration and its future in his *The Coming Prince.* They would discover it is not worth the risk to sheepishly follow Jean Monnet's nebulous vision of a federal Europe.

THE BETRAYAL AT LISBON

After the "betrayal at Lisbon," there were more calls for a referendum on the European Constitution Mark II. According to The Daily Telegraph, academics, diplomats and politicians united to demand a vote in all the 27 member states. The group of Conservatives eurosceptics, including the Socialists Liberals and Green, as well as Derek Scott, a former economic adviser to Tony Blair, issued this letter: "The adoption of this far reaching document without referendum would further decrease the legitimacy of the EU and seriously damage democracy in Europe." The Daily Mail summed up the autocratic performance of the European leaders in its editorial. Under the title *Democrats who despise the voters,"* the paper argued that the EU leaders claimed to be democrats, yet they united in their contempt for the voters who gave them their power. Lisbon was supposed to create a stronger Europe. But what kind of strength is built on such arrogance." The pompous European leaders have fulfilled Sir Robert Anderson's view of democracy: "Democracy not despotism is the goal towards which civilisation is tending. But democracy in its full development is one of the surest roads to despotism..." What a perfect reference to the European Project and its institutions!

THE "COWARD" EUROPEAN LEADERS

The then Irish Premier, Bertie Ahern, exposed the moral and intellectual bankruptcy behind the whole EU project when he rebuked the British Premier and the 25 EU leaders who attempted to force the shady EU treaty down the throats of their people. Mr Ahern lamented: "I think it's a bit upsetting to see many countries running away from giving their people an opportunity. If you believe in something why not let your people have a say." He continued: "I think the Irish people should take the opportunity to show the rest of Europe that they believe in the cause – and perhaps others shouldn't be afraid of it." The Irish 'disappointed' Bertie Ahern. They rejected the Lisbon Treaty.

Without the slightest hint of the implications of the EU project, and with only a superficial knowledge of European integration, the rest of the EU leaders lacked the confidence to make the case for the existence of the European project and its "unreadable" Constitution. European and British politicians "hide" behind their majority votes in their national Parliaments to impose abominable treaties on the voters. What a shame! We must not be surprised by the authoritarian attitude of the EU leaders. In the eyes of the architect of the European project, opinion of the masses must be ignored. The "obstinate" Monnet never believed in sovereignty. Let me quote his own words again: "Europe of sovereign states was incapable of, despite its leaders' goodwill, of reaching the sensible decisions that were needed for the common good. It would be quite another matter, however, once the power of decision was entrusted to institutions serving the general interest and applying the will of the majority in a system of common rules...... Like our provinces in the past, our nations today must learn to live together under common rules and institutions freely arrived at. *The sovereign nations of the past can no longer solve the problems of the present: they cannot ensure their own progress or control their own future. And the community itself is only a stage on the way to the organised world of tomorrow."* (Emphasis mine)

The truth is that had the Irish Premier examined what an Irishman wrote about European integration and its future prospects before the European Union evolved from the wreckage of the Second World War, he would have dropped the Lisbon Treaty into a sewerage, thus saving the Irish Republic a costly referendum. Bertie Ahern would have withdrawn Ireland from the European Union as his legacy before leaving office. Ireland might have gained from its relationship with the European project. However, the Irish people would be far better off remaining "poor" in their Island than receiving "gifts" from Brussels. For the European

Project is a "Trojan Horse" for Britons and the Irish. "Beware of the Greece even when they offer gifts." It is the end that crowns the work. The future of the European Union is dark as predicted by the "Seer of Dublin.

EU PRESIDENT: A SHADOW OF THE EMPEROR OF THE REVIVED ROMAN EMPIRE

The European leaders, having displayed utter contempt for the electorates who feed them, exposed their ignorance about the purpose of their own project. With their cunning moves to fool the masses, they unconsciously fulfilled what the "Seer of Dublin," over 128 years ago, wrote about the character of their project. And the repackaged European Constitution (the so-called reformed EU treaty), which creates a new position of an EU President, has also paved the way for the "Seer's" prediction about the dark future of Europe to be fulfilled.

The "Seer" wrote about the career of the coming King of Europe: Let us review his words: *"There would be a time when it* (the political alliance of European nations) *is no longer a confederacy of nations bound together by treaty, with a Napoleon rising up in the midst of them and struggling for supremacy; but a confederacy of kings who are the lieutenants of one great Kaiser, a man whose transcendent greatness would secure to him an undisputed pre-eminence And this is the man whom the Dragon will single out to administer his awful power on earth in days to come."* This is the picture of the most influential diplomat Europe and the world would adore. He will lead Europe to the Promised Land of Peace and Prosperity. The portrait of the EU President, which the brilliant Dr. Anderson painted in the 19th century, has become a reality in the 21st century with the Lisbon Treaty.

ANTIOCHUS EPIPHANES: A MAGNIFIED PICTURE OF THE POWERFUL EU PRESIDENT TO COME

Denis MacShane, in his article, "Europe needs the leadership and ability of Blair", confirmed Sir Robert Anderson's description of the powerful man who is about to lead Europe. Writing to support Tony Blair's candidacy for the Presidency of Europe, the former Minister of Europe in the Labour Government, outlined some of the qualities needed of the new commanding man in Europe: "The new president", he stated, "will have to be a statesman, a crafty diplomat, a soother of European quarrels, competent at managing the tedious minutiae of EU business, able to speak two or three languages and a father figure who can make the EU popular again. In short, rather more qualities are needed than those required to be manager of England's football team, secretary general of the United Nations, or Archbishop of Canterbury."

Mr. MacShane descriptions of the qualities needed of the EU President were described by Sir Anderson in 1881. Writing about the coming Prince of Europe, Dr Anderson stated: "By the sheer force of transcendent genius the man of prophecy will gain a place of undisputed pre-eminence in the world. A strange crisis marks his coming. The true King of Men must have an extraordinary combination of great qualities. He must be a scholar, a statesman, a man of unflinching courage and irrepressible enterprise, full of resources....The opportunity too must synchronise with his advent. The HOUR is coming and the MAN." These were some of the qualities of Antiochus Epiphanes, the Syrian King, the profane persecutor of God's people, who used trickery and soothing words to come to power. He also desecrated the Temple of God. The Real Powerful Man of Europe would be a magnified picture of Antiochus Epiphanes. I would remind Mr. MacShane, that just as Antiochus Epiphanes and his army were defeated by the Maccabees, so would the coming powerful emperor of Europe (of which the EU President is his shadow) and his "forces" be crushed by the "Rolling Stone" at the appointed time.

Dr. Anderson warned it would be degradation for Britain to participate in the "vile confederacy of the latter days", and that Britons would not be saved by joining the dreadful political alliance of European countries. Had MacShane examined the works of the great Anglicanised Irishman of Scotch extraction, he would not have recommended Tony Blair for the EU highest office.

By ignoring the electorates, the "despots" in Europe have again confirmed what Sir Robert Anderson wrote about "democracy". I repeat the words of the "Seer of Dublin": "Democracy, not despotism is the goal towards which civilisation is tending, But democracy in its full development is one of the surest roads to despotism". In the 21st century, Europe would yearn for *The Coming Prince* just as how in the 20th century Europeans, after the First World War, yearned for Dr Anderson's *The Silence of God.* At the appointed time the smiles on European leaders would turn into tears. The joy of British politicians for "selling" Britons to "slave traders" in Jean Monnet's "slave market" in Brussels would turn into sorrow, and their happiness would turn into sadness.

THE CRITICAL QUESTION AND THE "UNKNOWN TRUTH"

Before the "Last Supper at Lisbon", where Gordon Brown betrayed Britain "over vegetable crepe, grilled sole with saffron rice, chocolate cake and strawberries and washed down with Cartuxa wine", Camilla Cavendish posed a significant question in her article, *We must stand up to this cynical stitch-up.* She posed the question: "Why what was intended to be a free-trading zone is steadily granting itself the power to legislate in almost every area of national life"? The Columnist then reminded us: "When the European Economic Community was set up, justice and home affairs were kept separate as was foreign policy. Yet the new EU treaty waves those principles aside. Nation states will lose control of policing and justice matters. These were matters for sovereign states" (The Times 19 October 2007).

The answer is simple. The Frenchman, Jean Monnet, plotted a federal Europe to bring to pass what the Prince of Detectives had already written about a confederation of European nations which would be developed from an European crisis. The Knight Commander (of the Order) of Bath made this prediction before the French architect himself was born. So, we must not be surprised of how an economic community of six European nations has now developed into a political union of 27 nations. With this "unknown truth" having been made "known" today, Britons and Europeans should not be surprised by the EU dictatorship. It must happen to fulfil the word of the "Seer of Dublin."

At this point I would encourage those who sincerely desire to know the "unknown and awkward truth" about the European Union and its future to examine the works of Sir Robert Anderson. The distinguished public servant of Great Britain warned the British people would not be saved if they joined a political union of European nations. For the future of the European confederacy is dark. The sons and daughters of Great Britain must therefore leave Monnet's "Titanic" which is about to sink. If we procrastinate our withdrawal from the "crooked" European confederacy, we will leave traces of regrets behind our heels. The sun of procrastination never sets on man. The "EU Titanic" was destined to "sink". I repeat: if the passengers on the Titanic had known that the "unsinkable" ship would sink on its maiden voyage; would they have boarded the luxurious ship?

WORDS OF WISDOM

In so far as the fortunes of the European project is concerned, I would urge the EU leaders to reflect on Sir Robert Anderson's words of wisdom: "If a knowledge of the past be important, a knowledge of the future must be of far higher value still, in enlarging the mind and raising it above the littlenesses produced by a narrow and unenlightened contemplation of the present." Europe's so-called success story of "Enlargement" is irrelevant. The question is: "Where will the "Enlargement" end? What is the future of the European Union? Pascal Lamy, a former EU Commissioner, posed this question: "Can we be hopeful of Europe's future?" (Financial Times 21 March 2007).

In view of the concern raised Pascal Lamy, and coupled with the wise words of Sir Robert Anderson, and considering the fact that the future is mankind's greatest challenge, it is vital for the British and the Irish to know the future prospects of the European Union before they decide whether their future lie in Europe or not. The dream of a pleasure trip on the "Unsinkable" Titanic turned into a nightmare. It is not "safe" to be on the "Euro Titanic."

BRUSSELS' DAY OF RECKONING

The European leaders might have congratulated themselves on a 'job well done'. The reality is that they deceived the masses to deceive themselves. They have opened the gate for that "awful Being," spoken of by the "Seer", to enter the political scene in Europe to terrorise Europeans and mankind. The Emperor of Europe would be the chief terrorist – a brutal dictator the world has ever known. It would end in tears when the deception of all deceptions is perpetrated on Europeans and the "globalised society."

In his article, "*There will be a day of reckoning for the dictatorship of Brussels*," Charles Moore, former Editor of The Daily Telegraph, brought the message home. He wrote: "The EU project now resembles the state of the eastern European Communists after 1968, when party members gave up believing in their doctrine and just settled for comfortable jobs. They shored up their power and ignored their unpopularity. After 20 years, it all collapsed, because people started to take down the Berlin Wall, and no one dared stop them. The EU is not such a sharp oppression as was Soviet Commission, but it is similar in this respect – it tries wherever possible to avoid the democratic judgement of the people it rules. When that judgement does come, therefore, it will be merciless" (The Daily Telegraph October 2007).

And Simon Jenkins also made a similar point in his searching article *This broken promise is part of a wider fear of democracy*. After tearing into shreds Gordon Brown's argument for not calling a referendum on the fraudulent Lisbon Treaty because of his so-called 'red-lines' and 'opt-outs' clauses, Mr Jenkins concluded his commentary with these prophetic words: "The Truth is that Brown has joined Europe's other leaders in a most alarming development, a collective flight from democracy because it scares them. This is not a pretty sight. If people cannot decide how they are to be ruled, why should they obey the rulers? It is a question that always ends in tears" (The Guardian 24 October 2007). And so shall it be. The dream trip on Monnet's "luxurious boat" would end in tears.

Brian Sewell, in his article, "Why our voices must be heard" (Evening Standard 3 June 2003), wrote about how, since 1975, when Britain voted in a referendum to remain in the European Economic Community, the British people have had no further say on their involvement with the European project. "The 1975 debate was hotly debated", he wrote. "The nation had the opportunity to be well informed in the debate that preceded the referendum. No debate of such intensity has happened since. Deprived of any further opportunities to vote on European matters, the nation has become steadily less well-informed. Maastricht was a well kept secret...Without the stimulus of debate we have been denied information; without the stimulus of a referendum at any further stage in the development of the EU, we have slipped into ignorance, indifference and mistrust. All governments since 1975 wanted it this way: "Leave it for us". He added: "Any empire that embraces too many nations, cultures, languages and economies cannot be held together in perpetuity. I doubt if a united Europe will last long. Like the Titanic, the EU will become a universal symbol of hubris?"

Indeed, "United Europe" will not last long. This would certainly be the case with the world first non imperial empire when its powerful and charismatic Emperor is crowned in accordance with the Lisbon Treaty. On his ascension to the throne of Europe, the political 'Show Man' will reign for only 7 years. For the "Stone cut without human hands" will strike the human statute from its toes of clay and iron to its head of gold, and they will become like chaff from the summer threshing floors. There will be no trace of it. That would be the end of the European Union – the revived Roman Empire (Daniel 2:35).

Prime Minister Brown blindly followed the 'children' of Monnet to force their opinion on the Lisbon Treaty on British people. Sir Robert Anderson writes: "Opinions have taken the place of convictions, and the result is a liberality which is the offspring, not of humility and love, but of indifference or doubt. Opinions are our own, and should not be firmly held. The man who would force his opinions on others is a boor. He who would die for his opinions is a fool. Truth is divine; and is worth living for and dying for..."

THE "THEFT OF DEMOCRACY"
THE PATRIOT POWELL: "UK IS NOT FREE"

Gordon Brown, who had no mandate to sell the sovereign rights of the British people to undemocratic institutions in Brussels that have no political legitimacy, should have listened to the voice of the statesman, Tony Benn. In Mr Benn's article, *Don't deny voters rights*, the former Labour politician writes: "Electors are sovereign. They only lend their power for up to 5 years to MPs they elect. To transfer that power to those we don't elect is a theft of democratic rights" (*The Sun*).

Enoch Powell, the true British patriot, declared in 1992: "What the EEC (now the EU) is bent upon has nothing to do with free trade or free anything. It is a naked assertion of the will to power, the will to create a unified state to which, instead of our national organs of representation and government, we are all to be subordinated." Powell observed: "A nation is free externally in the sense that all laws, policies, and acts of government generally which affect its citizens are made by its own institutions. In a nation "free" in the sense, no laws will be made, or taxes imposed, or judgements judged by an external authority...but the UK is not free, since its laws may now be defined, its taxes imposed, and its policies laid down by an external authority, namely the institutions of EC". And on the floor of the House of Commons (which has now become the "House of Indulgence") the Patriot Powell cried out: "I did not become a member of our sovereign Parliament to see that sovereignty abated or transferred." (Source: *The Principality and Power of Europe* – Adrian Hilton)

Enoch Powell's conviction of the deception behind the Common Market and his stand against the transfer of British sovereignty to strangers in Europe have shamed those unprincipled politicians who placed their selfish interests above the sovereign rights of Britons who lent them their power to govern temporarily. Some of these politicians are 'lambs' when campaigning for votes. And when the voters give them their power they turn into "wolves in sheep's clothing" to "devour" them. With the Lisbon Treaty the day of reckoning is fast approaching.

THE "DEATH WARRANT" OF EUROPE AND THE WORLD

Portugal ended its "successful" EU presidency with the formal signing of the EU Treaty. On 13 December 2007 the EU leaders signed the so-called new Reformed Treaty. The British Prime Minister who claimed the Treaty was good for Britain could not attend the official ceremony to sign the "historic" document that would have marked a "significant" period in his premiership. Gordon Brown claimed a meeting with a Commons Committee prevented him to attend the grand ceremony. The Financial Times commented on Brown's absence at Lisbon in its editorial. Under the title, *Absent friend: The prime minister's Lisbon trip risks pleasing no one,"* the paper reported: "It is pity the prime reason, that he must attend the House of Commons liaison committee would merit respect except that the date for signing the Lisbon treaty has long been known. Even if it is true, a half competent government bureaucracy should have negotiated any diary conflict away... This illustrates the muddle-headed ambivalence of a man who doesn't know which gallery to play to. Is he a eurosceptic hero, to be hailed by Britain's euro-phobic tabloid press? Or is he a doughty fighter, struggling in many fronts to please all? If the latter, he risks pleasing no one."

Stephen Glover also commented on Euro's "Absent friend". In his article, *Mr. Brown, Europe and an exquisite example of having one's cake and NOT eating it,* he quoted the words of a senior EU diplomat: "Mr Brown will end up with the worst of all worlds. To anti-Europeans he's simply run away and accepted the signing of the treaty. To pro-Europeans he has simply refused to stand his ground and fight." Neither side will think better of Mr Brown for shunning the ceremony. He appears evasive, shifty and uncertain". The Columnist continued: "Our principal concern should not be the ups and downs of Mr Brown's prime ministership. If a government promises a referendum on the European Constitution, it is morally obliged to offer the electorate the same means of expressing its approval about another treaty that amounts to the same thing. Almost everyone, apart from Mr Brown and the Cabinet, can see this is the case. It is a question of integrity."

Mr. Glover concluded: "He may rue the day that he set his face against a referendum, just as he will surely regret postponing a General election when he appeared to have the country at his feet....What can be said with certainty is that by partially disowning a treaty which he has described as being good for Britain, Gordon Brown makes himself look ridiculous. Even Euro-sceptics would have respected him if he had had the courage of his convictions, and attended the signing of the European treaty in Lisbon".

EU AND HYPOCRISY

Even before the "historic" day - when the Treaty of Lisbon was signed - the vanity of the EU was again exposed. The European leaders struggled to justify holding two summits in Lisbon and Brussels instead of Lisbon alone to reduce carbon dioxide emissions from their planes to save the "planet." The Eco-Warriors in Brussels failed in their contribution to save Mother Earth as they increased their "carbon footprints" by flying to Brussels for another summit after the "Lisbon Treachery" in Portugal.

Secondly, Germany and France attempted to slip the EU Flag, the EU anthem, and the Euro into the reformed EU treaty. Arch-federalist, the haughty Valerie Giscard d'Estaing, boasted that the flag and the anthem would be "annexed" to the treaty. According to the plan, championed by Germany, the EU flag, anthem and motto, as well as the euro and Europe Day (May 9) will continue to be symbols of common membership of citizens of the European Union. Germany the "toes of iron", were supported by Belgium, Bulgaria, Greece, Spain, Italy, Cyprus, Lithuania, Malta, Austria, Portugal, Romania, Slovenia and the Slovak Republic- mostly the "toes of clay". Britain and Ireland as well as France and other countries refused to sign fearing it was a backdoor of reopening the debate on the discredited constitution which the voters in France and the Netherlands rejected in 2005. In the end, Germany forced the European Union Flag and anthem into the reformed EU Treaty as a subsidiary text. To conceal their ultimate goal of creating a United States of Europe with a constitution, the EU flag and anthem - the symbols of nationhood - were excluded from the text of the Treaty which was agreed in Lisbon to prevent the document being classified an European Constitution.

On 27 January 2007, Victoria Ayling commented on this issue in a letter to The Daily Telegraph. She stated: "At the last minute, Germany included the European Union Flag and anthem into the Reformed Treaty as a declaration. Previously, after scrutinising it, the Commons European Select Committee declared the Reformed Treaty exactly the same as the Constitution, but without symbols and without the music. By the back door these have been added. How can Gordon Brown continue to deny us a referendum?" Without a surprise, on 9 October 2008, the "employees" of the "European Rubber Stamp Factory" (ERSF) voted overwhelmingly to make the display of the EU Flag compulsory in the European Parliament, and the appearance of the EU symbol (a ring of 12 gold stars) on official documents compulsory. In addition, the pagan European Anthem – "Ode to Joy" – should be played at all important meetings. They then confirmed "9 May" (the day Robert Schuman laid the foundation stone for a United States of Europe) as Europe's Day. The "employees" at "ERSF" even suggested that "9 May" should become a 'real European public holiday.' I ask the question: Why did the European Parliamentarians fail to mention the "Schuman Caveat"? - the crucial advice the first President of the European Parliament offered to Europeans concerning the survival of the European Project.

THE "PATRIOTIC" GERMANS AND THE "UNPATRIOTIC" BRITONS

So far as the adoption of the EU Flag and Anthem are concerned, the Germans, in particular, were being 'patriotic'. They were desperate to fulfil the hazy vision of their 'father', Konrad Adenauer, a signatory to the Treaty of Rome. After the First World War this German Chancellor dreamt of a United States of Europe which would be completed when Britain joins the economic integration of West Germany, France, Belgium, Luxembourg and Holland. The question is: "Do Germans and the Members of the European Parliament and European citizens understand the significance of the European flag and Anthem?

Unfortunately, being the "normal" practice of British politicians, who blindly follow the "children" of Konrad Adenauer and Jean Monnet, the patriotic *Sun* newspaper reported how the Labour Government's Foreign Office secretly stock-piled about 107 EU flags to be hoisted on official buildings at the appropriate time. Had the Foreign Secretary, David Miliband, understood the meaning of the EU emblem and what Sir Robert Anderson wrote about the future of political Europe, he would have burnt the European flags. The Germans, by forcing the European flag and anthem on Europeans, unconsciously became agents to bring to pass what Sir Robert Anderson recorded on European integration, its character and future prospects when the German Statesman, Konrad Adenauer, was 6 years old. In the next chapter I would share with you what the European Flag signifies.

We know on 13 December 2007, the British Prime Minister arrived late at Lisbon to sign the dreadful Lisbon Treaty. With his signature, Gordon Brown disposed powers that don't belong to him to unelected and unaccountable commissioners in Brussels. Had Gordon Brown known the significance of the Lisbon Treaty, he would not have travelled to Lisbon, thus reducing his carbon footprints to help save Mother Earth. After Mr. Brown had sold Britons to the "wolves" in Brussels, he insisted he would not allow the British people to vote on the despicable document that would make them "slaves" in Monnet's "slave market" in Brussels. Somehow, the Prime Minister felt Great Britain was his personal property and could treat Britons as "servants"– imposing his opinions on them. The Premier should have pondered on the words of the brilliant British public servant. "Opinions are our own and we should not hold them firmly. The man who forces his opinions on others is a boor. And he who dies for his opinions is a fool..."

EMPTY AND PERILOUS BOASTING

After the Treaty of Lisbon was approved by the European leaders, Hans Gert Pottering, the proud President of the European Parliament, who, attempted to "bully" Britain to agree to the text for the new Reformed EU Treaty, boasted: "At the start of the year there was still talk of an insurmountable crisis for the EU. Today the EU is emerging from this crisis stronger – as has often been the case in previous cycles of crises and self-doubt". With this remark, the German politician found himself in a "land of delusion." If Mr Pottering had known what an Irishman published about his European project and its destiny when his "father," Konrad Adenauer, was 6-years old, and had the German analysed the advice the first President of the European Parliament offered to Europeans regarding the survival of the European Enterprise, he would have kept mute and ran away from the European Parliament (leaving his coat behind) to mourn over Germany and its European allies.

The same arrogant "chief executive" of the "European Rubber Stamp Factory" boasted in a full page poster in the Financial Times what he declared on Euro News about how the EU would influence a favourable outcome for the ratification of the repackaged Constitution by national parliaments. He stated: "The European Parliament approves of the treaty, and we'll give advice and exercise our influence with a view to getting a "yes" from all the national parliaments in the European nations too, so it comes into force at the start of 2009, a few days before the European elections in June 2009" (Source Financial Times 14 December 2007). Did they succeed? Ireland rejected the Lisbon Treaty. And what happened? The Germans and the French led the sycophant European leaders to bully the Irish people to vote again – all in the "spirit of democracy."

The fact is the more Hans-Gert Pottering and his allies attempted to influence national Parliaments to impose the despicable European Constitution on their voters, the more they unconsciously assisted to bring to pass what the "Seer of Dublin" wrote about the future of Europe. More importantly, the German politicians, in their zeal to push the Lisbon Treaty through, despite the fact that voters in Ireland had rejected it, were unconsciously acting as agents to give credence to the Book of Daniel which German Rationalists, in the eighteen century, labelled it a fraud – a religious novel – which was written after the events had already taken place.

After Mr Brown signed away Britain's sovereignty to Brussels, he was greeted with the following headlines in national newspapers.

- "PM signs EU Treaty: We shall never surrender ....Even if you have, Mr Brown. (The Sun).
- "Mr Bean signs away our freedom...cynical betrayal of Britain to Europe (Daily Express).
- Frederick Forsyth, in his article, *Freedom is stolen by burglar Brown*, writes: "Showing the moral cowardice that we have come to expect, Gordon Brown flew to Lisbon.....to sign away another huge chunk of our right to govern ourselves, and most appropriately he did it like a thief in the night...." Mr Forsyth added this significant statement: "We should not kid ourselves about the real significance of this text. It is the true foundation stone of the coming multi-region federal nation/state of Europe. What is truly impressive is not just the creation of one president and one foreign minister; nor yet the abrogation of another 50 national competences from Westminster to Brussels. It is this constitution, absorbing into itself all previous treaties, is self-amending. What that means is that it empowers Brussels to pass further laws, with Britain heavily outvoted on every one, without ever consulting you, or me again. It is a huge enabling act."

Frederick Forsyth suggested: "There could be another alternative to Britain's relationship with the European Union: which is to switch to mutual consent with our partners to active membership of the European Economic Area. This would offer us about 90 percent of the benefits of EU membership but only 10 percent of the burdens, the reverse of the present. If the British electorate could understand this, they would probably vote for it en masse. But if they were panicked into thinking the choice was between poverty, isolation and mass employment or the status quo, then an opposite choice would be a forgone conclusion" (*Daily Express* 14 December 2007).

Since 1975, Politicians have been instilling unnecessary fear into Britons - that they would be "isolated", "lose their jobs" and "starve" if they decline to board Monnet's "luxurious Titanic." The truth is that these politicians have no clue what the European Union is for. About 68 years before the European Union was born, the "Prophet of Linden Gardens" warned it would be "degradation" for Britain to participate in an European confederacy which would evolve from an European crisis. Whatever the servant of the British Crown wrote about European confederacy has come to pass. So, the "Seer's" prediction of the bleak future of Europe would surely come to pass. When? I do not know. But it would surely happen just as the sun rises in the morning and sets in the evening. The Lisbon Treaty has created the platform for its fulfilment. It was written of Sir Robert Anderson: "His views are worthy of the utmost respect and consideration.... Those who came into close contact...knew what a kindly heart he had...He did not follow in the beaten track of received opinions."

PRESIDENT SARKOZY AND POLITICAL EUROPE

Few hours after Gordon Brown handed over Britons to Brussels (a country that has little that unites it, and for more than 6 months could not form a government because of internal political squabbles) the Prime Minister joined forces with President Sarkozy to hand more powers to Brussels. The French President suggested a "Reflection Group", dubbed "wise men", to pursue an European dream. It was recommended that the former Spanish Premier, the socialist Felipe Gonzalez, known for his fervent advocate for a United States of Europe – lead the Group. Whilst Prime Minister Brown was claiming the "Wise men" were banned from looking forward at further "institutional reforms," President Sarkozy declared the task of the "Wise men" was to discover "the new European dream."

Nicolas Sarkozy, like his "obstinate Father," Jean Monnet, stated: "I want a politically integrated Europe." The group was to examine what shape the EU should take between 2020 and 2030. This should not surprise us. For Sarkozy was fulfilling the blurred vision of Jean Monnet and the German Economist, Walter Hallstein, who was once an European Commission President. According to Jean Monnet: "Once a Common Market has been created, then a political union will come naturally." And Walter Hallstein also proudly proclaimed: "Make no mistake, we are not in business, we are in politics. We are building the United States of Europe." It is therefore wishful thinking for British politicians to entertain the idea that Britain must be at the "heart of Europe" to reform the European Union. No one can reform Jean Monnet's project in Europe. You either board the "Sinking Titanic," or you disembark.

On 15 December 2007, *The Sun* commented on the treachery of the repackaged EU Constitution. In a leading article *"A new betrayal"*, the patriotic newspaper reported: "The arrogance of the EU leaders – and our own Prime Minister – is breathtaking. With the ink still drying on the treacherous Treaty of Lisbon, they sign us up to a **NEW** vision of Europe that could further emasculate our Parliament." The hilariously-dubbed Brussels "group of the wise" will plot even closer ties than those disgracefully agreed on Thursday. Surely Gordon Brown can no longer dismiss this threat to our sovereignty. Yet his spokesman says: "His view is this is a fuss about nothing. The real important thing is to focus on real issues that matter to people." The bloody nerve! Remember none of this was approved by Europe's voters. The French and Dutch rejected it. So would we, given the chance. Believe us, Prime Minister, this DOES matter to people. You deny it at your peril."

I would add: "Ignorant" politicians, who were "green" on European integration, were playing on the 'ignorance' of the masses by using their superficial knowledge on European integration to impose their opinions on the European project on a "deluded" public. British politicians, in their 'blind' enthusiasm for the European Project, blindly followed the 'children' of Jean Monnet and Konrad Adenauer, to help fulfil Sir Robert Anderson's prophetic word about the future of Europe. "Knowledge is power; ignorance is weakness".

It is time British politicians did their "homework" on European integration rather than swallowing the crumbs thrown from Brussels. Had they studied what their own "father" published about a political alliance of European nations and its future, they would not have "crawled" to please "Princess" Angela of Germany and "Prince" Nicholas of France. Sadly, the Labour politicians and their supporters have exposed their 'ignorance' and "weakness." It is an irony that President Sarkozy, who has no understanding of the significance of the European Union save what Jean Monnet plotted to create a federal Europe, should dictate to a British Prime Minister who should have known better about the European Project.

THE FRENCH SHOULD NOT BOAST ABOUT JEAN MONNET AND EU

We should not have been surprised by Nicolas Sarkozy's "initiative" for a "politically integrated Europe." Firstly, the French president was reflecting the significance of his name "Nicolas", which means "lording over the people." *"Nico"* means 'conquer'; and *"laos"* means the 'people'. Secondly, Sarkozy was eagerly following the distorted vision of Jean Monnet, who hated national sovereignty and vetoes. The truth is that if the Euro "wise men" - together with Nicolas Sarkozy, Angela Merkel, Jose Socrates, Romano Prodi, Jose Manuel Barroso, Gordon Brown and all the "toes of iron and clay" want to know the actual purpose of the European Project and its future prospects, they should ignore Jean Monnet's vision of European Community and analyse what the Prince of Detectives wrote about European integration before the First World War.

The truth is that the European Union was not created to solve the problems of Globalisation, Immigration, Poverty, Climate Change (The Modern Religion of Mother Earth), Energy Crisis and Terrorism. After all, the "Chief Terrorist" to terrorise Europe and the world would be installed by the "toes of iron and clay" of the world's first non imperial empire. The "unknown truth" is: the European Union was created by the French so that an Irishman's prophetic word about a political union of European nations and its future would be fulfilled. The French and the Germans should not boast about Konrad Adenauer and Jean Monnet for being the founding fathers of the European Union – the so-called the "rarest of all political phenomena."

The EU leaders would have been better-informed on their project had they studied the works of the 'wise' Irishman. For Jean Monnet's vision, "There would be no peace in Europe without a United States of Europe", was an illusion. It was an imagination clouded in error. For, the well-educated Irishman writes: "*There is no element of cohesion in error. Among the children of error there is no bond of unity save such as depends on common hostility to truth*". This is the character of the European Union – a divided and undemocratic political alliance of nations that is "hostile" to truth. The EU emblem testifies to this uncomfortable truth about the character of the European Union – a project whose "directors" are not accountable to its "shareholders."

On 17 December 2007, Gordon Brown reported to Parliament his controversial late trip to Lisbon where he signed the EU Treaty alone. David Cameron, the Leader of the Conservative Party, attacked the Prime Minister's "dithering" over his delay in going to Lisbon to endorse the crooked treaty. Mr. Cameron accused Mr Brown of being "shifty" and "untrustworthy" for surrendering more powers to strangers in Brussels without a referendum which the Labour Party had earlier promised in the 2005 General Election. Other Members of Parliament ridiculed Mr. Brown as "surly," "incompetent" and "discourteous" over how he ignored other EU leaders. The Prime Minister shocked the Parliamentarians without making any reference to his signing of the Treaty. Mr. Brown, in his defence, accused the Conservative Party of being "obsessed" with the EU Treaty. He also attacked Cameron of being "all slogans and absolutely no substance". The "ferocious beasts" snarled at each other in the 'political jungle of wild beasts.'

What did Brown mean by accusing the Conservative Party of being "obsessed" with the Lisbon Treaty? This particular accusation actually exposed Gordon Brown's ignorance about the purpose of the European Union and its Lisbon Treaty. Why shouldn't the Conservative Party be "obsessed" with a corrupt treaty which was designed to usurp the sovereignty of the British people? The "widely-read" Gordon Brown would have been "obsessed" with an "unreadable" document that forces Britons into "slavery" in Brussels had he read what a brilliant son of a Presbyterian wrote about European integration and its future before the French founding fathers of European Community were conceived.

GORDON BROWN: THE "OBSTINATE JUROR"

Despite the cries of Britons to have a say on the Lisbon Treaty, Mr. Brown dismissed their calls for a referendum on the controversial change to EU structures brought about by the Lisbon Treaty. He insisted a popular vote was not needed as if he was better-informed on European integration than the public. Clashing with Conservative leader, David Cameron, in the House of Commons, Mr. Brown said: "If this was a constitutional treaty, we would hold a referendum. But the constitutional concept was abandoned." By ignoring what all the European leaders had said about the Lisbon Treaty as being fundamentally the same as the European Constitution which was rejected by the French and the Dutch in 2005, Gordon Brown insulted the intelligence of the British people. He behaved like an obstinate juror who puts his back against the wall and refuses to accept the evidence.

THE ABSURDITY OF ALL ABSURDITIES

The question is: "When did Gordon Brown become an expert on European integration to impose his opinions on Britons who dislike being ruled by strangers whom they have not elected and are not accountable to them? Supporters of the Lisbon Treaty, including the former prime minister, Tony Blair, and Jim Murphy, the then Minister of Europe, suggested that calling a referendum on the Treaty would have been "absurd." Indeed, the absurdity of all absurdities was an "unelected" Prime Minister, who is not well-informed on the European Project, transferring powers that don't belong to him to unelected and unaccountable aliens in Europe who have no clue what the European Union is for. How fair was Gordon Brown to the British people whom he ignored their cries for a vote on a document that would have a profound impact on their lives. Yet, in his major speech at the Labour Party Conference, held in Manchester on 23 September 2008, which was billed as a speech to save his premiership, Gordon Brown constantly talked about "fairness" – a "Fair Britain," a "Fair Society" – a cause worth fighting for." The fact is words are vague and valueless if they do not serve as portraits of deeds.

Through ignorance, Gordon Brown crawled before arrogant EU leaders, who despise democracy, to win recognition. What a pity! How could a British Prime Minister, who should have known better about the significance of European integration, blindly followed the 'children' of Jean Monnet like sheep through a gap to board Monnet's *Titanic* which was doomed to sink before its construction began on 9 May 1950. "Knowledge is power; ignorance is weakness," says Gordon Brown's "Forgotten father." I repeat: Had the "intelligent" Brown examined what his brilliant "father," Sir Robert Anderson, published about political Europe he would have called for a referendum on the Lisbon Treaty and advised the British people to reject it. Sir Robert Anderson was a Man of Substance, a Man of Extraordinary vision. He was an intellectual among intellectuals, a 'giant' among 'giants', a theologian among theologians, and a servant among servants. The awkward truth is that none of the EU leaders, together with their supporters at home and away, who have taken Europeans, Britons and the Irish for granted, would have qualified to stoop and untie the bootstraps of The Knight Commander (of the Order) of Bath. Facts are stubborn, independent and unyielding.

BRITONS DENIED REFERENDUM ON THE LISBON TREATY

There is no doubt majority of British people oppose to the EU's remorseless expansion of power. They hate how the EU has been controlling their lives. They knew the Lisbon Treaty was the biggest issue facing their country since it would transfer more powers to undemocratic institutions in Brussels whose officials are unaccountable to no one, and enjoy immunity from prosecution. So, on 27 February 2008, about 3000 Britons marched to the British Parliament to lobby their MPs to vote for a referendum on the Lisbon Treaty. In the face of this protest, Gordon Brown closed his ears to the cry of the masses who wanted to vote on a document that would consign them into "slavery" in Europe. Despite the flaws in the Lisbon Treaty, which the Foreign Affairs Committee in Parliament brought to the attention of the public, Gordon Brown still ignored the findings of the Committee which is dominated by members of his own Labour Party. What became of the "humble" and "listening" Prime Minister?

THE DAY DEMOCRACY GAVE WAY TO "TYRANNY" IN BRITAIN

On 5 March 2008, Gordon Brown, who "schemed" to gain power, "bullied" the Labour Party to reject the public's call for a referendum on the Lisbon Treaty. "Unprincipled" and "greedy" politicians in the "House of Expenses and Shame" voted to transfer powers that don't belong to them to strangers in Brussels who have no idea what the European Union is for, and whom the British people have no right to question their stewardship.

The Government won the crucial vote on the referendum by 311 to 248. 29 Labour MPs defied their party line and voted for a referendum, as did 15 Liberal Democrat MPs. 50 Lib Dem MPs abstained in the vote, as instructed by their leader Nick Clegg. 15 Labour MPs abstained, and 3 Conservative MPs voted against a referendum. It was a "theft of democracy" because politicians had no right to transfer powers bestowed on them temporarily to strangers in a foreign land without the permission of the electorate. It was a day when 'selfish' politicians, who place ambition over principle, played "politics" with the destiny of Great Britain. Sir Robert Anderson wrote: *"The test of a man is not what he does, but what, with the principle he holds, he would do, and if this be true of individuals, it is still more intensely true with communities."* It is clear the sort of politicians who govern Great Britain in the 21st century. They trample on the voters who put them into power.

After the "smeargate," Prime Minister Brown called for politics in Britain to be "cleaned up," Was British politics "dirty" prior to the "smeargate? Part of the "dirty politics" was how politicians "schemed" to prevent the British people from voting on the Lisbon Treaty – a document that transfers their powers to aliens in Brussels.

THE HOUSE OF LORDS AND THE LISBON TREATY

After the House of Commons accepted the Lisbon Treaty, the bill to ratify it the "unreadable" Constitution of Europe was referred to the House of Lords to debate on it. On 11 June 2008 - the House of Lords voted 280 to 218 to prevent a referendum on the Lisbon Treaty - killing off any hope of the Labour Party honouring its manifesto pledge to hold a referendum. The "unprincipled" Liberal Democrats, who also supported a referendum at the 2005 General Election, and abstained in the House of Commons' vote, voted against a referendum in the House of Lords. If they had not done so, the referendum would have been passed. The "Dirty politics" was on display.

If indeed, the Lisbon Treaty is good for Britain, as suggested by Gordon Brown and his "principal disciples" (David Miliband and Jim Murphy), why didn't they allow Britons to make that decision for themselves? The answer is simple: they were scared of defeat in the ballot box. The Labour Government was even pleased that a High Court rejected Stuart Wheeler's law suit to force Gordon Brown to give Britons a say on the monstrous Lisbon Treaty which Ireland rejected it in a popular vote. The arena for the EU "experts" (Gordon Brown, David Miliband and Jim Murphy) to demonstrate their skills was not on the "judgement seat" in the House of Commons, but in the "witness box" at Wembley Stadium to be confronted with the "unknown truth' and the "forgotten truth" about European integration.

Daily Mail commented on the Lisbon treaty in its editorial: "Although all three main parties unequivocally promised a referendum on the new European Constitution in their election manifesto, only the Tories have voted according to their word. It is a story of deceit and betrayal that brings shame on our rulers and shakes our faith in British democracy. The truth (as most European leaders boast) is that it's identical in almost every particular – from appointing a full-time president and foreign minister to the wholesale abolition of national vetoes and the creation of a shared defence and foreign policy. Crucially, the Treaty also establishes the EU as an independent legal entity, with the power to amend its own rules and sign treaties in its own right, without reference to national parliaments. Indeed, it's no exaggeration to say that Lisbon takes a cudgel to our sovereignty and our right to choose who govern us. The Lib Dems are no less contemptible. First they abstained in the Commons, despite their pledge that ratification must be subject to a referendum of the British people. Then…in the Lords, they joined Labour in crushing all hopes of a referendum."

We should not be surprised by the despicable behaviour of unprincipled politicians who insulted the voters. In showing contempt for the people who gave them their power, and in trampling on the voters who feed them, they were unconsciously bringing to fruition what the learned servant of the British Crown wrote about the character of political Europe and its dark future. The Treaty of Lisbon has provided the avenue for its fulfilment.

EUROPEAN UNION IS A DICTATORSHIP: IT IS MORALLY BANKRUPT, INTELLECTUALLY BANKRUPT AND SPIRITUALLY BANKRUPT.
THE EU IS A BODY WITHOUT A "SOUL"; A CORPSE "UNFIT FOR PURPOSE" YET "FIT FOR PURPOSE"

Hans-Gert Pottering, the German President of the European Parliament, with his superficial knowledge on European integration, had the audacity to warn Britons: "Britain will surrender." The insolent German politician could "bully the Germans to board Monnet's luxurious "Titanic" which is steaming towards an "ice-berg." However, the arrogant German was not qualified to have interfered in the affairs of Britons - except dictating to British politicians who have 'sold' their 'souls' to the 'children' of Monnet and Adenauer. What does the German know about European integration save it was his "Father," Konrad Adenauer, who, after the First World War, called for an organic integration of European nations and declared: "In a future United States of Europe, I saw great hope for Europe and thus Germany"? I repeat: had Mr. Pottering, examined the advice the first President of the European Parliament offered to Europeans concerning the survival of the European Enterprise, he would have realised that the European Union is a body without a "soul" – a "corpse" - which is unfit for purpose; yet 'fit for the purpose'. A word to the wise is enough.

The Portuguese Labour Government promised a referendum on the EU Constitution. The British Labour government also promised a referendum. Yet, the British Prime Minister joined the French President to dictate to the Portuguese Prime Minister not to call the referendum his government had promised on a constitution which would transfer powers from the Portuguese to unaccountable commissioners in Brussels. It is a pity that a British Prime Minister should follow blindly French President Sarkozy who is not well-informed on the significance of the EU project, save the fact that it was his 'father' - the "obstinate" and "smuggler" Jean Monnet - who constructed the "European Titanic.

It has been the habit of Gordon Brown to patronise EU leaders. He once sang the praises of his "hero,"' Jose Manuel Barroso, on how "privileged" it was for him to have signed the Lisbon Treaty. Had Gordon Brown analysed the works of his "Forgotten Father,' he would have dropped the Lisbon Treaty into a dust-bin and advised Barroso to run away from Brussels. Unfortunately, due to ignorance, British politicians lacked the confidence to confront the "bullies" in Brussels not to interfere in the affairs of Great Britain. Having transferred powers that don't belong to them to strangers in Brussels, they are scared to argue for Britain's withdrawal from the European Union. "Knowledge is power, ignorance is weakness," declared the eminent Victorian.

It is clear to honest men and women, that the EU is a corrupt dictatorship. The EU is morally bankrupt. The EU is intellectually bankrupt. The EU is spiritually bankrupt – "unfit for purpose"; and yet "fit for the purpose." The autocratic EU leaders have dug their "graves" with the Lisbon Treaty. Frederick Forsyth made the point: "In America candidates raise their own funds, the Europeans, of course, rifle the pockets of the taxpayers who will not in anyway be consulted or involved. What a shoddy contrast between a democracy and what the EU is making us become. And how shaming, that in creating their democracy, the Americans copied the British." The European leaders have no shame just like their "patron," Jean Monnet, who stole someone's wife in "broad daylight." A seed produces its kind.

Prime Minister Gordon Brown, by denying the British people a referendum on the controversial Lisbon EU Treaty exhibited utter contempt for the very people whom he claimed he would listen to. This was utter hypocrisy. He who shows contempt deserves contempt. Great Britain does not belong to selfish and unprincipled politicians who place their personal ambitions and party unity above the interest of the masses who lent them their power for only 5 years. If they believed in the European Project and its Lisbon Treaty, why couldn't they make their case publicly? "Cowards" and less-informed politicians on European integration: they hide behind their parliamentary majority to ignore the demands of the British people just to please the 'children' of Konrad Adenauer and Jean Monnet. The day is at hand when politicians would realise their folly. Since 1960's, the British people have been deceived and dragged to board Monnet's sinking ship. "Selfish" and "unpatriotic" politicians have no twinges of conscience to ignore the concerns of the voters who feed them. In their craftiness, they have paved the way to be deceived by the King of Europe who is on the horizon.

Now, Brown, Clegg and their supporters, who claim they are better-informed on European integration than the voters, should answer the following questions:

- How many politicians knew the true significance of the EU symbol of 12 gold stars on a blue background?
- How many politicians knew the advice the first President of the European President

offered to Europeans concerning the survival of the European Enterprise?

- How many politicians knew the native of Dublin who predicted Britain's membership of a political Europe about 92 years before Britain first applied in 1963 to join the Common Market?
- How many politicians knew the Irishman who predicted Turkey's membership of the EU before Turkey first applied to join the EU in 1963?
- How many politicians knew the British public servant who, before the First World War, recorded that Belgium, Italy, France, Austria, Germany, Portugal and Spain would join a confederation of European nations with France and Germany?
- How many politicians knew the Prince of Detectives who predicted that a political alliance of European nations would be the next major political feature in history after the restoration of the Jews to Palestine? All these predictions were made before The Balfour Declaration in 1917, before the First World War broke out in 1914 and even before Political Zionism was launched in 1897 by Theodor Herzl.

The lack of knowledge of the significance European integration has sapped the confidence of British politicians to confront the 'bullies' in Brussels, that Britain does not need the European Union. Monnet's project would certainly collapse at the appointed time. Let us remember the words of Brian Sewell: *"Any empire that embraces too many nations, cultures, languages and economies cannot be held together in perpetuity. I doubt if a united Europe will last long. Like the Titanic, the EU will become a universal symbol of hubris?*

Commenting on the political storm over the controversial EU Treaty which left the Conservative, Labour and Liberal-Democrats Parties troubled and divided, Green MEP, Dr Caroline Lucas, said: "Political leaders throughout Europe have shown extraordinary arrogance and disregard towards their citizens in refusing to hold referendum on the Treaty, as well as in trying to pass off what is essentially a repackaged Constitution as a new "Lisbon Treaty." Even one of the key architects of the original text, Valery Giscard D'Estaing, has admitted that the proposals in the original constitutional treaty are practically unchanged. As he says: "they have simply been dispersed through the old treaties in the form of amendments." Dr Lucas added: "I don't oppose the principle of a constitution. But I oppose this particular one – and the Treaty which reproduces it – because EU citizens deserve better."

Christopher Booker also commented on the position the Members of Parliament took to reject the call for a referendum on the Lisbon Treaty. Within his article, *MPs stand firm on their own irrelevance,* Mr. Booker writes: "The spectacle of 311 MPs endorsing Gordon Brown's lie that the Lisbon Treaty is not a repackaged version of the EU's rejected constitution - to justify breaking the promise of a referendum on which they were all elected - was degrading." He explained how politicians have deliberately hidden the extent of the power they have already surrendered to Brussels. He also revealed how manufacturers of an anti-depressant drug, Seroxat, could not be taken to court for concealing evidence that it might drive people to suicide. The reason was due to a loophole in the law which emanated from Brussels. The law was ill-drafted. Nevertheless, our impotent politicians have no authority to amend laws from their masters in Brussels (The Sunday Telegraph, 9 March 2008). It's a pity that British politicians have ignored the extraordinary vision of their "father" - The Prince of Detectives to become "slaves" in Jean Monnet's "dungeon" in Brussels.

Macer Hall argued in the Daily Express, "The great European referendum debate ended up being a tawdry and vacuous spectacle. Rarely have defining moments in this nation's history been so forgettable. In a string of shamelessly self-regarding and pledges speeches, MPs of all parties shrugged aside their manifesto insisting the issue was a matter of the primacy of the Commons." At times common sense has not been common in the House of Commons.

The *Economist* also argued, "Reneging on what many see as a promise to have a referendum on substantial institutional change in Brussels comes at a bad time for politicians generally. Scandals over party funding and MPs' perks have damaged public trust in Westminster. Denying people a chance to vote also seems to contradict the oft-professed desire to push power downwards."

The British people were deceived in 1975 to join a Common Market. This Economic Community has now turned into a political Union, whose headquarters in Brussels impose laws on most aspects of our lives. Yet politicians, who have been intoxicated with power, would not allow the public a say on an issue which affects their lives. The British people deserve better. In 1992 the Patriot Powell declared: "What the EEC (now the EU) is bent upon has nothing to do with free trade or free anything. It is a naked assertion of the will to power, the will to create a United States of Europe which, instead of our national organs of representation and government, we are all to be subordinated."

And I repeat the Patriot Powell's observation of Britain's relationship with Jean Monnet's project: "A nation is free externally in the sense that all laws, policies, and acts of government generally which affect its citizens are made by its own institutions. In a nation "free" in the sense, no laws will be made, or taxes imposed, or judgements judged by an external authority...but the UK is not free, since its laws may now be defined, its taxes imposed, and its policies laid down by an external authority, namely the institutions of EC (now the EU)". And on the floor of the House of Commons the "Prophet" Enoch cried out: "I did not become a member of our sovereign Parliament to see that sovereignty abated or transferred" (Source: *Principality and Power of Europe* – Adrian Hilton)

We must not be surprised by the autocratic behaviour of EU leaders and the deceit British governments have perpetrated upon the British people. Firstly, these politicians were following the foot-steps of their 'father' – the 'obstinate' Jean Monnet, who had no shame in "smuggling" a beautiful married Italian woman to Moscow for a quick divorce and marriage. Secondly, in forcing the 'unreadable' Lisbon Treaty down the throats of the masses, European and British politicians have unconsciously paved the way for Sir Robert Anderson's prediction of the "vile" character of the European Union and its dark future to be fulfilled.

It is unfortunate that a British Prime Minister would ignore the extraordinary bright vision of his own brilliant "father" to follow the blurred vision of the French man Jean Monnet. Sadly, through ignorance British politicians are forcing Britons to embark on Monnet's doomed "Titanic." In the 20th century (1912), the Great Titanic started well on its maiden voyage from Southampton to New York. The passengers took luxurious items with them to enjoy the trip of their life time. But did they arrive safely? The passengers who perished on the Titanic would not have joined the ship if they had known the vessel would sink. The tragedy of Titanic should be a lesson to British politicians who are pushing Britons to board Monnet's "Vessel of doom."

WE MUST NOT BETRAY SUCCEEDING GENERATIONS

Nicola Roberts of *Girls Aloud*, writing for The Sun newspaper on the Lisbon Treaty, stated: "Young people are the ones who will have to deal with the consequences of this EU treaty...Personally I'm against the signing up under the terms being suggested because it means we will be handing over so many powers to unelected representatives in Brussels.....Do we really want to end up living in a country where we can't make our own decisions based on what is best for Britain?

The issue is: Why have politicians failed to educate the youth about the true significance of the European Union and its Lisbon Treaty? If the future belongs to our sons and daughters, then they deserve to know the extent to which the European Union would affect their lives. We should not allow the bureaucrats in Brussels and British politicians to "poison" the youth with misleading information about the European Union.

The Patriotic SUN newspaper, in its campaign for a referendum on the abominable EU treaty, which was designed to fool Europeans, rightly pointed out that the EU reformed treaty would seize the sovereignty of the British people and consign Britain to a puppet state – a province of Brussels. In 1881, the 'giant' Anderson predicted that Britain would become a ***province*** of an European Empire if it joins a confederation of European nations which would evolve from an European crisis**.**

I conclude this chapter by sharing with you Peter Hitchens' comments on the unreadable Lisbon Treaty and the character of the European Project, and why Britons would not starve outside the European Union. Mr Hitchens writes: "This is too frightening and too important to ignore any longer. If we don't act now Britain would become a neglected outstation of the European Superstate, stripped of our nationhood, powerless to decide who lives here, controlled by laws we don't make and can't change, ruled by a government we cannot throw out. The European Union is interested in your liberty and your money even if you don't care about it. Its decisions affect your life, even if you don't realise it."

For example, the potential cost of disposing our rubbish was an initiative of EU Directives. Mr Hitchens (observing the lukewarm attitude of the Conservative Party to its commitment to call for a referendum on the Lisbon Treaty even when the treaty is ratified by Parliament) added: "Political elites in all the parties love the EU, not because it is good for the country, but because it is good for them. They love its regular service of gravy trains, carrying failed Ministers off to a life of high salaries, big expenses and huge pensions, plus an almost total absence of responsibility. They don't mind at all that it deprives them of the power to do very much. They are for most part, short of ideas and lazy and happy to be able to pass the buck to Brussels while enjoying their pay and perks."

Peter Hitchens concluded his article: "British people have a way of ignoring the Continent, then finding out just in time that what happens before matters - Dunkirk being the most recent example. We probably won't get another Dunkirk to warn us. By the time it is clear to everyone what has happened it will be too late." The columnist then posed this question: "How will we be able to look our children and grandchildren in the face when they ask: What did you do to stop Britain being taken away by a foreign power?" (The Mail on Sunday 4 November 2007).

Mr Hitchens was proved right as various reports emerged on how Members of European Parliaments were fiddling their expenses: Witness the following headlines:

- *Cameron forces resignation of the Tories leader's in Brussels after expenses scandal*
- *Perks, Privileges and Power: the lifestyle to which MEPs have become accustom* to (The Times 6 June 2008)
- Tory chief quits over £445,000 expenses row (Daily Mirror)
- *Headache for Tories as more are caught on the expenses gravy train* (Daily Mail 9 June 2008)

And Leo McKinstry, in his essay, "*We elect our MPs to serve us, not to get bloated on expenses,*" reported: "Westminster and Brussels are rife with financial deception and the serial abuse of taxpayers' money." He commented on how a Labour MEP paid

£30000 to his gay partner to be his secretary in Brussels and another Tory MEP paying taxpayers' money into family business. And on 30 March 2009, Mr Mckinstry, again, commented on how some Members of Parliament abused their positions to rip-off the taxpayer. In his article, "*This is naked greed and hypocrisy on a grotesque scale,*" he writes: "The sense of rampart decadence has been highlighted by the extraordinary news that the husband of Home Secretary…..has used her House of Commons allowance to pay for "adult" films." He added: "Only in a truly sick political system would the taxpayer be expected to subsidise this kind of viewing on satellite television… Parliament has been degraded, rules bent and ethical standards obliterated. Naked avarice has replaced any concept of morality as the political elite ruthlessly plunder public coffers for private gain."(Daily Express). And Melanie Phillips summed it up in her column headed: *Is there no end to the outrageous ruses MPs dream up to fleece the taxpayer? In any other job, they'd be jailed.* She wrote: "Shamelessness in Parliament appears to be a truly bottomless well… Another Government minister had to put his hands up to yet another expenses fiddle….By any normal standards, it is outrageous for an MP to justify using taxpayers' money to fund his parents' house as if it is his own second home….Especially at a time of growing economic hardship, these expenses scams are intolerable. While MPs fiddle, democracy slowly but inexorably burns" (*Daily Mail* 23 March 2009).

On the issue of our membership of the European Union, the servant of the British Crown warned Britain would not be saved by participating in the "vile confederacy of the latter days." British and Irish politicians must not ignore the counsel of the "Seer of Dublin." They must withdraw Britain and Ireland from the abominable European Project, and become "isolated" in Europe. For the future of Europe, according to the "Prophet of Linden Gardens," is dark.

It is not late for us to leave the European Union. We only need politicians with moral fibre and conviction - selfless politicians who really love their country and do not follow the path of least resistant - to pull Britons and the Irish from the "EU Titanic" which is about to sink. The officials in Brussels have NO legitimate right whatsoever to force the majority of Britons, who do not want to be ruled by "strangers" in Europe, to love the European Union and become "adopted children" of Jean Monnet, the first honorary citizen of Europe. Ruth Lea writes: "A looser relationship, based on trade and co-operation, rather than full political and economic integration, is consistently the option of the British people." Why should "greedy" and "unpatriotic" politicians drag Britons to board Monnet's "EU Titanic" which was doomed before its construction began in 1950?

GREAT BRITAIN MUST RENEGOTIATE ITS RELATIONSHIP WITH THE EUROPEAN UNION

The "David" of Britain and the "Goliath" of Europe

In her essay, *The little dirty secret is that our MPs hardly matter* (Daily Mail 9 June 2008), Melanie Phillips writes: "The EU is fundamentally anti-democratic project based on the belief that the individual nation is the source of the ills of the world and that by contrast supra-national institutions offer the solution to all its problems. The absence of democratic accountability is now corrupting not just European politics but our own. She added: "Whatever happens to the constitutional treaty in Ireland or anywhere else, Britain must now re-negotiate its relationship with the EU. The politician who does so will be a hero to the nation. The issue is quite simply whether democracy in Britain has a future at all. It could not be more fundamental. If Cameron were to say he would renegotiate Britain's place in Europe, he would immediately establish himself as a statesman of the first rank."

According to a survey published in January 2009, majority of Britons want looser relationship with the European Union. The patriotic Sun newspaper reported on this survey in its 12 January 2009 edition. In a column titled ***2 in 3 say dump EU***, The Sun stated: "Only 22 percent favoured the current relationship with Brussels. But 48 percent want looser ties and another 16 percent want the UK to withdraw completely from the EU. A total of 64 percent are against Britain joining the euro, compared with 24 percent who want to adopt the currency." In the light of this survey, and coupled with the fact that Brussels has become a burden on Britons (for the EU CAP costs British taxpayers £10.3 billion a year (Daily Express 30 March 2009), would "little David" gather the political courage to confront the "Philistine Giant" and "kill" it with the "stone" provided by the Knight Commander? Or political cowardice would restrain "David" of Britain from the challenge to take on EU, the "Goliath" of Europe, to wrestle Britons from the "monster"?

I would quote the words of the "spiritual god-father" of EU to confirm Melanie Phillips' assertion that the European Union is 'anti-democratic project based on the belief that the individual nation is the source of the ills of the world and that by contrast supra-national institutions offer the solution to all its problems." Jean Monnet, crystallising his vision of a federal Europe, recorded: "*But time is passing, and Europe is moving only slowly on the course to which she is so deeply committed .... We cannot stop ... the community we have created is not an end in itself... Like the provinces of the past, our nations must learn to live together under common rules and institutions freely arrived at. The sovereign nations of the past can no longer solve the problems of the present; they cannot ensure their own progress or control their own future. And the community itself is only a stage on the way to the organized world of tomorrow."(*Jean Monnet Memoirs 1978 page 524*)*

Prince, which was released in 1957, the very year the Treaty of Rome was signed, the "spiritual god-father" of EU would have realised that he was a "poor slave" toiling to fulfil an Irishman's extraordinary vision of European Community. Britain should leave the European Union. Britons don't need Monnet's autocratic philosophy. The French hero would not have qualified to stoop and polish the boots of The Knight Commander (of the Order) of Bath. The Knight was a man of peace who never shirked a fight. He was a "literary recluse" who never raised the flag of truce before a foe. As 'children' of the Great Knight, we must also not shirk the fight for our release from bondage in Brussels. We must be silent no more.

SUMMARY:
THE TREATY OF LISBON AND THE EMPEROR OF THE EUROPEAN EMPIRE

I would borrow an extract from Sir Robert's *The Coming Prince* that describes the characteristics of the powerful Emperor who will guide Europe to its "glory." The Lisbon Treaty (with its provision for a President of Europe who will sign international treaties on behalf of Europeans) has paved the way for the brutal dictator to emerge to mesmerise Europeans and the rest of the world.

"WHAT is it that all Europe is looking for?" The words are quoted from a leading article in the *Times* newspaper, on the... finding of Agamemnon's tomb. "It is the KING OF MEN, the great head of the Hellenic race, the man whom a thousand galleys and a hundred thousand men submitted to on a simple recognition of his personal qualities, and obeyed for ten long years...The man who can challenge for his own the shield of Agamemnon, now waiting for the challenge, is the true Emperor of the East, and the easiest escape from our present difficulties."(*The Times*, Monday, 18 December, 1876). Dr. Anderson continued: "The realization of this dream will be the fulfilment of prophecy... A man of transcendent greatness... never fails to leave his mark upon his times. And the true King of Men must have an extraordinary combination of great qualities. He must be "a scholar, a statesman, and a man of unflinching courage and irrepressible enterprise, full of resources, and ready to look in the face of a rival or a foe." Dr Anderson added: "The opportunity too must synchronize with his advent. But the voice of prophecy is clear, that the HOUR is coming, and the MAN."

This MAN is the last Caesar of the revived Roman Empire. Remember how Paul Henri-Spaak addressed European Assembly: "We do not want another committee. We have too many already. What we want is a man of sufficient stature to hold the allegiance of all people, and to lift us out of the economic morass in which we are sinking. Send us such a man and he be god or the devil, we will receive him." And after the Treaty of Rome was signed in 1957, Spaak told his friends: 'Do you think we have today been putting the first stone of a new Roman Empire, and this time without firing a shot?' We all felt like Romans that day." (Source: TIME 5 June 2005: *The Decline and fall of Rome* by Michael Elliot)

"His views are worthy of the utmost respect and consideration ...and the well being of Ireland was to him a matter standing above politics in the ordinary sense.

Chapter 14

IF YOU WANT TO KNOW THE "VALUES" THE EUROPEAN UNION REPRESENTS, LOOK AT HER "BEAUTIFUL FACE" - THE EUROPEAN EMBLEM

"Rationalism in its most subtle phase is leavening society. The universities are its chief seminaries. The pulpit is its platform. Some of the most popular religious leaders are amongst its apostles. No class is safe from its influence." **(The Coming Prince RA)**

In the previous chapter we learnt how the Germans plotted to introduce the European Flag and Anthem into the European Constitution, codenamed the Lisbon Treaty. We know the European Flag and its symbol and the European Anthem were all excluded from the original text of the Lisbon Treaty to prevent the document classified as an European Constitution, and thereby avoiding the need of national referenda which European leaders were scared of. This was revealed in David Miliband's address to the "House of Shame": "It is good that the symbols, flags and anthem, which distracted attention from the discussion of the European Constitutional treaty, are done away with so that we can focus on what will make the EU useful to this country jobs, climate change and energy – the issues that matter to ordinary people."

The Foreign Secretary just poured out empty words to fool the masses about the European Flag and its symbol and anthem. For the European Parliament endorsed the German plot to introduce these items into the European Constitution with this statement: "Symbols are vital elements of any communication process. They convey an emotional image of the underlying values of the organisation they represent." We must, therefore, ask the question: what sort of "values" do the EU symbol – a ring of 12 gold star - represent?

Signs and symbols have meaning. Road Signs guide motorists to drive safely. For example, if a motorist, unknowingly, drives through a "One Way " street, or turns left instead of right, it is likely he could clash with another vehicle. So, just as road signs are vital to motorists, so must we also not ignore the EU symbol. For our understanding of the European emblem would help us identify the "values" the European Union represents and so guide our relationship with the European Project.

A nation's flag is the pride of its citizens. It identifies and affirms its existence among nations. For example, when a nation is conquered, its national flag is removed and replaced with that of the conqueror. When, in 2003, American soldiers led the invasion of Iraq and "won the war" by removing Saddam Hussein from power, the victorious Americans, initially, installed the American Flag. Later on it was removed to dispel the notion that they had 'conquered' Iraq. Americans wanted to be seen as "liberators."

The European Flag, with its emblem of a circle of 12 gold stars, is the "Face of EU." Our understanding of the significance of this emblem, which is the "pride of Europe," would reveal the "values" Jean Monnet's project represents. In this respect, I would briefly share with you what the circle of 12 gold stars on a blue background signifies. I hope the clarification would help Britons, the Irish and Europeans who have the European emblem on their Driving Licences, Car Registration Plates, Passports and Identity Cards, to realise what they are carrying. For us to appreciate the real significance of the EU Flag, and not to be deceived by the distorted meaning provided by the EU bureaucrats, we need to answer the following questions:

- Who suggested an European flag?
- Who designed the European flag?
- What inspired the designer to select a circle of 12 gold stars?
- Who was the Director of the Flag Institute who selected the flag?
- Who was the Secretary General of the Council of Europe who approved the European flag and its symbol of a circle of 12 gold stars?
- Why did he select this particular design because there were other designs he could have chosen from?

OFFICIAL INTERPRETATION OF EUROPEAN EMBLEM

Before we deal with the above questions, let us first examine the official explanation for the EU symbol and the history behind the adoption of the EU Flag. According to European Union publications, "The European flag is the symbol not only of the European Union but also of Europe's unity and identity in a wider sense. The circle of 12 gold stars represents solidarity and harmony between the peoples of Europe. The number of stars has nothing to do with the number of Member States. There are twelve stars because the number twelve is traditionally the symbol of perfection, completeness and unity. The flag therefore remains unchanged regardless of EU Enlargement."

The explanation continues: "The history of the flag goes back to 1955. At that time the European Union existed only in the form of the European Coal and Steel Community with just six members. But a separate body with larger membership – the Council of Europe – had been set up several years earlier and was busy defending human rights and promoting European culture. The Council of Europe adopted the present design, a circle of 12 gold Stars on a blue background, for its own use. The Council then encouraged other European institutions to adopt the same flag. In 1983 the European Parliament took up the call."

The above explanation of the European emblem is simplistic and inconsistent with the meaning the designer of the European flag attributed to the insignia of a crown of 12 gold stars. Was it a deliberate attempt to prevent Europeans from knowing the source of the emblem, or it was through ignorance?

THE SOURCE OF THE EUROPEAN EMBLEM

Let us deal with the facts surrounding the European flag and its symbol. In 1949, Paul G.M. Levi, a Jew, who became a Roman Catholic Theologian and a Professor at the Roman Catholic University of Leuven (Belgium), was appointed director of the Cultural Department of the Board of Europe. In 1955 this Catholic Priest (according to the leading German Newspaper *Die Welt*), came up with the concept of European flag. Levi, fascinated by the holy virgin with the stars around her head, proposed to the Secretary General of Board of Europe, Earl Benvenuti, to choose the symbol of Mary. When the members of parliament later agreed to his request, and selected a flag with the so-called Marian symbol, Levi said: "How on earth is it possible. We just rediscovered the introit of the new Mass of Mary's Assumption!"

The truth is that the European Flag was designed by the German artist, Arsene Heitz. He was inspired by the imagery of the Virgin Mary with a crown of 12 stars. Heitz's design was among other designs which were submitted to the European Council. The Council adopted Heitz's drawing after a competition was initiated in 1950. The Flag was officially adopted by the Council of Europe in 1955. It was Heitz himself who revealed to a French magazine the reason for his inspiration. At that time he was reading the history of the Blessed Virgin's apparitions in Paris' Rue du Bac, known today as the Virgin of the Miraculous Medal. According to the artist, he thought of the 12 stars in a circle on a blue background, exactly the way it is represented in traditional iconography of this image of the Immaculate Conception."

When the Flag was adopted, Professor Paredes stated. "That's a lot of coincidences, so henceforth it should not be difficult for us to discover in the folds of the European flag the smile and affection of our Mother, the Queen of Europe, ready to lend a hand in that great challenge that St Peter's successor has proposed to us to re-Christianise the Old Continent with the example of our lives and the testimony of our words." It is clear; the emblem on the European flag was "inspired" by the halo of 12 stars that appear around the woman in Revelation 12.

Commenting on the European flag in his book, *The Principality and Power of Europe,* Adrian Hilton writes: "Dr William Crampton, the Director of the flag institute, confirmed that it was Leon Marchal, a Secretary General of the Council of Europe, the supreme partisan of the Virgin Mary, who suggested the number 12. And when the Council of Europe's stained – glass window was unveiled on 11 December 1955 to coincide with the Roman Catholic Feast of the Immaculate Conception of Mary, Marchal said: "it's wonderful that we have got back to the new introit Mass of the Assumption, it's the *corona stellarum duodecim* (the crown of the 12 stars) of the Woman of the Apocalypse." When the EU membership increased to 15, a suggestion was made that the 12 stars should be increased to 15 for each star to represent a member state just like the American flag. The proposal was rejected. It was confirmed that the "12 stars" could not be changed, for they were as constant as they were drawn from chapter 12 of the Book of Revelation.

THE ROMAN CATHOLIC CHURCH AND THE EU SYMBOL

The Roman Catholic Church claims the woman with a crown of 12 stars in Revelation 12 represents the Blessed Virgin Mary, the "Mother of God" - the co-redeemer. In September 1958, Archbishop Montini of Milan (later Pope Pius XII) released on the mountain Serenissima a 20 meter high statue of Mary and called it "Our Beloved Lady, Ruler of Europe." Pope Pius XII called Mary "Mother of all Nations," and on 3 March 1953 called for a reunion of nations. Bishop Dr. Graber declared on 9 September 1978: "I've asked for a Marian European International.... We pray and ask in silence that the western world one day will be as it was: an IMPERIUM MARIANUM."

And without any surprise, Cardinal Miloslav Vlk from Czech Republic, who was once the head of the Council of Bishops Conferences of Europe, confirmed that the European flag has Catholic influence behind it. In an interview for *Aktualne.cz*, Ludvik Hradilek writes: "Vlk links the European Union's flag to Christian values. The flag consisting of twelve stars on a blue background was admittedly inspired by the Bible. In Vlk's view the circle of stars refers to the twelve-star halo of the Virgin Mary. Cardinal Vlk was quick to mention the flag was adopted on December 8, a day which celebrates the feast of the Immaculate Conception of Virgin Mary. The EU flag bears a striking similarity of the image of Virgin Mary, says Cardinal Vlk." (Czech News 9 January 2009).

The Cardinal proudly stated it was Catholic politicians, Alcide De Gasperi of Italy, Robert Schuman of France, and Konrad Adenauer of Germany, who came up with the idea of "unified Europe." Why didn't the Cardinal mention Jean Monnet, the principal architect of European Community? Was Cardinal Vlk aware that it was an Irish Protestant who predicted a political union of European nations before the Catholic Schuman, who was once put on a fast track to sainthood, was born in 1886?

THE DISTORTION OF "SCRIPTURAL TRUTH"

From what we have learnt about the EU symbol, and in view of the comments provided by the Catholic Church and Leon Marchal, the Secretary General of the European Council who adopted the European flag, it is clear, the official explanation of the EU emblem contradicts with what actually inspired the artist to produce the design the European Union adopted. So, the European Union's claim that the EU symbol has no religious connotation is FALSE in view of what Arsene Heitz, the artist who designed the European Flag, said about his work. After all, it was not the bureaucrats in Brussels who designed the symbol for the European flag. Therefore, European leaders cannot put their own interpretation on the circle of 12 gold stars that appears on the European flag. The EU officials should have produced their own symbol.

The undoubted fact is the European Union is atheistic. It has no room for God. It is "hostile" to Christianity, and therefore does not want Jean Monnet's Project to be associated with anything which is biblical, godly or Christian. But the reality is the EU is Useless to God and the Lord Jesus Christ. The Lord does not need the EU. Yet, the EU is "Useful" to the Lord Jesus Christ because; our Divine Lord needs the EU for His "purpose." A word to the wise is enough.

Anyway, the bureaucrats in Brussels should not worry about the "religious" meaning the Roman Catholic Church has placed on the EU symbol. The Catholic artist, Arsene Heitz, claimed to have been motivated by the imagery in Revelation 12 to produce a circle of 12 stars on a blue background. And this symbol was eventually adopted by the Council of Europe as its emblem. The scriptural truth is that the circle of 12 gold stars, purported to be the crown of 12 stars on the "woman of the apocalypse," has nothing to do with the Virgin Mary or Christian values.

WHO IS THE WOMAN WITH A CROWN OF 12 STARS?

Let us examine whether the Catholic Church's interpretation of "the crown of 12 stars on the woman" in Revelation 12:1 is accurate and consistent with the principle of interpreting Scripture with Scripture. According to Roman Catholic doctrine, the EU symbol is associated with the woman with a crown of 12 stars in chapter 12 of the Book of Revelation, and this woman is the Blessed Virgin Mary. This Catholic explanation of the "Woman of the Apocalypse" is based on a loose reading and superficial examination of the full text recorded in Revelation 12.

Let us read a portion of Revelation 12 and analyse the meaning of the text: *"A great and wondrous sign appeared in heaven: a woman clothed with the sun, with the moon under her feet and a crown of twelve stars on her head. She was pregnant and cried out in pain as she was about to give birth. Then another sign appeared in heaven an enormous dragon with seven heads and ten horns and seven crowns on his heads. His tail swept a third of the stars out of the sky and flung them to the earth. The dragon stood in front of the woman who was about to give birth, so that he might devour her child the moment it was born. She gave birth to a son, male child, who will rule all the nations with an iron sceptre. And her child was snatched up to God and to his throne. The woman fled into the desert to a place prepared for her by God, where she might be taken care of for 1260 days....When the dragon saw that he had been hurled to the earth, he pursued the woman who had given birth to the male child. The woman was given the two wings of a great eagle, so that she might fly to the place prepared for her in the desert, where she would be taken care of for a time, times and half a time, out of the serpent reach...Then the dragon was enraged at the woman and went off to make war against the rest of her offspring - those who obey God's commandments and hold to the testimony of Jesus. And the dragon stood on the shore of the sea."*

You don't have to be a Professor of Theology or a Bishop, neither an Archbishop nor a Cardinal or a Pope to realise that the "woman" in Revelation 12 is not related to the Blessed Virgin Mary and neither does the "male child" relate to the Lord Jesus Christ. A careful examination of the full text would confirm it. According to this passage of Scripture, this "woman," - who is clothed with the sun, with the moon under her feet - fled into the desert to a place prepared for her by God where she might be taken care of for 1260 days. This same "woman" was given the two wings of a great eagle, so that she might fly to the place prepared for her in the desert, where she would be taken care of for a time, times and half a time, out of the serpent's reach (Rev 12:14).

To understand this scripture, we need common sense and the application of the principle of "interpreting scripture with scripture" - not interpreting scripture with our own opinions and prejudices. In this respect, we must analyse Joseph's dream of the sun and moon and eleven stars bowing down to him. This is recorded in Genesis 37:9. And we must also examine the Old Testament Books of Isaiah and Daniel.

to pass and he sent and signified it by his angel unto his servant John........Write the things which thou hast seen, and the things which are, and the things which shall be hereafter." (Revelation 1, 19 KJ)

The issue is the Roman Catholic Church "worships" Blessed Virgin Mary. They have attempted to place her on an equal footing with the Lord Jesus Christ as "Co-Redeemer." Because of this practice and dogma, the Church of Rome has distorted the Scriptural truth in Revelation 12 to suit its doctrine by suggesting that the "pregnant woman" about to deliver a "man-child" in this portion of Scriptures refers to Virgin Mary about to deliver her "Son" - the Lord Jesus Christ. Since Mary never flee to a desert to be sustained for 1260 days during her pregnancy, how could Catholic theologians associate this "woman" in Revelation 12 with the Blessed Virgin Mary? The truth is that none of the 4 Gospels (Matthew, Mark, Luke and John) mentions an escape of the pregnant Mary into a desert to be protected for 42 months. And since there is no historical record about Mary seeking refuge in wilderness for 1260 days, there is no basis for the "Woman of the Apocalypse" to be associated with the Blessed Virgin Mary.

What is wrong with the Church of Rome? The Roman Catholic Church, at times, teaches error. A careful study of Daniel 7:23-27, Daniel 9:27, Daniel 12:5-7 and Revelation 13:5-8 where " a time, times half a time" - 3½ years and 42 months are mentioned - would reveal that the 1260 days and 42 months recorded in Revelation 12 relate to the 3½ year period of persecution of the saints - the faithful children of God. It is clear from these texts, that the woman in Revelation 12 who fled into the desert to be nourished for 1260 is not the Blessed Virgin Mary. The Woman as seen in Isaiah 66 represents God's Children. And the 'man-child' who was snatched up to God and to his throne (Rev. 12:5) does not refer to the Lord Jesus Christ either.

The "Woman of the apocalypse"- first mentioned in Isaiah 66 as "Zion" - symbolises the children of God. And the "Man-child" represents 'overcomers' - the faithful Christians and Jews - who would be raptured into heaven to escape the terror of the coming King of Europe - the "Man of Lawlessness - the "Son of Perdition." Witness the promise the Lord Jesus Christ gave to the *Church in Philadelphia*: "I know you have little strength, yet you did not deny my name....Since you have kept my command to endure patiently, I will also keep you from the hour of trial that is going to come upon the whole world to test those who live on the earth..." (Revelation 3:8-10). This "hour of trial" is the great tribulation the Lord Jesus Christ spoke about in Matthew 24 and Luke 21. And the *Church in Philadelphia* (the "Church of brotherly love") represents the true Church of Christ which would be taken away before the beginning of the 1260 days of untold persecution of the saints – when the King of Europe violates the 7-year peace treaty with Israel and its Arab neighbours and claims the whole world should worship him as "god" (Daniel 9:27).

chapter 12 of the Book of Revelation, and this woman is the Blessed Virgin Mary. This Catholic explanation of the "Woman of the Apocalypse" is based on a loose reading and superficial examination of the full text recorded in Revelation 12.

Let us read a portion of Revelation 12 and analyse the meaning of the text: *"A great and wondrous sign appeared in heaven: a woman clothed with the sun, with the moon under her feet and a crown of twelve stars on her head. She was pregnant and cried out in pain as she was about to give birth. Then another sign appeared in heaven an enormous dragon with seven heads and ten horns and seven crowns on his heads. His tail swept a third of the stars out of the sky and flung them to the earth. The dragon stood in front of the woman who was about to give birth, so that he might devour her child the moment it was born. She gave birth to a son, male child, who will rule all the nations with an iron sceptre. And her child was snatched up to God and to his throne. The woman fled into the desert to a place prepared for her by God, where she might be taken care of for 1260 days....When the dragon saw that he had been hurled to the earth, he pursued the woman who had given birth to the male child. The woman was given the two wings of a great eagle, so that she might fly to the place prepared for her in the desert, where she would be taken care of for a time, times and half a time, out of the serpent reach...Then the dragon was enraged at the woman and went off to make war against the rest of her offspring - those who obey God's commandments and hold to the testimony of Jesus. And the dragon stood on the shore of the sea."*

You don't have to be a Professor of Theology or a Bishop, neither an Archbishop nor a Cardinal or a Pope to realise that the "woman" in Revelation 12 is not related to the Blessed Virgin Mary and neither does the "male child" relate to the Lord Jesus Christ. A careful examination of the full text would confirm it. According to this passage of Scripture, this "woman," - who is clothed with the sun, with the moon under her feet - fled into the desert to a place prepared for her by God where she might be taken care of for 1260 days. This same "woman" was given the two wings of a great eagle, so that she might fly to the place prepared for her in the desert, where she would be taken care of for a time, times and half a time, out of the serpent's reach (Rev 12:14).

To understand this scripture, we need common sense and the application of the principle of "interpreting scripture with scripture" - not interpreting scripture with our own opinions and prejudices. In this respect, we must analyse Joseph's dream of the sun and moon and eleven stars bowing down to him. This is recorded in Genesis 37:9. And we must also examine the Old Testament Books of Isaiah and Daniel.

Joseph's Dream

On the significance of Joseph's dream and its relevance to understanding the implication of the woman with a crown of 12 stars, let me share with you Witness Lee's commentary on the subject in the *Holy Bible Recovery Version: "This woman is clothed with the sun, and the moon underneath her feet, and on her head a crown of twelve stars." In Genesis 37:9 Joseph in his dream saw the sun, the moon, and the eleven stars, signifying his father, his mother, and his eleven brothers. There the sun, the moon, and the eleven stars, plus Joseph himself, signified the totality of God's people on the earth. Based on the principle of that dream the sun, the moon, and the twelve stars here must signify the totality of God's people on earth, which is symbolised here by a woman. Most of her being is clothed with the sun. The sun signifies God's people in the New Testament age. Before Christ came to the world, it was the dark night of the Old Testament age. When Christ as the rising sun came from on high (Luke 1:78), the age of the sun came. Before that, it was the age of the moon, which signifies God's people in the Old Testament time. The moon is underneath the feet of the woman, for the age of the moon was the age of the law, which should not be exalted as the stars are. The stars, which signify the patriarchs, God's people before the law was given, are on her head as a crown. All God's people in these three ages, who constitute this woman, are light bearers. Hence, she is the bright woman shining throughout all generations. The child here, being a man-child (12:5) signifies the stronger part of God's people...."*

The "Male-child"

In Isaiah 66: 7- 9 we read: "Before she travailed, she gave birth; before her pain came, she delivered a *male child.* Who has heard such a thing? Who has seen such things? Shall the earth be made to give birth in one day? Or shall a nation be born at once? For as soon as *Zion travailed*, she gave birth to her children. Shall I bring to the time of birth, and not cause delivery?" says the Lord. (NKJV Emphasis mine). In this text it is clear the woman who gave birth to a "male child" is "Zion" the nation of Israel. And in Revelation 12:1-5 we also read of a pregnant woman who cried out in pain as she was about to give birth to a "male child." If the woman in Isaiah 66 was not Blessed Virgin (for it could not have been her), on what grounds does the woman in Revelation 12 become Blessed Virgin Mary, if we interpret Scripture with Scripture?

In Daniel 7:25 we read: "He (the Man of Lawlessness - the coming emperor of the revived Roman Empire) will speak against the Most High and oppress his saints and try to change set times and the laws. The saints will be handed over to him for a time, times and half a time." The phrase *"a time, times and half a time"*- which means 42 months or 3½ years or 1260days - is also associated with the pregnant woman in Revelation 12.

Here are questions for Vatican and Roman Catholic theologians who subscribe to the theory that the "Woman" in Revelation 12 refers to the Blessed Virgin Mary:

- "Was the Virgin Mary, during her pregnancy and in her life-time, ever given the two wings of an eagle to fly to a place to be nurtured for 3½ years?
- What is the significance of the enormous red dragon with 7 heads and 10 horns and 7 crowns that stood in front of the woman?
- Did such a monster ever confront Virgin Mary when she was pregnant with the Lord Jesus Christ?

THE SIGNIFICANCE OF THE "WOMAN OF THE APOCALYPSE"

A full explanation of Revelation 12 would require another book. So, in other not to digress further from the main theme of this chapter, I would provide a brief explanation of the significance of "the woman with a crown of 12 stars." In the Bible the number 12 stands for completeness in eternity and God's eternal administration. "The woman with a crown of 12 stars" represents the totality of God's people on earth - the Jews and Christians who would experience the Great Tribulation - the 3½ years of persecution at the hands of the last Emperor of the revived Roman Empire – the "beast from the sea"- who is also described as the "Man of Lawlessness." The "male-child" represents the overcomers – those faithful servants of the Lord who would be taken away before the Great Tribulation.

The issue is: if the "woman" in Revelation 12 represents the Virgin Mary, as alleged by the Roman Catholic Church, then this is the pressing question Pope Benedict XVI and his Catholic theologians must answer: "When Mary was pregnant with the Lord Jesus Christ, did she escape into a desert to be taken care of for 1260days? (Revelation 12:6). And how would the Catholic Church explain the text: "*When the dragon saw that he had been hurled to the earth, he pursued the woman who had given birth to the male child. The woman was given the two wings of a great eagle, so that she might fly to the place prepared for her in the desert, where she would be taken care of for a time, times and half a time out of the serpent reach*" (Revelation 12:13-14). If the "woman" in this text was Blessed Virgin Mary, then the Catholic Church must answer this question: was the pregnant Mary ever pursued by an enormous red dragon with seven heads and ten horns and seven crowns on his head? (Rev 12: 2-4). And I repeat: did Virgin Mary ever fly into a desert with two wings of an eagle to be cared of for a time, times and half a time?

We must remember the Book of Revelation is not about historical records. This last Book of the Bible, primarily, speaks of contemporary and future events. Witness the text in the opening chapter of the Book: "*The Revelation of Jesus Christ, which God gave unto him (John), to show unto his servants things which must shortly come to pass and he sent and signified it by his angel unto his servant John........Write the things which thou hast seen, and the things which are, and the things which shall be hereafter."* (Revelation 1, 19 KJ)

The issue is the Roman Catholic Church "worships" Blessed Virgin Mary. They have attempted to place her on an equal footing with the Lord Jesus Christ as "Co-Redeemer." Because of this practice and dogma, the Church of Rome has distorted the Scriptural truth in Revelation 12 to suit its doctrine by suggesting that the "pregnant woman" about to deliver a "man-child" in this portion of Scriptures refers to Virgin Mary about to deliver her "Son" - the Lord Jesus Christ. Since Mary never flee to a desert to be sustained for 1260 days during her pregnancy, how could Catholic theologians associate this "woman" in Revelation 12 with the Blessed Virgin Mary? The truth is that none of the 4 Gospels (Matthew, Mark, Luke and John) mentions an escape of the pregnant Mary into a desert to be protected for 42 months. And since there is no historical record about Mary seeking refuge in wilderness for 1260 days, there is no basis for the "Woman of the Apocalypse" to be associated with the Blessed Virgin Mary.

What is wrong with the Church of Rome? The Roman Catholic Church, at times, teaches error. A careful study of Daniel 7:23-27, Daniel 9:27, Daniel 12:5-7 and Revelation 13:5-8 where " a time, times half a time" - 3½ years and 42 months are mentioned - would reveal that the 1260 days and 42 months recorded in Revelation 12 relate to the 3½ year period of persecution of the saints - the faithful children of God. It is clear from these texts, that the woman in Revelation 12 who fled into the desert to be nourished for 1260 is not the Blessed Virgin Mary. The Woman as seen in Isaiah 66 represents God's Children. And the 'man-child' who was snatched up to God and to his throne (Rev. 12:5) does not refer to the Lord Jesus Christ either.

The "Woman of the apocalypse"- first mentioned in Isaiah 66 as "Zion" - symbolises the children of God. And the "Man-child" represents 'overcomers' - the faithful Christians and Jews - who would be raptured into heaven to escape the terror of the coming King of Europe - the "Man of Lawlessness - the "Son of Perdition." Witness the promise the Lord Jesus Christ gave to the *Church in Philadelphia*: "I know you have little strength, yet you did not deny my name....Since you have kept my command to endure patiently, I will also keep you from the hour of trial that is going to come upon the whole world to test those who live on the earth..." (Revelation 3:8-10). This "hour of trial" is the great tribulation the Lord Jesus Christ spoke about in Matthew 24 and Luke 21. And the *Church in Philadelphia* (the "Church of brotherly love") represents the true Church of Christ which would be taken away before the beginning of the 1260 days of untold persecution of the saints – when the King of Europe violates the 7-year peace treaty with Israel and its Arab neighbours and claims the whole world should worship him as "god" (Daniel 9:27).

EU SYMBOL: A "DISTORTION" OF "DISTORTION"

With this simple explanation before us, and again, using our common sense to analyse the text in Revelation 12, it is apparent that the meaning the Roman Catholic Church has attributed to the woman with a crown of 12 stars is plagued with error – a "distortion" of scriptural truth. The Catholic Church has, therefore, committed a grave theological blunder by associating "the woman of the Apocalypse" with Virgin Mary. It is this same Catholic Church that committed the blunder of all blunders by endorsing *The New Jerusalem Bible* which claims the Book of Daniel is an "edifying fiction." I repeat: What is wrong with the Roman Catholic Church?

I would make a point. Europe was consecrated to the Virgin Mary in the 14th century. Why such a consecration? After all, the name "Europe" was derived from a Greek mythical woman, called Europa, who was abducted and seduced by a pagan god, Zeus. So, had the hierarchy of the Roman Catholic Church had any respect for Blessed Virgin Mary, Vatican would not have associated the Mother of the Lord Jesus Christ with the Continent of Europe. The Roman Catholic Church, with its support for the European Union, is leading the 1.2billion Catholics astray to "worship" the "beast with 10 horns" when it enters the political scene in Europe.

For example, before the first Irish referendum that rejected the Lisbon Treaty in June 2008, Pope Benedict XVI pleaded with the Irish electorate to adopt the monstrous Lisbon Treaty which has no room for the Lord Jesus Christ. And without a surprise, the Catholic Archbishop of Dublin, Diarmuid Martin, urged Irish Christians to contribute to a "better Europe." He addressed his congregation: "The future of European integration will not in the first place be the result of a treaty or of new political structures,...Europe must become a Europe of peoples; a Europe of peoples which are different yet capable of living together in unity and solidarity. As Irish Christians we cannot and ought not flee from the challenges of shaping the Europe of the future. Christians make their contribution to a better Europe in a spirit of respect and dialogue." (Source: *Leading cleric in call for 'a better Europe'* - Irish Independent 20 April 2009).

Had the Archbishop of Dublin read what a native of Dublin, a Protestant Barrister from Trinity College, wrote about European integration and its future prospects before the Catholic founding fathers of the European Union, Jean Monnet and Robert Schuman, were born, he would not have encouraged his Irish Catholics to contribute to a project that has rejected God and the Lord Jesus Christ.

From what we have learnt, it is clear the Roman Catholic Church has distorted the meaning of the Woman of the Apocalypse. And the European Union - by claiming their symbol of a ring of twelve gold stars "represents solidarity and harmony among the peoples of Europe - has also distorted the "distorted" meaning attributed to its emblem. This means, the EU symbol represents "distortion" of a "distortion." Because, the meaning the Catholic artist attributed to his design of a circle of 12 gold stars is in itself a distortion of Scriptural truth. Hence, "distortion" is the "emotional image that underlines the values the European Union represents." Which means, the EU Flag, which is the "face" of the European Union, depicts falsehood and deceit. We can, rightly, conclude that the European Flag is a reflection of the "vile" character of Jean Monnet's project. It is, therefore, not surprising that the whole European project is built on deceit. Frederick Forsyth explained it in his article *EU made by deceit and lies.* He writes: "The EU is a legitimise government by trickery and deceit. The trouble is, once you adopt and legitimise government by trickery and deceit, corruption in public life follows as night does day" (*Daily Express,* 11 April 2008).

I have already stated that when the European Constitution was repackaged as the Lisbon Treaty, the European Flag with its emblem of a circle of 12 gold stars, and its pagan anthem, "Ode de Joy", were not included in the Treaty to prevent the document classified as an European Constitution to avoid referendums in the 27 member states. But what happened on 13 July 2009 when the new session of the European Parliament was formally opened in Strasbourg after the June 2009 European Elections which less than 40 per cent of the EU citizens bothered to vote? According to David Charter, *The Times* correspondent in Strasbourg, "1000 troops from strong Eurocorps garrison - consisting of soldiers from France, Germany, Belgium, Spain and Luxembourg - raised the gold-starred blue EU flag." The European anthem, Beethoven's Ninth Symphony, was also played to grace the occasion.

What further proof do Europeans need to convince them that "Deceit" is ingrained in the very DNA of the European Project?An extract from Lelia O'Flaherty's letter to the Editor of The Irish Times on this same issue – the hoisting of the European Flag and the playing of the European anthem in Strasbourg - confirms the vile character of the European Union. She reminded the Irish public that when Bertie Ahern, the former Irish Prime Minister, signed the Treaty of Lisbon in December 2007, he told the Irish people "that the anthem of the EU and the EU flag – symbols of EU statehood – would be 'dropped' in order to allay the fears of the people who feared the increasing power of the European Union." She goes on: "Yet when the new European Parliament session opened in Strasbourg....a detachment of combat troops, from various EU member-states led the ceremony and raised an EU flag – twice the size of the national flags around it ....These troops then stood to attention to a full orchestra and choral rendition of *Ode to Joy*, which is the European anthem. So much for Mr Ahern's assurances and promises..." (*The Irish Times* 17 July 2009).

In summary, the European Emblem - a ring of 12 gold stars on a blue background - speaks volumes about the vile "values" that are associated with the European Project: dictatorship, corruption, hostility to democratic principles, pornography, nepotism, bribery and fraud. Why should Britons and the Irish "swear allegiance' to the EU Flag which is an emblem of error and distortion to become 'adopted children' of the 'smuggler' Jean Monnet - the architect of the European Project? Why should Britons associate themselves with "falsehood" when the Labour Government secretly stockpiled European flags to be hoisted on some buildings in Britain? Our "Forgotten Father" warned us about the character of political Europe before the seeds of European Union were sown in 1950.

Those of us who carry the EU symbol on the Licence Plates of our cars, Driving Licences and Passports should now know what we are carrying. Are you proud to associate your self with the European symbol?

Chapter 15

REPUBLIC OF IRELAND AND THE LISBON TREATY AND FRANCE'S EU PRESIDENCY

"Truths may seem to us irreconcilable only because our finite minds cannot understand the infinite; and we must never allow our faulty apprehension of the eternal counsels of God to hinder unquestioning faith in the words of Holy Scripture"
(Forgotten Truths – RA)

On 12 June 2008, the Irish voted overwhelmingly by 53.4% to 46.6% to reject the Lisbon Treaty. Prior to the vote, the Irish government, together with businessmen, spent millions to seek a "Yes" vote. Also, European politicians, led by the President of the European Commission, Jose Manuel Barroso, intimidated the Irish to accept the Treaty. All the EU experts threatened, cajoled, blackmailed and frightened the Irish that their economy, which had been propped up by Brussels, would collapse if they voted "No." And secondly, a "No" vote would cast Ireland into "utter darkness" in Europe. However, the prudent Irish ignored the 'experts' and dumped the crooked Treaty of Lisbon.

Jose Manuel Barroso, the "Buffoon of Brussels", who insulted Britons that they 'don't matter,' was accused of interfering with Irish business when he suggested that there was "no plan B" if the referendum was not carried by Ireland, and "it would have a very negative effect for the EU." The Sinn Fein Member of European Parliament, who opposed the Lisbon Treaty, said his remarks were "unhelpful" and could "backfire" on the yes campaign. According to the MEP, "Once you enter into the territory of saying: 'if you don't vote for this catastrophe will follow,' then I think that's coercive and I don't think it is of any assistance to a good democratic debate."

Even Pope Benedict XVI, the "Green Pope", supported the Lisbon Treaty. The spiritual leader of 1.2 billion Roman Catholics cried to Irish Catholics to vote 'Yes' to an European Constitution that has no room for God. Is it not strange for a "Vicar of Christ" to support the European Union that has no room for Christ? We should not be surprised by the Catholic Church's support for the godless European Project. For the Material Babylon and the Religious Babylon would "share the same bed." The

Lord Jesus Christ revealed the fate of the "odd-couple" to Apostle John in Revelation 17. We will examine this in detail when we discuss "The Woman and the Beast" in Appendix 1.

Pope Benedict must realise that the Lisbon Treaty will pave the way for the powerful man who will lead the "true world political authority." This last Caesar of the revived Roman Empire would be "universally recognised and vested with the effective power to ensure security for all." The question is: would the world be secured under the leadership of this powerful man? The Pope's suggestion in his Encyclical Letter, Charity in Truth, which was released on 7 July 2009 to coincide with the Group of 8 summit in Italy - the meeting of the leaders of the world's biggest economies - will surely come to pass.

According to EU rules governing the adoption of the Lisbon Treaty, all the 27 countries must ratify the Treaty to become legally binding. And yet when Ireland dumped the document Jose Manuel Barroso claimed the treaty was "not dead." As jubilant "No" campaigners celebrated in Dublin, the Conservative Party in England suggested the treaty should be declared dead. They called on Gordon Brown to abandon ratification of the Treaty by the UK. But David Miliband, the Foreign Secretary, retorted that while it was important to respect the Irish result, there should also be a "British view" on the treaty, as expressed in the ratification bill then going through Parliament. Miliband declared: "I think it is right that we follow the view that each country must see the ratification process to a conclusion. I believe it is right that we continue with our process and take up the Irish offer of further discussions about the next steps forward."

To justify the Labour Government's refusal for not calling a referendum on the Lisbon Treaty, David Miliband said: "18 countries have now passed the reform treaty...each country must see the ratification process to a conclusion...there needs to be a British view as well as an Irish view." This was a silly talk. This suggestion by a British Foreign Secretary, who does not understand the significance of European integration, was disingenuous. To begin with: did the British people have a say on the "vile" Lisbon Treaty that would make them slaves in Monnet's "slave market" in Europe? Was it not arrogant and selfish politicians who adopted the Lisbon Treaty in the House of Shame? If the Lisbon Treaty were of any benefit to the British people, as suggested by David Miliband, it was Britons who should have made the decision to endorse the treaty in a popular vote, not imposed on them by "ignorant" politicians who blindly follow the "sons" and "daughters" of Jean Monnet and Konrad Adenauer.

When the French and the Dutch rejected the original European Constitution did Miliband's Labour Party, under Tony Blair, continue with the ratification of the Constitution? Did Tony Blair allow the British people to vote in a referendum he had promised? The Labour Party claimed it was not necessary since the constitution had already been rejected. So why did Miliband dictate to Britons that ratification of the Lisbon Treaty should go ahead even though the Irish had also rejected it. This is the normal practice of politicians. They pursue policies that suit their agenda. They talk about democracy, and yet they are "enemies" of democratic principles.

The fact is the selfish British politicians in the "House of Sleaze" ignored Britons who put them in the House of Commons where common sense is not always common. The greedy politicians decided to follow the orders of their masters in Brussels and ratified the unreadable Lisbon Treaty without popular consent. I would again remind the "double-standards" politicians of the wise words the selfless servant of the British Crown recorded: "The true test of a man is not what he does, but what, with the principles he holds, he would do, and if this be true of individuals, it is still more intensely true of communities."

David Cameron, the Leader of the Conservative Party, said he was "delighted" by the result of the Irish referendum. Cameron requested Gordon Brown to abandon the ratification process in Britain by saying: "People in Ireland have sent the clearest possible message that they do not want this treaty, they do not want this constitution…By all rights now it should be declared dead. The French said "no" to it, the Dutch said "no" to it, then it was brought back and the only people who have been given a chance to pass judgment on it, the Irish, have now said 'no' to it….The elites in Brussels have got to listen to people in Europe who do not want endless powers being passed from nation states to Brussels. They do not want these endless constitutions and treaties."

OBAMA ADMINISTRATION AND BRITAIN AND EUROPE

In his article, *A limp excuse for Tory foreign policy*, Philip Stephens writes: "Britain's influence in Washington depends on its capacity to shape events in Europe…On the big issues of the times – Iran, Afghanistan, climate change and the rest – it (Barack Obama administration) wants to deal with a more coherent, cohesive Europe. France is returning to full participation in the NATO alliance. The last thing Mr. Obama wants, one adviser informs me, is for Britain simultaneously to loosen its relationship with the EU." (Financial Times 17 February 2009) On 3 March 2009, Mr. Stephens wrote about Britain's "special relationship' with America in an article captioned "*The way to reset a once-special relationship.*" He concluded his writing with this remark: "If Britain wants to be heard in the White House, surely it must show it has real clout in Europe."

To begin with President Obama and his administration are not experts on European integration. For this reason, Britain's foreign policy on Europe should not be influenced by how President Obama and his Washington politicians view Jean Monnet's vision of a United States of Europe. Secondly, Britain does not need to have any "clout in Europe" to be heard in the White House. It is rather the White House that must consult "10 Downing Street" to gain a better understanding of Jean Monnet's fuzzy vision of a federal Europe. Unfortunately, 10 Downing Street has yet to learn what the "Prince of Scotland Yard" published about Europe and its future. I would urge American politicians in the Republican Party and the Democratic Party to do their 'homework' on the implication of the development of the European Union by examining the works of Sir Robert Anderson before they construct their foreign policy on Europe. They should ignore the significance of the Freedom Medal President Kennedy gave to Jean Monnet in 1963. They should also ignore the importance of the Grenville Clarke Prize Dr Henry Kissinger presented to Monnet in 1975.

The question is: would a Cameron Conservative Government have the political courage to withdraw the Lisbon Treaty from Rome, tear the crooked document into pieces to set Britons free from "bondage in Brussels? Britons are crying for strong leadership. They need a politician with conviction not a "calculating" politician. Britons want a selfless politician whose vision is based on reality - a politician who does not follow the whims of other politicians, a politician who listens to the voice of the masses and cares about their plight, a politician with guts to confront the "bullies" in Brussels and "slay" them with the "sword" of the Knight Commander (of the Order) of Bath. On Europe, Britain should not blindly follow the view of Washington politicians. American politicians, like their counterparts in Europe and Ireland, have only a superficial understanding of why the European Union evolved from the debris of the Second World War.

The "dictators" in Brussels (the "know-all-EU bureaucrats") are immune to public opinion. Like their "obstinate" father, Jean Monnet, they always want their way. When the Danes voted "No" to reject the Maastricht Treaty in 1992, they did not accept the verdict. They forced the Danes to vote again. When they voted "Yes" they accepted the verdict. In 2001 when the Irish rejected the Nice Treaty, they did not accept the verdict. They were forced to vote again. When the Irish voted "Yes" they accepted the verdict. In 2005 when the French and the Dutch rejected the original EU Constitution, which should have resulted in its demise, the despots in Brussels ignored the verdict. They repackaged the dumped Constitution and attempted to force it on the masses. Unprincipled politicians pushed the ratification of the Lisbon Treaty through their respective parliaments where they were guaranteed safe passages.

THE "EVIL" NATURE OF THE EUROPEAN UNION

Ireland, the only country bound by its constitution to give its citizens a say on the Lisbon Treaty, rejected it. Would the EU dictators burry the Lisbon Treaty? Certainly not! This was evident from the various comments made by some

European politicians. The political elites, including Gordon Brown, pledged to continue ratification of the Lisbon Treaty regardless of the Irish "No" vote. In the end the European leaders forced the Irish people to vote again. The only European leader who suggested the Lisbon Treaty was dead was the Czech President Vaclav Klaus. Nicolas Sarkozy decided to fly to Prague to influence the Czechs to endorse the Treaty to fulfil the 'vision' of his 'father' – Jean Monnet.

Let us examine some of the comments made by European leaders and politicians in response to Ireland's rejection of the European Constitution:

- Jean-Pierre Jouyet, French secretary of state for European affairs, said: "I don't think you can say the treaty of Lisbon is dead even if the ratification process will be delayed."
- German Foreign Minister, Frank-Walter Steinmeier, declared: "I am convinced that we need this treaty. Therefore we are sticking with our goal for it to come into force. The ratification process must continue." (*Reuters*, 14 June 2008).
- German Interior Minister, Wolfgang Schaeuble, joined the chorus: "Of course we have to take the Irish referendum seriously. But a few million Irish cannot decide on behalf of 495 million Europeans," *(Welle* 15 June 2008) [Question: "Did the 495 million Europeans have a say on that monstrous document?]
- Axel Schafer, SPD leader in the Bundestag, claimed: "We think it is a real cheek that the country that has benefited most from the EU should do this. There is no other Europe than this treaty. With all respect for the Irish vote, we cannot allow the huge majority of Europe to be duped by a minority of a minority." (*Irish Times* 14 June 2008) [The real "cheek" is arrogant politicians ignoring the democratic decision of the Irish and bullying them to revote on a document they had already rejected. A reminder: an Irishman predicted that Europe would be 'duped' by its powerful leader who is on the horizon. The Treaty of Lisbon, which is Europe's most precious document, would hasten the arrival of the King of Europe]
- Lopez Garrido, Spanish secretary of state for EU affairs, joined the bandwagon: "The treaty will be applied, albeit a few months late" *(Forbes 15 June)*
- Jose Manuel Barroso followed the sheep: "The Treaty is not dead. The Treaty is alive, and we will try to work to find a solution." (Press Conference 14 June 2008) [Question: "Is the "Buffoon of Brussels" aware that the EU is only alive in his sight, whereas, in reality, the EU is a "corpse"?]
- Giulio Tremonti, Italian finance minister, said: "Citizens are transmitting signals of fear and uncertainty. You can say it's not rational, but we

need to react because they are signs of difficulties with the democratic process." (*Financial Times* 16 June 2008). What is irrational is ignorant politicians imposing their shallow views on European integration on the people who pay for their lavish lifestyle.

- Italian President, Giorgio Napolitano, voiced his opinion: "Now is the time for a courageous choice by those who want coherent progress in building Europe, leaving out those who despite solemn signed pledges, threaten to block it." (*Irish Times*). The fact is the European Union is built on the "sand of deceit." The "coming hurricane" will blow it away.
- Belgian Prime Minister, Yves Leterme, commented: "In no case should the Union be stopped in its tracks. We need to examine the existing possibilities to assure in any case the entry into force of the Treaty and to associate Ireland with it.*"(AFP, 14 June 2008).* The fact is the European Union is in "its tracks" to ruin.
- Finnish Foreign Minister, Dr. Alexander Stubb, said: "The treaty is not dead. The EU is in constant crisis management. We go from one crisis to another and finally we find a solution**."** (*Deutsche Welle, 16 June2008*) I respond: "In the eyes of political elites the Lisbon Treaty is not dead. In reality, the EU is a "dead body." For the "EU Titanic" was doomed before its construction began on 9 May 1950.
- Polish Prime Minister, Donald Tusk, claimed: "We shall effectively look for ways to ensure it comes into force. Irrespective of the results of the referendum in Ireland, I think that we can deliver an optimistic message - Europe will find a way of implementing this treaty" *(BBC,* 13 June 2008***).*** Finding a way to implement the Lisbon Treaty is the rush to pave the way for the Irish Barrister's prediction of the dark future of Europe to come to pass.

In an interview with *Le Monde,* the former pompous President of the European Parliament, Hans-Gert Pottering, declared: "The Irish "no" cannot be the last word." Having conceded that there is an element of euroscepticism in Europe, the German stated: "I meet a lot of people, especially in Germany, and my impression is that they want a strong Europe, while rejecting a bureaucratic Europe...For my part, I think the ratification process must continue and I am delighted that the British Prime Minister Gordon Brown has announced his intention to see it to the end." I respond: Had Gordon Brown examined what his brilliant "father" wrote about political Europe and its future, he would not have signed the Lisbon Treaty.

On 16 June 2008, it was reported the President of the European Parliament made a "biased" remark about Ireland's decision to dump the Lisbon Treaty. He said he would appeal to the EU Summit which was held on 20 June 2008 to take all steps to push the treaty through. "Our goal remains the entry of the treaty into law by 2009," he said. When Gerrard Batten of UKIP responded to his remark, he was shut down. Mr Batten said: "When I tried to raise a point of order based on a Parliamentary rule that allowed me to reply, I was deliberately and blatantly refused the microphone to speak." The European Union is a political dictatorship - hostile to democratic principles.

According to Gordon Brown, the Irish needed "a short period of reflection" for them to "put forward their proposal" of how to re-vote to endorse a treaty they had rejected. William Hague, the Shadow Foreign Secretary, responded to Brown's comments: "Shouldn't this government show some true leadership in Europe and state plainly and sincerely that Britain will suspend ratification in this country immediately." The issue is: would William Hague and his Conservative Party show "true leadership" by allowing Britons to vote on the Lisbon Treaty whether the Irish had already rejected or ratified it before they form the next British Government?

Reacting to the arrogance of the EU leaders, and the dithering attitude of Gordon Brown towards the Irish veto against the Lisbon Treaty, Declan Ganley, a prominent Irish entrepreneur who spearheaded the campaign against the Lisbon Treaty, addressed the British people: "You cannot ratify this treaty. We have said "no" and, if you do, we are not going to take it lying down... This treaty is dead. The Irish people have exercised their veto. It cannot be ratified." Mr. Ganley also urged a referendum in Britain. The *Irish Times*, reporting on the issue, quoted Ganley as saying: "It appears that you (Britons) have a government that not only denies you a voice, but ignores the voice of my country." What an indictment on Gordon Brown's Labour Government that ignored the voice of the British people to have a say on a treaty that transfers powers from politicians they have elected to foreigners in Brussels who are not responsible to anyone.

The Czech President, Vaclav Klaus, responded to the aggressive behaviour of the French and German politicians towards the Irish with this comment: "The EU cannot ignore its own rules. The Lisbon Treaty has been roundly and democratically rejected by Ireland, and therefore cannot come into force. Any attempt to ignore this fact and make recourse to pressure and political manipulation to move the treaty forward would have disastrous consequences for Europe." (*El Pais* newspaper) Without any doubt, the European Union would experience "disastrous consequences" whether the Republic of Ireland adopts the Lisbon Treaty or dumps it again in its second referendum,

THE TYRANT OF ALL TYRANTS

Finally, Giscard d'Estaing told *Irish Times* that Ireland would not be allowed to kill the Lisbon Treaty. The French author of the European Constitution admitted that unlike his original constitution which was rejected by his own people, the Lisbon Treaty had been carefully drafted to confuse the public. "What was done in the Lisbon Treaty, and deliberately, was to mix everything up. If you look for the passages on institutions, they're in different places." An opinion poll in France newspaper *Liberation* indicated that 44 percent of the French people wanted Ireland to vote again. 26 percent wanted the ratification to proceed without Ireland. But a quarter wanted the Lisbon Treaty abandoned. Were the French and the Dutch forced to vote again when they dumped d'Estaing's European Constitution? Treat others as you would like to be treated. The haughty Giscard d'Estaing even went to the extent of suggesting that future referendums would be ignored whether they are held in Ireland or elsewhere. What an European dictatorship!

And another French man, Jean-Dominique Giuliani, Chairman of Robert Schuman Foundation in Paris, also dismissed the notion of referendum on EU issues. Arguing in favour of the Lisbon Treaty, he said: "There is no particular need for national referendums on European issues. Those who ask for referendums want to vote against the EU and their own government. Referendums are really populist procedures. People use them to answer different questions – not the actual referendum questions." Giuliani went on to pose silly questions: "Did Margaret Thatcher ask by referendum to be allowed to carry social reforms? Did Winston Churchill ask the English people to engage his country against Hitler? No. They all went to parliament, to have a debate and make the best decision. That is also what Sarkozy, Brown and Merkel did."

I respond. Firstly, the Chairman of Robert Schuman Foundation, should first examine the advice Schuman offered to Europeans concerning the survival of the European Project to know the fate of Europe. Secondly, if "people who ask for referendums want to vote against the EU and their own governments," don't they have the legitimate and democratic rights to do so? Why should selfish politicians force their shallow opinions on the people who feed them and drag them to board a "luxurious boat" which is about to sink? The fact is Margaret Thatcher, John Major, Tony Blair, Gordon Brown, Nicholas Sarkozy and Angela Merkel, together with all the politicians in Britain, Europe and Ireland are not properly informed of the significance of Jean Monnet's vision of a united (federal) Europe to deny their people a vote on a document that would consign them into 'slavery' in Brussels.

The fact is the Lisbon Treaty transfers more powers from sovereign nations to undemocratic institutions that are not accountable to any one. Politicians have no powers to transfer powers that don't belong to them to aliens without seeking authority from the people who finance their living. Politicians have become "dictators." They have vested interests in the European Project - to enrich themselves at the expense of the taxpayers. Had politicians examined what Sir Robert Anderson wrote about Jean Monnet's vision of a federal Europe, they would have had a different perspective of the European project.

On the Lisbon Treaty, *Open Europe's* Director, Lorraine Mullally, rightly argued that the Treaty "is bad news for Europe. It is a myth that the EU Lisbon Treaty will strengthen democracy in Europe." The reality is the Lisbon Treaty would pave the way for the "Seer of Dublin's" prediction of the gloomy future of Europe to be fulfilled. The Lisbon Treaty would welcome the tyrant of all tyrants. Europeans and the rest of the world would "worship" the charismatic King of Europe. But it would end in tears.

From the various 'hostile' comments made in response to Ireland's' rejection of the Lisbon Treaty, save the support of the Czech President, it is obvious the EU is not a democratic project. Most of the EU leaders have become 'despots' – 'enemies' of democracy. We should not be surprised by the authoritarian attitude of politicians. Prophecy must be fulfilled. European and British politicians, who have lost all concepts of what democracy means, have no shame in ignoring and bullying the very people who subsidise their living. They behave just like their 'obstinate father,' Jean Monnet. By their autocratic attitude, the EU leaders have confirmed the "vile" character of the European project as predicted by the "Seer of Dublin."

In his article, "*Ten reasons to get rid of the European Union,*" Fjordman commented on the European leaders' stance on the Irish. He stated: "The EU fails to consult its citizens and insults them when doing so. The Irish referendum in 2008 on the proposed EU Constitution (Lisbon Treaty) is a powerful testimony to the evil nature of the European Union. Before the referendum, a number of EU leaders made it perfectly clear that the Lisbon Treaty was virtually identical to the European Constitution which had been rejected by Dutch and French voters in 2005. Fjordman, by highlighting the "evil nature" of the European Union in his critique, confirmed the Irishman's prophetic description of political Europe - "the vile confederacy of the latter days."

At this point I would repeat the words the "Seer of Dublin" used to describe the character of political Europe which has been confirmed by EU's democratic deficit and the arrogance of European leaders who impose their views on the electorate:

- "Democracy, not despotism, is the goal towards which civilisation is tending. But democracy in its full development is one of the surest roads to despotism."
- "The true test of a man is not what he does, but what, with the principles he holds, he would do, and if this be true of individuals, it is still more intensely true of communities."
- "Opinions have taken the place of convictions, and the result is a liberality which is the offspring, not of humility and love, but of indifference or doubt. Opinions are our own, and should not be firmly held. ....The man who would force his opinions on others is a boor. He who would die for his opinions is a fool."

- "There is no element of cohesion in error. Among the children of error there is no bond of unity save such as depends on common hostility to truth." This is the "mirror" from which European leaders should see themselves.

THE IRISH AND THE AMERICANS AND THE EUROPEAN UNION

With his limited knowledge on European integration, John Brutton, the EU Ambassador to the United States of America, warned the Irish that their rejection of the Lisbon Treaty could inhibit US investment in Ireland by raising fears that Irish people were turning away from the European Union. According to the former Irish Prime Minister, Americans' reaction to the referendum result was overwhelmingly negative. He told Irish Times: "Americans I have met on both sides of the political aisle and in business and academic life are all baffled by the decision the Irish electorate took to reject the Lisbon Treaty, which was signed by the Irish Government on their behalf...Americans had come to assume that Ireland was completely committed to the European Union and that its Government was at the heart of European decision-making and that had created the climate in which Americans were more inclined to invest in Ireland because it was seen as being at the heart of the European Union." Mr. Brutton continued: "Now for the second time to reject an EU treaty which the Irish Government had agreed, Americans seem to see as somehow turning away from the European Union and they don't understand why that would be the case."

If Americans didn't understand why the Irish rejected the Lisbon Treaty, they should study what an Irishman published about European integration: how it would develop, its nature and future prospects before the European Union came into existence. The Irish, unconsciously, acted wisely by dumping the monstrous Treaty that turns the European Union into the government of Europe and would make Ireland a province of Europe with no control over their destiny. The brutal truth is that Ireland would make a momentous mistake if they ignore what the "Sage of Ulster" recorded about the bleak future of Europe and adopt the Lisbon Treaty.

According to Mr. Brutton, although it was a mistake to interpret the Irish referendum result as a rejection of the EU, such a view could take hold in US boardrooms unless "serious public diplomacy" is undertaken. He added: "Clearly, companies that have already invested in Ireland and are doing well there are not going to be influenced by this sort of thing because they have their own independent sources of information, but I would expect that companies that are looking at a number of countries for the first time might be influenced by it."

In Mr Brutton's view, there was a consensus of support for European integration across the American political spectrum. He stated: "The entire mainstream of political, strategic and economic thinking - both in the Republican Party and in the Democratic

Party - is strongly favourable to a strong European Union. It's only on the extreme fringes of one of the parties - and very much on the fringe - that one would find any other opinion. Americans I meet who would be very conservative, or very liberal, all agreed that the European Union is a good thing and that it's important for the stability of the United States and the stability of the world. So it would be a great mistake for people to think that any difficulty for the European Union is liable to be welcomed in the United States," (Source: John Brutton: sees a need for 'diplomacy' in US boardrooms DENIS STAUNTON in Washington)

To begin with: companies that invest in Ireland should be aware that the future of Europe is not bright, and therefore the future of Ireland cannot rest in the European Union whose future is dark. I would encourage Directors of American companies to undertake independent research about the future prospects of the European Union before getting excited about Jean Monnet's project. In this respect, I urge them to investigate what the brilliant Irish lawyer recorded about European confederacy and its future before Jean Monnet, the principal architect of the European Project, was even conceived in 1888.

DO AMERICAN POLITICIANS AND BUSINESSMEN UNDERSTAND THE SIGNIFICANCE OF EUROPEAN INTEGRATION?

The fact is businessmen and politicians in all the American Political Parties, who regard the European Union as a "good thing", have only a shallow understanding of European integration. Do American politicians know the prospect of "That Thing" in Brussels? Americans delude themselves by harbouring the impression that the European Union is a "good thing" that would contribute to the stability of America and the rest of world. Had Americans scrutinised the works of the "Sage of Ulster," they would have had a different perspective of the political union of European nations. As a result, they would have hailed Ireland's rejection of the Lisbon Treaty as the best thing to have happened in European and American politics.

The fact that most Americans have a favourable view of the European Union does not necessarily make the European Union a "viable business" worth investing in it. Which American would invest his Dollars in a company whose accounts have not been approved for 14 consecutive years because of fraud and financial irregularities, and whose managers are 'morose' and uncertain of the future prospects of the company? Would Financial Experts in Wall Street recommend such a "fraudulent company" to potential investors?

The Irish should ignore the views of those Americans who are in love with the European Union. They lack understanding of the implication of European integration. It is not always advisable and profitable to follow the view of the majority. For the "Seer of Dublin" writes: "Listening to the discordant voices that abound on every side, men are content to give heed only to the points on which the greater number appears to be agreed; and even these are held in sufferance till some new voice is raised to challenge them." Majority of American business men and politicians may have a favourable impression of the European phenomenon. That should not influence the British and the Irish to have a favourable view of European Union. Because, these Americans, just like their colleagues in Britain, Europe and Ireland, are not properly informed of the implications of the European Project.

KENNETH CLARKE ON PRESIDENT OBAMA'S POTENTIAL VIEWS ON BRITAIN'S RELATIONSHIP WITH THE EUROPEAN UNION

Let us examine the irrelevance of Kenneth Clarke's speech at Nottingham University, where he commented on the risk of US snubbing eurosceptic Conservative Government. According to Mr. Clarke, "Obama doesn't want his strongest European ally led by a rightwing nationalist, he wants them to be a key player inside Europe, and he'll start looking at whoever in Germany or France if we start being isolationist....I think the need to be working with Obama will influence my party on Europe...It is still firmly eurosceptic but it's now moderate, harmless euroscepticism. It's a bit silly sometimes, like which group do you join in the European Parliament, but full-blooded stuff like renegotiating the treaty of accession is as dead as dodo." Without any surprise, Caroline Flint, the then Europe Minister, praised Mr Clarke for "serving a warning" to David Cameron: "It's a straightforward test for David Cameron: give up your policy on Europe, as Ken Clarke says, or give up the special relationship," (Source: Financial Times 22 January 2009).

I respond. To begin with: Kenneth Clarke does not hold monopoly of scholarship on European integration. And the "lazy" Caroline Flint is not qualified to lecture Britons on European Union. When did these politicians become experts on European integration to impose their opinions on Monnet's project on Britons? Clarke and Flint have contributed nothing of substance to the European Debate save their infatuation with Jean Monnet's vision of a "federated Europe," and their propensity to munch the crumbs their masters in Brussels throw down. Secondly, Britain's so-called "Special Relationship" with the United States should not be maintained at the expense of Americans dragging Britons to board Jean Monnet's doomed Titanic. Britain's long-term relationship with the European Union should not be determined by President Obama's estimation of the European Project. Britain's future in Europe should be decided on what the prominent Victorian wrote about European integration and the warning the Prince of Detectives gave to Britain. Britain's relationship with the European Union should not be influenced by the views of the "Washington Trinity" – President Barack Obama, Vice President Joseph Biden and Secretary of State Hillary Clinton. These American politicians might not have liked what I have recorded. The fact is they are not experts on European integration. They have no idea why the European Union evolved from the wreckage of the Second World War.

PRESIDENT OBAMA AND TURKEY AND THE EUROPEAN UNION AND IRELAND

I do not know President Barack Obama's strategic views on the European Project save his support for Turkey's membership of Jean Monnet's project. At an EU-US Summit in Prague on 5 April 2009, President Obama told European leaders: "Moving forward towards Turkish membership in the EU would be an important signal of your (EU) commitment to this agenda and ensure that we continue to anchor Turkey firmly in Europe." His comments incurred the "wrath" of Sarkozy. According to the French President it was the business of EU member states to decide on Turkish entry. He stressed his opposition to Turkey's membership of the European Union by declaring on French Television: "I have always been opposed to this entry...I still am and I think I can say that the immense majority of member states shares the position of France...Turkey is a very great country, an ally of Europe, an ally of the United States. It will stay a privileged partner. My position hasn't changed and it won't change."

President Obama responded with a rebuke. Addressing the Turkish Parliament in Ankara, he reiterated his support for Turkey's membership of the European Union: "Let me be clear: the United States strongly supports Turkey's bid to become a member of the European Union", Obama stressed. "We speak not as members of the EU, but as close friends of Turkey and Europe... And Turkish membership would broaden and strengthen Europe's foundation once more."

Americans are also close friends of the Irish. There are about 40million Irish-Americans. If President Obama considered it necessary to support Turkey's membership of the European Union, why didn't he, as the world's leading democrat, deemed it necessary during the 2009 St Patrick's Day celebration at the White House to advise Brian Cowen, the Irish Prime Minister, and the European Union to respect the democratic decision of the Irish people in rejecting the Lisbon Treaty – a document that would transfer more powers from the Irish Parliament to Commissioners in Brussels who are not accountable to the Irish people? Having supported Turkey's membership of the European Union, would the American President and Leader of the Democratic Party also support the democratic decision of the people of Ireland? Would it be interference in the internal affairs of the Irish people?

OBAMA AND THE PRINCIPAL OF NATIONAL SOVEREIGNTY

In July 2009, President Obama visited Moscow to strike a deal on arms control with the Russian President Dmitry Medvedev. During his visit the American President spoke of "America's interest in an international system that advances cooperation while respecting the sovereignty of all nations." Obama added: "State sovereignty must be a cornerstone of international order. Just as all states should have the right to choose their leaders, states must have the right to boarders that are secure, and to their own foreign policies. That is true for Russia, just as it is true for the United States. Any system that cedes those rights will lead to anarchy." If Obama believes in "state sovereignty", while didn't he openly support Ireland's decision to reject the Lisbon Treaty – a document that would eventually turn Ireland, a sovereign nation, into a province of Europe without the Irish people having any control over their borders and foreign policies?

Nile Gardiner commented on President Obama's remarks on "state sovereignty" in his article *"Barack Obama should become a Eurosceptic."* According to Gardiner, Obama's comments on national sovereignty "were extraordinary" from "a president who is known as a strong supporter of supranational institutions...Not only did they (Obama's remarks) contradict his own administration's zealous willingness to cede sovereignty by treaty in key areas to international organisations such as the United Nations, but they directly went against the Obama team's rabid support for the idea of a federal Europe." Mr Gardiner continued: "Obama heads the most pro-European U.S administration in modern times, backing every single aspect of EU integration, including the Treaty of Lisbon, the European Security and Defence Policy, and the Common Foreign and Security Policy....If President Obama seriously believes the words he is uttering in lofty tones about the freedom of nation states to choose their own leaders and decide their own foreign policies, he should end his administration's support for Euro federalism, and instead back the principal of national sovereignty in Europe. The creation of a federal Europe is fundamentally undemocratic as well as a massive threat to the future of the Anglo-American Special relationship and the broader transatlantic alliance." The Political commentator concluded his analysis of Obama's speech with this significant statement: "President Obama should be encouraged to join the ranks of the Eurosceptics. There is no American national interest in backing the creation of a European superstate that will almost certainly oppose the United States on the world stage rather than work with it. Nor are U.S. interests served by a weakened alliance with her closet ally – stripped of key aspects of national sovereignty within a federal Europe. The sooner the Obama White House wakes up to this reality, and actually practices what it preaches, the better for both Britain and America."

GREAT BRITAIN AND THE "WASHINGTON TRINITY"

Would President Barack Obama and his Vice President Joe Biden and Secretary of State Hillary Clinton invest their hard earned Dollars in a company whose financial accounts have not been approved by its own auditors for 14 consecutive years due to financial irregularities? Would the "Washington Trinity" join a Board of Directors who are "morose" and "uncertain" of the future prospects of their business, and at the same time ignore the interest of its shareholders? Before the

European Union evolved from the ashes of World War II, the Prince of Detectives at Scotland Yard, whose voice echoed across the Pond, warned Britain would not be saved by joining a political alliance of European nations. The "Washington Trinity" and all Americans must reflect on the warning from the "Seer of Dublin."

According to a report by Denis Staunton, which was published in the Irish Times, Mrs Hillary Clinton, the US Secretary of State, claimed: "Deeper European political integration, including the enhanced EU foreign policy role envisages in the Lisbon Treaty, are in the United States national interest." In her view, "There would be advantages in having an interlocutor who represented decisions taken by the EU... We (the United States) want a strong Europe. We want a strong transatlantic alliance....Obama administration welcomes actions that strengthens Europe and relations among European nations, a commitment on the part of Europe to be a full participant and leader in a lot of ...global challenges." (Irish Times 20 March 2009). Does Mrs Clinton understand the implication of a "Strong Europe"? Does she know the "Strong Man" who will lead "Strong Europe"?

Because President Obama and his leading lieutenants – Vice President Joe Biden and Secretary of State Hillary Clinton - favour a politically integrated Europe, David Miliband, the Labour Foreign Secretary, seized on this to attack William Hague, the Shadow Foreign Secretary, for suggesting that a Conservative Government would give the British people the opportunity to vote on the "unreadable" Lisbon Treaty which the Labour Government forced it on Britons.

In his article *"Hague's EU policy would be suicidal for Britain,"* Miliband writes: "Mr Hague's political gamesmanship risks destroying our special relationship with the US. President Obama has said very clearly that, 'America has no better partner than Europe. Now is the time to join together, through constant co-operation, strong institutions, shared sacrifice and a global commitment to progress.' Secretary of State Clinton has looked to Europe for active partnership....If Britain moves itself to the margins of Europe I can draw no other conclusion from my work with the US administration than Britain's special relationship with the US will become a piece of historic nostalgia - dusty bunting hauled out to modern official occasions, not the lifeblood of our everyday diplomatic thinking." Miliband concludes his article: "His (William Hague's) current approach threatens a unique double whammy: bad for Europe and bad for Britain." (*Spectator* 9 May 2009)

Nile Gardiner, Director of the Margaret Thatcher Centre for Freedom at the Heritage Foundation in Washington, rightly described Miliband's article "bizarre" - a piece of writing which is "an example of political scaremongering at its worst, a poorly penned attempt to justify a failed European policy that is undermining Britain's position as a sovereign nation as well as her ability to act effectively as a world power."

With his hostile attack on Hague, and by suggesting four reasons why the Conservative Party's decision to impede the Lisbon Treaty would be a dangerous policy and suicidal for Britain, Miliband exposed his own ignorance about the significance of European integration. Had the Foreign Secretary done his homework on European integration, by studying what a brilliant British public servant wrote about Europe and its future, he would have learnt that Britain would rather commit a national suicide by committing her future to the European project. On the issue of Britain's special relationship with the United States, that should not be maintained at the expense of "selfish" and greedy British politicians blindly following the views of President Barack Obama, Vice President Joe Biden and Secretary of State Hillary Clinton. If the "Washington Trinity" are attracted to Jean Monnet's "luxurious Titanic" and would like to lead Americans to board the doomed boat, that should be their decision. Does Britain's special relationship with America imply that the British people should blindly follow Americans into a ditch?

Before the "Washington Trinity" guide Americans to board the "European Titanic," I would encourage them to investigate what the head of the Criminal Investigation Department at Scotland Yard recorded about a political union of European nations and its destiny before the European Union came into existence. The result of this investigation would help the Obama administration define America's relationship with the European Union, and to consider how many telephone lines President Obama and his administration would need to contact Europe. In the 19th century, clergymen in America and politicians in Washington respected the views of the Prince of Detectives. Would Americans, in the 21st century, ignore what Sir Robert Anderson published about the destiny of Europe and join the "European Titanic"?

THE EUROPEAN UNION FEARS ITS OWN PEOPLE

John Bolton, former United States Ambassador to the United Nations, rightly laid bare the autocratic character of the European project. In his article, Europe and the United States after Lisbon, Mr Bolton writes: "Pro-EU leaders in Europe are pushing headlong into nondemocratic—perhaps even antidemocratic—territory, and Americans are missing a very real threat to the transatlantic alliance....EU leaders will never construct an effective transnational Europe by consistently avoiding the judgment of the people. The leaders may not like what the voters think, and they may not obtain the kind of EU they really want, but continuing to thwart the people only builds up resentment and distrust that could frustrate their entire project." He continued: "They (The EU leaders) have actively snuffed out proposals to hold referendums and had to accept one in Ireland only because the constitution there unambiguously required it. Fear of popular voting indicates fear of the people, hardly a good sign for the EU project... Not only do EU leaders seek to prevent referendums, they sneer at the outcome when it goes "the wrong way." Fortunately or unfortunately, this should be the case to fulfil the Ulsterman's prophetic word about the character of an European confederacy that would evolve from an European crisis.

At the time of writing, the Lisbon Treaty has not been ratified by all the EU member-states to become legally binding. However, whether the Treaty of Lisbon is adopted or rejected, it would make no difference to the fate of the European Project. The European Union would continue to grow. Its leaders would eventually enthrone the last powerful Emperor of the revived Roman Empire - the brutal dictator who will deceive Europe and the world, and lead the European Empire to its fateful end as predicted by the "Seer of Dublin." Had the so-called EU "big four" - "Princess" Angela of Germany, "Prince" Nicolas of France, the 'saviour' Gordon of Britain and the 'Prince' of Brussels, Barroso, studied what the wise Irishman published regarding European integration and its destiny, they would have trembled at the sight of the Irish Flag. They would not have compelled the Irish to revote on the Lisbon Treaty, and neither would they have suggested that the ratification of the Lisbon Treaty should proceed.

In the light of the prophetic word delivered by the "Prophet of Linden Gardens" regarding the fate of Europe, Ireland and Great Britain would not be saved if they remain in the Union. The Irish must not yield to pressure and threats of 'Isolation in Europe' to adopt the Lisbon Treaty. Republic of Ireland and Great Britain must leave the 'abominable' European Project. For a "political tsunami" is destined to blow away Monnet's "magnificent Titanic" leaving no traces of the wreckage. This would surely happen at the appointed time.

If the "good manners" of the "sons" and "daughters" of the "Anglicanised-Irishman of Scotch extraction" influence them to ignore the advice of their "well-informed father" and remain on board Monnet's "lavish Titanic," they would regret their decision. I repeat: the 'unsinkable' Titanic of the 20th century started well on its maiden trip from Southampton to New York. Did it reach its destination safely? Did the passengers enjoy the trip? European Union - the biggest economic market in the world and the "rarest of all political phenomena in history - is the "Titanic" of the 21st century. The European Vessel - with its "luxurious Cargo" of European Flag, European Anthem, the Euro, European Central Bank, European Court of Justice, European Parliament, Common Agricultural and Fisheries Policies, Enlargement Policy and European Constitution (the Lisbon Treaty) - might have started well on its journey to the "Promised Land of Carbon-Free." The question is: would this "Colossal Titanic" reach its destination safely?" European leaders: Remember the maxim: "*Finis opus coronat.*" – The end crowns the work.

EU SUMMIT AFTER THE EU CRISIS DUE TO IRELAND'S REJECTION OF THE LISBON TREATY

An EU summit was held on 19 and 20 June 2008 to discuss the Irish 'problem' – the rejection of the Lisbon Treaty. According to reports, Nicolas Sarkozy blamed Peter Mandelson, the then European Union Trade Commissioner (who became Lord Mandelson in Gordon Brown's Labour Cabinet) for the fall of the Treaty in Ireland. At a press conference in Paris, according to the Evening Standard report, when the French President was asked if EU Commission President, Jose Manuel Barroso, was responsible for the Irish "No" vote, Nicolas Sarkozy, instead, took a swipe at Mandelson with this remark: "A child dies of starvation every 30 seconds and the Commissioner wanted to reduce European agriculture production by 21 percent during World Trade Organisation talks. This was counter productive." Mandelson deflected the attack: "Well, my shoulders are broad enough and my skin is thick to take this. I'm told that Mr Sarkozy has nothing against me personally."

It was claimed Peter Mandelson angered some Irish citizens during the Lisbon referendum campaign and that contributed to the rejection of the Treaty. For Mandelson's "treason," he incurred the 'wrath' of Sarkozy who was desperate for the Lisbon Treaty to be ratified by all EU countries during his EU Presidency. Sarkozy made the attack on Mandelson as EU leaders put pressure on Ireland to find a way to ratify the Treaty. Brian Cowen's government was given until October 2008 to develop plans for how to proceed with the 'stalemate' in Europe's march to glory. What a pity! How could Peter Mandelson, a "son" of a man of substance - the real genius who wrote about European integration and its future before Sarkozy's 'father,' Jean Monnet, the principal architect of the European Project, was born, - allow himself to be criticised by a "son" of Monnet who has no idea what the European Union is for?

A QUESTION FOR PRESIDENT SARKOZY

According to *Le Canard Enchaine*, Sarkozy was furious with the Irish following the "No" vote. They are "bloody fools", he told aides. "They have been stuffing their faces at Europe's expense for years and now they dump us in the s***." He also claimed issues that contributed to the rejection of the Treaty were concerns over euthanasia, abortion and the world trade talks. Sarkozy then signalled that the Irish would be forced to hold a second referendum. This was sheer arrogance cloaked in ignorance about the real purpose of the European Union and its destiny. Was President Sarkozy aware that an Irishman wrote about European Community before his 'father,' Jean Monnet, was conceived?

And the former Danish Foreign Minister, Uffe Ellemann-Jensen, also argued in

La Libre Belgique that, "Ireland should do the rest of Europe a favour and leave the EU." The truth is that Ireland - irrespective of what they have gained from their EU membership - does not need the European Union to survive. Had Irish and British politicians, in 1972, examined the 18th edition of their 'father's' classic work on European integration and its future prospects, they would not have joined the Common Market in 1973. It is not late for Ireland and Britain to leave the European Union. This would be an awkward decision for the Irish people to make. But the reality is Jean Monnet's *Titanic* is plunging into the sea bed. It was doomed before its construction began on 9 May 1950. The Irish must heed the warning of their "Forgotten father."

President Nicolas Sarkozy warned Ireland was jeopardising EU hopes of enlarging the Union to admit Croatia and, eventually, Turkey. He declared: "Without the Treaty of Lisbon there won't be any enlargement. You can't say no to reforms and yes to enlargement." This was a strange comment. How could a politician who was not keen on Turkey's membership of the European Union suggested that Ireland's rejection of the Lisbon Treaty would prevent Turkey and other European nations from joining the EU? This was disingenuous. President Sarkozy, temporarily became a "champion" for Turkey's membership of the European Union, of which the Irish became a stumbling block. I would ask the French President this question: "Who recorded Turkey's membership of a political union of European nations before Turkey first applied to join the European Community in 1963?

Sarkozy, later on, exposed his "double-standards" on Turkey's membership of the European Union. We have learnt how the French President rebuked the American President for urging the European Union to accept Turkey into their Club. President Sarkozy declared on French Television: "I have been working hand-in-hand with President Obama but when it comes to the European Union it is up to member states of the European Union to decide (on membership). I have always been opposed to this entry and I remain opposed." If Sarkozy has been opposing Turkey's entry into the European Union, why did the French president suggest that Turkey's membership of the European Union would be jeopardised without the Lisbon Treaty?

"POLITICAL COURAGE" OR "POLITICAL COWARDICE"

Courage confronts; it does not abscond

After the European leaders struggled to agree to a formal position on the issue of the ratification of the Lisbon Treaty, they honoured Gordon Brown for joining them in their plot to "bully" Ireland to adopt the corrupt Treaty. Sarkozy praised Brown - the "obstinate juror": "I want to thank you for demonstrating political courage by leading the ratification of the treaty." Was it really a "political courage" or "political cowardice"? A British Prime minister with no democratic mandate, signs away powers that don't belong to him to unelected and unaccountable commissioners who have no understanding of what they are doing in Brussels. How could it be a "political courage" for a British prime minister who refused the British people a vote on a document that would make them 'slaves' in Jean Monnet's "slave market" in Brussels?

If the 'super-hero' and 'magician' Gordon Brown - a man of 'Political courage'- actually believed the Lisbon Treaty was good for Britain, why didn't he have the political courage to allow Britons to make that decision for themselves? In 2004, Gordon Brown declared: "If we secure a treaty that is acceptable for Britain, then I believe we can also put it successfully to the British people." Why did he renegade on that promise and pushed the corrupt Treaty through Parliament? Gordon Brown hid behind the Labour Party's majority in the "House of Shame," and with the connivance of the unprincipled Liberal Democrats, forced the Treaty of Lisbon down the throats of Britons. This was not an exhibition of 'political courage' but a demonstration of 'political cowardice.' A man of courage confronts; he does not abscond. "The true test of a man is not what he does, but what, with the principles he holds, he would do..." writes Sir Robert Anderson, the courageous Prince of Detectives, a man of peace who never shirked a fight.

The fact is Gordon Brown was scared of losing a popular vote on the Lisbon Treaty. He, probably, had the impression that if the British people rejected the Treaty, it would undermine his position as a Prime Minister - the office he had laboured for. The question is: "When did Gordon Brown become an expert on European integration to dictate to Britons about the merits of the European Union? The simple truth is that Brown and his followers are not well-informed on the significance of Jean Monnet's project, and in particular the true implications of the Lisbon Treaty. In their ignorance, the selfish and greedy politicians ignored the cries of the multitude who lent them their power, and decided to crawl before "Prince" Nicholas of France, "Princess" Angela of Germany and the "Prince" of Brussels – Jose Manuel Barroso. What a pity!

THE FRENCH EU PRESIDENCY AND THE IRISH "PROBLEM"

On 1 July 2008, French President Nicolas Sarkozy took over the 6-months rotating Presidency of the European Union. Among Sarkozy's objectives were: a common EU immigration policy, a common European defence policy independent of NATO, a common European energy policy, the creation of a Mediterranean Union and the salvaging of the Lisbon Treaty.

Before France formally occupied the "hot-seat" in Europe to steer the European "Titanic" through the "turbulent waters", Financial Times described the President of France a "heckler" and "divisive." In an article entitled "Accusations and discord mark power handover" (FT July 2 2008), Tony Barber writes: "Disunity and recrimination marked the start of France's European Union presidency...as Nicolas Sarkozy exchanged accusations with the European Commission over world trade talks. The French president denounced Peter Mandelson, the EU Trade Commissioner...for allegedly selling out EU farmers."

In his address to the European Parliament in Strasbourg to mark the beginning of France's presidency, President Sarkozy told the assembly the possibility of multi-tier Europe - with the integrationists in the fast lane and the others in a slow lane. Sarkozy declared; "One day, unfortunately, we will have that multi-speed or multi-tier Europe. But it could only be a last resort. Let's think before we leave anyone behind" (Financial Times 11 July 2008). Outlining his vision for Europe, the French President attempted to undermine the integrity of Mr. Kaczynski, the Polish President. The Pole, initially, refused to sign the Lisbon Treaty because he considered it pointless due to its rejection in Ireland. Sarkozy claimed: "He (Kaczynski) negotiated the Lisbon Treaty. He gave his word. You must abide by your word. It's not a question of politics; it's a question of morals." The question is: "Was it morally sound for European leaders to enforce the Lisbon Treaty on their people – a document that would dictate how they conduct their lives? Was it an exhibition of democratic principle or a demonstration of political dictatorship?

In his attempt to justify his slur on the Polish president, President Sarkozy contended: "This is not blackmail. In Europe we don't blackmail, it's a question of consistency, honesty and logic. Everyone must be on board in the European Union. This is what the French Presidency will work for." This raises the question: If the French President's comments were not intended to blackmail President Kaczynski, what were they for? Is it logical for 27 European leaders, who have no idea what the European Union is for and have no clue where their project is heading towards, to decide the fate of almost 500 million people by forcing them to board a "luxurious boat" which is about to sink? Where was the "honesty" when the proud Valery Giscard d'Estaing boasted it was the rejected European Constitution that was repacked to fool the masses to prevent referendums? Has the EU got any credibility? This is a "Public Limited Company" whose accounts have not been sanctioned by its own Auditors for 14 successive years because of fraud and financial mismanagement. Under normal business practice the "EU PLC' should have been struck off and banned from "trading." However, the "EU PLC" is above European law. That is the concept of democracy in Europe.

On the issue of Ireland's rejection of the Lisbon Treaty, Sarkozy told the European Parliamentarians: "The problem is this. We need not to offend our Irish colleagues. But at the same time we need to know how and under what treaty we are going to be organising the European elections in 2009." He warned: "It is either Lisbon or Nice - there can be no more institutional conferences," saying Ireland's rejection must not lead to "some sort of institutional soap opera... There will not be any new treaty."

In order to apply maximum pressure on the Irish, Sarkozy wrongly claimed that future enlargement of the European Union was impossible without the Lisbon Treaty. He said: "No Lisbon, no enlargement." His suggestion was rejected by the European Commission and the UK Foreign Office, and the Czech Deputy Prime Minister Alexandr Vondra who said: "It simply is not true - the enlargement can go ahead even without the treaty. It's kind of a lie. It's not impossible. It's about the political will." The Polish President, Lech Kaczynski, added pressure on Ireland to vote again by calling Sarkozy on the phone and telling him that Poland would only ratify the Lisbon Treaty once Ireland has. German Chancellor Angela Merkel offered Nicolas Sarkozy her full support to push the Lisbon Treaty down the throats of the masses. To please his masters, Jose Manuel Barroso supported Sarkozy's stance on Ireland by saying: "We must make a collective effort to finish the process of ratification... Once the process is completed, we can talk with our Irish friends. If you want to go fast, go alone. If you want to go far, go together." Does Barroso, the political scientists, understand the purpose of the European Union? Does he know the fate of the world's first non imperial empire?

Alain Lamassoure, French Member of European Parliament and close advisor to Nicolas Sarkozy, insulted the intelligence of the Irish people by suggesting that Ireland was wrong to hold a referendum, which is "a tool for dictators." He also warned Ireland could spark a major crisis capable of splitting the EU if it cannot ratify the Lisbon Treaty. He rejected the idea that French pressure to ratify the Lisbon Treaty, despite the Irish "No" vote, was capable of splitting the Union. "It is not us that run the risk of splitting the Union," the French said. "If the other 26 ratify and Ireland is the only country not to ratify it is up to Ireland to say we are ready to split the Union, to kick off a huge crisis in the Union." This raises a legitimate question: did the European leaders of the 26 member states of the EU give their electorate the chance to vote on the Lisbon Treaty? No. They were terrified that the people who put them into power would reject the European Constitution to wreck their selfish ambitions.

THE FOUNDING FATHER OF EUROPEAN COMMUNITY HATED NATIONAL SOVEREIGNTY

It was obvious President Sarkozy and his "lieutenants" were desperate to fulfil the vision of their "patron"- Jean Monnet. For the "spiritual god-father" of the European Union hated the idea of national sovereignty. Monnet's vision was the surrendering of national sovereignties to centralized institutions that are not accountable to anyone. This is evident from his Memoirs. Witness Monnet's words: *"I have no doubt, for my part that a confederation will one day lead to a federation. But for the moment, is it possible to go further? I cannot say that it is. Meanwhile, the confederation would have the very great advantage of assuring public opinion in our countries that they have joined an entity which is not only economic but political and that they are therefore part of something bigger than any of their countries alone".* Monnet added: *"Europe of sovereign states was incapable of, despite its leaders' good-*

will, of reaching the sensible decisions that were needed for the common good. It would be quite another matter, however, once the power of decision was entrusted to institutions serving the general interest and applying the will of the majority in a system of common rules" (Source : Jean Monnet Memoirs 1978).

Let us now examine Monnet's closing statement in his Memoirs: *"But time is passing, and Europe is moving only slowly on the course to which she is so deeply committed.... We cannot stop ...the community we have created is not an end in itself...Like the provinces of the past, our nations must learn to live together under common rules and institutions freely arrived at. The sovereign nations of the past can no longer solve the problems of the present; they cannot ensure their own progress or control their own future. And the community itself is only a stage on the way to the organized world of tomorrow."* Sarkozy has been inspired by this vision to make sure of its fulfilment.

And Jose Manuel Barroso confirmed that Monnet's vision guides the European project. In an article for *TIME*, the president of European Commission stated: "Monnet's idea of European unity was seized upon by Robert Schuman and Konrad Adenauer....The power of Monnet's gradualist vision means that it still serves as a blueprint for European integration." It is time Barroso and his experts realised that Jean Monnet's vision of a united Europe was to fulfil the extraordinary vision of the Irish prophet – Sir Robert Anderson.

PRESIDENT SARKOZY'S FACT-FINDING MISSION TO IRELAND ON 21 JULY 2008

In his zeal to force the Lisbon Treaty on the Irish people so that the vision of his 'father' might be realised, the "faithful son" of Monnet went to Dublin on 21 July 2008 for a 'fact-finding-mission' – to establish why the Irish rejected the Lisbon Treaty. The so-called "fact-finding" mission was a subtle attempt to pressurise Brian Cowen to force the Irish to vote again. Even before his visit, President Sarkozy, determined to push ahead with his ambitious programme for deeper political integration, demanded that the Irish should vote again on the Lisbon Treaty. His outburst was greeted with fury in Ireland. It was considered "deeply insulting." Hundreds of protesters welcomed the French President with placards shouting: "No means No" to exhibit their anger at his remark that Ireland re-vote to reverse their "No" decision. However, Ireland's Europe Affairs Minister Dick Roche told Newstalk radio: "It is far, far too early to be talking about a referendum or about some specific policy to go forward."

In Dublin, the French president denied suggesting that the Irish must vote again on the Lisbon Treaty. According to Sarkozy, he "respected the outcome of the Irish referendum," but welcomed the fact that the ratification process was continuing in other member states and emphasized his commitment to the treaty. Sarkozy insisted the purpose of his visit to Ireland was to "listen and understand" the reasons Irish voters rejected the treaty. "To come to Ireland would be to meddle and not to come would be indifferent," Sarkozy announced at a news conference. "What would you, the Irish press do, rather meddling or indifference? We don't have a miracle solution that can be found at the wave of the wand...We want the Irish people to feel that their choice has been respected, has been listened to, but we also want people to realize that most of the EU member states have ratified the Lisbon Treaty." However, anti-treaty campaigners insisted that the European Union could not demand a second vote just because it did not like the result of the first one.

The truth is that had President Sarkozy respected Ireland's democratic decision on the Lisbon Treaty, his "fact-finding" mission to Ireland would not have been necessary. The case was simple. This Irish rejected the Lisbon Treaty in a popular vote. The French President had no business visiting Ireland, save his intention of finding ways to undermine the democratic decision of the Irish. There were rules that governed the ratification of the Treaty. All the 27 EU member states must approve it to become enforceable. The fact is Sarkozy and his EU partners 'disrespected' the Irish. Had the EU leaders respected their own rules, they would have abandoned the Lisbon Treaty the minute Ireland rejected the repackaged European Constitution.

Sarkozy and his "disciples" in Europe must realise that all their efforts to implement the Lisbon Treaty were to bring into fruition what the "Seer of Dublin" wrote about the preparation of the stage for the King of Europe to enter the political scene to lead Europe and the world to its destiny. Sir Robert Anderson recorded: "Through the gradual unfolding it may be, of influences; even now in operation; or far more probably as the outcome of some great European crisis in the future, this confederation of (European) nations shall be developed, *and thus the stage will be prepared on which shall appear that awful Being, the great leader of men in the eventful days which are to close the era of Gentile supremacy.*" (Emphasis mine). The Treaty of Lisbon is preparing the stage for the arrival of the "awful Being."

It would be appropriate, at this point, to borrow an extract from Leo Mckinstry's article "*Why Britain should stick up for Ireland against Euro bullies*" (Daily Express 24 July 2008). The columnist reiterated the fact that "the overwhelming Irish "No" vote should have sounded the death knell of the EU's Lisbon Treaty, which proposes to expand the power of Brussels at the expense of the member states." He added: "with their instinctive contempt for democracy, the EU's bosses ....decided to press on with the ratification of the treaty, brazenly ignoring the verdict of the Irish people. In any properly accountable political institution, a decision like that of Ireland would be respected. EU rules clearly stipulate that each treaty must be unanimously approved by the member states, so any objection from an individual nation should bring the ratification process to a halt. But the EU has never been a remotely accountable body. Gripped by its federalist ideology, controlled by a vast, unelected bureaucracy, it regards its own rules as expendable when they interfere with its project of creating a United States of Europe. In this profoundly undemocratic culture

it is the Irish, not the EU politicians, who are expected to change their minds."
The European leaders, by intimidating Ireland to change its decision on the Lisbon Treaty, demonstrated its lack of principles, and unconsciously confirmed the nature of their project as described by the Irish prophet. Dr Anderson described political Europe "the vile confederacy of the latter days" According to the Irishman, "The true test of a man is not what he does, but what, with the principles he holds, he would do, and if this be true of individuals, it is still more intensely true of communities." With their anti-democratic behaviour the European Union abandoned its own principles to confirm Sir Robert Anderson view of democracy. He recorded: "Democracy, not despotism is the goal towards which civilization is tending. But democracy in its full development is one of the surest roads to despotism."

EUROPEAN UNION MINI SUMMIT IN PARIS: 15-16 OCTOBER 2008

This summit was planned primarily to plot how Ireland would be forced to vote again on the Lisbon Treaty. However, it was dominated by the global financial crisis which the European Leaders could not foresee. The manner they approached the crisis, once again, exposed the EU as a divided Kingdom with mixed people. The 'rebellious' Irish kicked off the disunity by guaranteeing a scheme that would protect Ireland's major banks from collapsing. The British government and officials in Brussels were incensed by Ireland's unilateral action that put pressure on other EU countries to adopt the same tactics to prevent money flooding into Irish banks. On Saturday, October 4, 2008, President Sarkozy hosted a meeting of G8 leaders. He declared that co-ordination was paramount. "What is of essence is that Europe should exist and respond with one voice," said Sarkozy. But just after the meeting, German Chancellor Angela Merkel snubbed the talk of EU co-operation.

On Sunday, October 5, 2008, the German Government also took steps to guarantee all private bank deposits with German Banks. The Greeks followed to shore up their bank deposits. The Danes, the Italians and the Dutch joined. "Eschewing co-ordination," European countries opted for what The New York Times described as an "ugly disarray" of "self-interested policies to protect their citizens and banks first." (Source: THE AUSTRALIAN: "Europe still a tower of Babel, not one voice" October 2008)

EMPTY BOASTING

According to The Independent newspaper, Sarkozy told the EU summit: "For the first time in financial history, it is plans worked out in the EU which have inspired the measures taken in other countries of the world, including the US. Europe has shown leadership in dealing with the crisis and I welcome this." However, Sarkozy was reported to be 'furious' that the media portrayed the EU proposals as a British blueprint. Sarkozy had the opportunity to revenge. The French President was the politician who congratulated Gordon Brown for having the political courage to force the Lisbon Treaty down the throats of Britons. The same Sarkozy, who praised Gordon Brown's initiative to "save" the world from economic collapse, was the same man who attacked Gordon Brown on one of his schemes to save the British economy from ruin. Sarkozy, on French Television, criticised Gordon Brown's reduction of VAT from 17½% to 15% by saying it had "absolutely not worked." And that such a tiny reduction would not motivate Britons to spend more if "they are scared of their future." Sarkozy pointed out that France would not adopt Brown's economic tactics that would plunge Britain into further debt.

We must ask the questions: what right has Sarkozy to criticise the economic policy of British Government, save his misguided belief the French knows best about European integration? After all, did European leaders have the foresight to predict the financial crisis? Did they foresee the 'Financial storm' on the horizon, or they were taken by surprise? The reality is political leaders around the globe always react to circumstances. They are not in control of events. The Mother of all crisis - economic crisis, political crisis, energy crisis, security crisis and religious crisis - is about to engulf Europe and the world. No one can prevent the economic and political hurricanes which are on the horizon to terminate the powers of human governments.

THE RESULT OF THE SUMMIT

Due to the priority given to the financial crisis, European leaders decided to postpone any 'solution' to the 'Irish crisis' until the next EU summit in December 2008. However, pressure was further exerted on the Irish Prime Minister, Brian Cowen, to call for a second referendum. French Prime Minister, François Fillon, using the global financial crisis to justify the adoption of the Lisbon Treaty, cried out, "There is no doubt that the crisis shows how important it is for Europe to have a strong and stable presidency. The Treaty creates a stable presidency role and brings us closer to this goal. We need strong institutions that can react to events. It is up to the Irish to make up their minds on what role Europe can play in the economic crisis and draw the consequences from that." And Spanish centre-right MEP Íñigo Méndez de Vigo also attacked the Irish: "You're not going to stop us. We'll go ahead [with the Lisbon Treaty]. There are ways to do it. This is the history of the EU. If compromise is not possible, the others will go ahead. To me it is shocking that a government that held a referendum and failed is still in office. A government that puts a question to a referendum and loses has to resign: that's democracy." (Irish Times, Open Europe Blog 16 October 2008). Democracy also means the democratic decision of the Irish people to dump the Lisbon Treaty must be respected.

I repeat: the crisis of all crisis is about to dawn on Europe and mankind. The Lisbon Treaty has paved the way for the powerful leader of Europe to enter the political scene to 'solve' all the financial and political crisis, and then initiate the crisis of all crisis. The 2007-2009 global financial crisis that resulted in the collapse and nationalisation of financial institutions, liquidation of companies and the repossession of peoples' homes, as well as the Middle East crisis in December 2008 that resulted in the deaths of over 1000 people in Gaza were just signs of the "Tsunami Crisis" that is about to cause the havoc of all havocs on planet earth.

And here I will quote the words the "Seer of Dublin" borrowed from an article in the 1876 edition of The Times which could be attributed to the advent of the "strong man" who would enter the political scene to lead Europe: "What is that all Europe is looking for?" the "Seer" writes. "It is the King of Men; the great head of Hellenic race. The true King of Men must have an extraordinary combination of great qualities. He must be a scholar, a statesman, a man of unflinching courage and irrepressible enterprise, full of resources, and ready to look in the face of a rival or a foe. The opportunity too must synchronize with his advent. But the voice of prophecy is clear. The HOUR is coming, and the Man...a strange crisis marks his course.... The Coming Prince is presented as the head of the revived Roman Empire of the future." Let us remember, Jose Manuel Barroso, the President of European Commission, described the European Union the "first non imperial empire."

On the financial and economic crisis that caused anxiety among men, let us observe what the Lord Jesus Christ revealed to Apostle John over 2000 years ago: *"Woe! Woe! O great city, O Babylon, city of power! In one hour your doom has come! The merchants of the earth will weep and mourn over her because no-one buys their cargoes any more---cargoes of gold, silver, precious stones and pearls; fine linen, purple, silk and scarlet cloth; every sort of citron wood, and articles of every kind of ivory, costly wood, bronze, iron and marble; cargoes of cinnamon and spice, of incense, myrrh and frankincense, of wine and olive oil, fine flour, and wheat; cattle and sheep; horses and carriages; and bodies and souls of men." They will say, "The fruit you longed for is gone from you. All your riches and splendour have vanished, never to be recovered. The merchants who sold these things and gained their wealth from her will stand far off, terrified at her torment. They will weep and mourn and cry out: "Woe! Woe. O great city, dressed in fine linen, purple and scarlet, and glittering with gold, precious stones and purple! In one hour such great wealth has been brought to ruin...Woe! Woe, O great city, where all who had ships on the sea became rich through her wealth! In one hour she has been brought to ruin...."* (Revelation 18:10-19) At the appointed time the economies of all nations would collapse never to be restored. This would surely happen. We have just seen the sign.

EU SUMMIT: 11-12 DECEMBER 2008

Before the EU Summit which was held in December 2008, the Irish Prime Minister Brian Cowen, assured his European counterparts he would present a plan on how his government will settle the Lisbon issue. The fateful day arrived on 12

December 2008 for the European leaders to decide the fate of Ireland's relationship with the Lisbon Treaty. At the end of a two day summit that ended France's EU Presidency, the European leaders forced the Irish to ratify the Treaty before the end of 2009 so that the Treaty of Lisbon could be in force by 2010. Brian Cowen, cowed by pressure, eventually bowed to call another referendum on a document his people had already rejected. **According to the Irish Prime Minister, he won a series of concessions for the Irish people that merited another vote on the Treaty. One of the major concessions was that Ireland could maintain its Commissioner if the Irish people adopted the Lisbon Treaty.** Other concessions were Ireland's ability to set its own policies on taxation and on other social and ethical issues, such as abortion. Ireland would also be guaranteed of its military neutrality.

At the end of the summit, Brian Cowen agreed in principle to hold a second referendum on the Lisbon Treaty sometime in October 2009 provided all the guarantees given to Ireland would be legally binding. He stated: "The change in the commission arrangements so that Ireland keeps its commissioner is hugely significant….on the basis of the agreement….and on condition of our being able to satisfactorily put guarantees in place, I have said I would be prepared to return to the public….to seek their approval of it." He added: "I made it clear that a satisfactory response to the concerns of the Irish people is essential. On the basis of what we have agreed ….I am confident that we are on the right track….I'd like to emphasis that this is a national issue of huge importance to Ireland, clearly over and above party politics" (*The Irish Times* 13 December 2008).

Brian Cowen received "applause" from President Sarkozy for being "brave" to succumb to pressure to force his people to vote again on the Lisbon Treaty. Was it bravery or cowardice? Had Brian Cowen studied what his "Forgotten father" published on European Union; its nature and future prospects before Sarkozy's "father" – Jean Monnet – was conceived, he would have snubbed the summit in Brussels and withdrawn Ireland from the European Union. "Knowledge is power; ignorance is weakness", says Mr. Cowen's brilliant "father." Because of lack of knowledge on the significance of the European project, the Irish Prime Minister had to crawl before the "children" of Jean Monnet and Konrad Adenauer. What a pity! The "son" of a man of substance, who had an extraordinary vision of political Europe and its destiny, seeking favours from the "blind children" of Monnet and Adenauer who have no clue what the European project is for. I would remind the Irish Prime Minister, it was written of his "father'" - the scholar from Trinity College who, in the 19th century, wrote about European integration and its destiny - that "His views are worthy of the utmost respect and consideration…. and the well being of Ireland was to him a matter standing above politics in the ordinary sense."

SARKOZY'S "SUCCESSES"

President Sarkozy's EU Presidency was described as a "success" for forcing Ireland to vote on a document they had rejected in a popular vote, and for taking "the initiative during the conflict between Russia and Georgia (flying to Moscow without invitation) to broker a ceasefire. The French President ended his European presidency with this word to the European Parliament: "I tried to change Europe, but Europe changed me." (Financial Times 21 December 2008)

Launching his party's campaign for the 2009 European Elections in France, President Sarkozy once again boasted of his achievements during France's EU Presidency. This was revealed in an article, *"Sarkozy seeks to covert eurosceptics,"* which was published in the 6 May 2009 edition of the Financial Times. Sarkozy outlined his accomplishments: "If Georgia was not wiped off the map, if we got a ceasefire in Gaza and if Europe did not succumb to 'every man for himself' when the banking system threatened to go into melt down, it is because France took up its responsibilities when it had the EU presidency." According to the report, Sarkozy "sought to overcome his country's divisions over the merits of the European Union." He told the French who were losing interest in Jean Monnet's project: "We have to make the choice to be the plaything of events or actors in our own country. France cannot succeed without Europe."

RESPONSES TO THE DEAL THAT FORCED IRELAND TO VOTE AGAIN ON THE LISBON TREATY

European leaders' hostile attitude towards Ireland's rejection of the Lisbon Treaty prompted Declan Ganley, Chairman of Libertas, to rebuke the arrogant politicians with this remark: "The Irish government and the powerful elite in Brussels are showing utter contempt for the democratic decision of the Irish people in rejecting the Lisbon Treaty. Not one sentence will change in a new version. Some non-legally binding texts will be added in an attempt to fool the people. They tried this with the French, they tried with the Dutch, and they are trying with the Irish. It's time to put a stop to this bullying."

On BBC 2 Newsnight programme aired on 11 December 2008, Kirsty Wark interviewed Mr. Ganley on the European Union's decision to force the Irish to rerun their referendum vote on the Lisbon Treaty, and what his political party, Libertas, hopes to achieve. Mr. Ganley made this statement: "This elite in Brussels is so detached it cannot take no for answer……This Brussels as we have today has no ears to listen to the people." He ended the interview with this significant word: "If it (the European Union) is not democratic, it is not going to work, it is going to fail."

Mr. Ganley would be pleased to know it was his "Forgotten Father" who wrote about European Union, its nature and destiny before the French founding fathers of European Community, Jean Monnet and Robert Schuman, were even conceived. After describing political Europe "the vile confederacy of the latter days." Sir Robert Anderson warned of the gloomy future of Europe. The Lisbon Treaty, which the Irish rejected, is the "key" that would open the door for his prediction of the depressing future of Europe to be fulfilled. So, in view of what the "Seer of Dublin" recorded about European Union in the 19th century before the so-called "political phenomenon" and the "Quiet Miracle" manifested in the 20th century, what would Ganley and his Libertas Party do? Would they ignore the warning of their "father" and follow Jean Monnet's vision of a federal Europe? It was written of Mr Ganley's "father": "His views are worthy of the utmost respect and consideration ...and the well-being of Ireland was to him a matter standing above politics in the ordinary sense."

THE REACTION TO THE "BULLYING" OF THE IRISH

- William Hague, Shadow Foreign Secretary, attacked Gordon Brown in his part for putting pressure on Ireland to vote again. He said: "Trying to force the Lisbon Treaty down the Irish people's throats again is not only a dangerous distraction from what really matters, the economy, climate change and energy. It is profoundly undemocratic."
- Mary Lou MacDonald, a Member of the European Parliament for Dublin and Sinn Fein's national chairperson, reacted to the deal brokered in Brussels with this remark: "On 12 June 2008, almost one million people rejected the Lisbon Treaty with a turnout that was higher than in the second Nice referendum. Opinion poll after opinion poll ... demonstrated that people were deeply concerned with key aspects of the treaty. Issues of democracy, neutrality, public services, workers' rights, tax, sovereignty and international trade were at the heart of the "No" vote... Ratifying the Lisbon Treaty would give away Ireland's automatic right to a commissioner and not dealt with the more fundamental issues."

Ms MacDonald continued: "The broader issue of the EU's democratic deficit, its erosion of workers' rights and public services, its emerging foreign and defence policy agendas, and its promotion of free trade over fair trade will not be addressed. The high-handed and arrogant approach of the Government.... shows a complete lack of respect for the democratic will of the people. Re-running the referendum on the Lisbon Treaty would be a denial of democracy. It is no different to a defeated government re-running a general election in the hope that the voters would change their mind." (*Irish Times* 22 December 2008) The "daughter" of the "Seer of Dublin" unconsciously echoed what her brilliant "father" recorded about "democracy" and the "vile" character of the European Union.

- Doug Bandow, Senior Fellow at Cato Institute and former Special Assistant to President Reagan, also commented on the lack of respect European leaders showed to the democratic decision of the Irish in rejecting the Lisbon Treaty. In his incisive article, *Sarko's Folly,* he writes: "When the issue is consolidating power in Brussels, the European Union never gives up.....The most striking feature about the controversy over the treaty is not whether it deserves ratification. Lisbon offers a complicated restructuring of the EU that concentrates more power in Brussels. The decision is for the Europeans to make, based on their assessment of the proper role for continental government. Most extraordinary is the effort being waged to ensure that the common people who pay the bills have virtually no say in the form of government under which they live. Nations and governments typically rely on referenda to ratify constitutions. But not in the European Union......It's a sad day for democracy when Europe's politicians gang up on their citizens, rather than trying to win over their trust." (Source: *The National Interest* 24 December 2008)

Prior to the summit at Brussels, Patricia Mckenna, Chairperson of *People Movement* - the group that campaigned against the Lisbon Treaty in Ireland - commented on the strategy to fool the Irish people to vote again on the Lisbon Treaty. She made this significant statement: "Declarations on tax, abortion and neutrality are a devious ploy designed to dupe Irish voters into believing that our government have somehow obtained concessions from other EU states on the Lisbon Treaty..... Declarations, unlike protocols are not a legal part of a treaty and thus holding a second referendum on Lisbon will in legal terms mean voting on the exact same treaty rejected by the voters in June. She continued: "The government parties, supported by the main opposition parties, are displaying utter contempt for the decision of the voters..... Plans to hold a second referendum without any changes to the Lisbon Treaty are an affront to the democratic process.... It is patently clear that the purpose of any second referendum will be to reverse the result of the first vote without the substantive issues of concern being addressed. She concluded: "The most democratic course of action would be to consult all the peoples of the EU to see what kind of EU people really want but the political establishment both here and in Brussels fear the voice of their voters."

- Frank Keoghan, Secretary of *People Movement*, also expressed his concern over the double standards at the core of the EU Project. He stated: "When the people of France and the Netherlands voted to reject the EU Constitution, their governments requested that ratification should stop because of the unanimity requirement for treaties to come into force. But the Irish government chose to ignore the democratic decision of

> the Irish people and began conniving with other EU leaders in order to find a way of circumventing the referendum result." After delivering a letter to President Sarkozy, the Secretary declared: "This process has culminated in the Taoiseach (the Irish Prime Minister) travelling to Brussels....to be told by EU leaders how to solve the 'Irish question.' It is plain, that irrespective of the rules of the EU, there is one rule for the big member states (the "toes of iron") and another for the smaller ones (the "toes of clay") and that all the EU leaders are now guilty of corrupting democracy in an increasing post-democratic era for the European Union."

The "corrupting of democracy" in the European Union should not surprise the Irish. For the "Prophet of Ireland" wrote about how democracy, the goal towards which civilisation is tending, tends to become one of the surest roads to despotism."

THE EUROPEAN UNION SUMMIT IN BRUSSELS 18 – 19 JUNE 2009
The Irish to revote in October 2009 on the same Lisbon Treaty they rejected in June 2008

After a two-day summit in Brussels which ended on 19 June 2009, Republic of Ireland was granted legal assurance that the Treaty of Lisbon, if ratified by the Irish in another referendum, would not undermine Irish policies on tax, abortion and military neutrality.. Satisfied with the so-called 'legal guarantees," Brian Cowen declared: "I feel we will be in a position to hold a second referendum at the start of October....I am confident that we now have a solid basis to go to the Irish people and ask them to ratify the Treaty so that Europe can move forward." Cowen claimed that the initial rejection of the Treaty of Lisbon created "considerable doubt in the minds of business people at home and abroad about the Irish people's commitment to Europe. That doubt is the last thing we need at a time when, more than ever, we want to protect and sustain jobs."

The reality is, Cowen's intention was to exploit the economic crisis in Ireland to instil fear into the Irish that the European Union would abandon them to sink into economic abyss if they abandon the Treaty of Lisbon – the Constitution of Europe. This was evident from Cowen's comments which were reported in the Irish Times. He claimed, "it would be politically naïve to assume that there would be no "political consequences or effect" to a 'No' vote in the second referendum..... it's time we had a debate about the sort of Ireland we want in Europe, not the sort of Europe we feel best suits Ireland....Ireland could not survive the current economic crisis without our membership of the euro zone and the availability of resources from the European Central Bank. That is a fact over the last 12 months." I repeat: had the

Irish Premier studied what his brilliant "father" recorded about political Europe and its future, he would have leant that Ireland's future does not lie in Europe. He would have had the courage to confront the bullies in Europe, tear the Lisbon Treaty into pieces and campaigned vigorously for Ireland's withdrawal from the European Union. Cowen's "father" - the Lawyer with Sanctified Logic- wrote: "Knowledge is power; ignorance is weakness." Because of Cowen's ignorance about the true significance of the European Project, the Irish Premier was frightened to confront the "bullies" in Brussels that the Irish had already rejected the Lisbon Treaty and that was the end of the issue.

Commenting on the Brussels' summit, *Open Europe* stated; "what actually happened at the summit was that "EU leaders agreed to attach a series of 'declarations' as a protocol to the Treaty after the second Irish referendum once it is already in force, but the text of the conclusions of the summit notes that: "The Protocol will clarify but not change either the content or the application of the Treaty of Lisbon."

The Czech Prime Minister Jan Fischer confirmed it: "It is an explanatory clarifying text which changes neither a dot nor comma of the Lisbon Treaty." And Patricia Mckenna, former Green MEP, responded that the 'legal guarantees' given to Ireland were nothing more than a "ludicrous charade" and that the public had been given the false impression of legal certainty when this didn't exist. This was because the treaty had not changed "one iota" and would be interpreted by the European Court of Justice." (*Irish Times* 22 June 2009).

And the Socialist MEP Joe Higgins also repeated at a press conference that the EU summit was an "elaborate charade" meant to distract attention from the key issues. He stated: "The debate on the Lisbon Treaty has yet to be held because we've been dealing with side issues....The reasons why people voted 'No' to the treaty have not been addressed or rectified, and for that reason, once that message gets across to people, I don't think they are going to change their vote." (Irish Times 20 June 2009).

Aengus O Snodaigh, Sinn Fein spokesman on European affairs, summed up the "treachery' at Brussels. In his article, *"Clarified Lisbon Treaty the very same."* he writes: "But have we any changes to the text of the Lisbon Treaty itself? Will any aspect of the treaty's implementation in Ireland or across the EU be altered? Have the substantial concerns of the electorate on issues such as Ireland's loss of influence, militarisation and neutrality, workers' rights and public services, international trade deals, nuclear power and the developing world been addressed? The straight answer to all of these questions is "No." He goes on: "Brush aside all the meaningless rhetoric about legally binding guarantees – the decision of the heads of state, agreed last Friday, is nothing more than a series of clarifications of some aspects of the Lisbon Treaty. It does not alter the text of the treaty in any way. Nor

does it change the impact that the treaty will have on Ireland. So when we come to vote on the Lisbon Treaty in October (2009) we will be voting on exactly the same treaty, with exactly the same consequences for Ireland and the EU, as we did on June 12th, 2008. (Irish Times 25 June 2009)
Finally, I will urge the reader to reflect on these extracts from Bruce Arnold's perceptive article *Government has abandoned democracy to get a 'Yes' vote:* He writes; "Micheal Martin and Brian Cowen returned from the EU meeting ...on 19 June with a terrible mess of potage. They will try to sell this mess to the Irish people .... and it will inevitably involve further misrepresentation of the facts...The EU meeting they attended was designed to involve Europe in an entirely domestic Irish issue: that of Ireland deciding on its future in Europe. The EU should not be so involved; it is not its decision, it is ours. Yet Europe, at the top of its totalitarian structure, is up to its neck in such involvement, already committing huge sums of money to pervert democracy in the one country among 27 that can hold back this surge, this tidal wave of pernicious autocracy."

Mr Arnold goes on: "The legal guarantees are worthless and do not change the treaty. However, they had the desired effect. A number of foolish and misguided public figures, respected for talk shows on television, selling groceries, writing poetry, went public and said they would vote 'Yes'..... There is growing government determination to run the referendum campaign with huge, illegal support from the EU, preventing people from knowing what is in the treaty and what it means. ......We have to decide, for ourselves and for other benighted member states who have been denied any process of deciding these questions democratically, whether we want to create a super-power and ever afterwards to be subservient to it.

Bruce Arnold then reminds the Irish people and cautions them: "After 800 years of servile possession by outside powers, we are surrendering to a new servility and a new constitutional overlordship. Our citizenship would be secondary to European citizenship. The rights and duties would change. It would amount to a constitutional revolution throughout the EU and all its member states. We would lose power. Large member states - Germany, France, Italy and Britain - would gain hugely. Our voting strength in Europe would go below 1pc of the total European vote. We would not "choose", only "suggest" our commissioner... Any improvement in the EU parliament's power would be at the loss of power to the Dail...." (*The Irish Independent* 27 June 2009)

And *Open Europe* confirmed Bruce Arnold's remarks: "Despite promises from the Irish government that they would not force people to vote on exactly the same text a second time around, the deal reached at the EU summit... makes no change whatsoever to the text of the Treaty, meaning Irish voters will be voting on exactly the same text they rejected last year."

In England, Gordon Brown and David Cameron - who were playing "hide and seek" politics with the destiny of Britain - clashed in the British "House of Shame" over the 'clarifications' given to Ireland on the Lisbon Treaty. Brown also stressed that the 'guarantees' given to Ireland would "clarify but not change" the Lisbon Treaty, and that the new protocol would in no way alter the relationship between the EU and member states. Brown, the "obstinate juror", said: "To be absolutely clear, the Heads of State or Government have declared: the Protocol will in no way alter the relationship between the EU and its Member States. The sole purpose of the Protocol will be to give full Treaty status to the clarifications set out in the decision to meet the concerns of the Irish people. The Protocol will clarify but not change either the content or the application of the Treaty of Lisbon".

Brown added, "They have received their clarifications. It will be set out in a protocol. It will come to all Houses of Parliament, at the next accession treaty, when that has to be confirmed by these Houses of Parliament." Cameron responded, "Why are Irish voters being forced to give their views twice when the British people haven't been asked for their views once?" The fact is Gordon Brown and his selfish politicians in the "House of Sleaze" were not interested in the interest of the British people who feed them.

The influential Wall Street Journal also commented on the pressure Brussels put on the Irish to revote on the Lisbon Treaty. According to its editorial: "In some countries they rig votes, in the European Union they repeat votes to get the desired result.... To justify a revote, EU leaders put on a big show at last week's summit, giving the impression of tough negotiations in which Dublin supposedly won important concessions...Oh really? According to the EU summit's own conclusions, the protocol 'will clarify but not change either the content or the application of the Treaty of Lisbon.' So the Irish will vote on the same text they previously rejected by a seven-percentage-point margin despite assurances by their government as recently as last month that this would not happen."

And Adrian Michaels in the *Telegraph* writes, "If democracy is about listening to the people, then Iran isn't the only place where things have got a bit strained. A year ago, 53 per cent of Irish voters declined to ratify the substantial increase of the European Union's powers... Yet in early October (2009), the country will be holding another referendum, in which the people will be given a chance to come up with a better answer. (Source: *Open Europe*)

Open Europe, in collaboration with the Institute for Free Enterprise in Berlin, published a poll which showed that 77 percent of Germans want to be given a say on the Lisbon Treaty in a national referendum. Commenting on this poll, Open Europe Director Lorraine Mullally stated: "This poll clearly shows that it is not only the Irish who want to be consulted on the Lisbon Treaty. This Treaty transfers significant powers from the national to the EU level, and German voters want to be given a say." "Politicians claim they want to see more debate about the EU at national level, and yet they have conspired to deny voters a say on the Lisbon Treaty. Research shows that referendums on European issues significantly improve the public's interest in and knowledge of the EU - so referendums should be encouraged, not avoided at all costs." And "If politicians want people to connect with the EU, they should give them a say on the big issues like Treaty change. The public are crying out to be consulted - it is time to stop pretending that politicians know best, and inject some democracy into EU politics."

We must now ask the questions:

1. Why does the European Union ignore the democratic decisions of its citizens?
2. Why did European leaders prevent the citizens of 26 EU Member States from expressing their views on the Lisbon Treaty?

The answers are simple.

- Firstly, to bring to pass what the "Seer of Dublin", Sir Robert Anderson, wrote about the character of political Europe. He described it "the vile confederacy of the latter days."
- And secondly, so that the Lisbon Treaty would pave the way for the Irish "Prophet's prediction of the future of Europe to be fulfilled.

I would emphasise: no one can reform the European Union. The "luxurious EU Titanic" was destined to sink beneath the ways even before its principal architect, Jean Monnet, was born. So, Europeans should not be surprised when the former German Foreign Minister Joschka Fischer criticised the judgement of the German Constitutional Court by saying: "Europe will, despite numerous setbacks and crises, continue to progress as an alliance of states in a state of integration, whether Karlsruhe likes it or not".(Source: Open Europe *Die Zeit*)

THE IRISH MUST NOT PANIC. THEY MUST IGNORE THREATS OF "ISOLATION" AND BECOMING "SECOND CLASS" CITIZENS IN THE EUROPEAN EMPIRE AND REJECT THE LISBON TREATY

According to Charlie McCreevy, Ireland's EU commissioner, the Irish people had had a period of time to reflect about the Lisbon Treaty, and in his "humble opinion the ordinary people of Ireland know a damn sight more about the intricacies of the European framework than nearly all the members of the other 27 states." The former Irish finance minister defended the holding of referendums in Ireland by saying, "We might not like the result on occasion...but that's democracy and we should not be ashamed of it." (Source: The Irish Times 27 June 2009 *EU leader's attitude to No vote realistic* by Harry Mc Gee).

Indeed, the Irish must not be ashamed for rejecting the Lisbon Treaty in June 2008. They acted wisely – unconsciously acting on the warning their "father" gave to England about the danger of participating in a political alliance of European nations. The Irish must, therefore, ignore the threat from the senior German Socialist MEP Jo Leinen, that Ireland risks being relegated to a "second class" nation if it again rejects the Lisbon Treaty in another referendum. According to this "son" of Konrad Adenauer, "If there is a 'No' vote in Ireland I think we are likely to see a two-speed Europe emerge, with Ireland being in what might be called the 'second class'. Those in 'first class' will forge ahead in policy areas such as foreign affairs, justice and energy while the Irish will fall back." He added, the Irish people "have to ask themselves if they want to be isolated from the rest of the EU or to be integrated into the EU" and that the Irish must vote 'Yes' if they wish to continue to benefit from the "protective umbrella" that the EU provides." This was just bullying.

Why should this German politician, who has no understanding of the real significance of the European project and its destiny, dictate to the Irish to adopt the crooked Lisbon Treaty? Had the German Jo Leinen examined what the Irish graduate from Trinity College published about political Europe and its future when the first German Chancellor Konrad Adenauer was only six years, he would have trembled and dared not warned Ireland of becoming "isolated" in the "second class" cabin of Jean Monnet's "European Titanic" which is heading towards an "iceberg."

The people of Ireland must not panic. They should rather reflect on the warning their "father" - Sir Robert Anderson - recorded concerning the destiny of Europe and reject the Lisbon Treaty - a legal document that would turn an independent and sovereign Ireland into a province of a federal Europe ruled by strangers. Before European Union was born in the 20th centry, Sir Robert Anderson warned in the 19th century, that England would become a "province" of Europe if it joined a confederation of European nations which would evolve from an European crisis. I repeat what was written of the "Sage of Ulster": *"His views are worthy of the utmost respect and consideration....The well-being of Ireland was to him a matter standing above politics in the ordinary sense."* Jean Monnet, the French hero and the "god" of Europe, would not have qualified to polish the boots of the "Irish Giant."

From what we have leant about the hostile attitude European leaders exhibited towards the democratic will of the Irish electorate, and coupled with their tendency to muzzle the masses from expressing their views of the direction of the European Project, it is clear, the EU is a Dictatorship – hostile to democracy. This was evident from the comments the former German Foreign Minister Joschka Fischer made in response to the judgement the German Constitutional Court made on the Lisbon Treaty that delayed the ratification of the Treaty in Germany. The pompous Fischer said: "Europe will, despite numerous setbacks and crises, continue to progress as an alliance of states in a state of integration, whether Karlsruhe likes it or not". Was it not sheer arrogance and contempt for the rule of law?

It is clear:
The EU is Extremely Useful to the Political Elites who Manage it.
The EU is Extremely Useless to the People who Subsidise it.

The mind-set of those who control the "European Project" confirms what the "Seer of Dublin" wrote about the character of political Europe and "democracy." On Democracy, Dr Anderson penned these words: "Democracy, not despotism is the goal towards which civilisation is tending. But democracy in its full development is one of the surest roads to despotism. First, the revolution; then the plebiscite; then the despot." On the character of Europe, the "Seer" described it "the vile confederacy of the latter days."

ARROGANT EUROPEAN POLITICIANS HAVE NO SHAME

The awkward truth is that European leaders and politicians have no shame in ignoring the democratic decisions of the people who finance their lavish lifestyles. This is not surprising. For the attitude of European politicians who support the European Project is a reflection of the "selfish" character of their "hero," Jean Monnet. For this French architect of the European project had no shame in forcing a married woman, with a child, to leave her husband. Because the woman could not divorce her Italian husband in Italy, the "obstinate" Monnet repeated the story of Zeus and *Europa*. The "spiritual godfather" of European Community - the first honorary citizen of Europe- like Zeus, "abducted" the beautiful Silvia to Moscow for a quick divorce and re-marriage. The Greek Mythology became a reality in Moscow.

THE UNCOMFORTABLE TRUTH AND THE CRITICAL QUESTION - WOULD THE IRISH BE SAVED IN JEAN MONNET'S "LUXURIOUS BOAT"?

I will repeat: the Irish, by rejecting the Lisbon Treaty on 12 June 2008, unconsciously "reacted" to the warning their "father" offered to Britain about the fate of political Europe. If the Irish ignore the warning from the "Sage of Ulster" and adopt the Lisbon Treaty in another referendum, not only would they "betray" their "Patron", but would commit the blunder of all blunders by sacrificing their freedom and liberty on the "altar of intimidation." This is the uncomfortable truth the Irish people must wrestle with. So, before the "sons" and "daughters" of the "Seer of Dublin" revote on the Lisbon Treaty they must scrutinise what their brilliant 'father' published about the development of a confederation of European nations and its future before the European Union was born.

It is the end that crowns the work. Is the future of Europe bright or dark? Which means, whatever economic benefits the Irish might have gained from their membership of the European Union should not compel them to commit their future to a political project which, according to their "Father", has a bleak future. The Lisbon Treaty (as I have mentioned it many times) paves the way for Sir Robert

Anderson's prediction of the dark future of Europe to be fulfilled. A word to the wise is enough.

In view of Sir Robert Anderson's extraordinary vision about the European Project, and his prediction of the future of Europe which is bound to be fulfilled, It was, therefore, ridiculous, for the insolent Daniel Cohn-Bendit, the Franco-German Green MEP, to have criticised the Irish for rejecting the Lisbon Treaty. Had the euro-fanatic Cohn-Bendit studied the works of Sir Robert Anderson, he would not have humiliated his "children" with this remark: "They (the Irish) know how much they depend on the European Central Bank; that their policy of low corporate tax didn't save them; that the only thing saving them from the mess they're in is European protection..." (The Irish Times 17 April 2009).

We must ask the following questions:

- Is the European Union itself protected?
- How secured is Jean Monnet's Luxurious Boat" on the stormy seas of Europe?
- Does the arrogant Cohn-Bendit know the destination of the "European Titanic"?

The European leaders, in their devious attempt to force the European Constitution (so-called the Lisbon Treaty) on Europeans, were not being bold and clever. They, unconsciously, speeded up the process that would lead to the demise of their European Empire – the descent of the "stone cut without human hands" to crush the magnificent human statue from its toes of baked clay and iron and scatter them like chaff on a threshing-floor in the summer (Daniel 2:31-34). A word to the wise is enough.

According to Catherine Day, Secretary General of European Commission, Ireland's reputation was "tarnished" within the EU and the wider world for rejecting the Lisbon Treaty. She argued that this lost "reputation" could possibly be redeemed if Ireland were to ratify the Lisbon Treaty. She stressed Ireland had benefited immensely from EU membership and had powers and weight it would never have had outside the European Union. The fact is had the political elites who control the European Project and the wider world had had any sense of fairness, they would have condemned the European leaders for bullying "little" Ireland to vote again on a document they had already rejected. Europeans with sense of fairness would have rather applauded Ireland for being an EU country that offered its citizens their democratic and legitimate right to vote on a Treaty that would transfer more powers from their elected politicians to unelected strangers who are not accountable to them and are unable to remove them from power. European leaders should be ashamed of themselves for bullying "little" Ireland.

The question is: has the European Union got any sound reputation in the sight

of serious men? The European Project lacks democratic legitimacy and political accountability. For example, less than 46 percent of Europeans bothered to vote in the 2009 European Elections. In some countries less than 40 percent voted.
It was the Vice President of the European Commission, Ms. Wallstrom, who voiced her concern on how the Lisbon Treaty was forced upon the masses. According to this official, the European Council prepared a readable version of the Jargon-filled Reform Treaty but refused her requests to publish it until the treaty had been ratified by all the 27 members of the European Union. Her indictment was that everything that takes place behind closed doors was not good for Europe. What a "devious" Euro-project! Was it not the same Ms. Wallstrom who posted pornographic posters on the Internet to cite interest in the European Project? What kind of reputation has the EU got? The EU is "unfit for purpose", yet "fit for the purpose." A word to the wise is enough.

EUROPEAN LEADERS SHOULD "GO BACK TO SCHOOL"

In October 2008, when Ms Wallstrom commented on Ireland's rejection of the Lisbon Treaty, she suggested that EU national governments should "go back to school" to learn how to communicate EU values effectively. In her attempt to dismiss the result of the Irish referendum that dumped the Lisbon Treaty, the Vice President of the European Commission said the problem had "not been one of getting the information out there, but there being too much information, disinformation." According to her many of the arguments put forward by the "Anti-Lisbon Treaty campaigners" had been emotional ones to which the pro-Lisbon side "never had a counter argument."

I would remind Ms. Wallstrom that on the issue of "disinformation" the European Union is the "expert" in this field. A typical example is how European leaders have distorted the meaning of the European symbol – a circle of 12 gold stars on a blue background. I suggest Ms. Wallstrom and her boss, Jose Manuel Barroso, and all the political elites in Europe should "go back to school" to study the actual meaning of the EU symbol. Having obtained their "degree" in this basic subject - "EU Symbolism" - they would be qualified to examine the classic works of the scholar from Dublin's Trinity College to gain a proper understanding of the European project. In other words, European leaders and bureaucrats in Brussels should first acquire sound education on European integration, based on what the Learned Barrister from Dublin published on European Confederacy, before they attempt to educate Europeans on "Monnet's gradualist vision," which according to Jose Manuel Barroso, "still serves as the blueprint of European integration today." (*TIME* 31 October 2006).

IRELAND – A "DAVID" AND A "SMALL AXE" AND EU – THE "GOLIATH" AND THE "BIG TREE")

In an article for the Daily Express titled, *Brown joins EU plot to make Irish hold another treaty vote,* political editor Macer Hall, reported on how former French president, Valery Giscard d'Estaing, suggested on 19 June 2008 that the Irish should hold another referendum. According to the author of the Lisbon Treaty, "A country that represents 0.7 per cent of the European population cannot decide for others." This was sheer arrogance bedded in ignorance. Ireland is a "small axe" that can easily 'cut down' the EU – 'the big tree', provided the Irish people would wield the 'small axe' (The "unknown truth" about EU and its future) which their brilliant 'father' provided before the seed of the "Big tree" (EU) was planted on 9 May 1950 by Robert Schuman. Ireland is a "David" that can easily slay the "Philistine giant," the "Goliath EU." But would the Irish have the courage to throw the "small stone in their sling" at the "European Goliath"? Eamon de Valera rightly said; "We (the Irish) realise that small as were our physical resources, there were spiritual ones which were of great value; and we never doubted that our nation, though a small one, in the material sense, could play a very important part in international affairs." Indeed, the Irish have played a major role in international affairs. For it was an Irishman who, about 68 years before the rebirth of the nation of Israel, recorded that the Jews would be restored to Palestine, and the next major political feature in history after the "phenomenon of Israel" would be a confederation of European nations that would develop through an European crisis.

LITTLE IRELAND IS "UNIQUE"

The bitter truth for the 26 EU member states to swallow is that "Little Ireland" is "unique" among them. I repeat: it was an Irishman who wrote about Monnet's "gradualist vision" of a federal Europe, how it would develop from an European crisis; its character and future prospects before "Mister Europe" himself was born. The Irish must be proud. But unfortunately, Irish politicians were not aware of this truth; otherwise they might not have signed the Treaty of Maastricht in 1992. For it was this Treaty that went beyond the economic goals of the European Common Market to lay the foundation for political integration of European nations. The Irish must jump off the EU "Luxurious Titanic" before it sinks. I repeat: the European leaders, in their diabolical attempt to torment Ireland to adopt the European Constitution (The Lisbon Treaty) which they had already thrown out, were unconsciously rushing the arrival of the brutal dictator who will initiate a global financial crisis, economic crisis, political crisis, and social and religious crisis the world has never witnessed. The "Seer of Dublin" described this coming dictator the "awful Being" who will, initially deceive Europe and the rest of the world, and later terrorise men to close the era of Gentile supremacy on earth. This WILL SURELY HAPPEN just as the sun gives us light in the day, and the moon and the stars provide us with light at night. (You may read Daniel 9:27, Matthew 24, 2 Thessalonians 2:1-12, Revelation 13, 17 and 18).

IRELAND WIIL COMMIT NATIONAL SUICIDE IF THEY KEEP THE EUROPEAN "TROJAN HORSE"

Before Ireland voted again on the Lisbon Treaty, some politicians and commentators and academics adopted scare tactics to frighten the Irish electorate to vote 'Yes' to adopt the document they had already rejected. For example, in an article titled *Martin stresses import of second Lisbon poll* (Irish Times 28 February 2009), Marie O'Halloran commented on a special debate on Ireland and Europe. According to the report, Ireland's Minister for Foreign Affairs, Michael Martin, told the Irish people: "If Ireland rejects the Lisbon Treaty in the next referendum it would cast a fundamental shadow of doubt over our commitment to the European Union." Mr Martin warned another "No" vote would put Ireland into "genuinely uncharted waters at a time of severe and worldwide economic turbulence, and that opponents of the Treaty would risk "driving Ireland into a cul-de-sac." According to the article, Brigid Laffan, the Jean Monnet Professor of European Politics and Principal of the UCD College of Human Sciences, stated the next referendum "is about Ireland's relationship with Europe and whether we're in or out, and it's as stark as that." And Associate Professor Richard Sinnott of UCD, claimed research had shown that "the more people know about the EU the more they support it." Really!

The reality is that if the Irish get to know more about the European Union - what their brilliant "father" wrote about political Europe, its character and future prospects - the more they will reject the European project. And the more they will realise that the future of Ireland does not lie in Jean Monnet's vision of a "federated Europe." Unfortunately, the Irish are not aware of what the native of Dublin recorded about political Europe in the 19th century before the European Union evolved in the 20th century from the debris of the Second World War. I repeat: the citizens of the Republic of Ireland would commit the blunder of all blunders if they bow to pressure and intimidation to adopt the Lisbon Treaty. The European Union is a "Trojan horse" designed by the French Statesman, Jean Monnet, and approved by the German Chancellor, Dr. Konrad Adenauer. Ireland and Britain must return this "beautiful horse" to "Prince" Nicolas of France and "Princess" Angela of Germany, and allow the French and the Germans to pursue the vision of their patrons to its fateful end. "Fear the Greeks even when they offer gifts."

THE "LISBON BLACKMAIL" AND THE IGNORANCE OF CHRISTIAN LEADERS

The effort to force the Irish to embrace the Lisbon Treaty took another cynical twist. In May 2009, religious leaders in Europe met the President of the European Commission, Jose Manuel Barroso, and the then President of the European Parliament, Hans-Gert Pottering, to discuss the global financial crisis and other ethical issues. The two powerful men in Europe took advantage of the meeting to blackmail Ireland to accept the Lisbon Treaty. According to Barroso, one of the purposes of such meetings is to highlight how it is important in Europe to keep freedom of religion and also the freedom not to have a religion. The German President of the European Parliament then threatened the clerics, imams, vicars, cardinals, archbishops, bishops, grand muttis and rabbis who attended the meeting, that without the Lisbon Treaty they would have no place in the European project.

Bruno Waterfield, reporting on this meeting on his website under the title *God Crisis, the Lisbon EU Treaty and the Irish,* stated: "European Parliament President Hans-Gert Pottering used an EU-sponsored event dedicated to 'inter-religious' dialogue to suggest that without the Lisbon Treaty such a dialogue could not be guaranteed in the future. According to Pottering, "If the Lisbon Treaty should not come into force, with new leaderships in the commission and parliament, they could abolish this dialogue because legally it is not binding. With the Treaty of Lisbon when it comes into force, and this is Ireland's responsibility, then this inter-religious dialogue is legally for all the EU institutions." Was the German politician implying that Christianity would have no place in the European Project unless the Lisbon Treaty is forced on Europeans? We must ask: do Christians need any dialogue with the European Union that is anti-God and anti-Christ? Do Christian leaders and the Rabbis who attended the meeting understand the impact the Lisbon Treaty would have on faithful Christians and Jews?

After the meeting, the Archbishop of Dublin, Diarmuid Martin, suggested that Ireland rejected the Lisbon Treaty in the first referendum due to "a lack of understanding and difficulties in understanding." According to this spiritual leader of Catholics in Ireland, European partners should help explain the document and that the Irish need to realise the importance of Europe. On the other hand Europeans should also appreciate Ireland's importance to the European Union. (Source: *Irish archbishop calls for Lisbon treaty clarifications* by Jim Brusden 11 May 2009)

To begin with: the European project is atheistic. It has no room for God and the Lord Jesus Christ. And secondly, Archbishop Martin should rather have explained the spiritual significance of the European Union and its Lisbon Treaty to the Irish. It was, therefore, beyond belief that the Archbishop of Dublin and other Christian leaders attended a meeting chaired by politicians, and received lectures from Barroso and Pottering who have no idea what the European Union is for, and who do not understand the real import of the Lisbon Treaty. How could Christian leaders have belittled themselves by receiving lectures from the President of the European Parliament about how the Lisbon Treaty would somehow benefit Christians?

Had Archbishop Martin of Dublin and his fellow Christian leaders done their homework on European integration by studying the Books of Daniel and Revelation and St Paul's Second Epistle to the Thessalonians, and what Sir Robert Anderson, the Barrister from Dublin, recorded in his *The Coming Prince* about Europe and its future, they would have learnt that the Lisbon Treaty rather paves the way for the "Man of Lawlessness" to enter the political scene and persecute the faithful Jews and Christians. In fact, Christian leaders who attended the inter-religious meeting in Brussels demonstrated utter ignorance of what Sacred Scriptures teach about the restoration of the "dead" Roman Empire and the return of the Lord Jesus Christ as the "stone cut without human hands to crush the great human statue from its toes of baked clay and iron to its head of gold without leaving any traces." (Daniel 2:31-35).

I urge Christians in Ireland to ignore the Christian leaders who have sold their souls to the European Project. They have demonstrated lack of understanding of what the Bible teaches about the destruction of all worldly powers and the establishment of God's Kingdom on earth. The Irish should also dismiss the comments made by Hans-Gert Pottering. It was just a blackmail to frighten the Irish electorate to adopt the Lisbon Treaty. The fate of Ireland does not rest in the European Union. The Irish should rather devote their time and energy in studying what the Irish intellectual wrote about political integration of European nations, its character and future prospects when Pottering's patron, Dr. Konrad Adenauer, a founding father of European Community, was only six years. I repeat: the Irish would commit a national suicide if they follow their Church leaders and politicians to board Jean Monnet's "European Titanic" which was doomed before it set sail from Paris on 9 May 1950.

THE REAL PURPOSE OF THE LISBON TREATY

The popular view among politicians and political commentators is that the Lisbon Treaty was designed to make the European Union function smoothly and effectively, and also to make it easier for more countries to join the biggest economic market in the world. This is a superficial analysis of the Treaty's significance. The real purpose of the Treaty of Lisbon, without Europeans and the rest of the world knowing it, is to create the platform for the coronation of the King of Men, the Emperor of Europe, the "Awful Being," Sir Robert Anderson wrote about in *The Coming Prince.* The Emperor of Europe would be the political genius to lead Europe and mankind to their destiny. It is important for the Irish people to examine what their "Forgotten Father" published about political Europe and its destiny before surrendering their sovereignty to strangers in Brussels.

"DIVISION": THE TRADEMARK OF EU WAS ON DISPLAY IN BRUSSELS

Before and after the summit that was held to force Ireland to vote again on the Lisbon Treaty, diplomatic row erupted between Britain and Germany. German politicians ridiculed and attacked Gordon Brown's strategy of saving Britain and the world from the global financial crisis – a crisis none of the politicians saw it coming. Mr. Steinbruck, the German Finance Minister, described Gordon Brown's Labour Government's borrow-and-spend strategy as "crass." He ridiculed and rubbished the temporary 2.5 percent reduction in VAT. He said: "Are you really going to buy a DVD player because it now costs £39.10 instead of £39.90? All this will do is raise Britain's debt to a level that will take a whole generation to work off. The same people who would never touch deficit spending are now tossing around billions. In reference to the economist Keynes, Mr. Steinbruck described Mr. Brown's approach as "crass Keynesianism." Gordon Brown responded: "I do not want to get involved in what is clearly internal German politics, because they have a coalition with different political parties."

The row intensified when a second senior German politician contradicted Mr. Brown and called his borrowing plans the result of a complete failure of Labour policy. Steffen Kampeter, budget spokesman for Mrs. Merkel's Christian Democrats, said: "Peter Steinbruck's comments have nothing whatsoever to do with internal German politics as Prime Minister Brown has suggested. In questioning the British Government's approach, Peter Steinsbruck is exactly expressing the views of the German coalition."

And on 13 December 2008, the German Ambassador to Britain, Georg Boomgaarden, explained why Germany did not share Gordon Brown's view on how to solve the global financial crisis. Writing for *The Mail on Sunday*, the diplomat gave reasons for dismissing Mr. Brown's strategy. Firstly, there was no "housing market bubble" in Germany. Inflation was low. The Germans were prudent with their finances. They save about 13 percent of their disposable income with banks whereas individual savings in the United Kingdom is almost zero. Germans do not have huge credit card debts. Most importantly, Germany has trade surplus unlike Britain which is heavily in debt. (*The Mail on Sunday* 14 December 2008)

Here is another division that erupted among European leaders. *De Morgen* reported that the French President challenged the legitimacy of the Czech Presidency - may be, due to President Vaclav Klaus' refusal to fly the EU flag over Prague castle. According to Czech Head of State, "the EU flag doesn't fly at the seats of the Heads of State of Italy, Belgium, Lithuania, Sweden or the United Kingdom." Sarkozy was, perhaps, also "angry" at the Czech President's hostility towards the Lisbon Treaty – a Treaty which, in the eyes of the French, would finally bring into fruition the federal vision of their "hero" - Jean Monnet. According to *AFP* report, the then Czech Prime Minister, Mirek Topolanek, said: "The Lisbon Treaty is not expressly one of the priorities of our presidency." Mr. Topolanek suggested it would not be "fatal" if the Lisbon Treaty was not ratified by the Czech Republic during its EU Presidency. The Presidency ended in June 2009. The Treaty was approved by the Czech Parliament waiting for the signature of the Czech President and another possible challenge to the ratification of the Treaty.

The Czech Prime Minister criticised the Lisbon Treaty by telling the European Parliament, the document "is a bit worse than the Nice Treaty." He then "comforted" them: "I negotiated this text on behalf of the Czech Republic, we approved it. I signed it and I will vote for it." He admitted his people would reject the Treaty if there were to be a referendum on it. The Czech Premier then exposed the vile character of the European Project when he declared: "The fact of telling all member states that they are obliged to ratify a document and that they do not have the right to decide for themselves is quite absurd." (Euractiv EU Observer 15 January 2009). Mr Topolanek statement reveals how politicians treat the electorate with contempt.

THE "CONFRONTATION" BETWEEN FRANCE AND THE CZECH REPUBLIC

We know President Sarkozy "reluctantly" passed the baton of EU Presidency over to the Czech Republic. In Sarkozy's view a small nation like the Czech Republic, which is outside the eurozone and has not ratified the Lisbon Treaty, was not fit to 'captain' Monett's "Magnificent Titanic." When the Czech took over the EU "hot seat," the relationship between Prague and France began to deteriorate. It was not surprising when Sarkozy, in his attempt to be patriotic and exhibit his contempt for the Czech Republic, suggested that French car manufactures operating in other EU countries such as the Czech Republic and Slovakia, should return to France. He said: "If you build a Renault plant in India to sell Renault to Indians that is justified, but if you build a factory, without saying the company's name in the Czech Republic to sell cars in France, that is not justified."

Mr Mirek Topolanek, reacted angrily: "As the Prime Minister of the Czech Republic I do not understand the argument that it is unjustifiable to manufacture cars for the French market in the Czech Republic. The attempt to use the financial crisis to introduce such forms of protectionism and protective measures may slow and threaten the revival of the European economy. He added: "If someone wanted to really jeopardise the ratification of the Lisbon Treaty, he could not have chosen a better way and a better time."

Sarkozy's remark undermines the very principle governing the European Project

– free trade and free movement of people in a Single European Market. On 13 February 2009, the Financial Times commented on Sarkozy's rhetoric in a leading article titled *"Protectionism could sink the EU."* According to the paper, the European Union should provide "defences against the mutating virus of protectionism....The global financial crisis "is no excuse for beggar-thy-neighbour policies ......typified by President Sarkozy's outrageous call for French carmakers to repatriate their production from east European assembly plants to France..... The success of the EU is a result of its hybrid personality: part intergovernmental and part federal. Its traditional glue has been economic integration and the single market." The article concluded: "If Brussels fails to reassert authority in policing the single market, the EU risks being pulled apart. This Union needs a strong commission." The truth is that the Strong Man to lead Europe to its "glorious Paradise" of peace and prosperity is on his way.

President Sarkozy's obsession to control the direction of his "father's" project, prompted President Vaclav Klaus to criticise the supranational objective of the whole European project. Mr. Klaus took a swipe at Sarkozy: "I know he wants to remain in the post of EU President, it's very human...It's not necessary to be hyper-active and to organize an European summit every week end to have a good European Presidency." Klaus vowed to "do everything possible" to prevent the ratification of the Lisbon Treaty in the Czech Parliament (Source: *Open Europe*).

On 19 February 2009, President Klaus delivered his first address to the European Parliament in Brussels. He criticised the European Union for ignoring the voters and grabbing powers from sovereign nations. He compared supporters of deeper political integration of European nations to the era of the communist Soviet Union where dissent was not tolerated.

In an article titled *MEPs walk out as Czech President Scorns their 'democratic deficit,* Joishua Chaffin quoted President Klaus: "Here, only one single alternative is being promoted and those who dare thinking about a different option are labelled as enemies of European integration. Not so long ago, in our part of Europe we lived in a political system that permitted no alternatives." (*Financial Times* 20 February 2009). The sycophants at the "European Rubber Stamp Factory" who are hostile to democratic principles exhibited their character by booing the President and walking out of the chamber. What a shame! The Members of European Parliament do not want to be criticised, yet they are blended with the terms of accusation. A typical example was the leaked report that revealed their "systematic abuses of parliamentary allowances that enabled them to pocket more than £1m in profits from a single five-year term (*The Sunday Times* 22 February 2009)

In May 2009, the Senate in the Czech Republic approved the Lisbon Treaty, leaving the Head of State Vaclav Klaus to sign it. According to the report, the Senate accepted the treaty partly because it would improve their country's image among the EU member states. At this point, I would remind the Czechs that they won their independence from Austria-Hungary in 1918, the year Sir Robert Anderson passed away. Would the Czech Republic ignore the "Seer of Dublin's" warning about the dark future of Europe to adopt the Lisbon Treaty to become "slaves" in Brussels and perish on Monnet's "European Titanic"? After all, the former Prime Minister of Czech Republic, Mirek Topolanek, questioned the merits of the Lisbon Treaty. After ridiculing the blue-print of Europe as worse than the Nice Treaty, he declared the people of Czech would reject the Lisbon Treaty in a referendum.

REACTION TO GERMANY'S COURT RULING ON THE LISBON TREATY

On 30 June 2009, the highest court in Germany ruled that the Lisbon Treaty was compatible with German law, but demanded changes to domestic legislation before the treaty can be formally ratified. *Open Europe* summarised the wide-spread coverage given to the German Constitutional Court's judgement on the compatibility of the Lisbon Treaty with the German Constitution:

- *Handelsblatt* : "For the Court there is only one real basis for democracy in the EU: the national Parliaments"
- *Der Spiegel*: while "Brussels celebrates the judgement", the German Constitutional Court has expressed concern over the EU's democratic deficit. It notes that in the ruling the judges have formulated strict legal limits for future decisions regarding the EU, adding that if these were to be breached, "future EU law will be declared inapplicable in Germany".
- *Sueddeutsche* note that the Court has ruled that the German government must first get the approval of the German Parliament on EU decisions in Brussels which affect core German state competences. Commission President Jose Manuel Barroso was quoted saying "I welcome the judgement", but *Der Spiegel* argues: "It is hard to understand the reason for the Euro-rejoicing."
- *FAZ* described the court case as a "loud wake up call", explaining that "as the legal challenge was initiated by both the centre-right Bavarian CSU party and the far left, the large coalition in between has been caught sleeping when it comes to European politics."

And according to an article published in the 1 July 2009 edition of *The Irish Times*, Germany's highest court dismissed constitutional challenges to the Lisbon Treaty but called for ratification to be delayed until the rights of the German parliament in EU-decision making are strengthened. The article reported that on the ruling, the constitutional court vice-president Andreas Vosskuhle said: "The German constitution permits transfer of sovereign powers to an inter-states body like the EU, but does not permit entry to a European federal state. The Treaty of Lisbon changes nothing in that Bundestag remains the representative organ of the German people."

On 13 July 2009, Wolfgang Munchau also commented on the court's ruling in the Financial Times. In his article titled *"A damning verdict for European unity"*, Mr Munchau writes: "There was a collective sigh of relief in Brussels…when Germany's constitutional court ruled that the Lisbon Treaty was consistent with German law." On the most significant aspect of the ruling the columnists reported: " the court has given an explicit opinion on the question of European integration… The court said member states must have sovereignty in the following areas: criminal law, police, military operations, fiscal policy, social policy, education, culture, media, and relations with religious groups. In other words, European integration ends with the Lisbon Treaty." He concluded his piece with this significant statement which could have implications for the Irish: "The court's judgment reflects the nationalistic, post-Bismark era political mood in Berlin at the moment. At the very least, anyone locked in a monetary union with Germany should be very worried."

The Sun newspaper also commented on the ruling in its Editorial. Under the title "EU arrogance", the Patriotic Sun said, according to Germany's most powerful judges, "the loathed EU Constitution is not worth the paper it is written on." The judges ruled Brussels would be acting illegally if it tried to seize sovereign powers from member states." The court even considered the EU Parliament as an undemocratic body – pointing out that it does not even have a proper Opposition. And so according to the ruling: "Only elected governments have the right to decide economic, defence or foreign policy. That means NO European Army. NO control over criminal law, NO meddling in our police, welfare, education or media policies." (*The Sun* 14 July 2009)

Reacting to the expected German court ruling, Jan Techau, an EU expert at the German Council of Foreign affairs, made this simplistic comments: "This message could help the Lisbon Treaty in Ireland. Given that the entire Lisbon Treaty itself was affirmed by the court, the view in Ireland may be that what's good for Germany can't be bad for Ireland."(Source *Bloomberg Press*) Is it really the case that what is good for Germany is good for Ireland? The fortune of Germany is inseparably bound to the fate of the European Union. But does the destiny of Ireland lie in the European Union whose future remains uncertain? Had the EU expert examined what an Irish lawyer wrote about Europe and its future, he would not have made that suggestion.

"EU'S UGLY TRADEMARK"

Before the German court's ruling, Open Europe's poll of German voters found that 77 percent wanted to have a say on the Lisbon Treaty that would transfer more powers from German politicians to institutions they have no control of. Yet, despite this popular view and the court's ruling, Germany's ex-foreign Minister Joschka Fischer portrayed political elite's hostility to democracy and their lack of respect for the rule of law by shouting: "Europe will, despite numerous setbacks and crises, continue to progress as an alliance of states in the process of integration whether the court likes it or not." *The Sun* responded to this remark in its leading article of 14 July 2009: "Such high-handed contempt is now the EU's ugly trademark. Arrogant Eurocrats simply don't take No for an answer. That's why they forced the Danish people to vote twice over the Euro. They trampled on the express wishes of France and Holland to reject the constitution. Now they have insultingly ordered the Irish people to reverse" their June 2008 decision on the Lisbon Treaty.

The question is: why did German politicians, who talked about democracy, impose the Lisbon Treaty on Germans? They were scared the Lisbon Treaty, which has Angela Merkel's 'finger prints' on it, would be rejected. This is supported by the comments made by the EU Internal Markets Commissioner Charlie McCreevy: "When Irish people rejected the Lisbon Treaty a year ago, the initial reaction ranged from shock to horror to temper to vexation. That would be the view of a lot of the people who live in the Brussels beltway. On the other hand, all of the political leaders know quite well that if the similar question was put to their electorate by a referendum, the answer in 95 per cent of the countries would probably have been 'No' as well." (*Irish Times* 27 June 2009)

THE DESTINY OF GERMANY IS LINKED TO THE EUROPEAN PROJECT

Indeed, Germany's constitutional court ruling on the Lisbon Treaty – a document that confers legal personality on the European Union - as being compatible with German law was not surprising. As *Open Europe's* Director, Lorraine Mullally, put it: "Nobody realistically expected the court to rule against Lisbon." The reality is the fate of Germany is locked up in a Federal Europe. This is evident from the writings of the first German Chancellor, Dr Konrad Adenauer. In his memoirs Dr Adenauer recorded: "After the First World War, I advocated a plan for an organic integration of the French, Belgian, and German economies for the safeguarding of a durable peace...The unification of Europe seemed far more feasible now than in the 1920's... The idea of international cooperation between peoples must succeed ...*In a future United States of Europe I saw great hope for Europe and thus for Germany.* We had to try to remind France, Holland, Belgium, and the other European countries that they are and will remain forever our neighbours..." (Memoirs 1945-1953)

Adenauer added: "In the long run the French and Belgian demand for security can only be met by the economic integration of Western Germany, France, Belgium, Luxembourg and Holland. *If Britain, too, were to decide to participate in this economic integration, we would be much closer to the ultimate goal of a union of States of Western Europe"* (31 October 1945)....."A union between France and Germany would give new life and vigour to a Europe that is seriously ill. It would have an immense psychological and material influence and would liberate powers that are sure to save Europe. I believe this is the only way of achieving the unity of Europe" (7 March 1950). (Emphasis mine)

In view of Konrad Adenauer's vision about Germany's future, it was not surprising that German foreign minister Frank Walter Steinmeier welcomed the German's court decision that the Lisbon Treaty does not undermine German's constitution, and the German Joschka Fischer also pouring contempt on German Court by saying: "Europe will...continue to progress as an alliance of states in the process of integration whether the court likes it or not." The fact is the destiny of Germany is tied to the European Project. Divorce from this so-called "unique phenomenon" would be impossible for the Germans. Had German politicians examined the works of the Irish Barrister - what he published concerning the destiny of Europe, when the first German Chancellor was only six years, they would have shivered at the sight of the European Project.

DID IRELAND GAIN HER INDEPENDENCE FROM BRITAIN TO BE DRAGGED INTO "SLAVERY" IN BRUSSELS?

Before concluding this chapter, I would share with the Irish a significant portion of Bruce Arnold's article "History warns us about the risks of ceding power to EU." (*Irish Independent* 11 July 2009). Mr Arnold quoted Eamon de Valera's "prophetic" word to the Irish people when he returned from Strasbourg in 1955 where he attended a meeting about the construction of Europe's future. Eamon de Valera "bluntly told the Dail on June 12 1955 that Ireland would end up losing its freedom and independence if it joined any European federation. He continued: *"We (the Irish) realise that small as were our physical resources, there were spiritual ones which were of great value; and we never doubted that our nation, though a small one, in the material sense, could play a very important part in international affairs...We did not strive to get out of that British domination of our affairs by outside force, or we did not get out of that position to get into a worse one."* According to Bruce Arnold, Eamon de Valera's address "was a core-value speech, remarkably prophetic in ranging forward in time that is, today, quite astonishing."

Indeed, de Valera's speech was an echo of the warning the "Seer of Dublin" offered to Britain about them joining a confederation of European nations. If Britain would not be saved in a political Europe, as the "Seer" recorded - a year before Eamon de Valera was born in 1882 - would "small" Ireland be saved in Europe? Sir Robert Anderson did not expect his native land to participate in "the vile confederacy of the latter days." Eamon de Valera rightly said: *"Our nation (Ireland), though a small one, in the material sense, could play a very important part in international affairs."* And truly, it was an Irishman, who predicted that a political union of European nations would develop through an European crisis before Jean Monnet, the French master builder of European Construction, was even conceived in 1888. It was this same Irishman who wrote about the restoration of the Jews to Palestine even before Theodor Herzl formed the Zionist Movement in 1896 to "call for the establishment of a Jewish state in any available territory to which the majority of European Jewry would immigrate."

THE 'FORESIGHTS' OF JEAN MONNET, THE FRENCH STATESMAN, AND SIR ROBERT ANDERSON, THE IRISH LAWYER AND DETECTIVE

Let us examine, briefly, the visions of Jean Monnet (the French master builder of European Community) and Sir Robert Anderson (the Irish scholar) to establish who was a true visionary and a true prophet.

Jean Monnet: The "Revolutionary", The "prophet" and the "practical apostle of European unity"

In 1943, after the Second World War plunged Europe into deep economic crisis, Jean Monnet declared: "I have always believed that Europe will be established through crisis and not the sum of the outcome of those *crisis*." In his memoirs, Monnet, who has been described as a "prophet", the "practical apostle of European unity" and a "revolutionary", writes: "I have no doubt, for my part that a *confederation* will one day lead to a *federation*. But for the moment, is it possible to go further? I cannot say that it is. Meanwhile, the *confederation* would have the very great advantage of assuring public opinion in our countries that they have joined an entity which is not only economic but political, and that they are therefore part of something bigger than any of their countries alone." (Source: Jean Monnet Memoirs 1978)

Sir Robert Anderson: Irish scholar and the "Seer of Dublin"

Even before the term "Zionism" was coined in 1890 by the Jewish thinker, Nathan Birnbaum, and before the Zionist Movement was formed by Theodor Herzl in 1896, and before the First World War started in 1914, and before Jean Monnet, the 'spiritual godfather of EU,' was born in 1888, the Irish scholar, who became the Prince of Scotland Yard, recorded in his *The Coming Prince*: "Through the gradual unfolding....or far more probably as the outcome of some great European crisis in the future, this *confederation of nations* [a political alliance of European nations] *shall be developed.....*"

The Barrister from Dublin's Trinity College recorded that this union of European nations would be the next major political feature in history after the restoration of the Jews to Palestine. The nation of Israel was reborn on 14 May 1948, and the European Union was born on 9 May 1950 with The Schuman Plan exactly as the Irishman had predicted.

I appeal to the reader to examine the words of the French man (Jean Monnet) and the Irish man (Sir Robert Anderson) and consider which of them were from a true "prophet" and a "revolutionary," in so far as the birth of the European Union and the creation of the state of Israel are concerned. I would now put this question before the Irish and Britons: "Would you follow Jean Monnet's vision of a federal Europe or Sir Robert Anderson's vision of a "vile" European confederacy with a dark future and withdraw from the European Union?

I will conclude this chapter by urging the Irish to ignore Jose Manuel Barroso's "threat" that if they reject the Lisbon Treaty they would not have an automatic right to appoint an Irish Commissioner to "labour" in Jean Monnet's project. For in an interview with *The Irish Times*, which was published on 14 July 2009, the "Buffoon of Brussels" put pressure on the Irish electorate to embrace the rejected Lisbon Treaty. "With Lisbon it would always be possible to have one commissioner per member state," says the President of European Commission. "If you keep Nice then member states will not have the possibility to send a member to the commission all the time. So that is an important argument to vote for Lisbon I believe."

Was that all the argument Barroso could offer to convince the Irish electorate to embrace a document they had already rejected? The question is: why should an Irish Commissioner be a significant reason for the Irish to adopt the Lisbon Treaty? Of what significant use would an Irish Commissioner be to the Irish? After all, every EU Commissioner is obliged to promote the interest and values of the EU, not those of member states.

The argument the President of European Commission put forward was shallow and insignificant. For it exposed Barroso's superficial knowledge of the whole European Enterprise and his ignorance of the real significance of the Lisbon Treaty – the last "piece" that fits the "European Jig-Saw Puzzle." The former Portuguese Prime Minister and Constitutional Lawyer must "consult" the Barrister from Trinity College to gain a better understanding of the European Project and its prospects.

The stark choice before the Irish electorate on the second Lisbon referendum is whether they will follow the vision of Jean Monnet or the vision of their brilliant "father" – Sir Robert Anderson. It was written of Sir Robert Anderson, that "the well-being of Ireland was to him a matter standing above politics in the ordinary sense." The Irish and Britons must take seriously the warning the Prince of Detectives gave concerning the future of political Europe and dismiss Barroso's threat and ignore Jean Monnet's vision of a federal Europe. Sir Robert Anderson was the "giant" who, in 1892, "slaughtered" Darwin's "bulldog" – Professor Thomas Huxley.

Sir Robert Anderson K.C.B, LLD

"His views are worthy of the utmost respect and consideration ...and the well-being of Ireland was to him a matter standing above politics in the ordinary sense."

Dr. Anderson writes: "There would be a time when it is no longer a confederacy of nations bound together by treaty, with a Napolean rising up in the midst of them and struggling for Supremacy; but a confederacy of kings who are the lieutenants of one great Kaiser, a man whose transcendent greatness has secured to him an undisputed pre-eminence..."I say nations, not kingdoms, advisedly, for though they will ultimately be kingdoms, that is , under monarchical government, yet before the advent of the Kaiser (the new Emperor of the European Empire) such may not be the case.....This division of the Roman earth will take place before his appearance......but whether a year, a decade or a century...we do not know" (*The Coming Prince* 1881). [This was the picture of the European Union and its Powerful President which the "Seer of Dublin" painted in the 19th century before they became a reality in the 21st century. The Lisbon Treaty, signed on 13 December 2007, paves the way for the advent and coronation of the Powerful Caesar of the Revived Roman Empire]

CHAPTER 16

THE "SEER OF DUBLIN" AND THE EUROPEAN UNION

"A Lawyer with Sanctified Logic"

"...He was a man whose genius for comradeship was by no means the least of his many endowments. To many it was inevitable he should be known only as the stalwart defender of the Faith, the clear expositor, the zealous champion of Christian causes, the keen conversationalist, the distinguished public servant.....

In his consuming passion for what he regarded as vital to the Christian faith, he was often compelled to appear dogmatic to the point of unsympathy, and narrow-minded to the point of sheer unaccomodating.....He stood out as champion of the unpopular view of things, he both received and gave hard blows. No one could give harder.... "

But this was the role thrust upon him. If he must fight, he fought as a knight of God and a very perfect gentleman; so that those who opposed him, and finally gave up as 'hopeless', rode off with a fine appreciation of the character of their opponent.

Never for a single moment, did he betray the slightest bitterness towards an opponent... those who were privileged to know him at close quarters will ever think of him, in yet warmer terms, as one of the most devoted, humble, and kindly of men, and one of the staunchest of friends." (Rev. J J Stuart Holden MA DD)

"Zeal and piety and scholarship afford no proof of shrewdness and wisdom even in the affairs of daily life, and they are quite compatible with ignorance and error in the sphere of spiritual truth." (Pseudo-Criticism RA)

We have been informed by experts on European integration that one of the great achievements in the history of European Union occurred just before the end of 2007. It was the expansion of the Schengen Zone from 15 member countries to 24 European countries which took place on 21 December 2007. This development created a "border-free zone" from Estonia to Portugal – granting about 400 million citizens of 24 European nations the opportunity to travel freely within a radius of about 2500 miles without passport.

The Financial Times commented on the significance of this expansion. In its leading article entitled *"Schengen at 24 Border-free travel is a great achievement but not cost-free,* the editorial reported: "Border free travel has been one of the great practical bonuses of the European Union for its citizens since the establishment of the Schengen Zone in 1995. Passport free movement is now a reality from Estonia to Portugal and from Greece to Denmark with Norway and Iceland thrown in for good measure...That is no small achievement, one that gives meaning to the concept of European integration. Only UK, Ireland, Cyprus, Bulgaria and Romania are outside the Zone....Scrapping internal borders means agreeing on a common visa policy...."

POPE JOHN PAUL II AND EUROPEAN UNITY

The Schengen Zone expansion, which created a border-free zone in parts of the continent of Europe, was in line with a Catholic Pope's vision of a United States of Europe. This Pope advocated for a united Europe in a speech to the European Parliament. In page 37 of *The Principality and Power of Europe,* Adrian Hilton writes, "While visiting Austria in 1983, Pope John Paul II spoke out against the 'national and artificial borders' all over Europe." He added: "Europeans should overcome the menacing international confrontations of states and alliances, and create a new united Europe from the Atlantic to the Urals". In 1988, the Pope continued this theme when he addressed the European Parliament in Strasbourg; an occasion at which many asked why a perceived spiritual leader was addressing the issues of political unity. The Sunday Telegraph summed up the Pope's plans for the 'evangelisation': He (Pope John Paul II) is calmly preparing to assume the mantle which he solemnly believes to be his Divine Right – that of new Holy Roman Emperor, reigning from the Urials to the Atlantic."

EUROPEAN ROMAN CATHOLICS FULFILLING THE PROPHETIC WORD OF AN IRISH PROTESTANT

Pope John Paul II, in his request for a "united Europe," echoed the vision of a "federated Europe" dreamt by Roman Catholic politicians. The reality is Pope John Paul II, like most Catholic Popes and the Catholic pioneers of European integration, namely Alcide de Gasperi, Paul Henri-Spaak, Konrad Adenauer, Jean

Monnet and Robert Schuman, unconsciously, became agents to bring to pass what an Irish Protestant published regarding the future of Europe.

Peter Hitchens provided a sombre commentary on the Schengen Expansion. In an article headed *Britain, the final frontier....but not much longer,* he writes: "Almost silently, a disaster happened across the European continent...Hundreds of miles of frontiers were torn down. There is now no border control anywhere between the Channel Tunnel and the Balkans...the EU, now the true government of the territories formerly known as Britain, is utterly dedicated to what it calls 'free movement.' Mr Hitchens concluded: "As long as Britain remains a member of the European Union, It will be under relentless pressure to join the 1995 Schengen Agreement, and it will find it increasingly difficult to maintain the threadbare controls it possesses. The abolition of this country, especially all the good things about it, continues apace. *Will nobody act to stop it?"* (Emphasis mine. The Mail on Sunday 23 December 2007)

The question is: should Great Britain bow to pressure from the 'children' of Jean Monnet and Konrad Adenauer to join the 'Schengen Club'? The answer is "NO." We must not surrender our sovereignty to strangers in Brussels. We can stop the 'abolition of our great country' with the 'sword of truth' to slain the European 'monster'. Our 'forgotten father,' Sir Robert Anderson, wrote about borderless Europe before the First World War erupted. He warned Britain would degrade itself by joining "the vile confederacy of the latter days." Whatever Dr Anderson recorded in relation to political Europe has been fulfilled. We must use the 'sharp sword' of the Knight Commander to 'slay' the 'beast' in Brussels to free ourselves from its clutches.

DR. ROBERT ANDERSON ON CARDINAL HENRY NEWMAN AND PROFESSOR THOMAS HUXLEY

I urge Pope Benedict XVI and his Catholic theologians, as well as fashionable Protestant theologians, politicians, political commentators, scientists, sceptics, atheists and agnostics to examine what the Irish Protestant, who was a contemporary of Cardinal Newman and Prime Minister William Gladstone, wrote about European integration – about thirty six years after John Henry Newman's conversion to Roman Catholicism. For the record, Dr Anderson dismissed Cardinal Newman's defence of the Roman Catholic dogma of Transubstantiation as "abnegation of reason." You may read Dr Anderson's commentaries on the errors of Catholic doctrines on Holy Communion, Infant Baptism, Priestly Celibacy and Papal Supremacy in his *The Buddha of Christendom* and *The Bible or the Church.*

Dr Anderson also ridiculed Professor Huxley's excitement about Darwin's Theory of Evolution. Describing Darwin's theory as purely an hypothesis, the Lawyer with "Sanctified Logic" wrote: "Besides being absolutely without evidence to give it external support, this hypothesis cannot support itself internally - cannot be framed into a coherent thought. It is one of those illegitimate symbolic conceptions so continually mistaken for legitimate symbolic conceptions, because they remain untested. Immediately an attempt is made to elaborate the idea into anything like a definite shape, it proves to be a pseud-idea, admitting of no definite shape." (Pages 7-8 of *A Doubter's Doubts About Science and Religion")*

Let us, again, listen to the prophetic 'voice' of the Protestant Anderson on European integration: *"Next to the restoration of the Jews to Palestine, the most prominent political feature of the future is the division of the Roman earth....If there be any element of political diseases by which nations are afflicted, Europe will inevitably pass through another crisis. That there should be a commonwealth of nations living side by side at peace was a conception that nothing in the history of the world could have suggested....It is impossible to foretell how far kingdoms may be consolidated, and boundaries may be changed.....In forecasting the fulfilment of these.. we are dealing with events which, while they may occur within the lifetime of living men, may yet be delayed for centuries....we may rest content with the certainty that...their fulfilment will be clear, not merely to minds educated in mysticism, but to all who are capable of observing public facts....."*

The Protestant went on to predict the birth of the European Union: "*Through the gradual unfolding it may be of influences even now in operation; or far more probably as the outcome of some great European crisis in the future. This confederation of [European] nations shall be developed ..."* He concluded his forecast by describing the dark future of Europe. The Irish Protestant also put this question to his compatriots: "May we not indulge the hope that however far our nation may lapse in evil days to come from the high place which, with all her faults, she has held as the champion of freedom and of truth, she would be saved from the degradation of participating in the *vile confederacy of the latter days?" (*Emphasis mine*)*

THE "FORGOTTEN IRISH PROTESTANT" SPEAKS TODAY

In 2004, Pope Benedict XVI objected to Turkey's membership of the European Union. In 2006 the same Pope Benedict changed his mind and called for Turkey to be welcomed into the European Club. And before Tony Blair converted to Catholicism, the former British Prime Minister championed the cause of Turkey's membership of the European Union. It may interest Pope Benedict XVI and Tony Blair (now a devout Catholic), that over 128 years ago the Protestant Anderson mentioned Turkey as a member of a political union of European nations. And one hundred years after the "Sage of Ulster" listed Greece as a member of an European confederacy, Greece also joined the European Community in 1981.

A question for Pope Benedict XVI and his Cardinals: "Had John Henry Newman, thirty seven years after his elevation to the position of Cardinal in the Catholic hierarchy, predicted the European Union and then listed Turkey, England, Greece, Italy, Spain, Belgium, Austria and Portugal as members of this political alliance, would Vatican not have been proud of Cardinal Newman and considered his 'extraordinary forecast' about European integration as one of the 'miracles' of the century which should be included in Newman's Curriculum Vitae to boost his chances of becoming Britain's first saint for nearly 40 years?

Perhaps, Pope Benedict XVI and his Catholic Cardinals and all the experts in Vatican are not aware of the works of Protestant Anderson. I, therefore, encourage the Catholic Church to study the following books of the literary recluse: *The Coming Prince, Daniel in the Critic's Den, The Silence of God, The Buddha of Christendom, The Bible or the Church, The Bible and Modern Criticism, A Doubter's Doubts about Science and Religion* and *Pseudo-Criticism* for the benefit of the 1.2billion Roman Catholics. If the Almighty used a donkey to rebuke a Gentile prophet on His behalf (Numbers 22:21-33), how much more an intellectual among intellectuals. So, the Roman Catholic Church and its theologians should bury their pride and learn from the Protestant Anderson. Christianity is not a 'competition business.' It is about co-operation among Christians to build the Body of Christ for the Glory of His Holy Name. The Church of Rome cannot claim monopoly of scholarship on Sacred Scriptures. If anything, the Church of Rome distorts some of them. Remember the words of the Lord Jesus Christ: "God has hidden these things from the wise and the learned, and revealed them to little children, for this was His good pleasure" (Luke 10:21).

Here is an extract from a letter a Roman Catholic Monk, Father Ignatius, O.S.R, wrote to Dr. Anderson in response to a correspondence from the Protestant: "It is most kind of you to write to me in so brotherly a way and to send me your pamphlet. Indeed what you and I believe in common far exceeds in grandeur and importance the smaller details respecting which we may differ. I have read your *Coming Prince* with much pleasure and profit, and now shall read... your book on *Modern Criticism,*

Believe me your affectionate brother in our Lord Jesus.

"Ignatius, O. S. B, Monk"

Would Pope Benedict XVI and his 1.2billion followers read *The Coming Prince* and *The Bible and Modern Criticism?* The world is waiting for a response.

THE PROPHETIC VOICE OF THE PROTESTANT ANDERSON

Concerning the development of the European Union, the following words and phrases have been associated with the Project: "Crisis, Peace, Unity, Boundary, Region, Province, Confederation, Political adventure, Empire, Treaty, Biggest political alliance, "Largest Trading Block", "Rarest of all political phenomena in history"; "Global super-power of world-historic importance, second to none in economic clout", "Napolean" , "Vile", "Corruption", "Fraud", "Nepotism", "Bribery", "Pornography" and "Deception".

It may interest you to know, that in the 19th century the Protestant Anderson used the same and similar words and phrases listed above to describe a political alliance of European nations that would arise after the restoration of the Jews to Palestine. We know the state of Israel was created in Palestine in May 1948. Two years later, in May 1950, the European Union was born with the Schuman Plan.

Let us examine some of the words and Phrases which are associated with the European Union, and compare them with the words and phrases Sir Robert Anderson used to describe a confederation of European nations:

1"**Crisis" and "Peace"**:
In 1943, Jean Monnet, the "practical apostle of European unity," declared: "I have always believed that Europe will be established through **crisis** and not the sum of the outcome of those crises." He added: "There will be no **peace** in Europe if the states of Europe rebuild themselves on the basis of national sovereignty."

In a Special Report on the 50th Anniversary of the Treaty of Rome, *TIME* Magazine reported: "Europe's development from the Great Depression of World War II has been a "Quiet Miracle" of fifty years of peace and prosperity." And according to European Union publications, "The historical roots of the European Union lie in the Second World War."

2. "**Political adventure"**
Former French Prime Minster, Dominique de Villepin, described the European Union "the greatest political adventure of the last century" (Financial Times). *Newsweek* magazine described the European Union, "a global super-power of world-historic importance, second to none in economic clout." And Francois Duchene, Biographer of Jean Monnet, writes: The European Union is "the rarest of all political phenomena in history." And Dr. Ulrich Beck, Professor for Sociology at the University of Munich and the London School of Economics, also confirmed the "uniqueness" of the European Union. In his article, *Nation-state politics can only fail the problems of the modern world*, the German scholar writes, "Europe remains to be understood and conceptualised. This historically unique form of international community cannot be explained in terms of the traditional concepts of methodological nationalism...Cosmopolitan Europe was consciously conceived and launched after the second World War" (The Guardian 15 January 2008)

In *The European Union From Jean Monnet to the Euro*, which was a collection of essays drawn from the lectures of the Baker Conference at Ohio University, Dean J Kotlowski, Assistant Professor of History at Salisbury State University in Maryland, writes: "The transformation of Europe since the end of World War II has been astounding. In 1945, a battle-scarred continent lay in ruins. Today, it has achieved a level of integration, prosperity, and stability that few people could have anticipated. The life and career of the French statesman Jean Monnet and the recent adoption of the "euro" as Europe's common currency represent the book-ends of this five-decade metamorphosis."

3. **"Confederation"**

In his article, *Unloved and mistrusted, even by the French at 50*, Niall Fergusson, Professor of History at Harvard University, writes: "The custom union has become a (still imperfect) single market. Yet at root remains not the federal super-state of conservative nightmares, but a ***confederation*** whose primary concern is trade." (Daily Telegraph 25 March 2007).

Jean Monnet, the master builder of the European Project, used the word "confederation" in his memoirs: Writing about his vision of a federal Europe, the French "hero" recorded: "I have no doubt, for my part, that a ***confederation*** will one day lead to a ***federation***....the ***confederation*** would have the very great advantage of assuring public opinion in our countries that they have joined an entity which is not only economic but political, and that they are therefore part of something bigger than any of their countries alone."

President Charles de Gaulle also used the word "***confederation.***" Irene Finel-Honigman, Adjunct Professor in the MBA Programme at John Hopkins University, and a former Visiting Professor at Columbia University School of International and Public Affairs and Chair of Foreign Languages at New School University, who served in the Clinton administration as Senior Adviser, finance policy and EMU initiatives at the U.S Department of commerce, writes: "De Gaulle believed that Europe would become a ***confederation*** but only within a long-term historical political framework." The Professor quotes de Gaulle: "I don't exclude, far later, a ***confederation*** which would be the crowning point of a patient effort to bring forth a common policy, common diplomacy, common security at the end of a long period when the six nations have become accustomed to living together." (Source: *The European Union From Jean Monnet to the Euro* page 94)

The words of Sir Robert Anderson:

Let us now read what Sir Robert Anderson recorded about political Europe: "Through the gradual unfolding....or far more probably as the outcome of some great ***European crisis*** in the future, this ***confederation*** of [European] nations shall be developed....That there should be a commonwealth of nations living side by side at ***peace*** was a conception which nothing in the history of men would have suggested"

Let us review The Marshall Plan which confirms Sir Robert Anderson's prediction that a political alliance of European nations would develop through an European crisis:

"On 5 June 1947, US Secretary of State, George G. Marshall, outlined at Harvard University what has become known as the Marshall Plan. After the Second World War, Europe was devastated. The continent had nothing to sell. The economy was in shambles. United States offered 20billion dollars to help. "In considering the requirements for the rehabilitation of Europe – the loss of lives, the destruction of cities, factories, mines, railways.....Machinery has fallen into disrepair or obsolete, banks, insurance companies, and shipping companies disappeared. Confidence in the local currency disappeared. Breakdown of business structure in Europe was complete. Town and city industries were not producing adequate goods to exchange with the food-producing farmer. Raw materials and fuel were in short supply. The farmer or the peasant could not find the goods for sale which he desired to purchase. So the sale of his farm produce for money which he cannot use seemed to him unprofitable transaction.

The truth was: Europe requirements for foreign food and other essential products from America were so much greater than her ability to pay that she must have substantial help or face economic, social and political deterioration of a grave character..."Our policy is directed not against any country...Such assistance, I am convinced, must not be on a piecemeal basis as various crises develop......

The initiative must come from Europe."_(Source: *Congressional Record, 30 June 1947)* The initiative resulted in the launching of The Schuman Plan which created the European Coal and Steel Community which subsequently developed into the European Union. It is clear The Marshal Plan highlighted the European crisis through which an economic and political union of European nations developed exactly as Sir Robert Anderson predicted in 1881.

4. "Boundaries"

On 3 September 2006, The Sunday Telegraph reported on an EU initiative to ***change the boundaries*** of member countries. In an article titled *New EU map makes Kent part of same 'nation; as France,* Jasper Copping and Melissa Kite wrote: "A German led 'conspiracy of cartographers' stands accused of trying to use a new EU directive to give Brussels the powers to ***change national boundaries***.....This, according to the Tories, could be the first step of a Berlin-inspired master plan to create a United States of Europe divided, not into states, but instead a series of transnational regions, the templates for which have been drawn...They seek to break Britain into regions that cross national boundaries. A German minister said: "There is the great hope underlying the goal of a united Europe that we can permanently overcome our borders."

Witness what Sir Robert Anderson recorded concerning European integration: "It is impossible to foretell how far ***kingdoms may be consolidated and boundaries may be changed***.....We must rest content with the certainty that their fulfilment will be clear to all who are capable of observing public facts..."

5. "Province"

In William Rees-Mogg's article, *If Scotland got its vote, then so should we,* he writes: "Certainly, the English people, however much they might object to becoming one of the western ***provinces of the European Empire***, will be allowed no chance to decide the matter for themselves. It is extraordinary how many Scots are involved in the end game of English Independence..." (*The Times*, 17 September 2007)

- In a leading article on Gordon Brown's handling of the Lisbon Treaty, Daily Mail reported: "Labour's plan to sign the European treaty - without referendum - threatens to reduce Britain to a ***patchwork of regions,*** run by Brussels. If that happens, the unionist cause is surely lost. (Daily Mail, 15 August 2007)
- Professor Anthony Coughlan, Secretary for The National Platform EU Research & Information Centre and Senior Lecturer Emeritus in Social Policy at Trinity College in Dublin, wrote: "Lisbon [Treaty] would reduce Ireland and the other Member States to the constitutional status of ***provincial states*** in a Federation, like Virginia inside the Federal USA or Bavaria inside Federal Germany..."
- In his article, *Will Europe's spoilt children put us to shame by saying No to the EU Empire,* Peter Hitchens writes: "To the secret horror of the real rulers of Europe, one tiny country is letting its people vote on whether it should give up its independence for ever. The other 26 members of the Franco-German Empire have meekly agreed to accept their new status as ***provinces***" (The Mail on Sunday, 25 May 2008).
- Leo Mckinstry, in his essay, *National spirits are high yet Brown is about to sell our soul to Brussels,* also writes: "The commissars of the EU utterly despise traditional concepts of national identity and independence, believing that all borders must be removed as we are forced to submit to governance by a new federal superstate. In their view, France and England should disappear as sovereign entities, becoming nothing more than the ***provinces of the EU's new empire***." (Daily Express)
- Melanie Phillips, in her essay, *Contempt, apathy and lies - why Britain is crying for our own 'pitbull with lipstick,'* writes: "Middle Britain mourns that its country is being transformed by mass immigration. It is demon-

ized for saying so. It is aghast that it no longer governs itself but is becoming a ***province of Euroland;*** it is scorned as xenophobic" (Daily Mail 7 September 2008).

- On the subject, *Should our kids swear loyalty oath*, Phil Jones sent this letter to a newspaper: "Britishness" will soon be a totally meaningless concept – as British nationality changes to European nationality under the Lisbon Treaty, and the UK, France, Germany, etc become ***provinces in a federal state*** with the EU as central government." (*London Lite,* 12 March 2008)
- A literature provided by the United Kingdom Independence Party read: "This (Lisbon) Treaty will further destroy our sovereignty and reduce Britain to a mere ***province*** of the United States of Europe."

In the 19th century, Sir Robert Anderson recorded that England would become a province of an European Empire, if it participated in a political union of European nations. Let us read what the "Seer" wrote in his *The Coming Prince*: "Between these kingdoms and the Roman Empire....But some latitude must probably be allowed as to ***boundaries,*** otherwise we should have to choose between two equally improbable alternatives, namely, either our own nation shall have sunk to the position of ***a province*** or Ireland...."

Is it not amazing that the very word - ***"province"*** - Sir Robert used to describe the status of England if it joined a confederation of European nations, has been used in the 21st century to describe England's position if Britain remains in the European Union? What about Republic of Ireland if it adopts the Lisbon Treaty and commits its future to the European Union? Would Ireland not become another "province" of a federal Europe?

6. "Treaty"

It is well known the European Union has progressed through a series of Treaties. To name a few: The Treaty of Paris, The Treaty of Rome, The Nice Treaty, the Maastricht Treaty and the Lisbon Treaty which would crown the European Project by making it a legal personality with a powerful EU President and a Foreign Minister who will manage EU Embassies around the world.

Sir Robert Anderson wrote about this particular "Treaty" that makes a provision for an EU President, a powerful leader, who would exercise 'awesome' powers. Observe the words of the "Seer of Dublin": "There would be a time when it is no longer a confederacy of nations bound together by ***treaty***, with a Napoleon rising up in the midst of them and struggling for supremacy; but a ***confederacy of kings*** who are the lieutenants of one ***great Kaiser***, a man whose transcendent greatness would secure to him an undisputed pre-eminence." This is the picture of the European Empire and its influential Emperor who would emerge to lead Europe to the 'Promised Land of Peace and Prosperity.' Dr Anderson painted this picture in the 19th century before it became a reality in the 21st century. And we wait for its final fulfilment when the charismatic "Kaiser" enters the political landscape to begin his reign with a 7-year Peace Treaty between the Jews and their Arab neighbours. He will violate this 'Peace-Deal' after three and half years.

7. "Napolean"

The 'hyperactive' French President, Nicholas Sarkozy, who had a "successful" EU Presidency in 2008, has been compared to the French Emperor, Napolean. In an article entitled *Irish lead resistance to France's new Napolean*, Frederick Forsyth writes: "I am becoming much impressed by similarity between France's new mini-emperor and a predecessor in that role, one Napolean Bonaparte. Both were small. Both enjoyed multiple marriages. Both were not actually French by parentage. Both lusted for a unified continental Europe with France firmly in charge" (*Daily Express* 25 July 2008).

On 26 March 2008, *The Sun* newspaper recorded in its editorial: "It would be a mistake to underestimate this new **Napolean.** Sarkozy wants France to become leaders of the European Union with a European army to back it up. He needs Britain's cooperation to make his plan work. We would be mad to sign away our military independence by folding the best armed forces in the world into a ramshackle, Brussels run Dad's army."

On 22 January 2009, a column in *The Independent* newspaper read, "*The new Napolean? Small men. Big ideas. Glamorous wives. The similarities between Nicolas Sarkozy and Napolean are uncanny – and now have been explored in a book by France's foremost political commentator.*" Commenting on this book, John Lichfield writes: "Sarkozy resembles Napolean: bold and enigmatic, devastating and vulnerable….M. Sarkozy, authoritarian and iconoclastic, morally conservative and politically reformist, is therefore a 21st-century reincarnation of the First Consul: a "Bonaparte in a suit." They both set out to make sure that France was never the same again. Both see themselves as the rebuilders of a great but fragile nation…"

Let us observe what Sir Robert Anderson wrote in *The Coming Prince*: "There would be a time when it (the confederation of European nations) is no longer a confederacy of nations bound together by treaty, with a **Napolean** rising up in the midst of them and struggling for supremacy; but a confederacy of kings who are the lieutenants of one great Kaiser…"

8. "Empire"

In an article titled *The Decline and Fall of Rome,* Michael Elliot writes: "On the BBC TV series *"The Poisoned Chalice"* a few years ago, an aide to Belgian Foreign Minister Paul-Henri Spaak recalled the mood (after the signing of the Treaty of

Rome in 1957): "Spaak turned to us and said: "Do you think we have today been putting the first stone of a new **Roman Empire,** and this time without firing a shot? We all felt like Romans that day?" (Source: TIME, June 13, 2005).

Jose Manuel Barroso, the "Buffoon of Brussels," also boasted about the European Union being the first "**non-imperial Empire.**" And an American author, Parag Khanna, also associated the European Union with the Roman Empire. According to this scholar, the European Union is the world's most popular and ***successful empire***. In the 2 February 2008 edition of The Guardian, the newspaper produced a portrait of five EU leaders dressed like Roman Emperors. Beneath this picture was the inscription: "While Britain frets about EU expansion, Europe is overtaking its rivals to become the world's most successful **empire**: US scholar Parag Khanna on the rise of the new Rome". [Emphasis Mine]

Sir Robert Anderson, having foretold the development of a confederation of European nations, also recorded that the coming King of Men would be the 'head' of the revived ***Roman Empire."*** So, the European Union, becoming the foundation stone of a "new Roman Empire" as suggested by Paul Spaak in 1957, and the European Union being the first "non-imperial Empire" as claimed by Jose Manuel Barroso, and the European Union becoming "the world's most successful empire" as suggested by the scholar Parag Khanna, should not be surprising. Politicians and Scholars should not shout about it. The European Union is, indeed, the revived Roman Empire in its infancy. For the Irish Barrister with "sanctified logic" and an extraordinary insight and mental power, wrote about the European Empire, about 70 years, before European Community was born.

9."Vile","Pornography","Fraud", "Bribery" and "Corruption"

European leaders, in their desperation to motivate Europeans to love the European project, used nude posters and pornographic film to get their attention. We also know the accounts of the European Union have not been approved by its Auditors for 14 consecutive years because of error, fraud and financial mismanagement. This prompted Ian Pearson, the Treasury's Economic Secretary, to declare that the European Union's inability to get its accounts in order is "entirely unacceptable.... It is simply not good enough that the majority of the EU budget suffers from a level of error that is material."

And it is a common knowledge that the European Parliament has become a 'den' of corruption. Some Members of the European Parliament have been fiddling with their expenses whiles the Parliament refuses to publish details of the mis-use of taxpayers' money. This headline, *MEPs 'expenses abuse' hushed up by Brussels,* is an eloquent testimony. It was reported: "A secret internal inquiry by European Parliament found widespread abuse of expenses by MEPs employing fictitious staff or unqualified family members...The audit was kept secret by the Parliament and only shown to MEPs on request. The explosive inquiry centres on misuse of the annual parliamentary assistance allowance of £130000 available to all 785 MEPs to pay staff - a total of more than £100million. These misdemeanours, obviously, portray the EU in a dreadful light." (The Times, 21 February 2008).

On 27 April 2008, *The Sunday Times* also exposed another incidence of corruption in the European Project. In an article titled *Ousted for exposing 'scam' of EU Chief,* the paper reported that a British whistleblower, who exposed alleged corruption at an European aid Agency, faced the sack after he had informed EU fraud investigations that his boss was involved in the scam. Mr. Battersby uncovered evidence that the agency's former director... who became the energy minister of the West African Country, Mali, approved the award of lucrative European Union contracts to a company which he had a financial interest. Terry Battersby, from Manchester, was removed from his job as head of information technology at the Brussels based Centre for the Development of Enterprise (CDE) and placed on a short-term contract."

The "Vile" EU

The extremely unpleasant character of the European Union was, again, demonstrated in an art Exhibition held in Rome in 2007 to celebrate the 50th anniversary of the Treaty of Rome. Austria's contribution was the "erotic artist Schiele" - a naked woman with legs apart waiting for anyone to walk in". This pornographic image portrays how the European Union is morally and intellectually bankrupt of ideas to promote their Project. The nude art was revealed in the 22 March 2007 edition of The Times in a column titled *"Europeans make an exhibition of themselves."*

And commenting on the character of the European Union on his website, Tomasinabromleytzq made these significant observations: "The EU has placed itself in opposition to the United States. It has inveigled itself so deeply into the lives of its citizens, so deeply embedded itself into every aspect of life, that everything a person does is regulated in some way by the EU. Most of these laws are EU-inspired regulations prescribing the details of how activities are to be carried out." He added: "Sooner or later the sheer volume of regulations will start to affect people culturally. Our culture is slowly being eroded and destroyed by this ***vile institution,*** our national identities removed, our freedoms erased, and the end result? Inevitably, it will be war, but before that will be a morass of dull, lifeless existence for millions of people shorn of everything that once made their nations great......"(15 March 2008)

It is clear the European project is morally corrupt. Notice the word ***"vile"*** in the above commentary and compare it with Sir Robert Anderson's writing about Europe. In the 19th century, the Irishman used the same word - "vile" - to portray the character of the political Europe that would evolve from an European crisis. He described it ***"the vile confederacy of the latter days."***

From what we have learnt about the development of the European Union, let us, again, examine the words and phrases Sir Robert Anderson used in his prediction of a confederation of European nations that would arise from an European crisis and draw our conclusion about the sort of person Dr. Anderson was. I quote the words of the man from Dublin:

"Next to the restoration of the ***Jews to Palestine,*** the most ***prominent political feature of the future*** is the partition of Roman earth. If there be any element of periodicity in the political diseases by which nations are afflicted, ***Europe*** will inevitable pass through another ***crisis.*** That there should be a ***commonwealth of nations living side by side at peace*** was a conception that nothing in the history of the world could have suggested....It is impossible to foretell how far ***kingdoms may become consolidated and boundaries may be changed***...In forecasting the fulfilment of these...we are dealing with events which, while they may occur within the lifetime of living men, may yet ***be delayed for centuries***... we may rest content with the certainty that....their fulfilment will be clear...to all who are capable of ***observing public facts.*** .....Trough the gradual unfolding, it may be of influences even now in operation; or far more probably as the outcome of some great ***European crisis in the future. This confederation of (European) nations shall be developed,*** and thus the stage will be prepared on which shall appear that awful Being, the great leader of men in the eventful days which are to close the era of Gentile supremacy..."

If the development of the European Union has been a "Quiet Miracle" as TIME magazine suggested, how would TIME describe Sir Robert Anderson who wrote about this "Quiet Miracle" about 70 years before the "Quiet Miracle" manifested? Is it not extraordinary, that the very words Sir Robert used in the 19th century in connection with a confederation of European nations which would develop through an European crisis have been used in the 21st century to describe the European Union which evolved from the economic crisis brought about by the Second World War?

In his essay, *The Man from Cognac Jean Monnet and Anglo-American Mindset,* Henry H. H. Remark, Professor of Comparative Literature, Germanic and West European Studies at Indiana University paid tribute to Jean Monnet. He writes: "....how this unlikely person with an unlikely education from an unlikely corner of France was able to achieve, against all odds, what nobody else has been able to do since Charlemagne: the functioning structure of a European Community (EC). Not alone certainly, but without him it would not have happened. And the longer I plunged into this....unique phenomenon, the more surprised......I have been to discover how instrumental....the Anglo-American model and reality have been for

Monnet in laying the groundwork for a federated Europe." Professor Remark goes on with his adulation of Monnet: "What extraordinary combination of personality and circumstances drove this singular, inconspicuous and ultimately, against all odds, so productive provincial French Cognac salesman with his Anglo-Saxon propensities to become the progenitor of the European Community?

Here is the "Unknown secret" of Jean Monnet's achievement. The French Statesman, unconsciously, toiled to become the "progenitor of the European Community" to bring to pass what an Irish Barrister wrote about political integration of European nations and its future prospects before Monnet himself, "the salesman of European Community," was born in 1888. The question is: how would Historians, political scientists and political commentators and experts on European integration describe the scholar from Dublin's Trinity College who, in his teenage years, worked briefly in a brewery?

SIR ROBERT ANDERSON'S PROPHETIC WORD ABOUT BRITAIN

Sir Robert Anderson foresaw Great Britain, which had been the "champion of freedom and of truth," would fall in the wicked days to come. The "Seer" posed the question: "May we not indulge the hope, that however far our *nation may lapse in evil days to come* from the high place which, with all her faults, she has held as the champion of freedom and of truth, she will be saved from the degradation of participating in the *vile confederation of the latter days?"* (Emphasis mine) Historical and contemporary events have justified his prediction. Later on I would provide a catalogue of evidence that confirms Sir Robert's prophetic word about "Broken and Damged Britain."

Summary

- Is it not "incredible" that an Irish Protestant could foretell with certainty how a political alliance of European nations would develop through a crisis?
- Is it not astonishing that a Presbyterian could predict the character of the European Union and its future even before its Roman Catholic Founding Fathers – Jean Monnet and Robert Schuman – were born in 1888 and 1886?
- Is it not remarkable for the Protestant Anderson to forecast with certainty, even before the Zionist Movement was launched in 1897, that the Jews would be restored to Palestine, and the next major political feature in history after the rebirth of Israel would be a confederation of European nations?
- Had the Protestant from Dublin, an "Anglicanised-Irishman of Scotch extraction," been a Roman Catholic convert like John Henry Newman,

> he would have easily qualified for sainthood. The Vatican would have hailed the 'Catholic Anderson' the "Saint of Saints" and a Doctor of the Church. The Pope would have arranged for the remains of Dr Anderson to be exhumed from Kensal Green Cemetery to a 'posh' tomb in Rome.

Whatever your denomination, I would encourage you to study *"The Coming Prince."* You would appreciate, in detail, how most of the words and phrases Dr Anderson used in the 19th century to describe a confederation of European nations and its character have been employed in the 21st century to portray the European Union. You would also, learn that the Lisbon Treaty has smoothed the path for the "Seer's" prediction of the future of Europe to be fulfilled. For this Treaty has made the provision for the *"awful Being"* to be crowned as the last Caesar of the revived Roman Empire.

The reality is whoever becomes the President of Europe, would be a shadow of the coming "awful Being." Sir Robert Anderson even described the qualities of this "political genius" who will lead Europe to "glory". In pages 191 and 193 of *The Coming Prince*, the Lawyer with "sanctified logic" writes: "The True King of Men must have an extraordinary combination of great qualities. He must be a scholar, a **statesman**, a man of unflinching courage and irrepressible enterprise, full of resources…a general and a **diplomatist."** Compare this description with the qualities Denis MacShane, former Europe Minister, suggested would be needed by the President of Europe. In his article, *Europe needs the leadership and ability of Blair,* MacShane outlines the values expected of the EU President: "The new president of Europe will have to be a **statesman,** a crafty **diplomat,** a soother of European quarrels, competent at managing the tedious minutiae of EU business, able to speak two or three languages and a father-figure who can make the EU popular again." (Financial Times 11 February 2008). Question: Does MacShane's Blair know the future of Europe?

THE "UNPATRIOTIC" BRITISH AND IRISH POLITICIANS AND THE "PATRIOTIC" FRENCH AND GERMAN POLITICIANS

In examining the progress of the European Union - especially the repackaging of the rejected EU Constitution as a new EU Treaty - we saw the finger prints of France and Germany on that diabolical document. Angela Merkel and Nicholas Sarkozy initiated the process of deception. Without any doubt the Germans and the French are dictating the direction of the European Project to become a United States of Europe. When the Lisbon Treaty was rejected by Ireland, President Sarkozy, with the support of Chancellor Angela Merkel of Germany, insisted the ratification process should continue for the Treaty to be adopted.

The French and German politicians were being patriotic. They were committed to fulfilling the dream of their patrons – Jean Monnet and Konrad Adenauer. These European statesmen advocated for a "federated Europe." French and German politicians were conscious of what they were doing, and yet did not understand what they were doing. They were unconsciously bringing into fruition what Dr. Robert Anderson recorded about the "vision" of Monnet and Adenauer and its destiny.

This leads to the question: "Why were British and Irish politicians not being 'patriotic' in following the extraordinary vision of their own 'father' – Sir Robert Anderson - and withdrew from the European Union? Strangely, they preferred to become 'adopted children' of strangers. For example, the British Identity Card, which was unveiled by the Labour Government, had no room for the British Flag. Instead it contained the EU symbol – a bull which represents the Greek pagan god Zeus who transformed himself into a white beast to abduct and seduce *Europa*. Secondly, the Labour Government allowed an European Union regulation that makes it legal to display the European symbol and the letter GB on the left side of car number plates, but illegal to display the British flag. The public was not informed of this 'illegal practice' with the result that some motorists displayed the British flag on their number plates without knowing they were breaking the law.

This prompted Dr Bob Spink, a Member of Parliament, demanding to know how many drivers had been penalised for an offence they did not know they were committing. Dr Spink stated: "This affair illustrates the growing power of the European Union over our lives. It is also a betrayal of motorists who didn't know they were breaking the law. It shows yet again that what governments say and what they do are often miles apart" (Source: The Mail on Sunday 26 October 2008 *Labour hasn't legalized British flags on number plates.....seven years after saying it would*). It is clear British politicians have been lacking the confidence to promote their own country. What a pity! A prophet is of no honour in his own country and among his own people.

Because of the impact the evolution of the European Union would have, not only on the British and Irish people, but also on the entire human race, and in view of the extraordinary contribution Sir Robert Anderson made to this important subject, I would pause for awhile to introduce the "Anglicanised-Irishman of Scotch extraction" to the world. This would offer the British and the Irish the opportunity to decide whether the works of Sir Robert Anderson should be taken seriously, or ignored as irrelevant writings from an 'ignorant' man. I believe the works of the "Seer of Dublin" would also help Americans and their politicians to evaluate their relationship with the European Union.

The Literary Recluse –
"God's Barrister"

"Through the gradual unfolding, it may be, of influences even now in operation; or far more probably as the outcome of some great European crisis in the future, this confederation of [European] nations* shall be developed, and thus the stage will be prepared on which shall appear that awful Being, the great leader of men in the eventful days which are to close the era of Gentile supremacy."

"I say nations, not kingdoms, advisedly, for though they will ultimately be kingdoms, that is, under monarchical government, yet before the advent of the Kaiser (the Emperor of the revived Roman Empire) such may not be the case...This division of the Roman earth will take place before his appearance...but whether a year, or decade or a century....we do not know."

The Lisbon Treaty (The European Constitution) paves the way for the advent of the "Kaiser."

Dr Robert Anderson listed England, Greece, Portugal and Turkey as members of European confederacy 94 years before Britain joined the European Economic Community in 1973, and 100 years before Greece joined in 1981, and 96 years before Portugal submitted it application to join, and 94 years before Turkey first applied for membership of European Community in 1963. The Prince of Scotland Yard warned of Britain's participation in the European confederacy.

Chapter 17

WHO WAS THE ANGLICANISED IRISHMAN OF SCOTCH EXTRACTION?"

"A Special subject in a school's curriculum is often ignored, as not being essential to "a liberal education"; and prophecy neglected by many a Christian as being unnecessary to "assurance of salvation." But such neglect is perilous in these days of subtle attacks upon the Bible; when we are confronted by both the sceptical crusade of the Higher Criticism, and the steadily increasing influence of Romanism. And the study of prophecy will prove a safeguard against these apostasies. For no Christian who pursues it intelligently, and understands the Divine 'plan of the ages', which it unfolds, will be imposed upon by "the learned ignorance" of the Critics.... And the present-day decline of Protestantism in England is due to no change in the historic apostasy of Christendom, but to weakening of faith in Holy Writ. For when the devout religionist begins to lose confidence in the Bible, he is apt to fall back upon "the Church"

(RA)

Sceptics know the cost of every product but not their value. So, before the pompous liberal intellectuals and the shallow "book–knowledge scientists" who assert a belief in God and religion is an intellectual nonsense and backwardness, and the European politicians, who claimed it would have been a "serious mistake," a "divisive" and "absurd" to have mentioned God and Christianity in the European constitution dismiss Sir Robert Anderson as perhaps an uninformed man or a "nutcase", I shall introduce him to you from his memoirs, *The Lighter Side of My Official Life,"* from his book , *Sidelight of Home Rule,* from *The Police Review and Gossip June 14, 1901),* from *The Cassell's Saturday Journal* and from his Biography *Sir Robert Anderson and Lady Agnes Anderson.* The biography was published in 1947 by his son, A P Moore-Anderson – a year before the Jews were restored to Palestine, and three years before the European Union was born.

Robert Anderson was born on 29 May 1841 in Dublin. His father, Matthew Anderson, was a lawyer of considerable reputation. For nearly 50 years he was Crown Solicitor for the County and City of Dublin. He was in charge of the Fenian prosecutions from 1865-1867. Robert Anderson described himself an "Anglicanised

Irishman of Scotch extraction". "My forebears", he writes, "were among the Scotch colonists who made Ulster what it is. An ancestor of my mother, and an ancestor of my wife's mother, won fame in the siege of Derry."

Robert Anderson was privately educated in Dublin, Paris and Boulogne. When Anderson left school, a rich and sonless friend of his father, who owned one of the famous Dublin breweries, introduced him into his business with "the generous intention of making a fortune." Within a year young Anderson was promoted to be a Cashier. After eighteen months he decided to quit, for he recognised his talents did not rest in book-keeping. At the age of eighteen he entered Trinity College in Dublin. In 1862 he graduated BA with Moderatorship and Medal. In 1870 he joined the English Bar, being called at the Middle Temple. He did not engage in court practice in England. In 1875 he was awarded the LLD. He was keen on rugby and football.

Anderson was brought up in a devout Christian home. At the age of 19, with the support of his sister, he accepted the Lord Jesus Christ after he had heard Dr John Hall preaching. The preacher confronted the teenage Anderson: "I tell you as a minister of Christ and in His name that there is a life for you here and now if you will accept Him. Will you accept Christ or will you reject Him?" After a considerable long pause, young Anderson responded: "In God's name I will accept Christ." He confessed: "I turned homeward with the peace of God filling my heart." This happened in 1860 – the year the agnostic Professor Huxley became a "celebrity" because of his clash with Bishop Wilberforce over Darwin's Theory of Evolution. Anderson himself became a lay preacher. He wrote about seventeen Christian books. Some of them were translated into many foreign languages. The Lord used Dr Anderson's work to win many souls.

In 1863, the young barrister was admitted to the Irish Bar and served on the legal circuit. About this time, the Fenians, a secret society which was attempting to overthrow British rule in Ireland, was in operation. Robert Anderson became involved in interrogating prisoners and preparing legal briefs. This was his introduction into police work." *The Cassell's Saturday Journal,* which was published on 11 June 1892, gave us the detail: "At the Spring assizes in 1867, the Fenian rising took place, and 200 or 300 prisoners were marched into the yard at Dublin Castle and solemnly committed for trial on the charge of high treason...The Attorney General telegraphed for Dr Anderson, instructing him, to inquire into each case in order to advise the Crown which of the prisoners were worth sending for trial. An extraordinary sequence of events during 1867 led to the barrister being retained during greater part of the year at a professional fee to help the Government in various ways at the Castle. Then the Clerkenwell explosion occurred, and Lord Mayo asked the young advocate to proceed to London to investigate matters connected with the Fenian outrage on the spot."

Concerning this explosion, it is recorded that Dr Anderson gave a warning to the London Police – information which they did ignore. In page 37 of his biography, Moore Anderson quoted extracts from his father's obituary notice which was published in *The Times* of 18 November 1918: "His (Dr Anderson's) special knowledge of the ways of Irish political conspiracy became known in high official circles not only in Dublin but in London. After the famous Clerkenwell explosion in 1867—a warning of which he was able to transmit beforehand to the London Police, although they failed to make use of the information—one of the results of what he himself termed the unreasoning panic that followed was the organisation of a Secret Service department of the police, and he was invited to take charge of it. But it only remained in existence for three months, and he was about to return to the Irish Bar when he was requested to take charge of Irish business at the Home Office. In this capacity he had a good deal to do with the surveillance of the Fenian conspirators (Irish and American-Irish) whose plots gave some anxiety to the Government in the years 1869 and 1870."

In 1873 Dr. Anderson married Lady Agnes Alexander Moore, who was a sister of the Earl of Drogheda. In this year, Dr Anderson was asked by the Home Secretary, Mr Hardy (Later Lord Crankbrook), to go to the Home Office to organise the Department and to deal with political crime. He also acted as Secretary to several government Commissions - among them were Royal Commission on Loss of Life at Sea and Royal Observatory of Edinburgh Commission. In 1877 the Home Secretary offered Dr Anderson a temporary position as Secretary of the Prison Commission on passing of the Prison Act in July 1877. While still Secretary to the Prison Commission, he was retained by the Irish government to look after their interests in London – sometimes helping the Chief Secretary for Ireland and the Home Secretary. He was also responsible to the Secretary of State in relation to political crime in general.

His first family home in London was at 7 Kensington Gore, South Kensington almost in the shadow of the Royal Albert Hall. Four years later he moved to 39 Linden Gardens on the north of Hyde Park. He lived there until his death. He had four sons and one daughter. According to Moore Anderson, his father was proud of being a Londoner and of the amenities of the Capital in respect of its public parks. Moore Anderson writes: "...The London life had great attractions for him (Dr Anderson), especially the House of Commons, where his friendship with Captain Gosset, then Assistant Sergeant-at-Arms, gave him access to "Gosset's Room", which was in reality a sort of social club. Invitations were extended (with the exception of two or three relatives) only to MPs. In this way my father was brought into touch with all the by-play of the House, and met the elite of its members."

As a committed Christian with a profound knowledge of the Bible, some of Dr. Anderson's friends in the Church of England urged him to accept appointment as a lay preacher in the Church in order that he might have further opportunities to help them. He once preached in Eldon Parish Church.

In page 47 of his biography, Moore-Anderson writes. "An attack was made in 1910 in consequence of Sir Robert having mentioned in *Blackwood* that he was author of certain articles on the American Fenians published anonymously in *The Times* as far back as 1887. They were entitled "*Behind the scenes in America.*" In this case he was accused of having acted in a way contrary to the rules and traditions of the Civil Service. The fact that one of the articles exposed a plot to bring about a dynamite explosion in Westminster Abbey at the time of Queen Victoria's Jubilee might, one would think, have excused any breach of official propriety had such been indeed committed. But naturally the wild Irishmen in the House were out for his scalp and demanded the withdrawal of his pension....the responsible Minister, instead of defending him, contended himself with appeasing his opponents by making light of the whole matter and minimising the service he had rendered to the State."

Dr Anderson received many letters of sympathy and encouragement. This is a quote from one of the sympathisers, a Scottish Lawyer, Mr R. R. Stewart: "To speak of a faithful and able servant of his country, who unsparingly gave himself to his service in work most trying and involving danger to his own life, during a perturbed time which it is difficult for any one who did not live through it to understand or even to credit - in the way in which you have been spoken of - is a lasting disgrace to British statesmanship."

Moore Anderson further recorded: "An article in Black and White on *The Detectives who Frustrated the Dynamite Plot (in 1896),* said: "In Dr. Anderson's appearance there is more of the man of peace than of the terror of conspirators. Yet it is certain that he has been a conspicuous success in his high office, thanks to his analytical mind, his keen reasoning powers, and his 'scent' for the right trial...." And Chief-Inspector Melville, the head of the Special Division of the Scotland Yard, said: "Dr. Anderson has been described and fitly as the ideal detective of real life, yet he bears but little resemblance to those of the novelists' creation...His power of close and rapid reasoning from facts and his marvellous quickness in seizing on the essential points in difficult cases are at once the wonder and admiration of the men under his control. Naturally, he is discreet, silent and reserved man; his training has made him even more so, but no officer who has yet presided over the affairs of the C.I.D. can boast of being more popular or more genuinely respected by his subordinates."

Dr Anderson at Scotland Yard and Jack-the Ripper Case

On 1 September 1888 (about two months before Jean Monnet was born) Dr. Anderson was summoned to Scotland Yard in London to serve as Chief of the Criminal Investigation Department. When he was appointed to head the Scotland Yard, a horse and police groom were placed at his disposal. He usually rode to his office. But because of his love for keeping fit, Dr Anderson occasionally walked to work. As an Assistant Commissioner of Police he earned £1250 per annum. Sir Richard Mayne, the London Police Commissioner, gave Dr. Anderson access to the detective department. He soon gained "the confidence and goodwill of the officers. He got to know all that was worth knowing about their work."

When Dr. Anderson took charge of the complex Criminal Investigation Department, he and his staff dedicated themselves to matters relating to the prevention and detection of crime. The night before he assumed duty, the second Whitechapel murder was committed. The third occurred the night he left for a rest in Switzerland. On his return from holiday, he started reinvestigating the whole Jack-the-Ripper case. When the Chief Commissioner of Police, Mr Matthews, told Dr Anderson, "We hold you responsible to find the murderers", he replied: "I hold myself responsible to take all legitimate means to find him."

The so-called Jack-the-Ripper was found. Commenting on the case in his memoirs, *"The Lighter side of my official life,"* Dr Anderson records: "The people knew his guilt, and refused to give him up to justice.... If the Police had powers such as the French Police possess, the murderer would have been brought to justice....I will merely add that the only person who had ever had a good view of the murderer unhesitatingly identified the suspect the instant he was confronted with him; but he refused to give evidence against him." Dr Anderson concluded: "Having regard to the interest attaching to this [Jack-the Ripper] case, I am almost tempted to disclose the identity of the murderer and of the pressman who wrote the letter [about Jack-the Ripper which letter is preserved in the Police Museum at New Scotland Yard]. But no public benefit would result from such a course and the traditions of my old department would suffer." However, Dr Anderson stated the nationality of the murderer as a Polish-Jew. He qualified his description with this statement: "I am merely stating a definitely ascertained fact. And my words are meant to specify race, not religion."

Another terrible crime which the Assistant Commissioner of Metropolitan Police investigated, but which went unpunished, was the murder of Amelia Jeffs, at west Ham, in 1890. In this case also the identity of the murderer was believed to have been known, though it proved impossible to put him upon trial. There were a long list of cases which might be cited in which, largely owing to the skill of Dr Anderson, great criminals, such as Jabez Balfour, were brought to book. *Police*

Review records: "Of Dr Anderson's work at Scotland Yard, little is known or likely to be known to the public. Yet if public opinion was more alive than it is, there might be some chance of making that alteration in our methods of dealing with the criminal, which would end in what the Assistant Commissioner believes to be 'not only practicable, but easy' --- namely, the stamping out of professional organised crime."

During his reign at *SCOTLAND YARD* crime went down. Sir John Moylan, writing in the "*Scotland Yard and the Metropolitan Police,*" states: "The period 1890 to 1900 proved to be one during which there was an almost continuous decrease in crime....By signal successes in sensational cases, and by steady achievement in the less advertised everyday business of dealing with rogues in general, the C.I.D. built up in the nineties a world –wide reputation for efficiency in crime detection." According to Moore – Anderson, Sir Harry Furness, the famous artist, devoted a chapter of his book "*Some Victorian Men*" to the London Police. Sir Harry stated: "One of the hardest-working and most brilliant heads of the Criminal Investigation Department for many years was that eminent Victorian, Sir Robert Anderson, K.C.B."

Dr. Anderson and Americans

Before he took charge as the Head of the Criminal Investigation Department, staff were discouraged and demoralised. The crime returns for 1887 gave proof of that. The Commissioner's report for 1888 recorded that crime during the year has shown a decided tendency to increase. Such was the state of affairs when he entered on his new duties. From 1888 onwards crime reduced dramatically. He stated that no other large city in the world could show such results as these. And having regard to the huge population of London, and its peculiar characteristics, the safety of life in the metropolis was a standing miracle. I quote Dr. Anderson's own words to demonstrate the efficiency of the Police Force during his reign:

"one evening in the year after the Chicago Exhibition, I dined with some American gentlemen at the Hotel Cecil, and they gave me some astounding particulars of the number of homicides in that city. They mentioned 2,000 cases as having occurred in the previous year. I can scarcely believe such a tale, but that is not the point of my story. Presently they asked me how many murders we had in London in a year. ...I normal? Pleaded that London was three times as large as Chicago, and that facilities for crime increased in proportion to population: How many cases would they consider? After some discussion among themselves, the estimate they gave me was 200. I told them that the preceding year was the worst I had known, as we had twenty murders; but the average was fifteen or sixteen. They threw down knives and forks, and stared at me and at each other. My words travelled across the Atlantic, and I received several letters, including one from a prominent official in Washington, asking me if I had spoken seriously and by the book."

The Prince of Detectives continued: *"Though the Metropolitan Police deserve their need of praise for such results as these, a full explanation of them must be sought in the characteristics of our national life, and in the peculiar influences to which those characteristics are mainly due. But here I will deal only with the facts. In reply to questions in Parliament last year, the Home Secretary gave the following striking statistics. The murders in the Metropolis, he said, from the 1st of January, 1903, to the 30th of September, 1908, numbered 92, and among these there were only 10 "undiscovered crimes." Four of the 10, moreover, were deaths due to illegal operations; and such cases are murders only in a technical sense. This means six "undiscovered murders," or an average of one per annum, and this in a population that averaged more than 7,000,000 during the six years in question. It seems almost incredible, and I own that I should refuse to believe it if I had not personal knowledge of the care and accuracy with which the criminal statistics are compiled. And Mr. Herbert Gladstone added that, in some of the cases where no one was made amenable, the criminals were known to the Police, but evidence to justify an arrest was not obtainable."* When Dr. Anderson left the Scotland Yard, crime continued to fall.

The "Prince of Scotland" Yard and His War on Gambling

Among the legacies which Dr. Anderson's predecessor left him was a charge to wage war on "gaming-houses." He accepted the charge wholeheartedly. According to the Prince of Detectives, "gambling, a vice that springs from an illegitimate craving for money, does as much as drink to corrupt its votaries." There was abnormal growth of gambling clubs in London. There were West End Clubs frequented by "swells", middle-class clubs run by "snobs." He determined to begin at the top, for though the lower class clubs were far more the most mischievous, he decided he was not going to incur the taunt of chevying humble folk and leaving the "toffs" alone. He raided the most fashionable clubs and closed them down.

The gamblers decided to adopt new tactics by using the premises of a private house in the name of a lady of title and to arrange a weekly meeting there for gambling. Dr. Anderson adopted new tactics. Instead of maintaining secrecy, he announced his intention of raiding the place and the scheme collapsed. The Prince of Detectives and his forces then pursued the minor clubs scattered throughout London, and one after another all were successfully raided by the Police.

A journalist from the *Evening News and Post* interviewed Dr Anderson. This interview was published in the September 28, 1894 edition of *The Police Review and Parade Gossip* in a column titled A CHAT WITH THE PRINCE OF DETECTIVES AT SCOTLAND YARD. The "Prince" was asked whether Scotland Yard was now following in the footsteps of the French methods of dealing with criminals. Dr Anderson responded: "Oh, dear, no. There will be a very wide difference between our method and the French....You must understand that the Scotland Yard method must always differ widely from the French method, because our law is so different in these matters to that of France. For instance, using our representative as the *corpus vile* system on which to illustrate this difference in the system of the two countries: "You are walking along the streets of Paris, and are merely suspected as a criminal who has been in the hands of the Police on a previous occasion. The evidence against you may be of the flimsiest possible character - there may be really none at all - but you are seized all the same, and at once subjected to a searching scrutiny at the hands of the Police. Your measurements are taken, your finger-prints, etc., examined and you are not released until the authorities have satisfied themselves that they have made a mistake. Such a method is repugnant to British law and feeling. Here we cannot drag you to Scotland Yard and examine you in this summary fashion. If there is good reason to suspect you of being a criminal all that can be done is to charge you before a magistrate, and if the charge fails there is no way by which you can be subjected to examination for purposes of identification. We can only use our albums against you if you are remanded….." What a pity! In the 21st century British politicians -the "children" of Sir Robert Anderson - want Britain to adopt French laws because of their association with the European Union.

In page 56 of his biography, Moore-Anderson quoted a leading article in *The Times*, which was in response to an attack on Sir Robert by Irish members in the House: "It is greatly to be regretted that no official notice was taken of the gross attacks upon Mr Robert Anderson, the able and energetic Assistant Commissioner of Police who has the control of the Criminal Investigation Department, and to whose vigilance and activity it is undoubtedly due that so many detestable terrorist conspiracies have been nipped in the bud…. There can be no shadow of doubt that a great crime was being prepared in the bomb factory at Antwerp and that its execution was defeated by measures adopted by the C.I.D."

I have already mentioned that according to records, crime reduced in London during Dr. Anderson's reign at Scotland Yard. At the time when Conan Doyle was entertaining London with Sherlock Holmes stories, the Prince of Detectives and his staff were clearing out the metropolis of crime and criminals. Warren Wiersbe writes: "Dr Anderson tracked down myths and religious error, arrested and exposed it, with the same skill and courage that he displayed when he tracked down criminals."

Continuing with its tribute to the Head of the Criminal Investigation Department, *The Police Review and Parade Gossip* stated: "Dr. Anderson was regarded highly in his immediate official circle. His tenure of office was considered to be characterised by that comfortable placidity for which the majority of our public functionaries are remarkable. Moreover, his temperament, so admirably adapted to his social and religious proclivities, was not such as best fits one for the work of the C.I.D.

A Biblical scholar of repute, and a literary recluse, such as he is, would hardly be the man to take an active part in fighting the criminal classes of London. Discreet, silent, and reserved though he was, according to Major Arthur Griffith's estimate, he lacked one inestimable quality to success, as the director of the Detective staff of the most important Police Force in the world, and that was just the requisite kind of knowledge, of the world and of men...An acknowledged authority on our penal system, it was perhaps, hardly a looked-for choice on the part of Mr Home Secretary Matthews when Dr Anderson was transferred from Prisons Department to handle the reins at Scotland Yard."

Dr Anderson was described as a deep thinker and a student of prophecy, Biblical chronology, science and philosophy." He wrote several articles on "Criminals and crime". His article "*Morality by Act of Parliament*" was described a "hit." The lawyer published *A Doubter's Doubts about Science and Religion* anonymously. This attracted the attention of Mr William Gladstone, the then Prime Minister. Gladstone wrote to the author twice. (I will tell you more about this significant book).

In 1896, Dr Anderson was included in the New Year honours. The decoration of the Companionship of the Order of the Bath was bestowed on him at Windsor by Her Majesty Queen Victoria. When Sir Robert Anderson retired from the Criminal Investigation Department in 1901, the rank of K.C.B (Knight Commander) was bestowed on him by King Edward VII.

In his memoirs, Dr Anderson made this profound statement: "It is extraordinary how often it happens that very unique and costly things easily to be identified come into our hands and nobody asks question about them." The *Cassell's Saturday Journal,* in its article "*Dr Anderson at New Scotland*" stated: "There is no vindictive spirit in him, for Dr Anderson finds the pleasant part of his work in helping repentant criminals to reform."

Dr. Robert Anderson was intellectually brilliant. He was described as "a giant amongst giants and anything he wrote is worth having on one's library shelf..." The scholar among scholars held all his positions with distinction. In the midst of all his duties, the native of Dublin, who was a lawyer by profession, gained a profound knowledge of the Bible. He preached in various conferences. At a meeting at Cork, which he was invited at a few hours notice, Dr. Robert Anderson preached to about 500 people. When the meeting ended and the people were "dismissed" several times, they seemed unwilling to leave. He received invitations to preach in the United States and Canada. In 1906, Dr A. C Dixon, a Baptist Minister, wrote to Dr. Anderson: "...I was requested by five pastors – one Methodist, one Congregational, one Presbyterian and two Episcopalian to write to you and learn whether it would be possible for you to visit Boston and give series of lectures on the *The Bible and Modern Criticism.*" In the opinion of a reviewer in the New York Tribune, "*The Bible and Modern Criticism* is a work of singular lucidity of style and remarkable argumentative power.....which places critics as radical as Professor Cheyene or as conservative as Professor Driver on their defence before men of common sense." The Bishop of Durham wrote a notable appeal in the Preface to this classic work.

The Prince of Detectives was an author, teacher and defender of the Christian Faith. A Minute of the Victoria Institute, dated 22 December 1918, stated: "When Sir Robert Anderson was at leisure from official duties he undertook literary work in defence of Christian truth and the authority of Holy Scripture. The qualities which made him eminent in official life, together with his loyalty to truth and his incisive logic, rendered his advocacy of those cases weighty and influential." As a testimony to his work, the Rev WH Griffith Thomas, D.D, writing in *The Evangelical Christian,* stated: "Sir Robert Anderson's books are amongst the most valuable of our day, and will long abide as a testimony to the truth of the Gospel." And J. Arnold Fair, in writing the foreword to Sir Robert's book, *Redemption Truths,* records: "Sir Robert Anderson was a legally powerful man of the 19th century. He was head of the criminal investigation department of Scotland Yard and political crime adviser to the British Home Office. Not only was he in a God-given place of power, but he had an appreciation of authority. Could this be the reason that, in so much of Sir Robert Anderson's writing, he takes the position of an apologist? He believed and wrote that God's word is absolute truth to be trusted and lived. As an investigator of crime, he wanted only factual reality not fiction. He found this truth in the Lord Jesus Christ..."

In *A History of the Brethren Movement*, the Chartered Accountant, F Roy Coad, writes: "Sir Robert Anderson of Scotland Yard knocked down his Biblical opponents like ninepins.....Anderson wrote prolifically on religious matters, earning the (slightly depreciating) description from L E Elliot-Binns of "that doughty champion of popular Protestantism..."

Apart from the many Christian books Sir Robert Anderson published, he also wrote other non religious books such as *Criminals and Crime, Sidelights on the Home Rule Movement,* his memoirs, *The Lighter Side of my Official Life,* and many articles. According to his son, "My Father had wanted to write in more serious vein of his official life at a later date; but this was not to be."

The Police Review reported: "As an Ulsterman and a Presbyterian, Dr Anderson took naturally to theological controversy. As pronounced Evangelical, the Doctor found much to condemn in the methods and manner of all the Churches. Occasionally, Dr. Anderson preached at various Nonconformist churches in the West of London. "He possessed a dry humour and an incisive style. He was a critic of the higher criticism and of science falsely so-called. His correspondence with Professor Huxley of Oxford in *The Times* attracted considerable attention. Dr Anderson took up the controversy where Mr Gladstone left off, and scored several neat points against his doughty antagonist."

Dr Anderson on Evolution and Creationism Controversy: Thomas Huxley found wanting and Herbert Spencer dismissed

"*In the Dawn of Creation and Worship,* Prime Minister Gladstone sought to establish the claims of the book of Genesis to be a Divine revelation, by showing that the order of creation as there recorded has been so affirmed …by natural science that it may be taken as a demonstrated conclusion and established fact." Mr Gladstone suggested that science and Genesis were perfectly in accord as regards the order in which life appeared upon our globe. Professor Huxley sought to undermine Gladstone's assertion by arguing that natural science does not affirm the statement that birds were made on the fifth day, and everything that creepeth on the ground on the sixth day. Huxley misinterpreted sections of the Book of Leviticus to undermine Mr. Gladstone's claim. At this crucial point in the debate, Dr. Anderson stepped into the 'jungle' to rescue Gladstone from the "Jaws of Darwin's bulldog." Dr Anderson declared: "I agree in all essential points with Mr Gladstone, and I believe that the first chapter of Genesis and science are in accord.

This marked the beginning of a "confrontation" between the Knight himself and Professor Huxley, the Champion of Darwinism. I quote from Dr Anderson's *A Doubters Doubt about Science and Religion* in which he dismissed Darwinian Theory of Evolution and "slaughtered Darwin's "bulldog": "I (Anderson) challenged Mr Huxley on this subject in the columns of *The Times* newspaper. He (Huxley) sought to evade the issue by pleading that the real question involved was that of the supernatural versus evolution. This evoked a powerful letter from the Duke of Argyll, denouncing the reference to the supernatural as savouring of "bad science and worse philosophy," and warning Mr Huxley that in the new position in which he sought to take refuge "he would not have the support of the most eminent men of science in the United Kingdom." In a final letter I (Robert Anderson) restated the question, and again challenged Mr. Huxley either to establish or to abandon his contention that Genesis and science were in antagonism. His reply was a letter suggesting, in his grandest style, that the public were tired of the controversy. But it was not the public that were tired of it." Dr. Anderson added:: "The fact remains that Mr Gladstone's position stands unshaken. The fact remains that one who has had no equal in this age as a scientific controversialist entered the lists to attack it, and retired discomfited and discredited. Mr Gladstone's thesis, therefore, holds the field. "The order of creation as recorded in Genesis has been so affirmed in our time by natural science that it may be taken as a demonstrated conclusion and established fact."

Dr Anderson continued: "Are we then to conclude that when Genesis was written biological science was as enlightened and as far advanced as it is today? Or shall we adopt the more reasonable alternative, that the Mosaic narrative was a Divine revelation? All this of course will weigh nothing with men who have prejudged the question. First, there are the religious teachers of that school whose role it appears to be to import the raw material of German rationalism and to retail it with a veneer of British piety to suit the British market. And secondly, there are the scientists of the materialistic school, to whom the very name of God is intolerable......But it may be asked, what about evolution? The materialistic evolution of Herbert Spencer is as dead as its author. And even Darwin's more enlightened biological scheme is now discredited. For it is recognised that something more than Darwinism offers is needed to account for the phenomenon of life. The evolution hypothesis is thoroughly philosophical; and that it is all that can be said for it, for it is unproved and seemingly incapable of proof..."

Herbert Spencer was the philosopher who coined the phrase "*the survival of the Fittest.*" And Charles Darwin substituted "survival of the fittest" for his idea of "natural selection." Dr Anderson devoted a chapter in his *A Doubter's Doubt About Science and Religion* to dismiss Spencer's philosophy – the "hypothesis of special creation and the hypothesis of evolution." Under the title *Herbert Spencer's Scheme*, Dr. Anderson writes: Herbert Spencer will tell us that, "however regarded, the hypothesis of special creations turns out to be worthless - worthless by its derivation; worthless in its intrinsic incoherence; worthless as absolutely without evidence; worthless as not supplying an intellectual need; worthless as not satisfying a moral want. We must, therefore consider it as counting for nothing in opposition to any other hypothesis respecting the origin of organic beings." Dr Anderson continues: "Herbert Spencer proceeds to urge that a belief in creation is discredited by 'association with a special class of mistaken beliefs." Now this, of course, is a reference to the Mosaic account of the creation, and it is sufficiently answered by many men of competent attainments and of the highest intellectual capacity." The Knight Commander added: "No one ever saw a special creation." True: but a similar objection may be made to the hypothesis of evolution; and it has, in fact, been urged in these pages......"

"God's Barrister" concludes the chapter: "At a single plunge we have thus reached the level of blank atheism, which is the extreme depth of moral and intellectual degradation. 'The birth of the species and the individual' must equally be ascribed to "blind chance," "coercion" being appealed to, I suppose, to quell the inevitable "revolt of the understanding." And the strange religious propensities common to the race, whether civilised or savage, must also be suppressed; or, at all events, our *Penates* must be strictly limited to an effigy of our hairy quadru-manous ancestor with pointed ears, supplemented possibly by some "symbolic conception" of the primordial life-germ wrapped in cloud, and a copy of Herbert Spencer's *System of Philosophy* to guide and regulate the cult."

Footnote: *"The Gladstone and Huxley articles appeared in the nineteenth Century in the later months of 1885 and in January and February 1886. And Mr Gladstone's articles were in part reproduced in his Impregnable Rock of Holy Scripture. Dr Anderson's correspondence with Professor Huxley will be found in the Times of January 23 and 26 and February 1, 3, 4. 8, and 11 (1892). Dr. Anderson quoted an extract from a letter he received from Mr Gladstone after the Times correspondence closed: "As to the chapter itself (Genesis i), "I do not regard it merely as a defensible point in a circle of fortifications, but as a grand foundation of the entire fabric of the holy Scriptures."*

I diverted to provide this information on Evolution and Creationism for the following reasons;

- The Evolution and Creationism controversy resurfaced in 2008 as a result of the comments Reverend Professor Michael Weiss, a Royal Society scientist, made regarding teaching Creationism in science lessons.
- And secondly to remind the scientists, intellectuals and fashionable theologians who adore Charles Darwin, that the Champion of Darwinism, Professor Thomas Huxley, was 'knocked out' and humiliated by a scholar among scholars.

On this age-old controversy - Creationism and Science - Dr Anderson writes: "The question is not whether the Cosmogony teaches science, which no one asserts; but whether it is discredited by science, which no one has proved. And not even the testimony of such a scientist as Professor Dana in its defence will weigh as much with men of the world, as the fact that such a scientist as Huxley entered the lists to prove it in error and failed" (Pseudo Criticism page ix). My purpose of digression is to silence the arrogant scientists of the 21st century who sneer at Christians who believe in the Biblical account of creation.

SIR ROBERT ANDERSON: A MAN WITH KNOWLEDGE AND MENTAL POWER

Now, let us witness the following testimonies that reinforce the character and brilliance of Dr Robert Anderson. Dr James M Gray, former Professor of the Moody Bible Institute, writes: "Sir Robert Anderson is in some respects the most remarkable of current writers on religious subjects, whether we consider his personal history or the range and character of his works.....To sit at the feet of a man with such knowledge, mental power, courage and native wit, who is at the same time spirit taught, is for the true Christian one of the greatest privileges." And Dr J Stuart Holden of St Paul's Portman Square wrote: "From his writings I came to know something of the unfathomable content of the Gospel. From his life I came to know far more.....he was an example of the believers in word, in conversation, in charity, in spirit, in faith and in purity."

In the review of the first edition of his biography, the *Evangelical Christendom* writes:
"The Church of Christ owes a great debt to the memory of Sir Robert Anderson...... It is a great mistake to suppose that he was a narrow-minded man, or an opponent of legitimate criticism, or a mere unreasoning champion of orthodoxy. He had insight into the full-orbed Gospel, and his attachment to Christ amounted to a passion which sometimes - as for instance against the blasphemous "New Theology" teaching - found full display.....Sir Robert was a humble Christian of a most tender disposition as we were privileged to know by experience." And another review in *The Christian World* had this appreciation: "Ulster had a typical son in Sir Robert Anderson, whose strongly marked personality was familiar in strict evangelical circles for half a century. It was through several protective rinds that one had to pass to get to the simple pleasantness of the Christian father and friend. (He was outwardly) the keen, relentless Secret Service agent, the terror of Irish rebels; he was the "no-surrender" foe of Biblical criticism; he was the tireless speaker, preacher and writer for his faith. But when his day's fight was done he was lovable and much loved..."

Sir Robert Anderson: A Man of Peace who Never Shirks a Fight

I would now share with you how Dr Robert Anderson handled a "confrontation" between him and a British politician – Sir William Harcourt. This would highlight the character of the Prince of Detectives. In 1889, Sir William Harcourt - then a Leader of the Opposition - without checking his facts, attacked Dr Anderson for revealing official secrets to the *Times* newspaper. Dr Anderson recorded this incident in chapter 2 of his book, *Sidelight of Home Rule.*

According to Dr. Anderson, the Clerkenwell explosion which occurred in the winter of 1867 brought Fenianism to the front in England. Mr. Rebow, MP for Colchester, suggested that Le Caron, who had infiltrated the Fenians in America and obtained information about their activities, be placed in touch with someone representing the government. He was put in communication with Dr Anderson – Head of Criminal Investigation Department of Scotland Yard. His communication with Le Caron lasted for about twenty years and ended with Major Le Caron appearing as a witness before a Special Commission.

The Secret Service Agent recorded: "Our bargain was that while the information he afforded might be used by me freely in the public interest, his letters were to be deemed private. And so, when he decided, as he expressed it, "to testify for the *Times,"* he claimed in pursuance of this bargain, to have access to his letters in order to enable him to prepare his evidence. To this demand I acceded; and for doing so Sir William Harcourt declared war upon me. In reply to question in Parliament, on March 1, 1889, Mr. Henry Mathews, the Conservative Home Secretary, informed him that in this matter "I had acted without his knowledge or sanction." And he thereupon gave notice - "That on the Vote on Account relating to the Metropolitan Police he would call attention to the conduct of Mr Anderson in handing over confidential documents without leave from the Secretary of State, and its bearing upon his position as Assistant Commissioner of Police in charge of the Criminal Investigation Department."

Dr Anderson continued: "A fortnight later, speaking on a political platform in Lambeth, he (Mr Harcourt) used these words: "The confidential agent, the Commissioner of Police, the head of the Criminal Investigation Department, goes and hands over to an informer and to the agent of the *Times*, the secret papers of the Home Office without the consent of the Home Secretary. I should have liked to see a man in that position do such a thing under any of the predecessors of the Home Secretary. I know where he would have been today. It would not have been at Scotland Yard." This appeared in the newspapers of Wednesday, March 20, 1889.

According to the Police Commissioner, a friend from the House of Commons visited him with the news "that the whole business of the empire had been put aside in order to discuss my evil deeds," and that Sir William Harcourt, in particular, had attacked me fiercely." The object in calling Dr. Anderson was to warn him that his position was critical, and urged him to move to defend himself. The Prince of Scotland Yard responded: "A letter to the *Times* might roll back the tide of war. But would it embarrass the Secretary of State?" Dr Anderson was assured that "it would only help the Secretary of State." For his friend, who informed him about the case, was a personal, as well as a political friend of Mr. Matthews. On the basis of this assurance, Dr. Anderson went straight to the *Times* office and appealed to the editor to see a copy of the report of the debate in the House of Commons. It was given to him.

Dr. Anderson's relationship with Sir William Harcourt

Dr. Anderson recorded: "Sir William Harcourt's platform denunciations had not alarmed me. In the same connection he branded Sir Richard Webster as "a disgrace to the English Bar;" and nothing he said of me was quite as bad as that. That was "his way." But his words as leader of the Opposition in the House of Commons could not be treated lightly. And he had charged me, I learned, with "acting as a tout for the Times?" and "betraying the secrets of my Department," thus proving that I was "utterly useless in the office I held." Had he been Home Secretary, he declared, "a man in Mr. Anderson's position would not have remained twenty-four hours in Scotland Yard."

Disappointed by the behaviour of Sir William, Dr Anderson pointed out: "Though I am *a* man of peace I never shirk a fight, and this sort of thing was just what was best fitted to put me on my mettle." The Secret Service Agent continued: "So I took up my pen at once, and a couple of hours later I handed my apologia to the editor. Mr. Buckle was most sympathetic, and set himself to impress on me the gravity of the course I was taking. He urged me to hold back my letter till I had "slept over it." Dr. Anderson responded: "And give the lie twenty-four hours start?" "No." "I know what I am doing, and I fear nothing but delay."

The following morning, March 21, 1889, The Times published Dr. Anderson's letter, which according to the newspaper, "seems to stand out in striking contrast, for dignity of tone and straightforward statement, with the combination of recklessness and shiftiness displayed by his unscrupulous accusers."

" SIR W. HARCOURT AND MR. ANDERSON.
" To the Editor of the ' Times.'

SIR,

"It is an excellent rule that Civil servants of the Crown, when publicly attacked, should leave their defence in the hands of their Parliamentary chiefs. I have always observed that rule, and I have no intention of departing from it. But when acts done by me wholly outside the sphere of my official position are assigned as proof that I am unworthy of the office I have the honour to hold under Her Majesty's warrant, I must not shelter myself behind the Secretary of State, for whose generous defence of me in Parliament today I am most deeply grateful. It is my privilege, as it is clearly my duty, to put myself right with the public immediately.

"The proper method of doing so is, I admit, by appearing in the witness-box of the Commission Court, and I feel seriously aggrieved.

"As regards Sir W. Harcourt's criticisms upon the discharge of my official duties my mouth is closed. But I want to emphasize, and I am prepared to substantiate on oath, the fact asserted by Mr. Matthews that neither the Assistant Commissioner of Police nor the department which he controls has given help to the Times in the presentation of their case before the Commission.

" I am, etc.,

"R. ANDERSON.

" March 20."

According to Dr Anderson, "THE success of my Times letter was complete. In writing it I had a double purpose in view. I knew the importance of putting myself right with the public; but I wished also to make a covert appeal to Sir William Harcourt. For I had confidence in his fairness and generosity, and I wanted to recall to his memory matters which I felt sure he had forgotten. Here is his letter to me, to which I referred; and the only comment I need make upon it is to repeat that among the "modes of procedure" about which we differed, my arrangements with informants held a prominent place:

Sir William Harcourt's Letter to Dr. Anderson

> Private.
> "My DEAR ANDERSON,
> "I am sorry to find from your letter that you think I have not duly appreciated your indefatigable exertions in the disagreeable duty which has fallen to you. " I assure you that is altogether a mistake, and I pray you to dismiss it from your mind. "If we differ sometimes as to modes of procedure that is a thing which must be looked for. Pray go on as you have done in your useful work, and you may rely on entire sympathy and support from me. I am always most grateful for your reports and advice.
>
> "Yours truly,
> "W. V. HARCOURT."

From this story we have gained additional insight into the temperament of the man who, before the First World War, wrote about a political alliance of European nations and its future before the European Union evolved from the ashes of the Second World War. Would the Irish and the British take Dr Anderson seriously on what he recorded about European integration? In the 19th century, officials in Washington were impressed of Dr Anderson's fight against crime. Pastors in America invited him to preach to their congregation. In the 21st century, would politicians in Washington take the Prince of Detectives seriously on the warning he gave about the future of political Europe? And would pastors in America study his theological works for the benefit of their congregation?

Some of the Literary Works of Sir Robert Anderson

Despite his busy schedule - fighting and reducing crime in England - Dr Anderson had the time to write over 20 books on Theology and Political crime. I have seen original copies of the following works of the "Seer of Dublin" which I would like to share with you.

1. A Doubter's Doubts about Science and Religion

This book was first published in 1889 and the third edition was produced in 1924. In this work, God's Barrister argued against "Evolution." He dismissed The Darwinian Theory in the opening chapter of the book by raising the question: "How did life begin?" He goes on: "The first and greatest question relates, not to the phenomenon of life, but its origin. How did life begin? And here evolution affords no answer, and must stand aside. Let the existence of life be taken for granted, and evolution may explain the rest. But the sceptic takes nothing for granted. How did life begin? Science answers! In presence of a question which lies across the threshold of knowledge, science, the very personification of knowledge, turns agnostic and is dumb. "Creation" is the answer religion gives. The rejoinder which science ought to make is that life first sprang out of death, out of nothing; in a word, abiogenesis. Abiogenesis is merely a philosophic theory unsupported by even the faintest shred of evidence. But more than this, it is practically incapable of proof, for the problem implies the proof of a negative in circumstances which render the difficulties of such proof overwhelming."

Dr Anderson continues: "It is because science leads us back to an existence which never had a beginning, for want of any other term by which to designate it, we call it God." The Defender of the Christian Faith went on: "...Evolution – not as a hypothesis to account for the origin of species; but merely as a pretended explanation of the origin of life....we have found that......it is but a blind lane which leads nowhere.... First, Evolution is merely a philosophic theory, second, that it is unproven; Third it is inadequate and fourth...it is unnecessary, except of course those scientists who cling to any plank that will save them from having to acknowledge the existence of God. Regarded as a theory to account for life, evolution is the widest folly; but as an hypothesis to account for the varied forms of life, it claims a hearing on its merits...The man who can give no account of his own existence is a fool; and he who denies a God can give no account of his existence.....But philosophy is not folly, and folly has no right to call itself wisdom."

The Lawyer with "sanctified logic" continues: "Evolution assumes the existence of life; postulates it; as the scientist would say. No more is needed than one solitary germ of living matter. Indeed, to seek for more would be unphilosophical. But this primeval germ must be taken for granted. The sceptic will refuse to assign to it an origin which contradicts all our experience and surpasses our knowledge. The only hypothesis he can accept is that life has existed without any limitation of time; that the original life-germ was eternal and practically self-existent. And of course nothing could evolve from it which was not inherent. It must have been pregnant with all forms and developments of life with which the world is full. Moreover it is only ignorant conceit to maintain that evolution has reached its limits. If man has sprung from such an origin, we must suppose that, in the far-distant future, beings will be developed as superior to mankind as we ourselves are superior to the insects crawling on the earth. According to this hypothesis the latent capacities of the first life-germ were infinite, "capacities," remember, not tendencies. Unknowable force may account for tendencies, but it cannot create capacities. Not that this distinction will save us from the pillory. The philosopher will condemn the statement as unphilosophical----"a shaping of ignorance into the semblance of knowledge" and I know not what beside..."

Concluding *"How did life begin?"* Dr Anderson writes: **"**By what word, then, shall this "particle of living protoplasm" be called; this great First Cause; this Life-germ, eternal, self-existent, infinite in essential capacities? There is but one word known to human language adequate to designate it, and that word is GOD. Evolution - that is, Science - thus leads us to a point at which either we must blindly and with boundless credulity accept as fact something which is not only destitute of proof, but which is positively disproved by every test we are at present able to apply to it; or else we must recognise an existence which, disguise it as we may, means nothing less than God.

There is no escape from this dilemma. Our choice lies between these alternatives. The sceptic will at once reject the first; his acceptance of the second is, therefore, a necessity. Men whose minds are enslaved by a preconceived determination to refuse belief in God must be content here to stand like fools, owning their impotency to solve the elementary problem of existence, and, as humble disciples in the school of one Topsy, a negro slave-girl, dismissing the matter by the profound and sapient formula "I 'spect I grow'd" ! But the free thinker, unblinded by prejudice, will reject an alternative belief which is sheer credulity, and, unmoved by the sneers of pseudo-scientists and sham-philosophers, will honestly and fearlessly accept the goal to which his reason points, and there set up an altar to an unknown God."

"The irrationalism of infedilty": This is the theme of chapter 9 of *A Doubter's Doubts about Science and Religion.* On this subject Dr Anderson writes: "....If men would but use their brains, they would see that once we drift away from the anchorage of the old beliefs, nothing can save us from being drawn into the rapids which end in sheer agnosticism. This does not prove the truth of Christianity, but it exposes the untenableness of the infidel position.

These infidel books habitually assume that, if we refuse their nostrums, superstition is our only refuge. This is quite in keeping with the amazing conceit which characterises them. Wisdom was born with the Agnostics! They have monopolised the meagre stock of intelligence which the evolutionary process has as yet produced for the guidance of the race! But there are Christians in the world who have quite as much sense as they have, who detest superstition as much as they do, and who have far more experience in detecting fallacies and exposing frauds. And if such men are Christians it is not because they are too stupid to become infidels.

For faith is not superstition; and in presence of a Divine revelation unbelief betokens mental obliquity, if not moral degradation. Thoughtless people are betrayed into supposing that there is something very clever in "not believing." But in this life the formula: "I don't believe" more often betokens dull wittedness than shrewdness. It is the refrain of the stupidest man upon the jury. A mere negation of belief, moreover, is seldom possible; it generally implies belief in the alternative to what we reject.

The sceptic may hesitate, in order to examine the credentia of a revelation. But no one who has a settled creed ever hesitates at all. And the Atheist has such a creed; he believes that there is no God. If we do not believe a man to be honest, we usually believe him to be a fraud. If we refuse the testimony of witnesses about matters that are too plain and simple to allow of mere misapprehension or honest mistake, we must hold them to be impostors and rogues. And nothing less than this is implied in the position held by men like Herbert Spencer and Leslie Stephen.

But the infidel will deny that he impugns the integrity of the Apostles and Evangelists; he only questions their intelligence. He asks us to believe that they were so weak and credulous that their testimony to the miracles, for example, must be rejected. But the miracles were not rare incidences of dark-room seances; they were public events which occurred day by day, and usually in the presence of hostile critics. No person of ordinary intelligence, therefore, could have been mistaken as to the facts. What then do we know of the men on whose evidence we accept them? Their writings have been translated into every known language. They hold a unique place in the classic literature of the world, and the sublime morality and piety which pervade them command universal admiration. Certain it is therefore that if the New Testament is to be accounted for on natural principles, its authors must have been marvellously gifted, both intellectually and morally. And yet these are the men whose testimony is to be flung aside with contempt when they give a detailed description of events which happened in open day before their eyes. To talk of offering them a fool's pardon is absurd. If their narratives be false, we must give up all confidence in human nature, and write them down as an abnormally clever gang of abnormally profane impostors and hypocrites. But this alternative is more untenable than the other. It is absolutely certain that the men of the New Testament were neither scoundrels nor fools...."

The 'slaughter' of "Darwin's Bulldog"

In *A Doubter's Doubts about Science and Religion,* Dr Anderson exposed the 'ignorance' of Professor Huxley, whom Charles Darwin described as a brilliant scientist. In his communications with Professor Huxley, Dr Anderson referred to the Professor's last letter: "Mr Huxley wrote another letter, but it contained nothing save pretentious phrases about science and ungenerous sneers at those who believe the Bible. So far as this controversy (Creationism and Evolution) - that the Bible is discredited by science - is concerned he, Huxley, left his opponents in possession of the field. The fact asserted by Mr Gladstone remains established by this searching test. It is asserted, and it will still be asserted as unblushingly as if this correspondence had not taken place, that Genesis is proved false by the facts of science; whereas the testimony of science, whatever it be worth, confirms the Biblical order of creation."

On his 'fight' with "Darwin's bulldog," Dr Anderson records: "My object here is to beat off attacks which stumble or distress ignorant and weak-kneed believers. And to this end I have shown that Professor Huxley, the ablest and most bitter assailant of Genesis which this age has produced, has been met and routed upon ground of his own choosing. The first chapter of Genesis "was not written to teach science"; but not a single "fact of science" can be found to discredit it. This cannot be said of any one of the "religious books of the East" --- in this respect they are but a tangle of error and folly. Neither can it be said of any scientific book published before recent years. The "science" of the last generation is discredited by the discoveries of our own times..."

Dr Anderson wrote this book anonymously to imply how little value he placed on it. However, others appreciated it. Among them was Prime Minister W E Gladstone. Here is an extract of Gladstone's letter to the publisher:

> "*Dear Sir, I do not know whom I have the honour of addressing, but I wish to thank you for your Doubter's Doubt, and to say I have read it with great deal of sympathy, and concurrence in the main argument.....I presume to hope you will follow up the subjects of your volume with the same care, force, and exactitude which in it you have bestowed especially upon the treatment of the main argument.*
> *And*
> *I remain, dear Sir,*
> *Your faithful and obedient,*
> *W E GLADSTONE. 18 December 1889*

The Preface to *A Doubter's Doubt About Science and Religion* reads: "Extracts from Mr Gladstone's diary record that the December 18, 1889, was the occasion of Parnell's historic visit to Hawarden, and that the day was devoted to reviewing and reconsidering the whole Irish question, and discussing it with the Irish leader. And yet on that day Mr Gladstone found leisure to read my book, and to write to me about it. I should add that I had not sent it to him, nor was I aware that he possessed it." You may read the full letter in the book."

Charles Darwin described his friend, Professor Huxley, "The King of Men". Huxley, Darwin's bulldog, who is regarded as a brilliant scientist, was tamed by the Knight Commander.
Professor Richard Dawkins: A "clone" of Professor Thomas Huxley

On 21 May 2005, The Times newspaper published Professor Dawkin's article on Creationism and Evolution. In this article, *Creationism: God's gift to the ignorant,* the Oxford Professor wrote about "scientific logic" of evolution. In his attempt to defend Darwin's fable theory of Evolution, Dawkins branded Creationists "ignorant." The fact is Darwinian Theory of Evolution is Darwin's gift to the ignorant Pseudo-Scientists and "blind" Church Leaders who don't understand Sacred Scriptures, and have become "disciples" of Darwin.

In the 19th century, sneering at the integrity of the Bible was one of the trade marks of some Oxford Professors. The champion of the critics was Professor S R Driver. He attacked the Book of Daniel. So, Professor Dawkins' hostile attitude towards the Bible and Christians, and branding Bible-believers "ignorant" is not surprising. The 'Passionate Atheist' is just a 21st century 'clone' of the 19th century Professor Huxley. Thomas Huxley was fond of using pretentious phrases about science, and sneering at those who believed in the Bible. Had Professor Dawkins, who would have been in the "Paper-weight" division of the Evolution and Creationism Tournament, done his "homework" on this "Tournament," he would have learnt that Darwin's bulldog, Professor Huxley, was "put down" by Dr. Robert Anderson, The Champion of Darwinism was "knocked down" in the 19th century.

The pompous Dawkins - a carbon copy of the arrogant and "hypocrite" Huxley - should 'go back to school' to study the "Tournament" between Gladstone and Huxley, and the 'Tournament' between Huxley and Anderson, and then examine Professor Dana and Lord Kelvin's comments on Science and Creation to know the result of the contest. Dana was Huxley's "master." Lord Kelvin was a teacher whose "*dictum*" carried more weight than Huxley. Dr Anderson described Huxley the "most bitter assailant on Genesis and the Bible" his age has ever seen. In the 21st century it is Professor Dawkins, the atheist, who carries Huxley's "mantle." The fact is none of today's militant atheists, who attack the Bible and ridicule Christians, would have qualified to use the pen of the Knight Commander (of the Order) of Bath – the zealous Champion of Christian causes. Enough is enough from the arrogant and ignorant scientists of the 21st century who sneer at Christians. Professor Dawkins and his followers must realize that, "greatness has no definite measure. For if you compare it with one thing or another, it either increases or decreases. A ship that is big on a river is small on the sea; and a rudder that is big for one ship may be small for another."

In his *The Bible and Modern Criticism*, Dr Anderson writes: "Christianity is not a human religion, but a divine revelation of transcendental truths and facts that are of such a nature that no amount of mere human testimony could accredit it." He reminded the arch critic - Professor Driver of Oxford: "The Oxford infidelity of today is far in advance of German infidelity of half a century ago."

PROFESSOR THOMAS HUXLEY: WAS HE A "HYPOCRITE" OR A "FOOL"?

The "Disciples" of Charles Darwin and Thomas Huxley must answer this question: why did the agnostic Huxley, the Champion of Darwinism, and the ablest and most bitter assailant of Genesis, recommend that the Bible is the best medium of ethical instruction? In pages 150-151 of *T H Huxley: Scientist, Humanist and Educator,* Dr Cyril Bibby writes; "Because of his own agnosticism, Huxley had been forced to give a good deal of thought to the religious education of children....So far as the England of his time was concerned, he had no doubt that the best medium of ethical instruction was the Bible, and his ***Contemporary*** essay explained why ; Take the Bible as a whole; make the severest deduction which fair criticism can dictate for shortcoming and positive errors; eliminate, as a sensible lay-teacher would do, if left to himself, all that it is not desirable for children to occupy themselves with; and there still remain in this old literature a vast residuum of moral beauty and grandeur. And then consider the great historical fact that, for three centuries, this book has been woven into the life of all that is the best and noblest in English history, that it has become the national epic of Britain, and is as familiar to the noble and simple....."

Years later, Huxley justified his support of W H Smith's 'compromise' of allowing the reading of Bible in schools but not promoting any particular denomination in a letter to Edward Clodd. Huxley writes: "...though, for the last quarter of a century I have done all that lay in my power to oppose and destroy the idolatrous accretions of Judaism and Christianity, I have never had the slightest sympathy with those who....would throw the child away along with the bath---and when I was a member of the London School Board I fought for the retention of the Bible to the great scandal of some of my liberal friends who cannot make out to this day whether I was a hypocrite or simply a fool on that occasion. But my meaning was that the mass of the people should not be deprived of the one great Literature which is open to them----not shut out from the perception of their relation with the whole past history of civilised mankind." Dr Bibby went on: "Although it has been claimed that Huxley came to see that his support of Bible-reading was a mistake, eight months before his death (in 1895) he still did not repent of the compromise: Twenty years of reasonably good primary education is 'worth a mass,", he told Lord Farrer." The question remains: Why did Darwin's bulldog – a bitter enemy of the Book of Genesis – did not repent that he made a mistake of recommending the Bible to be used in schools? Did Huxley 'see the light' before he passed away?

In her Essay, *"Darwin's descendant"*, the Poet Ruth Pradel, the great-great-grandchild of Darwin, writes: "Darwin never said he was an atheist, only agnostic. He had two grounds for objecting to Christianity. One was lack of proof: he was a scientist to his marrow and the one thing he respected was evidence. The other was pain." (The Independent 12 December 2008). I ask the question: "Where is the scientific evidence and proof that man evolved? "The horse may have been developed from a pig-like animal, and man may be "descended from a hairy quadruped furnished with a tail and pointed ears," writes Dr Anderson. "But what direct proof is there that either the horse or the man was in fact, developed or evolved in this way? The answer must be, Absolutely none. It is a matter of inference only."

Ms Pradel says Darwin was an "agnostic." Was Darwin's claim sustainable? The title of chapter VIII of "A Doubter's Doubt About science and Religion" reads: "AN AGNOSTIC'S APOLOGY." In the opening paragraph Dr. Anderson writes: "The natural attitude of a thinking mind toward the supernatural is that of scepticism. Scepticism, not agnosticism. The sceptic halts at the cross-roads to take his bearings; but at sight of a cross-road the agnostic gives up his journey altogether. True scepticism connotes intellectual caution, but agnosticism is intellectual suicide." The scientific world celebrated the "Agnostic" Darwin's 200th birth day on 12 February 2009.

IGNORE DARWIN AND HONOUR ANDERSON

Scientists and the world now know the Irish scholar who exposed the fallacy of Darwin's theory of evolution, and then "knocked out" the Champion of Darwinism. Darwin's theory of Evolution is irrelevant in our generation. What are relevant in the 21st century is not Darwinism but the "Phenomenon of Israel," the Middle East Crisis and the "Quiet Miracle" – the European Union - and its future. For in the 19th century, Sir Robert Anderson, a faithful servant of the Lord Jesus Christ, wrote about all these "phenomena" and their future prospects before they materialised in the 20th century. Sir Robert Anderson and his works matter now. He deserves to be honoured and Darwin ignored. The British Secret Service Agent was the "Barrister of God" who defended the genuineness of the most marvelous manuscript in the Universe – the Book of Daniel – when it was under aggressive attacks by German infidels and English Professors in Oxford University. It would be appropriate, therefore, for the world to celebrate 29 May of every year, the birth day of Sir Robert Anderson, and mourn on 15 November of every year, the day the Great Knight departed.

OTHER LITERARY WORKS OF SIR ROBERT ANDERSON

2. *The Coming Prince*

This famous book offers solution to the much-discussed prophecy of the "Seventy Weeks" recorded in Daniel 9:24-27. In this work, Dr Robert Anderson calculated the exact date the Lord Jesus Christ rode on a donkey into Jerusalem and accepted the acclamation of the multitude that He was the Messiah. Dr Anderson also emphasised the Biblical truth that the nation of Israel would be restored to Palestine and the next major political feature in history after the rebirth of the nation of Israel would be a confederation of European nations. He published this book over a decade before Theodor Herzl, the father of Political Zionism, even outlined his vision for a Jewish state in 1896. The Knight Commander stated the prophecies of a restored Israel seemed to many people as incredible as predictions of the triumphs of steam and electricity would have appeared a century previously. Most importantly, Sir Robert also discussed the predicted division of the Roman earth (a subject of this chapter) about which so many guesses have been ventured by students of prophecy.

The Coming Prince was first published in 1881 before the founding Fathers of European Community – Robert Schuman and Jean Monnet - were born in 1886 and 1888. The third edition was published on 14 March 1889, the year Adolf Hitler, the Catalyst of European Community, was born, and 68 years before the Treaty of Rome was signed. The fifth edition was released in March 1895. The 14th edition was published in 1957 the year the Treaty of Rome was signed, and when Paul Henri Spaak claimed: "the first stone of a new Roman Empire" had been laid. The 15th and 16th editions were published in 1963 and 1967 the years Britain's applications to join the Common Market were vetoed by Charles de Gaulle. The 17th edition was published in 1969 the year President de Gaulle fell from power. The 18th edition was released in 1972 the year European Community Act was signed, and a year before Britain, Ireland and Denmark joined the European Economic Community. The 19th edition was published in 1975 the year Britain held a referendum to remain in the Common Market.

According to Dr Anderson's son, *The Coming Prince* "was written during very busy years, much of it late at night after "overtime" official work. The title refers to "the prince that shall come" of the ninth chapter of the Book of Daniel. The Lisbon Treaty signed on 13 December 2007 has opened the way for this powerful "Prince" to come and lead Europe and the rest of the world to their destiny.

Dr Anderson concluded *"The Coming Prince"* with these solemn words:

> "It was a calamity for the Church of God when the light of prophecy became dimmed in fruitless controversy, and the study of these visions, vouchsafed by God to warn, and guide, and cheer His saints in evil days, was dismissed as utterly unprofitable. They abound in promises which God designed to feed His people's faith and fire their zeal, and a special blessing rests on those who read, and hear, and cherish them. One of the most hopeful features of the present hour is the increasing interest they everywhere excite; and if these pages should avail to deepen or direct the enthusiasm even of a few in the study of a theme which is inexhaustible, the labour they have cost will be abundantly rewarded."

Testifying to the immense value of this work, *The Record* stated: "It deserves to be well and carefully studied." *The Christian* recorded: "There are few books on prophecy written in so fair and impartial in spirit." And Herbert Lockyer wrote: "The reprinting of this prophetic classic is most important at a time like this when men's hearts are failing them for fear. The only infallible antidote for perplexed hearts is an understanding of God's blueprint for the future, and this is why *The Coming Prince* is most valuable. Christians everywhere should not only invest in this indispensable volume, but thoroughly digest it for a divine understanding of our times and of those to follow."

Dr John Walvoord writes: "This classic interpretation of the book of Daniel, dealing with the prophecy of the ninth chapter in particular, has long been considered a standard volume in the field, often quoted, and original in its fresh exposition of Daniel's seventy weeks....This book belongs on the shelf of very pastor and layman intelligent in the study of the prophetic Word."

Dr Frederic A Tatford declared; "This is the ablest explanation of Daniel's seventy weeks and related subjects in existence." And according to Baptist Testimony: "Sir Robert Anderson is a giant amongst giants and anything he wrote is worth having on one's library shelf. This volume [The Coming Prince] concerns itself with Daniel's. Seventy weeks and the coming antichrist, and is considered the standard work on the subject."

I encourage Pope Benedict XVI and his theological panel in Vatican, the Archbishop of Canterbury and his Bishops in the Church of England, pastors and Christians of every denomination to read *The Coming Prince* and consider their attitude towards the European Union.

3. Daniel in the Critics Den

This book was first published on 14 October 1895. It was written to silence the German infidels and the super theologians, university Professors and clergymen who attacked the Book of Daniel as a religious novel – a literary fraud. The book was a reply to the Champion critic, Professor Driver of Oxford, and Dr. Dean Farrar, Archdeacon of Westminster. These Church of England scholars undermined the authenticity of the awe-inspiring prophetic Book of Daniel. Sir Robert Anderson refutes the charges against this Old Testament Book which were the characteristics of the late 19th century's "Higher Criticism" school – which alleged that the Book of Daniel suffered from late dating and other historical deficiencies. Sadly, the Roman Catholic Church's *New Jerusalem Bible* has adopted the discredited arguments of the infidels to suggest that the Book of Daniel is an "edifying fiction."

In the Preface to *Daniel in the critics den* the 'Barrister of God' opened his defence of Daniel with this statement: "The Daniel controversy has hitherto been regarded as the special preserve of the philologist. Who but he is qualified to decide what epoch any portion of the Hebrew Scriptures should be assigned? The claim, however, is based upon a fallacy. The whole question turns upon a simple issue of fact - "Was the book in existence before the days of Antiochus? If this be decided in the affirmative, its prophetic character is unquestionable."

Dr Anderson continued: "The appearance of Professor Driver's *Book of Daniel* marks the epoch in the Daniel controversy. Hitherto there has been no work in existence which English exponents of the sceptical hypothesis would accept as a fair and adequate expression of their views. But now the oracle has spoken. The most trusted champion of the Higher Criticism in England has formulated the case against the Book of Daniel; and if that case can be refuted – if it can be shown that its apparent force depends on a skilful presentation of doubtful evidence upon the one side, to the exclusion of overwhelming cogent evidence upon the other - the result ought to be an "end of controversy" on the whole question."

"God's Barrister" pressed his case: "Long accustomed to deal with evidence in difficult and intricate inquiries, I have set myself to investigate the genuineness of the Book of Daniel. And the results of my inquiry are here recorded...As regards my attitude towards criticism, I deprecate being misunderstood. Every book I have written gives proof of fearlessness in applying critical methods to the study of the Bible. But the Higher Criticism is a mere travesty of all true criticism. Secular writers are presumed to be trustworthy unless reason is found to discredit their testimony. But the Higher Criticism starts with the assumption that everything in scripture needs to be confirmed by external evidence. It reeks of its evil origin in German infidelity. My indictment of it, therefore, is not that it is criticism, but that it is criticism of a low and spurious type, akin to that for which the baser sort of "Old Bailey" fractioned is famed. True criticism seeks to elucidate the truth; the Higher Criticism aims at establishing prejudged results....It was the miraculous element in the book that set the whole pack of foreign sceptics in full cry. In this age of a silent heaven such men will not tolerate the idea that God ever intervened directly in the affairs of men."

Commenting on the so-called "violent errors" in chapter 6 of *Daniel in the critics den*, Dr Anderson writes: "The discovery of the hidden records of the court of Babylon cannot be much longer deferred, and when these shall have been brought to light we shall learn, perchance, on which side the folly lies - that of the believers or of the critics. And while an ignorant public is easily imposed upon by a parade of seeming scholarship, no one who is versed in the Daniel controversy can fail to recognise that fair and independent inquiry is absolutely wanting. Porphyry the Pagan it was who set the ball rolling long ago. After resting for centuries it was again put in motion by the rationalists. And now that the fashion has set towards scepticism, and "Higher Criticism" is supposed to denote higher culture, critic follows critic, like sheep through a gap."

In page 171 of the third edition of Dr Anderson's *In Defence* A *plea for the Faith*, he writes: "It is a canon of "criticism" with these men (Professor Driver and Dr Farrar, the Dean of Canterbury, and their colleagues at the University of Christendom) that no Biblical statement is ever to be accepted unless confirmed by some pagan authority..." So, how would the sceptics and critics account for the recent discovery of a tablet in the British Museum which confirms the existence of one of the officials in the court of king Nebuchadnezzar of Babylon?

In a newspaper column headed *Museum's tablet lends new weight to Biblical truth*, (The Times 11 July 2007), it was reported that a cuneiform inscription in a tablet dating from 595BC had been deciphered for the first time. It revealed a reference to an official at the court of Nebuchadnezzar that proves the historical existence of a figure mentioned in the Book of Jeremiah. This, according to the report, was rare evidence in a non-biblical source of a real person, other than kings, featured in the Bible. The tablet names a Babylonian official called Nebo-Sarsekim, who, according to Jeremiah XXXIX, was present in 587BC when Nebuchadnezzar marched against Jerusalem with his whole army and laid siege to it. This King Nebuchadnezzar is also mentioned in the Book of Daniel. And the opening chapter of the book describes how Daniel and three other young men from the Royal family in Judea were deported to serve in the court of Nebuchadnezzar.

Dr Jursa, who made this discovery while conducting research into officials at the Babylonian court, said: "It is very exciting and very surprising. Finding something like this tablet, where we see a person (King Nebuchadnezzar) making an everyday payment to a temple in Babylon and quoting the exact date, is quite extraordinary." It was Daniel who interpreted King Nebuchadnezzar's dream of a magnificent human image. This dream was the prophetic revelation of the rise and fall of all the major Empires from Babylonia to the Roman Empire and the revived Roman Empire – the European Union.

In defending the authenticity and the divine nature of the Book of Daniel, the Lawyer with sanctified logic stated: "Not one single new point against Daniel has been brought to light for a century. Every decade brings to light some new proofs of its genuineness and authenticity." True to his word, in the 21st century we have seen a new proof. It is a shame that the Roman Catholic Church has endorsed The New Jerusalem Bible that condemns the Book of Daniel as a literal fraud. What is wrong with this Roman Catholic Church? The truth is that the Catholic Theologians, who undermined the genuineness of the Book of Daniel, have produced no original work on the Daniel controversy. They just copied the errors of Professor Driver's denunciation of the Book of Daniel. Witness what Dr Anderson records in NOTE II (Page 191) of *In Defence: A plea for the Faith*: "Professor Driver's *Book of Daniel* ("Cambridge Bible" series), which is an expansion of the "Daniel" section of his *Introduction,* reproduces the farrago of "errors" and arguments which were formulated by Bertholdt just a century ago, and have been the stock-in-trade of the rationalists ever since. Archaeological discoveries have disposed of most of them, but still they serve their purpose....And even if they were all as weighty as most of them are frivolous, the Christian would brush them aside in view of the fulfilled prophecy of "the Seventy Weeks," and the fact that the book has been accredited by Christ."

Testifying for the value of *Daniel in the critics den, 'The Rock'* records: "If Sir Anderson has - as we believe he has - successfully refuted the charge as concerns the Book of Daniel, he has inferentially done so as concerns the whole Canon of the Scripture." *Church Family Newspaper* also gave evidence: "We sincerely trust it will have the extensive circulation it so well deserves. Few books expose with equal truth and vigour the fallacies of destructive criticism. *Daniel in the Critics Den* will be a welcome addition in the libraries of pastors, Bible teachers, or lay people desiring to reaffirm their confidence in the integrity of God's eternal Word." Commenting on Dr Anderson's book, *The Times* writes: "His apparently cogent elucidation of the vexed question of the Seventy Weeks." *Record* records: "The refutation of the critics is crushing. According to *English Churchman*, "It pulverises the latest attack on the Book of Daniel."

The spiritual leaders in the Roman Catholic Church who have sanctioned *The New Jerusalem Bible* should read *Daniel in the critics Den.* Pope Benedict XVI, even though he has read the works of Cardinal Newman, who was a contemporary of Dr Anderson, might not have been familiar with the works of the Presbyterian.

I appeal to the Pope to examine the writings of this fearless Champion of the Christian Faith. The Pontiff would be in the position to correct the supposedly "historical and language errors" associated with the Book of Daniel that make it an "edifying fiction."

In the 18th century German infidels attempted to discredit the Book of Daniel as a "forgery." And it is interesting to note that in the 21st century it was a German Chancellor, Angela Merkel, who unknowingly contrived to hasten the fulfilment of one of the major prophecies in the Book of Daniel. The German politician played the leading role in producing the Lisbon Treaty. This European Constitution makes provision for a powerful President of the European Union. This President, who would be appointed by EU leaders, is a picture of the future Emperor of the revived Roman Empire, the Man of Lawlessness, who will establish a 7-year peace treaty between the Jews and the Arabs. This Treaty would initiate the crisis of all crisis as predicted in Daniel 9:27 and Matthew 24:15 to end the European Empire to close the era of Gentile supremacy. God is WONDERFUL. His ways are mysterious

4. *Forgotten Truths*

This book was written in 1913. The theme is on the Hope of the Lord's Return. The Preface to the Second Edition reads: "The early demand for a new edition of "Forgotten Truths" gives proof that truths which have been let slip by so many are still cherished by not a few." The Bishop of Durham wrote to Dr Anderson: "What I have read has done what your writings always do for me. It has at once stimulated attention and challenged thought, often along quite fresh lines, and has everywhere braced and strengthened the faith of my soul in the divine character of Scripture...I hope to make it my companion..."

- In his Foreword to the 1980 edition of this work, which was published by Kregel Publications, J. Arnold Fair writes: "God chooses very special men to emphasise select truths. Almighty God still chooses the foolish things of the world to confound the wise that no flesh glory in His presence. As our Lord chose to use a scholarly Paul in emphasising the doctrines of the church, so He chose Sir Robert Anderson in the nineteenth century to re-emphasise the *Forgotten Truths*. As a foremost British barrister, Sir Robert Anderson desired to find and present the truth clearly and simply. His grasp of the scriptures, his intensive investigation, his wide acquaintance with godly, scholarly men such as Dr. Horatius Bonar and others, his extensive travelling which exposed him to much learning and most of all, the guidance of the Holy Spirit well qualified him to write this volume. In a day when truth to some has become relative and experience has seemingly been lifted to the throne of absolute judgement, the republishing of this work is necessary." He went on: "The author's staunch position that the Bible is the inerrant, infallible word of the living God shines through at every crack of a page". Mr Arnold Fair recommends the book to all who yearn for the truth.

Outlined below are some press notices of the First Edition:

- *Church Family Newspaper*: "We have read the book with pleasure and profit, and we firmly believe it to be the author's best work."
- *Evangelical Christendom:* "He handles great truths with the skill of a master mind....Making the Bible a complete compendium of God-breathed truth....There is something to be learned on every page."
- *The Sword and Trowel:* "A really grand book....It has not a dull line in it, or a superfluous paragraph, and it almost compels a second reading and frequent reference." Testifying to this book in *Things to Come,* Dr. R. W. Bullinger writes: "We wish the book may have a wide sphere both of usefulness and blessing....A fund should be opened to enable it to be sent to every preacher, every professor, and every modern critic."

5. The Bible and Modern Criticism

Dr Anderson published this work specifically to defend the Bible – and in particular the 5 Books of Moses. "God's Barrister" defended the integrity of the whole Bible against the highest critics. The second edition of this book was published in 1902. In this volume, the Lawyer with knowledge and mental power, again, defended the Book of Daniel by tearing into shreds the arguments the Oxford scholar, Professor Driver, raised against the Book of Daniel. Professor Driver copied the works of German rationalists who had earlier claimed the Book of Daniel was not a divine revelation, because it was written at a much later age than the 6th century in which the Book was actually written,

In page 46 of this work, the "Barrister of God" dismissed the leading expert of the English School of criticism with this remark: "To allow the critics to adjudicate upon the evidence they have themselves prepared would be quite as stupid and as dangerous as to permit the police to try the prisoners whose cases they bring into court. And yet this is, speaking generally, the attitude maintained by educated Englishmen towards every question raised in this (Daniel) controversy. It is intellectually as deplorable as that of the Irish Roman Catholic peasant who grovels before his priests and takes the law from his mouth...The critical attack upon Daniel not only destroys one of the great Messianic prophecies and impairs the authority of the New Testament, but impugns the teaching of the Lord Himself".

In page 136 Dr Anderson continues his defence of Sacred Scriptures. He confronted the German infidels with this rebuke: "The exaggerations of the German critics are the clearest proof that the crusade against Daniel was the outcome of prejudice or malice." Dr Anderson then dismissed the advocates of the "historical error" argument against the Book of Daniel with this ridicule: "This historical error is a blunder so glaring that a school boy might well be ashamed of it. And yet it is gravely adopted and reproduced by English ecclesiastics and Professors for the enlightenment of a much deluded public."

Is it not a shame, that over 100 years since Dr Anderson refuted the "historical error" argument that seeks to undermine the genuineness of the Book of Daniel, the Roman Catholic hierarchy has given its blessing to the *New Jerusalem Bible* which suggests the same discredited "historical errors" argument to undermine the divine character and the authenticity of the Book of Daniel? I, again, urge Pope Benedict XVI to correct the error in this Roman Catholic Bible for the sake of sound teaching to uphold the Integrity of our Lord Jesus Christ. For our Blessed Lord Himself put His Seal of Approval on the Book of Daniel when He made a specific reference to a prophetic word in Daniel 9:27:*"So, when you see standing in the holy place, 'the abomination that causes desolation', spoken of through the prophet Daniel…then let those who are in Judea flee to the mountains. (Matthew 24:15-16).* If this "Daniel" in Matthew 24:15 is not the same "Daniel" in Daniel 9:27, the Pope should tell the world which Daniel did the Lord Jesus Christ refer to?

European Union and the Book of Daniel

Dr Anderson continued his defence of the Book of Daniel: "Not a single new point against Daniel has been brought to light for a century. Every decade brings to light some new proofs of its genuineness and authenticity." And how true are his words, that in our generation, the development of the European Union has confirmed the divine nature of the Book of Daniel. It was from this Book that the Knight Commander predicted with absolute certainty that a political alliance of European nations shall be developed through an European crisis. And this political Union would be the next major political feature in history after the restoration of the Jews to Palestine".

Concerning the critics, Dr. Anderson writes: "Our quarrel with the Higher Criticism ….is not because it is criticism, but because it is purely destructive and therefore the lowest kind of criticism." He adds: "And while an intelligent scepticism will apply the severest tests to anything claiming to be a divine revelation, the rejection of it on a *priori* grounds is nothing but the dull stupidity of an ignorant unbelief."

Creationism Vs Evolution

In the opening paragraph of chapter 10 of *The Bible and Modern Criticism*, Dr Anderson writes: "Some there are who…love the Bible, and are assured that it is in the main Divine, but there is much in the Old Testament which unduly tries their faith. The creation story of Genesis," they would say, "is discredited by science." The Book of Jonah is incredible. The Book of Daniel can no longer be defended. The history of Israel is marked by moral difficulties which cannot be explained away. And so no one can now defend the correctness of Old Testament chronology."

Dr Anderson, again, dealt with the Creationism and Evolution controversy. He demolished all the arguments rained against the Old Testament Books. The most significant was his "destruction" of Darwin's Rotweiller, Professor Huxley. The Champion of Darwinism misinterpreted the significance of 'reptiles' in Leviticus xi in an attempt to discredit the Creation account of human origin in Genesis. Dr Anderson responded: "The fact remains that the word in Leviticus xi is wholly different from the word used in Genesis 1:24, whereas the validity of his (Huxley's) argument depends on its identity with it. And the argument is his, not mine. He it is who insists that Genesis 1, must be interpreted by Leviticus xi, and, adopting his canon of interpretation, I have shown that he is "hoist with his own petard." "God's Barrister" continued: "It is on petty points of this sort that the conventional attacks upon the Bible rest."

I would urge you to get a copy of the book. It would motivate you to have the confidence to confront the big-headed scientists of today who are blindly following the footsteps of Professor Huxley to discredit the Bible with Darwin's Evolution Theory. Darwin himself was not hostile to the Bible, unlike the insolent scientists of our flippant generation.

Before concluding *The Bible and Modern Criticism*, the Able Defender of the Christian Faith gave us an advice: "Treat your Bible as you would treat your friend. A friendship that cannot bear the strain of a misunderstanding does not deserve the name; nor a faith that gives way in presence of a difficulty. But with many the place the Bible holds resembles that not of a friend at all, but rather that of a mere acquaintance. For proofs that it is the Word of God are clear and abundant. But they do not lie open on the surface. Gold and diamonds are not picked up upon the highway: men need to dig for them. Even Nature hides her treasures from the trifler. God is a rewarder of them that seek Him diligently."

A note to the Sixth Edition of *The Bible and Modern Criticism* reads: "Copies of the Fifth Edition of this book were purchased for presentation to a thousand selected Public Libraries in this country, the Colonies, and the United States. And the letters of acknowledgement and thanks, which the courtesy of the donors has permitted me (Robert Anderson) to see, give gratifying proof of the appreciation with which this volume was received."

Some Press Notices of the First Edition

The Record: "it is full time that such a book as this was written....Sir R Anderson is well known to thoughtful readers as the writer of works of singular logical directness, and the present is justly styled by the Bishop of Durham, in a Preface of striking cogency, as well as beauty....We think we have said enough to prove to our readers that Sir R Anderson's treatment of this subject deserves a profound and prayerful study. He has seen, and plainly points out, what many even of true-hearted defenders of the faith have seen but imperfectly – that more, infinitely more is at stake than any literary question affecting the Bible..."

The English Churchman: "Valuable as the author's former works were, his latest volume excels them......*The Bible and Modern Criticism* should be read and digested by all thoughtful Christians, for its eloquent and scholarly testimony in favour of 'The Scriptures of truth' cannot fail to confirm believers and to assist waverers and all such as feel perplexed by the insidious reasoning of the New critics. We could wish that copies of Sir Robert Anderson's book were placed on the study shelves of all ministers and teachers of the Gospel, and presented to the libraries of our theological colleges."

The Church Missionary Intelligence: "A terse and vigorous style is a striking characteristic of this book....The book throughout is excellent reading, and is enlivened with apposite anecdotes which illustrate and elucidate the points urged."

Life of Faith: "The time has come for spiritual men to take a very decided position, and to use the plainest speech, in relation to criticism. Nothing is to be gained by delaying the inevitable issue of the conflict. We thank Sir Robert Anderson for his able, independent, and courageous witness."

The Witness: "Among the extending list of works from his able pen we have read none with more intense interest than this....It abounds in striking and peculiarly apt illustrations, and will repay more than once or twice."

The New York Tribune: "A work of singular lucidity of style and of remarkable argumentative power....He argues with cumulative force in this book, whether he is dealing with the proem in Genesis, the structural unity of the Pentateuch, the records of Jonah and Daniel, the history of Israel or the harmony of the Gospels, that the case of the Higher Critics must collapse unless they can succeed in discrediting the testimony of the chief witness, the Divine Master.....His brusqueness and racy invective are intellectually stimulative, although the Higher Critics and loose thinkers are irritated by his book, as is evident from the tone of some of the reviewers of it......Sir Robert Anderson has written a trenchant and straightforward book, which places critics, whether as radical as Prof. Cheyne or as conservative as Prof. Driver, on their defence before men of common sense."

Church Family Newspaper: "….. Those of our readers who cannot buy Sir Robert Anderson's book for themselves should enquire for it at the nearest free library, and not rest content until it is put into circulation there…..We doubt whether there is any other writer on this subject who can be considered equally successful in grasping the crucial points, and at the same time putting them before the general public in a concise and intelligent form."

The Bible League: "Sir Robert Anderson has rendered noble service to the cause of truth by the publication of this volume."

Daily Express: "Sir Robert Anderson handles the subject in a bold and original manner….He deals with all the main attacks which have been levelled against the Old Testament and the New. He flinches from none of them…. It is a book which should be placed in the library of all who are repelled by the methods of the critics."

Things to Come: "The book of the year."

The Christian: "We thank Sir Robert Anderson for devoting himself, heart and soul, to the good cause which here engages him. He shows, as we have many a time pointed out, that when studied with care, Holy Scripture justifies to the full all the claims which it makes of inspiration, integrity, and authority. He deals with many men and topics in this substantial volume, and in an appendix he discusses succinctly, but to good purpose, several important questions raised in the course of the book. We trust his pages will have many readers, and that his arguments will be brought under notice of such as have been unsettled in mind through disturbing criticism."

- *The News*: "This is the work for the present age. Sir Robert Anderson has rendered immense service by its publication. It should be widely circulated."

Indeed, *The Bible and Modern Criticism*, is the work for the 21st century. In this volume the literary recluse writes: "The microscope serves to make the wonders of nature seem all the more wonderful, and no criticism of scripture can be too searching and minute, if only it be intelligent and spiritual. Such criticism, moreover, is an antidote to the criticism of the sceptics. For if "knowledge is power, ignorance is weakness. And in no sphere is this more true than in the spiritual. But the knowledge that is wanting is the knowledge of Holy Scripture. For all scripture is profitable, that the man of God may be "ready at every point. And we cannot with impunity neglect large sections of Scripture which are inextricably interwoven with the rest."

6. In Defence - A Plea for the Faith

The third edition of this book was published in about 1907. This volume was addressed to "men of the world" from their own point of view. It was written from the standpoint of the "true scepticism which tests everything, not the sham sort which credulously accepts anything that tends to discredit the Bible. Sir Robert Anderson declared, "One who is a sceptic both by temperament and training can appreciate the difficulties of the honest truth seeker."

This book also deals with the Evolution and Creationism controversy. An extract from the Preface reads: "Spencerism is dead and Darwin discredited. But though biological theories which reigned supreme a few years ago have been abandoned or modified by "men of light and leading", their influences still prevail with the general public."

In chapter 1 of the book, Dr Anderson, again, raised the question: "How did life begin? And here evolution affords no answer, and must stand aside. Let the existence of life be taken for granted, and evolution may explain the rest. But the sceptic takes nothing for granted. How did life begin? Science answers--! In presence of a question which lies across the threshold of knowledge, science, the very personification of knowledge, turns agnostic and is dumb. "Creation" is the answer religion gives. The rejoinder which science ought to make is that life first sprang out of death, out of nothing; in a word, abiogenesis..."

In this book, Sir Robert Anderson mentioned the following prominent men: Darwin, Huxley, Tyndale, Kelvin, Herbert Spencer, Mark Twain, Sir Leslie Stephen, Harnack, A J Balfour, Max Muller. This indicates the scope of the discussion. In the opening paragraph of the last chapter of this work, the zealous champion of Christian causes writes: "Bible students nowadays seem to be haunted by the grim spectre of the "Higher Criticism." But if instead of running away from ghosts we face them boldly, our fears generally give place to feelings of contempt or indignation. And this is the experience of many who have fearlessly examined what are called "the assured results of modern criticism." The fact is these attacks upon the Bible originated with German rationalism formerly barred their acceptance by Christians of the English-speaking world. But in our day they have been accredited by distinguished scholars on both sides of the Atlantic, whose reputation for piety and reverence for things Divine is deemed a guarantee that they are legitimate." According to Dr Anderson, the German rationalists, eager to win the educated, decided "to bring the Bible down to the level of a purely human book, and therefore every feature savouring of what is called the supernatural had to be eliminated. All miracles had, of course, to be got rid off."

7. *Types in Hebrews*

An extract from the Preface, recorded by the publishers, reads: "The elucidation of the doctrine of the types, now entirely neglected, is an important problem for future theologians....There is much to be done if theology is to be cleared from the accusation that the study of Scriptural typology is neglected...This book is not a commentary on the Book of Hebrews. Its sole aim is to bring the light of the Old Testament types to bear on the main teachings of the Hebrews epistle and on certain passages which are often misinterpreted.

Hebrews has a special voice for us in the "trials of our own times" as Bishop Westcott mentions in his commentary. Those who take the sceptic's view of the Old Testament, primarily the Pentateuch, are joining the long line of individuals who are cheating themselves of the blessing of having the proper ammunition to fight the spiritual battles that are part of our everyday lives....Hebrews is misread by those who fail to recognise that the Christian revelation is based on the fact that God also is the originator of Judaism. To borrow a phrase from Lord Beaconsfield, the Hebrew Christian is a "completed Jew...." In the opening chapter, Sir Robert Anderson discusses the controversies concerning the authorship of Hebrews.

8. *Human Destiny:*

This book is about the controversial subjects: "hell", "Purgatory" and "what happens after Death." The ninth edition of this volume was published in July 1913. In the Preface to the second edition Dr Anderson writes: "In certain quarters the writer has been criticised for the severity of his criticisms upon the writing of others. But he sees no reason to modify his statements. In the wild field of literature upon the subject of these pages, the volumes quoted maintain a distinctive popularity. To ignore them would ...be impossible. Equally impossible would it be to handle them as they deserve, if considerations of the piety and eminence of their respective authors were permitted to intrude themselves......We are here dealing with books, not with men. In a sense, of course, they are inseparable; but generous minds will recognise that while the living man may be worthy of respect and deference, perchance of admiration, his book may be regarded as a dead thing, to which the dissecting knife of criticism may be ruthlessly applied..."

The title of the concluding chapter of *Human Destiny* reads: "The Question Answered." Dr Anderson writes: "To the reverent and refined there is something far more awful in the solemn measured language of Holy Writ upon the doom of the lost, than in all the word-pictures framed on it by facile pens or fluent tongues. These serve rather to repel, sometimes even to disgust. The outer darkness, the worm that never dies, the fire that is not quenched, the torment of the burning lake - all this may be but figurative language; but if so, the figures must represent realities still more terrible...."

He concludes with this significant text: "Man boasts of the proud but perilous dignity of an independent will. He used it in turning away from God. He may use it again in refusing to turn back to God. And what then? The gospel of a free pardon through the death of Christ is "preached in the whole creation under heaven." The amnesty has been proclaimed; and, because God is unwilling that any should perish, judgment waits. But if men despise the grace and reject the Saviour, the sure and inevitable alternative is PERDITION.

Strange it is that they who are most emphatic in asserting that God must give salvation to all men in the next world, are precisely those who dismiss as fanaticism the truth that He gives salvation here and now to those who seek Him. The Church of Rome denies grace altogether, and represents Divine love as dependent for its display on the human weakness of a traditional Jesus and the womanly tenderness of a traditional Mary. This conception of God has produced the coarse conventional hell of theology, which again has led to the creation of purgatory and masses for the dead, to alleviate the horrors of the system. In asserting the doctrine of justification by faith, the Reformation in great measure restored the lost truth of grace. Mariolatry and purgatory disappeared with the darkness which produced them, but the mediaeval hell remained. Protestantism, however, when separated from spiritual life, is a mere soulless body; and while the religious movement of the present century has deepened faith in the doctrines of the Reformation, those who have resisted its influences are either turning back to Rome or lapsing to infidelity. On the one side, we see a revival of the old errors of intercession for the dead and the power of "aeonian fire" to purify the soul. On the other side, the great truths of Christianity are dismissed as narrow cant; the mystery of Divine love to a lost world is degraded to the level of good-natured benevolence to erring creatures; sin is but human frailty, righteousness a myth, and judgment but the appointed means by which the lost of earth shall be fitted for the heaven to which their relationship to God entitles them. In a shallow, and, therefore, a sceptical age, this is the most popular religion. It vaunts itself as the outcome of increased enlightenment; in fact it is but the mingled ignorance and insolence of unbelief."

Testimonies: The great preacher, Charles Haddon Spurgeon, described Sir Robert's *Human Destiny*', "The most valuable contribution on the subject I have ever seen." According to *The Christian*, "The strength of this book lies in its fidelity to revelation, and its vigorous exposure of mere human speculations." *The Record* stated: "It is seldom that we take up a book that we wish it had been longer, but this is such a book." And *Christian Leader* recorded: "This masterly treatise .....ought to become a treasured handbook on the subject."

9. The Gospel and its Ministry

This book was published in 1876. Dr Anderson opened the Preface with this statement: "In these days men have left off faith. The spirit of the martyrs is not in them. Opinions have taken the place of convictions; and the result is a liberality which is the offspring, not of humility and love, but of indifference or doubt. Opinions are our own, and should not be too firmly held. Truth is divine; and is worth living for and dying for......in the last days the new light which men seek to dispel "the deepening gloom will not be wanting; but it will prove a wrecker's fire, though seemingly accredited as the beacon light of truth."

Dr Anderson stresses: "God has given us a revelation. And, while doubt still lingers around innumerable questions on which we crave knowledge, Divine certainty is our privilege in respect of all things that pertain unto life and godliness. The man who would force his opinion on others is a boor. He who would die for his opinions is a fool. But Christianity has not to do with *opinions.* It is founded on established facts and Divine truth; and faith based thereon is the heritage of the Church. Her martyrs knew the power of faith." The Knight continued: "We are not called upon to wear the martyr's crown, but it is ours to share the martyr's faith. We can have no toleration for the veiled scepticism which is passing for Christianity today. Agnosticism is Greek for ignorance, and ignorance is both shameful and sinful in the presence of a Divine revelation. The Christian is not ignorant; neither is he in doubt. We do not think this or that: we KNOW. "We know that the Son of God is come." "We know that He was manifested to take away our sins." "We know that we have passed from death unto life." "We know that if our earthly house were dissolved, we have a building of God, eternal in the heavens." "We know that when we shall appear we shall be like Him." Amen!

In the introductory chapter, Dr Anderson states the 'qualification' needed to proclaim the Gospel of Christ: "What God wants in those whom He will put in trust with the gospel, is not that they shall be polished and educated gentlemen, much less that they shall be coarse and ignorant boors; not that they shall be skilled in dogmatic theology, much less that they shall be unlearned in doctrine; not that they shall be brilliant and eloquent, much less that they shall be ungifted and dull. All He seeks is a fitting instrument upon whom the power of Christ can rest, an empty earthen vessel that He can fill with His priceless treasure. The man, whoever he may be, whether on the highest round of the social ladder, or the lowest, who can say with Paul, "Most gladly will I glory in infirmities, that the power of Christ may rest on me," and say it with unfeigned lips, and from a heart that has been taught it in the school of God, has gained the secret of this competency for the ministry of reconciliation."

On the chapter on GRACE, Dr Anderson writes: "But now about to come the world's great crisis - the most stupendous event in the history of man, the only event in the history of God! He had laid aside His glory, and come down into the scene. At His own door He had stood and knocked, but only to find it shut in His face. Turning them thence, He had wandered an outcast into the world which His power had made, but He wandered there unknown. His own received him not"; "the world knew Him not." As He had laid aside His glory, He now restrained His power, and yielded Himself to their guilty will. In return for pity He earned but scorn. Sowing kindness and benefits with a lavish hand, He reaped but cruelty and outrage. Manifesting grace He was given up to impious law without show of mercy or pretence of justice. Unfolding the boundless love of the mighty heart of God, He gained no response but bitterest hate from the hearts of men….."

In the Preparatory note to the thirteen edition of the *Gospel and Its Ministry*, Dr Anderson records that the book was written about thirty five years ago for a religious "Monthly". The latest edition was translated into Japanese. And in 1905 it was published by Fukuoaka, "and placed in the hands of all the native workers of the Church Missionary Society in Japan.

Testifying to this work**,** *The Christian* wrote**:** "A handbook of Evangelical truth… These essays contemplate the most stupendous subjects which can occupy human thought…..The chapters on "Grace" and "The Cross" are worth their weight in gold."

10. The Silence of God

This stimulating book was released in 1897. It explains how it seems heaven is not in existence and there is no God. Dr Anderson opens the volume with these words: "A silent Heaven is the greatest mystery of our existence. Some there are, indeed, for whom the problem has no perplexities…Societies, even in the great centres of our modern civilisation, is all too like a slave-ship, where, with the sounds of music and laughter and revelry on the upper deck, there mingle the groans of untold misery battened down below. Who can estimate the sorrow and suffering and wrong endured during a single round of the clock even in the favoured metropolis of highly favoured England? …..What mind is competent to grasp the sum of this entire great world's misery, heaped up day after day, year after year, century after century? Human hearts may plan, and human hands achieve, some little to alleviate it, and the strong and ready arm of human law may accomplish much in the protection of the weak and the punishment of the wicked. But as God - the light of moon and stars is not more cold and pitiless that He appears to be!…." Dr Anderson continues: "When we turn to Holy Writ this mystery of a silent Heaven, which is driving so many to infidelity, if not to atheism, seems to become insoluble…"

The Defender of the Christian Faith explained that the silence in Heaven "is not the silence of callous indifference or helpless weakness. The silence is the pledge and proof that the way is open for the guiltiest of mankind to draw near to God. When that silence is broken one day, it will mean the withdrawal of the amnesty; the end of the reign of grace; and the drawing of the day of wrath foretold in Scripture. God is silent now because He has spoken His last word of mercy and love in Christ. He is beseeching men to be reconciled (2 Cor. V. 20). The One to whom all judgement has been committed, and who will appear one day as the judge of all, is now the Saviour and is seated upon the Father's Throne in grace."

Dr Anderson noted: "Religion and Scepticism are rival competitors for popular favour. And yet there are many who, though conscious of longings too deep to be satisfied by mere religion, make choice of religion because they know of no other refuge from unbelief. And there are others again who, with too much knowledge for the sceptic's side, drift into scepticism in their recoil from priestcraft." He continues: "Infidelity trades upon the silence of heaven, the inaction of the Supreme. If there be a God, almighty and all-good, why does He not use His power and give proof of His goodness in the way men choose to expect Him? The answer usually offered by the Christian apologist fails either to silence the opponent or to satisfy the believer. And rightly so, for it is lacking not only in cogency but in sympathy. The God of the Bible is infinite both in power and in compassion; and in other ages His people had public proof of this. Why, then, is He so silent. The question is not why He does not *always* declare Himself, but why He *never* does so." Please continue reading from page 12 of *The Silence of God.*

The fifth edition of this exceptional work was published in 1899 when the Prince of Detectives was residing at 39 Linden Gardens in West London. Three editions of *The Silence of God* were published in a few weeks. The *New York Herald* described it: "a book which has astounded religious Europe."

Here are some extracts from the reviews of the book:
The Record: "A remarkable title, and it heralds a remarkable book....We are profoundly grateful for this most striking endeavour to move a terrible stumbling block out of the way of many. Seldom have we read a book so compelling in its logical directness."

The Christian Church: "This book sparkles with gems, and is from first to last so pre-eminently a word for the times."

New York Daily Tribune: "An ingenious and subtle attempt to meet scepticism on its own ground....A book which reveals deep learning, argumentative subtlety, and spiritual power."
Literature: "The Silence of God deals with a problem of inexhaustible interest."

The sixth and seventh editions of *The Silence of God* were published in 1903 and 1905. It became a source of hope during the First World War. A Danish version of the book titled, *Gud's Tavshed, was* published in 1917 by Mr J Fischmann. This writer hopes *The Coming Prince*, which foretold the development of the European Union and its future prospects, would become a source of light for our generation to appreciate the true purpose of Jean Monnet's vision of a federal Europe. And most importantly, *The Coming Prince* would help the British and the Irish people to decide whether their future lie in the European project which uses pornographic film and posters to promote its cause.

II. The Honour of His Name

This volume was first published in 1912. An extract from the Preface reads: "The title of this book, which is a quotation from the sixty-sixth Psalm – indicates not only its subject, but its aim.....While Bible students will greatly value this Appendix, I fear it will be neglected by the ordinary reader. And these pages need never have been written were it not that the New Testament is commonly treated in a similar fashion, the Book of Revelation being regarded as negligible Appendix to the Gospels and the Epistles. But the Patmos visions are divinely given to enable us by faith to behold what the beloved disciple saw when "in the Spirit on the Lord's day."

That some among them had "no knowledge of God" was the reproach the Apostle cast upon the Christians of Corinth. And were he with us today, might he not charge us with having no knowledge of the Lord of glory. For the Christian who accepts the opening vision of the Apocalypse as being a divine revelation of the Lord Jesus Christ as now enthroned in heaven, will need neither warning nor appeal to avoid all irreverent freedom in naming Him - to shun even the appearance of forgetting "the honour of His name." Dr Anderson listed 80 titles and names attributed to the Lord Jesus Christ. Just a few will do: God, Emmanuel, Son of God, Son of David, Cornerstone, Passover, Deliverer, Messiah, King, Saviour, Judge, High Priest, Alpha and Omega, Faithful and True, Lion of the Tribe of Judah, True Vine, "I am", Life, Bread, Lamb, Lord...."

Testifying to this book in *Things to come*, Rev E W Bullinger wrote: "Clear and vigorous in all that it so well says, our hope and desire is that this edition may lead to the issue of sixpenny edition. Then let some friend with plenty of money buy it in thousands, so that it may find its way into every pulpit and every pew." And the Bishop of Durham wrote: "I shall carry the impression of the book about with me everywhere."

12. *The Buddha of Christendom:*

According to Dr Anderson, this book is for the "Present crisis." In this work, the literary recluse covered a wide range of issues from Evolution and Creationism controversy to the claims made by the Roman Catholic Church. The book was updated and incorporated into *The Bible or the Church* and *A Doubters Doubt about Science and Religion.* I will share with you highlights of some of the issues he raised, and how a Roman Catholic intellectual attempted to drag Dr. Anderson into the Church of Rome.

THE THEORY OF EVOLUTION DISCUSSED IN THE BUDDHA OF CHRISTENDOM: (David Attenborough exposes his ignorance)

In the opening chapter of this book, Dr Anderson writes: "Neither the idealist nor the sceptic ever questioned the fact of his own existence. Here it is that knowledge begins; and at this point knowledge is absolute. I EXIST: this is a fact enthroned beyond the sphere where doubt is possible. But the question remains, how did I come to exist? I live: How did life begin? To say I am descended from a first man is no solution of it. Where did the first man come from? To reply that he was evolved or developed from a life-germ, is merely to put the difficulty back. How is the life-germ to be accounted for? The greatest living authority to whom we can appeal will tell us that "inanimate matter cannot become living except under the influence of matter already living. This, he (Lord Kelvin of British Association in Edinburgh) adds, "is a fact in science which seems to me as well ascertained as the law of gravitation...I am ready to accept as an article of faith in science, valid for all time and in all space, that life is produced by life and only by life"

The falseness of the alternative proposition – that life originally came from nowhere out of nothing - is apparent. Besides being absolutely without evidence to give it external support itself internally - cannot be framed into a coherent thought. It is one of those illegitimate symbolic conceptions because they remain untested. Immediately an attempt is made to elaborate the idea into anything like a definite shape, it proves to be a pseud-idea, admitting of no definite shape. It implies the establishment of a relation in thought between nothing and something - a relation of which one term is absent - an impossible relation. The case is one of those where men do not really believe, but rather *believe* they believe. For belief properly so called, implies a mental representation of the thing believed; and no such mental representation is here possible."

Dr Anderson then went on to dismiss Herbert Spencer's bland "philosophy" by refuting his claim. Spencer assumes that, at some time or other, "living matter must have arisen from not-living matter;" although his (Spencer's) own words so pitilessly expose the absurdity of the suggestion. For it involves a "pseud-idea"; and therefore, so he tells us, it cannot be believed, because "belief implies a mental representation of the thing believed, and no such representation is here possible."

The question before us is, not how the various developments of life can be explained, but how life itself can be accounted for. And this inquiry leads us abruptly to the startling conclusion that the human mind is incapable not only of believing, but even of *thinking* that life ever came except from life; or, in other words, that life ever had a beginning. But it may be urged, the only possible alternative to the hypothesis of evolution is that of creation; and Mr Spencer's argument, while clearly destructive of the one, is no less valid against the other. The objection is an intelligible one. All are agreed, of course that there...." I would not continue.

Dr Anderson opens Chapter 3 of *The Buddha of Christendom* with this statement "As soon as man grew distinct from the animal he became religious." No one gifted with a sense of humour could have gravely penned a suggestion so grotesque as this. That the remote descendant of an ape might become intelligent, philosophical, mathematical, musical, poetical, scientific - all this possibly we could understand; but why should he become *religious*? ....Charles Darwin himself admits that "a belief in all-pervading spiritual agencies seems to be universal". Accepting the conclusion, therefore, that man is by nature religious, the question remains, how can this fact be accounted for?

Please continue reading "*The Buddha of Christendom.*" You would be motivated to ignore the ignorant evolutionists. For example, Sir David Attenborough, the Darwinist, exposed his ignorance about the future of man in an article titled *Wanted, a young genius to be the next Darwin*. Attenborough writes: "....Darwin's was the cornerstone of all the wildlife films I've made, and I was delighted by the opportunity...to mark his place in history. But what of the future? There are many questions still to be answered. Will humans evolve? Or are we evolving? How will climate change, the possible extinction of hundreds of species of plants and animals through a process of decidedly unnatural selection, affect the balance of life on Earth?" .He goes on: "It baffles me that there are still people who reject the theory of evolution..." (The Daily Telegraph 3 March 2009).

Why should people accept an unproven theory as fact? If the agnostic Attenborough wants to know the future of man and our planet, he must consult the works of The Knight Commander with knowledge and mental power - the real genius - who wrote about European Union: how it would develop, its character and future prospects even before the French founding fathers of European Community - Jean Monnet and Robert Schuman – were conceived. Sir Robert Anderson's *Human Destiny* would enlighten Sir David Attenborough about the future of man. Charles Darwin and his Theory of Evolution are irrelevant in the 21st century. What is relevant in the 21st century are the works of Sir Robert Anderson which dismiss Darwin's fable theory of Evolution. Sir Robert Anderson's *The Coming Prince,* recorded the "Quiet Miracle" (EU) before the "Quiet Miracle" manifested.

"Romish Propagandism": Dr Anderson and the "Persistent Catholic"

Appendix II to *The Buddha of Christendom* is entitled "Romish Propagandism." In this section of the book, Dr. Anderson shares with us how a Roman Catholic intellectual attempted to convert him to Catholicism. The Prince of Detectives engaged in a series of correspondence with this Catholic scholar. Dr Anderson tells us how he responded to the Catholic and how the Catholic viewed him: "I wrote in terms which I supposed would be deemed final, and enclosed a copy of one of my books (The Gospel and its Ministry), which I referred as proof that I already possessed in Christ every blessing which he imagined "the Church" could give; and moreover that I was, from his point of view, a hopeless heretic."

This Catholic scholar felt Dr Anderson should be at "the right place" namely, the Roman Catholic Church. Towards the close of their correspondence, the "Persistent Catholic scholar" gave Dr. Anderson a copy of a Catholic treatise to show him how he (Anderson) has "grievously misjudged the Church." According to Dr Anderson, "His letter enclosing the book, gave me the first definite of what I naturally guessed, that his letters to me were part of a systematic effort to lead selected Protestants to make their submission to Rome.....Such are the methods by which the perverts to Rome are won."

The Catholic wrote another voluminous letter to Dr Anderson to which "God's Barrister" responded: "You refuse my appeal to the written Word of God, and point me to "the Church." But when I ask, "Why should I trust "the Church", you refer me to the written Word of God." "It amazes me", says Dr. Anderson, "that an intelligent man like you cannot see the inconsistency of such a position. Either "the Church" can justify its pretensions by an appeal to Scripture, or it cannot. If it cannot there is an end of the matter. If it can, then let us turn to Scripture and bow to its decision."

The stalwart defender of the Christian Faith did not respond to the last letter of the "Persistent Catholic." However, Dr. Anderson made this statement: "I am utterly at a loss to know what answer is possible to one who thus ignores or distorts both history and Scripture and honestly and earnestly believes in what he calls "the Church." Here I repeat are the arguments by which perverts to Rome are being won. Here, in its most advanced development, is the pestilently evil and profane view of "the Church," which is slowly but surely undermining Christianity in the Church of England at this moment." What an indictment on the clergy of Anglican Church who are running to Vatican. For what?

In Appendix IV, Dr. Anderson writes about "Bishops", "Deacons", "The Church", The "Virgin Mary Myth," "The Apostle Paul on Celibacy," "We have an Altar," "The Epistles of Ignatius," "Prevailing Irreverence in the use of the Lord's Name" and "Popular Hymnology." The True Defender of the Christian Faith declares: "If Rome has paramount claims to the position she assumes, it is being indisputably the most distinctive and advanced embodiment of the apostasy. When the historic Church adopted the pagan rite of baptism it ceased to have any moral right to be considered the Church of God; and when in a later age it gave up the Lordship and Headship of Christ its fall was complete. For if baptismal regeneration is unchristian, apostolic succession is anti-Christian. In "the Christian religion" the Church is everything. In Christianity the Church sinks to its true place as "a congregation of faithful men," and the great test of faithfulness is that the Lord Jesus Christ is all in all."

I encourage you to read *The Buddha of Christendom.* It would strengthen your Faith in the Bible to dismiss the disciples of Darwin and ignore Vatican's claim that the Roman Catholic Church is the true Church – the "Oracle of God."

13. *The Bible or the Church?*

This book was based on *The Buddha of Christendom.* In the Preface Dr. Anderson writes: "The greatest achievement in English history is a distinguished historian's estimate of the Reformation; but in this flippant and shallow age we seem to be letting slip what the Reformers won for us. For a national lapse toward superstition upon one hand, and rationalism upon the other, is one marked characteristics of the day. And altogether apart from religious controversy these movements deserve the earnest attention of the thoughtful. For the dethronement of the Bible eliminates the most important factor in the formation of our national character, and it is not easy to estimate the effect which this will have on the life of the people of this country."

What a prophetic word which is being fulfilled today in our nation. Britain is now a 'broken society". It faces moral collapse: teenage pregnancy and abortion, pornography, violence, drug addictions, suicide, anti-social behaviour, murders, falsehood in politics; Deception in sections of the media; false doctrine and sexual immoralities among the clergy and the laity, and Members of Parliament abusing their privileges to enrich themselves to the extent that politicians have accepted that the House of Commons, which has become the "House of Sleaze" needs clearing up.

It is appropriate, at this point, to quote Stephen Glover: "The Church of England like the BBC, has become timid organisation that is often frightened to take a public stand against moral excesses which it knows in its hearts are wrong. Both the director of the BBC and the Archbishop of Canterbury would be utterly incomprehensible figures to their predecessors of 50 years ago, let alone a hundred." (Source: Daily Mail 30 October 2008: *How could a man of such high morals preside over the BBC's descent into the gutter?).* I hope our politicians and church leaders will take notice of what Sir Robert Anderson wrote about Europe and Britain in *The Coming Prince.*

Before concluding the preface, Dr Anderson remarked: "The title *The Bible or the Church?* implicitly raises the question whether the Bible can still be accorded the place which it held with the Reformers as a Divine Revelation." In the first chapter of the book, Dr Anderson writes: "In the days of Pagan Rome the Church was on the side of the martyrs. But under Papal Rome the martyrs were the victims of "the Church."

Sir Robert Anderson on Cardinal Newman and the Catholic Eucharist

Dr Anderson took to task Cardinal Henry Newman's support of the Roman Catholic dogma of Transubstantiation. He records: "With reference to the dogma of Transubstantiation, Newman writes: "I had no difficulty in believing it as soon as I believed that the Catholic Roman Church was the oracle of God, and that she had declared this doctrine to be part of the original revelation." Transubstantiation, the Reformers maintain, "overthroweth the nature of a sacrament." "Simple and clear though this statement be, people fail to grasp its meaning. A sacrament is merely a sign or symbol to represent some spiritual reality. In the Eucharist, for example, the bread is bread and nothing more, but it represents the Lord's body. If therefore the bread be regarded as being in fact His body, it is no longer a "sacrament" at all."

Dr Anderson goes on, "But let us analyse Cardinal Newman's words. Why should we believe that a piece of bread is flesh, seeing that, judged by every possible test, it is not flesh but only bread? The Roman Catholic replies that we should believe it on the authority of the Church, for the Church is the oracle of God. But why, we demand again, should we believe the Church to be the oracle of God? We should believe it, the Roman Catholic tells us, because the Church is thus accredited by Holy Scripture. Is it not then our plain duty to test this claim by referring to the Scripture? "Certainly not," is the emphatic rejoinder; "that is Protestant heresy of the worst kind. For the Church is the oracle of God, and therefore the authoritative exponent of Scripture; and instead of using our own judgment or reason, we must accept the Church's teaching on the subject." To the enlightened this may be the highest wisdom; but to the benighted Protestant it bears a sinister resemblance to the artifice which, in another sphere, the vulgar describe as "ringing the changes." "Why, even of yourselves, judge ye not what is right?" the Lord demanded of the unbelieving Jews. But while faith is the highest exercise of reason, Newman's position is the complete abnegation of reason. "Come now, and let us reason together," was the Divine appeal to His people in the old time, even in days of apostasy. And coupled with that appeal was the Divine lament, "My people doth not consider." and the word is emphatic and significant. It means using their intelligence, and thinking for themselves, instead of blindly following their religious leaders, or in other words "obeying the voice of the Church."

That the Church is "the oracle of God" is a figment unsupported by evidence and disproved by facts. But no matter how able and pious a man may be, if he stultifies his reason by accepting it, he has "no difficulty in believing" that a piece of bread is the flesh of the Lord of Glory. In the same way he would have "no difficulty in believing" that this earth is not a planet but a fixed plane and the centre of the solar system; that the drivel contained in some parts of the Apocrypha was divinely inspired; and that the tortures of the Inquisition and the, fires of Smithfield were divinely sanctioned and blessed! Superstition such as this explains the advice which Pascal gave to those who found a difficulty in accepting the dogmas of the Church. Take to religion, he said in effect, "for that will make you stupid and enable you to believe."

Commenting on the *"Bible or the Church"*, Canon Teignmouth Shore, who was Chaplain-in-Ordinary to Queen Victoria and King Edward VII, wrote: "I saw the notice of your volume in *The Church Times*. It only shows how hard you have hit them. I need scarcely say how heartily I agree with you. The Church of England became Protestant at the Reformation, but the Bishops have by their cowardly connivance allowed her practices and doctrines as now taught by six-tenths of the clergy to become Roman Catholic...The Bishops snip off little bits of fringe here and there, when it is the whole pattern of the garment that is wrong." (What a prophetic word for today's Church of England's hierarchy! The Established Church has lost its way. It is plagued with divisions on homosexuality and ordination of women bishops. The Church of England gropes in darkness. It has become an object of irrelevance and ridicule).

The soldier, Field-Marshall Viscount Wolseley, forcibly expressed his opinion on *The Bible or the Church*: "It's Protestantism cannot be too strong for me; for it is not that I abhor all the absurd idolatry and customs appertaining to it that our fathers protested against and rid England of at the Reformation, but I have sublime contempt for the invertebrate creatures in trousers who try to take from our religion that healthy manliness which Protestantism engrafted upon our national Church."

Paolo Sarpi and the Roman Catholic Church

In Appendix III to *The Bible or the Church*, Dr Anderson reminds the world of the character of Roman Catholic Church by referring to Paolo Sarpi's ordeal at the hands of Papal Rome. Under the title *"Paolo Sarpi and the Council of Trent,"* the Zealot Champion of Christian Causes writes: "Of Paolo Sarpi it has been said that "there was no department of human knowledge about which he did not know everything that had been ascertained by others, and few to which he did not make substantial contributions." In truth, he seems to have been one of the most extraordinary men of his own or of any age. Born in Venice in 1552, he joined the Servites at thirteen years of age, and was immediately put forward as their champion at the great annual disputation in the Friar Church, where, before all the noble and great and wise of Venice, he held his own against all disputants. Five years later, at eighteen, he was appointed to the chair of Positive Theology at Mantua, and became private theologian to the Duke. In 1575 he returned to Venice, where he held the chairs of Philosophy and Mathematics in the monastery until, in 1579, he became a Principal of his Order. His high character, his intense piety, and his altogether phenomenal erudition and genius, secured for him the friendship of all who were best qualified to supply him with materials for his history of the Council of Trent.

His quarrel with the Vatican came later, and was brought about as follows: In 1606 the Senate of Venice, in order to secure his services, created for him the office of Theological Counsellor; and in the fierce struggle of that year between the Republic and the Pope, Paolo Sarpi was the adviser of the Senate. Paul V. launched his Bull of interdict and excommunication against Venice. Sarpi held that this action was ultra vires; and, acting on their Counsellor's advice, the Senate confronted and thwarted the Pope at every point. The Pope ordered the clergy to close the churches and suspend all services and sacraments. The Republic threatened to punish any priest who acted on the order. The Pope ordered the clergy to leave the country and repair to Rome. They were warned that if they attempted to act on the order they would be hanged at the frontier. The Pope was brought to his knees, and after pleading in vain for some way to save his dignity, he was compelled to issue another Bull, withdrawing the interdict; and this the Senate, acting on Sarpi's advice, would not permit to be read in the churches. Never since has any Pope dared to issue such an interdict.

Needless to say, the result was to make the Pope the bitter enemy of Paolo Sarpi. Having tried in vain every artifice to get him to Rome, he determined to be revenged by other means. Though, honours and money were pressed upon Sarpi, he refused to change his mode of life and while his days were spent in the public service, he insisted on returning nightly to his cell in the monastery. On the night of the 5th October, 1607, he was waylaid by assassins hired by Paul V (the "Vicar of Christ"), and left for dead within a few hundred yards of the monastery. But to the bitter disappointment of the Pope, and to the amazement of everybody, he recovered. For another fifteen years he continued his career of service to Venice and the world, and notwithstanding further Papal plots against his life, he died peacefully in his cell on the 15th January, 1623.

His fame may be judged by the fact that his death was formally reported to all the Courts of Europe, and that he was voted a State funeral and a public monument. But the malignity of the Vatican is undying. Plot after plot was hatched to desecrate the dead friar's tomb and scatter his ashes. Ten times those ashes were disturbed, and secretly reinterred to save them from the Papal emissaries; and for 270 years the decree of the Senate to erect a monument to his memory remained in abeyance. It was not till the 20th September, 1892, that, in pursuance of that decree, the statue which now stands in the Campo di Santa Fosca was unveiled in honour of that truly great and noble man". This is the Roman Catholic Church that claims to be the "Oracle of God." This is the Church of Rome that undermines the authenticity of the Book of Daniel and supports the European Union that has no room for the Lord Jesus Christ. What a contradiction! What a shame!

14. The Lord From Heaven

The second edition of this wonderful book was released in 1910. In the Preface, the Bishop of Durham writes: "The author explains how he had been asked on one occasion to mediate between the committee of a missionary society and some of their younger agents whose faith had been disturbed by….hostility to the truth of the Sonship of Christ. He had been unable to find a book which definitely meets their difficulties, and the thought of writing such a one was suggested to him. It is not controversial; it is a Bible study. And the question at issue was not merely the divinity of our Lord, now generally acknowledged, but His Deity. "Thou being a man makest Thyself God"; this was the charge for which the Jews threatened to stone Him…"After reading this book, Dr. Bullinger wrote: "I feel I have a fuller, better and deeper knowledge of my Lord and my God, and praise Him and bless you for it."

In the closing chapter of *The Lord From Heaven* Dr Anderson writes: "This is the age of His absence, but the coming age shall be characterised by His presence. Not an isolated event, albeit Scripture tells us that a series of manifestations of Christ will mark its course, but a new attitude towards men—immediate divine action both in blessing and in judgement. For while the covert atheism of these days of ours scoffs at the thought that the prayer which He Himself has put into our lips could ever be fulfilled, His believing people know that His Kingdom is certainly coming, and that His will shall be done on earth."

Testimonies:

Testifying to this work, Handley Dunelm writes; "The author handles his great theme with a penetration and force all his own, and at the same time with worshipping reverence, and with whole-hearted reliance on the Written Word. I pray our Master's blessing on this close study of the witnesses for the glory of Christ, done not by an official advocate of the faith, but by one long versed to weighty and difficult duties of civil law and order, accustomed through his whole life to the keenest of facts, and to the ruthless exposure of fallacy"

The Life of Faith: "We wish this book could be put into the hands of every divinity student in our land."

Evangelical Christendom: "Among the many valuable literary productions of the author, this volume is one of the most valuable."

The Sword and the Trowel: "Sound, strong, and to any open mind, convincing."

15. Redemption Truths

This book, also known as *"For us men"*, was first published in 1905. In his Foreword to the book, J Arnold Fair writes: "Like the pure pristine beauty of an unsoiled lily as it unfolds in the fruition and fragrance of God's creative purpose, so Sir Robert Anderson presents *Redemption Truths*. The gift of salvation is simply presented. The glory of Sonship is challengingly offered. The grandeur of eternity's splendour is shown". He continues, "*Redemption Truths* is a wonderful book to present to a new Christian. Here are many scriptural answers to the myriad of questions that flood a new believer's mind....This makes this book a valuable tool for the pastor, evangelist, and student of God's Word......One is captivated by scriptural principles presented with depth and practicality. As you mount his staircase of truths you will find them etched with personal experiences of inspiration and insights...."

In the Preface Dr Anderson writes: "This book is intended to help those who are seeking peace with God, or who desire to lead others into the way of life." In the opening chapter he writes: "...sin essentially is lawlessness; which means, not transgression of law, nor absence of law, but revolt against law - in a word, self-will. This is the very essence of sin." The Knight Commander added: "The truest test of a man is not conduct, but character; not what he does, but what he is. Human judgement must of course be guided by a man's acts and words. But God is not thus limited. Man judges character by conduct; God judges conduct by character. Therefore it is that "what is highly esteemed among men is abomination in the sight of God."

16. The Way

The second edition of this book was published in 1905. In the opening NOTE Dr Robert Anderson writes: "That another Edition of the "THE WAY' should be called for within a few weeks of its appearance is most gratifying to the Author." Explaining what it means to be a Christian, the Knight of God states: "In Christendom we are all Christians, for the Christian religion prevails.... The Christian religion has been a bitter opponent, and relentless persecutor of Christianity....the Christian is to use the world; but if he is betrayed into using it excessively, it becomes his master. And though mammon be a good servant, it is evil master.. ..For wealth will not buy health or peace of mind either. And without a good digestion and "a mind at leisure from itself" no amount of gold will enable anyone to enjoy life --- to "make merry sumptuously everyday." And so it has come to pass that princes have died broken-hearted, and millionaires have killed themselves." In our generation we continue to witness these tragedies.

The distinguished Victorian reminds us: "Suffering for Christ's sake refine and humble a man, but they never crush him...A Christian may seem to his fellow-man to be a fool. But it is one thing to be a fool, and quite another thing to seem to be a fool. The Christian acts in the presence with a view to the future." And in *The Coming Price* Dr Anderson emphasises: "If a knowledge of the past be important, a knowledge of the future is of far higher value still, in enlarging the mind and raising it above the littlenesses that is produced by a narrow and unenlightened contemplation of the present."

In summary: "THE WAY" throws light on many problems of the daily walk and warfare. According to *The Record,* "The work is one of a masculine and outspoken character, and well repays attention." *The Life of Faith* says: "The author deals with the problems of life in his own masterly manner." And *Christian Commonwealth* describes it to be "a real literary treasure.

17. Misunderstood Texts of the New Testament

This book was first published in 1916, two years before the Knight Commander departed. The work sheds light upon a number of difficult "misunderstood" passages in the New Testament. The title of the book aptly describes the purpose of the book - to correct distortions of some of the texts in the New Testament. According to Dr Anderson, a typical example is "love your enemies" sermon that was preached in a prominent metropolitan pulpit - a sermon to which the secular newspaper accorded an extraordinary measure of publicity. The Knight goes on: "He must be but a poor type of Christian who can regard without feelings of aversion, deliberate and deep, either the evil men who are directly responsible for the flendish crimes committed by our enemies in this (First World) war, or the mass of the German people who not only condone but sympathise with them...The main question here dealt with is a flagrant misuse of the Sermon on the Mount, which has discredited the sacred words in the estimation of multitudes, no authoritative voice having been raised to correct the error.

Some there are who, though sharing the views here expressed, will resent the statement of them by a layman. But if, when no other voice was available, "a dumb ass" was Divinely used to rebuke a prophet, surely, *faute de mieux,* "a mere layman" may rebuke a preacher...." Dr Anderson goes on to make this comment in the *Introductory Chapter:* "The words of God are like the works of God, in that we often need the microscope to enable us to appreciate them. And yet at times this element is of secondary importance. For, unless we understand the Divine scheme and purpose of the Bible as a whole, we cannot read even the New Testament intelligently....."

In the introductory note to this work Dr Anderson writes: "The Gospels are not, as infidels suppose, imperfect and often conflicting records of the life and ministry of "Jesus," but separate portraits, as it were, of the Lord Jesus Christ with reference to His various relationships and offices. This appears very strikingly when we compare the First Gospel with the Fourth. For the Fourth is the revelation of the Son of God, who came not to judge, but to save the world (John xii. 47); whereas the First records His advent and ministry as Israel's Messiah; and we scan it in vain for words of the kind we value in the Fourth - words which we, as Gentiles, can take to ourselves without reserve. This notable fact is not to be explained by suggesting that the Apostle Matthew was a narrow-minded Jew who refused to identify himself with the teaching of his Lord whenever it passed beyond the sphere of Jewish hopes and interests."

18. The Critics Criticised – Pseudo Criticism

This volume was first published in March 1904. In its Preface, the Secret Service Agent writes: "This book is an exposure of a false system of Biblical Criticism, by which "the Higher Criticism" has been discredited and almost supplanted". The Knight Commander dismissed Professor Driver's *Book of Genesis*, which treats Bible on Rationalistic principle. Dr. Anderson quoted Professor Driver's Introduction to his *Book of Genesis:* "We have found that, while there is no sufficient reason for doubting the existence and general historical character of the biographies of patriarchs, nevertheless much uncertainty must be allowed to attach the details of the narratives; which means that though the Rationalists have failed to discover any grounds for challenging the truth of the narrative, the Christian has no sufficient warrant for accepting it...there are no grounds for concluding that the Genesis narrative is not true, but in the absence of corroboration from pagan sources, we must not assume it's truth. For the testimony of the Bible must never be accorded any higher value than is allowed to the evidence of "informer" in our courts of justice, and therefore we are on the alert to find "sufficient reason for doubting it." (Today, in the 21st century, the apostate Church holds this view).

"God's Barrister" responded: "This sort of criticism is gratifying to the Rationalist; but a Christian naturally shrinks from it. And so, in the concluding section of his Introduction, Dr. Driver goes on to formulate the utterly unintelligible and wholly untenable compromise, in which writers of his school take refuge from the obvious consequences of their teaching. Although according to the writers whose views he adopts, Genesis is mainly a compilation of myths and legends, traceable ultimately to pagan sources, he earnestly insists upon "the inspiration of its authors." This may satisfy a scholar among his books, but it will not do with sensible men of the world. Such men care nothing for controversial subtleties about the inspiration of Scripture, but they will rightly hold that if inspiration be not a guarantee of truth, it may be classed with the superstitions of religion...."

Dr Anderson added: "The question is not whether the Cosmology teaches science, which no one asserts; but whether it is discredited by science, which no one has proved. And not even the testimony of such a scientist as Dana in its defence will weigh as much with men of the world, as the fact that such a scientist as Huxley entered the lists to prove it in error and failed...." The Knight went on to expose the ignorance of the proud Huxley: "As for the "Mosaic Cosmogony," if the Gladstone-Huxley tournament upon that question in the pages of the *Nineteenth Century* has failed to silence the silly cuckoo-cry about "the conflict between Science and Genesis," all discussion is idle. Mr Gladstone's thesis was that Science is perfectly in accord with Genesis as to the order in which life appeared on upon our globe. Upon one point only did Professor Huxley attempt to upset this, and that depended on interpreting "creeping things" in Genesis I, by the use of the word in Leviticus xi.29-31. "The merest Sunday School exegesis," he (Huxley) said, "suffices to prove that when Mosaic writer in Genesis i.24 speaks of creeping things, he means to include lizards among them," to which Dr. Anderson responded: "A sheer blunder, based on the chance reading of the English Bible; for there is no affinity between the word used in Genesis I, and that employed in Leviticus xi. But instead of apologising to the "Sunday School," Professor Huxley appealed to his "eminent friend Professor Dana" on the general question, and Professor Dana's answer was, "I believe that the first chapter of Genesis and Science are in accord."

In the Preface to *Pseudo-Criticism*, the Defender of the Christian Faith records: "The fact is that critics are so engrossed with what may be called the surface difficulties of Bible study, that they overlook difficulties of a far graver kind; difficulties which bring all fearless thinkers to the parting of the ways, compelling them to make choice between accepting the Bible as a Divine revelation, or giving up belief in Christianity." On the critics, the "Barrister of God" writes: "If we could get these pseudo-critics before any sort of competent tribunal, they would be "laughed out of court" in an hour." (*Pseudo Criticism* pages 18, 19).

In one of his works, Dr. Anderson writes: "Secular writers are presumed to be trustworthy unless reason is found to discredit their testimony. But the Higher Criticism starts with the assumption that everything in Scripture needs to be confirmed by external evidence. It reeks of its evil origin in German infidelity"

Testifying to *The Critics criticised–Pseudo-criticism*, *The Times* newspaper reported: "Sir Robert Anderson again levels his lance at rationalistic criticism."

The English Churchman declared: "It is a masterpiece of apologetics." And the Bishop of Durham also wrote: "I read the book through with the keenest interest, and I laid it down with the earnest hope that God would use it widely among precisely the men for whom it was written with such masterly force."

19. The Entail of the Covenant

This book was first published in 1914. Some of the contents were prophetic messages for Christian Churches in 21st century. In pages 10 and 11, the Zealous Champion of Christian Causes declares: *"The entail covenant is largely borne out by religious biography, and our churches are mainly composed of the pious children of Christian parents. If statements such as these should appear to be out of date today, it is not because the faithful Word has failed, but because the teaching of our churches is now so leavened with German scepticism that Christians are losing faith in Scripture, and as a natural result, they are losing hold on God. And the effects of the change are far–reaching, for they influence not only our Christian faith but our national character."* What a prophetic statement which is being fulfilled in America, Britain, Europe and the Western World that have rejected God and the Bible.

Dr Anderson referred to the address Rev. James Hamilton, the great preacher, delivered at the University of London: "The kind of teaching that was at one time imparted at the mother's knee, or from the lips of the father of the family, is largely a fast fading memory. 'Back to the Bible' should be a patriotic, as well as a religious cry; for the preservation of our liberties, and of our cherished institutions, depends much upon the maintenance of the Bible-taught heart-principles and stout convictions of our fathers."
On this book:
Times reported: "One more outcome of Sir Robert Anderson's close evangelical study of Scripture."

The Christian testified: "Sir Robert Anderson discusses the question of the salvation of the children of Christians in a way that will bring sheer and comfort to the heart of many.....In his own breezy fashion he states in plain commonsense

English a good many things for which readers will be thankful."

Life of Faith stated: "This is a book to delight a reviewer's heart-and a parent's.... the book should be bought, read and prayed over. The preacher will find many sermons in it....God bless this volume, and enable the honoured to give us more."

Here is an advice for British and American politicians. If they remove the Bible from their "institutions," they will "collapse." Trillions of Dollars and Pound Sterling pumped into our economies would not save us. I encourage politicians on both sides of the Atlantic to reflect on what Sir Robert Anderson shared with the Victorians: *"...The effects of this "Higher Criticism" are extremely grave. For it has dethroned the Bible in the home, and the good old practice of "family worship" is rapidly dying out. And great national interests are also involved. For who can doubt that the prosperity and power of the Protestant nations of the world are due to the influence of the Bible upon character and conduct....no one who is trained in the fear of God will fail in his duty to his neighbour, but will prove himself a good citizen. But the dethronement of the Bible leads practically to the dethronement of God; and in Germany and America, and now in England, the effects are declaring themselves in ways, and to an extent, well fitted to cause anxiety for the future."*

Are we anxious today? The "Seer" speaks today. The words the British public servant put down in the 19th century are being fulfilled in America and Britain of the 21st century. For example, on 8 March 2009, it was reported: "People who lose their jobs in the recession are to be offered specialist counselling for depression and anxiety. Around six million adults in the UK have depression or anxiety, with many of them receiving incapacity benefits, according to the Government. Sufferers will be referred to psychotherapists using an advice network in Jobcentres, doctors' surgeries and NHS Direct." According to the report, "The scheme, announced by Health Secretary Alan Johnson and Work and Pensions Secretary James Purnell, reflects Government fears that the downturn could drive up levels of mental illness and long-term unemployment."

On 28 March 2008, an article captioned *"Helping an anxious generations"* appeared in the Irish Times. The Social Affairs Correspondent, Carl O'Brien, reported: "Today's young people are growing up in a period of rapid change, uncertainty over the future, the absence of a clear set of ideals that transcend material prosperity, and contradictory messages regarding what's expected of them . . . While this generation seems to have more in terms of education and career opportunities, it's finding it harder to experience a sense of meaning, belonging and purpose in life."

And On 14 April 2009, this headline appeared in the Daily Mail: *"The anxious generation: 7 million Britons racked with worry over recession, crime, health and Big Brother state."* Under this headline Jenny Hope reported: "More than seven million Britons are living with anxiety problems, almost a million more than a decade

ago.... Two in three say the financial downturn has caused them to be anxious, fuelled by 24-hour news and 'worst case' images used by politicians. Mental health experts believe that fear and anxiety could actually make the economic crisis worse and result in a longer recession." The Correspondent cited a report from the Mental Health Foundation which said: "Knife crime, MRSA, bird flu and terrorism are among other issues contributing to a 'culture of fear'".
How do we help an "anxious generation"? "Back to the Bible" should be a patriotic, as well as a religious cry; for the preservation of our liberties, and of our cherished institutions, depends much upon the maintenance of the Bible-taught heart-principles and stout convictions of our fathers."

20. Spirit Manifestations And The Gift of Tongues.

In this 31-page booklet, Sir Robert Anderson warns Christians the dangers of depending on miracles, signs and wonders to authenticate their ministries and fellowship. In the opening page he writes; "The days we live in are intensely solemn. The stupid materialism of the science of yesterday has been exploded by the facts of Spiritualism, vouched for by some of our leading scientists of today. And the blind infidelity of the past has thus given place to a craving to get into touch with the realities of the unseen world." He adds: "This morbid influence has invaded the sphere of religious thought and life, and spiritual Christians even are being corrupted by it. It creates a tendency to make the great facts and truths of the divine revelation of Christianity subordinate to subjective spiritual manifestations, and to the emotions and experiences which such manifestations are fitted to produce. Among the many phases of this movement none is more striking than that of which the distinctive characteristic is what is termed "the gift of tongues."

In page 14 Dr. Anderson reminds us of the subtle character of the Devil. "The Satan of Scripture is very different from the mythical Devil of Christendom," he writes. "The devil devotes his power to making children naughty and grown-up people vicious...that awful being whose divinely given title is "the god of this world; not the instigator of its vices and its crimes, but the controller of its religion. Through ignorance of all this, people are deluded into assuming that any man who displays "spiritual powers," and is "a minister of righteousness" must be a minister of Christ. In these solemn days when the Christian dispensation is drawing to a close, and 'the professing Church' is drifting to its predicted doom, Satan is preparing the way for the supreme delusion of a travesty of the Incarnation. For the "Man of Sin" will be energised by him "with all power and signs and lying wonders to personate the Christ of God, and this to command the worship of mankind. What wonder it is then if he feigns to honour Christ, and bears testimony to His Advent."

Who is this "Man of Sin"? A picture could be seen in the new post of EU President which the wretched Lisbon Treaty has created. This head of the European Empire would speak with one voice for the member-states of the European Union. The maxim, "Many tongues one voice," would be displayed to the detriment of all.

In an article for *The Prophetic News,* Pastor F E Marsh provided this testimony: "Sir Robert Anderson was no visionary man, but a man of vision....one like Paul who has had a personal touch with Christ and who has responded to Him, who has not been disobedient to the heavenly vision....Those who came into close contact with this beloved servant of God know what a kindly heart he had and what a consistent Christian he was. He had a specially clear vision of God's Word. He did not follow in the beaten track of received opinions. He studied the Word under the Spirit's guidance for himself....Members of the Prophecy Investigation Society, especially the readers at its conferences, had to listen to something out of the ordinary, as he would often tilt over the edifices of their erection....We praise God for the faithfulness of Sir Robert's testimony, for the fragrance of his life, and the aroma of his friendship."

This was our brilliant "father," who wrote about European Union before it came into existence. Should we swap Sir Robert Anderson for Jean Monnet who had no understanding of the vision he toiled for?

21. Christ and Criticism

This is a short article Dr Anderson wrote to dismiss the critics of the Bible. He repeated the danger of eliminating the Bible from our society: "The rationalism of Germany at the close of the eighteenth century would accept the Bible only on the terms of bringing it down to the level of a human book, and the problem which had to be solved was to get rid of the element of miracle which pervades it. The effects of this "Higher Criticism" are extremely grave. For it has dethroned the Bible in the home, and the good, old practice of "family worship" is rapidly dying out. And great national interests also are involved. For who can doubt that the prosperity and power of the Protestant nations of the world are due to the influence of the Bible upon character and conduct? Races of men who for generations have been taught to think for themselves in matters of the highest moment will naturally excel in every sphere of effort or of enterprise. And more than this, no one who is trained in the fear of God will fail in his duty to his neighbour, but will prove himself a good citizen. But the dethronement of the Bible leads practically to the dethronement of God; and in Germany and America, and now in England, the effects of this are declaring themselves in ways, and to an extent, well fitted to cause anxiety for the future."

Dr Anderson added: "If a personal word may be pardoned in conclusion, the writer would appeal to every book he has written in proof that he is no champion of a rigid, traditional "orthodoxy." With a single limitation, he would advocate full and free criticism of Holy Scripture. And that one limitation is that the words of the Lord Jesus Christ shall be deemed a bar to criticism and "an end of controversy" on every subject expressly dealt with in His teaching. "The Son of God is come"; and by Him came both grace and TRUTH. And from His hand it is that we have received the Scriptures of the Old Testament".

22. *Unfulfilled Prophecy*

This was Sir Robert Anderson's last book. The notes were released on the Easter of 1917 a year before he passed away. The Defender of the Christian Faith published this volume in response to a request from the *Prophecy Investigation Society* to produce a manual on the prophetic vision of "The Seventy Weeks", which is recorded in Daniel 9:24-27.

In the Preface to *Unfulfilled Prophecy*, the Knight of God writes: Such a book would be a mere abridgement of *The Coming Prince* or *The Seventy Weeks of Daniel"*. He continues: "A Special subject in a school's curriculum is often ignored, as not being essential to "a liberal education"; and prophecy neglected by many a Christian as being unnecessary to "assurance of salvation." But such neglect is perilous in these days of subtle and sustained attacks upon the Bible; when we are confronted by both the sceptical crusade of the Higher Criticism, and the steadily increasing influence of Romanism. And the study of prophecy will prove a safeguard against both these apostasies. For no Christian who pursues it intelligently, and understands the Divine "plan of the ages", which it unfolds, will be imposed upon by "the learned ignorance" of the Critics. And the present-day decline of Protestantism in England is due to no change in the historic apostasy of Christendom, but to weakening of faith in Holy Writ. For when the devout religionist begins to lose confidence in the Bible, he is apt to fall back upon "the Church"

In the opening paragraph of chapter 2 of *Unfulfilled Prophecy*, the Knight records: The Hebrew Scriptures contain no Messianic prophecy that is simpler and more definite than this of the Seventy Weeks, and none better fitted to silence the infidel and convince the Jew. But its meaning and evidential value are lost in a bewildering maze of forced or fanciful interpretations. And this is the evil work of Christian expositors! The meaning of the language of the prophecy may be deemed matter for discussion; but no intelligent reader, whether he be Christian or Jew or Infidel, who will study it with an unbiased mind, can entertain an honest doubt as to what it says. Echoing the words of Daniel's prayer, the angel's message told him that not seventy years, but seventy weeks of years were decreed upon his people and his holy city, before they would enter into full Divine blessing. This era is divided into three portions, of seven weeks, sixty-two weeks, and one week, respectively. It dates from the issuing of a decree to build Jerusalem. From that event "unto Messiah the prince" there were to be 7+ 62 weeks. And after "the sixty-two weeks" the Messiah would be "cut off." The seventieth and last week of the era would be signalised by the advent of another Prince, who would make a seven years' covenant (or treaty) with the Jews; and in the middle of the week (i.e., after three years and a half), he would violate that treaty and suppress their Temple worship and the ordinances of their religion. All this is so plain that any intelligent child could understand it..."

To those Bible scholars who attacked the Book of Daniel as a religious fraud, and the hierarchy of the Catholic Church that has endorsed *The New Jerusalem Bible* which denies the Divine Revelation in the Book of Daniel, Sir Anderson has a word for you : "If you are a man of affairs and especially if you are a trained lawyer or an experienced juror, you are better fitted to deal with the Daniel controversy than the Hebraist, the professor or the ecclesiastic as such. The Christian who gives up Daniel at the bidding of the professor is both intellectually and morally on a level with the Roman Catholic peasant who blindly takes his creed from his priest." According to Dr Anderson, sham critics of Sacred Scriptures "are men who empty the works of watch into a bowl, and then after examining them in detail arrive at the sapient conclusion that presents no proof of unity of design."

The Lighter side of my Official life

This was Sir Robert Anderson's Memoirs. The opening paragraph reads: "Even in the case of people of distinction an autobiography is too often a blunder. In the case of commonplace folk it is generally an impertinence. And I am not so foolish as to suppose that the public would care to know anything about me save in relation to matters of public interest. Here, however, I am in a difficulty. Having regard to the position I held for so long at Whitehall, and in more recent times at Scotland Yard, I cannot even now write about the Secret Service, or police work in London, save with much reserve and under definite restraints. But it is constantly urged upon me that even the lighter side of official life in these spheres has a fascination for many people, and that I might say not a little which would interest and amuse the public; and it is with this modest aim therefore that, postponing graver " reminiscences " to a future date, I now take up my pen. By way of introduction I may describe myself as an Anglicanised Irishman of Scotch extraction. My "forebears " were among the Scotch colonists who made Ulster what it is...".

The Prince of Detectives concluded his Memoirs with these words: "I have already told how, when "in my teens," I relinquished a business career in order to enter Dublin University ; and I can still recall the delightful sense of rest and liberty I enjoyed the first day I spent in the quadrangles and park of Trinity College. I was reminded of that experience the day after my retirement from Scotland Yard, when I realised that at last I was freemaster of my own time, master of myself!

And now the time has come to lay down my pen and make my bow. The "graver reminiscences" alluded to in my introductory chapter may possibly have some historic interest, and prove of practical value to any who may hereafter be charged with duties such as those with which I was entrusted, first at Dublin Castle and afterwards at Whitehall. But the time for their publication has not arrived. And if this book fulfils the modest promise of its opening page I shall be content."

Testifying to this work, *Morning Post* declared: "Full of good anecdotes, and may be read with enjoyment from cover to cover." *The Times* reported: "The author guides us behind the scenes of the drama of criminal investigation....and he also gives us his candid opinion of various important official personages." *Scotsman* reported: 'The book's material gives it an interest such as only few volumes of reminiscences can claim, but it owes not a little to the manner in which it is written."

In the concluding chapter of Sir Robert Anderson's Biography, his son quoted the testimony the Rev, A C Dixon, D.D. recorded in *The Biblical Recorder:* "With the consciousness and courage of an Old Testament prophet, Sir Robert Anderson sounded the trumpet of alarm, and led the battler against the errors which he believed were destroying the fundamentals of Christianity. His lot to a large extent was loneliness of the man who seeks to be a prophet of God, faithfully proclaiming God's message without regard to results, not a leader following the line of least resistance and seeking to gather around him the largest number of followers. The age needs such men. May God multiply the number." To which I add: "Amen!"

It is recorded in his Biography, "Although the critics practically continued to ignore Dr Anderson as a mere layman, such opinions encouraged him in continually stressing the point that their proper place was in the witness-box as experts; and that they had no right to appoint themselves judge and jury into the bargain..."

Specially bound copies of several of the "theological" books of Sir Robert Anderson were graciously accepted by Their Majesties Queen Alexandra and Queen Mary, and some other members of the royal family." On 13 October 1918 The Knight of God preached in Trinity Presbyterian Church at Notting Hill. The Rev, Joseph Rorke thanked him. He mentioned the death of two members of his congregation, adding, "The veil which divides us from the eternal world seems at times almost transparent". Sir Robert replied: "It is a constant grief to me that I can take so little part in the service and ministries of the congregation; but this makes me all the more eager to give proof of my sympathy with you in the work of the Lord. Yes, death is busy in these days, not only on the battle-field, but here at home." The next morning the Knight Commander had a mild attack of influenza. He was not confined to bed. On 15 November he was feeling better and went out twice. According to his son, A. P Moore Anderson, "In the evening he sat writing and reading the Bible until half-past ten, when he went to bed. A few moments later the limitations of the earthly life were no more, and he had been called to the freer and more perfect service of the Lord towards which his steps had so long been set."

Even though Dr Anderson criticised some of the doctrines and practices of the Roman Catholic Church, especially his dismissal of Cardinal Newman's defence of the Catholic doctrine of Transubstantiation, his son recorded that Dr. Anderson had more in common with many a devout Roman Catholic than with "Modern Churchmen" who denied the Deity of Christ, and His atoning death. Moore-Anderson writes: "His (Dr Anderson's) personal touch with individuals in other Communions is exemplified by this letter from Father Ignatius: *"It is most kind of you to send me your pamphlet. Indeed what you and I believe in common far exceeds in grandeuer and importance the smaller details respecting which we may differ. I have read your Coming Prince with much pleasure and profit, and now shall read...your book on Modern Criticism. Believe me your affectionate brother in our Lord. Ignatius, O.S.B Monk*

THE HOME OFFICE OF YESTERDAY (1877) AND TODAY

In view of the catalogue of errors and administrative blunders that clouded the Home Office in 2006 and undermined the public confidence in this State Department, and which resulted in the public demanding the resignation of the then Secretary of State, Charles Clarke, it is worthwhile to recall Sir Robert Anderson's view of the Civil Service and the Home Office during his temporary association with them

In page 37 of his biography, More-Anderson writes: "My father had what he called an "intelligent aversion" to the Civil Service. And he did not entertain a high opinion of the Home Office of those days. In 1877 when he (Dr Anderson) first took a position at the Home Office, it was impressed upon him that the way to get on was to do as little as possible and do it quietly as possible. The ordinary work was light, and it was left to an industrious minority. The hours were from 11 am to 5pm – nominal 11 am and a punctual 5pm. Much of the time was given to luncheon, gossip and the newspaper, and there was plenty left for games and ragging. "

Dr. Anderson's impression of the Home Office and the Civil Service in 1877 was, unconsciously, confirmed by Dr John Reid, who succeeded Charles Clarke as the Home Secretary, and Mr Leo McKinstry, a newspaper columnist. Dr Reid was appointed by the Labour Government to sort out the mess in the Home Office. Giving his assessment of his new department to the House of Commons Home Affairs Parliamentary Committee, Dr Reid said: "Our system is not fit for purpose. It is inadequate in terms of its information technology, leadership, management, systems and processes."

And Leo Mckinstry summed up the state of our civil service in his article: *A SORRY BUSINESS: If any private company were as badly run as Britain's modern public sector, it would have gone bankrupt years ago.* The columnist reported: "Large swathes of our civic order now appear to be in administrative meltdown, whether it be the Child Support Agency, the exam boards or Criminal Records Bureau". He mentioned how some of our soldiers lacked proper equipment for war, and the failure of the Home Office to track down criminals. He continued: "In public offices throughout Britain, bureaucratic activities such as holding meetings, producing reports and attending seminars have become ends in itself." He made reference to the case of a senior civil servant who spent six months writing a single page of report on drugs policy." Mr Mckinstry asked the question: "What on earth is going on?" (*Daily Mail* Thursday, 1 June 2006). Sir Robert Anderson's "intelligent aversion to the Civil Service" in 1877 was confirmed in 2006.

In his *Story of Scotland Yard,* George Dilnot writes: "Sir Robert Anderson, after an honourable and distinguished service for many years, retired from the Criminal Investigation Department in 1901." His friend, Major-General J.C Russell, C.V.O, Equerry to King Edward VII, wrote to the Knight Commander: "I don't know whether to congratulate you or do console with the State....As a wretched item in the Commonwealth I feel that my person and goods are no longer so safe as they were."

Before I conclude this chapter, I would share with you an extract from the Foreword to Sir Robert Anderson's biography. This was written by Rev. J Stuart Holden, M.A. D.D: "He (Sir Robert Anderson) was a man whose genius for comradeship was by no means the least of his many endowments. To many it was inevitable he should be known only as the stalwart defender of the Faith, the clear expositor, the zealous champion of Christian causes, the keen conversationalist, the distinguished public servant.....in his consuming passion for what he regarded as vital to the Christian faith, he was often compelled to appear dogmatic to the point of unsympathy, and narrow-minded to the point of sheer unaccommodating.....He stood out as champion of the unpopular view of things, he both received and gave hard blows. No one could give harder. But this was the role thrust upon him. If he must fight, he fought as a knight of God and a very perfect gentleman; so that those who opposed him, and finally gave up as "hopeless", rode off with a fine appreciation of the character of their opponent...Never, for a single moment, did he betray the slightest bitterness of spirit toward an opponent....those who were privileged to know him at closer quarters will ever think of him, in yet warmer terms, as one of the most devoted, humble, and kindly of men, and one of the staunchest of friends...."

This was the "Seer of Dublin", the "Giant among Giants," an intellectual among intellectuals; a man who refuses to lift the flag of truce before a foe. Though he was "a man of peace", he "never shirked a fight." I struggle to find his match in Brussels – the headquarters of the European Project. Before the "Giant of Ireland" (Sir Robert Anderson) stands the "Giant of Europe" – the "obstinate" Jean Monnet with his fuzzy vision of a fused Europe. Let us put the two 'giants' on a scale and weigh them. And Jean Monnet would not have qualified to bow and polish the boots of the Knight Commander (of the order) of Bath.

DR. HENRY KISSINGER AND DR. ALEXANDER STUBB

In 1975 in Paris, Dr. Henry Kissinger presented the Grenville Clarke Prize to Jean Monnet for his contribution towards European integration. Had Dr Kissinger read the 19th Edition of Dr Anderson's *The Coming Prince,* which was released in 1975, he would have found no need to present the Grenville Clarke Prize to the French statesman. The American statesman, the former Secretary of State, would have thought twice before praising Monnet: "I want to tell you (Jean Monnet) that the men of the present generation who are in charge of political affairs regard your vision as well-founded. They see that it is on the point of being fulfilled as you originally conceived it. The creation of a united Europe seems imminent. The United States gives it full support." (Memoirs 1978 page 498). Again, had Dr. Kissinger examined *The Coming Prince*, he would have learnt that Monnet was a "labourer" who was toiling to bring to pass what an Irishman had already written about a political union of European nations.

On 17 July 2008, Dr Alexander Stubb, Finland's Foreign Minister, delivered a lecture at *Carnegie Endowment for International Peace.* The Theme was "Will the EU ever become a superpower?" Dr. Stubb extolled the strengths and weaknesses of the European Union. He told the distinguished audience: "We (Europeans) have the likes of kohl and Mitterand who understood why European integration was needed, because they had experienced World War II." Had the political scientist examined *The Coming Prince*, he would have learnt that a British Detective wrote about how a political union of European nations would develop even before the First World War. From this classic book, the former Member of European Parliament would have had a different perspective of European integration and its future prospects. Consequently, Dr Stubb would have become less excited about the European Union, now a "soft-power", becoming a "superpower" in the future. The "EU nerd" would have learnt that the British Detective, whose parents hailed from Scotland the birth place of Andrew Carnegie, predicted that the European Union would develop through a European crisis to become the next major political feature in history after the restoration of the Jews to Palestine. So, Dr. Stubb's comments: "There is no alternative to the European Union" was accurate. The European Union would, certainly, become a superpower as Dr. Stubb would like the EU to be. But what would be the end of this European "superpower"?

THE ROMAN CATHOLIC CHURCH AND ROBERT SCHUMAN AND CARDINAL HENRY NEWMAN AND SIR ROBERT ANDERSON

A Vatican official confirmed on 2 March 2004 that Robert Schuman of France was "on the path to sainthood, for being an authentic Roman Catholic and an example to all those responsible for the construction of Europe" (The Times 3 March 2004). And on Monday, December 20, 2004, The Times published another article on Schuman's sainthood titled *Saint-making Pope is ready to ditch the miracle clause.* In this article, Richard Owen writes: "Candidates for sainthood will be exonerated from the requirement to have performed a miracle under guidelines being considered by the Pope (the Late Pope John Paul II). The purpose of this miracle exemption clause, which, according to some in the Vatican, was "anachronistic" to "speed up the canonisation of the Pope's favourite candidates, including Mother Teresa of Calcutta.......It could also revive plans to beautify Robert Schuman, the French–born founder of the EU, shelved earlier....because of lack of evidence that anyone had been cured after praying to him."

The Vatican also considered making Cardinal Newman a Saint. According to reports, Reverend Jack Sullivan was miraculously healed of his "crippling back pain" after he had watched Cardinal Newman on television. On 25 April 2009, The Daily Telegraph reported that Cardinal Newman's beatified. In an article titled *English cardinal on path to sainthood after Vatican ruling*, Simon Caldwell reported: "The Vatican has cleared the way for the beatification of John Henry Newman....A theological panel agreed unanimously that the inexplicable healing of an American man bent double by a severe spinal disorder came as a result of praying to Newman for a miracle....However a second miracle will be required before he can be declared a saint for the miracle to be rubber-stamped by the cardinals of the Vatican's Congregation for the Causes of Sainthood, and the Pope's signature...."

In the process for Cardinal Newman's exaltation, the Catholic Church attempted to exhume Newman's remains from the grave he had requested to be re-buried, and transferred into a 'posh' grave befitting the status of a Catholic saint. It was Pope Leo XIII who, in 1879, made Henry Newman a Cardinal. The writings of Cardinal Newman continue to inspire Roman Catholics, especially Pope Benedict XVI.

We know Robert Schuman was put on a fast track to sainthood for being a founding father of European Community and an "authentic Catholic." Cardinal Newman is now on the path of Sainthood. I would raise a question: "Since the Pope and the Roman Catholic Church support the European Union, how would Pope Benedict XVI and the Catholic Church have described Cardinal Newman had he, before Robert Schuman was born in 1886, predicted that a political union of European nations would be the next major political feature in history after the restoration of the Jews to Palestine? (The nation of Israel was reborn in May 1948. The European Union was born in May 1950) If Cardinal Newman did not make this significant prediction, then we must ask the question: how would Vatican and Pope Benedict XVI describe Sir Robert Anderson who, before Schuman was born, confidently predicted that a political alliance of European nations would evolve from an European crisis?

Indeed, Cardinal Newman was a pious priest who produced volumes of Christian literature and Hymns. However, Sir Robert Anderson's theological works and their contribution towards the defence of the Christian Faith, which was under attack by German infidels and English theologians, were more significant. This is borne by the fact that some of Dr Anderson's works are still being reproduced today – especially his prophetic book, *The Coming Prince,* and *The Silence of God* which deals with the mystery of a "Silent God" - an Almighty God who does not seem to care in the midst of tragedies and evil that flourish in the world.

Sir Robert Anderson did not qualify for "beatification," perhaps, for being a Protestant and a fierce critic of some of the teachings and practices of the Roman Catholic Church. Nonetheless, as a devout Christian and the true Defender of the Christian Faith, Sir Robert Anderson did not need recognition from the Roman Catholic Church. "God's Barrister" was a saint before he passed away. According to Sacred Scriptures all faithful Jews and Christians are saints before they die (Daniel 7:25 Revelation 13:5-7). One does not become a saint after one's death if such a one was neither a faithful Jew nor a Christian before death. For this reason, the Catholic Church's practice of exalting a particular group of dead Catholics to the status of sainthood has no scriptural basis. The Bible says: "It is appointed unto man once to die, but after this the judgement" (Hebrews 9:27). Who knows who will be saved or condemned? It is only God. The Catholic Church cannot decide for God the destiny of the dead.

GREAT BRITAIN AND IRELAND SHOULD NOT IGNORE SIR ROBERT ANDERSON TO FOLLOW JEAN MONNET

The European Union would have a depressing impact on the lives of every soul on planet earth. Therefore, in view of what Sir Robert Anderson recorded about this European phenomenon before the European Union came into existence, I have spent some time to share with you a portion of Sir Robert's life and works. I hope what you have learnt about this devoted public servant of Great Britain and a faithful servant of the Lord Jesus Christ would help you to give a serious thought to what he published in *The Coming Prince* concerning Europe and its future.

Sir Robert Anderson had an extraordinary insight of world affairs. Great Britain and Ireland must not ignore his writings on European integration: *"This confederation of [European] nations shall be developed"*, says Sir Robert, *"and thus the stage will be prepared on which shall appear that awful Being – the great leader of men, in the eventful days which are to close the era of Gentile supremacy."* Since a prophet is of no honour in his own country and among his own people, I would appeal to Americans and Europeans, who desire to know the real purpose of the European Union and its prospects, to examine "The Coming Prince."

Dr. Konrad Adenauer, who was only six-years when Dr Anderson wrote about European integration, recorded these significant words in his memoirs: "The political goal, the political meaning of the European Coal and Steel Community, is infinitely larger than its economic purpose....I believe for the first time in history....countries want to renounce part of their sovereignty, voluntarily and without compulsion, in order to transfer the sovereignty to a supranational structure. In my opinion the European nation states had a past but no future...I regarded The Schuman Plan and the European Defence Community as preliminary steps to a political unification of Europe..." (12 July 1952). The fact is 'European nation' has a future, and this "future" should be the higher priority of Europeans. For "If a knowledge of the past be important," says Dr. Anderson, "a knowledge of the future must be of far higher value still, in enlarging the mind and raising it above the littlenesses which is produced by a narrow and unenlightened contemplation of the present." Angela Merkel and her European "brothers" and "sisters" should examine what the "Anglicanised Irishman of Scotch extraction" recorded about European integration. The Knight of God departed in 1918. About 34 years after his death the European Coal and Steel Community, the economic seed of the European Empire, was sown.

POLITICIANS AND POLITICAL COMMENTATORS MUST NOT IGNORE THE WARNING OF THE "SEER OF DUBLIN"

We have learnt what Sir Robert Anderson, the selfless servant of Her Majesty's Government, who did not collect his Knighthood from a "supermarket shelf," published concerning Europe and its future. Would politicians, political commentators and political scientists in America and Europe ignore the "Seer's" prophetic word concerning the destiny of Europe? The inhabitants of the 'Tiny Island' should not, under any circumstance, be lured by flattery or frightened by threat of "isolation" to jump into the "great sea" in Brussels. For in that "ocean" resides a "sea monster" with "7 heads" and "10 horns" (Revelation 13 and 17). A word to the wise is enough.

I would now give a reason why the British and the Irish should take the Prince of Detective's warning about the destiny of Europe seriously. Before the well-known Clerkenwell explosion occurred in 1867, Dr Anderson gave a warning to the London Police. Unfortunately they failed to make use of the information. Would British and Irish politicians of the 21st century also ignore Sir Robert's warning regarding the destiny of the European Union? Unfortunately, through ignorance, British politicians are financing the corrupt European project, whose accounts have not been approved for 14 consecutive years because of fraud. On 1 January 2007, the former British Foreign Secretary, Mrs Margaret Beckett, hailed the entry of Bulgaria and Romania into the European Club as good for Britain and Europe. "On what grounds?" we must ask. According to *The Great European Rip-off* by David Craig and Matthew Elliot, the European project costs every man, woman and child in Britain about £2000 a year. And what do we get in return? Nothing, save unnecessary laws and regulations and interference in our lives.

CHALLENGE TO JOSE MANUEL BARROSO – THE PRESIDENT OF EUROPEAN COMMISSION

Since the future of the European Union is dark, was it sensible for some British politicians and commentators to have suggested that Britain should join the eurozone to save itself from bankruptcy? And how irresponsible it was for the President of European Commission to have insulted the British people that those "who matter" in Britain would drag Britons into the eurozone. The political scientist from Portugal should 'go back to school' to learn what a brilliant British public servant wrote about European Integration before his French "hero," Jean Monnet, was conceived. In Barroso's wisdom a servant is greater than the master. The people "who matter" in Britain are Britons who, temporarily, delegated their powers to politicians. The people "who matter" in Britain are not the "selfish" politicians in the House of Commons who have vested interest in the European Project, and prevented the people who feed them to have a say on the Lisbon Treaty that would make them "slaves" in Brussels.

In an article *Pressure on UK to find shelter in the euro"* (*The Independent.* 30 January 2009), Sean O'Grady, Economics Editor, writes: "The President of the European Commission has hinted again that the pound should now join the eurozone. Jose Manuel Barroso, said that "Even the biggest states can't face these challenges alone", and that he would seek more coordinated EU action to deal with the financial crisis. He voiced his belief that more majority voting would help EU decision-making. Despite sterling's slide and the well-known problems in the UK banking system, Mr Barroso seemed as keen as ever to hint at his enthusiasm to see the pound in the European single currency" (The Independent 30 January 2009). The fact is Barroso has no clue what the European Union is for. Does he know the future of the Eurozone? It is time the "Buffoon of Brussels" kept quiet and stopped poking his nose into the affairs of Britons.

THE "BATTLE AT WEMBLEY"

Who is Barroso to put pressure on Britain to join the Eurozone? As an "expert" on European integration, Barroso's proper place is not on the "judgement seat" in Brussels, but in the "witness box" at Wembley Sports Stadium to be "cross-examined" by Britons. If Barroso believes the destiny of Britain lies in the European Union, I urge him to lead all his experts in Brussels including Jean Monnet Professors to appear in the "witness box" at Wembley to make the case for Jean Monnet's "gradualist vision of a united Europe that still serves as a blueprint for European integration today." I hope the "brave" Barroso, the "Prince of Brussels," who is fond of insulting Britons and criticising British politicians, would not ignore this invitation, but would exercise political courage to accept the challenge for the "Battle at Wembley."

After all, in October 2006, the President of the European Commission, comfortably, delivered the Hugo Young Lecture at Chatham House. His lecture was titled: *"Seeing through the Hallucination: Britain and Europe."* In September 2007, the same President of European Commission addressed the Liberal Democrat Annual Party Conference in Brighton. His speech was titled: *"Engagement with Europe: an opportunity, not a threat."* And in October 2007, Jose Manuel Barroso accepted invitation from Timothy Garton Ash and Kalypso Nikolaidis to speak to University Students of St Antony's College in Oxford. The theme of his lecture was: *"Europe and the challenges of globalisation."* In all his lectures the EU Chief extolled the achievements of the European Union and the challenges facing Jean Monnet's Project.

It would be political cowardice for the President of European Commission to ignore this open invitation to sell Jean Monnet's vision of European unity to "sceptical" Britons and the rest of the world. After all, before the June 2009 European elections, Barroso and his Commissioners spent millions of euro to encourage

Europeans to vote in numbers. The "Battle at Wembley" would give the President of European Commission and all his experts the opportunity to convince the British Euro-sceptics to love the European Union. After all, President Nicolas Sarkozy has called for "a real European debate," saying, "Europe cannot claim to be a living democracy if there are no debates." (Source: *Le Figaro* Open Europe 6 May 2009)

The "Seer of Dublin" "weeps" in the Arms of the Lord. He could not bear the sight of his native land, Ireland, and England, the country he loved and served with distinction, participating in a political union that has no room for the Lord Jesus Christ. The Knight Commander sobs, because the coming Emperor of the European Empire, which now includes Ireland and England (unless they withdraw from the European Union), would wage war against the Lord Jesus Christ. The charismatic and dynamic leader of Europe will oppose God and persecute the faithful servants of the Lord Jesus Christ who refuse to bow before his idol that would be set up in the Jerusalem Temple (Daniel 9:27. 2 Thessalonians 2:1-4, Revelation 13:5-8).

Presently, there are plans to rebuild the Temple. About 60 of the 90 sacred utensils needed for the Temple worship have been prepared. The 16 October 1989 edition of *TIME* magazine reported extensively on the strategy to reconstruct a new Temple in Jerusalem. The Word of God in Daniel 9:27 will certainly be fulfilled. *"Then he shall confirm a covenant with many for one week. But in the middle of the week, he will put an end to sacrifice and offering. And on the wing of the Temple he will set up an abomination that causes desolation, until the end that is decreed is poured out on him."*

Let us, again, listen to Sir Robert Anderson's concern about Britain before he departed: "May we not indulge the hope that however far our nation may lapse in evil days to come from the high place which, with all her faults, she has held as the champion of freedom and of truth, she will be saved from the degradation of participating in the vile confederacy of the later days?"

In his article, *IMMIGRATION,* Max Hastings lamented over an irrevocable shift in the character of Great Britain. He writes: "All the forces that hold us together for so long – empire, Monarchy, the Church, the memory of shared experience in two world wars – have been fading. Mr Hastings, unconsciously, echoed the sentiments of Sir Robert Anderson with this remark: "In truth, for all Britain's past follies and failures.....it is a society which has been one of the foremost, most creative and inventive on earth...and for all our problems, today by any measure this is one of the most successful societies on Earth" (Daily Mail 22 March 2005). This leads to the question: should our successful nation (despite its present economic difficulties caused by "selfish" and pompous politicians and greedy bankers with no foresight, and we, the irresponsible consumers) participate in the European Union which Sir Robert Anderson described it "The vile confederacy of the latter days?"

The uncomfortable truth is that Sir Robert Anderson has no equal among the 21st century fashionable intellectuals and aggressive atheists, who ridicule Christians that a belief in God is "intellectual nonsense." Which of these arrogant scholars could claim to have contributed more to our country and indeed to humanity than Sir Robert Anderson? I mentioned humanity, because it was the Knight Commander who defended the most mysterious Book in the universe, the Book of Daniel, when the German and English infidels attempted to discredit this Old Testament Book to undermine the Integrity of the Lord Jesus Christ. It is from the Book of Daniel that we trace the development of the European Union and its future. Again, Sir Robert Anderson was the first person on record to have calculated the prophetic date of the Lord Jesus' triumphal entry to Jerusalem – the first Palm Sunday which millions of Christians celebrate (Matthew 21:1-11, Mark 11:1-11; Luke 19:28-44 and John 12:12). This date was based on the prophetic word in Daniel 9:24-26. Sir Robert did not calculate this important date from his imagination as some liberal scholars suggest.

"God's Barrister" sought the assistance of the then Astronomer Royal at Greenwich, Sir George Airy, to calculate the date when the Persian King Artaxerxes issued the decree for the rebuilding of the walls and the city of Jerusalem (Nehemiah 2 (14 March 445BC) to the day the Lord Jesus Christ publicly accepted the homage of His disciples that He was the Promised Messiah (Luke 19 (6 April AD32) who came down to lay down His Life to take away the sins of the world (John 1:29; Genesis 5:1-29). Secondly, Sir Robert Anderson's classic, *The Silence of God,* was a source of comfort to many during the First World War. The book is still in print. In the 21st century, I hope Sir Robert's *The Coming Prince* would enlighten the minds of Christians and Jews about the fulfilment of the prophetic revelation in Daniel Chapter 2 and an understanding of the great vision of "70 Weeks," and becomes a blessing to those who yearn for a better understanding of the European Union and its future.

WAS SIR ROBERT ANDERSON A "DEMENTED DREAMER" AND AN "UTOPIAN", OR HE WAS A MAN OF SUBSTANCE WITH EXTRAORDINARY VISION?

Before I conclude this chapter, I would share with you the significance of a comment The Guardian columnist, Timothy Garton Ash, made concerning the European Union. On 1 January 2007, additional "toes of clay" (Bulgaria and Romania) were added to the "toes of baked clay and iron of the great human statue." The Oxford Professor recollected an event that led to the development of the European Union. In his article, *"Today's European Union is 27 states in search of a story,"* he writes: "As it (the EU) grows to 27 countries, the European Union is the most successful example of peaceful regime change in our time….Fifty years this March, at the height of the cold war, six western European-states established an European Economic Community by signing what came to be known as the Treaty of Rome. If you had told any of the signatories back in 1957 that in 2007 Europe would look as it does today, they would probably have dismissed you as a demented dreamer. And were Konrad Adenauer or Paul-Henri Spaak with us today, they would be saying: so you must be going to have a great celebration this March 25" (The Guardian, Thursday, 4 January 2007).

I ask the question: "Was Dr. Robert Anderson a "demented dreamer" when, in 1881, he predicted that a political union of European nations would be developed through a European crisis, and this political alliance would be the next major political feature in history after the restoration of the Jews to Palestine? Was the "Forgotten Victorian" a "dreamer" when he mentioned that Austria, Belgium, England, Greece, Italy, Portugal, Spain and Turkey would join this political union?

NEWSWEEK AND *TIME* MAGAZINES ON EUROPE'S 50TH BIRTHDAY

In March 2007, *NEWSWEEK* published a Special Report to mark the 50th Anniversary of the Treaty of Rome. The American magazine sang the praises of Jean Monnet's project: "Europe arose from the ashes of the Great Depression and World War II to become whole and free. Half a century ago, only an utopian would have predicted that, today, one can traverse Europe from Sicily to Sweden without encountering a border control….Europe is now a global superpower of world-historic importance, second to none in economic clout. It has constructed one of the most successful systems of government…which has brought unprecedented prosperity and security to Europe's people. It is the single most successful advance in voluntary international cooperation in modern history."

This leads to my questions: "Was Sir Robert Anderson an "utopian"? For before Jean Monnet, the master architect of European Construction, was born in 1888, the Irishman had already recorded with absolute confidence that a confederation of European nations would be the next major political feature in history after the restoration of the Jews to Palestine? Dr Anderson wrote: "To colonise a country is one thing, while to create a nation is another." The nation of Israel was reborn in May 1948, and the European Union was born in May 1950 with the Schuman Plan.

Was the British Secret Service Agent an "Utopian?" For before President John Kennedy and Dr. Henry Kissinger praised Monnet for his vision of European unity, and even before a German led conspiracy of cartographers were accused by the Conservative Party of trying to use a new EU Directive to give Brussels the powers to change national boundaries that sought to create a United States of Europe and break Britain into regions that cross national boundaries (Sunday Telegraph 3 September 2006), Dr Anderson had already written, with self-assurance, that there would be a consolidation of kingdoms in Europe which would result in the changing of boundaries to make England a province of an European Empire? I quote the "Seer of Dublin": *"It is impossible to foretell how far kingdoms may become consolidated and boundaries may be changed...We must rest content with the certainty that their fulfilment will be clear to all who are capable of observing public facts."* (The Coming Prince)

Secondly, if according to *TIME*, "Europe's development from the Great Depression and World War II has been a "Quiet Miracle," then how should we describe Sir Robert Anderson, who, before the First World War, predicted that a political alliance of European nations would be developed through an European crisis. The front cover of the 19 March 2007 edition of *TIME* read: "No one can see the future." We must, therefore ask the question: "How was Sir Robert Anderson able to predict with certainty, that a confederation of European nations would be the next major political phenomenon in history after the rebirth of Israel?" The European Union, now "a global super-power of world historic importance, second to none in economic clout," was born on 9 May 1950. The Knight Commander predicted these two political phenomena in history (the rebirth of the nation of Israel and the birth of the European Union) in 1881.

Again, if one could not have possibly envisaged over 50 years ago, that the 6 countries which formed the European Coal and Steel Community and signed the Treaty of Rome would develop into a political union of 27 members, how should Americans, Europeans and the rest of the world describe Sir Robert Anderson who, in the 19th century, predicted this European political phenomenon before the "Phenomenon" manifested in the 20th century? How would Brussels describe the Irishman who published these words concerning European integration about 77 years before the Treaty of Rome was signed in 1957: "Next to the restoration of the Jews to Palestine, the most prominent political feature of the future is the partition of Roman earth....In forecasting the fulfilment of these (a confederation of European nations) we are dealing with events which, while they may occur within the lifetime of living men, may yet be delayed for centuries...we may rest content with the certainty that....their fulfilment will be clear...to all who are capable of observing public facts."

The prominent Irishman, whose "sons" and "daughters" were bullied to vote again on a Treaty (the European Constitution) they had already rejected, continued: "....*Through the gradual unfolding it may be of influences even now in operation, or far more probably as the outcome of some great European crisis in the future. This confederation of nations shall be developed..."* The "Sage of Ulster" went on to predict the coming Emperor of European Empire, which the Lisbon Treaty has paved the way for his coronation: *"And thus the stage will be prepared on which shall appear that awful Being, the great leader of men in the eventful days which are to close the era of Gentile supremacy."*

I repeat: on 12 June 2008, the Irish acted wisely to dump the European Constitution that paves the way for the arrival of the "Awful Being" who will terrorise Europeans and the world. Would the Irish change their decision on the Lisbon Treaty? And would a Cameron Conservative Government in Britain withdraw the crooked Lisbon Treaty from Rome, burn it into ashes and release Britons from "bondage" in Brussels? Brussels is a Burden on Britons; and Britain needs a leader, who does not follow the path of least resistance, to set Britons free from 'slavery.'

I ask the question: "Would Americans, Europeans, Britons and the Irish describe the Knight Commander (of the Order) of Bath a "demented dreamer" and an "utopian"? The Prince of Scotland Yard was a man with an Extraordinary Foresight. The French statesman, the "obstinate" Jean Monnet, would not have qualified to polish the boots of the British Knight. The French should not gloat about Jean Omer Marie Gabriel Monnet.

THE KNIGHT TO REMEMBER

At this point I ask the reader: "On European integration: would you follow the vision of Jean Monnet, or the vision of Sir Robert Anderson? I look around at Home, in Britain, and Away, in America and Europe, and I struggle to find an opponent to face Sir Robert Anderson, the zealous Defender of the Christian Faith. If I have overlooked any credible opponent, I invite him to step into the ring to face the Knight. It was written of the Knight Commander, that in his days "he received blows but gave harder blows." One of the Knight's "deadly punches" stunned Professor Huxley. The Champion of Darwinism "crashed to the canvas." Great Britain and Ireland must be proud of their 'father. They must not be frightened by threats of "Isolation in Europe", and neither should they be influenced by Americans' favourable view of the European Union to enter and remain in the Eurozone. The Eurozone is a "deadly trap." It may seem bright outside, but inside is utter darkness. A white-washed tomb may be clean outside, but inside are worthless bones. A word to the wise is enough.

During Sir Robert Anderson's reign at Scotland Yard, crime in England reduced dramatically. His voice echoed across the Pond into Washington. What a Knight to remember! Unfortunately, Sir Robert's "children" in Ireland and Britain have "forsaken" him to become "slaves" to strangers in Brussels. What a pity for the 'sons" and "daughters" of a Man of Substance to become "adopted children" of a "Man of Straw" – who "abducted" a married woman to Moscow for a quick divorce and re-marriage. In truth: a prophet is of no honour in his own country and among his own people. "In abundance of water the fool is thirsty," says the late Bob Marley.

WHO STANDS FOR GOD?

I close this chapter by recalling the solemn plea Peter Lewis made to Church leaders to defend God against the onslaught from militant atheists who use "puerile and threadbare arguments" to condemn religion as evil. In his essay *WON'T ANYONE STAND UP FOR GOD?* Mr Lewis writes: "Atheists are on the march. The idea of God is under fire. The practice of religion is being condemned as a major source of evil." Christopher Hitchens claims "God is NOT Great." Mr Lewis continued: "I am astounded that in the face of so much aggressive atheist attack no one in the ranks of believers or in the Church has stood up to reply... Where are the Defenders of the Faith that they ridicule? Are our bishops and cardinals, our preachers, imams and rabbis too supine, too complacent or too scared to argue back? Have they no arguments? Why does the Pope not show that the Papacy can argue as well as act as a figurehead? The Church of England is mired in a squabble over homosexual priests....This lack of response is dangerous, especially in the eyes of young people seeking enlightenment."

Mr Lewis rightly stated: "It is not enough for complacent pastors to feed their dwindling flock with anodyne repetitions of old platitudes and the assurance that God is in Heaven waiting for them personally. People are too educated and sophisticated for the old messages." He concluded his indictment on Christian leaders and believers: "What are needed are speakers and writers of vision ready to address with open mind the questions and difficulties that would-be-believers meet in their spiritual searches, and to show up the blind spots and black holes of both religion and atheism. It is time for some honest debate."

The attack on God and the Bible in the 21st century is not surprising. The militant atheists and sceptics have nothing new to offer. They are following the German infidels and the champion critic, Professor S R Driver of Oxford University, who laboured to undermine the Bible. The unknown truth is that, in the 19th century, "God's Barrister" defended the Almighty God and His Word when the Bible was under attack by the rationalists and English clergymen. The issue had already been settled. I encourage militant atheists and agnostics and Church leaders and believers to examine the works of Sir Robert Anderson. He lived in an age when there were hostile attacks against God and the Bible. He took on the shallow critics, the sophisticated intellectuals at Oxford University, who copied the works of the Germans.

In 1902, the true Defender of the Christian Faith silenced the hostile enemies of God with this rebuke: "It is the fashion to assume that to attack the Bible gives proof not only of culture, but of mental vigour and freedom, and that its defenders are always narrow-minded and prejudiced." He went on: "Blank atheism is the extreme depth of moral and intellectual degradation." And the agnostics? he dismissed them by saying: "Agnosticism is Greek for Ignorance and ignorance is both shameful and sinful in the presence of a Divine revelation." And the critics of Sacred Scriptures? "God's Barrister" poured scorn on them: "Critics are men who empty the works of watch into a bowl, and then after examining them in detail arrive at the sapient conclusion that present no proof of unity of design." The Champion of Christian causes is still waiting in the ring for an opponent. Who takes up the challenge?

THERE IS A GOD:
NATURE HIDES HER TREASURES FROM THE TRIFLER

The shallow critics and aggressive atheists of the 21st century must be criticised. For the more they criticise the Bible and dismiss the existence of God, the more they expose their ignorance. For just before their eyes is the evidence of a living God and a trustworthy Bible that writes history before history is written. For the development of the morally and intellectually and spiritually bankrupt European Union – the so-called "the rarest of all phenomena in history" - was recorded in 1881 by a Christian before the European Union came into existence. This Christian, a Police Officer and a Secret Service Agent, was a student of the Bible. It was this faithful servant of Christ, not an atheist or Darwinist, who predicted the European project, its character and future prospects before, Jean Monnet, the Roman Catholic "spiritual godfather" of the godless European Union, was conceived.

The existence of the European Union as the "world's first non-imperial empire" proves the Bible is a supernatural Book. It has no equal. Which scientific book or computer predicted in the 19th century, that a confederation of European nations would develop through an European crisis, and this European confederacy would be the next major political feature in history after the restoration of the Jews to Palestine? The Secret Service Agent writes in *The Bible and Modern Criticism:* "Proofs that the Bible is the Word of God are clear and abundant. But they do not lie open on the surface. Gold and diamonds are not picked up upon the highway: men need to dig for them. Even Nature hides her treasures from the trifler. God is a rewarder of them that seek Him diligently."

"There is probably no God?" That was the slogan desperate atheists, led by the "clone of Huxley," painted on some London Buses. NO! There is God. For the "unknown" and "unseen" God has made Himself "known" and "seen" in the person of the Lord Jesus Christ. For the Blessed Lord, who boldly claims to be the way, the truth and life, declares: "Anyone who has seen Me has seen the Father" (John 14:8,9) "Blank atheism is the extreme depth of moral and intellectual degradation", says the lawyer with sanctified logic. I repeat the words of Rev A C Dixon that testifies Sir Robert Anderson's biblical scholarship: "With the consciousness and courage of an Old Testament prophet, he (Dr Anderson) sounded the trumpet of alarm, and led the battler against the errors which he believed were destroying the fundamentals of Christianity. His lot to a large extent was loneliness of the man who seeks to be a prophet of God, faithfully proclaiming God's message without regard to results, not a leader following the line of least resistance and seeking to gather around him the largest number of followers. The age needs such men. May God multiply the number." Amen!

The Knight of God" cried out: "The days we live in are intensely solemn. The stupid materialism of the science of yesterday has been exploded by the facts of Spiritualism, vouched for by some of our leading scientists of today. And the blind infidelity of the past has thus given place to a craving to get into touch with the realities of the unseen world. This morbid influence has invaded the sphere of religious thought and life, and spiritual Christians even are being corrupted by it... The speaking of tongues and miracles and signs and wonders..."

DARWINISM DISCREDITED
PROFESSOR HUXLEY - THE CHAMPION OF DARWINISM - "FLOORED"
AND THE CHURCH OF ENGLAND'S RIDICULOUS APOLOGY TO DARWIN

The "Evolution and Creationism" controversy rages on in the 21st century. The 'disciples' of Charles Darwin proudly celebrated the 200th birthday anniversary of their "hero". And the Church of England offered an absurd apology to Charles Darwin. I have, therefore, deemed it necessary to remind the scientific world and the Church of England of Sir Robert's Anderson's contribution to the Evolution and Creationism debate. In 1860, the Bishop of Oxford, Samuel Wilberforce, might have 'lost his fight' with Professor Huxley, the Champion of Darwinism. But does the world know that in about 1892, Dr. Anderson took part in the Creationism and Evolution Tournament and knocked out Huxley, the Champion of Darwinism? The Prince of Detectives of Scotland Yard tamed Darwin's bulldog.

I would repeat what the Biblical scholar of repute wrote about Darwin's Theory of Evolution: "The question is not whether the Cosmogony teaches science, which no one asserts; but whether it is discredited by science, which no one has proved. And not even the testimony of such a scientist as Dana in its defence will weigh as much with men of the world, as the fact that such a scientist as Huxley entered the lists to prove it in error and failed....The materialistic scheme of Herbert Spencer is as dead as its author. And even Darwin's more enlightened biological scheme is now discredited. For it is recognized that something more than Darwinism offers is needed to account for the phenomenon of life. The evolution hypothesis is thoroughly philosophical; and that is all that can be said for it, for it is unproved and seeming incapable of proof."

In his *A Doubter's Doubts about Science and Religion,* the fearless Defender of Christian Faith writes: "The first and greatest question relates, not to the phenomenon of life, but its origin. How did life begin? And here evolution affords no answer, and must stand aside. Let the existence of life be taken for granted, and evolution may explain the rest. But the sceptic takes nothing for granted. How did life begin? Science answers-----! In the presence of a question which lies across the threshold of knowledge, science, the very personification of knowledge, turns agnostic and is dumb. "Creation" is the answer religion gives.

The rejoinder which science ought to make is that life first sprang out of death, out of nothing; in a word, abiogenesis...First, Evolution is merely a philosophic theory, second, that it is unproven; third it is inadequate and fourth...it is unnecessary, except of course those scientists who cling to any plank that will save them from having to acknowledge the existence of God......Regarded as a theory to account for life, evolution is the widest folly; but as an hypothesis to account for the varied forms of life, it claims a hearing on its merits...The man who can give no account of his own existence is a fool; and he who denies a God can give no account of his existence." He added: "To establish the fact of spontaneous generation in a world teeming with life, would be as hopeless as the attempt to prove that the displacement of a table in a dark room crowded with people was caused without interference on their part."

Sir David Attenborough, the agnostic, who adores Charles Darwin and blames Genesis for the so-called environmental problems of our time (The Independent 31 January 2009), exposed his ignorance of Sacred Scriptures with his simplistic view of the Book of Genesis. It's ridiculous for Sir David to have suggested that Darwin's Theory of Evolution is not a theory but a fact. Sir David should prove beyond every reasonable doubt that Darwin's Theory of Evolution is a fact. He should also explain to mankind how life began, and how man, a living soul, with mind, conscience and will, evolved from a brute with no conscience. And if life evolves from a bacteria or a molecule, as he suggested on his Television documentary to 'glorify' Darwin, he must tell the world how that bacteria or molecule came into existence. The "most distinguished television naturalist" would have been in the Light-Weight" Division had he taken part in the Evolution and Creationism Tournament held in the 19th century. The celebrated David Attenborough should "go back to school" to study the works of the learned lawyer, the brilliant Sir

Robert Anderson, who knocked out the Heavyweight Champion of Darwinism – the Naturalist Professor Thomas Huxley.

THE CHURCH OF ENGLAND AND THE ROMAN CATHOLIC CHURCH AND CHARLES DARWIN'S THEORY OF EVOLUTION

In his *A Doubter's Doubt About Science and Religion*, the "Sage of Ulster" gave this warning: "Spencerism is dead and Darwin discredited. But though biological theories which reigned supreme a few years ago have been abandoned or modified by "men of light and leading," their influences still prevail with the general public..." The "Barrister of God" went on to explain how Charles Darwin could have made a better case. The "Prophet of Linden Gardens" writes: *"Darwin might, indeed, have stated the matter much more strongly. To call into existence a lowly organised form of life, endowed with latent capacities so wonderful, and so exquisitely adjusted that only when a certain stage of development is reached, the moral qualities spring into existence, immortality is attained, and there arises in the mind the idea of . . ."* I will not continue because this book is not about Evolution and Creationism. You may continue reading from page 17 of *A Doubter's Doubts About Science and Religion.*

Had the Church of England done its "home work" on the Evolution and Creationism controversy by studying the writings of the Theologian among Theologians, the hierarchy of the Established Church would not have made the weird apology: "Charles Darwin, 200 years from your birth [in 1809], the Church of England owes you an apology for misunderstanding you still. But the struggle for your reputation is not over yet, and the problem is not just your religious opponents but those who falsely claim you in support of their own interest." (Source: Daily Mail 14 September 2008).

Without any surprise, the Roman Catholic Church followed the Anglican Church to give credence to Darwin's discredited theory of evolution. In an article *Vatican buries the hatchet with Darwin* with a subtitle *Pope will not be endorsing Intelligent Design* (The Times 11 February 2009) Richard Owen writes: "The Vatican has admitted that Charles Darwin was on the right track when he claimed that Man descended from apes. A leading official declared that Darwin's theory of evolution was compatible with Christian faith, and could be traced to St Augustine and St Thomas Aquinas."

Firstly, the fact is that, the Archbishop of Canterbury and his Church of England, in their attempt to distance themselves from fundamentalist Christians, who believe in the Biblical account of the creation of the world in six literal days, exposed their lack of understanding of Sacred Scriptures and ignorance of historical facts concerning the Evolution and Creationism controversy. Secondly, the

Catholic Church does not believe in the Bible. It picks and chooses sections of Sacred Scriptures that suit its traditions and doctrine. So, Vatican's fascination with the theory of evolution that undermines the Integrity of Christ is not surprising. For the Catholic Bible – The New Jerusalem Bible - has already undermined the integrity of the Lord by claiming the Book of Daniel is a forgery. Whether Pope Benedict XVI endorses or rejects Intelligent Design is immaterial. The Pope should not be taken seriously. This is the "infallible" Pope who spoke against Turkey's membership of the European Union and later on changed his mind and pleaded for Turkey to be accepted. This is the German Pope who welcomed a priest who denied the Holocaust to enrage the German Chancellor.

What is relevant to Bible–believing Christians is what the Lord Jesus Christ taught the Pharisees in Matthew 19:4-7, and not what the "Pharisees" of today teach: *"Haven't you read, that at the beginning* ***the Creator*** *made them male and female, and said, 'For this reason a man will leave his father and mother and be united to his wife, and the two will become one flesh? So they are no longer two, but one. Therefore, What God has joined together, let no man separate."* How can this plain statement of our Blessed Lord be reconciled with the theory that man descended from a beast. This is sheer stupidity.

As I have already mentioned, Darwin's Theory of Evolution was discredited in the 19th century by a lawyer with sanctified logic. None of today's Catholic and Anglican theologians would have qualified to write with his pen. I would, therefore, urge Dr Rowan Williams, the Archbishop of Canterbury, Pope Benedict XVI, the spiritual head of 1.2billion Catholics, and all the Christian leaders who are scared of militant atheists, led by Professor Richard Dawkins, the 'clone' of Darwin's bulldog, Professor Huxley, to analyse the writings of Sir Robert Anderson. The works of this Stalwart Defender of the Christian Faith would provide them with ammunition to 'blow away' the shallow criticisms of the 'hostile enemies' of Genesis, and defend God and the Lord Jesus Christ. The confrontational atheists are just 'copies' of the pagan Porphyry.

The Lord Jesus Christ rose from the dead on the third day of His burial (Luke 24:7). The Lord of lords did not spend millions of years in the grave. The question is: would it have been impossible for the Blessed God (Mahalalel Genesis 5:15) to have created all things in 6 literal days? The Lord Jesus Christ claims to be the way, the truth and life. If, according to our Blessed Lord "All things are possible with God" (Mark 10:27), couldn't God have created all things in 6 literal days?

Dr Anderson's words have come to pass. Today, we have "Lisbon Scientists" – the so-called eminent scholars who have repackaged the discredited arguments on Evolution to blindfold the naïve to discredit the Book of Genesis. Without any surprise, the "Lisbon Theologians" in the Roman Catholic Church and the

Anglican Church are following Professor Huxley like sheep through a gap to worship Darwin to undermine the teachings of the Lord Jesus Christ. What a pity! The Heavyweight Champion of Darwinism was defeated in the 19th century. So, men of reason would ignore the "Paper-Weights" of the 21st century. Dr Anderson writes: "Scepticism is not a permanent resting-place for human reason.....and blank atheism....is the extreme depth of moral and intellectual degradation."

It is fitting I refer Church leaders to pages 93 to 94 of Sir Robert's *The Silence of God* - the book that astounded religious Europe in the 19th century: "But the Bible is more than a book-it is a revelation; and thus regarded, it is above the Church. We do not judge the Bible by the Church; we judge the Church and its teaching by the Bible. This is our safeguard against the ignorance and tyranny of priestcraft. But in our day those who deprecate most strongly the tyranny of the priest are precisely those who champion most loudly the tyranny of the professor and the pundit. The occupant of a University chair cannot fail to be eminent in the branch of knowledge in which he excels, and his value as a specialist is unquestionable. But he may be so utterly unspiritual, and withal so deficient in judgment and common sense, that his opinion may be worth less than that of an intelligent peasant or a Christian schoolboy. The fabric of the Bible, he tells us, is wholly unreliable, but some of its most unbelievable mysteries are truths Divinely revealed. But what claim has he to be listened to in such a case? The setting of the trinket is worthless, and most of its seeming gems are spurious, but here and there he indicates a diamond or a pearl. But the profoundest knowledge of mathematics or Oriental dialects does not qualify a man to judge of pearls and diamonds, Still less does it fit him to recognize spiritual truths."

Dr. Anderson goes on: "If the Bible has really been discredited by modern research, let us have the honesty to own the fact and the manliness to face its consequences. But if the Bible has not been thus discredited, if the results of modern research have been entirely in its favour, then let us show a bolder front in our stand for faith. And let faith and unbelief measure their distance once again....The Bible was written for honest hearts. It is addressed, moreover, to spiritual men. And what is the practical test of spirituality? "If any man think himself to be a prophet, or spiritual, let him acknowledge that the things which I write unto you are the commandments of the Lord" these words betoken, not the insolence of a priest, but the authority of an inspired apostle. It is as believers then, and in the spirit of faith, that we turn to the Epistles."

I would share with you additional testimonies which were published about the life and works of Sir Robert Anderson.

Reverend J. Chalmers: "His (Dr. Anderson's) ceaseless and fearless advocacy of the great essentials of the faith, and his utter devotion to his Lord, made an abiding impression on all who knew him; and I owe him much".

Bishop Taylor Smith: "Sir Robert always inspired and helped me."

W("Cairo") Bradley wrote to Dr Anderson's daughter: "Your father was a wonderful champion for the truth, and can ill be spared in these days when error seems rampant, and those who should hold forth the truth only seem to be watering it down." This testimony speaks to the 21st Church of England and all Christian leaders who have diluted Sacred Scriptures to court popularity.

Rev, E.L Langston: "Sir Robert has been an inspiration to us all in his strong adherence to the Word of God and his zeal for the truth."

Dr J H Townsend: "A Prince has fallen. He was a born leader; and with such intellectual gifts and deep learning in the scriptures he combined the lowliest humility in spiritual things."

A member of the Trinity (Notting Hill) congregation recorded: "It seems as though a personal friend had gone, for Sir Robert was one of the few men in whom I had absolute confidence….one who helped me to have an intelligent understanding of the faith I now hold".

A missionary in China testified: "How thankful I am that *Redemption Truths* ever came into my hands. It has helped me more than any book. I have read for many a day."

Another in Asia Minor recorded how he bought six of Sir Robert's books within a year, 'because a missionary needs absolute confidence in the Word of God:" (Source: Biography *Sir Robert Anderson and Lady Agnes Anderson* by A. P. Moore –Anderson)

WOULD SIR ROBERT ANDERSON WIN "PLAUDITS"?

Chris Giles, writing for the Financial Times on the 2007-2008 global financial crisis, stated: "Economic forecasters even the most bearish failed to foresee the full ramifications of the financial crisis but a few pundits win plaudits for spotting aspects of what was to come this year." Would Sir Robert Anderson win applause from Brussels for predicting how a political union of European nations would develop from an European crisis before the founding fathers of European Community were born?

John Thornhill reviewed Emmanuel Todd's book, *After Democracy*" in the 1 December 2008 edition of the Financial Times. In a column entitled *Europe urged to protect and survive,* he writes: "The financial crisis is convulsing politics in unexpected ways....Emmanuel Todd, the French historian, made a name for himself by predicting the collapse of the Soviet Union.".

From what we have learnt about Sir Robert Anderson, has the Prince of Detectives, made "a name for himself" by accurately predicting that a confederation of European nations would be the next major political feature in history after the restoration of the Jews to Palestine?

Has the Knight Commander (of the Order) of Bath made "a name for himself" by predicting that Austria, Belgium, England, France, Germany, Greece, Italy, Portugal and Spain would become some of the leading nations in a political union of European nations?

Has the former Assistant Commissioner of Metropolitan Police made "a name for himself" by predicting Turkey's membership of political Europe before Turkey first applied to join the European Community in 1963?

Finally, TIME Magazine says: "Europe's development from the Great Depression and World War II has been a Quiet Miracle." Has the Prince of Scotland Yard made "a name for himself" by predicting the "Quiet Miracle" in 1881 before the "Quiet Miracle" started to manifest in 1950?

THE CONCLUDING WORD:
THE KNIGHT COMMANDER CONFESSES HIS FAITH

I would now conclude my introduction of the "Unknown Victorian" - Sir Robert Anderson - by sharing with you how one of his numerous articles to a newspaper provoked a long debate among intellectuals and distinguished theologians. During this debate Sir Robert Anderson confessed his faith in the Lord Jesus Christ and how he became convinced that the Bible is the Word of God. This information is recorded in a book entitled *Should Clergymen Criticise the Bible?*

This particular 241-page book was published in November 1905. It was a result of a series of responses to Sir Robert Anderson's article, *The Search for Religious Truth,* which were published in the *Daily Mail.* The following personnel contributed to the discussion: Bishop Welldon, Bishop Wilkinson, The Dean of Ripon, Archdeacon Wilberforce, Professor S R Driver, Professor Kirkpatrick, Canon Sanday, Canon Mac'Coll, Sir Oliver Lodge, Father Ignatius, and many others.

Here is an extract from the Preface to *Should Clergyman Criticise the Bible?* This little book contains a selection of the more important and the more suggestive of the letters, which poured in thousands into the letter-box of the *Daily Mail* during the months of July, August, and September this year (1905). Had space permitted, at least two thousand additional letters, equally suggestive if in other respects less important, might have been added to the number here included, and even then not one-half of the total correspondence would have been absolved.... If I may add a word for this selection, it will be to point out that it includes so remarkable a series of judgements pronounced by the most distinguished of living scholars and theologians; so large a number of considered opinions offered by trained and responsible thinkers, both clerical and lay; and so many various and divergent views ably maintained by men and women of all classes, professions, and standpoints, that I venture to think the book may constitute a complete armoury of illustration and argument for any one approaching the important problem – *Should clergymen criticise the Bible?....* A. J. M B November 1905

How the discussion began

On July 10, 1905, the following article by Sir Robert Anderson, K.C.B, LLD., appeared in the *Daily Mail*, and on the 14th and 15th of the same month the letters by "Laicus" and "Rural Dean", here printed after Sir Robert Anderson's article, inaugurated a discussion which elicited the most various views, from thousands of thinkers, and was eventually closed on September the 7th 1905.

The search for Religious Truth
by Sir Robert Anderson K.C.B., L.L.D

"Have the modern Higher Critics ever heard of Ferdinard Christian Baur? Before most of them had left the nursery that most brilliant of scholars and critics accomplished precisely what they think should be attempted to-day – five-and-forty years after his death. There is not a single destructive article in the *Encyclopaedia Biblica* which might not have been written by any literary hack with Baur's works before him. He and the other notable men of the Tubingen school of half a century ago convinced "all people of culture" that, the New Testaments was a tissue of deceptions and forgeries."…..

Dr Anderson went to expose the naivety of eminent critics, including Professor Driver of Oxford. He dismissed Canon Driver's "untenable position". Dr Anderson writes: "And this is the position of Professor Driver, the most accredited champion of the Christian school of Higher Criticism in England. He holds that the Christ, whose imprimateur attests the books, was Divine, but that the books are priestly forgeries. And yet, *mirabile dictu,* they are inspired. "In the hands of Christian scholars," he says, "criticism presupposes the inspiration of the Old Testament." But true criticism presupposes nothing. Men who have reached faith through

scepticism counted the cost when entering on the path of criticism.."
Concluding his article, Dr Anderson stated: "The avowed Rationalist is entitled to respect, for he holds a position which is intellectually unassailable. But men who champion that position from within the camp of faith leave themselves open to the charge of being deficient either in honesty or in intelligence....To recommend the Higher Criticism as an antidote to Rationalism is homoeopathy gone mad. *If our churches are losing their hold upon the people, it is because common men turn away instinctively from what is unreal. Able or attractive preachers here and there may draw a crowd; but priestcraft and the Christianised Rationalism of the critics are alienating the masses. The pulpit is no longer a spiritual power. There is no doubt as to the gravity of the disease. But true remedy must be sought not in a development of the new theology, but in a return to the great truths which underline the Welsh revival."* (Emphasis mine). In response to this article, thousands of letters for "the case for criticism" and for "the case against criticism" of the Bible were sent to the Editor of the *Daily Mail.*

Sir Robert Anderson's Confession of Faith

Page 209 of *Should Clergyman criticise the Bible?* records how Sir Robert came to believe the Bible as the PURE WORD OF GOD. Here is the letter to the Editor. I have decided to produce the full text so that the scholars and atheists who attack the Bible may know that Sir Robert Anderson was not an "ignorant" man, and at the same time to strengthen the faith of Christians who are disturbed by Church leaders who attack the Holy Bible.

"As my name has come up so often in this correspondence, I venture to ask for another hearing. The special question you raise may be restated thus: May one who is a clergyman, in virtue of giving definite ordination pledges and singing the Thirty-Nine Articles, teach what is a violation of those pledges and that creed? Our answer to this will depend, surely, on our estimate, not of the Bible, but of the clergy. But the main question underlying the correspondence which has followed my article of July 10 relates to the character of the Bible, and especially of the Old Testament. That article was written avowedly from the man-of-the-world point of view, and therefore I confined myself to destructive criticism of the critics; but having regard to what others have written, may I deal with the Old Testament only, without repeating what I have already said about the New.

I began life by believing the Bible on the authority of my parents, my teachers, and "the Church." This I now admit, savoured of superstition. But in due course I passed through that crisis which thinking people generally experience, when all early beliefs are thrown into the crucible. And as the result my faith in Holy Scriptures became more firm, because more intelligent, than before. The true Christian does not make a fetish of a book, still less of "the Church," but he owns the Lord Jesus Christ, not only as his Saviour, but as his Teacher and Lord. And from his hands it is that we receive the Hebrew Scriptures, accredited as a Divine revelation. His entire ministry was expressly based on them, and His testimony to them was clear and explicit.

Here my faith rested till the study of the so-called "Higher Criticism" undermined it. For the critics reject the Lord's teaching as worthless, because, they say, He spoke only as a Jew of His own age, and because the Pentateuch, e.g., can be shown to be a priestly work of late date. Had my earnest study of the matter led me to accept these conclusions, I should have given up Christianity and fallen back upon the position of Dr. Harnack, of Berlin, and the other great thinkers who have the courage of their convictions.

But I have been led to reject both these main theses of the critics. As regards the Pentateuch, I am not certain whether its genuineness could be established before a purely secular tribunal; but I am clear that the "critical hypothesis" of its origin would be...."laughed out of court." It is demonstrably false. Which leads me to add that the question whether a clergyman is competent to be a critic in the true sense of the word depends mainly upon whether he has adequate experience in dealing with evidence and is versed in the science.

If, following a great example, I may "speak as a fool," I would in conclusion appeal to my books to give proof that my faith in the Bible does not depend upon ignoring "Biblical difficulties" of the kind which some of your correspondents parade with such pertness.

Final reply from Sir Robert Anderson

May I be allowed a parting word in this correspondence which has followed my article of eight weeks ago?

I accept unreservedly Professor Driver's statement of the character and aims of higher criticism, as given in his letter of August 23, and I concur in regarding such a system of Bible study as both legitimate and valuable. But I would emphasise the distinction between higher criticism as thus defined and its counterfeit which is working such mischief. The "Higher Criticism" (in inverted commas) is the acceptance of the "assured results" formulated by a certain school of foreign sceptics and rationalists who have used higher criticism as a cloak for attacking Holy Scriptures.

Let me illustrate my meaning. The Dean of Canterbury is a very distinguished higher critic, but as his study of the Hebrew Scriptures has led him to maintain their genuineness, he is an opponent of the "Higher Criticism."

The rationalists have established, by evidence which is full and clear, that the Pentateuch is a literary forgery of the age of the exile. And the layman is apt to suppose that what is thus established must be true. But the lawyer knows that it is not until a charge is established by evidence which is full and clear that any one is required to answer it in a court of justice. And the object of a judicial trial is to test the case thus established, and to hear what can be said on the other side. True criticism begins, therefore, precisely where the sham "Higher Criticism" pronounces judgment.

Professor Driver's "Introduction" would not have shaken my faith in the Hebrew Scriptures had I not supposed it was the outcome of an independent inquiry by an English Christian scholar. What saved me the discovery that it was merely the presentation of the "case for the prosecution," to the exclusion, as Professor Sayce and others have shown, of all of the Samaritan Pentateuch is an absolute bar to the rationalistic hypothesis for which Dr Driver stands sponsor.

But your limits of space check my pen. May I say, in conclusion, in reply to two of your correspondents, that when I appealed to the teaching of our Lord Jesus Christ as final, I was speaking only of the Old Testament? To maintain that He was Divine, and at the same time that He was ignorant and deceived, and yet that He demanded acceptance of His words as being the very words of God – this, I confess, is beyond me." Robert Anderson.

This was our brilliant Protestant "father" who wrote about European Union: how it would develop, its character and future prospects before the Catholic Founding Fathers of European Community – Jean Monnet and Robert Schuman – were born in 1888 and 1886.

Should Clergymen Criticise the Bible?

Here is a sample of the calibre of the scholars and theologians who contributed to the debate in the *Daily Mail*

In favour of criticising the Bible	Against Criticising the Bible
• Rev. W. Sanday, D.D., Canon of Christ Church, Oxford, and Lady Margaret Professor of Divinity	• Right Rev. T E Wilkinson D.D Anglican Bishop for Northern and Central Europe
• Rev. S. R. Driver, D.D., Canon of Christ Church, Oxford, and Regius Professor of Hebrew	• Right Rev, the Bishop of Ossory and Ferns
	• Ven. William Sinclair, D.D., Archdeacon of London
• Sir Oliver Lodge, LLD., F.R.S	• Father Ignatius, O. S. B
• Rev. A.F Kirkpatrick, D.D., Master of Selwyn College, Cambridge, and Lady Margaret's Professor of Divinity.	• H.W Garrod, M.A., Fellow of Merton College, Oxford
	• Rev. the Hon. James Adderley, M.A
• Ven. Basil Wilberforce, DD., Archdeacon of Westminster	• B.W I. Morton Liet,-General Indian Army
	• Rev. C. T Porter, D.D
• W.A Cox, M.A Fellow of St. John's College, Cambridge	
• T.E Rogers Chancellor of Bath and Wells	
• Frederick C. T. Bosanquet, Rector of Catherston, Dorset	

Matthew Anderson, the father of Sir Robert Anderson, was a lawyer of considerable reputation. For nearly 50 years he was crown solicitor for the County and City of Dublin. He had charge of Fenian persecutions in 1865 - 1867

Chapter 18

RELIGION AND POLITICS IN THE EUROPEAN UNION: THE TWO TRUTHS

"The God of revelation is the God of nature; and in the spiritual as in the natural sphere, there are difficulties which perplex and distress us. But though the word of God, like the works of God, may be full of mystery, it is wholly free from falsehood and folly **(The Bible and Modern Criticism - RA)**

We have already learnt that on 18 February 2005, The Times newspaper made this announcement in one of its columns: "*The EU truth has many faces....*" This was evident from the different views European politicians, political commentators, businessmen and ordinary citizens of the European "Empire" expressed on the first European Constitution which was rejected by the French and the Dutch in 2005. But the Christian Truth, which is the Holy Bible, has only ONE FACE: the Lord Jesus Christ, whom Sir Robert Anderson vigorously defended. The Lord Jesus is "The same yesterday, today and forever" Amen! (Hebrews 13:8).

The architects of the European Constitution had no room for the Precious Face of the Lord Jesus Christ. If the Lord of lords, the King of kings was not found worthy to be at the centre of the European Constitution, the Lord of Heaven and Earth will NOT plead to take the back seat at the EU Table. And if the Blessed Messiah was not considered worthy to sit at the top table, the "Beginning and the End" will NOT sit at the side table. The EU is NOT a Christian club as their own leading politicians and commentators have suggested.

After all, some politicians claim they *don't do God.* They also assert religion and abortion must be kept out of politics, because it is unhealthy to bring religion into the political process. Why should abortion and religion be kept out of politics? If it is unhealthy to bring religion into the political process, then Christians must not take part in politics, because the religious beliefs of Christians must reflect in every facet of their lives. Christians cannot build a wall between the expression of their religious beliefs at home and in business or in politics. Christianity is not a cult to be practised in secret. It is a declaration of belief in the Lord Jesus Christ as the Saviour of the world; and this belief should be articulated in the open not behind 'closed-doors.'

To a committed Christian, who believes in the Absolute Authority of the Bible, homosexuality and same-sex marriage have moral and religious dimensions just like abortion. The Bible does not condone homosexuality and abortion. On Abortion, Scripture says: *"In thy skirts is found the blood of the innocent poor..."* (Jeremiah 2:34). On same-sex relationships the Lord Jesus Christ made it clear of its non-existence in the plan of God. This was evident in the response our Divine Lord gave to the Pharisees concerning divorce. The Jewish religious leaders asked the Lord, "Is it lawful for a man to divorce his wife for any and every reason? The Lord Jesus, who was not a politician, replied: "Haven't you read that in the beginning the Creator made them male and female, and said, "For this reason a man will leave his father and mother and be united to his wife and the two will become one flesh? So they are no longer two, but one. Therefore what God had joined together, let no man separate" (Matthew 19:3-6).

DO POLITICIANS "DON'T DO GOD"?

If politicians find it expedient to bring homosexual issues into politics by fighting for the votes of the homosexual community, why should abortion and religion not enter the political arena? If abortion and religion should not be discussed in politics, then Christianity should be taken out of politics. This means Christianity should not feature in any of European Union's deliberations, particularly on the issue of Turkey's membership of Jean Monnet's project.

Because politicians "don't do God," they do not welcome religion into the political arena. Why? Because, at times the Laws of God may contradict the laws of politicians. And politicians do not want God to upstage them in their pursuit of votes. However, these same politicians "do God" and welcome religion into the political process, if the presence of God in the political arena could help their cause to win more votes to gain power. This fact was made plain in an article published in the Daily Mail on 30 March 2005. In a space entitled *"Oui to EU, say French churches,"* Ian Sparks writes: "A poll showed 53 percent are against the blue-print for a federal Europe......to confirm a trend towards rejection of the European constitution." The article further reported that Christian leaders in France, in a joint letter, urged the French people to vote for the ratification of the constitutional treaty. According to those church leaders, "The constitution deserves support because it respects human dignity, expands democratic procedures and recognises the contribution religion made to modern society."

The unnecessary intervention of 'blind' Christian leaders in the political process to influence French voters to adopt the old European constitution in their referendum, was a clear support for the politicians who were then campaigning for the electorate to vote "Yes." Furthermore, it was also a boost to the then French President. Because, according to the article, President Jacques Chirac, "in a desperate address to the French nation on Sunday (27 March 2005), urged the French to vote "Yes", saying, "The fate of France for decades to come depended on the referendum result."

I take issue with politicians who argue that abortion and religion must be kept out of politics. When Christian leaders in France entered the political process to influence the outcome of the French referendum on the rejected constitutional treaty - an interference that was designed to favour politicians who supported the European constitution - which politician in Britain and Europe, together with their supporters who claim abortion and religion must not enter the political arena, objected to the partisan interference of French church leaders in France's political process? But when, in Britain, religious leaders of Judaism, Christianity and Islam expressed their concern about the lax laws on abortion, and urged their followers to bring abortion into the political debate, politicians, led by the former prime minister, Tony Blair, objected to the interference of religion in British politics. What an exhibition of double-standards and blatant hypocrisy! When Pope Benedict XVI, with his support for the Lisbon Treaty, attempted to influence the result of the Irish referendum on the Lisbon Treaty, which politician criticised the leader of 1.2billion Christians for his interference in a political issue? It suited politicians so they kept quiet. Hypocrites! You cannot have it both ways.

In view of the arrogant position the European leaders adopted to eliminate God and Christianity from the European Constitution, why did Cardinal Murphy O'Connor suggest that the Church and the State should help Europe to grow? To grow from what to what? Some Church leaders have lost confidence in themselves to the extent that they blindly follow the blind world. An example is the 'Religion of Global Warming' which has attracted followers in the church. For example an Anglican Bishop, Dr. Gordon Mursell, jumped on the Green bandwagon, to criticise those who don't subscribe to the 'Cult of Climate Change.' The Bishop, who should have known better from scriptures, that it is not global warming that would destroy planet earth, compared sceptics of the "Green Cult" to an Austrian child abuser – Josef Fritzl. This was reported in a newspaper article, *Global warming sceptics are as bad as dungeon man – That's the astonishing view of Church of England bishop* (Daily Mail 3 June 2008). Why have some Church leaders and Christians become 'slaves' to a world that has no room for the Lord Jesus Christ? The answer is simple. They don't believe in the authority of the Bible. They believe in their own opinions. "Anyone who dies for his own opinion is a fool", says Sir Robert Anderson.

I repeat: Religious leaders and their views are welcomed into the political process only if such views could help politicians to win more votes to stay in power. But religious leaders and God are not needed in the political arena when their views could undermine politicians to loose power. On the issue of religion and politics, politicians should hold their breath. Because, so far as faithful Christians are concerned, the Lord Jesus Christ has already advised them to come out of the political Babylon and the religious Babylon (Revelation 18:4).

Politicians "Don't do God," and "God doesn't do sleaze," and "God is not selfish and incompetent." What are 'blind' men, whose glory is like the grass on the field that withers and thrown into the fire? What are men who have no control over events, and yet boast: "We can change the world and make the world a better place." Were politicians able to predict the 2007-2008 Global Financial crisis that turned them into headless chickens rolling around for solutions? The Omnipotent God declares: "I am God, and there is no other; I am God, and there is none like me. I make known the end from the beginning, from ancient times, what is to come. I say, My purpose will stand, and **I** will do all that I please." (Isaiah 46:9-10).

A PLEA TO BRITONS AND THE IRISH

I urge fellow Britons and the Irish to study the Book of Daniel with unprejudiced mind. Examine the prophetic messages about the *"Magnificent Human Image"* in chapter 2 of Daniel and the vision of the *"four cruel beasts from the sea"* recorded in chapter 7. Reconcile them with the visions of the *'beast from the sea"* in Revelation 13 and the vision of the *"beast with 7 heads and 7 horns"* in Revelation 17 to the development of the European Union. These Scriptures would throw a light on the European Project. You would be in a better position to appreciate what the European Union is for and its future. This would help you to decide how to associate yourself with "the biggest political alliance in the world and the biggest economic market at your doorstep".

Had the men and women who, in 1912, perished on the Titanic have known that the luxurious 'unsinkable' ship would sink on its maiden voyage from Southampton to New York, would they have boarded the vessel? The European Union might have started well on its journey to the 'carbon-free' land of peace and prosperity ⊠ showering billions of euros into member states to enhance their economies. If the end crowns the work, then what are the future prospects of this economic and political union of European nations? We must reflect on the saying: "Beware of the Greeks even when they offer gifts." The EU is the 'Trojan horse' of the 21st century. The British and the Irish must reject the 'horse'. Where is the 'Laocoon' in Britain and Ireland? Dr Anderson, the "Laocoon" of the 19th century, warned Britain about the deadly "Trojan horse" before it was even constructed. The 'lance" has been thrown at the side of this 'horse' and despite the "groaning" inside the "horse," Gordon Brown and Brian Cowen forced Britons and the Irish to 'celebrate' the wonderful gift from their masters in Brussels.

I would encourage you to analyse carefully chapter 11 of the Book of Daniel. You would appreciate the impact the career of the coming emperor of the European Empire would have on mankind. In the 3rd century AD, a pagan Greek philosopher, Porphyry, attempted to discredit the Book of Daniel as a forgery written in the 2nd century BC. In the 17th and 18th centuries German infidels followed the atheist Porphyry to undermine the divine character of the Book of Daniel. And in the 19th century some British theologians, led by Professor Driver of Oxford, also followed the German Rationalists to 'damage' the Book of Daniel. And today, 'Lisbon theologians' have also treaded the 'worn-out' path of the infidels to discredit this wonderful Old Testament Book. To Roman Catholics and their Jerusalem Bible (to borrow the words of Sir Robert Anderson), "the Book of Daniel is the merest fiction, differing from other fiction of the same kind by reason of the multiplicity of its inaccuracies and errors. Its history is but idle legend. Its miracles are but baseless fables. It is, in every part of it, a work of the imagination, "Avowed fiction" it calls it."

According to the Catholic Bible, the Book of Daniel was written between 167-164 BC during the persecution of the Jews by Antiochus Epiphanes, and there was no Daniel in existence save a sage "Daniel" who lived in the East. Hence, *The New Jerusalem Bible's* ridiculous conclusion that the Book of Daniel was an "edifying fiction." This leads to the question: Did the Lord Jesus Christ refer to a "fictitious Daniel" when he spoke of a "Prophet Daniel" in Matthew 24:15. When the Lord spoke about Abraham, Jonah, Moses, David did he refer to fictional characters in the Old Testament? And when the "scroll of the prophet Isaiah" was given to the Lord Jesus in the synagogue, did our Divine Lord read from a fictitious document written by an "unknown" Isaiah? (Luke 4:14-21) The Roman Catholic Church has cast a slur on the Divinity of the Lord Jesus Christ who endorsed the Book of Daniel in Matthew 24:15. Because of the treachery perpetrated in *The New Jerusalem Bible,* I would, in the second volume of this work, make a contribution towards the defence of the supernatural character of the Book of Daniel to uphold the Divine Integrity of our Blessed Lord.

A PLEA TO THE CITIZENS OF THE UNITED STATES OF AMERICA

Finally, I would exhort Americans to be vigilant about the growth of the European Union. Because, when the "king of Men", the last Emperor of the Revived Roman Empire, that *"awful Being",* emerges in Europe to lead the world with the support of the 10 powerful 'kings' of the provinces of the European Empire (Revelation 17:12-13), America would experience the consequences of the violation of the 7-year peace treaty the false messiah signed with Israel and its Arab neighbours at the beginning of his career.

We know from Scriptures that the counterfeit messiah, the Antichrist, will terminate the 7- year peace treaty within three and half years of his coronation. And we are aware that the 'beast from the earth', the degraded Jew, will command the Jews and the world to pay homage to the idol of Antichrist in the Jerusalem Temple (Daniel 9:27). For 42 months this charismatic and political genius would initiate the persecution of faithful Jews and Christians who would deny him homage (Revelation 13:5-8). And according to our Lord, this harassment of His followers would mark the beginning of the Great Tribulation He spoke about in Matthew 24:15-22: *"When you see the abomination of desolation, spoken of by Daniel the prophet, standing in the holy place, then let those who are in Judea flee to the mountains...For there will be great tribulation, such as has not been since the beginning of the world until this time, no, nor ever shall be."* .

THE WINGS OF AN EAGLE – A PLACE OF REFUGE FOR PERSECUTED CHRISTIANS

We will now examine how the Lord Jesus Christ would care for His persecuted saints, and the role the United States of America would play during the Great Tribulation. Let us recall what Apostle John saw in a vision: *"The woman was given the two wings of a great eagle, so that she might fly to the place prepared for her in the desert where she would be taken care of for a time, times and half a time "* (Revelation 12:14). "A time, times and half a time" implies three and half years or 42 months. I have already explained the "Woman" in this Scripture represents the faithful children of God, not the Blessed Virgin Mary.

It is clear from the passages in Revelation 12:4-6, Revelation 12:14, Revelation 13:5-8, Daniel 7:24-25, Daniel 9:27, Daniel 12:7 and Matthew 24:15, that the Great Tribulation would continue for 3½ years only, that is 42 months or 1260 days, and not 7 years or 1260 years. For the "Middle of the Week" of the "Vision of 70 Weeks" recorded in Daniel 9:24-27 makes it plain that the persecution of the saints by the Man of Lawlessness cannot be 7 years or 1260 years. Secondly, not all Christians would be raptured before the Great Tribulation. Only the few chosen overcomers would escape the persecution of Antichrist. Witness the Lord's words of comfort to the 'Philadelphians': "I know your works....you have a little strength, yet you have kept my word, and have not denied my name....Because you have kept my command, I also will keep you from the hour of trial which will come upon the whole world, to test those who dwell on the earth" (Revelation 3:8-10).

A careful examination of the Lord Jesus' 7 letters to the 7 Churches in Asia Minor would reveal that He made this solemn promise, "I will keep you from the hour of trial which will come upon the whole world, to test those who dwell on the earth", only to the *Church in Philadelphia* (The Church of Brotherly Love - Revelation 2 and 3). Some of us Christians would experience the terror of the Son of Perdition. But our Faithful Lord has prepared a place of refuge for those who would face the wrath of the "Man of Lawlessness" – the "Chief Terrorist." We must ask the question: Where would the persecuted Christians seek shelter? Notice the text in Revelation 12:14: *"The woman was given the two wings of a great eagle, so that she might fly to the place prepared for her to be taken care of for three and half years."* We know this "Woman" represents the loyal children of God not the Blessed Virgin Mary. Another question arises: What about the "The two wings of a great eagle?" They are symbolic from two perspectives. Let us find out what they represent. 'Eagle', the powerful bird of the air, signifies God's awesome power to deliver His people from the terror of the Man of Sin just as how the Almighty delivered the Israelites from bondage in Egypt and then rescued them from the terror of Pharaoh.

Secondly the 'eagle wings' have another symbolic expression. We know some countries have animals as their national symbols. For example, my country, England, has lion as its symbol. The *"Great eagle"* in the text gives us a clue of the place of refuge for the children of God who would face the wrath of Antichrist – the last Caesar of the revived Roman Empire. There are nations that have eagle as their national symbol. But of these nations, only the United States of America is the most powerful and religious. America is also the only dominant nation that fights for the interest of the nation of Israel – God's chosen people. I have already explained the position of the Jews in the Divine Plan of God. I would reiterate for further clarification.

JEWS ARE NOT BETTER THAN GENTILES

Because of their unfaithfulness to God, the Almighty scattered the Jews among the Gentile nations. The Omnipotent also predicted the Jews would suffer, yet He would bring them back to possess the land which their forefathers had occupied (Deuteronomy 30:1-5; Ezekiel 36:24). God spoke plainly to the prophet Ezekiel that it is not because He loves the Jews more than the Gentile nations, but for His own Name sake He will keep His Word. Hear the Voice of the Lord: "*...I had pity for mine holy name, which the house of Israel had profaned among the heathen, whither they went. Therefore say unto the house of Israel, Thus saith the Lord God; I do not do this for your sake, O house of Israel, but for mine holy name's sake, which ye have profaned among the heathen, whither ye went. And I will sanctify my great name, which was profaned among the heathen....and the heathen shall know that I am the Lord...*" (Ezekiel 36:21-23 KJ). So, the United States of America, by standing with the Jews, are consciously or unconsciously, supporting the cause of the Lord to fulfil His Word to uphold His Great Holy Name.

The United States of America may be the "great Satan" - an "evil country" with "evil people." Yet, despite its many faults and moral failings, just like all other nations on planet earth (for no nation could claim to be better and more righteous than America), it is the only powerful nation on earth, the majority of its citizens, fight for the Lord Jesus Christ as the Source of Creation. Other countries that seek the interest of the Lord Jesus Christ do not have eagle as their national symbol. They are not as commanding as the United States of America, with the resources to cater for the believers who would seek refuge from the wrath of the last Emperor of the Revived Roman Empire – the Terrorist of all Terrorists.

Secondly, the United States of America is the only powerful nation on earth the majority of its citizens are fighting heartily against Darwin's fable theory of evolution that undermines the Divine integrity of our Lord and Saviour Jesus Christ. If man evolved and was not created by God, then, Darwin's theory of Evolution clearly makes the Lord a 'liar.' For the Lord Jesus, in His response to the question the Pharisees raised about divorce, told them: "Haven't you read that at the beginning the Creator made them male and female, and said, "For this reason a man will leave his father and mother and be united to his wife, and the two will become one flesh" (Matthew 19:4-6).

That Americans are religious and predominantly Bible-believing Christians is no exaggeration. For example, on 19 January 2005, a title in the *Daily Express* newspaper read: "US school ban evolution lessons – Science pupils told religious alternative to Darwin." According to this article, children in the United States of America were being taught that Charles Darwin theory of evolution could be wrong. Campaigns were carried out in schools to present religious alternative to scientific teaching on evolution. The article further reported: "Dover High School in Pennsylvania took the lead....by becoming the first in US to include thinly - veiled hints - being taught as science in biology lessons - that God created the universe. The lessons claim evolution is only a patchy theory and mankind could have been created instead by a supernatural force using "intelligent design". The article concluded: "One TV opinion poll has shown nearly two-thirds of Americans favour teaching creationism alongside evolution. And on the Christian News Service website, the Reverend Mark Greech said: "It is a travesty of justice if God or supernatural explanations of science are summarily banned from the classroom."

THE POMPOUS SCIENTISTS

On 11 April 2005, an Editorial in Financial Times read: *"Fight for evolution: Creationism poses a growing threat to science teaching."* The opening paragraph of this leading article stated: "As the religious right strengthens its hold on US politics, the threat to teaching about evolution grows." According to this editorial, there was an assault on rational science. And this "assault is moving from schools to public education in a wider sense, some science centres and museums in southern states have refused to show big-screen Imax films that refer to evolution. They are boycotting titles such as Volcanoes of the Deep Sea, which suggests that life might have begun more than 3bn years ago …."

The plain truth is evolution is a theory NOT a fact. Question: "Where did life begin?" Evolution has no answer. I repeat the words of Dr Robert Anderson, who knocked out Professor Huxley – the Champion of Darwin's Theory of Evolution: "The man who cannot give no account of his own existence is a fool; and he who denies God can give no account of his existence." In the old time men whispered their folly within their own hearts; nowadays they proclaim it on the house-tops, or to translate the Oriental figure into its Western correlative, they publish it in printed books….Regarded as theory to account for life, evolution is the wildest folly, but as an hypothesis to account for the varied forms of life, it claims a hearing on its own merits."

In Page 7 of *A Doubter's Doubts About Science and Religion*, "God's Barrister" writes: "If the hypothesis of evolution be true, living matter must have arisen from not-living matter. Therefore life did originate thus, and the truth of evolution is established. Thus argue the professors and scientists. But the man who considers, reflects, hesitates, doubts, will call for the evidence; and finding there is none, he will reject the conclusion, and also, if necessary, the dependent hypothesis."

I encourage scientists to examine Dr. Anderson's *A Doubter's Doubts about science and Religion.* In this classic work, as I have mentioned many times, the Knight Commander "slaughtered" Darwin's 'bull-dog' - Professor Thomas Huxley.

I close this chapter by recalling what Dr. Konrad Adenauer, the first German Chancellor, spoke of America - the "Great Satan": "Germany must declare herself wholeheartedly for the Christian world of the West and all it stands for…The world must be convinced of American strength…The US has today perhaps the mightiest mission in history. In a human and historic sense America has a duty… to see that the light never goes out on our earth…I want to see a united Europe. Only then can my country be free. To that we need the help of the best Europeans of all – the Americans" (*TIME* 5 December 1949). Unfortunately, today, some Americans are deserting Christ to follow Charles Darwin. Darwin and his *On origin of Species* and *The Descent of Man* are irrelevant in the 21st century. What is relevant is Sir Robert Anderson's *The Silence of God, The Coming Prince, A Doubter's Doubts about Science and Religion, The Bible and Modern Criticism* and all his theological works.

Great Britain and America: listen to what Sir Robert Anderson wrote about your prosperity and power: "The effects of this "Higher Criticism" are extremely grave.

For it has dethroned the Bible in the home, and the good old practice of "family worship" is rapidly dying out. And great national interests also are involved. *For who can doubt that the prosperity and power of the Protestant nations of the world are due to the influence of the Bible upon character and conduct?* Races of men who for generations have been taught to think for themselves in matters of the highest moment will naturally excel in every sphere of effort or of enterprise. And more than this, no one who is trained in the fear of God will fail in his duty to his neighbour, but will prove himself a good citizen. *But the dethronement of the Bible leads practically to the dethronement of God; and in Germany and America, and now in England, the effects of this are declaring themselves in ways, and to an extent, well fitted to cause anxiety for the future."*

"Mr Huxley wrote another letter, but it contained nothing save pretentious phrases about science and ungenerous sneers at those who believe the Bible. So far as this controversy (Creationism and Evolution – that the Bible is discredited by science) is concerned he - Huxley - left his opponents in possession of the field. The fact asserted by Mr Gladstone remains established by this searching test. It is asserted, and it will still be asserted as unblushingly as if this correspondence had not taken place, that Genesis is proved false by the facts of science; whereas the testimony of science, whatever it be worth, confirms the Biblical order of creation."

Sir Robert Anderson: K.C.B LLD
An Intellectual among
Intellectuals

page 615

My object here is to beat off attacks which stumble or distress ignorant and weak-kneed believers. And to this end I have shown that Professor Huxley, the ablest and most bitter assailant of Genesis which this age has produced, has been met and routed upon ground of his own choosing. The first chapter of genesis "was not written to teach science"; but not a single "fact of science" can be found to discredit it. This cannot be said of any one of the "religious books of the East" - in this respect they are but a tangle of error and folly. Neither can it be said of any scientific book published before recent years. The "science" of the last generation is discredited by the discoveries of our own times."

Chapter 19

PLACE OF REFUGE FOR GOD'S PEOPLE DURING THE THREE AND HALF YEARS OF THE GREAT TRIBULATION

"He is the unchanging God with whom there is no variableness, neither shadow cast by turning. Therefore while with men the use of absolute power is often arbitrary it is never with God. No element of caprice even marks the exercise of sovereign grace."
(RA)

Apart from the United States of America, there is another place God has reserved for His people to seek shelter from the fury of the last Emperor of the revived Roman Empire. Like Antiochus Epiphanies, the despicable Syrian king who was a vicious enemy of the Jewish people, and who defiled the Temple in Jerusalem with the blood of a female pig and the idol of Zeus, so would the coming King of Men, the Emperor of the European Empire, also desecrate the Hebrew Temple in Jerusalem with his idol, and by replacing the sacrifice and offering in the Temple with his one world religion. This would be the worshipping of his statue, which the apostate Jew - the false prophet - would construct in the Temple. (Revelation 13:14-15).

We know the Man of Sin would exalt himself as God and claim the homage of all men. He would persecute those Jews who fail to subscribe to his 'global religion.' Hence the Lord's advice to the disciples: "When you (Jews) see the abomination of desolation, spoken of by Daniel the prophet, standing in the holy place ....then let those in Judea flee to the mountains. Let him who is on the housetop not go down to take anything out of his house. And let him who is in the field not go back to take his clothes......For then there will be great tribulation, such as has not been since the beginning of the world until this time, *no, nor ever shall be.* And unless those days were shortened, no flesh would be saved; but for the elect sake those days will be shortened" (Matthew 24:15-22).

In this Scripture the Lord Jesus Christ cautions the children of Israel to "flee to the mountains." These mountains would be a safe haven for the suffering Jews where the Lord would care for His afflicted people. The Lord Jesus revealed this 'escape of the Jews' to Apostle John in a vision: "*The woman fled into the desert to a place prepared for her by God, where she might be taken care of for one thousand two hundred and sixty days*", which is 42 months or three and half years (Revelation 12:6). In this text, "the Woman", who represents the children of Israel, was not given the two wings of a great eagle to fly. According to the Lord Jesus Christ, this "Woman", the Jewish people, must "flee to the mountains" (Matthew 24:16).

The question arises: where are these "mountains" which would be the hiding places for the devoted Jews to escape the terror of Antichrist, and to be nourished for three and half years? We get a clue from the Book of Daniel 11:36-42. This particular Scripture foretells the wrath of Antichrist, and where he would not be able to conquer. "And the king (Antichrist) shall do according to his will; and shall exalt himself, and magnify himself above every god, and shall speak marvellous things against the God of gods, and shall prosper till the indignation be accomplished: for that is determined shall be done.....And at the time of the end shall the king of the south (Egypt) push at him: and the king of the north (Syria) shall come against him like a whirlwind, with chariots, and with horsemen, and with many ships; and he shall enter into countries, and shall overflow and pass over. He shall enter the glorious land (Israel), and many countries shall be overthrown: *but these shall escape out of his hand, even Edom, and Moab, and the chief of the children of Ammon"*.

THE REFUGE IN PETRA

The kingdoms of Edom, Moab and Ammon are all in mountainous areas - east of the Jordan River. In Edom, there is a beautiful ancient city called Petra. Petra, which in Greek means "rock", is a city in the mountains of Edom- about 80 kilometres south of the Dead Sea. The city of Petra is carved out of the rocks of Edom. It is in this metropolis the suffering Jews would be preserved for 1260 days (3½ years) from the wrath of the 'chief terrorist.' This flight of the Jews to Petra would be a prophetic response to the advice the Lord Jesus Christ offered to the Jews: "...When you see the abomination of desolation (the image of Antichrist) spoken of by Daniel the prophet, standing in the holy place (the Temple)....Then let those who are in Judea flee to the mountains" (Matthew 24:15).

Dr, Howard E Esten, founder of "The King is Coming" (a Christian Broadcasting Network in America), who is now with the Lord, presented a detailed study on the significance of the city of Petra, and the role it would play in the last three and half years of this age. I encourage you to obtain materials on this subject. You would appreciate how God, before time began, prepared a sanctuary for His people to flee from the horror of the "Monster" - the Emperor of the world's first "non-imperial empire. "Before things happened, I pronounced them, says the Lord (Isaiah 48:5).

THREE OF THE SEVEN WONDERS OF THE WORLD

It may interest you to know that three of the "Seven Wonders of the world," which are the "Colloseum," "Petra" and "Christ the Redeemer," are associated with the final stages of the European Empire. Petra is the city where the Jews would seek refuge from the "Man of Lawlessness." Colloseum - a symbol on the Italian 5 Euro cents - reminds the world how the Romans persecuted the Jews and celebrated their victory with the construction of an amphitheatre. 'Christ the Redeemer' is the "Stone cut without human hands' that would strike the human statue from its toes of baked clay and iron to its head of gold and scatter them like chaff (Daniel 2:31-35).

Chapter 20

EU: "THE VILE CONFEDERACY OF THE LATTER DAYS"

"It is only the infidel who doubts that there is a destined limit to the course of "this present evil world. That God will one day put forth His power to ensure the triumph of the good, is in some sense a matter of course. The mystery of revelation is not that He will do this, but He delays to do it. Judged by public facts around us, He is an indifferent spectator of the unequal between good and evil upon earth...Vice and godlessness and violence and wrong are rampant upon every side, and yet the heavens above keep silence. The infidel appeals to the fact in proof that the Christian God is but a myth. The Christian finds in it a further proof that the God he worships is patient and longsuffering-patient because He is eternal, longsuffering because He is almighty, for wrath is a last resource with power. But the day is coming when our God shall come and shall not keep silence." **(The Coming Prince - RA)**

In this chapter we will focus on the character of the European Union as described by Sir Robert Anderson. Before that a word on the coming Prince of Europe and how the European Project would stumble to the "finishing post." On 1 July 2005, Tony Blair, succeeded the Luxembourg Prime Minister, Jeane Claude Juncker, as the next President of the European Union's six-month rotating presidency. On 23 June 2005, before Britain took over the position, Mr Blair addressed Members of the European Parliament. He outlined his vision for Europe: "A political Europe with a strong and caring social dimension, not only an economic market" - and an Europe that should embrace free markets, and face up to the challenges of globalisation, and an Europe which is committed to the enlargement of the Union."

Mr Blair, reiterating the economic and political crisis that confronted the European Union brought up the crucial issue facing the European Project- "leadership in Europe." He declared: "The debate about Europe should not be conducted by 'traditional insults.' This is not a time to accuse those who want Europe to change of betraying Europe....It is not a crisis of political institutions, it is a crisis of political leadership...The people are blowing the trumpets around the city walls...

The people of Europe are speaking to us. They are posing the questions. They are wanting our leadership. It is time we gave it to them."

Whatever the social, economic or political problems that would engulf the European Union, the EU Project would 'succeed'. It would "muddle through." The European Empire will survive and grow from strength to strength until its true leader emerges so that Scriptures would be fulfilled. To the citizens of Europe (as I have already stated) the vacuum of political leadership in the continent would be filled. The qualified leader may not appear in our life time. But at the appointed time, this great leader of Europe - the last emperor of the revived Roman Empire - would emerge on the political scene. The Lisbon Treaty has paved the way for his advent.

With his power and charisma, the King of Europe will demonstrate extraordinary intelligence and political skills. He will solve complex problems which the world has never witnessed before. The European Union would be convinced that their leader has eventually arrived. The 10 powerful 'Kings' of the Union will enthrone this *genius*, and delegate their powers and authority to him (Revelation 17:12-13) to lead Europe and the world to the *"promised land"* of peace, security, and economic prosperity. As the new European leader begins to solve the world's diverse problems, including the Middle East crisis, he would claim divine authority. With proud words he will blaspheme against God and the whole world would adore him, saying *"Who is like the beast? Who can make a war against him?* (Revelation 13:4-6).

But, the "king of men"- the counterfeit messiah, the Antichrist - would reveal his true colours as a false prince of peace, when he breaks his 7 year peace treaty with the nation of Israel, and then command all men to worship his image in the temple of Jerusalem (Daniel 9:27, Revelation 13:12). At the appointed time, the Lord Jesus Christ would destroy this *"Impostor"* with the breath of His Mouth (2 Thessalonians 2:8). The Lord would eventually cast the Son of Perdition and his followers into the lake of burning sulphur (Revelation 19:19-21). The Mother of all Deceptions would have taken place (Revelation 13:13-14). There would be wailing in the eternal hell fire.

This is the Pure Word - the ABSOLUTE TRUTH - which the Lord Jesus Christ has revealed to us in His Word – the Books of Daniel, Matthew and Revelation. The Lord says: "Heaven and earth shall pass away, but My Words shall not pass away" (Matthew 24:35). The day of reckoning is near. Let us share this message with our loved ones. Succeeding generations will bear witness of the schemes of the Great Deceiver. We must, therefore, help our children to recognise the "Beast with 7 heads and 10 horns" whenever he emerges from the "sea" (Revelation 13:1) and is enthroned by the ten powerful leaders of the Revived Roman Empire (Revelation 17:12-13).

We have learnt about the development and the fate of the European Union as foretold in Daniel 2:32-33, 40-45. I repeat: because of the accuracy of its prophecies, especially in chapter 11, the Book of Daniel has suffered hostile criticisms more than any other book of the Bible. Some theologians and philosophers and even bishops have described the Book of Daniel a literary fraud, which was written in the 2nd century BC after the events had already taken place. The Popular and the Reader's Editions of *The New Jerusalem Bible* and *The Good News Bible* have adopted this false position in their introduction to the Book of Daniel. In the next volume I will highlight the errors of the critics of Daniel that undermine the truthfulness of this precious Old Testament Book. Without any doubt, the Book of Daniel is a supernatural Book not an "edifying fiction" as suggested in the *The New Jerusalem Bible.*

The predictions concerning the development of the European Union, which have been outlined in the Book of Daniel, would be fulfilled just as how the prophetic revelation relating to the defeat of the Medo-Persian Empire by Alexander the Great, and his sudden death at the height of his power were all fulfilled to the letter (Daniel 7 & 8). The Prophetic message about the Revived Roman Empire – *The 10 toes partly of iron and partly of baked clay* (Daniel 2:31-33, 40-45) – will surely come to pass in the Precious Name of our Lord and Saviour Jesus Christ. Amen!

THE PROPHETIC VOICE OF SIR ROBERT ANDERSON

The Lisbon Treaty has created the influential position of EU President who would be a shadow of the powerful emperor of the European Empire. Whether this Treaty is adopted, revised or abandoned the Strong Man to lead Europe would still emerge to be crowned. I urge the reader to keep a close watch of the offices of the EU President and the EU High Representative with its international embassies so that you do not become a victim of the charisma and the guile of the coming cunning Emperor of the European Empire. He will be a 'super-hero' – a celebrity among celebrities. Newspapers, Television studios and Radio stations would fight to interview him.

The prophetic voice of Sir Robert Anderson about the European Union and its destiny is still vibrating since 1881: *"In forecasting the fulfilment of these....we are dealing with events which, while they may occur within the lifetime of living men, may yet be delayed for centuries...we may rest content with the certainty that...their fulfilment will be clear...to all who are capable of observing public facts...Through the gradual unfolding, it may be of influences even now in operation, or far more probably as the outcome of some great European crisis in the future...This confederation of (European) nations shall be developed and thus the stage will be prepared on which shall appear that awful Being, the great leader of men, in the eventful days which are to close the era of Gentile supremacy.....May we not indulge the hope that however far our nation may lapse in evil days to come from the high place which, with all her faults, she has held as the champion of freedom and of truth, she will be saved from the degradation of participating in the vile confederacy of the later days?"*

EUROPEAN UNION: "THE VILE CONFEDERACY OF THE LATTER DAYS"

Sir Robert Anderson's prophetic description of the "*vile*" character of political Europe was fulfilled just before Austria took over the EU presidency from Britain. On Friday December 30, 2005, a column in The Times read. *"Outrage as porn posters of the Queen 'promote' EU presidency….."* Within this column Roger Boyes reported: "PORNOGRAPHIC posters showing naked figures wearing masks portraying the Queen, President Chirac and President Bush …created fierce controversy in Austria on the eve of the country taking over the EU presidency from Britain….The George Bush figure is a woman model using the appropriate mask. She is seen bending over, with the Queen and President Chirac kneeling behind her. The Queen can be seen clutching up the hips of the George Bush character." The group sex scene was produced by a Spanish artist.

The second pornographic poster was by a Balkan artist. It depicted "a woman's spread thighs wearing blue knickers embroidered with the stars of Europe." The Austrian government financed the filthy posters with €1million (£680000) grant. According to this EU state, the degraded posters were part of an artistic project known as Europe-art, which was intended to promote interest in the European Union. Their "big idea" was that, a series of undressed figures in group sex scenes by artists from all member states of the European Union "would reflect the social and political diversity of the EU." What an "excellent idea" in our Age of Enlightenment.

That "Big-idea" (sexual images mounted on rotating boards in Austria) caused widespread protest. Even a tabloid newspaper *Krone Zeitung,* described the posters "Absolutely outrageous," and responded: "This will overshadow the beginning of our EU presidency." Gabi Burgstaller, governor of the Salzburg region, also commented on the poster which showed a "woman's spread thighs wearing blue knickers embroidered with the stars of Europe. He said, "The EU knickers are depraved and sexist and can only damage the European idea. However, an art critic, who helped to select the posters for the exhibition, hailed the pornographic posters with these words: "One could see the picture of the woman's crotch as an image that the EU is the new source of life for the world." Was this art expert sure of his comments? What "source of life" would the EU become? This was an exhibition of intellectual and moral bankruptcy.

EUROPEAN POLITICIANS ARE DESTITUDE OF IDEAS

We must ask the question: what was the purpose of the Austrian government exhibiting profane images that showed disrespect to the Queen of England and the Presidents of France and America? To stir up interest in the European Union for Austrians to subscribe to Jean Monnet's hazy vision of a federal Europe. The issue is: Austria is one of the most sceptical members of the European Union. The Austrian government was struggling to find ways of engaging the interest of its young people. Hence, the 'enlightened' EU state reached the 'wise' conclusion that the most effective way to influence the 'sceptics' in Austria and educate their "ignorant" youth about the European Construction was to catch their imagination with nude characters in group sex scene. What a "brilliant" idea from an EU presidency; and what an insult to the intelligence of the youth of Austria.

What have pornographic images of sex scenes got to do with raising awareness about European Union issues? For an EU presidency to use pornography as a tool to engage interest in Jean Monnet's project, demonstrates the plague of intellectual bankruptcy that has spread among the European Leaders. Had Austrian politicians examined what Sir Robert Anderson recorded about political Europe and its future, they would have known the actual purpose of European integration. This information would have helped them to educate Austrians about the European Union and its destiny. In other words, if the Austrian government seriously wanted to stir interest of its citizens in the European Union, its politicians should promote Sir Robert Anderson's *The Coming Prince.*

SEX SELLS IN POLITICS AND IN BUSINESS

The nude posters, which were sponsored by the Austrian government, were intended to be shown to European Union leaders when they visited Salzburg on January 27, 2006 for a conference entitled, "The Sound of Europe." But public disgust with the pornographic posters put pressure on the artists to remove the degraded images. The Austrian EU presidency, by financing pornographic posters as a means of generating interest in the European project, demonstrated the despicable character of Jean Monnet's project. And this, once again, fulfils Sir Robert Anderson's prophetic description of the nature of political Europe: "*The vile confederacy of the latter days.*" In our 'civilised' generation, sex sells in politics and in business. So, the Austrian Government adopted the "tried and tested marketing tool" to sell the European Union to Austrians. A boxing promoter once said, if it would take advertising naked women to fill a sports stadium for a boxing contest, he would employ such service.

A SEED PRODUCES ITS KIND

The depraved images of naked figures to promote interest in the European Union should not surprise us. For we know Europe was named after the Greek mythical Europa. The beautiful Europa rode naked on a beast that abducted her to a foreign land and seduced her. This beast was the Greek god Zeus. This imagery is commonly associated with the European Project. It is seen on the Greek 2 euro cents. And the Labour Government- blindly following the 'children' of Jean Monnet - incorporated the god Zeus in a form of a bull into the British identity cards. Did the Government really understand the significance of the EU symbol?

"SEDUCTION": DESPERATE SOLUTION TO SOLVE EU PROBLEMS

On 27 April 2006, the then 25 European Commissioners secretly met in Belgium to plan ways to "revitalise" the European Project and "define a positive agenda" for it. What was the plan? The Austria Foreign Minister, Hans Winkler, came up with a "brilliant" idea: "Seduction". This was the most excellent way to nurture a feeling for and an interest in Europe to discover its sensuous and cultural identity. And on Friday 28 April 2006, *The Times* reported the desperate move of European leaders in an article titled *EU tries seduction to rekindle voters' ardour.* Reporting from the European headquarters in Brussels, Anthony Browne stated: "As the European Union haemorrhage public support, the minds of top eurocrats are turning to seduction, and this time not just among themselves." The secret meeting was led by Austria which held the EU rotating presidency. Austria had been classified as the "most sexually satisfied nation on earth." So their idea was to sell "sex" to Europeans to rekindle love for Europe and its constitution which was then on a life-support machine.

According to the report, posters were planted in Vienna to promote Europe under a slogan "*Europe be inspired, Europe be seduced.*" Jiri Grusa, the president of International PEN Club...wrote an essay titled "Temptress Europe" to help stir interest in the campaign. According to his essay, "We owe Europe to a heavenly being from the time of the gods, when they took on a corporal form to seduce and make love to earthly maidens. Europe .....is the goddess of languages. She understands each and every one of us who understands her." This was a clear reference to the god Zeus who deceived and seduced *Europa*.

THE 'ABDUCTION OF EUROPA" RESTAGED:
The "Confession of a Rascal"

Is it not interesting and significant that' Jean Monnet, the "spiritual godfather" of the European Union,' the "first honorary citizen of Europe," and the "practical apostle of European unity," also "abducted" a woman to a foreign country for marriage? The Pride of France personally boasted of his 'notorious adventure' from France to Russia. In page 109 of his Memoirs, "Mister Europe" confesses his 'exploits': "It was an August evening in Paris, in 1929," says Monnet. "An Italian couple were among those having dinner with me. He was a businessman. That night, I saw his young wife for the first time. She was very beautiful. We forgot the other guests...I was forty years old, she was little more than twenty. We soon decided that we must be together for life. Many obstacles stood in the way. Silvia was married under Italian law, which forbade divorce. I looked into a number of solutions...I found that divorce and remarriage were possible under Soviet law. We decided on that as a solution. We met in Moscow on November 13, 1934, and everything went as simply as could be. Many years later Monseigneur Henri Donze, Bishop of Tarbes and Lourdes and a great friend of the family, married us in Lourdes itself" (Memoirs 1978). The "obstinate" Monnet had its way.

In pages 54 to 56 of Jean Monnet's Biography, Francois Duchene described in detail how Monnet schemed and took someone's wife. Duchene writes: "When Monnet left Shangai for the first time in July 1934....he was not simply returning to Europe and America, as he claimed, to complete his financial plans for China. His main interest in Moscow was to conduct perhaps the most important personal transaction of his life. This was to marry, on November 13, 1934, Silvia nee de Bondini, an Italian born in August 1907....." A lawyer, John J. McCloy, described Silvia as "the most beautiful" woman he had met. Duchene continued: "The difficulty was that the future Madame Monnet was married to someone else". Monnet met this married woman at a party in Paris in August 1929.

FROM EUROPE TO RUSSIA WITH LOVE: MONNET AND SILVIA

The fact is Jean Monnet had no shame for grabbing someone's wife. 'Mister Europe' openly declared that when he met the beautiful married Silvia at a dinner, "we forgot the other guests." According to Duchene, Silvia's husband, Francesco Giannini, who had married Silvia on 6 April 1929, was an employee of Monnet. Duchene added: "Divorce in the 1930s was a far cry from the routine affair it has since become. In Italy it was not recognised at all. Worse, Silvia and Francesco Gianni now had a daughter, Anna, born in April 1931." For five years (between August 1929 and November 1934) there was a long separation between Silvia and her husband. During this period, "Silvia Giannini and Jean Monnet tried and failed to secure an annulment of her marriage....Monnet finally planned his own marriage like a negotiation between great Powers. Monnet wanted the legitimacy of a big country behind his marriage. The couple could not marry in the United States because of residence qualifications." Duchene continued: "Monnet and his bride-to-be felt that divorce and marriage Reno-style lacked dignity. This left Moscow. Though Stalin's Moscow was a surprising venue", according to Duchene, "it had two signal advantages. It was possible, in Moscow, to obtain Russian citizenship and residence qualifications rapidly, and to divorce and remarry at once. "The actual divorce and wedding in Moscow were a lightning operation," said, Duchene. The Married Silvia Giannini, who had been staying in Switzerland with her mother and her Italian child, left for Moscow. "In a few days, she became a Soviet citizen. She then divorced without delay. That done, she and Monnet promptly married and left immediately for the United States and then proceeded to Shanghai in March 1935."

What a despicable episode surrounding the marriage of the first honorary citizen of Europe! Not every British citizen wants to become an 'adopted' child of the "smuggler" Jean Monnet. European citizenship cannot be imposed on Britons. European Citizenship, like all citizenship, should be acquired voluntarily not under compulsion.

TIME Magazine also provided additional insight into Monnet's adventure. In the 6 October 1961 edition of *TIME,* the American Magazine reported: "Monnet's personal life took an international turn. At a Paris dinner party ..., he met darkly handsome Silvia de Bondini, a painter and a wife of an Italian diplomat. Silvia soon left her husband; after 5 years of trying to obtain an Italian divorce, she was whisked to Moscow by Monnet, for quick Moscow divorce and wedding. The gay Gallic bachelor became a devoted family man." The couple had two daughters." Was this episode not a repetition of the mythical story which is illustrated on the Greek 2 Euro cents and seen outside the European Parliament?

It is interesting that the Continent of "Europe" derived its name from a fabled woman who was abducted by a pagan god. For the mythical Zeus whisked the beautiful *Europa* away to Crete. And Jean Monnet became the first "honorary citizen of Europe." In view of the 'sanctuary' Russia provided for Monnet to "successfully conduct" the most significant personal transaction in his career, it is clear the continent of Europe is 'indebted' to Russia for coming to the aid of their 'father' after America had 'rejected' him. It is therefore not surprising when President Nicholas Sarkozy, Jean Monnet's 'son', "joined Russia in condemning the Pentagon's plans to install missile defence bases in central Europe....and then backed President Dmitri Medvedev's previously ignored calls for a new pan-European security pact" (Source: The Guardian 15 November 2008 *Sarkozy backs Russian calls for pan-European security pact"*

Could Monnet's personal lifestyle be one of the reasons why Monnet and Schuman were not close associates as published in Monnet's biography? Unlike Monnet, Schuman was a "deeply religious" man. As a committed Christian he might, probably, have found it 'degrading' to be close to a man who had no scruples in 'stealing' someone's wife. Chancellor Konrad Adenauer described Schuman a "saint in business suit." And Jean Monnet himself applauded Schuman as an 'honest' politician whom "people will believe in whatever he says." Why were the Founding Fathers of European Community - Schuman and Monnet - not close? Was it Monnet's conduct - especially her marriage to a married woman -that pulled the 'deeply religious' Schuman away from him? Could this aspect of Monnet's life also be the reason why the Roman Catholic Church did not recommend him for sainthood, even though he was the master-brain behind the European Project? For Pope John Paul II put Robert Schuman on a fast track to sainthood for his contribution towards European unity despite the fact that Schuman only launched Monnet's plan for a united Europe.

I ask again: Why did the Roman Catholic Church fail to honour Jean Monnet? After all, he was also a Catholic. And he was the principal architect of European Construction and the "practical apostle of European unity" – a project the Catholic Church is passionate about. The Catholic Church itself has no shame in supporting the godless European Union. Was it not Pope Benedict XVI who pleaded with the Irish to adopt the anti-Christ Lisbon Treaty? The Church in Rome would repeat the history of the mythical Europa and Zeus as painted in Revelation 17.

Now let us return to how Austria's EU Presidency ended at the last European summit. The secret meeting concluded with an assignment for the European Commissioners "to find policies to rekindle enthusiasm for a Union whose original justification – cementing the peace after the Second World War - seems remote to most Europeans." The perplexing question is: after more than 50 years of its existence, European politicians are still searching for policies to revive interest in the legacy bequeath to them by their 'obstinate' father - Jean Monnet. The promotion of these big ideas: "Seduction of a naked woman by a pagan god" and "pornographic posters" to regenerate interest in the European Project - demonstrate how depraved and intellectually bankrupt the European Enterprise is. Sir Robert Anderson's prophetic description of the political alliance of European nations as "*the vile confederacy of the latter days*" has been fulfilled.

This is the European Union whose leading politicians and some of its citizens were proud to have seen God, the Lord Jesus Christ and Christianity removed from their proposed constitution. The Lord would not associate Himself with a project that uses pornographic materials to promote its cause. I repeat: God does not need the European Union. Yet, the Lord needs the *"Vile confederacy of the latter days"* to fulfil His prophetic word. The European Union is 'unfit for purpose'; yet the European Union is 'fit for purpose'. A word to the wise is enough. In the Appendix I will throw more light on the significance of the imagery which is illustrated on the Greek 2 Euro cents.

THE HYPOCRISY OF THE "VILE CONFEDERACY OF THE LATTER DAYS"

The bureaucrats in Brussels, in their zeal to prevent the so-called Global Warming that 'threatens' human existence, threatened to take legal action against car manufacturers who failed to cut carbon dioxide emissions. In an article titled *EU threat to legislate on reduced car exhaust emissions,* The Times Correspondent reported: "Herr Verheugen and Stavros Dimas, the Environment Commissioners, gave warning that if the sector did not honour its commitments, they would consider tabling legislation forcing car makers to meet target" (*The Times,* Wednesday 30 August 2006). Few days after this threat to car manufactures, the bureaucrats in Brussels were exposed of hypocrisy.

The EU's double standards were laid bare by a Member of the European Parliament. This was reported in the 8 September 2006 issue of the *Daily Mail* in an article titled *"The dirty secret of the Brussels limos."* According to a report published on 7 September 2006, the European Commission admitted that the limousines used by EU staff "create twice as much pollution as the limits Brussels is forcing on car makers." The report indicated that the EU Commission threatened to impose legislation to reduce carbon dioxide emission in new cars to 120 grammes per kilometre by 2013. However, the 85 vehicles used by the Commissioners and other senior staff produce more than 258 grammes. This information was brought to light by Mr Chris Davies, the environment spokesman for the Liberal Democrat Party in the European Parliament. Mr Davies said: "It's all deeply embarrassing. It is no longer acceptable for Brussels to insist that people should do as we say rather than do as we do. It is time we practised what we preach." It was the same Chris Davies who, in February 2008, exposed corruption among some members of the European Parliament. They claimed fictitious expenses for assistants and pocketed the money. What credibility has the European Union got to impose laws and penalties on car manufacturers who break their environmental laws? Is the European Union 'fit for purpose'?

The hypocritical and despicable character of the European project was once again exposed to fulfil the prophetic word of Sir Robert Anderson about political Europe. We recall that the European Parliament demanded the sacking of Rocco Bottiglione, a distinguished Catholic moral philosopher, when he expressed his Christian view: homosexuality is a sin. Despite his plea that he would not allow his religious inclination to influence his position as Commissioner for Justice, the Members of the European Parliament voted for his expulsion. The European leaders did not defend the Christian. Yet, when the same Members of the European Parliament demanded that the Union's offices in Strasbourg should be removed to Brussels to save money, the leaders of Europe rejected the demand. Because of national economic interest, Austria, which was then holding the EU Presidency, took the lead to block the democratic request of the EU Parliament.

This case was reported in the 25 May 2006 edition of the Financial Times. In an article captioned *Austria stifles debate on EU parliament,* the Brussels Correspondent wrote: Strasbourg's role as the hugely expensive second home of the European Parliament is ....to survive unscathed at a European summit. According to the report, the Austrian host of the summit warned that he would not allow "any debate on Strasbourg's future in spite of growing pressure from members of the European Parliament to move all their work to Brussels." Even a member of the European Parliament was warned by the Austrian chancellor that it "would be stupid to create a fuss on the subject." The "waste of money" issue the parliamentarian wanted to raise was not negotiable. It is something that could not be changed.

Was this episode a demonstration of true European democracy, or an exhibition of dictatorship? This is the two-faced European Union which claimed that it would have been an "absurdity" and a "serious mistake" to have mentioned God in the rejected European Constitution. This is a document which European leaders repackaged it with a "cosmetic surgery" and offered the "face-lift" to the "ignorant" citizens of Europe, Britain and Ireland. Demonstrating his contempt for democracy, the architect of the European Constitution," Mr Giscard d'Estaing, in an interview with the Financial Times, suggested that the people of France and the Netherlands should be given another chance to vote again with the hope that they would change their minds to adopt the failed constitution. His justification for a second referendum in France was that: "It is not France that has said no. It is 55 percent of the French people – 45 percent of the French people said yes." A second referendum was not necessary in France as President Sarkozy imposed the so-called new EU Treaty on the French people.

I would raise a question: had the 55 percent of the French voted "Yes" to accept the Constitution, would the "Father of the Constitution" have suggested a second referendum to allow the 45 percent to vote again? Definitely NOT! He would have rejoiced singing: "The French people have clearly spoken to adopt the Blue-print of Europe. This is a historic day – a new dawn for *Europa* – the beautiful Princess. We are in the fast lane; we are leaving the foot-draggers behind" – a possible swipe at the "foot-dragger" Britain. In any case European leaders had their chance to impose the corrupt EU treaty on the hapless Europeans and Britons. The reality is that, the European Union is a dictatorship - paving the way for the 'Tyrant' of all Tyrants to rule Europe and the world with an iron fist.

EUROPEAN TAX

Another big idea put forward by the Austrian EU presidency was the proposal for all the citizens of the European Union to pay a new tax to Brussels. A column in the 2 January 2006 edition of the *Daily Mail* read *Austria demands Euro tax to pay for Brussels.* According to the report, controversial plans to impose a tax burden on the citizens of Europe were proposed by the Austrian EU presidency. The Correspondent, Graeme Wilson, stated: "Proposals for an EU-wide tax were given new life by Austria....Austrian President Heinz Fischer gave his backing to the idea, though conceded it would face fierce opposition from countries like Britain." The President claimed there were good reasons for this idea. He told BBC Radio 4's World This Weekend programme, "If the EU had its own revenue, it would be easier to negotiate its budget and therefore I support the idea and we shall see how successful the idea will be". He cited the difficult negotiations that lead to the Budget deal for 2007 – 2013 as a justification to introduce the Euro tax to finance the construction of the corrupt European project.

The Austrian's Presidency also suggested other sources of tax revenue to finance the 'vile' EU. On Thursday January 19, 2006, an article with the title "Outcry over call for EU tax that will hit the City" appeared in the Daily Mail. Within this article, the political correspondent reported that the Austrian Chancellor, Wolgang Schuuessel, told members of the European Parliament that the budget for the European Union should be financed by "charges on international air travel and currency transactions." According to the report, this proposal was condemned by the British Treasury and the Financial Community in London, because "it would be disastrous for the City with business forced away from London to New York and the Far East." The consequence for such a tax would be an increase in air tickets which could affect holiday makers.

A Treasury spokesman responded to this tax proposal, which had the support of the EU Chief, by saying, "This would undermine the democratic legitimacy of public revenues, which can only come from scrutiny by national parliaments and through member states' control over tax decisions." And the then Shadow Europe Minister, Graham Brady, also responded: "The idea of EU taxes is completely unacceptable to the British people. This tax would be bad for the world economy as a whole. It would be particularly damaging for London and other British financial centers like Edinburgh, which would simply see their businesses move to New York or Tokyo. This is an ill-thought-through idea." Gary Titley, leader of the Labour MEP's, said: "A European tax is not acceptable...." And Matthew Elliot, chief executive of the Taxpayer's Alliance, also added his voice: "We've seen council tax rises, numerous stealth taxes, and now there's a threat we'll be forced to hand over more tax to politicians in Brussels. An EU tax would be bad for the British economy and an unacceptable burden on ordinary families."

Despite the financial mismanagement in Brussels that has resulted in their accounts not being approved for 14 consecutive years, the European Parliament planned to impose taxes on Europeans, the result of which could force British taxpayers paying more to the coffers of "That Thing" in Brussels. Kirsty Buchanan reported this plot in the 31 December 2006 edition of the *Sunday Express*. In a column titled "*Now EU wants a £510 income tax,*" the Deputy Political Editor wrote: "Brussels politicians have drawn up proposals to create a European income tax which would leave Britons shelling "£510 a year to the superstate." The idea behind this proposal on "personal and corporate tax was for Brussels not to rely much on national contributions to EU budget.

Commenting on this source of additional revenue to the treasury of Brussels, the UK Independence Party reminded the British public that they face a threat of a Brussels tax on their pay packets on top of ordinary tax. The Treasury pays a net £6billion a year to the European Union. John Whitaker of UKIP warned: "British taxpayers are already paying through the nose to fund the EU, the last thing they need is yet another tax. The EU is not directly accountable to the people of this country. To give these unelected bureaucrats power over tax is a massive step in the wrong direction. Most people see the EU wasting money left, right and centre. The last thing we need is them having more to pour down the drain. What economic sense is it that the £37.73billion or 49% of the EU budget is spent on farming which contributes less than 6% to the income of the EU?" Is this not "vile"? The EU benefits the political elite and not the voters. The corrupt EU exists to cater for the interest of the rich. But this would not go on indefinitely.

I repeat:
EU is Extremely Useful to the Political elites who Manage the Project.
EU is Extremely Useless to the People who Subsidise the Project

I ask the question: "What is the justification for the European Union to impose tax on Europeans whereas the European Court of Auditors has for the past 14 consecutive years failed to approve the European Union's Accounts because of fraud and errors?" On Monday, 4 November ***2005***, it was reported in the *Daily Mail* that, "The European Court of Auditors has consistently argued that it cannot approve the budget (then) standing at £68 billion a year, because there were insufficient controls over how a large part of the money was spent." The newspaper added. "The auditors have for the past decade raised questions regarding the spending of around 90 per cent of the entire EU budget. Poor control over transfers from Brussels to national capitals is at the heart of the problem." The situation prompted a comment from Gawain Towler, spokesman for the UK Independence Party: "Time and time again, we hear about fraud from the EU's Common Agricultural Policy budget. We are still not sure where this money goes. At least the court of auditors, which is perhaps the only honest EU institution, has the guts to say this." This information was published in a column headlined: "Auditors blast EU's lost billions."

Why, in spite of all the financial mismanagement in the EU, which has resulted in the lost of billions that could not be accounted for, should the Austrian Presidency propose that Europeans should pay tax to finance corruption? Not surprisingly, some Members of European Parliament were exposed as 'fraud.' On 21 February 2008, it was reported in British national papers how MEPs ripped off up to £100million from the European Parliament in fiddled expenses. It was a Liberal Democrat MEP, Chris Davies, who exposed the corrupt practices at the 'Euro Rubber-Stamp Factory' when he saw a secret report into a random audit at the EU Parliament. He examined the report under surveillance and refused to sign any confidential agreement preventing him to make his discovery public. Some MEPs claimed allowances for fictitious staff. One of them paid a "Christmas bonus" of 19 times an assistant's monthly salary. Some MEPs pocketed a £130000 allowances for employing assistants they never hired. Others hired low-paid secretaries and kept the rest of the money. This corruption at the heart of the European project prompted Matthew Elliot, director of the Taxpayers' Alliance, to declare: "MEPs pilfering our money like this is completely unacceptable."

I would encourage you to read Matthew Elliot and David Craig's book *The Great European Rip-off – How the corrupt, Wasteful EU is taking control of our lives.* This fascinating book will open your eyes on how the whole EU project is plagued with corruption, hypocrisy, incompetence and moral bankruptcy. You will learn that some Members of European Parliament spend some of their lavish allowances on prostitutes. In chapter 10, *The cradle of corruption*? the authors write: "...becoming an MEP is almost like being given a licence to fill your pockets at the taxpayers' expense. Claiming attendance allowances for meetings that MEPs don't attend, taking cash to pay employees who don't exist, making huge profits from over-generous travel allowances, dishonestly filling up your pension fund with taxpayers' money - all these appear to be accepted and even encouraged practices at the thoroughly discredited European parliament."

The "incompetent" European institutions have no moral credibility to impose taxes on Europeans and Britons. Yet, the pompous European politicians claimed it would have been "absurd," a "serious mistake" and "divisive" to have mentioned God and Christianity in their European Constitution. But is it not rather a gross absurdity, a serious mistake and divisive, for undemocratic institutions in Brussels, whose accounting practices are riddled with fraud and error, and who are not accountable even to the people they represent, to have rather contemplated imposing tax burden on the British people, to finance European projects riddled with fraud? We, Britons, hold our allegiance to our Queen and democratically elected politicians in the House of Commons. Sadly, since 1973 'selfish' British politicians have been transferring the sovereign rights of Britons to strangers in Brussels who are not accountable to Britons.

How ridiculous it was, that the same unaccountable bureaucrats in Brussels wanted to confront the then British Exchequer, Gordon Brown, (now europhile Prime Minister) over supposedly failure to comply with public borrowing rule (Financial Times Friday 6 January 2006), and how our Finance Minister had "failed to protect a million Equitable Life Policies" (The Times Monday 13 January 2006). Whatever the lapses of the British Chancellor, the bureaucrats in Brussels have no financial credibility whatsoever to investigate the failings of our Chancellor. Britain is a sovereign nation. It does not need strangers in Europe to interfere with its economic and political affairs. Unfortunately, due to the folly of 'selfish' politicians Great Britain has become accountable to unaccountable aliens in Brussels. What an irony! Brussels should concentrate on eradicating fraud and errors in its accounting practices.

It is now clear Gordon Brown has responded to Brussels' advice to become a 'team-player' to promote that abominable 'thing' in Brussels by imposing the Lisbon Treaty on Britons. For, before Gordon Brown took the keys to No 10 Downing Street, the EU Commission President warned him that when he becomes the Prime Minister and is eventually elevated to the EU High Table, he should abide by the "rules of the club." This was reported in the 6 July 2006 Edition of The Daily Telegraph. In a column headlined *"EU chief warns Brown to accept the 'club rules,"* the Chief Political Correspondent, Toby Helm, writes: "Jose Manuel Barroso..... fires a warning shot at the Chancellor saying that he must learn to behave like a team player if he is to have influence in Brussels as the next prime minister." According to the report, the President of the European Commission "argues that ....Mr Brown has not been one of the EU's big players - even at finance minister level - because of Britain's refusal to join the euro. This has left him in the outer circle of finance ministers....rather in the inner core of 12 euro group ministers whose countries have joined the single currency."

BRITONS DON'T NEED THE EURO

Brussels have taken Europeans for granted for too long. Great Britain and Ireland are 'unique' among the member-nations of the European Union. We must isolate ourselves from the corrupt EU. It was our brilliant 'Father', Sir Robert Anderson, who wrote about European integration: how it would develop from an European crisis, its character and future prospects before the 'rascal' Monnet – the 'hero' of Europe – was born. Britain should NOT join the Euro club for Britons to become "slaves" in Jean Monnet's 'slave market' in Brussels. Why should Britons remain in a "club" whose accounts have not been audited for over 14 years because they are riddled with fraud and error? After all, how well-informed is Jose Manuel

Barroso on the significance of European integration and its destiny to lecture Britons about Jean Monnet's vision of a united Europe. What right has Barroso, the "Buffoon of Brussels," got to insult Britons that the "people who matter" in Britain are the 'selfish' and unprincipled politicians who have vested interest in the corrupt European Project? Brussels matters to Barroso where his bread is buttered. Barroso's Eurozone does not matter to Britons.

The Eurozone may be a 'paradise.' In reality it is a zone of utter darkness. Shadow Chancellor George Oborne was hundred per cent right when he attacked Labour's 'euro-fanatics,' led by Peter Mandelson, and pledged the Conservative Party will never take Britain into the European single currency. Peter Oborne rightly stated it would be "suicidal" for Labour politicians to take Britain into the euro. In his essay, *"Mandy's scheming chums and their suicidal plot to take us into the euro,* Mr Oborne outlined many reasons why Britain should not join the European Single Currency. He writes: "...While the euro has certainly created some benefits for member countries, such as the abolition of currency transaction, these have been outweighed by one fundamental flaw: nations in the eurozone are forced to have the same interest rate regardless of their individual economic circumstances." He explained how interest rates have been manipulated to suit the German economy to the detriment of other nations including Ireland, France, Spain and Italy (Daily Mail 6 December 2008). Again, in his essay *"The pound may be in trouble but don't be fooled by the euro gloaters. Their bogus currency will never see its 20th birthday,* Mr Oborne explained how suicidal it would have been for the British economy during the 2008 recession, had Britain followed Tony Blair's enthusiasm for the euro and entered the eurozone (Daily Mail 2 January 2009).

I am not an economist, but common sense tells me you cannot apply the same interest rates in different countries with different economic and social priorities. The European single currency was a political not an economic project. Whatever the merits of the euro, the fact is the future of the European Union is VERY DARK. I repeat: the eurozone is a 'Pit of Utter Darkness.' Sir Robert Anderson has already warned Britain would not be saved in a political Europe. Which expert warned Britain of the 2007-2008 financial crisis? Would British politicians ignore the warning from the Secret Service Agent at Scotland Yard and remain in the European Union? After all, Germany and France use the European Union as a tool to serve their national interests. This was evident in Charles Grant's article, "*Unilateral Germany threatens to weaken Europe*" (Financial Times 15 December 2008).

If beef-eaters wanted to patronise a club which uses pornographic posters and film to stir interest in its activities so be it. It is no honour to sit at the high table of such beef-eaters club – a club, which, under normal business law, should have been struck off from the Register of Companies for failure to submit professionally audited Accounts for several years. Why should Britain join the euro and pay homage to a naked woman riding at the back of Zeus - a pagan god? (Revelation 17) Why should Great Britain join the euro and "visit" the amphitheatre where thousands of innocent souls and animals were slaughtered for fun?

The Colloseum, which is the portrait on the Italian 5 Euro cents, was inaugurated by Titus Vespasian. It was this Roman Prince who, in AD 70, led the Romans to destroy the Temple of God in Jerusalem. Prince Titus was a shadow of the powerful Emperor of the European Empire who is about to enter the political arena to 'save' Europe and bring 'peace' into the Middle East. The Lisbon Treaty has paved the way for the coronation of the King of Men.

The British people do not need financial lessons from the European Union that lacks financial discipline. At the end of a two day summit in June 2006, which ended Austria's 6 month rotating Presidency, the political leaders could not determine the future direction of their project. The summit was reported in the 17 and 18 June 2006 editions of the Financial Times. In an article titled "Europe summiteers duck the big issues," it was reported that the leaders "poured gallons of fudge" over the "biggest issues facing the then 25- member- club". The fact is "Fudge", "corruption" and "bullying" are the trade marks of EU. They are written in EU's DNA.

THE ARROGANCE IN BRUSSELS AND EUROPHILE POLITICIANS

In their meeting to find ways of making the European Union a credible Enterprise, the summit ducked the major issues confronting the Union namely, the then rejected European Constitution and the enlargement of the Union – especially Turkey's prospective membership. The host of the summit suggested which parts of the dumped constitution should be salvaged from the wreckage.

The Blue-print of Europe was initially hailed by the leaders of Europe as the beacon of light for Europe and the world. Why should parts of the discredited constitution be salvaged from the wreckage? In this same summit which was chaired by Austria, Tony Blair acknowledged that the European Union needed "a new set of values" to stop it grinding to a halt with 27 or more members. So, the host of the EU Summit, Wolfgang Schssel, suggested that the "Period of reflection", which was imposed after two of the EU founding members rejected the Constitution for Europe, should be extended. This would give them time to determine which sections of the Blue-print could be adopted – still without seeking the approval of those who rejected the constitution.

No wonder Nicolas Sarkozy, the then interior minister of France, in outlining his vision for Europe, suggested that "key elements of the failed constitution should be pushed through without a referendum. In his wisdom, Sarkozy "believed politicians in many countries could gain mandate to approve a slimmed down treaty through national parliaments rather than plebiscite. Sarkozy's ambition included long term powers for the European Commission President to select his team of commissioners of an advanced guard of countries to forge closer integration in key areas (Source: The Independent 9 September 2006- *Sarkozy outlines vision for radical EU reform)*. Is this democracy or autocracy?

The former Minister of Europe, Denis MacShane, was sympathetic to Sarkozy's short-sighted and autocratic view, that it is only Parliament that can decide the fate of Britons in the European Union. Mr MacShane, in his article, "*Europe: the issue that dare not speak its name*", tells us: "Sarkozy wants France to have a French commissioner in Brussels, but for this to happen a new treaty in 2009 will be needed." The Labour politician then went on to create the impression that if Britain did not get its act together and join the "herd" in the fast lane to the 'slaughter house,' "we risk being left behind to the ideas shaped in other EU capitals." This echoed the popular song of Europhiles: "Britons risk isolation in Europe because of their eurosceptism."

I would say: "It is not always safe to drive a fast car in a fast lane, particularly when drivers with fast cars in the "fast lane" are racing into a ditch they cannot see." It is sometimes sensible to withdraw from the "fast lane" to the "slow lane" to reach safely. Britain should not follow the "herd" to the slaughter house. I repeat: before the founding fathers of 'Cosmopolitan Europe' - Jean Monnet and Robert Schuman - were conceived, our "father," Sir Robert Anderson, warned it would be degradation for Britain to participate in "the vile (European) confederacy of the latter days."

According to Mr MacShane, the German Chancellor contemplated breathing life into the rejected constitution by considering adding "a reference to Christianity to please the Pope (The Independent 26 September 2006). This was a misguided approach. Whether Christianity were to have been mentioned in the European Constitution or not, to please or displease the Pope (the so-called "Vicar of Christ" who does not understand the significance of European integration), it would have made no difference to the character and destiny of the European Union. The Pope's support for the European Union is irrelevant save to those who blindly follow the Pope and subscribe to the Catholic Church's enthusiasm for the European project. As I have already mentioned, the European Union is NOT a Christian Club; the European Union has NEVER been a Christian Club, the European Union will never qualify to be a Christian Club. The Lord Jesus Christ does NOT need the European Union to promote His Gospel. Yet, the Lord needs the European Union for His own purpose which the 'blind' European leaders have no clue. It is time politicians and political commentators stopped associating that

'Vile Thing' in Europe with Christianity.

On the issue of reviving the 'corpse' (the European Constitution which was rejected by the French and the Dutch in 2005), Lord Chris Patten suggested that the dumped constitution could not be "revived in its present form." Having been invited by Romano Prodi, the then Italian Prime Minister, to join the 12-strong international Group of wise men to find an alternative to the rejected European Constitution, Lord Patten suggested that national Parliaments should have "an enhanced role." He then qualified his suggestion by saying, "He did not think a referendum would be necessary in Britain on constitution's successor." According to Lord Patten, he is "a strong opponent of referendums, in principle, which undermine Parliament...That said, any change in EU should be subject to debate." (The Times 22 September 2006).

I do not share Lord Patten's view. To begin with: politicians do not hold monopoly of scholarship on European integration. And the plain fact is that most politicians are not well-informed on the significance of "Jean Monnet's gradualist vision of European unity" which, according to Jose Manuel Barroso, "still serves as the blue-print for European integration today." Therefore, a debate on European Constitution, or any document that transfers powers from the British Parliament to foreigners should be followed by a referendum for the people to decide whether they prefer to be governed by laws enacted by unelected and unaccountable officials in Brussels. The British people elected members of Parliament to preserve their sovereignty. The British Parliament, therefore, exists for the interest of the British people not for the few greedy Politicians who have vested interests in the European Project. So, politicians have no right to surrender the sovereign rights of the people who feed them to strangers. It would be a "theft of democracy" for politicians to transfer powers that don't belong to them to the 'children' of Jean Monnet and Konrad Adenauer in Europe.

GERMAN EU PRESIDENCY IN 2007

When Germany took over the EU Presidency on 1 January 2007, one of its major goals was to plot and impose the rejected European Constitution on countries that have not voted for or against it. First, the German Foreign minister, Frank-Walter Stenmeier, commenting on the discarded Constitution, said: "The German EU presidency in 2007 intends to help make the EU more future-oriented.......With regard to the constitution we aim to restart process after a two-year period of reflection. The German Ambassador to Britain supported his compatriot: "We want to preserve significant portions of the document without a second referendum process." This was sheer arrogance. Why no referendum? Because, politicians are scared of the people who feed them.

The German Chancellor, Angela Merkel, confirmed the diabolical plan to impose the European Constitution on Europeans in her interview with the Financial Times. In her desire to 'pick' the Constitution from the "rubbish bin," "Princess Europa" remarked: "Of course we must respect the No vote in the French referendum. But the German presidency will not approach this from a minimalist position. There are also 18 countries that have already ratified the treaty and a few more countries that take a very positive attitude. We cannot simply ignore that fact. According to the report the German Chancellor did not like the term "mini-treaty" coined by the French politician, Nicolas Sarkozy (Financial Times 3 January 2007)

Majority of the EU countries might have endorsed the Treaty, as suggested by Angela Merkel. But the question is: did all the countries allow their citizens to vote on a document that would govern their lives –a document that was produced by political elites they had not elected and are not accountable to them? The truth is that the Lisbon Treaty was not democratically approved. It was 'Self-Centred' politicians who forced it on their citizens – treating them with contempt as if they, the politicians, know everything about European integration. The German government forced the constitution on the Germans just as how the Euro was forced on them. Now some Germans are crying for their beloved deutschmark. They don't want the Euro. When some Germans challenged the Lisbon Treaty in court, the Judges expressed a sceptical view of the document. Judge Di Fabio stated: "One has to look at things soberly: How much power does the Bundestag (*Germany's federal parliament*) still have?" A second Judge, Rudolf Mellinghoff, said he didn't really understand how Germany's parliament would benefit from handing over competencies to the European Union. The court had the view that the Lisbon Treaty would allow the EU to have a say in German criminal law. In the end the German Court ruled that the Lisbon Treaty is compatible with the German constitution.

EUROPEAN UNION LEADERS ARE 'DESPOTS'

There were rules governing the adoption of the European Constitution. For it to become enforceable, all the 27 member countries of the European Union must approve it in their Parliaments or by a popular vote in a referendum. In 2005, The French and the Netherlands rejected the European Constitution. It should have been abandoned. The arrogant politicians don't accept 'No' for answer. They 'know better' than the people who feed them. So, irrespective of the democratic decisions of the masses, politicians would ignore them in so far as such decisions do not suit their selfish agenda. If politicians believed in true democracy, and if they believed the European Constitution would be a good thing for Europeans why were they scared to give voters the opportunity to decide on its merits in a referendum, but decided to force it on them. The European Union leaders have

10, 2006). The copious legislations from Brussels that have drowned the British people confirm the words of Lord Denning, the Master of the Rolls: "No longer is European Law an incoming tide flowing up the estuaries of England. It is now like a tidal wave bringing down our sea walls and flowing inland over fields and houses, to the dismay of us all."

The noble Lord, Lord Campbell of Alloway, referred to a speech Lord Denning made in the House of Lords on 31 July 1986 about how much powers have been transferred from British Parliament to the European Court of Justice: "Acts of Parliament and decisions of our courts have been set aside and rendered invalid by decisions of the European Court, which is superior in all matters of EEC law not only to British Courts, including the House of Lords, but also to Parliament where their Acts past, present or future have been, can be and will be declared illegal by an overweening court sitting in a foreign capital. As we proceed with the completion of the internal market the powers and decisions of this supranational court will impinge more and more on every aspect of our national life, social, legal, political, business, labour, economic and, indeed, on our relations with countries in the rest of the world outside the EEC. Business and individuals will find themselves, unwittingly, breaking laws of which they have no knowledge and which have been made, not by their own Parliament in public, but by the institutions of the EEC meeting in private, probably after wheeling and dealing in secret". (Extract from Hansard Column 153-154 House of Lords Debate: European Union (Amendment) Bill - 29.4.08

Gunter Verheugen, the EU's Enterprise Commissioner, admitted that he was not succeeding in his drive to simplify EU laws. The Commissioner blamed some senior officials in Brussels for the failure. In an interview with the Financial Times, which was reported in an article titled *Uphill battle against Brussels bureaucracy,* Mr. Verheugen disclosed that some senior bureaucrats in Brussels had not adapted to "a new political culture." He says, "There is a view that the more regulations you have, the more rules you have, the more Europe you have. I don't share that view." According to the article, Mr Verheugen's criticism of Brussels bureaucracy incurred the wrath of many of the bureaucrats in Brussels to the extent that the president of the FFPE staff union demanded his apology or resignation. The Commissioner dismissed the call for his resignation. Is this an exhibition of democracy or autocracy? Where is the freedom of speech? Brussels does not want to be accused and criticised; yet, Brussels is blended with the terms of accusation and criticism.

EU: DECEIT AND LIES

In the 11 April 2008 edition of Daily Express, Frederick Forsyth summarised the 'vile' character of the European Union. In his article, *EU made by deceit and lies,* the Columnist mentioned three former EU leaders who were involved in financial scandals. He went on: "This is just the tip of the iceberg. The most EU-integrationist country in Europe, Belgium, has literally lost count of its corrupt politicians." Mr Forsyth then referred to Jean Monnet's scandalous idea of bringing his fuzzy vision of a fused Europe into reality. According to Monnet: "Europe's nation should be guided towards the superstate without their people understanding what is happening. This can be accompanied by successive steps, each disguised as having an economic purpose but which will eventually and irreversibly lead to federation." In Monnet's view the masses would be stupid to appreciate the deceit perpetrated on them. So, they should be tricked to sign away their freedom to unelected and accountable few to rule over them – a government by deceit." Mr. Forsyth continued: "The trouble is, once you adopt and legitimise government by trickery and deceit, corruption in public life follows as night does day."

A seed produces its kind. The "children" of Jean Monnet adopted their father's 'spirit of trickery" on the masses. They designed the Lisbon Treaty to 'steal' the sovereign rights of Europeans. The Columnist concluded: "Since 1997 the British people have been governed by trickery and deceit – and with intent. The culminating shames have been going to war tricked by a tissue of lies and selling our country into the Lisbon Treaty on the basis of yet more lies. This has been done by an army of MPs and peers, half still stupid and gullible...but the other half bought and paid for. And they affect the Union flag even as they betray it."

EU: THE "MONSTER" FROM THE "EUROPEAN SEA"

The European Project has become a burden on Britons. I don't need to list the sea of regulations and laws that have strangled us. An example is the "Recycling Fiasco" – the growing mountain of paper waste in Britain which was the result of EU landfill regulation. (The Mail on Sunday 4 January 2009). "The EU's red tape ties our hands again", was The Mail's leading article on the problem caused by busy-bodies in Brussels. The European Project has become a "monster" that frightens British politicians. Andrew Grice writes: "Europe is the sleeping giant of British politics. It often suits our leaders not to talk about it. Just when they think the issue is dead, a monster awakes, goes on the rampage, divides their parties and damages them in the eyes of the voters" (The Independent 17 June 2006). British politicians would have killed this 'monster,' ages ago, had they wielded the 'sword' the Knight Commander (of the order) of Bath provided in 1881 before this 'monster' evolved from the wreckage of the Second World War.

From what we have learnt about the European Union and its obsession of imposing penal rules and regulations on Britons, it is clear Sir Robert Anderson's description of the character of political Europe has been fulfilled. The Secret Service

Agent, the Prince of Scotland Yard, warned Britain would degrade herself by participating in a political alliance of European nations. The Prince of detectives described this political union the "vile confederacy of the latter days." Sir Winston Churchill, unconsciously, echoed the prophetic voice of The Knight Commander of (the Order of) Bath when he declared: "I love France and Belgium, but we must not allow ourselves to be pulled down to that level." Britain does NOT need the European Union to survive. If British politicians want to become 'adopted sons' and 'daughters' of Jean Monnet and Konrad Adenauer, they can either renounce their British citizenship and become French or German citizens, or obtain dual citizenship. They cannot force all Britons to become "children" of strangers in Europe. European citizenship cannot be imposed on Britons. It must be obtained voluntarily, not under compulsion or through trickery. Britons are not the property of politicians.

THE MISGUIDED POLITICAL ELITES IN BRUSSELS

The busy-bodies in Brussels have the impression that the more laws and regulations they impose on Europeans to choke them, the more closer they are in achieving their ultimate aim - the creation of a United States of Europe with a President in Brussels. The EU Enterprise Commissioner rightly described the misguided mission in Brussels: "There is a view that the more regulations you have, the more rules you have, the more Europe you have."

Because of superficial knowledge about the root of the European Union, the political elite in Brussels are blinded from perceiving what the future holds for their Enterprise. The Oxford Professor, Timothy Garton-Ash, confirmed this plight of the European project when he wrote about EU membership of Bulgaria and Romania. In his article, *Today's European Union is 27 states in search of a story,* he writes: "Everyone knows that, beneath the surface, political Europe is not in a party mood about itself. The Community is morose, ill-tempered and uncertain of its future direction. Individually, most Europeans live better than before, but collectively they don't feel good about their voluntary empire. Rarely has such a successful enterprise been so plagued with self-doubt" (The Guardian 4 January 2007).

The more Brussels attempt to make their "ever closer union" a reality, the more the *"ten toes"* invite the *"Stone"* to roll over them. In other words, in their zeal to create a federal Europe, the unaccountable officials in Brussels are preparing the ground for the *"Stone cut without human hands"* to strike the *"toes of baked clay and iron"* of the human statue to close the era of Gentile supremacy on earth. It was this fate of the revived Roman Empire that prompted Sir Robert Anderson to declare in 1881, that a political alliance of European nations would be the next major political feature in history after the restoration of the Jews to Palestine. And this European confederacy would welcome a charismatic man to lead it. And this 'political genius' would prove to be an "awful Being."

Question: Who is this "awful Being"? It is the King of Men who will plunge Europe and the rest of the world into the crisis of all crisis. I repeat: the Lisbon Treaty has paved the way for his advent. Had Gordon Brown known this truth, he would not have patronised European leaders that he was 'privileged' to sign the Lisbon Treaty. He would not have praised pompous European Commission President, Jose Manuel Barroso, that he was doing a "brilliant job". What kind of job? Is it the dragging of Britons to board Monnet's *Titanic* which is heading towards an 'ice-berg'?

Chapter 21

WHO IS IGNORANT ABOUT EUROPEAN INTEGRATION?

"We refuse to surrender Holy writ to the tender mercies of those who approach it with the ignorance of pagans and the animus of apostates" **(RA)**

Political commentators and most European politicians claim, "Poll after poll has shown the British have a greater level of ignorance and far greater level of hostility of all things about EU than any member states of the Union." On the issue of the supposedly "British ignorance" about the EU project, this writer, who is a British citizen, asks the following questions:

- How many of the political commentators and European politicians, who accuse Britons of "ignorance" about anything to do with the European Enterprise, knew of the crucial advice the first President of the European Parliament offered to Europeans concerning the survival of the European Enterprise?
- Which of the EU experts knew that before Britain and Ireland joined the European Economic Community in 1973, a British public servant, who was an Irishman, had already predicted over 90 years ahead that England would be a member of a confederation of European nations?
- Which European politician and political commentator knew that before the Founding Fathers of the European Union, Jean Monnet and Robert Schuman, were, born in 1888 and 1886, a Detective had already written that a "confederation of European nations" would certainly be developed through a great European crisis, and that Austria, Belgium, France, Germany, Greece, Italy, Portugal, Spain, and Turkey would become members of this confederacy? Is it not fair to suggest that the Irishman, who predicted the development of a political union of European nations and its character, also knew of the purpose of this political union and its future?

'LUXURIOUS CARGO'

I have already mentioned that the Lisbon Treaty, signed on 13 December 2007 in Portugal, has created the environment for the "Seer of Dublin's" prediction of the future of Europe to be fulfilled. It is time politicians and the commentators who are not properly informed on the significance of Jean Monnet's vision of a united (federal) Europe, stopped labelling the British people 'ignorant' about EU. After all, what is special about EU? It is a 'corrupt corporation' on the verge of 'bankruptcy.' For the European Enterprise is morally and intellectually and spiritually bankrupt. All its so-called 'achievements' namely, Enlargement, the Single Currency (the Euro), the Common Agricultural and Fishery Policies, the EU Flag, the EU Anthem, the European Central Bank and Parliament, the signing of the Kyoto Agreement to save the world from global warming, and the European Constitution (known as the Lisbon Treaty) are "luxurious cargo" on board the *Great Titanic* of the 21st century streaming towards an 'ice-berg. The awkward truth is that Jean Monnet's 'fantastic boat' was doomed before its construction began on 9 May 1950, and even before the designer of the boat himself was born.

EUROPEAN UNION: A JOURNEY WITHOUT DESTINATION?

In his book, *Why Europe will run the 21st century*, Mark Leonard, who is described as "one of UK's most visionary thinkers," writes: "Monnet's contribution was a vision of how not to have a vision......He let the fear of conflict drive European unity and left its goal vague, allowing everyone to feel that Europe was going their way. To this day, Europe is a journey with no final destination, a political system that shies away from the grand plans and concrete certainties that define American politics. Its lack of vision is the key to its strength."

If the European Union is "a journey with no final destination," then the question arises: how can a man start a journey without knowing his destination? Does this not exemplify extraordinary ignorance and the undertaking of an unnecessary risk? This illustration depicts Monnet's 'ignorance' about his 'European project.' The French architect of the European "Titanic" knew what he was doing, and yet did not understand what he was doing. A traveller who does not plan his journey, and does not know his destination could land anywhere. And how could a man have a mission without a vision? Vision propels mission to a destination. And mission without vision is just an illusion. "Where there is no vision the people perish" (Proverbs 29:18). The truth is that "Europe is a journey" with a final destination. The coming Emperor of the European Empire would lead Europe to its destination.

THE DESTINATION OF DECEPTION

According to Mark Leonard, Jean Monnet, the "Spiritual god-father of Europe", left the "goal" of European integration "vague". It is, therefore, not surprising that the "children" of Jean Monnet (the supporters of the European Union) are struggling to define precisely the purpose of the European Union and its future? Consider this remark from a former EU Trade Commissioner, Pascal Lamy: "Can we be hopeful of Europe's future?" (Financial Times, 21 March 2007) Here is Timothy Garton-Ash's response: "Everyone knows that, beneath the surface, political Europe is not in a party mood about itself. The Community is morose, ill-tempered and uncertain of its future direction. Individually, most Europeans live better than before, but collectively they don't feel good about their voluntary empire. Rarely has such a successful enterprise been so plagued with self-doubt."

Though the leaders of the European Union may not know the final destination of the European Boat, the "cruiser" would not land anywhere. The qualified 'Captain' of *Euro- Titanic*, the King of Men, will pilot the European *Titanic* to the "Shore of Deception". After all, the European Project was constructed on deception. We reap what we sow. The Lord says: "My people are destroyed for lack of knowledge" (Hosea 4:6). I urge the citizens of Europe and their politicians to examine Dr Anderson's *The Coming Prince* to learn more about Jean Monnet's vision of a federal Europe and its future

THE 'PLOT' BY JEAN MONNET AND KONRAD ADENAUER

In their book, *THE GREAT DECEPTION,* Christopher Booker and Richard North enlightened us: "In 1941, when most of Europe was under Nazi or Fascist rule, an obscure Italian ex-Communist, imprisoned on an Island of the Italian coast, set out his vision that, when World War Two was over, enlightened politicians should set about building a "United States of Europe". According to the authors, this ex-Communist, Altiero Spinelli, suggested that politicians "should quietly assemble all the essential ingredients of this new state, without revealing too openly what was their purpose. The people of Europe should not be directly consulted, until at last all was ready for the summoning of a "constituent assembly." Only then would the people be allowed to acclaim their new constitution by voting for it. This would thus mark, not the beginning of the process whereby a "United States of Europe" was created, but its culmination, to "crowning dream": the moment when the goal could finally be revealed."

Jean Monnet adopted similar tactics of "deception" when he shared the Schuman Plan with Konrad Adenauer. On 23 May 1950, Konrad Adenauer met Jean Monnet to discuss the Schuman Plan. Monnet expounded the idea of an economic merger of the coal and steel industries of France and Germany that would eventually lead to the creation of a federal Europe. After the explanation, Adenauer responded: "I was in complete agreement with the project he described to me." The German Chancellor continued: "There was agreement on the point that once the technical experts of six countries sat down together, the technical difficulties and differences of opinion would seem enormous to them and they would then proceed to discuss them in such detail that the whole plan was in danger of being talked to pieces." Monnet proposed that the countries participating in the conference, called in Paris on 20 June 1950, should send no technical expert. Rather, they should be represented by persons with a wide economic horizon and European convictions, and that "it was also necessary that these representatives be in a position to draft and discuss agreements in constitutional and international law." Adenauer supported Monnet's idea with this remark: "Monnet thought, and I agreed with him that only after the conference in Paris - which was to work as fast as possible - had reached a basic understanding on the scope of the High Authority of the Schuman Plan and on the outlines of the treaties to be concluded, and after the parliaments of the six countries had given their approval, should the field be open to technical experts." (Source: Adenauer Memoirs 1943-1953 pages 263-264*)*

The deceit and lack of transparency that surround the whole European project are recorded in Monnet's Memoir. In 1961 Macmillan visited President Kennedy. He was told the United States would support Britain's application to join the Common Market which would eventually lead to the political unification of European nations. Macmillan and Heath were aware of this fact, yet they made a conscious decision not to inform the British people. All along Britons were being told that they were joining a Common Market not a political union.

Christopher Booker and Dr Richard North exposed the treachery and irresponsible behaviour of Edward Heath. "Without any electoral mandate, having barely mentioned 'Europe' during the 1970 election campaign, on arriving in office Heath almost immediately applied for entry. What was presented as 'negotiations' were no more than a prolonged act of surrender, on everything from the Commonwealth to the CAP, summed up by Con O'Neill as 'swallow it whole and swallow it now.' Even more blatantly than in 1961, Heath persistently misrepresented Britain's membership of the Common Market as no more than a trading issue, when behind the scenes this was already being given the lie by the Werner and Davignon proposals for monetary and political union."

If you study Jean Monnet's Memoirs, you would learn that "Deception" was the foundation stone upon which the European Project was built. According to "Mr Know-all" Monnet, the sovereign nations were incapable of ensuring their own progress. So, the 'effective way to ensure their future prosperity and peace was to transfer their powers to a centralised institution and then live under common rules." With all these facts before us, some commentators and politicians claim the EU is not a political project. The masses have been deceived and being deceived. This 'Deception' would be the platform on which the *dead* Roman Empire would be resurrected. And the emperor of the European Empire would deceive Europeans. This "Deception", which led to the construction of the "rarest of all political phenomena" in history, fulfils Sir Robert Anderson's prophetic description of the character of political Europe: *"The Vile confederacy of the latter days"*. Would the world applaud Sir Robert Anderson for his foresight and accurate description of the character of the European Union, and his prediction of a political union of European nations being the next major political feature in history after the restoration of the Jews to Palestine?

I repeat Dr Anderson's prediction of the development of European Union: **"...** Through the gradual unfolding, it may be, of influences even now in operation; or far more probably as the outcome of some great European crisis in the future, this confederation of nations shall be developed and thus the stage will be prepared on which shall appear that awful Being, the great leader of men in the eventful days which are to close the era of Gentile supremacy...." The "awful Being" would be the King of Europe who will deceive Europeans and mankind. Europe would reap what they have sown. British and Irish politicians must reflect on the question Dr Anderson posed: *"May we not indulge the hope that however far our nation may lapse in evil days to come from the high place which, with all her faults, she has held as the champion of freedom and of truth, she will be saved from the degradation of participating in the vile confederacy of the latter days?*

Where was Jean Monnet when Dr Anderson penned his prediction about political Europe and its future? The French "spiritual god-father" of European Union had not even been conceived. Europe will certainly run the 21st century, as Mark Leonard argues in his, *"why europe will run the 21st century"*. The question is: who is qualified to lead Europe in its current state of confusion and division? None of the present leaders is capable of such a task. The political genius with extraordinary talent is on his way to lead the greatest political alliance in the world and the largest trading block in the 21st century to its destiny. The Lisbon Treaty has prepared the way for his arrival.

BRITAIN'S 'HOSTILITY' TO EUROPE

On the issue of the so-called British 'hostility' to the European Union, I would contend that Britons' scepticism to the European Union should not be construed as 'hostility' to Europeans. Britons don't hate Europeans. We prefer to trade with them, not to be ruled by strangers in Europe. The simple truth is that politicians deceived Britons to join the European Common Market, and they are still deceiving the British people about their relationship with the European Union. A typical example is how Gordon brown imposed the Lisbon Treaty on Britons. Majority of Britons don't want to be governed by aliens they have not elected, who are not accountable to them and cannot be removed from power by them. This is the simple common sense British politicians don't seem to appreciate. It is therefore disingenuous for the supporters of the European project to label eurosceptics as 'enemies' of Europe. Would those who blindly follow the 'children' of Monnet describe Jeijo Kemppinen an 'enemy' of Europe? He is a citizen of Finland and the European Union Ambassador to Britain who, in his first recorded interview with The Times, told Britons: "I don't love Europe. I love my family, I love my children, I love my dogs, but I don't love Europe." This same EU Ambassador boasted: "I am employed by Europe and I am lucky to work for an Institution I believe in" (The Times 7 November 2005).

According to Mr Kemppinen, he does not love Europe, but loves his dogs, and he is fortunate to be employed by Europe and to work for an Institution he believes in. Was this a joke, or a serious "sales presentation" from a professional salesman from Brussels who wanted to persuade his "sceptical customers" to buy his "product"? How could a professional car salesman tell a potential customer (a car renting company): "I don't like these particular cars I am selling; I don't like the models, but they would be good for your car renting business, so buy them?" Would this be a serious business presentation to a prospective customer?

If the EU Ambassador to "sceptical" Britain does not love Europe, why should Britons be forced to love Europe and become European citizens? Citizenship is acquired voluntarily not under compulsion. On June 23, 2006 *The Sun* reported that a plot was being hatched by Eurocrats to brainwash British kids as young as five on the merits of EU. Members of European Parliament considered plans to prepare students for their role as European citizens." It would be part of the curriculum, with TV lessons and pamphlets. In its Editorial, *The Sun* described the move of the "ferocious beasts" in the EU "jungle" as "cunning". In its leading article, *Poisonous EU,* the patriotic *Sun* newspaper reported: "Having been humiliated time after time in referendums, Brussels knows it cannot con sensible adults. So their propaganda campaign will start while children are still naive enough to believe in fairies." However, the desperate Brussels engineered to introduce misleading information about the true colour of the European project in propaganda booklets and DVD to indoctrinate innocent school children (*Daily Express* Thursday 4 January 2007: "EU 'propaganda aimed at pupils")

If the EU Ambassador to Britain loves his children more than Europe; if he loves his dogs more than Europe, why should the European Union attempt to use "brainwashing techniques of religious cults and fanatics" to force British kids to love Europe? And why should euro-phile political commentators, businessmen and politicians expect the "sceptical" British people to love the European Union - a Project constructed on deception? Why should the British people unconditionally love Europe? I urge you to read *The Great Deception* and *The Great European Rip-off.* They will help you to know more about the 'devilish' nature of the European Enterprise. Peter Hitchens of The Mail on Sunday describes *The Great Deception* "….a superb history of the EU and of Britain's relationship with it….every MP, every senior civil servant, every journalist with any claim to understanding the current state of the country, should read it." And Rodney Leach of *The Spectator* also writes: "a tour de force…a fascinating forensic history of the seen and unseen forces which have brought us to the present point." On *The Great European Rip-off, Spectator* writes: "The first serious work to deal in a thorough fashion with the incompetence, nepotism and waste that have defined New Labour in government….David Graig and Richard Brooks have performed an immense public service, and this horrifying book deserves a wide readership." And according to *Daily Telegraph*: "It is no exaggeration to say that if the right people read it, take it seriously, and take appropriate action, this book could not only save the taxpayer billions, it could save lives….This is a terrifying book, but a brilliant and necessary one.."

CHAPTER 22

EUROPEAN UNION AND 'PEACE' IN THE MIDDLE EAST

The "Puzzle" which couldn't be solved would be "solved"

Why is God so silent? How is it that Almighty power is passive in a world where sorrow and suffering prevail, and sin and wrong are rampart? To these difficulties enlightened faith can find an answer. But it does not lie upon the surface. It must be sought for as men dig for gold. And even when it has been grasped, and reason bows before the teaching of revelation, the cravings of the inner being still refuse to be satisfied, and "heart and flesh" cry out for the Living God."
(Pseudo-Criticism Sir Robert Anderson)

THE REHEARSAL OF THE MIDDLE EAST PEACE TREATY THE WORLD HAS BEEN WAITING FOR: A PICTURE OF THE BIBLE PROPHECY IN DANIEL 9:27 WHICH IS ABOUT TO BECOME A REALITY

I have already shared with you that the "Mother of all Deceptions" would be perpetrated by the great leader of men, that *"awful Being"*, who will be enthroned by the powerful "kings" of the revived Roman Empire. I will now share with you what would be the greatest "political success" story of all times, which the coming King of Europe would achieve. He will "end" the political crisis and the hostilities in the Middle East to bring "peace" between the Jews and their Arab neighbours. But how long would this "peace" last?

A "rehearsal" of this Middle East Peace treaty took place in 2005. On Tuesday 29 November 2005, the *Financial Times* published the result of a meeting between European Union, Israel and its Arab neighbours. In an article titled, *Middle East tension foils final Euromed declaration,* the paper reported: "The limits of the European Union's influence were ...laid bare when a summit with countries bordering the Mediterranean to the South and east failed to agree a final declaration." The summit was co-hosted by Tony Blair, the then British prime minister (who is now an envoy to the Middle East) and Jose Luis Rodriguez Zapatero, the prime minister of Spain. According to the report, all the member states of the European Union and their Euromed partners - Algeria, Egypt, Israel, Jordan, Lebanon, Morocco, the Palestinian Authority, Syria, Tunisia and Turkey – agreed to "a previously negotiated five-year work plan on extending "political pluralism," modernising the southern Mediterranean's economies and reducing illegal immigrants."

It was disclosed that the European Union supports the Euromed region with about £2.1 billion a year in grants and loans. However, none of the Arab heads of states invited to the meeting attended. Apart from Mr Recep Tayyip Erdogan, the Prime Minister of Turkey, and Mr Mahmoud Abbas, the Leader of the Palestinian Authority, the other invited Heads of States stayed away. The then Primer Minister of Israel, Ariel Sharon, did not attend either. The absentees sent their deputies and foreign ministers instead. The report further stated, "a dispute between Israel and its Arab neighbours foiled last-minute attempts to agree a final declaration for the summit. Israel "wanted the text to emphasise its pull-out from Gaza and objected to a reference to an Arab initiative." The summit could not achieve any meaningful purpose due to the absence of the Heads of states. After the co-chairmen (the British and Spanish Prime Ministers) concluded the meeting, an Israeli official declared: "This is not binding to all parties .... What was binding were the documents which were accepted by consensus, the code of conduct, and the five-year work plan."

The November 2005 Euromed summit, which was an attempt to initiate a peace deal between Israel and its Arab neighbours, was to mark the tenth anniversary of the Euro-Mediterranean Association. This Association was first launched in 1995 during Spain's first EU presidency. The organization consists of the then 25 member states of the European Union and 10 countries from the Southern Mediterranean region – Algeria, Egypt, Israel, Jordan, Lebanon, Morocco, the Palestinian Authority, Syria, Tunisia and Turkey. One of the major goals of this Association is to promote peace, security, political stability and democracy and to prevent terrorism. The failed Euro-Mediterranean summit was reported in the 1 December 2005 edition of *Financial Times* in a column titled: "Europe's muddled message to its neighbours."

Apart from the above failed initiatives, other attempts were being made by various bodies such as *The Arab League, Anna Lindh Foundation*, and *European Coalition for Israel* to end the conflict in the Middle East. For example, among the prime aims of the *European Coalition for Israel,* which is based in Brussels, are:

- To promote closer relations and understanding between Israel and the

European Union.

- To confront anti-Semitism in Europe and to educate people about its long, and tragic history in the continent.
- To support ways for peaceful coexistence between Jews and Arabs in Israel and the European Union.

TO EVERY PROBLEM THERE IS A SOLUTION

We have witnessed the failure of the Euromed summit in November 2005 by the European Union to secure a peace deal between Israel and the Palestinians; the United States' inability to encourage the Jews and the Palestinians to live in peace, and despite the introduction of the "Road Map", and from our own observations of the continuing violence in the Middle East, which have resulted in suicide bombings in Israel and military attacks against the Palestinians, it is clearly neither the European Union nor the United States of America, or the United Nations has a solution to end the protracted turmoil in the Mediterranean region. The bloodshed continues and properties are being destroyed. It seems the "Camp David" Conference, the "Oslo Accords of 1992", the "Road Map" initiative; the Euromed summit, and the numerous diplomatic peace conferences on the Middle East crisis have proved futile in resolving the ancient "blood-feud" between "two brothers" who are the descendants of Abraham through his sons Ishmael and Isaac. The cry for peace in the hostile Mediterranean Region continues. American and European politicians are still struggling to bring peace to the troubled Middle East. The world is searching for peace to the extent that the United Nations planned to invest trillions of dollars to solve problems facing humanity: poverty, famine, epidemic diseases, and terrorism – to bring peace on earth. Who is the genius to solve the problems of the world?

ISRAEL'S SEIGE OF GAZA

In 2006, the world witnessed how Israel besieged Gaza and cut its people off from electricity, terrified its children with sonic bombs and kidnapped about a quarter of Hamas government. This was Israel's response to the kidnapping of one of its soldiers and the killing of two of them. The confusion and the agony in the Middle East rage on. The world powers are impotent to prevent further bloodshed.

On 6 July 2006, Jonathan Steele commented in *The Guardian* on the failure of Europe to help resolve the conflict in the Middle East. In an article, *Europe's response to the siege of Gaza is shameful,* he writes: "Thank goodness for the Swiss. Alone in Europe, their government has dared to condemn what the Israelis are doing to Gaza. Israel violated the principle of proportionality, and took no precaution to protect civilians." According to the report, the position of the Swiss government "stands in contrast to the European Union's shamefully muted voice. The

Palestinians kill two soldiers and take one prisoner and, in response, power stations are blown up, sewage and water systems grind to a halt, bridges are destroyed, sonic bombs terrify children day and night, and all this is inflicted on a hungry people who are under siege...The EU's response? Vague expressions of "concern" and calls for restraint."

Mr Steele continued: "European impotence in the Israeli-Palestinian conflict is of course an ancient problem...The outcome of the current crisis is unclear. However it ends, the moment has surely come for Europe to break from its useless policy of backing the US and Israel." Before concluding his report, Mr Steele stated: "The EU should admit that the Palestinians have no partner for peace. They will only have one if Israel recognises Palestine's right to function.....Israel must renounce violence, in particular, the assassinations of Palestinian leaders.....The facts do not support the notion that Israel is "retaliating" to provocations. The article concluded: "There is a global audience which expects Europe to take the right stand. Whether Israel chooses to listen should not be the decisive factor."

THE LEBANON WAR:

THE CREDIBILITY OF EU AND THE "DISHONEST" AMERICA

The 34-day Lebanon War ended in August 2006. The cease fire was initiated by a United Nation's Resolution. Israel, which was supported by the United States of America, was perceived to have lost their "Reckless Adventure." Hizbollah, which was supported by Syria and Iran, was the victor. Hizbollah's victory was described in an article entitled: "*Hizbollah has redrawn the Middle East.*" The article noted: "Clearly Iran is the winner but its strategy can work only as long as Syria and Hizbollah are seen as legitimate champions of the Arab cause" (Financial Times 18 August 2006). In this same edition of the *Financial Times,* a letter was published in a column titled *EU has much to gain in lead role for Mideast.* The United States of America (then led by President George Bush) was accused for its blind support of Israel's disproportionate attacks on Lebanon. The writer, Mr Nasser, continued: "The US is no longer seen as an honest broker by the Arab world. The EU on the other hand, is seen to pursue much more balanced policies in the Middle East. Furthermore, the EU has the economic clout to apply pressure on both Palestinians and Israelis. Finally, the EU has much to gain by taking a leadership role in promoting peace and stability in its Southern neighbourhood. Therefore, it is time for the EU to move out of Washington shadow and play a leading role in reaching a fair and just solution to the source of most problems in the Middle East, namely the Israeli-Palestinian conflict."

On 21 August 2006, a report in Financial Times highlighted the lost cause of America in the Middle East conflict. Within an article captioned *America has emerged as a loser in the Middle East,* the paper noted: "As Israelis and Arabs continue their debate over who won and lost in Lebanon, one outcome already seems clear; America lost. According to the article, America's support for Israelis' invasion, and its refusal "to seek an early ceasefire may have had some marginal benefits for the US, such as the destruction of some of Hizbollah's military capability." However, in the end Washington's support for the war "have been a disaster." In summary: the outcome of the 34-day Lebanon War (from which Hizbollah emerged "victorious") finally exposed the impotence of America – its inability to solve the Israeli-Palestinian conflict. On the other hand, the European Union emerged as the credible political force with economic "clout" to be an honest broker to bring peace to the Middle East.

UNION FOR MEDITTERANEAN

It is interesting to note that in July 2008, President Sarkozy, the 'faithful son' of Jean Monnet, launched in Paris a Union for Mediterranean to speed up the process for ending the Israeli – Palestinian conflict. This new Organisation, which consists of more than 40 countries from the European Union, the Balkans, North Africa and Middle East, is to replace the Euro Mediterranean project, which was considered a failure. The headquarters of Union for Mediterranean would be based in Barcelona. As I have already stated, it is the coming King of Europe who would lead the negotiation to 'resolve' the crisis in the Middle East. So, Nicolas Sarkozy's idea of creating a new organisation to "inject fresh dynamism into EU-Mediterranean relations to replace the Barcelona Process" (Financial Times 5 November 2008) is "the step in the right direction."

THE "WEAK" AMERICA AND THE "STRONG" EUROPE

I agree with Mr Nasser that the United States of America has lost credibility in the eyes of the Muslim world (especially because of its irresponsible invasion of a sovereign country – Iraq), and it lacks the power to lead the world. This apparent weakness of the United States of America is not surprising. That the US has lost its economic and political power to lead the world and influence the peaceful settlement of the long dispute between Israel and its Arab neighbours is nothing new to be written about. For in *The Late Planet Earth,* which Hal Lindsey and C. C Carlson published in 1970, the writers predicted that America would be replaced by Europe as the world economic and political power. The book records: "The United States will not hold to its present position of leadership in the Western world. Financially, the future leader will be Western Europe....The military capability of the United States has already been neutralised. As the United States loses power, Western Europe will be forced to unite and become the standard–bearer of the Western world." It is interesting to notice that today, political commentators are confirming what had been written over three decades ago.

THE ROLE OF THE EU – THE 'HONEST BROKER'

Now that the European Union has replaced the United States of America as the "honest broker" to solve the Middle East crisis, the question arises: Would the European Union be able to end the blood-feud between the Jews and the Arabs to bring everlasting peace to that troubled region? Yes, the European Union would "solve" the Middle East conflict. However, this 'incredible feat' would not be achieved by the present crop of leaders in Europe. The powerful and charismatic leader of Europe, who is yet to be crowned, would bring the Israelis and the Palestinians to the final negotiating table to seal a peace deal. The world would respect this European leader for his 'successes'.

SOLUTION TO THE 'SOPHISTICATED' MIDDLE EAST CRISIS

We know the world is crying for a solution to the Middle East conflict. In response to the world-wide lamentation on the blood-shed in the Middle East, the CNN, on 23 September 2006, telecast a Global Summit on the Middle East crisis and the genocide in Darfour. The CNN's Chief International Correspondent, Christiane Amanpour, hosted the Clinton Global Initiative in New York which discussed how the quarrel in the Middle East could be solved, and how the genocide in Darfour could be halted. The Summit – *In the name of God* - was attended by the following distinguished personalities:

- George Mitchell, the former United States Senator (now President Obama's Middle East envoy)
- Dina Habib Powell, the United States Assistant Secretary of State.
- Rahmi-Khouri of American University of Beirut.
- Simon Peres, former Prime Minister of Israel.
- Her Majesty Queen Rania of Jordan.
- Ambassador Lakhder Brahimi, former United Nations Special Advisor and
- Bill Clinton, former President of the United States of America.

During the discussion, the Queen of Jordan and Ambassador Brahimi made significant statements that shed a light on how the intractable conflict between the Palestinians and the Israelis could be resolved. Ambassador Brahimi said: "....In the case of Palestine and Israel, this is one of the most complicated and difficult problems. The fundamental thing to know is that these two peoples will never solve the problems alone. They need outside help. And that outside help – let me say it bluntly is not available....The quartet (the European Union, the United States of America, the United Nations and Russia) make a statement and they go back home. They don't do much." Indeed, in the 25 September 2008 edition of The Independent, the newspaper confirmed the sentiments of Ambassador

Brahimi in an article titled *Quartet creating power vacuum in the Middle East.* The Paper reported that the international quartet - the United States, European Union, United Nations and Russia - was accused of creating a "vacuum of leadership" as the aid agencies complained that "visible progress" in the middle East had "failed to materialise."

Queen Rania of Jordan made this remarkable statement during the Global Summit: "There must be a "sophisticated approach." On November 27, 2008, the Financial Times reported another initiative taken to bring peace into the Middle East. In an article titled *Senior Israelis back Arab push for peace,* the paper reported: "A group of Israel's security officers launched a campaign to promote the Saudi-sponsored Arab peace initiative, in a fresh effort to help end 60 years of conflict in the Middle East. The Arab initiative offers Israel peace and normal relations with all Arab states in return for a full withdrawal from all land occupied in the 1967 war, including Palestinian territories and Syria's Golan Heights**...A** report by the Oxford Research Group, a UK think-tank, calls on the US and the European Union to put the peace initiative at the centre of Middle East Policy. The Plan calls for the creation of a Palestinian state with east Jerusalem as its capital."

Truly, the ancient blood-feud between the children of Ishmael and Isaac is a sophisticated problem that needs a sophisticated approach as stated by the Queen. I have already mentioned that the sophisticated man to solve the complicated Middle East crisis will come from the European Empire. The "outside help" which the Ambassador rightly identified as the prerequisite to solve the hostilities between the 'two brothers,' will be available. The political genius who will be installed by the "10 toes of the great human image," is the 'sophisticated' leader of Europe who will use his extraordinary diplomatic skills to broker a 'peace' deal between the Jews and the Arabs.

In summary: the promotion of political stability, peace and economic prosperity in the Middle East, which have become the burden of the European Union, Russia, the United States of America, the United Nations and the Clinton Global Initiative, would be established by the most powerful leader humanity has ever known. The world will love this "sophisticated" leader of Europe for his amazing achievements. But it would end in tears. The "honest broker" from the revived Roman Empire would turn out to be the greatest dishonest politician and brutal dictator the world has ever witnessed. He will terrorise mankind after he has broken the 7-year peace treaty between the Jews and their Arab neighbours.

THE MIDDLE EAST CRISIS: 2008 AND 2009

The year 2008 ended with the beginning of renewed hostilities between Israel and Hamas. And the year 2009 began with the continuation of the Middle East crisis: the invasion of Gaza by the Israelis.

The following newspaper headlines highlighted the crisis:

- "Gaza: 225 DEAD. Biggest Israel air strikes yet signal new phase in conflict" (The Sunday Telegraph, 28 December 2008).
- "Gaza mourns Israel targeted" (*Financial Times*, 30 December 2008).
- "Gaza protest Middle East Quartet urges immediate cease fire"
- Israel in 'all-out war with Gaza Militants" (31 December 2008).
- "Israel: No let-up. They defy International calls for ceasefire in Gaza" (*The Sun*, 1 January 2009)
- "Israel rejects ceasefire move as divisions emerge in leadership"
- "More troops mass on border"
- "Hamas rockets land 25 miles into Israel" (*The Guardian* 1 January 2009)
- "Israel snubs truce appeal and lurches towards ground war" (*Daily Mail*, 1 January 2009)
- "Israel tanks roll into Gaza to crush Hamas"
- "This operation won't be easy and it won't be short"
- "The militant Arab states are outraged. America stands behind Israel – but neither side get sucked into war" (*The Sunday Times*, 4 January 2009)
- "The Battle over Gaza": Provoked by Hamas rockets, Israel wrecks devastation on Gaza. As President-elect Obama stays mum, the stakes get even higher" (*TIME*, 12 January 2009).
- "Israel tanks roll in to storm Hamas rockets"
- "Olmert defies Brown's plea not to invade" (*The Mail on Sunday* 4 January 2009)
- "500 dead as Gaza crisis intensifies" (*the Londonpaper* (5 January 2009)
- "Family of 7 wiped out by an Israeli tank shell" (*London Lite* 5 January 2009)
- "Israel eyes control of Gaza's key sites."
- "Civilian death toll rises as plight worsens" (*Financial Times* 5 January 2009).

THE "PUZZLE" WHICH COULD NOT BE SOLVED WOULD BE "SOLVED." "PEACE" WOULD BE ESTABLISHED BETWEEN THE JEWS AND THE ARABS

Mark Almond, lecturer in modern history at Oriel College in Oxford, and a visiting professor in international relations at Bilkent University at Ankara in Turkey, produced a significant commentary on the 'Battle' between Israel and Hamas. In his article, *"Even Obama can't solve this,"* the professor analysed the dilemma facing the world: "Outsiders look on with baffled dismay as Israel's high-tech air force pounds crowded Palestinian tenements in Gaza. We are baffled, too, by why Hamas guerrillas have provoked such an attack on their own people by firing mortars into southern Israel. Sadly, both sides' actions make sense, even though neither can win this battle." The Lecturer continues: "But Israel's existence is guaranteed as much by US cash as US arms....Even if America could safely abandon the Middle East, Israelis have made it their home. A gruesome fight to the finish between Israelis determined to hold on to all the land they have now and Hamas-inspired Palestinians determined to recover everything lost since 1948 cannot be ruled out." The Oxford Professor concludes his critique with these solemn words: "Solving the Arab Israeli dispute is not an option for Obama. There is no basis for an agreement between the two sides, not in their current mood. Stopping the violence spreading is the only plausible goal. But that will not lead to real peace." (Daily Mail 1 January 2009).

The Israelis and the Palestinians want to live in peace. World leaders want peace in the Middle East. But since there is no basis for a peace agreement between the warring factions, as Professor Almond rightly analysed it for us, the following questions require answers:

- When would real peace be restored in the Middle East?
- Which diplomat would become the "peace-maker" to end the hostilities between the Jews and their Arab neighbours?
- How would the political genius achieve such a seemingly "impossible task"?

To answer these questions, we must consult the Prince of Detectives who, 36 years before the Balfour Declaration made a commitment to "the establishment in Palestine of a national home for the Jewish people," predicted that the Jews would be restored to Palestine, and the next major political feature in history after the rebirth of the nation of Israel would be a confederation of European nations. We know the nation of Israel was re-born on 14 May 1948 and the European Union was also born on 9 May 1950. If these two significant political events in the chronicles of history have been fulfilled, then it is reasonable to suggest that the Detective's prediction about how 'peace' would return to the Middle East would also come true. Indeed, as I have mentioned it many times, the Lisbon Treaty will pave the way for the political genius to enter the stage to bring 'peace' between the Jews and the Arabs. And this would fulfil God's Word in Daniel 9:27: "And he will confirm a covenant with many for one week. And in the middle of the weak he will put an end to sacrifice and offering. And on the wing of the temple, he will set up an abomination that causes desolation, until the end that is decreed is poured out on him." I have already explained the significance of this prophetic message with references to Matthew 24:15, Revelation 12, 13 and 17, and 2 Thessalonians 2:1-12). In view of the significance of this prophetic word, I confidently state: "A time will surely come when the Jews and the Palestinians would listen to the "chief negotiator" who would settle their dispute "peacefully."

THE SIGNS

A sign of how this "skilful negotiator" who will lead a Multi-National Middle East Peace Conference to solve the crisis in the Mediterranean Region was shown to us in the Iraq Study Group Report which was presented to the then US President, George Bush. *The Baker Report* recommended that United States' commitment to a two-state solution between the Israelis and the Palestinians could only be achieved when America engages in direct talks with the Arab nations – Iran, Syria and Lebanon. The cooperation of these Muslim countries would be needed to solve the ancient crisis in the Middle East.

- Another "sign" of how the political genius would "end" the hostilities between the two "brothers" was revealed to us in an article titled *Envoys play down ceasefire hopes* (*Financial Times* 5 January 2009). In this article, the reporters explained how "European and Arab officials stepped up diplomatic efforts to contain the Gaza crisis as Israel escalated its offensive against Hamas." They made this significant statement: *"According to French officials, Mr Sarkozy will be carrying concrete proposals on how France and Europe could offer guarantees of security to both sides and he is hoping that the relationship Paris has developed with Syria in recent months provides a channel of communication with Hamas, which Damascus backs."* Notice carefully the text: "France and Europe could offer guarantees of security to both sides" (the Jews and their Arab neighbours). This "guarantees of security" are exactly what the coming King of Europe would offer to the Israelis and the Arabs in a 7-year peace covenant he would establish with them.

Another "sign" was revealed in Adrian Michael's article - *Surprise news from the Middle East: People are starting to talk* (*The Daily Telegraph*, 11 March 2009). In this piece of writing we were informed:

- Obama Administration is determined to help bring peace in the Middle East. The US Secretary of State, Hillary Clinton, sent envoys to Damascus to seek the cooperation of the Syrians.
- Syrian President, Assad, to hold talks with Saudi Arabia's King Abdullah.
- Talks in Cairo between Fatah and Hamas, the two opposing camps vying for Palestinian support.
- "The 22 nations in the Arab League trying "to coalesce around a negotiation position that would see them all prepared to declare their recognition of Israel in return for the establishment of a Palestinian state."

SUMMARY

We must not be surprised at the increasing hostilities between the Jews and the Arabs, and the dispute concerning the city of Jerusalem. For the Bible predicted the current conflict in the Middle East and the control over Jerusalem. Let us listen to the Lord Almighty: "I am going to make Jerusalem a cup that sends all the surrounding peoples reeling; Judah will be besieged as well as Jerusalem. On that day, when all the nations of the earth are gathered against her, I will make Jerusalem an immovable rock for all the nations." (Zechariah 12: 2-3). In Daniel 9:27 the Lord revealed to Daniel that the conflict between the Jews and their Arab neighbours would be *"resolved"* not permanently, but for a brief period of 3½ years. And it is the last Emperor of the revived Roman Empire, who would be the "skilful negotiator" to bring 'peace' between the "two brothers."

Just as European leaders entered into a series of pacts with the Arab League to obtain favourable oil prices during the 1973 oil crisis, so would the coming Emperor of Europe establish a peace agreement by negotiating with the Arabs and all the various organisations that have been trying to end the hostilities in the Middle East. Under his leadership, the charismatic leader of Europe will bring peace, political stability and economic prosperity to the entire Mediterranean region. This is one of the most important goals of the European Union.

I have already mentioned that the "end" of the warfare between the Israelis and the Palestinians would lead to the fulfilment of Bible prophecy. It was about 538BC that God revealed this prophetic message of a temporary 'peace' between the Jews and the Arabs to Daniel: *"And after threescore and two weeks shall Messiah be cut off, but not for himself; and the people of the prince that shall come shall destroy the city and the sanctuary; and the end thereof shall be with a flood, and unto the end of the war desolations are determined. "And he shall confirm the covenant with many for one week; and in the midst of the week he shall cause the sacrifice and the oblation to cease, and for the overspreading of abomination he shall make it desolate even until the consummation, and that determined shall be poured upon the desolate"* (Daniel 9:27 KJ). Because of the impact the "end" of the Middle East Crisis would have on mankind, let us, again, analyse the significant words and phrases in the prophetic message. They are ***"he", "one week", "many",*** and ***"in the mist of the week."***

- The ***"he"*** is the coming Emperor of the Revived Roman Empire, the political genius, the "beast from the sea", the Antichrist, the Man of Lawlessness, the Man of Sin, the Son of Perdition. The shadows of this cruel dictator were: the despicable Syrian king, Antiochus Epiphanes, who persecuted and killed thousands of Jews and abolished their religion and desecrated their Temple with the blood of a swine. He also encouraged fornication in the Temple and erected an idol of Zeus on the

Temple altar. The next shadow was the Roman Prince, Titus Vespasian. He led Roman Legions to invade Judea, destroyed their Temple, killed thousands of Jews; captured some as slaves and scattered the rest. The European Union will repeat the "achievements" of Antiochus Epiphanes of Syria –a descendant of Alexander the Great's Grecian Empire and Prince Titus of Rome. The Lisbon Treaty has paved the way for the Coming King of Europe.

- The ***"one week"*** is the last 7 years of this age.
- The ***"many"*** refers to the nation of Israel, their Arab neighbours (Egypt, Iran, Kuwait, Lebanon, Saudi Arabia, Syria, and Turkey) and the Quartet (United Nations, the European Union, the United States of America, and Russia). The rest of the ***"many"*** are China, the Clinton Global Initiative, The Arab League and all the various organisations that have laboured to bring peace between the Jews and the Arabs.
- The ***"In the midst of the week"*** refers to the first three and half years of the 7-year peace treaty at which time the Emperor of Europe would violate the peace covenant.

A SEED OF DECEPTION YIELDS A FRUIT OF DECEPTION THE MOTHER OF ALL DECEPTIONS

At the end of the first 3½ years of the "7-year peace" agreement, the Emperor of the European Empire will instruct the Jews to stop worshipping in their Temple. Like Antiochus Epiphanes, the Man of Sin will abolish the Jewish religion; blasphemes the name of God; utter proud words; set up his idol in the Jerusalem Temple and demand homage for being the deity who has brought peace and prosperity to mankind. The world will follow the Son of Perdition because of the signs and wonders the apostate Jew, the "beast from the earth", would perform on his behalf. The faithful Jews and Christians who reject the call for homage to the 'god of Europe' would be persecuted (Revelation 13:8). This would be the Mother of all Deceptions that would be perpetrated on mankind.

The Antichrist's persecution of the *"rebels"* (the faithful Jews and Christians) would mark the beginning of the great tribulation the Lord Jesus Christ spoke about in Matthew 24:15- 22: "When ye therefore shall see the abomination of desolation, spoken of by Daniel the prophet, standing in the holy place....Then let them which be in Judea flee into the mountains. Let him which is on the housetop not come down to take anything out of his house. Neither let him which is in the field return back to take his clothes......for there shall be great tribulation, such as was not since the beginning of the world to this time, no, nor ever shall be. And except those days should be shortened, there should be no flesh saved; but for the elect's sake those days shall be shortened." Thereafter, there will be the final global war which would be waged in the Middle East, as nations march from the "upper North" to attack Israel to fulfil the Word of God in Zechariah 12:2-9.

THE "MOST POWERFUL MAN" IN BRITAIN

We will now discuss a significant event which was published in some of our newspapers. This incident confirmed Sir Robert Anderson's fears about "*The vile confederacy of the latter days*", and that "awful Being", the false messiah, who is about to enter the political stage to lead Europe and the rest of the world to the Promised Land of "Carbon-Free" - full of Peace and Prosperity.

A BBC Radio 4's Today programme conducted a survey among millions of its listeners to find out the most powerful man in Britain. The result of the survey which was titled *Who runs Britain?* was released on 2 January 2006. The person who won the contest was a foreigner, a Portuguese national, who heads the European Commission in Brussels. Not all the newspapers gave a prominent coverage to the outcome of this particular poll, which is very significant. On 3 January 2006, Daily Mail commented on the "extraordinary" result of the survey in a column entitled, *EU chief 'Britain's most powerful man'.* According to the report, "Jose Manuel Barroso, the European Commission President, came ahead of Tony Blair (the then British Prime Minister) and Gordon Brown (the then Chancellor of the Exchequer) in the survey to find out who has the most influence over our lives. More than a fifth of Radio Four listeners chose the EU's top bureaucrat, underscoring fears that unelected politicians in Brussels have more sway in Britain than those chosen through the ballot box. Mr Barroso oversees the team who dream up an array of EU directives, which are then enshrined in UK law."

The Daily Mail described how Roger Knapman, the then leader of the UK Independence Party, viewed the result of the survey. He congratulated the listeners for highlighting the overwhelming influence politicians in Brussels have on the British people. He said, "Seventy percent of our laws are now made in Brussels….. he (Jose Manuel Barroso), is now a bureaucrat perceived as the most important man in this country and that is quite shocking." The outcome of the study is important in so far as the eternal destiny of our nation, Great Britain, is concerned. It also has prophetic implications. It is a shadow of what is about to come upon our nation and the rest of the world. In this respect, I have borrowed extracts from Stephen Glover's article, *HURRAH FOR THE BBC! At least its listeners know who really runs Britain,* to help highlight the implications of the consequence of the Radio 4 Poll.

Mr Glover writes "….In one sense this was an amazing result. A person about whom most of us know practically nothing is accounted the most powerful man in our country by a well informed and knowledgeable people….Most of us know very little about Mr Barroso….He is unaccountable to Parliament. Months pass without our hearing or seeing him. And yet we have a dim sense that he is considerably more important to our lives than our elected prime minister." After describing the background of the President of the European Commission, Mr Glover refuted the Europhiles claim that the European Commission employs fewer people and "it is no more than a slimmed-down civil service." He continued: "It (the European Commission) is responsible for administering and implementing EU policies, which makes it much more powerful than a traditional civil service. If it employs relatively few people, that is because it does not need to employ many. The Commission issues directives to the civil servants of member states to carry out its wishes."

The Columnist reported how Mr Barroso and his 24 fellow Commissioners make all kinds of decisions on behalf of the British people without consulting them. An example he quoted was an important meeting of the World Trade Organisation in Hong Kong, which Britain was represented by an unelected Commissioner who is responsible to the European Parliament. Mr Glover continued: "Would our fathers have believed that an unelected Portuguese could be the most important person in our country? Obviously not! The idea would have seemed completely barmy to them. The odd thing is that it seems almost equally barmy to us. And yet, we have accepted it, or ...we have not resisted it. Perhaps we feel that ...Mr Barroso and his colleagues will withdraw from our lives to be replaced by much saner arrangements." To which the Mr Glover rightly declared, "I would not bet on it."

Mr Glover explained that despite the rejection of the European Constitution by two founder members of the European Project – France and Germany – there was little evidence that the European leaders had taken on board the concerns of their citizens about the direction of the "Project." He added: "Business has gone on as usual. The European caravan rolls on" to the extent that the leaders of Europe "produced a substantially enlarged budget, with Britain paying considerably more than it has previously. Our cherished leader Jose Manuel Barroso was cheering in the wings. More than 40 percent of the new budget will be spent on subsidising farmers, in spite of the objections of the British Government and the British people." He continued: "The EU continues to grow like some horrible organism, endlessly extending its powers in numerous unnoticed ways. Without a new Constitution, we are edging towards a European diplomatic service as well as an European army. A new European police college is already in place at Bramhill in Hampshire. We are moving towards the harmonising of our judicial system. Without anyone being consulted, the EU has recently agreed to set up a European space council to draw up an EU space programme to compete with the US."

Mr Glover continues with his report: "The examples of creeping federalism in every area of our lives are legion. It does not matter whether our leading politicians declare themselves against further European integration because it is taking place willy-nilly and without our say-so. We are seemingly unable to stop it." He concludes: "How fitting that the man who more than any other can be associated with this covert and inexorable process should be almost totally unknown to us and should rarely visit our shores. It took the best of 1000 years to set up a representative democracy that worked pretty well, and then we casually exchanged it for an unknown and unelected Portuguese and his fellow Commissioners. Thank God many Today listeners have the gumption to understand what has happened to us."

And not surprisingly, this "most powerful man in Britain" - the "Buffoon of Brussels"- had the impudence to order Tony Blair, a British Prime Minister, to ignore the concerns of the British people over the unreadable Lisbon Treaty which was designed to transfer more powers from elected and accountable politicians in the British Parliament to unelected and unaccountable busy-bodies in Brussels - the "EU jungle of wild beasts."

THE REHEARSAL OF THE RECOGNITION OF THE COMING PRINCE – THE MOST POWERFUL POLITICIAN TO 'SAVE' EUROPE AND MANKIND

Stephen Glover's article paints a prophetic picture of what is yet to take place in the political scene - the role of the coming world leader. That a foreigner, who heads the institutions of the European Union - upon which the "*dead*" Roman Empire would be "resurrected" - has become the most powerful man in our country, should not surprise us. The recognition of the majestic role of the European Chief, as the person who influences our lives more than our Prime Minister and the Chancellor of the Exchequer, should not confound us. Mr Glover puts it: "How a person (the European Commission President Barroso) of such comparatively limited attractions should have ended up as the most powerful man in Britain…….may appear something of a mystery..." This state of affairs in Britain and in Europe in general are the shadows of what would actually take place when the unknown political genius suddenly appears on the political landscape to 'end' the Middle East Crisis and set Europe 'free' from economic and political 'bondage'. The picture of the reign of this mysterious leader is the role of the European Commission President, who controls our lives with copious legislations from Brussels.

For example, on Friday, January 6, 2006, it was announced in the Financial Times: "*Brown faces EU censure over failure to comply with public borrowing rule.*" Under this headline Tobias Buck writes: "Gordon Brown, the chancellor of the exchequer, faces embarrassing censure from the European Commission….when Brussels will recommend the launch of an excessive deficit procedure against Britain for its failure to keep public borrowing below 3 percent of gross domestic product." According to the Correspondent the European Union Commission estimates Britain was close to breaking "the deficit ceiling enshrined in the European

Union Stability Pact for four years running...The UK is bound by the pact's provisions, even though it is not in the 12-member eurozone. However, unlike the governments that have adopted the single currency, Britain cannot be financially penalised..."

The question is: why should a British Chancellor of the Exchequer, chosen by the British people to administer their nation's finances, and who is accountable to the British Parliament, be accountable to unaccountable and unelected bureaucrats in European Institutions whose financial records have not been approved for 14 consecutive years because of error and fraud? It does not make sense. Yet it makes sense, because the 'selfish' British politicians have sold their souls to strangers in Brussels. To borrow the words of Bill Clinton: "This whole thing is a fairy tale – Give me a break."

Another Brussels' unnecessary interference in the affairs of Britons. British newspapers reported on an EU proposal to force employers to increase the minimum period of maternity leave from 14 to 18 weeks. This proposal, which would put additional burden on British businesses, prompted a rebuke from Pat McFadden, the employment minister. According to the article, *Ministers to fight Brussels' plans on maternity leave,* the minister "told peers that Britain would see any move to impose a 100 per cent pay requirement as a "red warning light." Mr McFadden said, the EU should avoid seeking to impose "prescriptive" common standards, rather than setting minimum base-lines on maternity pay and parental leave." (Financial Times 13 March 2009). The question is: why should Britain "fight Brussels on maternity leave pay?" Had British politicians not 'sold' their souls and Britons to Brussels, the "Children" of Jean Monnet would not have dared to impose laws on the British people.

The question still remains: "Why should our British democratic Parliament become subservient to undemocratic and unaccountable institutions in Brussels?" The answer is simple. British politicians have ignored the warning the British Secret Service Agent, Sir Robert Anderson, recorded concerning the character of political Europe and its destiny. The development of the European Union is a prophecy which is being fulfilled. Whatever is associated with this political and economic union has a spiritual significance which would have an impact on every soul. For example, we have, earlier, learnt the implications of two euro coins – the Greek 2 euro cents, which shows a picture of a naked woman sitting at the back of a beast, and the Italian 5 euro cents, which depicts a portrait of the Amphitheatre built by Emperor Vespasian in AD75 and inaugurated by his son, Titus Vespasian, in AD80.

Just as the "powerful" Barroso is an alien to Britons, so would the coming Emperor of Europe, who will be enthroned by the ten influential leaders of the European

Union (the *10 toes of the human image* in Daniel 7:24 and the 10 kings in Revelation 17:12-13) be an alien - an unknown charismatic and intelligent figure - who will jump onto the political scene. It is his ability to solve complex problems that would mesmerise "*the 10 toes*" to hand over their powers and authority to the 'political genius' to guide Europe and the world. Remember, according to Mark Leonard, *"Europe will run the 21st century."* So shall it be; but for a while (Revelation 17:12-13).

THE "AWFUL BEING" - THE KING OF MEN

European Union, the "rarest of all political phenomena," needs a powerful leader. So, the leaders of the revived Roman Empire would embrace the political genius who will grace our troubled world with his charisma, eloquence and extraordinary intelligence. In our "era of charisma" (where spin and rhetoric have replaced substance and reality, and politicians who lacked personality are rejected for not being "winning materials"), mankind would be mesmerised by the magnetism of the "King of Men". They will hail him as their "saviour" when he receives his crown in Europe. (Revelation 13:4). And all will end in tears when the "Kaiser" starts terrorising the world and persecuting those who refuse to honour him (Revelation 13:4). He would be the "Awful Being" Sir Robert Anderson referred to in his *The Coming Prince.*

At this point, I would like to share with you again an extract from a leading article in the 18 December 1876 edition of *The Times*, which prophetically described the attributes of the coming "saviour" of Europe: "What is it that all Europe is looking for? It is the KING OF MEN, the great head of the Hellenic race, the man whom a thousand galleys and a hundred thousand men submitted to on a single recognition of his personal qualities, and obeyed for ten long years. Here are his arms, his shield, and all his familiar accoutrements, as well as the sword and other weapons that had become in a manner part of his own natural frame.......The man who, as soon as he enters, can single out the shield of the KING OF MEN, and say, "That is Mine," must be the man to head the entire Greek race and the races mixed with it in their impending struggle with the remnant of the Asiatic power. It must be a true Philliellene, a scholar, a statesman, a man of unflinching courage and irrepressible enterprise, full of resources, and ready to look in the face of a rival or a foe.....The man who can challenge for his own the Shield of AGAMEMNON, now waiting for the challenge, is the true Emperor of the East, and our easiest escape route from our present difficulties." Sir Robert Anderson referred to this prophetic article in *The Coming Prince.*

True, the easiest escape from Europe's economic, political and security difficulties, and - especially the solution to the Middle East turmoil – would be made possible by the "Mighty king of Europe" who is on the horizon. The rehearsal of the advent of this last Emperor of the revived Roman Empire has now been staged in Britain. We wait for the reality of his presence and kingship.

The coronation of the charismatic King of Men would be the answer to Paul Henri-Spaak's prayer: *"We do not want another committee. We have too many already. What we want is a man of sufficient stature to hold the allegiance of all people, and to lift us out of the economic morass in which we are sinking. Send us such a man and he be god or the devil, we will receive him"* Spark, the Belgian statesman and President of the Consultative Assembly of the Council of Europe from 1949 -1951, was a close friend of the "rascal" Jean Monnet.

I do not know when this "Awful Being," the false messiah, will present himself to *"the 10 toes."* However, I know for certain that the "fake saviour" of the world will appear to deceive mankind to close the era of Gentile Supremacy on earth. The Word of the Lord in Matthew 24:15 would surely be fulfilled. This is one of the Scriptures that motivated Sir Robert Anderson in 1881 to write about Europe and its future, and as a result made this declaration: "In forecasting the fulfilment of these....we are dealing with events which, while they may occur within the lifetime of living men, may yet be delayed for centuries....we may rest content with the certainty that.....their fulfilment will be clear.....to all who are capable of observing public facts...."

As we ponder on Sir Robert Anderson's prophetic writing on European integration, let us also reflect on Apostle Paul's sombre words on the last Caesar: *"The coming of the lawless one* (the King of Men) *will be in accordance with the work of Satan displayed in all kinds of counterfeit miracles, signs and wonders, and in every sort of evil that deceives those who are perishing. They perish because they refused to love the truth and so be saved. For this reason God sends them a powerful delusion so that they will believe the lie and so that all will be condemned who have not believed the truth but have delighted in wickedness"* (2 Thessalonians 2:9-12).

Christians who are obsessed with "miracles, signs and wonders" should take notice of St Paul's warning. Our Lord Himself, in His Sermon on the Mount, cautioned His followers about "miracles, signs and "wonders": He told them, "Many will say to me on that day, 'Lord, Lord, did we not prophesy in your name and in your name drive out demons and perform many miracles?' Then I will tell them plainly, "I never knew you. Away from me, you evildoers!" (Matthew 7:22-23). And finally, the Lord Jesus Christ warned His disciples: "For false Christ and false prophets will appear and perform great signs and miracles to deceive even the elect..." (Matthew 24:24)

THE AGE OF DECEPTION

In our Age of Enlightenment, the shadows of deception swirl around us. Deception in the political system with false promises; deception in the economic system, with false accounting and dubious business practices; deception in the scientific world with bogus claims by so-called experts; deception in the pharmaceutical industry with "disease mongering"; deception in the literary industry with authors peddling falsehood about the Lord Jesus Christ; deception in sports with some athletes cheating with performance enhancing drugs; deception in the fashion industry where super models, who have enhanced their appearances with cosmetic surgeries, promote beauty products as if the use of such products contributed to their beauty. There are deceptions in the Television Industry to the extent that Children are being deceived. Pharmaceutical companies are producing drugs which don't work. On 26 February 2008 newspapers reported how millions of sufferers took useless antidepressant drugs. Manufacturers of these drugs withheld vital data about their products to gain approval.

We also witness deception in the Church – fake miracles, the duping of the congregation and the propagation of "sweet doctrines" to tickle the ears of the naive. The deceptions continue on and on and on. It is not surprising, how Christians stumble when confronted by atheists to explain their Faith. Andrew Sullivan reminded us in his searching article *"There's a new power in America – atheism. The faithless are a growing force as the churches duck the challenges of the age"* (The Sunday Times 15 March 2009). He writes: "In the arguments spawned by the new atheist wave, the Christian respondents have been underwhelming. As one evangelical noted in The Christian Science monitor..."being against gay marriage and being rhetorically pro-life will not make up for the fact that massive majorities of evangelicals can't articulate the Gospel with any coherence." He concludes: "It seems to me that American Christianity, despite so many resources, has ignored its intellectual responsibility. And atheists, if this continues much longer, will continue to pick up that slack."

THE PROPHETIC WORD OF SIR ROBERT ANDERSON

By virtue of Britain's membership of the European Union, let us, again, reflect on Sir Robert Anderson's prophetic word relating to the development of the political alliance of European nations:"....*Through the gradual unfolding, it may be, of influences even now in operation; or far more probably as the outcome of some great European crisis in the future, this confederation of (European) nations shall be developed, and thus the stage will be prepared on which shall appear that awful Being, the great leader of men in the eventful days which are to close the era of Gentile supremacy...That there should be a commonwealth of nations living side by side at peace, was a conception that nothing in the history of the world could have suggested ...That our nation shall have sunk to the position of a province, not even Ireland remaining under her sway....or else England which is to be numbered among the ten kingdoms will include the vast empire of which this island is the heart and centre. .....May we not indulge the hope that however far our nation may lapse in evil days to come from the high place which, with all her faults, she has held as the champion of freedom and of truth, she will be saved from the degradation of participating in the vile confederacy of the latter days?"*

We have learnt in *The Coming Prince,* that the Knight Commander (of the Order) of Bath foretold the restoration of the Jews to Palestine and the development of the European Union. If the Word of God has been fulfilled in the rebirth of Israel and the birth of EU, surely the same Word of God about the future of the *"Vile confederacy of nations"* would also be fulfilled. And it is being fulfilled before our eyes. We are waiting for the leaders of Europe to install their powerful leader to negotiate an "effective" peace deal between the Israelis and the Palestinians. The Lisbon Treaty which was designed to be unreadable to deceive Europeans will pave the way for the final fulfilment of God's Word – the appearance of the King of Deception. For this Treaty of Lisbon would make the EU a legal personality - qualified to sign treaties with other nations. The King of Europe, who will speak on behalf of all the citizens of the European Empire, will sign the 7-year peace deal between the Jews and the Arabs.

BRITAIN AND IRELAND MUST WITHDRAW FROM THE ABOMINABLE EU CLUB AND LEAVE THE FRENCH AND THE GERMANS TO PURSUE THE DREAM OF THEIR FATHERS – JEAN MONNET AND KONRAD ADENAUER. If we persist to follow blindly the 'children' of Monnet and Adenauer to board the "European Titanic," we would not be saved. The "Unsinkable EU Titanic" is destined to sink beneath the waves. A word to the wise is enough, and it takes a wise man to avert a prophecy. "Surely the Sovereign Lord does nothing without revealing His plan to his servants, the prophets" (Amos 3:7).

THE PATRIOT POWELL

In Britain, greedy and unpatriotic politicians are forcing Britons into "slavery" in Jean Monnet's "slave market" in Brussels. A typical example is the suggestion by some politicians and political commentators that Britain would be better off in the eurozone by swapping the Pound for Monnet's Euro. The eurozone is an "abyss of utter darkness". It is appropriate to remind British politicians of the prophetic word of the "Patriot Powell." In 1992, the "Prophet" Enoch addressed Britons: "What the EEC (now the EU) is bent upon has nothing to do with free trade or free anything. It is a naked assertion of the will to power, the will to create a united state to which, instead of our national organs of representation and government, we are all to be subordinated. A nation is free externally in the sense that all laws, policies, and acts of government generally which affect its citizens are made by its own institutions. In a nation "free" in this sense, no laws will be made, or taxes imposed, or judgements judged by an external authority...but the UK is not free, since its laws may now be defined, its taxes imposed, and its policies laid down by an external authority, namely the institutions of EC (now the EU)." And on the floor of the House of Commons (now the House of Indulgence) the Patriot Powell cried out with power: "I did not become a member of our sovereign Parliament to see that sovereignty abated or transferred" (Source: *Principality and Power of Europe* – Adrian Hilton)

THE FAITHFUL JUDGE AND A RIGHTEOUS JUDGE

God is faithful. He does not want any one to perish. The Lord always warns His people before He judges them. For example, before the general flood in the days of Noah, which is recorded in chapters 6 – 8 of the Book of Genesis, the Almighty, through Enoch, warned the wicked and immoral men to repent. The Lord waited patiently for 969 years before He destroyed all life on earth with the exception of 8 people - Noah and his family.

After the deluge, the Almighty continually spoke through His prophets to warn the children of Israel about impending judgement because of their rebellion. The Righteous Judge judged the sins of His people by using King Nebuchadnezzar to escort them into servitude in Babylon, the land of idols. Daniel was among the captives. And it was during this era of exile that God revealed to Nebuchadnezzar, in a dream, concerning the destiny of Israel and all the worldly powers that would succeed the Babylonian Empire. After Daniel had interpreted the dream of a dazzling human image, whose toes were partly of baked clay and partly of iron, Daniel addressed the Emperor of Babylon: *"The great God has shown the king what will take place in the future. The dream is true and the interpretation is trustworthy"* (Daniel 2:45).

THE SILENCE OF GOD

The Almighty God, after spoken through His prophets, came down in the Person of the Lord Jesus Christ to preach the Gospel of forgiveness of sin through repentance. In Matthew 24:15, our Divine Lord revealed the final sign that would mark the beginning of judgement on our corrupt, wicked and immoral generation. God has spoken His last Word. Heaven is now silent. The silence of God does not imply His indifference to our rebellion. The Lord is slow to anger. He is waiting for the appointed time to act. He has waited for over 2600 years. One day He will return in His Majestic Glory to crush the human statue from its "10 toes of baked clay and iron" to its head of gold and scatter them like chaff (Daniel 2:34-35).

The Omnipotent God has remained silent. Is God impotent as some infidels suggest? No. In the third edition of *The Silence of God*, which was published in 1898, Dr Robert Anderson stated: "A silent Heaven! Yes, but it is not the silence of callous indifference or helpless weakness; it is the silence of a great sabbatical rest, the silence of a peace which is absolute and profound - a silence which is the public pledge and proof that the way is open for the guiltiest of mankind to draw near to God. When faith murmurs, and unbelief revolts and men challenge the Supreme to break that silence and declare Himself, how little do they realise what the challenge means! It means the withdrawal of amnesty; it means the end of the reign of grace; it means the closing of the day of mercy and the dawning of the day of wrath." *The Silence of God* was a blessing to many during and after the First World War. Sir Robert's *The Coming Prince* would become a blessing to many in our generation as we witness the European Union – the "vile confederacy of the latter days" – rushing towards its destiny.

IT TAKES A WISE MAN TO AVERT A PROPHECY

We must be vigilant. We must open our eyes, our ears, our minds, our hearts, our soul and our spirit to the Word of God. The Holy Bible, a Library of Books, contains life. We have already seen a picture of what is about to take place. It takes a wise man to avert a prophecy. The people of Nineveh were wise. They repented at the preaching of Jonah. They saved themselves from the wrath of God. King Nebuchadnezzar of Babylon was a fool. His foolish pride blinded him from heeding to Daniel's advice to stop his wicked ways to save himself. God turned Nebuchadnezzar into an animal to live among the beasts in the fields. At the scheduled time the King of Babylon realised that the Heavens rule (Daniel 4).

King Belshazzar, the grandson of Nebuchadnezzar, was also a fool. He did not learn from the mistakes of his grandfather. He failed to humble himself before God. In his arrogance, he and his wives and concubines defiled the scared vessels stolen from the Jerusalem Temple by drinking from them. The last King of Babylon was put on a scale and found wanting. God removed him from power to close the era of the Babylonian Empire. God installed Darius the Mede to mark the beginning of the Medo-Persian Empire (Daniel 5) The Medo-Persian Empire subsequently fell to Alexander the Great, whose Grecian Empire was replaced by the Roman Empire. And the European Union is the revived Roman Empire.

The Lord is in control of events in the world. He used a dazzling human sculpture in Daniel chapter 2 to illustrate the history of human governments and their destiny. Which human being could have adopted such a figure to illustrate the history and fate of all the worldly powers? Witness Lee, the great Bible teacher, says: "Who could write such a Book – the Book of Daniel. The Bible is not only holy, but divine...It is stupid not to believe in the Bible." The Lord gives power to men to serve His purpose, and He takes it away at His pleasure. No one can withhold His Hands. Amen!

I exhort you to keep a close watch at the enlargement of the European Union by studying the Books of Daniel and Revelation. What I have shared with you may not happen in our life time. But they will all come to pass - may be in the days of our children or grandchildren. "The King of Men" (the counterfeit messiah) would appear to fulfil what the Lord predicted in Matthew 24:15-21 "...When you see standing in the holy place the abomination that causes desolation, spoken of through the prophet Daniel.....then let those who are in Judea flee to the mountains. Let no-one on the roof top go down to take anything out of the house... for there will be great distress, unequalled from the beginning of the world—and never to be equalled again..."

Whenever the "King of Men," "the beast from the sea" (Rev. 13:1), appears in your life time, please do not worship him. Do not receive his mark "666" (Revelation 13:18) even at the expense of losing your life. Because, at the appointed time, without the mark "666" on your right hand or on your forehead, *"no-one could buy or sell"* (Revelation 13:16-18). If you are tempted to save your life by accepting the mark of the "beast, you will lose your life. But if you lose your life by refusing the mark of the cunning "beast," you will save your life (Matthew 10:39).

THE SIGN OF WHAT IS TO COME

The sign of the "sign" is already with us. Witness this title in a newspaper article which appeared in the 9 January 2006 edition of the Daily Mail: *"Can't remember your PIN? Then you can forget about shopping."* In this article, Sean Poulter, the Consumer Affairs Correspondent, writes: "Shops and Supermarkets are already turning away customers who want to pay by plastic but cannot remember their personal identification number." At the time of writing, Banks were refusing to authorise payments made without the personal identification number. The Correspondent reported about a supermarket cashier who warned a customer "she would not be able to do her shopping in future if she could not remember her PIN." This was confirmed by Tesco's customer service helpline. (Tesco is one of the major supermarkets in Britain).

BRITISH IDENTITY CARDS

Secondly, let us consider the desperate attempt by the British Labour government to introduce Identity Cards in our nation. Examine this front page article in the 18 April 2006 edition of the Financial Times *"Labour races to introduce ID cards."* It was reported in this story that, "Labour plans to race forward with contentious identity cards scheme to ensure the multi-billion pound infrastructure is up and running before the next election, neutering a Tory pledge to scrap it." Why was the Labour government keen on this contentious project? The powerful leaders of European Union, who will enthrone "the beast from the sea," were behind the scheme.

So, it was not a surprise when, in September 2008. Jacqui Smith, the Home Secretary, unveiled the British identity card which had nothing to do with British identity. As usual, British politicians followed their masters in Brussels to produce an Identity Card that has the EU logo – a bull – incorporated in it. Labour's handiwork was greeted with these headlines: *Anger over ID card that fails to look British* (Daily Express, 26 September 2008). *Unveiled, the ID card (or is it an EU card?* (Daily Mail). According to Daily Mail newspaper, "The card revealed by Home Secretary, Jacqui Smith, features a picture of a bull above EU-style golden stars, while the coloured background is made up of hundreds of tiny letters spelling "EU." The bull is European pagan symbol drawn from Greek mythology. It depicts the Greek pagan god Zeus, who transformed himself into a white handsome beast to abduct *Europa*, daughter of the King of Tyre. Zeus carried *Europa* off to Crete, where he resumed his human form. *Europa* gave birth to a son, Minos. The Minoan civilisation is frequently considered the cradle of European culture. The Labour government may "not do God." However, they must realise that majority of Britons are not pagans for politicians to impose a pagan Identity card on them. We will learn more about this godless symbol, a woman on a beast, in the Appendix.

The Lord Jesus Christ warns us to watch for the coming "beast" so that we do not adore him by receiving his fatal number "666." Witness the caution: "If anyone worships the beast and his image and receives his mark on the forehead or on the right hand, he, too, will drink of the wine of God's fury, which has been poured full strength into the cup of his wrath. He will be tormented with burning sulphur in the presence of the holy angels and of the Lamb. And the smoke of their torment rises for ever and ever. There is no rest day or night for those who worship the beast and his image, or any one who receives the mark (666) of his name. This calls for patient endurance on the part of the saints who obey God's commandments and remain faithful to Jesus" (Revelation 14: 9-12). This is the Pure Word from the Lord Jesus Christ, the King of kings, the Lord of lords and the Lion of the Tribe of Judah, before Him every knee will bow. "See to it that you do not refuse him who speaks, if they did not escape when they refused him who warned them on earth, how much less will we, if we, turn away from him who warns us from heaven?" (Hebrews 12:25).

INSPIRATION FROM THE BOOK OF DANIEL

I conclude this chapter with a summary of some of the prophetic texts in the Book of Daniel which are relevant to our generation. This Old Testament Book, as we have learnt, predicted the reign of all the major Empires that would arise after the Babylonian Empire. It foretold the succession of the three empires - Medo-Persia, Greece and Rome. It also predicted in detail and with extraordinary accuracy the following historical and current events:

- Cyrus' defeat of the last Babylonian King, Belshazzar, and the reign of the Medo-Persian Empire (Daniel chapter 5)
- The defeat of the Medes and the Persians by the Greeks under Alexander the Great (Daniel 8:1-7)
- The sudden death of Alexander the Great at a young age at the height of his power (Daniel 8:8).
- The Division of Alexander the Great's Empire into 4 kingdoms (Daniel 8:8).
- The rise and fall of the wicked Syrian king, Antiochus Epiphanes, and his persecution of the Jews and the desecration of the Jewish Temple with an idol of the Greek god, Zeus (Daniel 8:9-12, 11:3-32)
- The Jewish revolt led by Judas Maccabeus; the defeat of the Syrian army by the Maccabees, and the reconsecration of the defiled Temple (Daniel 11:33-35). .
- The 2300 days from Antiochus invasion of Jerusalem in 170BC to the reconsecration of the Temple on 25 December 165BC (Daniel 8:13-14).
- The day of the first Palm Sunday - 6 April AD32 and the crucifixion of the Lord Jesus Christ (Daniel 9:25-26).
- The destruction of Jerusalem and its Temple in AD70 by Prince Titus Vespasian and his Roman army (Daniel 9:26).
- The revived Roman Empire and its destiny (Daniel 2:39-45).

Just as the Book of Daniel predicted all these historic events with startling accuracy, so has this same Book predicted in detail the development of the European Union which is signified by the *ten toes of baked clay and iron* of the stunning human effigy King Nebuchadnezzar saw in his dream (Daniel 2:40-43). Glory is to God. Before things happened, He announced them (Isaiah 48:5). Amen!

Chapter 23

THE SUPERNATURAL CHARACTER OF THE BIBLE: THE MYSTERIES HIDDEN IN THE FIRST GENERATION OF MANKIND AND THE 12 SONS OF JACOB

"To attempt to stifle criticism of Scripture by the cry that "the Bible is the word of God" only serves to excite distrust on the part of earnest-hearted inquiries. There never was an attack made upon the truth that could not be refuted. "Truth is one"; but error is in its very nature inconsistent, and therefore absurd. And while Divine truth is spiritual, and can only be spiritually discerned, human error is natural and can be met on its own ground. We cannot "reason" men into the kingdom of God, but by reasoning we can expose errors which prejudice them against it." **(The Bible and Modern Criticism RA)**

Before we end our journey of discovering the "Unknown Truth" and the "Forgotten Truth" about the European Union, I would like to share with you in this chapter why we must take the Bible seriously of its prediction about the European Union and its future. I will spend some time to use sections of the first Book of the Bible, Genesis, to demonstrate the supernatural character of the Bible. This would impress upon you, that what God has revealed in the Books of Daniel and Revelation about the European Union and its destiny would surely come to pass. This is a treasure you cannot pick on the street. You must dig deep for its recovery. In *The Bible and Modern Criticism,* Dr. Robert Anderson writes: "Proofs that the Bible is the word of God are clear and abundant. But they do not lie open on the surface. Gold and diamonds are not picked upon the highway; men need to dig for them. Even nature hides her treasures from the trifler. God is a rewarder of them that seek Him diligently".

The discovery of these "Treasures", which are hidden in chapters 5 and 49 of Genesis, will, once again, confirm the divine nature of the Bible, that the Author of this Library of 66 Books knows the end from the beginning. "Before things happened, He announced them" (Isaiah 48:5). The "Author" of the Holy Bible, therefore, writes history before history is written by men. Hence, God's revelation about the European Union and its destiny over 2600 years before the European Union came into existence. We have learnt that the European Union is the revival of the "dead" Roman Empire. Jose Manuel Barroso, the President of European Commission, has already confirmed it by describing the European Union "the world's first non-imperial empire."

THE HIDDEN TREASURE IN THE FIRST GENERATION OF MANKIND: FROM ADAM TO NOAH

The first four chapters of the Book of Genesis teach us about the creation, the fall of man, and how man began to cry to God (Genesis 4: 26). From chapter 6 we learn of the wickedness of men, the flood, the rescue of Noah and his family, Noah's sacrifice to God, the descendants of Noah, the construction of the Tower of Babel, God confusing human speech and scattering men and women over the earth. And finally, the call of Abraham from the land of idol worshippers to become the father of many nations. These events are popular because they are full of interesting incidents.

But Genesis chapter 5 is one of the chapters in the Bible we usually ignore. Some of us find it "boring" - just like the first 17 verses of the Book of Matthew. Why? Because, they are full of "this begat that, and that begat this." Moreover, these verses also contain some "awful" names which are difficult to pronounce. However, Genesis chapter 5 is a glorious chapter. It is full of revelation and riches. The "horrible" names in this chapter contain a "Priceless Jewel."

Before the general flood, we had a record of the first generation of mankind. This was the genealogy of Adam to Noah – a list of 10 names recorded in Genesis 5:1-29.
Adam begat Seth.
Seth begat Enosh
Enosh begat Kenan.
Kenan begat Mahalalel.
Mahalalel begat Jared.
Jared begat Enoch.
Enoch begat Methuselah.
Methuselah begat Lamech.
And Lamech begat Noah (Genesis 5:1-29 KJ).
These names are summarised in 2 Chronicles 1:1-4. We also find them in Luke 3:36-38.

Some of these names may sound "horrible" and difficult to pronounce. However, we will seek the Light of God to shine on them to reveal the *"Treasure"* which is hidden in the names. This revelation will, once again, confirm the supernatural character of the Bible as the source of Absolute Truth. The revelation will also strengthen the Faith of Christians to share the riches in the Bible with the nations of the world. It would also help Europeans to realise that Jean Monnet's vision of a united Europe was recorded over 2600 years ago.

THE SEARCH FOR THE HIDDEN TREASURE – THE PRICELESS JEWEL

Names in the Bible have meaning. In Hebrew tradition we can infer the meaning of a name from its root. For example, Elijah means "Yahweh is my God". Elisha means "God has granted salvation". Ishmael means "God hears." And Malachi means, "My messenger." We will now begin our "Treasure Hunt" by examining the meaning of the 10 names in Genesis 5:1-29 to help us discover the "Priceless Jewel."

1. ADAM

The Hebrew word "adam" is used for "man" in general. It is also the name of the first man. Adam means *"Man"*.

2. SETH

The Bible tells us Cain killed his brother Abel out of jealousy (Genesis 4:1-9). Later on Eve gave birth to another son. She named him Seth. Eve felt God had given her Seth to replace Abel. Scripture says: And Adam knew his wife again. And she gave birth to a son and called his name Seth, for she said, God has appointed me another seed instead of Abel, because Cain slew Him" (Genesis 4:25 HBRV). The name Seth implies *"Appointed."*

3. ENOSH

Enosh was the son of Seth. Enosh comes from a Hebrew word that means incurable wound, frail or mortal. The name Enosh means "Mortal". The Holy Bible Recovery Version confirms the meaning in its commentary on Genesis 4:26.

4. KENAN

Enosh gave birth to Kenan. The name *"Kenan"* is derived from a people called the Kenites. According to "THE OXFORD COMPANION TO THE BIBLE", "The kenites are portrayed in biblical tradition as staunch supporters of Israel and Yahweh who were never fully incorporated into Israelite society." It was foretold in the Book of Numbers that the Kenites would perish. The Bible says, when Balaam saw the Kenites, he uttered his oracle: "Your dwelling place is secure, your nest is set in a rock; yet you Kenites will be destroyed when Asshur takes you captive" (Numbers 24:21-22). That was the plight of the Kenites. The name Kenan implies *"Sorrow"*.

genealogy of the Saviour. But for brevity and not to digress much from the main theme of this book, we will focus on one of them. God wanted to demonstrate to mankind, that He alone knows the end from the beginning, and that whatever He has written in His Word would come to pass. This should encourage us to believe in His promises of judgement, eternal peace and prosperity (Isaiah 45:5-12).

In His Sovereign Will, the Almighty God deemed it necessary to reveal the exact years at which the descendants of Adam to Noah were born and passed away. Without such information we would not have known the fulfilment of the prophetic name Enoch gave to his son. The name Methuselah was based upon the revelation Enoch received from God, that the coming judgement on the rebellious men would not take place in the life time of his son. This means, God would judge the world after the death of Methuselah.

According to Genesis 5:28-29, Methuselah, the 8th generation of mankind, was *187 years* old when he gave birth to Lamech. Lamech, the 9th generation, was *182 years* when he brought forth Noah who became the 10th generation of mankind. Which means, Methuselah was *369 years* old when his grandson, Noah, was born. If Methuselah died at the age of *969 years* (Genesis 5:27), it means, Noah was then *600 years* old. And what happened on Noah's 600th birthday - the day Methuselah died? The Bible says: "In the six hundredth year of Noah's life....on that day the springs of the great deep burst forth, and the floodgates of the heavens were opened. And rain fell on the earth for forty days and forty nights. On that day Noah and his sons, Shem, Ham and Japheth, together with his wife and the wives of his three sons, entered the ark....Every living thing on the face of the earth was wiped out**.....**" (Genesis 7:11-13, 23)

METHUSELAH: THE PROPHETIC NAME FULFILLED

It is clear, that the day Methuselah died the floodgates of the heavens were opened. The corrupt inhabitants on planet earth (who were grumblers and fault-finders; who followed their own evil desires; who boast about themselves and flattered others for their own advantage), were judged (Jude 1:16). Hence, the judgement of the general flood fulfilled the prophetic significance of the name Methuselah - "*His death shall bring.*" Is the Bible not a wonderful Book without an equal? We can depend on its prophetic messages, especially the destiny of the European Union as revealed in Daniel chapter 2. Tim Irwin of St Helens, Merseyside, summed it up: "The test of time and history is that the Bible can be trusted for clear guidance in ethical issues. The problem is that our arrogant and self-indulgent post-modern society tries to remake God in its own image...." (*The Times* 2 March 2004).

THE SIGNIFICANCE OF NOAH'S AGE AT THE TIME OF THE FLOOD

We know the Almighty judged the world with a flood at Noah's 600th birthday. Noah's age at the time of the deluge was also significant in another aspect. It demonstrates how God acts according to Plan. The number 600 is composed of 6x10x10. Numbers in the Bible have symbolic significance. 6 is the number for man. And the number 10 stands for fullness, power and authority. The meaning of these numbers signifies that, God, by using the flood waters to destroy all life on earth when Noah was 600 years, was a demonstration of His Absolute Power and Authority (10x10) to man (6) (Genesis 7:20-23)

GOD IS PATIENT AND SLOW IN ANGER

We can deduce from what we have learnt so far, that from the day Methuselah was born, God waited patiently for *969 years* before destroying all life on earth – birds, livestock, wild animals and mankind - with the exception of 8 people and the creatures in the Ark Noah built. Since the ministry and the death and resurrection of our Lord Jesus Christ, the Almighty has been patient with our rebellion for over 2008 years. At the appointed time the Righteous Judge will pour His wrath on our corrupt, violent, blasphemous and sexually immoral world. This time the Almighty will not judge us with flood, but with an unquenchable fire (Revelation 20:15, 21:8).

Let us reflect on the Lord Jesus' prophetic word about our generation: *"As it was in the days of Noah, so it will be at the coming of the Son of man. For in the days before the flood, people were eating and drinking, marrying and giving in marriage, up to the day Noah entered the ark; and they knew nothing about what would happen until the flood came and took them away"* (Matthew 24:37-39). If we examine our lifestyles and consider how degraded we have become to the extent of claiming there is no Creator and that man just evolved from a brute with no conscience, are we not in the days of Noah? Today our society is plagued with pride, wickedness, violence, sexual immoralities and all the vices we can image. The Lord is about to judge our ungodly world. We see the signs of His coming: wars, rumours of wars, famines, fatal epidemic diseases, earthquakes in diverse places (Matthew 24) and financial and economic crisis (Revelation 18). The sign of all the signs is about to appear in Jerusalem. It would be visible when the Emperor of the revived Roman Empire breaks his 7-year peace treaty with Israel and her Arab neighbours (Daniel 9:27 and Matthew 24:15).

9. LAMECH

Let us examine what the name of the 9th generation of mankind stands for. Methuselah, the 8th generation, gave birth to a son whom he named Lamech

(Genesis 5:25). In Genesis 4:23 we read about a Lamech who made an astonishing confession to his two wives: "Adah and Ziliah, listen to me; wives of Lamech, hear my words: I have killed a man for wounding me, a young man for injuring me. If Cain is avenged seven times, then Lamech seventy-seven times." In Lamech's confession, we could detect the voice of a desperate man crying for comfort. The name Lamech serves as the root for the English word 'Lament" and 'despair.' Thus, "Lamech" implies "*despairing.*"

10. NOAH

Lamech named his son Noah. The name Noah means "*Comfort*". We get a clue from Genesis 5:25 which says, "When Lamech had lived 182 years, he had a son. He named him Noah and said, "He will *comfort* us in the labour and painful toil of our hands caused by the ground the Lord has cursed." *The Hodder Dictionary of Bible Themes* says: "The life of Noah (whose name means comfort demonstrates God's ability to save the righteous and destroy the ungodly."

THE DISCOVERY OF THE "HIDDEN TREASURE": THE "PRICELESS JEWEL"

We know the number 10 stands for fullness, power and authority. What, therefore, is the significance of the 10 names mentioned in Genesis 5:1-29? If we assemble the meaning of these names (Adam to Noah), we will appreciate their spiritual implications.

1. Adam	means	*Man*
2. Seth	means	*Appointed*
3. Enosh	means	*Mortal*
4. Kenan	means	*Sorrow*
5. Mahalalel	means	*The Blessed God*
6. Jared	means	*Shall come down*
7. Enoch	means	*Teaching*
8. Methuselah	means	*His death shall bring*
9. Lamech	means	*Despairing*
10. Noah	means	*Comfort*

Now let us read these 10 names with their meanings:
Man (Adam) is *Appointed* (Seth) *Mortal* (Enosh) *Sorrow* (Kenan) *The Blessed God* (Mahalalel) *Shall come down* (Jared) *Teaching* (Enoch) *His death shall bring* (Methuselah) the *Despairing* (Lamech) *Comfort or Rest* (Noah).

What is the implication of this statement? *"Man is an appointed mortal sorrow; the Blessed God shall come down teaching His death shall bring the despairing comfort or rest"*? Who in history has claimed that his death shall bring comfort or rest to the sinful man? Was it Moses, Aristotle, Alexander the Great, Plato, Confucius, Freud, Darwin, or any other religious or an eminent philosopher?

Let us listen to the voice of the Lord Jesus Christ:
"I am the good shepherd; I know my sheep and my sheep know me...and I lay down my life for the sheep" (John 10:14-15).

"I am the good shepherd, the good shepherd lays down his life for the sheep" (John 10:11).

"I lay down my life-only to take it up again. No-one takes it from me, but I lay it down of my own accord. I have authority to lay it down and authority to take it up again." (John 10:17-18)

"Come to me, all who are weary and burdened, and I will give you rest. Take my yoke upon you and learn from me, for I am gentle and humble in heart, and you will find rest (Noah) for your soul. For my yoke is easy and my burden is light" (Matthew 11:28-30).

From the above declarations our Divine Lord made about Himself, it is clear the statement constructed from the meaning of the 10 names of the first generation of mankind (from Adam to Noah) refers to the Lord Jesus Christ alone. This means, these 10 names are a revelation about the Lord Jesus Christ who came down to lay down His life for our salvation. He is the Lamb of God who takes away the sins of the world (John 1:29)

GOD'S RESPONSE TO THE FALLEN MAN

Genesis 4:26 tells us, *"Seth also had a son, and he named him, Enosh* (Mortal). *At that time men began to call on the name of the Lord."* According to this Scripture, when man disobeyed God and lost the Paradise of Eternal life, the mortal man began to seek his Creator. The loving and merciful God did not turn a deaf ear to the cry of the desperate, sinful man. The Almighty God immediately responded – that He, Himself, would come down to earth to sacrifice His life to save the fallen man from the consequences of his sin. In Genesis 4:26 man cried to God. And God responded in Genesis 5:1-29: *"Man is an appointed mortal sorrow; the Blessed God shall come down teaching that His death shall bring the despairing comfort or rest."* This statement is the summary of the Christian Gospel – the life, the ministry, the agony and the death and resurrection of the Lord Jesus Christ.

The prophet Isaiah spoke of this "Glorious Gospel" about 700 years before it was released in the New Testament. Witness the prophetic message: "He was despised and rejected by men, a man of sorrows, and familiar with suffering...He took up our infirmities and carried out our sorrow. ....He was oppressed and afflicted. He was pierced for our transgression, he was crushed for our iniquities; the punishment that brought us peace was upon him, and by his wounds we are healed...He was cut off from the land of the living; for the transgression of my people he was stricken (Isaiah 53:1- 8). And in about 538 years, before the Lord Jesus visited the earth to sacrifice His life for our redemption, God revealed to the prophet Daniel the exact day the Lord would reveal Himself to the Jews as the promised Messiah – riding on a donkey into Jerusalem. The Almighty also revealed the sacrificial death of the Lord Jesus Christ to the prophet Daniel: "*...After threescore and two weeks shall the Messiah be cut off but not for himself...*" (Daniel 9:26).

Let us examine what the Lord Jesus Christ spoke about His Ministry and sacrificial death:

- "...The bread of God is he who comes down from heaven and gives his life to the world...Your forefathers ate the manna in the desert, yet they died....I (Jesus) am the living bread that comes down from heaven" (John 6:33,51).
- "The reason my Father loves me is that I lay down my life...only to take it up again. No-one takes it from me, but I lay it down of my own accord. I have authority to lay it down and authority to take it again. This command I receive from my Father" (John 10:17-18).
- "I tell you the truth, if anyone keeps my word, he will never see death" (John 8:51).

Without any doubt, the Lord Jesus' testimonies to the Jews are consistent with the revelation in the genealogy of Adam to Noah (Genesis 5:1-29). The Lord Jesus Christ is the fulfilment of the significance of the first generation of mankind. It was the Lord Jesus Christ who came down from heaven to shed His blood at Calvary to save us - the mortal, sorrowful and desperate men - from our sins, and to give us eternal life, which is full of comfort and rest. In summary the genealogy of Adam to Noah was a portrait of the Lord Jesus Christ in the Old Testament that expresses His Humanity mingled with His Divinity. The Jews who believe in the Torah - the five Books of Moses - must believe in the Lord Jesus Christ as the Promised Messiah. Israel's Messiah has already come and He is about to return to Mount Zion.

JEWISH RABBIS:
Moses wrote about the Lord Jesus Christ

With the prophetic message in Genesis 5:1-29, how could some Jews and Jewish Rabbis claim: "We could not comprehend how the Promised Messiah from God should be crucified – die as a criminal?" But, the ministry and the fate of the

Messiah had already been foretold in chapter 5 of Genesis. This first Book of the Torah was not written by the 12 apostles of the Lord Jesus. Paul did not write them either. The Torah was written by Moses, the great Jewish prophet, who led the children of Israel from bondage in Egypt. Apart from Genesis chapter 5, God also revealed to the prophet Daniel the fate of the Saviour: *"The Messiah shall be cut off* (crucified), *but not for himself"* (Daniel 9:25-26).

Under divine inspiration Moses wrote the Books of Genesis, Exodus. Leviticus, Numbers and Deuteronomy. Let us listen to what the Lord Jesus told the unbelieving Jews: "You diligently study the Scriptures because you think that by them you possess eternal life. These are the Scriptures that testify about me, yet you refuse to come to me to have eternal life...If you believed Moses, you would believe in me, for he wrote about me" (John 5:39-40, 46). Truly, Moses wrote about the Lord Jesus Christ in Genesis 5:1-29: "Man (*Adam*) is Appointed (*Seth*) Mortal (*Enosh*) Sorrow (*Kenan*); The Blessed God (*Mahalalel*) shall come down (*Jared*) Teaching (*Enoch*) His death shall bring (*Methuselah*) the Despairing (*Lamech*) Comfort (*Noah*)."

THE PLAN OF GOD TO RESCUE THE FALLEN MAN
God answers the faithful before he calls on Him

In summary, when man disobeyed God under the deceitful influence of the Devil, he sinned. The immortal man lost his fellowship with God. God did not condemn man. Immediately, the merciful God put a plan in place to rescue the mortal man from the Devil. The Almighty God prophesised to the scheming Devil: *"I will put enmity between you and the woman, and between your offspring and hers; he will crush your head, and you will strike his heel"* (Genesis 3:15).

From what we have learnt, it is clear, that before men began to cry to God in Genesis 4:26, the Almighty had already answered them in Genesis 3:15, 21. According to Genesis 3:21, "the Jehovah God made coats of skin for Adam and his wife." God, by clothing Adam and his wife with coats of skin, implied He, God, shed blood. He killed a lamb and used its skin to make garments for the fallen couple. God's killing of a lamb to clothe the "nakedness" of Adam and Eve foreshadowed the substitution death of the Lord Jesus Christ, as the Lamb of God, who shed His blood at Calvary to redeem us from our sins (John 1:29). And while men were crying to God in Genesis 4:26, the Almighty responded in Genesis 5:1-29 to confirm His Word in Isaiah 65:23-24: "...They will not labour in vain......they are the seed of those blessed of Jehovah. And it will be that before they call, I will answer. Even while they are speaking, I will hear." Amen!

the surface. Gold and diamonds are not picked upon the highway; men need to dig for them. Even nature hides her treasures from the trifler. God is a rewarder of them that seek Him diligently." I would urge agnostics, atheists, humanists and all devout sceptics to approach the Bible with an open mind and sincere spirit to seek the truth. God rewards those who diligently seek Him.

We have now discovered the "Treasure" which was hidden in the genealogy of Adam to Noah in Genesis 5:7-29. This was the portrait of the sacrificial death of the Lord Jesus Christ destined to redeem us from our sins and to grant us eternal comfort and rest. The generation of Adam to Noah was therefore a picture of the summary of the Christian Gospel.

THE MYSTERY 'HIDDEN' IN THE TWELVE SONS OF JACOB

The experiences of the children of Israel in the Old testament was a picture of the Church

We will now attempt to discover another mystery which is hidden in Genesis. This is a message of comfort the patriarch Jacob delivered to us through his twelve sons - Reuben, Simeon, Levi, Judah, Zebulun, Issachar, Dan, Gad, Asher, Naphtali, Joseph and Benjamin. Upon these men the 12 tribes of Israel were established. And Genesis 49:1-28 is a record of how Jacob blessed his 12 sons. The order in which the patriarch blessed them is very significant with spiritual implications.

The 12 sons of Jacob became the ancestors of the twelve tribes of Israel. The Old Testament, which is a record of the history and experiences of the children of Israel, are full of pictures, types and shadows of the Lord Jesus Christ. And if the Church is the Body of Christ (Ephesians 4:12), then it implies, the history and adventure of the Jews recorded in the Torah, the Prophets and the Psalms are also pictures, types, and shadows of faithful Christians, who constitute the Church, which is the Body of Christ. In other words, the history of the Israelites is a picture of the Church, which is composed of believers in Christ. For example, when the children of Israel complained to Moses in the wilderness to provide them with water to drink, Moses cried to God for help. The Almighty instructed Moses: *"Pass on before the people, and take with you some of the elders of Israel; and take in your hand your staff with which you struck the River, and go. I will be standing before you there upon the rock in Horeb; and you shall strike the rock, and water will come out of it so that the people may drink. And Moses did so in the sight of the elders of Israel"* (Exodus 17: 1-6 HBRV).

Let us listen to what Apostle Paul had to say about this experience of the Jews: "All our fathers (the Israelites)....were baptised unto Moses in the cloud and in the sea", said Paul. "And all ate the same spiritual food. And all drank the same spiritual drink, for they drank of a spiritual rock which followed them, and the

rock was Christ" (1 Corinthians 1:1-4 HBRV). This text implies that the Israelites experienced the Lord Jesus Christ in a shadow form in the wilderness, just as how we Christians of today experience Christ in this "barren world of troubles". And Hebrews 3:5-6 also tells us: "Moses was faithful as a servant in all God's house, testifying to what would be said in the future. But Christ is faithful as a son over God's house. And we are his house (the church), if we hold on to our courage and hope of which we boast".

So, just as the nation of Israel was established on the 12 sons of Jacob, who became their ancestors. So have the 12 Apostles of Christ become our spiritual ancestors, For the Church was built on the leader of the Apostles, and our knowledge of the Lord Jesus Christ is based upon the teachings of the Apostles, and the *pictures* of the Lord in the Old Testament. For these reasons, therefore, Jacob's prophetical words about his 12 sons have a bearing on Christians.

THE "FOUR SINNERS"

We know from Scriptures the first four sons of Jacob –Reuben, Simeon, Levi and Judah – were sinners. Reuben defiled himself by sleeping with his father's concubines (Genesis 35:22). As a result of his immoral behaviour, Reuben lost his birthright (1 Chronicles 5:1). Simeon and Levi killed the men who raped their sister, Diana (Genesis 34:25-30). Judah also committed incest with Tamar, his daughter – in law (Genesis 38:15-18). However, Levi and Judah were transformed. Because of what the Levites did in Exodus 34:25-30, they were set apart to become the chosen tribe for the priesthood. And 1Chronicles 5:2 tells us: *"Judah prevailed among his brothers, and from him was the leader..."* The tribe of Judah became the line of kings.

THE SIGNIFICANCE OF THE NAMES OF THE 12 SONS OF JACOB

Just as the 10 names in the genealogy of Adam to Noah in chapter 5 of Genesis were meaningful, so were the names of the 12 sons of Jacob. Let us examine these names and consider their implications. Names in the Bible may reflect personal or national experience. They may also indicate future destiny. The root of the names of the 12 sons of Jacob stemmed from the circumstances surrounding their births. In other words, they were a reflection of the events that led to their deliveries.

1. REUBEN

Jacob did not love his wife Leah. When the Lord saw this, He opened her womb. But Rachel whom Jacob loved, because she was lovely in form and beautiful (Genesis 29:17), was barren. "Leah became pregnant and gave birth to a son. She named him Reuben, for she said, "It is because the Lord has seen my misery" (Genesis 29:32).The name "Reuben" means *"Heard my misery"*.

2. SIMEON

Leah conceived again. And when she gave birth to a son she said, "Because the Lord heard that I am not loved, he gave me this one too". So she named him Simeon" (Genesis 29:33). The name "Simeon" means *"One who hears"*.

3. LEVI

Leah gave birth to another son. She said, "Now at last my husband will become attached to me, because I have borne him three sons" (Genesis 29:34). The name "Levi" means *"Attached."*

4. JUDAH

Leah conceived again. When she gave birth to a son she said, "This time I will praise the Lord". So she named him Judah. Then she stopped having children" (Genesis 29:35). The name "Judah" means *"Praise."*

5. DAN

Rachel, whom Jacob loved, became jealous of her sister Leah. Because Rachel was having no children, she confronted Jacob: "Give me children, or I'll die". Jacob became angry and replied: "Am I in the place of God, who has kept you from having children?" Rachel then offered Jacob her servant Bilhah as a wife. Jacob slept with her. She became pregnant and bore him a son. Then Rachel said, *"God* has vindicated me; he has listened to my plea and given me a son" Because of this Rachel named him *Dan"* (Genesis 30:1-4). The name "Dan" implied *"Justice."*

6. NAPHTALI

Bilhah, the servant of Rachel, conceived and bore Jacob a second son. Rachel said, "I have had a great struggle with my sister, and I have won". So she named him Naphtali" (Genesis 30:7). The name "Naphtali" means *"My struggle."*

7. GAD

When Leah realised that she had stopped having children, she gave her maidservant, Zilpah, to Jacob as wife. Zilpah bore Jacob a son. Then Leah said, "What a good fortune!" So she named him Gad" (Genesis 30:9-10). The name "Gad" means *"Good fortune."*

8. ASHER

"Leah's servant Zilpah bore Jacob a second son. Then Leah said how happy I am! The women will call me happy". So she named him Asher (Genesis 30:12). The name "Asher" means *"Happy."*

9. ISSACHAR

Leah became pregnant herself and bore Jacob a fifth son. Then Leah said, "God has rewarded me for giving my maidservant to my husband". So she named him *Issachar"* (Genesis 30:17-18). The name "Issachar" sounds like the Hebrew word for *"reward."*

10. ZEBULUN

Leah conceived again and bore Jacob a sixth son. Then Leah said, "God has presented me with a precious gift. This time my husband will treat me with honour, because I have borne him six sons" (Genesis 30:19-20). The name "Zebulun" means *"Honour."*

11. JOSEPH

The Bible says: "...God remembered Rachel; he listened to her and opened her womb. She became pregnant and gave birth to a son and said, "God has taken away my disgrace". She named him Joseph, and said**,** May the Lord add to me another son" (Genesis 30:22-24). "Joseph" means *"May he add."*

12. BENJAMIN.

The circumstances surrounding the name given to Rachel's last born are very significant. We will spend time to examine them. According to the Bible,, one night Jacob wrestled with a stranger. When this man realised that he could not overpower Jacob, he touched the socket of Jacob's hip so that his hip was wrenched as he wrestled with the man. The stranger pleaded with Jacob to release him. Jacob replied, "I will not let you go unless you bless me." The alien asked Jacob his name. He answered: "Jacob". The stranger addressed Jacob: "Your name will no longer be Jacob, but *Israel,* because you have struggled with God and with men and have overcome. Thereafter he blessed Jacob (Genesis 32:22-29).

Later on God said to Jacob (now Israel): "I am Almighty God; be fruitful and increase in number. A nation and a community of nations will come from you, and kings will come from your body" (Genesis 35:11-12). Jacob and his family moved on from Bethel. While they were still some distance from Ephrath, the pregnant Rachel went into labour. "And as she was having great difficulty in child birth, the midwife said to her, "Don't be afraid, for you have another son. As she breathed her last - for she was dying---she named her son *Ben-Oni.* But his father named him *Benjamin"* (Genesis 35:16-18).

"SON OF MY TROUBLE"; "SON OF MY RIGHT HAND"

"Ben" is the Hebrew word for son. "Ben-Oni", the name Rachel gave to her last son, means *"Son of my trouble."* But, Israel (Jacob) changed this name to *Benjamin,* which means *"Son of my right hand."* The circumstances surrounding the birth of Jacob's last son, and the substitution of the name *Ben-Oni* with *Benjamin*, are of special significance. We will notice it when we establish the meaning of the 12 names of Jacob's sons.

In the Bible the number 12 signifies perfection or completeness in eternity, which implies God's Eternal Administration. We have learnt that the 12 tribes of Israel typify the Church – the congregation of God's people in the Old Testament, which is represented in the New Testament by the 12 Apostles. We also know the first 4 sons of Jacob – Reuben, Simeon, Levi and Judah – were sinners, and the number 4 is the earth number. Let us now reflect on the message the Patriarch Jacob left with the nation of Israel and the Church, as we assemble the meaning of the names of his 12 sons in the order in which he blessed them before he died. This is recorded in Genesis 48:1-28.

1. Reuben	means	Heard my misery
2. Simeon	means	One who hears
3. Levi	means	Attached
4. Judah	means	Praise
5. Zebulun	means	Honour
6. Issachar	means	Reward
7. Dan	means	Justice
8. Gad	means	Good fortune
9. Asher	means	Happy
10. Naphatali	means	My struggle
11. Joseph	means	May he add
12. Benjamin	means	Son of my right hand

THE MESSAGE OF COMFORT

When we construct the meaning of these 12 names, they offer us these comforting words:

"We are sinners (*Reuben, Simeon, Levi and Judah*) in the world.
In our **Misery,** You, God, are the **One who hears** us (R*euben* and *Simeon*).
When we **Attach** (*Levi*) ourselves to You with **Praise** (Judah) and **Honour** (*Zebulun*);
You **Reward** us (*Issachar*) with **Justice** (*Dan),* **Good Fortune** (*Gad),* and **Happiness** (*Asher*). And in our **Struggle** (Naphtali), **May You (God) Add** (*Joseph*) us to Your Son, who **sits at Your Right Hand** (*Benjamin*).

WHO SITS AT THE RIGHT HAND OF GOD?

Listen us examine what the Bible says:

- When Peter was miraculously released from his chains in prison, he went to the temple to preach to the house of Israel saying: "The God of our fathers raised up Jesus whom you murdered by hanging on a tree. Him God has exalted *to His right hand to be Prince and Saviour,* to give repentance to Israel and forgiveness *of sins"* (Acts. 5:30-31).
- Colossians 3:11 says: "If you were raised with Christ, seek those things which are above, where *Christ is sitting at the right hand of God."*
- Hebrews 11:12 tells us: "But this Man (Jesus), after He had offered one sacrifice for sins forever, *sat down at the right hand of God."*
- Apostle Peter teaches, "...Jesus Christ...has gone into heavens *and is at God's right hand*-with angels, authorities and power in submission to him" (1 Peter 3:21-22).
- David died and was buried. He did not ascend to heaven, and yet he said: "The Lord said to my Lord: *"Sit at my right hand* until I make your enemies a foot stool for your feet" (Acts. 2:34-35).
- Stephen was filled with the Holy Spirit when he was explaining the history of the Children of Israel to the Jewish leaders. Before he died from stoning, "He looked up to heaven and saw the glory of God, and *Jesus standing at the right hand of God.* Stephen told the crowd: "Look, I see heaven open, and the *Son of man standing at the right side of God"* (Acts. 7:54-56).

From the above Scriptures, it is clear that Benjamin, the 12th son of Jacob, whose name means *"son of my right hand,"* was a type, a picture and a shadow of the Lord Jesus Christ in the Old Testament. Benjamin's initially name was *"Ben-Oni."* His father changed it to *"Benjamin."* We must, therefore, examine the significance of Benjamin's first name - *"Ben-Oni"*- and how it relates to the Lord Jesus Christ.

THE LORD JESUS CHRIST AS "BEN-ONI" AND "BENJAMIN"

The humiliating and brutal death the Lord Jesus experienced at Calvary inflicted pain on His mother. Mary saw her innocent Son nailed to a wooden tree with a crown of thorns, and slowly bleeding to death in excruciating pain. Such a spectacle would send shivers through the heart of any loving mother. Mary's sorrowful experience beneath the cross fulfilled the prophetic message Simeon delivered to her when he held the baby Jesus in his arms: *"Sovereign Lord, as you have promised, you now dismiss your servant in peace. For my eyes have seen your salvation which you have prepared in the sight of all people, a light for revelation to the Gentiles and for glory to your people Israel....This Child is destined to cause the falling and rising of many in Israel, and to be a sign that will be spoken against, so that the thoughts of many hearts will be revealed. And a sword will pierce your own soul too"* (Luke 2:23-25). And on the cross, when the Lord Jesus saw His mother and the disciple whom He loved overwhelmed with grief, He comforted them with these words: *"Woman, behold thy son; Son, Behold thy mother"* (John 19:26-27).

We know Rachel experienced "great difficulty" during the delivery of her last son. On account of her pains, she named him *"Ben-Oni"*- meaning *"Son of my trouble."* So, just as Rachel's last son became a source of trouble for her, in type, the Lord Jesus' cruel death was a source of distress for His mother, Mary. The Lord Jesus Christ became *"Ben-Oni"* to Mary. We know Jacob changed the name "Ben-Oni" to "Benjamin" - meaning *"Son of my right hand."* We also know the Lord Jesus rose from the dead on the third day of His burial. And the Gospel tells us: "After the Lord Jesus had spoken to them (the disciples), he was taken up into heaven and he *sat at the right hand of God"* (Mark 16:19). From this Scripture we notice how the Lord Jesus Christ became *Benjamin* - "Son of my Right Hand." So, the Lord Jesus Christ, whose violent death was a source of pain to Mary *("Ben-Oni*), and who rose from the dead to sit at the Right Hand of God to become *"Benjamin,"* was the reality of Jacob's 12th son, Benjamin, whose first name was Ben-Oni.

JOSEPH WAS A "SHADOW" OF THE LORD JESUS CHRIST IN THE TORAH

When we read the implications of the names Jacob gave to his 12 sons, we noticed in the text that the name "Joseph," which means *"May He add,"* refers to God. And the name "Benjamin," which means, *"Son of my right hand,"* refers to the Lord Jesus Christ who sits at the Right Hand of God. But we also know from Scriptures, that Joseph was a type of the Lord Jesus Christ in the Old Testament. For example, Joseph was betrayed by his own brothers. They cast him into a pit like a dead sheep and sold him as a slave. The Lord Jesus was also betrayed by one of His own disciples, Judas, who sold him for thirty pieces of silver. The wife of Potiphar falsely accused Joseph of rape. The Lord Jesus was also wrongly accused of blasphemy. Joseph suffered at the hands of his own brothers. The Lord Jesus was also maltreated by His own people. At His trial before Pilate, the Roman Soldiers whipped and crowned the Lord with thorns. The Jews jeered at Him and cried for His crucifixion. Joseph's brothers cast him into a pit. In the end Joseph saved them from dying of hunger. Joseph addressed them: "You meant evil against me, but God meant it for good" (Genesis 50:20). In the same way, the Jews thought, by crucifying Jesus, they would get rid of a blasphemer and a rebel. However, the crucifixion of the Lord Jesus Christ and His Resurrection was destined to save us from our sins. This was foretold in Daniel 9:25-26: *"...And after three score and two weeks shall the Messiah be cut off, but not for Himself."*

Joseph became the Prime Minister of Egypt at the age of 30. He had the power to imprison his brothers who maltreated and sold him into slavery. But Joseph forgave his brothers when he revealed his identity to them in Egypt. Joseph assumed his leadership role at the age of 30 (Genesis 41:46-50). The Lord Jesus also began His public ministry at the age of about 30 (Luke 3:23). Like Joseph who forgave his cruel brothers (Genesis 45:5), so did Jesus, when He was dying on the cross, prayed to God to forgive those who persecuted him (Luke 23:24). Remember, Joseph wept privately when he was about to reveal himself to his brothers (Genesis 43:30-31). Jesus also wept over Jerusalem for two reasons. Firstly, the failure of the Jews to recognise that He was the Messiah they had been waiting for, when He rode on a donkey into Jerusalem. Jesus expected the Jews to have known that day, because it had been predicted in Daniel 9:25. Secondly, the Jews were also unaware that their city, Jerusalem, and its Temple would be destroyed. The Lord, again, expected them to have known this from Daniel 9:26. The Lord confirmed the siege and the destruction of Jerusalem in Luke 19:41-44.

THE LORD JESUS CHRIST IS GOD

It is clear from what we have learnt that, Joseph was a shadow or a picture of the Lord Jesus Christ in the Old Testament. But we also know the name "Joseph" means *"May He (God) add."* So, if Joseph was a picture of the Lord Jesus Christ in the Torah, and the same Joseph is referred to as "God", by virtue of the meaning of his name - *May God Add* - it, therefore, implies that the same Jesus whom Joseph typifies, is also a picture of God. The Lord Himself declares: "If you see Me you have seen the Father; I and the father are One" (John 10:38)

Let us illustrate this Divine Truth in a mathematical form:

Joseph's name	=	May He (God) add
Joseph typifies	=	Jesus
Therefore:		
Joseph (May He (God) add	=	Jesus
It follows		
Jesus	**=**	God. Amen! **(QED)**

It is on the basis of this divine truth Apostle John declares: "In the beginning was the *word,* and the *Word* was with God, and the *Word was God*...The *Word* became flesh *(Jesus)* and made his dwelling among us" (John 1:1, 14). It is obvious from this Scripture, that the Lord Jesus Christ was the ***Word.*** And He was with God. And He was God, who came to live among men (Divinity mingled with Humanity) to lay down His life for our redemption. This is consistent with the revelation in the genealogy of Adam to Noah: *"Man is appointed mortal sorrow. The Blessed God shall come down teaching; His death shall bring the despairing comfort"* (Genesis 5:1-28).

From these Scriptural truths, it is clear if we deny the Lord Jesus Christ - The Blessed God (*Mahalalel),* who came down *(Jared),* "and went about all Galilee teaching *(Enoch)* in ...Synagogues, preaching the gospel of the kingdom, and healing all kinds of sickness and all kinds of diseases among people" (Matthew 4:23), we deny the existence of God. If we ridicule the Lord Jesus Christ we mock God. If we blaspheme the Name and Person of the Lord Jesus Christ, we slander God. We dishonour our Maker. The Bible tells us, "Do not be deceived, God is not mocked; for whatever a man sows, that he will also reap" (Galatians 6:7). But, if we repent and accept the Lord Jesus Christ as our Saviour; and "confess our sins, he, who is God, is faithful and just and will forgive us our sins and purify us from all unrighteousness" *(*1 John 1:9). We shall have eternal life (John 6:40). The Lord Jesus Christ is God. Hallelujah! Make a decision today to accept Him and live by His Word. He has shed His Blood for every man and woman - rich or poor, strong or weak. Amen!

If the Lord Jesus Christ is the Blessed God (*Mahalalel),* who came down *(Jared*) in the flesh as the Messiah whose death brought us (*Methuselah)* comfort and rest (*Noah),* then we must know the cost of following the Messiah. It is expensive. For the Lord Himself tells us, in this world we will have troubles, but we must be of good cheer because He has overcome the world. Hence, His caution: if we want to follow Him we must deny ourselves and take up our cross. The Lord, again, warns that some of us would be put in prison and others would be killed (Revelation 2:10).

CHRISTIANITY IS A LABOUR

It is clear from the Lord, that Christianity is not easy. It is a labour. A labourer worths his pay. Our wages are not temporal; they are eternal life with Christ. But the narrow road that leads to eternal life is like the eye of a needle. This tiny path is crooked, full of "thorns" - which are ridicule, persecution and death. The pains we would experience from the "thorns" on the narrow road would cause some of us to shed blood and die. This experience is what the Almighty God revealed to us in the Covenant of Circumcision – the painful removal of our foreskins on the eighth day of our birth. (I would deal with the significance of the Covenant of Circumcision in a later volume)

Our "wages" of eternal life with the Lord Jesus Christ would be preceded by the three and half years of the Great Tribulation He described in Matthew chapter 24. We know after this three and half years of distress, the Lord would descend with His overcomers, who had already been ruptured, to clear the mess on planet earth. The clearing of the 'rubbish' would be the destruction of all human governments and their charismatic leader, the last Caesar of the revived Roman Empire. This would be preceded by the completion of a '4 colourful horse race'.

THE RACE OF THE 4 COLOURFUL HORSES

Today we are witnessing this remarkable 4-horse race. In the first lane is a White horse. In the second lane is a Red horse. In the third lane is a Black horse. And in the fourth lane is a Pale Horse. These four colourful horses are on the 'home stretch'– competing fiercely for the finishing line. As they head towards the finishing post, we could see the "jockeys" whipping their horses, and the galloping sounds of the horses becoming louder and louder.

THE SOUNDS OF THE 4 HORSES

The significance of the "Rider on the White Horse" is very important, since its symbolism has been associated with Antichrist. I will therefore spend some time to throw a light on this particular horse. We know the 4 coloured horses left their starting blocks when the Lord Jesus Christ, after he had ascended into heaven, opened the first four of the seven seals. In his vision Apostle John tells us: *".....I looked, and behold, a white horse. He who sat on it had a bow, and a crown was given to him, and he went out conquering and to conquer" (*Revelation 6:2"). Where was the arrow? It had already been shot at the enemy. The reward was the crown given to the Rider.

The Lord Jesus Christ defeated Satan on the cross at Calvary when He resurrected from the dead. When the Lord ascended into Heaven and opened the first seal, His disciples began to preach the Gospel to convert lost souls. On the Day of Pentecost, when the Church was established, the preaching of the Gospel saved 3000 souls. They were delivered from the Devil. Since then the Gospel has been spreading to convert souls for the Kingdom. The Gospel is being preached all over the world. Paul says; "I am not ashamed of the Gospel. It is power unto salvation." The Gospel is Glorious, and those who preached it are wearing the crown of glory, because it is this "Sword of the Spirit" – the Word – that destroys the Devil. The Word has the power to uproot the Devil. There is no shame in proclaiming the Gospel.

The Bible does not contradict itself; it interprets itself to compliment itself. Apostle John confirmed the Rider of the White Horse in this vision: "Now I saw heaven opened and behold a white horse. And he who sits on it was faithful and true, and in righteousness. He judges and makes war. The Rider was conquering. His head has many crowns. His name is called the Word of God. (Revelation 19:11-13). It is clear the Rider of the white horse is the Gospel. Hence, the sound of the White Horse is the Word of God, which is being preached and taught all over the world by priests, pastors, evangelists, and through books, radio and television broadcasting and the internet. White symbolises pure and clean, which means the Gospel is clean and pure. We must not contaminate it with our opinions.

The sound of the Red Horse is War. We read in our newspapers and watch on our television screens how wars are raging fiercely among nations resulting in the shedding of blood – bringing confusion, distress and unrest among men. A clear example was the invasion of Iraq by the United States of America and its principal ally, Britain, which resulted in the deaths of thousands of people including innocent children. The ongoing conflict in the Middle East between the Jews and the Palestinians has also caused the deaths of hundreds of people including innocent children. The invasion of Gaza in 2009 by the Israelis resulted in bloodshed and the destruction of properties. The Continent of Africa is plagued with tribal wars, political and religious conflicts in Somalia, Sudan, Nigeria, Zimbabwe and Congo. Thousands of lives have been lost.

The sound of the Black Horse is famine, poverty and fatal epidemic diseases, which have claimed the lives of millions of people around the world. The lost of these lives is the sound of the Pale Horse - death. Clear examples are the tribal conflicts and droughts in many parts of Africa – including Ethiopia, Sudan, Somalia that have resulted in poverty and famine. And epidemic diseases like AIDS have claimed millions of lives all over the world. On 26 January 2005, a headline in a Ghanaian newspaper, *Daily Graphic*, read: *"42 Million die of AIDS worldwide"* This 4-horse race is recorded in Revelation 6:1-8.

THE "TOES OF IRON" AND THE "TOES OF CLAY"

As we watch the 4-horse race, we also witness the appearance of the "10 toes of the magnificent human statue, which are partly iron and partly clay" (Daniel 2:33, 42-44). We know this is the development of the European Union. The emergence and the enlargement of these "10 toes of iron and clay" imply that the Antichrist, the "Man of Lawlessness," is about to enter the political scene to rule Europe and the world with the support of the 10 kings of the revived Roman Empire. Which means, the "stone cut without human hands" is about to descend to strike the human statue from its toes, and crush the whole colossal effigy of gold, silver, bronze and iron and clay and scatter them like a chaff on a threshing-floor in the summer without leaving a trace" (Daniel 2:34-35, 43-45).

THE BEGINNING OF SORROWS

We are also seeing the earth shaking from its place. On 26 December 2004, an underwater earthquake (tsunami) occurred in the Indian Ocean. The world suffered a terrible tragedy as furious waves wrecked havoc – spreading deaths across Asia.

- The Sunday Telegraph described the underwater earthquake: "THE DAY EARTH SHOOK" (2 January 2005).
- TIME magazine described the disaster: "...massive earthquake that

trembled the earth crust" (10 January 2005).

- THE TIMES newspaper described the tsunami in an article entitled *How earthquake jolted the planet.* The paper reported: "The earthquake responsible for the Asian tsunami was so powerful that it changed the local geography, shifting islands and the mainland of Sumatra by as much as 120ft. America seismologists said...The energy released by the quake was so huge that it may even have caused the Earth to wobble on its axis. Geophysicists are calling it a mega thrust, the term used for the most powerful of changes in the Earth's surface"(29 December 2004).
- On 3 January 2005, a column in Financial Times read: "The tsunami have left a tragedy of biblical proportions."

The above descriptions of the underwater earthquake that resulted in the death of over 200000 people across over ten countries, confirmed the infallible Word of the Almighty God. In Isaiah 13:1-13 we read: *"See, the day of the Lord is coming – a cruel day, with wrath and fierce anger to make the land desolate and destroy sinners within it....I will punish the world for its evil, the wicked for their sins. The stars of heaven and their constellation will not show their light. The rising sun will be darkened and the moon will not give its light. I will make the heavens tremble; and the earth will shake from its place_at the wrath of the Lord Almighty, in the day of his burning anger."* Indeed, we are witnessing great earthquakes that are shaking the earth from its place, famines and pestilences in various places. We see nations in anguish and perplexity at the roaring and tossing of the sea. We also see men fainting from terror, and gripped with apprehension of what is coming on the world (Luke 21:11, 25-26).

On 10 January 2005, TIME published a Special Report on the Tsunami tragedy. According to the report, "...The cause of the carnage was a massive earthquake that trembled the earth crust off the western coast of the Indian Ocean of the Indonesia island of Sumatra, setting off through the Ocean shockwaves that were felt more than 5000Km away on the coast of East Africa......Like no other natural disaster in living memory, the Asian tsunami induced a planetary torrent of sorrow." TIME described the whole catastrophe as, "The most powerful earthquake in 40 years quickly turned into one of the most disasters in a century." The ferocity of the waves, which were generated by the underwater earth quake, spread deaths across Andaman & Nicobar Islands, Bangladesh, Burma, India, Indonesia, Kenya, Maldives, Somalia, Seychelles Sri Lanka, Tanzania and Thailand.

Apart from the Asian tsunami, other earthquakes have already killed thousands of people. In an article, *Lessons of humility and compassion that come from disaster* (Daily Mail 3 January, 2005) Melanie Phillips writes: "There have been other disasters with comparable or even greater loss of life....In 1970, a Bangladesh cyclone left 500,000 dead; in 1965, an Indian drought wiped out 1.5 million people; in 1976, an earthquake in China caused 242800 fatalities. In 1755, the Lisbon earthquake which wiped out 60000 souls caused a seismic shudder throughout religious faith in Europe. In the 20th century, the massive slaughter of World War 1 undermined much Christian belief. And for many Jews and others, God died in the gas chambers at Auschwitz."

THE WORD OF THE LORD MUST COME TO PASS

The misfortunes we experience, the disasters we witness around us that have resulted in the deaths of millions from earthquakes, wars, famine and fatal epidemic diseases, should not cause Christians to doubt and question the existence of God. These catastrophes should rather strengthen our FAITH in the Lord Jesus Christ - the Blessed God *(Mahalalel),* who came down *(Jared)* to teach (*Enoch),*that His sacrificial death shall bring (*Methuselah)* eternal rest and comfort (*Noah*) to those who would believe in Him. The Lord Himself predicted over 2000 years ago, that there would be wars and rumours of wars - "Nation will rise against nation, and kingdom against kingdom. There will be great. famines and pestilences in various places, and fearful events and great signs. All these are the beginning of birth-pains" (Matthew 24:7-8, Mark 13:8 and Luke 21:10-11).

According to the Lord Jesus: "Heaven and earth will pass away, but My words will by no means pass away" (Matthew 24:35). So that His integrity and Omniscience would not be questioned by any man, all the tragedies the Lord Jesus Christ listed in the Gospels of Matthew, Mark and Luke must come to pass to confirm His Words will never pass away. And this would bear testimony that the universe was created through Him, and He Alone knows the end from the beginning. "*...Before things happen I announce them to you*", says the Lord" (Isaiah 48:5). Amen!

A HOPE TO THE WORLD?

A leading cultural historian, Felipe Fernandez-Armesto, commented on the Asian tsunami. In his attempt to offer hope to the pagan world, he blasphemed God. In his article, *We should still dare to hope* (Evening Standard, 31 December 2004), the learned historian writes: "It's characteristics of human nature that once we start getting gloomy, all our thoughts darken. The Indian Ocean tsunami seems to symbolise the intractability of nature and the inevitability of disaster. Neither God nor humans seem capable of getting the planet right. We are equally powerless in the face of catastrophes we cause for ourselves: wars and genocides..." The scholar goes on: "I am a congenital pessimist. I recommend pessimism to everyone: it is the only indemnity against disappointment.....Optimism condemns you to disillusionment whenever things go wrong, whereas the pessimist is gratified with even modest little successes and improvements."

I disagree with this intellectual. I do not share his "Philosophy of Pessimisms and Optimisms." It is we, the fallen human beings, who are incapable of getting the planet right, not God. The truth is that the pen, or whatever the learned cultural historian used to publish his comments on the underwater earthquake, was not an accident. Someone produced it. If the instrument the scholar used to write his article was not an "accident", how could the sun, the stars and the moon that give us heat and light be an accident? The truth is, God, who created the heavens and the earth, predicted that there would be wars, famines, fatal epidemic diseases and earthquakes in various places, before He visits the earth for the second time to judge the living and the dead (Revelation 20:11-15).

Whether it is God who causes disasters or the Devil who causes them, who are we to question the integrity of the One who created us from the dust of the ground. Since creation, God does what pleases Him. In chapter 28 of the Book of Deuteronomy, the Almighty, speaking through His servant Moses, described to His people, the children of Israel, the Blessings He would pour on them if they obeyed His commandments, and the Curses they would inherit if they disobeyed His Laws.

Let us witness how Moses finally described the curses the Israelites would experience if they rejected God: "The Lord will also bring on you every kind of sickness and disaster not recorded in this Book of the Law, until you are destroyed. You who were as numerous as the stars in the sky will be left but few in number, because you did not obey the Lord your God. Just as it pleased the Lord to make you prosper and increase in number, so it will please him to ruin and destroy you. You will be uprooted from the land you are entering to possess. Then the Lord will scatter you among all nations, from one end of the earth to the other" (Deuteronomy 28:61-64). Has the Lord been proved right?

Again, the Lord tells us: "I will have mercy on whom I will have mercy, and I will have compassion on whom I will have compassion" (Exodus 33:19).

- When the children of Israel rebelled against God, out of over 1,000,000 people who left slavery in Egypt to enter the Promised Land, only two made it - Joshua and Caleb. The rest perished in the wilderness.
- In the days of Enoch, which was the seventh generation of mankind, God warned the inhabitants of the earth that He would destroy the world because of their rebellion – wickedness and sexual immoralities. True to His word, in the tenth generation of mankind, which was the days of Noah, God used a general flood to destroy all life on the face of the earth with the exception of 8 people - Noah and his family (2 Peter 2:4-5).
- In the Book of Numbers we read how God sent His angel to kill 24000

> of His people in one night, when they disobeyed His command and engaged in sexual relationships with Moabite women.

God loves His creation. He is also a Righteous Judge who judges sin. The Eyes of God are too pure to look on evil. God only exercises patience for our sins. He cannot tolerate wrong (Habakkuk 1:13). Our human wisdom is foolishness in the sight of God (1 Corinthians 3:19). How could we question God with our flawed and limited human intelligence? The Word of God will always come to pass. He has predicted greater disasters to come upon our wicked and immoral generation; and so shall it be.

The Lord Jesus Christ tells us in the Book of Revelation that He will, one day, destroy a third of the world, and cause boils to swell on those who will bear the mark of the Beast – Antichrist. He will command locusts to invade the earth, not to harm the grass of the earth, or any green tree, but with a power like a scorpion to torture "those men who do not have the seal of God on their foreheads" (Revelation 9: 2-4). Today we do not want to die prematurely. We run away from death. We want to save the planet to save ourselves by reducing carbon dioxide in the atmosphere. But the Lord says, there will be a time when *"Men will seek death and will not find it; they will desire to die, and death will flee from them"* (Revelation 9:6).

A FALSE HOPE TO THE WORLD

The leading cultural historian offered the world a false hope with his Philosophy of Pessimisms and Optimisms. This intellectual may be "a congenital pessimist." And in a world of free speech, the cultural historian is entitled to blaspheme God as being impotent – "not capable of getting the planet right." He is also free to recommend pessimism to the world. The confused world that has no clue of what is happening and claims man evolved from a brute, may be grateful for his advice. But we, the Bible-believing Christians, would ignore the recommendation of the "congenital pessimist" scholar.

We are optimists. Our optimism is deeply rooted in the Lord of the heavens and of the earth, who assures us of our future with this statement: "Eye has not seen, nor ear heard, nor have entered into the heart of man the things which God has prepared for those who love him" (1 Corinthians 2:9). Our optimism is anchored in the "Root of David" - the Lord Jesus Christ (Revelation 22:16) - the Blessed God (*Mahalalel)* who claims with absolute authority: *"I am the resurrection and the life. He who believes in me will live, even though he dies; and whoever lives and believes in me will never die"* (John 11:25-26). The world should ponder on these words from the King of kings in the context of the tsunami tragedy, as well as all the other catastrophes that have claimed millions of lives – both young and old.

THE DESTINY OF THE INNOCENT

Whatever kind of death we observe and experience- through wars, earthquakes, famines and diseases - are not the real death. The actual death, which would be a separation from the Lord Jesus Christ into the lake of fire, would take place before the Judgement seat of the Lord Jesus Christ. If our names are not found in the Book of Life we would be cast into the lake of fire. So, if innocent adults and children have lost their lives through earthquakes, wars, famine and diseases, the Righteous Judge would not condemn them to hell to experience the real death.

The Lord Jesus Christ knows how every soul will leave this world to face Him on the judgement day. The manner of our death is insignificant. The important issue is: would our names be found in the Book of life? Daniel 12:1-2 says: "everyone whose name is found written in the book will be delivered. Multitudes who sleep in the dust of the earth will awake; some to everlasting life, others to shame and everlasting contempt." The record in the book of life would determine our eternal fate, not our deaths through earthquakes, wars, drowning in the sea, famine or deadly diseases. Most of the followers of the Lord Jesus Christ experienced gruesome deaths. For example, Stephen was stoned to death. Peter was crucified head downwards. The head of Paul was cut off. Emperor Nero burned Christians alive and offered them as meals to hungry lions. Yet these persecuted Christians are resting in the Arms of the Gracious Lord.

JUDGEMENT BEFORE THE LORD JESUS CHRIST

Let us listen to what the Lord revealed to Apostle John: "I saw the souls of those who have been beheaded because of their testimony for Jesus and because of the word of God. They had not worshipped the beast or his image and had not received his mark on their forehead. They came to life and reigned with Christ for a 1000 years" (Revelation 20:4). And let's reflect Apostle John's vision of what will take place before the Righteous Judge: "I saw a great white throne and Him who sat on it from whose face the earth and the heaven fled away.....And I saw the dead, small and great, standing before God, and books were opened. And another book was opened, which is the Book of Life. And the dead were judged according to their works, by the things which were written in the books. The sea gave up the dead who were in it, and Death and Hades delivered up the dead who were in them. And they were judged, each one according to his works. Then Death and Hades were cast into the lake of fire. This is the second death. And anyone not found in the Book of Life was cast into the lake of fire: (Revelation 20:11-15). "The cowardly, unbelieving, abominable, murderers, sexually immoral, sorcerers, idolaters, and all liars shall have their part in the lake which burns with fire and brimstone, which is the second death" (Revelation 21:8).

THE END OF PAIN, DEATH AND SORROW

Let us brood over what the Lord Jesus Christ revealed to Apostle John concerning those whose names were found in the Book of Life: "...I saw a new heaven and a new earth, for the first heaven and the first earth had passed away. Also there were no more seas (no more tsunamis)....And I heard a loud voice saying: "Behold, the tabernacle of God is with men, and He will dwell with them, and they shall be His People. God Himself will be with them and be their God. And God will wipe away every tear from their eyes; there will be no more death, nor sorrow, nor crying. There shall be no more pain, for the former things have passed away" (Revelation 21:1-4). Amen! All these Scriptures confirm the Word of the Lord Jesus Christ: "I am the resurrection and the life. He who believes in Me, though he may die, he shall live. And whoever lives and believes in Me shall never die" (John 11:23).

GOD IS GOD; NO ONE CAN QUESTION HIM
(The Lord is angry with all nations)

To the pessimist pagans who do not believe in the existence of God, and question His Omnipotence and loving-kindness, and to the doubting Christians and church leaders, who because of tragedies, are tempted to question the existence of God, I would share with you what the Almighty God declared through the prophet Isaiah:

- "The earth is defiled by its people. They have disobeyed the laws, violated the statutes and broken the everlasting covenant. Therefore a curse consumes the earth; its people must bear their guilt. Therefore, earth's inhabitants are burned up, and very few are left...... the beer is bitter to its drinkers. The ruined city lies desolate" (Isaiah 24:5-10).
- "...You nations listen; pay attention, you peoples! Let the earth hear, and all that is in it, the world, and all that comes out of it! The Lord is angry with all nations, his wrath is upon all their armies; He will totally destroy them, he will give them to the slaughter. Their slain will be thrown out, their dead bodies will send up a stench; the mountains will be soaked with their blood. All the stars of the heavens will be dissolved, and the sky rolled up like a scroll..." (Isaiah 34:1-4). Where is that "global warming" thing?
- "I am the Lord, and there is no other. I form the light and create darkness, I bring prosperity and create disaster; I, the Lord, do all these things...Woe to him who quarrels with his Maker, to him who is but a potsherd among the potsherds on the ground. Does the clay say to the potter, 'What are you making?' Does your work say, 'He has no hands?' Woe to him...Concerning things to come, do you question me about

> my children, or give me orders about the work of my hands? It is I who made the earth and created mankind upon it. My own hands stretched out the heavens; I marshalled their starry hosts……. Turn to me and be saved, all you ends of the earth; for I am God, and there is no other. By myself I have sworn, my mouth has uttered in all integrity a word that will not be revoked. Before me every knee will bow, by me every tongue will swear" (Isaiah 45:7-12, 21-24). Amen!

Now, let the doubting Christians, clergymen, bishops and Archbishops, who have been tempted to question the existence of God because of tragedies that affect innocent children, consider the implications of these Scriptures:

- Isaiah 7:14 predicted the birth of the Lord Jesus Christ: "…The Lord Himself shall give you a sign; Behold, a virgin shall conceive, and bear a son, and shall call his name Immanuel."
- Isaiah 9:6 supported the prediction of the birth of the Messiah with these words: "For unto us a child is born, unto us a son is given and the government shall be upon his shoulder, and his name shall be called Wonderful, Counsellor, the Mighty God, the Everlasting Father, the Prince of Prince."
- The Prophet Isaiah described in detail how the Messiah would suffer and die": *"He is despised and rejected of men; a man of sorrows and acquainted with grief…..he was wounded for our transgressions, he was bruised for our iniquities; the chastisement of our peace was upon him. ….He was oppressed, and he was afflicted, yet he did not open his mouth: he is brought as a lamb to the slaughter, and as a sheep before her shearers is dumb, so he opened not his mouth. He was taken from prison and from judgement…… for he was cut off out of the land of the living: for the transgression of my people was he stricken. And made his grave with the wicked…..he had done no violence, neither was any deceit in his mouth. Yet it pleased the Lord to bruise him* (Isaiah 53: 3 – 10).
- And in the marvellous Book of Daniel, the Angel Gabriel confirmed Isaiah's prophetic message about the "cutting off" (the crucifixion) of Christ: *"….After threescore and two weeks shall Messiah be cut off, but not for himself…"* (Daniel 9:27).
- The doubting Christians and church leaders must deal with this question:
- If the prophetic messages in chapters 7 and 9 in the Book of Isaiah about the virgin birth of Jesus have been fulfilled;
- If chapter 53 of the Book of Isaiah, which foretold the unjust trail of Christ, His condemnation to death, His agony, His humiliating, cruel and sacrificial death have all been fulfilled;
- Shouldn't the prophetic messages in the same Book of Isaiah about the

> disasters that would come upon our wicked, corrupt, immoral and blasphemous world, be fulfilled?

We should not select Scriptures that suit our thinking and prejudices. Let us listen to the Voice of the Lord Almighty: "…My thoughts are not your thoughts, neither are your ways my ways…As the heavens are higher than the earth, so are my ways higher than your ways and my thoughts than your thoughts. As the rain and the snow come down from heaven, and do not return to it without watering the earth and making it bud and flourish, so that it yields seed for the sower and bread for the eater, so is my word that goes out from my mouth; It will not return to me empty, but will accomplish what I desire and achieve the purpose for which I sent it" (Isaiah 55:8-11). Amen!

A WORD FOR THE ARROGANT INTELLECTUALS AND PROGRESSIVE CHURCH LEADERS AND THEOLOGIANS

The Lord has a word for the haughty intellectuals and politicians, who claim to know better than ordinary Christians, and so ridicule the Church, slander the Name of the Lord Jesus Christ, and gloat under the guise of "Freedom of speech": "God is dead"; "Belief in God and religion is intellectual nonsense." *"You have trusted in your wickedness and have said, 'No one sees me'. Your wisdom and knowledge mislead you when you say to yourself, 'I am, there is none besides me'. Disaster will come upon you, and you will not know how to conjure it away. A calamity will fall upon you that you cannot ward off with a ransom; a catastrophe you cannot foresee will suddenly come upon you"* (Isaiah 47:10-11). Did the arrogant politicians and scientists foresee the 2007-2008 economic hurricane that engulfed the economies of America and Great Britain?

The educated scientists, sociologists, theologians, political commentators and politicians, who sneer at the Lord Jesus Christ and claim there is no God, and boast of their human achievements, would plan in vain to prevent future hurricanes, earthquakes, wars, poverty, famine and epidemic diseases. We are limited to what we can do. Let us listen to the prophet Isaiah: *"All men are like grass, and all their glory is like the flowers of the field. The grass withers and the flowers fall, because the breath of the Lord blows on them. Surely the people are grass. The grass withers and the flowers fall, but the word of our God stands forever."* (Isaiah 40:6-7). Amen!

THE DAYS OF GOD'S WRATH AND VENGEANCE

As we look forward to seeing dreadful signs in the sun, the moon and the stars (Luke 21:25), the trees burning, great mountains burning with fire, creatures in the sea dying, ships being destroyed, waters poisoned, men dying from the poisoned water, and the moon, the sun and the stars becoming darkened, and men seeking to die and death eluding them to fulfil the Word of the Lord Jesus Christ in Revelation 8 and 9, we know the time is close for the Righteous Judge to pour His wrath on our rebellious generation.

Let us recall the comforting words the Patriarch Jacob left with the Jews and Christians.

> "Oh Lord, we are Sinners in this world.
> In our Misery You are the One who Hears us.
> When we Attach ourselves to you with Praise and Honour,
> You will Reward us with Justice, Good Fortune and Happiness.
> In our Struggle, May You (God) Add us to Your Son, who Sits at Your Right Hand". Amen!

The Lord Jesus Christ ("Benjamin") tells us without Him we can do nothing. So, He advises us:

> *"Come to me, all you who are weary*
> *And burdened, and I will give you rest.*
> *Take my yoke upon you and learn from me,*
> *For I am gentle and humble in heart,*
> *And you will find rest for your souls,*
> *For my yoke is easy and my burden is light"* (Matthew 11:28-30).

THE BIBLE'S "HIDDEN HARMONY"

I would now refer the reader to what Sir Robert Anderson, the ablest Defender of the Christian Faith, recorded in his *The Bible and Modern Criticism* to confirm the supernatural character of the Holy Bible: "What concerns us is the fact, first, that the chronology of the Old Testament is framed upon a system, and a system, moreover, which is not of human design; and secondly, that there is a mystic element in it..... The element of design is beyond question, and the clew to it is to be found in the history of the favoured people..... The covenant with Abraham is made the central date between the Creation and the Cross, and the ages measured back and forward from that epoch are each divided into two periods of equal length, but in inverse order. And the history of that people is marked throughout by cycles of "seventy weeks" of years.

- From the entrance into Canaan (B.C 1586-5) to the establishment of the monarchy (B.C. 1096) was 490 years.
- From the kingdom (B.C. 1096) to the Servitude to Babylon (B.C. 606) was *490 years.*
- From the conquest by Babylon the national history of Judah was suspended until the royal edict of Artaxerxes Longimanus of Persia ordered the rebuilding of the walls of Jerusalem, and restored the old polity of the Judges; and then began the **mystic era of** *490 years* which constitute the "seventy weeks" of Daniel's prophecy.
- And from the dedication of Solomon's temple (B.C. 1005) to the dedication of the second temple in the sixth year of Darius Hystaspis (B.C. 515) was also a period of *490 years.*

Dr Anderson continues: "Now all this is deduced from works written in different ages by men who had no plan or purpose of the kind in view. To attribute the results to chance is too silly for discussion, and no intelligent person will hesitate to conclude that the chronology of the Old Testament is part of a Divine plan, or "economy of times and seasons". I (Robert Anderson) deprecate the suggestion that the Christian's faith in the Bible depends on such incidental proofs of its "hidden harmony." But they are not altogether without value as an antidote to the scepticism of the critics."

I have taken the time to digress from the main theme of this book to share with you these scriptural truths to impress upon you, that whatever is written in the Books of Daniel and Revelation about the progress and destiny of the European Union would surely come to pass.

I close this chapter with an extract from the last chapter of *The Bible and Modern Criticism* to silence the liberal theologians and atheists, and to strengthen the faith of Christians. Under the titles: *"Competence of the Critics"* and *"Scepticism and Scholarship,"* the "Barrister of God" writes: "In the higher sense of the word a "critic" is a skilled and impartial judge - all that here in England we expect a judge to be. Its secondary meaning is that of a "harsh examiner," a hostile fault-finder. These sceptical writers belong to the second category. And let this be kept in view. We do not reject the ascertained results of true criticism. Our protest is against the assumptions of a criticism which is unsound in principle, and which is carried on by unsound methods. "We are prepared as Christian men to receive and welcome the fullest light of the new learning. We are not prepared to be dragged at the wheels of those who would give us a discredited Old Testament, an emasculated New Testament, a fallible Christ."

Dr. Anderson continues: "If therefore I may venture to combine practical counsel with this summary and retrospect, I would say, first, let no one be "browbeaten out of belief" by these attacks upon Holy Scripture. The Bible is not discredited because eminent scholars have turned against it in the camp of faith. The critics represent indeed that the scholarship of Christendom is with them. But the claim is absolutely unfounded. Their apparent pre-eminence is due largely to their being adepts in the art of what the Americans call "literary log-rolling." They are "a mutual admiration society." No one of them can raise a cry but that the whole party responds. And then the secular Press joins in. For the Press is with them. Naturally. For the newspapers represent "the world," and "the world" is never on the side of Divine truth."

"PIECES OF WOOD" FOR MEDITATION

- Pride is the mark of the impertinent.
- Life is sown to bear fruit.
- The Lord Jesus Christ is the best choice of man's security in life.
- The Lord Jesus Christ is the Universal Clock of times and seasons.
- The wheel of God's judgement spins at a snail's pace.
- Creation bears the indelible marks of the changeless decrees of God.
- In the midst of ridicule, persecution and death in the Lord Jesus Christ, we have eternal life.
- Belief is the voice of truth, and faith is its sound.
- Truth does not prevail in the world of darkness.
- In the world of darkness confusion breeds death.
-

Chapter 24
MORE OR LESS OR NONE OF EUROPE?

"Truth is one; but error is in its very nature inconsistent and therefore absurd. Truth is one, but when the circle of divine truth is broken, men soon forget its unity, and the segments that remain lie open to attack." (RA)

On 23 January 2006, Daily Mail reported on how Brussels had sought the help of Jacques Delors, a former EU Commission President, to salvage the European Union constitution which had been rejected by France and Holland. According to the newspaper, "Mr Delors….is known to blame Britain for the serious crisis over the constitution. He has said that many Europeans think the EU would be better if Britain had never joined..."

Secondly, Mr Prodi, another former European Commission President, unveiled a plan to speed up the integration of core European nations without Britain. On 16 April 2006, The Sunday Times reported: "*Prodi plan to leave Britain out in EU cold.*" According to the report, Prodi, who prides himself of taking Italy into the Euro-Zone, declared that "his priority was to forge alliance of "the countries most determined to push for a common European policy." "We need a strong relationship not just with France and Germany," he said, "but also with countries like Belgium and Luxembourg – but not the Netherlands." When euro-fanatic Prodi was asked whether his dream group would include Britain, he responded: "I believe it is difficult to include it (Britain) among countries which are pushing for more integration. Britain has decided not to hold a referendum on Europe so it has not approved the European position. Evidently, it believes in a policy which is more independent of the EU."

Delors and Prodi and their pompous politicians and commentators who label Britons "ignorant", must answer the following question:

- "Who, before the First World War, predicted that a political union of European nations would develop through an European crisis?
- Who predicted that a political alliance of European nations would be

the next major political feature in history after the restoration of the Jews to Palestine?

- Who listed Austria, Belgium, England, France, Greece, Germany, Italy, Portugal and Spain as members of a confederation of European nations, before the founding fathers of the European Community – Jean Monnet and Robert Schuman – were even conceived?"

Here is the answer: It was not an European. It was Dr Robert Anderson, an Irishman, who became an outstanding British public servant. He wrote about Europe and its future at his residence in London - 39 Linden Gardens.

The arch federalists - Prodi and Delors - should undertake a proper research on European Integration. Britain does not need the European Union to survive. Britain would be better off leaving *"the vile confederacy of the latter days,"* which was constructed on deception. Yes, Britain should "believe in a policy which is more independent of Europe." as suggested by Prodi. It is time the big-headed European politicians, who criticise Britain's position on the European Project, knew this truth. It was not the Frenchmen Aristide Briand, Jean Monnet and Robert Schuman, and neither the German Konrad Adenauer who first wrote about European integration. It was a Londoner, Sir Robert Anderson, who, before the French founding fathers of European Community were conceived, boldly predicted that a confederation of European nations would be the next major political feature in history after the restoration of the Jews to Palestine.

Do European politicians and statesmen, who think the European Union would be better off without Britain, know the destination of the European "Titanic"? Are European leaders not struggling to determine the direction of the European project, despite over 50 years of its existence? They laid their discredited Constitution on a Life Support Machine, and through deceit imposed it on the peoples of Europe as a new Treaty dubbed the Treaty of Lisbon.

THE CONFUSED EUROPEAN UNION

It is interesting to note how confused European politicians are about Britain's role in the European Union. Delors and Prodi claimed the European Union would be better off without Britain. On the other hand, the German Chancellor, Angel Merkel, flatters Britain by claiming, "We must have Britain on our side to make Europe work" (*The Times* 9 January 2007). The fact is the European Union will work with or without Britain. And with or without an European Constitution (the Lisbon Treaty), the European Union will work. The question is: where is the European Union heading towards? If the "European Community is morose, ill-tempered and uncertain of its future direction" as Timothy Garton Ash eloquently described it in his essay, *Today's European Union is 27 states in search of a story* (The Guardian 4 January 2007), why should Britain associate itself with a Project whose future is uncertain? Why should Britons invest in a "Public Limited Company" whose accounts have not been approved for 14 consecutive years due to fraud and financial mismanagement? It is only an ignorant fool who would buy shares in such a "dubious" company.

Because of the so-called threat from Climate Change, globalisation and the emerging economic giants from India and Asia, British politicians may have no where to escape but to Europe. That would be their decision. However, they cannot drag Britons to join them on Monnet's *Titanic* which is steaming towards an ice-berg. The Sovereignty of Britons belongs to the British people not a handful of "selfish" politicians who have vested interests in the European project and have no idea what the European Union is for. The consent of Britons must be sought before greedy politicians trade with their sovereign rights. The British people must ignore any soothing words from European politicians and withdraw from "That Thing" in Brussels.

We can "fish in the small island to catch cod" without necessarily throwing our net into the "deep sea". We risk being devoured by a "sea monster" with "7 heads" and "10 horns." Lord Willoughby rightly concluded: "Our country's best interests are best served outside the European Union." (Source: The Times 9 January 2007: *Tory peers defect to UK independence Party*). The French love the European Project. It was their 'father' – Jean Monnet who 'constructed' it. As the "Captain" of the doomed "Titanic," pride would prevent the French from abandoning their doomed "luxurious ship." It is their choice to pilot the "European Titanic" to its destination.

Britain's love for the European Union should not be unconditional. The destiny of Great Britain does not lie in the *"vile confederacy of the latter days"***,** as predicted by the eminent Victorian. It is time the "sons" and "daughters" of Sir Robert Anderson exalted their own 'Father,' and ignored Jean Monnet. For the Knight Commander (of the Order) of Bath has contributed more to Britain and the world - morally and spiritually - than the "Father of Europe" - Jean Monnet. I repeat: the French "giant" was only a "labourer" who toiled to bring to pass what the "decent" Irishman predicted concerning Europe and its future before he, Jean Monnet, was born. It is only the man in the street who would adore Jean Monnet for being the master-builder of the "European Titanic."

It is sad and ironic, that *Jean Monnet Centres of Excellence* have been scattered around Universities in the United Kingdom and Ireland to "brainwash" students. The brutal truth is that Sir Robert Anderson has offered more to Britain and the world than Jean Monnet. The Knight Commander published more than 20 general and theological books in addition to many articles that had great impact on the lives of millions. One of his articles, *The Search for Religious Truth,* which was published in *Daily Mail* on 10 July 1905, "inaugurated a discussion which elicited the most various views from thousands of scholars, theologians and thinkers" (Source: *Should Clergymen Criticise the Bible*).

I, once again, urge you to read Sir Robert Anderson's biography and examine four of his classics - *The Coming Prince* which predicted the European Union and its future, *A Doubter's Doubts about Science and Religion, Peudo-Criticism* and *The Buddha of Christendom* which deal with the Evolution and Creationism Controversy. In these books you would witness in detail how Dr. Anderson, the Champion of True Protestantism, dismissed Darwin's Theory of Evolution and "knocked out" Professor Thomas Huxley – the Champion of Darwinism.

MONNET'S ACHIEVEMENT IS A MYTH
"Americans: the best Europeans of all"

I look in vain for *Sir Robert Anderson Centres of Excellence* in British and Irish Universities. Why? Because, a prophet is of no honour in his own country and among his own people. Who is the "giant" in Europe to face the Irish "giant"? I repeat: so far as the development of the European Union and its future prospects are concerned, Jean Monnet unconsciously acted as an agent to fulfil what his 'unknown master' - the Prince of Detectives - wrote about European integration before the First World War. Jean Monnet would not have qualified to bow and polish the boots of the Knight.

The so-called 'achievements' of Jean Monnet are 'myths.' It is time, we, the British and the Irish raised up our heads, and with pride, exalt our brilliant father for the world to appreciate his contribution to mankind. We should not blindly follow Monnet's fuzzy vision of a 'fused' Europe. It is time our schools, colleges and universities learnt about Sir Robert Anderson K.C.B., LLD. We must be proud of what Sir Robert Anderson has done for our country and Christianity – the bedrock of Western Civilisation, which, according to one of the founding fathers of European Community, is the "soul of Europe."

It would be appropriate at this point to repeat the compliments the German Chancellor, Dr. Konrad Adenauer, paid to Americans after the "great Satan" had rescued Europe from its economic crisis after the Second World War: "Germany must declare herself wholeheartedly for the Christian world of the West and all it stands for", says the German Statesman. "The world must be convinced of American strength...The US has today perhaps the mightiest mission in history. In a human and historic sense America has a duty...to see that the light never goes out on our earth...I want to see a united Europe. Only then can my country be free. To that we need the help of the best Europeans of all – the Americans" (*TIME,* 5 December 1949).

Politicians in Britain and Ireland have a simple choice to make. They must either follow Sir Robert Anderson's extraordinary vision of European integration and withdraw from the European Union, or follow the "vague" vision of the French Statesman, Jean Monnet, to end up in the "euro-pit of darkness." Remember what *The Liverpool Post* wrote about the Knight Commander: "Sir Robert Anderson's views are worthy of the utmost respect and consideration." Would politicians ignore Sir Robert's vision of Europe's future?

It is appropriate, at this point, to repeat the following testimonies written in honour of Sir. Robert Anderson:

- Rev. J Stuart Holden, M.A., D.D described the faithful son of Ireland as: "The stalwart defender of the Christian Faith, the clear expositor, the zealous champion of Christian causes, the keen conversationalist, and the distinguished public servant."
- Sir Harry Furness, the famous artist, in his book, *Some Victorian Men*, described Sir Robert Anderson, K. G. B, as "an eminent Victorian, one of the hardest-working and most brilliant heads of the Criminal Investigation Department for many years."
- In *Chief Men among the Brethren,* which was compiled by Henry Pickering in 1918, the author writes: "W H Smith, on the floor of the House of Commons, stated that Sir Robert Anderson "had discharged his duties with great ability and perfect faithfulness to the public." And Raymond Blathwayt, in his *Great Thoughts*, recorded: "Sir Robert Anderson is one of the men to whom the country, without knowing it, owes a great deal." As an author his name will go down to generations yet unborn. His general books: *Criminals and Crime, Side Lights on the Home Rule Movement,* and *The lighter Side of my Official Life*, which dealt with "things Present," may not survive, but his theological volumes, dealing with "things eternal", will remain".

Sir John Moyland, in his *Scotland Yard and the Metropolitan Police,* writes: "the period 1890 to 1900 proved to be one during which there was an almost continuous decrease in crime....By signal successes in sensational cases, and by steady achievement in the less advertised everyday business of dealing with rogues in general, the C.I.D built up in the nineties a world-wide reputation for efficiency in crime detection".

In the 10 July 2008 edition of Daily Mail, Christopher Hudson reviewed *The Blackest Street* in a column headed "Hell on Earth". Mr Hudson writes: "...Violent crimes were rare (in Victorian times). According to the Old Bailey archives, between 1885 and 1895 only one murder occurred within the Old Nichol...Domestic violence was commonplace, but it stopped short of murder." The crime-ridden streets in the Victorian era "were safer than today's." This was the period when Sir Robert Anderson was the Assistant Commissioner of Metropolitan Police and the Head of the Criminal Investigation Department of Scotland Yard.

MORE, OR LESS OR NONE OF EUROPE?

Without any knowledge of Sir Robert Anderson's extraordinary vision of the development of the European Union, the bureaucrats in Brussels and political commentators who have no idea of the future prospects of the European project, and who claim the British people are the "most ignorant" about Europe, are forcing Monnet's blurred vision of a united Europe on Britons. What motivated Jose Manuel Barroso to assert that the British people could be persuaded, over a time, to embrace Europe unconditionally? This is my response to the "Buffoon of Brussels": "Over a time, the British people would recognise Sir Robert Anderson's vision of Europe. They will realise the deception perpetrated upon them by British politicians. Britons would be confronted with a choice: Either to leave the European Union or follow the "sons" and "daughters" of Jean Monnet to remain on the doomed "European Titanic."

On 9 May 2006, the European Union celebrated its 56thbirthday. In marking the anniversary, the President of the European Commission published a document titled, *Citizens Agenda for Europe.* The document states Europeans wanted "more of Europe." This declaration was intended to, some how; rekindle the flame of the European Project which was extinguished when France and the Netherlands rejected the European Constitution in 2005.

On 14 May 2006, The Sunday Telegraph commented on Mr Barroso's declaration: Europeans "want more of Europe." In an article titled *Mr Barroso believes more Europe will make us happy,* the newspaper expressed dismay by the statement of the President of European Commission, since the source of his evidence did not support his "more of Europe" claim. Because, surveys by Eurobarometer, which is the "instrument" Brussels uses to monitor public opinion on Europe, showed majority of Europeans do not support the European Project. *The Sunday Telegraph* Columnist, Christopher Booker, stated: "Particularly poignant was a study entitled The European Citizens and the Future of Europe part of which is headed "Near-zero knowledge and understanding of the functioning of the Union, its institutions and their role." Although this is the system of government responsible for many of the laws and policies which now govern our lives," Eurobarometer found that most people in Europe lacked knowledge about the European Project and its system of operation.

I ask the question: How credible was Barroso's claim that Europeans "wanted more of Europe," since the study (*The European Citizens and the Future of Europe*) concluded: "The institutional workings of the European Union and how decisions are taken is a matter of nearly complete ignorance." It was highlighted in the article that even most of the European politicians seemed "to understand the EU no better than anyone else, despite having handed over most of their powers to it."

Without any surprise, Dr. Ulrich Beck, professor of sociology at Munich's Ludwog-Maximilians University and London School of Economics, supported Barroso's view: "Europeans want more of Europe." In his article, "*This economic crisis cries out to be transformed into the founding of a new Europe,*" the German scholar writes: ".... If the EU did not exist, we would have to invent it today. Far from being a threat to national sovereignty at the beginning of the 21st century, the EU first makes it possible...... The pooled sovereignty of the EU provides the only hope for every nation and every citizen to live in freedom and peace. *Those who harm the union harm themselves.... Europe does not need less Europe - it needs more Europe.* The global crisis shows that monetary union cannot be achieved without political union." Professor Beck claims, "There can be no return to the national idyll. It is in all our interest for states to now abandon their nostalgic self-delusion." (Emphasis mine. Source: *The Guardian* 13 April 2009)

To begin with: had the German Professor done his "homework", he would have leant that the European Union was destined to exist. For an Irishman predicted a development of a political Union of European nations and its future even before the French Founding Fathers of European Community, Jean Monnet and Robert Schuman were born, and when the first Chancellor of West Germany, Dr. Konrad Adenauer, was only six years old.

And now the question: "Do Europeans need more or less or none of Europe?" Europeans may need more of Europe. So, it would be in the interest of the Germans and the French and the rest of the European countries to pool their sovereignties together and transfer the powers to govern themselves to undemocratic institutions in Brussels as Monnet suggested in his Memoirs. But it is not in the interest of Britons and the Irish to transfer their sovereignty to strangers to be ruled by aliens. Britons need less and none of the "vile" European project which only benefits the political elites, and is Extraordinarily Useless (EU) to the masses whose democratic decisions are always ignored. Professor Beck deludes himself with his claim: "Those who harm the European Union harm themselves." The reality is those who love the European Union and remain on the "luxurious EU Titanic" would eventually harm themselves. Because, Jean Monnet's "European Titanic" will sink. It was doomed before it set sail on 9 May 1950.

THE DESTINY OF EUROPEAN COMMUNITY

The issue of ignorance about the future of the European Union was raised in the 19 May 2006 edition of *The Times*. In an article titled *Europe will not go away, so let's start discussing its future,* Peter Riddell analysed some of the problems the then British Minister for Europe, Geoff Hoon, painted in a major speech in Berlin. Among the issues the minister raised were: the Enlargement of the "Empire" – how the European Union would accommodate new members; the fate of the European Constitution which was then on a "life-support machine"; Globalisation – the economic threat from China and India, Trade Protection, and Military Co-operation – how the European Union should deploy its military forces in times of conflicts in other countries.

In his speech Mr. Hoon recommended to Europeans Barroso's blueprint: "*The European Citizens and the Future of Europe.*" Before Peter Riddell's analysis, he lamented on how the main political parties in Britain: the Conservatives, New Labour and the Liberal Democrats, have avoided discussing Europe. In his analysis Mr Riddell revealed how the British Minister for Europe "placed less emphasis on the future organisation of the EU." Perhaps, in Mr Hoon's view, the future organisation of the European Project did not merit attention since the European Constitution had then been rejected by two of its founding members. He stressed that Britain would like the "*period of reflection*" to continue indefinitely. This "period of reflection" was advocated by the British government after the Blueprint of Europe was discarded by the French and the Dutch. Mr Hoon rather emphasised that focus should be placed on "Jobs, Security and Stability." What about the future of Europe? The end crowns the work. This means, the knowledge of the future prospects of the European Union is far important than anything else.

In his hazy imagination, the former Minister of Europe thought the draft Constitution of Europe was "dead" and those who were talking about its survival were "misleading alarmists" who were living in a fantasy world. Unfortunately for Mr Hoon, the "tyrants" in Brussels proved him wrong. For under the leadership of Angela Merkel, the Eurocrats, with the connivance of the European leaders, schemed and brought the 'dead' European constitution to life. The political analyst, Peter Riddell, concluded his analysis: "It is a classic British error to pretend that what we do not want to face will not occur. It is far better to start thinking now about the Future of EU."

In view of Mr Riddell's concluding analysis, we must ask these questions:

- How is it that 58 years after the birth of the European Union, European leaders do not know the future of their project, and they are yet to start thinking about it?

- Why is it that there is still a "near-zero knowledge and understanding of the project, its institutions and their role"? How is it that this "is a matter of nearly complete ignorance?"
- Why do most politicians in Europe "seem to understand the EU no better than anyone else (despite having handed over most of their powers to it)?"

I would, at this point, quote the question Minette Marrin posed in the 29 May 2005 edition of *The Sunday Times*: "Its getting hard to avoid the question: what is Europe for? This is the simple question which underlines the whole project but is rarely asked and rarely answered...If you ask Europhiles what the European project is for; they will respond with incredulity and perhaps even mild contempt...." Politicians cannot answer the question, because of their limited knowledge of the European Project. They are only familiar with: "Jean Monnet - the principal architect of European Construction; "The Schuman Plan," "The European Coal and Steel Community," The "Treaty of Rome," The "Nice Treaty," "The Single Market," "Enlargement" (the most successful foreign policy in history) the "EU Flag," the "EU Anthem," the "Euro," the dirty "CAP," the "European Central Bank," the "European Parliament," the "European Court of Justice," "Climate Change" and the new European Constitution – code-named "The Lisbon Treaty." With British politicians, their 'expertise" on European integration is the fallacy that "Britain must be at the heart of Europe to influence Europe" and "3 million jobs would be lost if Britain leaves the European Union." What a pity!

TO EVERY PROBLEM THERE IS A SOLUTION

It is obvious Europe has problems to resolve. The brain that gives birth to an idea must know its purpose. Since Europeans and their masters have a "near-zero" knowledge and understanding of the European Enterprise, it means they were not the "brains" behind the European Project. If they were the "brains," they would have known the purpose of their "brilliant idea"- the political union of European nations.

To every problem there is a solution. But where a particular problem cannot be solved, it means the requisite knowledge out of which the solution could be drawn has not yet been acquired. The answer to the protracted European problems lies in the "Brain" behind the European Union. The political leaders of Europe must identify this "Brain" for a solution. If Jean Monnet was the "master brain" behind the European Project, why have European politicians not consulted Monnet's works to know the future of Europe? For an architect of a project should be able to produce a blue-print that explains its workings and purpose to enable succeeding generations follow his vision.

THE SOLUTION

We have the European Union, a "Soft-Super-Power" and the biggest economic market on planet earth and the biggest donor of Aid; and yet the European Union has no credible leader to guide it through its difficulties. It is true Europe will not go away, with or without a Constitution. But the questions persist: What is Europe for? What is its future? And who would be qualified to lead the European Empire to its "paradise of carbon-free, prosperity and peace." The Lisbon Treaty has paved the way for the "Superman" – the King of Men – to be crowned. Dr. Anderson described this "Superman" the "awful Being" who will lead Europe to close the era of Gentile supremacy on earth.

If Europeans and their leaders are still struggling to determine what Europe is for and its future, I would encourage them to carefully examine Sir Robert Anderson's *The Coming Prince*. In this book, as I have already mentioned, the scholar among scholars predicted that a political alliance of European nations would be the next major political feature in history after the restoration of the Jews to Palestine. We know that two years after the rebirth of Israel in 1948, the European Union was born on 9 May 1950. And we know the stalwart defender of the Christian Faith described the political alliance of European nations *"the vile confederacy of the latter days"*. And he has been proved right. I don't need to list the catalogue of corruptions, fraud, hypocrisies and nepotism which are embedded in the very DNA of the EU project to justify his description of political Europe.

The truth is that the European project is morally bankrupt, intellectually bankrupt and spiritually bankrupt: It is godless and autocratic. It stifles the democratic voices of its people and uses pornography to promote its cause. European leaders lack the courage to make the case for EU's existence. Declan Ganley, who led the campaign against the Lisbon Treaty, responded to the bullying of the Irish to vote again on the rejected Treaty. He declared on BBC Today Programme: "What we are seeing here is an absolute contempt for the democratic process being shown by unaccountable elites in Brussels....A higher percentage of the Irish electorate voted "No" to this [Lisbon] Treaty than American electorate voted for Barack Obama. I don't hear calls for another election there." European leaders should reflect on Dr Anderson's vision on democracy: "Democracy, not despotism is the goal towards which civilization is tending towards. But democracy in its full development is one of the surest ways to despotism."

At this point I would remind the pompous politicians, who ridicule Christians and claim the European Union would be better off without Christ, that it was not an atheist, but a committed Christian who launched the European project on 9 May 1950. The question is: have European politicians paid heed to the advice this founding father of European Community, the "honest" politician, offered to

Europe concerning the survival of the European project? Later on I would share with you that critical advice. I repeat the question Dr Anderson posed to Britons: "....May we not indulge the hope that however far our nation may lapse in evil days to come from the high place, which with all her faults, she has held as the champion of freedom and of truth, she will be saved from the degradation of participating in the ***vile confederacy of the latter days?"*** Have the *"evil days"* come upon us in Britain? I will examine this prophetic word later on.

It was the "Real Brain" behind the European Project who revealed what Europe is for and its destiny to Sir Robert Anderson. I have already mentioned that this faithful servant of Christ published the prophetic revelation concerning the European Union and the rebirth of Israel before the First and Second World Wars. Apparently, in the eyes of men, the European Union evolved from the ashes of the Second World War – the great European crisis - just as Sir Robert Anderson predicted. But, in reality, in the sight of God, the European Union was concealed in the great human statue the King of Babylon saw in a dream about 604BC.

The "toes" of this human statue were partly of baked clay and partly of iron. That was the European Union – the revived Roman Empire - which the President of European Commission, Jose Manuel Barroso, confirmed it with this statement: "Unlike old super-state empires, the EU was based on a voluntary surrender of sovereignty, not military conquests. What we have is the first non-imperial empire. We are a very special construction unique in history. Sometimes I like to compare the EU as a creation to the organisation of empire. We have the dimension of empire" (*The Daily Telegraph* 11 July 2007). Was the surrendering of national sovereignties to unelected institutions in Brussels, whose officials are not responsible to anyone, voluntary or under 'compulsion' and deceit? Were Britons consulted before their politicians imposed on them The Treaties of Nice, Maastricht and Lisbon that transfer more powers from the British Parliament to Brussels?

We must answer the question. "Who was the "Real Brain," who gave the revelation relating to the progress of a political union of European nations to Dr. Robert Anderson?" The Author of the Bible, the God Almighty, whom European politicians claimed it would have been an "absurdity," "divisive" and a "serious mistake" to have mentioned Him in the Constitution of Europe. The Lord does not need the European Union to proclaim His Gospel. Yet, the Lord needs the European Union to fulfil His Word to enable Him to come down as a "stone" to crush the magnificent statue from its toes of baked clay and iron to its head of gold. Amen! (Daniel 2:34-35). This is the purpose of the existence of the European Union.

Chapter 25

IT IS EITHER THE VISION OF JEAN MONNET OR THE VISION OF THE "SEER OF DUBLIN"

"It is necessary for the comer unto God to believe that He exists, and that He is a rewarder of them that seek Him out. Men do not find pearls upon the open beach, or nuggets of gold upon the public road. Even in this world the principle of "the narrow way" prevails. And it is only the few who find it. Even in the mundane sphere, success is not for the trifler or the faddist. But while in this world the diligent seeker is often thwarted, and sometimes crushed, it is never so with God: He never says, "Seek ye Me in vain." **(RA)**

In so far as the future of the European Union is concerned, I will share with you an advice from Joan Bakewell's article on why we should take history seriously. In her critique, *History repeats itself, when you don't know any*, Ms Bakewell writes: "The dangers of ignorance are on every hand. Who can take a measured view of the Israeli conflict without at least a cursory knowledge of The Balfour Declaration, the British Mandate and the Arab/Israeli wars of 1967, 73, and 82. How can a leading politician be expected to make wise judgements in the Middle East when he is clearly not familiar with the Sykes Picot Agreement of 1916, by which France and England secretly agreed to carve up Iraq, Syria, and the Lebanon between them. History is the shadow between every news headline, every government initiative, every impulse to rebellion and subversion. We neglect it at our peril." She continued: "History is the very essence of our thoughts about who we are, setting the parameters of national identity by telling where we came from. All our current crises - issues of asylum seekers, overcrowded prisons, wayward children, national sovereignty, European unity - become more tractable when we examine their history." (*The Independent* Friday 7 July 2006)

In the context of our subject, let us follow Joan Bakewell's advice to re-examine the following questions again:

- Where did the European Union come from?

- What is the purpose of the European Union?
- Who will lead Europe to solve its economic, social, security and religious problems?
- What is the future of the European Union?
- What is the ultimate benefit for the 500 million European consumers in the biggest trading block in the world?

REMEMBER THE VOICE OF SIR ROBERT ANDERSON: WE IGNORE THE PRINCE OF DETECTIVES AT OUR PERIL

To answer the above questions, we must refer to the reliable historical records about the European Union, not what Jean Monnet recorded in his memoirs and then left the goal of European unity "vague." We must depend on what the servant of Christ, Sir Robert Anderson, a lawyer with forensic skills and remorseless logic, wrote before the architect of European Construction, Jean Monnet, stepped into the world. The Knight Commander (of the order) of Bath was described as a man who "rendered noble service to the cause of truth". He was known as "Mr Valiant for the truth." It was him who recorded in *The Coming Prince*, that the next prominent political feature in history after the gathering of the Jews to Palestine would be a confederation of European nations. He stated: "Through the gradual unfolding, it may be of influences even now in operation; or far more probably as the outcome of some great European crisis in the future; this confederation of [European] nations shall be developed, and thus the stage will be prepared on which shall appear that awful Being, the great leader of men in the eventful days which are to close the era of Gentile Supremacy."

When *The Coming Prince* was first published in 1881, the first German Chancellor, who, after the first World, advocated for a United States of Europe, was about 6 years old.

- The 14th edition of *The Coming Prince* was published in 1957 the year the Treaty of Rome was signed to establish the European Economic Community which laid the foundation for the "first non-imperial empire" in history.
- The third edition of *The Coming Prince* was published on 14 March 1889 – the year Adolf Hitler was born, and when the "Father of Europe", Jean Monnet, was only a year old.
- The fifth edition of *The Coming Prince* was published in 1895 when Jean Monnet was a teenager of fourteen years.
- The 15th and 16th editions of *The Coming Prince* were published in 1963 and 1967 the years in which Monnet's compatriot, President Charles de Gaulle, vetoed Britain's applications to join the Common Market. It was also in 1963 when President Kennedy adored Monnet for his 'achieve-

ments'. Had Charles De Gaulle read this edition he would have learnt the true purpose of the European Common Market and its dark future. And had British politicians studied what their 'Father' recorded about European confederacy and its future prospects, they would not have bothered to apply to join the Common Market. They would have saved themselves humiliation from the pompous de Gaulle.

- In 1969 Charles de Gaulle fell from power. That same year the 17th edition of the Knight Commander's extraordinary work on political Europe was released.

In 1972, the 18th edition of *The Coming Prince* was published. Had British politicians read this particular edition, they would not have signed the European Community Act 1972, and the British people would have saved themselves from the "tragedy" of joining the Common Market in 1973.

In 1975, two years after Britain had confirmed its membership of the Common Market in a referendum, the 19th edition of *The Coming Prince* was released. Again, had British politicians studied this edition, they would have learnt of the warning Dr. Anderson gave to Britain concerning the dark future of political Europe. And Had American politicians also read this edition of *The Coming Prince,* they would not have presented the Grenville Prize to Jean Monnet, and Dr Henry Kissinger would have ignored Jean Monnet and ridiculed his vision of a united Europe.

- The 20th edition of *The Coming Prince* was published in 1977. Had John Major and Mrs Margaret Thatcher studied this work, they would have known where the destiny of the European Economic Community lies. They would have had a different perspective of the European Project and not signed the Maastricht Treaty and the Single European Act to drag Britons into "slavery" in Europe, and the Conservative Government would have prevented the economic blunder they caused by joining the European Exchange Rate Mechanism in 1990, and then forced to withdraw from the programme in 1992 after the pound had come under pressure from currency speculators. And had the House of Commons seen a copy of *The Coming Prince,* succeeding British governments would not have made the mistake of committing the future of Great Britain to the vile European project. Indeed, Tony Blair and Gordon Brown would have withdrawn Britain from the European Union had the architects of New Labour read what an Assistant Commissioner of Metropolitan Police recorded on political Europe.

BRITISH POLITICIANS: REPEAL THE EUROPEAN COMMUNITIES ACT 1972

The destiny of Great Britain does NOT lie in the European Union with a gloomy future. Britain is not the property of politicians at "home" and "away" in Europe. British politicians must repeal the European Communities ACT 1972 and release Britons from bondage. According to a poll conducted for BBC2's Daily Politics programme by ComRes between the 13th March and 16th March 2009, 55% of Britons wanted to leave the European Union. 84% want a referendum before new powers are transferred to the European Union. The survey revealed that Britons preferred only close trading links with the European Union not to be controlled by strangers. Despite the economic crisis that resulted in over 2million Britons being unemployed, the majority of Britons rejected the idea of joining the Eurozone – to replace the Pound with Monnet's currency, the Euro. And on the issue of whether Britain has benefited from its membership of the European Union, only 44% agreed with 51% disagreeing. It is time pompous and self-centred politicians realised that they cannot force majority of the British people to become adopted "sons" and "daughters" of Jean Monnet.

Europeans are committed to the vision of their 'Patrons' - Jean Monnet and Konrad Adenauer. They hope to reach the Promised Land of "Carbon Free," where peace and prosperity prevail. The British and the Irish are "unique." Our "Father" warned us about the fate of Monnet's project. We must not procrastinate our withdrawal from the European Union. If we postpone it, we will leave traces of regrets behind our heels. For the strife to procrastinate is the stride to fail.

Chapter 26

THE SOUL OF EUROPE AND THE "SCHUMAN CAVEAT"

"Who made God? the solution is to be found, not in attempting to answer the question, but exposing its absurdity. "Science," Lord Kelvin declares, "positively affirms creative power." And it is because science leads us back to an existence which never had a beginning that for want of any other term by which to designate it, we call it God...."
(*A Doubter's Doubts about Science and Religion.* RA)

We will examine a piece of a "jig-saw puzzle" in the European Construction. This "Piece" is the advice Robert Schuman, the politician who launched the European Project, offered to Europeans. I term this "advice" "The Schuman Caveat." Before we conduct this vital examination, I would share with you what the biographer of Jean Monnet, Francois Duchene, wrote about Robert Schuman's attitude towards the European Project, and his relationship with the master-builder of the Project, Jean Omer Marie Gabriel Monnet.

Duchene writes: "Monnet and Schuman are odd couple, paired by history rather than by any personal compatibility.....Schuman was still wary in May 1950. In the first place he was wary on principle. On top of that, he and Monnet were not at one on supranationality. For Schuman, the plan existed to solve the immediate Franco-German problem. For Monnet, it was the first step to a united Europe. Schuman accepted supranationality for the plan because there was no alternative, *but he was not committed.* Schuman was very different from Monnet. He was "*a deeply religious bachelor...*" When Schuman was once having a launch with Monnet, Monnet told Schuman: "*You have a great asset. You look honest....I am not joking. You look honest. It is a priceless asset as a politician. People will believe what you say.*" Schuman responded to the compliment by describing Monnet "*very obstinate, but plays fair*". According to Duchene, "Some associates felt Monnet and Schuman were never really close". [Emphasis mine]

This section of Monnet's biography is very interesting and significant. It sheds

an important light on the entire European Project. We must ask the following questions:
Why was Robert Schuman, a founding father of European Community, not committed to the idea of "Supranationality" – a political union of European nations?
Why was Schuman "wary" on the principle of supranationality?
Why did Jean Monnet describe Robert Schuman an "honest politician whom people would believe what ever he said"? Was this the reason why the "obstinate" Monnet prevailed upon the 'honest' Schuman to sell his plan of a Federal Europe that would be evolved from the economic instrument – the European Coal and Steel Community?

If Schuman, who was described as a "deeply religious bachelor" and an "honest politician", was "wary" about the idea of a United States of Europe, and was not committed to the design of supranationality, for he thought the whole plan was "to solve the immediate Franco-German problem" of hostility," could it be the case, that as a committed Christian, Schuman felt in his spirit that the scheme for a federal Europe, planned by Monnet, was somehow not feasible or unscriptural? We could determine Schuman's thoughts on European integration from his address to the European Parliament in March 1958 and what he recorded in his last book.

THE "SCHUMAN PLAN" AND THE "SCHUMAN CAVEAT"

In the "Introduction" to this book, I mentioned how historians, politicians and political commentators have rightly given prominence to "The Schuman Plan" which eventually brought into being the European Union of the 21st century. Jose Manuel Barroso also referred to "The Schuman Plan" in his "Hugo Young Memorial Lecture" at Chatham House. The President of European Commission, again, referred to "The Schuman Plan" when he extolled the virtues of his "hero," Jean Monnet, in the 60th Anniversary edition of *TIME* magazine. Mr Barroso writes: "Monnet's idea of European unity was seized upon by French Foreign Minister Robert Schuman and German Chancellor Konrad Adenauer....The power of Monnet's gradualist vision means that it still serves as a blue-print for European integration today."

Why did the President of European Commission fail to mention "The Schuman Advice?" For the "honest" Schuman warned Europeans about the survival of the European Enterprise. Strangely, European politicians have ignored this vital advice. In his address to the European Parliament on 19 March 1958, Schuman, a devout Roman Catholic, told the Parliamentarians: "All the European Countries are permeated by Christian Civilization. *It is the soul of Europe which must be restored to it."* In other words, according to one of the Founding Fathers of the European Community, "Christian Civilization" is the "Soul" of Europe. [Emphasis mine]

Angela Merkel, once spoke of the need to find the "Soul of Europe". Had the German Chancellor done her "homework," she would have known that the committed Christian who launched the European Union on 9 May 1950 had already spoken and written about the "Soul of Europe,"

"THE SCHUMAN PLAN"

In launching the European Coal and Steel Community, which laid the foundation for a federal Europe, Robert Schuman declared: "Europe will not be made all at once, or according to a single plan. It will be built through concrete achievements which first create a de facto solidarity. The coming together of the nations of Europe requires the elimination of the age-old opposition of France and Germany. Any action taken must in the first place concern these two countries....The pooling of [France and Germany] coal and steel production should immediately provide for the setting up of a common foundation for economic development as a first step in the federation of Europe."

"THE SCHUMAN CAVEAT"

Robert Schuman did not issue a "blank cheque" to Europeans when he unveiled Monnet's plan for a federal Europe. He "crossed" the "Euro-cheque" with a "caveat": The 'caveat' is recorded in his last book, *pour l'Europe*, which was published in the 1960's. Schuman stressed the significance of the restoration of the "Soul of Europe" into Jean Monnet's plan for a United States of Europe. The "saint in business suit" recorded: "*This togetherness [of peoples] cannot and should not remain an economic and technical undertaking. It must be given a soul. Europe will not live and will not be saved except to the degree in which it has awareness of itself and of its responsibilities, when it returns to the Christian principles of solidarity and fraternity*" (Source: "Faith illuminated his political action" by Edoardo Zin). In Schuman's estimation, the European Construction should not be a political and economic project only. It must be governed by Christian principles of solidarity and fraternity which are the "Soul of Europe."

A CONSPIRACY OF SILENCE OR IGNORANCE?

I ask the question: "Why have politicians, journalists, political commentators, and political intellectuals failed to give prominence to Schuman's "Advice" concerning the survival of the European Community? After all, Jean Monnet, the "spiritual godfather" of European unity, described Robert Schuman an "honest" politician whom people would "believe in whatever he said." I ask again: "Why have European leaders ignored the 'advice' the 'honest' Schuman offered to Europe concerning the survival of the European Project?

In view of Monnet's endorsement of Schuman's character, as an "honest" politician, I ask the question again: "Why have historians, politicians and political commentators ignored the "The Schuman Caveat"? Is it a conspiracy of silence to eliminate God and Christianity from the European Enterprise, or it is ignorance? Whatever it is, Christianity was not mentioned in the Constitution of Europe? Some Members of the European Parliament cried it would have been an "absurdity", "a serious mistake" and "divisive" to have mentioned God and Christianity in the Blue-print for a federal Europe. Political commentators and leading politicians, including Tony Blair, reiterated that European Union is not a Christian club. Without any surprise, David Miliband, the atheist, jumped on the anti-Christian bandwagon by disparaging the role of Christianity in the Euro-project. Championing Turkey's membership of the European Union in his first major speech to a Labour Party meeting, Miliband declared: "Europe can't be a "closed Christian club."

I have already mentioned that the Foreign Secretary's view is misplaced. Europe is not in any way a Christian club. The EU has never been a Christian Club. The EU will never be a Christian club and the EU does not deserve to be a Christian club. After all, European leaders and bureaucrats in Brussels have already rejected the "godly advice" the "honest" politician offered to Europeans concerning the survival of the European Union. It was, therefore, ridiculous for David Miliband to have associated Christianity with that "godless thing" in Brussels. The Lord Jesus Christ does not need the EU, yet the Lord needs the EU for HIS purpose. A word to the wise is enough.

THE EUROPEAN UNION IS A "CORPSE"; IT HAS NO "SOUL"

If we consider the "advice" Robert Schuman presented to European Parliamentarians on 19 March 1958, and what he recorded in his last book: -"*This togetherness [of peoples] cannot and should not remain an economic and technical undertaking alone; it must be given a soul. Europe will not live and will not be saved except to the degree in which it has awareness of itself and of its responsibilities, when it returns to the Christian principles of solidarity and fraternity*" - it becomes clear that, since the European Project has no room for Christian principles in its Constitution, the European Union has no 'Soul.'

A body without a soul is a corpse, because its mind and will and conscience do not function. Has the European Constitution got a soul?

- Where in the Lisbon Treaty do we find "The Christian principles of solidarity and fraternity" which was advocated by the "honest" Robert Schuman? When the Catholic Rocco Buttiglione expressed his Christian view: "I may think of homosexuality as a sin, but it has no effect unless

faith out of public life." Stark calls Europe's new religion hedonism, "and says it is why Europe is dying. No Western European country is having enough babies to replace its current population. And Rocco Buttiglione, Italy's Culture Minister, who was denied office in the European Commission because of his Christian views on same-sex relationships and marriage, calls the new European religion, "a nihilistic fundamentalism against truth." (Source: *Israel & Christians Today.* UK Spring 2006 Edition).

EXHIBITION OF IGNORANCE AND FOOLISH PRIDE

Was the French foreign minister, Robert Schuman, who was Prime Minister for a brief period, naïve, when, after the Treaty of Rome was signed in 1957, advised the European Parliament that the *soul of Europe,* which is the Christian principles of solidarity and fraternity, must be restored to Europe? European politicians, who claimed it would have been an "absurdity" and a "serious mistake" and "divisive" to have mentioned God and Christianity in the European Constitution, have clearly demonstrated their ignorance about the survival of their own Project. These politicians, who boast of monopoly of scholarship on European integration, and yet not well-informed of the real significance of the European Union, should bury their foolish pride.

For example in an article "Dealing with NO" – which was a commentary on Ireland's rejection of the Lisbon Treaty, Charles Grant, director of the Centre for European Reform, writes: "The yes campaign failed to provide good reason for supporting a document that promised mere technical changes to E.U institutions. Richer and better educated people tended to vote for the treaty, while working-class Irish mostly opposed it. A similar social division over attitudes to the EU is apparent in many European countries: (*TIME* June 30-July 7, 2008")'

The question is: to what extent are the "educated" and the "rich" better-informed on the implications of the European project than the "less-educated" and poor men in the street? On the significance of European integration, the educated and the rich are less-informed just like the "poor working-class." Had the so-called educated and the rich been well-educated on the significance of European integration and its future prospects, they would not have supported the European Union and its Lisbon Treaty – a document that paves the way for the dark future of Europe to be fulfilled, as predicted by the "Seer of Dublin." The uncomfortable truth is that Jean Monnet's *EU Titanic* is heading towards an iceberg. The Lisbon Treaty would provide the "experienced Captain" to pilot the luxurious vessel to its fatal destination.

Let us now revisit the assertion, that it would have been an 'absurdity' and a 'serious mistake' to have mentioned God and Christianity in the European Constitution.

It is only a fool who says in his heart "there is no God" (Psalm 14:1). Dr Robert Anderson writes: 'Proofs that the Bible is the Word of God are clear and abundant. But they do not lie open on the surface. Gold and diamonds are not picked upon the highway; men need to dig for them. Even Nature hides her treasures from the trifler. God is a "rewarder of them that seek Him diligently." He adds: "The success of the sceptical movement" in the eighteen century (especially the German rationalists who attacked the Bible and their English supporters) was "not due to the strength of the attack, but to the weakness of the defence."

And this is the case in the 21st century – where Church leaders lack the spiritual insight to defend God and the Bible, and so quailed before the so-called sophisticated intellectuals – the militant atheists led by the "Archbishop of Atheism," Professor Richard Dawkins, who is a "clone" of Professor Thomas Huxley - "Darwin's bulldog."

THE LORD JESUS CHRIST IS AN "EXTREMIST"

The Lord Jesus Christ tells us: "Without Me you can do nothing." Without the Lord the EU would do nothing, save its ability to fool the masses with development projects whiles "sucking their blood**."** The European Union has rejected God, the Lord Jesus Christ and Christianity. They have no room in the Constitution of Europe. Witness the words of Christ: "Whoever acknowledges me before men, I will acknowledge him before my Father in Heaven. But whoever disowns me before men, I will disown him before my Father in heaven" (Matthew 10:32-33). "He who is not with me is against me; and he who is against me scatters". "If anyone is ashamed of me and my words in this adulterous and sinful generation, the Son of Man will be ashamed of him when he comes in his Father's glory with the holy angels" (Mark 8:38). The Lord Jesus declares: "The Father loves the Son and has placed everything in his hands. Whoever believes in the Son has eternal life. But whoever rejects the Son will not see life, for God's wrath remains on him" (John 3:35-36). These are EXTREME statements from the Lord Jesus Christ. It is an EXTREME position the King of kings has taken.

We, the Bible–believing Christians, are not ashamed to follow the "extreme" teachings of the Lord of lords and the King of kings. We care less if "blind" men label us "Fundamentalists" or "Extreme Right-Wing." If the Master praises, what are mortal men. After all, our Divine Lord was mocked, spat upon and unjustly treated. The world may ridicule us as "fundamentalists." We gratefully accept the compliment. Indeed, we are "Fundamentalists" because we believe in the FUNDAMENTAL TRUTHS in the Holy Bible. We don't belong to the "mainstream" that has diluted the Word of God to please men. We are not politicians who occupy the Centre-Ground. We are not interested to occupy the "Left of Centre", neither the "Right of Centre" nor the "Middle-Ground." We are not

"Middle of the Road" politicians, who are neither hot nor cold. We are not "Sea-Saw politicians" (SSP) who are always at the mercy of the Pendulum of Public Opinion (POPO). We are not in the political arena to camouflage voters to win their votes and ignore their legitimate and democratic demands. We, the followers of the Lord Jesus Christ, are only interested to proclaim the fundamental truths of the Gospel of Christ to win souls for Christ to please our Lord and Saviour. We are not here to twist truth to win votes. We are not politicians to do whatever it takes to appease men to become popular.

We care less about public opinion. Christians are not scared of genuine criticism. In *A doubter's Doubts about Science and religion*, Dr Anderson, the literary recluse, and a theologian among theologians, writes: "True scepticism is that which honestly test everything, and is a genuine aid to faith. Sham scepticism is that which credulously accepts anything that tends to discredit the Bible." So, "we refuse to surrender Holy Writ to the tender mercies of those who approach it with the ignorance of pagans and the animus of apostates."

THE PLAIN AND UNCOMFORTABLE TRUTH ABOUT EUROPEAN UNION

I urge my fellow Britons, the citizens of the Republic of Ireland, Europeans and Americans who support the European Union to strive to know the fundamental truth about Jean Monnet's project that has no space for the Lord Jesus Christ. The plain and inconvenient truth is that it was neither a philosopher, nor an atheist, or a political scientist from a prestigious university, who predicted that the birth of a political union of European nations would follow the rebirth of the nation of Israel. It was a Christian, a learned lawyer, and an illustrious British public servant, who, with absolute confidence predicted that a confederation of European nations would be the next major political feature in history after the restoration of the Jews to Palestine. The Bible-believer Dr. Anderson, who made this extraordinary prediction, was not "naïve." He was well-informed. None of today's "blind pigmies," who sneer at Christianity, would have qualified to write with his pen. It is, therefore, an exhibition of gross ignorance and silly pride for European politicians to dismiss any notion of mentioning God and Christianity in their European Constitution, and to gloat about what Jean Monnet has given to Europe.

I repeat: God does NOT need the "vile" EU. Yet, the Lord needs the corrupt EU to bring His Word to pass. Amen!
I repeat: the EU is Extraordinarily Useful to the politicians who control it.
I repeat: the EU is Extraordinarily Useless to the citizens who subsidise it.

THE WHOLE WORLD HAS BEEN DUPED

The fact is the whole world has been duped about the status of Jean Monnet. The French statesman, the European giant, was no 'genius.' He might have been a hero to the French and Jose Manuel Barroso and his followers in Brussels. In reality, Monnet was only a 'poor slave' who laboured to fulfil the vision of his 'Irish master' he never knew. The political elites in Europe should bury their irrational pride which is cloak in ignorance about the significance of European integration.

According to *New York Herald*, Dr Anderson's *The Silence of God* "astounded religious Europe" in the late 19th century and the early 20th century. Today, in our 21st century Age of Enlightenment, Dr Anderson's *The Coming Prince* would educate the godless European Union that has no room for the Lord Jesus Christ. After the First World War there was a huge demand for *The Coming Prince*. In response to the cry, the tenth and eleventh editions of the prophetic book were published. If you desire to know the truth about Jean Monnet's vision of a united (federal) Europe, and for the truth to set you free from bondage in Brussels, I would encourage you to get a copy of *"The Coming Prince"* from Kregel Publications in America.

Chapter 27

THE "SEER OF DUBLIN" SPEAKS TODAY: BRITAIN HAS "LAPSED IN EVIL DAYS"

"The rationalism of Germany at the close of the 18th century would accept the Bible only on the terms of bringing it down to the level of a human book, and the problem which had to be solved was to get rid of the element of miracle which pervades it The effects of this "Higher Criticism" are extremely grave. For it has dethroned the Bible in the home, and the good old practice of "family worship" is rapidly dying out. And great national interests also are involved. For who can doubt that the prosperity and power of the Protestant nations of the world are due to the influence of the Bible upon character and conduct? Races of men who for generations have been taught to think for themselves in matters of the highest moment will naturally excel in every sphere of effort or of enterprise. And more than this, no one who is trained in the fear of God will fail in his duty to his neighbour, but will prove himself a good citizen. But the dethronement of the Bible leads practically to the dethronement of God; and in Germany and America, and now in England, the effects of this are declaring themselves in ways, and to an extent, well fitted to cause anxiety for the future"

(Pseudo-Criticism RA)

The Prince of Detectives at Scotland Yard Speaks Today About the European Union and Great Britain

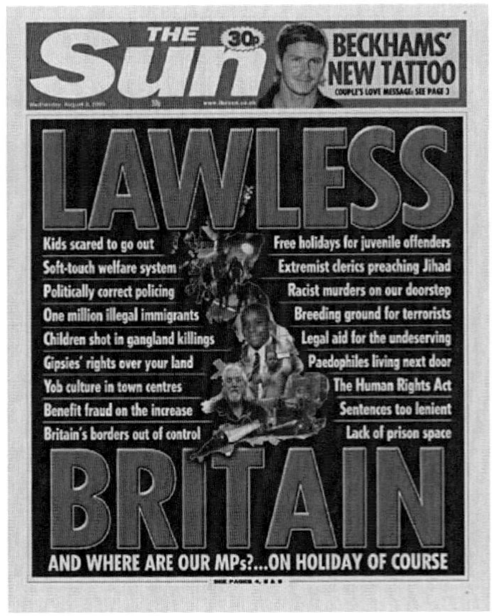

THE Sun 30p

BECKHAMS' NEW TATTOO

LAWLESS

Kids scared to go out
Soft-touch welfare system
Politically correct policing
One million illegal immigrants
Children shot in gangland killings
Gipsies' rights over your land
Yob culture in town centres
Benefit fraud on the increase
Britain's borders out of control

Free holidays for juvenile offenders
Extremist clerics preaching Jihad
Racist murders on our doorstep
Breeding ground for terrorists
Legal aid for the undeserving
Paedophiles living next door
The Human Rights Act
Sentences too lenient
Lack of prison space

BRITAIN

AND WHERE ARE OUR MPs?...ON HOLIDAY OF COURSE

Through the outcome of some great ***European crisis in the future***, ***this confederation of nations shall be developed,*** and thus the stage will be prepared on which shall appear that ***awful Being***, the great leader of men in the eventful days which are to close the era of Gentile supremacy.... May we not indulge the hope that however far our ***nation may lapse in evil days to come*** from the high place which, with all her faults, she has held as the champion freedom and of truth, she will be saved from the ***degradation of participating in the vile confederacy of the latter days***?" (The Coming Prince 1881, 39 Linden Gardens, London)

THE KNIGHT OF GOD'S PROPHETIC WORD ABOUT GREAT BRITAIN

I have already shared with you how Sir Robert Anderson's prophetic description of the character of the European Union - being "*The vile confederacy of the latter days*"- has been fulfilled. What about the Knight Commander's prophetic word about the state of our nation? The Prince of Scotland Yard foresaw that Great Britain, which had been the "Champion of freedom and of truth", would "lapse in evil days to come." I repeat the question he posed "May we not indulge the hope that however far our nation *may lapse in evil days* to come from the high place which, with all her faults, she has held as the champion of freedom and of truth, she will be saved from the degradation of participating in the vile confederacy of the latter days?"

His word has come to pass. The following newspaper articles confirm the prophetic word of the Prince of Detectives.

- On 11 November 2005, it was reported in the Daily Mail, that according to "a state-funded sex group, parents have no right to judge what is best for their children. Under the title *Parents don't know what's best for a child, says charity,* Social Affairs Correspondent, Steve Doughty, explained how a mother was fighting for the right to be told if her two daughters are being given advice on sexual matters. According to the report, the mother wanted "to overturn what she calls the "horrifying" government policy which allows girls under 16 to terminate a pregnancy without their parents knowing." The same edition of Daily Mail revealed how a leading academic angered children's campaigners by claiming sexual relationships between pupils and teachers could sometimes be "positive." In an article entitled *Teacher-pupil affairs can be a good thing, says academic,* Educational Correspondent, Sarah Harris, described how a "senior education lecturer at Sheffield University, who married her own former teacher", was of the view that pupils are not exploited in sexual relationships with their teachers. According to this University lecturer, "1,500 pupil-staff relationships develop every year." In her research paper, the academic concludes: an "erotic charge" can often be characteristic of good teaching." Clearly, we see evidence of a lapse society where government and academic institutions promote and condone fornication. Now girls, without advice from their General Practioners, can get a pill on the counter to abort. (Daily Mail 10 December 2008)
- On 11 November 2004, the *Metro* newspaper reported about a woman teacher who "admitted having a lesbian fling with a 15-year-old pupil."
- On 24 March 2006, an article titled *Violent pornography blamed for quadruple rape by 14-year-old boy* appeared in The Times: According to the article, a boy lured girls from playground and forced them to commit sex act. In the "opinion of the adolescent forensic psychiatrist who examined the teenager, the boy was inspired to carry out the offences by the violent sexual images he has seen. He had been exposed to extreme and crude pornographic material at the time of these offences." It was reported that this boy had been expelled from school because of his use of "foul language". His mother often lost track of him. The Judge sentenced the teen-age. He told the boy his behaviour was "intolerable," and said: "There is clear evidence in this case of social controls breaking down."
- On 28 June 2006, a column in the Daily Mail confirmed the social breakdown in our society: Under the depressing title, *"Traditional families are hit by declining morals, say mother,"* Rebecca Camber writes: "Family life is under attack from declining moral values and the increas-

> ing number of single parents." A survey reported that almost two-thirds blamed the Government, which "doesn't like traditional family set-ups and seems to favour single and working mums. And "a quarter of mothers claimed the traditional family structure is under attack from the increasing numbers of unmarried couples and same-sex parents."

In the 10 July 2006 edition of Daily Express, Leo McKinstry also highlighted the collapse in the social fabric of Britain. In his essay, "*Why are murder rates on the increase in this once civilised country?"* Mr Mckinstry writes: "One of the most alarming developments of our recent history has been the transformation of Britain from a tranquil, relatively crime-free society into a dangerous, violent place." The columnist quoted what the anthropologist, Geoffrey Gorer, spoke in 1955. "The English are certainly among the most peaceful, gentle, courteous, and orderly populations that the civilised world has ever seen." Mr McKinstry continued: "Half a century later, it would be absurd to use those words about modern Britain, where savagery, aggression and law-breaking are endemic. We have been turned from the land of harmony into a land of fear. Tragically, under Labour's supine regime, the slide into disorder is accelerating...Cases of murder and manslaughter have gone up by almost a quarter...the number of homicide victims has averaged 737 per year since 1997, compared to 601 from 1990 to 1997." Sir Robert Anderson's prophetic word has been fulfilled.

Charles Moore, The Daily Telegraph Columnist, also wrote about how it is becoming difficult to share the Gospel of Christ with prisoners in Britain. In his article "*No faith in prisons means there's no hope for prisoners*", he shared with readers how the teaching of the virtue of heterosexual marriage to prisoners could be considered "discriminatory" against homosexuality. He stated: "Prison may protect the public, but at present it does not succeed in getting criminals to go straight.... without the religious element, there is so little success in helping prisoners lead new lives." Mr Moore continued, "Someone called the Area Psychologist of the Prison Service" objected to the Christian belief that "the root of offending is in individual sin." The ground of her objection was: such a Christian concept "lacks basis in specific scientific research." Mr Moore quoted what this Psychologist wrote to support her objection to the Christian concept of sin in human nature: "The place of anti-social behaviour in the concept of good and evil, god [she kept God lower case] and the devil may not encourage self-responsibility in a manner which enables the individual to make sophisticated choices when faced with complex situations in their lives." According to this "expert," the promotion of the unique virtue of heterosexual marriage was "discriminatory" against "homosexuality." The Christian charity InnerChange was refused accreditation to proclaim the Gospel of Christ to Prisoners.

On 21 July 2006, Daily Mail also commented on the banning of the Inner

Change's Christian message from British Prisons. Under the title, *"Axed for being 'too Christian', the prison course proven to help criminals change their ways,"* Luke Salkeid reported that a Religious Scheme for prisoners was scrapped "in case it offends men from other faiths and homosexuals. The organisers of the Christian initiative in prisons were told "their traditional message was discriminatory and did not conform to 'diversity, policy." A spokesman for independent think tank Civitas voiced his displeasure: "This is absolutely wrong. The Government is always saying we need to reform prisoners, and then when someone does something that actually works, it gets stopped. "The people running this course were doing far more good than the equal opportunity jobsworths who have put a stop to it. It's a disgrace".

It was further disclosed that the decision to prohibit the Christian message in the prisons was implemented "less than a year after it was announced that prisoners were to be allowed to have altars in their cells for witchcraft ceremonies. They can burn incense, keep Tarot cards and runestones and wear robes and religious jewellery. Governors have been told to put paganism on an equal footing with Christianity and other major faiths." According to the report, no prisoner objected to the Christian message. The Muslim Council, one of the major Faiths in Britain, was not against the Message. They said: "As the scheme was voluntary, we see no problem at all. If it meant prisoners were being helped to reform using Christian values, then that has to be a good thing – for them and for society as a whole. Where is the harm in trying to stop prisoners reoffending."

Concerning the freedom of information, the Labour Government planned to make it costly for the public to seek information. The stifling of access to information was highlighted in a newspaper article titled *"Freedom of information refusals 'set to increase."* Within this article Nicholas Timmins, Public Policy Editor, writes: "One in seven of all freedom of information requests - and potentially many of the most important, are set to be ruled out by the government, the campaign for Freedom of Information warned." (Financial Times 17 October 2006).

And Paul Caulfield highlighted Britain's slide towards dictatorship in a letter which was published in the 18 October 2006 edition of the Daily Express. Under the title *"Arrogant leaders are destroying all our freedoms."* Mr Caulfield writes: "...Democracy is now just a thin veneer. The only democratic process we are permitted is a vote every few years. We are now prevented from expressing many of our opinions by a mire of legislation that has criminalised much of everyday life. Christianity is being suppressed. Christmas lights, Nativity plays and carol concerts are banned. Even wearing a crucifix at work is banned." This is all in the name of "the Human Rights Act, which states that freedom can be waived for the protection of the rights and freedom of others."

On Thursday 19 October 2006, the novelist and the polemicist, Henry Porter, summarised the assault on personal freedom in Britain in *The Independent* Newspaper. In his essay, "*We're all suspects now,"* he writes: "Don't get me wrong, we do not live in a police state or a big brother society – yet....The trouble is that it's happening so very quietly, so very discreetly that few really see it.
"

- "We used to believe in innocent until quilt was proved right. Not any longer...."
- We used to believe that there should be no punishment without a court deciding the law had been broken, and that every defendant had the right to know the evidence against him. Not any longer...."
- We used to believe that an Englishman's home was his castle. Not any longer..."
- We used to believe in the right to be tried by jury. Not any longer..."
- We used to believe there was a good reason not to allow hearsay evidence in court. Not any longer..."
- We used to believe in free speech, but not any longer....."
- We used to believe that our private communications were sacrosanct. Not any longer..."

Mr Porter continued: "Cumulatively, these small barely noticed reductions in our rights add up to the greatest attack on liberty in the last hundred years." And commenting on the possible introduction of identity cards in Britain (a project which the autocratic EU is behind it) the novelist enlightened us on how much of our freedom would be restricted. He explained that each adult would be required "to provide 49 pieces of information about themselves....If you refuse to submit to what is called, *without irony,* enrolment, you will face fines of up to £2500. The government is deadly serious about this thing because of simple truth. They want to know ...everything there is to know about you..."

And on Thursday 28 December 2006, *The Independent* summed it all up with a dazzling front cover title *WHAT FREEDOM OF INFORMATION? 40% of requests under right-to-know laws are rejected – and it is likely to get worse. All these were refused."* The newspaper listed numerous requests refused. Inside *The Independent* was an article titled "Ministers are accused of scuppering right to know legislation." In this article Robert Verkaik, Law Editor, summarised in detail some of the requests which officials have denied.

We live in the days where there is "a dangerous credibility gap" between our politicians and the public. For according to a survey by the Committee on Standards in Public Life, majority of the British people have lost faith in the political system because politicians are perceived to be lairs and seldom admit their mistakes. Within an article captioned "*Disillusioned voters turn their backs on politics,"* Kirsty

Walker reported that the public have lost trust in politicians. "Some even believe that politicians siphon off public money to boost their own salaries and benefits." A report, based on work-shops with voters, which was submitted to the Electoral Commissioner, said: "Cynicism about politics and politicians was widespread among participants. There was a strong sense that politicians and parties had become disconnected from the electorate. They are also distrustful of politicians and cynical about conventional politics, but many of them believe the problems of the existing system could be overcome by systematic reform." (Daily Mail 18 October 2006). In 2007 and 2008 all the political parties were engulfed with "sleaze" allegations which prompted resignations and investigations.

I would share with you a catalogue of headlines and reports that fulfil the "*lapse in evil days*" in Britain which was spoken of by Sir Robert Anderson in 1881:

- According to Mori poll published in *The Sun* on 23 January 2006, Britain has become an "Anxious" nation. People are concerned about internet pornography, chatroom perverts, drugs abuse, bad behaviour and crime.
- A charity claimed "Parents do not know what is best for their children." Girls under 16 terminate pregnancies without their parents knowing (*Daily Mail* 11 November 2006). The morning - after pills are given out like smarties to under age schoolgirls to prevent pregnancies.
- In June 2006, an English teacher was given 12 month suspended sentence after admitting sleeping with a boy after he turned 16.
- School nurses were told to supply contraceptives to girls and arrange abortions for teenagers without their parents' knowledge. And it was reported in Daily Mail on 8 September 2006, that schools should teach abortion benefits. And according to ministers' advisers, such education should be compulsory (7 September 2006).
- There was outrage over condoms for 13-year olds (*The Sun,* 20 June 2006).
- Task force are being sent into primary schools to tackle the rise of inappropriate sexual behaviour in young pupils (*The Daily Telegraph,* 18 July 2006).
- "Teen abortions up despite £130m campaign" (*Daily Mail,* 24 November 2006*)*.
- "Young Britons top the Euro cocaine league."
- "*Pupils' lesson on sex with animals"*. School children were asked to discuss sex with corpses and animals during a religious studies lesson *(Metro,* 17 January 2003).
- "Desperate man has sex with hedgehog" (*The Sun,* 16 September 2006).
- Paedophiles were setting up orphanages in overseas so that fellow per-

verts could indulge in their evil deeds.

- "Three drove 80KM to have sex with corpse": The *Metro* reported on Friday 8 September 2006 that three men caught digging up a grave were trying to have sex with a lifeless body – after seeing the dead woman's pretty picture in a newspaper.
- Cash to halt sex diseases epidemic pays NHS debt (Evening Standard 19 July 2006)
- *"The betrayal of Christianity in our schools":* It was revealed in this article that many children don't know the Lord's Prayer. They were being taught that all religions are equal. And it was also published that a former Tory Education secretary said in 1991 that religious education should not be designed to convert pupils, or to urge a particular religion or religious belief on pupils (*The Sun,* 18 June 1997). What should religious education do? I ask the question.
- A headline in an evening London paper read, "Even animals are better parents than us" (12 September 2006).

An article in the 19 October 2006 edition of the Daily Express read: *The school that lets pupils smoke at 14.* The newspaper reported: "A school was accused of "politically correct idiocy"...for allowing pupils as young as 14 to smoke during break times." The head of the school encouraged such illegal practice by providing smoking areas for children who are under 16 to smoke. But what was bizarre was that the school prevented the drinking of fizzing drinks and teachers, who were adults, were banned from "lighting up."

Is it not beyond belief that a school encouraged children to smoke, because some of them were addicted to cigarettes? The Chairman of the Campaign for Real Education, Nick Seaton, said: "Adults are surrendering their authority to the kids – it seems that the school has got everything upside down." Indeed, some things in Britain have been turned upside down. For example, in a Christian country, where the cross of Christ, which is not offensive to other religious faiths, has been banned in certain sectors of our society for being offensive to non Christians.

- A teacher, fed up with violence and anarchy in the classroom, cried out, "Don't blame us. It's the fault of you rotten parents! (*Daily Mail,* 24 November 2006).
- "11 year-olds will be taught that sex outside marriage is fine....You don't have to be married to have a strong and supportive relationship"(*Daily Mail,* 1 March 2008)
- "Decline in marriage is destroying our pupils: They're too mixed up to learn; they've more eating disorders; they're more prone to suicide (*Daily Mail,* 19 March 2008).
- "Teach under-11s 'pleasure of gay sex' say researchers" (*Daily Mail,*

September 2008). This raises the question: "Is sexual intercourse a recreational activity to be enjoyed by infants?"

In February 2009, the British media reported the story of a 13 year old boy who was thought to have fathered a child with a girl aged 15 years (the actual father was also a 15-year old boy). Amanda Platell commented on this 'tragic incident' in her article, *Smug liberals, morality and 13-year-old 'babyfather.'* She writes "...For their predicament is testament to the moral collapse that is the true legacy of a liberal establishment that has imposed its own values ...on the British people for the past four decades. For this establishment, marriage and the nuclear family are dead, community is irrelevant, individual responsibility counts for nothing, the State will always pick up the tab and the only sin is to be judgmental. Children must never be told that they're not emotionally mature enough for sex, but must be given every possible help with contraception. Sex education is imposed on younger and younger children...the devastation created by this moral decay is evident not only in the ever-increasing numbers of fractured and dysfunctional families...for many teenagers and even-pre-teens in Britain today, having sex is of no greater consequence than sneezing...The morning after pill is handed out like Smarties. It was announced GPs will even be paid bonuses for persuading teenagers to go on to long-lasting contraception (which their parents often won't even know about)" (*Daily Mail,* 14 February 2009).

CRIMINAL ACTIVITIES

- Murder rates on increase in our once civilised country (Daily Express 10 July 2006).
- "Father is killed by teenage gun gang" (Evening Standard 23 August 2006).
- "A–level pupil; beaten to death by two young drunks" (*Daily Mail* 4 August 2006).
- "Girl knifed to death at top public school" (*London Lite,* 15 September 2006).
- "Three girls are chased and stabbed by man who argued with them on a bus" (Daily Mail 25 August 2006).
- "Girl 10, stabbed mum over skin on cocoa" (16 September 2006).
- 40% of criminals are now left off with slap on wrist" (*Daily Express,* 24 November 2006)
- "280 killers and paedos at large, two more murders flee jail. And STILL Reid (the Home Secretary) says...I KNOW NOTHING" (*The Sun,* Thursday 11 March 2007).
- "Reid under fire: Ministers knew of crime debacle" (*The Independent,* Thursday 11 March 2007).
- "Broken Britain: 30 Gun crimes a day" (*The Sun*)
- "19 teen murders...still just a fine for carrying knife (*The Sun* 8 July 2008).
- "London stabbings 20th teenage victim is killed in capital. Four stabbed

to death in a single day" (*Evening Standard,* 11 July 2008).

- "One child killing another child....What does that say about society? Where were the parents? What were they doing?" (*The Mail on Sunday,* 21 December 2008)
- A leading article in the 19 July 2008 edition of the *Financial Times* read: "Repairing Britain's damaged society." According to this influential paper, "British society is not broken, but it is damaged. It will need a series of complex local interventions, not the rebadging of ideological policies that aim to solve phantom general problems."
- Stephen Glover summed it up in his article: "What sort of society have we become when a good Samaritan is kicked to death and a suicidal man jeered by a mob?" (Daily Mail 2 October 2008). He writes: "Our society has produced amoral, feral young men who do not have any quaint concepts like 'right' and 'wrong.'
- In her essay, Life in Yob Britain where even a nun cannot walk safely, Julie Welch, a Social Commentator, writes: "A frail elderly nun was mugged for her handbag in broad daylight, yards from the door of her convent. These are all heartless, cynical crimes that seem to exemplify this country today. And these crimes are only extreme examples of what makes life in Britain so unpleasant right now. The rest is Essence Of Yob – drunkenness, petty vandalism, your car getting sprayed on. Drug-dealing, gun-related nuisance, harassment, foul-mouthed abuse: burglaries are up, fuelled by the burgeoning credit crunch, break-ins increased by 4 percent, fatal stabbings increased, 18 percent rise in robberies involving knives. Fraud and forgery offences were up by 16percent. On average 239 women and girls were arrested every day for violent offences, often fuelled by alcohol." She concluded: "Over the course of the past decade or so we've become so used to, or intimidated by, this kind of behaviour that some of it just doesn't impinge on our radar any more. How has the country been allowed to get to the state where drunken violence and foul-mouthed abuse is tolerated and ignored? Where is the voice of authority that you can respect....Right now it seems we're no longer going to hell in a hand-cart. It's already drawn up at its destination" (Daily Express, 5 February 2009).
- The cover story of the 28 March 2009 edition of the Daily Mail read: "As teenage thug gets life for murdering schoolboy, victim's parents deliver their damning verdict on modern Britain. This country of anger and fear." The paper reported how a teenage murdered a 16-year. The parents of the victim' -Barry and Margaret Mizen - pleaded for Britain to stop itself becoming a country of 'selfishness, anger and fear...This is a country of civility, fair play and with traditional values. Things have got to change."

SOLUTION TO "BROKEN" OR "DAMAGED" BRITAIN

We must ask the question: "What is the solution to a "Broken" or "Damaged" Britain? How do we repair a "damaged Britain"? And how has Britain "been allowed to get to the state where drunken violence and foul-mouthed abuse is tolerated and ignored?" How do we change and return to civility and our traditional values?

For the answers, let us listen to the prophetic voice of the eminent Victorian who wrote about European Union and its future before the European Union came into existence: "*In this flippant and shallow age we seem to be letting slip what the Reformers won for us...For the dethronement of the Bible eliminates the most important factor in the formation of our national character, and it is not easy to estimate the effect which this will have on the life of the people of this country.....The rationalism of Germany at the close of the 18th century would accept the Bible only on the terms of bringing it down to the level of a human book, and the problem which had to be solved was to get rid of the element of miracle which pervades it.*

The effects of this "Higher Criticism" are extremely grave. For it has dethroned the Bible in the home, and the good old practice of "family worship" is rapidly dying out. And great national interests also are involved. For who can doubt that the prosperity and power of the Protestant nations of the world are due to the influences of the Bible upon character and conduct? Races of men who for generations have been taught to think for themselves in matters of the highest moment will naturally excel in every sphere of effort or of enterprise. And more than this, no one who is trained in the fear of God will fail in his duty to his neighbour, but will prove himself a good citizen. But the dethronement of the Bible leads practically to the dethronement of God; and in Germany and America, and now in England, the effects of this are declaring themselves in ways, and to an extent, well fitted to cause anxiety for the future"

Sir Robert recorded that the dethronement of the Bible leads to the dethronement of God in England, and this is "well fitted to cause anxiety for the future." On 14 April 2009, a headline in the Daily Mail read: "7 million in the anxious generation." Under this headline the paper reported: "Mental health experts believe that increased fear and anxiety could actually make economic crisis worse." Another headline in The Independent read: *Britain is becoming a more fearful place – and the economy is paying the price."* Under this headline Jeremy Laurence, Health Editor, reported: "Britain is becoming a more fearful nation with rising levels of anxiety and depression that are fuelling the economic crisis by undermining confidence. "In February 2009, the Office for National Statistics published figures showing a 12 percent rise in the rate of anxiety disorders in the UK between 1993 and 2007, equivalent to 800,000 more sufferers." Have we not dethroned the Bible and dethroned God in our nation? We are reaping the fruits of what we have sown – We have become "Anxious Generation". The prophetic word of Sir Robert Anderson has come to pass.

Britain has lapsed. The "evil days" are upon us where "criminals are counselled, not punished. School children 'understood' not disciplined. Family breakdown rewarded not condemned. And the result is a nastiness that's destroying Britain." (Source: *The evil of niceness* Kenneth Minogue, Daily 28 March 2009). No amount of political and economic initiatives would save our nation from sinking into the mud. Great Britain must return to the Bible to save itself. In *Entail of the Covenant*, Sir Robert Anderson writes: *"Back to the Bible' should be a patriotic, as well as a religious cry; for the preservation of our liberties, and of our cherished institutions, depends much upon the maintenance of the Bible-taught heart-principles and stout convictions of our fathers."* The Bible is the only solution to our problems. Without the Lord Jesus Christ we can do nothing. Let's prove Him wrong by ignoring Him.

THE LAPSE IN THE CHURCH
ARCHBISHOP OF CANTERBURY: A "CLONE" OF PROFESSOR DRIVER OF OXFORD

- Seventy Church of England Ministers admit they no longer believe in God (*The Sunday Times,* 30 November 1997)
- Third of clergy do not believe in Virgin Birth, and some priests are embarrassed to talk about hell (*The Sunday Times,* 17 July 1999)
- "Promiscuity may not be immoral, says bishop" (*The Times* 24 July 1999).
- "Priest raped us in orgy says nun" (*The Times* 24 January 2006).
- Father flash (a Roman Catholic priest) in hiding as cousin reveals pregnancy (The Times 24 August 2006)
- "Pope draws line under Irish sex abuse scandal" (*The Times,* 27 April 2004)
- Homosexual clergy can marry but should not have sex (*The Times,* 25 July 2005).
- "Evangelical pastor leaves wife for man" (*The Times,* 30 September 1999).
- "Jail warning for child porn vicar" (*Daily Express,* 9 September 2006).
- "Bishop banned from pulpit for swearing" (*The Sunday Times* 27 August 2006).
- "Vicar jailed after sex with girl, aged 13" (*Metro* 30 May 2003.*)*.
- Roman Catholic Church faces 140 abuse claims... *(Daily Mail* 3 August 2006). Boys raped and beaten. One was drugged and attacked after Christmas party.
- Pope sacks Church leader over sex abuse (*The Daily Telegraph,* 21 May 2006).
- Church blessing for a homosexual vicar (*The Daily Telegraph,* 22 December 2005)
- According to the Archbishop of Canterbury, homosexual clergy dispute will split the Church of England apart (*Daily Mail* 25 June 2006).
- "The Archbishop who undermines Christian values......He does not

understand the moral void that exists today." (*Daily Express* 28 February 2008)

Archbishop "fails to promote Christ" (*The Daily Telegraph,* 16 July 2008). What a depression headline? According to Dr Williams, the Christian doctrine of Trinity is "difficult, sometimes offensive to Muslims." Should Christians abandon their core belief in God the Father, God the Son and God the Holy Spirit and then apologise for it? This is ridiculous.

Just as Professor Driver of Oxford and Dr Dean Farrar, an Anglican clergyman, attacked the Book of Daniel to undermine the genuineness of this marvellous Old Testament Book, and by so doing discredited the Lord Jesus Christ, so has Dr Rowan Williams, the Archbishop of Canterbury, in his many theological writings and pronouncements have undermined the Bible and Christianity. It was the habit of some Church of England theologians in the 19th century to undermine Christianity and the Bible by blindly following the German infidels. It is, therefore, not surprising when Theologian Dr Williams undermines Christianity with university knowledge and his own opinions. Dr Williams is just a 'clone' of the Anglican clergyman – Professor S R Driver, who was an occupant of a chair in the University of Oxford. This Anglican Theologian copied the works of German rationalists to undermine the Book of Daniel. History is repeating itself. The "Pseudo-Lisbon-Theologians" of this age have nothing new to offer. Theologians are needed in Universities and Seminaries which have become the cemeteries for the Gospel of Christ. Theologians are not useful to the "Living Body of Christ." A clergyman who is subsidised to defend Christianity rather undermines it. What a pity!

SHOULD CLERGYMEN CRITICISE THE BIBLE?

At this point I would share with you an extract from a letter "Laicus" wrote to the Editor of the *Daily Mail* on 14 July 1905 in response to Sir Robert Anderson's article: *"The Search For Religious Truth"*

"SIR, - In your issue of Monday (10 July 1905) Sir Robert Anderson raised a question of the most vital importance to the great religious bodies of this country, and, although promptly challenged, I noticed that Sir Robert still sticks to his point.... that point seems to resolve itself into the question - Should the clergy criticise the Bible?

Is it permissible, it would lead one to ask, for a Christian minister to subject the Scriptures to the same tests that an expert would apply to an ancient manuscript or Assyrian tablet? Are we, as a Christian nation, for one moment to allow our religious teachers to "search the Scriptures" in a sceptical mood? Is it not their assumption of the sacred ministry an outward and visible sign of their acquiescence in the ancient faith of the Christian Church, and does not their position as Christian ministers preclude their stepping down from the sure platform of settled conviction into the arena of conflicting doubt? Are we, in short, to allow our ministers of religion first to take upon themselves authority to teach, and then, only then, to consider what it is they are or not going to teach

It is impossible to exaggerate the importance of these questions. A wave of scepticism is sweeping over the country. People are becoming increasingly indifferent to their religious duties. It has been estimated that fifty thousand persons spend a fine Sunday on the River Thames. The churches of London, if filled, would only hold one-tenth of the known church-people of the metropolis, but the majority of the churches are never filled.

Only this week a well-known clergyman draws attention to the increasing practice of those people who do go to church of walking out before the sermon. Last Sunday I was at a famous West End Church, and it almost emptied during the singing of the hymn before the sermon. Where were the people going? To walk in the park I am told, and I can quite believe it. But why do they leave the church at all at that point? Because in my opinion, they are impatient of discipline and indifferent to instruction. Because, as they actually say, no one knows quite what to believe nowadays-some persons still teach what is no longer believed, and others have begun to teach what many have not yet learnt to believe.

Nothing is certain, and Faith is in flux. And not a little of this do we owe to the clergy of the Church itself. Canon Henson declares the Gospel evidence of Christ's physical resurrection to be worthless. Dr. Sanday-a great scholar and divine-has stated that the incidents of Christ's temptation "are on the face of them not historical facts." The Bishop of Birmingham-Dr. Gore-has admitted that the historical evidence of our Lord's birth of a virgin "does not compel belief."

As to the ascension and the physical going up of a material body, Archdeacon Wilberforce has pointed out that "What is up in Galilee is down at the antipodes." The Bishop of Winchester has demolished the accepted version of the Gift of Tongues at Pentecost. And the whole position of belief in the Bible was given away by the Bishop of Birmingham when he said that "Prophetic inspiration is consistent with erroneous prediction."

"Laicus" continues: "Of what profit is all this criticism? These great divines only agree to differ. Some reject what others accept, and *vice versa*. On the field of criticism canon Henson and Dr. Gore are at daggers drawn. When doctors differ, who shall decide?

If in practice, then, the results of such criticism are clearly not re-settlement but unsettlement, are the Christian people of this country justified in revolting against a clergy who pick the Faith to pieces bit by bit/ are they entitled to demand that their ministers of religion shall leave their biblical gerrymandering alone and get to their Christian business?.

I submit, sir, with all due deference, that it is high time for the people of Christian England to come forward and speak out fearlessly on the this vitally important matter; and give no uncertain answer to this fateful question for England and Christianity: Shall the clergy be allowed to pick the Bible to pieces?"

And this is an extract from "Rural Dean's letter dated 15 July 1905: "These modern critics are so misusing the acids of their mordant science that the hitherto impregnable rock of Holy Scriptures is in danger of dissolving and crumbling away.... Thee Bishop does not believe in some of the incidents of the Crucifixion, and that in his view the miracles of the New Testament, with the exception of Christ's Virgin Birth, Divinity, resurrection, and Ascension, may be explained away as "ideas not coincident with fact." If this be the leading given to us by a Christian Bishop, wither shall we follow, and where, at last, shall we arrive." (Pleas read the various arguments in *Should Clergymen Criticise the Bible?)*

Is it any surprise that in 2009, over 104 years since the above letters were written; the Church of England has rejected Christ and His account of creation and has accepted the agnostic Charles Darwin's Theory of Evolution? I, again, urge Dr. Rowan Williams and his "disciples" in the Church of England to study Dr. Robert Anderson's *A Doubter's Doubts About Science and Religion, Psuedo-Criticism* and *The Buddha of Christendom"* for an enlightenment on the "Evolution and Creationism" controversy

-THE FAILURE OF "BLIND" CHURCH LEADERS

It was the responsibility of the spiritual leaders of the Established Churches – the Church of England and the Roman Catholic Church – to have advised our political leaders of the spiritual implications of the European Union. Unfortunately these leaders have no clue of what is going on in Brussels and the impact the European Union would have on mankind. Since our Church leaders do not believe in the absolute authority of the Bible, they lack the knowledge to guide our politicians. Some priests consider parts of the Bible "boring" and out of date. Even some bishops and theologians of the Church in Rome do not believe the Book of Daniel is a divine revelation. For the Roman Catholic Bible, *The New Jerusalem Bible – The Popular and The Readers' Editions-* claim the Book of Daniel is an "edifying fiction." The same Catholic Church teaches the Book of Revelation does not tell us about the end of the world. Why wouldn't the Church of Rome be blind to the spiritual significance of the European Union, since the truth concerning this political union was recorded in the Books of Daniel and Revelation thousands of years ago?

CONFUSION IN THE ROMAN CATHOLIC CHURCH

The "blindness" of Vatican to the scriptural truth about the European Union and its dark future has resulted in its confusion and division over Turkey's membership of the European Union. The leaders of the Roman Catholic Church do not know whether to support or object to Turkey's membership of the political phenomenon of the 21st century. In 2004 Pope Benedict XVI, then a Cardinal and the Defender of the Catholic Faith, objected to Turkey's membership of the European Union. In 2006 Cardinal Cormac Murphy-O'Connor, the then spiritual head of the Catholic Church in England and Wales, suggested that Turkey should be banned from the European Union (Daily Mail 22 September 2006). However, in December 2006 the Spiritual Head of the Catholic Church became a diplomat and decided to support Turkey's membership of the European Union to the delight of the prime minister of Turkey. Pope Benedict's change of position on Turkey's membership of the European Union earned him the label: "flip-flop" Pope (*TIME* 25 December 2006-1 January 2007).

SHOULD THE CHURCH AND THE STATE HELP THE EUROPEAN UNION TO GROW?

On 21 July 2007, The Times published an edited version of a lecture Cardinal Murphy-O'Connor delivered at Cumberland Lodge. His address was summarised in an article, *Church and State should help Europe to grow.* According to the Cardinal, "The European Union is a conscious attempt to transcend national loyalties and to foster a new "European" identity based on common values. But Europe's slow and painful birth has involved an attempt to brush under the carpet the continent's Christian heritage." The spiritual leader then suggested: "recognising Christianity's role in Europe's history could save the European project and reinvigorate democracy for the new century."

Why should a Christian leader lecture Eurocrats who have made a conscious decision to exclude the Lord Jesus Christ from its constitution? The European project has no room for God. The State has no place for the Lord Jesus Christ. Some of the laws of the state undermine the teachings of Christ. This raises the question: "How could the Church of Christ team up with a "godless" State to help a "godless" Europe to grow? After all, European leaders have ignored the godly advice the first President of the European Parliament, who was a committed Roman Catholic, offered to them concerning the survival of the European Enterprise. Had the Catholic Cardinal studied the Book of Daniel, he would have learnt that "the 10 toes of the human image would be crushed by a stone cut without human hands". How would the Catholic Cardinal know the truth about the European Project, when the Roman Catholic Bible – *The New Jerusalem Bible* – teaches that the Book of Daniel is a literary fraud – pregnant with "historical errors" and "inaccuracies?" Had Cardinal Cormac Murphy-O'Connor read *The Coming Prince* by the Protestant Anderson, who wrote about the European Union before the Catholic founding fathers of European Community were born, he would have reminded his audience that the European Project, without the Lord Jesus Christ, would eventually collapse.

CARDINAL'S DISTORTION OF THE PARABLE OF THE LEAVEN

Unfortunately, in his lecture, Cardinal Murphy O'Connor misinterpreted the *Parable of the Leaven* with a mechanical interpretation of the significance of "leaven." According to the Cardinal, "The gospels offer the more modest, but no less vital, metaphor of the leaven in the dough, the unseen agent that enlivens and animates society from within... The Church understood as leaven does not rule but serves." Had the Cardinal applied the principle of interpreting Scripture with Scripture, he would not have made the spiritual blunder of associating the Church with "leaven." "Leaven" in scriptural terms denotes evil: hypocrisy, licentiousness, and liberalism. During His ministry on earth, the Lord Jesus Christ warned His disciples against the leaven of the Pharisees, the Leaven of the Sadducees and the Herodians. The Old Testament tells us God advised the Jews to eat unleavened bread: "Three times a year you are to celebrate a festival to me. Celebrate the Feast of Unleavened Bread; for seven days eat bread made without yeast, as I commanded you. Do this at the appointed time in the month of Abib, for this month you came out of Egypt." (Exodus 23:14-15)

In the Parable of the leaven, which Cardinal Cormac Murphy-O'Connor referred to, the Lord Jesus Christ speaks of a woman who secretly hides leaven in three measures of meal until the whole loaf was leavened. The leaven in the Parable signifies heretical teachings and evil practices. Is it not clear how various Christian denominations have mixed the Scriptures and the teachings of Christ with their own dogmas? Why did the *"woman"* hide the leaven? We are not to "hide" the gospel. The Lord Jesus Christ taught the disciples to proclaim on the mountain top and in daylight what He had taught them in secret. The "woman" in the Parable of the Leaven in Matthew 13:33 represents the apostate church. The same "woman" is the Jezebel we find in Revelation 2:18-21 where the Lord addressed the "Church in Thyatira." The Christian Church should leave the European Union alone to meet its destiny. Nothing would prevent Monnet's "European Titanic" from sinking beneath the waves.

Reports in the media and our own practical experiences have confirmed Sir Robert Anderson's fears about Britain. To begin with, in September 2006, British newspapers reported on how schools would no longer teach children what is wrong and right. In a column headlined "Teaching right and wrong is scrapped" (*Daily Mail 31 July 2006*), the correspondent, James Tozer, reported that the British National

Curriculum would be changed so that teachers would merely have to help children develop "secured values and beliefs." There would be no education about Britain's cultural heritage. In Britain today people live in fear. Violence among our youth has spread over our nation. Why? Because we have failed to use the Christian Gospel – the bedrock of our civilisation - to teach them eternal truths from falsehood.

The days have arrived, when our nation, once a champion of freedom and of truth, has abandoned its Christian heritage by not educating our children on what is 'Right' and "Wrong." Even the Archbishop of Canterbury, the spiritual leader of the Established Church of England, who is supposed to defend the Bible and Christianity, in his desire to appease the "disciples of Darwin," and to be seen as a progressive intellectual, claimed the Truth about Creation, which is recorded in the Book of Genesis, should not be taught in schools. Why? Shouldn't our children be taught that it was God who created the heavens and the earth, and that man is His handiwork not a creature of accident? Did man descend from ape as suggested by Darwin? Had Dr Rowan Williams, the 'thinker and sophisticated intellectual,' done his homework on Darwin's Theory of Evolution by studying *"A Doubters Doubts about Science and Religion", "The Bible and Modern Criticism"* and *"Pseudo-Criticism,"* he would have learnt how the brilliant Dr. Anderson, an intellectual among intellectuals, tamed 'Darwin's bull-dog,' - the "hypocrite" Professor Thomas Henry Huxley - the most important High Priest of Darwin's Evolutionary Theory.

The Archbishop of Canterbury and his fashionable clergy and Bishops should reflect on this extract from Dr. Anderson's *The Silence of God; "No generous mind would willingly insult a man's religion, whether he be Christian or Jew, Mahometan or Buddhist. But when "religious" men pose as sceptics and critics, they come out into the open, and forfeit all "right of sanctuary." Courtesy is due to the religious man who stands behind the labarum of his creed. Courtesy is no less due to the agnostic who refuses faith in all that lies outside the sphere of sense or demonstration. But what shall be said for those who discard belief in the supernatural while they claim to be the true exponents of a system which has the supernatural as its only basis; or who deprecate belief in the inspiration of the Scriptures, while they profess to hold and teach that to which, apart from inspiration in the strictest sense, none but the credulous would listen?...These men pretend to mental superiority; but we only need to tear away the lion's skin they masquerade in to find exactly what we might expect! Here is a dilemma from which there is no escape.......*

.......The Christian and. the infidel cannot both be right, yet both are entitled to respect, for the one position is logically as unassailable as the other. But what shall be said for the unbelieving Christian, or the Christianised infidel? If he be dishonest he is almost bad enough for a gaol; if he be honest he is almost weak enough for an asylum. The weak deserve our pity; the wicked our contempt. And their claim to be freethink-

ers, their affectation of intellectual superiority, give proof that with the majority the more generous alternative is the true one. The old Jewish proverb about straining out a gnat and swallowing a camel well describes their attempt to combine the most fastidious scepticism with the blindest faith. These modern Sadducees talk "as though wisdom were born with them"; whereas, in fact, like their prototypes of old, they are the stupid advocates of an impossible compromise.....The Bible is not infallible, but the Church is infallible, and upon the authority of the Church our faith can find a sure foundation. But how do we know that the Church is to be trusted? The ready answer is, we know it upon the authority of the Bible. That is to say, we trust the Bible on the authority of the Church, and we trust the Church on the authority of the Bible! It is a bad case of "the confidence trick." But, it will be said, is it not to the Church that we owe the Bible?

But the Bible is more than a book - it is a revelation; and thus regarded, it is above the Church. We do not judge the Bible by the Church; we judge the Church and its teaching by the Bible. This is our safeguard against the ignorance and tyranny of priestcraft. But in our day those who deprecate most strongly the tyranny of the priest are precisely those who champion most loudly the tyranny of the professor and the pundit."

Today, some Church leaders lack the confidence to state publicly the Eternal Truths in the Sacred Scriptures. They are scared of trendy intellectuals. They are afraid of offending people. What a shame! The Lord Jesus Christ, who is the TRUTH, proclaimed: "At the beginning the Creator made them male and female." According to our Blessed Lord, male and female did not "evolve" (Matthew 19: 4-6). Despite this Eternal Truth from the lips of our Divine Lord, the Church of England has bowed to Darwin's hypothesis of Evolution and apologised to the agnostic Darwin (Matthew 19:4-6). I repeat the words of God's Barrister: "The man who can give no account of his own existence is a fool; and he who denies a God can give no account of his existence....Regarded as a theory to account for life, evolution is the wildest folly; but as an hypothesis to account for the varied forms of life, it claims a hearing on its merits" (*A Doubter's Doubts about Science and Religion"*). I encourage church leaders to read this book and *The Bible and Modern Criticism*. They will have the confidence to defend the Bible and the Christian Faith.

LAPSE IN BRITISH SOCIETY: THE "EVIL DAYS" ARE UPON US

The Archbishop of Canterbury, Dr Rowan Williams, commented on the lapse in our British society with a plea for a ban on all advertisements that are corrupting our children. On Monday 18 September, the London evening newspaper, which is aimed at young people, adorned its front page with this message: *Ban the ads destroying childhood: Archbishop launches crusade for the family.* Under this headline, Jason Beattie reported: "Dr Williams spoke out amid fears that modern commercial pressures are destroying childhood. According to the Archbishop, there was an "enormous problem", because advertising companies and retailers were forcing children to become consumers before they were ready. The report noted that, the Archbishop intervened as a result of an inquiry launched by the Children's Society. This enquiry revealed that there were growing levels of depression among the young. About one in ten young people were identified with "mental health problems, including self-harm and clinical depression." And it was later revealed that a girl of 4, who suffered from stress and depression, was prescribed to take pills. What has become of Great Britain?

Following the concern the public raised on how some television advertisements have had negative influence on our children, this message was published on the *Messageboard* in the London Lite: "Protect children from our material world." (19 September 2006). This issue, and the decline in moral values in our society, summarise how the "lapse in evil days", spoken of by Sir Robert Anderson in the 19th century, have crept upon us in the 21st century.

The Labour Government was accused over pornographic advertising campaign which featured young holiday makers in sexually explicit modes. According to a Report, published in a column titled *Passport to degradation,* Martin Delgado writes; "The four advertisements are aimed at 16 to 24 year-olds to highlight the fact that first-time passport applications will now take longer following the Government's controversial decision to introduce compulsory interviews. But the sleazy images appear to encourage sex-acts with strangers - at a time when …the Department of Health was spending millions of pounds trying to reduce Britain's high rate of unwanted pregnancies and sexually transmitted infections." One picture showed a man in sunglasses frolicking in the sea with two girls and saying: "Shame u didn't get UR passport m8…"

The profane advertisement prompted this response from Michaela Aston: "Given the latest surge in abortion rates and the epidemic of sexually transmitted diseases in the UK, it is irresponsible of the Home Office to produce adverts aimed at young people which blatantly give the message that holidays are only about sex". Politicians claim they "don't make moral judgement". So, it might not be a "big deal" if a government encouraged the young to have sex with strangers. After all, the European Union, which British politicians have fallen in love with, used pornographic film and posters to "win customers" for the largest economic market in the world. Without any surprise, the Labour Government, destitute of confidence and ideas, blindly followed European politicians.

The British Broadcasting Corporation's attitude towards the Holy Bible sums up how "evil days" have crept upon Britain. Kings and Queens of our nation have sworn on the Bible to defend its teaching. Yet, the BBC suggested that they would allow the Holy Bible to be thrown into a dustbin on a TV comedy show, but not the Koran. BBC admitted: "We are biased". It was reported in the newspapers that The "Biased Broadcasting Corporation" is "dominated by trendy, left-leaning liberals who are biased against Christianity and in favour of multiculturalism." (*The Mail on Sunday,* 22 October 2006).

The same BBC televised a show that depicted the Lord Jesus Christ as a homosexual in a nappy. The Directors justified their blasphemous programme despite about 60,000 complaints. The BBC also showed a misleading film about the Queen which resulted in one of its executives losing his job. Since then, the BBC has perpetrating deceptions on the public. Melanie Phillips summarised how the BBC has lapsed. In her column, *"Faked footage, rigged votes and a culture of bias. No wonder we've lost faith in the BBC,"* she writes: "The Wyatt report highlighted a sorry catalogue of misjudgements, poor practice and ineffective systems that led Mr Fincham to make false claim about the Queen." The BBC reputation for integrity was "hit by ... revelations of fakery and frauds that it perpetrated upon the public by such iconic Shows as "Blue Peter," "Children In Need" and "Comic Relief." The columnist continued: "At the heart of the BBC's own identity crisis lies Britain's loss of belief in itself as a nation. That has expressed itself in the onslaught by the Left-wing intelligentsia on core British and western values, including the belief that there is no such thing as truth or objectivity and that everything is instead a matter of subjective opinion" (*Daily Mail,* 8 October 2007).

On human opinion, Sir Robert Anderson writes: "Opinions have taken the place of convictions; and the result is a liberality which is the offspring not of humility and love, but of indifference or doubt. Opinions are our own and should not be too firmly held.... The man who would force his opinions on others is a boor. He who would die for his opinions is a fool. But Christianity has not to do with opinions. It is founded on established facts and Divine truth...Truth is worth living for and dying for."

In October 2008, the British Broadcasting Corporation (BBC) was criticised for allowing its Radio 2 Show to broadcast a series of obscene phone calls on the air .An elderly man and his grand daughter were subjected to lewd abuse – all in the name of entertainment. The public revolt on the filth that was pumped into the atmosphere resulted in the resignations of one of its presenters and two officials, and the suspension of its highly paid presenter.

Melanie Phillips commented on this despicable episode in her column. Under the title, *Gloating cruelty, foul vulgarity and a BBC that has lost all sense of shame,* she writes: "What kind of degraded cultural universe are we all now living in? What possible justification can there be for this vile behaviour, let alone putting it on air? How can the gratuitous harassment of an elderly man by foul obscenities about his granddaughter be considered public entertainment.....The issue here is not just the use of profanities, but the cruelty and indeed sadism in the desire to torment an unsuspecting elderly man and his family." Commenting on the "brutality" that is shown on our TV, the Columnist reported: "Watching other people show distress, incompetence or mediocrity and then seeing them humiliated for exhibiting these characteristics apparently entertains audience by making them feel superior. "What kind of society have we become in which enough people gain vicarious pleasure or entrainment from such displays to persuade cynical TV executives they can make huge profits from them?

"GUTLESS" LEADERS LEADING BRITAIN

Another evidence of 'lapses' in Britain. Dress code instituted by the British Airways prevented the display of Christian cross around the neck. Some politicians, Bishops, Muslim, Jewish and other religious leaders expressed their outrage at such a ban of Christian symbol. In its editorial of 25 November 2006, The Daily Telegraph states: "British Airways is not the only company to issue politically correct guidelines that discriminate against Christians."

Amanda Platell also reported on how political and religious leaders in Britain reacted to the "Great BA cross revolt." In her article, "*Deafening silence of our gutless leaders,*" she explained that these leaders were mute to criticise British Airways for their action. She writes: "All claim to be Christians. All say they are defenders of British values. But none spoke. Have we ever had a more gutless bunch of individuals leading this country? It was left instead to the Uganda born Archbishop of York, Dr John Sentamu, to speak for the silent majority in this country when he attacked BA for turning its back on our nation's Christian heritage." The columnist concluded: "We have leaders who are so frightened of offending minority faiths – and so desperate to indulge every whim – that they have forgotten they are elected to serve the many not the few. We may not be a church-going nation, but we are a Christian one. And there has never been a greater need for strong moral leadership than now" (Daily Mail 25 November 2006).

The "evil days" have come upon our nation. Truly, the prophetic word of Sir Robert Anderson has been fulfilled. Great Britain has lapsed with no sense of what is right or wrong. And not surprisingly, Major Pruw Boswell, who was reported to be a practising Roman Catholic, ordered that prayers should be banned before council meetings in one of Britain's oldest boroughs to "allay fears they may offend other religions." The Daily Express reported this news in an article titled "*Council axes Christian prayers after 600 years. You guess it...in case it offends other faiths.*" Mark Reynolds writes: "For 600 years, vicars had opened proceedings at Totnes Town Council in Devon with a prayer to ask God's help in making the right decisions. Every meeting was closed with a rendition of the Lord's Prayer. But this monthly prayers have now been axed after officials claimed the blessing may offend councillors who follow other faiths or are atheists." I ask again: "What has become of the Christian nation – Great Britain?" Some of us have decided to ignore the Almighty God whose commandments and Laws were the foundation stone upon which Britain was built.

Majority of Britons call themselves Christians. The fact that Church buildings, which are governed by "blind" men, are empty is not the yard-stick to measure how Christian our nation is. Christianity is not measured by how many millions of people visit Cathedrals on Sundays and sing "Hallelujah" in imposing or wretched buildings. The Lord Jesus Christ is still building the Church which He shed His Precious Blood for. His Church is not magnificent Cathedrals, nor dilapidated buildings in street corners. It is an organic body of men and women who have "forsaken" the world and are following His teachings in spirit and in truth.

Our lapsed society was, again, highlighted in a newspaper article titled *A society out of control* (Daily Mail 18 January 2008). In this article James Slack and Liz Hull reported: "A Judge warned that an obsession with rights had created a society "bedevilled by feral youths." Judge Ian Trigger spoke out amid a wave of anger over the murder of devoted family man Garry Newlove in a vicious gang attack. He also attacked the policy of releasing violent offenders on bail. According to the report, Cheshire Chief Constable, Peter Fahy, complained of a tide of drunkenness, coupled with extended opening hours that had left police struggling to cope with violent youths. Even middle-class children from decent families were being sucked into 'extremes of violence' by alcohol.

Judge Trigger warned of a generation apparently out of control. He declared: "It is the fault of politicians, that bail is so readily granted, rather than judges or magistrates. Parliament and its woeful and indeed dreadful concentration on rights forgets duties and responsibilities...We are living in a society bedevilled by wild feral youths...It is time for parents to resume control over their offspring. It is time for parents to teach values and respect to their children, value and respect for other people and not to allow their offspring to engage in selfish and irresponsible behaviour...It is time for community and faith leaders to condemn the prevalent violence on our streets rather than excuse or condone it and it is time for sentencers to send a clear warning that violence will not be tolerated."

It was reported in our national newspapers how sex offenders were cleared to teach in schools; foreign criminals set loose to re-offend; plans to legalise the killing of the terminally ill. And on 18 January 2006, the *Daily Mail* highlighted our lapsed society in its leading article "*Pimps charter*": "declassification of cannabis"; "24-hour drinking"; "Potential explosion of "casino gambling"; "Proliferation of den for prostitutes"; "Reformers plan to legalise mini-brothers under their risibly named 'co-ordinated prostitution strategy - up to three women will be able to ply their trade in flats and houses everywhere, without fear of prosecution."

Our nation has lapsed. The evil days have come upon us as eloquently predicted by Scotland Yard Chief Detective. On the subject of *Criminals and Crime*, the Prince of Detectives, who was also a Secretary to the Prison Commission, wrote: "There should be as much liberty and opportunity for mental and moral improvement as compatible with discipline; and prisons should be open to all the influences of Christianity, not only to official religious services. "*It is scandalous nothing short of a scandal that in a Christian and Protestant country the inmates of our goals should know nothing of religion save what comes to them officially like the water and the gas. To turn from the soul to the intellect; what means are now available to develop and excite a prisoner's mental powers*? I repeat Sir Robert Anderson's significant statement: "The dethronement of the Bible eliminates the most important factor in the formation of our national character, and it is not easy to estimate the effect which this will have on the life of the people of this country."

The Established Church has also fallen. It has become irrelevant to the extent that a Christian launched an attack on its leadership. The Times Religious Correspondent, Ruth Gledhill, reported this incident in an article titled "*Anglican leaders are losing their way.*" She writes: "The head of the Church Army ... launched a surprising attack on the Church of England, accusing it of losing faith in Christian fundamentals. According to Captain Philip Johnson, newly converted Christians preferred to share their new found faith with friends in Pubs and on the internet than going to sit in empty church buildings, And the Church, "seen as increasingly irrelevant," is "led by people who no longer seemed to believe in the Gospel tenets of their faith" (The Times 13 July 2006). The clergy in the Church of England have become disciples of Darwin. What a shame! The Anglican Church should reflect on Sir Robert Anderson's words: "illumination is much needed at this moment, when the church is honeycombed by scepticism –a scepticism, moreover which is the outcome, not of fuller knowledge or matured thought, but of intellectual conceit and levity which are the marked characteristics of the age."

How is the mighty falling? Great Britain has abdicated its position as the "champion of freedom and of truth" to champion falsehood in our political system and the Established Churches. Christianity is on the verge of being criminalised as Melanie Phillips described it in her essay "*How Britain is turning Christianity into a crime*". Commenting on an evangelist who was arrested for handing out Bible verses about homosexuality, she writes: "How long will it be before Christianity becomes illegal in Britain? This is no longer the utterly absurd and offensive question that on first blush it would appear to be...Christianity is fast becoming the creed that dare not speak its name. It is being written out of the national script by ideologues seeking to hasten its disappearance....Local authorities and government bodies are systematically bullying Christianity out of existence by refusing to fund Christian voluntary groups on the grounds that to be Christian means that they are not committed to "diversity". She continued: "The 'diversity' agenda... is a fig-leaf for an attack on Christianity.....But Christianity is still the official religion of this country. All its institutions, its history and its culture are suffused with it; Britain would lose its identity, its values and its cohesion without it. But minority rights are now being wielded against it like a wrecking ball."

She concludes: "Christianity is being steadily removed from the public sphere. Various councils have banned Christmas on the grounds that it is 'too Christian' and therefore offensive to people of other faiths, and replacing it with meaningless 'winter festivals.' This attack on Christianity is not merely something that seems straight out of Alice In Wonderland. It is not merely a threat to freedom of speech and religious expression. It is a fundamental onslaught on the national identity and bedrock value of this country—and as such will destroy those freedoms which Christianity itself first created" *(Daily Mail,* 7 September 2006*)*.

The beginning of 2007 was greeted with a poll which suggested that Britain has lapsed. *"Britain in gloom"* was the headline in a column of the *Daily Mail.* According to the survey, the year 2006 was a bad year for Britain and things would get worse. Rebecca Camber reported, though many of the British people were upbeat about their own prospects, "more than half think the nation has had a miserable five years. In a pessimistic outlook, those surveyed blamed rising immigration, yobbish behaviour, rudeness and bad language for the nation demise...53% believed it would be a worse place in five years' time. More than a quarter were not proud to be British." (*Daily Mail* Monday 1 January 2007*)*.

WHY "FILTHY" BRITAIN?

Tom Utley summed up how Britain has lapsed in his essay *"I'm not too religious.... but is Mr Blair now so arrogant he believes his morality takes precedence over God's."* (*Daily Mail,* Friday January 5, 2007). Mr Utley writes: "Christians, Muslims and Jews who take their religions seriously don't have to look far in modern Britain to find dozens of developments to appal them: filth every night on the TV, drunks on the streets, abortion on demand, an epidemic of teenage pregnancies, mass fornication and marital breakdown...Seen from the pulpit, ours is a nation sunk in moral depravity, beyond hope of Earthly redemption". Mr Utley continued: "...In our easy-going, decadent liberal democracy: we have no laws - or at least none....which force them.... to behave as individuals in ways that affront their consciences or the teachings of their faith."

The columnist further commented on the Labour Government's attempt to introduce the Sexual Orientation Regulation 2006 – a legislation which would make it illegal for anyone who provides goods, services, facilities or education to discriminate against others on the grounds of their sexual preferences – heterosexual, homosexual or bisexual. This is a legislation which provoked Christians that they were being forced to act in contrast to their faith. The Catholic Church was concerned with the Government plans that it threatened to shut down its nine adoption and fostering agencies rather than putting children into the care of same-sex couples. Mr Utley concluded his critique of the governments plans to impose their notion of morality on the masses by stressing that, the government by its action was "gratuitously offending religious sensibilities...Why does the Government think it worthwhile to stir up ill-feeling in this way? Has Tony Blair become so arrogant after ten years that he really believes his version of morality must take precedence over God's?" The man who could not "do God" in office is now "doing God" out of office.

On the lapse of "freedom" in Britain, Daily Mail raised this question in its Editorial: *A free nation?* "Time was, in this cradle of democracy when we took it for granted that we had an inalienable right to honest opinion. No longer it seems". You may read the rest of the leading article. And just before the year 2006 closed, The Independent adorned its front cover with this question: *"WHAT FREEDOM OF INFORMATION?"- 40% of requests under right-to-know laws are rejected – and its likely to get worse. All were refused.* Finally, a Labour Party supporter, Chris Atkins, gave a damning verdict on Tony Blair's assault on personal freedom. In an essay titled, *We now live in a land where we are all prisoners,* Mr Atkins writes: "Today, in Tony Blair's Britain...we have witnessed a breath-taking erosion of civil liberties. The truth is we are fast becoming Orwellian state, our every movement watched, our behaviour monitored, and our freedom curtailed...Our civil liberties enshrined in British law since the Magna Charta, are being whittled away." He added: "This shift away from individual freedom towards state power has happened slowly and almost without us noticing" (Daily Mail).

"BROKEN BRITAIN"

What has become of Great Britain? A nation which, according to Sir Robert Anderson, was once "the champion of freedom and of truth" has descended into a nation where freedom of information is being denied and truth cast to the ground. The moral fabric of our nation has disintegrated to the extent that multiple abortions among young people are considered to be a lifestyle choice. Abortion is now a method of birth control. The result: more than a quarter of British people are not proud to be British. What a pity!

Ian Duncan-Smith, a former Conservative Party Leader, produced a document which concluded that the British society has "broken but could be fixed." In a

Special report published in The Sunday Telegraph, he writes: "I have visited many of Britain's most deprived and fractured communities and seen levels of breakdown that have appalled and angered me. In the fourth largest economy in the world, too many people live in dysfunctional homes, trapped on benefits. Too many communities are blighted by crime, alcohol and drug addiction, and debt." Gang warfare has resulted in a series of teenage stabbings and shootings in our cities. This is "a stark illustration of a broken society." Mr Duncan-Smith continued: "As the fabric of society has crumbled at the margins, what has been left behind is an underclass, where life is characterised by dependency, addiction, debt and family breakdown. This is an underclass in which a child born into poverty today is more likely to remain in poverty than any time since the late 1960s"

And Bruce Anderson supported Ian Duncan-Smith's findings. In a newspaper article titled "*Duncan-Smith has got it right: family breakdown is at the heart of social ills,*" the columnist writes: "The family is a social multiplier. Where families held together, difficulties were surmounted. Where families disintegrated difficulties grew. Britain has the highest rate of single-motherhood in Europe, which is why we also have the highest prison population."

LAPSE IN THE BRITISH PARLIAMENT
THE EXPENSES SCANDAL IN THE HOUSE OF COMMONS

On 8 May 2009, the front page of *The Daily Telegraph* read: "The truth about the Cabinet's expenses." This was the beginning of a series of revelations about how British politicians abused their privileges to enrich themselves at the expense of the taxpayers. The following headlines appeared in the Telegraph and other national newspapers:

- "Tricks of the trade, from shifting 'second homes' to profiting after taxpayer-funded renovations."
- "The 1.7 million property empire built on the back of the MPs' expenses system."
- "MP who claimed £16,000 for mortgage that did not exist."
- "The Tories and taxpayers' money."
- "The justice minister, his home and the convicted landlord."
- "Claims for three different properties in a year."
- "Grant my expenses, or I may be facing divorce, minister pleaded."
- "Millionaire minister received £100,000 to help pay mortgage."
- "Fees office allowed MPs to make inflated claims."
- "Support for the major parties fall as 2 in 3 voters doubt integrity of MPs."
- "Cover-up: the Labour MP and his daughter's cut-price flat deal."
- "I'll quit over mortgage cash, says Labour MP."
- "Absolutely outrageous: Cabinet engulfed by expenses storm…" (*Daily*

Mail 8 May 2009).

- "Expenses sensation: It stinks. One greedy MP even claimed for sack of manure." *(The Sun, 9 May 2009)*
- "Speaker's scapegoat: Official who signed off MPs' expenses didn't even have a qualification in accountancy." (*The Mail on Sunday* 10 May 2009).
- "House of Shame: The revelations about MPs' expenses – from the foreign secretary's pram to the justice secretary's free kitchen – undermine their moral authority. After blocking any attempts to reform MPs' pay over the past three years, can parliament now redeem itself." (*The Observer* 10 May 2009)
- "As politicians get a help line to cope with public fury over lavish claims.... MPs vote for £16m more expenses." (*Sunday Express* 10 May 2009).
- "Labour 'will stop cheats standing at the election." (*Daily Mail* 20 May 2009.)
- "Tory who claimed £1.600 for his duck pond is told to quit." (Daily Mail 22 May 2009).
- "Shamed politicians cost taxpayers £150,000 each by staying for a year" (*The Daily Telegraph* 29 May 2009).
- "Three MPs agree to stand down in bout of bloodletting over expenses" (*Financial Times* 29 May 2009)
- "Cheats 'wont' get seats in the Lords" (*Daily Mail* 30 May 2009).
- "Cameron: phantom mortgage MPs must face fraud charges...I'm ashamed by what's happened....the swimming pools, duck ponds and moats" (*The Daily Telegraph* 30 May 2009)
- "End pay-offs to MPs shamed into leaving, says Lib Dems." (*The Daily Telegraph* 30 May 2009)
- "Gardiner queried necessity of the work he was asked to carry out."

In its leading article, *"A scandal at the heart of our democracy,"* The Telegraph's editorial states: "The systematic misappropriation by MPs of the allowance paid to defray the expense of keeping a second home is one of the great scandals of modern public life...MPs maintained they are all acting within the rules, but that is only because they set the rules and enforce them. It is arguable that some have acted beyond the rules...It is clear many MPs regarded the money as theirs to be claimed whether it was proper to do so or not."

In its leading article, *"Dissolve this rotten Parliament before it corrupts public life altogether,"* The Mail reports: "This Parliament has now lost all moral and political authority and ought, by rights, to dissolve itself. It is now not only the Government that has ceased to deserve our trust. So many members of the House of Commons have disgraced themselves so completely that their right to make laws for the rest of us has evaporated. Nothing comparable has happened to British politics in modern times. The revelations of surreptitious greed – sometimes pathetic, sometimes outrageous, often both at the same time – are uniquely damaging......The

Mother of all Parliaments has been transformed into a personal wealth-creation scheme on the moral level of Las Vegas. Both major parties have played their part in the transformation of politics into a well-paid and comfortable career for people who probably could not succeed in any other field. *Both have done this as the European Union has hovered power from Westminster to Brussels, leaving British governments with little to decide and not all that much to divide the parties.* The editorial concludes: "We cannot expect Parliament to hold the executive to account, in every sense of the word. Now is the time to do so. The people can and must recapture Westminster from the careerists and the cheats." Emphasis mine. (*The Mail on Sunday,* 10 May 2009)

In an article titled, *"These scams are atrocious. Worse is the lack of remorse,"* Andrew Rawnsley writes: "The expenses racket shows how politicians have lost touch with any ethical bearings and even any sense of self-preservation...If politicians do not arrive at the Commons corrupt, there is clearly a culture in Parliament that is corrupting. Disgraceful scams for milking the taxpayer have become encoded in the DNA of many parliamentarians. One reason is cowardice....Politicians are further stripped of any moral authority to guide the country. How can they now talk about the disgraceful behaviour of bankers or demand sacrifices from voters to cope with the recession?" *(The Observer* 10 May 2009)

- In its leading article, *Greedy MPs must be forced to give us value for money,* the paper reports: "The astonishing claims in allowances and expenses have revealed a malignancy at the heart of Westminster that must be cut out. The evidence revealing how MPs reward themselves has turned the House of Commons into a laughing stock.....Parliament is the cradle of our democracy where MPs are supposed to defend our liberty not line their pockets with taxpayers' money..." (Sunday Express 10 May 2009)
- The editorial of the *News of the World* read: "Real expense is the cost to our democracy." The paper reports: "Of course MPs insist they are claiming expenses within the rules. When your actions are morally indefensible you seek any excuse and hope the gullible will be convinced. But the level of public anger at Westminster reveals that the UK electorate is far from gullible. ...The amount that our MPs have milked from us to live in style is bad enough. But the greatest damage done is to our democracy. They have reduced the mother of Parliaments to a sick comedy of errors."
- The leading article of the 9 May 2009 edition of *The Sun* states: "Claim excuse: It is the pathetic claims that are most humiliating...It is the greedy claims that are the most outrageous...Have they no sense of honour? Or in public life all about ripping off the taxpayer to the max? All parties share blame for the greed at Westminster...Not all MPs are on the make. But Mr Brown's Cabinet are giving all politicians a bad name. The Westminster trough needs to be put away."

Additional newspaper headlines on the expenses scandal:

- "Peers face historic suspension over bribes" (*Daily Mail* 15 May 2009). According to the newspaper, the House of Lords privileges committee found two Labour peers guilty of misconduct. These men were prepared to accept money to influence amendments to Government legislation.
- "EXCLUSIVE: Monarch tells PM of grave concern over MPs' expenses. THE QUEEN 'IS DEEPLY TROUBLED.' (*The Mail on Sunday* 17 may 2009)
- "The shaming of Parliament As police are called in to probe expenses scandal and the revelations continue, MPs fear tide of revulsion among voters" (Front page *The Independent* 9 May 2009)
- "There can be no justification for this abuse of expenses. MPs should put up their hands and throw their efforts behind reform." (Editorial)
- "After all those claims for mortgages, moats and lavish furnishings, a new revelation.....SCANDALS OF MPs' TRAVEL EXPENSES" (Daily Mail 25 May 2009).
- "Remorseful peer says he fiddled expenses." (*The Sunday Times* 31 May 2009) It was reported "a Labour peer and former chairman of the party...admitted he "fiddled" for not being paid a salary." The Member of the House of Lords, who lived outside London, claimed up to £18000 in a year for an overnight subsistence when he had actually stayed with friends for free or had even returned to his home.
- "Labour MP claimed £5 for church donation." It was reported a Labour politician was refused a £5 claim he requested. His receipt for the claim for the contribution he made during a memorial service for dead soldiers read: "Battle of Britain church service Sunday 17.09.05 £5 contribution to offertory on behalf of..." (*The Sunday Times* 31 May 2009)

Commenting on the expenses scandal on Sky News, Sir Alistair Graham, the former chairman of the Committee on Standards in Public Life, said MPs had shown 'a lack of moral leadership' by 'stretching the rules to the furthest limit for what looks like personal benefit. I think a culture developed in the House of Commons that it was legitimate to play the system to maximise your income."

This headline, "Shameless: Ministers brazen out expenses scandal and even blame the media," appeared in the Daily Express of 9 May 2009. In its leading article, "*The shameful corruption of a parliament in decline,"* the paper reports: "After the collapse of Labour's political mission, ministers are utterly fixated upon the trappings of power. The details of their resort to the public purse for private purposes comprise the mostly shocking inventory of corruption published in modern times. Cabinet ministers on £140,000 salaries have used taxpayer's money to fund hundreds of items that have nothing to do with parliamentary duties...It is no use the mainstream parties lecturing voters about the folly of backing extremists if they cannot show they are worth backing themselves." Without any surprise, the "shameless" politicians, who sold Britons to Brussels by forcing the Lisbon Treaty on the British people, imported the "spirit" of Jean Monnet - "shamelessness" - into British politics. For Jean Monnet, the "spiritual god-father" of the European Union, had no shame in "stealing" someone's wife.

"Dishonour among thieving MPs." This was the headline for the *Daily Mail* editorial. The leading article states, "Little wonder MPs of all colours fought so doggedly to stop their expenses from being made public, and passed a law to keep their various addresses secret – their covering the tracks of the likes of….who flipped her second homes allowance three times a year... The days of MPs using expenses to steal from the taxpayer are over. If they can't see that, they shouldn't be allowed within a million miles of the levers of power."

Peter Mckay, in his article, "*The cheats poisoning politics,*" writes: "We're pawns in their tawdry schemes, financing everything from their house extensions to packets of Tampax. It would be good if we could have the worst offenders arrested, charged with fraud and by-elections held in their constituencies…." (*Daily Mail* 11 May 2009).

In a Daily Telegraph editorial captioned, "*MPs are there to serve, not to be self-serving,*" the paper reports: "If members of Parliament cannot live without someone else paying for their dining chairs, barbecue sets, garden hoses and 75p bath sponges…then we have a simple suggestion: don't run for Parliament. Politicians are not doing us an honour by sitting on the green benches; we are doing them an honour by investing in them the power to make decisions about our daily lives as our elected representatives. Too few appear to grasp the point."

In her article, "*Our democracy going down the plughole with Home Secretary's dirty bath water,*" Melanie Phillips writes: "Torrent revelations about our grasping MPs and their fraudulent expenses claims shows no sign of slowing. Elected members across the political divides have been exposed as greedy, taxpayer-cheating chancers whose skill for exploiting their own lax expenses rules is matched only by their warped sense of entitlement to top up a salary which – at £64766 – they claim is far too low." (*Daily Mail* 11 May 2009)

On 11 May 2009, *Evening Standard* published an article titled, "*MPs finally eat humble pie.*" Under this heading Joe Murphy, Paul Waugh and Nicholas Cecil, write: "Shamed MPs and ministers finally admitted they were in the wrong over expenses." The correspondents shared with readers the following comments made by some of the politicians:

- Cabinet Minister Ed Miliband confessed: "There has been abuse... we've let people down."
- Tory Shadow Commons Leader Alan Duncan said: "All MPs should be ashamed of themselves."
- Tony Wright, the Labour Chairman of the Public Administration Committee, went further: "This is not victim-hood that is going on here. They were people who were clearly....actively screwing the system. What we have been seeing is a kind of masterclass in ingenuity in how to exploit an overgenerous and insufficiently scrutinized system."
- David Cameron, the Conservative Partly Leader, added: "We need a big acknowledgement that we are sorry that this happened and it needs to change. We need collectively to say, 'this system was wrong, we took part in it, we too operated it. It's no good enough to say 'I obeyed the rules....It's not just about the Government, it's about every party. Let's clean up the system." (*Evening Standard* 11 May 2009)
- **On 13 May 2009,** a column in The Sun read**;** *"Sack half our MPs....the lazy, greedy ones."*

Sir Alistair Graham commented on the expenses scandal. In his article, "*The festering scandal of MPs' expenses must be sorted out once and for all."* He writes: "Surely we have a right to expect our MPs to have a sense of right and wrong – particularly when it comes to claiming financial benefits that are awarded on trust. For too long, too many MPs have been abusing the taxpayer by unethically claiming parliamentary allowances to enhance what they see as an inadequate salary" (*The Mail on Sunday* 29 March 2009).

The fact is Members of Parliament should rather have taken an 80 percent pay cut. They have transferred most of their powers to Brussels. As a result, about 80 percent of our laws come from undemocratic and unaccountable institutions in Brussels. British politicians have little to do in Parliament. Consequently, they spend their time in the House of Indulgence devising schemes to rob the masses who feed them. If Members of Parliament felt their salaries were inadequate for serving the British people, why didn't they leave the House of Commons and sought better jobs elsewhere?

This leads me to share with you an extract from Melanie Phillips' article *"No wonder our MPs turned to crime. They gave up their real job long ago."* She describes how the major political parties (Conservatives, Labour and Liberal Democrats) had failed to address the two most important issues facing the country - mass immigration and the European Union. "These issues are fundamental to the very identity of the country and its ability to govern itself at all." She goes on: "Indeed, their neglect can even be said to have contributed in no small measure to the expenses scandal. This is because parliamentary democracy itself has become steadily emptied of meaning and purpose, leaving a vacuum which has been filled by corruption. For more than three decades, Parliament has become increasingly powerless.....the British Parliament has progressively surrendered its powers of national self-government to Europe, which has reduced the cradle of democracy to the status of little more than Westminster Regional Council." (*Daily Mail* 18 May 2009).

And Camilla Cavendish also reported on one of the causes of public hostility to the expenses scandal. In her article *"Our powerless MPs, overwhelmed with trivia,"* she writes: "Public outrage isn't just about expenses: it's that politicians have blithely handed over authority to the EU and quangocrats....The readiness of politicians to relinquish power amazes me. Take the European constitution, now rebranded as the Lisbon treaty. I read all the drafts of that document, spoke to lawyers and became convinced that its calculated opacity was a charter for the creeping takeover of national policy by bureaucrats and judges.... I met others who hadn't even read the document.... Many decent MPs are dismayed at being lumped together with the crooks. But one of the reasons public anger goes a lot deeper .... is because we feel we can no longer change our laws by voting out politicians. The EU machine marches on, constraining everything from the future of the Post Office to what vitamins we can take. The promised referendum on the Lisbon treaty has been ditched. The quango nanny state has acquired a momentum of its own. Politicians have given away powers that they held in trust for the people. They cannot be altogether surprised if people now lump them all together in impotent fury." (*The Times* May 2009).

THE END OF THE GRAVY TRAIN

In its leading article, *"A swamp of greed funded by your taxes," The Mail on Sunday* made this comment: "The institutionalised corruption in claims for MPs' housing allowances is practically limitless. Hardly a weak goes by without another instance of creative fiddling being revealed. The most striking thing about these exposures is not what is illegal, but what is legal. Private Sector workers and businessmen who behaved in this way would be sacked or prosecuted..."

On 13 May 2009, the front page of Daily Mail read: *"After claims for pools, chandeliers and that moat, Cameron's ultimatum to Tory MPs: Repay the cash or I'll kick you out. Payback Time."* The paper reported: "The Westminster gravy train was finally driven off the rails... after David Cameron ordered Tory MPs to pay back their 'excessive' expenses claims. The furious Conservative leader told senior shadow ministers and party grandees...to write out cheques for thousands of pounds. He warned any who refused that they would be thrown out of the party."

THE PRIME MINISTER'S APOLOGY AND HYPOCISY OF POLITICIANS

On 13 May 2009, the *London Lite* adorned its front page with this text: "Brown: We are all very sorry." The Prime Minister apologised on behalf of all the political parties for robbing the British people. Gordon Brown, in his attempt to assuage the public anger at the misappropriation of taxpayers' money, said: "... I think what people want to see is a system that is reformed, politics seen to be serving the public interest, people recognising that as a country we depend on trust in our political system and trust in the people who actually are in offices of authority and influence, and they have a duty to show that that trust is deserved."

On 29 May 2009, the Prime Minister followed his apology by sending letters to British households. He again apologised for the corruption in the House of Commons. I received a copy of the 2-page letter. The opening paragraphs read: "I know that people are angry about MPs' expenses. I apologise – on behalf of all parties – that the political system has let you and the public down. Whatever party they belong to, MPs should never have spent taxpayers' money on clearing their moats or swimming pools, or paying phantom mortgages – and it's even worse at a time when ordinary families are worried about the impact of the recession." The Prime Minister went on to attack the policies of Conservative Party and cynically urged voters to vote for his Labour Party in the June 2009 European Elections. Every page of Mr Brown's letter reads: "Vote Labour Thursday 4 June."

Gordon Brown was accused of "hypocrisy" for exploiting the crisis. Opposition parties called the letter a crude attempt to cash in on the scandal. Tory Party Chairman Eric Pickles said: "Gordon Brown is clearly unable to ditch his obsession with scoring cheap political points. We have a Prime Minister who cares more about attacking the Tory party and creating dividing lines than reforming the expenses system and getting the country out of this economic mess. "(*Daily Mail* 30 May 2009).

On 31 May, 2009, Gordon Brown outlined his vision of cleaning the "filth" in the House of Commons. In his "sermon" on Parliamentary Expenses Scandal on *The Andrew Marr Show* on BBC 1, the Prime Minister told the British people that the scandal 'offends my Presbyterian conscience....I was brought up in a home where integrity mattered." Where was Mr Brown's "Presbyterian Conscience", when he consciously ignored the British people's request for a referendum on the Lisbon Treaty? Gordon Brown showed no respect for the democratic demand of the masses to have a say on a document that would govern their lives. The Prime Minister should have apologised for leading the "House of Fiddlers and Embezzlers" to force the Lisbon Treaty on Britons. By ratifying the despicable Lisbon Treaty in the "House of Shame" to please President Nicolas Sarkozy and Chancellor Angela Merkel, Gordon Brown and his greedy and unprincipled politicians "stole" the democratic rights of the British people and transferred powers that don't belong to them to undemocratic and corrupt institutions in Brussels to rule over Britain. The "theft" of the democratic rights of Britons was more serious than discredited politicians fiddling with their expenses. Because, we, the British people, have no power to remove from power the "children" of Jean Monnet and Konrad Adenauer who control our lives with unnecessary laws and regulations. An example is the silly EU's Working Time Directive (WTD) which limits the working hours per week to 48. And according to John Black, president of *The Royal College of Surgeons*, such a regulation would put patients' lives at risk.

Mr Black warned, "Unless the Government comes to its senses, the result will be catastrophic for the NHS, with patient safety on a knife-edge, surgeons not being properly trained, waiting lists going up again and even hospitals closing.....Over the past ten years there has been a driving-down of the hours worked by junior doctors as, bit by bit, the working time directive has come into force. We have already reached the point where patients' health has been endangered. There is a serious risk of units in hospitals having to close to emergencies, with resulting chaos, not to mention the danger and inconvenience brought about by patients going long distances to a hospital that has enough staff to stay open. This is truly a nightmare, and I despair that the Government will not take action " (Source: *The Mail on Sunday* 31 May 2009 *Europe's 48-hour working week will be 'catastrophe' for patients, says UK's top surgeon.*) I would remind Gordon Brown that before the European Union was born in 1950, a Presbyterian had already warned in 1881 that Britain would not be saved by participating in "the vile confederacy of European nations."

On 17 May 2009, before Gordon Brown's "sermon" on the expenses scandal on BBC 1, Nick Clegg had already commented on the issue on *The Andrew Marr Show*. The Liberal Democrat Party leader told the audience: "One of the reasons people are so angry about all these revelations about MPs' expenses is that they feel powerless and they now think MPs are going to act as judge and jury on their own failings, That's why I think that for those MPs who have clearly been shown, proved, to have done something wrong - particularly those that are then suspended in the House of Commons - there should be a mechanism where a small number of people in the constituency can say 'I don't want this MP to carry on... People reading about these revelations ask themselves a very simple question: if I did something like this at work I would be out, I'd be sacked.....And they cannot understand why there seems to be no way that they, the people, who are the boss, cannot exercise that kind of right over MPs who are supposed to be serving them."

The issue is: if Nick Clegg believes that the people are the "boss," why didn't he and his Party support the people's call for a referendum on the Lisbon Treaty that transfers the peoples' power to aliens in Europe? Were the British people not powerless to have a say on that treacherous document? On the ratification of the Lisbon Treaty in the "House of Fiddlers", didn't the degraded politicians in the British Parliament act as "Judge and Jury"? Did the Liberal Democrats in the House of Commons and the House of Lords act honourably on the issue?

Peter Oborne's article, *"Make them pay the money back, sack the spivs who let them get away with it – and put the thieves on trial,"* sums up the tragedy that befell on the Mother of all Parliaments in May 2009. He writes: "People would seek to become MPs or government ministers not out of self-interest and personal greed, but because they wanted to serve the nation. The key reward was never financial. Rather, it was measured in terms of honour. This admirable motive drove all the greatest parliamentarians in our history: Oliver Cromwell, William Pitt the Elder, Gladstone and Winston Churchill. These men were respected for their self-sacrifice and exceptional high standards of ethics." He goes on: "Nobody can say any longer that our politicians are motivated by honesty, duty or patriotism.... They have been exposed as ordinary criminal conspiracy whose primary purpose is to defraud the taxpayer and serve the vested interest of a venal political class.... The shocking truth is that, with the handful of gleaming exceptions, almost all ministers and MPs are caught up in the scam including the Prime Minister, the Chancellor, the Home Secretary and the Speaker of the House of Commons. Gone are those values of decency and integrity, to be replaced by a squalid system of institutionalised corruption and private self-enrichment."

Mr Oborne continues with his indictment on the gluttonous politicians: "It is no exaggeration to say that this is a national disaster of the first order. Nor does this moral and financial corruption merely infect the Government. Voting out Gordon Brown's stinking New Labour administration would not make the faintest difference. The stench of greed, cheating and dishonesty spreads into the opposition parties.... Labour, Tory and Liberal Democrat have conspired together to feather their nests and steal money from the public. This means that the fundamental division in British politics is now no longer between Tory and Labour. Instead, it is between a greedy venal and corrupt political class - and the great mass of ordinary decent people. MPs and ministers have known about this rotten state of affairs for years, which is why they fought to the bitter end to keep their expenses claims secret.... Politicians are now held in public contempt, and rightly so because so many of them have been exposed as liars and thieves. Trust in British democracy stands at its lowest point since the First Reform Act of 1832." (*Daily Mail* 9 May 2009).

The voters gave their verdict on the expenses scandal: "We are fed up with all this disgusting behaviour" (*The Independent* 9 May 2009). And according to a BPIX poll for the 17 May 2009 edition of *The Mail on Sunday*, about 38 percent of the electorate demanded that Prime Minister Brown should dissolve Parliament and call a General Election. The poll emphasised how voters were angry over politicians who abused their expenses. And if they had their way, "five politicians would have faced criminal charges."

LORD CAREY'S CONDEMNATION OF ABUSE OF PARLIAMENTARY PRIVILEGES

The indignity of Members of Parliament fiddling with their parliamentary allowances prompted Lord Carey, the former Archbishop of Canterbury, to condemn the "culture of abuse" surrounding MPs' expenses. In his article for the *News of the World,* he writes: "MPs of all parties have exploited the Westminster system of allowances and expenses.. ....The moral authority of Parliament is at its lowest ebb in living memory. The latest revelations show it was not just a few MPs with their noses in the trough, but a culture of abuse. It is not just the clawing greed of painstaking claims for such minor items as tampons, barbecue sets and bathrobes, but also the egregious way some have transferred allowances from one second property to another – enabling them to refurbish homes at public expense, then sell them for profit," Lord Carey adds, "Let us not forget there was a time when to become an MP was seen as a noble and honourable way of serving your country. Ask yourself now whether men or women of integrity from whatever walk of life will want to touch political office. Instead of well-qualified people from outside the political system, our politicians of the future are all likely to have climbed the greasy pole from within by working as researchers or lobbyists."

THE RESIGNATION OF THE SPEAKER OF THE HOUSE OF COMMONS

On 19 May 2009, the Speaker of the House of Commons, Michael Martin, who had been accused of blocking reforms of the expenses culture, and even threatened a legal action against the person who revealed the expenses scandal to *The Daily Telegraph,* offered to stand down: He addressed the "House of Fiddlers and Zombies": "In order that unity can be maintained I have decided that I will relinquish office on Sunday June 21."

The Speakers resignation announcement provoked the following headlines:

- "A very British revolution: First speaker forced out in 300 years in 33 second speech."
- "MPs urged to repay profits from sale of second homes"
- "Tory claims £2000 for ex-wife's home on day he moves out."
- "Ministers cared only for perks of power, says Boothroyd."(*The Daily Telegraph* 20 May 2009).
- In its editorial, The Telegraph writes: "The resignation of Michael Martin as Speaker marks the latest stage of a very British revolution.... His fate is symbolic of the rottenness of a political system that was once

> the envy of the world. That system now lies broken and demoralised. With its sovereignty already dissipated by the power of the European Union, the role of the House in scrutinising legislation has been further undermined by the placing of time limits on all debates; the hours it sits have shrunk, the chamber is often virtually empty, and MPs routinely fail to articulate the concerns and aspirations of the people who elect them.."The "Speaker's abrupt exit", according to the Evening Standard of 19 May 2009, "paved the way for commons clean-up."

In his article, *"So will the frauds and charlatans follow suit?"* Peter Oborne writes: "...It is certainly true that he (the Speaker) was the symbol of the culture of criminality and corruption that has disgraced the British Parliament...The reputation of Parliament will remain in the gutter until they - the squalid collection of MPs who have been cheating the taxpayer - quit office too." He concludes: "We need to create a new generation of decent and honest men and women who will not disgrace the great traditions of the British Parliament – as so many of today's generation have done." (*Daily Mail* 20 May 2009).
The Daily Telegraph recorded the comments of the following politicians:

- Gordon Brown (Prime Minister): *"It is a bit like a lot of people in a lifeboat slinging one person out in the hope that the water won't now lap. Westminster cannot operate like some gentleman's club where the members make up the rules."*
- Betty Boothroyd (Former Speaker): *"The Commons must bear a collective guilt in this."*
- Nigel Evans (Conservative MP for Ribble Valley): *"We should have a period of reflection, not running around like headless chickens."*
- Paul Flyn (Labour MP for Newport West): *"He (the Speaker) could have gone with a great deal more dignity last week if he had got the message."*
- Douglas Carswell (Conservative MP for Harwich and Clacton): *"You can't clean up a cesspit without doing some unpleasant things."*
- David Cameron (Leader of the conservative Party): *"What people really want is the chance to go out and put their cross in a box for the politicians they want."*

Edward Heathcoat Amory commented on the behaviour of the Chancellor of the Exchequer. Under the title *"Chancellor of Hypocrisy.... declared war on tax evasion in his Budget. How can he stay in office when he's guilty of evading tax himself?"* he writes: "....Of all the disgraceful revelations....perhaps the most disturbing was the discovery that the moral and upright Chancellor of the Exchequer, the man who has talked about the need to abide not only by the letter but also the spirit of tax legislation, has been playing every dodgy trick in the book to avoid paying a penny of it himself." He continues: "The saga of the Chancellor's tax avoidance was revealed because his expenses claims showed that he'd 'flipped' his designated second home – the one on which he could claim running costs from the tax taxpayer – four times in four years." The Chancellor went to the extent of billing "the taxpayer for £1400 to pay an accountant to advise him on how to keep his microscopic tax bill even smaller." He concludes; "If there were any justice, the Chancellor would be sacked...But as an old Scottish colleague of an increasingly weak and isolated Prime Minister, he knows where many of the bodies are buried, and it's unlikely the Prime Minister will take the political risk of moving him." (*Daily Mail* 28 May 2009)

I conclude with Daily Mail's comment on the political corruption. Under the title "*Exit Martin, but now the hard work begins,*" the editorial reports: "All Parties have agreed on an immediate reform of the expenses system....Some may regard it as extraordinary that it has taken this long for the Government to come to the conclusion that MPs cannot be trusted to set and regulate their own 'pay and rations....MPs need to appreciate that Mr Martin's resignation is not an excuse for them to sweep the grave issues facing the Commons under its capacious carpets. For all its failings, Speaker Martin was a symptom, rather than a cause, of Westminster's woes." According to the leading article, instead of the Speaker urging reform of the expenses system, "he stood the way." The commentary concludes: "There is a great deal to be done, and the concern remains that the current crop of MPs are not the ones to do it. They chose Mr Martin in the first place. They got the Speaker they deserved. Which is why his departure does not address the profound moral and political failure of the House of Commons as a whole." (Editorial 20 May 2009).

WHY THE LAPSE IN THE BRITISH PARLIAMENT?

It is clear from the newspaper commentaries on the political earthquake that erupted from the misappropriation of taxpayers' money in the House of Commons, that the reputation of the Mother of all Parliaments was soiled. We must ask the question: "Why the lapse in the House of Commons?" Answer: to bring to pass what the Prince of Detectives wrote about the "evil days" that would come upon Britain.

POLITICIANS AND THE ASSISTANT COMMISSIONER OF METROPOLITAN POLICE

The selfish politicians, who failed in their stewardship of Britain's finances, must reflect on the wise sayings of the selfless servant of the British Crown, Sir Robert Anderson, who did not collect his Knighthood from a grocery shop:

- "The true test of a man is not what he does, but what, with the principles he holds, he would do, and if this be true of individuals, it is still more intensely true of communities."

- "The dethronement of the Bible eliminates the most important factor in the formation of our national character, and it is not easy to estimate the effect which this will have on the life of the people of this country."

Have our politicians not thrown away the Bible and God from the British Parliament? And what has been the result? The reputation of the House of Honour, built on godly principles, was dragged into the mud. This fact is supported by Peter Oborne's article *"The man who must take the blame for this culture of lies and corruption."* He writes: "Like the 18th century aristocracy, today's strutting political class has used its privileged position at the centre of power to steal from the taxpayer, thus enriching themselves at the expense of the rest of us. It has evolved one set of very lax rules for itself and another for the rest of us. It is morally and financially corrupt. Yet, bizarrely, this political class believes that it has a monopoly on virtue and wisdom....Not mere that, but it is wholly contemptuous of the values and beliefs of ordinary people. Its members are convinced that the rest of us are bigoted, xenophobic, racists, intolerant and nasty. The political class finds itself literally unable to understand the values that appear admirable to most people, such as honesty, patriotism and religious observance..."

THE SOURCE OF PROSPERITY AND POWER OF PROTESTANT NATIONS

In the light of Peter Oborne's critique, politicians in the "House of Shame" must reflect on the wise words of the Assistant Commissioner of Metropolitan Police: ""The effects of 'Higher Criticism of the Bible' are extremely grave. For it has dethroned the Bible in the home, and the good old practice of "family worship" is rapidly dying out. And great national interests also are involved. For who can doubt that the prosperity and power of the Protestant nations of the world are due to the influence of the Bible upon character and conduct? Races of men who for generations have been taught to think for themselves in matters of the highest moment will naturally excel in every sphere of effort or of enterprise. And more than this, no one who is trained in the fear of God will fail in his duty to his neighbour, but will prove himself a good citizen. But the dethronement of the Bible leads practically to the dethronement of God; and in Germany and America, and now in England, the effects of this are declaring themselves in ways, and to an extent, well fitted to cause anxiety for the future..... The teaching of our churches is now so leavened with German scepticism that Christians are losing faith in Scripture, and as a natural result, they are losing hold on God. And the effects of the change are far–reaching, for they influence not only our Christian faith but our national character. "The kind of teaching that was at one time imparted at the mother's knee, or from the lips of the father of the family, is largely a fast fading

memory. 'Back to the Bible' should be a patriotic, as well as a religious cry; for the preservation of our liberties, and of our cherished institutions, depends much upon the maintenance of the Bible-taught heart-principles and stout convictions of our fathers."
Is it not sad, that the executives of the British Broadcasting Corporation would let the Bible be thrown into a dustbin on a TV comedy show, but not the Koran? Britain is still a Christian country established on godly values before the politicians of the 21st century were born. The "Lapse" in our British Parliament is due to the fact that our elected representatives have undermined the Judeo-Christian values upon which our institutions were built. They have produced ungodly laws that undermine the teachings of the Holy Bible. For example, politicians encourage school children to fornicate and abort by making it legal for pupils to collect contraceptive pills from the counter and then kill babies in their wombs without the knowledge of their parents.

And we, the voters, have encouraged our representatives to destroy our Christian values with immoral laws. Some of us support abortion on recreation grounds. Even the Church of England subscribe to Charles Darwin's silly theory that man evolved from a brute, thereby impugning the integrity of the Lord Jesus Christ.

Witness Stephen Glover's comments in his article titled *Bare-faced lies and why we let all politicians get away with them:* "Politicians are addicted to lying because they believe that telling the truth in a difficult situation, or apologising involves a loss of face. They understand that we may see through their deceptions but they calculate that we will not mind very much as long as we reap the benefits of their lies. Politicians would think twice about telling lies if they feared they would be punished for it....We have entered into a dishonest contract with our rulers, tolerating a degree of deception so long as the economy continues to grow, and we are at least half competently governed." (*Daily Mail* 10 October 2007).

The behaviour of our elected representatives is a reflection of what we are. We deserve the politicians who have raided our treasury. Melanie Phillips confirmed it in her column. Under the title, *"MPs bleating. Brown and Cameron using the crisis for their own cynical ends. What none of them gets is....IT'S THE MORALITY, STUPID,"* she writes: "For personal accountability, in the form of paying a price for one's misdeeds, is essential to a moral sense. It is the breakdown of such accountability at all levels in our society that has caused the values free-for-all of which our MPs have shown themselves to be such spectacular exemplars. For years.... the Church has spinelessly gone along with this wider non-judgmental culture of self-gratification which has turned morality on its head and undermined the cultural foundations of this nation. It is no accident that the churchmen who have spoken up in support of the expenses disclosures, the former Archbishop of Canterbury Lord Carey and the Bishop of Rochester Michael Nazir-Ali, have both criticised the Church for conniving at society's moral and cultural disintegration. Dr Williams (the Archbishop of Canterbury) by contrast....exemplifies the moral confusion of the age, which increasingly lets wrongdoers off the hook while punishing instead their victims or those who blow the whistle. This society has accordingly got the Parliament it deserves. And we won't put Parliament right until and unless we arrest the slide in our wider culture." She concludes: "...the only political platform that will address the parliamentary crisis is also one of moral regeneration, upholding the historic ethical principles of this nation and its right and duty to govern itself with those principles. It's the morality, stupid." (*Daily Mail* 25 May 2009).

Let us listen to what God, over 2700 years ago, spoke through the Prophet Isaiah to his people: "Your silver has become dross, your choice wine is diluted with water. Your rulers are rebels, companion of thieves; they all love bribes and chase after gifts. They do not defend the cause of the fatherless, the widow's case does not come before them....I (the Lord) will make boys their officials; mere children will govern them. People will oppress each other – man against man, neighbour against neighbour. The young will rise up against the old, the base against the honourable. A man will seize one of his brothers at his father's home, and say, "You have a cloak, you be our leader; take charge of this heap of ruins!" But in that day he will cry out, "I have no food or clothing in my house; do not make me the leader of the people." (Isaiah 1:22-23, 3:4-7)

We must all repent of our sins and return to the Lord for forgiveness and rebuild our nation on godly values to restore Great Britain to its glory. According to Brother Joseph, "Repentance is the music of the soul which involves the studying of the melodic sounds of self – denial." The Bible says: "If my people, who are called by my name, will humble themselves and pray and seek my face and turn from their wicked ways, then will I hear from heaven and will forgive their sin and will heal their land." (2 Chronicles 7:14).

I boldly declare: "Our broken society cannot be fixed with economic instruments alone. "Back to the Bible" is the sane solution to our problems. If the Bible is cast into the "dust-bin," and politicians ignore the teachings of the Lord Jesus Christ, their economic measures to fix "broken Britain" and our "rotten Parliament" would turn into blunt instruments. "Without me you can do nothing", says the Lord of lords and the King of kings. Let politicians and political intellectuals prove the Lord wrong by ignoring Him. This is the challenge to the "anti-God fanatics" who sneer at Christianity.

The popular "anthem" of our age is: "Change, Change," "Reform, Reform." "Times have changed; we must move with the times of the world to remove the Bible, God and Christianity from our progressive society." The reality is that if we follow the times of the world, we shall fumble in darkness. Bible-believing Christians do not move with

the times of the world. The significance of Joshua's victory over the Amorites - the day when "The sun stopped in the midst of the sky and delayed going down about a full day" (Joshua 10:13) - is a warning to the children of God not to move with the times of the world otherwise darkness would overshadow them. I have explained the significance of this miraculous event in my book *Understanding Jesus*.
What has become of Great Britain? A nation Sir Robert Anderson described as the "champion of freedom and of truth," has abandoned its cherished Christian traditions. What has become of Great Britain? The problem lies, primarily, with the Church. We, Christians, have failed to become the "light" for our nation. We have compromised with the world and ignored the Bible. Witness the words of Sir Robert Anderson: "The scepticism of the day may be clearly traced to the rationalism which almost swamped the religious life of Germany. But the chief cause of that apostasy has never been fully recognised. Not even in the darkest periods of the history of Christendom had the character and authority of the Bible ever been questioned. It was always regarded as the inspired word of God, the supreme and infallible guide in all questions of faith and morals. But just as apostate Jews in a preceding age had "made the word of God of none effect by their traditions," so also did apostate Christians" (*The Bible and Modern Criticism*). Had our Church leaders been spiritually enlightened in the knowledge of Truth, as enshrined in the Bible, our politicians would not have taken any major decision that affects the character and destiny of our nation without at least seeking their opinion. Unfortunately, the blind is following the blind. The Pharisees of today's religious Babylon are following the Sadducees of today's political Babylon.

HAS EUROPE BECOME THE "LAND OF CAPTIVITY" FOR BRITONS?

We have fallen. The "evil days" spoken of by the "Seer of Dublin" have come upon our nation. Britain is "broken; our Parliament is in "ruins" because we have forsaken God to worship the agnostic Charles Darwin whose image is on our national currency. Sir Robert Anderson, who destroyed "Darwin's bulldog", "weeps." If we do not repent of our sins and return to the merciful God for forgiveness, we will not escape His judgement. Our nation will be "carried away into captivity" for our rebellion. Europe would become our "Babylon." The signs are clear. Most of our laws originate from Brussels. We must remember what happened to the rebellious Jews. They were carried away into servitude in Babylon to serve pagan Kings for 70 years (Jeremiah 25:1-11). God is not a respector of persons. He uses the same scale to measure His people.

In *Great Britain has fallen*, pastor Wale Babatunde of World Harvest Christian Centre gives us an incisive account of how our nation has deviated from the righteous path our forefathers laid down for us. He explained how we could restore our fortunes. Testifying to the value of this book, Dr Robert E Smith of Total Outreach for Christ Ministries in Little Rock, Arkansas, USA, writes: "This treatment of historical facts concerning the fall of Great Britain is both educational and burdensome. However, it leaves us with a greater expectation of total restoration to a glory not seen before. I recommend this book to all who are concerned for Great Britain's share in the divine economy of God."

I will conclude this chapter by sharing with you, again, Sir Robert Anderson's prophetic word about our attitude towards the Bible: "The dethronement of the Bible eliminates the most important factor in the formation of our national character, and it is not easy to estimate the effect which this will have on the life of the people of this country....It is not on the side of vagueness that the creeds of our British Churches are in fault, and men who boast of being free thinkers would deserve more respect if they showed their independence by refusing to subscribe, than by undermining the doctrines they are both pledged and subsidised to defend and teach. But what concerns us ...is the indisputable fact that rationalism in its most subtle phase is leavening society. The universities are its chief seminaries. The pulpit is its platform. Some of the most popular religious leaders are among its apostles. No class is safe from its influence....If the authority of the Scriptures be unshaken, vital truths may be lost by one generation, and recovered by the next; but if that be *touched,* the foundation of all truth is undermined, and all power of recovery is gone." The able Defender of the Christian Faith added: "Illumination is much needed at this moment, when the church is honeycombed by scepticism – a scepticism, moreover which is the outcome, not of fuller knowledge or matured thought, but of intellectual conceit and levity which are the marked characteristics of the age."

In his *The Gospel and its Ministry*, the "Knight of God" exhorts Christians: "The Gospel will bear the test of the severest metaphysical inquiry, but it is addressed to plain people, and not to metaphysicians; and we may be certain that the doctrine of faith is not a subtle difficulty, but a truth within the reach of all... We are not called to wear the martyr's crown, but it is ours to share the martyr's faith. We can have no toleration for the veiled scepticism which is passing for Christianity today. Agnosticism is Greek for ignorance and ignorance is both shameful and sinful in the presence of a Divine revelation. The Christian is not ignorant; neither is he in doubt. "We do not think this or that; we KNOW". We know the Son of God has come. "We know that He was manifested to take away our sins... We know that we have passed from death unto life. We know that if our earthly house were dissolved, we have a building of God, eternal in the heavenly...We know that when He shall appear we shall be like Him." Amen! This was the humble man who wrote about European Union, its character and future before the French Founding fathers of European Community – Jean Monet and Robert Schuman – were born.

SIR ROBERT ANDERSON: A MAN OF SUBSTANCE

Great Britain and Ireland witness what was written of our "Forgotten father": "... Dr Anderson was a man whose genius for comradeship was by no means the least of his many endowments. To many it was inevitable he should be known only as the stalwart defender of the Faith, the clear expositor, the zealous champion of Christian causes, the keen conversationalist, the distinguished public servant..... in his consuming passion for what he regarded as vital to the Christian faith, he was often compelled to appear dogmatic to the point of unsympathy, and narrow-minded to the point of sheer unaccommodating.....He stood out as champion of the unpopular view of things, he both received and gave hard blows. No one could give harder. ...But this was the role thrust upon him. If he must fight, he fought as a knight of God and a very perfect gentleman; so that those who opposed him, and finally gave up as "hopeless," rode off with a fine appreciation of the character of their opponent. Never for a single moment, did he betray the slightest bitterness towards an opponent...those who were privileged to know him at close quarters will ever think of him, in yet warmer terms, as one of the most devoted, humble, and kindly of men, and one of the staunchest of friends." We must be proud of the Knight Commander of (the Order of) Bath.

Chapter 28
THE 4 PROPHETIC 7's

"Religion and Scepticism are rival competitors for popular favour, and yet there are many who, though conscious of longings too deep to be satisfied by mere religion, make choice of religion because they know of no other refuge from unbelief. And there are others again who, "with too much knowledge for the sceptic's side," drift into scepticism in their recoil from priestcraft.... Christianity delivers us not only from scepticism on the one hand, but from superstition on the other. " **(The Silence of God RA)**

In this chapter we will, again, examine a scriptural truth to confirm that what we have learnt about the European Union and its future would surely come to pass. Before we proceed, I would stress this significant point. In the Bible numbers have symbolic meaning. The number 2 stands for Witness. 3 stands for the Triune God. 4 is the earth number. 7 stands for perfection and completeness. The earth number, which is 4, is associated with events that relate to our planet.

We have already learnt that the last 7 years of this age would begin when the King of Men, the coming Emperor of the revived Roman Empire, signs a 7-year peace treaty with Israel and its Arab neighbours. We know this political genius would break the peace covenant after three and half years. He will claim to be God and command the world to worship his image installed in the Jerusalem temple by the "beast from the earth" – the apostate Jew. We know the penalty for not joining this one world religion - the persecution of the faithful Jews and Christians. This would mark the beginning of the Great Tribulation the Lord Jesus Christ spoke about in Matthew 24:15 -16: *"When you see the abomination of desolation, spoken of by Daniel the prophet, standing in the holy place....Then let those who are in Judea flee to the mountains: Let him who is on the housetop not come down to take anything out of his house....For then there will be great tribulation, such has not been since the beginning of the world until this time, no, nor ever shall be."*

THE OTHER SETS OF 7'S

The 7-year peace treaty, which the "Man of Lawlessness" would sign with "many" (Daniel 9:27), was foretold in about 538BC. This is the first 7 of the 4 prophetic 7's that relate to the Great Tribulation that would engulf mankind to terminate the era of human governments. What are the other 3 sets of 7? They are:

- The 7 Seals recorded in chapters 4 – 7 of the Book of Revelation.
- The 7 Trumpets recorded in chapters 8 – 11 of the Book of Revelation, and
- The 7 Bowls recorded in chapter 16 of the Book of Revelation.

These 4 sets of 7's, which are associated with the Great Tribulation on planet earth, are in accordance with the Sovereign Will of God. We must remember the dazzling human statue Nebuchadnezzar saw in his dream represents the history and destiny of the **4 major Empires** that have ruled the earth since the servitude of the Jews in Babylon. This magnificent statue was divided into 4 sections of 4 different metals. Daniel also had a vision which was parallel to Nebuchadnezzar's dream. In the case of Daniel he saw **4 cruel** beasts which represented the respective characters of the **4 world Empires** – Babylonia, Medo-Persia, Greece and Rome. These were symbolised by **4 metals** of the great human image - gold, silver, bronze and iron.

"The Heavens rule." That was the confession the King of Babylon, the head of world powers, made after the Lord had humbled him to dwell in the forest like a beast. "The Heavens rule." This is the central message in the Book of Daniel (Daniel 4:34-37). It is the Almighty God, not 'hindsight' politicians and scientists, who is in control over the affairs of men until the Lord Jesus Christ returns as a "Stone cut without human hands" to crush all human governments. The Book of Daniel is about the destiny of Israel on earth, the crucifixion of Christ on earth, and the return of Christ on earth. For this reason, the number 4, which is the earth number, is scattered in this Old Testament Book.

For example:

- When Shadrach, Meshach and Abednego were cast into the burning furnace for not bowing to the golden statue of King Nebuchadnezzar, another person "like the Son of the God's" joined the three Hebrews to become **4 people** in the blazing fire (Daniel 3:20-25).
- In chapter 7 of the Book of Daniel, the prophet saw a vision of **4 nasty beasts** coming out of the sea. The first three beasts looked like a lion with eagle wings, a bear and a leopard. These ferocious beasts corresponded to the empires of Babylon, Medo-Persia and Greece respec-

tively. The 4th **beast** had no name. It was a hideous animal with large iron teeth which corresponds to the Roman Empire.

- In chapter 8 Daniel saw in a vision a fierce struggle between a two-horned ram and a male goat. The goat had a conspicuous horn. And when the horn was suddenly broken, **4 great horns** rose from the place of the broken horn. The conspicuous horn represented Alexander the Great. The **4 horns** represented the **4 generals** who succeeded Alexander the Great (the Male goat) after his sudden death. It was these **4 generals** – Cassander, Lysimacus, Selecius and Ptolemy – who divided Alexander's Grecian Empire into **4 kingdoms** of Macedonia and Greece, Asia Minor, Syria and Egypt.
- In about 538BC, Daniel saw the marvellous vision of '70 Weeks.' This particular vision is regarded as the greatest of all prophetic visions concerning the crucifixion of Christ and the judgement on earth. This vision of "70 Weeks," which is the key to understanding all the prophecies relating to the destiny of Israel, the public declaration of the Messiah, His crucifixion, the destruction of the Jerusalem Temple by the Roman Prince, Titus Vespasian, and the appearance of the last Prince of the Revived Roman Empire who will deceive mankind, has **4 main sections**:

1. The first section of the "Vision of 70 Weeks" covers a period of 7 weeks of years (49years) from the date King Artaxerxes of Persia issued the royal edict to Nehemiah to return to Jerusalem to rebuild the city and its walls. The walls were destroyed by King Nebuchadnezzar in about 586BC.
2. The second section of the prophetic revelation covers a period of "62 weeks of years" (434 years) from the completion of the rebuilding of Jerusalem and its walls and gates to the public declaration of the Lord Jesus Christ as the Messiah during His triumphal entry to Jerusalem, and His crucifixion about a week later.
3. The third section of "1 Week" (7 years) marks the beginning of Antichrist's 7-year peace treaty with the Jews and the Arab nations. This section is divided into two periods of 3½ years each.
4. The first **3½ years** is the period during which the last Caesar of the European Empire deceives the world by posing as the prince of peace. He portrays himself as the messiah to solve the economic, political, religious and security problems that have plagued the world. The last **3½ years** is the second phase of his career. The fake messiah demonstrates his true colour as a brutal dictator and the Chief terrorist. After violating the 7-year peace covenant, he forces the world to worship his idol in the Jerusalem Temple. The "Man of Lawlessness", known as the "Son of Perdition," proclaims himself as god. He blasphemes the Lord

of Heaven. He starts persecuting the faithful Jews and Christians. This marks the beginning of the 42-months of the great tribulation which the Lord Jesus Christ spoke about in Matthew 24:15-17. It is also recorded in Daniel 7:25, Daniel 12:7; and in Revelation 12:6, 14, Revelation 13:5-7 and 2 Thessalonians 2:1-4.

Without the Book of Revelation our understanding of the prophetic Book of Daniel, which is filled with the number **4**, would not be complete. In *Daniel speaks today* C. Ernest Tatham writes: "There is a marvellous harmony in the prophetic Word, as well as in every other part of the inspired Message of God. One prophecy casts its light upon another, and we need the contribution of every single part in order to have a comprehensive view of the whole." God did not give His revelation to a single person.

This is borne by the fact that when Daniel was struggling to understand the visions he had seen, and what would be the outcome, the Almighty told him: "Go your way, Daniel, because the words are closed up and sealed until the time of the end. Many will be purified, made spotless and refined, but the wicked will continue to be wicked. None of the wicked will understand, but those who are wise will understand" (Daniel 12:8-10). However, when John had seen all the visions recorded in the Book of Revelation, the Lord told him: "Do not seal up the words of the prophecy of this book, because the time is near. Let him who does wrong continue to do wrong; let him who is vile continue to be vile; let him who does right continue to do right; and let him who is holy continue to be holy " (Revelation 22:10-11).

The "open" Book of Revelation unlocks the mysteries in the "closed" Book of Daniel. By divine providence, the Book of Revelation, which compliments the Book of Daniel, and which completes God's revelation about His Eternal Administration, is filled with the numbers **7** and 12. For example in the Book of Revelation we read about:

- 7 Churches, 7 golden lampstands, 7 stars, 7 Kings, A beast with 7 heads, A woman who sits on 7 Hills.
- 7 Angels, 7 Spirits. A red dragon with 7 heads and 7 crowns
- 7 Seals, 7 Trumpets, 7 Bowls of God's wrath, 7 Plagues.
- A woman with a crown of 12 Stars, Gates with 12 walls, 12 Angels at the Gates, 12 foundations, 12,000 stadia, 12 Apostles of the Lamb, 12 Tribes of Israel.

The number 4 is the earth number. The number 7 is the perfect number which stands for completeness in time. And the number 12 stands for completeness in eternity which represents God's Eternal Administration. It is, therefore, clear, that the consistency with which the number 4 is associated with all the events that are related to planet earth, and the numbers 7 and 12 which are associated with God's complete revelation and His Eternal Administration in the Book of Revelation, which is the last Book of the Bible, are all a demonstration of Divine Providence. This perfectly illustrates the Divine inspiration behind the 66 Books of the Bible. How could the Book of Daniel be an *"edifying fiction"* as suggested in the Catholic Bible -*The New Jerusalem Bible*? Liberal theologians, bishops and priests support this ridiculous and unscriptural view in the Roman Catholic Bible. How could a fictitious book - a literary fraud - fit into the pattern of prophetic truths in the Sacred Scriptures?

According to the Greek philosopher, Aristotle, numbers are the principle of all things. Why? Because, numbers and numerical laws are written in the well organised universe and its solar system. Since God is the God of order, it is clear the consistency with which the earth number 4 is associated with all the prophetic visions that relate to the destiny of mankind and the human governments on earth, demonstrates how the Book of Daniel was written under divine inspiration to bear witness of the Omnipotence and Omniscience of God, in designing the universe. This proves how the Almighty controls all things in heaven and on earth.

THE UNIQUE ATTRIBUTE OF THE ALMIGHTY GOD

In *All things For Good*, the seventeenth century author, Thomas Watson, writes: "God is the great Disposer of all events and issues. He sets everything working. "His Kingdom ruleth over all" (Psalm 103:19)...Things in the world are not governed by second causes, by the counsel of men, by the stars and planets, but by divine providence. Providence is the queen and governess of the world. There are three things in providence: God's foreknowing, God's determining, and God's directing all things to their periods and events....That which is by some called chance is nothing else but the result of providence." The Almighty God says: *"Before things happened I announced them to you...How can I let myself be defamed. I will not yield my glory to another"* (Isaiah 48:5, 11). This is the UNIQUE attribute of the Almighty God. He sees the end from the beginning. The Theory of Evolution, which has led to Militant Atheism, is Darwin's great gift to fools and ignorant scientists and intellectuals who scorn Christianity.

Here is a simple question for the liberal theologians and pompous intellectuals who only read the black letters in the Bible, and claim it is "intellectual backwardness" to believe in God and religion. "Using your super intelligence and scientific knowledge, explain to the world what is written in 1 Chronicles 1:1-3: *"Adam, Seth, Enosh, Kenan, Mahalalel, Jared, Enoch, Methuselah, Lamech, Noah?"* The world is waiting for an answer.

THE ROMAN CATHOLIC CHURCH AND THE BOOK OF DANIEL AND THEIR "GIFT OF SCRIPTURE"

Finally, in the interest of Roman Catholic seminarians and university students and the laity, I appeal to Pope Benedict XVI to declare to the 1.2billion Roman Catholics whether the Book of Daniel is an "edifying fiction" or a Divine Revelation? Is the Book of Daniel a literary fraud written in the second century BC as suggested in *The New Jerusalem Bible?* The Roman Catholic hierarchy has endorsed this "blasphemous" Bible with its seal of Imprimatur.

In the Roman Catholic booklet - *The Gift of Scripture* - which was supposed to enlighten Roman Catholic Bishops, reference was made to the two apocalyptic books of the Bible – The Book of Daniel and the Book of Revelation. On the Book of Revelation, the document makes specific reference to the writer – "one called John." But on the Book of Daniel there was no specific mention of its author. *The Gift of Scripture* just states: "Standing on the threshold of the New Testament, the Book of Daniel though placed among the prophets by Christian usage, is a unique book, which contains enigmatic visions. It was written for a persecuted people to assure them of God's unending care, and reassures the oppressed and persecuted in any age that evil cannot finally triumph. This is a new kind of writing, known as 'apocalyptic,' which will also be found in the New Testament Book of Revelation (*The Jewish people).* The book speaks of the coming of the kingdom of God (Daniel 2:44) and proclaims the reward of resurrection for those who are faithful (Daniel 12:1-3). It prepares for the coming of Christ."

To begin with, this is a superficial summary of the Book of Daniel. At least a reference should have been made of the great vision of "70 Weeks." Why was it omitted? In the case of the Book of Revelation, "one John" was mentioned as the author. In the case of the Book of Daniel, the name of the author was not mentioned. Why? The Pope should tell the world who wrote the Book of Daniel? In view of the Jerusalem Bible's claim that the Book of Daniel was written during the days of Antiochus Epiphanes, Pope Benedict should also clarify the statement: "Standing on the threshold of the New Testament...." The Pope should broadcast on the Internet when the Book of Daniel was written?

If the Book of Daniel is an "edifying fiction," a literary fraud, as suggested by the Catholic Bible, then how could a fictitious book be classified as part of God's Word – the Holy Bible? How could a fictitious Book (assuming it was written in 200BC as claimed by the pagan Porphyry and liberal theologians) accurately predict the date of the Lord Jesus' Triumphal entry into Jerusalem – 6 April AD32? How could such a fabricated book predict the crucifixion of Christ before the Lord Jesus was even born? And how could a fictional book forecast the destruction of Jerusalem and its Temple before Titus Vespasian, the Roman Prince who led the invasion, was born to destroy Jerusalem and its Temple in 70AD – about 38 years after the death of Christ? (Daniel 9:25-26). And how could such an invented Book of Daniel forecast the development of the European Union – "the rarest of all political phenomena in history?"

On the other hand, if Pope Benedict XVI accepts that the Book of Daniel is a Divine Revelation, then the "Introduction to the Book of Daniel" in *The New Jerusalem Bible* must be amended for the sake of TRUTH. The Roman Catholic Church cannot play "politics" with Sacred Scriptures. The Book of Daniel is either a forgery or a supernatural book. The world is waiting for a clear answer from the Pope, who was once the Defender of Roman Catholic Doctrine.

In his defence of the Book of Daniel, "God's Barrister" writes: "The inadequacy of the reasons put forward for rejecting Daniel clearly indicate that there is a potent reason of another kind in the background. It was the miraculous element in the book that set the whole pack of foreign sceptics in full cry. In this age of silent heaven such men will not tolerate the idea than God ever intervened directly in the affairs of men" (*Daniel in the critics den).*

God writes history in advance. The Almighty announced the development of the European Union and its destiny to the world over 2600 years before the European Union came into existence. We wait for the future king of the Disunited European Kingdom of mixed people who are not united (Daniel 2:41-43) to be fulfilled. For the Lord declares: *"My thoughts are not your thoughts, neither are your ways my ways. As the heavens are higher than the earth, so are my ways higher than your ways, and my thoughts than your thoughts. As the rain and snow come down from heaven, and do not return to it without watering the earth and making it bud and flourish, so that it yields seed for the sower and bread for the eater, so is my word that goes out from my mouth. It will not return to me empty, but will accomplish what I desire and achieve the purpose for which I sent it."* (Isaiah 55:8-11).

Soon, the King of Europe would emerge. On 13 December 2007, in the city of Lisbon, European leaders signed the document that would welcome the Great Emperor of Europe – the political whiz kid who will "save" Europe. The arrival of this genius, I repeat: would be the answer to Paul Henri-Spaak's "prayer": "We do not want another committee. We have too many already. What we want is a man of sufficient stature to hold the allegiance of all people, and to lift us out of the economic morass in which we are sinking. Send us such a man and he be god or the devil, we will receive him."

DOES THE FUTURE OF BRITAIN AND IRELAND LIE IN THE EUROPEAN UNION?

We can conclude from what we have learnt that the future of Great Britain and Ireland does not lie in the European Union. And it is ridiculous for politicians to suggest that Britain and Ireland must be at the "heart of Europe." What is the "heart of Europe?" The heart is the life centre of man. But man is a living being only when his conscience operates to use his mind and exercise his will. Conscience, mind and will constitutes the soul of man. In simple terms the Soul of man is the life of man. We can conclude that HEART = SOUL. The Lord Jesus tells us: "What will it profit a man to gain the whole world and suffer the loss of his soul."

If we examine the advice the "honest" Robert Schuman offered to Europeans concerning the survival of the European Enterprise, it becomes clear that the "Soul of Europe" is the Christian principles of solidarity and fraternity. Since the Lord Jesus Christ and Christian principles have no room in the European Project, we can rightly conclude the European Union has no "Soul." The EU is a dead body. How can Britain and Ireland be at the "heart of a corpse?" Yet, British and Irish politicians claim they want their countries to be at the "heart of EU" (a Corpse) to reform it. Some commentators claim, "Britain is now remote from the centre of European power than ever." What a "ridiculous" statement! What power can a "corpse" display?

In his article, *"All politicians are in denial, it's the state that needs cutting, not taxes"* (*Daily Mail* 12 November 2008), Peter Oborne writes: "One of the basic rules of politics is that when all major politicians agree on any given issue, they are – almost always – by definition wrong." Applying this "basic rule" to the issue of Britain's membership of the European Union – whereby all the major political parties agree that the future of Britain lies in the European Union – we reach this conclusion: leaders of the Labour Party, Conservative Party and the Liberal Democrats are all wrong. In this case they are 1000 per cent wrong. Britain's future does not rest in the European Union. Britain would not be saved in a political Europe as predicted by the Assistant Commissioner of Metropolitan Police – Sir Robert Anderson.

In the Appendix to this volume, I will share with you in detail the significance of the Greek 2 Euro cents – *Europa* riding on a bull. This is the subject of chapter 17 of the Book of Revelation – "a woman riding on a beast with 10 horns and 7 heads". We will know more about the "*awful Being*" Sir Robert Anderson referred to in his prophetic word about the European confederacy.

538 BC - THE VISION OF "70 WEEKS" (DANIEL 9:24-27) THE DESTINY OF ISRAEL AND ALL HUMAN GOVERNMENTS THE CLIMAX OF HISTORY

13 March 445BC → The Decree to restore and rebuild Jerusalem and its walls (Nehemiah 2:1-8)

7 WEEK: S (7x7 Years — 49 years

396BC → Completion of the rebuilding Jerusalem and its walls in difficult times (Daniel 9:25)

62 WEEI KS (7x62 Years — 434 years

"Messiah cut off but not for Himself (crucifixion of Jesus) (Daniel 9:26) — 6 APRIL AD32 → The "Messiah the Prince" The First Palm Sunday (Luke 19:28-44)

483x360 days 173880

*The Age of Mystery
*The Age of Grace
*The Age of the Church
(The Lord Jesus Christ is secretly preparing His Bride for a wedding feast)

JESUS OPENS THE FIRST 4 SEALS:
THE 4 COLOUR-HORSE RACE (Rev. 6:1-8)
1. The White Horse - The preaching of the Gospel
2. The Red Horse - Wars, resulting in bloodshed
3. The Black Horse - Famine, Poverty & Pestilences
4. The Pale Horse - Deaths from wars, famine & fatal epidermic diseases (e,g AIDS)

Israel is experiencing "a hardening in part until the full number of the Gentiles has come in" (Romans 11:25)

AD 70 - Titus, a Roman Prince, destroyed Jerusalem and its Temple as recorded in Daniel 9:27 and confirmed by Jesus in Luke 19:43-44.
* May 1948 The nation of Israel reborn as predicted in Jeremiah 30:1-3.
*Middle East crisis - Jerusalem becoming a cup that sends all surrounding nations reeling (Zech. 12:1-3)

THE SHADOWS OF ANTICHRIST (JOHN 4:1-3)
*Men blaspheme God & slander His Name
*Men mock Jesus, ridicule His virgin birth and Resurrection. They ridicule His Cross.
Pagans mock, persecute and kill Christians

A GAP OVER 2005 YRS - UNKNOWN PERIOD

THE FULFILMENT OF THE PROPHETIC MESSAGES IN THE PARABLES OF:
* The Tares and theWheat
*The Mustard Seed
* The Leaven -recorded in Matt. 13:24-33

THE RELIGIOUS BABYLON - THE APOSTATE CHURCH - THE GREAT PROSTITUTE (Rev.17)
*The Harlot teaches false doctrines- e'g homosexulaity and same-sex marriage.
*False believers in the Church - the Tares
THE MATERIAL BABYLON - THE POLITICAL SYSTEM (Rev.18). Introduce policies and laws that undermine the precepts of the Bible

PROPHETIC MESSAGES IN JESUS' 7 LETTERS TO THE 7 CHURCHES IN ASIA MINOR FULFILLED (Revelation 2 & 3
1. *EPHESUS* - Church that has lost its first love.
2. *SMYRNA* - The Suffering Church.
3. *Pergamos* - The compromised Church - A Church married to the world.
4. *THYATIRA* - The Apostate Church - full of evil practices and heretical teachings.
5. *SARDIS* - THE Dead Church
6. *PHILADELPHIA* - The Church of Brotherly Love
7. *LAODICEA* - The Luke-warm Church - The blind church full of pride and materialism

THE DEVELOPMENT OF THE EUROPEAN UNION
The foundation stone of the Revived Roman Empire. The seed of the Revived Roman Empire was sown in 1952 (ECSC). 10 powerful leaders will give their power to Antichrist to rule.

APPENDICES

APPENDIX I
THE WOMAN AND THE BEAST

The Rape of Europa- The image on Greek 2 euro cents

Europa abducted by Zeus. Antiochus Epiphanes desecrated the Temple in Jerusalem by erecting the statue of Zeus on its altar. The Wicked Syrian King also sprinkled the blood of a female pig in the Holy Place.

"The reformation was not merely a revival, it was a revolt. And ecclesiastical supremacy was the bondage from which those brave and noble men delivered us. That Church which is vital unity of the body of Christ Rome confounds with the visible Church on earth---the public organisation entrusted to human administration. But more than this, the Church on earth, which according to Scripture, is the congregation of the faithful, the Romish system represents as an authority to govern the faithful with power to control not only their acts but their beliefs.."(The Bible or the Church – RA)

The illustration on the Greek 2 euro cents (a woman riding on a beast) is a vision Apostle John saw. This vision is recorded in chapter 17 of the Book of Revelation.

In this vision John saw a beast with 7 heads and 10 horns. The 7 heads are 7 hills on which the woman sits. The 7 heads are 7 Kings. 5 have fallen. One is not; the other is yet to come. The 10 horns are 10 Kings.

We have already learnt that the splendour of Greece and the greatness of Rome are the foundations of Western civilisation. We know the cultures of Europe and the world, in general, are influenced by the civilisations of Greece and Rome. For example, the English language, the most common medium of communication, has its root in Greek and Latin. Our political and legal systems have their origin in Greek and Roman traditions.

We have read of a Spanish politician who once said it is upon the euro currency the European Empire would be built. And so should it be. The end crowns the work. We must ask the question: How would this magnificent European Empire (now 27 countries) end? If the European Union is built on Greek and Roman civilisations, then let us put a special "powerful microscope" on the Greek 2 euro cents to examine it in detail the significance of this coin and its implications for Europe and the world. I have selected this particular Greek euro coin, because the woman on it has a special relationship with the continent of Europe. The portrait on this "civilised" Greek 2 euro cent is a naked woman called *Europa*, sitting on a beast. We know this beast was the Greek god Zeus who turned into a handsome white bull to deceive *Europa* and seduced her. The Continent of Europe was named after *Europa*.

THE VISION OF A WOMAN RIDING ON A BEAST

Thomas Watson, in his *"All things For Good,"* writes: "Providence is the queen and governess of the world. There are three things in providence: God's foreknowing, God's determining, and God's directing all things to their periods and events... That which is by some called chance is nothing else but the result of providence." Therefore, it is not by chance that the sketch on the Greek 2 euro cents – a naked woman on a beast – is painted in the last book of the Bible. For Revelation 17 tells us about a vision of a woman riding on a beast. And this "woman" would be exposed for what she is. Apostle John saw this prophetic image in about 96AD after he had been banished to the Island of Patmos. It was the era when Domitian, the younger brother of Prince Titus, was the Roman Emperor. In this vision, John, the disciple whom Christ loved, saw *"a great prostitute who sits on many waters. With her the kings of the earth (*the political system*) committed adultery and the inhabitants of the earth were intoxicated with the wine of her adulteries."* John also saw a woman sitting on a scarlet beast covered with blasphemous names. This beast had "7 heads" and "10 horns." The woman was dressed in purple and scarlet and was glittering with gold, precious stones and pearls. She held a golden cup in her hand filled with abominable things. This title was written on her forehead:

MYSTERY
BABYLON THE GREAT
THE MOTHER OF PROSTITUTES
AND OF THE ABOMINATIONS OF THE EARTH (Rev. 17:3-5).

The sight of this *woman* shocked John. The angel soothed his fears by saying, "I will explain to you the mystery of the woman and of the beast she rides, which has "*seven heads and ten horns*". The beast, which you saw, "*once was, now is not, and will come out of the Abyss and go to his destruction*". The inhabitants of the earth whose names have not been written in the book of life from the creation of the world will be astonished when they see the beast, because "*he once was, now is not, and yet will come.*" "This calls for a mind with wisdom," the Angel said. "*The seven heads are seven hills* on which the woman sits. They are also seven kings. Five have fallen, one is, the other has not yet come; but when he does come, he must remain for a little while. The *beast who once was, and is not,* is an eighth king. He belongs to the seven and is going to his destruction. *The ten horns you saw are ten kings* who have not yet received a kingdom, but who for one hour will receive authority as kings along with the beast. They have one purpose and will give their power and authority to the beast. They will make war against the Lamb, but the Lamb will overcome them because he is Lord of lords and King of kings – and with him will be his called, chosen and faithful followers (Revelation 17:6-14).

THE FATE OF THE "PROSTITUTE" AND THE IMPLICATIONS OF REVELATION 17

The angel explained to John: "The waters you saw, where the prostitute sits, are peoples, multitudes, nations and languages. *The beast and the ten horns* you saw will hate the prostitute. They will bring her to ruin and leave her naked; they will eat her flesh and burn her with fire. For God has put it into their hearts to accomplish his purpose by agreeing to give their power to rule, until God's words are fulfilled. *The woman you saw is the great city that rules over the kings of the earth.*" There are two different women in Revelation 17. One is a *"Prostitute"* who rides on a "Beast". The other is "*The great city,*" This particular "woman", "The great city", is different in nature from the *"Prostitute"* that rides on the "Beast". However, these two "Women" are related.

I will now examine the practical implications of this Scripture, in so far as the European Union is concerned, by first identifying the "Woman," *the great city,* that rules over the kings of the earth (Revelation 17:18). But before I reveal this *"great city,"* I would like to say a word about the Book of Revelation.

REVELATION: THE BOOK OF SIGNS AND SYMBOLS

The opening chapter of the Book of Revelation states: "The Revelation of Jesus Christ, which God gave unto him, to show unto his servant things which must surely come to pass; and he sent and signified it by his angel unto his servants…." (Revelation 1:1KJ). The phrase, "and signified it," indicates that Apostle John used signs, symbols and figures of speech in writing this precious and "mysterious" Book to describe the message from the vision the Lord Jesus Christ revealed to him. Hence, the Book of Revelation is full of signs and symbols. This means, for us to appreciate this "unusual" Book, we must understand the symbols and the signs it contains. When we establish their meaning, we must believe them literally. That is, we must interpret the Book of Revelation both symbolically and literally.

For example, Revelation 20:1-2 tells us of an angel who "seized the dragon, that ancient serpent…..and bound him into the Abyss." In this text: "the dragon, that ancient serpent" symbolises the subtlety and cruelty of Satan. It is obvious the angel did not seize a literal, creeping animal and bound it into a deep hole. And Revelation 19:7 says: *"For the wedding of the Lamb has come and his bride has made herself ready".* This text does not refer to a literal four –footed animal (lamb) which is going to marry a woman. It is the Lord Jesus Christ (the Lamb of God) who is going to have a glorious re-union with all those who believed in Him. These believers constitute the Church, which would become the "Bride" of Christ. For in the Parable of the Ten Virgins the Lord Jesus referred to Himself as the Bridegroom (Matthew 25:1-13). A bridegroom must have a bride. The Church is the "Bride" of Christ.

WHAT IS THE "GREAT CITY"?

With this background of information, let us now identify *"The great city that rules over the kings of the earth"* (Revelation 17:8). In chapter 2 of the Book of Daniel we learnt that only 4 major Empires have ruled on earth since the captivity of the Jews in Babylon which began in about 606BC. These empires were Babylon, whose king was Nebuchadnezzar; Medo-Persia, which was initially ruled by Darius and Cyrus; Greece, which was governed by Alexander the Great, and finally Rome, which was ruled by the Caesars. In Daniel 7:3-8 these 4 Empires were respectively symbolised by 4 beasts: Lion, Leopard, Bear and a frightening cruel creature with iron teeth. And in chapter 2 of the Book of Daniel we also discovered that the Empires of Babylon, Medo-Persia, Greece and Rome were represented by Gold, Silver, bronze and Iron respectively.

We know the number 4 is the earth number. Solomon confirms it: "Four things on earth are small (Ants, coneys, locusts and lizards) yet they are extremely wise (Proverbs 30:24-28). And we are aware that 4 Empires have ruled the world since the Jews were exiled to Babylon. From the spiritual stand point there would be no 5th empire. The fourth empire to control the world, which was the Roman Empire, is still in "existence" in the form of the European Union. We discovered from our study of the development of the European Union, that the whole world is influenced by the Roman culture, which is a composition of the cultures of Greece, the Medes and the Persians and the Babylonians.

Now the question arises: from which city did this fourth and last Empire ruled over the earth? The Lord revealed it to us in Revelation 17:9. This scripture gives us a clue: "The seven heads are the seven hills on which the woman sits." This text is symbolic, because there is no a literal woman who sits on 7 hills. Therefore, if we could identify a city that has been built on 7 hills, we would be able to identify this particular city mentioned in the Book of Revelation. According to Encyclopaedia Britannica, "The ancient city of Rome began as a small village on the banks of the River Tiber in Italy. Rome was built besides this River on what are known as the seven hills. These seven hills are: "Palatine, Capitoline, Aventine, Caelian, Equiline, Viminal and Quirinal."

THE CITY OF ROME AND THE 7 CAESARS

Before we attempt to identify the "woman who sits on these seven hills", I would like to mention that there are other cities built on seven hills. For example, Rio de Janeiro was built on seven hills. But in the context of the revelation given to Apostle John (as we shall discover during our study) no other city fits the description than the city of Rome. And we must also remember Apostle John wrote the Book of Revelation during the era of the Roman Empire. So, John used a symbolic language to identify the city of Rome, whose Kings persecuted Jews and Christians. It is therefore clear from the symbolic expression, that, the *"Woman who sits on these seven hills"* is the city of Rome. Revelation 17:10 also tells us: "They are also seven kings. Five have fallen, one is, the other has not yet come, but when he does come, he must remain for a little while." For us to appreciate this crucial Scripture, we need the Light of God and our knowledge of history. We have established that the "Great city" in Revelation 17:18 is the city of Rome which is built on "seven hills." Who are the "seven kings" mentioned in this Scripture? Obviously, the "seven kings" described in the text are associated with seven Emperors of the Roman Empire who ruled the earth from the city of Rome. These Emperors were seven Caesars. It is the word *"Fallen"* in Revelation 17:10 that helps to confirm that the *seven kings* were seven Caesars of Rome, and not seven different kingdoms or empires.

The word *"Fallen"* which is associated with the *"seven kings"* suggests that these Caesars experienced unnatural death. Scriptural passages in Judges 3:24-25 and 2 Samuel 1:10, 25, 27 help to confirm it. In 2 Samuel 1:9-10 a young Amalekite went to David with the news of the death of king Saul. When he saw Saul leaning on his spear, with chariots around him, the king pleaded with the man: *"Stand over me and kill me! I am in the throes of death, but I am still alive".* Witness how the Amalekite described Saul's death to David: "I stood over him and killed him, because I knew that after he had *fallen* he could not survive". Jonathan, the son of Saul, was also killed. And 2 Samuel 1:25 described his unnatural death: "How the mighty have *fallen in battle*! Jonathan lies slain on your heights". Applying the principle of interpreting scripture with scripture, we can conclude that, the five kings who have "fallen" in Revelation 17:10 refer to these five Caesars who did not die naturally. They committed suicide or were murdered – Julius Caesar, Tiberius, Caligula, Claudius and Nero.

Up to the time Apostle John was exiled to the Island of Patmos, where he wrote the Book of Revelation, 12 prominent Caesars had ruled the Roman Empire. They were:

- **Julius Caesar (45-44BC)**
- Augustus (31BC-AD14)
- **Tiberius (14-37AD)**
- **Caligula (37-41AD)**
- **Claudius (41-54AD)**
- **NERO (54 – 68AD)**
- Galba (68-69)
- Otho (69AD)
- Vitellus (69AD)
- Vespasian (69-79AD)
- Titus (79-81AD)
- And ***Domitian***(81-96AD).

But in Revelation 17:10 only seven Caesars were referred to. However, these seven Caesars include the Caesar of the revived Roman Empire, the Man of Lawlessness, who will appear at the beginning of the final 7 years of our generation (Daniel 9:27) to become the thirteenth Caesar. The Son of Perdition would "mysteriously" become the fourteenth Caesar. We shall discover this in Revelation 17:11.

THE FIVE "FALLEN" KINGS

The text: "Five have fallen" in Revelation 17:10 refers to the five wicked Caesars, who did not die naturally. They committed suicide or were murdered before the Book of Revelation was written after AD90. These five *"Fallen kings"* were: Julius Caesar, Tiberius, Caligula, Claudius and Nero. It is important for us to examine briefly how these Caesars reigned and died. This information would help us to understand the career of the last Caesar (the King of Men) - how he would reign and pass away as predicted in Revelation 19:19-20. The character of the last Caesar of the revived Roman Empire would be a reflection of the following Caesars who preceded him namely, Julius Caesar, Tiberius, Caligula, Claudius, Nero and Domitian.

1. Julius Caesar (45-44BC)

Julius Caesar was a great soldier who turned into a dictator. In Rome, he was treated as though he was a god. Julius seemed to have claimed to be divine. The Romans erected his statue in one of_their temples. Underneath this effigy was the inscription: *"To the Unconquerable God."*

Julius Caesar fought many battles. He had wanted to rival the achievements of the Greek Warrior, Alexander the Great. After one of his victories in Asia, Caesar sent back the haughty message: *"Veni, Vidi, Vici"*, meaning *"I came, I saw, I conquered"*. The noble families in Rome hated Caesar. Some were jealous of him. Consequently they plotted his down fall. At a meeting in the Roman Parliament on 15 March 44BC, Marcus Brutus, a noble man, stabbed Caesar to death.

2. Tiberius (AD41-37)

During the reign of Augustus Caesar from 63BC to AD14 our Lord Jesus was born (Luke 2:1-7). When Augustus died in AD14 his step-son, Tiberius, succeeded him. The Romans disliked the reign of Tiberius. He was a suspicious man who was afraid about plots to kill him. When Tiberius discovered that Sejanus was plotting his death, he ordered the Senate to put him on trial. After his conviction, Tiberius decreed the execution of Sejanus, his friends and family members.

Tiberius, like all the Roman Emperors, lived in paranoid fear of his life. He had many innocent people sent to exile. He commanded some to commit suicide or be executed just because he considered them threatening. Quarrels erupted in Tiberius' family about who would succeed him. The Emperor spent the last five years of his reign in retirement in the island of Capri. According to *"What a way to go,"* a book which describes how some famous people died, Tiberius also experienced unnatural death. "He suffocated under a pile of bed linen, hastily placed upon him when he showed signs of recovery from a collapse that his well-known successor Gaius Caligula had wrongly assumed to be fatal." The Lord Jesus was crucified in about AD32 during the reign of Tiberius.

3. Caligula (AD37-41)

Caligula was the nick name of the Emperor Gaius Caesar. He was the grand nephew of Emperor Tiberius. When he was a boy he wore soldiers' boots. Because of this the soldiers nicknamed him Caligula, which means *"Little Boot."* Caligula became Emperor in AD37 at the age of 25. He started his reign well. He allowed the Romans a considerable freedom and let political exiles returned to Rome. Caligula insisted he was god. He demanded people should kiss his feet, flatter and adore him as Jupiter. Caligula was a cruel tyrant for the rest of his life. He killed those whom he disliked, and murdered senators for their property and wives. He considered making his horse a consul. In AD41 one of the imperial guards murdered him.

4. Claudius (AD41-54)

Claudius succeeded Caligula after his death on 1 January AD41. In the beginning some people regarded Claudius as a clumsy and weak minded person. Actually, he was very shrewd. He exhibited compassion by admitting Gaul's into the Senate and in the way he treated slaves. He demonstrated his intelligence by writing several books. Claudius expanded the Roman Empire. He invaded and conquered and colonised Britain in AD43. He also took over North Africa. Claudius extended Roman citizenship to a number of colonies and encouraged the founding of new colonies.

However, many Romans despised Claudius because of his wickedness. It is thought he even executed some senators. Claudius married about four times. His third wife, Messalina, was put to death for conspiring against him. The Romans plotted his assassination. The fourth wife of Claudius was said to have poisoned him to hasten the succession of her son, Nero. Claudius was declared a god after his death.

5. Nero (AD54-68)

In the context of our study, the reign of Caesar Nero is significant because of the role Nero's devilish spirit, which is now in the Abyss, would play when the last Caesar of the revived Roman Empire enters the political scene. For this reason we will examine Emperor Nero closely. According to Revelation 17:10, Nero was the fifth Caesar. Caesar Nero's number is 666, which is represented by the Hebrew letters of the name Caesar Nero.

When Nero came into power there were great expectations among the Romans that a new Golden Age for Rome has dawn. Nero started well. His advisers managed to keep him away from the evil influence of his mother. Later Nero became wicked. His mother, Agrippina, married Emperor Claudius in AD49. Even though Claudius himself had a son named Brittanicus, Agrippina put pressure on her husband to adopt her son, Nero, to succeed him. Agrippina schemed for his son to marry Octavia, Claudius daughter. This would strengthen the position of Nero to become the next Emperor. Eventually, in AD54, Agrippina poisoned her husband and Nero took the imperial crown.

Nero's mother, on realising that she could exercise no influence in the Empire, threatened to support Brittanicus' claim to the throne. Nero arranged for Brittanicus to be poisoned, and his mother killed by soldiers. From this period

Nero became evil. He fell under the spell of another ambitious and ruthless woman, Poppaea. Nero had frequent disputes with the Senate. Disasters began to overtake the Roman Empire. In AD64 a great fire destroyed almost the whole city of Rome. The historian Tacitus suggested Nero blamed the Christian Community for the fire. Nero started to persecute the Christians. According to other sources Nero's persecution of Christians resulted in the death of Apostles Peter and Paul.

When Nero started to rebuild the city of Rome, he constructed a magnificent palace for himself. The Romans could not bear the tax burden Nero had imposed on them to finance his projects. The people began to plot his downfall. When Nero discovered the plan in AD65, he killed all the conspirators. He killed his own tutor, Seneca, and the poet, Lucan. In AD68, the generals in Gaul and Spain rebelled against Nero. Eventually the Roman Parliament (the Senate) appointed Galba, the governor of Spain, as the Emperor. The Senate also passed death sentence on Nero. When Nero realised that soldiers were about to capture him to be executed, he committed suicide. The appearance of Nero in the Roman Empire was hailed as a New Golden Age for Rome. And so would the emergence of the charismatic leader of Europe mark the beginning of a New Dawn in European history. This political genius, who will "solve" all the complicated problems facing Europe, will crown his success with a "permanent peace" deal between the Jews and the Arabs.

6. *Domitian (AD81-96)

Domitian was crowned Emperor in AD81. He was a son of Emperor Vespasian. His elder brother was Titus, the Prince who led the destruction of Jerusalem and its Temple in AD70 to fulfil the prophetic word in Daniel 9:26. It was this Titus Vespasian, who, in AD80, inaugurated the Amphitheatre built by his Father. The portrait of the Colloseum, a symbol of bloodshed, is painted on the Italian 5 Euro cents. Titus' destruction of the temple and his persecution of the Jews also fulfilled the Lord's prophetic word about the fate of the Jews and their Temple (Luke 19:43-44). Like Tiberius, Caligula and Nero, Domitian was also a wicked despot. He commanded the Romans to build statues of himself, and insisted people refer to him as "lord and god".

The Roman Senate feared Domitian who became suspicious of them. When Domitian noticed that members of the Senate had plotted to kill him, he put some of them on trial for treason. Those found guilty were killed. After their death Domitian would confiscate their assets for the treasury of the Empire. During the last three years of his reign the Romans had to live through a period of terror. Domitian surrounded himself with personal body guards. He was murdered by a man named Stephanus in a plot that involved Domitian's own relative.

Apostle John wrote the Book of Revelation in about AD90. Since Domitian reigned from AD81-96, it is obvious Domitian, who succeeded Nero, was alive when John published Revelation. This was the reason why in Revelation 17:10 John stated, "*There are seven kings* (that is seven Caesars*) five have fallen, One is, the other has not yet come....*" This *"One is"* was a reference to Emperor Domitian. John did not mention the name of this Caesar because he was still alive. John adopted the same tactic to name the "beast" by using his number "666" (Revelation 13:18).

7. Antichrist - the last Caesar of the revived Roman Empire- (Daniel 9:27)

The seventh Caesar would be the Antichrist, the coming leader of the European Empire. He is *"the other has not yet come; but when he does come, he must remain for a while"* in Revelation 17:10**.** We know from Daniel 9:27 that Antichrist would rule for a short period. He will start his reign with a 7-year peace treaty between the nation of Israel and its Arab neighbours. The King of Europe, will promise the Jews peace and freedom to worship God in their Temple.

Like Nero, who came into power amid great expectation among the Romans that a New Golden Age has dawn, so would the emergence of the last Emperor of Europe into the political scene be regarded as a New Golden Age of Peace and Prosperity for the world - especially since this Caesar would 'end' the Middle East conflict. Europe would live in peace; but for how long. Like Claudius, this last Caesar of the revived Roman Empire would be very shrewd. He would demonstrate extraordinary intelligence and military might and invade other countries.

We already know within three and half years of his reign, this Emperor, the Antichrist, will break the peace treaty with the Jews. The King of Men, like the arrogant Julius Caesar, will also exalt himself; utter proud words and blaspheme God. Just as the Romans built a statue of Julius Caesar in one of their temples and worshipped it as god, and just as Domitian also commanded the Romans to build a statue of him in their temple, so would the coming false prophet (the apostate Jew) instruct the citizens of the revived Roman Empire to erect an image of the last Caesar in the Jerusalem temple for the world to adore it. (Revelation 13:14).

Like Julius Caesar and all the Caesars who claimed to be god, the King of Europe will also assert his deity. Like Nero who executed Christians, the Emperor of the revived Roman Empire will also kill the faithful Jews and Christians who refuse to honour his image. And just as the Romans regarded Julius Caesar as divine, and an unconquerable god, so would the citizens of the European Empire worship their Emperor as god. When the spirit of Nero (*666*) revives the slain Emperor, the blind world would sing the praises of the "resurrected" Antichrist: "Who is like the beast?" they will sing. "Who can make war against him?" they will dance. (Revelation 13:4).

The brutal Domitian, who was on the imperial throne when John wrote the Book of Revelation, insisted people should worship him as god. During the last three years of Domitian's reign, the Romans lived in fear. Similarly, the last Caesar, like the wicked Domitian, would also command the world to worship him as god – an act of abomination before the Almighty (Daniel 9:27). And just as the Romans dreaded the last three years of Domitian's reign, so would the citizens of the revived Roman Empire live in fear during the final three and half years of the reign of their Emperor (Revelation 13:4-8).

It is clear from Scriptures and historical perspective, that Antichrist, the seventh Caesar, would be the composition of the characteristics of all the Roman Caesars who were arrogant and cruel dictators - who claimed to be God, and killed all those they disliked. Finally, just as all the impious Caesars experienced unnatural deaths, so would the last Caesar. The "*Beast from the sea*" would also face an abnormal death. For the Lord Jesus Christ will cast the "Man of Lawlessness" into the lake of fire to burn forever. He will share the destiny of Satan and the false prophet (Revelation 20:10). It is this King of Europe Sir Robert Anderson described as the "awful Being" in his *The Coming Prince.* This is the man who will lead the world to close the era of Gentile supremacy on earth. If whatever Sir Robert Anderson recorded about a political union of European nations has come to pass, it is certain what he wrote about the "awful Being" will also be fulfilled. It will surely happen.

THE "MARVELLOUS COUNTERFEIT RESURRECTION" OF ANTICHRIST

Revelation 17:11 says: *"The beast who once was, and now is not, is an eighth king, He belongs to the seven, and he is going to his destruction."* Let us examine what this passage of Scripture teaches us:

- What is the "Beast who once was"? We know this "beast" is the Antichrist, who will come out of the "Mediterranean Sea" (Rev. 13:1) – one of the nations in Europe. It is clear from Daniel 9:27, Matthew 24:15 and 2 Thessalonians 2:4, that the "beast," the "Man of lawlessness," has not yet stepped into the political arena.

The question remains: who does this beast, "who once was," refer to? Revelation 13:18 tells us the number of the beast, which is "666", is the number of a man. Who is this man with the number "666"? The great Bible teacher, Witness Lee, explains in the commentary section of the Holy Bible Recovery Version that the number represented by the Hebrew letters of the name Caesar Nero is 666. Apostle John wrote the Book of Revelation when Rome was ruling the world with iron fist. John did not mention the name of Nero. He indicated it with a number. Hence, his words: "....no one may buy or sell except one who has the mark or the name of the beast, or the number of his name. Here is wisdom. Let him who has understanding calculate the number of the beast, for it is the number of a man. His number is 666" (Revelation 13:17-18).

History tells us Caesar Nero was a monster. He ordered the execution of Apostle Paul. He crucified Apostle Peter. It was this "ferocious beast" - Nero - who burned Christians alive and offered some as meal to hungry lions. Hence, the *"beast who once was"* clearly refers to the brutal Caesar Nero when he was in power.

- *"The beast....and now is not"* in Revelation 17:11 implies that when John was writing the Book of Revelation, Caesar Nero, the nasty beast, had already died. Nero was murdered in AD68. John wrote the Book of Revelation in about AD90.
- *"The beast....is an eighth king. He belongs to the seven and is going to his destruction."* This text reveals that Antichrist would be the seventh and "Perfect" Caesar of the revived Roman Empire, which is now being built on the European Union. The "Man of Lawlessness" would also be the "Eighth Caesar".

For us to appreciate this revelation, we need to examine Revelation 13:3 which says: *"One of the heads of the beast seemed to have had a fatal wound, but the fatal wound had been healed. The whole world was astonished and followed the beast."* From this text we notice Antichrist, the "beast," would be killed and then "rise" from the "dead." It would be the spirit of Nero, the 5th Caesar, whose number is "666", and who is still in the abyss, which would resuscitate the slain Antichrist. Thus, Antichrist, the last and seventh Caesar of the revived Roman Empire, would then become the "Eighth Caesar." This explains the text: "He (Antichrist) is an eighth king. He belongs to the seven...." (Revelation 17:11).

The "resurrected" Antichrist would bring the number of Caesars to 14. The number 14 is made of 7 + 7. The number 7 signifies completeness. This means, at the close of this age, when the revived Roman Empire comes to an end, there would be no more Caesars to rule the world. Remember, the stone cut without human hands will roll to crush the human statue from its toes of clay and iron to its head of gold (Daniel 2:35).

THE ROLE OF THE SPIRIT OF CAESAR NERO (666)

Let us examine closely the significant role the spirit of cruel Nero, which is in the Abyss, would play in the "resurrection" of Antichrist. Revelation 17:10 says: "*There are seven kings, five have fallen, one is, and the other has not yet come....*" From the "Five kings who have fallen", Emperor Nero was the 5th Caesar. We know the ***"One is"*** refers to Emperor Domitian. Since Domitian was alive when John recorded Revelation, the Apostle did not mention his name. Antichrist would be the 7th Caesar, who is referred to in the text as *"the other has not yet come."* When Antichrist returns to life from his fatal wound, as described in Revelation 13:3, he will become the 8th Caesar. Before his "death" Antichrist was the 7th Caesar. After his "death" and "resurrection" he becomes the 8th Caesar. This would be the imitation of the Real Resurrection of the Lord Jesus Christ, which took place on the first day of the week (Matthew 28:1), which is the 8th day of the second week.

In the Bible the number 5 signifies responsibility. The number 7 signifies perfection or completeness. And the number 8 signifies resurrection – a new beginning. So, from our knowledge of symbolic meaning of these numbers, we notice that it would be the responsibility of the spirit of Caesar Nero (the 5th Caesar) whose number is 666, to "resurrect" the "dead" Antichrist (the last and perfect Caesar (7)). It is by virtue of the role the spirit of Nero would play in "resurrecting" Antichrist, that is why the number of Antichrist is also "666" (Revelation 13:17-18).

THE FAKE RESURRECTION THAT AMAZES THE WORLD TO WORSHIP THE LAST CAESAR OF THE REVIVED ROMAN EMPIRE

We have established that after Antichrist's bogus "resurrection", he would become the 8th Caesar. This is why Revelation 17:11 tells us: *"He (Antichrist) is an eighth king, He belongs to the seven…"* (Revelation 17:11). Antichrist's "resurrection" would stun the world to the extent that men would begin to worship him. (Revelation 13:3). And this would mark a new beginning (8) for the "Man of Lawlessness" as he assumes the status of a deity. His reign would be brief. The Lord Jesus Christ will cast the Son of Perdition into the lake of fire after the three and half years of the Great Tribulation. This is why scripture tells us: "The beast who once was (Caesar Nero -666), and now is not (Nero was not alive when John wrote Revelation***),*** is an eighth king (the resurrected Antichrist***).*** He belongs to the seventh (Antichrist - the *last* Caesar after Domitian), and is going out to his destruction" (The Lord Jesus Christ will condemn Antichrist into the lake of fire Revelation 17:11).

SUMMARY

Let us review what we have discussed so far: Antichrist, the "Beast", the last Emperor of the revived Roman Empire, the Man of Lawlessness, would be the 7th Caesar. After his "death" the "Son of Perdition" would be "resurrected" by the spirit of the 5th Caesar, Nero, to become the 8th Caesar. Antichrist's imitation of the Resurrection of the Lord Jesus Christ would astonish the world for people to adore him (Revelation 13:3-4). This Scripture reveals how Antichrist would be honoured as god, just as the Romans worshipped their Caesars as gods.

Energised by Satan, and imbued with the spirit of brutal Nero, the "Man of Lawlessness" would be the carbon copy of the "Dragon" – an incarnate of the Devil. This is why the Antichrist - with the composite spirit of Nero and the Devil - would be capable of displaying extraordinary intelligence and charisma. He would be the Rock Star of all Rock Stars, the celebrity of all celebrities. Men and women would yearn for his autograph. This 7th Caesar, animated by the spirit of the 5th Caesar, Nero, would be the impious Caesar the world has ever known. He would be the "father" of all terrorists.

The King of Men, the "awful Being," will have deeper understanding of world politics. It is his extraordinary personality, intelligence and fluency that would mesmerise the leaders and the citizens of the European Empire to follow him. Because of his devilish attributes, Antichrist will display unusual arrogance. Antichrist (like Titus of Rome and Antiochus Epiphanes of Syria (the despicable king who killed hundreds of Jews and desecrated their Temple and caused so much destruction) will also utter proud words, blaspheme God and kill the faithful Jews and Christians who refuse to honour him. The "Man of lawlessness" will also desecrate the temple in Jerusalem by demanding worship of his idol placed in the holy Place by the apostate Jew. Remember, in about 132AD, the wicked Hadrian of Rome erected a pagan god on the ruins of the Temple to provoke the Jews.

ANTICHRIST (THE BEAST) HAS NO DESIRE FOR WOMEN

Daniel 11:36-37 predicted that the Antichrist would do what ever pleases him. He will exalt himself above God and every body. He will have no desire for women. This means, the *"Man of Sin"* – the coming King of Men, who will lead the "Global Society," would be a proud celibate or a charismatic sodomite. This is the man the world has been waiting for to solve its economic, political, security and religious problems.

A PORTRIAT OF THE LAST CAESAR OF THE REVIVED ROMAN EMPIRE

I will, again, refer to the article regarding the Greek legendary hero, Agamemnon, which The Times newspaper published it in 1876. This item was not about Antichrist, yet in describing the qualities of Agamemnon, that piece of writing prophetically described the attributes of the coming King of Europe, who is about to lead the revived Roman Empire to the paradise of peace and prosperity. Let us read a portion of the thesis: ".....What is it that all Europe is looking for? It is the King of Men, the great head of the Hellenic race, the man whom a thousand galleys and a hundred thousand men submitted to on a simple recognition of his personal qualities, and obeyed for ten long years...The man who, as soon as he enters, can single out the shield of the King of Men, and say, "That is mine", must be the man to head the entire Greek race and the races mixed with it in their impending struggle with the remnant of the Asiatic Power. He must be a scholar, a statesman, a man of unflinching courage and irrepressible enterprise, full of resources, and ready to look in the face of a rival or foe...... The man who can challenge for his own the shield of AGAMEMNON, now waiting for the challenge, is the true Emperor of the East, and our easiest escape from our present difficulties."

It is interesting to note in this writing, that the "King of Men" Europe is looking for to deliver Europeans from their "present difficulties" (Financial and economic crisis, terrorist threats, Climate Change, Immigration, Energy, etc) is associated with the nation of modern Greece. And the Bible also tells us, the "beast" (Antichrist) who is "coming out of the sea" (one of the Gentile nations in Europe*)* "resembles a leopard" (Revelation 13:1:-2). And according to Daniel 7:4 the leopard, a swift beast, was the symbol of the Grecian Empire which had Alexander the Great as its head. It is clear from The Times' article we have read, which has been confirmed by the language of Scripture in Revelation 13:1-2, that the coming powerful world leader would, to some extent, directly or indirectly, be associated with the nation of Greece - a member-state of the European Union. Sir Robert Anderson predicted Greece's membership of an European confederacy about 100 years before Greece joined the European Community in 1981.

Because of the personal qualities of the "*King of Men*"- his unflinching courage and irresistible enterprise and resources - scripture rightly tells us: "All the inhabitants of the earth will worship the beast - all whose names have not been written in the book of life belonging to the Lamb (the Lord Jesus Christ)....He who has an ear, let him hear" (Revelation 18:8-9). This is a sombre warning. We must open our eyes, our ears, our minds, our hearts and spirit to understand the development of the European Union and its implications. Daniel prophetically described how the coming *"king of Men"*, the false prince of peace, would disregard God and cause destruction in the land of Israel. The prophet also described how the "Man of Lawlessness" would invade other countries. But the "Beast" (Antichrist) will finally go into destruction (Revelation 17:8-11). At the end of his short reign (Daniel 9:27), the Lord Jesus Christ will destroy the "beast", with the breath of His Mouth (2 Thessalonians 2:8).

THE BEAST WITH "10 HORNS" AND "7 HEADS"

According to Revelation 17:12-13, the *"beast"* John saw in his vision had "10 horns and 7 heads." It was explained to John: "The *ten horns* you saw are the *ten kings* who have not yet received a kingdom, but who for one hour will receive authority as kings along with the beast. They have one purpose and will give their *power and authority to the beast."*

Let us find out what this Scripture teaches us. In the Bible a "horn" is an emblem of political power. We learn this from Zechariah 1:18. In this scripture the prophet saw a vision of "four horns." When he asked the angel for an explanation, the angel answered: *"These are the horns that scattered Judah, Israel and Jerusalem......"* Were literal horns responsible for the dispersal of the children of Israel over the face of the earth? No. It was the Empires that ruled the world in succession that persecuted, killed and scattered the Jews across the globe.

We know from the prophetic passages in chapter 2 of the Book of Daniel that it was the Babylonians, the Greeks and the Romans who persecuted the Jews. For example, it was the Roman Prince, Titus Vespasian who, in AD 70, invaded Judea, destroyed the Temple in Jerusalem, killed thousands of Jews and took some as slaves. Another brutal Caesar, Emperor Hadrian, completed the rout by killing thousands of Jews and attempted to wipe them from the face of the earth by renaming Judea *Syria Palestina.*

The *"ten horns"* mentioned in Revelation 17:12-13 correspond to the *ten toes* of the magnificent human image king Nebuchadnezzar saw in his dream (Daniel 2:42-43). We have already learnt that the *"ten toes"* of the statue, which were partly of iron and partly of baked clay.....partly strong and partly brittle (Daniel 2:42-43), represent the powerful and the weak, and the rich and the poor member-states of a *"divided kingdom"* with mixed people, who are not united (Daniel 2:41-42). And we have already established that this *kingdom* would be the revived Roman Empire, which is in its infancy as the European Union. Even the Belgian statesman, Paul Henri-Spaak, confirmed that the European Economic Community would lead to the revival of the dead Roman Empire. After the signing the Treaty of Rome in 1957, Spaak told a friend: "Do you think we have today been putting the first stone of a new Roman Empire, and this time without firing a shot? We all felt like Romans that day." (Source: Article *"The Decline and Fall of Rome"* by Michael Elliot - *TIME* 13 June 2005) And in 2007, Jose Manuel Barroso, the President of the European Commission, confirmed Spaak's view when he declared to the world that the European Union is the world's first "non imperial empire."

We know the European Union is a "united kingdom" of 27 different nations with a Parliament, a common Currency, a Common Agricultural Policy, a Common Fishery Policy, a Central Bank, a Court of Justice, a flag, an anthem and a Constitution yet to be adopted to make the EU a legal personality with powers to sign treaties on behalf of member states. However, in reality, the European Union is a *"divided kingdom"* of small and big nations, weak and powerful nations, poor and rich nations of mixed people with different languages and cultures.

THE 10 HORNS ARE THE 10 POWERFUL KINGS OF THE REVIVED ROMAN EMPIRE

If Scripture interprets itself, then by implication the *"ten horns which are the ten kings"* in Revelation 17:12-13 would be the ten powerful leaders from the ten regions or provinces that would emerge from the revived Roman Empire. And it is these ten leaders who would be one with Antichrist before he signs the 7-year peace covenant with Israel and her Arab neighbours and all the institutions that are fighting for peace in the Middle East (Daniel 9:27). And what would be the purpose of the alliance between the ten influential leaders of the European kingdom and the "Man of Lawlessness"? To oppose God, blaspheme God, slanders His holy Name, and oppress the faithful Jews and Christians (Revelation 13:5-7 Daniel 7:19- 22, 24-25).

Today, we witness the "carbon copies" of Antichrist. They are the enlightened and sophisticated men who blaspheme the Lord Jesus Christ, slander His Holy Name, and portray Him as a homosexual in a nappy. These shallow intellectuals mock the Lord's Virgin Birth and Resurrection. We read and watch how authors, comedians, artists, pop stars, actors, television companies, film producers and tourist centres blaspheme the Lord Jesus Christ in the name of "Freedom of speech and expression". We read and hear about how Christians are being persecuted and killed in certain parts of the world.

Michael Gove highlighted the plight of Christians in his article "Remember Jesus? He is that baby they all forgot in the Parable of Tussauds". He stated: "In China, Vietnam, Laos, Nigeria, Sudan, Egypt and Indonesia, Christians are variously imprisoned for their faith, tortured, have their families broken up, the public expression of their faith banned, their homes and churches burnt…" (The Times 24 December 2004). We also witness how the political systems of the world enact laws and promote policies that undermine the commandments of God.

We know from history how the Jews have been persecuted and killed. The Holocaust was a grim example. It was preceded by Hadrian's "holocaust." And now we read in our newspapers how the President of Iran threatened that the Jews should be wiped out from the face of the earth. This announcement should not have surprised anyone. An attempt to wipe out the Jews would certainly be made by the forces from the "North." I will share with you, in the next Appendix, how the former US President, George Bush, should have responded to the personal letter the Iranian President delivered to him. He raised the issue of the "Phenomenon of Israel."

Dr John Hagee, pastor of Cornerstone Church in San Antonio, Texas, shared with us the plight of the Jews in his article "Battle for Jerusalem." According to

Dr Hagee, "Jerusalem means "City of peace", but it has known more wars, more bloodshed, more tears, and more terror than any city on earth. It has been conquered and re-conquered 38 times by the Babylonians, Greeks, Romans, Crusaders and Ottomans, yet it stands today as a testimony to the faithfulness of God to preserve the sacred city" *(Source: Israel and Christian today).*

We, the Bible-believing Christians, are not surprised of the tidal waves of ridicules and persecutions that Christians in certain parts of the world have experienced. Our Divine Lord predicted: some of *"You (Christians) will be handed over to be persecuted and put to death, and you will be hated by all nations because of me"* (Matthew 24:9). In view of this prophetic word from the Lord, faithful Christians are not shocked of the activities of the prototypes of Antichrist. We regard the current "persecutions" by the infidels as a "rehearsal" – a picture of the real persecution we would face when the "Man of Lawlessness," the "King of Men", sits on his majestic throne in the revived Roman Empire to begin his 7-year reign to close the era of Gentile supremacy on earth.

THE TEMPORARY REIGN OF ANTICHRIST AND THE 10 POWERFUL LEADERS IN THE EUROPEAN EMPIRE

Revelation 17:12 tells us about "*The ten horns ....who for one hour will receive authority as kings with the beast.*" We know the "Beast" in this text is the last Caesar of the revived Roman Empire. The "ten horns" are the ten commanding leaders of the European Empire. Let us now establish what the "One hour" in the text signifies. One hour is 60 minutes, which is composed of 6x10. In the Bible 6 is the number of man, and 10 indicates power, authority and fullness. Hence, this "one hour" in Revelation 17:12 signifies that the 10 leaders of the revived Roman Empire would be powerful men. They will exercise great authority and influence. But their reign would endure for a short time.

These 10 dominant leaders in the European Empire are the "ten horns" who would have one mind and purpose. They will delegate their power and authority to Antichrist (the beast) to rule Europe and the world. These European leaders would bow to the Son of Perdition, who would have already convinced the "ten horns" of his supernatural intelligence and ability to solve the problems that have plagued Europe and the rest of the world.

A LESSON FOR CHRISTIANS

According to Revelation 17:14, the "ten horns, which are the ten kings, will make *a* war against the Lamb, but the Lamb will overcome them with His called, chosen and faithful_followers." It is clear the faithful Jews and Christians would be harassed by the European Empire. The persecution of the children of God was revealed to the prophet Daniel: Let us listen to Daniel: "Then I wanted to know the true meaning of the fourth beast, which was different from all the other beasts and most terrifying, with its iron teeth and bronze claws – the beast that crushed and devoured its victims and trampled underfoot whatever was left. I also wanted to know about the ten horns on its head and about the other horn that came up, before which three of them fell – the horn that looked more imposing than the others and that had eyes and a mouth that spoke boastfully. *As I watched, this horn was waging war against the saints and defeating them, until the Ancient of Days came and pronounced judgement in favour of the saints of the Most High, and the time came when they possessed the kingdom."* (Daniel 7: 19-22).

In Revelation 17:14 we learnt that the Lord will destroy the European Empire with His called and chosen followers. "Chosen" is mentioned after "called". Let us relate this text to what the Lord said in Matthew 22:14: "Many are called, but few are chosen," to establish the significance of this relationship. The message is clear. The Lord Jesus Christ would not invite all those who profess to be Christians to join Him in His final war with Antichrist and the kingdoms of the world. Only the few overcomers would be chosen. These were members of *"The Church in Philadelphia"* (The Church of Brotherly love), who remained faithful to the Lord. Because of their faithfulness, the Lord Jesus promised them: "Since you have kept my command to endure patiently, I will also keep you from the hour of trial that is going to come upon the whole world to test those who live on the earth" (Revelation 3:10). The "hour of trial" is the 3½ years of the great tribulation the Lord spoke about in Matthew 24.

Here is another lesson. The Lord Jesus will invite only the chosen overcomers to join Him in the Marriage Supper of the Lamb. And these few will reign with the Lord for a thousand years (Revelation 20:4). After this period Satan would be released from the Abyss and then cast into the lake of burning sulphur where the false prophet and Antichrist had been thrown. The unbelievers would also be judged and cast into the lake of fire (Revelation 20:10-15). This is the Word of the Lord. Amen!

Just as the Maccabees defeated the Syrian forces of Antiochus Epiphanes, so would the Lord Jesus Christ lead His overcomers to defeat the "Man of Lawlessness" and his followers, and cast them into the lake of fire. Vengeance belongs to the Lord. He will repay those who have ridiculed Him. Apostle Paul warns: "Do not be deceived, God is not mocked; for whatever a man sows, that he will also reap" (Galatians 6:7). "All mankind will come and bow down before me", says the Lord. "And they will go out and look upon the dead bodies of those who rebelled against me; their worm will not die; nor will their fire be quenched; and they will be loathsome to all mankind" (Isaiah 66:23-24). Amen!

WHO IS THE "GREAT PROSTITUTE"?

Let us return to our Scripture – Revelation 17. I have already mentioned there are "two women" in this passage of scripture. These "women" are different, but they are "relatives". We have already established the identity of the first woman. She is the Great City of Rome, which is built on seven hills - Aventine, Caelian, Capitoline, Esquiline, Palatine, Quirinal and Viminal (Revelation 17:9). I will now attempt to unveil the personality of the second woman. Revelation 17:1-2 tells us, this "*woman*" is "the great prostitute, who sits on many waters, with her the kings of the earth committed adultery and the inhabitants of the earth were intoxicated with the wine of her adultery".

To locate this particular *woman*, we need to ascertain the significance of the key words in the passage. They are: "Prostitute", "Waters", "Kings", "Adultery" and "Wine".

- A "*prostitute*" is an unmarried woman who fornicates. She indulges in sexual relationships with different men for her livelihood.
- "*Waters*" in the Bible signify the corrupt and politically unstable world.
- "*Kings*" represent the political systems and powers of the world.
- "*Adultery*" signifies an unholy alliance with the world. In the Bible, adultery and fornication are used both in their literal and spiritual senses. For example in Isaiah 1:21 the Lord tells the prophet: "See how the faithful city (Jerusalem) has become a harlot. She once was full of justice; righteousness used to dwell in her –but now murderers". In Jeremiah 3:9 we read: "Because Israel's immorality mattered so little to her, she defiled the land and committed adultery with stone and wood." And the prophet Ezekiel describes in detail the spiritual adultery of Israel (Ezekiel chapter 16).

Knowledge is Liquor: it intoxicates

- Finally, let us find out what the "*Wine*" signifies? Our behaviour are prompted by the knowledge we hold and exercise. For an example, Accountants, Lawyers, Engineers and Medical surgeons perform their duties by the application of the respective professional knowledge they have acquired. Likewise, all artisans provide their services under the influence of the skills they have acquired. If a person has not studied Medicine how could he operate on a patient who needs Heart Surgery? How could one prepare a Consolidated Profit and Loss Accounts, Balance Sheets and Cash Flow Statements if such a one lacked accountancy knowledge? How could one successfully prosecute or defend a suspected criminal if such a one has had no legal education and training? How could you prepare a nuclear bomb if you lacked knowledge and training in nuclear physics? It is clear we act on knowledge, and knowledge influences our behaviour just as the actions of a drunkard are influenced by the amount of alcohol he has consumed. We can conclude that knowledge is liquor; it intoxicates. Therefore, *"wine"* in this Scriptural passage signifies "knowledge" or "doctrine."

From the symbolic significance of the various items which are associated with this second woman, the "Great prostitute", we can conclude that this "woman" is the apostate church (the Churches in Pergamus and Thyatira). The degraded church is married to the political institutions of the world. They have led the servants of Christ to commit sexual immoralities. (Revelation 2:18-29). In her unholy alliance with the political systems (which is spiritual adultery), the apostate church has influenced her own congregation and the world with false doctrine (polluted knowledge) to undermine the True Word of God - the Holy Bible. With arrogance, the polluted church places her own traditions and teachings on equal footing with Sacred Scriptures.

THE APOSTATE CHURCH: THE COUNTERFEIT BRIDE OF CHRIST

According to Revelation 17:4-5, "The woman (the great prostitute) was dressed in purple and scarlet and was glittering with gold and precious stones and pearls. She held a golden cup in her hand, filled with abominable things and the filth of her adulteries. This title was written on her forehead:

MYSTERY
BABYLON THE GREAT
THE MOTHER OF PROSTITUTES
AND OF THE ABOMINATIONS OF THE EARTH.

What does the glorious appearance of the *"Great Prostitute"* signify? In Revelation 21 we read that the Holy City, the New Jerusalem, as a bride of Christ, is beautifully dressed for her husband "with very precious jewel, like jasper, clear as crystal." (Revelation 21:11). The foundations of the walls of this Holy City were decorated with every kind of precious stone. The wall was made of jasper, and the city of pure gold. The twelve gates were pearls, each gate made of a single pearl. The great street of the city was of pure gold, like transparent glass.

We notice the apostate church is also dressed with the same precious materials that were used to build the New Jerusalem, the Beautiful Bride of Christ. This symbolises that the corrupted church, the *"Great prostitute"*, has an appearance of the true Church – the Bride of the Lamb (Revelation 19:7). This means, outwardly, the apostate church professes to believe in the Bible and the Lord Jesus Christ, yet inwardly she is not. In reality, she has forsaken the Lord Jesus Christ for the political system. As a result, this church has become polluted. She is filled with hypocrisy, corruption, materialism, greed, heretical teachings and sexual immoralities.

Some of the priests and bishops in the degraded church are sodomites and paedophiles. They engage in sexual relationships with their congregation. The apostate church also recognises and promotes lesbianism, and blesses same-sex marriages. And the sad spectacle is that some of them sexually abuse boys even in the church, and the Church hierarchy conceals their evil deeds.

The confusion in the renegade church has reached the level where its blind leaders, who only read the black letters in the Bible, claim to know better than the Lord Jesus Christ and His Apostles, who referred to God as "Our Father." The tainted Church proudly claims it is not appropriate to refer to God as Man. Why? Because, a masculine imagery of the Almighty would encourage men to beat their wives. What an exhibition of spiritual ignorance! A true Christian would not beat his wife. The Bible advises us: "Husbands…be considerate as you live with your wives, and treat them with respect as the weaker partner and as heirs with you of the gracious gift of life, so that nothing will hinder your prayers" (1 Peter 2:7). Only a degraded man beats his wife. "Wife-beating" has nothing to do with the gender of God. Another misguided Liberal Church leader in America also claims the Lord is a woman. The religious Babylon blindly follows the foot steps of her husband - the political Babylon. No wonder the contaminated Church has become irrelevant and the pews continue to be empty.

Without any doubt, the stained church approves the very sinful practices the Bible condemns. She is the counterfeit bride of Christ, for she is actually married to the political Babylon which shares the same values with her. Is there any difference between the apostate church and the political institutions of the world? Since both of them have colluded to undermine the Word of God, they will share the same fate when the Lord returns to sit on His White Throne to judge the living and the dead.

That, the soiled church, "Babylon the Great, is the Mother of prostitutes," implies "She" has daughters who are also prostitutes. These "little harlots" are the various denominations and cults that are also married to the political systems of the world to undermine the Sacred Scriptures. A seed produces its kind. These "Little prostitutes", like their "Mother", pretend to follow the Lord. In reality, they have rejected the Lord Jesus Christ. The "little whores" also undermine the Word of God. They are also filled with greed, materialism, hypocrisy, corruption, and sexual immoralities. They propagate false doctrines to deceive the naive. They claim sodomy is compatible with the Gospel. How? In the Gospel the Lord Jesus Christ states plainly: *"At the beginning the Creator made them male and female….a man will leave his father and mother and be united to his wife, and the two will become one flesh"* (Matthew 19;4-5).

Despite the plain teaching of the Lord Jesus Christ about human relationship, the apostate church claims a man can have sexual intercourse with a man, a woman can have sexual intercourse with a woman, a man can marry a man, and a woman can marry a woman. The "Little prostitutes" and their "Mother" have leavened the "Fine flour for the three measures of Meal." These "Prostitutes" belong to the Churches in Ephesus, Pergamos, Thyatira. Sardis and Laodicea to whom the Lord warned: *"I will strike her children dead...."* (Revelation 2:18-23). And *"Because you are luke-warm ---neither hot nor cold - I am about to spit you out of my mouth...you are wretched, pitiful, poor, blind and naked..."* (Rev.3:16-17).

The ruined Church, by encouraging her members to engage in sexual immoralities on the basis of false teachings, has clearly revealed her adulterous relationships with the kings of the earth, and how the inhabitants of the earth have become intoxicated with the wine of her adultery. Through the ecumenical movement, the "little whores" are now yearning to return to the 'womb' of their Mother to wait for their doom as predicted in Isaiah 47 – the fall of Babylon.

We must remember how the Lord Jesus Christ confronted the Pharisees (the pious religious leaders) and the teachers of the law (the sophisticated intellectuals): *"You hypocrites! Isaiah was right when he prophesised about you: "These people honour me with their lips, but their hearts are far from me. They worship me in vain; their teachings are but rules taught by men"* (Matthew 15:7-9). Today, in the changing modern world, where the slogan is: "change", "reform or you die", it is the opinion of intellectuals that prevails in the church, not the Sacred Scriptures. The truth is that the True Church does not need "Lisbon Theologians". Theologians are needed in Universities and Seminaries – the "cemeteries" for Sacred Scriptures.

THE DESTINY OF THE GREAT PROSTITUTE AND HER DAUGHTERS

Finally, in Revelation 17:6, the Lord explained to Apostle John the career of the "Beast" and the "10 horns": *"The beast and the ten horns you saw will hate the prostitute. They will bring her to ruin and leave her naked; they will eat her flesh and burn her with fire. For God has put in their hearts to accomplish his purpose...."* We know the "Beast" is the Antichrist, and the "10 horns" are the ten influential leaders of the revived Roman Empire. This Scripture clearly predicts that during the last three and half years of this generation, the "Man of Lawlessness" and the ten influential leaders in the European Empire would join forces to destroy the apostate church and her daughters. This "Task Force" would expose the hypocrisy, corruption, evil practices and the sexual immoralities that have prevailed in the degraded church. However, the faithful Lord would protect those in the *Church in Thyatira* who have not held to the teaching of the polluted church, "and have not learned Satan's so-called deep secrets" (Revelation 2:24).

A PICTURE OF WHAT IS TO COME

On Tuesday 10 January 2006, a prophetic picture of the destruction of the apostate church by the "beast" and the "10 horns" was illustrated in *The Times*. The "picture" was painted in a space titled *Church must lose its £17 million tax break.* The newspaper reported that the Roman Catholic Church in Spain was "embroiled in a dispute over a bill for millions of pounds of unpaid tax." According to the report, the Church has not paid Value Added Tax for over 25 years because of an agreement the Vatican made with Madrid. This agreement helped the Church to save about £17million a year. We were informed that the European Commission (a symbol of the "ten toes") threatened Spain with a court action if "it does not close the loophole and abide by the same VAT laws as the rest of the European Union."

We can detect from this information that the European Union is not prepared to offer any favours to the Roman Catholic Church. In the eyes of the European Union, the Church of Rome should not enjoy any preferential treatment. The European Union wants Spain to "violate" its "25-year covenant" with the Vatican. This is a sign of what is to come when the charismatic Emperor of the European Empire flouts the 7-year covenant with *"many"* (Daniel 9:27), and then fulfils the prophetic word in Revelation 17:16-17. *"And the ten horns which you saw on the beast, these will hate the harlot, make her desolate and naked, eat her flesh and burn her with fire. For God has put it into their hearts to fulfil His purpose, to be of one mind, and to give their kingdom to the beast, until the words of God are fulfilled."* It takes a wise man to avert a prophecy.

The Lord Jesus Christ would use the Emperor of Europe to demonstrate to the world that He was not *"married"* to the apostate church and her *"daughters."* Why? because, the "woman" and her "daughters" were harlots. A harlot has no husband. The degraded church is not the bride of Christ. The Bridegroom removed the lampstand in the locality of the apostate church, when "She lost her first love for the Bridegroom (Revelation 2:4-5). The Bridegroom also spat the apostate church from His mouth, when He realised that His supposedly wife was of no use, but an adulteress (Revelation 3:15-16).

The Catholic Bishops have undermined the Divinity of the Book of Revelation with their comments in their "Gift of Scripture." The Catholic Church, by refuting the apocalyptic prophecies in the Book of Revelation, and by teaching that the symbolic language in Revelation must be taken for what it is (as if it is has no relevance), and that we should not expect to discover in the Book of Revelation details about the end of the world, is leading the 1.2 billion Catholics astray. If the Catholic bishops claim we must respect the Book of Revelation for what it is, then Scripture exposes the *Church in Thyatira* for what it is. (Revelation 2:18-26).

THE BIBLE OR THE CHURCH?

Enough is enough from the hierarchy of the Roman Catholic Church. This human organisation with a 'Chairman for life' has assumed unnecessary authority over the Bible to undermine the Books of Genesis, Daniel and Revelation with their traditions of infant baptism, purgatory, prayer for the dead, manufacturing of saints and praying through dead men. Some theologians in the Vatican were even tempted to rehabilitate the "evil" Judas to undermine the Gospel. Remember what the Lord Jesus Christ told the Pharisees – the pious religious leaders who made their phylacteries wide and the tassels on their garments long (Matthew 23:5): "You have let go of the commands of God and are holding on to the traditions of men……Thus you nullify the word of God by your tradition that you have handed down" (Mark 7:8, 13). And the Lord went on to advise us to be conscious of the "leaven of the Pharisees and that of Herod" (Mark 8:15); and "to be on our guard against the leaven of the Sadducees" (Matthew 16:6), and "not be carried away by all kinds of strange teaching" (Hebrews 13:9).

Apostle Peter also warned us about false teachers: "There were also false prophets among the people, just as there will be false teachers among you. They will secretly introduce destructive heresies, even denying the sovereign Lord who bought them - bringing swift destruction on themselves" (2 Peter 2:1). And before the Lord returns to judge us, He finally warned us: *"Watch out that no one deceives you"* (Matthew 24:4).

Despite the teachings of our Divine Lord, a Roman Catholic priest, Father John Corapi, who is also a theologian, proclaimed on Eternal Word Television Network (EWTN) on 29 January 2006, that there is no Bible without sacred tradition and "Majesterium of the Roman Catholic Church." According to this priest/theologian, the "Authentic Majesterium of the Church" is the "Holy Father – the Pope, who is the successor of St Peter, in union with the Catholic bishops "teaching the same thing in its essence."

This is the Catholic doctrine Pope John Paul II expounded in his *Faith and Reason*: the Encyclical Letter the Supreme Pontiff delivered to Catholic Bishops in 1998. He writes: "There are also signs of a resurgence of *fideism*, which fails to recognise the importance of rational knowledge and philosophical discourse for the understanding of faith, indeed, for the very possibility of belief in God. One currently widespread symptom of this fideistic tendency is "biblicism" which tends to make the reading and exegesis of Sacred Scripture the sole criterion of truth. In consequence, the word of God is identified with Sacred Scripture alone, thus eliminating the doctrine of the Church which the Second Vatican Council stressed quite specifically. ...Sacred Tradition and Sacred Scripture comprise a single sacred deposit of the word of God entrusted to the Church, Embracing this deposit and united with their pastors, the People of God remain always faithful to the teaching of the Apostles. Scripture, therefore, is not the Church's sole point of reference. The supreme rule of her faith derives from the unity which the Spirit has created between Sacred Tradition, Sacred Scripture and the Magisterium of the Church in a reciprocity which means that none of the three can survive without the other, Moreover, one should not underestimate the danger inherent in seeking to derive the truth of Sacred Scripture from the use of one method alone, ignoring the need for a more comprehensive exegesis which enables the exegete, together with whole Church, to arrive at the full sense of the texts". This is FALSE teaching. In the 19th century, Sir Robert Anderson exposed this Catholic ERROR in his *The Buddha of Christendom.*

What kind of Church's doctrine did Pope John Paul II refer to? Is it that of the human organization whose headquarters is in Rome with a life time "President," or the men and women who have been called out from the "sea" (the corrupt world) to form the organic Body of Christ with Christ ALONE as the HEAD? The question is: "Is it the Bible (Sacred Scriptures), or the doctrines and traditions of the Church in Rome, we must honour? Was it not a Roman Catholic Pope, Paul V, the "successor of Peter", who in the 16th century, plotted to kill Paolo Sarpi and helped to desecrate Sarpi's tomb after his death? Would Apostle Peter have plotted someone's death and hired a mob to desecrate his tomb? What about the Inquisition and the Crusaders?

If the Majesterium of the Roman Catholic Church, is the "third person" of the "infallible and Blessed Holy Catholic Trinity" of Sacred Scripture, Sacred Tradition and The Majesterium, are we compelled to believe what the Roman Catholic Bible – *The New Jerusalem Bible* – says about the Book of Daniel? This Catholic Bible teaches that the Book of Daniel is an "edifying fiction"? Is it true this Old Testament Book is a religious novel which was written between 167BC and 164 BC after the events described in the Book had already taken place? Are we to dismiss what the Lord tells us in Matthew 24:15 about "*the abomination that causes desolation spoken of through the prophet Daniel*"?

The Lord Jesus Christ has already warned us: "Be on your guard against the leaven of the Pharisees, which is hypocrisy. There is nothing concealed that will not be disclosed, or hidden that will not be made known" (Luke 12:1-2).The hierarchy of the Roman Catholic Church is not be taken seriously. It preys on the ignorance of Christians who have put their Bibles in a locker to gather dust. Through laziness they refuse to study the Holy Scriptures and have thus become victims of deceptive doctrines by liberal and "Lisbon theologians", Cardinals, Archbishops, Bishops, Priests and Pastors.

The Roman Catholic Church cannot put its human traditions on equal footing with Sacred Scriptures. This is sheer arrogance – the absurdity of all absurdities. I urge you to read Sir Robert Anderson's *"The Bible or the Church"*, which is an updated version of *The Buddha of Christendom*, to appreciate some of the false teachings of the Roman Catholic Church.

CHRYSOSTOM AND AUGUSTINE ON SACRED SCRIPTURES

At this point I would refer Roman Catholic Theologians to pages 43-45 of Sir Robert Anderson's *The Bible or the Church.* He quoted what the famous Greek Father, Chrysostom, and the Latin Father, Augustine, wrote about the Scriptures. Dr. Anderson began by stating: "The Christian turns to the Bible to hear in it the voice of his living Saviour and Master and Lord, who, by the Holy Spirit, sent down from heaven to that very end, "speaks" in and through the Word, "to the soul which closes not itself against it." But the founder of this religious system is the dead Buddha of nineteen centuries ago, the pure waters of whose teaching are now dissipated in "the troubled estuary rolled backward and forward by the varying tide" of the opinions of the Fathers, and "rendered brackish by the continued contact with the bitter waters" of a corrupt and apostate Church."

"God's Barrister" continued: "Let those who thus appeal to the Fathers hear the Fathers. No one among them is held in higher esteem than Chrysostom. The most famous of the Greek Fathers, he has been canonised by the Roman Church; and both Greek and Roman Churches celebrate his festival. And with abundant reason. For he lived a pure and floble life in an age when this much-vaunted "primitive Church" was characterised by shameless profligacy and corruption. On Scriptures. here is Chrysostom's testimony;

"And why does he bid all Christians at that time to betake themselves to the Scriptures? Because at that time, when heresy hath got possession of those Churches, there can be no proof of true Christianity, nor any other refuge for Christians wishing to know the true faith but the Divine Scriptures. For before it was shown in many ways which was the Church of Christ, and which heathenism; but now it is known in no way to those who wish to ascertain which is the true Church of Christ, but only through the Scriptures. Why? Because all those things which are properly Christ's in the truth, those heresies have also in their schism: Churches alike, the Holy Scripture alike, bishops alike, and the other orders of clergy, baptism alike, the Eucharist alike, and everything else; nay, even Christ Himself. Therefore, if any one wishes to ascertain which is the true Church of Christ, whence can he ascertain it, in the confusion arising from so great a simili-

tude, but only by the Scriptures? ...... Therefore the Lord, knowing that such a confusion of things would take place in the last days, commands on that account, that the Christians who are in Christianity, and desirous of availing themselves of the strength of the true faith, should betake themselves to nothing else but the Scriptures; otherwise, if they should look to other things they shall stumble and perish, not understanding which is the true Church." Dr Anderson stated: "These were the words of the most famous of the Greek Fathers."

The 'Barrister of God' continued: "Now let us hear the testimony of Augustine, the most famous of the Latin Fathers." He says: *"I declare unto you that the Holy Scriptures which are called canonical, are the only books in the world to which I have learned to pay such honour and reverence, that I most firmly believe that none of their authors has committed any error therein. Other authors are read by me with the persuasion that however they may excel in holiness and learning, what they write is not true because they write it, but because they can prove it to be true either by Scripture or reason."* Dr Robert Anderson added: In "all things that pertain to life and godliness" the words of Holy Writ are so simple and clear that a little child can grasp their meaning. Thus the apostle could write to Timothy, "From a child thou hast known the Holy Scriptures which are able to make thee wise unto salvation."

In the Preface to *The Buddha of Christendom*, the able defender of the Christian Faith writes: "The Reformation has been well described as "the greatest achievement in English history".....It was the main purpose of the then rulers of the church...to put prominently forward the supremacy of the Bible. Rome maintains the supremacy of "the Church": it is the foundation of her entire system. The Reformers rejected the pretensions of the Church, and made the Bible the supreme standard of authority. This was the vital question at issue in the sixteenth century: it is the vital question at issue today..." In chapter 4, the Knight of God dismisses the papal doctrine that teaches the Pope is the successor of St Peter. Dr Anderson asserted there is no "evidence" to support the claim. The scholar among scholars went on to comment on the Catholic concept of the Pope being the "Vicar of Christ". The Prince of Detectives writes: "...the story that Peter was ever Bishop of Rome is the merest legend and absolutely inconsistent with his office of Apostle; and thirdly, that the figment of his having had a position of supreme authority in the Church is exploded by the very Scripture to which appeal is made in its support..." He added: "Such is the foundation upon which rests the claim of the Pope to be the Vicar of Christ on earth. And yet his pretensions are acknowledged, not merely by ignorant peasants and superstitious women, but by educated and sensible men; by men reputed to be thinkers and scholars; by some even who are trained lawyers, holding high judicial offices. How is this phenomenon to be accounted for?" You may continue reading the book.

HENRY VIII AND THE ROMAN CATHOLIC CHURCH

In page 89 of *The Buddha of Christendom,* the "Knight of God" deals with Henry VIII's relationship with Vatican. He writes: "Roman Catholics seek to discredit the movement in England by representing Henry as its leader. But they are on dangerous ground. They forget that it was from the Pope that Henry obtained the title of "Defender of the Faith." Immorality and hypocrisy were no bar to papal favour. Let them paint the King as black as they can, and brand him as hypocrite and scoundrel, the fact remains that he was no worse than the man who then sat in "the chair of St. Peter." The vices of Henry VIII were of a kind that the Church habitually condoned. But what shall be said of Paul III? This "Vicar of Christ on earth" so far from being ashamed of his immoralities, flaunted them in the face of the world. The Duchies of Parma and Piacenza he conferred upon his illegitimate son Lewis, and he made provision for two of his grandsons, although they were schoolboys in their teens, by appointing them Cardinals. These things need to be remembered in these days when the salaried servants of the church of the Reformation are trying to undermine the work of the Reformation..." What a prophetic word for the Archbishop of Canterbury, Dr. Rowan Williams, and his 'disciples' in the Church of England and those Anglican priests who have left the Church of England for the Church of Rome. And in pages 256 and 257 of *The Buddha of Christendom*, the stalwart defender of the Christian Faith writes: "In the days of Pagan Rome, the Church was entirely on the side of the martyrs. In the days of papal Rome the martyrs were victims of the "Church" in its apostasy...."

YOU DON'T HAVE TO BE A THEOLOGIAN, A POPE, AN ARCHBISHOP OR A PRIEST TO UNDERSTAND THE BIBLE

According to Sacred Scriptures, Moses was the first person to write about the Lord Jesus Christ thousands of years before the Lord was born. Moses was neither a pope, nor a theologian. Isaiah predicted the miraculous virgin birth of our Lord about 700 years before it was fulfilled. He also recorded a graphic detail of how the Lord would suffer before His crucifixion. Isaiah was neither a pope nor a theologian. Jeremiah had no linguistic skills. He was neither a pope, nor a bishop, or a theologian. Yet he wrote about the 70 years of the Jewish captivity in Babylon before Nebuchadnezzar attacked Jerusalem to deport the Jews to Babylon.

Matthew was not a theologian when he wrote the Gospel that bears his name. None of the other evangelists was a theologian. Luke was a physician not a theologian or a pope. Apostle Paul was a Pharisee, a highly educated lawyer, yet he tells us: "I want you to know...that the gospel I preached is not something that man made up. I did not receive it from any man, nor was I taught it; rather, I received it by revelation from Jesus Christ" (Galatians 1:11-12). The message is clear: We don't need education in seminaries or prestigious universities to collect hundreds of alphabets before our names to understand the Scriptures. According to Apostle Paul we need the "Spirit of Wisdom and revelation from the Lord Jesus Christ to enable us know better" (Ephesians 1:17-18). Theological education could even become a stumbling block to our understanding of the Scriptures. For example, the Lord Jesus Christ exposed the 'ignorance' of the highly educated 'theologian', Nicodemus, when He told this Pharisee, a member of the Jewish ruling council: "You are Israel's teacher and do not understand these things" – that "No one can see the kingdom of God unless he is born again" (John 3:1-10).

We should not be mesmerised by the number of academic qualifications a priest, an Archbishop or a theologian has acquired. Bible scholars do know everything about the Bible. Bible scholarship does not guarantee understanding of the Bible. Some scholars teach falsehood, just as how Dr. Farrah, a Dean of Canterbury, and Professor Driver of Oxford, an Anglican clergyman, laboured in vain with "skilful presentation of doubtful evidence" to undermine the supernatural character of the Book of Daniel. Sir Robert Anderson, a lay Christian, tore their arguments into pieces to defend and uphold the divine nature of the Book. Strangely, Catholic theologians have applied Professor Driver's discredited arguments to claim in *The New Jerusalem Bible* (both the Popular and Reader's Editions), that the Book of Daniel is an "Edifying fiction." I quote verbatim the words of Sir Robert Anderson: "With the ignorance of Pagans and the animus of apostates they perverted the Scriptures and tore them to pieces." (*Daniel in the Critics' Den).*

And in his *The Gospel and Its Ministry*, the "Prophet of Linden Gardens" writes: "What God wants in those whom He will put in trust with the Gospel, is not that they shall be polished and educated gentlemen, much less that they shall be coarse and ignorant boors; not that they shall be skilled in dogmatic theology, much less that they shall be unlearned in doctrine; not that they shall be brilliant and eloquent, much less that they shall be ungifted and dull. All He seeks is a fitting instrument upon whom the power of Christ can rest; an empty earthen vessel that He can fill with His priceless treasure. The man whoever he may be, whether on the higher round of the social ladder, or the lowest, who can say with Paul, "Most gladly will I glory in infirmities, that the power of Christ may rest on me, and say it with unfeigned lips, and from a heart that has been taught it in the school of God, has gained the secret of this competency for the ministry of reconciliation."

CHRISTIANS: COME OUT OF BABYLON

The Lord Jesus Christ is merciful and faithful. By virtue of His love and compassion, our Divine Lord warned His followers to end their relationship with the religious and political Babylons. Witness the words of the King of kings: *"Come out of her, my people, so that you will not share in her sins, so that you will not receive any of her plagues; for her sins are pilled up to heaven, and God has remembered her crimes....in one day her plagues will overtake her: death, mourning and famine. She will be consumed by fire, for mighty is the Lord God who judges her"* (Revelation 18:4-8).

Revelation 18 also tells us about the end of human pleasures and entertainment as well as the destruction of the economic systems of the world (the material Babylon), which is the husband of the apostate church: "Woe! Woe, O great city, O Babylon, city of power," declares the Sovereign Lord. "In one hour your doom has come!" The merchants of the earth will weep and mourn her because no one buys their cargoes any more – cargoes of gold, silver, precious stones and pearls; fine linen, purple, silk and scarlet cloth; every sort of citron wood, and articles of every kind made of ivory, costly wood, bronze, iron and marble; cargoes of cinnamon and spice, of incense, myrrh and frankincense, of wine and olive oil, of fine flour and wheat; cattle and sheep; horses and carriages; and bodies and souls of men...The great city of Babylon will be thrown down, never to be found again. The music of harpists and musicians, flute players and trumpeters will never be heard again. No workman of any trade will ever be found in you again...By your magic spell all the nations were led astray. In her was found the blood of prophets and of the saints and all who have been killed". And the Lord tells His saints (not the few "manufactured" in Vatican): "Rejoice over her, O heaven! Rejoice, saints and apostles and prophets. God has judged her for the way she treated you" (Revelation 18:20).

The 2007–2009 global financial crisis that resulted in the collapse of businesses, the nationalisation of financial institutions, the unprecedented fall in the value of shares and properties were only the signs of the mother of all political and economic hurricanes that are about to engulf the "Global Society" to terminate the reign of all human governments. When, I do not know. But I know it will surely come to pass. It shall begin three and half years after the coronation of the last Caesar of the revived Roman Empire.

Among the developed nations that experienced the "Financial Storm," America and Britain, in particular, suffered severely. For example, the value of British Pound Sterling fell dramatically. The American Government had to pump billions into the American Economy. Why? Could it be that the prosperity and security America and Britain once enjoyed are about to evaporate forever for turning their backs against God on whose Commandments these nations were built? For Sir Robert Anderson penned these words in the nineteen century: "For who can doubt that the prosperity and power of the Protestant nations of the world are due to the influence of the Bible upon character and conduct.....The dethronement of the Bible leads practically to the dethronement of God; and in Germany and America, and now in England, the effects of this are declaring themselves in ways, and to an extent, well fitted to cause anxiety for the future."

Since the Lord Himself would repay the infidels, who have taken advantage of their entitlement to freedom of speech to sneer at Him and persecute His followers, I urge Bible-believing Christians to ignore the ignorant fools. For the fool has said in his heart there is no God (Psalm 141); and yet evidence of God's existence are around us. These "fools" are men who take their "expensive designer" wrist watches; open them, remove the contents, display them in bowls and reach the 'wise' conclusion that there was no unity of design. Their "designer watches" fell from the air. No one manufactured them. This is the wisdom of our Age of Enlightenment where Darwin's discredited Theory of Evolution reigns supreme.

We should not even protest when pagans and "disciples" of Darwin deliberately mock our Faith and slander our Lord to provoke us. We must show restraint. The more the heathens and the ignorant ridicule Christians and blaspheme the Lord Jesus Christ, the more the fools dig their own pit for their destruction. Faithful Christians are the Body of Christ. Whatever ridicule and persecution they experience are direct attack on the Lord Himself. The Lord Jesus Christ is more than capable of defending Himself. He tells us vengeance is Mine. The Lord will repay His enemies at the appointed time. Let us be patient. Heaven is silent, but not a silence of indifference.

In the light of the warning the Lord gave concerning the fate of the two Babylons, Christians should not harbour the impression that we can enter the political Babylon to change its system of government. The truth is that if we are not careful, the political Babylon would rather mould us. Remember what happened to Rocco Buttiglione in the European Union. *"The Members of the European Parliament spitefully rejected* (him) *because he, a devout Catholic, believes homosexuality is a sin and dares to say that marriage is the best environment in which to bring up children"* (*Daily Mail* Editorial Comment*)*. By asserting his Christian moral values, Rocco Buttiglione was denied the position of European Justice Commissioner in the European Union.

POLITICIANS "DON'T DO GOD"
THE POLITICAL BABYLON IS NOT THE ARENA FOR THE EXHIBITION OF TRUE CHRISTIANITY

A Christian's attempt to enter the political Babylon to apply his Christian values to change its secular values, which are inconsistent with Scriptures, would be fruitless. This fact was confirmed in an article *"Why politicians don't do God when it comes to fighting elections."* (*Financial Times,* 27 December 2004). According to this article, the British population has become secular to the extent that religious beliefs of the Members of Parliament could become stumbling blocks to winning the minds of the electorate. The report states, "...Ministers whose faith precludes them from implementing an aspect of government policy are expected to exempt themselves from that role rather than campaign to change that policy on religious grounds.....politicians' religious convictions appear more likely to antagonise the electorate than to seduce it..."

If religious convictions could become political liabilities in the political arena, which could result in the lost of votes and loss of power to govern the political Babylon, how could a Christian politician promotes his or her Christian values in the political Babylon? Could a Christian politician argue in the political theatre, which is dominated by non-committed Christians and atheists, to change its laws that undermine Sacred Scriptures? Such a politician would be voted down in the democratic process.

Today, it is legal in the political Babylon to fornicate and commit adultery. It is also legal for a man to marry a man, and a woman to marry a woman. But the Holy Writ, the Christian Manifesto, does not approve such human relationships. On abortion, it is legal in the political Babylon to "kill" an unborn baby in the womb. Children can collect pills from the counter to abort but are not allowed to collect cigarettes from the counter for health reasons. On abortion the Bible says: "*...You have even taught wicked women your ways. Also on your skirts is found the lifeblood of the innocent poor. You did not find them breaking in, but killed them because of all these things*" (Jeremiah 2:33-34 HBRV).

How many Christian politicians have succeeded in preventing the political Babylon from legalising sexual intercourse between the same sexes? How many Christian politicians have succeeded in preventing the political Babylon to make it illegal for a man to marry a man and for a woman to marry a woman? How many Christian politicians have succeeded in preventing the political Babylon to make it illegal to terminate pregnancy on recreational grounds, not for medical reasons? Even the political Babylon rules that parents should not be consulted when their young daughters wanted to abort a foetus. Yet, the same political Babylon wants parents to be responsible for the antisocial behaviour of their children.

We must take the advice our Divine Lord offered us: "Come out of her (the political Babylon), my people, so that you will not share in her sins, so that you will not receive any of her plagues; for her sins are piled up in heaven, and God has remembered her crimes....She (Babylon) will be consumed by fire, for mighty is the Lord God who judges her" (Revelation 18:4, 8). It takes a wise man to avert a prophecy.

To gain a deeper understanding of the subject of this Appendix, I urge you to study chapters 13, 17 and 18 of the Book of Revelation. There is an eternal reward for your labour. Because, in the opening chapter of Revelation, the Lord Jesus Christ makes this promise: "Blessed is the one who reads the words of this prophecy, and blessed are those who hear it and take to heart what is written in it, because the time is short" (Revelation 1:3). And in the closing chapter, the Gracious Lord confirmed His earlier promise: *"Behold, I am coming soon! Blessed is he who keeps the words of the prophecy in this book"* (Revelation 22:7).

FREEDOM TO CHOOSE: BUT NOT FREEDOM TO CHOOSE THE CONSEQUENCES OF OUR CHOICES

Pagans may depend on human intelligence rather than spiritual faith to claim their right to choose to believe in God or not. Atheists would chant: "God is dead." "No-God, atheism is freedom." "Belief in religion is intellectual nonsense and backwardness." How intelligent are the pompous atheists. What serious works have they produced to help humanity, save their sneering at Christians? Human intelligence is foolishness in the sight of God. None of these so-called intellectuals would have qualified to use the pen of Sir Robert Anderson. It was this scholar among scholars who routed the Champion of Darwinism. He 'slaughtered' 'Darwin's bull-dog,' - the "hypocrite" Professor Thomas Huxley.

We are free to eat whatever food we crave for. However, we are not free to choose the consequences of our bad eating habits. Similarly, we can exercise our free will and freedom to choose not to believe in God, and to ridicule the Lord Jesus Christ as a homosexual in a nappy. However, our free will would not give us the freedom to choose the consequences of our choices – to deny the Lord Jesus Christ and blaspheme His Holy Name and Divine Personality. I would, therefore, urge pagans, agnostics, humanists, and all sceptics to be open – minded. They should use their free will and freedom to seek the truth by studying the Bible independently and with unprejudiced mind. You will know the truth; and the truth will set you free in the Precious Name of the Lord Jesus Christ, who sacrificed His life to redeem us from the consequences of our sins.

The Lord Jesus Christ is the Only One in history who was born purposely to lay down His life to redeem us. Let us listen to the Lord: "I tell you the truth; I am the gate for the sheep...whoever enters through me will be saved. He will come in and go out, and find pasture....I am the good shepherd. The good shepherd lays down his life for the sheep" (John 10:7-11). Who, from time began, has claimed to have laid down his or her life for the world?

The Book of Daniel foretold the sacrificial death of the Messiah about 538 years before the Lord Jesus Himself was born. Witness the prophetic message that was delivered to Daniel: *"....Sixty two weeks* (that is 434 years) *after the rebuilding of the city* (Jerusalem) *and its walls, the Messiah shall be cut off, but not for Himself...."* (Daniel 9:25 -26). I have already shared with you this prophetic revelation about the crucifixion of the Messiah. The mystery was hidden in the genealogy of Adam to Noah recorded in chapter 5 of Genesis.

SUMMARY: PROPHECIES FULFILLED AND PROPHECY YET TO BE FULFILLED BY THE EUROPEAN UNION

In 587BC, King Nebuchadnezzar of Babylon attacked Judea and destroyed the Temple in Jerusalem. He looted the Holy Place of its treasures and so defiled the Temple of God. We know the head of gold of the human statue which Nebuchadnezzar saw in his dream represents the Babylonian Empire.

- In 168BC, Antiochus Epiphanes of Syria also attacked Jerusalem. He killed thousands of Jews. He abolished the Jewish religion and custom of circumcision. He also defiled the Temple with the blood of a female pig. He polluted the Altar by erecting on it the image of the Greek god, Zeus. The portrait of Zeus turned into a beast is depicted on the Greek 2 euro-cents. Antiochus' kingdom descended from Alexander the Great's Grecian Empire which was symbolised by the abdomen and thighs of bronze of the dazzling human statue.
- In 70AD, the Roman Prince, Titus Vespasian, led an army to invade Judea. They killed thousands of Jews; plundered the Temple of its riches and destroyed it to fulfil the prophetic word in Daniel 9:26. The Empire of Rome is symbolised by the two legs of iron of the great human statue. It is this Roman Prince who, in AD80, inaugurated the Colloseum which his father, Emperor Vespasian, started to build in AD75 with Jewish slaves. This Amphitheatre was the grave yard of slaves and Christians. This symbol of blood-shed is the portrait on the Italian 5 euro-cents.

At this point, it is apparent that the Temple of God in Jerusalem has been defiled three times by the head of gold of the human statue (Babylon), by the abdomen and thighs of bronze of the human statue (Greece), and by the two legs of iron of the human statue (Rome). The Jerusalem Temple would be defiled again for the fourth time to fulfil the prophetic word in Daniel 9:27. Remember, the earth number is 4.

The final desecration of the Temple would be performed by the leader of the *ten toes of iron and baked clay* of the great human image. This last Caesar of the revived Roman Empire would force the world to worship his idol which would be set up in the Temple under the guidance of the false prophet (Revelation 13:11-12, 2 Thessalonians 2:3-4). And as we have learnt already, the "awful Being", the King of Men, would start to kill those who refuse to worship his image. And this would initiate the beginning of the great tribulation the Lord Jesus Christ spoke about in Matthew 24:15-12: "*So when you see standing in the holy place, the abomination that causes desolation, spoken of through the prophet Daniel.....then let those who are in Judea flee to the mountains. Let no-one on the roof of his house go down to take anything out of the house.....For then there will be great distress, unequalled from the beginning of the world until now.*"

EUROPEAN UNION: THE CLIMAX OF HISTORY

Finally, the magnificent human statue - "Babylon the Great"- would be destroyed from the sole of its feet to the crown of its head. For the Book of Daniel tells us that while King Nebuchadnezzar was watching the brilliant statue, "a stone cut out without hands struck the image on its feet of iron and clay, and broke them into pieces. Then the iron, the clay, the bronze, the silver, and the gold were crushed together, and became like chaff from the summer threshing floors; the wind carried them away so that no trace of them was found. And the stone that struck the statue became a great mountain and filled the whole earth" (Daniel 2:34-35). This closes the history of human government - the end of "Gentile Supremacy" - which Sir Robert Anderson wrote about in *The Coming Prince.*

It was Sir Robert's concern of the fate of the "10 toes" of the great human statue that prompted him to raise the question of Britain's participation in the political alliance of European nations after he had prophetically described this political union the "vile confederacy of the latter days." Sir Winston Churchill was absolutely right when, in January 1952, he privately told his doctor: "I love France and Belgium but we should not allow ourselves to be brought to that level."

The Knight of Peace who Never Shirks a Fight

A this point I will repeat the prophetic words of the "Seer of Dublin," - the able defender of the Holy Bible - who "knocked out" the Champion of Darwinism: "This confederation of [European] nations shall be developed, and thus the stage will be prepared on which shall appear that "awful Being," the great leader of men, in the eventful days which are to close the era of Gentile Supremacy.... May we not indulge the hope that however far our nation may lapse in evil days to come from the high place which, with all her faults, she has held as the champion of freedom and of truth, she will be saved from the degradation of participating in the vile confederacy of the latter days?"

I would, again, remind European leaders, that in their attempt to force the Lisbon Treaty on the masses who feed them, they were unconsciously helping to bring to pass Sir Robert Anderson's prediction of the dark future of Europe. For the Lisbon Treaty would pave the way for the "awful Being" to be crowned by European leaders to lead the world to its destiny. I repeat: it was not an accident that Ireland was the only EU country to have voted on the Lisbon Treaty and rejected it. The Irish, unconsciously, paid heed to the warning their "Forgotten Father" gave to Britain. Would the "sons" and "daughters" of the "Seer of Dublin" change their minds to adopt the Lisbon Treaty to please the "children" of Jean Monnet and Konrad Adenauer?

BRITAIN AND IRELAND: LEARN FROM THE FATE OF THE "UNSINKABLE" TITANIC

The future of Great Britain and Ireland does not lie in the European Union. The British and the Irish people must leave Jean Monnet's luxurious *Titanic* heading towards an ice-berg, According to a Channel 4 TV Documentary on the "Unsinkable Titanic," which was aired on 3 November 2008, it was a catalogue of misjudgements, human errors and misfortune that sealed the fate of the largest ship of its day. The patriotic *Sun* newspaper reported on this documentary in an article titled *Row sank Titanic.* John Cole stated: "The Titanic disaster could have been prevented if its radio operator had not been RUDE...Jack Philips had a row with his counterpart on the nearest ship who tried to warn him of ice in the area." Philips told Cyril Evans of the SS California; "Shut up." Angry Evans switched off his radio equipment." Within ten minutes the Titanic hit an iceberg and 1523 people died.

Would Britain and Ireland ignore the warning Sir Robert Anderson recorded about the fate of the European Union? The EU is the "Unsinkable Titanic" of our generation. Would ignorance and silly pride blind politicians to ignore Sir Robert's warning and drag Britons and the Irish to board Jean Monnet's luxurious ship which is heading towards an iceberg? We must be silent no more. We must leave the European Union.

According to Open Europe Press summary dated 12 January 2009, "ComRes poll commissioned by the Campaign for an Independent Britain, shows that 75 percent of people think the EU is out of touch with voters, 65 percent think the UK gets an unfair deal from the EU, 75 percent think UK politicians do not stand up for their interests in Europe, 71 percent think there should be a referendum on whether the UK remains in the EU, and 83 percent disagree that EU law should override national law." Why are we still financing the European Union – "the vile confederacy of the latter days?" Our brilliant "father," the Assistant Commissioner of Metropolitan Police, the Prince of Detectives, warned Britain the consequences of joining the European confederacy.

I close this appendix with an illustration to summarise the significance of the portrait on the Greek 2 euro cents in so far as chapter 17 of the Book of Revelation is concerned –

THE WOMAN AND THE BEAST (Revelation 17)

THE WOMAN SITS ON 7 HILLS OF THE GREAT CITY OF ROME

Rome is built on the following 7 Hills:

1. The Palatime
2. The Capitoline
3. The Aventine
4. The Caelian
5. The Equiline
6. The Viminal
7. The Quirinal

The Treaty of the European Economic Community (EEC) was signed in Rome on 25/3/57. The EEC has developed into the European Union - the foundation stone upon which the *dead* Roman Empire would be restored.

A Greek Euro coin has a portrait of a woman (Europa) sitting at the back of a Bull (The Greek god - Zeus turned itself into a bull to carry Europa across a sea)

Horst Schaffranek - a German Bible teacher - in his booklet: *"Farewell to Europe" wrote: "On one Euro coin you can see an undressed girl sitting on a bull. That is not only a figure from Greek Nythology; the last great earthly power is being manifested in this picture, and it will reveal itself just as soon as God will allow it".*

THE BEAST HAS 7 HEADS & 10 HORNS

7 KINGS

The 7 kings represent 7 Caesars of Rome who committed suiicide or were murdered:

1. Julius Caesar
2. Tiberius
3. Caligula
4. Claudius
5. NERO *(666)*
6. Domitian (is)
7. Antichrist

8. Antichrist

*The spirit of Caesar Nero, which is in the Abyss, will resuscitate the slain Antichrist. The 7th Caesar would now become the 8th Caesar. The world would marvel.

*Domitian was alive when John wrote Revelation in about AD90. He is the *"one is"*

10 KINGS

The 10 kings are the 10 powerful leaders of the reformed Roman Empire, of which the European Union is its foundation stone.

These 10 leaders would give their power to Antichrist to rule thw world

After Antichrist has broken his 7 year peace treaty with Israel, He will order the world to worship his idol in the Jerusalem Temple. And He will kill the Jews and Christians who would refuse to worship his image.

The Lord Jesus Christ will cast Antichrist into the llake of fire to experiemce an unnatural death just like the Caesars before him, who committed suicide/murdered

Appendix II

THE IRANIAN PRESIDENT ON THE PHENOMENON OF ISRAEL AND THE MIDDLE EAST CRISIS

"No book can be written in behalf of the Bible like the Bible itself. Man's defences are man's word; they may help to beat off attacks, they draw out some portion of its meaning. The Bible is God's word, and through it God the Holy Ghost, who spake it speaks to the soul which closes not itself against it." (**The Coming Prince RA**)

I would briefly share with you another plain truth in the Bible – the coming invasion of Israel by world powers, and why no human being can put a question mark against the existence of the state of Israel. Some were shocked when the President of Iran suggested that Israel should be "wiped off the map." He told the world: "The Zionist regime is a rotten, dried tree that will be eliminated by one storm." A Holocaust Conference was held in 2006 to reject Hitler's slaughter of millions of Jews. The world shouldn't be surprised by President Ahmadinejad's comments and the Holocaust denial. The Bible is clear about how Israel would be invaded by Persia (now Iran) together with the nations from the upper North - Russia and China.

Let us listen to what the Lord spoke about this military invasion through the prophet Ezekiel: "The word of the Lord came to me: Son of man, set your face against Gog, of the land of Magog, the chief prince of Rosch (Northern Russia) Meshech (Moscow) and Tubal (Tobolssk); prophesy…..This is what the Sovereign LORD says…..your horses, your horsemen fully armed, and a great horde with large and small shields, all of them brandishing their swords. Persia (Iran), Cush (Ethiopia) and Put (Libya) will be with them, all with shields and helmets, also Gomer (Germany) with all its troops, and Beth Togarmah (Armenia) from the far north with all its troops--Get ready; be prepared about you…After many days you will be called to arms. In future years you will invade a land that has recovered from war, whose people were gathered from many nations to the mountains of Israel, which has long been desolate. They have been brought out from the nations, and now all of them live in safety. You and all your troops and the many nations with you will go up, advancing like a storm; you will be like a cloud covering the land..." (Ezekiel 38:1-9)

I have referred to the above scripture to prove that the Bible publishes history before history is recorded. An example of this is the development of European Union and its future prospects which were published in the Book of Daniel thousands of years before the European Union came into existence.

The 34-Day Lebanon War in 2006 and the 22-day Gaza War in 2009 were just dips in the ocean. After the "Gaza Truce," world leaders called for measures "to secure a permanent peace settlement" between the "two brothers." This would not happen now. The Middle East would be plagued with more conflicts until the final battle to close the era of Gentile supremacy on earth. This subject is outside the scope of this book. However, I will make brief comments on the Middle East Politics because the European Union will play a significant role in the final negotiation that would bring "peace" between the Jews and the Arabs.

According to the 17 November 2008 edition of *TIME* magazine, Barack Obama's US Presidential election victory "generates new hope and greater expectation." Prominent among the "new hope" was the solution to the Middle East conflict – the unceasing hostilities between the Jews and the Arabs. Here are the comments made by Archbishop Desmond Tutu of South Africa, Mohamed ElBaradei, the Egyptian Director General of International Atomic Energy Agency (IAEA) and David Miliband, Britain's Foreign Secretary, on the Middle East crisis.

Archbishop Tutu: "A new era has dawned for Africa and the entire world....Obama's election has given hope to people everywhere that change is possible, that this debilitating status quo of a polarized world of "them and us" can change.....The world now expects the new President to bring viable initiatives for peace in the Middle East..."

David Miliband: "When he spoke in Berlin on July 24, 2008, Senator Obama pledged to work with Europe in a spirit of constant co-operation....our highest priority must be to meet the current challenges in the global economy...addressing the threat of climate change...commitment to tackle violent extremism. And third we must make the search for a comprehensive settlement in the Middle East a top priority..."

Mohamed ElBaradei: "The President-elect is an African-American Christian with a Muslim father who lived across many continents from humble beginnings. This sends a powerful message to the rest of the world about the need for diversity and build bridges....to create a world at peace with itself....I also hope that conditions will be created soon for direct U.S–Iran negotiations which are key for durable peace and security in the Middle East."

The same Middle East issue was raised by European leaders in their letter to the then President-elect. In an article, *Europe has fallen in love with America again because of Barack Obama,* William Horsley of BBC News writes "France's President Nicolas Sarkozy said the world was "spellbound" by Barack Obama's brilliance in the campaign. He promised that ties between Europe and America would be re-energised. And the Europeans have bold ideas about how to do that. They want "a partnership of equals" to resolve the urgent challenges, like the world financial crisis and bringing peace to the Middle East." This raises the question: Would any of the current world leaders succeed in bringing peace to the Middle East? Who is capable of achieving that feat?

THE "PHENOMENON OF ISRAEL"

The creation of the state of Israel in Palestine has, perhaps, contributed to the "hundred years of war" in the Middle East. In May 2006, the Iranian President, Mahmoud Ahmadinejad, delivered an open letter to President George Bush. He queried the state of Israel with this remark: "*...Young people, university students and ordinary people have asked many questions about the phenomenon of Israel. I am sure you are familiar with some of them. Throughout history, many countries have been occupied, but I think the establishment of a new country with a new people is a phenomenon that is exclusive to our times. Students are saying that 60 years ago such a country did not exist. They show old documents and globes and say, try as we have, we have not been able to find a country named Israel....*"

The "Phenomenon of Israel" might have been "exclusive to our times," yet it should not have surprised any one. On this issue, it would have been helpful had President Bush reminded the Iranian President, that 15 years before Theodor Herzl, the Father of Political Zionism, outlined his vision of a Jewish State in 1896, a British public servant had already predicted the restoration of the Jews to Palestine, and that the rebirth of the state of Israel would be followed by another political phenomenon in history – a confederation of European nations. This information would have impressed President Ahmadinejad that the establishment of a country named Israel was not an accident; it was destined to happen.

In his letter, the Iranian President made references to Jewish prophets Abraham, Moses, Joseph, Ishmael, Isaac and others. President Bush should have seized the opportunity to share with the Iranian President what the prophet Moses *(Musa)* and other Hebrew prophets wrote about the children of Israel and their destiny. In this respect, President Bush should have explained to President Ahmadinejad the prophetic messages in the Books of Deuteronomy, Ezekiel, Zechariah, the Psalms and Amos that relate to the children of Israel. President Ahmadinejad and the rest of the world would have learnt it was God who, over thousands of years ago, handed over the children of Israel to the King of Babylon and other Gentile nations (Daniel 1:1-3) to punish them and scatter them around the earth for their national sin. And it was the same God who also promised to bring the "stubborn" Jews back to their homeland. President Bush could have quoted the relevant Scriptures that deal with the dispersal of the Jews and their return to occupy their land.

For example, the Prophet Moses (*Musa*), who is recognised by Muslims as one of the five Major Prophets, warned the Israelites: "If you do not carefully follow all the words of this law...you who were numerous as stars in the sky will be left but few in number, because you did not obey the Lord your God. Just as it pleased the Lord to make you prosper and increase in number, so it will please him to ruin and destroy you. You will be uprooted from the land you are entering to possess. Then the Lord will scatter you among all nations. From one end of the earth to the other....Among these nations you will find no repose, no resting place for the sole of your foot....You will live in constant suspense, filled with dread both night and day, never sure of your life..." (Deuteronomy 28: 58-66).

And concerning the restoration of the Jews to their home land, the Prophet Amos recorded what the Lord said: "I (God) will bring back the captives of My people Israel: they shall build the waste cities and inhabit them; they shall plant vineyards and drink wine from them; they shall make gardens and eat from them. I will plant them in their land, and no longer shall they be pulled up from the land I have given them..." (Amos 9:14-15).

SHALL A NATION BE BORN AT ONCE?

Our Muslim brothers and sisters believe in the prophet Ezekiel (*Dhulkifl*). President Bush could have referred President Ahmadinejad to this significant passage in Ezekiel 36:22-24: "Therefore (Ezekiel) say to the house of Israel, thus says the Lord God." I do not do this for your sake, O house of Israel, but for My name's sake, which you have profaned among the nations wherever you went. And I will sanctify My great name, which you have profaned among the nations, which you have profaned in their midst; and the nations shall know that I am the Lord... when I am hallowed in you before their eyes...For I will take you from among the nations, gather you out of all countries and bring you into your own land."

President Bush could have included in his response the song of the Prophet David (*Daud*) about God's promise to save the Jews: *"If I (God) forget you, O Jerusalem, may my right hand forget its skill. May my tongue cling to the roof of my mouth if I do not remember you, if I do not consider Jerusalem my highest joy."* (Psalms 137:5-6). The President could have concluded his reply with Isaiah (*Ishaia*) 66:7-10: "Before she travailed, she gave birth; before her pain came, she delivered a male child. Who has heard such a thing? Shall the earth be made to give birth in one day?

Or shall a nation be born at once? For as soon as Zion travailed, She gave birth to her children...Shall I (God) who cause delivery shut up the womb? Rejoice with Jerusalem, and be glad with her, all you who love her."

Such a letter to President Ahmadinejad would have helped him to gain a different perspective of the "Phenomenon of Israel" – that "people who have come from far areas of the world" to Palestine is a Bible prophecy fulfilled. And that God, by restoring the Jews to Palestine, did not exalt the children of Israel above the Gentiles. The Jews were no better than other races. God brought the Israelites to Palestine for the sake of His Holy Name - to keep His promise as clearly described in Ezekiel 36:22-24. After all, the name "Palestine" was coined from "*Syria Palestina.*" Emperor Hadrian of Rome despised the Jews for their rebellion. In his attempt to remove the Jewish nation and its people from memory, the wicked Hadrian eliminated Judea from the map and renamed the area *Syria Palestina.*

The Scriptures I have shared with you should have settled the dispute between the Israelis and their Arab neighbours. Muslims and Jews are all descendants of Abraham through his sons Ishmael and Isaac. They should have lived in peace. So, why the "blood feud?" Please read chapters 16 and 17 of the Book of Genesis, written by Moses (*Musa*), for an answer. The "blood-feud" would continue to its climax as prophesised. Would we be wise to avert the prophecy which is yet to be fulfilled?

After the Lebanon War in 2006, there was a pause. The hostilities between "Ishmael" and "Isaac" resumed in 2009. Israel invaded Gaza in response to Hamas firing missiles into their southern cities. The invasion resulted in over 1300 deaths in Palestine. *Economist* and *TIME* magazines provided commentaries on the conflict. The *Economist*, in its leading article, *The hundred years' war. Why Arabs and Jews still fight in Palestine,* recorded: "The Jews and Arabs of Palestine have been fighting off and on for 100 years. In 1909 the mostly Russian socialist idealists of the Zionist movement set up an armed group, Hasomer, to protect their new farms and villages in Palestine from Arab marauders. Since then has come the dismal march of wars –1948, 1956, 1967, 1973, 1982, 2006 and now 2009—each shared by blood and fire into the conflicting myths and memories of the two sides."

For us to understand the significance of the "100-years war," and why Arabs and Jews still fight in Palestine, we must examine how the Prince of Detectives was able to predict with certainty that the Jews would be restored to Palestine and the next major political feature in history after the "Phenomenon of Israel" would be the development of a confederation of European nations. The Assistant Commissioner of Metropolitan Police made this forecast even before the terms "Zionist" and "Zionism" and "Political Zionism" were coined in 1890 and 1892 respectively by Nathan Birnbaum, a native of Vienna, and a contemporary of Theodor Herzl, the Founding Father of Zionist Movement.

TIME's report on the Gaza conflict was also published in an article titled "*Why Israel Can't Win.*" Among other things, Tim Mcgirk writes: "As much as any other nation on earth, Israel is based on a dream: the aspiration to establish a home for the Jews in the birthplace of their ancestors. To a remarkable extent, that dream has been fulfilled, as Israel has grown into the most modern and democratic country in the Middle East and a dependable American ally. A strong, confident Israel is in American's interest, but so is one that can find peace with its neighbours, cooperate with the Arabs to contain common threats and, most important, reach a just and lasting solution with the Palestinians. But accomplishing that will require Israel and its defenders to confront excruciating dilemmas: How do you make peace with those who don't seem to want it? How do you win a war when the other side believes time is on its side? And what would true security, in a hostile neighbourhood populated with enemies, actually look like? As is always true in the Middle East, there are no easy answers but it's never been more vital that Israel start looking for them."

The truth is that the declaration of an Independent State of Israel by David Ben Gurion on 14 May 1948 was not "based on a dream" just like any other nation as suggested in Tim Mcgirk's article. The creation of a home for the children of Israel in the birthplace of their ancestors is not a dream come true. It was the fulfillment of a specific prediction Sir Robert Anderson made, about 68 years, before it happened.

I will now make a brief commentary on the re-establishment of the Jews onto the soil of Palestine after they had been without a home for over 2000 years. Without any doubt, the conflict in the Middle East primarily stems from Israel's rebirth. Had it not been the restoration of the Jews to Palestine, the hostilities between the Jews and the Arabs would, probably, not have arisen. It is clear the creation of the state of Israel in the 20th century has been a major political phenomenon in the history of mankind. And President Ahmadinejad rightly mentioned the "Phenomenon of Israel" in his letter to President George W Bush. This "Phenomenon of Israel" is exactly what Sir Robert Anderson predicted in 1881 before it materialised in 1948. And his prediction of a confederation of European nations becoming the next political phenomenon in history after the rebirth of Israel was also fulfilled on 9 May 1950 when Robert Shuman laid the foundation of a federal Europe with an economic plan that created the European Coal and Steel Community.

DID THE JEWS STEAL ARAB LAND?

Robert Fisk, in his article, *"How can you trust the cowardly BBC?"* writes: "Anyone who has read the history of Zionism will be aware that its aim was to dispossess the Arabs and take over Palestine. Why else are Zionists continuing to steal Arab land for Jews only, against all international law? (*The Independent* 16 April 2009). I ask the question: How would Fisk reconcile his claim - the 'stealing' of Arab land in Palestine by the Jews - with the fact that before the founding father of Political Zionism, Theodor Herzl, outlined his vision of a Jewish State in 1896, and even before the term "Zionism" was coined in 1892, Sir Robert Anderson had already written that the Jews would be restored to Palestine, and the next major political phenomenon in history would be a political union of European nations which would develop through an European crisis?

I hold no brief for the "criminal activities" of the Jews. However, no human being, and no organisation on planet earth can query the existence of the State of Israel. The destiny of the Jewish people is not at the mercy of any politician or organisation. The fate of the children of Israel is in the hands of the ONE who uprooted them from their land and restored them. Witness what God told Solomon after he had completed the Temple in Jerusalem: "I have heard your prayer and have chosen this place for myself as a temple for sacrifice.....But if you (Solomon) turn away and forsake the decrees and commands I have given you and go off to serve other gods and worship them, then *I will uproot Israel from my land, which I have given them, and will reject this temple which I have consecrated for my Name.* I will make it a byword and an object of ridicule. And though this temple is now so imposing, all who pass by will be appalled and say, 'Why has the Lord done such a thing to this land and to this temple? People will answer, 'Because they have forsaken the Lord, the God of their fathers, who brought them out of Egypt, and have embraced other gods, worshipping and serving them - that is why he brought this disaster on them." (Emphasis mine 2 Chronicles 7:12, 19-22).

THE STRUGGLE OVER JERUSALEM

Jerusalem is a city revered by Jews, Christians and Muslims. The sign that Jerusalem would become a "thorn in the flesh of Gentile nations," as foretold in the Book of Ezekiel, was unveiled in an election of a new Major for Jerusalem. In an article entitled *"Secular Jerusalem Major ends orthodox dominance"* (*Evening Standard* 12 November 2008), Ed Harris writes: "Jerusalem was....coming to terms with a new Major, a secular businessman who has ended five years of ultra-orthodox Jewish control of one of the world's most complex cities." He concludes his report with this comment: "The status of Jerusalem is one of the most hotly-contested issues in Israeli-Palestinian negotiations. Israelis see the city as their capital, while Palestinians want to locate the capital of a future state in the east of the city – which Israel occupied in the 1967 Israeli-Arab war. Mr Barkat (the new Major) opposes any division of the city and supports building thousands more apartments for Israelis in the disputed part of the city, a policy certain to anger Palestinians." Tim Mcgirk also reported: "Both the Israelis and the Palestinians claim it (Jerusalem) as their capital. Muslims and Jewish holy places occupy the same space. Some people call for the city to be placed under third-party supervision" (TIME 19 January 2009).

The struggle over Jerusalem would continue. The world should now listen to what the Almighty God declared thousands of years ago: "I am going to make Jerusalem a cup that sends all the surrounding peoples reeling. Judah will be besieged as well as Jerusalem. On that day, when all the nations of the earth are gathered against her, I will make Jerusalem an immovable rock for all the nations. All who try to move it will injure themselves. On that day I will strike every horse with panic and its rider with madness...I will keep a watchful eye over the house of Judah, but I will blind all the horses of the nations. Then the leaders of Judah will say in their hearts, "The people of Jerusalem are strong, because the Lord Almighty is their God" (Zechariah 12:2-5).

And the Prophet Joel also recorded what the Lord told him about His land and the final war in the Middle East: "In those days and at that time when I (God) restore the fortunes of Judah and Jerusalem, I will gather all nations and bring them down to the valley of Jehoshaphat. There I will enter into judgment against them concerning my inheritance, my people Israel, for they scattered my people among the nations and divided up my land. They cast lots for my people and traded boys for prostitutes; they sold girls for wine that they might drink" (Joel 3:1-3) Would men dare to divide God's land? It takes a wise man to avert a prophecy.

It was these scriptures, together with what is written in the Books of Daniel *(Danyal)* and Revelation, that influenced Sir Robert Anderson to predict with certainty that the Jews would return to Palestine and the next major political event in history, after the rebirth of Israel, would be a political union of European nations. On the critical issue of peace and security in the Middle East, neither the International Peace Quartet of EU, USA, Russia and United Nations nor the Arab League could prevent further blood-shed between the "two brothers" until the last Emperor of the revived Roman Empire is crowned. "Peace" would be restored in the Middle East but for how long. I have mentioned it many times, that the Lisbon Treaty has paved the way for the powerful and charismatic Emperor of Europe to enter the political scene to use his extraordinary diplomatic skills to broker a "peace-deal" between "Isaac" and "Ishmael." If even the Lisbon Treaty were to be abandoned, the political genius would still emerge to lead Europe and the world to negotiate a "permanent peace" deal between the Jews and the Arabs.

If Sir Robert Anderson's predictions of the restoration of the Jews to Palestine and the development of a political alliance of European nations have been fulfilled, it is likely what he wrote about the future of Europe and the fate of Israel would also come to pass. In *The Coming Prince*, the Knight Commander writes: *"The Hour is coming and the Man...the opportunity must synchronise with his advent."* Indeed, the "Hour" is upon us. The global economic crisis and the unresolved conflict between the Jews and the Arabs are events that are unfolding to pave the way for the arrival of the "Prince of Europe."

In the 10th edition of *The Coming Prince,* which was released in 1915 during the First World War, Sir Robert Anderson made a reference to the destiny of the children of Israel in Palestine. In the Preface to this edition, the Prince of Detectives writes: "The Coming Prince has been out of print for more than a year; for it seemed inadvisable to reissue it during the War. But the War has apparently created an increased interest in the prophecies of Daniel; and as this book is therefore in demand, it has been decided to publish a new edition without further delay. Not that these pages contain any sensational "Armageddon" theories. For "a place called in the Hebrew tongue Armageddon" is situated neither in France nor in Flanders, but in Palestine; and the *future of the land and people of the covenant* (the Israelites) *will be a main issue in the great battle which is yet to be fought on that historic plain."* (Emphasis mine).

Since the release of the 10th edition of *The Coming Prince*, series of wars have been waged between the Jews and the Arabs in the land of Palestine. But the war of all wars is yet to be waged. What would be the outcome? First, I urge you to get a copy of *The Coming Prince* from Kregel Publications in America, and then examine the Books of Ezekiel, Daniel, Zechariah and Revelation. God rewards those who earnestly seek Him (Hebrews 11:6).

APPENDIX III

CORRECTING THE "MISTAKES" OF GEORGE BUSH – THE 43RD PRESIDENT OF THE UNITED STATES OF AMERICA

During his 8-year presidency, George W Bush was perceived to have tarnished the image of the United States of America by leading Americans to invade Iraq. It was an adventure that resulted in the deaths of thousands of people and the destruction of property. President Bush compounded his "mistake" by incarcerating suspected terrorists at Guantanamo Bay detention camp where some of them were "tortured."

During the 2008 US Presidential campaign, Mr Barack Obama promised to restore the dignity of America by righting the "wrongs" of President Bush. True to his word, when Mr Obama entered the White House in January 2009, the new President began to correct the "mistakes" of his predecessor. President Obama promised to withdraw American troops from Iraq within a reasonable time to end the occupation. He also ordered the closure of Guantanamo Bay. He threw out Bush's "divisive policy" on embryo stem cell research. As a result, he overruled federal funding on this controversial research by signing an executive order to allow public money to be used for research that scientists claim could help prevent some deadly diseases. Obama's bold move was greeted with the following headlines in British newspapers:

- "Fears of brain drain to US as Obama lifts Bush's ban stem-cell research funding" (*The Times* 9 March 2009)
- "Obama go-ahead for stem cell funds" (*Financial Times* 10 March 2009).
- "Obama gives green light to stem cell research" (Daily Mail 10 March 2009).
- "US scientists relieved as Obama lifts ban on stem cell research" (*The Guardian* 10 march 2009).
- "Obama lifts ban on funding of stem cell research" (*The Daily Telegraph* 10 March 2009). In this article, it was reported: "In a thinly-veiled criti-

cism of former President George W Bush, Mr Obama promised to restore 'scientific integrity' to government." According to the President, his decision "would be based on facts not ideology." To the applause at a White House gathering of leading genetics, campaigners and Congressmen from Democratic and the Republican Parties, President Obama declared: "We will also vigorously support scientists who pursue this research. And we will aim for America to lead the world in the discoveries it one day may yield."

- Professor Richard Dawkins, the Archbishop of Atheism and a "clone" of Darwin's bulldog - the "hypocrite" Professor Thomas Huxley - congratulated Barack Obama for overturning George Bush's ban on funding stem-cell research (Source: *Daily Mail* 2 April 2009,*"Pope is dim for saying condoms increase Aids claims Dawkins"*)

Another correction of Bush's "mistakes" was the easing of the restrictions the former President introduced to "prevent US-based relatives sending more than $1,200 per year to Cuba and allow one visit every three years to immediate family" (*The Daily Telegraph* 11 March 2009). The Obama administration also replaced George Bush's slogan, "War on Terror," with a 'respectable' catchphrase: "Overseas Contingency Operation."

PRESIDENT OBAMA'S INTERVIEW ON AL-ARABIYA

Finally, President Obama, corrected another "mistake" of President Bush by offering a hand of friendship to the Iranians who were isolated by his predecessor. This was evident in his first interview with Al-Arabiya Arab TV Network. In this interview, President Obama told the world about his vision of US relationship with Iran and how America would help to promote peace between the Jews and the Arabs. To prevent misquoting the American President, I have reproduced part of the transcript of the interview posted on the website of Al Arabia News Channel.

Question: "President Bush framed the war on terror conceptually in a way that was very broad, "war on terror," and used sometimes certain terminology.....You've always framed it in a different way, specifically against one group called al Qaeda and their collaborators.."

THE PRESIDENT: "I think that you're making a very important point. And that is that the language we use matters. And what we need to understand is, is that there are extremist organisations - whether Muslim or any other faith in the past - that will use faith as a justification for violence. We cannot paint with a broad brush a faith as a consequence of the violence that is done in that faith's name. And so you will, I think, see our administration be very clear in distinguishing between organizations like al Qaeda - that espouse violence, espouse terror and act on it - and people who may disagree with my administration and certain actions, or may have a particular viewpoint in terms of how their countries should develop. We can have legitimate disagreements but still be respectful. I cannot respect terrorist organizations that would kill innocent civilians and we will hunt them down. But to the broader Muslim world what we are going to be offering is a hand of friendship."

Question: "Will the United States ever live with a nuclear Iran? And if not, how far are you going in the direction of preventing it?"

THE PRESIDENT: "You know, I said during the campaign that it is very important for us to make sure that we are using all the tools of U.S. power, including diplomacy, in our relationship with Iran. Now, the Iranian people are a great people, and Persian civilization is a great civilization. Iran has acted in ways that's not conducive to peace and prosperity in the region: their threats against Israel; their pursuit of a nuclear weapon which could potentially set off an arms race in the region that would make everybody less safe; their support of terrorist organizations in the past - none of these things have been helpful.

But I do think that it is important for us to be willing to talk to Iran, to express very clearly where our differences are, but where there are potential avenues for progress. And we will over the next several months be laying out our general framework and approach. And as I said during my inauguration speech, if countries like Iran are willing to unclench their fist, they will find an extended hand from us."

ON PEACE BETWEEN THE ISRAELIS AND THE PALESTINIANS

Question: Sir, you just met with your personal envoy to the Middle East, Senator Mitchell. Obviously, his first task is to consolidate the cease-fire. But beyond that you've been saying that you want to pursue actively and aggressively peacemaking between the Palestinians and the Israelis. Tell us a little bit about how do you see your personal role, because, you know, if the President of the United States is not involved, nothing happens - as the history of peace making shows. Will you be proposing ideas, pitching proposals, parameters, as one of your predecessors did? Or just urging the parties to come up with their own resolutions, as your immediate predecessor did?

THE PRESIDENT: "Well, I think the most important thing is for the United States to get engaged right away. And George Mitchell is somebody of enormous stature. He is one of the few people who have international experience brokering peace deals. And so what I told him is start by listening, because all too often the United States starts by dictating - in the past on some of these issues - and we don't always know all the factors that are involved. So, let's listen. He's going to be speaking to all the major parties involved. And he will then report back to me. From there we will formulate a specific response.

Ultimately, we cannot tell either the Israelis or the Palestinians what's best for them. They're going to have to make some decisions. But I do believe that the moment is ripe for both sides to realise that the path they are on is one that is not going to result in prosperity and security for their people. And that instead, it's time to return to the negotiating table."

And it's going to be difficult; it's going to take time. I don't want to prejudge many of these issues, and I want to make sure that expectations are not raised so that we think that this is going to be resolved in a few months. But if we start the steady progress on these issues, I'm absolutely confident that the United States - working in tandem with the European Union, with Russia, with all the Arab states in the region - I'm absolutely certain that we can make significant progress."

ANOTHER BUSH'S "MISTAKE" WHICH PRESIDENT OBAMA MUST CORRECT

It is clear from President Obama's interview with the Arab News Channel, that the Leader of the Free world and the most powerful man on earth wants to improve US relationship with the Arab world which President Bush soiled it. President Obama is also eager to help resolve the conflict between the Jews and the Arabs. In this respect, I would remind the President to correct another significant "mistake" George Bush made. President Ahmadinejad raised important issues in his May 2006 open letter to President Bush. He queried the legitimacy of the Iraq war and then demanded explanation of the "Phenomenon of Israel." Unfortunately, President Bush did not explain the "Phenomenon of Israel" to the President of Iran.

Here is an extract from the open letter: *"Young people, university students, and ordinary people have many questions about the phenomenon of Israel. I am sure you are familiar with some of them. Throughout history, many countries have been occupied, but I think the establishment of a new country with a new people, is a new phenomenon that is exclusive to our times. Students are saying that 60 years ago such a country did not exist. They show old documents and globes and say try as we have, we have not been able to find a country named Israel.*
I tell them to study the history of WWI and II. One of my students told me that during WWII, which more than tens of millions of people perished in, news about the war, was quickly disseminated by the warring parties. Each touted their victories and the most recent battlefront defeat of the other party. After the war they claimed that six million Jews had been killed. Six million people that were surely related to at

least two million families. Again let us assume that these events are true. ***Does that logically translate into the establishment of the state of Israel in the Middle East or support for such a state? How can this phenomenon be rationalized or explained?"*** (Emphasis mine)

President Ahmadinejad made references to some of the prophets in the Holy Bible, including the Lord Jesus Christ. He noted: *"If Prophet Abraham, Isaac, Jacob, Ishmael, Joseph, or Jesus Christ (Peace Be Upon Him) were with us today, how would they have judged such behaviour? Will we be given a role to play in the promised world, where justice will become universal and Jesus Christ (Peace Be Upon Him) will be present? Will they even accept us?*

We know President Obama wants to lead America and the rest of the world to end the violence in the Middle East to bring peace between the Palestinians and the Israelis. To show his commitment to this noble cause, the President appointed Senator George Mitchell, a man of "enormous stature," as his Middle East Envoy. At a Press Conference at the White House, President Obama, again, stressed his determination to pursue for peace in the troubled Mediterranean Region. He told Americans: "What we do know is this – that the status quo is unsustainable; that it is critical for us to advance a two-state solution where Israelis and Palestinians can live side by side in their own states with peace and security."

In May 2009, President Obama welcomed the Israeli Prime Minster, Benjamin Netanyahu, to the White House. They discussed the Israeli-Palestinian conflict. The President reiterated his commitment to the Middle East peace process by emphasising that there should be a Palestinian state living side by side with the Israelis.

OBAMA AND THE HOLY BIBLE AND THE "PHENOMENON OF ISRAEL"

In the light of Obama's commitment to peace between the Israelis and the Palestinians, it is necessary for the President to deal with the query concerning the "Phenomenon of Israel". It was President Ahmadinejad of Iran who raised this issue in an open letter to Obama's predecessor, President George Bush. On this query – the restoration of the Jews to Palestine and the creation of the state of Israel – the Iranian President has unclenched his fist by demanding an explanation. He expects an "extended hand" from the American President - an explanation of the "Phenomenon of Israel."

The Holy Bible is not silent on the "Phenomenon of Israel." In front of millions around the globe, Mr Barack Hussein Obama swore on the Holy Bible to become the 44th President of the United States of America. President Ahmadinejad, in his letter to George Bush, rightly referred to Moses as a prophet. Since President Obama and his politicians in Washington want to engage with the Iranian President, and not to isolate the Islamic Republic of Iran, it is therefore proper for President Obama to refer the Iranian President to what the Prophet Moses (*Musa*) and other prophets in the Bible wrote concerning the children of Israel – how they would be dispersed and be gathered back to the land of their ancestors.

I have provided some scriptural passages in the previous appendix which could help President Obama to frame his response and explain the "Phenomenon of Israel" to the President of the Islamic Republic of Iran and the rest of the Middle East Quartet - the European Union, Russia and the United Nations. President Obama's open response to President Ahmadinejad's query would correct the "mistake" President George Bush made by not explaining the "Phenomenon of Israel" to the President of Iran. The world media are looking forward to commenting on President Obama's letter.

THE RESTORATION OF THE CHILDREN OF ISRAEL

I close this appendix by stressing that the destiny of Israel is not in the hands of politicians and commentators. It is not in the hands of Americans or Europeans. It is neither in the hands of the Jews themselves nor in the hands of the United Nations. The fate of Israel is the Hands of the Mighty One who scattered the Jews around the globe and brought them back to their land. At His own scheduled time the Lord will restore the fortunes of Israel – not because God loves the Jews more than other men, but for the sake of His Holy Name (Ezekiel 36:22-23).

God mysteriously revealed the restoration of the children of Israel in the opening verse of the Book of Zechariah. Zechariah 1:1 reads: "In the eighth month of the second year of Darius, the word of the Lord came to the prophet Zechariah son of Berekiah, the son of Iddo. According to this scripture Zechariah, who was born during the Jewish captivity in Babylon to a priestly family, was the son of Berekiah and the grandson of Iddo. Just as the ten names in Genesis 5, which describe the first generation of mankind (the genealogy of Adam to Noah), convey a message, like wise the three names mentioned in Zechariah 1:1 are also pregnant with a message. In Hebrew the name Zechariah means "Jehovah will remember." The name Berekiah means "Jehovah will bless." And the name Iddo means "at an appointed time." Hence, the significance of these three names is that "Jehovah will remember, and Jehovah will bless (His people) at the appointed time." I repeat: no human being or organisation can question the existence of the State of Israel.

PIECES OF WOOD FOR MEDITATION

- Truth moves on the wheels of facts.
- Life is a texture of truisms of woven fabrics of acts of realities.
- Misunderstanding besmears the spirit of reconciliation.
- A dying man is a desperate man, and a desperate man is a despaired soul.
- When the soul of man is despaired, the desperate spirit of Satan besieges the despaired man.

Index

C

Y

Z

• In his zeal to unite Europe to create a "federated Europe", Jean Monnet, the chief architect of European Construction, unconsciously, toiled to bring to pass what an Irish scholar wrote about Europe and its future before he (Monnet) was born in 1888.

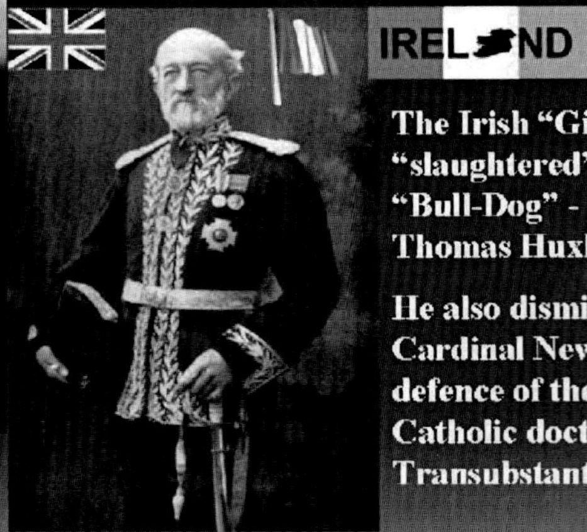

The Irish "Giant" who "slaughtered" Darwin's "Bull-Dog" - Professor Thomas Huxley.

He also dismissed Cardinal Newman's defence of the Roman Catholic doctrine of Transubstantiation.

Intellectually, Spiritually and Morally, the "Labourer" Monnet, the Pride of France, would not have qualified to stoop and untie the bootstraps of the Knight Commander– the Pride of Ireland.

TRINITY COLLEGE, DUBLIN

K.C.B, BA (with a Medal) LLD: A Lawyer with Sanctified Logic

"....His views are worthy of the utmost respect and consideration....and the well being of Ireland was to him a matter standing above politics in the ordinary sense."